ON THE MORMON FRONTIER

The Diary of Hosea Stout
1844–1889

HOSEA STOUT
1810-1889
From a photograph, about 1852

ON THE
MORMON FRONTIER

Volume One
1844–1848

EDITED BY
JUANITA BROOKS

UNIVERSITY OF UTAH PRESS
UTAH STATE HISTORICAL SOCIETY
Salt Lake City

The Defiance House Man colophon is a registered trademark of the University of
Utah Press. It is based upon a four-foot-tall, Ancient Puebloan pictograph (late PIII)
near Glen Canyon, Utah.

12 11 10 09 08   1 2 3 4 5

LIBRARY OF CONGRESS CATALOGING-IN-PUBLICATION DATA

Stout, Hosea, 1810–1889.
    On the Mormon frontier : the diary of Hosea Stout 1844–1889 / edited
by Juanita Brooks.
         p. cm.
    Includes index.
    Originally published: 1964.
    ISBN 978-0-87480-945-9 (pbk. : alk. paper)   1. Stout, Hosea, 1810–
1889—Diaries.   2. Mormon pioneers—Utah—Diaries.   3. Legislators—
Utah—Diaries.   4. Mormon Church—Utah—History—19th century—Sources.
5. Mormon Church—Illinois—Nauvoo—History—19th century—Sources.
6. Utah—History—19th century—Sources.   7. Nauvoo (Ill.)—History—19th
century—Sources.   I. Brooks, Juanita, 1898-1989.   II. Title.
    F826.S76A3 2009
    289.3092—dc22
    [B]   2009007236

Cover painting of Hosea Stout © 2008 by Paul H. Davis. Used by permission.

Printed and bound by Sheridan Books, Inc., Ann Arbor, Michigan.

ON THE MORMON FRONTIER

Contents

Illustrations

ON THE MORMON FRONTIER

Preface

Of the Mormon diaries available to scholars, perhaps there is none which so adequately mirrors the times and locale of the writer and his people over such an extended period as does the diary of Hosea Stout. Unlike some other diarists, Hosea Stout held positions of responsibility in church, civic, and governmental organizations, and so was able to observe and record events of great moment.

At various times he was an officer in the militia in Illinois and Utah, chief of police at Nauvoo, Illinois, and Winter Quarters on the Missouri River, attorney general of the State of Deseret and the Territory of Utah, United States district attorney for Utah, and president of the house of the Utah Territorial Legislature. These associations with the highest ecclesiastical and civil authorities permitted Stout to inscribe in his diary conversations and transactions which were outside the knowledge of many diarists. Nowhere is this better exemplified than in the proceedings of the territorial legislature. Hosea Stout's writings offer a more detailed account of the affairs of the legislative assembly than is provided in the official published *Journals* of that body. And while Stout as a diarist is not as colorful as John D. Lee, he was more faithful in making daily entries in his diary and was given to greater accuracy and fewer flights of fancy. These qualities in addition to his keen powers of observation make his diary, in the words of Dale L. Morgan, ". . . one of the most magnificent windows upon Mormon history ever opened . . . [the publication of which] will place before the world an enduring contribution to American history. . . ."

Along with the editor of this diary, Dale L. Morgan is one of the best qualified individuals to judge its value. It was he who "discovered" it in 1941 while working on the Utah Writer's Project of the WPA. Mr. Morgan, cooperating with Lafayette Lee, a grandson of Hosea Stout, and Mrs. Dean Palmer, a granddaughter, had the diary copied. Periodically over several years, Mr. Morgan worked at obtaining an accurate typescript from which this work is produced.

Copies of the diary eventually found their way into libraries where they came to the attention of scholars who have cited it extensively. Finally in 1957, Dr. A. R. Mortensen, then director of the Utah State Historical Society, obtained from Mrs. Palmer all but two small diaries for the Society. The first volume, covering the period 1844-45, was located in the Historian's Library of The Church of Jesus Christ of Latter-day Saints. Through the efforts of Earl E. Olson, librarian, a microfilm of this volume was obtained for the use of Juanita Brooks, the editor. The last diary for 1869 is a recent gift to the Society from a great-granddaughter, Mrs. Josephine Di Pastena.

For more than two years, Mrs. Brooks as an employee of the Utah State Historical Society worked diligently to edit these priceless volumes. And when, in 1962, the end appeared almost in sight, the funds of the Society were exhausted. Turning to the members and friends of the Society and the Stout family, the director of the Society was able to raise sufficient funds to see the project through.

Members of the Stout family especially are to be congratulated for their interest and support in this project. They have insisted that the diary be published in its entirety. In order to comply with the family's desires and in order to reduce the whole to a manageable size, the Utah State Historical Society published in Volume XXX, 1962, of the *Utah Historical Quarterly*, Hosea Stout's autobiography. It was edited by a great-grandson, Reed Stout, and is available in booklet form.

The autobiography is made up of two parts. One was written in 1844 in response to a request by Mormon Church authorities that each member of the Quorum of the Seventy, an organization with which Stout was affiliated, should write a brief account of his life; the second portion of the autobiography is longer and more detailed. It was written during the bitter winter of 1846-47 while the Mormons were camped on the bank of the Missouri River at Winter Quarters. Night after night, after returning from his tour of duty as chief of police, Hosea wrote of his childhood, his life in a Shaker school, his apprenticeship as a farm hand, his determined effort to gain an education, and his struggle to support himself while a young man.

The daily journal of Hosea picks up his life where his autobiography terminates. The Utah State Historical Society in association with the University of Utah Press is privileged to be able to publish this diary. The Society gives recognition to the excellent cooperation and efforts of many organizations and individuals who have made this publication possible but are too numerous to name. To these persons the Society extends its sincerest appreciation.

Everett L. Cooley
Utah State Historical Society
Salt Lake City, Utah

ON THE MORMON FRONTIER

Introduction

As the diary of Samuel Pepys (1633-1703) mirrored the life of London in the late 1660's—the great fire, the pestilence, the shifts of power, the coronation ceremonies—so the diary of Hosea Stout illuminates the history of the Mormons. Beginning in Nauvoo in the fall of 1844, the diary continues with unbroken sequence for seventeen years, the account of Mormon activities as seen by a loyal member who, as chief of police and ranking officer in the military organization, is close to the policy-making and executive groups. In his autobiography, Hosea Stout graphically portrays his early years until his life's story unfolds in his diary.

Hosea Stout was born September 18, 1810, in Mercer County, then the backwoods of Kentucky. His parents, Joseph Stout and Anna Smith, were first cousins, their mothers being sisters. Hosea was the eighth of twelve children, five of whom died young. By 1814 poor health and poverty had forced his parents to place Hosea and his four sisters in a Shaker home, where, with other unfortunate or orphaned children, they were provided with food, clothing, shelter, and education. Here Hosea was kept with the boys and given a rigid schedule of training, entirely removed from all association with his parents or sisters.

After nearly four years of living with the Shakers, Hosea was afraid of his father and so terrified at the thought of going home that he had to be taken by force. He soon adjusted, however, and had a normal home life until his fourteenth year, when his mother died. After that time he supported himself by doing farm work under one master or another, attending school whenever possible, and managing for himself as best he could.

In the face of great difficulty, Hosea did get a fair education for that time and place; at twenty-two he secured a position teaching school on the Ox Bow Prairie in Putnam County, Illinois. From there he was called to join a company of volunteers to fight the Indians, but his military service was limited to one expedition. In 1833 he joined his older sister Anna and her husband, Benjamin Jones, in the lumber business. Mr. Jones, a member of the Mormon Church, tried without success to convert him to that faith. Later that year when Charles C. Rich came to proselyte in the area, Hosea was so impressed that he soon found himself defending the doctrine before his neighbors.

In 1834 he met Joseph Smith, Hyrum Smith, Lyman Wight, and other leading Mormons of Zion's Camp as they passed en route to Jackson County, Missouri, from Kirtland, Ohio. Hosea wrote that "The effect of their preaching was powerful on me . . . and it was all that I could do to refrain from going. Elder Jones and I let them have one yoke of oxen. Elder Charles C. Rich went with them."

Here his autobiography comes to an abrupt end; the notation "to be continued" indicates that the author intended to finish it. A quotation from the sketch done for the Eleventh Seventies Quorum fills in the gap: "He remained in company with Benjamin Jones and Samuel Hadlock until in the fall of 1836. Then he went to Tazewell County . . . where he went into the carpenter business in company with Benjamin Jones until August 1837 when he and Mr. Jones and several more families who had also sold out for the same purpose went to Caldwell County, Missouri, for the purpose of being gathered with and associating with the Latter Day Saints, where he purchased 200 acres of good tilable [sic] land and built him a house and commenced operating a farm. There he became acquainted with and married Surmantha Peck, the daughter of Benjamin and Phebe Peck, on the 7th day of January 1838. On the 25th day of August following, he was baptized into the Church of Jesus Christ of Latter Day Saints by Elder Charles C. Rich."

The Church of Jesus Christ of Latter-day Saints, commonly called the Mormon Church, was organized in western New York on April 6, 1830. The youthful leader, Joseph Smith, maintained that in answer to prayer, God the Father and Jesus Christ His Son appeared in a vision and told him that the true church was no longer upon the earth. If he proved faithful, he might be the instrument through whom it would be restored.

Soon thereafter young Smith was directed to some ancient records which had been buried in the Hill Cumorah near Palmyra, New York, from which he claimed to have translated the Book of Mormon, a history of the Indian tribes in the Americas. Beginning with only six members, the new church grew with amazing rapidity. Soon it was moved to Kirtland, Ohio, where for a time its adherents prospered and built a temple. Then, because of financial difficulties and frictions with their neighbors, the leaders decided to move westward again, this time to Missouri.

The "Saints" settled first in Jackson County. Here they were to claim their "inheritance" as God's favored children; here they were to establish their Zion, build their temple, and be ready for the Second Advent, for they shared the general belief that the Millennium was about to dawn. The Missourians, on the other hand, resented the Mormon's confident, possessive attitude, their religious zeal, even their thrift and industry. Resentment was fanned into violence, and the Mormons were literally driven from Jackson County. Nowhere in their persecutions did they suffer worse indignities—whippings, tar-and-featherings, mass drivings—than they did here, not to mention the plundering and burning of property.

The citizens of adjoining Clay County offered the refugees temporary shelter, but urged them to go elsewhere for permanent homes. The Mormons then moved to sparsely settled Caldwell and Clay counties, where they again set about clearing land. Now in the majority, they resolved to defend themselves and repay in kind.

To this end they organized the Danite Band, with which Hosea Stout and his brother Allen at once became affiliated. Since the very existence of this group has been a matter of some dispute and since his association with it had such a far-reaching effect upon the life of Hosea Stout, we should consider it here briefly.

The actual date of the inception of this organization is not found, but it was sometime near the end of June 1838. Allen Stout wrote of it: ". . . they [Missourians] swore to some lies and some truths which were calculated to encite [sic] the Gentiles against us in so much that mobs began to rise and commit depredations till we were forced to resort to arms in order to save ourselves and our property. The Church organized under captains of Tens, Fifties, One Hundreds and One Thousands. This made the inhabitants mad to see us making ready to defend ourselves. They called our organization THE DANITE BAND. I belonged to the 3rd Fifty led by Reynolds Cahoon."

July 4, 1838, was the occasion for an elaborate celebration at Far West. Sidney Rigdon, the orator of the day, made an eloquent speech in which he recounted the Mormons' past troubles and announced that, while they would not be aggressors, they would defend their rights with their lives, and if attacked would resist their enemies with gun and sword. The first violence broke out on election day, August 6, at Gallatin, when a crowd of Missourians tried to keep the Mormons from voting. The result was a free-for-all fight in which clubs and knives were wielded and men on both sides were injured.

By mid-August Oliver B. Huntington wrote that "Every day, almost, brought fresh news of some new outrage and outbreak on one side, and the next would be a signal revenge or victory on the other." He justified the retaliation of the Danite Band: "Remember that they [the Missourians] were the aggressors, and commenced upon our innocent and unoffending brethren, burned their houses, drove off their cattle, plundered their property . . . . So we thought it was no more than right to pay them in their own coin, which we done the best we knew how, and be sure we knew how as well as they . . . ."

Conditions reached a climax when word came to Far West that three Mormons had been taken captive and were to be executed at sunrise. This was on October 25. A posse was at once assigned to go to their assistance. David A. Pattén, their "Captain Fear-naught," was in command, with Charles C. Rich over one contingent, and under him Hosea Stout. The encounter is known as the Battle of Crooked River, in which three Mormons were killed (one being their leader) and several Missourians killed or wounded.

Immediately upon word of this battle, Governor Lilburn W. Boggs issued his famous order that "the Mormons must be exterminated or driven from the state." Three days later an armed band, taking license from this, attacked a small Mormon village at Haun's Mill and massacred seventeen men and two young boys. Joseph Smith then decided that he and other leaders should surrender rather than defend Far West by force of arms.

October 31, 1838, really marked the end of the Danite Band. All were ordered to bring whatever loot they had taken to a central place where it could not be identified with any specific person. Joseph Smith and several of the leaders surrendered and were confined in Liberty Jail, and those who had participated in the Battle of Crooked River fled into the unsettled stretches of Iowa to the north. All other Mormons were forced to give up their arms and property holdings except what they could load into their wagons, and to leave the state. By this time winter was upon them, and since many of the people had no means by which they could move, more than two hundred of the "better-to-do" Saints signed a pledge that they would pool their resources and unite to be sure that all who wished to leave might do so. They withdrew back across the Mississippi River to build their new homes at Commerce, Illinois, which they renamed Nauvoo.

In the minds of the Missourians, the twenty-eight men who fled north were the Danites, and their absence removed the stigma from other members. Some of the Danite leaders had turned state's evidence; others had scattered. Charles C. Rich and Hosea Stout were among those who fled, and for three months were absent from their wives. Surmantha Stout, never strong, was so weakened by malnutrition and exposure in her wanderings that she died on November 29, 1839, and was buried in Lee County, Iowa.

Hosea now moved to Nauvoo, where on March 8, 1840, he was appointed clerk of the High Council, or policy-making body of the church. On May 16 he was made a second lieutenant in the Mormon army, the Nauvoo Legion. On November 29, 1840, he married Louisa Taylor, daughter of William and Elizabeth Taylor, and they built a home in Nauvoo.

The story of the building of Nauvoo is a dramatic one. Mormons from all parts of the immediate area and from the East, and converts from the British Isles and other European nations flocked there in such numbers that in a period less than six years a village of a few families had become a city of 20,000 inhabitants. Homes, large and small, were built; public buildings included the Masonic Hall which was dedicated on April 5, 1844, the Seventies Hall completed in 1845, the Nauvoo House, and an arsenal. Most important, the massive stone Nauvoo Temple was almost up to the square. During all this time, Hosea was an active public worker. When on December 29, 1843, forty men were selected to act as police in Nauvoo, his name was third on the list. By the time his diary opens, he had been advanced to the position of chief of police.

In the meantime two changes had been introduced into the Mormon Church which were destined to affect profoundly the lives and fortunes of all its members. The first of these was the doctrine of "Celestial Marriage," or plurality of wives. Although Joseph Smith had discussed this principle earlier with a few intimate associates, it had never been presented as doctrine, and all intimations that he had taken extra wives were strongly denied.

On April 5, 1841, Joseph Smith took his first admitted plural wife, Louisa Beaman, the ceremony being performed by Joseph Bates Noble. Before the end of 1842, with the cooperation of a few confidants, he had persuaded several other girls to marry him. The principle was written as a revelation on July 12, 1843, and soon thereafter was read to a gathering of the Twelve Apostles. Of their number, three opposed it openly. Others had already been initiated and had taken at least one extra wife.

It was inevitable that word of the practice should leak out and that opposition to it should grow. By June 7, 1844, sentiment had reached the point where a group of dissident members published a paper, the *Expositor*, declaring that Joseph Smith was living in polygamy and accusing him of sin and deceit. The city council of Nauvoo promptly declared this paper to be a nuisance and ordered it destroyed. This action resulted in the arrest and imprisonment of several authorities of the Mormon Church and culminated in the murder of Joseph and Hyrum Smith at Carthage Jail.

Those of the faithful who had accepted the "principle" continued to preach and practice it in secret. In this diary the reference to "eternal exaltation" and the discussion of "spiritual matters" refer to Stout's indoctrination by John D. Lee, Charles C. Rich, and others. So great was the secrecy that Hosea did not record his marriages in his diary but referred to them as social gatherings at which Amasa Lyman was present to perform the ceremony, and John D. Lee and other friends stood as witnesses. His nights spent with his wife, Miranda Bennett, were entered in the record as "on patrol guard with Brother Allen Weeks." Weeks was married to two of Miranda's sisters.

The second innovation grew out of the belief, then current among many sects, in the immediacy of the Millennium, or the Second Advent of Jesus Christ. The Mormons believed that they were to establish the Kingdom of God upon the earth— an actual, physical kingdom with a temple to which He might come. To implement this, the Council of Fifty was organized. Though the initial revelation on the subject was received on April 7, 1842, the organization was not completed with its full membership until March 4, 1844. This also was a secret organization, the activities of which have found little place in Mormon history in spite of the fact that it was probably the most important group in the whole organization.

The men set apart to establish the Kingdom were "practical men of the earth" trained in useful crafts of all kinds, and men so dedicated that they would place their responsibility to the church ahead of their own personal welfare. Designated by John D. Lee as the YTFIF, or *fifty* spelled backwards, this group decided upon general policy, determined to complete the Nauvoo Temple, planned and executed the general evacuation of Nauvoo, and carried their authority to the colonization of the West. Each new settlement was spearheaded by members of the Council of Fifty. Although Hosea Stout was not a member until 1871, he was on occasion called in to report to that body.

Men like George Miller, Alpheus Cutler, Reynolds Cahoon, John Scott, James Emmett, and others who had been called by their Prophet Joseph Smith and made members of the Council of Fifty, found it sometimes difficult to give unquestioning obedience to Brigham Young. As a result, some of them left the church. Others still fired by the spark they had received from their earlier leader remained loyal and never refused to answer any call or to make any sacrifice necessary for the good of the church.

The actual power of the Council of Fifty can only be appreciated by noting that these men held the key offices in both church and civil government where Mormons were in control.[1]

Joseph and Hyrum Smith were assassinated at Carthage Jail on June 27, 1844, leaving the church without an official head. Sidney Rigdon, first counselor to Joseph Smith, and Brigham Young, president of the Twelve Apostles, were rivals for leadership of the church. Each presented his claim before a general conference of the members, on August 8, 1844. Many diarists recorded that "the mantle of Joseph fell upon Brigham." At any rate, he was sustained by an overwhelming majority in his capacity as president of the Council of Twelve Apostles.

Hosea Stout's affiliation with the Nauvoo Legion and its role in Mormon history were so important that it seems appropriate to give a brief background of that organization:

The Nauvoo Legion was an independent body of the Illinois State Militia, authorized by special acts passed by the Illinois Legislature. The original act approved December 16, 1840, and effective the first Monday in February 1841, provided that the Nauvoo City Council might organize the inhabitants of the city, subject to military duty under the laws of the state. The officers of the Legion were commissioned by the governor. The members were required to perform the same amount of military duty as the regular state militia and were placed at the disposal of the mayor of the city and the governor of the state in executing the laws. There were only six companies when first organized; but in September of 1841, the ranks had increased to 1,490 men; and at the time of Joseph Smith's death in 1844, the Legion numbered about 5,000 men.

On February 8, 1841, the city council of Nauvoo activated the Legion in a remarkable document which varied widely from existing military practice. Signed by John C. Bennett, mayor, and James Sloan, recorder, it gave new powers to the "Court Martial," and in the second section provided that "The Legion shall be and is hereby divided into two cohorts; the horse troops to constitute the second cohort." The name "cohort," actually one of the ten sub-elements of a legion in the army of ancient Rome, was at that time and still remains unknown in the American military system.

In this first organization Hosea Stout was a captain in the second cohort, but had risen in rank until at the opening of his diary he was a colonel.[2]

The Stout diary opens on October 4, 1844, as the tensions between Mormons and the "mobocrats," as Mormons called their enemies, were mounting. As chief of police, as well as an officer in the Legion, Hosea was responsible for the personal safety of the leaders and the general welfare of the members.

Hosea Stout was thirty-four years of age, the father of two living sons: William Hosea born April 16, 1843, and Hyrum B., born July 4, 1844. His first

1. See Klaus Hansen, "The Kingdom of God," (M.A. Thesis, Brigham Young University, 1958); also Robert G. Cleland and Juanita Brooks, eds., *A Mormon Chronicle: The Diaries of John D. Lee, 1848-1876* (2 vols., San Marino, 1955), I.

2. For a complete and scholarly account of the Nauvoo Legion see Hamilton Gardner, "Utah Territorial Militia" (MS, Utah State Historical Society).

child, Lydia Sarah, had died on November 13, 1842, at the age of eleven months. Members of the family often mentioned in the diaries were his younger brother, Allen Joseph; his older sister, Anna; and her husband, Benjamin Jones. The mother of his first wife (Surmantha Peck), Phoebe Crosby Peck Knight, and her second husband, Joseph Knight, were also referred to often, as were the family of his second wife (Louisa Taylor): Allen, Joseph, and Pleasant Green, her brothers; William, her father; as well as her sister, Julia, wife of Isaac Allred.

The diary of Hosea Stout has been divided into two volumes. Volume I records conflicts in Nauvoo that culminated in the Mormon exodus from that city, their crossing of the Mississippi River, their muddy trek to Winter Quarters, their two winters spent in that temporary city, and their long journey across the Plains to Utah ending with Stout's arrival in the Valley of the Great Salt Lake, in 1848.

Volume II continues with an interesting combination of private and public affairs. The author, a member of the legislature, gives details of laws under consideration whether passed or rejected, of court cases, of missionary undertakings, of the "Mormon War," of the emigration problems, and of the policies under the theocracy as established by Brigham Young.

The diary ends abruptly just before Hosea is called to the Cotton Mission of southern Utah in the fall of 1861. After that date only sketchy notations for the year 1869 remain. The intervening eight years and the remaining nineteen years of his life are sketched briefly from other sources.

Every attempt has been made to reproduce this diary exactly as it is with no change of construction, spelling, or punctuation. Hosea wrote for the most part in a clear, legible hand, but sometimes in the midst of daily pressures, he misspelled a word or left a letter off the end. These volumes bring to the reader the original as nearly as it is possible for the printed word to reproduce the written one.

Juanita Brooks
St. George, Utah

PART I

October 4, 1844 to May 14, 1845

OCTOBER 4, 1844 TO MAY 14, 1845

Part I

This part of the diary covers the period from October 4, 1844, to May 14, 1845, inclusive, while momentous events were taking place within the Mormon community. On June 27, 1844, the Mormon Prophet, Joseph Smith, had been martyred at Carthage, Illinois; on August 8 following, Brigham Young had been sustained by the people as their leader. Hosea Stout was chief of police in Nauvoo and a colonel in the Nauvoo Legion. His account shows the mounting tensions between the Mormons and their neighbors.

October 4, 1844 Friday. I was ordained an Elder in the Quorum of Seventies[1] on the night of the fourth day of October, 1844, under the hands of Benjamin L. Clapp, Samuel Brown and Henry Jacobs, Presidents in the quorum of Seventies.

Oct 5th. Attended the Court of Inquiry and assessment of fines, which was held at the Seventies Hall for the 5th Regt, 2nd Cohort Nauvoo Legion, and in the evening met with the Police.

Oct 6th, 7th & 8th. attended the General Conference on the 8th the Eleventh Quorum of Seventies were organized at the Conference and I was appointed one of the Presidents of said Quorum upon the nomination of President Brigham

---

1. The Quorum of the Seventy of the Mormon Church had its foundation in the Bible. See Numbers 11:16-17; Luke 9:3; also Luke 10:1-8.

Each quorum which was organized in the Mormon Church consisted of seventy members, of whom seven were designated as presidents, one being senior president. Hosea Stout belonged to the Eleventh Quorum in Nauvoo with Jesse P. Harmon, Hosea Stout, Waldo D. Littlefield, Alvin Horr, Jonathan Browning, Alfred Brown, and William L. Cutler, presidents.

Presiding over the Quorums of the Seventy of the Mormon Church at the time of the October conference of 1844 were Joseph Young, Levi W. Hancock, Daniel S. Miles, Jedediah M. Grant, Zera Pulsipher, and Henry Herriman. Prior to this conference, James Foster was one of the seven presidents but "was dropped and cut off by the council of the Seventies, and the following spring (1845) Albert P. Rockwood was called to fill the vacancy, caused by his removal." Andrew Jenson, ed., [Church of Jesus Christ of Latter-day Saints], *Historical Record*, V (July, 1886), 81-83.

In the early organization of the Mormon Church, the Quorums of Seventy were very active. By January of 1846, thirty-three such quorums had been organized. Andrew Jenson, *Church Chronology, A Record of Important Events Pertaining to The Church of Jesus Christ of Latter-day Saints* (Salt Lake City, 1899), 28.

Young[2] and was ordained to that office under the hands of Presidents Brigham Young and Amasa Lyman.[3]

Oct 9the. At home untill in the evening then went to the meeting of the Police and at dark went to a publick Concert of vocal and instrumental music at the Masonic Hall,[4] was agreeable entertained untill about 9 at night and then stood guard with Br. J. D. Lee[5] untill 12 o'clock P.M.

Oct 10the. At home untill evening and then went to the meeting of the Police and at dark met with the Quorum of High Priests at the request of President Brigham Young who taught on the powers and authority of the High Priests and Seventies, in relation to their jurisdiction over each other and the proper order of sending the Gospel to the nations, &c, and about half past 10 came home.

Oct 11th. At home, was unwell at 5 o'clock met with the police, at dark went on guard and at 12 at night came home.

Oct 12. at home, at 5 o'clock met with the police, at dark met with the 11th Quorum of Seventies at the Seventies Hall the Third and Sixth Quorums was also there.

---

2. Brigham Young, at this time forty-three years old, was acting-president of the Mormon Church. Born in Windham County, Vermont, June 1, 1801, he grew up with little formal education, but was trained in carpentry. Baptized in April 1832, he soon became an important figure in the new church. In 1835 he was made an apostle and before 1844 had been advanced to president of that quorum.

After the death of Joseph Smith, both Young and Sidney Rigdon claimed the right of leadership, and at a general meeting of the membership held August 8, 1844, Brigham Young was sustained by an overwhelming majority. He assumed leadership but was not formally sustained as president of the church until December 27, 1847, when he was presented to the congregation at Kanesville, Iowa, having previously been accepted by the Council of the Twelve Apostles. He served until his death on August 29, 1877. Although a number of books have been written on Brigham Young, no definitive biography has yet appeared.

3. Amasa Mason Lyman, born March 30, 1813, in Grafton, New Hampshire, joined the Mormons in 1832. In 1838 he was a member of the military organization at Far West. In 1842 Lyman was made an apostle and in 1844 a member of the Council of Fifty. Among the first to accept "Celestial Marriage" he performed many such marriage ceremonies secretly in Nauvoo.

Lyman came to Utah in 1847, helped to establish San Bernardino in California, and continued to be active in the church until 1870, when he was excommunicated for teaching false doctrine. He died February 4, 1877. See Andrew Jenson, *Latter-day Saint Biographical Encyclopedia* (4 vols., Salt Lake City, 1901-1936), III, 96.

4. Quite a number of prominent Mormons had become Masons before Nauvoo was established, among them Hyrum Smith, Heber C. Kimball, Newel K. Whitney, and John C. Bennett. On October 15, 1841, a dispensation was issued to George Miller as worshipful master, John D. Parker as senior warden, and Lucius A. Scovil as junior warden to form a lodge in Nauvoo. On March 15, 1842, the Nauvoo Lodge of Freemasons was established. Subsequently two additional lodges, Nye and Helm, were established in Nauvoo. Also, dispensations were issued for the Mormons to establish lodges in Montrose and Keokuk, Iowa, which were chartered respectively as the Rising Sun Lodge and the Eagle Lodge.

The Masonic Temple at Nauvoo, said to be the finest in the area, was dedicated April 5, 1844, with Erastus Snow giving the dedicatory speech. The building was used for many public meetings. See Everett R. Turnbull, *The Rise and Progress of Freemasonry in Illinois, 1783-1952* . . . ([Harrisburg], 1952), 129-30; also E. Cecil McGavin, *Mormonism and Masonry* (Salt Lake City, 1956), 88-121.

5. John D. Lee was born in Kaskaskia, Illinois, September 12, 1812, and joined the Mormons in 1838. During the first years of this record, he and Hosea Stout were closely associated. In 1844 Lee became a secretary for Brigham Young; after the exodus from Nauvoo he also kept the records, among them the minutes of the Council of Fifty. In 1850 he was called to help colonize southern Utah.

On March 23, 1877, Lee was executed at Mountain Meadows for his part in the massacre which occurred there on September 11, 1857. See Robert G. Cleland and Juanita Brooks, eds., *A Mormon Chronicle: The Diaries of John D. Lee, 1848-1876* (2 vols., San Marino, 1955); also Juanita Brooks, *John Doyle Lee, Zealot—Pioneer Builder—Scapegoat* (Glendale, 1961).

President Brigham Young attended and taught on the duties of the Seventies and High Priests as on the evening of the 10th inst. in the High Priests Quorum.

Oct 13. Sunday at home all day my wife was very sick.

Oct 14th & 15th. at home till 5 o'clock then met with the police, came home at dark.

Oct 16th. In the morning went to see a lot of 100 muskets, at the request of Genl Rich,[6] which were at Col Turley's,[7] which had just been purchased at New Orleans for the Nauvoo Legion, by Br Turley then came home and 5 went to the police and came home at dark.

Oct 17. Worked for Allen Tayler, at 5 met police and came home an hour after dark.

Oct 18. at home. was unwell with a cold. Gen Dunham[8] came to get a list of the names of some men who were needed at the Carthage Court   there was a melting snow falling to day very fast, which covered the ground about six or seven inches deep.

Oct 19. At home till in the evening, went to the meeting of the Seventies. no buisness done.

Oct 20 Sunday. Went to the meeting of the Seventies at their Hall.   done buisness at 12 adjourned till 2 and met again and proceeded to buisness again, in the mien time there was a request sent in from Gen Rich for some preperations to be made for the brethren who had to go to Carthage to court in the morning, whereupon there was thirty teams raised to go and carry the brethren there and all were to await the order of the Court. This was in the case against the brethren who had been bound over to the Court for riot for executing the orders of the Mayor to destroy the "Nauvoo Expositor" which had been declared a nuisance by the City Council After the meeting I had orders from Genl Rich to raise 100 minute men who were held in readiness to act as occasion required and who were wanted in the morning to go to Court. Which order I executed and came home about ten at night.

Oct 21. Earley in the morning I went to the Seventies Hall as agreed the evening before to assist in sending to Carthage according to the arraingements the day before came home in the fore noon & settled with Jesse D. Hunter[9] about noon met with the police as usual and came home about 9 at night.

---

6. Charles Coulson Rich, who had a profound effect upon the life of Hosea Stout, was born August 21, 1809, in Campbell County, Kentucky. He joined the Mormon Church in 1832 and became an apostle in 1849. In 1844 he became one of the Council of Fifty and in that capacity helped to colonize both San Bernardino, California, and Bear Lake Valley, Utah-Idaho. He died October 24, 1880, in Paris, Idaho. See John Henry Evans, *Charles Coulson Rich: Pioneer Builder of the West* (New York, 1936).

7. Theodore Turley, a clockmaker and gunsmith by trade, had been ordered to help secure guns for the Mormons after they had been disarmed in June previous. Born April 10, 1800, Turley was among the first converts to Mormonism and had followed their fortunes from place to place. He built the first house in Nauvoo and became a lieutenant colonel in the Nauvoo Legion. He died at Beaver, Utah, August 22, 1872.

8. Jonathan Dunham, known as "Black Hawk" among his fellows at Far West, had been a captain of a Danite group called the "Fur Company." In Nauvoo he was named "High Policeman" over the forty men who were selected on December 29, 1843. On June 8, 1844, he was made acting-major general of the Nauvoo Legion, with Stephen Markham and Hosea Stout as acting-brigadier generals over the first and second cohorts, respectively. Dunham was called from Nauvoo to go on a mission to the Indians, where he died July 28, 1845.

9. Jesse D. Hunter had been a close associate of Hosea Stout during the earlier troubles in Missouri and appears often in this record until 1846. At that time he enlisted in the Mormon Battalion and, accompanied by his wife, made his way to San Diego. Here his wife died in childbirth, but the child survived. Hunter settled in San Bernardino where he lived the remainder of his life.

Oct 22 T. Went down in town stoped Allen Stout's who came home with me came by B. Jones, and brought home some corn & at 5 met the police as usual came home about 9 in the evening.

Oct. 23 W. In the morning went to see Lee [*sic*] Genl Rich to learn the news from Carthage. There was none received. Came home and crouted away my cabbage met the police as usual (while there I understood there was an appointment out for the Eagles to meet that night [crossed out in original]) came home after dark

Oct 24 T. In the morning heard from Carthage and went to see Genl Rich, who sent me to Brother Coolidges[10] to a Council of the officers of the Legion and others in relation to affairs at Carthage, the brethren who had gone there as before related having came home the evening before, heard a letter read from the Governor authorizing the Lieutenant General of the Legion to call out the Legion to protect the Court at Carthage and suppress all mobs which might rise in Hancock County, if necessary.

At that time the mob was geathering at Carthage very fast with the express purpose of depriving the brethren from having the benefits of a fair trial and also to deprive the grand jury from hearing those who had assassinated Brothers Joseph and Hyrum Smith; for they had sworn that they would murder any one who dared to appear against them and had sought to take the life of one man, named Daniels,[11] who was present at the time the murder was committed and he narrowly escaped with his life to Nauvoo where he now is.

---

10. Joseph W. Coolidge was at this time acting as administrator of Joseph Smith's estate. A member of the Council of Fifty and a sergeant major in the Nauvoo Legion, he had participated in the destruction of the *Nauvoo Expositor* press. Coolidge was a carpenter by trade, his specialty being the making of doors and window sashes. His name is not found among those who came to Utah.

11. William M. Daniels was at Carthage with the crowd outside the jail when Joseph Smith was killed. On July 4, 1844, he made an affidavit which concluded: "That your said affiant saw Joseph Smith leap from the window of the jail, and that one of the company picked him up and placed him against the well curb and several shot him, Col. Williams exclaiming, 'Shoot him!' and further your affiant saith not." *The Latter-day Saints' Millennial Star,* XXIV (Liverpool, 1862), 695.

Daniels' name appears as author of a pamphlet, *Correct Account of the Murder of Generals Joseph and Hyrum Smith at Carthage,* . . . published by John Taylor at Nauvoo in 1845. On page 18 of the account it says that when one of the assassins would have severed the prophet's head from his body, a light, sudden and intense, burst from the heavens. "This light, in its appearance and potency, baffles all powers of description. The arm of the ruffian . . . fell powerless; the muskets of the four, who fired, fell to the ground, and they all stood like marble statues, not having the power to move a single limb of their bodies." This paragraph is quoted almost verbatim in *The Martyrs* by Lyman O. Littlefield (Salt Lake City, 1882), 81.

When Daniels was questioned in court, he denied having written the pamphlet; he said he had never seen it, in fact, but admitted having talked to Lyman Littlefield about the incident. Without being specific, Daniels indicated that he did not say all that was printed. Governor Thomas Ford said that the story was not supported by other witnesses. He totally discredited Daniels whole testimony. Thomas Ford, *A History of Illinois* . . . (Chicago, 1854), 368.

For a summary of the incident and a denial of the story of the light, see B. H. Roberts, *A Comprehensive History of The Church of Jesus Christ of Latter-day Saints* (6 vols., Salt Lake City, 1930), II, 332-34. Roberts says: "This William M. Daniels after the tragedy at Carthage joined the Church, but soon after the trial dropped out of sight . . . our church writings . . . are singularly silent respecting Daniels; also as to Brackenbury, about whom less is known."

After William Smith was excommunicated from the church, he wrote a long letter to the *Sangamo Journal* (Springfield, Illinois), under date of September 24, 1846, which was printed in the issue of November 5 following. In the letter Smith accused the church leaders of having ordered several men to be put out of the way, among them this man Daniels: "He [Daniels] returned to Nauvoo after the court was over; some of Brigham's guard was heard to say that it was best to save Daniel's soul while he was in the faith . . . [and put him] where he can tell no lies, or recall his former statement. . . ."

It was decided by the Council that the Legion be put in immediate readiness for actual service and I was ordered to call out my Regiment forthwith which I did and at 4 o'clock P.M. at the Stand reviewed it and examined the arms and equipments and made returns of the situation it was in to Gen Rich, at dark, from thence I went in company with Gen Rich to see Gen Miller,[12] where we held another council in relation to affairs at Carthage. We then went to Brother Cooledge's and Taylor's[13] and some other places and learned how matters was going at Carthage. We then came back to General Miller's when I was concluded to send with the deputy Sheriff to court at his request, a Posse of 30 men to guard the witnesses above referred to, against the violence of the mob. It was then concluded that I should procure 5 waggons to convey the 30 men to Carthage who were to meet at Brother T. Turley's in the morning at sunrise, I then went in company with Brother Cyrus Daniels and engaged the waggons as was decided upon and came home about 11 o'clock at night.

October 25th. I went in the morning to Turley's to assist in sending the 30 men to Carthage, as before decided. When I got there I learned that they had received additional inteligence from Carthage upon which they had concluded to send a Posse of only [4] men who were now gone. I then came home and in the evening met with the Police and at dark went to hear John A. Forgess preach, he was one of those who had left the Church in the dissension which Sidney Rigdon[14] had occasioned.

He endeavored to show that Joseph Smith was a fallen prophet and that Sidney was a prophet in his place, in his opening remarks he said that any one who wished to make any remarks after he was done should have the oppertunity when Brother Earsley followed & showed that according Sidneys own teaching Joseph was not fallen and finaly confounded him in all his points of doctrine against Br. Joseph and the Twelve and sustained the present organization of the Church under the administration of the Leaders. after meeting I came home about 12 at night.

Oct 26th S. In the morning went to mill home at Noon met the police as usual, at dark went to hear a debate between the said Forgess and Brother Earsley, at which Forgess was again Beaten.

---

12. At this time George Miller was the general in command of the mounted cohort of the Nauvoo Legion. Born November 25, 1794, in Orange County, Virginia, Miller met Joseph Smith in 1839 and was instantly converted. He came to Nauvoo where he was one of the most trusted and able of the prophet's friends. After the death of Edward Partridge on January 15, 1841, Miller was made presiding bishop of the church, and in 1844 he and Newel K. Whitney were named trustees-in-trust for all the property of the church.

Miller tells in some detail of his break with Brigham Young and his final withdrawal from the church. He joined Lyman Wight in Texas, where he remained only a short time, then returned to visit briefly with James J. Strang in Wisconsin. He died in 1856 as he was en route to California. For a part of Miller's diaries and some letters see H. W. Mills, "De Tal Palo Tal Astilla [A Chip Off the Old Block]," *Annual Publications Historical Society of Southern California,* X (1917), Part III, 86-157.

13. John Taylor served as editor of many L.D.S. publications both in America and England. Born at Milnthorpe, Westmorland, England, November 1, 1808, Taylor came to Canada, where he was converted to Mormonism in 1836. From that time he was an effective proselyter and defender of the faith. At the death of Brigham Young in 1877, Taylor became president of the Mormon Church. See Brigham Henry Roberts, *The Life of John Taylor, Third President of the Church of Jesus Christ of Latter-day Saints* (Salt Lake City, 1892).

14. Sidney Rigdon, born in Pennsylvania, February 19, 1893, was converted to Mormonism in 1830. During the early years of the church he was most helpful. In 1833 he became the first counselor in the presidency. In 1842 a coldness developed between him and Joseph Smith because of polygamy, but an understanding was reached not long before the prophet's death. Disappointed that the congregation rejected his claim to leadership, Rigdon established a church of his own. See Dale L. Morgan, "Bibliography of the Church of Jesus Christ of Latter-day Saints — Strangites," *Western Humanities Review,* V (Winter, 1950-1951), 43.

Oct 27. Sunday. At ten A.M. went to a meeting of the Eagles at the Masonic Hall, from thence to the meeting at the Stand and at 2 in the evening met with the meeting of the Seventies it was here arrainged the each Quorum should meet one night in succession at the Seventies Hall that each Quorum might have an opportunity to transact their own buisness, came home at dark.

Oct 28th M. At home till evening met police and came home at dark.

Oct 29 T. In the forenoon went with my wife to the store and at 2 in the evening met with the eagles at the Masonic Hall and came home at dark.

Oct 30 W. In the morning went to see President Brigham Young on the subject of G.G.E.D.,[15] which he disapproved. Wrote in the after met the police as usual and at dark met with the E made a speech and after some remarks by others it was concluded not to have any more meetings at present came home about ten at night.

October 31 T. Worked at home till in the evening met the police as usual came home about 7 o'clock at night.

Nov 1 F. Worked the roads, in the evening met the police at dark went on guard with J. D. Lee, came home at 12 at night.

Nov 2 S. Worked the roads (met the police as usual [crossed out]) at home in the afternoon.

Nov 3 Sunday. At home till in the evening then went to the meeting of the Seventies after which I went on guard at H. C. Kimball's[16] with Br. Lee., Came home at 12.

Nov 4 M. Today was the Presidential election and the brethren all concluded to vote for Polk and Dallas for President and Vice President of the United States however, it was with peculiar feelings that I went to the polls. I thought of the man whom we had elected as the man of our choice for president of the United States: our Beloved Prophet Joseph Smith whose voice seemed yet to sound in the air, teaching this nation the way they might be saved and the means to pursue to avoid a disunion and overthrow of our Government. I well remembered the never to be forgotten 27 of June, 1844 when fell a sacrifice to the violence of a mob while the constituted authorities of this State winked at their deeds after the honors of the govornor and faith of the State had been pledged for his protection and his blood is now to be seen on the floor of the jail at Carthage where it cries to God for vengeance on this Nation who rejoice at his fall.

It is no wonder then that it was with little confidence that I took part in the election for I could but vote for those, who, if they had not approved of the murder

---

15. The letters "G.G.E.D." seem to refer to the "Eagles." From the reference on October 23, 27, and 29, the group that met was of a secret nature. In this paragraph he designates it as the "E." A parallel entry in the "Journal History" (Church of Jesus Christ of Latter-day Saints Historian's Library, Salt Lake City), October 30, 1844, ties in the discontinuance of the meetings with the disapproval of Brigham Young.

16. Heber Chase Kimball, one of the most colorful characters of Mormondom, was born June 14, 1801, at Sheldon, Vermont. He was a blacksmith and potter by trade and was also an excellent proselyter for his church, baptizing thousands in England. Though he accepted plural marriage with reluctance, he became the most married man in the church. On December 5, 1847, when Brigham Young was formally named as president of the Mormon Church, Kimball was made his first counselor, which position he held for the remainder of his life. He died in June 1868. See Orson F. Whitney, *Life of Heber C. Kimball, an Apostle: Father and Founder of the British Mission* (Salt Lake City, 1888).

of our own candidate had remained silent and each party was willing to truckle to us for our votes and say all is well it was a dreadful alternative truly the corruption of this nation is great. After the election I met the police and we had a reorganization and came home about dark.

November 5th T. Went to mill in the morning, at home till in the evening. met the Police as usual, Stood guard at Br Brigham Youngs, came home at 2 in the morning.

Nov 6th W. At home till evening met the police as usual came home after dark.

Nov 7th T. Went round through the City on patroll duty with other police men and came home about 3 P.M. — very sick with a head ache went to bed and at dark got up and went to the meeting of the Eleventh Quorum of Seventies at the Hall. taught on the necessity of looking up and keeping our genealogy and organizing the Quorum more perfectly and was followed by several other brethren on the same subject adjourned about ½ past 9 and patroled with other policemen till 2 and then stood guard at Br Brigham's till day and came home about sun rise.

Nov 8th F. At home met with the Police as usual came home a little after dark.

Nov 9th S. In the morning went to the Mansion House to pay taxes from thence went to the City Council at 10 to lay the case of the police before them, from thence met the police as usual, came home at dark, then went on guard at Br. Brigham's was relieved at 12 then patrolled till day with other policemen and then came home.

Nov 10th. Sunday. At home in the evening met the police as usual, and at dark went to the meeting of the seventies at the Hall Br George A. Smith[17] taught came home at about 10.

Nov 11th M. At 9 met with a General Council at the Masonic Hall, composed of the Twelve, the High Council of the Church, Trustee in Trust of the Church, Mayor of the City[18] the police and some of the officers of the Legion, to take into consideration the general welfare of the City and regulate the Police &c when it was agreed that the Trustees in Trust for the Church should pay the police all that was due them from the City and redeem or buy up all the Treasurer's orders which had been issued to pay the police heretofore, also, that there be 400 policemen raised in the City and that it be guarded in future by said police force, at 12 adjourned one hour and met again and continued in Council till dark I then went home not being very well.

---

17. George Albert Smith, cousin of Joseph Smith, was born June 26, 1817, in New York. He early became active in the Mormon Church, being made an apostle at the age of twenty-two. In 1844 he became a member of the Council of Fifty.

In 1850 George A. Smith was put in charge of the colonization of the southern part of Utah, and thus became known as "The Father of the Southern Mission." He succeeded Heber C. Kimball as first counselor to Brigham Young, which position he held until his death in 1875.

18. The mayor of Nauvoo at this time was Daniel Spencer, who had been appointed by the city council to fill the unexpired term of Joseph Smith. Born at West Stockbridge, Massachusetts, July 20, 1794, he was a man of wealth before he joined the Mormons. Soon after his arrival in Nauvoo, he was made a member of the High Council. See Edward Tullidge, *History of Salt Lake City* (Salt Lake City, 1886), 166-70.

At the time of the journal entry the Nauvoo Stake was presided over by John Smith with Charles C. Rich as his only counselor. The High Council consisted of Samuel Bent; James Allred; Lewis Dunbar Wilson; George W. Harris; William Huntington, Sr.; Newel Knight; Alpheus Cutler; Aaron Johnson; Henry G. Sherwood; Thomas Grover; Ezra T. Benson; and David Fullmer; with Hosea Stout as clerk. The trustees-in-trust were George Miller and Newel K. Whitney.

Nov 12th T. At home til in the evening met police as usual came home one hour after dark

Nov 13th W. Went down in Town in the morning, came home and met police at Col Harmon's at which place the police were to meet in future came home at dark, and then went on guard at Bro Brighams and came home about 2 o'clock A.M.

Nov 14th T. Worked at home till evening met the police as usual, home a little after dark.

Nov 15th F. Was at home till evening, met the police as usual and at dark stood guard Br Brigham Youngs at which place there was a consultation held with Br Young and others about building the Arsenal & carrying on the public work pertaining thereto and the best method to pursue. Came off guard at one, and patrolled till 3 with Br Lee and others came home very sick with the headache.

Nov 16th S. In the morning Dr. Barnhisel came to my house had some talk about the murder of Brother Joseph and Hyrum let him have several numbers of the old Star & Messenger & advocate was still very unwell in the evening met the police came home at dark, and went down in Town with Br A. Lytle Came home at 10.

Nov 17th Sunday. At home till in the evening met police as usual came home at 8.

Nov 18th M. At home till evening met the police as usual. patrolled on the bank of the river till one was with T. Rich and others came home about ½ past one.

Nov 19th T. At home, in evening met police as usual, at dark went to a meeting at the Seventies Hall which was met for purpose of making up a school to teach the Sword exercise by a Mr. Stanley[19] and signed one Scholar came home about one hour after dark.

Nov 20 W. At home, wife had a quilting, met police as usual, and went on patroll guard with Harmon, Arnold, Hamilton & others; came home about 12.

Nov 21 T. At home, met police as usual, at dark met with the Eleventh Quorum of Seventies, then stood guard at Br Brighams till 12 and then came home.

Nov 22 F. At home, met police, came home a little after, unwell.

Nov 23 S. At home writing for Col. J. H. Hale,[20] met police came home after dark.

---

19. The *Nauvoo Neighbor* for December 11, 1844, carried an announcement that "Mr. H. Stanley, a gentleman recently from the north, is now in this city giving instruction in the Art of Fencing to such as wish. His skill and moderate terms, render the opportunity highly favorable to such as wish to manoeuvre in the cuts, thrusts, and salutes with grace, precision and dexterity."

20. Jonathan H. Hale was born January 30, 1800. He joined the Mormon Church early; he served as treasurer of the Kirtland Camp which was planned March 10, 1838, by the Seventies in Kirtland as a means to move their quorum and others of the faithful to Missouri to join the prophet and other leaders. The Kirtland Camp started July 5. "It consisted of 515 souls, namely, 249 males and 266 females. They had 27 tents, 59 wagons, 97 horses, 22 oxen, 69 cows and 1 bull." The camp arrived at Adam-ondi-Ahman, Daviess County, on October 4, 1838, "at the time the persecutions were raging against the Saints in Missouri, and about a month later the whole Mormon population . . . were forced, by the mob, to vacate Adam-ondi-Ahman and remove to Far West." Jenson, *Historical Record,* VII (July, 1888), 593, 603.

Oliver B. Huntington wrote of Jonathan Hale as one of the most influential men at Far West "who initiated me into the mystic rites of the Sons of Dan." At Council Bluffs, Iowa, Hale with Newel K. Whitney and Daniel Spencer were assigned to handle the $5,860 which Parley P. Pratt had collected from the Mormon Battalion.

Jonathan Hale died at Council Bluffs, September 4, 1846. Within a week his wife and two daughters also died, leaving three sons and one daughter to go to Utah alone. See Heber Q. Hale, *Bishop Jonathan H. Hale of Nauvoo . . .* (Salt Lake City, 1938).

Nov 24 Sunday. At home, met the police as usual, at dark went to a meeting of the Seventies at the Hall and came home about 9 o'clock.

Nov 25 M. At home, in the evening met the police and at dark went to a meeting of the Presidents of the Seventies at Br Chandler Holbrooks, and was agreeably entertained by Prest Jos Young, after which all the rest of the Presidents told their feelings and testified of their faith and confidence in the present organization of the Church under the Twelve; came home about Nine.

Nov 26 & 27. Was at home till evening, and met police as usual, on the evening of the 27 patroled with Benj Jones.

Nov 28 T. Was at home, wife very sick, met police, at home at dark.

Nov 29 F. At home, met police, patroled with Bro A. Lytle and M. D. Hamilton at home at 10.

Nov 30 S. In the morning went to the fencing school but being very unwell came home again.

Dec 1 Sunday. At home, in the evening met the police, came home about 9 o'clock.

Dec 2 M. At home, in after noon went down in town, met police, at dark met with the Presidents of the Seventies at Br C. Holbrooks, came home about 9.

Dec 3 T. At home, went down in town, came home, met police, gave them some instruction relative to their duty, patroled on the hill with some other policemen.

Dec 4 W. Atended fencing school near the Temple, met police, at dark met the fencing school at Seventies Hall, came home about 9.

Dec 5 T. At home there was an election at my house in Allen J. Stout's company, [of the Nauvoo Legion], after, I went down in town, met police, at dark met with the Nauvoo Lodge. There was an election of officers took place and I was elected Secratary of the Lodge, after which I patrolled on the hill with several policemen, home at 2.

Dec 6 F. At home, met police, at dark met met with the Lodge, was duly installed and took my place as Secratary of the same, came home at 9. there was a wet snow falling this evening which was, in the morning 4½ inches.

Dec 7 S. At home, met police, at dark went to Lodge, came home about 11 o'c.

Dec 8 Sunday. At home, met police came home at 7 o'c.

Dec 9 M. Wrote at Lodge, came home, met police, went to Lodge at dark, came home at 10.

Dec 10 T. Wrote at Lodge home at 3 met police. (met Lodge at dark, came home at [crossed out]) at dark went to trades meeting at Lodge, home at 12 o'clock.

Dec 11 W & 12 T. Wrote at Lodge came home at 3 met police, at dark met with the Lodge, came home about 10 o'clock.

Dec 13 F. At home, met police and Lodge.

Dec 14 S. Went to the City Council there was an ordinance passed by the Council Chartering the "Seventies Library and Institute Association."[21] Came home at 3, met police and Lodge; afterwards patroled on the hill with Hunter, and others.

---

21. The Seventies' Library and Institute Association was established to promote the arts and sciences and to provide reading matter and schooling for the members of the quorum that they might become more effective missionaries.

Dec 15 Sunday. Went to the meeting of the Seventies, home at 3 met police.

Dec 16 M. Wrote at the Lodge home at 3 met police and Lodge as usual.

Dec 17, 18, 19. At home, met police & Lodge.

Dec 20 F. Wrote at the Lodge, met police and attended the Lodge at dark. Home at 10.

Dec 21 S. Worked at home met police and Lodge as usual.

Dec 22 Sunday. Met with the Quorums of Seventies at their Hall. Attend to procuring subscribers for the Seventies Library and Institute Association. Came home about 2 and met the police as usual, then went to Brother Lee's at dark obtained a share in the Seventies hall,[22] home at 9.

Dec 24 T. Went to write at Lodge was unable to write, was with Br Lee, met police at dark attended the meeting of the Stock holders of the Seventies Library and Institute Association, for the purpose of holding an election of the Board of 7 trustees of said Association. G. A. Smith, Amasa Lyman, John D. Lee, Joseph Young,[23] L. W. Hancock,[24] Albert Carrington,[25] and Jas M. Monroe[26] said Board of Trustees, came home at 9.

---

22. The Library and Institute Association was authorized to sell shares to its members at five dollars per share, each man being expected to purchase at least one share. This custom was continued after the Mormons' arrival in the Salt Lake Valley.

23. Joseph Young, an elder brother of Brigham Young, was born April 7, 1797, in Massachusetts. He joined the Mormon Church in 1832, and was a member of Zion's Camp which was organized by the Prophet Joseph Smith in the spring of 1834 in Kirtland, Ohio, to assist the Saints who had been driven out of Jackson County, Missouri, into Clay County. By the time the men had arrived in Missouri, the camp numbered about 200, and the inhabitants of western Missouri were "deeply prejudiced and excited by their arrival." Missouri Governor Daniel Dunklin was unwilling to fulfill his obligations to the exiled Mormons, and the camp was disbanded June 24, 1834. For a full account of Zion's Camp, see Roberts, *Comprehensive History*, I, 358-60, 364, 370. See also, Jenson, *Historical Record*, VII (June, 1888), 577-91.

Young was a survivor of the Haun's Mill massacre in Missouri. In Nauvoo he was made senior president over all of the Seventies in the church, and in honor of his position his fellow members built him a fine home. See John D. Lee, *Mormonism Unveiled: The Life and Confessions of . . . John D. Lee . . .* (St. Louis, 1877), 156.

24. Levi W. Hancock, born April 7, 1803, in Massachusetts, joined the Mormon Church soon after it was organized in 1830. A cabinet-maker by trade, he followed the church from Kirtland through the march of Zion's Camp to Missouri, where he was active in defending his people. He signed both the order for Oliver Cowdery and his associates to leave Far West and the covenant pledging his means to help the poor to evacuate that place.

Hancock became one of the first seven presidents of the Seventies, and in this position was the only one of the presiding authorities to join the Mormon Battalion. He had been the fife major in the Nauvoo Band and was also in Company "E" of the Mormon Battalion, as well as the chaplain for the Mormon group.

Coming to Utah with the first of the Mormon Battalion, Levi Hancock soon afterward moved to Provo. He was the delegate from Utah County to the first legislative assembly. He lived in various towns in southern Utah, and died in Washington, Washington County, Utah, in 1882.

25. Albert Carrington was one of the few college graduates to join the Mormon Church during its early years. He had graduated from Dartmouth College in 1833, when he was twenty years old, and had taught school and studied law in Pennsylvania. He joined the Mormon Church in 1841 and later moved to Nauvoo, arriving there just before the martyrdom. As a member of the Council of Fifty, Carrington shared the responsibilities of the exodus to Great Salt Lake with Brigham Young's pioneer company and returned east with President Young to bring out his own family in 1848.

Though he filled missions and held other responsible positions, most of his life in the church was spent as clerk and assistant to Brigham Young, an office he held for more than twenty years. Albert Carrington served a term in the state penitentiary, along with George Q. Cannon and others, for polygamy. In 1885 he was excommunicated from the church but was reinstated before his death in 1889.

26. James M. Monroe was baptized a member of the Mormon Church on October 3, 1841, and soon thereafter went on a six-month mission. On August 22, 1842, Monroe opened a school

Dec 25 W. Christmas wrote at Lodge met police and Lodge as usual.

Dec 26. At home. in afternoon met with the Seventies at the Dedication of their hall met the police at dark met the eleventh Quorum of Seventies, home at 9 o'clock.

Dec 27 F. At home, in the afternoon met the Seventies at the Dedication as before met the police, at dark met at the 70's Hall with a General Council of the whole Authorities of Nauvoo to take into consideration the affairs of our City as it was before the Legislature and give our representatives[27] instruction. Came home about 11 o'clock.

Dec 28 S. Wrote at the Lodge met police and Lodge as usual.

Dec 29 Sunday. At home met police came home about 11 o'clock P.M.

Dec 30 M. Today was the 5th day of the Dedication of the Seventies Hall and the day that the Tenth and Eleventh Quorums met, myself and wife went we had an agreeable time, was well entertained under the instruction of the Twelve. It was a time long to be remembered. The dedication took 7 days. Two Quorums met each day until all the Quorums were through there was then fifteen Quorums, or about 1000 members belonging to the Seventies all who were heralds of salvation to the nations, to wind up the Law and seal up the Testimony. It was well calculated to awaken our minds to a sense of our duty. Came home about 5 o'clock P.M. and then met the police and Lodge as usual.

Dec 31 T. At home, met police & Lodge as usual.

January 1 1845 Wednesday. today was the beginning of another year & God grant that it may not prove as omnious to to the Saints as the year just gone. I went to the 70's Hall again and about 2 o'clock came home and then met the police and Lodge as usual.

Jan 2 Thursday. Wrote at Lodge came home at 2 met police & Lodge as usual.

Jan 3 F. Went on a visit with my wife to see (her sister at [crossed out]) Isaac Allred's. Came with her home and then met the police and Lodge as usual, came home at 8.

Jan 4th S. At home sick about 2 o'clock George D. Grant came after me and said that Brother J. D. Hunter was taken up on some charge and wanted me he was one of the police I went he was found not to be guilty. I plead his case before A. Johnson Esq which caused some to have feelings at me but it turned out to be an evil

---

in Nauvoo, his first roll showing thirty-seven students. In November he advertised that he would teach reading, writing, and spelling for $2.00 and grammar, arithmetic, geography, and philosophy for $3.00. Following this, his roll includes names of quite a number of adults. Monroe's journal through April and May of 1845 contains many interesting items regarding conditions in Nauvoo. James M. Monroe, "Diary [1841-1845]" (microfilm, Utah State Historical Society; original, Coe collection, Yale University).

That Monroe was held in esteem in Nauvoo is shown by the fact that he was appointed a regent of the University of Nauvoo on December 14, 1844, and a member of the board of trustees of the Seventies' Library and Institute Association on Decmber 25.

27. Representatives from Hancock County in the Illinois Legislature in 1844 were Almon W. Babbitt and Jacob B. Backenstos.

plot laid to injure the credit of the police. At dark Brigham met police at 70 H [Seventies' Hall] gave instruction.

5 Sunday. Went to meeting at the Stand President Brigham Young taught on the necessity of having more order & against the progress of iniquity, and exhorted the brethren to rise up en masse and put down the thieving, bad-houses, swearing disorderly conduct of the boys, gambling, retailing spiritious Liquors, bogus making, and such like abominations which was practiced in our midst by our enemies who, after they could not live among us any longer would go out to the world and publish all these things upon us, He severly rebuked the civil authorities of the City for their want of energy in the discharge of their duty and said that if we did not as a people up root such things from our midst they would up root us and we would have to leave before we had done the things the Lord had commanded us to do, in the evening met the police as usual.

6, 7, 8. Wrote at the Lodge met police & Lodge as usuall on the evening of the 8th met at the Seventies Hall. with the Twelve, High Council and (City [crossed out]) City Officers to hold a caucus to nominate the officers for the next City Council. The Twelve spoke at length on the subject and unanimously declined serving in any capacity in the City Council, because they were anxious to attend to the affairs of the Church and not be brought under the persecting hands of their enemies untill the Temple was finished and we had our endowment. After which on motion of Orson Spencer Esq.[28] the Twelve were appointed a nominating Committee and were to nominate the candidates for office when, after a Short absence they declared the following nominations to wit: Orson Spencer Esq. for Mayor. Daniel Spencer C. C. Rich, N. K. Whitney[29] and G. W. Harris[30] for Aldermen and Phinehas

---

28. Orson Spencer was one of the most scholarly of the members of the early Mormon Church. Born March 14, 1802, in Massachusetts, he was graduated from Union College in Schenectady, New York, in 1824, and from Theological College at Hamilton, New York, in 1829. Spencer labored in the ministry until his conversion to the Mormon Church in 1841. He served as an alderman in Nauvoo; he wrote reports and letters regarding the death of the prophet and his brother. For further information on Spencer see Vol. I, Part 3, footnote 35.

29. Newel K. Whitney was born in Marlborough, Windham County, Vermont, on February 5, 1795. He joined the Mormon Church in 1830 and was very helpful and generous to the young prophet. In December 1831, he was called to be the bishop of one of the wards and was then called to be the presiding bishop of the church. He was also a member of the Council of Fifty.

After the death of Joseph Smith, Whitney and George Miller were appointed trustees-in-trust for the church; and after Miller's withdrawal, Whitney acted alone. When the Council of the Twelve set out for the Salt Lake Valley in 1847, Whitney and Isaac Morley were left in charge of the Saints at Winter Quarters. Newel Whitney died in Salt Lake City, September 23, 1850.

30. George W. Harris, a carriage- and wagon-maker in Nauvoo, appears often in this record. Twice Hosea Stout refers to him as "being a member of my family," but the connection is not made clear since Harris was thirty years his senior.

George W. Harris, born April 1, 1780, was fifty-four years old when he joined the Mormons in 1834. At Far West he was active in the Danite organization; he married Lucinda Pendleton Morgan (widow of the Masonic martyr William Morgan), who had been sealed to Joseph Smith. Harris held many positions in Nauvoo. When the body of the Saints moved west in 1848, he remained in Kanesville, Iowa, where he was the president of the High Council. In 1852 Brigham Young ordered all members to come to Salt Lake City, but George W. Harris did not comply. He was excommunicated from the church October 7, 1860, and died later that year.

Richards,[31] W. W. Phelps,[32] James Sloan[33] Edward Hunter,[34] Jonathan C. Wright,[35] John Pack,[36] George Miller, Samuel Bent,[37] and David Fullmer[38] for Councillors. All of whom were unanimously accepted by the caucus after some remarks   next

---

31. Phineas (Phinehas) Richards, father of Franklin D. Richards, born November 15, 1788, at Hopkinton, Massachusetts, had been a member of the High Council at Kirtland, Ohio, and was at this time a member of the Nauvoo City Council. He came to Utah in 1848 and was made a member of the first High Council in Salt Lake City. He served as a senator in the legislative assembly of the State of Deseret. Richards was a carpenter and joiner by trade. He died in Salt Lake City, November 25, 1874.

32. William Wines Phelps led a checkered career as a Mormon, being twice excommunicated and twice reinstated. Born February 17, 1792, at Hanover, New Jersey, he was baptized in 1831, after a special revelation to Joseph Smith. A printer by trade, Phelps published the *Evening and Morning Star* at Independence, Jackson County, Missouri, in 1832.

In 1838 Phelps protested some of the activities of the Danites at Far West, and with Oliver Cowdery, Lyman E. Johnson, David Whitmer, and John Whitmer, was excommunicated from the church and forced to leave the area. By 1841 the differences were resolved, and Phelps was reinstated by special request of the prophet.

In Nauvoo, Phelps became a member of the city council and the Council of Fifty, and following the death of Joseph Smith supported Brigham Young. In 1845 he was one of those tried for *treason* by the State of Illinois but was acquitted.

William Phelps came to Utah in 1848 in Brigham Young's company and became very active in public affairs. He accompanied Parley P. Pratt in his explorations of southern Utah. He served as a justice of the peace, a notary public, and a legislator — for a time he was a senator in the State of Deseret. He died in Salt Lake City, March 7, 1872.

Phelps will be remembered as the writer of many Mormon songs and hymns, nineteen of which are still in the *Hymns, Church of Jesus Christ of Latter-day Saints* (Salt Lake City, 1961).

33. James Sloan was born October 28, 1792, in Ireland. He was in Far West in 1838, for on July 21 of that year William Swartzell described the ceremony by which eleven men were made members of the Danite Band, himself among them: "We then stepped off a few paces, for the purpose of choosing our captain. I suggested brother James Sloan. . . . We proceeded to elect Brother Sloan . . . by acclamation and uplifted hands." William Swartzell, *Mormonism Exposed* . . . (Pekin, Ohio, 1840), 23 (microfilm, Utah State Historical Society).

Sloan was made the first city recorder at Nauvoo and general recorder for the church in 1841. He was clerk for Pottawattamie County, Iowa, in 1848. He came to Utah in 1850, where he was associated with the printing and publishing business.

34. Edward Hunter, born June 22, 1793, in Pennsylvania, was forty-seven years old when he joined the Mormon Church. Hunter was a successful farmer, tanner, and currier who sold all his holdings and came to Nauvoo, where he gave liberally to the church. A member of the Council of Fifty, the city council, and police force, he was also a bishop.

In 1847 Hunter brought his own company to Utah. Appointed presiding bishop over all the church in 1851, Hunter initiated the Perpetual Emigrating Fund. He died October 16, 1883.

35. Jonathan Calkins Wright was born November 29, 1808, in New York, and joined the church in 1843. After the death of John P. Greene on July 10, 1844, Wright was made city marshal in Nauvoo. He came to Utah in 1850 and settled in Box Elder County, where he served as probate judge, county clerk, county recorder, prosecuting attorney, superintendent of schools, and member of the legislature for twenty-one years. He died November 8, 1880.

36. John Pack, born in Canada, May 20, 1809, was baptized into the Mormon Church in 1836, just in time to become an active participant in the Missouri troubles. In Nauvoo Pack was a member of the Council of Fifty, the Nauvoo Legion, the Old Police, and was mentioned often in the diaries of his contemporaries.

Pack came to Utah with the pioneer group of 1847 and returned to bring his family out the next year. Later he was sent to help colonize Carson Valley, Nevada, returning to Utah at the time of the "Mormon War." Pack died in 1885.

37. Samuel Bent, born July 19, 1778, at Barre, Massachusetts, was baptized a Mormon in January 1833. He lived at Kirtland, came to Missouri with Zion's Camp, and shared in the persecutions there. At one time he was severely whipped by a mob.

In Nauvoo, Bent was a member of the Council of Fifty, the High Council, and the Nauvoo Legion. During the exodus he was appointed to preside over the settlement at Garden Grove, where he died on August 16, 1846.

38. David Fullmer was born July 7, 1803, in Pennsylvania. Active in the church in Ohio, Missouri, and Illinois, he was a member of the police force, the High Council, and at the death of Samuel Bent, became president of the Garden Grove settlement.

In 1850 Fullmer came to Utah with the Edward Hunter company and settled in the Salt Lake Sixth Ward. A farmer by occupation Fullmer died October 21, 1879.

Tuesday the 14th inst. was appointed as a day for a General meeting of the people at the Stand to take into consideration the nominations as above. I cam home about 10 o'clock.

9th T. Today the Police had jointly made a dinner at which all the police and their wives were to attend the Twelve and Father John Smith were also invited we met at 2 o'clock P.M. at Brs Dunn and Tufts and a large turnout most of the Twelve were present we had an agreeable time all were well pleased and joy good feeling prevailed throughout. We continued our meetin untill 12 o'clock A.M. and came home rejoicing

10th F. At home. met police & Lodge.

11th S. Went to the City Council to present a petition from the police which was granted in part, was appointed Judge of the coming election for municipal officers, by the City Council, which was to be held on the first Monday in February next. came home at 2, and then met Police & Lodge.

12th Sunday. At home. Met Police home. 7

13th M. Wrote at the Lodge, met police and at dark met the Presidents of Seventies.

14th T. Wrote at the Lodge, today commenced going to a writing school at 10 o'clock and at one o'clock met at the Stand as appointed on the 8 inst. and the same persons nominated then were also nominated & accepted. I came home and then met Police & Lodge.

January 15th 1845. At home till one o'clock, went to writing school, met police and Lodge as usual.

16th T. Was a cold rainy day in the morning went to the Mayor's office, then to the writing school, then to police and at dark met the 11th Quorum at the Seventies Hall and took up a subscription for Prest Joseph Young home at 8 o'clock.

17 F. At 11 o'clock went to the Mayor's then to the writing school which was held at the Lodge then to Police and at dark to the Lodge then home at 10½ o'clock.

18 S. At home with President J. P. Harmon assisting him in making out a short biographical scetch of his life At one o'clock went to the Seventies Hall where there was a meeting of some 200 police just raised and met for instructions then met police and Lodge.

January 19th 1845 Sunday. Went to the meeting of the Seventies at the Hall and in the eveing met the police and gave them some instructions in relation to the appointment of City officers by the City Council after the next Municipal election; and the policy for them to pursue in relation thereto. President B. Young met with us and gave us good instructions on our duty All was well satisfied and seemed determined to continue to discharge the duties of policement and abide council. I came home at 8 o'clock.

January 20th 1845 Monday. Went as a witness to a trial between Brothers Coultrin and Matthews, thence at one o'clock to the writing school. then to the police and Lodge as usual home at 12 o'clock.

21st T. At home in forenoon, then went to the writing school at one o'clock, then went to the police & Lodge, home at 11 o'clock P.M.

22 W. Went down on the flat to rent a house went to the writing school then to the police and Lodge, home at 9 o'clock.

23 T. Went down on the flat as before then went to the writing school, as before then met the police and at dark met with the 11 quorum at my house, and taught at some length on the necessity of being united and giving heed to council, being prepared for the endowment the order of the judgement &c. took up a subscription for br J. Young had a good meeting.

January 24th 1845 Friday. In the morning went down to the river came home about 11 o'clock A.M. then went to the writing school, then to the police, then to the Lodge and came home at 9½ o'clock.

25th S. At home in the forenoon, then went to attend a trial before Esqr Wells,[39] for Benjn Jones who was sued and was unable to attend. the trial was adjourned one week. I came home and then went down to the Lodge where the 500 new police-men were to meet, from thence to the police, & then to the Lodge as usuall home at 8 o'c.

26th Sunday. In the forenoon met with the Seventies at their Hall; came home about one, then met with the police and at 8 o'c went to Br. B. Youngs who wished to see me on some police buisness, received instructions from him on police duty.

January 27th 1845 Monday. At home in the forenoon on buisness with some of the police, then went to the writing school, then to the police, & at dark went to a meeting of the presidents of the Seventies at the Hall. had a good meeting. teaching by President Brigham & Joseph Young and others.

28 T. In the morning went to Col. Hale's to make some arraingements for the Municipal election on Monday next. came home and wrote for President Harmon till one, then went to the writing school, then to the police then to the Lodge at dark as usual, home at 10 o'c.

29 W. In the morning David Fullmer came to my house to learn something about the High Council records as they were wanted for W. Richards[40] in writing the Church History, which was arrainged by myself and Br Fullmer at Br Richards. I then went down on the flat and came home about 2 o'c then went to the police, and at dark met with the 11 Quorum at Br Jos. Murdock's Came home about 10 o'clock.

30th, T. In the forenoon wrote for Prest. Harmon, when Brs Scovil[41] & Worthen came to me desiring that I would join with them and others and form a mechanical

39. Daniel H. Wells was a resident of the area when the Mormons purchased the land around Commerce, Illinois, and established Nauvoo. Before Wells joined the church he was elected alderman, a regent of the university, and a brigadier general in the Nauvoo Legion. Baptized in August 1846, he participated in the battle at Nauvoo.

In Utah, Wells was in command of the forces during the "Mormon War"; he served as mayor of Salt Lake City from 1866 to 1876; and he was counselor to Brigham Young from 1857 to 1877. See Bryant S. Hinckley, *Daniel Hanmer Wells* (Salt Lake City, 1942).

40. Willard Richards joined the church in 1837 and was ordained an apostle in 1840. He was private secretary to Joseph Smith and general historian for the Mormon Church. Although Richards was in the Carthage Jail when Joseph and Hyrum Smith were murdered, he escaped injury.

Richards became secretary to Brigham Young and continued as historian, keeping a daily account of general church activities until his death on March 11, 1854. From 1847 he also acted as counselor to Brigham Young. See Claire Noall, *Intimate Disciple: A Portrait of Willard Richards . . .* (Salt Lake City, 1957).

41. Lucius N. Scovil came west to Missouri with the Kirtland Camp in 1838, bringing with him his wife and two children. In Nauvoo he operated a bakery and confectionary. A promi-

and mercantile association the condition of which may be given hereafter. I concluded to join with them and went with Br Worthen to see some other brethren on the subject, and at two o'clock P.M. met with a General Council of the Authorities of the City & Church, held at the Mason Hall, for the purpose of consulting the best method for us to pursue in relation to the course the Legislature has taken in repealing our Charter, which they had granted to us for the term of perpetual succession the repeal of which was not only cruel and tyrannical but unprecedented in all civilized nations it was thought best to hold on to the Charter and if necessary appeal from them to the Supreme Courts of the United States And to this end there was a committee appointed to confer with the most able and Learned legal men on the subject.

Br George Miller informed the council that he had received propositions from a friend of his in offering to have a petition sent to Congress to have a tract of land set up to us and we organized into a territorial government of our own, with the privilege of making our own laws, not however to be repungent to the laws of the United States. The matter will most likely be spoken of hereafter.

After the Council broke up I went to the police from there to the Lodge as usual, then came home about 9 o'c.

31 F. At home in the forenoon. at one o'c met at the Seventies Hall with some others for the purpose of forming a mercantile & mechanical Association[42] as mentioned yesterday when it was concluded to to form an Association as aforesaid. the meetin proceeded to elect 12 trustees, who were to govern the Association; whose names were Daniel Carn,[43] Samuel Bent, Shadrach Roundy,[44] C. C. Rich, John D. Lee, L. N. Scovil, Joseph Worthen, Joseph Horn, Hosea Stout, Edward Hunter, Gustavius Williams, and Charles A. Davis. The said Trustees appointed next Tuesday at 9 o'c at the Masonic Hall, to meet to proceed to buisness. there was a good

---

nent Mason, Scovil was in charge of erecting the Masonic Hall in Nauvoo, and for a time was a representative of the Eagle Lodge at Keokuk, Iowa.

On April 10, 1845, Brigham Young wrote that "We advised Lucius N. Scovil, keeper of the lodge, to suspend the work of that institution . . ." See McGavin, *Mormonism and Masonry*, 88.

In Utah, Scovil settled at Provo where he served as the first clerk of the county court, as postmaster, and as justice of the peace. He died at Springville in 1906.

42. The Mercantile and Mechanical Association mentioned here was an attempt to muster all forces for group action. The Mormons had earlier experimented with collective living in a "United Order," but had been forced to abandon it. The action here enabled the leaders to press into use wagons, teams, or goods as they were needed for the group benefit, either for defense against their enemies or for making the move west.

43. Daniel Carn's name appears often in these pages. Because about 1854, by some accident, it was printed Daniel *Garn* and thereafter appeared that way, there has been some difficulty in securing biographical data.

Daniel Carn was born December 13, 1802, at St. Clair, Bedford County, Pennsylvania. He appears in Mormon history at Far West in 1838, for he signed the open letter ordering Oliver Cowdery and others to leave *forthwith*, and he was a temporary prisoner for participation in the Battle of Crooked River.

In 1842 Carn was a bishop in Nauvoo; in 1843 he was one of the Old Police; in 1846 he was a bishop at Winter Quarters. During the 1848 emigration he was captain of fifty in Brigham Young's company. A photostat of the early land drawing of the Salt Lake Valley shows his signature in a neat, small hand as "Daniel Carn."

From 1852 to 1854 Carn was president of the German Mission, bringing with him 484 Saints on his return. From this time on, his name appears as *Garn*, which occasioned his heirs some confusion in the settlement of his estate. He died April 20, 1872.

44. Shadrach Roundy was born January 1, 1789. In 1833 Joseph Smith sought shelter in his home; in 1838 Roundy was in Far West with the body of the church. At Nauvoo he was made a member of the Council of Fifty and a member of the prophet's bodyguard. In Utah he was bishop of the Sixteenth Ward in Salt Lake County. He died July 4, 1872.

spirit manifested by all present. from thence I went to the police and at dark to the Lodge as usual and came home at about 9 o'c.

February 1st Saturday. At home till 4 o'c then went to a fencing school composed of the police, then went to police meeting and Lodge as usual home at 9 o'c.

2nd Sunday. Went to the meeting of the Seventies at the Hall, met police then came home, and met with Presidents Jesse P. Harmon Alvin Horr & Alfred Brown at my house we had a good time our minds were occupied on the best manner to pursue to unite our Quorum and prepare them for the endowment and agreed to meet here every Sabath evening and thus cultivate a spirit of perfect union among ourselves & thus be prepared to teach our quorum with one heart and mind in meekness we broke up about 9 o'c.

February 3rd 1845 Monday. Today I attended the Municipal election as one of the Judges of the same as mentioned on the 11th of January last there was about 850 votes polled and the persons nominated by the Twelve on the 8th of January was unanimously elected without a dissenting voice the greatest union and peace prevailed that I ever knew before in the place at an election came home about dark.

4th T. In the morning met with the board of Trustees as appointed on the 31st inst and learning that the order of the Association differed from the arrangements then making by the Twelve in some points the matter was laid over untill a proper knowledge of the same could be had and if it should be thought improper to let the matter rest where it is from thence met police, and at dark met with the Trades meeting, and came home about 9 o'c.

5th W. At home in the forenoon then went to see T. Rich on some old buisness which was discussed and again laid over then went to fencing school. then met police, and at dark there was a meeting at my house of the 11 quorum. we then attended to the buisness of the Quorum as usual.

6th T. At home in the forenoon then went to see T. Rich again on same buisness. which was not settled as it should be. Then went to fencing school, then met police, then met with the Lodge came home at 10 o'c-

February the 7th 1845 Friday. In the morning went to see Brother S. Bent and C. C. Rich to regulate some matters in relation to the Mercantile & Mechanical Association as mentioned the 31st. inst. We concluded to lay the matter before the Committee appointed by the Twelve to regulate such matters which was to set for today at 10 o'c. at Elder John Taylor's we accordingly went there and laid it before them which they gave some instructions about and the matter rests there. from thence I went to the fencing school, thence to police and thence to the Lodge and came home at 10 o'c.

8th S. In the morning I went to the City Council to have some buisness transacted for the police as it was the time that the old Council went out and the Council elected last Monday took their seat, and consequently all the officers who received their appointments by said Council were to be reappointed or others put in their place. I succeeded as follows. in having tr [transfer] appointments conferred on the old police Lorenzo Clark was appointed supervisor of streets of the first Ward. J. P. Harmon of the 2 Ward Benjn Jones the 3 ward the old Supervisor to have the supervision of the whole and also the 4th Ward. And Benjn Boyce Constable of the 1st Ward E. J. Sabin the second Ward Howard Egan[45] the third Ward & D. M. Repsher the fourth ward the constables were likewise appointed fire wardens of their respective wards Daniel Carn flour inspector for the City with privilege of having agents Jesse P. Harmon was also appointed Pound Master, John D. Lee Warf master.

I was much pleased with the good feeling manifested towards the old Police by the Council, who seemed willing to extend the hand of patronage to us after we had spent the winter thus far without any renumeration, and kept up the guard to the satisfaction of the Twelve and other authorities and now they in return were willing to put some buisness into our hands to afford us a small compensation for our support. it also was an encouragement to us to persevere in the discharge of our duty as policemen.

In the evening I met with the police and reported to them what had been done at the Council, and the course I had pursued to to ward them they were all well satisfied & unanimously gave me a vote of thanks for the interest I had taken in their behalf and all warmly assured me that they would be governed by me as heretofore in all matters. To stand at the head of so worthy and honorable a company of brethren who possess the inteligence which they do and hold so honorable a standing in society as they, who are willing to be dictated by me in all cases without a dissenting voice in a matter of so vital importance as the safety of the Temple & the lives of the Twelve at this critical & trying time places me in a position and responsibility which is more easy to be imagined than described & to know that I am approved of by them is a satisfaction added to a consciousness that I am in the discharge of my duty which I hope I may always be in possession of. I went from the police to the Lodge and came home about 10 o'clock.

9th Sunday. in the morning went to the meeting of the Seventies at the Hall my brother Allen J. Stout was ordained a President of the Nineteenth Quorum of Seventies. I came home about 2 o'c P.M. & in the evening met with the police and then met with Presidents J. P. Harmon and Alford Brown at my house for social and brotherly conversation as on last Sunday.

10th M. In the morning I went to the Lodge to get some papers relative to the war last June and in the evening met police then went to the Lodge then home at 9 o'c.

February 11th Tuesday. At home wrote a scetch of my life for the 11th Quorum of Seventies as mentioned on the 7th Nov last. at 4 o'clock went to fencing school and then met the police then went to the Lodge home at 9 o'c.

12th W. Went to a trial. A man named John C. Elliot[46] who had been engaged in the murder of Joseph and Hyrum, came in town and put up with William Marks,[47]

---

45. Howard Egan was born June 15, 1815, in Ireland. In his youth he became a sailor, but upon his return home in 1842, he was converted to Mormonism.
In Nauvoo, Egan made rope and cordage and became a member of the Old Police and the Nauvoo Legion. He came west with the 1847 pioneers. Many of Egan's experiences are preserved in a book which was evidently written from dictation or copied from notes kept by James Monroe. See Howard Egan, *Pioneering the West* (Salt Lake City, 1917).

46. The *Nauvoo Neighbor* describes the arrest of John C. Elliot much as it is given here, except that it says John Scott made out and signed the affidavit, supported by the signature of Benjamin Brackenbury. "When they came to court it was supposed that Brackenbury's testimony would corroborate Daniels', but Hay represents their testimony as conflicting, and because of jealousy Brackenbury contradicted in his evidence all that Daniels had sworn to. Hay also represents that Brackenbury brought out the story of the martyrdom in a series of paintings that were "badly executed." Roberts, *Comprehensive History*, II, 333.
Elliot was one of the band who stormed the Carthage Jail and murdered the Smith brothers. Though he was locked up briefly, he was soon acquitted.

47. In Kirtland, Ohio, in 1838 William Marks had been the subject of a special revelation. In Nauvoo he was president of the stake from 1839 to 1844. Though he was suspected of being

who done all he could to secret him but he was found out and arrested and brot before A. Johnson, D. H. Wells & Isaac Higbee and examined found guilty and sent by the Sheriff who was present to Carthage (jail [crossed out]) to lay in the lonesome jail which he had stained with the best blood in the world. As soon as he was arrested Marks used all his influence to notify the mob and raise an excitement against us & Several Lawyers and other men from Warsaw came to his trial and used every stratagem in their power to get him (clear [crossed out]) discharged one of the Lawyers gave the Court to understand that if they committed him to jail that it might cause some of our best men to be slain, thus threatening us with a mob if we attempted to put the Law in force against wilful murderers, but the Court took a bold and decided stand in favor of the laws, from thence I met with the police and at dark met the 11th Quorum at my house, we had a good meeting. I taught at some length on the duties of Seventies and other matters.

13th Thursday. At home writing for the 11th Quorum in the forenoon. When Brother John Kay came after me to go to Brother Turley's to consult on the safety of some of the Twelve whose lives were sought, from thence went to the police and Lodge home at 9 o'c.

14th F. At home in the forenoon writing my history. and at 4 o'clock went to the fencing school thence to the police & Lodge home at 9 o'c today Lucretia Fisher[48] came to live with me.

15th S. At home till 4 o'c then went to the fencing school, then to the police and Lodge, home at 9 o'clock

16th Sunday. At home wrote Alvin Horr's life for the Seventies, met with the police as usual home at dark

17th M. Went with wife to Dibbles & then to A. J. Stouts and at one o'clock went to a meeting at the Stand which was held to take some action in relation to building a dam in the Mississippi River & other purposes for giving employment to the poor from thence went with Br Lee to the fencing school had some talk on the way with him on eternal exaltation met police & Lodge home at 9 o'c.

February the 18th 1845 Tuesday. At 9 o'clock met with the Board of 12 Trustees of the Mercantile & Mechanical Association as organized on the 31st of January last as they had received instructions to proceed to buisness, all the Board were present Elder Taylor and some others met with us and gave us the necessary instruction requested, that inasmuch as Br Bent, Rich & Hunter of our Board was appointed in the Board of 12 who were called the Living Constitution[49] that we would release

---

a traitor to the prophet, he was still the first counselor in the presidency and president of the Council of Fifty at the time of the martyrdom.

Since he had supported Sidney Rigdon's claim to leadership, Marks was excommunicated on October 6, 1844. He later affiliated himself with the James J. Strang faction briefly; then he became first counselor to Joseph Smith, III, in the Reorganized Church of Jesus Christ of Latter Day Saints.

48. Lucretia Fisher lived in the home two months before she was married to Stout. This plan was sometimes followed to see if the two wives would be compatible, and also to determine whether or not the second was attracted to the husband sufficiently to become his wife. The Stout family Bible gives the wedding date as April 20, 1845.

49. "The Living Constitution" was an inner circle of the Council of Fifty, evidently the policy-making arm of that organization, of whose deliberations no record was kept. See Lee, *Confessions*, 173.

Under the same date in the official minutes of the meeting, Stout wrote: ". . . John Taylor and Theodore Turley were called the Living Constitution and were present." This identifies five of the members. Hosea Stout, Miscellaneous Notes 1829-1869 (typescript, Utah State Historical Society; original, LaFayette Lee, Salt Lake City), 200.

them from our Board which was done, and Levi W. Hancock, Erastus Snow,[50] and James Mendenhall were appointed in their place, The Board then proceeded to business, and Daniel Carns was chosen President of the Board, and a committee of three to wit H. Stout, E. Snow, and D. Horn[51] were then appointed to draft some rules of government, for the Association and then the Board adjourned untill Wednesday at 9 o'clock and the committee appointed tomorrow at 9 o'clock to meet to transact the business committed to them   from thence I went to the fencing school thence to the police, thence to the Lodge home at 9 oc.

19th W. At 9 o'clock met the committee as appointed the day before. was engaged with them untill 4 o'clock, then met the fencing school, thence to the police, thence to the meeting of the Eleventh Quorum at my house. had a good meeting though there were but few met all seemed to be of one mind and willing to abide council and discharge the duty which may be required of them. [Written along the margin] See April 1st 1845.

20th T. Met the Board as mentioned on the 18th inst. all were present the committee made report of a form of government which was accepted without a dissenting voice. The Board then proceeded to draft some bye Laws which were accepted. I was appointed General Secratary of the Association and of the Board by the unanimous vote of the same. From thence went to the fencing school, thence to the police thence to the Lodge, thence home about 10 o'c.

21st Friday. At home till 3, then went to fencing school, then to the police & Lodge. home at 9 o'c.

22 S. In the morning went to Br J. P. Harmon's there met Bishop Miller, when we three went to the Temple while consulting on matters pertaining to our safety and also the manner to pursue to rid ourselves of traitors who are in our midst seeking our lives. from thence Brother Harmon & myself went to Br C. C. Rich's and talked the same matter over again while we were all going down at the flat. Br Rich went to the High Council and we went to the Lodge room and locked ourselves up and talked over some particular matters reletive to our Eternal exaltation in the Kingdom of God and the absolute necessity of the brethren's being united and maintaining our integrity to each other. We both were highly pleased with our interview and went on our way rejoicing. I then met with President L. W. Hancock, who went with me to my house talking on the things of the Kingdom as with Br Harmon. after we had eaten our dinner there we went down on the flat continuing the conversation as before, and parted and I went to the police and at dark went to the meeting of the Eleventh Quorum at the Hall as that was the time for the regular meeting of that Quorum at the Hall we had a good meeting. I delivered two short discourses and was followed by President Harmon Child's & others Came home at 9 o'clock.

23rd Sunday. In the forenoon went with my wife to a meeting at Bishop Hales Elder Dunham preached. Sister Smith the mother of Joseph the Prophet and Seer was there. She spoke to the congregation and told her feelings and the trials and

---

50. Erastus Snow was born November 9, 1818, in Vermont. He joined the Mormon Church in 1833 and was thereafter active as a missionary and a builder. He came to Utah in 1847, keeping a careful diary en route, which has not yet been published.

In 1848 Snow brought his families west; in 1849 he was made an apostle and a member of the Council of Fifty. The next two years Snow spent as a missionary in the Scandinavian countries, where he made many converts. In 1861 he was placed in charge of the Cotton Mission in southern Utah, which position he held until his death on May 27, 1888.

51. This is evidently an error on the part of Hosea Stout. In the group were Daniel Carn and Joseph Horne, either of whom might well have served on this committee — but no D. Horn.

troubles she had passed through in establishing the Church of Christ and the persecutions & afflictions which her sons & husband had passed through and the cruel and unheard of martyrdom of Joseph & Hyrum which had took place so lately. and exhorted the brethren & sisters to be faithful and bring up their children in the way they should go and not have them running about in the streets as was too much allowed now.

all were deeply affected with the remarks of this "Mother," of the "mothers in Israel" for she spoke with the most feeling and heart broken manner of the troubles she had passed through From meeting we came home and in the evening we went to Isaac Allred's where I left her and met with police from thence I went to Seventies Conference at the Hall at dark but the Hall being so crowded with the vast number who had assembled I could not get in so I went back to Br Allreds & when I got there I found that my wife had went with her sister Julia Ann Allred to a meeting at Brother Gully's. I went there where I arrived just as meeting commenced. Elder L. Gee preached and was followed by Elder I. Allred. After meeting we returned to Brother Allreds home where we came about 9 o'clock. When we came home Sister Williams was there who wished to make it a home at my house.

24th M. In the forenoon went down to the Masonic Hall and met with the Trustees of the Association. after the Board had assembled, the Stock books were opened for subscriptions and several subscribed stock, and other business was entered into after which I was appointed Treasurer of the Assoication. from thence I went to Br Hancocks from thence I came home from thence went to the fencing school, from thence went to police held a council with them relative to enlarging the number did not come to any conclusion but we appointed tomorrow evening at an hour before sun down to meet again to determine on the matter. I then went to the Lodge and came home about 9 o'c.

February 25th 1845 Tuesday. At 9 o'clock went to take a list of Br Worthens property for the Association from thence went to A. J. Stout's had some talk with him about the seal of the Covenant, from thence we both went to the police and when we came there I was informed by some of them that there was suspicious characters seen in town this evening, who, it was supposed by Br Turley, were making arraingements to form a company of mobocrats and waylay President Brigham Young, Heber C. Kimball and some other brethren, who had gone to Macedonia, about 25 miles off, the day before and were expected to return home tonight. there was nothing positive however. But knowing the evil intentions of some false brethren in our midst who were connected with the mob and had been heard to swear they would take the lives of these men We immediately determined to take efficient measures for the protection of the brethren. Accordingly I gave orders for all the police, who could procure horses and the necessary equipments to go and prepare acordingly and be back to the police quarters (as the shortest [crossed out]) soon as possible; armed in the best manner for defense and also to raise such others as were willing to go with us whereupon they nearly all dispersed, for that purpose, this was about one hour by sun. In the mein time General Rich came near by and I called him to me and informed him what was going on, and likewise what my intentions were in case the brethren should be attacted either before or after we should join them, which he approved. We immediately agreed that he should go and see Br Turley and find out the particulars and also get such other information & advice as he could. While I was still making every preparation to fit out the company. In a short time he returned accompanied by Elder John Taylor one of the Twelve, who informed me the Brethren did not intend to come home to night. and consequently they would not be in danger of being attacted to night. He advised me to take six or eight men and go and see if all was right with the brethren at Macedonia. Brs Taylor & Rich then went home and in a few minutes. Lorenzo Clark, one of the police returned, and informed me that it had been reported to him that the brethren were arrested At Macedonia. This created considerable excitement. I immediately dispached him with news to Elder Taylor and another to Genl Rich. During which time the brethren began to geather in, and in a short time there was a pretty large company all well armed & equiped impatient for the word to march. When Elder Taylor heard the report of B. Clark, he called a council to which I was notified to appear. All the information relative to the report was there elicited. which proved the report to be groundless. At the suggestion of Elder Willard Richards one of the Twelve, the Council instructed me to take the number propsed by Elder Taylor and go and inform the brethren at Macedonia that they would be pleased to have them take breakfast in Nauvoo tomorrow morning.

From the Council I returned to the company all who were waiting with great anxiety, the result of the council. I then delivered the command of the police up to Daniel Carn with instructions to keep a close guard until I returned after which I selected seven men to go with me to Macedonia as mentioned above namely Jesse P. Harmon, Andrew Lytle, Simeon A. Dunn, Howard Egan of the police and William H. Kimball, Josh S. Hollman, and Robert T. Burton. We then started and I stopped at my house to put on some more clothes and get some arms. Untill then my wife had heard nothing of the matter & knew not that I was going. (I came [crossed out]) I stoped but a few moments and left at 9 o'clock. We had a very pleasant journey, The night was warm and clear, the moon rose about ten o'clock & shone with a most beautiful lustre on the wide extended prairies which we had to cross. The roads were very muddy most of the way which made it fatiguing for the horses.

About two-thirds of the way there we passed a house where lived a man by the name of Jones a most confirmed and busy mobocrat. it was one o'clock, they were still up and had a light in the house and there were two horses fastened to the fence saddled. It was thought by the company that it was some who were seen in Nauvoo before we left which confirmed our suspicions. We had no further difficulty. When we had come to the subarbs of Macedonia Br Holman and my self went to Br Andrew Perkins and sent the company in town to seek for the brethren. We expected that some of them would be at Br Perkins' but when we came there we found that they were all in town so we went there and found our company and the brethren all at Br Benjn Johnsons they were very glad to see us and had been looking for us. Br Brigham had set up untill one o'clock looking for us for it was revealed to him that something was wrong. but he did not know what he told the brethren that we would come out before day. it was half past two when we got there. We delivered the message sent to them by the Council (to whom [crossed out]) however Br Brigham concluded not to start until morning. so after putting up and feeding our horses we all laid down and took a short sleep.

In the morning, after we had eaten breakfast, we all prepared & started home, accompanied by about 20 brethren, from Macedonia, who came with us about five miles, to assist us if we should be attacted by any mobocrats lying in wait. We had no difficulty on the road. In the morning when we started the day was warm & clear, but it soon began to cloud up and when we had come within about ten miles of Nauvoo it began to rain, which soon turned to snow, which fell very fast in large flakes accompanied by a driving west wind blowing in our faces made it very disagreeable. We came to Nauvoo about 3 o'clock P.M. and after escorting them all to their several Homes, we went our way. So the designs of our enemies were frustrated. I came home about four o'clock and that night there was a meeting of the Eleventh Quorum at my house.

27th T. In the forenoon went to the printing office from thence to the Lodge to receive subscriptions for Stock for the Association from thence came by Worthen's home thence to fencing school, thence to police and Lodge at home at 9 o'clock P.M.

28th F. In the morning went to Worthen's & went with him G. Williams Wooley's and some other places to receive subscriptions for Stock in the Association. came home and went to the fencing school, police, & Lodge. Sat in council with the officers of the Lodge about the manner to adopt in relation to the fees, &c came home at 9 o'clock P.M.

March the 1st Saturday. At or about home until three o'clock went to fencing school police and Lodge home at 9, raining.

2 Sunday. At home till in the evening then met with the police came home at 7 o'clock P.M.

3 M. went to the printing office and paid 25 dollars on a/c then went to Lodge to receive subscriptions for stock for the Association then came by Worthens home at 2 o'c then went to the fencing school, police and Lodge as usual came home at 9 o'clock. P.M.

4 Tuesday. Went to meeting of the Association at the Hall received some subscriptions for Stock, from thence went to fencing school, & police then came home at dark.

5th W. In the morning down to the Uper landing on the river to see about establishing a grocery for the Steam Boats & passengers did not effect anything positive came home about noon then went to the fencing school. and from there went with G. A. Smith to see President B. Young who was very sick. from there I went with the police to Schussler's brewry where we all got what beer we could drink then detailed the guard and came in company with President L. W. Hancock to the meeting of the Eleventh Quorum at my house where we had a good meeting and broke up at 9 o'clock P.M.

6th Thursday. In the morning went to Avery's came home by B. Jones' — in a short time Grant came to my house, had a settlement with him bought some cloth &c. In the afternoon took a coat pattern to the Taylors, and then started to the upper stone quiry to buy some lime, met William Backenstos who told me that there was a warrant out for me and not knowing what evil there might be intended against me I went to W. Richards' who knew nothing about it had some talk with him about affairs with the mob, police, and the troubles in Missouri &c. and then went down on Parly and Main Streets, but could hear nothing more of the warrant, so I got in a waggon and went to the stone quiry and engaged what lime I wanted of Br. Boyce then went down to the printing office and other places, then to the fencing school, & police, from thence went to the Lodge it was a regular Communication, home at 9

7th F. In the morning went to Turley's to get a pistol repaired from thence went with Br Scovil to the Mansion then to see Br Major[52] who was painting the scenery of the murder of Joseph & Hyrum at Carthage, thence I went to Br Harmons and got a Stand and came home about 2 o'c after which I met with the police & Lodge. home at 9 o'c.

---

52. William W. Major was a native of England, born in 1804. He joined the Mormon Church in 1842 and arrived at Nauvoo in 1844, not long before the martyrdom of Joseph and Hyrum Smith. In addition to the pictures mentioned here, he made sketches of the scenery along the route to Utah. These pictures were later exhibited throughout the territory. Major died October 2, 1854, while on a mission to England.

8th S. Worked at home untill evening then met police and Lodge home at 10 o'clock.

9 Sunday. At home was very unwell with a sick headache confined to bed

10th M. In the morning went to Brother Horne's and there met Br Mendenhall and we went to see Br Gulley about joining the Association with his store which he agreed to do if it was council from the Twelve. we then went to see Br John Taylor on the subject and he not being at home, we went to the stone query for the Water power Company at the place where the dam is to be built in the river about one mile below Town things were going on well from thence we came back and he went home & I to see Br Taylor and on my way I met Br Carn and he went with me, and in a few moments we met Br Taylor and laid the matter of Gulley's store before him which he approved, we agreed then to call the Board of Controll to gether tomorrow at 4 o'c we went up the river and he went home & I went to Br Mendenhall's soap works and from there I went by the Lodge, home and in the evening went to the police and Lodge after which I came with Br Worthen to see and notify several of the Board of the meeting, and came home about 10½ o'c.

11 T. In the morning I went to Br Mendenhall's to take a list of his goods which he was to put into Association and I got through about 2 o'clock and then went to see Br Gulley from thence I went to the Hall to meet the Board of controll The Board decided to put goods up at Gully's store. from there I went to the police and Lodge and came home about 10 o'clock.

12 W. In the morning went to Br Mendenhalls to assist in removing his goods to Gully's store then went to the mansion House and then went and had a settlement with N Knight after which I went and helped Gully put up the goods and then went to Br Mendenhalls again and traded for some nails &c then went to the stand saw President Young & agreed to meet him at his house at 7 o'clock tomorrow morning I then came home and went to the police Brs. H. C. Kimball and B. Young met with us and gave us some good instructions for about one hour after dark. I then went to the meeting of the Eleventh Quorum at my house, when I came I found the meeting about half out they not knowing what kept me, but I told the reason and we had a good meeting afterwards.

13 T. In the morning I went to see Prest Young (as above mentioned [crossed out]) he informed me that (Br [crossed out]) Mr. Brackenberry,[53] whom the mob was trying to arrest for false swearing, but in reality were trying to get some advantage of him in order to destroy his testimony as he was a witness against the murderers of Br. Joseph and Hyrum, was going to go before the justice of the peace

53. Benjamin Brackenbury, referred to in footnotes 11 and 46, was able to elude his pursuers with the help of his Mormon friends.
Oliver B. Huntington's diary tells the story:
Benjamin Brackenbury was arrested (in the Bar room) upon a charge of perjury, by virtue of a writt issued in a little place called Agusta situate in the southeast part of the county. The design of the enemies were to destroy his testimony in relation to the murder of the Smiths.
The Constables attention was drawn by a clamor from the crowd who had designedly gathered to rescue him, believing and knowing his life in danger when once in the hands of the mob. While this was going on, the moment offered so favourable I slipped Brackenberg out, and into a back room through another back door, and so he disappeared entirely. Oh, how mean the Mr. Officer felt on soon seeing himself left entirely alone. (Oliver B. Huntington, Journal 1842-1900 [3 vols., typescript, Utah State Historical Society], I, 55.)
Brackenbury was in Utah in 1849, but little else is known of him.

at Augusta to whom the warrant was returnable and have his trial and he wanted six men to go with him to protect him against the mob, so I set about raising the men, in doing which I went to several parts of town. About the time I had accomplished it I fell in company with Br C. C. Rich who told me that he was going to a meeting about 5 miles below town and desired me to go with him. And I then came home and prepared myself and met Br Rich as we had before agreed and we then went to meeting at Evans Ward 6 miles down the river. It was a meeting got up for the purpose of organizing the Sisters into an Association according to their several occupations for the purpose of promoting the cause of home industry and manufacturing the necessary articles for their own use without being dependent on the stores for all that we need. When we came there we found the house crowded full waiting for us it was now two o'clock, P.M. Meeting was opened by Br Rich when he proceeded to explain the benefits arising from such an order of things, and the order which was instituted in Nauvoo, after he was done speaking I followed by making a few remarks on the subject, and was followed by Br Bell The organization was then went into and they all with one accord joined in the Association and were classed according to their several occupations and each class appointed three of their number to superintend and manage the business for the class There was not a dissenting voice all seemed truly as a "band of Sisters." We then came to town and he went home & I went to meet with the police from thence to the Lodge and came home about 10 o'clock P.M.

March 14th 1845 Friday. Wrote at home till 10 o'c went down in town met with Major Bills had some conversation about military matters. at one o'clock went to a meeting of the New Police under Col Markham, at the Masonic Hall they were organizing into companies of ten with a Captain at the head of each company, but after some discussion it was concluded to organize the whole community of Saints in this County into Quorums of 12 deacons and have a Bishop at their head and they could thus administer in the lesser offices of the Church and preserve order without a charter, as the Legislature had taken away our Charter and deprived us of our Republican rights We also agreed not to do any more military duty and licensed ministers of the Gospel were not Compelled to by the Laws of the State. After meeting I sent the names of Lorenzo Clark, E. J. Sabin, Benjamin Jones and Jesse P. Harmon to the County Commissioners Court at Carthage to have them appointed Supervisors of the first, Second, third and fourth Wards as road districts since the Charter is repealed. I then went to the police and we there made some new arrangements about the guard I then went to the Lodge and came home at ten o'c.

S 15. Wrote at home till noon, then went down in town, then to the fencing school, then to the police. The men who went with Brackenberry had now returned. he had not come to trial, the other party not being ready, but he offered to admit the charge and give Bonds for his appearance at next court which is all that the justice of the peace could require if they had went to trial, but he would not do it so determined were they to have a chance to collect and be ready to offer voilence to him. The trial was adjourned and this evening we had to raise another company to go with him again so we did accordingly and was to meet in the morning at 8 o'clock at this place to prepare to go. from thence I went to the Lodge and came home at 9 o'clock P.M.

16 Sunday. At 8 o'clock I went to police quarters to fit out the company as mentioned yesterday and was engaged at it till about 3 o'clock when they started after which I met with the police and came home at dark.

17 M. In the forenoon went to L. R. Foster's and had him to take a Dagueratype likeness of myself this was given me by the Old Police as a token of regard for

me as their Captain. from there I went to several places on the flat then to Br
J. Knight, Sr., then to the police and then went with Major Lee to Br Free's they
were very sick from there I went to the Lodge and came home at 10 o'clock
It was a very cold windy night.

March 18th 1845 Tuesday. At home writing Met Police & Lodge home at 10
o'clock.

19 Wednesday. At home till in the evening, met the police and at dark stood guard
at Br Brigham Young's. had some talk with him about settling the interior of
the country between the head waters of the Arkansas and the head waters of the
Colerado of the West.[54] home at 8 o'c A. M.

20 T. At home writing till in the evening and then met the police and then went
to the Lodge home at 10 o'c.

21 F. In the morning went with my wife to Isaac Allreds on a visit to see her sister
& I met with Br C. C. Rich, and was with him untill noon talking about the exaltation to be obtained by being faithful, &c. In the meintime we went up to the upper
end of Town I then went to Br John Higbee's & then came down to the printing office
and then went and helped my wife carry her child home. then met police and Lodge
& home at 10 o'c.

22 S. At home untill noon then went down to the river for wood was at Joseph
Knight's then met with the police, this evening elder J. Taylor sent a company
under the commands of A. C. Brewer,[55] to meet with us, wishing them to abide my
instructions. They were composed of the hands in the printing office principally
and he desired to have one of the old police to be at his house every night where
one or more of Capt Brewers men would be to guard Elder Taylor and the police-

---

54. Under this same date Brigham Young noted that he had discussed with Hosea Stout
possibilities "in regard to the saints settling the country near the headwaters of the Colorado of
the West." B. H. Roberts, ed., *History of the Church of Jesus Christ of Latter-day Saints* . . .
(7 vols., Salt Lake City, 1902-1932), VII, 387. (Hereafter cited as Roberts, *Documentary History*.)

At this time there was a general interest in the geography of this region. The *Nauvoo Neighbor* carried regular articles describing the Intermountain and Pacific Coast areas. The issue
of January 9, 1845, carried the account of the John C. Frémont exploration and the announcement that on September 31, 1844, Frémont had reached "the great Salt Lake of Northern
Mexico."

Much of the Mormon interest in the West stemmed from earlier predictions of Joseph Smith
that they would move to some region in the Rocky Mountains. In addition to those from the
regular Mormon sources, one from the "Autobiography" of Mosiah L. Hancock is interesting.
It tells how Joseph Smith came into the carpenter shop of Levi W. Hancock, and taking a
map he said: "Now, I will show you the travels of this people." Smith then traced a line westward through Iowa and said, "Here you will make a place for the winter; and here you will
travel North and to the South, and to the East and to the West; and you will become a great
and wealthy people in that land. But, the United States will not receive you with the laws which
God desires you to live, and you will have to go where the Nephites lost their power . . ."
Mosiah Lyman Hancock, "Autobiography [1834-1907]" (microfilm, Utah State Historical
Society), 21.

55. This A. C. Brewer, who was working at the printing press in Nauvoo, is evidently
Ariah C. Brower in the later official records. Brower was born January 13, 1817, at Phelps,
New York. He came west in 1848 as a captain of ten in the John Taylor company. At that
time Brower's family consisted of his wife Margaret (aged twenty-eight) and three children.
The account book of Paddy Sessions shows that the youngest of these was delivered at Winter
Quarters for a fee of $2.00.

In 1849 Brower lived on a farm in Big Cottonwood, Salt Lake County, adjoining that of
John D. Lee on the east. In 1851 he leased this farm to Albert K. Thurber. That same year
Brower printed a *Mormon Way Bill to the Gold Mines*, describing the route from Pacific Springs
to California.

men who would be there could direct them what to do if any attact should be made on him, from there I went to the Lodge home at 10 o'c.

23 Sunday. In the forenoon I went with my wife to Br Benjamin Jones' and at 2 o'clock I went to Charles C. Rich's leaving my wife at Jones'. I had been notified by Br. Rich (himself come to his house, that myself and some [crossed out]) that a committee had been appointed to write a history of the Nauvoo Legion for Elder Willard Richards who was wrighting the Church history. The committee was composed of Charles C. Rich, A. P. Rockwood, Theodore Turley, and myself. We met and proceeded to business untill about 8 o'clock and then sent the report by Turley to Richards for approval or disapproval I then after having some conversation with Br Rich on some particular matters of the kingdom came home.

24th M. At home writing untill 2 o'clock then went down in town and had a talk with Br J. D. Lee on his temporal affairs then went to the police and then to Lodge at 10 o'c home.

25 T. In the forenoon went to John Higbees and made some arrangements with him and his wife about helping me procure from thence I went down the river bank to try and buy some wood & stopped at the printing office then went to the police. Br Brigham Young met with us and informed us that it is in contemplation to incorporate one mile Square of the City so as to include the Temple Nauvoo House and other public property which could be done according to the Statute Laws of Illinois and thus keep up a legal police for the protection of our lives and property. in the mein-time Genl Rich came in & informed me that the history of the Legion as we had wrote it was accepted and we were requested to meet again to night at his house to write more and continue it from time (to time [crossed out]) untill the same should be completed. I then came to his house & we proceeded with the history and I came home at 9 o'clock.

March 26th 1845 Wednesday. Wrote at home untill noon then went to the Lodge and wrote the minutes of the last two meetings from thence I went to Petty's gun smith shop to get a brace of pistols made and then went to the police and then went with Br Daniel Carns to Br Jones and took supper and we then went to Br Rich's to continue the history of the Legion. about nine o'clock we adjourned after the committee had appointed me to finish the history. & when I came home I found F. M. Edwards at my house, who had returned to Nauvoo for council he was one who had been led away by James Emmett[56] to the wilderness.

March 27th 1845 Thursday. In the morning I went down to town by the request of the Shoe makers' Association to do some business for them after which I saw and had a talk with Br Lee who gave me some light on some spiritual matters I then went to Brother Willard Richard's to see about the history of the Legion, and from thence I went to see General Miller on the same subject from thence I went to see Genl Rich and went with him to my house and after dinner I went to the police and we all went to Leonard Schussler's Brewery and got what Beer we could drink and as we were coming back I stopped at Br Joseph Knight's and had some conversation with my mother-in-law. I then came home a little after dark.

March the 28th 1845 Friday. At home writing the history of the Legion untill 2 o'clock then by C. C. Rich's to the police, and from thence to the Lodge and home about 10 o'clock.

29 S. In the forenoon I went to John Higbee's from thence to A. J. Stout's and at 2 o'clock went to the Masonic Hall to meet with the Lodge to attend to the funeral

---

56. For a full story of the Emmett Expedition, see Dale L. Morgan, ed., "Reminiscences of James Holt: A Narrative of the Emmett Company," *Utah Historical Quarterly*, XXIII (January, April, 1955), 1-33, 151-79.

obsequies of John P. Smith, a Master Mason, and there the Lodge formed the procession at 3 o'clock and marched to the stand where we were addressed by Br Orson Hyde.[57] at 4 o'c we then marched to the burying ground where we arrived about sun set, we then returned to the Lodge and commenced work on the third degree, and at 10 I came home.

30th Sunday. In the fore noon I went with my wife to meeting at the Stand. Elder A. W. Babbitt[58] spoke & was followed by President Young from meeting we came home and at 4 o'clock P.M. I went to the police with G. D. Grant & John Kay who came to my house, from thence I came by B. Jones'. with Warren Smith part of the way, and at Jones' I met with S. H. Earl, and he came home with me about dark, and I went with him to see Br Isaac Morley[59] and about 9 o'clock came home & he went to Brother Jones' again.

31st M. Was at home, having my house plastered, untill 4 o'clock then met with the police & Lodge and came, by Br Richards home about 10 o'clock.

1st April T. At home having my house plastered untill in the afternoon went down in town & then went to Br John D. Lee's while there Bro Meechem presented me with a letter it was from Elder W. Richards in answer to one I had sent him on the 19th of February last. Elder Richards some time previous had proposed to me to pay the police some forty dollars as he felt for their welfare, & I told him it would not be their feelings to receive it from him but he persisted in his desire to relieve them some what and requested me to lay the matter before them and inform him what he should do. & I accordingly did so and they all as with common consent declared that it was improper to receive assistance from him or any one of the Twelve and that they felt it their duty to guard them and the Temple without remuneration from them as it was a Church matter. But least Brother Richards might feel himself treated with contempt in their refusal they all agreed to present him with a fancy Bed Stead as a token of their respect for him and that I should write him

---

57. Orson Hyde, born January 8, 1805, joined the Mormon Church in 1831 and in 1835 was made an apostle. He filled several missions before joining the group at Far West. Here for a time Hyde had been estranged but was received back into fellowship by Joseph Smith at Nauvoo.

In 1848 Hyde was left in charge of affairs at Kanesville, Iowa, with George A. Smith and Ezra T. Benson as his counselors. Here they set up a printing shop and published the *Frontier Guardian*, the first issue of which appeared February 7, 1849. It ran until 1852, when the site was evacuated by the Mormons.

Orson Hyde colonized Fort Supply in the Green River area, organized Carson Valley in Nevada, and later took a group to Sanpete County, Utah. His final home was at Spring City, Utah, where he died November 28, 1878. Hyde's name appears often in this record.

58. Almon W. Babbitt, born October 1, 1813, joined the church soon after its organization. In 1834 he was a member of Zion's Camp; in 1835 he was made one of the First Quorum of Seventy. In 1840 his fellowship was withdrawn, but he was soon reinstated and appointed to preside over the Kirtland Stake in 1841.

In 1842 Babbitt moved to Illinois and settled at Macedonia, near Nauvoo. In 1844 he was elected to the state legislature from Hancock County, and along with Jacob B. Backenstos, was instrumental in securing the charter for the City of Nauvoo.

In 1846 Babbitt was appointed, with Joseph L. Heywood and John S. Fullmer, to take charge of the property of the Saints at Nauvoo, and participated in the battle of Nauvoo in which the last of the Mormons were forced to leave. His name appears often in this record. Discussion of Babbitt's later life and death will be included in Volume II.

59. Isaac Morley, an early convert to Mormonism, was first counselor to Bishop Edward Partridge, the first bishop of the Church of Jesus Christ of Latter-day Saints, from 1831 to 1840. In 1838 he was ordained a patriarch, which position he held until his death. He came to Utah in 1848, bringing in his wagon the records of the church and some precious items from the Nauvoo Temple. Morley served as a senator in the general assembly of the State of Deseret. In 1851 he held a seat in the legislative council of Utah Territory, as a councilor from Sanpete County.

a line expressing their good feelings for him and the Twelve, which was to be presented with the Bed-Stead which letter read as follows (it should have been inserted on the 19th of February last.)

"February 19th, 1845

Elder Willard Richards,

Beloved Brother:—

This is to inform you that I have laid the matter before the "Old Police" relative to the relief which you kindly offered them, which they unanimously declined to recieve, considering as they do that it is their bounden duty not only to sustain you & all the Twelve, temporally as well as spiritually; but guard you also against the voilence of midnight assassins, who stalk abroad, as wolves in sheeps clothing, without having you put to any expense or trouble for us.

We deem it a sufficient remuneration for us from the Twelve, to be thought worthy, to be entrusted with your lives; & consequently the salvation of the Church, when wicked men are continually arrayed against you; who seek thereby to thwart the purposes of God. Hence it would not be proper for us to receive temporal assistance from you.

Be assured that the "Old Police" have the most unfeigned love and respect for you, and duly appreciate your kind offer & as a small token of their respect, have sent the Bed stead, which accompanies these lines; which I hope you will receive as such, while I have the honor to be your most sincere friend and Brother in the

New Covenant,
Elder W. Richards   (Signed) Hosea Stout
Done in behalf of the "Old Police."

When the letter and bed stead was presented it came entirely unexpected to him but he said we would hear from him hereafter but we heard nothing more untill today upon the receipt of this letter which was as follows:

March 31st, 1845.

Col. Hosea Stout

Beloved Brother

Permit me, at this late hour, to apologize to you, and through you to those dear brethren, the "Old Police" of Nauvoo, for a seeming carelessness on my part, in not responding to your philanthropic communication of the 19th ultimo, at an earlier date.

Nothing but a press of business could have prevented a timely acknowledgement of your kind favor, which has scearce been absent from my mind for a moment, but I have many little cares for the publick weal, I mean the brethren, the Kingdom of Saints, and will attend to all as fast as time permits.

Accept this appology, *dear*, with my thanks, and my blessings, and my prayers, which shall ever ascend to Heaven in your behalf. I received your *"token of respect*, the *Bed-Stead"* with all the thot, warmth of feeling and friendship with which it was presented, and although you may be a little coveteous, inasmuch as the giver is more blessed than the receiver, yet the blessing shall be multiplied on your heads an hundred fold.

The "Old Police" are God's Noblemen.
Watchmen in Zion; Go on in your labors of love, and you shall stand in the Towers on the walls of the Holy City. *"shall see eye to eye"* shall

encompass the peaceful habitation of the saints at a glance, when your enemies shall be no more, and your joy shall be full; and although you may be disturbed of your rest for a little season, yet bye and bye you shall rest in peace, your sleep shall be sweet unto you, & you shall say it is enough we have seen the salvation of the Most High & we want for no good thing.

God bless the "Old Police" forever, Amen.

I remain your brother in the Kingdom of watching and Praying.
Col Hosea Stout.   Willard Richards.

From Br Lee's I went to Police and read the letter to them They were all well pleased with the spirit which manifested to wards us. From thence I came home about dark.

2nd W. I was at home untill noon having my upper room plastered then went to assist Worthen borrowed some money which we got of the Trustee in Trust, was with Genl Rich until time to meet the police, where I went and then came home at dark.

3rd T. In the morning I went to the Temple and was roughly accosted by Brs Cahoon & Cutler[60] about a circumstance which took place last night at the Temple. They said that the Old Police had beat a man almost to death in the Temple. To which I replied I was glad of it and that I had given orders to that effect in case anyone should be found in the Temple after night and they had only done as they were told, or ordered, that they had been imposed upon long enough while on duty and I was determined to bear it no longer. This created considerable warmth of feelings in them and the bye standers, however after they understood the matter they seemed satisfied and said the guard only done their duty from thence I went to John Higbees from thence to Gullys store, and there met with Br Carn and told him the circumstance at the Temple and we concluded to lay the matter before President Brigham Young and get his advice, as we went we met Brother H. C. Kimball and while relating the matter to him Brother Brigham came to us and we related the matter to him and he approved of the proceedings of the Police and said he wanted us to still guard the Temple after which he & Br. Kimball went to the Temple to regulate the matters there which was done to our satisfaction and justification. I went from thence to Br Turleys, and from thence to see Br Harmon and from thence to the Lodge to a regular communication at 4 o'clock, from thence home at 8 o'clock P.M.

4th Friday. Was in and about home untill evening, and then went to police and Lodge home about 10 o'clock P. M.

5th S. In the fore noon I went to John Higbee's and at One o'clock met the police to inspect their arms and then took them out and trained them awhile and then

---

60. Reynolds Cahoon and Alpheus Cutler, both members of the Council of Fifty, had been commissioned by Joseph Smith before his death to make certain that the Nauvoo Temple was finished. They had pushed the work with such vigor that some authorities complained.

Reynolds Cahoon, born April 30, 1790, at Cambridge, New York, joined the church on October 12, 1830, and had for years been closely associated with the Mormon Prophet. At Far West he served under David Patten of the Danite Band. Cahoon came to Utah in 1848 and settled in Murray, where he died April 29, 1861. See Stella Cahoon Shurtleff and Brent F. Cahoon, *Reynolds Cahoon and His Stalwart Sons* (Salt Lake City, 1960).

Alpheus Cutler, who had been a bodyguard for Joseph Smith, did not agree with Brigham Young and was excommunicated in 1851. He died in 1864 in Fremont County, Iowa. Cutler founded a small church of his own which had headquarters in Minnesota. Included in the membership was Louis Denna (Dana), an Indian chief who had done missionary work under Joseph Smith.

marched to the Mansion House from thence to the Printing office & there A. C. Brewer joined with us and we then went to L. Schussler's Brewery and got what Beer we wanted to drink after which we marched back to our quarters and after making some arraingements to defend the conference which was to commence tomorrow, against the violence of our enemies who had threatened to break it up, I went to the Lodge do some business home at 8 o'clock.

6th Sunday.   GENERAL CONFERENCE

This was General Conference and I was instructed to keep the "Old Police" in readiness to suppress any riot or breach of the peace which might happen there had bein threats from our enemies that Conference should be broke up. The day went off quietly no disturbance, except Dr. Charles[61] from Warsaw who came and was taking notes for the "Warsaw Signal" — he pretended to be our friend but in reality he was a secret enemy lurking in our midst in the afternoon he was invited to leave which made him so mad that he did not take any more notes that day In the evening met the police and then went to John Higbees and came home a little after dark and about 9 or 10 o'clock Br Arnold and Thos Williams[62] came to my house and informed me that three of the mobocrats from Pontusuc was in the City at a Mr. Smith's, and wished to know what to do about it. I went with them to Temple Guard and while some went after Col Markham & others I went to consult Genl Rich and get his mind he was in bed and after he got up we had a talking he was taken with some kind of a spasm and fainted and fell against me and down on the floor groaning as a dying man. this caused great alarm for his family was afraid some one in disguise had come in my name and taken his life but he was well again in a few moments after putting him to bed and after we had come to a conclusion on the subject I returned to the Temple and reported to let them alone till morning came home at 2 o'clock A.M.

April 7th 1845 Monday. At 9 o'clock A.M. I went to the Conference and the cold wind blowing the dust in clouds on the congregation the Conference was removed to another part in among the hills. In the forenoon Dr. Charles made complaint that he had been insulted by some boys and abruptly demanded to know if this people tolerated such things of which President Young satisfied him that they did not. In a short time he came back again making more bitter complaints than

---

61. Dr. John F. Charles had been elected to the Illinois Assembly largely by the Mormon vote and because of this had worked for the adoption of the Nauvoo Charter. Two years later when he ran for the Senate, the Mormons withdrew their support and Charles was defeated. He was now working for the *Warsaw Signal*, a paper which was generally anti-Mormon. His complaint that he was insulted by some boys had reference to the activities of the "Whittlers."

Oliver B. Huntington, then a teen-age boy wrote: "I belonged to the 'Whittling Society' and the 6th of April helped whittle doctor Charle of Warsaw out of town. He was a real Mormon eater. That was an order established in place of the city Charter, which had unjustly been taken from us. That was the acting authority of the city, upon poor devils, and would soon run them out of town without touching them, for no one liked the sight of ½ dozen large knives whittling about their ears and not a word said." Oliver B. Huntington, Journal, I, 56.

62. The name of Thomas (Tom) S. Williams appears often in this record and in other diaries of the period. At this time he was a member of the Nauvoo police, was an expert horseman, and as a fearless defender of his people was often sent as a messenger or trusted with dangerous missions.

In 1846 Williams joined the Mormon Battalion as second sergeant under Captain Nelson Higgens of Company "D." He took with him his wife, Albina, and two children, Ephraim and Caroline. A second daughter was born at Pueblo, Colorado. Williams arrived with his family in the Valley of the Great Salt Lake on July 29, 1847, five days behind the pioneer group. Details of his later activities and death appear in Volume II.

ever. President Young then called for me and requested me to protect him from further insults and ferret out the names of the boys who insulted him I conducted him to the Mansion House & informed Br Pack what had happened to him and he promised to see him duly protected and I came back; and conference being adjd for noon I came home and in the afternoon accompanied my wife to meeting after which I went with her to a Grand Concert of Vocal & instrumental Music at the Concert Hall at 6 o'c P.M. we were well entertained untill about 11 o'clock and came home —

8th T. Attended conference as before and in the evening went to the concert and home at 11 o'c.

9th W. Attended seventies Conference at the Stand, Met 11th Quorum in the afternoon near the Stand and in the Evening accompanied my wife to the Concert again. Home at 11 o'clock P.M.

10 T. At home untill about one o'clock P.M. then accompanied my wife to Prest Harmons, & I went to the Lodge & Printing office, thence to Br Turley's & A. J. Stout, and back to Harmon's and went then with my wife to the Masonic Hall and after attending to the police the "Old Police" who had been invited to by the proprietors, went to see an exhibition of the scenery of the Murder of Brs Joseph & Hyrum at Carthage also of Jesus raising Lazerus and other like Paintings it was an entertaining display of art. we came home about 9 o'c.

11th Friday. In the morning before breakfast went to the upper landing for wood came by John Higbee's and rode with Brs B. Young & Rockwell[63] to Hendrix's thence home and wrote untill about 5 o'c P.M. then met police had a good and lively meeting then went to Allen Stouts & home at 8 o'c.

12th S. At home untill about 2 o'clock and then went with my wife to the Masonic Hall to a feast of beer and cakes prepared by the old police. The Old police and wives and some of the Twelve were present We had a joyful time as much cakes & beer as we could eat and drink we broke up about 9 o'clock P. M. & I then came home.

April 13th 1845 Sunday. In the forenoon went to meeting at the Stand there was some officers there with writs for Br Young & others. the U. S. Martial was one Elder Taylor spoke on the Stand give them to understand that if they made an attempt to serve the writs it would cost them their lives & also told them how they had murdered two of our best men while under a civil process and the authorities of the State pledged for their safety & that we would submit to no more such outrages on our lives and liberties. In the afternoon I went to the Seventies hall from thence to the police and came home about 8 o'c.

14th M. Worked at home until 3 o'c then went to the Temple and Petty's shop for pistols then to the Police and done business at the M. Hall untill about 8 — came home by the Temple stayed with the guard came home at 9 o'c.

---

63. Orrin Porter Rockwell, one of the colorful figures of Mormondom, was born June 28, 1813, in Belcher, Massachusetts, and joined the Mormon Church in 1830. A self-appointed bodyguard for Joseph Smith, "Port" took literally the promise that, if he did not cut his hair, his enemies should not have power over him. All his life he wore it long and braided. Rockwell was also a bodyguard for Brigham Young. For years he served as sheriff and marshal and kept a mail station near the Point of the Mountain, Salt Lake County, where the Utah State Prison now stands. He died June 9, 1878. For a critical review see Charles Kelly and Hoffman Birney, *Holy Murder* (New York, 1934), also Nicholas Van Alfen, "Porter Rockwell and the Mormon Frontier" (Master's thesis, Brigham Young University, Provo, Utah, 1939).

April 15th 1845 Tuesday. I was at home untill about 11 o'clock went to B. Jones and was there taken very sick went to bed and about 4 o'clock got up and went to the police from thence to Br Turleys to make some arraingements about the old police in relation to the incorporation of the City as mentioned on the 25th of last March. home at 8 o'c.

16th W. In the morning I went to see Genl Rich about the "Old Police" as with Br Turley last evening from thence I went to see Br J. D. Lee to have him assist me with the Old Police Regulations as above but he being sick could not attend with me I then came home an at 4 o'clock P.M. met with the President and Trustees of the Town incorporation, whose names are: Alpheus Cutler, Orson Spencer C. C. Rich T. Turley & D. Fullmer. They appointed the "Old Police" to be the regular police of the Town and I was appointed Captain of the same and I succeeded in having Br Lee appointed one of the Assessors & Collectors of the Town. I then came home about dark.

17th T. In the morning I went to Harmon's shop to get a Table made thence to the Printing office thence up to Blazzard's saw pit-for lumber for the table thence to A. J. Stout's and stayed there untill 3 o'c thence to Br Lee's who was still sick, thence to the Lodge to a Regular Communication thence met with the Police & came by Br Lee's again home at dark.

18 F. Worked in my garden untill 12 and then went to Lodge at one, then went to seventies Hall to see Br Lee, then came to Br Harmons' and got him to detail the guard as I was very sick I then came home a little while before dark.

April 19th 1845 Saturday. In the morning I was sent for by Brother Lee who wanted to see me. I went there and done some business with him and then went to Genl Rich's to meet the Committee to write the Nauvoo Legion but they not coming I came home about 11 and in the evening met with police came home after dark & just after I had gone to bed Thos L. Edwards Sr. came who had been with Emmett in the wilderness he was in a sad condition said he wanted counsel to know what to do.

20th Sunday. In the morning myself and wife Lucretia Fisher[64] went to Br John D. Lee's to a Social meeting we came there about 9 o'c we had a good and friendly meeting Prest A Lyman, Br Lee & wife & others were present. we came from there by the Temple to B Jones & in the after noon my wife & I went to meeting, & then we all came home & I met the police and came home a little after dark.

April 21st 1845 Monday. In the morning I went to the Temple & met with Dana[65] went to Brother Harmon's with him to a council from there to Brigham's and went with Br Shumway to the uper landing for wood, then came to A. J. Stout's

---

64. The Stout family Bible gives this as the date of Hosea's marriage to Lucretia Fisher. Amasa Lyman performed the ceremony. John D. Lee stood as witness, as Stout had done for him the day before, when he noted that "I was sent for by Brother Lee . . . . I went there and done some business with him." Lee's diary for April 19, 1845, says: ". . . Louisa Free was also admitted, taking upon her my name. On the same day Caroline Williams was registered on my list . . . ." John D. Lee, "Diary [Winter 1845-1846]" (unpublished, L.D.S. Historian's Library).

65. Louis Dana (also Denna) was an Indian chief who had been converted to Mormonism by Dimick B. Huntington and made an elder by Joseph Smith to preach to his people. Oliver B. Huntington wrote in detail of this Indian — both of his conversion and his activities at the court where J. C. Elliot was tried. Oliver B. Huntington, Journal, I, 59.

Because of the efforts of Brigham Young to court Dana's favor, his name appears several times in this record. Dana preferred to stay with Alpheus Cutler. See David T. Jones, *Vintonia*, V (Vinton, Iowa, 1945), 341.

then came home went with my wife to Roberts, for crocks then came to B Jones took dinner wife came home and I went to Temple to do business for the "Old Police" came home & met police & after detailing some on particular patroll duty came home at dark.

22 Tuesday. at home untill after noon went down in Town and met police home at 9 o'c.

23 W. In the morning went with my wife to Isaac Allred's & A. J. Stouts on a visit & I went to J. Higbee's, then to see Mrs. Clyde gave her some counsel relative to her situation, then went to Father Knights had some talk with Sarah[66] came thence to Allen's then went to police and then came with Br Shumway to Lyon's store for wine he was going away. I then went and took my wife home a little after dark.

24th T. In the morning went to printing office then went with G. D. Grant up the river for some wood and came home at noon and in the evening met the police and came home at dark. very wet boisterous day.

[The following entries for 25th and 26th were crossed out and rewritten below.]

25th 1845 F. In the morning I went with G. D Grant after wood above town on the river came home at noon and in the evening met the police it was a very wet day home at dark.

26th S. In the morning went with my wife to the meat market, and meeting with G. W. Langley on the way we came home and went down on the flat and saw several police on business met with Kay and Daniels made some police arrangements, & met Joel Terry at the Mansion went home with him took dinner & agreed to take him under my instruction in things pertaining to the Kingdom of God. we went to the Temple & I meeting with Brother L. N. Scovil we went to J. P. Harmon's, & I stopped there untill evening met police, and gave them some instructions relative to the proper order of things then came home a little after dark.

25th 1845 F. In the morning I went to see Warren Smith on police duty and came home & went down on the flat to see Brs Daniels & Kay had a talk with them on police opperations and afterwards met the police & came home at dark met genl Rich on my way and went with him home & then to Warren Smith's and went on patrol duty with him Daniels Kay and others, and came home about 10 o'clock.

26th S. In the morning went with my wife to the meat market, and meeting with G. W. Langley on the way we came home and went down on the flat and saw several police on business met with Kay and Daniels made some police arrangements, & met Joel Terry at the Mansion went home with him took dinner & agreed to take him under my instruction in things pertaining to the Kingdom of God. we went to the Temple & I meeting with Brother L. N. Scovil we went to J. P. Harmon's, & I stopped there untill evening met police, and gave them some instructions relative to the proper order of things then came home a little after dark.

27th Sunday. I went with my wife to meeting at the Stand Elders Babbitt and Taylor preached. Old Father Cowles one of Law's apostates was there, a company of boys assembled to whistle him out of Town but I prevented them. I came home and in the evening went to police, on my way was informed that the old man had been whistled out[67] immediately after meeting. I met police & came home before dark.

---

66. Sarah was a sister of Hosea Stout's first wife, Surmantha Peck. She later became a plural wife of Charles C. Rich.

67. Among the many references to the activities of the Whittlers, this one is quite specific and indicates that there might have been good reason to disband the group.

April 28th 1845 Monday. At home untill noon then met with the Lodge & at 4 o'clock met the Police & had a meeting & all told their feelings we had a good time & love and union prevailed. I came home at 9 o'c.

29th. In the morning I went with my wife to the grave yard & came home and went down on the flat about one o'clock went to the Printing office, and then met with the police home at 9 o'clock.

30th W. We went down to the Lodge at one o'clock, and at four o'clock met with the Eleventh Quorum at the Masonic Hall and at 6 o'clock met the police as usual; home at 9 o'clock.

May the 1st Thursday. In the morning wrote Alfred Brown's history and was in and about home untill noon went to see Br Turley on some business for the Police and went to the Lodge at 4 o'clock it was R. Communication then met the police and came home about 9 o'clock.

May the 2nd 1845 Friday. In the fore noon I went to Worthen's & the Temple, then down on the flat and at one o'clock met with the Lodge and then went round about Town with G. W. Langley and met the police and came home before dark a little.

May 3rd S. In the morning went to B Jones' stayed till 11 o'clock then went down to the Lodge & at one o'clock then went to Petty's shop and got a brace of pistols then came to the police and then came home about dark.

4th Sunday.[68] In the forenoon went to meeting with my wife and heard Brigham Young preach came home and after dinner went to meeting again and then met the police and at dark went on guard at Brigham Youngs untill 12 o'clock P.M. then patroled round by the Temple home with Joel Terry came home about 8 o'clock A. M.

5th M. In the forenoon went to see General Rich about establishing a picket guard on all the roads leading from Nauvoo to keep our enemies from passing to and from Nauvoo. we made the arrangement and I came home about noon and went to the Lodge and afterwards went with Col. John Scott[69] to see after some of our

---

I joined the whistling and whittling band . . . from what we could learn, some of them [Gentiles] were interested in taking the life of the Prophet. We were . . . directed to keep an eye on the "Black Ducks." We generally tried to do our duty and we succeeded in baging some game. I was about to give some instances, but forbear by saying In no case did I ever help to engage in whittling any one down to make them cross the great river unless they were known to be lurking around the Prophet's premises quite late . . . . In extreme cases when we knew a man to be a mobber, and who still sought the life of the Prophet, we would use our rail. We generally had four boys to a rail — the rail would be flat on the bottom and was three cornered; on the top it was terribly sharp — fixed to suit the aggravating circumstances. Four boys generally knew how to manage the rail. We all had our knives and cut timbers to whittle and make rails from, and knew what tunes to whistle. (Hancock, "Autobiography," 26.)

68. On this day Hosea Stout issued to his wife, Louisa Taylor, an official appointment "to the office of First Assistant to the Colonel of the Fifth Regiment, Second Cohort, Nauvoo Legion of the state of Illinois," in which she was ordered to "carefully and diligently discharge the duties of said office, by doing and performing all manner of things thereunto belonging . . . ." Stout, Miscellaneous Notes, 73.

We can only conjecture as to whether, after taking a second wife, Stout gave his first this appointment to placate her feelings and give her assurance of her status, or whether the office carried a cash recompense for the labor of keeping his uniforms in order.

69. John Scott was born May 6, 1811, in Armagh, Ireland. At Far West he was one of the mounted band of Danites. In Nauvoo Scott was a colonel in the Nauvoo Legion in charge of the artillery, and it was his business to transport the cannon to Utah.

enemies who were lurking about Town, then met police and came home before dark.

May 6th T. I was home untill noon and <u>met with the Lodge at 1 o'clock</u> then met with the police, the Twelve was present home a little after dark.

7th W. At home untill noon. Br Kay came to my house we went down on the flat together I gave him a double barreled pistol. <u>I went to the Lodge at one,</u> and at 5 o'clock met with a general convention of the officers of the Nauvoo Legion to regulate matters in case we should be attacked by our enemies. I was appointed to act as Brigadier General 2nd Cohort then met police and came home before dark.

May the 8th 1845 Thursday. In the morning I went with J. B. Nobles[70] to see John Bills to regulate matters pertaining to the 2nd Cohort we came home and I went down on the flat and then went to General Rich's to meet the committee to write the history of the Legion from thence I met with the police and then came home before dark.

9th F. In the morning went with my wife to A. J. Stout's and other places on the flat and came home at 12 o'c, and <u>I went to the Lodge at 1 o'c</u> and then met with the police. Elder Taylor came and desired us to take a boat around Night's mill dam for Ivins we went and did so, and then went to the Temple to be sworn into office; but was too late. I then came home about dark very sick with a head ache

10th S. At home untill noon, then went on the flat, & brought home some cheese & butter and then met the police and came home about 11 o'clock.

May 11th 1845 Sunday. Went to meeting at the Stand and came home at noon and after dinner went back to meeting, and then met the police came home about dark.

12th M. In the morning I went to the meat market for some provisions and came home, and Joseph Worthen came to my house and we rode down on the flat to see Kay & Daniels when I came with Kay to see some men on the hill & then went back & I went with Daniels to see a man about some money we then went down Mulholland Street onto the flat again and I went to see Father Knight and also had an interview with Bishop Carn & went back to Father Knight's, and then <u>went to the Lodge at one o'clock</u> and then met with the police at the Temple where we were all sworn into office as policemen of the Town of Nauvoo as before mentioned from thence I went to the Masonic Hall to meet with the officers of the Fifth Regiment and gave them some instructions pertaining to their duty in case we should have any difficulty with the mob at Court. I then started home and stoped at Br Lee's awile and again started home and in a few minutes met Brs Brigham & Lorenzo Young, and after some conversation I went home with Br Brigham, and while there Br C. Daniels and some other police men came there who was on the hunt of some men

---

As an early member of the Council of Fifty, Scott was willing to accept his responsibilities in the exodus, but insisted that he had his authority from Joseph Smith directly and did not want to take orders from any not his superiors. Scott came to Utah in 1847 and settled in Mill Creek, Salt Lake County. He died in 1876 at Millville, Utah. Further notes on his activities will appear in Volume II.

70. Joseph Bates Noble was born January 14, 1810, in Massachusetts. He became a member of the Mormon Church in 1832 and was made one of the First Quorum of the Seventy at Kirtland. In 1834 he traveled to Missouri with Zion's Camp.

Noble was one of those who was miraculously healed during the plague year at Nauvoo. He performed the first plural marriage in the church, sealing Louisa Beaman to Joseph Smith on April 5, 1841. Roberts, *Comprehensive History*, II, 102. Noble came to Utah in the J. M. Grant company of 1847. He died August 17, 1901.

by the name of Hodges[71] who were suspected of being guilty of murdering a man in the Iowa. after some conversation with them I went with them We found some men from Iowa who had come over after them and did not know what to do so we all went on the hunt. We first went to see Col. Markham. who had been in pursuit of them, and he came with us. We then went and raised some more men and went where it was said they were and found them. They refused to be taken untill day light, so we guarded the house untill day, when they gave themselves up and was conducted away by Col Markham. I, after serving a search warrant on them & another house for stolen goods, went to Father Knights and took breakfast, being allmost worn down with fatigue.

13th T. I then went to Dr Turley's and got a horse & buggy and in Company with Kay went and done some business with some brethren from Mississippi I then went home and after dinnr we went on the flat and <u>at one o'clock I met the Lodge</u> after which. I was round in Town untill time to meet the police which I did and at dark met the officers of the fourth Regt and taught as I did the officers last evening came home at 10 c...

May the 14th 1845 Wednesday. At home untill 11 o'clock, then went to Br. Turley's & then went to other places and <u>at one o'clock met with the Lodge</u> and at 2 o'clock met the Committee to write the History of the Legion at General Rich's & at 6 o'clock met the police, & came home at dark.

---

71. The Hodge family were evidently members of the Mormon Church. The father, Abraham C. Hodge, is listed as a "Pioneer" among the Old Police; and it would seem that, in spite of all the misfortune which befell his sons, he remained with the church. On June 18, 1848, he was made a lieutenant colonel in Brigham Young's company.

Amos C. Hodge is listed second on the roll of the bodyguards for Joseph Smith. Lorenzo D. Young, a companion of Rich, Stout, and others as they fled from Far West, wrote that a Brother Hodge was wounded at the battle of Crooked River and later as they were traveling along ". . . a man named Irvine Hodge overtook us . . . . He informed us . . . [that] a troop of sixty cavalry [were] in pursuit; . . ." James Amasa Little, "Biography of Lorenzo Dow Young," *Utah Historical Quarterly*, XIV (1946), 56, 58.

PART II

May 15, 1845 to February 9, 1846

MAY 15, 1845 TO FEBRUARY 9, 1846

Part II

This part of the diary covers the period from May 15, 1845, to February 9, 1846, inclusive. It opens with the story of complications following a murder committed by Mormon boys and continues with incidents of violence and reprisal until the whole area was in such a state of civil war that the Mormons promised to leave the vicinity in the spring if they were allowed to live in peace during the winter. This part ends when Hosea Stout and his family land on the western bank of the Mississippi River.

May 15th 1845, Thursday. To Day was kept by the Church in fasting & prayer. At 9 o'clock I went on the flat, as the trial of the Hodges came off to day before Esqurs. Johnson & Higbee. Just as the parties were ready to examine the witnesses the Shiriff from Lee County Iowa, presented an endictment against them from the Lee County Circuit Court, which after considerable debate by the Lawyers, the Court decided to be valid and the prisoners were committed and after taking Council with their lawyers thy consented to go immediately to Iowa and went accordingly[1]

---

1. The story of the offense and fate of the Hodge brothers has been told and retold with varying interpretations. An account appeared in the *Illinois State Register* (Springfield), May 23, 1845; and the *Niles National Register* (Baltimore), July 26, 1845, carried two articles.

Books which carry rather detailed accounts include: Edward Bonney, *The Banditti of the Prairies* . . . (Chicago, [1850]). Bonney was the sheriff in Iowa where the murder was committed. He tells of the trial of the Hodge brothers and of his attempts to track down and capture Tom Brown, the one he considered most responsible.

John Bowes, *Mormonism Exposed* . . . (London, 1851). This pamphlet of sixty-five pages tells the story of the Hodge murder as related by William Arrowsmith, who was living near Nauvoo at the time and was married to a sister of John Taylor.

Elnathan C. Gavitt, *Crumbs from my Saddlebags; or Reminiscences of Pioneer Life* (Toledo, 1884). This book tells of the murder, the trial, and the execution.

Colonel J. M. Reid, *Sketches and Anecdotes of the Old Settlers and New Comers, The Mormon Bandits and Danite Band* (Keokuk, Iowa, 1876). Although he wrote thirty years after the events he chronicles, the author evidently had access to the county records, for he names the judge, the jury, the witnesses, and even the sheriff's escort. His account of the execution as well as the trial is detailed.

From these accounts it would seem that William and Stephen Hodge were living with their brother Amos on the outskirts of Nauvoo. John Miller, a German Mennonite, with his family and a son-in-law, Mr. Lieza (spelled also Liesy, Liese, and Liecy) had built a home near Montrose, Iowa. It was believed that these people had a large amount of money. Tom Brown and the Hodge brothers crossed the river, and in an attempted robbery became involved

There was a great excitement about this murder in Iowa and our enemies taking the advantage of us endeavoured to lay this thing to the Mormons and when they found that those men were in Nauvoo, raised a hue & cry that we were harboring the murderers and that it was no use to come after them, this was when there was an excitement up against us as Court time was near and our enemies sought every opportunity [to] raise evil reports against us, hence the people of Iowa was jealous and expected we would not let the men go, but when the Court decided against them and they being conveyed by the police to Madison the same evening, they saw we were willing to do justice by all and they all as with one accord declared that we were abused and misrepresented so the matter turned in our favor and they instead of being our enemies as the mob intended became our friends.

I then met the police and came home at dark.

16th Friday. In the forenoon went down on the flat and was with other police-men untill one o'clock then met with the Lodge and police

17th S. In the morning I went down on the flat and at one o'clock met with the Lodge & police as usual and at dark met in Council at the Seventies Hall with the authorities to take into consideration the best method for the brethren to pursue who had to attend Court at Carthage next week. after Council I came home about 11 o'clock

18th Sunday. Before meeting time Genl Rich came to my house to make some arraingements with me, relative to our opperations in case we should be attacted by our enemies, while the brethren were at Court and as he was one of the jury[2] he had to be absent and it was necessary for me to act in his place & the mob intended to do something in order to have us commit our selves as a people that they might have a pretext to call out the militia against us so after we had made the necessary arrangements we went to meeting at the Stand & I in time of meeting collected eight brethren who were lately from the South[3] and after giving them the necessary instructions sent them out in different parts of the County to spy out the plans & designs of the mob After meeting I went to Br B. Jones' and took dinner and returned to meeting in the after noon after which I met the police & came home at dark.

May the 19th 1845 Monday. In the fore noon I went to A. J. Stout's & thence to Br Joseph Knight's and at one met the Lodge after which I was with Br H. Egan

---

in a fight in which Miller was killed and Lieza fatally wounded. Hearing a noise in an adjoining room, the attackers became frightened and fled without any loot.

The alarm was sounded and neighbors and officers crowded to the scene. Tracks to the river indicated that three men had been involved; a dropped cap was identified as belonging to Stephen Hodge. The Hodge brothers were arrested as told here by Stout; the descriptions given by the wounded Lieza would seem to identify the one who killed Miller as Tom Brown, and the one who struggled with him as William Hodge.

Friends of the Hodges insisted that the younger man, Stephen, was only an accessory as he stood watch guarding the boat, that the knife embedded in Miller's chest belonged to Brown, and that Brown was responsible for the whole expedition. Reid, *Sketches and Anecdotes*, said that the Hodge boys remained calm and asserted their innocence to the last.

An interesting comment was written by James M. Monroe, schoolteacher in Nauvoo, under date of May 12, 1845: "I have heard today that two men had been murdered by our people a short distance from here and whether it is the fact or not it will be so reported and we shall have to suffer for it; indeed the course pursued in this city of late *seems to have invited persecution.* [Italics ed.] All it wants now to raise a fuss is that some writs should be made out and sent in here after the Twelve." James M. Monroe, "Diary," 123.

2. Charles C. Rich was on the panel of jurors but was released. No Mormon was allowed to serve.

3. These were the "brethren from Mississippi" referred to on May 13. Being strangers in the area, they would not be recognized as Mormons and hence could be effective spies.

and met the police, and came home at dark and then went to the Temple as I had heard that there were suspicions that some evil was intended but nothing serious occurred I then went by Br C. C. Rich's and came home about 11 o'clock.

20th T. In the morning I. went with my wife to the Store and came home and then went to see Bishop Miller, who had sent for me who was at the Temple. he wanted to See me about the guard at the Temple, I then went to Allen J. Stout's and at one o'clock met the Lodge after which I met the police as usual and came home at dark —

21st W. I went down by the Temple to A. J. Stout and met the Lodge & police as usual home at dark

22nd Thursday. In the fore noon I went with my wife to B. Jones, on a visit & came home and then met the police and came home at dark.

23 F. In the fore noon I went down to the Temple and saw John Kay working in the Temple[4] and had a long talk with him and matters concerning police duty and other business came home and after dinner met the Lodge & police as usual & came home about one hour after dark.

May the 24th 1845 Saturday. This morning at 6 o'clock the cap Stone of the Temple was to be laid by the Twelve Myself and wife went It was a very cold & disagreeable morning the wind was in the N.E. We were present and beheld it laid the band of music was present and played some appropriate airs when the cerimony of laying the Stone was performed by the Twelve, when all the congregation Shouted hosanna to the Most High God for his preserving care over us in delivering us out of the hands of our enemies thus far It was a beautiful sight to behold the Surrounding country from the top of this Splendid edifice erected to the name of the Most High God. How different the Scene this morning from the day the foundation Stone was laid under the hands of the Prophet Joseph Smith at the head of the Nauvoo Legion & Sidney Rigdon at his right hand as his spokesman I remembered the flow of eloquence which gladdened the harts of the Saints on that day as he addressed the vast assemblage. But now our Prophet has fell a martyr to the cause, Sealed his testimony with his blood, and Sidney has turned a traitor to the cause of God and is now blaspheming against that same Prophet to which he was appointed a Spokesman and has this day been proved a false prophet, in the eyes of all the Saints, for he has prophesied that the walls of the Temple would never be completed, which was done to our great Joy which seemed this morning to be full, after the Stone was laid President Brigham Young observed to the saints present that this was the Seventh day, the day in which the Lord finished the work of creation & rested so we this day had finished the work of wall of the Temple and he would say to them to rest also that it was the Jewish Sabath & he would release all those who were working. on the Temple from labor this day and said also that all the Saints who felt to keep to day sacred to the name of the Lord could do so too but Said they could do as they saw proper. We then came home about 7½ o'clock. and at one o'clock met the Lodge & police as usual and came home at dark.

25th Sunday. Went with my wife to meeting at at noon went to Benjn Jones' and took dinner. We then went back to meeting again after which we came home and I went on the flat and met with the police and at dark patroled with Egan, Daniels Kay & other policemen, on the flat. and upper landing. and was out all night.

---

4. The Mormon need for guns is pointed up here by the fact that John Kay was drilling out a six-pound cannon and preparing it for service. Roberts, *Comprehensive History*, VII, 417.

May the 26th 1845 Monday. Earley in the morning I went in Company with George D. Grant to see Brs Heber C Kimball & Brigham Young. they taught us some principals of the Kingdom about the law of consecration.[5] I then went to Allen J. Stouts and heard that the Ware house at the upper landing was broken open last night and Bryants & Egan's goods stolen[6] and I with other police-men were on the look out for the goods. at one o'clock met the Lodge & the police & at dark met in Council with. B. Young, H. C. Kimball, A. Lyman G. A. Smith, D. Carn, H. Egan G. D. Grant C. Daniels John Kay, at the Masonic Hall, and came home at 11- o'clock at night —

27th T. In the morning Early met at the Hall agan with the Same as last night. we remained there all day I met the police in the evening and came home at 11 o'clock at night.

28th W. Earley in the morning I went to the Hall again on business and at one ' o'clock met with the Lodge & came home and in the evening met the police, and came home at dark.

29th T. In the morning Thos L. Edwards came to my house wanted to know how I felt towards him I told him. I then went to the meat market came home, and met the Lodge and police as usual and came home at dark.

30th F. Early this morning I went to Br Sabin took breakfast and had some talk with him on the Spiritual Kingdom & came by Benjamin Jones, & then came home & then went to the Temple and saw Br Daniels & Kay then I went in company with Br H. C. Kimball who wanted me to see [and] Br Scovil which I did in the evening. I went from the Temple to see Br Egan & then came home and in the evening met the police and came home a little after dark.

31st S. Wrote at home in the morning then went down to Jos Knights then met the Lodge and police as usual home at dark.

June 1st Sunday. In the fore noon I went to meeting with my wife & came home and after dinner I went to meeting again & then came home & met the police & came home at dark

2nd M. In the morning Brs Mathews & Thomas came to see me about raising a company of Southern Brethren for my regiment I gave them some instructions on the Subject I then went to see Br Brigham from thence to Brother Knight and then met the Lodge and police as usual & came home at dark.

3rd T. In the morning went to see L. D. Driggs and at 9 o'clock met the Lodge and at one went to see the scenery of the Carthage murder exhebeted at the Masonic Hall, & then met the police home at dark

4th W. At home till evening & J. Sabin & here on a visit met the police home at dark.

---

5. The Mormons had first taught the "Law of Consecration" in 1831, as a communal way of life in which all Saints should consecrate their property to the church in order that all should be equal. Although the Mormons early learned that they could not live this doctrine, church leaders did preach that the needs of the church as a whole must be placed before individual needs. The effort here was to institute a cooperative program for building wagons for the exodus.

6. The *Nauvoo Neighbor* of this date reported the theft of several hundred dollars' worth of goods and added, "The thieves have as yet escaped detection." The owners were Mormons.

5th T. In the morning went to see Genl Rich then to the Temple then to the Lodge at 9 o'clock and then to the Masonic Hall & then home and met police as usual came home at dark

June the 6th 1845 Friday. Worked at home untill noon & then went to the Lodge & police as usual, came home at dark.

7th S. In the morning went down on the flat & got some fish & came home accompanied by Bishop D. Carn and after dinner we went down again & I met the Lodge at one, after which I went to Davis' landing on the river and bought some pine Lumber with James H. Glines who bought some beer and brought it to the Hall for the police with me and after having a good drink I came home at dark.

8th Sunday. In the forenoon I went to meeting with my wife at the Stand and came home at noon and in the evening met with the Seventies Conference at their hall or nearby there met the police and came home about dark.

9th M. Br Lewis D. Wilson came to see me before I was up. After breakfast I went to [Samuel] Gully's Store and at one met the Lodge and then came home & afterwards met the police & came home at dark.

10th T. In the morning I set out some cabbage plants and then went to see Br Willis and came home and after dinner met the Lodge and then went with Br Carn to the Temple and saw Br Brigham about the ferry. then met the police and came home at dark

11th W. In the morning I went with my wife to look at the Temple and came home and met the Lodge at one, and at 4 o'clock met the Eleventh Quorum of Seventies at the Masonic Hall and then met the police and came home at dark —

12th T. This was fast day. I was at home untill about 2 o'clock then went on the flat by way of the Temple met the Lodge at 4 then met the police & then saw Brigham who gave me advice about police duty home at 10 o'c

June the 13th 1845 Friday. In the forenoon I went to the Temple and in Company with Elders Kimball, A Lyman Parker & Roundy went on the top of the attic Story and had a delightful view of the surrounding country, after which I had an interview with Br Harmon and then went to see Br Turly and then saw W. Hickman[7] then went to Father Knights then met the Lodge at 2 o'clock then met the police and came home a little after dark.

14 S. Early this morning I went to S. D. Driggs came home & then went down on the flat by the Temple and at 2 o'clock met the Lodge & then met the police and came home at dark —

15th Sunday. In the forenoon went to meeting at the Stand came home & after dinner went back to meeting heard Wm Smith[8] preach his claims to the Church

---

7. William Hickman, born April 16, 1815, in Warren County, Kentucky, had married early and moved west into Iowa before the Mormons came to Nauvoo. He was already a well-known frontiersman before he joined the church in 1840.

In the exodus out of Nauvoo, Hickman was in John Scott's company; he did not come west with the 1848 emigration, but was a sheriff in Kanesville, Iowa, as he was after 1852 in Utah. In 1872, William Hickman became alienated from the church and published the book, *Brigham's Destroying Angel, . . .* (New York, 1872), in which he gave details of several murders with which he had been connected. He died July 21, 1883, in Wyoming.

8. William Smith, eldest brother of Joseph and Hyrum, was born March 13, 1811, in Windsor County, Vermont. He was baptized into the church in 1831, but several times was estranged from his brother. Twice he was excommunicated but restored to membership later.

& was followed by O. Hyde then met police and after some conversation with some of the police on the Subject came home at 9 o'c

June the 16 1845 Monday. In the morning went to the meat market also saw S. Earl on some business came home had some business with C. Canfield then went & Saw Br Lee at the brick yard then went down in Town on the flat saw D. Carn on Main Street on police duty and took dinner with Br Dunn and met the Lodge at 2 o'clock then saw Br Lee again for Br Langley and met the police and then went to See Br Young at his house then went to Br Harmons & we went with Br McArthur to the Temple to instruct the guard and then I came home about 10 o'clock.

17th T. In the fore noon Saw James Pace on buisness then went down to the river with J. D. Lee & others to load timber for Br Joseph Youngs house met the Lodge & police as usual had some talk with John Parker on police matters then saw O. Hyde & others on the Same business and then came home about ½ past 10 o'clock

18th W. In the morning met Br Lee at the brick yard and went with him to the Temple from thence home with him and I went to A. J. Stout, and at 2 o'clock met the police. after which after notifying some ones of them to tarry we held a council at which I expressed my feeling more fully than usual as did the rest also home at 11 o

19th T. At 9 o'c met Carn, Egan & Roundy to do some business in temporal matters and then went to Father Knights to see him on some matters which Br Binley had to communicate to me about the police then met the Lodge and police & then went to Br Brigham's who gave me instructions about the police & after having some talk with Egan & Harmon I came home about 11 o'clock.

20th F. In the morning went to John T. Barnetts to give a list of my property to the assessor came home and met in council with the Same police as on the 18th except L. W. Hancock at the Masonic Hall then went to Father Knight on the same business as before & then met the Lodge & police as usual then went and saw Br Young and patroled with Egan, Parker, Carns, Harmon & D. McArthur untill 12 o'clock and came home it being a very warm, still, rainy night. I was wet.

21 S. At home untill noon & met the Lodge at 2 o'clock then went up to the upper landing with Egan Saw John S. Higbee & Charles Allen on business then met the police then went to see Br Brigham and then came home at 9 o'c.

22 Sunday. In the fore noon went to meeting at the Stand and there Saw Allen Weeks about his friend whom he introduced to me it was a rainy day and the meeting broke up I came home and then went back but it being Still wet I went on the flat to the Seventies meeting at the Hall then met the police after which I patrolled untill day light in company with Egan, Harmon, Carn Parker &c and came home about the dawning of the day

---

In 1842 and 1843, William Smith was a member of the Illinois Legislature, where he was eloquent in defense of the Nauvoo Charter. He was in the East when his brothers were killed.

On May 11, 1845, James Monroe wrote: "I then went up to the stand and found William Smith preaching. He did not seem to approve the harsh measures now going on to get rid of our enemies, but advised the Saints to leave judgment in the hands of God, and continue the mild law-abiding course we had hitherto taken. He seemed determined to live up to his privilege and stand in his place, let what would come." James M. Monroe, "Diary," 121.

Smith had previously been made a patriarch in the church, and Monroe was his scribe.

June the 23rd 1845 Monday. In the morning I went with my wife and others to see the Temple and arsnal then went to Isaac Alred and I went to Allen Stouts and at 2 o'clock met the Lodge and police then came home at dark

24 T. this morning before day I got up and went to the Temple to see to the guard and when I got there I was informed that one of the Hodges[9] was murdered I went to the place and found it to be So he had been knocked down & then stabed 4 times in his left Side with his own knife and left and he got up and ran away directing his course to Brigham Youngs to have him lay hands on him he fell dead with a rod or so of his door. Allen Stout & John Scott first saw him he said he knew who had killed him but could not tell when I came he was laying in a horrible situation dead & covered in blood and a jury holding an inquest over his dead body but no trace could be had of those who had killed him at daylight I went with others to the place where he had been killed & found his knife a Short distance therefrom as if it had been thrown away as the man had fled. from thence I went to Allen Stouts & then came home about breakfast time & took a short nap and about 9 o'clock went home with Allen Weeks where I Stayed untill 12 then went to the Temple Saw Harmon & then went to Allen Stouts and took another Sleep as I was very much worn out then met the police and came home with Shumway and then I came home a little after **Dark.**

June the 25th 1845 Wednesday. At home Br Shumway came to see me and about 10 o'clock went to lay hands on Phineas Young who was sick I came home. and after dinner went with my wife to See Sister Sabin who was very low I then went to the Lodge at 2 and at 4 met the police as usual. the Twelve also met with us to council on some matters then agitating the Town[10] Brother William Smith addressed us and was followed by Br Brigham; we were dismissed about dark I then Saw and had an interview with Br Lee and came home about ½ past ten —

26th T. In the fore noon I went to Br Allen Weeks Stayed there untill 11 o'clock then went down to Br Knight's, and took dinner and met the Lodge at 2 then went to the printing office and down Main Street and met the police and came home at dark and learning that Sister Sabin was very Sick I went with my wife to visit her we came home about midnight —

27th F. Wrote at home untill noon and then met the Lodge and police as usual then came home and went on patrol guard untill 12 and went to bed at Brigham's and Stayed till morning.

---

9. Under the sign M U R D E R!!! the *Nauvoo Neighbor* of July 6, 1845, offered a reward of $200 to anyone giving information which would lead to the arrest of those who had killed Irvin Hodge on the streets of Nauvoo on the 23rd of June. It was signed by M. R. Deming, Sheriff of Hancock County. No one ever claimed the reward.

The *Illinois State Register* for July 4, 1845, quoting the *Quincy Herald,* told how Hodge was called out of his house, knocked down with a club, and then stabbed with his own knife. ". . . he lived a short time after he was discovered, said he knew the person who committed the deed, but would not name him because he was a friend."

Allen J. Stout, Hosea's younger brother, was standing guard with John Scott at the home of Brigham Young. He reported that just before time for change, he heard a cry followed by the sound of dull blows, as if someone were beating an animal. They ran toward the place and met Irvin Hodge staggering, wounded in the back with a knife. It was so dark that they did not see the assailant. Allen J. Stout, "Journal [1816-1889]" (typescript, Utah State Historical Society; original, L. D. S. Church Historian's Library), 16.

10. The "matter which was agitating the town" grew out of a difficulty between William Smith and one of the policemen, Elbridge Tufts. From the entry in Roberts, *Documentary History,* VII, 428-29, it would seem that William Smith had demanded the release of an unnamed prisoner, and when he was refused, had attacked the officer.

28 S. Took breakfast at Allen Stout's and then came home and worked till noon and then met the Lodge and police then went to A. Weeks then to Sabins and then came home about ten o'clock —

29th Sunday. In the fore noon went to meeting to the Stand which was now moved to the old place west of the Temple B. E. T. Benson[11] Spoke & was followed by Prest B. Young. I came home and met the police and then went to see Br Young and then came home at 10 o'clock

June the 30th 1845 Monday. In the morning went to Allen Weeks and I then went to A. Stout's and then after Seeing Amasa Lyman I went to the Lodge and being very Sick with a head ache came home and at 6 o'clock met the police at the Temple and then went to the Music Hall from there I went in company with Br A. Lyman & Charles Shumway to Br Shumway's house and in a Short time Br Scovil came, & also Br Allen Weeks & wife and two of her Sisters We had a short address from Br Lyman and after drinking what wine we wanted we dismissed all being very much edified with the remarks of Elder Lyman,[12] the company then dispersed & I Staid in company with Br Shumway that night on watch & came home early in the morning.

July 1st Tuesday. This day there was a grand concert for the Police at the Masonic Hall it commenced at ten o'clock myself & wife & L. Fisher went we had also the 12 and other authorities with us, and was also provided with as much beer, wine, cakes &c as we could eat and drink. We had a very entertaining time all was peace, good feelings, and brotherly love no discord or contention among us. It lasted untill about 6 o'clock P. M. when we dismissed I came home.

2 Wednesday. This morning G. W. Langley came to my house & we went to the Hall and round on the flat till two and then met the Lodge and police I then went to see Sister Sabin who was sick night unto death from thence to Allen Weeks and there entered into the[13] [blank] and came home about day light in the morning.

July the 3 1845 Thursday. This morning I went down on the flat an at 9 o'clock met the Lodge and then went on the Hill to the Shoe Shop and at 2 o'clock met in Council at the Hall with President B. Young & G. A. Smith and the officers of the Lodge and the officers of Helm Lodge relative to our two Lodges joining together it was not decided then. At 4 o'clock the Lodge met again being a Regular Communication and there the matter of the Lodges were discussed and refered to Scovil Roundy & my-self to Settle afterwards I met the police & spoke at considerable length to them on the Subject & necessity of their keeping their selves out of all

---

11. Ezra Taft Benson was born February 22, 1811, in Mendon, Massachusetts. He was a member of the High Council at Nauvoo. At this entry he had filled a mission to the East and brought a large company of Saints from the Boston area. He now worked on the temple, stood guard at night with the Nauvoo police, and was made a member of the Council of Fifty. On July 16, 1846, he was ordained an apostle to take the place of John E. Page, who had been excommunicated.

Benson was one of the pioneer group of 1847, returning on August 2 with O. P. Rockwell to meet the incoming migration. In 1848 he brought his family to Utah. Here he helped to organize the government of the State of Deseret and served as a member of the legislature for many years. He was connected with the settlement of Tooele and Cache counties before he died September 3, 1869, at Ogden, Utah.

12. The Stout family Bible gives this as the date of the marriage of Hosea Stout and Marinda Bennett, making her his plural wife. She was born August 26, 1826, at Bedford, Tennessee. Many of the plural marriages of this time were performed by Amasa Lyman.

13. This entry indicates the date when the marriage was consummated, and thereafter Hosea's weekly visits to his wife Marinda Bennett are indicated as "standing guard" or "on parole guard with Brother Weeks."

bad company and mantaining an upright & dignafied course before the people after which I went to B. Youngs and Saw him to get council on Some matters and Br Lee coming I Staid with him a while and after ward we got in conversation with B. Young on the doctrine of Christ's mission in the world and at 11- o'clock I came home.

4th.[14] This morning at 8 o'clock I went to the Hall to meet with Some of the police and was there untill 12 o'c and went round on the flat then met the Lodge & police and at dark went to the Music Hall to a Concert given for the benefit of the "Old Police" and came home at 11 o'clock.

5th S. Went to the Masonic Hall at 10 o'clock & took dinner at Father Knight's and at 2 o'clock met the Lodge then the police came home at dark very lame from a hurt on my foot.

6th Sunday. Went to meeting at the Stand heard Wm Smith & H. C. Kimball preach came home and after dinner went to meeting again from there to the police then came home at dark and went to See Allen Weeks and was on guard all night came home early in the morning.

July 7th 1845 Monday. This morning I went down by the Temple to the flat and then went to see Br. Campbell[15] and engraver & Br Maudsley Portrait Painter, to have the likeness of myself & wife taken and engraved on stone, or in other words have a Stone cut of our likeness taken to be Lithographed. from thence I went to the Lodge, then to the burying ground to Seek for the grave of Little Lydia my daughter I then came home and then met the police & came home at about 10 o'clock.

July 8th T. this morning Br Shumway & Langley came to see me and we went to the Masonic Hall & I went to Father Knight, and took dinner then met the Lodge and after went to Maudsley's then met the Police and came home at 9½ o'c

9th W. This morning I went to Br Maudsley's. again from thence to Br Campbell's and took dinner then went to the Lodge then met the Eleventh at the Same place then met the police and came home at dark.

10th T. This was a fast day. & I went to See Sister Sabin who was yet very sick from thence to Br Weeks. and from thence, in company with Br L. W. Hancock, to the Stand to meeting and heard Brigham Speak on the policy of preserving our health and condemned the present system of Doctors, &c I went from meeting to Father Knight an took dinner then met the Lodge and police and came home at dark and then went on (Patrol guard) with Br Weeks and came home at day break.

11 F. this morning went to the Shoe Shop & got a pair of boots and came home and then went to Maudsley's again & got my likeness, then went to Father Knight. and at 2 met the Lodge then went to the Temple for some Lithograph paper and then went to the police and came home about 9 o'clock —

---

14. July 4, 1845, was not celebrated in Nauvoo this year, except for the concert that night at the music hall. Instead, the people went about their regular duties, with an extra number helping on the temple. Since the death of their leaders and the failure to bring any of the assassins to justice, the Mormons felt that this was a land of depotism rather than one of freedom.

15. This is Robert L. Campbell who was born January 21, 1825, baptized in 1842, and arrived in Nauvoo in early 1845. He did some engraving and later did clerical work with Patriarch John Smith and Apostle Willard Richards. He came west with the 1848 migration and continued in clerical work all his life.

The lithograph made at this time is now in the possession of a grandson, LaFayette Lee. (Copies are in the Utah State Historical Society and the Henry E. Huntington Library.)

12th S. This morning I met some of the police at the Stand to regulate some seats for ourselves and then went to Father Knight and took dinner and then met the Lodge and police and came home at dark.

13th Sunday. This was a very wet disagreeable day untill noon when the rain ceased and I went to the Temple and from thence to the Masonic Hall and met the Police and came home about dark.

14th M. Went down on the flats this morning & fell in company with General Rich on the way and had some talk with him he desired to see me again and I went to the Hall saw D. D. Yearsly on my way conversed on merchantile business, the Lodge met at 9 o'clock from thence I went to Br Campbell's thence to Maudsleys and took dinner at Allen J. Stouts. and met the Lodge again at 2 o'clock, then went on the hill to the Shoe Shop got a pair of shoes and then took them to Br Maudsley and Started to the police met with Br John E. Page[16] and he came with me to the Hill & spoke to the police on the Subject of having a house built. for himself for which the police subscribed very liberally I then came home and went to Br Sabins & Sister Sabin who had long been sick was dead from thence I went to Br Weeks' and was on guard all night which turned out to be a very wet rainy night I came home in the morning a little after sunrise

Tuesday July 15th 1845. This morning I went to the upper stone house to by some groceries of Oliver. fell in Company with D. McArthur who was with me we came by his house Stayed awhile and came home & after dinner went to Br Tufts who was very sick and after Laying hands on him I went to the Lodge after which I went to Yearsley's Store then met the police and came home with Br Shumway and then came home at about dark.

16th W. This morning about 10 o'clock I went to Petty's Shop to get a pair of bullet molds made and then went in company with Amasa Lyman to Br Hewett's to see dead bodies of the two Hodges who had been hung at Burlington but they had been taken to the grave yard before we got there. I then came with Br Turley down to Allen Stout's and I went to Br Maudsleys and from there to the Lodge

---

16. John E. Page was a member of the Council of Twelve Apostles of the church, having been ordained in 1839 at Far West. Previous to this appointment he had filled several important missions for the church. In 1835 he had "converted upwards of six hundred persons in Canada" and brought them in a group to join the Kirtland Camp. With the other apostles, he had been absent at the time of the martyrdom, and at his return he had supported Brigham Young as leader.

His request here on July 14, 1845, would have been no surprise for the *Nauvoo Neighbor* of July 9, preceding, had carried the following announcement:

HO! The Temple, The Nauvoo House
and My House

Let no private interest obstruct the progress of the Temple or Nauvoo House; yet it is obvious to all the church that I should have a home as much as other men and something to sustain me and my family while we serve them in our capacity and if the Saints and others design to help in this matter it is imperatively necessary it should be done soon, if done at all this season.

While the masons are employed on the Nauvoo House you can bring on the materials for my house, stone, brick, lumber, etc. that all things may be ready for the masons when they can be had. A word to the wise is sufficient.

Please hear us and attend to your call in due season, that we may have a house to shield off the chilling blast of winter.

Respectfully your servant,
John E. Page

By the next February, when the leaders left Nauvoo, he was out of harmony with his fellow apostles, and on the 6th of that month was "disfellowshiped." On July 16, 1846, Page was excommunicated, and Ezra T. Benson was appointed to fill his place in the quorum.

and then went with Br Langley to John S. Higbee and then met the Police and came home at dark.

17 T. This morning I went to the Arsnal to help put on the timbers for the roof, took dinner at Jones' went back to the Arsnal & at 4 o'clock met the Lodge at a regular Communication. then met the police came home at dark and patrolled with James Pace about 2 hours on Parly Street then came home.

18 F. this was a rainy morning, after dinner I went to the Lodge then met the police and came home at dark accompanied by Brs Egan & Shumway and brought home some wine and after supper I returned with Br Egan to the flat and came home about ½ past eleven o'clock.

Saturday. July 19th 1845. Earley this morning I went to Warthan's to get a horse & buggy and went with my wife and child to the Steam mill about a mile below Nauvoo to get some lumber and came home about noon. after dinner took the horse & buggy home and went to the Lodge. then went to John S. Higbee's then met the police and came home and went to see Allen Weeks and stood patrol guard all night came home in the morning about sun rise.

Sunday 20th. Went to meeting in the fore noon Elder Orson Pratt[17] spoke and was followed by B. Young's and others after which Elder Taylor Spoke and mentioned about the dissatisfaction which was caused by the two Hodges who were hung at Burlington being buried here that he had been requested to mention it there was remarks made for & against them remaining the vote being put to the congregation it was almost unanimously decided that they should not remain in our burying ground.

I came home and and in the evening met the police and after the duty was over Spoke about one hour on certain principles where called forth by a circumstance taking place last night at the Temple by Some persons forcing themselves in the Temple abruptly without autharity from the police guard. after which I came home about 9 o'c —

M. 21st. This day there was an exehibition of animals in town & the Police were invited to go free it commenced at one o'clock In the forenoon I was down on the flat making preperations for the police to go to the Show. First about the time the Show was to commence there came a hard north wind which blew down the canvass and completely frustrated the calculations of the Show men. it was followed by rain. There was a large concourse of people assembled to See the Show the Seventies Hall was crouded to over flowing during the storm and the Street was still full of people who still remained So anxious were they to See. after the winds had somewhat subsided the Show men began to regulate the waggons to still make an exibition as well as they could. there were crouds of people who. without respect to order or decency who crouded on to the canvass &c of the Show men and rendered it impossible to do any thing for them when the police took it up and tryed to inforce order which they did after having first to nock down some three or four which raise a great excitement about it some for & some against the police at length the Show commenced and we had a tolerable time though it was raining most of the time. The police were invited free after the show I met at the police quarters as usual and came home about half past 6 o'clock very sick

---

17. Orson Pratt, one of the most intellectual and influential leaders of the Mormon Church, was baptized on his nineteenth birthday, September 19, 1830. From that day on he filled many missions and wrote much in defense of his faith. In 1835 Pratt was ordained an apostle; in 1844 he was made a member of the Council of Fifty. He crossed the Atlantic Ocean sixteen times on missions for the church. In addition to some fifteen religious pamphlets, he published scientific books on mathematics, astrology, and calculus. He died on October 3, 1881.

Tuesday July the 22. This morning Br Langley came to my house and we went to the Temple and went on the top and "viewed the Land Scape over" and about noon I went to Allen Stouts then. Saw Br Harris who expressed his good feelings to me and the police for our good & efficient course we had taken yesterday and in former times wishing me God Speed. I then went by the printing office to the Temple and came home and after supper met the police. Br Young met with us and gave us some good advice relative to our duty I then came home and went on guard as on last Saturday night and came home about Sun up

W. 23. Went down on the flat and Temple with Brs Langley & Shumway met police. Saw Prest B. Young in the after noon on matters relating to groceries and such like abominable things home at dark.

T. 24. This morning I went to Br. Brigham Young's with the police a greed on last night to pile his lumber to dry from thence we went to the Stand to fix our seats I then went to A. J. Stout's and took dinner and from thence went to the grave yard with W. D. Huntington[18] the Sexton to hunt the grave of my child we dug up two graves but they were not the one. We did not find it. I came home and met the police & came home accompanied by Br Shumway & P. Young and after taking some wine I went home with Shumway and then went on patrol guard as on Tuesday night & came home before day.

F. 25. In the fore noon I went down to S. Gulley's to get some apples and flour, came home and after dinner met the Lodge and police and came home at dark.

S 26. This morning I went to Br McArthur's & with him to the Lower Steam mill for lumber for my house & came home and after dinner met the Lodge & police, came home at dark.

Sunday July the 27th 1845. Went to meeting at the Stand Br. Brigham preached after some business had been done about the Nauvoo House at noon Br A. Lyman came home with me and took dinner & we then went back to meeting and at 2 o'clock I went to the Seventie's conference at the Hall, and after some general business was done the different Quorums met Seperately. I met with the 11th from thence met the police and then came home and went to A. Weeks then to Horn's Store for candles came home at about 10 o'c

M. 28th. Br. Langley came to my house for me to go home with him to See Sister Vear whose husband was sick I went and returned home about 9 o'clock and after dinner went to the Lodge and then met the police and came home at dark

T. 29th. In the morning Andrew Lytle came here and I went with him to the flat and went to see Egan & Kay then came home and after dinner went to the Lodge and then met the police and came home at dark about which time Br Egan came

18. William D. Huntington, father of Dimick and Oliver B. and also of two daughters who became wives of Joseph Smith, was born March 28, 1784, in New Hampshire. He was baptized in 1835 and joined the Mormon Church at Kirtland where his home was always a refuge for the prophet. Although he lost heavily in the Kirtland bank, he remained loyal through all the persecutions.

In Nauvoo, Huntington was a fifer in the band, a stone cutter on the temple, and sexton. He prepared the bodies of Joseph and Hyrum Smith for burial, supervised the interment, and later was in charge of moving them to a new location. The *Nauvoo Neighbor* carried a weekly report of the work of the sexton, which included the names, ages, and cause of death of those for whom he dug graves. After the exodus Huntington had charge of commissary and provisions for the camp. He died at Mount Pisgah in 1846.

with a buggy after me to go to a small party at his house to celebrate his wife's birth day. I went we had a most agreeable entertainment and had a very delicious Supper well served up, plenty of wine & beer & other good drinks. the feast was mostly entertained with music, (i.e.), three violins bass viol and horn, with occasional Singing and agreeable conversation Br William Clayton, Wm Pitt,[19] Hutchison, Smithie & Kay were the musicians. We continued untill about half past twelve o'clock at night when we dismissed and went away I have been to but few such agreeable parties in my life where a few were assembled together with the same good feelings of friendship. All seemed of one heart & partook of the enjoyment of the good things and comforts of [life] with that dignaty which bespoke that they knew how to appreciate the blessings of God in the way that he designed we should. May they all have many more such good & happy nights. I came home at day light.

W. 30th. In the morning Br Clark came to my house and I went with him to Warthan's and I then went to the Temple and from thence to Levi Stewart's and took dinner and then went to the Lodge & from thence to Br Turley's to get some meat and came home and then met the police and came home at dark.

T. 31. This morning Br Berry came to my house to lay stone in my cellar. I went to Warthan's to get some meat and after dinner went to the Lodge & then met the police and came home at dark.

August the 1st F. To day I had several of the police to wit Clark, Pace, Glines, Sabin, A. J. Stout to come & dig at my cellar untill noon and then they went home and at evening I met the police and came home by Warthans and gave him a lesson on his duty, got some meat & came home at 9 o'c

2 S. Wrote for Br Harwood before breakfast & was at home untill evening attending to my cellar digging untill evening then met the police on my way home met A. C. Brewer had a long talk he told me about 1500 waggons &c I got home about dark —

3 Sunday. Went to meeting at the Stand in the fore noon. President Young preached he warned the saints to awake from their lethargy in which they seemed to be at present and said that if they did not we should be blown to the four winds & many other things. after meeting I came home accompanied by Bishop Carn & my brother and took dinner went to meeting again and from thence to the police meeting and it was this evening that the police unanimously agreed to make & present Prest Brigham Young a carriage suitable to his rank & station in the Kingdom of God. I came home and went on guard as on the last night I was out on guard and came home in the morning about light.

W. 4th. This morning I took my spy glass to Br Shumway who was going on a mission came home and set the masons to work at my cellar wall and then went to the Temple to the election and voted and came home accompanied by Br C. Daniels and after dinner I went to the Lodge and Br Knight's and then met the police and went to see Brigham Young on some police business and then came home and went on patrol guard with a number of police near the Temple saw Brs

---

19. William Pitt and his band were all converted at the same time as a result of the missionary work of Wilford Woodruff and Heber C. Kimball in England. They emigrated as a group and always maintained their identity as a unit. William Pitt composed a special "Capstone March" for the ceremony in Nauvoo. During the exodus they gave concerts at some of the settlements and camps. In Utah they usually appeared in holiday parades. William Pitt died February 21, 1873, in Salt Lake City.

Bigler & Everett who was on guard and at their request gave them some instructions on the duty of guards which they seemed to receive. I came home about 11 o'clock —

T. 5. This morning I went to get some help about my cellar and was at home till after dinner and met the Lodge and police and came home at dark

August the 6th 1845 Wednesday. At 8 o'clock this morning I met with a number of the police in council at the M Hall President B. Young was present and gave us a charge we all seemed to be of one heart and mind. I then went to the upper landing with Egan & Kay and went with them down the river to the ferry they went across and I went to A. Stout's and then came home and at evening met the police and came home and went to see Scenery of the assassination of Joseph & Hyrum exhibited and came to A. Weeks and was out all night & came home at dawn of day.

T. 7th. Was engaged in procuring help & materials to build my cellar untill in the evening then went to the Lodge at 4 o'clock to a regular communication then met the police and home at dark

F. 8th. this morning I was very unwell & was at home untill time to meet the Lodge at 2 o'c Still attending to the work at the cellar &c I met the Lodge then went to Father Knight's then met the police and came home before dark rainy

S. 9th. Still attending to the work at my cellar I met the Lodge at 2 o'clock then went and got lumber for a door frame then met the police and came to the Temple & Saw father Cutler about removing certain nuisance &c and met D. Wilson as I came home & had some talk about our police duty & came home about ½ past nine o'clock.

Sunday 10th. Went to the Stand to meeting and at intermission I went with a number of other police and some of the band on the top of the belfrey of the Temple and the musicians played some beautiful airs to the congregation as they were dismissed we came down and I came home accompanied by Brs Pace & Grant of the police. after dinner we went to the Seventies conference from thence to the police and I then came home and went on patroll guard round the Temple was with A. Weeks. the latter part of the night. came home at day light

11 M. Was at home attending to my house untill after dinner then went to the Lodge, and police then went to see B. Young on business came home at dark.

12th T. At 9 o'clock went to a council of the Twelve at Br Richards and was there untill noon came home and met the Lodge and police and after Some other business about Emmett came home about. dark very rainy.

13th W. To day the police assembled near the temple at 7 o'clock A.M. to fill up a cellar which had been dug by Dr Foster[20] there was a large company of other brethren came to assist we worked till 12 o'clock hauling sand and throwing into the cellar in the afternoon we met to level the sand in the cellar and had a joyful time. At 3 o'clock I met the Lodge then met the police and came home about dark.

---

20. Dr. Robert D. Foster became interested in Mormonism through Sidney Rigdon, who was one of his patients. Foster was baptized in 1841 and moved to Nauvoo, where he was made surgeon general in the Nauvoo Legion.

He had purchased considerable property in Nauvoo and planned to erect a home on the hill near the temple. The fact that the Mormon leaders objected to this and that Foster himself was opposed to the doctrine of "Celestial Marriage" combined to put him so out of harmony that on March 4, 1844, Joseph Smith publicly branded him as a traitor. Already embittered, Foster now became such an open and active opponent that after the martyrdom the Mormon people held him responsible in part for it.

T. 14th. Fast day. In the morning went to See about brick for my house, then went to meeting at the Stand from there to the flat ~~met the Lodge at 2 o'clock~~ and as usual and came home about dark and went on guard by Weeks again and came home in the morning after day light.

August the 15th 1845 Friday. In the morning I went to the Hall to meet Levi Stewart on business and from thence to the upper Landing saw Br Higbee and C. Allen. done some business in relation to temporal matters of the police then came Down by Levi Stewarts. & saw Br J. D. Parker about a coat and then came home by A. Weeks to see about _____. and then came home and in the evening went to the police came home at dusk and after dark went to lay hands on Br Colemere who is very sick came home about ½ after 9.

16th S. This morning I went to Masonic Hall to meet the police at 8 o'clock. They met to tell their feelings to each other and their determinations I was taken very sick. At ½ past one we adjourned till tomorrow at 2 o'clock as only about half had spoken and I came home just able to walk and was confined to my bed all that evening was sick all night.

17th Sunday. Not very well yet. Went to the Stand to meeting. W. Smith[21] [spoke on] what he called the first Chapter of the Epistle of St William and was followed

---

Roberts, *Documentary History*, VII, gives several examples which show the strong feeling that existed against this man. His appearance in the town, always heavily guarded, was enough to start a riot. A letter to County Sheriff Deming requested that Foster transact his business in Nauvoo by agent to avoid any violence. When Foster came into the town a few days later, a delegation of nine women called upon him, ordering him to leave before night lest there should be further bloodshed.

On October 25, 1845, Foster was aboard the steamer *Sarah Ann* when it docked at the Nauvoo wharf, and at once there was such a riot between his men and the Mormons on the pier that the captain was forced to pull away without unloading his cargo. Even then some shots were exchanged. Roberts, *Documentary History*, VII, 169, 176, 486.

In the light of these facts, it is easy to understand Stout's statement that "we had a joyful time," and also the willingness of townspeople to help fill up the excavation.

21. William Smith had grown more and more critical of the policies of Brigham Young. Three days after the incidents recorded here, Smith wrote a long letter to J. C. Little in Washington, D. C., of which the following is an excerpt:

City of Joseph Augt 20, 1845

Dear Bro Little

It has been some time since I have seen you . . . , but I have thought often of you and the pleasant acquaintance I found in your place . . . .

Now for Nauvoo . . . the subject of Rigdonism is nearly dead now, and I hope the spiritual wife doctrine with it, both in and out of the church. What will come next the Lord only knows. The saints here are generally well and are working diligently in building up the Temple and Nauvoo House though they are mostly very poor . . . .

Nauvoo is not the place for poor people. As there is such an immense number of them here already and there must be great suffering among them. I find that I cannot live here, . . . the people are so poor.

There seems to be a severe influence working against me and the Smith family in this place, which makes our situation very unpleasant . . . .

. . . I hope you will always remember me in your prayers.

Your afflicted but devoted Brother
William Smith

Original is in the possession of Mr. J. C. Little, Morgan, Utah; typescript, Utah State Historical Society.

William Smith was dropped from his position in the church on October 6, 1845, and the next week (October 12) was excommunicated. For a time he associated himself with the Strangites; later he joined the Reorganized Church of Jesus Christ of Latter Day Saints. Occasionally he wrote letters in criticism of Brigham Young or of the church policy in general. Some of these were published and then answered in the *Frontier Guardian.*

by Elder John Taylor to which William showed considerable feelings after meeting I went and took dinner with A. J. Stout. and then met the police at 2 o'clock we had a good meeting untill about 6 all seemed well united and determined to go ahead after police I went to Allen's again and then came home and went home with Allen Week's and from there to the Temple on guard and came home a short time before day light.

August the 18th 1845 Monday. Went Earley to see Br Wilson to do some hauling for me. then went to John S Higbee's to take Sister Bennett after a bonnet came home and went with my wife there also for a bonnet came home and after dinner went down to the Lodge & on my way Br George A. Smith spoke to me about setting a guard at the Nauvoo House which I agreed to do. he said he would gave three dollars pr night to have it guarded. after the Lodge was over I remained there untill the police met after the guard was detailed the police went to W. P. Lyon's to raise some timber for him on his building. from there I went to the Nauvoo House with the guard which I had detailed there and saw it commenced all things was right I then came to A. J. Stout and took Supper and then came to Br J. P Harmons and after some talk, he and Br. L. W. Hancock came home with me after I had come home Br Hancock having his fiddle played on it for about one hour and a half to our satisfaction. We had an agreeable evening about 10 o'clock they went home & I to bed.

19th T. This morning at 8 o'clock I met with a number of the police at the Masonic Hall we had a good meeting which lasted till noon. I then went to A. J. Stouts & took dinner and then to Maudsley's and met the Lodge & police and came home and went on guard with J. D. Parker & J. Worthan untill near midnight and then came home.

20th W. Very wet rainy morning. Earley this morning A man by the name of Ralphs was killed by lightning I was at home working at my window glass & also wrote the history of Abraham Stephens life, and then went to the Lodge and then met the police and came home about dark.

21st T. Went to Jos Warthans for a Buggy came home met the Lodge at 2 o'clock & at 4 also it being a regular communication. Then met the police and came home about dark and went on guard at the Temple, & came home about dawn of day.

F. 22nd. Went to Warthans & got a horse & buggy & took my wife to Br Maudsley's to have her portrait taken came home at 12 and then went to the Lodge Then to the Nauvoo House with Br Daniels and then met the police, then went and saw B. Young, at Lorenzo Young's about our police duty and also some cast iron shafts for cannon. home at dark.

S. 23rd. I went this morning to see Br B. Young and went with him to Br Maudsley to have his likeness taken, I went then to the Masonic Hall and met in council with Brs Roundy, Parker, Daniels & Stephens of the Police and adjourned at one o'clock and I came home very sick. fell in company with Thos. S. Edwards on my way home & at his request taught him matters concerning what constitutes the Priesthood, when I came home I went to bed and was unable to set up any more that day was sick all night.

Sunday 24th. I was still weak and feeble about 8 o'clock Br Scott came after me to go to Col Rockwoods[22] to meet the Committee to make out the history of the

---

22. Albert Perry Rockwood was born June 9, 1805, at Holliston, Massachusetts. He was baptized at Kirtland, Ohio, by Brigham Young on July 25, 1837, and soon thereafter, the two

Nauvoo Legion I went & at ten we went to meeting at the Stand. Br B. Young preached on several subjects I came home and after dinner went to the Stand to a business meeting where matters relative to the Nauvoo house and other matters of local interest was taken up from there I went to the police and then came home & went with Allen Weeks on guard again & came home in the morning

25th. M. Went to the Temple then to A. J. Stout then to Br. Knight and met the Lodge at 2 and at 3 met the committee to write the history of the Legion, then met the police and then after some running about I went to the Temple and then went on patrol guard with Parker Roundy Warthan Pace 2 of the Mechams & Langly, [*sic*] was out nearly all night. came home and went to bed at 3½ o'c

26th T. Markham came to my house this morning with papers containing the history of the Legion I was very unwell and kept my bed untill noon then went to Br Pace's and we went to A. J. Stouts, then to the Lodge & police I came home at dark.

27th W. Still unwell. Was writing the history of the Legion till about ten, then went to Br Richards to take that which I had written. F. M. Edwards came to my house just before I had started and wanted to know my mind concerning him which I did not give. I went from Richards' to the Lodge room to get some papers concerning the war in June 1844, for Br Richards, and then went to A. J. Stout's & went to bed about 3 hours being worn down, then met the Lodge and police and came home & went on guard with A Weeks again. home at day

August the 28th 1845 Thursday. Still very unwell. Early in the morning wrote the Biographical history of Lewis Mecham then went to A. J. Stouts and at 2 met the Lodge and then the police and then came home by A. Weeks & got some pork about dark.

29 F. Some better this morning. After writing a while I met with the Lodge at 9 o'c then went to W. Richards and saw B. Young & laid some matters of police before him and had his instructions thereon then came home and thus started to the police fell in company with P. Dibble went with him near the Temple and met with I [Ira] Miles & F. M. Edwards we all went to Grub & Richie's Store and took a good bate of watter mellons. Edwards & I then went to the Masonic Hall to meet with the police. J. S. [Joshua Sawyer] Holman Brought a load of mellons to the police they had a good mess and several left. I came home at dark.

30th S. I am now quite well. In the morning I went to Warthan's and got a buggy & took my wife to J. Higbee to get a bonnett and then we went to Maudsley's to have her likeness drawn, then came home and I took the buggy home and met the Lodge & police & came home at dark.

---

went as companions on a mission to the Eastern States. In 1842 he was captain of Joseph Smith's "life guards," a drill officer for the Nauvoo Legion, and finally became a general in that organization. In the exodus from Nauvoo he was a captain of fifty; at Garden Grove he was put in charge of bridge building. From 1845 until his death, he was one of the first presidents of Seventies for the whole church.

As Brigham Young's first adopted son, Rockwood enjoyed many privileges and responsibilities, one that he was placed in charge of all the family during the 1848 emigration. In Utah he was warden of the territorial prison for fifteen years, the first fish commissioner, director of the Deseret Agricultural and Manufacturing Society, and a member of the legislature from 1851 until his death. He died on November 25, 1879, in Sugarhouse Ward, Salt Lake City.

31st Sunday. I went to meeting at the Stand Br P. P. Pratt[23] spoke having lately returned home from the East, then went and took dinner with Br J. D. Lee, then met at the Seventies Hall, then went to the Temple and went to the top of the Steeple with Br Scovil & Langley then went to Weeks took supper & met the police at the Temple as we had agreed to meet there after, then went to Weeks' again. and staid till about nine o'clock then went with him to the Temple and met some other of the police & we then removed a nuisance which took till about 12 o'c I then came home.

September 1 M. About nine o'clock I met with B. Young & L. N. Scovil in the Masonic Hall & made some arrangements with him in letting him have some articles to finish his house He then taught us some what concerning the future destiny of the church. I then came to the Temple and then home and at 2 met the Lodge and then met the police and then took Br Pace and went and brought a trunk to my house from the Hall where came about dark.

2 T. Wrote the Biographical history of Joseph Clements then went to Allen Stout's then to Br Campbell's & had my likeness taken to be put in a Scenery representing Joseph Smith addressing the Nauvoo Legion on the 18th of June 1844. it is to be taken in military uniform[24] I then went to the Lodge & then to the police and then to Br Sabins & who gave me some earthen ware as a mark of respect I then came home it was a little after dark

3 W. Br Lewis Mecham came here this morning & I wrote & finished his Biographical History & then Br C. Shumway came & after a short time we went to Allen J. Stout's then to the Nauvoo House & then to the Temple. & then to a mead shop and took a drink on our way round town I was giving him some instructions relative to police duty and the principals to be governed by to prevent being decieved & imposed upon by false hearted men I left him there & I went home with H. Peck and took dinner then went to the Lodge and then to J. Knight. then to the Temple to meet the police but as there was a storm rising I went with some others of the police to Warthan's meat Shop and staid till the storm was over. This was one of the severest hail storms I ever saw It rained very fast and the hail fell in large lumps and was blown with such force that all the windows in the North and West of the houses in the city I believe was broken It lasted about an hour, after the hail had done falling & the rain somewhat ceased I went to the Temple and the guard being detailed by Br Harmon, I then came home it still raining very fast when I came home it being dark I found that all the glass in the North and west of my house was broken except a few in the west which were shielded by a shade tree and the storm had beat in at the windows but no injury further was done.

---

23. Parley Parker Pratt was one of the most effective proselyters of early Mormondom. Born April 12, 1807, in Burlington, Otsego County, New York, he joined the Mormon Church in 1830 and thereafter spent much of his time as a missionary.

In 1835 Pratt was made an apostle. He shared in the persecutions of Missouri, being imprisoned without trial for eight months, but escaped July 4, 1839. In 1840 Pratt went with others to England, where they began publication of the periodical, *The Millennial Star*. He returned in 1842, only to be sent on another mission, this time to the Eastern States.

He came to Utah in the fall of 1847; in 1849 he was sent on an exploring mission to southern Utah. Most of his time was spent in either preaching or writing for the church, his best-known pamphlets being *A Voice of Warning* and *A Key to Theology*. Many of his hymns are still sung by Mormon congregations.

On May 13, 1857, Parley P. Pratt was stabbed to death in Arkansas by a Hector McLean, whose former wife had become a plural wife of Pratt's. Pratt was buried near the spot where he fell. His grave, for many years unmarked, now bears a simple headstone.

24. This picture was widely exhibited later in Mormon settlements as a part of a lecture on the early history of the church.

4 W. At home in the fore noon & went to Shumway's & got a six shooter Brs Eagan & C. Allen came here I went down in town with them and saw B. Young and then met the Lodge at 4 o'c then met the police & and [*sic*] the Eleventh Quorum at the Temple both met at 6 o'c Warthan then came and brought me home in a buggy & then took me down to see B. Young who gave me the advice which I wanted. We then came to the Temple & I stoped there and patroled with Egan & Kay & Stephens and came home at 11½ o'clock

5 F. Went down in Town met with C. C. Rich and was with him till, 2 o'clock. He told me some of his proceedings in relation to some matters which I was concerned in &c &c I left him and went to the Lodge then to John Lytles an run Some bullets and then went to the Temple & met the police & then went home about dark & then went to A. Weeks and went on patrol guard with Weeks Sabin Langley & W. Smith and was out till 11 o'c

6th S. Earley went to Warthans and got his horse & buggy and took my wife to the Widow Casto's and got some apples, then came home and met the Lodge and then went to A. Stout's and then to the police & then to A. Weeks. home at day light.

7th Sunday. Went with my wife to meeting at the Stand & at intermission met with the Eleventh Quorum & made arrangements for a feast next Saturday. came home from meeting with my wife and, then met the police and then came home and went with Warthan around through the city saw B. Young he told me to see to the picket guard out of the city as the mob was threatning again came home at 11 o'c.

8th M. This morning I went with my wife to the Store and then to the tailors, then to the rope works with Langly & Stout, to see Br Egan but did not see him, and at 2 o'clock met the Lodge and at 5 met some officers of the Legion at Coolidges' to see about the painting of the scenery of Joseph the Prophet addressing the Nauvoo Legion on the 18th day of June 1844. The officers were dissatisfied with the plan for Br. Dibble was about put in the like ness of officers who were not present & also some men who were to be put in conspicuous places on the scenery who were not officers and moreover betrayed the prophet & patriarch to death & also other men who had disgraced their calling as officers to all of these things I made objections and declared I would not be seen portrayed in a group of such men for it would be a disgrace to my children and roughly handled the characters of certain characters in our midst after which the matter was laid over for future consideration I then met the police & went with Br Harmon and laid hands on Br A. Weeks who was very sick then we went to Br Shumways and laid hands on him he was very sick also then to my house and took supper and went to B. Youngs to see him but he was gone to bed being unwell, then to A. Stouts, then to the Temple & saw C Allen he gave me some tithing in stockings & gloves I then came home at 11 o'clock at night.

9th F. Went Early this morning to see B. Young, he (also met the Lodge at 9 o'c) was very unwell, gave him some presents, in stockings & gloves. then went to the Temple with Jos Warthan and got his horse & buggy and went with Br Harmon to Major Bills about 4 miles East of the Temple to give him some orders respecting regulating a picket guard in that quarter as there is some signs of Mobocracy rising up we took dinner there and came home by way of Br C. Allen & then I took the horse & buggy home and came home and met the police and then went with Br

Harmon & Horr to see a boy look in a "peep Stone,"[25] for some money which he said he could see hid up in the ground, he would look and we would dig but he found no money he said it would move as we approached it, I came home about ten oclock at night.

September the 10th 1845 Wednesday. Went to the Temple then to the Committee house and saw H. C. Kimball and gave him some presents and after some conversation about the Law of God I went to the Temple and got in his buggy and rode with him to Allen J. Stouts who came home with me to help me bring some articles which I got from S. Gully and after dinner we went down by the Temple & to the Lodge at 2, o'clock, and I then met with the Police & some officers of the Legion at the Stand to consult on the matter of the painting as refered to on the 8th the matter was related by Br Dibble who stated his reasons for the course he had taken when I again spoke at length on the position I took on the 8th and was followed by by others after which the thing was agreed to be left to the officers concerned to say what was right about it I then detailed the police guard and then went to A. Weeks with C. C. Rich and laid hands on him we then went to C. Shumway who was also sick then I came home it was a little after dark.

11th Thursday. Early went to Warthan meat Shop and got some beef and saw S. Earl on my way who told me that the mob had commenced burning houses at Lima.[26] What will be next God only knows. I then went down by the Temple to see A. J. Stout & then went to see Col Turley and while there I recieved orders from General Rich in person to have the Cohort put in readiness to repel an attact in a minutes notice. Col Turley and I then went to put the orders in execution and came to my house, and took dinner & then went down on the flat on the same business. I then went with Br J. P. Harmon and went with him on the same business and then after going to the Masonic Hall to see the state of the cannon I went to the Temple to meet the police and then came home and went on guard at A. Week as previous. home at 12 o'c

12th F. Went to A. J. Stouts after some flour, heard that the mob was still burning houses at Lima and that they had burned 5 yesterday. and then went to the Temple saw Br Harmon about the military affairs in prospect, then went with him down to Turley's saw him on the same subject. We were not well satisfied with the shape of matters for we suspected that those who betrayed Joseph & Hyrum was now trying to sway an influence in the affairs pertaining to the military in case of a war with the mob. I went from there to Allen Stout's and eat dinner and while eating recieved orders from genl Rich to meet him at the Masonic Hall which I did and he told me what was done in council We were to let the mob burn for the time being the houses of the Saints, and not make war on them. I felt better satisfied when I saw for I learned that those men were not using an influence in the councils as I expected for they were not admitted in council I went there to the Lodge then to the Temple then home and reloaded my pistols & then went to the police and

25. A current belief was that lost or buried treasure might be located by the use of a peep stone. Quite a number of such stones are now on display, along with other Indian artifacts, in the museum at Binghampton, New York. They all have common characteristics: each is flat, smooth, and of unusual color or design, and each has a hole made by artificial means in the larger end. If the stone is oblong, it often has a hole in each end. It would seem that these stones were originally used by ancient Indian tribes as good luck charms or embellishments suspended around the neck, wrist, or ankle.

26. The story of the burning of homes in the village of Lima has been told by many Mormon writers and diarists. "Isaac Morley presided at the village and had advised non-resistance, whereupon about one hundred and seventy-five houses were burned to the ground and the families forced to flee for their lives." Ford, *History of Illinois*, 405-7.

while detailing the guard Col Scott told me that I was wanted to go to W. Richards
to a council. I went and found H. C. Kimball W. Richards, G. A. Smith, G. Miller
A. H. Perkins C. C. Rich J. Scott Brigham Young did not come because it commenced raining very hard. I then learned that the mob were still burning houses
and that 400 teames had gone down to move the Saints to the city who had their
houses burnt up. I then came home through the rain & wind about 10 o'clock when
I came home.

13th S. Was unwell this morning The 11th Quorum had a feast to day at the Seventies Hall at which the 12 & first presidents of the Seventies were invited. I went and
took my family we had a day of feasting and enjoyment in the fore noon I learned
that the mob were still burning houses I came home and then went to the police
and then had a talk with Br Langley then came home soon after dark.

14th Sunday. Went with my wife to meeting at the Stand H. C. Kimball & B. Young
preached about the mob burning houses and gave the Saints advice what to do
under the present trying circumstances, at inter-mission I met the Eleventh Quorum
near the Stand,[27] and then in the afternoon attended meeting. it was a business
meeting and all who were not in good fellowship were not allowed to be present
and the police in keeping them away had to flog three who were determined to
stay. I remained there till time to meet the police saw B. Young who told me to
see Genl Rich about business which he had to do, after police meeting I went with
Col Scott to see Rich after some consultation with them we concluded that it was
best to post a guard below the City to prevent any person from going in or out
to correspond with the mob as some were trying to make a difficulty in the name
of the mormons we then went to see Br E. Everett who was to post the guard. Scott
& I. then went to B. Young's & saw him and then I came home about 10 o'c.

15th M. At 7 o'clock met with the police at B. Young's to build him a Stable and
at 9 o'clock met at the Masonic Hall with B. Young C. C. Rich, S. Markham, G.
Miller A. P. Rockwood G. W. Langley, D. Carn J. Scott, T. Turley, D. McArthur
&c officers of the Legion to hold a council on the subject of defence against the
mob it was then decided that the Legion be put in immediate readiness for defence
and that I should be Brig Genl of the 2nd Cohort I then was summoned to go with
Langley, Parker & A. Lytle to Genl Millers We went and then adjourned to the
Masonic Hall and wated an hour and was told by Miller that the subject of our
meeting was laid over, I then went to the Nauvoo House Store and got some soap
I came home, at 2 o'clock and then went to see Brs Shumway and Weeks who were
sick and then went to the shoe shop then to the police and home at dark.

16th T. The mob are still burning houses worse than ever at 8 o'clock I met the
fifth Regiment at the Masonic Hall, and organized them for the defence of the
Saints according to the decision yesterday, the Question being put they unanimousley
voted that I should be their Brigadier General the Regiment was then by T. Turley
acting Colonel I then went and saw B. Young at his house and complained about
the practice of having the police taken away for other business without my knowledge and thwarting my opperations &c & then went to A. J. Stout's and took dinner
about 12 o'c From thence I went to the Hall again and met the First Regiment under
Col Scott and had it organized and inspected as the other was in the fore noon
I then went to Willard Richards to a council and saw Genl Miller who had taken
some of the police to do business for him. He insisted on having them & I demured

---

27. "The Stand" was a platform upon which the authorities sat at their outdoor meetings,
while the audience sat on benches of split logs or on the grass. This portable meetinghouse
was moved from place to place according to the weather.

We then left it to Brigham Young, who decided that he did not want any one to intercept the arrangements of the police, for they was his men and were to be let alone. Just as I came there I learned that a party of the mob had pursued and came very near overtaking Col Backenstos[28] our sheriff, who had gone down among them, to restore peace with the intention of killing him. But he fortunately met with the assistance of two men[29] one of whom upon his orders fired and killed one man, who proved to be the famous mobocrat Captain F. Worrell, who was sergeant of the guard at the jail when Joseph [and] Hyrum were assassinated at Carthage and was leagued with the assassins and had the guards guns loaded with blank cartrages. Thus fell one of the that fiendish gang of desperadoes & one of the worst enemies we had who was a ready tool to be sent by Col Levi Williams, the leader of the mob to execute his nafarious purposes. they took him into one of their waggons and all retreated This saved the life of the sheriff I went from thence to the Temple and there it was decided that There be a guard kept night & day around the Temple and that no stranger be allowed to come within the Square of the Temple Lot, and also that there be 4 large lanterns made for the purpose and placed about 25 feet from each corner of the Temple to keep a light by night for the convenience of the guard I immediately gave orders to have the lanturns made and then met the police as usual and detailed a regular Temple guard and put them under the command of Duncan McArthur, and then ordered Capt J. D. Hunter to guard the Nauvoo House with a part of his fur Company[30] and thus relieve the "old Police somewhat Just after dark Genl Miller went with a party of about one hundred men with the sheriff to take his family from Carthage to Nauvoo as she was in the hands of the mob party. I went from the Temple to Br. Harmon's & then went with him to A. Stouts and saw Genl Brigham Young who gave us orders to stop the firing of guns after night we then went home with him to see if the cannon was allright which were taken to his house finding it was we went to Br Harmons and Br J. H. Glines took a horse & buggy and brought me home at 11 o'clock.

17th W. Early this morning I recieved orders from Genl Rich to call the 2nd Cohort out to meet at the Square North East of the Temple at 10'clock A. M. I immediately gave orders to the several Colonels to that effect I then went to the Shoe shop and ordered a belt and rigging to carry pistols in I then went to the Masonic

---

28. Jacob Backenstos was not a Mormon, but was always friendly to the Mormon people. He had moved into Hancock County because his friend, Stephen A. Douglas, had been appointed to hold court there. Of him Governor Ford said:

Backintos [sic] was a smart-looking, shrewd, cunning plausible man, of such easy manners that he was likely to have a great influence with the Mormons. In due time Judge Douglas appointed him to be the clerk of the circuit court, and this gave him almost absolute power with that people in all political contests. In 1844, Backintos and a Mormon elder [Almon W. Babbitt] were elected to the legislature; and in 1845 he was elected sheriff, in place of Gen. Deming; and finally, to reward him for his great public services, he was appointed a captain of a rifle company in the United States army. But being just now regarded as the political leader of the Mormons, Backintos was hated with a sincere and thorough hatred by the opposite party. (*Ibid.*, 408.)

29. The two men who helped the sheriff were Orrin Porter Rockwell and Return Jackson Redden, with Rockwell firing the fatal shot. *Ibid.*, 409, also Roberts, *Documentary History*, VII, 446-47.

30. The term "Fur Company" had been coined during the 1838-39 troubles in Missouri. It referred to two or three small bands of mounted horsemen who went disguised on raiding expeditions from which they secured horses, cattle, or at times goods. They were especially avid in their search for firearms. Quite a number of writers, both Mormon and non-Mormon mention the fur companies by name. It is interesting to note that although the Danites had been disbanded and the name dropped, the "Fur Company" should continue.

Hall to meet the 4th Regt at 8 o'clock and other business I then went to Br. Dibble's and shaved and then went to the parade ground when the Legion & was formed and organized. as followes to wit Major Genl Charles C. Rich in command of the Legion The First Cohort was nearly all gone with General Miller as aforesaid and was not present. The Second Cohort was under my command. Previous to taking command I appointed David Candland to be my Clerk. who took his place as such There was three Regiments on the ground to wit The first Regiment under Col Scott, The 4th under Col Harmon and the 5th under Col Turley After the proper arraingements were made the Cohort was formed into A Hallow Square and Lieutenant General Brigham Young then into the Square and addressed the officers & soldiers as follows to wit: — It is my wish that every man from the age of 16 to 100 be enlisted in these companies & that Gen Rich continue the charge of the same & see that every man is armed & equipd as the Law directs & as the sheriff as ordered & be ready for any event that may happen. I am composed nor has the late disturbance had any effect upon me. I want this holloings. beating of drums & firing of Guns should cease the Police have their orders from this time to arrest every man or boy in our street found guilty of these acts or any one walking our street after night detain them till daylight & stripping off their clothes show whether they are male or female I am going to propos to J. B. Backenstos that he make every man a Deputy then we may sally forth with our writs in our pockets in any number & arrest these Mobbers when you shoot be sure & shoot right If you die — die like Deming[31] in the defence of your country's rights when we meet Deming's in another world he will [be] happy in the death he died God grant you may all live & die in the defence of your country's rights keep your Guns to yourselves trust no one & when you shoot take a good aim — Majr Genl Rich enquired if the officers & soldiers were willing to hearken to the counsel given to which he us also all the Regts responded Hie — Col Markham called for 50 men for a reinforcement to our comrades already out he failed in getting his compliment they having no horses he further said if a man owning horses refused to let them go he would mark that man — Brigr Stout said Let him be marked with a mark not soon forgotten & take his horse any how. The Corps were dismissed by Gen Rich at 12 — to meet at 2 P M. from thence I went to Gen'l Rich's to dine while there we agred to place certain companies upon picket guards to wit one about 4 miles above town — another at or near John Bills or Suffacools about 4 or 5 miles East of town the other on the Carthage Road near Joseph Farm from thence I returned to meet the Legion at 2 o'clock — the several Regts were as in the morning on the ground as also Col Hale with the 3 Reg who took his post in the line I detailed Capt O M. Allen with his compy from the 5 Reg up the river — Capt Bair from the 4 to guard near Bills & Suffoccools — Capt Kay of the 5 Reg — to guard near Lotts[32] Farm — with orders to let no man except he prove himself a friend if a

---

31. Miner R. Deming, the sheriff of Hancock County, offered a reward in the *Nauvoo Neighbor* July 6, 1845, for information which would lead to the arrest of the assassins of Irvin (also called Ervin and Irvine) Hodge. Although not a Mormon, Deming defended them upon occasion. And in one such attempt of violence against the Mormons, Deming shot and killed the leader of the mob, Dr. Samuel Marshall, who had assaulted him. Deming was arraigned on charge of murder, but died before he could be brought into court. This was on September 10, 1845, just a week before Brigham Young's comment was made. His death intensified the anti-Mormon feeling in the area and was in part responsible for this added mobilization of Mormon forces.

32. Cornelius P. Lott joined the Mormon Church in Bridgewater, Luzerne County, Pennsylvania, before 1834. He moved first to Kirtland and then to Missouri, where he became a leader in the Danite band. The *Elders Journal* for August 1838, reported that Jared Carter, Sampson Avard, and Cornelius P. Lott were generals before whom the military band passed in review at the celebration on July 4 preceding. Benjamin F. Johnson, *My Life's Review* (Independence,

spy bring him into Town. at 4 A. M. I gave order for Col Scott to select 30 men from the 1 Reg to be stationd near the Mansion House Barn to keep guard night & day till further orders also 30 from the 3. Reg under Col Hale to be stationd in Squire Spencer Barn east of the Temple to be stationed as the other till further orders — order that at the tolling of the Temple Bell every man know it as an alarm & repair forthwith armed & equipd to the parade ground at ½ past 4-o clock The Legion were dismissed to meet at 9-o clock on the parade ground next morning I went to meet the police at the temple & Capt Hunter & McRaes Two Compy met at the Stand I gave by invitation an address to the Two compy assembled & then went & detailed the Police guard at this moment by express I I was called to Council at Br Richards I met the compy commanded by Gen'l Miller just returned & who were in council at the house of Dr Richards he reported that on their entering Carthage they were fired upon by the mob who instantly fled the families which they designed to rescue were all fled except Mrs Deming, wife of the late Genl Deming she thought the recent death of her husband might appease the wrath of the mob against her and her family. The mob attempted to burn their own houses in order to lay it on the possee but the sheriff threatened to put the town to the sword if they did which caused them to desist. They then went towards Warsaw and on on reaching a point midway they were informed they were informed of new depredations by the mob. The sheriff then sent his family to Nauvoo under a small guard and proceeded to the scene of the mobbers. The mobbers saw them coming and took to flight the posse pursuing with orders to arrest them if possible if not to fire upon them. After pursuing them for some distance the posse fired upon them and killed two and wounded it is believed others. This was on Bear Creek about 2 o'clock this afternoon the possee then came to Nauvoo where they arrived about dark performing a forced march of about 65 miles in about 20 hours. After the council I had some conversation with B. Young relative to a man by the name of _____ who was in the _____ fur company. After relating the circumstances He gave his opinion and I saw Capts Hunter & McRae we went [half page left blank]

Thursday Sepbr 18. 1845. met with the Legion this morning at 9 A. M. as on yesterday the 4 Regts were present as aforesaid — report from the 2 Reg. was made that they had met & organized ready for service & had elected Capt Henry Herriman Leiu Col. of the same in place of Philamer [Philander?] Colton who showed a negligence in the service of his regiments — reports from the different guards — were all well — several prisoners were sent in — having failed to satisfy the guard but were dismissed. at 12 o'clock Gen Rich dismissed the Legion with orders for all companies except those occupying the several posts aforesaid, to be in readiness for actual service at a moments warning & that they immediately repair to the ground they now occupied At firing of the artillery it shall be the signal of alarm after which I went home — took dinner at ½ past 1 o clock David Candland my clerk came & wrote the address of Leui Gen Brigham Young at ½ past three Gen Rich came from thence I went with him to see Charles Shumway who is still very sick from there we went down to the Temple to meet with the police

Missouri, 1947) devotes Chapter III to his activities as a Danite and on page 38 describes a raid under Cornelius P. Lott.

In 1842 Lott moved onto Joseph Smith's farm, four miles east of Nauvoo on the Carthage road, managed this farm and purchased land adjoining it. On September 20, 1843, his daughter was sealed to Joseph Smith. In 1846 Lott left Nauvoo with the general exodus. At Winter Quarters he married Phoebe Crosby Peck Knight (Hosea's mother-in-law), her husband, Joseph Knight having died there. In 1848 the Lotts came to Salt Lake Valley, where Cornelius Lott was placed in charge of the Church Farm, located on the site of the present Forest Dale Golf Course. Lott died in 1850. See Joseph M. Tanner, *A Biographical Sketch of John Riggs Murdock* (Salt Lake City, 1909), 103-6.

at 5 o clock — Capt Hunter & McRae of the Fur Comp'y were dispatched on an expedition to reconnoitr the enemy lines near Carthage — After detailing the police guards I received orders from Gen Rich to raise 20 men well armed & equiped to be sent in 3 wagons to assist the Brethren on Camp creek which I did from the 1st & 4 regts under the command of Howard Egan of the old Police this was done from reports brought in that the mob were about to commit their depredation on that settlement I then went home about dark being unwell about dark

F. 19. Early this morning before I was dressed I received by express orders from Gen Rich to repair forthwith to the parade ground which I did but still very unwell from thence I went to the Arsenal were the Gun was fired I had an interview with Gen Rich from thence to the parade ground where I saw Capt Hunter & McRae who had returned from their expedition who reported that they went on the borders of Carthage in the night but finding the town closely guarded did not enter — arrived in their former quarters about day-break they perform a very necessary & useful expedition and all was well & satisfactory the Legion appeared officered as before — the 2 Reg. took its place in the line under the command of Lieu Col Herriman. the 6 Reg. also our Silver Grays composed of the Fathers in Israel took its place under the command of Col. Titus Billings at ½ past 8 o clock Lieui Gen B. Young appeared on the ground & after all the commisond officers were formed in an hollow square — he addressed them as follow I want to know if a likelihood existed of getting the men called for by Gen Miller — at this moment the express arrived from Bear Creek with advice from Gen Miller to send them aid — he continued his remarks Gen Young ordered all waggons to be pressed — let your men be dismissed for refreshment. preserve your companies for encampments on the ground. As Signals — we will have the flag hoisted and then let all men be on the ground as a flag with strips is hoisted it is a signal for all commissioned officers to meet in council at Gen Miller's house — we intend shortly to have a light at night on the top of the temple which can be seen for miles — the white flag is for the mustering of men — dismiss you men for breakfast & by that time a messenger may be here from the Lower Country Let every man going out as an officer when he sends back not send back advice to us but for counsel for instance Gen Miller sends word to have 600 men sent to him & cannon here & cannon there all before day light just as though a thing of that kind could be done in a moment if he was not a sensible man I should call him a fool to act no wiser he must not think to counsel us for we and the men & horses have feelings the same as he as I want every man to be tender to his horse Backenstos needs our counsel to keep the peace I would advise the officers to preserve the lives of your men do not rashly expose them because the life of a good man is worth 20 of the mob — & if life is once gone it is not brought back. Backenstos advises us not to meddle with any body property but my counsel is to take enough property to sustain life and keep your lives in your hands I am for letting the mob go home if they will and then we can have the law upon them and let them come to the Gallows were they ought to be or else in the Penetenary — the mob would rather fight now then give up — expose no lives for life is not restored there is a chance to take the evil doers in a day they think not off if Gen Miller or any man think they have more wisdom then I have let them come and advise & I will go out & fight but if not let them be satisfied to have counsel from us — Gen Miller just wants his memory jogged & he would see were he is acting & that he must be subject to us here for we know what is best and not him he has Sheriff Backenstos there but it will not do to listen to ever[y] suggestion he make but he himself must use prudence. I am the Counsel or Genl in the field and I am going to direct the affair — our council room must be fixed and we will be on near the Parade ground — let teams be pressed in all readiness to have the brethrens conveyed where ever they may want to go to protect our brethren I would much rather be in the brush on foot than on horseback. Let us have fun brethren we have worked hard all summer we have enough to eat for 2 years let have a good time I bless you all in the name of Israel God. Amen he then left the ground I then rode down with my clerk down to see Mr Maudsley whose is at work for me I made an agreement with him for the Painting of a portrait — from thence I drove to clements he was not at home. Maj Lee informed of an accident which at 11 o clock on the parade ground of a man being shot by name unknown the man name was Phippins that was shot (from [crossed out]) thence to our Quartermaster Nobles to procure a Marquee for my accomodation from this we drove home I went to bed my clerk went home to return at 1 o clock took dinner and at 1- oclock my clerk came for me & proceeded to the ground. Quartermaster Noble who reported his success in obtaining a Marquee — the Soldiers made & making all preparation for an encampment on the parade ground — at 3 oclock my marquee was raised — at ½ past 5 oclock I went down to the Temple detailed the Police to their several posts — reports all well — I returned to my Marquee at ½ past 7. I went in compy with my clerk to the council Chamber where I met Gen Rich. I they learned by express from Gen Miller — that he was marching with his troops for Carthage — his to forward his march to the half way house in the morning about [one line left blank]

I received orders from Gen Rich to have 50 waggons — with 8 men in each besides Teamster well armed & equiped and one 6 pounder with ammunition & necessary ac- coutrement to march in the morning by 6 oclock precisely — to form a junction with Gen Miller to (carry out the decision of of council to take [crossed out]). I went to supper with Col Turley at Br Clark store. I returned to my Marquee — and met in Council with the officers of the Regts Council of War assembled at 9 o clock at night — after the decission that each Col strive to his utmost to raise the requisite teams and that all Col see there men in readiness for march I then went back to the council chamber with Gen Rich Andrew H Perkins appeared before the council as one of the committee appointed to treat with the Mob Party he made the following report that he had met with the committee from the mob The terms of Peace which they offered us — were about as follows if we would enter into bonds — that if by the 1st day of April next leave this state — & all things that appertained to them — & pledge all the property of the church for the performance of the same we shall live in peace this winter I also learned that the Spirit of the mob appeared to be broken and that the counties around were in our favour it was also decided by Leiu Gen Brigham Young that Col Hale take the command of the reinforce- ment to be sent out to act in concert with Gen Miller reports from Capt Egan com- pany from Camp creek all well. no he did not apprehend any danger from the mob in that quarter. he was waiting for further orders — Gen Young recieved a letter from Gen Miller & Backenstos requesting the aforesaid reinforcement & further that the mob were quelld in that quarter as far as burning is concerned for the present. We had an agreeable council & many interesting subjects were talked over After which President Brigham Young requested the Council to unite with him in prayer for the success of our troops &c which they did [one fourth page left blank] I returned to my Marquee after a short time Leui Gen Brigham Young Gen Rich & other of the 12 Paid me a visit in my Marquee — Friend Hutchinson with violin in hand Capt Kay gave some choice songs & tunes beside other little comforts in the midst of our encampment after a cessation of our merriment we lay down to rest & snatch a few moments of rest — but finding myself unwell I went home where I arrived about one o clock A m I got up & got here on the ground at my marquee about sun rise and assisted in fitting the expedition ready for the march — but sent only 200 men a large force being deemed unnecessary — at about 6 o clock the white flag was for the first time hoisted as a signal for mustering — I went to the council chamber returned to the ground in company with Leui Gen Young & Gen Rich who were on the ground till the troop started — from thence I went to take Breakfast with Gen Rich — returned to my marquee and found all thing moving well. Gen Rich reports the mob consider themselves whipped but mean to strve & make one more attempt bye & bye — I attend to the business of the Legion — at about 12 o clock I took my glass & ascended in company with Capt McRae the Tower of the Temple & by the assistance of my glass I had a fair & unbounded view of the wide spread carpet of creation it a scene which makes an impression not soon forgotten for the eye stretches & beholds the handy work of the world's Creator — I descended from the lofty height & returned to my marquee were Col. Scott reported that the Hiram Kimball our Mail Carrier with his guard were assaulted in the most inhuman manner their lives threatened & by submitting from an absolute to a sound whipping were permitted to make their way for nauvoo under penalty of death if as ever again seen in Keokuk

September the 20th 1845 Saturday. at about 2 o clock My Quartermaster brought a good cooked supply of the eatables at ½ past 3 o clock Capt Jesse B Hunter dispatched his company to reconnoitre the lines of the enemy about — at ½ past 5 Leui Gen Brigham Young drove on the ground and after the officers & soldiers had formed themselves into a square Heber C. Kimball addressed the soldiers as follows — I do not apprehend I shall make many remarks on this occasion but I want do I do it by way of consolation to the friend of the deceased[33] — I know it is not good to meddle with other person guns so with the things of the Gosple ought not to be meddled with I would rather be shot a thousand times than do as the mob are doing he as died a martyr and he shall (die [crossed out]) recieve a martyr crown I do not wish any thing I have said by way of reproof to any body — you have done well since this disgraceful mob you will continue still in your spiritual & temporal salvation we set up the standard of King Emanuel continue to do your duty you shall recieve your crown the deceased will come forth with the Martyred Prophet he is better to die as he as than do the things the mob are doing — I long for a land were we can plant & inhabit I am weary of it do you love it I wish I were out of it the brethren have done right so [in] some cases and if we had the chance we do right every time Luei Gen. Brigham Young — said he laid hands on the deceased the day he was [shot] that he felt to pronounce a Martyr blessings & the blessing of a Martyr crown in he as died in the cause of Mobocracy I feel to sympathize with this Father Phippins he died but he desired to live for the same cause as we do he shall come forth in the first resurrection I am for work & preach too live long upon the earth. God bless you all men he gave order for the Artillery stationed in his yard immediately in no wise delay God bless you Amen — Gen Rich The troops are now dismissed as far as being under command. let the strict obedience be your constant motto from the Highest officers to the lowest keep yourself ready for immediate use stack up your (grain [crossed out]) wood clean ready & you will want it bye & bye — Brigr Gen Stout wish the teams stayed on the ground as also be particular about your signals — the encampment broke up & dispersed to their homes I returned to my Marquee and partook of a good repast provided by our worthy Quartermaster Bates Noble a man of the right stripe — The guards are to be continued at their respective station as before and that a guard be placed on the banks of the rivers — our kind neighbor in whose yard my Marquee was pitched gave me a bottle of wine — drank his health & wish him

----

33. This is the Phippen boy who had been accidentally shot by his own men a few days earlier.

& lots of wine in California — I must here relate an incident worthy of recording for the striking contrast it affords — Mr Hamilton of Carthage A Tavern Keeper, was sent express by the Mob party to treat with our people when he arrived here he was perfectly ashamed of his despatches which bore the requisition for us to surrender all & leave the state by next April he returned having accomplished nothing last night the embassy for the mob — returns home finds his house occupied by our troops & he turns to & feeds them & do as good as man can want so great a change is truly a very remarkable coincidence as also the fact that no one mob man can be found in all Hancock County — who own the Lands & the fruits Ah —

Sunday Sept 21. 1845. After supper we amused ourselves in my Marquee with a pleasing varieties at 8 o clock Capt McRae started on a expedition with his company to reconnoitre the enemy line about 8 or 10 miles south   about 11 o clock he returned report favourable Capt McRae & company returned from their expedition about 2 o clock all well

4 o clock Col. Hale & Compy returned from Warsaw.[34] 5 o clock I left the Marquee & went home after a short time I returned to my Marquee and whence I went to Gen Rich and received orders for the recalling of the out post guards — I gave them as follows — one for Capt Egan stationed at Camp creek one at near Lotts — as also all guards now on posts — My Quartermaster Bates Nobles provided a most excellent Breakfast of which myself & staff partook of the same   our Friend Hutchinson performed the necessary office of Trimmar he is also recognised as an aid & musician in Kay Staff — the order for recalling Capt Egan & Guard was sent out by Bingham — Capt O. M. Allen & guard were recalled from their station up the river & at head quarters were dismissed till further orders for day time — but the night watch to be continued as before. I took my wife to the meeting at the stand   I returned to my Marquee and attended to such duties as demanded my attention (at 3 o clock gave some general orders for my quarter master Noble to be executed [crossed out])   I again returned to the stand after meeting took my wife home I immediately returned to my Marquee by Allen Weeks. at ½ past 4 oclock Capt McRae with 20 men left [to] reconnoitre the enemy line on the south I issued orders for the quartermaster Noble to station guard over my Marquee, also East of the parade ground one at the butchery &c   about this time Cyrus Daniels came to me & reported of a plan which he had devised to watch & regulate some matters north of Town up the river & requested me that George Langley & such others as he might select should go with him — granted.

took supper at ½ past 6 at Br Boyce — whose lady had kindly volunteered her services to cook for me & staff. Maj' Gen Rich gave me orders to call out the

---

34. George Miller wrote a detailed account of this military expedition. See Mills, "De Tal Palo Tal Astilla," *Annual Publications . . . Southern California*, X, 86-157.

John D. Lee, who accompanied Colonel J. H. Hale wrote his version:
. . . a detachment of about 400 men under the command of Col. J. H. Hale and myself marched to a place called Midway tavern where we joined Gen. Millers troops as a reinforcement   At this point a council was held by the officers and we decided that the troops should be divided into 3 divisions this being done we were soon on the march again — the Artillery which consisted of 4 pieces of good Ordinance was placed immediately in the rear of the advance guard — leaving the infantry to form the rear — About sunset we entered the town of Warsaw . . . Finding no opposition what ever we concluded to divide the company into 2 divisions sending the artillery & infantry the prairie route under the command of Col Hales & myself This move was made in order to scour out the county on the east while General Miller who had command of the cavalry raked the river yet nothing was to be seen we all arrived home about 4 o'clock in the morning almost cold enough to warm . . . .

The excerpt ends here with the sentence unfinished, but the account makes clear the fact that the governor would be forced to take drastic action to maintain the peace. Lee, "Diary," 58.

4 & 5 Reg probably then amounting to 400 men 100 of whom was to be mounted & forthwith be marched to Carthage to protect the place and the 20 men Gen Miller had left there previously to guard and protect the place — this was occasioned by report that the mob were now gathering into Carthage — I immediately gave orders to Cols to have the same executed forthwith about 40 or 50 men mounted & equiped were dispatched under command of Col. Markham we continued making preparations to send out the remainder of the troops in waggons under command Col Scott — he presently informed me that his wife lye dangerously sick — Gen Rich then proposed my going — to which I consented I left the Marquee to see my horses saddled — Maj. Gen Rich leaving with Lieu Gen Young as to the expediency of my going — declared by him not to be policy — just at this moment. the Lieu Gen — came on the ground and said that the alarm was a false one & ordered the dismissal of the troops reserving only guards to be stationed on the river under the command of A Farnham I believe G W. Langley returned & reported that he had went with Cyrus Daniels & others as above mentioned. (at ½ past 4 o clock Capt McRae left in company with 20 men to reconnoitre in the South. I issued order to my Quartermaster to see a guard stationed on the Marquee ground & at the East side of the parade grounds one at the Butcherry &c.

Monday Sept 22. (I went to the Butchery & found thing in a bad condition I was occupied in arranging this & the Commisarry department [crossed out in original]) and that in attempting to execute the arraingements thy were fired upon and Cyrus Daniels was shot though the right arm just above the elbow. Whereupon myself and Br Nobles went with him to assist him home. We however did not find him till he had traveled to Col Turleys. When we got there we found him in a desperate condition his arm was shattered to atoms the ball passed just above the elbow & both bones were broken & his arm in a sling We had to tear his coat to pieces to get it off of him after which Br Turley set the bones as well as he could & then Dr. J. M. Barnhisel was sent for who undone his arm & set it over again. During which time he suffered the most excrutiating pain. A ball passed through Langley hat at the same time I returned to my Marquee with G Langley about 2 o clock on my return I found a part of Capt McRae Comp-y had returned & reports that they had brought [line blank] Egan comp'y in part came in under Capt R Thompson reserving 6 men to make observation reports all well Egan to be home at Day break I then went to Allen Weeks & stayed till day all well. about day Capt McRae came home. I went to the butchery & found thing in an uproar occupied in arranging this & the Commisary department — occupied all the morning in seeing these matters arranged — returned and took dinner about ½ past 3 o clock Gen Rich came to Marquee and reported that the Twelve had appointed my clerk to accompany a delegation to Macomb which was attended to by him—I was engaged in making arrangements for my new Marquee in company with my Quartermaster Nobles — about ½ past 3 o clock I recieved orders from Gen Rich to raise 40 men in waggons under Col Parker to guard the citizens of Laharpe against the Mob in that quarter also about the same number under Capt A Farnham to guard Macedonia in consequence of the absence of the officers & men from my Quarters it was with great difficulty and exertion the companies were raised & fitted out however the company under Col Parker left about Sun-down that under Capt Farnham left about dusk for Macedonia after the Companies had started the officers and soldiers (were assem [crossed out]) of those left on the ground were assembled to whom I gave a general course of instructions how to proceeds in raising companies in future so as to prevent the difficulty and the confusion we experienced this Evening recommending the Cols to have some one stationed near my Quarter ready at all times to convey news to them more speedily that orders may be dispatched & done forth with — to which they immediately attended to — after detailing a guard to be on the river under George Langley — also a guard S. E. of town I then retired to rest in the Marquee —

Tuesday Septr 23. 1845. Arose about 5 this morning went with Capts Hunter & McRae to Lathorp' Store & made arrangements thre for the necessary provision for my Marquee — took Breakfast at 8 o clock then made some arrangements with Col Rockwood relative to doing some butchering up the River at 9 o clock I left the Marquee with Gen Rich for my home — returned at 10 o clock. I called the Cols & officers & gave them instructions relative to the Commisary department so as to avoid all impositions in the distribution of Rations Tarried till dinner — after which I took my Quartermaster — to visit the sick Police — and went home returned at 4 o clock, had some conversation with Majr Lee relative to my New Marquee. about 6 Elder P Pratt introduced 2 Indians of the Sou Tribe & committed them to my charge & that their wants should be attended to & supplied from my Marquee. After supper Levi Hancock amused with tunes on his Violin at 8 they laid down to sleep I went home.

Wednesday Sept 24. I came to my marquee about 6 o clock. I was introduced to George Herring a Mohawk Chief — he speak good English and converses freely on all subjects understand the Customs of the Whites well. he also put up at the Marquee & made it his home — also some 4 or 5 others who came in after Breakfast I was busy in making preparations to go to Carthage for my trial it having been decided by the Council that we should go this day as it will appear in its proper place — about 9 o clock Lieu Gen Brigham Young H. C Kimball Willard Richards P P Pratt & J Taylor came to my Marquee & were introduced to the Red men — about ½ past 9 I started in company with the Twelve & a number of other Gentlemen for Carthage — left Col Harmon in command — ¼ past 1 o clock we arrived at Carthage — we visited the Jail wherein the Murder of our Prophet & Patriarch was committed The marks were the balls penetrated are still visible as also the blood on the floor it was scene which called forth feelings of horror — we were called from this place by word that the court was ready to proceed with the trial — we then ushrred into the sherriffs office. Names called and answered to — to wit Daniel Spencer W W Phelps John Taylor Orson Spencer Chas Rich Wm Clayton Willard Richards Edward Hunter Reynolds Cahoon Alpheus Cutler Hosea Stout.[35] we were then taken to the office of T. L. Barnes & E. A Bedell Esqurs and Anthony Barkman whose name was to the affadavit upon which the writ was issued was sworn. Upon investigation it appeared that the witness had been suborned had signed & sworn to two affadavits written by George Backman, he did not know any of the defendants named, had sworn to to both affidavits upon reports & was decieved is sorry for what he had done &c There being no cause of action what ever the Court discharged the defendants. the writs were issued by E. F. Smith, Capt of the Carthage Greys and was in command at the time Joseph & Hyrum was martered. After we were discharged we went back to the shiriff's office and after some arrangements with the sheriff we prepared to come home. When we had came about four or five miles from Carthage we met an express, Br. C. Lott, by which we were informed that a Committee of the Citizens of Quincy had arrived in Nauvoo "requesting us to communicate in writing our disposition and intention at this time, particularly with regard to moving to some place where the pecular organization of our church will not be likely to engender so much strife and contention as so unhapily exhists at this time in Hancock & some of the adjoining counties." We all drove up near to President B. Young and heard the report as above and then pro-

---

35. In addition to the men named here, the list included Stephen Markham, Jonathan Dunham, Dimick B. Huntington, and John Scott.

ceeded on our way home where we arrived about at 6 o clock a black set of men as it was a very warm & dusty day and our faces looked like we were painted black. We drove up on the parade ground before my marquee and Genl Young addressed them in a short speech thanking those who had attended us and then the croud dispersed. I then washed my self and took supper and then went with J. D. Hunter and A. McRae to Lathrop's store and took up some goods and then returned to my marquee about 10 o'clock and gave orders to Col Harmon to prepare teams for Laharp by daylight and then went home and returned to the marquee about 12 o'clock and stayed till morning.

Thursday the 25 Sept 1845. Attended to my official duty till 7 o'clock then took breakfast, at 8 commenced arranging the teams for Laharp & Camp Creek they started at 9 o'clock under the command of Col Harmon nothing of any particular importance occured till dinner after which I rode out & went home and returned to the marque and laid down and rested myself a little and then at 5 left the marque for home and returned again & stayed all night.

Friday 26th. I arose this morning very unwell and went home & returned after a short time A part of the guard left at Carthage returned this morning and reports that the mob are assembling & that they are unsafe. At 11 o'clock Col Turley came and told me he wanted to go after Dr Levi Richards to attend on C. Daniels as his arm seemed to be worse I dispatched Nobles for the doctor — took dinner — after which I recieved orders from Gen Rich to raise 20 volunteers for Carthage as a Relief to our troops stationed there — at about 4 o clock The company under command of Col Harmon arrived from Laharpe accompanied by between 40 & 50 teams loaded with grain &c called into the centre of the Square and were addressed by Lieu Gen Young the object of calling you together and of gathering you from your houses & farms to a place where you have none is because we have been called out by the sherriff to guard you so far as we have done by fifties here & there — our men are sick & afflicted, their horses are run we can go out no longer — the committee which we have appointed have done well, they have been industrious. I would advise those having teams to keep them constantly going bring in your grain first. Shock up your corn — your straw & all your fodder taking care of — let those having rails lend them to your brethren & make smaller fretos for hay & cattle, Gribs[36] & things necessary — I refer you to our proclamation as to what we intend to do — I never intend to winter in the United States except on a visit we do not owe this country a single Sermon we calculated to go all the while for I do not intend to Stay in such an Hell of a Hole and if this bee your mind signify it by saying Hie — which was loudly responded to by the assembly — they are continually accusing us of stealing they horses & cattle — I wish some of the brethren would steal & kill them I will venture to guess as a Yankee we will have the best winter we ever had I expect you will really enjoy yourself — An old Farmer here enquired what would be done with those that were not Mormons to which our Lieu Gen replied treat him the same as Mormons — Parley P Pratt motioned all men not known as any thing else be called Mormons — The Gen proceeded & said we have been peaceful inclined yet nothing appeases the Mob they are angry they know not what with but I know it is because the kingdom of God is set up we have done the best we could They are as corrupt as Hell from the president down clean through the priest and the people are all as corrupt as the Devil I will leave them and God grant I may live to get to some place of peace

---

36. Fretos and Gribs (cribs?) were v-shaped, latticed containers for hay, built so that the cattle could eat between the slats and the pile would automatically settle to the bottom. These provided food with little waste.

health and safety If you are on patrol under the Sherriff do not touch any one Goods and the mob shall be cursed for their dishonesty — but we will be at peace I will be at peace and treat them well and they may do their own preaching we do not owe them a sermon nor this nation a mile of travelling we will see who will judge the earth and show them with what judgment they shall be judged if we was sure the Gov. & had the courage & spunk of a flea we should have no need of this parade but we have all the time been cursed with Governors & other officers not worth having and Jacob B Backenstos is the only man that as ever stood up for equal rights & if he goes right we will make a great man of him yet awhile — he then left the ground. I went & met with the old police and gave them a lecture therein showing the necessity of abstaining from the use of ardent Spirits showing the result thereof. returned to my Marquee — took supper — left with Gen Rich to assist in getting the Carthage expedition under March after which I attended a General Conference of the officers of the 2. Cohort in Col Harmons' Marquee — at 11 o clock Capt Egan left with his company for Carthage at 12 our Conference broke up I then left in Company with Capt Hunter

Saturday Morning . . Sept 27th. I arose about 7 — I immediately went on the Parade ground and attended to the Organization of the Teams for an expedition under the command of Col Herriman for Laharpe & Camp Creek this took the greater part of the morning. I then went home after a short stay I returned to my Marquee were I learned from Gen Rich that a meeting of the Old police and officers of the 2 cohort was to be held at the Masonic Hall at 3 o clock P M also to raise 6 Horsemen to assist Capt Egan at Carthage also to notify the Col of the meeting at the Masonic Hall. dispatched R Cliff to call them together — I then rode down down to the Hall. The meeting was addressed by Amasa Lyman in the absence of the Lieu Gen whose appropriate remarks prepared us for the still further remarks of our Gen who presently made his appearance and addressed us as follows

News has reached us from Squire Bedell & Capt Rose who had started to see the Governor[37] — that they met Genl Hardin with about 200 men at Rushville and that to morrow noon he would be in Carthage — so much for this now for my subject To the Police & officers I would say — I have been asked for counsel what we should do and how things would be done and conducted & report as reached me of feelings existing among these bodies of men — It may be all comprehended in this there is an evident lack of humility & faith among you — you have partaken to much of the spirit of the world not that I would say you have disobey counsel you have shown yourselves ready at all times to do this — but I can for see that a reckless spirit is creeping in among you that should one of your best friends come across you without thought or meditation you would up & shoot him and thereby rid of one good man and he fall a sacrifice to your envy hatred & malice this is wrong it must not be — I know it is my duty to discern

---

37. Governor Ford, upon learning of conditions in Hancock County, met with General J. J. Hardin, Major William B. Warren, Attorney General John A. McDougall, and Judge Stephen A. Douglas. According to Governor Ford:

   It was agreed that these gentlemen should proceed to Hancock in all haste, with whatever forces had been raised, few or many, and put an end to these disorders. It was now apparent that neither party in Hancock could be trusted with the power to keep the peace. It was also agreed that all these gentlemen should unite their influence with mine to induce the Mormons to leave the state. Gen. Hardin lost no time in raising three or four hundred volunteers, and when he got to Carthage he found a Mormon guard in possession of the courthouse. This force he ordered to disband and disburse in fifteen minutes. The plundering parties of Mormons were stopped in their ravages. The fugitive anti-Mormons were recalled to their homes, and all parties above four in number on either side were prohibited from assembling and marching over the country. (Ford, *History of Illinois*, 410.)

between truth & error — it also our duty to discern and discriminate in the same way we ought to be able to understand the rights & liberties of one another and not seek to infringe upon another and by so doing we move every man in his own sphere On the contrary I leave it to you whether you have not giving way to folly in many instances and have showed yourselves departing from the spirit of God and nourishing the spirit of folly — for instance when I passed through the street I will see some 6 or 7 men of the Old Police talking & making fun highly amused themselves — strangers passing them unheeded and I will walk up to them and tell them that a stranger has just passed them I have no sooner spoken to them than they have gone instantly to see the stranger and his business there but why should they need the spur and need to be told of their duty continually they should ever be on the look-out all over town and seeing every stranger in town and why he is here for you are the safe guard of this people After orders had been given to the old police I have gone to the Temple and found them mixed with strangers when the orders were for all strangers to be kept from the Temple Square I am aware that your Unity is great you are attached to one another and are ready to obey my counsel and have done as I have said & counseled yet I have said and now fore-seen that by following in this way it will lead you to be the deadly enemy of each other in one year from this time it as already led you to the use of ardent spirits and I know this from your breath when I have met you and I know that the Spirit of God cannot rest upon a man who is filled with Whiskey for the kingdom of God cannot be built up by Unholy things for purity must exist in the upholders of this kingdom and we must now cleanse ourselves from every impure thing nor need a man expect for the conferring of blessings & powers from God who is now habitually used to the things which are unholy and impure — we must arrive to all blessings & powers by our good works — you must try to be united in all your movement hard feelings must cease it will not do they must cease and let the principle of love and charity take place this must be done and we must attend to our prayers and be humble and attend to your family duty and by so doing a good spirit will take place of a spirit of folly & malice for I know if we are allowed to stay here the winter it will be a miracle indeed for the enemies are seeking to annoy us & aggravate us to retaliation & should we have to do it will have a great amount of sufferings we must let your prayers be offered continually to God that we may be sustained here this winter — If hardness does creep in among you I know what course to pursue with you we shall have to take you into the Temple & there give you your endowment together and send you on a five years missions to the Islands of the sea and that would soften our hearts and we would find it necessary to call on the name of the Lord least we be devoured by our enemies & where there is not a Latter Day Saint on the land — this will I know make a man come to his feelings and he would see the necessity of steadying yourselves by the Wisdom of God cause you to act manfully — carefully & prayerfully — I want every man to know his place and know enough to act in his own place and sphere and let me tell you that I and those in connection with me will counsell with me with me [*sic*] will watch over you and so let those who are under you be counselled by you and so all things move in harmony and in good order & I pray that God will forgive you and let your hearts be humbled one towards another leave off your whiskey — I am and ever intend to be the Master of my passions & not the subject thereof so you must be the master of your passions — and not be the slave of passions in themselves so degrading & entirely debasing — some may say I am in the habits of taking snuff and Tea yet I am no slave to these passions and can leave these off if they make my brother affronted — if ever we live to see the kingdom of God set up we shall see the judgment poured out upon that man who seeks to overthrow the kingdom for righteousness shall be put to line — I would also caution you against using the name of God in vain it as been used to much and will be with us like the Ancients of old they forbade them the frequent use of the same — for I tell you the time is coming when that man uses the name of the Lord is used the penalty will be affixed and immediately be executed on the spot why should we use it in our private & public conversation — the Ancients have giving us an example of reverencing then had for the name of the Deity by calling the priesthood not after God but after Melchisedec it must be held sacred nor must it be the common practice from this time & henceforth — if we do not purify ourselves we shall yet be devoured by our enemies — even if we are gathered into the wilderness he will there destroy them either by famine or by Indians who will be brought upon us & thereby destroyed let Col Scott — see the artillery placed in a secure place & kept from sight &c &c — God bless you all amen —

Returned from the meeting to the parade ground attended to the raising of 6 men horsemen for Carthage — to the relief of Capt Egan already stationed there — after which took supper from thence I went home

Sunday Sept. 28. I returned to my Marquee assisted in raising the teams for Laharpe and Camp creek for the purpose of bringing the families and grain into the City — they were then accordingly dispatched under the command of Col Herriman — I then had a counsel with Gen Rich on the plan and the policy of guarding the City it was decided that this be given into the hands of Capts Hunter & McRae and that they be responsible for the good performance of the same and all things connected therewith be under their control — consequently all out standing guards were called in and disbanded — The teams under command of Col. Scott did not appear on the ground in time for the intended purpose and they were sent to haul wood for the police and the troops who were unable to procure it otherwise — after which I rode in company with Capt Hunter on the East and South Skirts of the City to see and obtain the best place to station guards — returned home about 1 oclock took my dinner then went home with Capt [J.D.] Hunter in Company with George L. M Herring Br Herring Edward Whiteseye — Peter Cooper And Moses [Otis][38] to partake of a dinner prepared for us by the kindness of Capt Hunter's Lady — & we had a complete jollification and then went with George Herring to see Cyrus Daniels who is still very unwell returned to the Marquee & found all well I then went still in company with G Herring to see Charles Shumway who still very unwell from there we went to My house stayed a short time and returned to my Marquee — dispatched two waggons to meet Capt Egan's & his Troops who were on the road from Carthage a foot — Saw Gen Rich and gave him a full report of my proceedings through the day to which he gave his entire approbation Gave orders to have 50 teams for the purpose of working the road near the Temple or as it is known the Hill Road. About 9 o clock we attended to prayers by the Clerk — Capt Egan & troops arrived and reports the number of troops now in Carthage under the command of Gen Hardin of the Illinois Volunteers to be about 320 men who are sent by the Governor to maintain & be the efficient arms of the Law as he published in his general Orders to Hancock county — God grant it may prove as he as published — The weather

---

38. Since the Book of Mormon purports to be a history of the origin of the American Indians, the leaders of the church early sent missionaries to some western tribes. The conversion of Louis Dana has already been noted.

On September 23, Stout had mentioned meeting two Indians of the "Sou" tribe, and on the day following was introduced to George Herring, a Mohawk chief. Of the present company — George L. M. Herring; his brother, Joseph Herring; Edward Whitesye; Peter Cooper; and Moses Otis — the two Herring brothers appear most often in this record. Brigham Young evidently courted them because of their knowledge of the land to the west and their potential value as guides and interpreters.

during the day was disagreeable owing to the drizzly state of the atmosphere about time for rest a strong West wind came up & well nigh overset my marquee I then went into the Tent of Col Harmon and retired to rest it continue to rain the most of the night and when we awoke in the morning the water stood ankle deep

Monday Sept 29. This morning the weather presented a very lowery aspect and threatened a storm never the less the teams appeared on the ground and repaired to the ground for the purpose as afore stated under Col. Harmon for some time My Clerk & Myself were busily engaged in arranging the reports of the different Regts the time they had been engaged as a posse Commitatus & other expenses connected therewith to be laid before the County Commissioners Court whose sessions commenced today at Carthage — as by Law we were entitled to pay for the services so rendered to the County in Maintaining the supremacy of the Law. As General Hardin as prohibited in his general orders 4 men being together armed deeming his troops quite sufficient to quell all further disturbance and maintain the supremacy of the Law in conformity to the above we discontinued our Camping for the present — I then release my clerk for the present to give him liberty to transact his private business (As the present aspect of affairs to all Law & order citizens of course portended a season of peace as the future will show) I then went into council with the Twelve and other authorities of the Church at Br D. Spencer's with G.L.M. Herring and his comerades, which council only consisted an introduction to the feeling and mind of his people towards us and some circumstances relative to our removal from hence. We had an interesting interview with them for an hour or two I then went home to look somewhat to my temporal affairs for the first time since I had been called out to duty. When I got there I found Br. Sabin had commenced to finish laying up my brick as before agreed upon and all things doing as well as could be expected. Capt. McRae came and took dinner with me & we then went to the Marque again which was now totally occupied by our "red friends" and then in company with G.L.M. Herring we rode to the printing office and bought him a book of mormon from thence we went to see C. Daniels again who was not any better, then came back to the marque again and then met the police at the Stand and gave the instructions which had been given by President Young to me and others on the 27th in relation to spiriteous liquor & to them which was gladly recieved and all with uplifted hands covenanted to obey the same. and then after returning to the Marque again went home to enjoy domestic happiness again for one night.

Tuesday Sept 30th. At 7 o'clock A. M. went to the parade ground to see about fitting out teams to work the road and on the Temple as agreed the day before. and also to send Col Scott with the Teams of his Regiment to Thresh wheat on Camp Creek and then Started home and on my way learned from the out guards that General Hardin and his troops were now entering into Town without leave or notice. I went home then to the parade ground to be ready for any orders which might be sent to me, but learning that General Rich was on the flat I went to the Seventies Hall where the Council of 50 were in Session. when I arrived there I was informed by Prest Jos Young that Rich had gone on the hill, I then went to the Temple & there met him while he was telling me what was to be done Backenstos & Judge Douglas one of General Hardin's aids rode up and was introduced by Backenstos and we all trooped off down to Elder Taylor's and met in council with the 12, Douglas informed them that he was sent by his General to notify them that he desired an interview with the Twelve to which they consented to grant at the prade ground which place he now was formed.

I was then sent to look up some witnesses to testify against the house burning mob and also to escort Douglas to his General; which I did and then made the necessary arraingements to procure the witnesses as aforesaid. About this time the Twelve & others came in their buggy's to the ground and was introduced to Genl Hardin, who Showed his authority for coming here and told his intentions of mintaining the "Supremacy of the Law" as he called it. He also said that there had been compaints made to him while at Carthage about two men being missing one in Nauvoo named Wilcox and the other between Carthage and Appanoose named Debonair[39] and that he intended to have an effectual and thoroug search made here for them that it was somewhat Strange that a man should leave so large and populous a City as this and no body see him and in a scarcastic manner insinuated that we had been guilty of their death, after which the Twelve returned back & I went home and in a Short time Captains Hunter & McRae came and took dinner with me and then we went to A. Weeks to get Mirinda to wash for my wife from thence to quarters again and there heard that Hardin's troops had search the Temple through out even in the dome for the dead bodies also the Masonic Hall was searched from the garrett to the cellar. they then went to Mansion House Barn as said that they wanted to search it as Col Scott had Stationed troops there as they thought to conceal the bodies aforesaid to which Col Scott consented after requiring them not to steal any thing else to which they agreed. they searched it in the Hay mow & all other apartments after they were done Col Scott told them that they were fools to suppose that we would hide dead men in the Hay &c when the river was so near which seemed to in some degree to shame his barefaced impertinence for in reality they only wanted to find our cannon[40] &c as we had good reason to believe and Deprive us of our means of defence and then we could be more easy brought to bow in Submission their unjust mandates. It may be seen that I have no confidence in them since our leaders were martered by the Gov. and his men

How rediculous and contemptible the idea that rational men as we are should be supposed to murder men under the excitement which now prevailed against us when the mob and State authorities both Sught a pretext to form an alliance against us and then in warm weather hide them in Hay mows and Masonic Hall and even in the Temple where more than one hundred men were at work and that in all parts of it at once & we expect not to be found out. Their object was too obvious & I feel indignant at the idea & also think of the "Honor of Governor Ford and the plighted faith of the State" to Joseph & Hyrum's protection while

39. The report of General Hardin on October 4, 1845, said that about September 16 Phineas Wilcox went to Nauvoo with a load of wheat to be ground. He stayed at the home of a friend, Ebenezer Jennings. Mrs Jennings warned Wilcox that he would be taken for a spy. Next day Wilcox went with Jennings to visit the Temple, but was not admitted. As they left the Temple they met three men. One of them told Jennings that he had heard that Wilcox was a spy. The other two took Wilcox to the Masonic Hall. He did not return to the Jennings home and Jennings never saw him again.

The "Debonair" referred to was Andrew Daubenheyer, who lived near Camp Creek and was known to be an active anti-Mormon. On the 18th of September he started to Carthage with a two-horse wagon-load of provisions, which, it is said, were intended for the rioters. On the evening of the 20th he left Carthage on horseback for his home, which he never reached; but on the morning of the 21st his horse came home without him. On his road home was an encampment of the sheriff's *posse* . . . . Search being afterwards made, his body was found buried near the place of encampment. (*Illinois State Register*, October 17, 1845. See also Ford, *History of Illinois*, 409.)

40. Of paramount concern among the Mormons was the securing and keeping of arms. They found many ways of hiding them: in a wagon box covered with straw and referred to as "the old sow and little pigs"; in a hole in the midst of a cornfield; in an excavation over which a pile of lumber was stacked. Roberts, *Documentary History*, VII, 448, tells the story of the search, but attributed the statement that "they must think we were fools to bury dead men in a stable when it was so easy to throw them into the river, which was only a few rods off," to Almon W. Babbitt rather than Scott.

he could lock them in jail and then with draw his forces to insult us, in his weak administered, & "Brief authority," in Nauvoo while his compeers could assassinate them in cold blood in despite of the "Carthage Grey" Guard loaded with "Blank Cartrages" as we know they were To all Such men officers and governments I can truly say that it is my hearts desire and prayer to God for Christ's and his kingdom's and people's sake that they may be speedily damned to the lowest degredation of Hell. But ceace my feelings & be calm. I then went to the flat with J. B. Nobles in a Buggy to the printing office & to Allen Stouts, then to the police, then to the Marque & took Supper & then home a little after dark and Staid about two hours and went to Shumway's who was not much better then to A. Weeks and there found that [Marinda] was gone to set up at Br Lewis' whose son was dead I went to bed and sept soundly till about two hours before day, when [Marinda] came to my bed and put [her] cold hand on my forehead which awoke me then came to bed and at day break I got up and came home[41]

Wednesday, October the 1 1845. At 7 o'clock I went to the parade ground as usual and started the teams to work on the road and Temple again and then went to the printing office with G.L.M. Herring and got there just as Hardin's troops had marched up and formed before the office. I then went in to Elder Taylor's house where the 12 & others were in council with Hardin and his officers

He seemed to think that he could do nothing for us that if he marched his troops away the mob would rise again and if we defended ourselves as he said we had a right to do the mob would raise forces enough to overwhelm us at once, but never said any thing about the protecting arm of Government. His conclusion of the whole matter was that if we did not give the public some convincing tokens that it was our determination to leave here in the Spring that nothing could Save us from being totally over whelmed.

What patriotic protection for an officer sent by the governor to maintain the "Supremacy of the Law" from there the troops all marched to the Temple and all went through and round about it and I & Herrin followed on to the Temple to witness their manouvers I there found that they had took Br. Caleb Baldwin prisoner to make him account for the exit of Wilcox because Mr Jennings had complained that Baldwin had said that he was a Spy, from here after we had grown tired of witnessing the imprudence and ill manners of the troops in the Temple and on it Hering & I came home and then took dinner and went back he to the marque & to the Temple, the troops having returned to their encampment, from the Temple I started down the hill and met Br Baldwin who informed me that they had set him at liberty as they could get no pretext against him & that they were then inquiring after me as the Captain of the Police, and thought I had best look out for myself, so I rode down to the bank of the river and came to Br D. Carn and left word with his wife how matters were going and then went to John Binley's and put up my horse and sent him to see Col Harmon and inform him what was going on, and I staid there and at Father Knight untill dark and then took my horse and rode up to Allen Weeks with Capt McRae and took them to my house and after finding out by sending Weeks in that no one had been there I went in and informed my wife what was done and then took a trunk which had some articles which I wanted with us we then returned to Weeks again where I remained all night in peace

Thursday October 2nd 1845. Earley this morning I sent Weeks down in town to learn what was going on & inform me. But before he returned the troops

---

41. The blank spaces here refer, of course, to Stout's plural wife, Marinda Bennett, whose name he dared not write in.

passed up Mulholland Street on their way back to Carthage they were Singing and hollowing & making use of the most insulting and imprudent language to grate on the feelings of the Saints which they could which Showed the goodness and patriotism of this "efficient arm of the Law" So kindly Sent by the Govorner to insult and abuse us as he did last year under the name of protection & Law. After the troops had passed Capt McRae & Charles Allen came here said that they had not heard any thing more of me being demanded. I went with them then to the Marque and there met with Thomas Rich who came home with me and I remained there till 4 o'clock P. M. and then met the police at the Temple from thence went to Allen Weeks' again & Stayed till morning.

Friday October 3rd 1845. Came home about Sun rise and nothing particular transpired till 3 o'clock I then took my horse and went to Warthan's and there Saw Br Roundy who informed me that he had orders from President B. Young to raise and fit out a company of one hundred for emegrating to Calaforna and that he was allowed to take the old Police, from thence I went further on and met Capt Hunter and informed him what Roundy had said and asked him what he thought of it he said he did not know what to think, we then went to the Temple from thence to see Br J. D. Lee who was present when the orders were given to Roundy.[42] His opinion was that President Young was dissatisfied with the old Police and that was the cause of his new arraingement with them. We then went to Hunters quarters at the Masonic Hall, from thence to the Temple & came home about dark.

Saturday Oct 4th 1845. Earley this morning I was awoke by Br J. Butterfield who told me that the cows had broke into my garden I got up and found my cabbage nearly all destroyed by them It was a disagreeable rainy morning. I wrote in my Journal till 9 then went to Ripley's and took my horse back to him, and then went to S. Roundys & there got in his son's Buggy and he brought me home about noon wrote in my Journal till 3 and then went to the Temple & Saw Hunter, Turly & others conversed about the old police Turly think it all right with Brigham & the police. I then met the police and came home at dark & with Mr G.L.M. Herring and 3 others of his company. We had an entertaining evening George understands the Policy of this government well is well acquainted with many of its rulers at Washington his talk is interesting and agreeable —

Sunday October 5th 1845. Went with my wife to meeting in the Temple this fore noon. Elder Taylor Spoke at length on our present prospects and the Satisfaction of going to Calaforna & being redeemed from oppression & legal mobocracy &c which was very interesting. Came home about 2 and after dinner went back and heard the arraingements about the ten Companies organized for Calafornia & gave Roundy a list of the old police and others for his Company as aforesaid, then met the police had a talk with Hunter & McArthur about the Seal of the Covenant and left Hunter at Warthan's Shop and came home at dark, and my clerk Br Candland came and we wrote in my journal till bed time.

Monday Octr the 6th 1845. This was the first day of conference which was held in the which commenced at 10 in the morning. I went with my wife, there was about 4,000 persons present within the walls of the Temple and a large concourse

---

42. The orders referred to appear to require a company of only one hundred men to emigrate to California. On the day before, October 2, the church leaders received a letter from General Hardin, Major W. B. Warren, Stephen A. Douglas, and J. A. McDougal containing the information they had discussed with the delegates from nine counties, who said that they would "agree to restrain and with-hold all further violence, and that you [the Mormons] may be permitted to depart in peace next spring." *Ibid.*, VII, 450-53.

of people without. At 12 we came home, and took dinner, we then back at 2 P. M. This after noon the authorities were presented to the Conference for their approval or disapproval in passing the Twelve When it came to William Smith the Conference disapproved of him both as one of the Twelve and also for Patriarch of the Church. At 5 o'clock I met the police and my wife came home. After the police guard was detailed Genl Rich came to me and told me that Elder H. C. Kimball wanted me to hand him a list of the old police and I ordered the Clerk to do it then went home with A. Weeks and brought Some thing home in a trunk about dark and then took Supper and went to the Lodge at 7 o'clock and not being well came home about 10'clock.

Tuesday Oct 7th 1845. Was very unwell this morning & not able to go to the meeting of the Seventies at 7 o'clock A. M. However at 10 o'clock and in the after noon I went to Allen Weeks and while there I found the some of Hardin's troops had come into town and went into different parts. some had went to where Col Scott had some artilery covered in some corn fodder and put a guard round the lot evidently with the intention of taking it away but Scott put a guard in side with orders to let no man touch it His guard increased so fast that they soon thought proper to go away and let it alone, Another part of them went and took Daniel Smith & another man as they said for Stealing but I do not know how it is about the matter they were took off by them. When Genl Rich found that they were coming in with out leave and most likely had writs against the 12 & others he gave orders for every man at the Temple to go and get his arms and be prepared for the worst, This created a great stir and conference was dispenced with till tomorrow. When I came to the Square the people had assembled in considerable numbers but in a Short time we had word to disperse and be ready at a moments warning as the troops had passed out of town. At 5 met the police and then come home Br Arnold was with me. Then went to Allen Weeks and Staid all night as I did not like to be at home at that time not knowing but they were Seeking me also as well as some others.

Wednesday Octr 8th 1845. Earley this morning I got up and went to Genl Rich's and took breakfast and learned the news He told me that there was some who were now taking cattle &c from our enemies and was raising thereby considerable excitement and wanted me to find out about it & have it Stoped. I then went to the Stand and met Hunter & McRae's companies and laid the matter before them they all promised to assist me in putting a Stop to such opperations. I then Spoke to them about their using Spiriteous liquor and for bade the use of it among them and ordered the captains to drop any man from the company who would or had used it since it was put down before. He then retired. Capt Hunter then dropped one man who had been drunk the night before I then went to the meeting of the Seventies in the Temple and then attended the conference and at noon Col Scott came home with me and took dinner and went to conference again, and at 5 met the police I Spoke on the policy of preparing for Calaforna. I then came home at dusk L. D. Wilson with me and he went home & I took the book of my Quorum and Started to a meeting of the same at Br Dustin Amy's. On my way hither I learned that the mob party had found the man By the name of Debanair whom Hardin Said was missing, was found found buried in the bottom of a ditch made for a Sod fence and they now swore that the mormons in that Settlement should atone for it. I went to the meeting and left the books and went to Genl Rich's to report to him about the matter but he was not at home, So I went to the meeting again, and then went to W. Richards and found the 12 in council and after waiting a while went in and reported in a few minutes Genl Rich came and the thing was talked over[43] and I went back to Br Amy's and Saw the brethren a Short time and then Started for home and met D. Carn who informed me that I was wanted at the M. Hall by Genl Rich. I went and was engaged in making arraingements to have Hunter's company at the Hall untill about 12 or one o'clock and then came home.

Thursday Oct. 9th 1845. I arose Earley and went to the Hall again and assisted in preparing for Hunters Company as aforesaid. I then went with Genl Rich to Br J. Knights and took breakfast — from thence to the Printing Office from thence to the Temple. and then Saw A Weeks about his relations over the river &c also James McLelland & others going with us to Calafornia Br Egan & I then came to my house and after a little he went home & I took dinner at 12. (Wife said Lucretia was gone) I then went to the Hall again to see Hunter all was right there, then went to Br Jos Hutchings and he Shaved me then met the police from thence went to Weeks & took [blank] to the Concert Held at the Hall and was well entertained till 8 or 9 o'clock and then returned to Weeks and staid till morning and came home about Sun rise.

Friday Octr 10th 1845. This morning heard that troops were coming here from Quincy and that the people there were trying to shoot Backenstos & Swear that he shall not get away alive. Went to Harmons and took him and went to see Daniels who is no better, then to Campbell's & so round to the Hall and there selected a Temple guard out of Hunter company & regulated the Commissary department. While there recieved orders from the Lieutenant General by A. P. Rockwood to have the Second Cohort ready to be called out at a moments warning — for them not to be far from home and to rally as usual at the hoisting of the flag at the Temple, for them not to give up their gains to our enemies but first to Shoot. I then went home very sick with the head ache & went to bed and lay till Br James Pace came after me in a Buggy to take me to the police which he did though I was hardly able to sit up from there I came home about dark Still very Sick. Br D. Candland[44] my clerk came here to write out my journal for me which he did untill about 11 o'clock P.M. I was some better after taking Some nourishments. Br Joseph Holbrook & Col Hale now came in and left me orders from Genl Rich for me to have the men of the Second Cohort congregated in convenient parts of town by Regiments or otherwise, and there beseech the Lord for his delivering hand to be extended towards us as from all appearance our enemies were determined to fall upon us, also to have our arms so as to be got in a moment. For we were determined not to let them come in and arrest and take away our men to be murdered in cold blood as had been done. If they should try it we were determined to cut them off from the face of the earth though we all should be exter-

43. The subject of discussion was evidently general strategy in keeping the guns in the Mormons' possession from the hands of their enemies. Writing under the same date (October 9, 1845) Norton Jacob said, "This night at 12 o'clock I was called to come immediately to the Temple. Col. Scott and 12 or 15 others were there. We went to work and prepared a place behind some large piles of lumber and stowed away our four pieces of artillery, having heard that General Hardin's posse were coming in from Carthage to demand all the persons that were in command of the sheriff's posse in the late disturbances. If they were not given up they would immediately make war upon the city." Edward and Ruth S. Jacob, eds., *The Record of Norton Jacob* (Salt Lake City, 1949), 11.

44. The original diaries from September 17 to October 10, 1845, are written by David C. Candland, with occasional blanks evidently left for Stout to fill in later. These additions in Stout's hand are very easily recognized, as are sentences inserted at various times. For example, on the night of September 21 the clerk wrote: "I then went to Allen Weeks" and Stout added between the lines "stayed till day all well" to indicate his satisfaction at spending the night with his wife, Marinda Bennett.

minated by a government who were always so ready to Sanction the doings and acts of the mob I first went to the Temple then to the Masonic Hall and then to Col Harmons and learned that Rich had given the necessary orders to all the Colonels so I returned to the Hall again and Staid till one o'clock Huntr and others retired to evade the search of our enemies, then went to Rich's Saw him and he thought I had best be concealed so I made arraingements with him to send for me in the event I should be needed in case of an attact. I then sent my Clerk home who had been with me and went to Allen Weeks & there went to bed in his cellar room & Rich was to send me the news &c as it might be necessary from time to time

Saturday Octr 11th 1845. I was awake this morning about one hour by sun by my clerk who had agreed to meet me at that time and assist me in writing my journal while I had to secrete myself. About half past ten A. M. we came to the place where I released him from on the morning of the 29th of September & from that time to this I had kept notes myself so I released him and sent him away that he might learn and send me word what was going on and I amused my self to the best advantage and also wrote in my journal untill 12 when Weeks came home and informed me that all was well as yet but that General Rich Said for me to lay low & keep dark. In my seclusion from the public gaze & the Society of my fellow soldiers whom it was my lot to lead on to fight the battles of the Lord in case of an attack my mind was wrapped up in the contemplation of the future destany of the House of Israel, and I asked my Self why this seclusion of myself from the knowledge of even my friends who knew not where I was, in an hour when it seemed I was actually needed to head the armies of Israel. When an army of Saints were met together to Supplicate the Lord our God for deliverance would they not ask one another where is our general who was always with us & why is he not here to strengthen us as in former times. I reflected upon it and beheld that the Safety and welfare of this people demanded it for should our enemies come in as we expected & find me and some others whom they also hated they would we expected arrest us & take us to Carthage as is usual and to Suffer us to be taken away the Saints were determined not to suffer hence it would lead to a resistance of what they would term law. and this would bring down the indignation of a goverment upon us who delights in Shedding the blood of prophets and cause many of the Saints to be Slain and the residue driven out into the wilderness. I thought of the tender ties of nature at home of my little ones who prattle round me in childish loveliness when I come in but now they know not where I am or what will be my destiny before we see each other again. I thought how I have So often seen the Prophet Joseph hide from his enemies when our Safety demanded it. I thought how they also took him through treachery and slew him and Said is this my fate, am I to be also torn from every thing that is Sacred as he was and treacherously Slain and Said to my self that I would not give my self up Save it was to redeem my people and Should they attempt to arrest me I felt determined to Sell my life life as dear as I could and try and convince our enemies that the blook [blood] of the Saints was not as easily Shed as was our Prophets & Patriarch

I felt that I had served my maker as well as I knew and was willing to hide and wait the full time of the Lord But in the event of a battle I was resolved to come forth as a lion from his thicket and roar upon our enemies as did the People of God always and trust to him for the result So I am composed and as yet fear no evil

This passed away the day in the evening Br. Langley & my Brother came in and saw me and said all was well as yet just after dark we took Supper & Langley went with me to Genl Rich's to see if he had any intelligence for me; but he was not at home. So we came to my house my folks were all well & in good Spirits. After Staying awhile with them we returned to Genl Rich's again who had not come home yet Langley then went home & I to my hiding place again at about nine or ten o'clock Nothing of importance happened till morning.

Sunday Octr 12th 1845. Earley this morning I got up and went to see Genl Rich who informed me that he had sent home the troops with orders for them to keep them selves in readiness in case of an alarm and that there had been no writs in yet that there was no appearance of danger at this time We went then to Br Hutchings and he shaved us and then to his house and took breakfast We then went by the Temple to the Masonic Hall all was right there. We then Sent some spys towards Bear Creek & other parts where we thought the mob were geathered and then went to his house again and I there met my clerk who was in search of me to See if I wanted him so I went with him to Weeks and got my journal & papers and then came home & he went to do Some Special business for me When I came home I learned that Br Daniel S. Miles one of the First Presidents of the Seventies was dead He died at Josiah Butterfields. he came to conference and was taken Sick last Sunday at meeting. He was a fine clever jolly man. In the troubles in Missouri he was a Captain of ten and I belonged to his company part of the time — My wife not being very well I Staid & wrote in my journal at home till 2 o'clock and then went to the after noon meeting at the Temple.

The business of this after noon was taken up in organizing companies for Calaforna or the West. I was now apprised for the first time that I was appointed to lead a company myself. President B. Young Stated that as the "Old Police was attached to me that it was my right to have them This was glad tidings to all the Police who immediately came to me this was about 5 o'clock so the police all left the Temple and met near by and I had the guard detailed and after making Some arraingements relative to joining a company I came home Stopping at Weeks & Sabins on my way. I then went to see Br F Harwood who was very Sick and then came home & wrote in my journal till nine o'clock.

Pleasant Green Taylor, my wife's brother came to live with me this evening with the expectation of staying untill we move and on the road

Monday Oct 13th 1845. Wrote in Journal then went to the flat raising & making preparation for the Company Saw several of the Police & at 2 came home, wrote in journal till 4 & then met the police and came home at dark and wrote in my journal till ten o'clock P. M.

Tuesday Octr 14th 1845. Before day this morning Brs Hunter & Warthan came to my house on their way to their hiding place. Hunter wanted me to go in the morning to the Hall to see how the picket guard was doing in his absence and also make such arrangements an I thought necessary to keep up the guard till he could be with them accordingly at 7 o'clock I went and found the guard very much confused and disorganized and did not attend to their business very punctually I then regulated matters to the best advantage I could and at 10 met the Lodge during its Session Br Langley was taken very Sick with the ague & I had to take him home, & then hearing that some of the governors "Moblitia" had come in Town again I went to See Genl Rich but he was in the country I then went to Hutchings. and Stayed awhile and then met with the Company in the cellar of the Temple to organize and make Some preperations for our Contemplated journey next Spring and came home and went with Br A. Brown to See John Robinson who was going with us we then came home & I went to bed at 8 o'clock.

Wednesday Octr 15th 1845. Went to Weeks' Saw him then to the Lodge at 10 o'clock then to the Printing office and then home at 2 o'clock and then wrote in my journal till 4 o'clock and then met the police and came home at dark.

T. 16th. Saw Col Scott about fitting out our company met the Lodge & came home met the police and came home at dark

Friday Octr 17th 1845. Met the Lodge at 10 o'clock then came home at 3 o'clock and went to Allen Weeks and there Staid till morning.

Saturday Octr 18th 1845. Came home before day. All was well. Went to see Br Campbell and met the Company at one o'clock at the Masonic Hall. Made preperations for fitting out &c then went See Hunter and came with him to my house all was well. We then went to the Temple and he home & I to Langley's & Staid all night.

Sunday. 19th. This morning about 3 o'clock Hunter came and waked me up and we went down the river to look at some timber for boards & came back & went to my house about day. and took breakfast and then went to See a timber lot to make arraingements to build some graineries to put corn in for our company and then came home & went to meeting at the Temple. To day some letters were read from William Smith abusing the 12 and the church. The matter was refered to the Saints and he was disfellowshiped from the church and turned over to the hands of God after meeting I went home with Allen Weeks and took dinner met the police and came home accompanied by George Herring who Staid all night.

Monday Octr the 20th 1845. This morning a lot of teams met at my house to go with some hands to cut draw some timber for cribs &c for grain. I then went to the flat and the Lodge and then came home at one o'clock and wrote in my journal till near three o'clock and then went to the Temple in company with Hunter & some others who came here and met the police and came home at about 8 o'clock.

Tuesday Octr 21st 1845. Hunter met at my house this morning to make arraingements set the company hands at work. I then went to Br W. Richards who wanted to See me He wanted me to Send a policeman there to day to be on hands in case any thing should happen There was a council to be there and Jas Arlington Bennett was to be present and it was also Court week and people was very liable to disturb them so I went to the Masonic Hall and sent D. McArthur who was at work there. I then went to see Langley & then went in a Buggy with Col Scott about Seven miles below here to see Br Pettitt. We came back about 2 o'clock and learning that some of the troops was in from Carthage, we went to Br J. Knight & Scott left me there & then went home and I Staid there till time to meet the police and went and met them as usual. We had a general meeting again on the Subject of being more punctual to attend to our duty &c I then went to Lathrop's Store and Warthan told me that there was a writ out for me & others. I then came home about an hour after Dark

Wednesday Octr 22nd 1845. Met at the Masonic Hall at about 8 o'clock with Hunter & others to See about the hands of the company going over the river after waggon timber which we done and have got the waggon Shop Started I then went with Hunter to See other ones of the company to have them commence work at which I was engaged till time to meet the police. and met them as usual & then went to Allen Weeks and Staid all night and came home about Sun rise

Thursday Octr the 23rd 1845. Hunter came and we went to Lathrops there to see about raising a new guard by making a levy of 3 men out of each company which is organized for emigration and returned home again at noon took dinner and then went down on the flat and met the police and then came home and then went Down to Langley's and he not being at home so I waited for him a short time when S. Perry came on the want of me to go to a council at Elder John Taylor's so I went and there learned that we were going to call out the troops to guard the country round and protect it from the depredations of the men whom the governr had sent here to maintain the "Supremacy of the Law" So I went and made arraingements to call out the troops and then went to Langleys and Staid all night.

Friday Octr 24th 1845. Went Earley and took breakfast at Hunter's and then went to the parade ground and met the troops as before mentioned and about 8 o'clock got them under way I took command of a company & went towards Carthage and Stopped on the large mound about half way there and flanked the company to the right and left for about six miles. Col J. D. Parker took a company and went in the direction of Camp-Creek and flanked so as to meet my men & Col Turley went down the river & flanked so as to protect that part then the whole country was guarded We had an entertaining time of it about one o'clock I called in the men and flanked them again after about an hours time which they were there. About half past 3 I called them in again and returned to Nauvoo where I arrived about 5 o'clock and after dismissing the men went and met the police and then went in company with Hunter to Joseph Knights and took Supper and then we went to Elder Taylor's to a council and after arraingements were made for the guard tomorrow I went with B. Young & H. C. Kimball & some of the police to the Hall and there attended to some business & after that went home where I arrived about one o'clock

Saturday Octr 25th 1845. Met at the parade ground at 7 o'clock and to command of the Same company and all hands went forth on the prairie as on yesterday. We were out as before and had a joyful time of it. All was peace yet at court. In the after noon I got word from Carthage that the court had adjourned till Monday & that it was the intention of the officers of the court to leave Backenstos in Carthage and all them to come into Nauvoo So about 3 o'clock Major Warren who had command of the governor's troops at Carthage came along as I before had been informed. He was accompanied by the judge and other officers of the court. They drove up and he demanded in an angry manner of us to know what we were there for. We told him nothing but to convey news to & from Nauvoo to Carthage. He accused us of being there for treasonable purposes and contrary to his orders and such like impertinence all of which we denied for we were not armed (as he could See) He then complained that we were armed with Side arms. We then demanded of him to know if it was wrong for us to carry private arms to which he answered that it was not but said it was not Politic for us to carry them when he was here to keep the peace for it would raise the prejudice & excitement of our enemies. To which I told him that I had carried private arms ever since 2 of our men had been murdered in jail by them under the protection of the govorner. All we said only made him more angry. He then stood up in his buggy and counted all the men he could see which was fifteen and called them 15 parties of men and asked the judge if he did not think that it was a war like appearance he said it was and after some insinuations was cast that he would do something he drove not however till he had taken my name. In about one hour Col Backenstos and all the brethren who was in Carthage came up to us on their way to Nauvoo Backenstos was in the hands of H. W. Miller[45] the Coriner. We then went

45. Henry W. Miller, a carpenter and builder, had worked on the Nauvoo House and the temple. Born May 1, 1807, in New York, he had been baptized into the church in 1839. In Nauvoo he was a member of the High Council. On January 20, 1846, when the last preparations were being made for leaving Nauvoo, Miller was named along with A. W. Babbitt, John S. Fullmer, and John M. Bernhisel to act as a committee to dispose of the property of the Saints, the proceeds to be used to outfit those who otherwise would not be able to leave. In 1848 Miller and Andrew Perkins were asked to carry a petition from the people of Kanesville asking for

to Nauvoo where we arrived at about 6 o'clock. After dismissing the men I went to the Masonic Hall and met the police & also the Emegrating company which met at Sun down. I then made a few remarks to the company and appointed tomorrow evening for them to meet again I went with Hunter & A. J. Stout to John Brinley's and took supper which had been prepared for us by his wife. We then went to the Mansion House and there met with some of the 12 and the officers of the Court & Major Warren & heard their ideas. The Major thought we did not pay that respect to him which was due to one who had been Sent here to restore peace. There was much said on both sides. Elder Taylor gave his opinion of them very Severely & told them that they were but a legalized mob. Warren took great umbrage at this and went into another room & I went in company with some others to guard President Young to John Taylors and then went home it was then very late at night. —

Sunday Octr 26th 1845. Went to the parade ground at 7 o'clock to stop the troops from geathering and then went to meeting at the Temple. and then came home at noon & found my wife sick. Hunter was with me. After dinner we went to the Temple again and met the police and then went with the police to the Masonic Hall and met the Emegrating company and had a good meeting and arrainged tomorrow for work & then went to Allen Weeks and staid all night.

Monday Octr 27th 1845. Came home before Sunrise, and after breakfast went to the Masonic Hall to Start the hands to work in the Company. We started one company of hands to work up the river under Chandler Rogers & and also attended to regulating the concern and then went with Hunter & got some goods from Lathrop for Herring & his friends amounting to twenty dollars. and then came to my house and took dinner and then went to see about raising a new guard and met the police and then went to Hunters & Staid all night

Tuesday Octr 28th 1845. At 7 o'clock went to the Hall to set the company to work and was engaged at arrainging matters untill about noon and then went home accompanied with Hunter and took dinner and then went and done some more business & met the police and then went to Hunters and took supper and then we came home again & there staid all night

Wednesday Octr 29th 1845. We went to the Hall at 7 o'clock as before and then after taking a horse of James McGraw to winter for his use I came home for a Saddle & bridle. Still with Hunter. It was about one o'clock and staid till about 3 o'clock and then went to the flat and then met the police & then went to Hunters and met in council with Joseph & George Herring & Hunter in relation to their missions. They then explained to Hunter & myself the nature of their mission to us and their standing at home. which was not understood by us heretofore. It was quite an important and interesting council. & I expect will yet make a great alteration in their affairs and ours after the council was over I & Hunter went to A. P. Rockwood's and told the result of the council and he was of our opinion.

I then came home & found that Amanda Taylor, my wife's youngest sister who had been for Eleven days sick was dead & all the family in mourning I came home about nine o'clock.

---

a post office at that place. A little later he was sent as representative from Kanesville to the Iowa Legislature.

Miller came to Utah in 1852 and went with the C. C. Rich-Amasa Lyman company to San Bernardino, and on his return in 1858, settled briefly at Beaver Dam, Arizona. He moved to St. George where he was a lawyer, farmer, and stock raiser, as well as a carpenter until he died in October 1885.

Thursday Octr 30th 1845. Met with the company hands at the Hall as usual and then went to see Br. B. Young on the busines of last night. and agreed to meet him at A. P. Rockwoods and then went to do some business for the Company and then took Langley, Hunter & S. Herring with me to Rockwoods as before mentioned to council & after remaining there about till noon & making the necessary arangements for the Herrings and all to the Satisfaction of all concerned I went with George Herring & Hunter to make arraingements for George to go home and then came home about 3 o'clock and took dinner and met the police and then went to see H. G. Sherewood[46] who had returned home from his mission with with Jas Emmett. he reported all well but Emmett was yet as untempered morter. I came home about 9 o'clock.

Friday October 31st 1845. Met at the Hall as usual with the hands and at noon went home and then went to see D. McArthur in the woods   all was well. <u>I then came back home again and took dinner then met the police as usual and appointed L. N. Scovil, G. W. Langley and Lorenzo Clark to stand at Brigham Young's as a regular guard and Allen J. Stout & Wilber J. Earl as a regular guard at H. C. Kimball's. This was done to Save time in the company as it disqualified those who had been on guard from work the next day. and these men had business to attend to in the Lodge which kept them from working regular in the company, so it was thought best to detail those who could not do regular work to stand guard and release the rest for the time being as we was now doing our best to prepare to be off earley in the Spring with the first who Should go west</u> I then came home & went to Jas McLelland's & back at 8 o'clock

Saturday November 1st. Went to the Hall at 7½ o'clock as usual and then went with Hunter to see how Chandler Rogers was doing. He was choping wood with a company of hands above town all was well We then went to see how Duncan McArthur was doing he was also choping wood East of town on Br John Robinson's Land with a company of hands. He was doing well. The company was at this time doing well and all was agreed as far as I knew and in a most flourishing condition. We then went to my house and took dinner and then we went to Br Maudsley's and then met the police and at dark met the company meeting at the Hall. We had a goodly number present and all was in good Spirits and ready to do any thing which I thought best. the reports from the different working companies was good and the best of feelings prevailed. I then came home at 9 o'clock.

Sunday Nov. 2nd 1845. This morning I went in company with Hunter, C. Allen & D. M. Repsher in a buggy to look at a ten acre lot of land about 4 miles below the city. It was a lot of Land put into the company by Br Boss. It was a good lot and had good waggon timber on it & was of great service to us.

We came back & I went to the Temple just as meeting was dismissed. I then fell in company with Levi W. Hancock who came home with me and we took dinner and Staid there till 4 o'clock and then went to the police and after detailing the guard I went to Allen Weeks & staid all night.

---

46. Henry G. Sherwood held many positions of trust in the Mormon Church. One of those healed by Joseph Smith on that "day of healings," July 22, 1839, Sherwood was soon after appointed as salesman and authorized "to price, exhibit, contract, and sell town lots in Commerce," with $200 being the minimum and $500 the maximum price charged. In 1841 Sherwood was made marshal in Nauvoo; in 1843 he was a member of the High Council. During the exodus he was one of the purchasing commissary for the camp and also the general surveyor.

Sherwood came with the pioneers to the Valley of the Great Salt Lake, where again he was a member of the High Council and a surveyor. In 1852 he surveyed the property purchased at San Bernardino. For a time he was agent for the Pony Express in Salt Lake City, but returned to San Bernardino, where he died in 1862.

Monday Nov. 3rd 1845. I came home this morning before day and took break-fast and met the hands at the Hall at 7½ o'clock as usual and was engaged there till noon in matters pertaing to the company and then came home and took dinner & then Saw John Kay about commencing work at gun Smithing who agreed to arainge and Start the Shop, I then went to see Br John Lytle & about his black smith Shop who agreed to have his shop used for company purposes and for forg-ing gun breeches &c but all of it amounted to nothing for I was disappointed in both.

I then went to the police and Saw the two Herring about their going home and then came home and A. Patten came to my house and made Some arraingements for his company.

Tuesday Nov. 4th 1845. This morning the teams met at my hous at Sun rise to go to Bear-Creek for corn. I went to the Hall as before to attend to company mat-ters & while was told that Brs Parker & Roundy were some what dissatisfied about some thing which had been done by some of the officers of the Lodge. I met in the Lodge at 9 o'clock and then went to G. W. Langley's and from thence to J. D. Hunters and took dinner & he & my self then went and saw Peter Haws[47] and made a bargain with him for the use of his Steam Mill 4 miles below here to Saw the Lumber for our waggons. This was very convenient for my company as it was so near to the Lot of Land alluded to (yesterday [crossed out]) day before yesterday We then went to Joel Edmunds' and then met the police and then went to Br. Henry P. Sherwoods' and got the Six Shooter which I lent him previous to his mission with James Emmett. it was in good order. I then came home at dark.

Wednesday Nov. 5th 1845. Went to the Hall at 7½ as before and Sent Jas McGaw with Jas Woolsey up the river to ascertain what had become of Urban V. Stewart & G. W. Hickerson who had been up the river after a raft They had been gone about ten days & had not been heard of They were to have been back in 3 days when they left home and their wives were very uneasy about them least they had fell into the hands of the mob.

I Staid at the Hall till about noon and McGaw & Woolsey came back and reported that Stewart and Hickerson were on their way down the river & all was well I then went on horse back to see how Chandler Rogers & his company of wood choppers came on, who were chopping wood up the river all was well I then went to where Duncan McArther was chopping wood, with a company on John Robin-son's land East of the City. All was well there also.

I then went home and from thence to the police and let Hunter have my horse and went to Allen Weeks and from thence to B. Gardner's and to A. Patten's on company business and then home at 8 o'clock

Thursday Nov. 6th 1845. This morning the teams met at my house at 6 o'clock A. M. to go to Bear Creek again for corn. After breakfast I went to the Hall in company with J. D. Hunter who had come to my house this morning and met the Lodge at 9 o'clock then went to John Robinson's to see him on business pertaining to the company & then came by where McArthur was chopping wood as before from thence home and then met the police and then met the Lodge again at 6 o'clock P. M it was a regular Communication and after the Lodge was adjourned I went

---

47. Peter Haws, an early Canadian convert to the church, had been named by Joseph Smith as one to help build the temple, which he did by going to the Wisconsin pineries to get out lumber which he later prepared on his steam sawmill. One of the first members of the Council of Fifty, he put all that he had at the disposal of the church.

In 1846 Haws was appointed purchasing commissary for the first fifty families in the exodus. In 1854 he moved to Nevada, settling on a branch of the Humboldt River, where he raised grain, vegetables, and cattle for the overland emigrants. After three successful years here, he moved on into California, where he died in 1862.

to the meeting of the 11th Quorum of Seventies at Br D. Amy's and from thence home at 8½ o'clock P. M.

Friday Nov. 7 1845. This morning teams met at my house again   I then went to the Hall as was usual and was busy there till noon & then went with Hunter to procure a Shelling machine to Shell Some corn for the company & then went & took dinner with Hunter and was on the flat till four o'clock and then met the police and then went with Hunter to see President Brigham Young who was found at W. Richards'   Huntr had some business with him after which I went home where I arrived at 6 o'clock.

Saturday Nov. 8th 1845. This morning went to the Hall and attended to business as usual.   at noon I went and took dinner at J. D. Hunter's met the police and at dark went with Hunter to James Porter's who joined my company and put in the use of his Steam mill.   came home at 8 o'c.

Sunday Nov. 9th 1845. Went Earley to the Temple & Hall to See about some sheep   from thence to Hunter's & with him to the Hall and then to the Temple to see Brigham Young who gave instructions about sending for iron and then went home and took dinner in company with Hunter from thence to the police and to the Hall to issue some meet for the hands and after seeing Brigham Young I staid all night at G. W. Langley's

Monday Nov. 10th 1845. Got up earley and went to J. Knights & took breakfast and went to the Hall to start the hands and teams to work.   The coal pit which was burning was done.   In the after noon I came home and then went to Allen Weeks & from thence to the police and came home at dark.

Tuesday Nov. 11th 1845. This morning some hand met at my house and after regulating matters for them to go to work I went down to the Hall at 9 o'clock where I was engaged as formerly until noon and then went with S. Gully to see Br. Fuller to try and loan some money of him for the company & to procure iron to set the smiths to work but did not succeed so after taking dinner with him I returned to the Hall and from thence to the steam mill and there saw A. P. Rockwood who wanted us to grind for the Temple Committee or rent them the mill.   after some proposals on each side the matter was left to the Council of the church. The matter of the City & police guard being on my company was then taken up and also our tithing and he agreed to lay the matter before the council and have them say what is right concerning us.   I then went with   C. Allen to see Sister Clyde who was in some difficulty for the want of some instructions from thence we went to the police where I again saw Br Rockwood about the Mill & he proposed giving a certain price per bushel for grain which was acceded to on our part   I then went home at dark & from to Jas McLellands & S. D. Driggs in company with P. G. Taylor on company business home again

Wednesday Nov 12th 1845. After regulating some company work at home I went to John Robinson's an from thence to the Hall and after regulating affair some there I went to Hunter's and from thence to the Steam Mill and saw our company boat land with it loaded with axeltrees from there I went to Hunter again and took dinner   After dinner Hunter & I went to the Hall on company business & there had a talk with John Scott about Cyrus Daniels Andrew Lytle & others who it appeared had a spirit of Dissatisfaction at the policy of our company affairs & some other matters and then after some conversation with R. J. Redding[48] who was there in the Lodge room I went to the police and then home and staid a few moments and went to Charles Allen's and then to Allen Weeks and staid all night.

Thursday Nov. 13th 1845. Came home this morning at about three o'clock and wrote in my journal untill day and after breakfast went to the Hall and then to the uper Steam mill to see and assist in drawing axletree timber to the Hall & then returned to the Hall. About noon Br Peter Hawes came to the Hall to see me about the sawing of our waggon timber at the lower steam mill for there was a difficulty between his hands and mine in relation to the dividing the lumber which had amounted to some hard feelings So after going to Col John Scotts & taking dinner I went with Br Hawes to his mill and had the matter arrainged satisfactory on both sides it only was a misunderstanding. I then returned with him and met the police about sun set. My brother A. J. Stout told me there that Elder Heber C. Kimball & the Twelve was not satisfied with the procedings of the different companies who were doing business on a common stock principal which was not right. I then went home a little after dark. To night the moon was allmost totally eclipsed on her northern limbs about dusk it was a beautiful sight and it spread a dark and dismal gloom over the bright and clear night & seemed to shroud all nature in deep mourning. I never felt such a desolate sensation in my life at the changes of nature.

Friday Nov. 14th 1845. This morning I went to J. D. Hunter's & saw him about what my brother told me in relation to the common stock business of the companies so we concluded to reduce all the opperations of my company to business like principals in all the features where in it partook of common stock principals which [it] did in some things although we had not yet entered into particular mode of business; but had gone ahead at work at any thing which we thought best for the general good of the company and all things were in an exceeding prosperous condition and far in advance of the anticipations of the most sanguine. After we had concluded as above mentioned we went to the upper Steam Mill now at our control & laid the matter before them & showed them the reasons which thing met their feeling and they all concured in the same. We then went to the Hall and laid the matter before the hands there which likewise met their sanction. I then went home & took dinner at 3 o'clock & then met the police and went home with Hunter & took supper and then went with him to B. Young's to stand guard, but he not being at home we went to W. Richard's where he was and on our way home with him we all went by the Masonic Hall to an exebition of the Paintings of the Scenery

---

48. Return Jackson Redden, often spelled "Redding," was a prominent figure in the Nauvoo period of Mormon history. He was known as a fighter for the "cause." Born September 26, 1817, in Ohio, he joined the Mormons in 1841. Bold and fearless, Redden was a "private detective" and bodyguard for Joseph Smith. After Smith's death Redden had been with O. P. Rockwell when Franklin A. Worrell, the leader of the mob, was shot. Redden had also engaged in a fight with Dr. Robert D. Foster's men on October 25, 1845.

Redden was with the 1847 pioneer group which came to Utah, and is often mentioned by William Clayton and Howard Egan as a "faithful, praiseworthy, man, who works for the good of the camp." He was always in the vanguard. He first located the Cache Cave, near Logan, Utah, which was called Redden's Cave in his honor.

Redden brought his family to Utah in 1848. He staked out the route from Salt Lake City via the Humboldt River to California, and made a map and an outline of the watering places and distances which he published in the *Deseret News* (Salt Lake City), December 1, 1863. In 1849 Redden moved his family to Carson Valley, Nevada, and set up a business. It was reported that he advised all Mormons traveling that route to paint the tips of their oxen's horns red, so that they would be recognized as friends as soon as they drove up.

With the approach of Johnston's Army in 1858, Redden returned to Utah, where he remained acting as justice of the peace in Tooele and Summit counties and later serving as U. S. marshal. He died August 30, 1891, in Hoytsville, Summit County, Utah.

of the assassination of Joseph & Hyrum at Carthage & also of Joseph addressing the Nauvoo Legion on the 17th day of June 1844. It was an entertaining time and we staid till about 9 o'clock and then we went home with him and staid till mid-night and then went home with Hunter staid all night.

Saturday Nov. 15th 1845. This morning I went earley to take a letter to O. M. Allen from B. Young After breakfast I went to the Hall on business as was usual and was engaged till evening and met the police & then came home a little after dark.

Sunday Nov. 16th 1845. Went to meeting at the Stand Heber & Brigham spoke. They taught on the principal of the Companies not going into common stock business as Allen had informed me on Friday eveing.

At inter-mission I went in company with Alfred Brown & wife and Eveline Robinson up in the Temple & to the top of the steeple and had a fine and romantic view of the surrounding country.

We came down & I attended the afternoon meeting which was devoted to company business. It commenced a cold rain in time of meeting from there I went to B. Jones' and took dinner & then met the police and there was informed that Br Edmund Durfee had been shot dead by the mob on Bear Creek

The mob had set some straw on fire which would communicate with his barn & he on discovering the fire ran in company with some other brethern to put it out and was fired upon by the mob who concealed in the darkness one ball went through his breast and he died in a few moments. He had been driven into the City by the mob during their house burning in September last & had gone down there in company with some other brethren to take care of his grain and thus fell a martyr to his religion

I went to see. He was in a heart rending condition all steeped in his gore and his numerous family all weeping around him. The scene is one not to be forgotten. He was one of the oldes[t] in the church having been in the church almost from its rise and had passed through all the persecutions & vicissitudes of the Church & was a faithful Brother.

From this melancholy scene I went to the meeting of my company at the Hall and then went to Hunters and staid all night. It was still raining very hard & I got very wet & cold.

Monday Nov. 17th 1845. This morning was very unpleasant in consequence of the rain the night before Hunter & I went to rent a house for some of our company to live in We then went to W. Hewett and got a buggy and then went to my house and took dinner and Hunter took my horse and went home & I took the Buggy and went to Alfred Browns' and took Evelina Robison home it being still very muddy. I then came home and took my wife down to the Temple and again ascended the Steeple which was the first time which she had ever been up. I then took her home and came back to the police and then went home.

Tuesday Nov. 18th 1845. Went to the Hall as usual and was there engaged in business all day; then met the police while there Br R. Cahoon came to me and expressed some dissatisfaction towards me for saying he had been consenting to Joseph & Hyrum being given up at the time they were murdered. I told him what I had heard and so the matter rested for the present. I then went home and took supper and went to Allen Weeks and staid all night.

Wednesday Nov. 19th 1845. Went to the Hall on business as before & also met with the Lodge was engaged there till noon and took dinner at J. D. Hunters and then started to the Temple and saw met the police then saw Alfred Brown at his house. I then went home at dark.

Thursday Nov. 20th 1845. Went to the Hall as usual & then met with the Lodge Saw R. Campbell who took a profile likeness of myself and J. D. Hunter then came home & gave the books of the Eleventh Quorum to Aaron Rager who I had appointed to be Clerk pro tem in my place in the Quorum untill my business allowed me to attend to it my self. To day Marinda Bennett came to live at my house and made it her home. Met the police as usual & then went to the Lodge again at 6 o'clock it was a regular Communication then came home at 9 o'clock.

Friday Nov 21 1845. This morning I went with my wife to the Store to buy some cotton thread and from thence to the Hall then to see McLean who was printing Lithographic copies of my likeness, but he had ran to St Louis and disappointed me. I then came to the Hall and staid at the Hall till one o'clock and went to Hunters and took dinner and then went to the Steam Mill and then by the Hall again to the police and then started home and stopped at A. Browns and took supper and then went home after dark.

Saturday Nov 22 1845. This morning Br Alfred Brown came to my house and I went with him to John Robinson's where staid untill after dinner We had a long conversation with him about the doctrine of Eternal exaltation and then came home and went to the Hall then to A. J. Stout's & met the police then home and then to A. Weeks & staid all night.

Sunday Nov. 23rd 1845. Came home before sun up. J. D. Hunter came here earley & we went to the Temple & then to his house and staid there till time to meet the police and from the police to the meeting of the Company at the Hall and then home

Monday Nov. 24th 1845. Went to the Hall & Lodge and was engaged in company business all day. Met the police and then went to B. Young's and staid till Eleven o'clock to see him about John Robinson's [daughter] and then went home.

Tuesday Nov. 25 1845. Went to the Hall as usual & appointed John Scott & D. M. Repsher each Captain of ten in the emigrating company and then went home at one o'clock P. M. and took dinner and staid there. Hunter & wife came there and took supper. I then met the police and then went with Hunter to D. McArthur's and appointed him a Captain of another ten and went home at 7 o'clock.

Wednesday Nov 26. Went to the Hall as before and appointed James Pace a Captain and then Hunter & I went to my house & took dinner and went to Asa Barton's and appointed him also a captain of ten. We went to the Hall again and to the police and I with Br Harmon went to a meeting of the Presidents of Seventies at J. D. Lee's & there I saw J. M. Grant[49] take his place as one of the first Presidents of Seventies from thence I went to A. J. Stouts & staid all night.

---

49. Jedediah Morgan Grant was born February 21, 1816, in Windsor, Broome County, New York; was baptized in 1833; and at the age of eighteen went west with Zion's Camp. He worked on the temple at Kirtland and filled many missions. At the age of thirty, Grant was made one of the first presidents of the Seventies.

Grant came to Utah in 1847, became the first mayor of Salt Lake City, and later superintendent of Public Works. In 1849 he was appointed brigadier general of the Nauvoo Legion, and in 1854 he was made an apostle and second counselor to Brigham Young. Grant initiated the great reform of 1856, and in his zeal for the cause impaired his health and died that year. Morgan County, Utah, was named for him.

Thursday Nov. 27th 1845. I came home at day light and went to the Hall at 9 o'clock, and then went to J. D. Hunters and was taken with a spell of sick head-ache so after appointing Hunter to detail the police guard I went home and staid all night.

Friday Nov. 28. 1845. Went to the Hall and Lodge and staid there till noon and took dinner at A. J. Stout's and went from there to the police and then met with the Eleventh Quorum of Seventies at Dustin Amy's and came home at 9 o'clock.

Saturday Nov. 29. 1845. Went to the Hall & Lodge as before & then went to R. Campbell's to have him work at my profile again and then went home with Hunter and took dinner He had a quilting and a good dinner we then went to the Hall again and I met the police and came home at dark.

Sunday Nov. 30th 1845. Went to the meeting of the Seventies at the Temple at 9 o'clock and then went home & staid till evening met the police & then went to the Company meeting at the Hall and then to A Weeks & staid all night.

Monday Dec 1, 1845. Went to Hunters at day light & took breakfast and attended to get some company hands to work who were to meet there this morning for the purpose of cutting wood up the river & then to the Hall and then to the foundry with Hunter & bought a pair of and irons We then came to my house & took din-ner from thence to the Temple & to the Hall again & met police & came home at dark.

Tuesday Decr 2nd 1845. Went to the Hall Saw John Scott about the dissatis-faction of some of the police took dinner with Hunter & went to the Hall again met police, home at dark.

Wednesday Decr 3 1845. This morning I went with G. W. Langley to see about having some timber out and wood cut on the company wood lot 4 miles below here came back & went to the Hall & then went home & met the police and home again at dark

Thursday Decr 4th 1845. I was very sick with the head ache this morning. Went to the Temple & saw Jos Warthan on the way who desired to have an understanding with me about matters which he had been dissatisfied with me about took dinner at A. J. Stouts. and there learned that he had a son born unto him yesterday which was his second son he called his name Allen J. Stout Jr. went to Hall, to police & to Lodge at 6 o'c it was a R. C. [Regular Communication] Come at 9 o'c

Friday Decr 5th 1845. I went to the Hall this morning as usual: but when I came I found the waggon shop in confusion about the price of wages & many other matters of dissatisfaction which had been brewing for some time. In fact matters had got to such a pass among some of the old police that I could hardly suggest an idea which was not some exceptions taken to it & some had even gone so far as to join some other companies in a clandestine way and kept the same from me & at the same time was working in my company because they said I was doing better than the company to which they had attached themselves and not content with that they were using their influence to have others do the same and thus spreading the seeds of discord & disunion in the midst of this once happy and united company. There was hardly a move which I could make but some one would either leave or threaten to leave the company. The guard was also on the wane & it seemed that the very genius of contention was about to prevail. There would also be some one or two dissatisfied every time I would appoint a captain of ten. So it appeared this morning that the matter had come to its achme. So I went to reconciling the difficulties again and as fast as I would reconcile one another would become dissatisfied whereupon I concluded to call the captains together to night at dark and have these differences adjusted and the price of wages settled and thus it ended for the present. I then went to Hunters to see him about what had happened at the Hall this morning but he not being at home I was there left to contemplate on the situation of the company alone. I plainley saw that it all had originated from a spirit of dissention which was in the old police and I concluded to fall back on my former rights and deal with all offenders as was our custom in such cases and informed Hunter of the same who approved of my resolution. We then met the police and then to the Hall and met with the Captains of my company (who were thirteen in number)

When we were ready for business I told them that I had no intention to regulate wages settle difficulties but was resolved to stand on my on rights privileges and that the way I was going to do was to drop every one of the company who had been using his influence against it all those who had joined other companies should not work in mine to continue the Spirit of disunion as they had done and ordered the captains to see to it in their respective companies or I would hold them accountable for the neglect that if they and all of their companies or any one of them did not like my policy they could leave the company in welcome and I would allow them what was right for what they had done if they went in peace that inasmuch as we were appointed to guard the city I intended to perform that part of my duty if everything else remained undone & that I was determined to have men of integraty and such as would remain so to assist me to perform this most responsible part of my duty as it respected the old police who were disaffected I told them that I would not detail them any more on guard untill they made satisfaction for what they had done or showed good reason for the course which they had pursued.

After I was done the captains all spoke and also all in the house about twenty in all and said that they were glad I had taken the course I had & that they would support me in it to the utmost of their ability

The names of the old police who we considered disaffected that night were Jesse P Harmon Daniel Carn Andrew & John Lytle & M. D. Hambleton and no others were mentioned or intended to be in the move which was taken at that time after the meeting was over I went home at 9 o'c.

Saturday Dec 6th 1845. Went to the Hall this morning as usual when I got there D. M. Repsher was settling with M. D. Hambleton accord in to last nights decision He denied allmost all that we alleged Said he had joined Roundy's company and had come back into mine again. We paid him off and let him go I then went to Hunters & took dinner and then returned to the Hall again and all being right I then went with Hunter to Edmunds Shop on the hill and found that all was right there. We then went to the police meeting. When I came there I found all the disaffected police present. They had heard what was done last night and was determined not to abide the decision so they came and reported that they were ready to go on guard.

The word had gone out that we had cut of all the police who did not belong to my company & some others had got the idea that they were cut of also So all those who felt themselves cut off were there and manifested in their looks the bitterest hostilites. When I came I saw how matters were & I detailed the guard and withdrew and left them & when they found I was gone then let out their feelings & showed that they too disaffected and were in a clandestine way were against me. I took this method of leaving them which they all were arrayed at once to force themselves on guard to draw out their feelings which it did most effectually for they brayed out some bitter imprecation against me when they found I was gone & some even Said that they could count numbers with me, that is they thought that they had the Strongest party & could thus mantain the guard.

I went to S. H. Earl to see him on company business and from thence to Alfred Brown's and then came home at dark

Sunday Decr 7th 1845. This morning there was a light snow on the ground which had fell last night I started to the Temple to a meeting of the Seventies and met Hunter & his wife coming to my house & I went back with them. When I returned I found Br A Patten who had come to see me on matters respecting purchasing some iron & other things so after transacting the business with him & Hunter went to his Brotherinlaw's I went to the Temple & found that the meeting had been moved to the Music Hall and adjourned till 2 o'clock P. M. I saw some of the guard at the Temple who told me that the disaffected police were still raging about as usual I went from thence to the Music Hall where there was still a large company of Saints who had not dispersed and fell in company with Br John D Lee who wanted to see me as he had been informed that he was one who had been cut off from the police last Friday night and he was very much dissatisfied with me about that and some other things which he had heard which had caused him to think that I was not his friend. We talked the matter over as we went to his house and continued the same while there and untill we had returned to the Temple & then went into it and continued our conversation untill time to meet the Seventies which resulted in his being convinced that the things which he was dissatisfied with me about was entireley false and that instead of being his enemy was a friend instead of cutting him off from the police had not done anything about his case but had considered him one of my strongest friends but he plainley saw that those who were making feelings between us were equally our enemies & thus ended the difference between us.

I remained at the Temple awhile and some of the disaffected police were there who had been saying that they were anxious to have a talk with me but none of them even hinted the thing to me & never had in all their pretended grievances but when I asked and any of them what their feelings were about these things they would allways say it was all well

J. D. Hunter came and I went home with him and took dinner and we then met the police Some or nearly all the disaffected police met again and reported ready for guard as usual & as though nothing had happened thus showing that they did not regard my authority and treated these matters contempteously but I detailed the guard and paid no respect to them or let on as I knew that they were present. After which just as we were going away Daniel Carn asked me in presence of all the rest if he was needed on guard to night to which I replied I did not as the guard was made out. He then desired to know if he was wanted on guard any more I told him that under the present circumstances he was not. He then wanted to know why & I told him & he said he was not guilty and wanted a meeting called to have the matter settled & I told him it was a matter between him and me & I was ready to settle all difficulties myself &c and continued our talk to the Masonic Hall where I was going to a company meeting when we got there we appointed a time to settle & have an understanding of our differences and parted He manifested a good spirit which convinced me that he was not confederate with the rest. I then met with the company in the Hall and done the necessary business and went home at 9 o'c

Monday Decr 8th 1845. Went to the Hall and was there nearly all day and in the evening met the police and saw Br J. P. Harmon who told me that he wanted to have a talk with me which was the first lisp that ever came from him to me about the police dissention. I told him I would be at the Temple tomorrow and see him I went home at dark. After I had been home a short time Br S. Gully came & brought me some leather.

Tuesday Decr 9th 1845. Went to the Hall and in company with John Scott & J. D. Hunter had a talk with Daniel Carn. He related his grievances and told all the causes of dissatisfaction which he had against me and after he was through I explained the matter as they were and showed him reasons for doing as I did and also wherein he was mistaken which convinced him and he was satisfied and all causes of hardness were removed between us. Hunter & I then went to Allen J Stout's and took dinner & then we went to the Temple and Saw and had a talk with Br J. P. Harmon relative to his dissension from the police and the course I had taken in regard to him. He told all the causes of grievances which he said he had against me which was simply this He said that he had understood that I had put him in John Scott's company of ten which he thought was not treating him with proper respect & He had thought for sometime that I had not been as familiar with him as usual. Upon which consideration he had joined Roundy's company without letting me know it thus forsaking me with out giving me notice that he was dissatisfied He said it was all nothing to have feelings about. I told him I had not put him in Scotts ten neither was I ever inclined in my feelings to treat him coldly he said it might all be his own private feelings without any cause but still he manifested no disposition to be reconciled. I thought he was wilful in his dissension and verily believe that he is now engaged in a crusade of evil against me with others who have an aspiring spirit to rise on my ruins which thing I will venture to predict will yet manifest its self in the sight of all the Saints but I will say but little about that now as it will transpire fast enough. But if this disposition for wicked men to rise on the ruins of others would stop at that I would be willing to fall a sacrafise to them if it would let those above me alone but let the future reveal its own history. I left Br Harmon, after showing him all the intentions which I had for the course I had taken just as I found him as I thought wilfully dissatisfied from here Hunter went home & I to the Hall from there I started in company with A. J. Stout to the police and on our way we met Brs B. Young & O Hyde and Br Young told me that it was decided in council for me to go on a mission to England and wanted to know what I thought of it I told him I was ready to do any thing which was counciled for me to do and then parted with them & went to the police and then Hunter & I went to my house where we came about dark.

Wednesday Decr 10th 1845. Went to the Temple and there saw President Brigham Young again who wanted to know what my feelings were relative to going to England I told him I had no other feelings than to obey council He told me that it would be the best thing that I could do and that it would be the cause of giving me more power and exaltation than any thing else.
 I then went with Hunter who had come to the Temple, to Allen Weeks and from there to A. Patten's and then home & to S. D. Driggs, and then went to police and from there I went to A. Weeks and staid all night.

Thursday Decr 11th 1845. Came home earley this mornin and after Breakfast went to Moses Gay's and got a pair of boots and went to the Hall and then Hunter & I went to S. Maudsley's and to A. J. Stout's and then home and took dinner & then to Boice and got a pair of shoes and to M. Gay's and then took the shoes to S. Maudsley's and then met the police and then to Allen Stout's and then came home at about 8½ o'clock.

Friday Decr 12th 1845. Went to the Hall & to Lodge and from thence to the Temple to settle some accounts there and then to Hunters and took dinner and

went to Hall & came home & then met police & met 11th Quorum & came home at
8½ o'c.

Saturday Decr 13th 1845. Went to Dustin Amy's for some tin ware & there saw
D. Candland about the endowment[50] as he had been through and went from there
to the Temple & to the Hall & to Allen Stout's and then came home and not being well
went to bed & got up and went to the police and then met the Captains of ten
at the Hall & thence went and staid all night at Allen Stout's.

Sunday Decr 14th 1845. Went with Alfred Brown to John Robinson's but he,
not being at home we came back and took dinner at my house. J. D. Hunter & wife
also were there, we then went to the police and from there to the company meeting
at the Hall and came home at 8 o'c

Monday Decr 15th 1845. This morning at 8 o'clock I went with my wife to the
Temple to recieve our endowment and was there untill near noon before we commenced recieving it & was engaged untill evening in recieving it   When we came
out the police was assembled together and I detailed the guard and came home at
dark.

Tuesday Decr 16th 1845. Went to the Temple at 7 o'clock a.m. was engaged
there all day in assisting in the work of the endowment, took dinner at B. Jones'
met the police & staid at A. Weeks all night

Wednesday Decr 17th 1845. Went to the Temple at 7 again and assisted in
preparing watter for the washing.[51] was there till near noon went home for dinner J. S. Higbee came home with me and took dinner and then went to the Temple
again and assisted as before, detailed the police guard and came home at nine o'clock.

Thursday Decr 18th 1845. Went to the Temple and worked as yesterday took
dinner at B. Jones' This morning I got Jones to Bring my wife & Marinda Bennett
to the Temple as Marinda was to have her endowment today which she did
    It was a very cold & windy day After dinner Jones took the women home &
I returned to the Temple and detailed the guard and worked in the Temple awhile
and went home at 8½ o'clock

Friday Decr 19th 1845. Went to the Temple and was engaged as before. About
10 o'clock I went to the Hall & Saw some of the old Police who were to recieve
their endowment tomorrow and then went to Jos Knights and notified Sarah Peck
that she was to recieve hers tomorrow & took dinner at A. Stouts. & to the Temple
and then to police & worked in the Temple awhile and came home at nine o'clock

Saturday Decr 20th 1845. Went to the Temple as before At 9 o'clock my wife
came to the Temple with her mother who had come for her endowment. Today
my brother Allen and Sister Anna Jones and her husband Benjn Jones recieved
their endowment
    I met the police as usual and then went to the Hall to attend a meeting of the
Captains of my company but there not being enough to form a Quorum we adjd
sine Die and I went to Allen J. Stout's and staid all night.

Sunday Decr 21st 1845. This morning I came home before sun up and about
Eleven o'clock I and my wife went to Allen J. Stouts on a visit. and took dinner

---

50. The temple ceremony is called "The Endowment," a promise of blessings and a gift
of power which Mormons believe each member should receive. The first of these endowments
was given on December 10, 1845.

51. The "washing" is a part of the endowment ceremony, a symbolic cleansing of body
and spirit.

an then went to a meeting in the Temple at two o'clock which was the first time which we ever met in a meeting of the Holy order.[52]   After meeting we came down and I detailed the guard and then came home with my wife and went to a meeting of my company at the Hall and arrainged the hands and teams to cut and draw wood to the upper Steam Mill and then came home at about eight o'clock —

Monday Decr 22 1845. Went to work at the Temple at 7 as on last week. At one o'clock went to the M. [Moses] Gay's for shoes & boots, and then to Bice's for boots & then to W. Edwards for a vest and then back to the Temple about 3 o'clock and worked there till evening and then met the police and came home at dark

Tuesday Decr 23 1845. Went to the Temple at 7 as before and took breakfast at B. Jones' and then went back to the Temple & at ten o'clock went to the Hall and met the Lodge and then to the Temple again and then to see some of the Temple Hands who owed the Lodge and settled with them.

About two o'clock a company of the governor's troops came in the city with a United States writ for some of 12 and came to the Temple and while they were there not knowing what to do Br William Miller[53] & G. D. Grant came down out of the Temple and started to Brigham carriage and as they were going Br Grant called Br Miller President Young & asked him if he did not want to take a ride and the officer hearing what was said immediately arrested Br Miller and took him down to the Mansion House and from thence to Carthage not knowing but they had Br Young until they had got there.

I worked in the Temple untill evening and met the police and then came home and Br James Pace came with me & brought some bleached cotton and let me have 24 yards to make me & my wife robes and other garments. It was bought for me by his Br W. Pace for which may he be blessed.

Wednesday Decr 24th 1845. Went to the Temple before 7 o'clock to work as before. At Eleven my wife came to the Temple to cut out our robes and other garments. Miller came home from Carthage The officer's never knew but what they had President Young until they got there and a man by the name of G. W. Thacher [Thatcher] who knew him well informed them of their mistake whereupon his lawyer demanded his release which was granted & he left them immediately

In the evening I met the police and then went home about dark.

Thursday Decr 25, 1845. Went to the Temple about 9 o'clock to work as before and at 2 o'clock returned home and then went with my wife to a dinner at Joseph Taylor's where we had been previously invited After dinner I returned to the

---

52. Of this meeting, Brigham Young wrote: ". . . a meeting was held in the Temple today of those who had received the ordinances. Seventy-five persons were present. The sacrament was administered by Father John Smith and Bishop George Miller. Elder George A. Smith and Heber C. Kimball preached, and others made a few remarks confirming what had been said. Elder John Taylor was mouth in prayer. Meeting dismissed at 2 p.m." Roberts, *Documentary History*, VII, 557.

53. This "Bogus Brigham" incident has been widely told in Mormon history. William Miller, the chief actor, was born February 8, 1814, and joined the Mormons in 1834. In 1838 he was a participant in the election-day fight at Gallatin, Missouri. At Far West he saved the printing press by placing it in a hole over which large poles were laid, and on top of that a stack of hay was piled. He was one of those who signed the covenant to help the poor leave Missouri.

Miller came to Utah in 1849 with his own company, and for a time was employed hauling freight for the Gentile merchants, Livingston & Kinkead. He settled first west of Jordan, Utah, but later moved to Springville, Utah, where he became president of Utah Stake. He died August 7, 1875.

Temple and in the evening met the police and then went to Allen J Stouts & staid all night.

Friday Decr 26th 1845. Went to the Temple at sun up. To day there was no work done at the endowment. There was officers in for some of the 12 and others who were intending to search the Temple for those who they wanted. At 9 o'clock I went home for my breakfast and got and Loaded my pistols and took them and returned to the Temple.

When I came to the Temple I found all the hands engaged in the endowment in a meeting. President Young called a meeting and concluded not to work for a few days and also made new arraingements about the order of business. I then went to the Hall and from there came home very unwell with the sick head ache in the evening met the police and came home at dark.

Saturday Decr 27th 1845. Met the Lodge at 9 o'clock and then went & took dinner at Hunters and in the evening met the police and home at dark

Sunday Decr 28th 1845. To day I was at home all day sick and in the evening met the police and from thence to the Hall to a company meeting

I laid before the company the necessity of increasing the guard which was according to instructions I had received from B. Young. the company all agreed to it and all reported ready to go the next day except a few whom we reserved to carry on the waggon business. So by this move all business in the company was suspended in consequence of the cursed rascality of a legalized mob sent here to vex us by our Govenor. About 9 o'clock I came home.

Monday Decr 29th 1845. This morning I went to the Stand where all those of the company were to meet to regulate the guard. I doubled the Temple guard and sent quite a number of men to patrol the City by night and day and to keep a good look out for strangers and then went to the Hall and then met the Lodge and then in company with J. D. Hunter & Morgan Phelps came home and took dinner after which we rode out by Doyle's and up the river & 30' up to the Temple and there met all the guards in the evening. They were to meet at the Temple every evening All was well and after regulating the guard and police I came home at dark

Tuesday Decr 30th 1845. Went to Br Patten's and then saw Br Charles Shumway. He had been informed that he was cut off from the Police & I showed him why those reports had been set afloat by those who were my enemies to turn him against me. From there I went to the Temple and was informed that President Young wanted to see me & had dispached a messenger for me so I went up to his room in the Temple. He wanted me to raise an additional guard of fifty horse men kept on hands which I immediately went to raising.

When I had got about twenty men raised and mounted captain Morgan[54] and about Eight or ten men passed by They had come into the city with some writs for some of the brethren and were going round through the City saying they were hunting some hogs which D. Hibbard[55] said he had lost.

We all went after him going in squads of six or eight men We met them in every turn of the streets and some were after them all the while & every place that they went some times they would seperate but we kept close on them at last they

---

54. Captain James D. Morgan commanded a company of Quincy (Illinois) riflemen. He joined the Union forces in the Civil War, where he rose to the rank of general.

55. Davidson Hibbard had been a landowner here before the Mormons arrived and sold property to them. During the spring just past, James M. Monroe had at different times "procured books on Phrenology from Mrs. Hibbard." On this date "Four dragoons came in from Carthage and searched for hogs said to have been stolen from Mr. Hibbard." *Ibid.*, VII, 556.

wanted to know what we ment We told them we were hunting stolen property &c The captain tried to ascertain if we ment to insult him we told him we did not but that he had a man by the name of Hill in his company who was guilty of murder & House burning and we intended to wach him. They then proceeded to Carthage where they were stationed & we followed them to the edge of the city and there I organized them guards into Squads of six men each and appointed a captain over each Squad & sent them through town and to meet at the Temple in the evening Hunter & I then proceeded to the Temple and made report of what had been done which was satisfactory I then went to Br Hall[56] to have my Horse Shod and returned to the Temple and arrainged the guard and police for the night and came home at dark

To day Hunter & I got each a horse which had been put into our posession by Br A. Patten They proved to be good horses for our business.

Wednesday Dec 31 1845. Met the Horse guard at the Temple at Eight o'clock a.m. and dispached them on patrol guard in Squads and then went to the Hall for to transact some company business for Patten and Stevens and then (to R. Campbell's with Hunter [crossed out]) came home for dinner and then met Hunter at the Temple and we then went to the Campbell's and then to the police and came home at dark.

Thursday January 1st 1846. This was a very warm rainy day and very disagreeable. I was at home & very sick with the headache. In the evening I went to the Temple and met with the Horse and police guards and came home at dark.

Friday January 2nd 1846. Met the guards at the Temple at 8 and went in a body and patroled through Hibbards & Doyle's woods and round Moffat's farm and then sent the guards home in Squads and came home at noon, took dinner and met the guards at the Temple at 2 o'clock and then rode in a body down to the Mansion and then up the river to the uper end of the city and round to the East Side of the city and came to the Temple again and then met the police & arrainged the guard for the night and went home about dark —

---

56. William Hall was converted to Mormonism by Samuel Lake and baptized by him on March 16, 1840. Hall moved to Nauvoo where he operated a blacksmith shop. Evidently he early protested against some of the policies of the church, for he wrote with bitterness of the constant demands for donations, public work, and tithing.

Hall left Nauvoo with the early group in 1846. On March 14, 1846, John D. Lee as clerk for Brigham Young wrote:

Some time to day Wm Hall left camp with his team for the Desmoines river to bring forward a load for A J Stout At Indian creek one of his horses sickened with bloating and cholick Elder Hall & Luallen Mantle layed hands on him & he recovered immediately & went on about 2 miles when he was again attacked much more violently than before they tried to give him medicine but could not succeed the horse layed on his side with his foot over his ear Ruben Strong said he beleived there was life in him yet, and proposed to lay hands on him but some doubted whether it was right to lay hands on a horse or not Elder Hall replied the Prophet Joel has said that in the last days the Lord would pour out his spirit upon all flesh & this satisfied the Brethren & Elder Wm Hall R R Strong L Mantle Jos Chaplain Martin Potter & one more laid hands on the horse and commanded the unclean and foul Spirit of what ever name or nature to depart and go to Warsaw and trouble the Saints no more when the horse rolled twice over in great distress sprang to his feet squealed vomited & purged next morning was harnessed to a load of about 12 hundred & performed his part as usual. (John D. Lee, "Plan and Inventory of the Camp of the Saints . . . [February 1, 1846-June 8, 1846]" [typescript, Utah State Historical Society; original, L.D.S. Historian's Library]. Hereafter cited as Lee, "Camp of the Saints.")

Saturday Jany 3rd 1846. Met at the Temple with the guards at 8½ o'clock and sent out patrol guards in Squads & then went home with Hunter ̲t̲o̲ ̲t̲h̲e̲ ̲L̲o̲d̲g̲e̲ and from thence to R. Campbell's Settled with him and let him have a watch and took dinner at A. J. Stout's and met the troops at 3 o'clock and all marched to the Mansion & up Parley Street East to Green Street and thence North to Mulholland Street and then back to the Temple and met the police and regulated the guards and with Hunter made report to Brigham and came home at dark quite sick

Sunday Jany 4th 1846. Met the guards at 8½ as before & sent Some Squads out. ̲J̲o̲h̲n̲ ̲S̲c̲o̲t̲t̲ ̲t̲o̲l̲d̲ ̲m̲e̲ ̲o̲f̲ ̲a̲ ̲c̲o̲n̲c̲o̲c̲t̲i̲o̲n̲ ̲t̲o̲ ̲t̲r̲y̲ ̲a̲n̲d̲ ̲g̲e̲t̲ ̲m̲e̲ ̲o̲u̲t̲ ̲o̲f̲ ̲t̲h̲e̲ ̲L̲o̲d̲g̲e̲ ̲a̲s̲ ̲S̲e̲c̲r̲e̲-̲ ̲t̲a̲r̲y̲ at 12 I came home accompanied with Hunter & took dinner and Met the guards at 3 o'clock and rode down below Hibbards and wattered our horses and came back to the Temple and regulated the guard and met the police and came home when I came I found Sisters Jane and Martha Bennett on a visit to see my wife

Monday Jany 5th 1846. Met the guard at the Temple at 8½ o'clock and regulated the guard for the day and ̲w̲e̲n̲t̲ ̲t̲o̲ ̲t̲h̲e̲ ̲H̲a̲l̲l̲ ̲a̲n̲d̲ ̲m̲e̲t̲ ̲t̲h̲e̲ ̲L̲o̲d̲g̲e̲ ̲a̲t̲ ̲E̲l̲e̲v̲e̲n̲ ̲o̲'̲c̲l̲o̲c̲k̲ Saw Hunter who let me have Seven and a half dollars and then came home and took dinner and met the guard again at three o'clock and rode down the river and through Doyle's pasture and so on round and then by my house and on to the Temple and met the police and regulated the guard for the night and then came home at dark

Tuesday Jany 6th 1846. Went with my wife to the store and also met the guards at 8½ o'clock and regulated the guard for the day & then came with my wife home and returned to the Temple and met Hunter We then came to my house and took dinner and then returned to the Temple and from thence to Foundry and Saw them casting which was the first time I ever saw this opperation. We returned to the Temple and met the guard at 3 o'clock and rode around to the East and passed D. H. Wells' and so on down back by my house & to the Temple and regulated the guards and police for the night and then went to Robert Campbell's to see him about painting for us and then to Elder John Taylor's where we had been cited to appear with John Scott to settle some difficulty which had arisen with Cyrus Daniels[57]

It was done in presence of Brigham Young, Heber C. Kimball & John Taylor of the Quorum of the 12. The matter was droped and all concerned agreed to lay

---

57. Cyrus Daniels had been suffering intensely with his shattered arm for more than three months, and evidently felt that he had been neglected. On September 21 Hosea recorded that "Cyrus Daniels reported of a plan which he had devised to watch & regulate some matters north of Town up the river," which seemed to be a raid of some kind. Only George W. Langley was mentioned by name as being an accessory, though others were involved. Daniels had borne the brunt of the failure.

Definite biographical data on this man has not yet been found. In 1832 he accompanied Thomas B. Marsh to Kirtland, traveling horseback; on February 7, 1839, in an attempt to help Joseph Smith and his companions escape from Liberty Jail, Daniels had taken two of the guards, one under each arm, and run down the stairs with them, barely escaping a shot from another guard. Jenson, *Historical Record*, VII (January, 1888), 18, 455.

Marsh was listed with the group at Far West who ordered Oliver Cowdery to leave forthwith, and he was among those who went out from Nauvoo to the Wisconsin pineries to bring out lumber for the temple.

After the injury here referred to, Daniels did not take active part. The only evidence found that he came to Utah is an article by Waldo Littlefield published in 1880, which explains Daniels' crippled arm as a possible result of the attempted prison-break. *Ibid.*, VII (July, 1888), 668.

aside all hardness. Elder Taylor then invited us to a Supper which was prepared in the most Sumptious Style. He had a feast at his house that evening. After Supper I came home at about Eight o'clock.

Wednesday Jany 7th 1846. Met the guard at the Temple at 8½ o'clock as before. About the time the guard was paraded D. H. Wells came to me and told me that one of his horses were gone & requested me to have the guard to hunt for it He offered five dollars if we found it & if it was stolen he offered ten if we found it. The guard went out to look for it in all parts of the Town I then met the Lodge at nine o'clock While there Wells came & told me he had found his horse which had been taken up and gave me three dollars for our trouble although he found the horse himself

At one o'clock I came home & took dinner and met the guards again at three. We rode to the river above the uper steam mill and then down to Main Street and down Main Street to Hodgkiss Street thence West to the river or near it & there detailed the guard for the night & then down the river to Main Street again and thence to the Temple and met the police and came home at dark.

Thursday, January 8th 1846. (Went to see a stove to buy) Met the guard as before and rode down the river below Hibbards and wattered the Horses and I then met with the Lodge and then to B Jones' and to the Temple & came home A. J. Stout came there in the mein time After dinner met the guard as usual at 3 & rode North East to the edge of the city & regulated the guard & police & came home before dark.

This evening William Taylor came across the prairie from the North of Carthage & said he saw seven men going from towards Appanoose towards Carthage with a cannon and bearing a large red flag. The cannon was drawn by four horses.

Friday January 9th 1846. Met the guard as usual We rode below Hibbard on the river as before and wattered our Horses and regulated the guard for the day as was our custom I then went to the Lodge and then came home. John Scott was with me. After dinner we returned to the Temple at three to meet the guard as usual

Scott was raising about twenty or thirty men to go to Carthage tomorrow to attend a meeting of the (citizens) of Hancock County to appoint delegates to meet a convention at Springfield to nominate a (Democratic) candidate for goverrner at the next election next August.

When we came to the Temple some what a considerable number of the guard were assembled and among them was William Hibbard son of the old man Hibbard. He was evidently come as a spy. When I saw him I told Scott that we must "bounce a stone off of his head."[58] to which he agreed we prepared accordingly & I got an opportunity & hit him on the back of his head which came very near taking his life. But few knew any thing about what was the matter he left the ground out of his senses when he came to himself he could not tell what had happened to him &c

Just as the guard was formed a man came to me who said he had lost two horses last night and supposed they had been stolen & was yet in the North part of town and agreed to pay three dollars to the guard if they would search this evening for them which they did by going in companies but did not find the horses. After the companies were then dispersed to search for the horses I met the police & then sent my horse home and went home with Allen J. Stout & he and I went to

---

58. The expression "to bounce a rock off his head," was colloquial in southern Nevada, without any suggestion that it might be put into effect as it was in this instance.

Thomas Rich's and we all three patrolled on the flat untill about Eight and I went home with Allen & Staid all night. —

Saturday, Jany 10th 1846. This morning I went to the Temple at 6½ o'clock and from there to B. Jones' & took breakfast and then met the company who were to meet here for carthage as mentioned yesterday and then went home and got my horse & met the guards as usual and rode to the uper steam Mill and wattered and regulated the guard and then met the Lodge at 9 o'clock and started home at Twelve and was informed by Elisha Hoops that the mob were making preparations at Warsaw for another campaign against us. I went on home and after dinner met the guard at three as usual and as I & Hunter had business with Hecock & Loomis I put the guard under D. McArthur. Near sun down the guard returned from their excurtion & I regulated it for the night and met the police and started for home & on my way met Scott & his company returning from Carthage All was well Anties made no resistance & the mormons carried the day. I came home at dark.

Sunday Jany 11th 1846. Met the guard as usual and rode to Hiram Kimball's Landing[59] and wattered and then regulated the guard for the day and dismissed them till 3 and then went to the Temple to a public meeting in the Second Story but the congregation was so numerous that it would not contain them and so I went to Benjn Jones' and from thence to Archabald Kerr's and from thence by the Temple, home at one o'clock and took dinner & then Met the guard at 3 as usual and rode below Hibbards as before mentioned and wattered our horses and from thence to the Masonic Hall and regulated the guard for the night and then came home about a half an hour before sundown.

Monday Jany 12th 1846. This morning about 2 o'clock A. m. I was awoke by Joseph Taylor who had come from the Temple to let me know that the troops from Carthage were coming in and I immediately arose and went to the Temple and found some of the guard present The Twelve were some of them up and on the ground and so I sent out spies to see where they had gone to. Near daylight I was informed that they had taken Andrew Colton[60] and sent him to carthage and

---

59. Hiram Kimball was living in the neighborhood of Commerce, Illinois, when the Mormons began to buy property there. He sold them some large tracts. Although for a time not a member of the church, Kimball was friendly to the people. In 1842 he was a member of the municipal court, and during one of their sessions, Joseph Smith received and wrote a special revelation, which he handed to Kimball. It was to the effect that "Hiram Kimball has been insinuating evil and forming evil opinions against you with others; and if he continues in them, he and they shall be accursed . . . ." Roberts, *Documentary History*, V, 12.

In June 1843 Joseph Smith was brought before the municipal court, of which Hiram Kimball was one of the justices, and acquitted of charges made against him. In 1844 when Joseph Smith and his brother Hyrum had crossed the river intending to flee to the west, Emma wrote her husband to the effect that some of his friends, among them Hiram Kimball, had criticized him, comparing him to the unfaithful shepherd who abandoned his flock when the wolves came. The fact that because of this letter Joseph Smith returned to his death made many members consider Kimball a traitor.

Stout's actions in riding up the river to Kimball's Landing and around by the home of Hibbard, an acknowledged apostate, would indicate that both men were suspect. Kimball later declared his loyalty and demonstrated it at the battle of Nauvoo where he helped to protect the few remaining Mormons, receiving a slight wound with a musket ball across his forehead.

In 1856 Kimball was in Salt Lake City, and received the mail contract from Independence, Missouri, to Salt Lake City. This was canceled by the government prior to the sending of Johnston's Army.

60. Of this incident Norton Jacob wrote under date of January 11, 1846:

This evening a number of such scoundrels, under the character of government troops, went to the house of Brother Andrew Colton in the midst of the night and took him out of his bed, under a charge of horse stealing. They went also to Brother Eatman's stable and broke it open looking for the stolen horse, but found him not. But they took

a party remained till day for what we knew not. In the mein time I had sent for all the guard to be called together at the Temple and there be ready for an emergency. and also sent Capt D. McArthur with a company to watch their movements, They went down on the flat after breakfast and began to enquire of the children for certain men as was their custom at the same time Col Scott was watching them. They were very insolent and insulting They passed by the Temple & I and Hunter & some more joined the company who was watching them & they threw out some insults about us for keeping after them. At last we told them that we considered our selves abused and insulted by them for coming in the way that they did & that no gentleman would do it. and also that before we would have the city thrown into an alarm as they had caused it to be by their frequent military displays of power which was altogether unconstitutional & uncalled for, we would resist them & that the next time they attempted to patroll our streets by night we would be the death of them for we had rather die than be treated with such tyranny as we had been by Major Warren and his troops and many more thing we said for we had come to the conclusion that we would shoot the next set of armed men who came in our midst with out giving us notice of their coming which they would if they were men who respected the right of others

After which they put for carthage & we continued our guarding till about noon and then dismissed them till three and I went Hunters and took dinner & met the guard at 3 and rode down the river & wattered as heretofore and regulated the guard and policy for to night and then went near my house & dismissed the troops and went home and saw my family and then went with Hunter to the Store & to Temple & Allen Stout's and then to J. D. Hunter's and to the Temple where I intended to stay all night. all was now peace

I remained in the Temple all night.

Tuesday Jany 13th 1846. This morning I arose before day and remained in the Temple untill 8½ o'clock when the guard met nothing of importance transpired during the night After the guard had assembled I regulated it for the day and went to the Hall & to Campbell's & then back to the Temple at ten o'clock and met with the Council of fifty.[61] This is the first time which ever I met with that Council.

The subject of our removal West was discussed & I was well entertained. From the Council I went home accompanied by J. D. Hunter & Cyrus Daniels & took dinner Br Daniels' arm was now so that he could walk out.

From thence I went to the Temple again and met the guard and we rode out on the Carthage rode about four miles On our way out we regulated the guard and police for the night. From the Carthage road we went to the North to the Laharp rode and back to the city and dismissed the guard and went home and left my horse and went to Allen J. Stouts and Staid all night

Wednesday Jany 14th 1846. Went to the Temple at day light and took breakfast and met the guard as usual We rode down to the river at the lower stow or ferry and down the river to the foot of Main Street and wattered our horses and dismissed the guard and met the Lodge and then went home about Eleven o'clock. While I was there Col Scott and wife came to my house. Just as dinner was ready an express came from the Temple for me forthwith whereupon Scott and I went

their prisoner off to Carthage. The police were soon in pursuit; and some of the rascals who stayed till morning were driven off by our police and were told by Captain Stout that if they came back and were found running through the streets at night he would kill them; and left the city in great rage. (Jacob and Jacob, *Norton Jacob*, 15.)

61. The Council of Fifty had been active since March 1844. Hosea was not yet a member of the council, but was called in here and later to report progress in getting wagons ready for the evacuation.

immediately with out waiting for dinner. I was there notified by President B. Young to send spies out in different parts of the country to watch and report the proceedings of the mob —

I committed the business of sending spies out in Iowa to Sanford Porter[62] who lives in Iowa he was to send some three or four in different directions to watch their movements and let us know when anythings is going on among them against us.

When the guard had assembled we rode to the upper Steam Mill and wattered our horses & then rode round and through the North part of the City and regulated the guard & police and sent my horse home & after assisting Hunter to be Sealed to Lydia Edmunds I went home with Allen Weeks and staid all night

Thursday Jany 15th 1846. This morning I came to the Temple before day and found all well I remained there till 8½ o'clock and met the guard as before we rode down the river and wattered our horses as we had previously done and then returned to the Masonic Hall and dismissed the guard after had made arraingements for the day. After which I met with the Company which had assembled at ten.

We had a meeting of the captains of tens last night at the Hall and they were instructed [to] notify their companies to meet as aforesaid for the purpose of ascertaing their situation and readiness to emigrate to the West immediately. There was a large assemblage after I had made the necessary arraingements I went Home. Hunter was with me & took dinner. While eating dinner two of the guard came & informed us that there were Strangers in the city so we immediately went to the Temple but nothing of importance transpired till the guard met at three we rode East & came in on Parly Street regulated the guard & police and I Stopped at home & put on an under garment for the first time to wear it[63] & then met the Lodge at six it was a Regular Communication then went to the Temple & Staid all night

Friday Jany 16th 1846. I remained at the Temple & took breakfast and at Eight and a half o'clock and then met the guard as usual & we rode direct North to the River and down on the beach to the foot of Main Street & regulated the guard for the day as we came down. From thence to the Masonic Hall and dismissed the guard and met the Lodge at ten and then came home by way of the Temple where I arrived about noon & Met the guard at 3 as usual and regulated it for the night also the police and then came home about four we did not ride out this evening because it was a very disagreeable time the Snow and wind was blowing hard from the North East.

Saturday Jany 17th 1846. Met the guard as usual and sent them out under Capt D. McArthur after detailing the guard for the day & I Staid at the Temple until one o'clock on business of the guard then went home Scott was with me & we took dinner & met the guard at 3. We rode below Hibbards again and wattered our

---

62. Sanford Porter was one of the most faithful members of the Mormon Church at that time, and also most respected among non-members. Born in Massachusetts, March 17, 1790, he was baptized in 1831 and followed the fortunes of the church from Kirtland, Ohio, through the Missouri troubles. He was the father of a large family, all of whom were active in and loyal to the church. Living across the line in Iowa, he escaped many of the difficulties of Nauvoo.

Porter followed the pioneer group to Utah in the fall of 1847 with the Charles C. Rich company, and the next season he sent back teams and supplies to meet the immigrants and lighten their loads. In Utah, Porter settled first at Millcreek, then moved to Centerville, where he served as bishop. Later he moved to Morgan County and established Porterville, named for him. He was a sawyer and a farmer. Porter died February 7, 1873.

63. A modern version of this garment is worn by all who have obtained their endowments in the Mormon temple.

horses and regulated the guard for the night & I came home by the Temple about dark

Sunday Jany 18th 1846. Met the guard as usual. Lorenzo Young reported to the guard that he had lost some five or six head of cattle last night I sent the guard in search of them for the[y] thought they were stolen & then heard the report from Br. Patten who had been to Carthage as a spy & then went to A. J. Stouts and there learned from some of the guard that they had found the cattle near Hibbard's. From there I came home at Eleven and there remained untill three and then met the guard as before. We rode up the river three or four miles to look at a lot of timber which had been procured by M. Johnson for the guard we came in on the North East part of town & I came home before dark

Monday Jany 19th 1846. Met the guard as usual and put them under Capt Scott who rode out with them & I remained with Hunter & some others at the Temple untill ten and then met the council of fifty as on last Monday It was there decided among other things that the Capt of the different emegrating companies should arrainge & prepare as many of their men to Start for the West and leave their families as could with [out] leaving them to suffer At three met the guard again and rode down the river regulated the guard for the night and delivered a Speech to them on the nature and office of their calling and then dismissed them and came home and then went to the Temple and met the capt of my emegrating company on some business & about Eleven o'clock came home.

Tuesday Jany 20th 1846. This was a very disagreeable morning and the wind & snow drove furiously from the North East. I met the guard & paraded them in the Temple cellar on foot and regulated the guard for the day & dismissed them & remained at the temple till one and came home Hunter came with me & took dinner and returned to the guard at three. Paraded in the cellar again and regulated it for the night and was presented with a letter by C. Rogers from Br Franklin R. Tower who had been sent as a Spy to Warsaw it Stated in Substance that They were forming Secret Societys to make arraingements to make a Simultanius attact on Nauvoo and the Temple both by land and water and at the Same time to have the officers to attempt the arrest of Some of the 12 & others. That they had Spies here who gave them news daily and that he had reason to believe that one of the guard was a Spy. That my life was to be taken by them if it could be & also the Twelve. that he was a member of their lodges and yet unsuspected.

I took the letter & read it to Brigham Young and informed him of the circumstances relative thereto from there I came home a little after dark the driving snow still falling fast from the North East. and staid awhile & went to the Temple and staid all night

Wednesday Jany 21st 1846. Staid at the Temple untill 8½ o'c and met the guard and after regulating it for the day put in under Capt B. Jones & I remained there and then came home & took my wife to the Temple She came to accompany Lucretia Fisher who was going down to get her endowment we was there untill dark and then came home but I regulated the guard at three and sent them out under Capt Scott. I remained at home untill about eight o'clock when an express came from the Temple stating that some men had come into town under suspicious circumstances & also that some writs had been sent in by two Strangers one for me & one for Elder Orson Hyde I immediately went to the Temple it proved a false alarm. I remained there all night all was well in the morning

Thursday Jany 22nd 1846. Met the guard on foot in the Temple cellar at 8½ and made new regulations as follows that each company should furnish six men each day to guard in the day time except the company which was on guard the night before & the ones which was to go on that night for the guarding was done at night by companies one company at a time in succession, a part of the guard is to stand at the Temple and part patroll the city & suburbs, one half on guard at a time and relieved by the other half at noon & midnight. after the above regulations I appointed Elam Luddington[64] to be Seargent of the guard at the Temple he was to see that the guard done its duty & kept its post &c & also that the patrol guard report to him when I am absent. I then went to the Hall & from thence to the upper Steam mill with Hunter and wattered our horses and then we went by C. Allens to my house & took dinner & met the guard at three as usual in the cellar & regulated it for the night and then started for home. Scott was with me just as I was going I met F. R. Tower who was on his way home from Warsaw — I had not time to talk with him so we parted to meet again in the morning & I went home & came to the Temple at dark and met with a company of Saints in the Temple for prayer we were dressed in *our robes which was the first time I ever met to pray according to the order of the priesthood.* About 8 o'clock I went to Allen Weeks and staid all night.

Friday Jany 23 1846. This morning I came to the Temple at seven o'clock and found all well and met the guard at Eight and a half o'clock and regulated it for the day and then had an interview with Br F. R. Tower as mentioned last night. He informed how the mob intended to opperate but I shall not relate it now for I will see how they come out in their plans He let me know that they had singled me out as an object of their revenge and was determined to take my life. They are also now trying to hire some daring person to secretly assassinate some of the Twelve. They have also some spies here who gives them news every day After he had made his report he also made it to Prest B. Young H. C. Kimball & A. Lyman & some of my company. I still remained at the Temple and about one o'clock Hunter & I went to my house and saw how matters were there (and also to notify my wife to be ready to go to the Temple to recieve our anointing sealing & further endowment but [crossed out]) [three lines blank]

We then came back to the Temple & I remained there till three & met the guard and regulated it for the night and then went home again (to prepare as above but found matters no better [crossed out]) I came to the Temple again and remained there all night

Saturday Jan 24th 1846. Arose about sun up quite sick Met the guard as usual in the cellar & spoke at length to them on the necessity of keeping ourselves humble and prayerful before the Lord & also to keep ourselves in order when we meet together to attend to the business of our calling which was unanimously recieved by the company whereupon it was also then agreed to hence forth open our meetings by prayer and supplication to the Lord to protect us and the things which we are intrusted with and deliver us from our enemies

I remained at the Temple untill about one and then in company with J. D. Hunter went home and took dinner & returned to the guard at three as before. Meeting was opened by prayer by Duncan McArthur The guard was then regulated for the night and I went up in the Temple and wrote in my journal. To day

---

64. Elam Luddington was at this time a member of the Nauvoo police. Later he joined the Mormon Battalion. Since he had both his wife and his mother along, he was permitted to go with Captain James Brown to take the sick and most of the women to winter at Pueblo, Colorado. Luddington's name appears in the diaries of Robert Bliss, John Steele, and Henry W. Bigler.

Luddington and his family returned to Utah in the fall of 1847. On January 9, 1851, he was elected city marshal in the first municipal organization. In 1853 Luddington was one of thirteen missionaries called to the Orient.

at ten there was a general meeting of the Saints in the second story of the Temple to elect new trustees in trust for the church & other purposes and Almon W. Babbitt Jos. L. Haywood and John S. Fulmer were elected Trustees in trust for the church and John M. Barnhisel[65]

I went from the guard home again I felt depressed in spirit and went to bed and laid untill sundown and again rode down to the Temple for it was not safe for me to stay at home at night because of my enemies. I sent my horse home by one of the guard and went up in the Temple and staid all night About one o'clock laid down to rest & slept well till day —

Sunday Jany 25th 1846. Went home very earley and took breakfast and returned to the Temple to meet the guard after detailing the guard for the day Br G. W. Langley came to me and demanded of me to call the old Police together to themselves as there was something to settle, they met in the Temple cellar He was dissatisfied at my proceeding in some instances and in particular because I had appointed E. Luddington sergeant of the guard at the Temple and swore in absolute terms that he would not submit to it but said the rest of the police might do as they pleased. He said many hard & inflamatory things about my course in the guard which was calculated to disaffect those who were well disposed to do their duty but said he was a friend to me I considered it nothing more nor less than absolute and wilful dissension and an attact on the discharge of my duty. There was much said by different ones but none came out against me but some were somewhat disaffected at first others were decidedly against him and sustained me in the course I had taken. The more which was said about it I saw that the police thought the less of what he said. However after a long time I spoke on the subject of their disaffection and told them the fatal consequences thereof and warned them to ceace their bickerings murmering backbiting evil speakings about one another or they would be torn asunder and scattered to the four winds (as police) and fall away from the faith. All but Langley were melted into tears amost and some asked my pardon for what they had said Langley remained inveterate as ever there was other things which he had done as he said there which proved that he had been my secret enemy for a long time. After the matter had been thus discussed I proposed for all those who felt perfectly satisfied with me as matters now stood and would sustain me even unto death to give their names to the clerk which they all did & Langley among among the rest. But he immediately went to doing all that he could against me by Sowering the mind of Genl C. Rich about some things which had called forth his name in our talk I went home and took dinner and met the guard at three as usual and adressed them at some length on the things which were coming to pass and the responsibility of the guard and also warned them to beware of evil Spirits and men among them who would lead their minds away from their duty &c. The spirit of God rested down upon us and the whole house was melted into tears. after I was done Speaking we joined in prayer by Br A. Patten. I then detailed the guard and went home before dark and had a difficulty settled at home as before refered to[66] after which I felt at rest My mind had been so burthened & my Spirits depressed at what had taken place in the police At the unfaithfulness of Langley whom I had taken so much pains to learn to govern and be a man of influence and befriended so long and now was so ungrateful as to leave me in trouble that I was almost down sick.

I went to bed and rested well all night

---

65. As the blank space would indicate, Stout did not complete this entry. He should have added ". . . and Henry W. Miller trustees for the building of the Nauvoo House."

66. The entry on January 23 clearly indicates that there was dissension among his wives, which meant that they could not enter the temple.

Monday Jany 26th 1846. This morning met the guard as usual and regulated it for the day and there learned that Genl Rich was displeased at me I saw him & in company with Scott & Hunter Satisfied him that I was his friend and had not been using an influence against him. His mind had been soured by G. W. Langley who was now doing all he could against me.

I remained at the Temple untill about ten and then with Hunter came home and Staid awhile and then returned to the Temple and was there till three & met the guard as usual and then Staid at the Temple all night. Nothing of importance transpired more than usual I retired to rest at one o'clock.

Tuesday Jany 27th 1846. Arose Earley and took breakfast at the Temple Met the guard as usual. came home at ten Hunter & came to my house all was well We Staid awhile & returned to the Temple made some arraingements with W. O. Clark about Spies &c over the river in Iowa. Took dinner at S. [Stephen] M. St John's Met the guard as usual at three regulated it for the night and came home at about five, and Staid all night.

Wednesday Jany 28th 1846. Met the guard at the Temple cellar as usual and regulated it for the day and then had a talk with James Pace and warned him against the Spirit of dissension which had prevailed in the "old Police" and Showed him how to detect it & then was with Hunter, Scott, & C. Allen at the Temple untill about Eleven o'clock when I recieved news that some 6 or 8 of the govorner's troops (moblitia) had come in town again. I sent some of the guard to watch their movements & then went up in the Temple and informed Brigham Young of their arrival. I remained there a short time and then went down again & was informed that they had left for Pontoosuc where they had quartered some troops. Met the guard as usual and then apointed Eight o'clock A. M. and three and a half in the evening for the times of meeting the guard and then regulated the guard & police as usual for the night and then came up in the Temple again before dark a short time and staid all night

Thursday Jany 29th 1846. Met the guard at Eight o'clock and regulated it for the day. This was a very wet and disagreeable day & I posted all the city guard in and around the Temple to keep them out of the Storm and also to have them where they could be come at in case they were needed for I had learned that Majr Warren & some troops & a man from Warsaw was in the city and had not learned their business. About nine o'clock I returned up in the Temple again. About one I learned that there were twelve of the troops in the city. I remained in the Temple all day & met the guard as usual and regulated it for the night and then went home a little before dark. It was very wet & muddy and still raining.

Friday Jany 30th 1846. Warm foggy morning. Some appearance of clearing off. I met the guard as usual and regulated it for the day and then went to the printing office and made arraingements for some books then to the Lodge & the waggon shop and then to the Temple and then with C. Allen I went home & took dinner and then met the guard and then saw Br Alpheus Cutler who wanted to see me. He informed me that a company was organized to steal our waggons as fast as we got them done to prevent us from moving west. I then gave him a full statement of the nature of the dissension in the "Old Police" He had a better understanding of it than any man which I had before talked with and seemed to comprehend the Spirit by which they were actuated and informed me of evil plotting against me which I had not heard of and also that my life was threatned by some in very positive terms. I felt that he was my friend.

I went from the Temple to Hunters & returned to the Temple after supper and staid all night.

Saturday Jany 31 1846. Arose at 6½ o'clock all was well   Prest J. P. Harmon notified me that the Eleventh Quorum was going to have their endowment to day and wanted me and wife to attend   I went home and brought her down and after staying awhile went with John Scott to see Br A. Cutler about the dissension of the Police and wanted him to and have the matter laid in a proper manner before the Twelve   This was about noon.   I think some thing is wrong in the minds of the Twelve in relation to this matter but how it appears to them I know not.   But I feel that I have done my duty in protecting their lives from their enemies both from within and without which thing has brought down the indignation of the mob and also false brethren upon me & my life is threatened by both and diligently sought for as I walk in the streets but whether I live or die I am determined to sustain the Twelve and the Authorities of this kingdom although I feel that some very un- expected catastrophe is going to happen because of false brethren

I went up in the Temple again at one, and remained there untill about 3 then sent my wife home and met the guard and regulated it & Police for the night and came home and staid all night.

Sunday Feb 1 1846. Met the guard at 8 as usual and regulated it for the day and then went to the printing office with A. J. Stout & W. J. Earl and got for them two sets of the Times & Seasons[67] and then came to the Temple and home and remained there untill time to go to the guard and then took my little Son Hosea to Ben Jones' and left him and met the guard and regulated it for the night and came home at dark. & staid all night —

Monday February 2nd 1846. Went with my wife to the Temple to be Sealed but there was no sealing going on to day.   Hunter & I saw & had a talk with B. Young about the Police. He said he was satisfied with me in some things that Some said he thought I was wrong in.   He gave us good instruction in relation to governing men & Said he wanted me to stand in the place I now hold after we get to the West   After he was done instructing us he blessed us in the name of the Lord.

I came home with my wife at noon and while eating dinner John Scott came for me and said that we must be ready to leave for the west by next thursday. So we went to the Temple and saw B. Young and then Scott went over the river to procure boats & lead for the journey & Hunter and I went to the river also to procure boats and then met the guard and regulated it for the night & then met with the Capt of the emegrating companies & was there informed that we must put every thing in our companies in readiness to be used on demand   I then met some of our captains and made the necessary arraingements as above, & then went up to the Temple & saw Br Kimball who told us that we might bring our wives to the Temple to night and have them Sealed which we did & came home at 9½ o'clock

Tuesday Feb 3 1846. Met the guard as usual and regulated it for the day, and apointed B. Jones & R. Stevens[68] to see & regulate all the Boats preparitory to our

---

67. The *Times and Seasons* was first published in November 1839, at Nauvoo, Illinois. At that time it was the only paper in Hancock County. It was edited by Don Carlos Smith, youngest brother of the Prophet Joseph, and Ebenezer Robinson. Smith died on August 7, 1841, and Robert T. Thompson took his place for a short time. In November 1842, John Taylor became editor and Wilford Woodruff, business manager. Except for a short period during which Joseph Smith acted as editor, the paper continued under this management until it was discontinued at the time of the Mormon exodus, the last issue appearing on February 15, 1846.

68. Roswell Stevens was born October 17, 1807, in upper Canada. In 1834 he was con- verted to Mormonism and baptized by John P. Greene. Later he moved to Missouri, where he settled in Daviess County, and so missed some of the conflicts in Far West and in Caldwell County. Stevens was one of the "better-to-do" who helped to manage the evacuation of Mis- souri and pledged his means to that end.

crossing the river then had a talk with G. W. Langley relative to the difficulty in which we settled with good feelings to each other, & was engaged there and at the Hall untill noon & then came home and then went to the Temple & was there untill three & a half and met the guard and Police & regulated it for the night The police expressed their satisfaction at the settlement which I had made with Langley I then went up in the Temple and found all right and then came home & packed up my books & staid all night. While up in the Temple I had a talk with Br J. P. Harmon relative to his dissension from the police. Matters was settled to the satisfaction of us both.

Wednesday Feb. 4th 1846. Met the guard as usual and regulated it for the day and made regulations with E. Green about some tents and after making some regulations about the guard &c I came home Hunter was with me. We then went to Asa Barton's and got his waggon & team for the west & then came home and took dinner and then went to the Temple and made some regulations on our way about some waggons for our exit West. We met the guard at 3½ and regulated it for the night and came home at dark and assisted my folks in packing up our goods untill bed time.

Thursday Feb. 5th 1846. Met the guard as usual & regulated it for the day & then went to the Hall and other places on the flat regulating matters for the move West, and then came on the Hill and home. all was right The people was busy at my house preparing to start Hunter & I then went to the river at Kimball's landing to see how Capt Jones came on preparing the boats for crossing the river all was well and the boats was in a forward state for use.

We then went to Hunter's and took dinner and met the guard at 3½ and regulated it for the night and then made arraingements with Capt Jones to take about twenty of the guard and cross over the river to Montrose and bring two boats which were there from Nashville on this side to be ready for further orders. I then came Home and packed goods till bed time.

Friday Feb 6th 1846. Met the guard as usual and regulated it for the day and then went with J. D. Hunter up in the Temple to see Prest B. Young to learn what to do next. He gave us orders to notify all the Capt of the Emegration Companies to cause their extra teams to meet at the Masonic Hall in the morning where he could dictate the lading thereof and also ordered me to collect all the extra men in the different companies & organize them into a body of troops ready to March (on foot) whenever they were needed. I was engaged in executing the above orders untill one o'clock and then went with John Scott to see Br B. Willis about his daughter who Scott was engaged to and Willis was opposed to the match we then went to my house & took dinner and then went to the Temple and was there at three and met the guard as usual and also had quite a large number of men besides assembled who were ready to be organized as above After giving them the necessary instructions I came home and prepared to move untill bed time.

At Nauvoo, Stevens was given responsible positions. In 1846 he left his wife and five children to enlist in the Mormon Battalion, where he served as a private in Company "E." At Santa Fe he was detailed to go with the sick to Pueblo, Colorado, but instead returned to Winter Quarters with John D. Lee and Howard Egan. Here he was appointed to look after the welfare of the families of the absent Battalion men.

A member of the 1847 pioneer group, Stevens went with Amasa Lyman, Thomas Woolsey, and John H. Tippetts to meet the sick detachment and guide them from Pueblo to the Valley of the Great Salt Lake. In Utah, Stevens helped to pioneer a number of settlements, ending at Bluff, San Juan County, where he died May 4, 1880.

Saturday Feb 7th 1846. Met the guard as before and regulated it for the day also at the same time the troops met preparatory to their marching and after giving them some more instructions I went to the Hall where Br Young was to meet the Teams There was a very poor turn out of teams From there I then came home and prepared some more to leave and at three met the guard & troops as usual there was near two hundred men present from there came home and after dark a short time John Scott came to see me about preparing the cannon We then went to see Brigham on the subject. He gave us orders to raise and prepare baggage waggons for the cannon & troops and as all things necessary for a start I came home at ten o'c

Sunday Feb 8th 1846. Met the guard and troops as usual and returned home at ten and Staid there till three and met the guard again as usual.

There was a meeting at the Stand West of the Temple to day at which the Twelve delivered their last discourse before leaving for the West. I returned home from guard & went to packing my goods again for a move & sent two waggons loaded with my goods & other things for our journey, to the river under the management of Robert C. Moore who agreed to go with and see to have them taken care of untill I came over and I went to Allen Weeks & took him along with me & went to the ferry and saw my waggons safe on board of the ferry boat and then went by Allen Weeks' and from thence to Elizabeth Taylor's my wife's mother where my wife had gone to stay all night as all our things were sent over the river

On our way to the river Br. Weeks told me that he had been sealed to Br John D. Lee and also had at the same time had Malissa Bennett sealed to him also [blank] Bennett to him — I staid with my wife till morning

Monday Feb 9th 1846. Met the guard as usual at 8 and was then busy in arrainging matters of business untill noon when my wife & family Started to the river and Stopped at J. D. Hunters' and staid awhile & I went to Mother Taylor's and took dinner and then took leave of them all not expecting to see them any more untill we all meet in the West and then went to Hunters and sent him to meet the guard in my place and I went with my family to the river to cross over into Iowa. We waited awhile for a boat at length we went on board of an old small boat and started over. The wind being quite high & the river very ruff. While on the watter I beheld the most heart rending and dangerous scenes that I was ever called to wittness When about half across the river there was a man and two Boy in a Skiff coming from one of the the islands with a load of wood the Skiff was loaded down allmost to the top and upon coming out in the open water began to fill by the waves running over the top The man did not understand how to manage a watter craft & kept it with the side to the waves. He began to throw out the wood to the windward which hung on the edge of the Skiff and only made it fill faster The Boys were fritened at every wave and would Scream at the Startling approach of death. At this time our boat was but a short distance below and opposite to them.

I endeavored to have him turn his Skiff towards our boat and come to us which would have made him perfectly Safe; but he heeded not any thing that was Said. In a few minutes after passing us & but a Short distance his Skiff Swamped and drifted on the water without sinking however

All on our Boat Stood petrified as it were at the passing scene while the Screemes of the boys for help thrilled through every heart. We expected them every moment to go to the bottom A short distance behind us was another larger ferry boat coming over with two waggons, two yokes of oxen and about twenty people on board. This boat Saw the Situation of those in the Skiff and turned down Stream a little & took them in & Saved them from a watery grave About the time that we thought them all safe on board the boat and felt relieved from our anxiety and was going on our way we were called to behold a tenfold more melancholy event transpire. We were alarmed by the Schrieks & cries of the men women & children on the boat All seemed to screem and cry & becken to us to come to them in the hiest state of alarm in a moment we Saw that their boat was sinking in the middle of the river and were imploring us in the fear of instant death to come to their rescue. They made every sign token cry scream gesture and manifestation of distress that I had ever saw in my life and would rise on the waggons & edge of the boat and continue these distressing tokins of their situation untill they were disheartened and their voice would pine away in the utter hopelessness of being Saved they gave themselves up to a watery grave and all was hushed and the boat went down. In a few minutes we saw them scattered on the surface of the watter lik so many wild fowls in Silent & frightful anticipations of soon leaving this world of fears & disappointments Some were on feather beads sticks of wood, lumber or any thing they coud get holt of and were tossed & Sported on the water at the mercy of the cold and unrelenting waves which Seemed to vie with each other which should treat their frightened visitors with the most rude and deathly reception. Some climbed on the top of the waggon which did not go quite under and were more comfortable while the cows & oxen on board were seen Swiming to the shore from whence they came

It was some time before any relief came to them A Boat which was crossing over empty came to them and with Some Skiffs & Sail boats Succeeded in Saving them and not one of them were lost though Some were So near gone that they coul not speak

When the boat first began to Sink we attempted to turn our boat and go to their relief but on attempting to turn our boat come very near Sinking and we were obliged to desist and abandon the idea of rendering them any assistance We were coming into a part of the river where the waves ran higher and instead of saving them we found that we were also near going to the bottom also whereupon we made for the shore on an adjacent island which we made just in time to Save ourselves Had the shore have been much farther there is no doubt but we must have Sank in the deep Swift currant which swept to the very Shore I succeeded in landing my family on the island to my great joy though in a very bleak and cold island amid mud and a thick under wood. My wife and oldest son both just able to walk. We stook there & and contemplated the sad spectacle of our brethren & sisters strugling in death & our own narrow escape from the same fate Fatigued and worn out with my family sick we proceeded down the shores of the island to the camp which at length we reached in a desolate situation the brethren rendered us all the comfort in their power while those from the sunken boat also landed allmost chilled to death excited the liveliest simpathy in every breast

While beholding this melancholy Scene I remembered the revelation which Said the Lord had cursed the watters in the Last Days and Said in my heart it was verily true This was not all the disasters which were in our midst for in the time of our difficulty in the watter the Temple took fire in the roof from the centre stove pipe and came very near burning down and the news was spread over the city that a boat had sunk with me and my family on it and that we were drownd and the Temple on Fire at the same time which created an unusual excitement The people ran to the river & Temple in confusion. By great & uncommon exertions the fire was extinguished not however before the roof was burndd about 12 feet square And after the people had learned that no one was drowned the excitement ceased and the city was again quiet.

It seemed that the destroyer brooded over the land and water at this time & was in a fair way to be triumphant

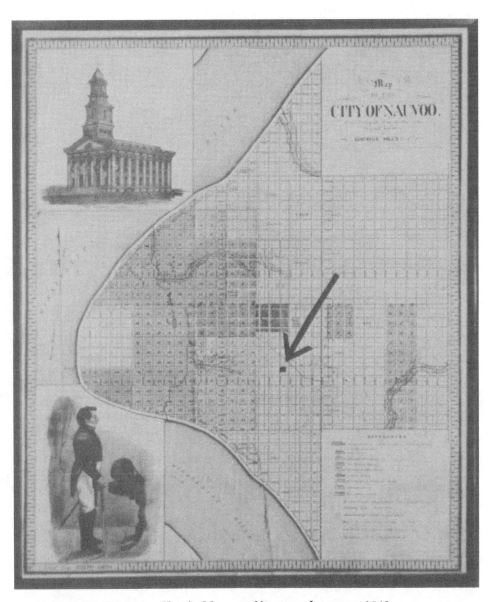

GUSTAVAS HILL'S MAP OF NAUVOO, ILLINOIS, 1843
The arrow indicates the location of Hosea Stout's home. The deed records of Nauvoo show that Hosea's lot was two-thirds of an acre and had an assessed valuation of sixty-five dollars.

NAUVOO, ILLINOIS, ABOUT 1846
One of the few known daguerreotypes of the city
as it appeared before the destruction of the temple

I understood after wards that the way the Boat came to sink was by a rude boy spitting ambear[69] in an ox's eye which cause him to jump over board and his mate in his flouncing kicked off one of the bottom planks of the boat one yoke of oxen which were fastened to one of the waggon's were drowned.

When I came to the camp I stopped at the tent of John S. Higbee where he was encamped with a company of ten pioneers & there prepared for the night by erecting a temporary tent out of bed clothes at this time my wife was hardly able to set up and my little son was sick with a very high fever and would not even notice any thin that was going on.

About dark Captains Charles Allen and Elam Luddington's with their companies came over and camped. Nothing more of importance transpired to night The fever went down on my boy and he was better

---

69. Brigham Young, writing under this same date said, "A filthy, wicked man squirted some tobacco juice into the eyes of one of the oxen attached to Thomas Grover's wagon, which immediately plunged into the river, dragging another ox with him, and as he was going over-board he tore off one of the side boards, which caused the water to flow into the flatboat, and as they approached the shore the boat sank to the bottom, before all the men could leap off. Several of the brethren were picked up in an exhausted condition. Two oxen were drowned and a few things floated away and were lost. The wagon was drawn out of the river with its contents damaged." Roberts, *Documentary History*, VII, 582.

In the South the word "ambear" refers to whiskey.

PART III

February 10 to September 22, 1846

FEBRUARY 10, 1846 TO SEPTEMBER 22, 1846

Part III

This third part of the diary includes the journey from the Mississippi River crossing at Nauvoo to the settlement at Winter Quarters, the inclusive dates being February 10 to September 22, 1846.

A number of other diaries parallel this. Among them are those of John D. Lee, William Clayton, and Willard Richards. Norton Jacobs made some significant entries after he caught up with the emigration, as did John Laub, John Pulsipher, Wandell Mace, and William Hall. In The Women of Mormondom, *edited by Edward W. Tullidge (New York, 1877); also (Salt Lake City, 1957), Eliza R. Snow has written some vivid details of this community on wheels.*

Tuesday Feb. 10 1846. This morning I arose before day and went to the city again and met the guard at 8 o'clock All was right. I made more arraingements for sending other companies across the river and appointed D. M. Repsher Sergeant of the guard as I could not be there to attend to it myself. About noon I returned to my family and continued with them untill morning without any thing of importance transpiring.

Wednesday Feb. 11th 1846. This morning I was very unwell with a sick headache. Remained in camp all day attending to the affairs of the troops Nothing of importance ocured

Thursday Feb. 12th 1846. Went to the city Earley and met the guard at eight o'clock and then went round to see to matters pertaining to the companies untill noon all was well in the City returned over to camp At two was informed that some of the Carthage troops were in the city with writs for some of the brethren and me among the rest whereupon I called out all the troops belonging to our camp and agreed that if any of them came across the river after any of us as we were informed they intended that we would put them to death rather than be Harrassed as we had been after we had started to leave their cursed & corrupt government and also established a line of skiffs across the river to recieve the intelligence necessary the more readily. I remained in camp making the above regulations untill evening. In the mein time Br Jones & Lee's families came to my tent which we had just raised to the great relief of my family who had been to this time in the open prairie exposed to the wind & weather. I then regulated the guard for the night and staid in camp till morning.

Friday Feb 13th 1846. Slept well in my tent All was well this morning Called out the troops and gave them instructions about the order to be observed in the camp and also gave it as an order for them to assemble at the sound of the bugle. About ten o'clock I went in company with Br John D. Lee to the camp on Sugar Creek This was near to the place where I lived at the time my wife (Surmantha) died and was the place of many a mournful hour to me in days gone by when by her death I was deprived of all and the last bosom friend which I then had on earth in whom I could implicitly confide. On our way to the camp I passed by her grave which was near to the road I found the paling still round it which I put there seven years ago as a last token of respect due to her untill the first resurrection not dreaming of the plan of redemption which was so soon to be revealed through the now martyred prophet Joseph. How little did I then think that in so short a space of time as a work of redemption for her whom I then thought Saved in the celestial kingdom I should be married twice more to her who was now dead through the administration and kind office of the one who took her place in the flesh. When I left this place I went disconsolate and alone mourning her untimely death and my own lonesome condition But I went to Nauvoo to keep the commandments of God and my history from that time to this will show the scenes of peril and want which I went through to roll forth the kingdom. But now the time for me to leave this gentile world of oppression & tyrranny had come and I was now on my way to the remnant of the Lord in the wilderness to pass yet again through new scenes of want and peril Then I was alone and but little know to my brethren & to his prophet. But by a succession of dangerous & continual scene & of a life devoted to the Exution department of this kingdom from that time to this has brought me to where I am at the Head of the Army of Israel which was raised by my own individual influence and was now marching forth from the gentiles under my command subject to the Head of the Church

These things came flitting across my mind when I approached her grave and the land so full of gone by reflections and I exclaimed in my mind "O Lord keep me in the way I should go that my exaltation may be shore Instead of being deprived of my last bosom friend I now had three equally dear and confiding to me;

From her grave I proceeded to the camp and found the Saints comfortably situated on the bottom land on Sugar Creek on either side of the St Francisville road They were in good spirits but anxious to be on their way to the wilderness. I came in camp at one o'clock After tarrying awhile in camp I returned to my camp again where I arrived at three and a half o'clock and found all well. This evening Elder Parley P. Pratt crossed the river with his family and effects and camped within our grounds that night and proceded to Sugar Creek Camp in the morning About dark I called the troops together by sound of the bugle and regulated the guard for the after which nothing more of importance took place that night.

Saturday Feb. 14th 1846. This morning there was a pretty deep snow on the ground and still falling very fast accompanied by a high North wind So comfortable was my tent that not one of us who were in it knew any thing of the snow storm untill we looked out the next morning. But there were many families that night in our camp & waggons without covers who were recieving the driving snow amid their women & children & also their goods which rendered their condition truly uncomfortable

I remained in camp all day and in the evening called out the guard as before & regulated it for the night. The driving snow continued to fall all day and abated late in the evening & was melted fast rendering the the traveling very bad.

Sunday Feb 15th 1846. After regulating the guard I went to Nauvoo as I had been informed that there could not be any waggons procured to carry the public muskets in & I thought that I could make a raise of one. When I landed on the other side of the river I met President Brigham Young just ready to go aboard of this boat to cross over from Nauvoo to the camp He told me to send the rest of the guard over also as soon as possible Accordingly I proceeded to the Temple and sent out orders to the different captains to proceed forthwith accross the river and from thence to Br Noah T Guyman's[1] to raise a team there belonging to Robert Johnson After much ado and persuasion he agreed to go & I staid untill he was ready to start and came with him to the Temple and took in about one hundred muskets and while loading them Genl Rich came with a man and a team also for the muskets so I took my load and left him to bring on the rest and then started to the river While going down the hill west of the Temple my horse being very unruly broke his bridle bits and I leaped off as soon as possible but not before he was near full speed which threw me heels over head down the hill in the watter & sand but not materially hurt otherwise. I proceeded to the river & crossed over and there found Br. Young just ready to start to the other camp who told me to come on with four or five companies I then set all hands to preparing to move leaving Hunter in charge at the camp till morning. We started about four o'clock and over took Brigham at the hill 2½ miles from the river about dark His teams could not get up the hill without doubling them He was there at work in the mud assisting the teamsters we also assisted them up and they went on and we were a long time getting up as all our teams had to be doubled also. It was now some time in the night and very cold and the women & children cold and disagreeable. After getting on the hill we proceeded to camp and found Brigham[2] just driving to his fire on the East side of Sugar Creek which we called Kedron we also encamped west of him also on the East of the brook.

It was about Eleven o'clock when we was through and ready for rest After posting out the guard we retired to rest untill morning.

Monday Feb. 16th 1846. This morning I called out the troops and made arrangements for the day guard and appointed Capt Charles Allen to act as Sergeant of the guard and also instructed the troop not to defile the camp as was too much the case but remember the law of Moses in such cases wherein the Lord would turn away from them and abandon them to their enemies if they did not [observe] the proper prescribed rules of cleanliness accordingly men were set apart to make the necessary preperations to observe the same.[3] Our camp was formed on the curved bank of the Creek forming a large circle the centre of which was reserved for a parade ground & other public camp purposes. Our horses oxen and cows in the rear of our waggons immediately on the bank.

About two o'clock I had a white flag raised in front of my tent, as a token of peace but it refused to waive in the air notwithstanding there was a light breeze which seemed to say that it would not proclaim peace in the United States when there was nought but oppression and tyrranny towards the people of God by the

---

1. Noah Thomas Guyman was born June 30, 1819, in North Carolina. He had joined the Mormon Church early and came from Kirtland to Far West, Missouri. He was one of those who pledged to help the poor leave that state. In Nauvoo he did not belong to the Legion but was a member of the Quorum of the Seventy.

Guyman came to Utah in 1850 with his parents, two wives, and three children, and settled at Springville. In 1855 he brought in the second company of immigrants for that season, consisting of fifty-eight wagons. He died at Orangeville, Emery County, Utah, on January 7, 1911.

2. Under the same date John D. Lee wrote: "After much anxiety and desire Prest. B. Young crossed & drove into camp at about 8 O'Clock at night. on the 15th inst.

"The day following was spent in arranging and regulating the Tents & camp Pres B Young having about 15 waggons and 50 persons in No. of his own family." Lee, "Camp of the Saints," 1.

3. The laws of cleanliness to the Israelites under Moses commanded that each person should be responsible for burying his own excreta far from camp. The Mormons early adopted the rule while traveling of "Gents to the Right and Ladies to the Left." At any camp of more than a few days, temporary facilities were set up with trenches always in the same direction from the camp. Deut. 23:12-15.

rulers of this government and the Saints fleeing from her borders to the wilderness for safety and refuge from her iron yoke.

About four or five o'clock Br Chase came into camp with two loads of powder and other articles for the use of the troops and by order of President Brigham Young it was delivered into the hands of myself & Col Markham Captain of the pioneers & he desired me to take it in charge accordingly I placed it in the centre of the public ground in the circle of our encampment and placed a strong guard over it. About sundown I called out the troops and regulated the night guard and then detailed a regular guard over the ammunition whose [duty] it was to guard it day & night after which I called out all the mounted men together and organized them into a company of horse and appointed J. D. Huntr Captain.

After the above regulations were made I called Chandler Rogers, D. McArthur, Charles Allen & J. D. Hunter together in my tent and after giving them the necessary instructions and informed them of what I wanted and consulted them about the same & proceeded to appoint four Captains of fifties as our troops now numbered 20 companies of ten. I appointed Chandler Rogers Capt of the first fifty Benjamin Jones of the Second, Charles Allen of the third and Duncan McArthur of the fourth fifty After which I retired to rest it being now very late at night. In the night a tree which hung over Capt [Elam] Luddington's Company commenced giving away and just give them notice to get out of the way with their waggons before it fell In getting his waggons away Capt. Luddington got his hand mashed very badly

Some time in the night Elder John Taylor arrived in camp with his family and effects in comming down Sugar Creek hill and near the camp one of his waggons upset and very badly hurt a young man & woman.

Tuesday Feb 17th 1846. Guard met as usual & I reported to the different Captains of the appointments of Captains of fifties. Each fifty respectively accepted the same At ½ past nine A. M. B. Young called the whole Ca[m]p of Israel together on the Guard ground and addressed them in relation to their organization and being ready for a move &c and also gave them instruction in relation to order in camp and the course for us to pursue on our journey and then made complaint about the negligence of the Gard that was out last night. He then made regulations for the pioneers to see to having Corn & Hay brought into the camp and ordered me to build pens for the same & take charge of the commissary department which I did and set Capt Jones to build the pens & appointed George W. Harris one of the high council who had come into my family to be commissary genral of our little army. Capt Duncan McArthur was Sergent of the Gard to day to continue for twenty four hours.

To day the public arms which were in camp were delivered into my charge and also a baggage waggon to draw them in and I put them under the guard which kept the powder and appointed S. Gully to see to having them put in good order and seperate those which were in good order from those which were not and pack them in the waggon ready for moving which he proceeded to do

Awhile before night I in company with Capt J. D. Hunter &[c] looked [picked?] out location to post the Gards as we wished to post them in a manner to encircle the whole encampment, and had made arrangements with S. Markham to Gard the West side of Sugar Creek and I the East Side accordingly we went and found that it took fourteen men on Gard at once, which being releaved every two hours makes it necessary to use Eighty four Men to Gard each night while the Gard was assembled, B. Young came to the gard & requested us to cover the Guns, and then counceled me to put tried men to Gard the Powder. Nothing more of importance occured to night

Wednesday Feby 18th 1846. Regulated the Gard and appointed Captn C Rogers officer of the day. about 9 A.M. B. Young called a meeting of the whole camp together at the Bridge and addressed them again on the subject of organizing and being ready to move, and also to save our provisions such as flour and meat &c which could not be procured in the wilderness; After the meeting I procured six tents for the use of my company and gave them to the four captains of Fifties, and to J. D. Hunter, and kept one myself as the one I had was not big enough for me

About 3 A. M. Col. Scott arrived in camp with the Artilery[4] and about fifty men encamped on the South of my tent, the whole forming a semicircle of about forty rods diameter our whole number of troops now amounted to about two hundred and fifty men besides teamsters & others necessary to be along In the evening I arrainged the guard as usual

Thursday Feby 19th 1846. This morning there was a snow storm falling fast from the N. All was peace in the Camp. At about 8 or 9 A. M. I called the Captains of 50 & 10s together and reproved them for a spirit of insubordination which was becoming manifest but no hard feelings existed. After which I spread another Tent over the one I had befor which was larger and made it much more convenient, I then took out the other. Nothing more of importance took place to night, the snow was still falling fast.

Friday Feby 20th 1846. This morning the storm was over but very cold. I was in camp until three doing business as usual, when the Captains of 100 & 50 & 10 were called together at the bridge and notified to make out a report of every thing in camp, such as the amount of provisions, seed, grain, farming utencils and armes, also the Number of Souls, Horses & cattle so that the provision and Grain for the camp may be distributed equally; And Isreal numbered before we start to move which I proceeded to do immediately.

In the evening there was a disturbance took place by som refusing to comply with the rules of the commissary. It was by those disaffected Police who were trying to spread there dissensions in the Camp of Isreal which they had practised against me all winter but they were hissed down by the people and left to shame. They even impeached Br Harris in their murmurings with injustice and partiality. nothing more of consequence occured to night

Saturday Feby 21st 1846. The weather was clear & cold this morning. The commissary department had order this morning for Br Harris requested all the Captains to make a written report to him of the number beasts to be fed, before he would [let] them have any corn which brought things more in order. It did not take as much corn to supply the wants of the camp this morning as usual, for some would lay up corn and needlessly waist it, whereas they would not now be allowed to take only enough to do them.

The spirit of confusion, so plainly manifested last evening was thus stoped, and equal justice took place and all seemed satisfied. I called the Captains of 50 together and gave them instructions about the working of the Gard in order as some dissatisfaction was manifested in consequence of irregularity in calling out the Gard. After which nothing more of importance took place until the afternoon when another meeting was called at the Bridge for the purpose of asserta[in]ing among other things who had come and brought there famalies without being counciled so to do, and the Captains of Emigrating companies were requested to make report of the same to the Genl council. Nothing more of importance took place to night

Sunday Feby 22nd 1846. This morning all was right, about 8 o'clock there was another meeting called at the Bridge for the purpose of makeing regulation about procurring Grain &c for the camp & other camp regulations. In the evening Col.

---

4. The artillery consisted of two six-pounders, one three-pounder, and one short twelve-pound cannon. Roberts, *Documentary History*, VII, 592.

Turley came to my qua[r]ters to assertain the number of Waggon makers and
Black Smiths in camp, as it was the intention to set them to work while we lay
here, This evening Brigham came home in good health and spirrits as usual.

Monday Morning Feb 23rd 1846. This morning about 9½ oclock another
meeting was called at the Bridge for the same purpose as the ones preceding. Immediately after a council was called of the Twelve and Captains of 100 by which it
was determined to start 50 teams on to the next camp and for some of the pioneers
and such others as might be appointed to go before them and purchase provisions
and grain for the camp and also to prepare the roads.

While the council was in session intelligence was brought in that a man by the
name of Abner Blackburn[5] had been shot by accident.

I afterwards learned that a man by the name Benjn Stewart had shot him
He took up a pistol which lay near by and pointing it at the unfortunate man
who was shot the man told him that the pistol was loaded and not to shoot him but
Stewart Seemed to not know what he said not even as much as to understand what
was said but fired direct at Blackburn and the ball passed into his thigh and severely
wounded him but I think not dangerously. The man who was shot belonged to
my brother Allen J. Stout's company and it took place in front of his tent and
across the fire When my brother discovered what was done he kicked Stewart
out of camp for it was a palpable violation of orders for any man to even handle
another's arms much less to fire one. After the council was over I called out all
the guard and gave them a severe reprimand for their disobedience of orders & want
of discipline and their practice of firing guns in camp which had been so often
forbid

I then sharply reprimanded the Sergeant of the guard for not being more
strict and resolute in relation to the orders of the guard. because they would
allow them to leave their posts or kindle and keep fires up while on duty which was
also forbid often

After I had done I called on Elder H. G. Sherwood & G. W. Harris of the
High council who sustained me in all I had done & said after which I enjoined
it on all the guard who saw any such orders broken in future to kick the offender
out of the camp which they agreed to do & after making arrangements to set several
men to work to preparing some baggage and gun waggons I dismissed the men

In a short time after the men were dismissed Br Roswell Stevens, who had been
set apart with several other men to get timber for waggon bows, went into the
woods for the same when a man fired a gun and missing the tree he shot at the
ball came close by their heads, whereup Br Stevens, without saying a word to the
man ran to him and gave him a severe flogging.

The man I afterwards learned belonged to Capt Shadrach Roundy's[6] company
Nothing more to night.

---

5. Abner Blackburn, who later joined the Mormon Battalion, was sent with the sick detachment to Pueblo and from thence followed the Mormon pioneer group into Salt Lake Valley
in 1847. On August 9 of that year, he was sent as one of a group of men to accompany Captain
James Brown to California to collect the pay of the Mormon Battalion.

Always on the frontier Blackburn helped to establish the "Mormon Station" in Carson Valley
— selling out after a season or two to John and Enoch Reese, who renamed the place "Reese's
Station." After 1850 Blackburn seems to have remained in California. He died at San Bernardino.

6. Shadrach Roundy was born January 1, 1789. He had joined the church very early, and
his home was a shelter for Joseph Smith in 1833. He became a member of the prophet's bodyguard, accompanying him on many trips, and was always near to protect him. He was active
in the troubles at Far West, being one to sign the covenant to help the poor move away. He
was also an early member of the Council of Fifty.

Roundy came to Utah with the 1847 pioneer group and was made one of the first members
of the High Council in the valley. He was bishop of the Salt Lake Sixteenth Ward from 1849-56.
He died July 4, 1872.

Tuesday Feb. 24th 1846. This morning there was another snow which fell last night. Nothing of importance took place to day more than preparing waggons for the anticipated start.

The 50 teams which were to move to day did not go because of the snow storm.

Wednesday Feb. 25th 1846. At 9 o'clock this morning another meeting was called at the Bridge but was removed in one of the deep ravines to find shelter from the cold wind. For it was now very cold even more so than was common this winter.

At this meeting Br Young spoke in behalf of the guard and sustained them in the discharge of their duty against those, who had disregarded them here and had sworn that they would go where they pleased despite of the guard and those who had acted so with the guard were present he gave them a severe repramand and declared that himself nor any other man had any right or exclusive priviledge to pass or repass the guard and that he would do his duty was he on guard and come what would and that he would know no man who had not the counter sign[7]

He also gave other instructions to us as a guard pointing out our duty. He also said that he was going to morrow Bishop Miller left after meeting with his company. I was engaged most part of the day in preparing to be off with Br B. Young In the evening I called out the guard and forbid any one from leaving the camp without my knowledge and also warned the Capt of tens not to let any of their teams be taken out of camp as some intended to get off with their teams clandestinely and return to Nauvoo & leave us without our baggage teams which thing I was determined not to allow. Nothing more to night.

Thursday Feb. 26 1846. This morning we were all preparing to move about ten miles up Sugar Creek but did not go because of the cold wether

In the afternoon I went in company with my wife Louisa to make a visit to see the grave of Surmantha, which was the first time that ever she saw the grave of her whom she had commenced to redeem. We returned before night.

Friday Feb. 27 1846. Nothing of importance took place to day I sent to Nauvoo & brought my cook stove table & some other articles to my tent & put up the stove which I found to be very convenient and comfortable to my family for they had suffered much from cold in the tent whereas the stove kept it as warm as need be even in the coldest wether I was in camp all day all went off well to day

Saturday Feb. 28th 1846. To day Captains Bent, Spencer, Snow and Shumway's Companies went to the next camping ground on Sugar Creek where a job of work was taken which was all that took place today of any importance. —

Sunday March 1st 1846. At ten a council was called again at which instructions were given for the camp to be ready to start immediately to the next camp up sugar

---

7. This entry shows the growing differences between George Miller and Brigham Young. Under this same date, Brigham Young wrote in his journal: ". . . this great 'I' and little 'you' I cannot bear, if the guard consider the Twelve as privileged characters they must consider the high council also, and if the high council, the high priests, etc., and we should all be privileged characters; and what is the use of any guard? None at all. When I want to pass the guard I will go to the sergeant and get the password, and I want all the brethren to do the same. Let no man crowd upon the guard and let the guard know no man as a privileged character."

The day before Brigham Young had written: "Evening, I met with Elders Heber C. Kimball and Willard Richards at his tent, to investigate some disaffection which existed between Bishop Miller and the guards which proved to be a misunderstanding." "Journal History," February 24, 1846.

Miller's account differs somewhat from the above. See Mills, "De Tal Palo Tal Astilla," *Annual Publications . . . Southern California*, X, 106.

Creek about 4 miles on a strait line. After the council I went and made preperations to start and also gave orders to the guards to do likewise

About one all being ready and waiting for the Twelve (who were detained
because some of their men & horses were in Nauvoo visiting) I gave orders for
all the ox teams to move on and for the horse team to wait the motion of the Twelve
I should have said also that the men taried. We waited accordingly untill four
o'clock and the families becoming very impatient in waiting I permited all the
teams who had them in to also go on & encamp while we yet taried

President B. Young was now ready to move and only waiting the return of his
men & horses from the City It was a beautiful fine clear warm day and great
numbers of the brethren & Sisters came to the camp visiting, About an hour by
Sun, the men & horses returning from Nauvoo President Young was ready to start
& we all set out on our journey leaving Elder John Taylor behind who was not
yet ready to start. We had a good road on the dividing ridge between Sugar Creek
and the Des Moines. I left in camp four companies behind amounting in all to
men Sufficient to guard themselves against any emergency which might occur to
wit Capt Gulley & Dillie because they had not teams sufficient to move with and
Capt L. H. Calkins because one of his horses was in Nauvoo and Capt O. M. Allen
to Strengthen them in case any thing should happen & they be molested. The road
as we went was about six miles. We arrived at the camp about the last dawn of day
without any thing material transpiring. I found my tent piched on a ridge in the edge
of the prairie in a very inhospitable place and the guard also placed as near me
as was convenient but my family was as comfortable as could be expected. The
main camp was down in the low ground in the timber to get to which from where
we were there was a very steep and dangerous hill to go down in the dark. After
super I went to a council at the tent of President B. Young wherein it was determined to move on tomorrow to the next camp four miles above Farmington at which
place Bishop Miller had taken a job of work and was there doing it. At this place
there was also some men at work making rails. After returning from council I
made arraingements to send back after those companies which I had left back
at Sugar Creek camp to day. accordingly I detailed Capt Duncan McArthur with
his fifty to stay and bring them up to this place & I would leave some one else to
assist in like manner at the next camp if circumstances permited after which I
retired to rest at about half past eleven o'clock at night.

Monday March 2nd 1846. This morning the camp moved on leaving Br Bent
and those who had previously come here to finish the work which they had commenced. President B. Young and those who had gone down the hill crossed over
this part of Sugar Creek taking a very rough road but I took the guard and kept
the same dividing ridges which we had followed last evening and thus Saved myself
the trouble of crossing this stream at such a bad place but sent a guard of about
ten men under J. D. Hunter to accompany President Young on the road and render
him the necessary assistance which he might need

The guard and also many other teams which took the road that I did kept
entirely to the left that is took the extreme left hand roads and thus escaped or in
other words went round many very bad places which the others had to pass through
and by this means they got ahead of nearly all the camp We had a very bad
road all day & often at hills & difficult places to cross branches I saw teams standing
waiting for those forward to pass over which were a mile long & often at hills
teams would stall and have to be rolled up by hand thus making it both laborious
for the men who were on foot, and also slow for the teams to be thus detained for
each other. It was a beautiful country but no way dissimilar from the western
prairie country.

About two o'clock I had advanced on horse back before the forward team then
traveling & not knowing it to be so & finding the roads by their appearance had

not been traveled to day I began to conclud that we had taken a wrong road so I pushed on untill I came to a house and upon inquiry found it right. I felt very much concerned about it for it would be a serious matter to have some two hundred teams lead astray for they were scattered over not less than five miles along the road.

A small mistake of this kind would take a whole day to rectify it with all the teams. After leaving the house where I enquired the road I passed along a high ridge in the timber & then came down a steep hill to a considerable stream and proceeded a short distance and came to a house and there found Col S. Markham, Capt. Darby & Capt C. Allen who I did not know was in my advance untill now. They were now looking for corn & fodder for the camp to night but could get but little at any reasonable price. Col Markham whose duty it was to select ground to camp on sent me back about a quarter of a mile to stop the teams at the creek untill he ascertained whether he could procure food for the cattle & horses for the night or not & if he could we were to stop in a field immediately where they would thus be stoped. I went back & had not been there long before the advance teams drove up & I stoped them & word coming from Markham for us to turn in to the field & there encamp for the night we did so, but not however before I and Col A. P Rockwood who acted for President Young in forming his camp had selected & settled the order of the camp. It was a beautiful piece of ground in timbered land and had the timber cut down and piled up in log heaps & dry the use of which the owner gave us gratis. It was very convenient for our fires

The camp was formed so that the guard encompassed the most essential parts of it for they formed in a long line & had thus to only guard their own rear and thus guarded also the camp. We had to night but a scant allowance of food for our teams. The weather was warm & pleasant

Tuesday March the 3rd 1846. The weather continued to be warm and pleasant. & horse food scarce — At nine o'clock the President called a meeting and spoke on the proper order of traveling and reproved the camp as a general thing for the disorder in which they had traveled hitherto Immediately after meeting the camp commenced moving. After seeing matters start in proper order I went on leaving Hunter in command & had went but a little ways on the road ere I came to the river Des-Moines, it was a beautiful stream with a rock bed but appeared very narrow after being so long accustomed to the broad rolling Mississippi. the road was now good dry & level. immediately on the bank of the river I soon passed the advanc teams again and overtook the Artillery which had encamped the night before about three miles behind us and taking an early start came in ahead of our camp. Here Br Gillett of the Artillery accompanied me and we rode on to Farmington where we arrived at 12 where I stoped and traded for some articles which I need and then we went on. It is situated on the river the site is level and not very romantic but rather dull looking and I should think sickly. When we went into the store there were a group of men standing by who manifested every symptom which looks could to pick a fuss with us but I was armed with 2 Six shooters & a large Bowie knife all in sight which they eyed very close and when I came near any of them they would give me a wide birth

But when the waggons came along one of Br Rogers' boys drove his team by accident over a hog and killed it The owner who saw it was about to bleed it and so make use of it not appearing to think the least hard of it when some of these bye Standers interfeared & swore that he ought to have pay for it and thus commenced a parly Some of the brethren thought it no more than right also and some thought not and thus matters were when Hunter came up and saw what was going on he ordered the teams to move on and told the people that they might think themselves well off to get the hog dead for they generally took the hog also whereupon the teams drove off and that ended the matter. Some of the men made some remarks about Hunters arms & he gave them to understand that they could be used very easy if he was molested which entirely put to rest the hog Scrape[8]

We proceeded on to the camp where we arrived at two o'clock it being now three & a half miles The roads along here was uncommonly bad both rough & muddy Here I found Bishop Miller at work with his company. He had cleared and fenced a field wherein the camp was to stop & had also with the help of the pioneers a pen filled with corn which we very much needed. I selected a place for the guard & Gillett another for the Artillery to encamp in the field. but we soon found that the selections we had made would have to be occupied by President Young & others. So we selected another in an adjoining woods which was a beautiful level thick set with Sugar maple. We were told by the brethren who were at work that the owner of the land did not permit any to encamp without the field but we thought as all the best ground within was or be taken up that we would venture to "take the responsibility" and piched our tents accordingly when our teams came up which was about four o'clock After the teams had drove up and we all properly encamped the owner of the land came and seemed well satisfied and told us we were welcome to use any timber in the woods except the green & even that if we needed it. but to leave such as would make saw logs or be useful for timber for which I thinked him & promised that all should be as he desired but that I would see that no green timber was cut as there was plenty of dry.

About dark met the council where it was decided to stay here to morrow after which I called a council of my officers to make arrangements to send for Capt Gully & Dillie, as they were yet unable to move on and there decided to send back one yoke of oxen which we thought would enable them to over take us perhaps before we started and then wrote a letter to them instructing them how to proceed and how to dispose of the property which they had which was not needed on our campaign. Nothing more.

Wednesday March 4th 1846. Earley this morning I sent the yoke of oxen to Gully & Dillie as decided last night. The wether was very clear and warm. At nine a meeting was called and instructions given by President Young in relation to our further move. Capt Samuel Gulley came in camp in advance of his company and had exchanged his horse for oxen which I was very glad to hear as I supposed that it would enable them to proceed on with[out] being further delayed. He seemed well pleased with the arraingements I had made relative to his company but did not meet the oxen I had sent to his relief or if he did he knew not where they were going. To day a man by the name Giles Wells came in camp who was an old school mate of J. D. Huntr who introduced me to him as Col Wells. He was intelligent and despised Sectarians, was a Deist in principal, friendly and was willing for us to enjoy our opinions & let us alone. I also saw a Mr Lundy who I once knew in Tazewell County Illinois when I was a boy he seemed glad to see me. made himself known to me, but seemed to care nothing about whether we were right or not in our principals His capacity was but ordinary

Several of our company traded their horses for oxen today.

About noon I called out the guard & spoke to them at considerable length on the policy of working our way and thus relieve the Church from the expense of supporting us when we were not traveling and also on the prospects of our further move to which all agreed. Immediately after the meeting Charles Allen Capt of the third fifty called his men together with out my knowledge and delivered an inflammatory speech against what I had said and declared that he would not work neither would he recieve orders from me but go himself to the President and there

---

8. This "hog scrape" gives credence to some legends of Mormon aggressiveness and preparedness to fight.

recieve his orders and more things said he against the course I had pursued knowing at the same time that I was acting in due subordination to the proper authorities

Some drank into his spirit. He even took a vote of the company whether he should go to Brigham or not and they all voted that he should go. Some to sustain & others to see what he would effect & they came to me and informed me what was going on and desired to know what to do There was but a few in favor of him But more of him hereafter as he will most surely be guilty of yet more insubordinate acts if he does not speedily turn to his duty.

This evening I concluded that as the companies were now generally less that their full number to disband some and fill up the rest with their men

Capt Wilber J. Earl came to me and desired to resign as he said that he could not attend to the duties of the company and see to his wife. I excepted his resignation and ordered Capt Jones his Capt of Fifty to regulate it accordingly. Capt Earl was dissatisfied all the way with his company and often wished to give it up. About dark I called out all the Captains and there had a general council on the propriety of thus disbanding some of the companies to fill up the rest and also spoke to them on the propriety of the thing which I had taught to day to which they all acknowledged to be right and Capt. C. Allen also suported me They unanimously agreed to cast lots who should resign. The lots to resign fell on Chandler Rogers Capt of the 1st fifty for we intended to lessen our fifty also Capt. Allen J. Stout Thomas Woolsey, L. H. Calkins all on whom the lot fell seemed perfectly satisfied.

I then told them all to remain as they were untill they could be disposed of without confusion. While the business of casting lots were going on I recieved orders to appear forthwith at head quarters I went and was there ordered to have the guard ready to be divided into four divisions as it was decided to have the camp move in four Companies and a portion of the guard in each company and also was notified to to be ready to start in the morning with the part of the guard which was to accompany the first company which entirely destroyed or done away the necessity of reducing the guard to three companies of fifty so I came home and notified the captains that that had been done was null & void and also of the arraingements of the camp and for them to govern themselves accordingly. I then wrote in my journal till Eleven o'clock.

Thursday March the 5th 1846. This morning at 9 o'clock another meeting was called by the President and orders given for the first company to proceeded on their journey as previously arrainged and I made ready to act accordingly. They commenced to move off and I waited for them all to start befor I commenced marching the guard I was ready with the first and fourth fifties leaving the second and third as ordered last night At ten o'clock supposing that the camp was all off I gave orders for the guard to march they did so but they were before some of the camp and Artillery. We had not proceded more than one mile before one of Bishop Whitney's[9] Alxetrees broke and left his waggon in the road. It was at this mill

---

9. Newel K. Whitney was born on February 5, 1795, in Marlborough, Windham County, Vermont. In 1830 he was living in Kirtland, Ohio. Upon Joseph Smith's first visit there in February 1831, he greeted Whitney by name, instantly converting him, and stayed at his home for a few weeks.

Whitney was made bishop of all the church in Kirtland. Here he gave freely of his means to the erection of the Kirtland Temple, and was present at its dedication. He continued in this position in Nauvoo, where he was one of the first to hear and accept the doctrine of "Celestial Marriage," copying the original revelation and keeping the copy safe. On July 27, 1842, he performed the ceremony uniting his seventeen-year-old daughter, Sarah Ann, to Joseph Smith in marriage.

After the death of Joseph Smith, Whitney was made trustee-in-trust for the church, which position he held until the end of his life. He died on September 23, 1850, in Salt Lake City.

at the mouth of the Creek on which we were encamped We had the worst kind of a road narrow full of short deep hollows muddy and verry killing to the teams

At 12 o'clock we came to the little town of Bonaparte situated on the low lands on the bank of the Des-Moines it hat not many charmes for me in its general appearance I could not see as it differed much from Farmington.   There was a splendid Mill on the Des Moines in this town. The mill dam was built entirely across the river with lock to pass boats up or down

The River was beautiful and had a good ford with a rock bottom and was for a river of its size very convenient for travellors to ford at this time   after I crossed over I proceeded along the level muddy bottom road up the river which was full of waggons and teams standing still which was a sure indication of some difficulty ahead Not far up the river I came to a distillery owned by a Mr Bateman The road here took up a large ravine or branch and then in a short distance went up the river hill Here I discovered the reason why the teams on the bottom were waiting for the hill was litterally fill up with waggons some stalled others the teams could scarce draw It was deep white oak clay land & the waggons cut dow[n] the road might almost be called impassable I went on and when I came to the top of the hill I found it no better.

There was a thick under wood in the timber which prevented waggons from going out of the road It was thus for about two miles & the worst road by far that we had yet passed. At the edge of the prairie lives a man by the name of Neil he is an uncle to Genl C. C. Rich I stopped at his house for I had been introduced to him by Br Rich at the last camp and was there making the necessary inquiries about the road and entirely in advance of the whole company (being horse back) when President Young drove up in his buggy and requested me to enquire for corn I then did so Mr Neil asked 15 cents per bushel I then reported it to the President and went on to the next house & there enquired again but finding Mr. Neils corn cheapest the President bought some there and fed his teams on the prairie about one mile from Mr. Neil's. While feeding a load of corn came up which had been previously arrainged the day before and there left for the camp to feed their teams as they passed At 6 o'clock the President proceeded on to the next encampment which was yet seven miles As soon as my forward teams had eaten I started also to camp & and passed many teams on the road which were give out in passing the bad roads thus far. The road on a head was on a high prairie and was dry & good The teams traveled over without much difficulty. The Artillery and Elder Heber C. Kimball and many others encamped on the road their teams being unable to proceed further that night. I came to camp about dark and found Col Rockwood laying out the camping ground on a flat level prairie and so I proposed to him for me to locate on the other side of the Creek (Indian Creek) to which he consented. I done so which saved me the trouble of crossing it in the dark on a rough pole bridge

When the President came up he did not like Rockwood's location & he removed his tent to an adjacent woods hard by and piched his tent on a dry rolling piece of land on the bank of the creek. After my teams came up I went with Hunter to Brigham's tent to learn the orders of the night and then regulated the guard for the night and went to rest at twelve. Many of the guard did not come here to night.

Friday March 6th 1846. The weather was clear pleasant & warm to day. Sent some teams for corn & some men went out to work for some meat and corn. I staid all day in camp. My wife was very sick to day with a pain in her right side. To day some of Gully's men overtook us and reported that he had got his waggon up to the camp below Bonaparte and had there fell in company with his wife and left his company and declared that he would have nothing more to do with it and advised his men also to attach themselves to other companies or take any course which they thought proper He now complained that he was not used well. He

LOUISA TAYLOR

1819-1853

Second wife of Hosea, she was married to him in Nauvoo and became the mother of eight of his children. She died while Hosea was on his China mission

ALLEN J. STOUT

1815-1889

Younger than Hosea, he shared many of his brother's characteristics. There remained a strong attachment between the brothers throughout their lives

KANESVILLE (COUNCIL BLUFFS), IOWA

Sketched by Fredrick H. Piercy in 1853. The town was built by the Saints in 1846 as a stopping place across the Mississippi River from Winter Quarters. By the time this sketch was made, the site had been abandoned.

never even sent word to me by his men who he knew were coming to me to let me
know what he had done but took the things out of the waggon and left it by the
road side without any arraingements to either let me know it or to bring it himself
In fine he most disgracefully deserted his post and proved himself unworthy to
be trusted.

After I had learned the situation of affairs from his men we had come in
camp I sent Rowland Shannon & Joseph Taylor with three yoke of oxen to bring
up the waggon. They started about four o'clock P. M. with orders never to return
untill they brought it up They proceeded forthwith and returned before day the
next morning traveling all night. The found the waggon by the road side and
Gully in the camp He kept his yoke of oxen thus entirely abandoning the guard.
All day to day teams were coming into camp which had not been able to come
last night Capt B. Jones & C Allen also came up today

They did not wait for the companies which they were to accompany because
they did not organize as they were directed and so the guard did not want to have
any thing to do with them. To night Capt C. Allen gave us another specimen of
his Stubborn and insoubordinate Spirit for when his men were called on to stand
their regular turn on guard he preemptorially refused to let one go saying that
they was too tired. which if it was true it was equally true with the rest Nothing
more took place tonight.

Saturday March the 7th 1846. This morning orders came for the camp to move
and we all made arraingements accordingly. We expected to go only about seven
miles where we expected to make a lot of rails. I here had to leave part of the
guard some to finish some work and Capt Duncan McArthur of the fourth fifty
because I had to take three yoke of his oxen to put on the big waggon which I
had brought up last night. I only took Capt Jones & the second fifty

It was a fine clear pleasant day & good roads We started at eleven o'clock
and traveled fast and easy. About one o'clock I came to the place in advance of the
guard where the rails were to be made and found Col Rockwood locating the camp.
He set apart a beautiful ridge for me to encamp where I pitched my tent as for
many days but about the time that President Brigham Young came up he recieved
a letter from Col Scott of the Artillery who went on yesterday informing him of
better prospects where he was he concluded to go on at this time most of his
company & the Band were already located and knew nothing of his new arraingements. This threw every thing into confusion

Some of the guard without my knowledge went on and Brighams Company
as soon as they learned that he had gone on also struck their tents & went on.

When I had learned how matters had turned also went on with the guard.
We proceded along a bad road to the place where Scott was encamped. This was
at Richeson's Point and fifty-five miles from Nauvoo. We came here about dark
and encamped

The Band staid back at the place I had put up at today. Today my wife was
so much afflicted with a pain in her right side that she was unable to set up in
the waggon and we had to make a bed for her to lie in but notwithstanding all
of our care the traveling to day injured her very much Here I found Scott who
had taken a job of rails and I agreed to help him. All else passed off well to
day We found feed scarce but I sold a bed stead which I had along for eight bushels
of corn which made a feed for the guard tonight.

Sunday March the 8th 1846. The weather this morning was very dry, warm,
and pleasant. My wife was very sick yet. I went before breakfast to see Col Scott
& also to locate and prepare a meeting ground and also sent a team for hay. At
Eleven o'clock meeting commenced there being a number of gentiles present. Elder

J. M. Grant preached. I staid awhile at meeting and then went in company with J. D. Hunter rode out to G. Miller's camp three and a half miles ahead on the other side of Fox river. Here we had been informed that Bishop Miller had collected and stored one hundred and seventy five bushels of corn for the camp which the President concluded to draw to Richardsons Point rather that go to it [*sic*] as the ground was better to camp on than Fox river bottom and he expected to stay there several days. When we came to the camp we found Orson Pratt there who had gone ahead contrary to orders but Miller Shumway and some others had taken what corn was left and gone on leaving President Young and his company to shift for themselves. We also found President Young & Heber C. Kimball who had come to this place to see how it looked. They were not well pleased at what had been done but they said nothing. We all came back together and about half way home we met Capt Charles Allen in advance of his fifty We told him what was done and he turned his Company back He & C. [Chandler] Rogers Capt of the First 50 had just arrived and supposing the camp would move on had concluded to go to Millers camp to night. not knowing that we would stay where we were for several days but they returned. no more this evening.

Monday March 9th 1846. My wife still continued to be afflicted with her side. Sent off some hands to make rails. At ten was called to a council at Brigham Young's tent It was there required for me to ascertain how many men in the guard could go over the mountains without going back to Nauvoo and for all those whose circumstances required it should return home and report the same as soon as possible. It was also decided to light up the loads of the Artillery by burying up the ball & shot in the ground and getting them some other time. In the afternoon Captains Samuel Bent, C. C. Rich, Peter Hawes, and S. Roundy with some of the pioneers came up from the camp at Big run below Bonaparte

    This evening I sold my table for a hog and divided it out to the guard. It made about one mess for them all. About dark in company with Hunter & C Rogers rode out for exercise. Then called out the guard and spoke on the subject of our going to the mountains & the strict necessity of subordination.

Tuesday March 10th 1846. It was intended to send some teams on to day; but it clouded up earley and began to rain and turned out to be a wet rainy day. My tent leaked badly all day & I was troubled to keep our selves and thing dry At night we had trouble by our beds getting wet thus endangering my sick wife While making down the beds a quail came fluttering in the top of the tent and lit down in the tent door & I picked it up with out any trouble which reminded me of the children of Israel but nowing it was not sent in wrath I had it cooked and it proved a blessing instead of a cursing as their quails did The rain continued and it was Eleven o'clock before we could lay down and then we were rained on all night. To day I was in and about my tent all day.

Wednesday March 11th 1846. The weather was warm & raining and the ground extreemly muddy I was in camp untill evening and then rode out a short distance with Hunter and also rode round through the encampment While out we came across H. G. Sherwood surveying & taking the points of the compass from certain objects where the cannon balls had been buried while there Mr Richardson came also and he told him that Elder Sherwood had been takeing an observation to find out the distance to Nauvoo and found it to be fifty five miles and a quarter to a certain spot designated which he was so much taken up with the idea of having the correct distance that he went more than a half a mile in the rain and mud and packed a stone and had it buried there to mark the place which also served Br Sherwoods purpose as well as his and left no suspicion of what was done[10]

To night our beds and furniture was all wet and my wife still sick with a pain in her side Some time in the night the weather cleared off. But the roads were almost impassable no more

Thursday March the 12th 1846. Nothing of importance took place to day. I rode out for exercise with Hunter and wrote a letter to Elizabeth Taylor my mother-in-law. The ground was still wet and muddy. no time for travelling.

Friday March the 13th 1846. Better weather overhead, but muddy roads Rode out for exercise with Hunter in the timber to the west of the camp and when I came back was sent for by President B. Young to make some arraingements about dividing the guard as spoken of at Big Run. And then a council was called at which it was decided best for all those whose families were left behind & stood in need of their husbands for them to go back to Nauvoo in case they wanted to. After the council I called out the guard and laid the matter of returning home to the men and explained the matter to them. Nothing more of importance took place to night.

Saturday March the 14th 1846. To day was spent in making out a return of all the guard, as required yesterday. It was done by the companies coming by number commencing at the first company, and giving their names and also whether they would go back home or procede on to the Mountains We were engaged at it nearly all day. It was also required by the authorities to keep all the teams that is for none of the teams to go back: but to have them valued and the owner thereof to take an order for the amount on the trustees in Nauvoo and thus keep up our strength of teams as the whole camp was entirely too heavily loaded. The waggons and teams were valued by Lorenzo Young and Steven Markham who were appointed by Brigham Young to do it for the whole camp.

This was a new corner to most of the guard for but few of them was looking for it Some murmered at the idea of leaving us their teams one man swore that he would not give up his fathers team but would sooner poisin their horses so we

---

10. John D. Lee reported that on March 9, 1846, "This afternoon the Council instructed Capt Scott of the Artillery to cache about 24 hundred lbs of ball in this vicinity . . . ."

It was March 14 before Lee found time to enter the full description of the ammunition cache for the record, and then he inferred that other items were also buried. Lee's description bears out Stout's suggestion of the great pains taken by Sherwood to make the location definite:

Certain deposits near Vorree (viz) beginning at an augur hole in the west side of a white oak tree near the roots, running thence with the needle pointing 80° degrees N L 130 links to a black oak tree — thence 39 links to another black oak tree thence 23 links to a mound with a pit on the side of said mound making in all 192 links in a direct line from said white oak tree — thence from said mound S with the needle pointing 10 degrees E. L. & 135 links to a stone about 15 inches long & about 7 to 9 set in the ground on the east side near the root of a forked black oak Tree forked near the ground.

Witness:
John Scott
John Farnham
George D. Johnson
Joel Terry
Warren Snow
Henry G. Shearwood
Surveyors

The use of the word "Vorree" in the above has interesting implications, since Vorree, Wisconsin, was the headquarters of the Strangite branch of the Mormon Church. At another time an elder rebuked an evil spirit, commanding it to depart at once and go to Vorree, evidently the home of the devils. Lee, "Camp of the Saints," 21-22.

put them under guard and sent him home. About thirty of the guard returned home out of one hundred & eighty men. About dark Hunter & I went to William Claytons tent about one mile from ours to have him draw the orders for the waggon's and teams on the trustees in Nauvoo. It was some time in the night before he got done. It was now pitch dark and a bad road but he sent a man with a lantern to light us to the edge of the prairie after which we thought we could go comfortably but had to wade a considerable distance in deep mud and water in the rain which was now falling fast We went or rather waded to President B. Youngs tent with the orders and left them there to have him & Bishop N. K. Whitney sign them. There learned that Aaron Rager, who had told me that he had been to B. Young & got council to take the team which he had & go back after his family, had told me an infernal lie for Brigham said he did not give him any such council. So I took the team into my own charge and he went into Brigham's company without any feelings being manifested

Sunday March the 15th 1846. Several of the guard and others returned to Nauvoo this morning, & several and in fact the majority of the guard who had reported to return gave up the idea and resolved to go untill they had fulfilled their mission and were regularly discharged by the order of the camp regulation.[11]

I called a meeting of the Guard in a hollow North of the camp in the timber and taught them on the disorder resulting from persons continually running to President B. Young for advice & council about matters which has already been laid down for some were in the habit of doing so I was also compelled to speak again about Charles Allen Capt of the 3rd 50 for he here commenced another system of disobedience. As in the first place on Flat rock run he would not work neither allow his men to do so now in as much as he concluded to work he took jobs of work and done them with his own men and kept the pay and even went so far as to exact money from those who were under the necessity of using any thing which he had they procured and his men often told me that he kept the money that he got and never let them have any of it all of which caused great dissatisfaction in the guard. He not content with thus instilling a spirit of insubordination among us but he also set up a line of grumbling at every that was done and would frequently go to B Young for council when my council did not suit him but in no instance did he ever get council different from what I give not withstanding it did not stop his grumbling so on this occasion I took up his course of conduct and exposed it to the guard & let them know that I disapproved it as much as they and also told them that he had the Spirit dissension and warned them not to partake of it and for those who were under his command to leave him forth with if he did not Speedily retract and return to his duty. which they all agreed to do.

At Eleven o'clock a general meeting was held by the camp. Elders H. G. Sherwood and Truman Gillett preached. The meeting was attended by a number of Gentiles. I did not attend the meeting but was engaged at company business the rest part of the day. It was a very windy day my tent blew down several times.

In the evening I had a meeting of Archd Beers[12] Company the same company which S. Gully had made such a display with. They seemed to have caught his Spirit and disappointed the expectations of all who depended on them.

---

11. On March 17 John D. Lee noted that twenty-nine members of the guard had been reported by Hosea Stout as "having been faithful in camp and honorably discharged & to return to Nauvoo within a day or two." On the same day Captain Scott of the artillery handed in the names of seven men, and Captain Markham of the pioneers the names of nineteen more, all of whom were "honorably released" and sent back to Nauvoo without their teams. Instead they carried orders on the trustees there for others of equal value to be supplied. Lee carefully entered every name on the record. *Ibid.,* 25.

12. The handwriting of Stout's diary is so dim on this line that the first letter of the last name is almost illegible. It seems to be Archibald Beers, who appears later in the account.

Some of them stubbornly vindicated their tardy course which caused me to give them a severe repramand & lay down the rules in pointed terms before they would come to the proper Spirit but at last they all agreed to do their duty henceforth cherfully and promtly and all was order and quiet. No more to night.

Monday March the 16th 1846. I was in camp to day. Saw and had a talk with Capt C. Allen about what I said about him yesterday the matter was Straitened up in good feelings & he agreed to act in due subordination hereafter. The guard was most all out at work to day. Hunter & I took a walk for exercise to the west in the timber to day in the afternoon.

This evening at dark a meeting was appointed at Dr Richards tent for W. J. Earl to preach a Methodist Sermon. At dark the meeting assembled and also some Gentiles who heard that a Methodist was to preach and among them some methodist. So it was thought best not to have him preach as it would give occasion for them to have hard feeling at us thus to preach Methodism in mockery to their religion. The meeting was passed off by Br Lee calling for the methodist as he said he understood that one was to be there. The Gentiles supposing the preacher to be really a methodist considered it a disappointment on his part and all past off well

From assembly at Richards I called out the guard to a meeting of the same in the little prairie North of the camp and there spoke "long & loud" on the nature of keeping order & council & the atonement for shedding inocent blood also had it understood that Capt Allen & myself had Settled the matter between us & he expressed publickly his determination to abide council hereafter and all was thus made right.[13] no more tonight.

Tuesday March the 17th 1846. Today it was intended to start again on our journey but was prevented by the death of Edwin Little. He died from being over done on the road, as I heard He was buried at the place spoken of where the stone was put in the ground as mentioned on the 11th of March.[14] Hunter & I rode out today on the road about four miles to see what state they were in for traveling and it to be good. When we came back President Young told me that the man who owned the land which we were encamped on was trying to make a fuss about the trees which the horses nawed but it never amounted to any thing of importance. I was in camp the rest of the day and nothing of importance took [place].

(Minutes of Wednesday lost)

Thursday March 19th 1846. Today the camp moved again. Amasa Lyman & Theodore Turley staid not being ready for want of teams. & I left Capt L. H. Calkins and his company to stay with them and come on when they did. We went about

13. Rumors of trouble in the camp had evidently been carried back to Nauvoo, for on this date (March 16, 1846) John D. Lee wrote a letter from the Twelve Apostles to the trustees in Nauvoo saying: "Brigham Young is not murdered; John Taylor has not apostatized; Hosea Stout has not mutinized; the guards have committed no insurrections, and we can say with the utmost confidence, that we do not believe that so large a company ever camped together so long . . . , as this has, with so much good feeling, contentedness, kindness, benevolence, charity and brotherly love as has been, and is still, manifested among this Camp, . . ." "Journal History," March 16, 1846.

14. Of this burial, John D. Lee writes: "Richardson's Point, Monday March 18, '46 Edwin Little died at 20 min past 7 this A M and was buried on the divide between Fox & Chequest Rivers beginning at a beginning at a black oak tree that forked near the ground with the letters S T on the east side thence East needle pointing 74 deg N 40 links in a direct line toward a white oak tree marked S T on the west side about 140 links from said black oak tree as aforesaid and immediately west of the grave of Sidney Tanners child that was buried 17 Mar 1846." Lee, "Camp of the Saints," 26. Edwin Little was a nephew of Brigham Young.

fifteen miles to day. The road was mostly prairie and tolerable good. I went on ahead on horse back with some others and looked out the best ways to get around mud holes We had some times to open fences. The country here began to show that we were leaving the settlements for the farms were more scattering and newly made. To night we came to S. Roundy's company. They were encamped on a widow's farm. She wanted pay for the wood we used. although she did not own the land However she got nothing.

Roundy was gone to Nauvoo. Andrew & John Lytle & James Pace were here. To day some of the guard had to help Jeremiah Willie's team draw his load. They done it by attaching a rope to the waggon tongue to draw by.

Friday March 20th 1846. This morning the camp started earley. It was clear and cold. I sent Capt Charles Allen with some men to go before the camp & prepare the roads as we did yesterday. The teams started in confusion this morning & would try to rush by each other on level prairie. We overtook the Artillery and Orson Pratt this forenoon.

At 12 we came to Fox river and found a good bridge across it built by the inhabitants. We crossed over and found a good camping place and waited here untill Capt Averett[15] went on to look for another as he said there was one three miles ahead. He sent word for us to come on. We started but found the roads almost impassable About half way to the camping place we struck the old Mormon trail. This was the trail which we made when I in company with 27 others fled from Far West Mo into the wilderness to escape the vengeance of the mob under executive authority of Gov Boggs in 1838 when the saints were expelled from that state It was with peculiar feeling that I saw this old trail It was yet to be saw although a public road now occupied the same ground but was not much traveled. At 4 we came to the camping place It was half a mile from the road We had to go over a wet miry prairie to camp through which most of the teams stalled. The teams were coming untill dark. The fire broke out from some of the fires & came very near burning up some of the tents & waggons but by great exertions it was extinguished without any damage being done. It was near night before President Young came up

Saturday March 21st 1846. This morning some of the teams began to move earley but had great difficulty in getting out into the road because of the deep mud. One of President Young waggons had the toungue broke out at Fox river and was left and he did not go on but went back with some others to mend it and bring it up. Jesse D Hunter & I went along. and the principal part of the guard waited untill we returned but their families and teams mostly went on the men only waiting. We came to Fox river at Twelve. When we returned to camp the Omni-

15. Elijah and Elisha Averett were twins, born December 10, 1810. Both served in the Black Hawk War in Illinois; both were converted to Mormonism in 1835, moved to Nauvoo, and worked as stone masons on the temple there. They were members of the "New Police."

At the time of the exodus from Nauvoo, Elisha went ahead with Stephen Markham in the George Miller company as a captain of fifty. Elijah was captain of ten.

Elijah wrote in his journal: "I was told to take my ten . . . and feary the brethren across the Mississippi River, which I did until President Young came to cross, and he told me to go with him which I did. He camped at Sugar Creek. When most of the people had crossed the River, he organized the camp. I was appointed Captain of the third fifty of Pioneers." Elijah Averett, "Journal [1810-?]" (typescript, Utah State Historical Society), 11.

As captain of the third fifty, Elijah directed the erection of the stone abutments for nine bridges, moving ahead of the main migration across Iowa, along with the George Miller group. Averett came to Utah in 1851, lived at Manti for ten years, and moved to the Dixie Mission in southern Utah in 1861. Here he worked as a stone mason, building the fort at Pipe Spring and working on the St. George Temple. His oldest son, Elijah, Jr., was killed by Indians in the Pariah area. Elijah, Sr., lived his closing years in Springerville, Arizona.

bus[16] & some 4 or 5 other waggons were yet there. I then sent on the foot guard and then proceeded with the horsemen and traveled about a mile and got word the toungue of the Omnibus was broken whereupon I returned with the horsemen to assist in reparing it but it was soon lashed together again with ropes so as to answer the purpose and we then went on again performing as we rode some Danite evolutions[17] of horsemanship as practised in the War in Davis County Missouri in the fall of 1838. We crossed a prairie about 12 miles on a good lope. It was a rich level prairie and on the Mormon trail

We found one of Richards teams stalled in a deep ravine about half across and help it out. After we passed some other teams came along and in helping them across William Clyde got his arm broke. The road was good and dry

We came to the camp before night and made fires. We camped on a large branch I piched my tent under the hill in a good place. All the waggons came in before dark. It rained a little in the night.

Sunday March the 22nd 1846. This was a dark wet & a drizzly morning and a very bad time for traveling. I here sent off and bought ten bushels of corn and paid the cash for it About ten I started. The creek was a deep pitch on both sides and bad for the teams to pass. The roads passed through a rough ridge & bluffs of Chariton about 4 miles We came to the Chariton river at noon. This stream had deep steep & sandy banks. I found the teams crossing They had to let the waggons down the pitch by ropes attached to the hind end of the waggons and thus enabled the teams to let the waggons down more easy. It was now raining. The teams were all day crossing as above mentioned Here while the waggon was waiting to cross the river Henry B. Jacobs'[18] wife was confined and had a child & no harm happened to her not withstanding the inclement weather.

---

16. The *Omnibus* was a very large carriage owned by Brigham Young often mentioned by name in the records of many diarists of the company.

17. These "Danite evolutions of horsemanship" are mentioned several times by Stout, Lee, and other contemporary writers. Some were used in southern Utah as a part of parades and celebrations as late as the 1860's.

18. Henry Bailey Jacobs was born in Jefferson County, New York, and joined the Mormon Church in 1832. In 1838 he moved to Missouri, where he served as justice of the peace in Richmond. He also signed the covenant to help the poor leave the state.

On March 7, 1841, Jacobs married Zina Diantha Huntington and a few months later accompanied John D. Lee on a mission to Tennessee. On October 27, 1841, Zina was "sealed" to Joseph Smith for eternity, her brother Dimick officiating. Her son, Zebulon Jacobs, was born on January 2, 1842, and she continued to live with her husband. In 1843 Henry Jacobs was called on another mission, this time to New York with Zina's brother Oliver Huntington as companion. They were gone six months, during which time Oliver kept a daily record.

On his return to Nauvoo, Jacobs again joined his wife and was active in the church, working on the temple and other public buildings. On October 4, 1844, he was made a member of the Quorum of the Seventy. On February 9, 1846, just before she left Nauvoo, Zina D. Huntington Jacobs was sealed to Joseph Smith in the Nauvoo Temple, with Brigham Young acting as proxy and her husband standing as witness.

The Jacobs family traveled with the migrating group, her second son, Chariton Jacobs, being born as recorded by Stout and others. They made a temporary home at Mount Pisgah, where Zina's father was left in charge.

Again Jacobs was called on a mission, this time to England; again his companion was Oliver B. Huntington, his brother-in-law. At the end of one year Jacobs returned, joining W. W. Phelps in the East, whence he had gone to secure a printing press. Upon their arrival at Winter Quarters in November 1847, both men were excommunicated from the church for bringing along plural wives. They were later rebaptized.

In the meantime Jacob's father-in-law, William Huntington, had died, and Zina had been moved to Winter Quarters. She now renounced Jacobs and joined the family of Brigham Young, traveling west in 1848 in a wagon provided by him and driven by her brother Oliver.

Jacobs came west in the same general migration, but in the Perkins company. He evidently brought his plural wife, Sarah Taylor, with him. On January 26, 1851, he was disfellowshipped from his quorum and later excommunicated from the church. He moved to California, where

The bottom on the other side was a flat level & now wet land and floded with water by the rain on which I found encamped the companies of C. C. Rich, C. Shumway, Elder Taylor and some others who had gone on ahead of us. After we came over we went up on the hill which was very steep & high and now deep mud in the road and there encamped on the ridge which now in its wildness presented a beautiful camping ground It was thick set with white ok timber. We filled the ridge with our tents & waggons for perhaps half a mile. No more to night

Monday March the 23rd 1846. Today was warm dark rainy and muddy. We had no corn for our horses and cattle but President Young had purched some 4 miles back and sent some of my teams to draw it to camp & when it came he gave us half of it It made but one feed for us of four years to a beast. I rode out on the road with Hunter & Anderson and found it to be very muddy travelling. Lorenzo Snow and his company went on today. George Miller & his company who were now 8 miles ahead also moved on. This was contrary to council & it was decided that if they did not stop they should be cut off from the camp and their names not known in the "Camp of Israel."[19]

Tuesday March the 24th 1846. Today was a chilling rain and snow all day. The mud was very deep in camp being tramped up by the beasts. No feed in camp today for the beasts and also more than half the men out of provisions

I went to B. Youngs quarters today and Rockwood told me that Capt C. Allen had reported to him that I had a vacant waggon, which was the one that Capt Robert Collins used for a baggage wagon for his company. I told him it was not so but that Capt Allen had said so because he had a private pique against that company and wanted to brake it up. But I told him that I could let them have one and accordingly let the one which Capt Coons used in his company

Before I took the waggon I levied on the provisions which he and Capt Collins had. It made a waggon Load and furnished two pounds to each person in the guard I then disbanded their companies.

In the after noon met in Council at B. Youngs quarters & wrote a letter to Mother Elizabeth Taylor. Thomas Tidwell killed two deers and after giving one fourth to B. Young I distributed it to the guard it made them a good mess and came very opportunely for they were out of meat A man came in camp today & and wanted to join the church & guard but believing him to be a Spy rejected him & set William Hall to watch him his name was Devlin at dark called out the guard and spoke to them as usual no more

Wednesday March 25th 1846. There was a handsome snow covering the deep mud this morning. The weather cold and windy Provisions scarce no horse feed but Col Rockwood brought 150 pounds of flour to the guard which was distributed among them which was a great relief to us. No word from Miller & those ahead. We had another deer killed in the guard to day. After dinner I was not well. No more to day.

Thursday March the 26th 1846. Perfectly clear, windy and muddy today. President B. Young called a council of the Captains of tens fifties and hundreds

---

he lived for some years. Oliver B. Huntington wrote that "Friday May 8, 1880, . . . Henry Jacobs came from California to spend the remainder of his days with his sons [Zebulon and Chariton] in Salt Lake, by their request." He was rebaptized on February 2, 1886.

19. On this date William Clayton, clerk of the camp, recorded: "I wrote a letter to them [Miller's Company] saying that if they did not wait or return to organize, the camp would organize without [them] and they be disfellowshipped." William Clayton, *William Clayton's Journal: A Daily Record of the Journey of the Original Company of "Mormon" Pioneers from Nauvoo, Illinois to the Valley of the Great Salt Lake* (Salt Lake City, 1921), 9.

this morning and reproved them for their want of order and unwise course in sending men out to buy corn and bidding against each other & raising the price of corn. That before Bishop Miller came here corn was a drug at 15 cents per bushel and now it was 20 & 25 cents & sometimes more. That he felt to withdraw fellowship from the Bishop That he was going against council.

That he had recieved no answer from him yet. After which he sent another messenger to him to learn what he was doing. At ten in the morning another council was called of the Captains of tens fifties and hundreds at Col Scotts quarters to talk over and make calculations about organizing the camp in due form which had never as yet been done. but could not organize because the camp could not be got together.

It was then councilled for us to take jobs of work when we could to get something to live upon. It was also decided here to send a company of men on to the Platte country to take jobs of work and also to lay up grain for the camp while it was moving on. After Council Capt C. Allen took a job of making 2,000 nails and I sent Capt Morgan Phelps to do it with his men and also detailed O. M. Allen with his company to set up and burn a coal pit for the camp. Also sent a number of men out to look out for & take jobs of work.

Just after council (about one) Bishop Miller, O. Pratt and others came into camp. All was said to be made right on the part of Miller and a good understanding entered into and he complied with the requisitions of the council.

This evening Br Lee told me that the course which I took at Sugar Creek with G. Miller when he forced the guard was approved by the President.[20] No more today.

Friday March the 27th 1846. This morning the ground was frozen & a boisterous wind blowing. Went to W. Richard's tent on business for J. Champlin & W. Hall relative to their teams which they wanted to take back. Champlin had come from home here to get his team It had been receipted to the church but he had not recieved it and was the same team which his son had threatned to poison as mentioned at Richardson's Point.

When I returned from Richards tent I was informed that B. W. Wilson was about to desert so I went to see his brother H. H. Wilson who denied knowing any thing about it although the tent was in his keeping and his brother's trunk & things gone I accused him of being accessary to it himself and took his horse and put it under guard to keep him from leaving in my absence for I was going to a council as you will soon learn & just ready to start. I put his horse under the charge of Capt. D. McArthur untill I returned. and told H. H. Wilson that I would hold him accountable to let me know where his brother had gone which he said he could not do but some of the men present said that he knew all about it. He got into a rage & threatened to fight & then went to where his brother had gone It was to his brother L. D. Wilson's[21] tent and was actually making arraingements to escape. I then took his horse also and put it under McArthur and then went on to the council at ten.

This council was on Shoal Creek seven miles on ahead and all the officers and councillers went along for the purpose of having an organization of the whole

20. This refers to the incident of February 24, when George Miller challenged the guard's authority to keep him from crossing the bridge without giving the password. Miller accused Stout of ordering the guard to kill him and throw his body into the ravine below.

21. Of the three Wilson brothers mentioned here, Lewis Dunbar Wilson is best known in the ranks of the Mormon Church. See footnote 11 in Volume I, Part 2. Three days before the incident here recorded, he was appointed to supervise the making of rails at Garden Grove.

Henry H. Wilson later became counselor to Bishop Silas Richards in the Little Cottonwood Ward, later known as the Union Ward in Salt Lake County. Of the younger brother, B.W., nothing additional has been found.

camp. While on the way I fell in company with Charles Shumway who voluntarily told me that he had been induced to believe that I was wrong in the matter of the dissension of the "Old Police" and that he was compelled to believe so from the tales which had been told him about me by those whom he supposed to be good men of the police and that he had also blamed me in the case of Langley for he believed his stories but that in all these things he had learned that the men in whom he had so much confidence were aspiring to over through [throw] me to rise on my own ruins. That he had taken Langley into his own company and done all that he could for him and he had turned against him also when he was innocent but that they had made all right between themselves now &c. That he was happy to confess these things and let me know that he was as good a friend to me as ever he was. The roads was uncommonly wet and miry mostly through the prairie. We met Bishop Miller & others after we had gone a little more than half way coming to our camp & they turned back and we all went into their camp together. We arrived at their camp at half past 12. It was scattered on either side of the creek and the main boddy was camped about one mile on the other side of the creek Miller's camp was yet seven miles on

We were very friendly recieved and corn furnished for our horses and also preperations made for our dinners. I took dinner with G. A. Smith with some ten or twelve more and President B. Young among the rest. We had a good dinner composed of baked beans & ham coffee & other necessary articles to grace the meal It was a welcome repast to me for I was very hungry.

At two o'clock we went into council at Br E. Averett's tent and proceeded to the organization which consisted of six companies of 50 or three of hundreds and was organized as follows. Each company of 100 had a Captain and each company of 50 had also a Captain and one President who presided over the affairs of the company and one Contractor and one commissary and one Clerk. William Clayton was appointed General Clerk for the whole Camp. The first hundred was composed of Brigham Young's & Heber C. Kimball fifties and Ezra T. Benson appointed Capt. B. Young President, A P Rockwood Capt. J. D. Lee Clerk H. G. Sherwood Leading commissary or Contractor Chas Kenada [Kennedy] issuing commissary.

Heber C. Kimball President second 50 and Stephen Markham Captain, J. M. Grant Issuing Commissary. David D. Yearsley Contractor John Pack Clerk

The second hundred was composed of Parley P. Pratt's and Peter Haws Companies and Haws Company had the Band attached to it here It was officered as follows Father John Smith Captain, Parley P. Pratt President of the First fifty John Harvey Captain Nathan Tanner[22] Issuing Commissary, William H. Edwards Contractor and Lorenzo Snow Clerk Peter Haws President of the Second 50. Howard Egan Captain Orson B. Adams Issuing Commissary and Peter Hawes was also appointed Contractor, and George Hales Clerk.

The third hundred was composed of John Taylor's and George Millers Companies and was officered as follows. Saml Bent Captain. John Taylor President of the first 50 & C. C. Rich Captain James Allred[23] Issuing Commissary Joseph

---

22. Nathan Tanner was born May 14, 1815, in New York, and was baptized a Mormon in 1831. At the age of nineteen he joined the Zion's Camp trek west. In Missouri he was so active in defense of the church that he was known at Far West as a real "minuteman." His name is on the list of those who pledged to help the poor leave Missouri. At Nauvoo he helped with public works and with the defense of the city.

Tanner came to Utah with the immigration of 1848 and engaged in farming and freighting. His home was at Little Cottonwood. He died September 10, 1910, at Granger, Utah, the last survivor of Zion's Camp.

23. James Allred was born January 22, 1794, in North Carolina. He joined the Mormon Church September 10, 1832, was active in Kirtland, and came west with Zion's Camp in 1834. In 1840 he was kidnapped by a Missouri mob, imprisoned and threatened, but not

Warthan Contractor. and John Oakley Clerk. George Miller President Second 50 Charles Crisman Captain Isaac Alred Commissary & Samuel Gully Contractor and Asael Lathrop Clerk.

Such was the organization as near I could get it at the time. The pioneers and Guard were to be equally distributed amongst the different 50 and I had orders accordingly. I forgot to mention in the proper place that B. Young was appointed General Superintendant of the whole camp

It was then adjourned till next Monday at Shariton Ford. About half past 4 I started home in company with the rest of the brethren from our camp where we arrived about dark on My way home I had a talk with Br Lorenzo Young about our travels on this road when we fled from Missouri & also he spoke of his good feelings towards me and that he felt for me when he considered the precarious and dangerous duties of the office of my calling That he had often felt for me when he considered what I had to go through. We also talked over the time when we passed through here and he & I had a falling out and some words passed between us but said he had not laid anything up against me on account of it.

When I came home I found that McArthur had kept the Wilson's horses as I told him and they were both here as mad as they could be to be comfortable. H. H. Wilson declared that he would have the matter before Brigham. But I, after showing him the nature of the case, satisfied him and both of them said that I done right. but B. W. Wilson after being councilled by both myself & Brigham not did go home afterwards grumbling.

Saturday March 28th 1846. The weather was cold windy & cloudy & the ground froze John L. Butler & Jas Cummings started to James Emmett with a letter for him to start with his company and meet us at fort Larame. I was engaged in arrainging the guard in order to have it distributed among the different companies of fifties as decided yesterday and had a meeting in the morning to that effect. Most of those of the guard who had their families with them into different fifties as other families At dark I went to Brighams tent to meet in council but there was no business

Sunday March the 29th 1846. This morning a considerable number of the guard returned home and among the rest was Br John Groesbeck one of my teamsters & Joseph Taylor my brother-in-law They both went by my advice and not untill I told them that it was best for them. They had both been faithful & true to me & I expect to remember them for good. I was in camp all day Some of the guard seemed very much dissatisfied at the last order of the council on them. I was informed by Br S. M. St John that some traps had been stolen from a trapper in this neighbourhood by some of the brethren & that it was like to make difficulty with some but afterwards learned that Capt E E [two lines left blank][24] had stolen

---

whipped as were his three companions, Benjamin Boyce, Alanson Brown, and Noah Rogers. He was a member of the special bodyguard for Joseph Smith and served also on the High Council in Nauvoo. After the martyrdom he took his wagon to Carthage and brought home the wounded John Taylor. He brought his family to Utah in 1851 and founded Spring City, Sanpete County, where he was known as "Father Allred" until his death on June 10, 1876.

24. The official story of this is as follows:

A boy by the name of Edmund Whiting shot an otter at the bend of the river; he afterwards discovered that the otter was caught in a trap; he took off the skin and carried it to the camp, leaving the trap on the bank. In the course of the day, the trapper, who lived a short distance off, came into camp and stated that he had eight traps set in the neighborhood, and had lost six of them . . . . In the evening the Council heard what the boy had done with the otter skin, and called him into the post office with the skin . . . . The Council . . . instructed him to go early in the morning and bring the trap and take it and the skin to the trapper in company with Brother Stephen Markham. President Young instructed Brother Markham to say to the man that if one

two and it had been proven on him and would have been put on the public record to his disgrace had it not been for the respect they had for   About dark I went to council at Dr. Richards tent & it was there arrainged for me to go into the first fifty and form the sixth company called the guard company and take the remnant of the "Old Police" with me which with the teamster & others amounted to about twenty men which I divided into two companies the old police in one and the teamsters into another

Monday March the 30th 1846. This morning B. Jones went from the guard to the second fifty. My Brother Allen went out pedling to day & I sent some articles by him which he traded to good advantage. At ten a council was convened at B. Youngs tent in pursuant to adjournment on the 27th instant but as there was more than could get into the tent it was adjourned to the woods. Asabel A. Lathrop reported that he had been on grand river and the people's feelings were good towards us. The different companies of ten then made their reports which need not be mentioned here. The Artillery under Col John Scott was placed in the first fifty. At two the council adjourned.

After council I was engaged in arrainging the affairs of the guard and my own concerns to suit the order to distribute them   Called out the guard at dark & made arraingements for them to meet in the morning to go into the different fifties as might be directed.

This evening Edward P. Duzett the celebrated brass drummer arrived here from Nauvoo with his family   He had been sent for by the President   in crossing the Chariton his waggon up set and turned everything he had in it into the watter but none I believe was lost. no more tonight.

Tuesday March the 31st 1846. This morning I drew corn from Brigham's commissary for my horses & cows. & for my two companies   Capt O. M. Allen with his company of guard went in to Hawes fifty. & Capt. Robert Collins & his company went into Bishop Miller's fifty — after which Hunter & I went on the other side of the Chariton and down the bank and found the place where I had encamped when fleeing from Missouri   It was but a short distance from the road   The place looked very natural. this was the place where Br L. Young my self & some others had a falling out.   There was an Indian camp about a half mile below in a thick woods   Hunter & I went to the place   It yet showed signs of their camp or rather their town   We came home about one o'clock & was at home the rest of the afternoon.   At dark we went to Brighams tent as usual to council but there was not any thing of importance going on. The mail came in tonight I believe & I recieved a speech from the Honorable Joseph P. Hoge[25] of Galena Illinois delivered in the House of Representatives, on the claim of the United States to the Oragon urging the absolute necessaty of taking military possession of it and bidding defiance to Great Britain & her pompious bravado — (Speech delivered at Washington)

Wednesday April the first 1846. This morning was clear warm & pleasant Orders came earley for the camp to move and we were preparing accordingly. Some of the men went out & found a bee tree & cut it but got but little honey. Br Samuel Thomas was at my tent sick & I had him to move. At about one we started. The road was very much settled but got soft in some places. Several waggons broke down but none of mine.

---

of his traps were found in the camp within one thousand miles of that place, it should be sent back to him with the man that took it." (Preston Nibley, *Exodus to Greatness* [Salt Lake City, 1947], 143-44.)

25. Joseph P. Hoge had acted as attorney for Joseph Smith. As a result of the Mormon vote, he had been elected to Congress in August 1843.

We went to Shoal Creek at the place we held the council on the 27th and encamped It was on the edge of the prairie. The first 50 encamped in a hollow square but was laid out too little for my company to camp in so I encamped close by. There was none but the first 50 & Band moved to day. I arrainged it with Rockwood for each company to do the guarding one night in succession & my two companies each one night would have to do duty one night in each week. The first company was to stand guard on Sunday This was a great relief to my men for they would now have to do duty only two nights in a week whereas they had it to do every night before

Thursday April the second 1846. Recieved orders from Rockwood to send 4 men ten miles to make rails also to send some men to prepare a forge for the black-smith and then sent the cattle off to brouse and regulated other necessary business for the camp as we were going to stay here to day.

Br J. D. Lee shot at an elk but did not kill it. At ten another council was called & convened in a hazel rough below the camp. It was decided to cross the Missouri river at Banks ferry a letter was read from Br Hyde at Nauvoo. all was well there. William Smith was doing all he could against us

President Young said in talking about him that he had become satisfied that William was in the murder with the Hodges in Iowa for which two were hung as before mentioned[26] That Amos Hodge was also accessary.

It was councilled for the poor in Nauvoo to move as far this way as they can and take farms and live as well as they can untill they can be provided for. The Second 50 & the Artillery came in today & went on seven or eight miles.

After council, I was at my tent till in the evening & then with Hunter took a walk in the timber adjoining to look at the country It was a beautiful woods of Burr oak & a very rich loose & sandy soil. We returned home about sun down and found the waggons sent for flour had returned the teams for corn came in before dark. the rail makers also done their job.

About 8 o'clock Rockwood came and gave orders to have me put out a stronger guard that is eight men at a time and for me to furnish four of them out of my company so I went with him and raised 7 men[27] and put them in under Lorenzo Clark who was to keep a sharp lookout and see that the guard done their duty untill one o'clock at which time they were to be relieved. I posted them so as to encompass the whole of the first fifty including our cattle & horses which were fastened out side of the square & had one man in the square to keep all right there. He also reported that strangers were in camp near dark and that President Young wanted search made to see if they had put up in camp

After the guard was posted we went and searched every tent. President Young was not satisfied with the arraingements of the guard last night and had ordered it thus. After the above regulations was done I went into my tent and wrote into my journal till one o'clock as I was going to relieve the guard at that time and

26. The enmity between William Smith and Brigham Young reached a new climax with this accusation. Smith and others had inferred that Irvin Hodge had been killed by order of the police or the Council of Fifty.

William Hall listened to this speech of Brigham Young and wrote later in his book ". . . that William Smith, the patriarch, was out of town three miles where he was giving blessings all day and staid all night." William Hall, *The Abominations of Mormonism Exposed* . . . (Cincinnati, 1852), 33.

Smith was at that time a patriarch in the Mormon Church and James Monroe was the clerk who wrote the blessings. The James M. Monroe, "Diary" supports Hall's statement.

27. On this date William Clayton wrote that, "the portion of the guard detailed to our company joined with us, being Orvil M. Allen and eight men. They reported themselves destitute of everything and said they had lived a week on corn meal gruel, Stout and Hunter having made them serve as their bodyguard and used them very hard." Clayton, *Journal,* 12.

relieved but once tonight. It was a cold cloudy night and a boisterous East wind
blowing which seemed as though it would blow the tent down. At one I relieved
and put the guard for the latter part of the night under Levi Stewart

Friday April the 3rd 1846. This was a dark cloudy morning and a heavy East
wind blowing and the appearance of rain and presented a dreary looking time for
traveling. notwithstanding the camp commenced moving before sunrise. All was
hurry and bustle for every one started as soon as they could get ready without
waiting for the rest. All started before breakfast I waited as was my custom
with the guard, untill the rest of the 50 was gone before I started but I was off by
seven o'clock. The road ran on a ridge and of course was very crooked. The
ground was very soft Some of the heavy waggons cut in deep & was uncommonly
hard on the teams.

By nine o'clock however we came to the camp of H. C. Kimball & the Artillery
a distance of five miles & found them all well It was in a point of timber on one
of the prongs of Shoal Creek.

We went on without making any halt about two or three miles further and
came to Bishop Miller's camp also on another prong of Shoal Creek. This is the
first time that we had been up with him since he left Flat rock run on the other
side of the Des Moines. They were all doing well. This was about ten o'clock
Here we let our teams bait a while.

While here it commenced raining in showers with every appearance of rainy
wether. About half past one I started on having a ten mile prairie before us. I
was on horse back and rode across in two hours. Shortly after we started across
the prairie it commenced a regular rain which continued all night. When I got
across I with some others who was with me built up some fires on a branch of
Locus creek & warmed ourselves. But when Rockwood came he concluded that we
had best camp further back as the teams would be tired. So I went with him back
about one mile and there met President Young when after some considerable deliber-
ation we turned about half a mile to the right to a point of timber and encamped
which we called hickery Grove because most of the timber was hickery. This was
a hard day for my wife and was very sick at night. The teams were coming in all
the evening and many laid out in the prairie unable to cross for the road was very
soft After regulating the guard I went to bed earley. The wind blew uncommonly
hard and beat the rain into the tents but we rested well In some of the tents the
watter ran into the tents and the people in them were completely soaked in morning.

Saturday April the 4th 1846. This was a dark gloomy drizzly morning & the
ground was flooded with water & the mud deep throughout the camp. but all
else was well. After breakfast Rockwood came to me and ordered guards to be
placed round the camp so as to prevent cattle and horses from escaping which
I done. There was not any thing of importance going on to day more than sending
back teams to assist those who had to stop on the prairie last night. President
Young visited my tent twice to day. the last time with Rockwood and came to
enquire into the way and manner the guarding was done. Rockwood gave him
an account of the manner it had been done since we left the Chariton which he said
was all right. He then said that he wanted me to attend to it on the same principles
which I had done heretofore and call on all the men in the fifty to do duty in
equal proportion

J. W. Binley took a job of making rails to day for my men for bacon which
came very seasonable for they were out of meat

In the evening I commenced guarding according to the President's instructions It did not suit the people very well It was a rainy day. My wife was very
sick with pleurasy

Sunday April the 5th 1846. This was a fine clear morning and the ground froze a little It was clear & warm all day. and very pleasant.

Today Allen Stout's wife came to my tent they had been in the prairie during the storm in their waggon We all sent off our cattle to brouse not having any thing to feed them with.

I took a long walk today with Hunter to the North of the camp We went over roling prairie of very rich soil & came to a beautiful grove of [trees] which had all been killed by the fire & presented a striking sensation of destroyed lovliness & made us think on the destruction of our enemies. We then passed through some timber and took a circuitous rout to the road in advance of the camp & found Elder John Taylor moving to our astonishment for we did not think that any one would again presume to go in advance of our President & Leader after what had been said about Bishop Miller & others

The roads had just began to settle & his waggons cut in to the hubs in some places rendering the road almost impassable for any one else to pass He had been on the prairie during the storm. We then came into camp & there remained till evening I then regulated the guard at dark after which I called out my company of teamsters & gave them instructions on their duty. & then gave the Old Police company their instructions on the nature of their duty. My wife was better this evening. no more to night.

Monday April the 6th 1846. This was of all mornings the most dismal dark and rainy after such a fine day as yesterday was. President Young concluded to move on to Locus Creek about three miles for the purpose of new pasture & brouse as the brous & pasture was all gone here Accordingly he started very earley before breakfast The roads were so bad that he doubled his teams and made two trips. but I thought I could go at one without doubling as I had not yet stalled This day capped the climax of all days for travelling The road was the worst that I had yet witnessed up hill & down through sloughs on spouty oak ridges and deep marshes raining hard the creek rising. the horses would sometimes sink to their bellies on the ridges teams stall going down hill. We worked and toiled more than half the day and had at last to leave some of our waggons and double teams before we could get through. At length however we arived at Locus Creek 3 miles & found it a narrow deep stream and muddy banks There was a good bridge built by the pioneers. I camped just across it on a fine ridge & a good place President Young camp with the 50 some two hundred yards below on a level piece of bottom which was before night cut up and tramped into deep mud by the horses & cattle I had decidedly the best ground It was allotted me by Rockwood whose duty it was to order the manner of encampments.

Immediately upon my arrival I recieved orders from Col Rockwood have a coal pit up and set on fire tonight notwithstanding it was still raining hard and the men wet through and worn out and fatigued and hungry for they had to toil and labor to help the teams along in the mud & rain They went however cherfully to work & put up the coal pit & had it set on fire that night according to orders

This morning a company of my men went earley to finish a job of rails They worked all day in the rain & finished it and overtook us at dark all dripping wet and merry. At dark I put out the guard as usual Here we found good brouse & pasture for our horses and cattle. After I laid down a wind arose which came very near blowing down my tent for I had not put on stay ropes thinking that the thick timber would secure it against wind I had to get out of my bed and hold it along time in the wind and rain which [b]eat upon me untill I was wet thoroughly nor could I leave to secure it because it would blow down. however some of Capt

Meeks[28] men came to my assistance at length & fastened it with ropes & relieved me. It blew up a very hard storm accompanied by thunder & lightning and hard rain.

Tuesday April the 7th 1846. Cold windy morning a little snow and a slight freeze. The creek was rising very fast and already near to the bridge. A part of Brighams cattle was across a slough and full of watter and they completely watter bound. but they were well supplied with brouse and done very well untill the water fell. I sent my stock over the bridge to a good place to brouse and graze. The water came up to the bridge & it had to be braced to keep it from floating off. Rockwood came and told me today that I could have the priviledge of sending out as many hunters as I saw proper.

President B. Young came to my tent to day and staid an hour or two. Bought a large knife today of J Carpenter for 1.10 in cash for a hunting knife. had my little one horse waggon repaired today. Sent 6 men to make rails The winds were high and bousterous today. In the evening I regulated the guard as usual and made out a full list of all the men in the fifty able to do duty and commenced detailing the guard by it for the first time

Wednesday April the 8th 1846. I sent of two me[n] to hunt today but they killed nothing. Got some blacksmith work done & over hauled my loads to give them air and was in camp all day. President B. Young J. D. Hunter and others went towards grand river to look at the roads. In the evening I regulated the guard as usual My wife was almost dead today with the pleurasy.

Thursday April the 9th 1846. cloudy morning. Sent of[f] some more hunters this morning. Elder John Taylor was moving his company across the creek all day today. and encamped about one & half miles on ahead of us. At noon it commenced raining again for a rarity but no wind of consequence My wife continued to be sick she took medicine (Lobelia) today and was better at night. John W. Binley came back from Medicine Creek whither he had been to get work but did not get any but reported better roads I wrote in my journal in the afternoon and at night regulated the guard as usual No more.

Friday April the 10th 1846. It rained hard all night The creek was almost full this morning & the wind blowing hard We expected to have to move out of the bottom on account of the watter but did not.

At ten President Young came to my tent & there called the people togeather and gave them some instructions relative to their duty and required them to be subject to the order of the guard when called on and also advised each captain of ten to appoint a teacher in his company to see that each man attended to his duty in Spiritual matters. whereupon I appointed Br George W. Harris in my company he being of my family. The President then proposed a council of all the captains of tens and other officers in his 50 and all others who were present to be held at Dr W. Richards which was agreed to by the congregation The council immediately assembled and the following decisions made To send teams on to Grand river where grain could be had and recruit them up a little and then come back and bring us on for we would remain here or when the teams came back for us to

28. William Meeks was born in Indiana in 1815. His name appears in these records as a horseman and scout. He came to Utah in 1852 in Captain Nisonger's company. He was an early settler of Provo, where he was living in 1858. In 1863 he was in Pine Valley, Washington County, Utah, getting out lumber. James G. Bleak's report of November 1870 states that "business is prospering in the new Pariah settlement under the Presidency of William Meeks."

Later Meeks set up a dairy at the foot of Boulder Mountain and shipped butter and cheese in wagon loads via Nephi to Salt Lake City and Ogden. Some of his sons set up a cattle ranch in Canada.

take a North course untill we came into Iowa again and there make a settlement and then go to the Missouri river and make another and then cross over the river & make another settlement

This was done to give the poore in Nauvoo & elsewhere a chance to come to a place where they could make a living for the time being. Also to send men on to Grand river to work for such thing as we needed Decided also to record the names of those who disobey orders & to send back and bring those companies who were in our rear for they had not teams enough to keep up Before dark I regulated the guard as usual and came home at nine o'clock & found Levi North & Thos S. Johnson there who had come for some goods which they wanted of Hunter & I. which we let them have & they went a satisfied as they said My wife to night came very near dying with the pleurasy & I set up till eleven o'clock.

Saturday April the 11th 1846. Cold windy morning with a sleight freeze. I sent Capt Lorenzo Clark with his company to repair a bridge on ahead he went with some others of the fifty Sent off the cattle & horses to brouse down the creek & then went a hunting with Hunter to the brousing and below cattle was doing well. Some of my men went off to make some boards & some to cleaning the publick guns in my charge I had them all over hauled and cleaned I returned from hunting about one and wrote in my journal untill evening and then regulated the guard as usual & came home at dark

Sunday April the 12th 1846. Cold Cloudy & windy wether. Today there was a council at Heber's camp three miles back I did not go but remained in camp all day being unwell with something like the piles cattle & horses was sent off to brouse as usual. Bishop Miller & his company passed by and camped on the side hill just above us I regulated the guard as usual

Monday April the 13th 1846. This was a warm pleasant day Capt Lorenzo Clark's company that is the old police were taken and put in another place for the purpose attending to the wants and necessities of President B. Young

Br G. L. Colemere came to me this morning and informed me of certain evil plotting against me and gave me the names of some of the principal ones He did as a friend to me & had got his knowledge unknown to them for they had not told him any thing about it. Captain William Weeks and his company comprising all my teamsters started to work today on Grand river leaving me one man of the the company so the Army was now reduced to one man &c

About three o'clock I recieved orders to remove to the top of the hill about one mile distance where the fifty were going to all move. We had to double our teams in order to get out of the mudy bottom We went at three trips and got the last load up at dark This evening my little son Hiram was dangerously sick

I regulated the guard to night according to the order of the encampment and it took twelve men to guard. I was up till twelve.

Tuesday April the 14th 1846. Cold windy cloudy weather this morning My wife and child some better. Sent off the horses & cattle to brouse & graze

There was a number of teams sent back three miles today to bring up Heber's company and the Band I sent a yoke of oxen. I went a hunting with Allen J. Stout we killed two plovers and a snake.

We came back & I then went with Hunter to geather ground nuts which the low lands abounded we got a basket full They are good to eat raw we tried to use them as a substitute for potatoes but they will not do. Heber & the Band came up and encamped on the same ridge which we were on It formed a beautiful sight to see so many waggons & tents together and could be seen for miles on the prairie. I was unwell in the evening Regulated the guard as usual

Capt Edmund Ellsworth[29] would not furnish any of his men & the Artillery which had come up and camped by us did not want to furnish any guards They were not satisfied with the order of things in the fifty It was a hard matter to raise a guard to night.

My wife was worse to night President B Young came to my tent and laid hands on her.

Wednesday April the 15 1846. The weather was clear & cool I sent off the stock to brouse as usual This morning Col Scott & A. P. Rockwood had quite a sharp talk about their right & rank[30] and Rockwood's jurisdiction over Scott & he was not willing to comply with the orders of Rockwood not believing them to be legal & refused to furnish men for guard on his order as was mentioned last night. Much was said by both and the matter was left where it was. A short time after that Rockwood informed Hunter & I that Hunter had been appointed in company with C. Shumway to go on a mission to the Cherokees & to see Lewis Dana & George L. M. Herring and &c which appointment was done upon his nomination

I was very sick today with a disentary & had strong symtoms of having a hard spell of sickness

Capt George Miller & John Taylor went on to day with their companies to day in the fore noon

I had a long interview with John Scott today relative to the situation of & the order of the guard he said he felt towards me as well as ever & that he intended to keep his covenant with me which we once made to stand by each other in our rights & rank in military affairs &c He did not like Rockwood manner of doing business &c and that he would not submit to it. The fact is there was none of the old Mormon brethren who had been used to stand against our enemies who were

I felt to withdraw from under his rule although it would seperate me from Brigham untill a change of his officers should take place

To day Lorenzo Clark, captain of the old Police company which was refered to on the 13th instant was taken out of his company to drive a team for President Young I believe and Samuel Williams appointed capt in his place He was not of the police but before night the company was incorporated in to Capt. Ellsworth Company which was the fourth Company of Brighams fifty Thus the distinction of the old Police was entirely done away & we could say according to the prophecy of Joseph "Where is the old Police" &c I regulated the guard as usual Col Scott still refusing to furnish any help on the order of Rockwood I had hard work to get men enough.

---

29. Edmund Ellsworth, a son-in-law of Brigham Young, was born July 1, 1819, in New York State. He was baptized into the Mormon Church in 1840, made a Seventy in 1843, and came to Utah with the pioneer company of 1847.

As a lumberman, he was influential in the building operations in the new territory. In 1856 he brought the first company of handcart pioneers across the plains; in 1857 he was stationed on the ferry at the Platte River. He was a member of the military during the Mormon War. Ellsworth was superintendent of construction on the Utah Northern Railroad and an alderman in the Salt Lake City government.

In an attempt to avoid arrest for polygamy, Ellsworth moved to Arizona, but was caught at Prescott and served a term for unlawful co-habitation. He died at Showlow, Arizona, December 29, 1893.

30. Like George Miller, John Scott found it difficult to give prompt and unquestioning obedience to the commands of Brigham Young, especially when they were issued by Albert P. Rockwood. Both Miller and Scott had been appointed to the Council of Fifty by Joseph Smith, so considered themselves equal in rank and authority to Brigham Young and higher than A. P. Rockwood.

Thursday April the 16th 1846. The weather is warm clear & pleasant our fifty moved to day & also Heber's   we went on a ridge to the north in a zig zag road about six miles I had one more waggon & team today than I had teamsters driving my wife's team my self.   It was the first time on the journey that I was obliged to drive a team.   Col Scott sent me a man to drive a team but he did not go far before he left the team and went on leaving us to get along the best we could but we had no difficulty for my teamsters drove the odd team with theirs.   We camped in the prairie where we stoped at one o'clock

We had no feed for our stock but what they could graze on the prairie This evening Rockwood informed me that Scott had agreed to do the guarding himself untill his men had all taken their regular turn and that I was releaced untill then from any guarding duty.

About dark the wind rose very high and blew all night which caused my wife to suffer much from cold

Friday April the 17th 1846. Moved on the teams started earley   It was very clear & very cold and windy   We went on a ridge again. one of our oxen give out & we left him in the prairie.   The camp took two roads today one went to a place which P. P. Pratt called Paridise & the other to a place called Pleasant Point where also Brighams company camped.   I came there at two o'clock and all was well   Nothing more of importance tonight.

Saturday April the 18th 1846. The weather was warm clear and pleasant. Sent off the cattle to feed as usual and they filled themselves quite full today.

There was a General council called of the different Captains & other officers today in the timber at Pleasant Point   The object of which was to ascertain who were prepared to cross the Mountains as it was determined that those who were ready should go The different Captains made a report of their availables and the amount of provisions now on hands. The Twelve were to determine who could go upon the reports.   I made a report of the situation to Rockwood in detail after council and the nature of my waggons and teams   I was at this time entirely out of provisions & so was Hunter

After the Council was over I sent Hunter & Green Taylor out a hunting and also gave them some books for them to sell if they should meet with any inhabitants and by us some provisions.   No more tonight.

Sunday April the 19th 1846. Clear, cool, wind, but pleasant today   Sent of the cattle as usual. There was a meeting at ten in a beautiful place which had been previously prepared in the timber   President Young taught on the contemplated order of the journey and some principles of economy necessary to be observed by those who travel over the Mountains.   He also spoke of adopting a rule to use one half pound of flour for each person per day and laying in accordingly which was sanctioned by vote but some thought it too small an allowance.   Bishop G. Miller said he could do on one quarter of a pound per day   That his family had used 6,000 pounds since they left Nauvoo.   That he was strong and hearty and could out travel any horse in camp[31] &c   He was followed by Lorenzo Young who said in

---

31. Under the same date John D. Lee gave a long and detailed account of this meeting, particularly of the speeches of Brigham Young and Heber C. Kimball. He included also Bishop Miller's boast that he could outrun any horse in camp and added Lorenzo Young's answer: ". . . if Bishop Miller could live on 4 oz of flour for 24 hours he has made very bad use of the flour that he started with as he has said that he laid in 6000 lbs of flour and has used it up within 140 miles journey . . . . I do it merely to impress upon the minds of this camp the reality of being reduced to this scanty allowance . . . don't let the bump of Ideality get so high & be carried away in anticipation to that extent that you will venture to take a journey of 12 months upon the scanty allowance of 4 ounces per day as Bro. Miller would feign make you believe . . . ." Lee, "Camp of the Saints," 40.

reply that he did not wonder if the Bishop could out travel any horse in camp if he had used so much bread stuff in so short a time but he advised those who could do on so little to try it awhile before they started &c. Br E. T. Benson said he would try it for he did not know what he could do &c

To day there was much said about me going on the journey even Br John D. Lee seemed to manifest a disposition to interfear with my private arraingements relative to my waggons but I shall refrain from saying any thing on the subject. at present.

The mail arrived today from Nauvoo with 306 letters and papers Two of which were to me. One from Asa Barton & one from Joseph Taylor and Benj. Dobson.

About dark Hunter & Green came home They did not kill anything but they sold three books and bought some bacon which was a great relief to us for we were suffering for want of something to eat.

Monday April the 20th 1846. There was a council today at ten o'clock A. M. at which there was a letter read from Br J. C. Wright then I think in Cincinnati which among other things stated that Sidney Rigdon & his prophet shop was about down & that old Austin Cowles[32] was seting himself up for some great one. He termed the "old one eyed prophet" which I thought was very applicable for him There was also some news papers read giving an account of the saying of the world about us and also Thomas C. Sharp's[33] account of the endowment which was a most rediculous & willful perversion of the truth but he has evidently been taught some thing of the true order by some traiterous apostate. After which reports were made by the different captains of ten of their availables. While this was going on I left the Council very sick.

After Council John D. Lee called on me to make a report to him of all my waggons but when I commenced he went from me without giving me a hearing & so that matter ended. President Young then told me to report my waggons & teams and also to enlist & fit out all the young men that I could and take with me as it was determined that I should go. Those men were to go to the settlements and work for a fit out. I told him that I had reported my teams to Col Rockwood which he said was right. He said also for me to send my disposable goods to the settlements and sell them for provisions which I did but my goods were not taken as no pedlars went from this place. This evening I regulated the guard again as Scotts tour was out. To day Col Scott with some of his men started to the settlements to work & also some others.

Tuesday April the 21st 1846. The weather was warm & cloudy. To day we moved about 8 miles to the next piece of timber over a level flat & wet prairie. It rained some as we traveled making it very uncomfortable traveling. I was very unwell.

The camp was first put on the first side of the creek, but the grass took fire as the sun shone out and came near running through Bishop Millers company

---

32. Austin Cowles had been a trusted friend of Joseph Smith. He was first counselor to William Marks in the Nauvoo Stake Presidency, Charles C. Rich being second counselor. They were among the select group to whom the revelation on "Celestial Marriage" was read. Father Cowles accepted it, his daughter Elvira A. becoming a wife of Joseph Smith. Jenson, *Historical Record*, VI (May, 1887), 234.

In 1844 Austin Cowles had left the Mormons to act as first counselor to William Law in a new church.

33. In 1840 Thomas C. Sharp purchased the press at Warsaw which was publishing the *Western World*. He changed the name to the *Warsaw Signal*, a bitterly anti-Mormon publication which the Mormons said was "replete with the most glaring falsehoods." Sharp consistently advocated driving the Mormons from Illinois. After the death of Joseph Smith, Sharp was indicted by the grand jury as one who was responsible, but he was acquitted. He later changed the name of his paper to the *Warsaw Gazette*, which he was still publishing in the 1880's.

where there was two loads of powder but by great exertion & much excitement the fire was extinguished and the camp moved by order of President Young to the other side of the creek & put on the burnt prairie. Some of the hunters killed two wild hogs this evening hence the creek was called hog creek. Lewis Mecham came to me and told me this evening that he was my friend and had as good feelings for me as ever & so had his brother Moses & spoke in favor of some more of the old police who were in the company when it was removed from me at Locus Creek. I thought very little of what he said for when I left Locus Creek there was not one of them but declined driving one of my teams as an act of accommodation to me after they had been requested to do it by Col Rockwood. They well knowing I had a waggon & team for which I had no driver & they were only requested to drive for the day hence such empty protestations of friendship and good will towards me after deserting me in time of need & trouble looked very mean & groveling & made me think less of him than ever. I regulated the guard this evening I was very tired and sick this evening.

Wednesday April the 22nd 1846. The weather was warm, sultry with a damp heavy air & broken clouds Earley this morning the camp commenced moving. At 8 o'clock and just as we were going to start Louisa was taken sick and delivered of a daughter and we called its name Louisa. This was my first born in the wilderness as some of the old prophets once said and from the situation of our dwelling might be called a "Prairie chicken" We did not go to day in consequence of her being confined but herded our cattle as usual when we did not travil Most of the camp went today The prairie was set on fire today in the afternoon on the other side of the creek & I & some others went & set the grass so as to set a long string of fire which the wind drove furiously along as though it would devour every thing before it presenting a scene "fearfully grand" Allen Stout & his father-in-law came up today

In the evening it clouded up & rained uncommonly hard & wet our beds some were very wet but no harm done.

Thursday April the 23rd 1846. This was a dark heavy windy wet morning The fire was out I was up earley. Hunter and I went & saw Br Daniel Spencer and got some flour for we were out and in a suffering condition for provision. To day I weighed my children & Allen his. Hosea weighed 33 pounds Hyrum 15. and Louisa 8 pounds. Allen's Charles weighed 30 pounds. I went a hunting with J. D. Hunter down the creek but killed nothing. In the after noon it clouded up and rained hard again & cleared off beautifully again in a short after dark

This evening Col Scott returned from the settlements on Grand river. The Artillery being encamped here. He informed us that he came very near being mobbed & that the inhabitants manifested a very hostile spirit & that he thought they intended to give us trouble yet. He seemed considerably agitated on the subject His men were down there at work & he expected that they would be driven away immediately.

Friday April the 24th 1846. Today was clear warm & dry. I sent Allen & the two gun waggons on today & Hunter & I tarried This was done because there was not team enough to go all together. They were to go to the next timber or good camping place & send the teams back for us. Col Scott with the Artillery also moved on. The ox which we left in the prairie give out was brought on today by Charles Hales. This added strenght to our teams which were now too weak for our loading

There was many passed by today I was in camp all day. After dark a short time the boys came back with the teams for us.

Saturday April the 25th 1846. Today we moved on to the place where Allen was encamped a distance of about 8 miles. John W. Binley had returned from Grand river last night on my riding mare and put up in Heber's company and this morning Archibald Patten seized on her as his own property and told such a sentimental *bach* [batch] *of infernal* lies that he induced Br Heber to have him keep her for the time being but more of it hereafter —

This was a cold, windy, disagreeable day and the roads were very bad & some what hilly. I came in about 12 & the ox teams about 2 or 3. We encamped on the branch in the timber where we found Br Charles Shumway who professed great friendship to me. We talked over the gone by days of perils & suffering we had passed through which would have been a satisfaction had such friendship been real!!! My wife was getting along well & my afflicted family seemed to be in a fair way to be in good health. but while while here I discovered my children were taking the whooping-cough

This seemed to draw back the dark curtain of coming evil on my family which I so anxiously anticipated would be now so soon entirely withdrawn. The fatal consequences of which will be revealed a few pages hence.

There was a warm and moderate rain fell to night without any wind which hurried the tender grass so much needed.

Sunday April the 26th 1846. It was warm pleasant and cloudy, raining a little at times. Warren Snow, one of Col Scotts men in the Artillery & some hands came from Grand River. They stated that they had been ordered from Grand river by a mob & also some of the pioneers

They expected a general out-break against us by the Missourians immediately & seemed very much disconcerted. About Eleven o'clock Jesse D. Hunter went on & I and Allen tarried untill he sent back the teams. About one o'clock Chas Dalton & Nathan Young came back from the camp with six yoke of oxen after me & Col Scott. They had been sent for us by President B. Young knowing us to be in want of teams They staid all night.

Monday April the 27th 1846. To day was a warm, showery day Young & Dalton's cattle were strayed this morning. Job Hall returned with my cattle & for me this morning. He was thoroughly wet having come all the way in the rain. About one o'clock we started in the raind mud & mire. The roads would have been good had it not been for the incessant rains & continual travial, which made it nearly impassible We arrived in camp at four P. M. about five or six miles

This was what was called "the farm" then but was afterwards called "Garden Grove". When I came to the edge of the timber I found a number of men at work clearing & cutting house logs. It was a pleasantly situated place from the first appearance and presnted a beautiful thick wood of tall shell bark hickory the soil uncommonly rich & so loose now that our teams could but draw their loads through Farther in the timber commenced white oak land & a harder soil where I found the camp. All seemed to be engaged at work I had already been classed in a company of plough makers along with Hunter & a number of others

Business here seemed to be on the common stock order and all that a man had to do was to go to work. where he was told asking no questions[34]

---

34 Stout had missed the meeting on April 25, so did not know of the decision to open up a farm. John D. Lee kept careful minutes which were later incorporated into the "Journal History" of the church.

Jenson records: "On the 24th of April [1846] a place for a settlement was selected on Grand River, to which the name of Garden Grove was given. At the council, which was held two days after, three hundred and fifty-nine laboring men were reported in camp, besides trading commissaries and herdsmen. From these one hundred were selected to make rails, under the superintendence of C. C. Rich, James Pace, Lewis D. Wilson and Stephen Markham. Ten,

I was well pleased with the good order and businesslike appearance which the camp had assumed so quick in this "Magic City of the Woods" as it seemed to be. When I drove up Col Rockwood showed me my camping place adjoining Hunter a short distance from the rest or General Camp.

I was busily engaged untill dark pitching my tent and preparing for the night which was a very warm still and rainy one.

Tuesday April the 28th 1846. This was a warm drizzly morning and very disagreeable the mud from one end of the camp to the other was so deep that it was almost impossible to get around

The people were however generally at work. After breakfast Hunter and I went to see A. Patten about my mare as before refered to. He seemed to be determined to act the raskal. He said he would do as "old Boss Says" meaning Brigham and this was about all we could get out of him. At length he said he had promised to move Br Perry on here and he would use all the property which he got last winter to move him and he said it would take it all This Br Perry had put his property out of his hands to keep it from being used for the poor and the man would not give it up and after several fruitless trials he at last wanted me to take it up which I would not do unless he would let me have all that it was worth which he did and so I set Patten at it as my agent He procured a considerable amount & I let him have enough to pay him for his trouble & also let Br Perry have a large amount as much and even more that Patten thought was his due at the time for it was with great reluctance that I got him to pay him his last payment because he said it was too much but now that he had as good as stolen my mare which was a part of the property he was very benevolent & said that it would take all the property thus procured to move him after which I might have a part. To which I replied that he was only my agent and had nothing to do with Perry only as I ordered him and that I was the man to move him if any one was to do it on that property that I had a letter from Perry to that effect which showed that he did not look for him to move him and in as much as it took all the property to move Perry I demanded not only the mare but also all that he had which was a waggon & team to move him & I was determined to have it forthwith. This brought him to a stand & the matter here rested awhile. When I came to him again and showed him a letter from perry that confirmed what I said he said that the fact was Perry had enough allready and was willing to give up the mare and say that Perry did not merit any more help. Which showed that he only made Perry a pretext to wrest from me my mare and did not intend to help him at the time, which was worse than stealing and took this oppertunity to do it for he thought that there was such a prejudice now against me that I could not help myself.

After we had got through with Br Patten we went down on the bottom about a mile below camp to help Br Hill put a saw log on a pit for he wanted to saw it into inch plank for Brighams waggons and came back with a turn of the sick head ache.

About ten one of the cannon came in camp which Col Scott sent in by the oxen which Dalton & Young brought there to help him & me in camp but did not see fit to come himself

The weather was pleasant this after-noon. That I might have no further trouble about the mare with patten we laid it before Br Heber C. Kimball for Patten was willing to tell the truth now so the matter was considered by him &

under James Allred, were appointed to build fences; forty-eight, under Father John Smith [the father of the prophet] to build houses; twelve, under Jacob Peart, to dig wells, ten, under A. P. Rockwood, to build bridges. The remainder, under the direction of Daniel Spencer, to be employed in clearing land, plowing and planting." Jenson, *Historical Record*, VIII (August 1889), 885-86.

he saw Brigham & they decided that we should keep what we had for Perry had enough. Thus ended this matter now.

I was now out of meal & flour & went all round camp and could not get any for cash except of Br Henry Herryman [Herriman]. The people would not sell flour when they knew we were starving & some sick. The weather was dark and disagreeable this evening.

Wednesday April the 29th 1846. This was an uncommonly wet rainy, muddy, miry disagreeable day. Very wet night last night the ground flooded in water At twelve there was a general council called of all the men in camp to acertain who could go to the West for it was determined now to send 100 men without any families across the Mountians in time to put in as earley a crop as possible and to this end Br Orson Pratt made a report of the amount of thing necessary for a fit out for one hundred It was also determined by this council to instruct the Trustees at Nauvoo to sell the Temple and also the Kirtland House [Nauvoo House?] for the simple reason that we were going so far away that they not be of any service to us and the money was needed to help the poor away from among the Gentiles

The weather was good and the men went to work. I went with a set of hands to survey the North field and was out till near dark This field was never fenced.

Thursday April the 30th 1846. Cool damp dark foggy morning I worked some at plough making but not being well came home. Shadrach Roundy started to Nauvoo at 12 & is very sanguine that Babbitt is a good man and will do right in the things committed to him as Trustee but we will see. Br John D. Lee told me all was right and that the prejudice against Hunter & me would soon pass off that Brigham wanted to try us to see if we would stand in adversity and evil as well as good times.

Today there was a requisition made from President Young by Col Rockwood for the two men which Col Scott had sent here with the cannon, to go to the settlements to work as all the men were sent who could possibly leave, but they did not think that they could be required to go only by Scotts order for he had forbid them positively not to recieve orders from any one but himself. The question was with them whether Scotts orders could be countermanded only through him by a superior officer and the matter was refered to myself & Hunter merely as a matter of opinion when we declared that to us President Young's ordered always countermanded every thing else as he holds the Keys of the Kingdom and that he allways disobeyed every thing for him & so we had taught our men to deal with our orders upon which they went and left the cannon. I mention this for reasons which may be hereafter given.

This evening I wrote three letters for Br John D. Lee as he was over run with business one was to Captain Hendrix Great Chief of the Stockbridge tribe, one to Lewis Dana and one to George M. Herring a Mohawk They were to be sent by Brs G. W. Langley and C. Shumway I got through about ten at night and went home

Friday May the 1st 1846. Foggy, muddy, miry, wet wether; too bad Langley and Shumway started on their mission mentioned last night and Jessee D. Hunter & Job Hall & others to Grand river to work for Rockwood had called on Hunter to go there to hew timber. I was round the camp today & done but little only explored the windings of the creek & visited the bridge now in progress of building. Anna Jones came in today she had no word from Benjamin Jones her husband since he went to the settlements to peddle. Their things were yet at Pleasant Point on Medicine Creek & she wanted them brought on here.

Saturday May the 2nd 1846. Sent James Allred & Green Taylor to Pleasant Point after Jones things with an ox team which left me and Hunter's family destitute of any help for my men were now gone and I had to herd cattle today though I was scarcely able to walk It was a lonesome day to me after being so much accustomed to the hum of public life to be in the prairie confined to a herd of cattle and sick at that I came in before night almost fainting with the sick headache. In fact during my stay here I was almost confined to my bed & some times felt that my constitution was giving away.

Sunday May the 3rd 1846. Br Samuel Thomas, one of the guard who had been sick all the way, died last night & was buried today

At ten o'clock there was a meeting Orson Spencer[35] preached and was followed by President Young who taught on the duty of this camp which was to do the things which were immediately before us and that was now to make a farm here for this was the will of the Lord to us now after which he said something about the Lord leading this camp in a way which we knew not as we had so often read For said he who ever thought that the Lord would lead us through Iowa & into Missouri & then back into Ioway again He said he knew that the Lord lead us and he did not care for the consequences as long as the presence of the Lord was with us Another meeting was appointed in the afternoon which was prevented by a hard rain

About dark President Young called a council of all the Captains in the camp near his tent at which Br H. G. Sherwood & others were appointed to go on and look out another location and then regulated the work for tomorrow and decided that this field must be fenced before we go any further. At dark I went on guard & staid till one o'clock relieved by Keneda [Charles Kennedy]

Monday May the 4th 1846. This morning I was called out of my bed by Col Rockwood to go to work after being up untill one and having a sick family to attend to the rest of the night. The weather was clear and cool. I went to girdling timber with Br Benson. The boys came back with Jone's things today. I did not work in the afternoon because I was out of provisions however I got some flour from Br Thomas Grover[36] before night & some meat from the Commissary.

Tuesday May the 5th 1846. Clear, Cool, drying weather road some better Girdled timber with Benjn Jones and W. J. Earl. In the evening we had another thunder storm and hard rain.

---

35. Orson Spencer immediately moved his family to Nauvoo when his brother Daniel converted and baptized him into the Mormon Church.

At the time of the exodus Orson Spencer moved with the first group, but under the hardships and exposure his wife grew ill and died, leaving him with six small children. At the time of this entry she had been dead for just two weeks (March 12, 1846).

Within a short time Spencer was called to fill a mission to England, where he presided over the mission and published *The Millennial Star*. Upon his return he was made chancellor of the University of Deseret (1850). In 1855 he was sent to St. Louis to edit the *St. Louis Luminary*, but poor health and strenuous duties resulted in his death on October 15, 1855. See also Vol. I, Part 1, footnote 28.

36. Thomas Grover was born July 22, 1807, in New York. He became a Mormon in 1834, and helped to build the temple at Kirtland. He was a member of the High Council in Kirtland, Far West, and Nauvoo. He became a bodyguard for Joseph Smith, helped to rescue him several times, and was in many ways so helpful that the prophet presented him with a sword in appreciation.

It was Grover's wagon which had the accident in the river of which Stout wrote so vividly. Later he was superintendent of the ferry at the Platte River, and remained behind to ferry all the companies across. He came in with the company of C. C. Rich.

In the fall of 1848, Grover went to California with about thirty men on the "Gold Mission." He worked in the gold mines and collected $20,000 in gold dust for tithing from men in the mines. His home was in Farmington, Utah, where he died February 19, 1886.

Wednesday May the 6th 1846. Clear and warm again. Had nothing to eat again. Hunted for flour till noon but got none Worked in the after noon.

About 4 o'clock there came another storm and the wind blew from the south. East to the North West at first but it shifted entirely around before it was done It blew like a huricane the trees fell all round the camp some close to my tent one fell on one of Br Lee's Mules and some on some cows. We had to hold up my tent in the storm for my wife and child was sick and it seemed that it would blow down every moment but no harm was done. At dark it came off cleare and warm. I had nothing to eat now

Thursday May the 7th 1846. Warm still and cloudy. We have nothing to eat yet. This morning Br Ephraim Green's wife was brought in to camp from Grand river dead & was buried here About nine o'clock I got parched meal enough to make one mess

Took a walk over the bridge with W. J. Earl both being very lonesome.

Last night Erastus H. Derby was caught in bed with a certain girl in camp and a lot of boys upset the waggon putting them to an uncommon nonpluss and disappointment. The girl afterwards threw a cup of hot coffee in the face and eyes of a young man whom she suspected to be engaged in it and almost scalded his eyes out.[37] I understand that Derby has since denied the faith and went off whining into Missouri.

Friday May the 8th 1846. Clear & cool good weather. This fore noon I assisted Br E. T. Benson to hew some timber to be sawed into plank to fix his waggons to move on West. In the after noon was not able to be out. The mail came in to day from Nauvoo bringing news that Br O. P. Rockwell had been taken prisoner in Nauvoo and taken to Carthage but have not learned the particulars I suspect that there has been some treachery used by some or he could not have been taken as it seems to me.

Good clear dry weather. I was sick in the fore noon. In the after noon I went out in company with Benjn Jones into the wood being very lonesome and was talking over our feelings when I was sent for and informed that my little son Hyrum was dying. I returned immediately home and found the poor little afflicted child in the last agonies of death. He died in my arms about four o'clock. This was the second child which I had lost both dying in my arms. He died with the hooping cough & black canker He had worn down ever since he first took it as before mentioned. I shall not attempt to say anything about my feelings at this time because my family is still afflicted. My wife is yet unable to go about & little Hosea my only son now is wearing down with the same complaint and what will be the end thereof. I have fearful forboding of coming evil on my family yet We are truly desolate & and afflicted and entirely destitute of any thing even to eat much less to nourish the sick & just able to go about my self. Arrainge-ments were made to bury him this evening.

Business was lively at this time. There was a long string of log houses now being put up on the East & on the west of the farm for the accommodation of those who were going to stay which gave the appearance of a civilized country again.

Sunday May the 10th 1846. Warm clear and dry weather.

Attended to the funeral obsequeys of my child about ten or Eleven o'clock

---

37. Of this incident John D. Lee wrote: "Thursday May '46 . . . the next morning Emiline Haws beleiving & pretending that Benjamin Denton was concerned in upsetting the waggon the previous evening threatened revenge & while at breakfast about 8 o'clock threw a cup of boiling coffee in his face which penetrated his eyes Doct Sprague was immediately called to his assistance, & conclude it doubtful whether he would ever see again." Lee, "Camp of the Saints," 60-61.

About the same time meeting commenced Jeddediah M. Grant spoke on the first principles of the gospel. There was quite a number of Gentile men & women here today at meeting & hence his sermon I was at meeting a short time and went home. There was another meeting in the after noon. President B. Young spoke on the subject of the ownership of the Farm least there might be some difficulty about it hereafter. It was however voted by the congregation that as it was made by those who were going on for the benefit of the poor who should follow that those who go on should own it subject to the Presidency who should be left in charge of affairs here.

Monday May the 11th 1846. I was uncommonly sick this morning & had some bodily symtoms of being confined with a hard spell of sickness consequently by the advice of Doctor Chandler Rogers I consented to take a regular course of Lobelia.[38] This was the first time ever I had taken it. & it made me so weak & nervous that I could not raise my head and my stomach so irritable that I could not take all that was designed for me It however helped me. William Hunter came from grand river with some meal for me which was indeed greatly needed

Tuesday May the 12th 1846. I was very sick and feeble yet. Jesse D. Hunter came home from Grand river to day with the teams which we sent there from Locus Creek by J. W. Binley to fed on corn and prepared for the journey but instead of that he had rode the horses down & they came back much reduced instead of being improved. In fact I learned from Hunter what had been reported ever since he was gone, that is he was acting the rascall in every thing he went about. Instead of making reports to me as he was to as he had charge of my men he reported to President Young & endeavoured thus to make court to him by running by me & telling my men all the time that it was understood between him & me & that he was recieving letters of instructions from me from time to time which was a most palpable lie When Hunter went down there he settled all difficulties between him and the men as he did not wish the work to be stayed notwithstanding Binley's rascality but more hereafter I was able to walk to the East of the farm today and my health and strength improving A part of the camp commenced to move today and crossed the bridge and most of the ballance were preparing to go. About dark it clouded up and rained again to the great anoyance of those who intended to move

Wednesday May the 13th 1846. Most of the camp moved on to day Just as President Young was starting[39] he called at my tent and enquired into my & Hunter's circumstances & we told him He then said for us to do the best we could to move on and he would send back for us as soon as he could and that he wanted me to continue to keep charge of the public arms

This entirely broke up our arraingements for there had been nothing said to me or Hunter about what was required of us & we were like to be left here without any requisition upon us by the authorities in the event of which we intended to tarry here and raise a crop as our means were now about exhausted, but this order made it obligatory on us to go on so we had to calculate accordingly My health was better to day

I sent Green Taylor & William C. McLelland back today with the two waggons which I moved here in leaving me without any but the gun waggons to move in

---

38. Lobelia is an herb that was widely used as an emetic and purgative. Dr. Priddy Meeks administered it for many ills and spoke of it as "that blessed Lobelia," but its reactions were so violent that most doctors soon discontinued its use.

39. Brigham Young left the beginnings of a settlement at Garden Grove under the direction of Samuel Bent, David Fullmer, and Aaron Johnson, while he moved ahead to establish another stopping place.

& they were full of the publick arms hence I was in a poor situation to move. In the evening it rained again William H. Edwards died today. He was one of the pioneers and was appointed Contractor for the first 50 in the Second hundred as organized at or near Chariton on the 27th of March last. He was one of the "old Police at the time that it was first organized under Joseph Smith Mayor and Johnathan Dunham High Police man in December 1843 and served as such untill he was led away with James Emmett in his uncouncilled exit to the wilderness in the fall of 1844. He was in all the troubles in June when our prophet & patriarch Joseph & Hyrum was assassinated & stood firm in all these difficulties I have faced the the chilling blast many a winter night with him in Nauvoo guarding the city against our foes from within & without. He left Emmett and returned to Nauvoo in 1845 and seemed willing to do his duty faithfully from that time till his death This was a wet night.

Thursday May the 14th 1846. Cold North wind today & cloudy but clear in the afternoon

This last requisition of President Young yesterday made it necessary for Hunter and me to calculate fast so we concluded for him to go to Grand river again for another supply of provisions before we went on and he accordingly started to day in the meintime I was to keep every thing right in camp as well as I could although I was yet very weak and feeble.

Friday, Saturday, Sunday, and Monday the 15 - 16th, 17th and 18th of May. the weather was clear cool & dry and I was in and about the camp nothing of importance took place except now and then some starting on who had found their lost cattle

Tuesday May the 19th 1846. The weather was still clear & cool as before I had concluded to put projections on the gun waggons if I could so as to thus make room for me to move as that would help accordingly I laid the thing before (Genl. C. C. Rich)[40] who agreed to help me but he did not neither did he seem to take much interest in it any way and I was not able to work & so it turned out that it was not done Had Rich used his influence he might have done it for he had a number of hands with him and some were carpenters but he would not turn them out as I would have done had he been in my place however it matters not.

Wednesday May the 20th 1846. Rainy all day. Teams arrived here for William Weeks[41] & others who had been left here but none for me & Hunter which looked

---

40. Here Hosea Stout has clearly written the name of "Genl. C. C. Rich," and then in a different colored ink and evidently at a later date, drawn a line through it as though to blot it out.

41. William Weeks, the architect of the Nauvoo Temple, was born April 11, 1810 (one source gives the year as 1813), at Martha's Vineyard Dukes County Massachusetts. Nothing has been learned of his background or training, but in 1841 he drew the plans for the temple, subject to the approval of Joseph Smith. He also designed the baptismal font and carved the first of the twelve oxen which supported it, leaving the others for Elijah Fordham to do.

Weeks was present at the capstone ceremony and was one of the first to receive his endowments after the temple was finished. When he left with the exodus, the finish work on the temple was left for Truman O. Angell.

Lee mentions him as being present at a Brigham Young family meeting, where he was singled out for special attention. Here Stout infers that the leader is more solicitous for the welfare of Weeks than for that of the law enforcement officers. Weeks traveled west in the Jedediah M. Grant company, arriving in the valley in September 1847. During the fall he became dissatisfied with the restrictions and left, without the consent of the local authorities. He spent the winter in the Ogden area because he could not stand "so much bondage." In the

very much like we were forgotten. Late this evening J. D. Hunter returned from Grand river with our provision. He found Binley & my men and also all the hands there at variance again and very much dissatisfied upon which he let Capt William Meeks & Allen Talley & some more of my men know how he had treated me and agreed to let them deal with him which they did that night and all his rascality was exposed and they ralleyed on him without reserve.

It appeared that F. R. Tower was also as bad as Binley for he was his clerk & both had been in the habit of getting drunk on the hard earnings of the boys and had proven themselves consumate villians after which by the consent of Hunter Captain Meeks & all the rest of my men returned home after their families leaving Binly & Tower to settle with those who were left. They were a set of faithful men to me even to the last & they shall be gratefully rembered by me yet when circumstances will allow.

This F. R. Tower is the same one that I sent to Warsaw last winter as a spy and ever since he has manifested strong symtoms of the "Big Head" which I fear will yet prove fatal to him.

Thursday May the 21st 1846. Still raining yet but ceased after breakfast after which Hunter & I took a long walk on the road towards the next camp consulting in the mein time the most expedient course for us to pursue.

It was at last arrainged for him to go on and for me to tarry untill he sent for me unless Brigham should send before he got there. As all my waggons were gone now I put up another tent as I had a public one which was very fortunate for me as I need more room. In the evening it clouded up and rained and blew very hard the wind continued all night

Friday May the 22nd 1846. The creek was very high this morning and the ground flooded by the rain

About ten o'clock Hunter started taking one of the gun waggons with him & leaving one which was all the waggon now left me & it full of guns.

Saturday, Sunday, Monday & Tuesday the 23rd, 24th 25th & 26th of May. I was in and about home weak and feeble & just able to look after my cows and horses. No news of importance.

During this time my little & only son Hosea seemed to be growing worse & his cough seemed to be settling on his lungs I repaired little Hyrum's grave on Tuesday as I expected to start soon & never see it again.

Wednesday May the 27th 1846. This evening we had an unusual hard rain storm The water came down in torrents wetting almost every thing in the tents which made my child worse

In the midst of the rain & gross darkness Pleasant Green Taylor, my wife's brother came to the tent wet thoroughly. It was very unexpected to us. He said that his mother and all his folks were eight miles from here and on their way to the next farm. He said also that there was a war between the United States and Mexico and a great excitement in the state about raising troops to March to the relief of General Taylor in Texas who had already had two battles with the Mexicans. I confess that I was glad to learn of war against the United States

---

spring with three other families, he started back for the states. They met the large Mormon emigration near Chimney Rock, but Weeks did not go to visit with Brigham Young.

According to Lee: ". . . fear Seased hold of Wm Weeks, from the fact that he had made way with Team & waggon that had been left in his care by Pres. B. Y. . . ." Cleland and Brooks, *A Mormon Chronicle*, I, 53.

At the general conference in the Salt Lake Valley, October 29, 1848, William Weeks was excommunicated from the church. He is not to be confused with "Captain William Meeks" in the same day's entry. See footnote 28 preceding.

and was in hopes that it might never end untill they were entirely destroyed for they had driven us into the wilderness & was now laughing at our calamities.

Thursday May the 28th 1846. The weather was warm & pleasant with broken clouds. Job Hall & William Taylor returned with the teams after Hunter had arrived in safety to the next camp. So we immediately set about being off About ten o'clock we started and went eight or nine miles and camped in the prairie. It rained some to night but not so as to distress us.

Today my wife was able to walk a short distance and occasionally ride on horse back which was the first time she was able to move otherwise than in a bed made down in a waggon

It seemed like new life to see her even thus recovering from a long sickness.

Friday May the 29th 1846. We started earley this morning. Nothing of importance took place untill noon. The roads thus far were quite muddy About noon we took a road leading to the right and went 8 or 9 miles and encamped for the night and was over taken on the way by F. R. Tower & M. H. Peck who were going to the next camp to get some council from President Young. Tower was going to exculpate himself and J. W. Binley from the odium of their conduct as before refered to He was sure of succeeding for he spoke very sarcastically to me about it which showed that he treated the feelings of those concerned with utter contempt for thus daring to sencure his conduct. I will now say in advance that when he came to Brigham and made an attempt to justify Binley Brigham very sternly asked him if he took up for Binley and would not even hear him but told him that Binley was an infernal scoundrell and not to undertake to plead his cause to him This Tower said himself to Hunter He applied for privilege to work on grand river this summer and fit himself out which Brigham readily granted and he returned Since then I have not heard from him.

These men went on being on horse back It was a beautiful country where we encamped tonight.

Saturday May the 30th 1846. We started on this morning and went about one mile along a very bad road and met Peck & Tower returning. They said that had been twelve miles on ahead and over took a man with a waggon & team and learned that this road went to the Raccoon Fork of the Des Moines to a garrison.

We returned back immediately & met two more waggons coming who had been led off by seeing us on this road. About two o'clock we got back to the right road again thus we lost one day and about 18 miles travail. We here met my wife's mother & all her people and many more of my old neighbours in Nauvoo The meeting of which was quite joyful.

We traveled on untill near night & encamped in the prairie. Tonight Allen Taylor's wife was delivered of a child. All was wright however in the morning.

Sunday May the 31st 1846. This morning all was well & I concluded to go on to camp on horse back it being about 15 miles for I had understood that President Young was going on tomorrow & I wanted to see him before he went on to know what he wanted me to do next as I had now fulfilled his last order to me which was to come on I started about 9 o'clock and came into camp about twelve and found the Saints at meeting all seemed cheerful

This was a wet disagreeable evening All things in relation to Hunter and myself were about as usual

This evening Br Noah Rogers died. He was a captain of ten in the guard He returned home to Nauvoo from a three years mission last winter to the Sandwic islands He was a good man and a faithful captain while under me in the guard. I staid at Benjamin Jones all night.

Monday June the 1st 1846. It rained and blew very hard till noon and then ceased. My family came in the evening. They camped last night on a hill in the prairie and had a very disagreeable time of it. I went to the North of this place to hunt a location with Chandler Rogers and came back and went East with Hunter and there found one to suit me

It was in a beautiful grove of small hickory and formed a pleasant shade and was a delightful place. Here Hunter and myself intended to build & put in a crop such as would come to maturity at this late time of planting.

This place was called Mount Pisgah and the main settlement was situated on a long ridge running North & South. To the west was a large deep valley or bottom land of good prairie and was now being plowed & planted while all the adjoining glades and groves were teeming with men & cattle engaged in the busy hum of improving and planting The whole woods & prairie seemed alive to business & a continual streem of emegration pouring in which looked like the entire country would be inhabited as a city in a short time

Tuesday June the 2nd 1846. President Young started to day to the Council Bluffs. Some of his teams however were gone before about four miles and encamped. He did not say any thing to us as to what we must do. So we went to arraingeing matters for farming in good earnest

About noon General Charles C. Rich came to me with a written order signed by Brigham as Lieutenant General ordering him to take the public arms into his possession and put them in good order and send them on by "Col Stout or some trusty officer" He wanted to know what I could do I told him the situation of my family and circumstances and he thought it could not be required of me to leave my family under such circumstances and thus released me from going & I then went and showed him the guns and desired him to take them away. He had a like order to take the artillery from Scott.

I confess that I did not understand the object of this move neither did I care for it released me from all public care and responsibility and I felt like a free man with nothing on my mind but to contrive how to take care of my family for the best Accordingly Hunter and myself went and laid the foundation of a house a piece on our beautiful location and was going to move to it as soon as our cattle could be found. But however before our cattle were found President Young having returned to this place came to see us. He wanted us to go on with the guns and leave our families here and wanted to know what we could do about it We told him we were always ready to obey him, and would do any thing which our circumstances would permit He then enquired into our situation very particularly & found us to be very destitute, and after giving Hunter some money as he had none told us to buy provision for our families untill we could return and come as soon as we could and left us. Here again we were entirely disconcerted and now all together gave up the idea of raising a crop and it seemed that it was designed by some over ruling power that we should not "Sow nor reap" neither enjoy the peace and happiness of a private life any more. We saw nothing but a long train of public cares and responsibility hanging over us for we knew it would not end at the Bluffs.

Wednesday June the 3rd 1846. This morning Br George W. Harris left me and went on because matters took such a turn that he thought it would be to long & uncertain to wait for us to go.

In the evening with Br Miles Anderson I went to where Brigham was encamped four miles on ahead to see him about how to arrainge for my family. He told me to bring them along or any part of them if I could for it would save having to send back for them and that Genl Rich had orders from him to fit me out so I came home and commenced to fix to go as soon as I could.

Thursday June the 4th 1846. I went to see General Rich this morning about the waggons for the guns and having lumber sawed for preparing them according to Brigham's orders and was engaged at it most of the day. Alen Stout went to the settlements today with his father-in-law Miles Anderson and was going to stay there and take care of some cattle for him untill he went to Nauvoo after his family when Anderson would bring him on. I sent B. Jones along to Bring up a yoke of church oxen which were there to draw the gun waggons.

Friday June the 5th 1846. Was hunting after some one to saw some lumber today as we had prepared logs and trying to obtain help from Rich who never even used his influence to assist me much less fit me out as Br Brigham had ordered him.

Saturday June the 6th 1846. Was after Br Rich again to no purpose for he still evaded any help or using any influence However I got some lumber sawed and commenced work at my waggons.

Sunday June the 7th 1846. Was at meeting Br O. Hyde was there and spoke to the people Most of the time was taken up in procuring teams & means to fit out the Twelve This was according to council But there was nothing said about the guns and I plainly saw that Br Rich did not intend to do any thing for me

It appeared that he thought that I was obliged to take them any how & if I got no help it would only be my own trouble.

Monday, Tuesday, and Wednesday the 8th, 9th and 10th of June. I was engaged in preparing the waggons.

Thursday June the 11th 1846. Today Br Robert Johnson owner of one of the gun waggons came after it. I went to see Genl Rich about it. He said it could not go and for me to fix it for the guns so we had and had the guns put into it and covered over with plank screwed on over the bed. It was done in good order when Br Rich had it given up and all our work was lost and we left in a worse fix than ever we now had but one waggon for guns

Friday June 12th 1846. A man by the name of John T. Gurthrie came here today. He was a brother-in-law to Adam Perry as mentioned before in relation to the property which Patten had endevered to wrest from me at Garden Grove. He also came to get some more & went to the Presidency[42] about it whereupon Hunter & myself were cited to trial forth with. We let him tell his own story and did not make any reply But after some insinuations being thrown out by the Presidency that we had acted dishonestly They concluded that they had no jurisdiction in the case. After it was over I told them that we did not care what decision they made any how for we did not intend to make any plea because the matter had been acted upon by Brigham & Heber and we would not give away to anything that they might decide upon untill it went there again. I then told the particulars to Br Rich who seemed well satisfied but notwithstanding he went secretly and advised Gurthrie to write to Brigham about it I mention this because it appeared to me in every move that Br Rich made while I was here that he was my secret enemy and doing all that he could against me which I consider a very ungrateful thing for I had always been his strong friend and was always ready to step forward to help advance him even when it militated against me as it often did But let him prosper in it.

Today a company of Gentiles came in and it created a great excitement as all the guns lay in the yard by my tent but we covered them up and placed a guard

---

42. The presidency here referred to consisted of William Huntington, Ezra T. Benson, and Charles C. Rich who had been left to preside over the settlement of Mount Pisgah. During the stay there an epidemic broke out which took many lives, William Huntington's among them.

over them They came to see if we were preparing for war as they they had heard but went off well satisfied that we were not.

Benjamin Jones returned from grand river to day The cattle which he went after had also been brought in the mein by S. H. Earl and were given up to Seeley Owen by Br Rich and thus disappointed me again Owen had put them into the church & tryed to get them back from Brigham & failed but was more successful with Br Rich after Brigham was gone.

Saturday June the 13th 1846. I had an opportunity of going to the Bluffs today as a man named John Van Cott was going on and had an empty waggon & two yoke of cattle but my cows were strayed which prevented me from going. In the evening I laid the foundation of another house as I intended to leave my family in it and go on with the guns. But when I concluded thus & told Br Rich about it he seemed pleased & I suspected some evil again which put me to my studdies to know how to ascertain how to find out as you will see I did soon.

Sunday June the 14th 1846. Went to meeting today There was considerable said about the brethren stealing when it was voted to put down all who did

Monday June the 15th 1846. Today I concluded to go in two waggon accordingly I put all the gns [guns] in one & some of my things & the ballance of them in another General Rich had let me have another waggon since he gave up the one to Johnson So when I concluded thus and had arrainged my affairs to go I told General Rich what I had done which brought out the thing I was after last Saturday. for as soon as I told him he seemed surprised and disappointed and told me that he had hoped that if I could take all the guns in one waggon and go on that he could have the other for Elder W Woodruff this explained the whole matter He had been urging me to go on with the guns in one waggon and leave my family in the other which he thought I was going to do and as soon as I was gone intended to take the other waggon away from my wife and leave my family without any shelter but a tent which would not shield them from the storm and all this to be done in my absence In fact I have good reasons to believe that he intended to take the tent also but he did not acknowledge that to me Had I not have suspected some rascality I should have left my family and that was what induced me to undertake to move to such a disadvantage

I thought it best to move from hill to hill with my family and effects if it should take me all summer rather than to leave them in Pisgah where such a friend could take some unknown advantage of them

I have spoken thus about him but it is contrary to my custom notwithstanding I wish him well and only want to keep myself where he can have no power over me and let him rise or fall on his own merits I am even willing to befriend him yet as I so often have done but never to trust myself in his power I am now perfectly satisfied that he is a most secret and an inveterate enemy of mine and for what reason I know not. His course did put me back a long time and prevented me from executing the orders of Brigham and caused me to go through the most deep affliction all the way to the Bluffs Now that I have said what I have about him I will say that I shall notice how he prospers hereafter and see if all is well

Tuesday June the 16th 1846. Today I intended to start but my oxen were gone so Hunter & I had a settlement about our property as he was going to stay and we did not know when we would meet again. I wrote a letter to Allen Stout and all was ready to start in the morning.

Wednesday June the 17th 1846. This morning I was ready to start. I traded for a little one horse waggon before I went which was of great service to me in my crouded situation. I had no one to drive team for me. The way I had to start was to borrow a harness of Hunter and one of his boys went with me to the next timber about four miles and then I had to come back with the Harness, and one of the girls drove the one horse waggon When I crossed the bridge I met with Henry Hepker who lent me a chain. He was in company with Br Titus Billings and they were going on and agreed to help me

The prospect seemed to brighten a little but was dark enough yet for I had no driver & three waggons and not very well and not more than three days provisions on hands. After some arraingements with Billings & Nebeker I went on the four miles and encamped but on the way the big bolt of the gun waggon broke and gave me new trouble however the waggon kept together and no other injury was done.

Thursday June the 18th 1846. Today I got the bolt mended again and all things ready to move on.

Friday June the 19th 1846. This morning I went back to the bridge to see what became of Br Billings and company as I could not find them & was now waiting for them but when I got there I learned that they had gone ahead so I was again disappointed I then went back and Br John H. Tippetts who was camped near me kindly let me have a one horse harness and sent a boy with me about 8 or 9 miles ahead to another good camping place accordingly we thus set out and on our way was overtaken by a black boy named Peter Manning who wanted to drive a team for some one who would take him to the Bluffs and I took him in This was a great relief to me as I was unable to see to the cattle and horses and do what was necessary on the journey for I was very feeble and liable to lay myself up if I continued to over exert myself. I now only wanted a one horse harness to be ready for a tolerable move. I will say here that my cows which had strayed at Pisgah and prevented me from going with Br Van Cott had never been yet found & I had to go on with out them We came to the creek before mentioned & found no one there. We put up here & then boy went back with the borrowed harness I found Peter a great help to me.

In the evening some four or five waggons drove up and among the rest was Br John Dailey who said there was another good camping place three miles ahead where I intended to camp tomorrow night.

Saturday June the 20th 1846. This morning I went some three miles to Henry Mours [Mowers] camp to see Br. S. Wixom to try and get some meal for hunger began to grin hard around us but I got none and was now entirely out and knew not where the next meal would come from so my wife went to preparing our dinner which might be properly called our "ultimatum" It consisted of a small portion of seed beans & a little bacon boild and made into soup we had flour enough to set it out & in fact we this last time as it seemed had a more luxurious & sumptious table than usual which made to a stranger an appearance of plenty. Just as it was ready Elder Henry G. Sherwood & Jas W Cummings rode up very hungry I invited them to stop and turn out their horses & rest and take dinner to which they readily consented little thinking that they were going to help make away with all I had and then leave me in this wild & desolate place to risk the kind hand of Providence for the next. We had a joyful time and plenty to eat but none left They were on their return to Nauvoo after their families in case they did not meet them on their way. Br Jas W Cummings was now on his return from the mission with John L. Butler to James Emmett as mentioned on the 25th of last march at the Chariton, Br Cummings reported that when he got there he found that Emmett was absent having gone to some of the neighbouring Indians to trade off some horses and consequently he had no trouble with him. But some of his company were yet strong advocates for him & some as hard against him among the latter was his wife who was tired of his oppression & tyranny.

The two parties were about equally divided. Some of the party however having gone before to the settlements near or above Fort Leavenworth. They managed to get all of those who were yet there to move down to where we were to cross the Missouri at the Bluffs not however without considerable opposition from Emmetts adherents. Suffise it to say that they all left and came off and brought every thing with them and left Emmett to guess at what had happened & follow on or do whatever else he thought best. They had all come to the Council Bluffs & Emmett followed on and was here striped of his kingdom and him & all his followers put under Bishop Miller and sent on to Grand Island. Thus ended the reign of this man who sought to divide and to lead off the Saints &c

After our "ultimatum" was ultimately used up & we had all joyfully feasted & enjoyed ourselves sufficiently they went on & I also prepared to go by attaching my little waggon to one of my large ones for the want of a harness & one of the girls took charge of the horses Thus arranged we started slowly on our way. Previously to our starting however I made out to procure of those who had encamped here last night some bread stuff to last a day or so. We started about three o'clock leaving them here for their waggon was broke down. Dailey had lied most shamefully about there being a good camping place three miles ahead for we traveled on untill night & went about eight miles & encamped in the praire and no signs of timber yet

Sunday June the 21st 1846. We started very earley this morning on our way we met Thomas Williams, who was on his way from the Council Bluffs to Pisgah with an express to Genl Rich. He said that it was to raise men to send over the Mountains. That it was contemplated to raise a guard of four hundred men, a sufficient number, as it was deemed, to protect those who were moving, against the depredations of the Indians and this was the object of the express There could not be the requisite number raised at the Bluffs because there had not a sufficient number come on & hence the express. They intended to go on in time to put in wheat this fall.

We traveled on very steady untill about noon and came to a beautiful little grove in the midst of a boundless praire as it looked Here we found Br Billings and those who were with him encamped They had stoped to wash and fix up and so we overtook them. The prairie which we had last passed was 15 or 20 miles across. Mostly a level good road.

We put up here for the day & found Br Billings and most of those with him very kind and accomodating and more especially when they found that we were sick and afflicted as we were

In the evening Brs Orson Spencer & C. Shelton came on and encamped here also. which made a very large company.

Monday June the 22nd 1846. This morning we all went on and made a good days's travel going perhaps 18 or 20 miles. We crossed the Little Platte to day and went on two or three miles and encamped in the prairie on a small stream.

Tuesday June the 23rd 1846. We also made a good days travel to day and came to the Nodaway and there encamped

We passed by Henry W. Miller's company to day who were encamped while they went down to the settlements to trade for provisions. Here we saw several Indians which was the first that we had seen since we left Nauvoo Today was a dark day at times raining some but good for traveling.

Wednesday June the 24th 1846. We lay up to day it being a wet day. In the evening Bunnell & Clark drove up in the rain with their companies. this now made a very large encampment

Thursday June the 25th 1846. The weather was still heavy and like for rain There was quite a number of Indians came to camp to day some we fed They were all friendly

Little Hosea was all this time on the decline and the laying on of hands seemed to do but little or no good but to day we concluded to call in all the men & women who had had their endowment and have the ordinance performed according to the Holy order & with the signs of the Priesthood Accordingly we did so in my tent Br Spencer taking the lead which seemed to do some good for the child was better afterwards & we felt incouraged that he thus seemed to appear to be under the influence of the ordinances of the Priesthood and we now had hope again that he would yet be delivered from from the power of the destroyer. But our hopes were destined to be of short duration for in the evening there came one of the hardest rains that had been this summer.

The water came in torrents & the wind blew hard. In a few minutes our tent was down & the water ran through the waggon covers and thus every thing we had was wet almost before we knew it.

The beds were also wet and Hosea was soon discovered by his mother to be lying in water so fast did it come in on the bed. He was immediately taken worse and thus our last hopes for him vanished

The rain continued an hour or so and before dark the Nodaway was out of its banks notwithstanding it is a stream That is very deep being about twenty feet banks. The bridge across it is about 8 or nine feet below the surface of the level ground and it was thought by us before this rise that the water would never come up to the bridge. At dark the bottom was like one continued sea and some of the tents and waggons standing in the water.

Friday June the 26th 1846. To day the weather was cloudy & sun-shine alternately The Nodaway had not fallen much. The ground yet flooded and the whole camp seemed to be driping in water.

There was many friendly Indians came & went to day. My child was more dangerously ill. Br William Clayton came here from the Bluffs going to Pisgah & Thomas Williams on his return from Pisgah to the Bluffs both water bound

Br Clayton crossed by flotting his things over in his waggon bed & swimming his horses which took a long time for there could be but little taken in at once & Williams swam his horse & thus both crossed to day. There was a continual crossing of the Indians all day swimming their horses which seemed to be but little disadvantage to them to come to a stream out of its banks.

The stream before night had fallen some five or six feet.

Saturday June the 27th 1846. Clear and warm. My child was still worse The water falling very slowly. It had not yet uncovered the bridge

Some of the brethren went today to the next creek about four miles to see what was the prospect of crossing there and found it much larger than the Nodaway and still rising and the bridge either gone or damaged so that we could not cross on it

There was plenty of Indians here today They were going to the Buffalo country to kill their winter meat It is about one hundred miles and among the Souix Indians with whom all other tribes are at war These are Pottawottamies & Musquakas. They not only expect to kill all the buffalo they can but also all the Souix. So it is a war expidition as well as a buffalo hunt.

My child seemed strangely affected to night after laying hands on him we found him to [be] troubled with evil spirits who I knew now were determined on his destruction He would show all signs of wrath to wards me & his mother and appearantly try to talk. His looks were demoniac accopanied by the most frightful gestures I ever saw in a child. His strength was greater than in the days of his health.

At times I felt almost to cowl at his fierce ghastly & horrid look and even felt to withdraw from the painful scene for truly the powers of darkness now prevailed here. We were shut up in the waggon with nothing to behold or contemplate but this devoted child thus writhing under the power of the destroyer It was now late in the night & he getting worse when we came to the conclusion to lay hands on him again that the powers of darkness might be rebuked if he could not be raised up. Thus alone my wife & me over our only and dearest son struggled in sorrow and affliction with this last determination that we would not yield with the portion of the Priesthood which we had to the evil spirits After laying hands on him and rebuking the evil spirits he took a Different course He ceased to manifest a desire to talk & his ghastly and frightful gestures and with a set and determined eye gazed at me as if concious of what had been done

We thus beheld him a long time until finally he became easy and went to sleep Late at night we went to sleep also leaving a burning candle in the waggon.

Sunday June the 28th 1846. I awoke very early this morning and immediately discovered my child to be dying. He seemed perfectly easy and now had given up to the struggle of death and lay breathing out his life sweetly. The evil spirits had entirely left him and he now had his natural, easy, pleasant, calm and usual appearance but death was in his countenance and his little spirit now in the enjoyment of its own body only seemed loth to give it up as almost every one seemed involuntary to observe who was present. He gradually and slowly declined untill forty minutes after seven when its spirit took its leave of its body without any appearant pain but seemed to go to sleep.

Thus died my only son and one too on whom I had placed my own name and was truly the dearest object of my heart. Gone too in the midst of affliction sorrow & disappointment In the wild solitary wilderness. Surrounded by every discouraging circumstance that is calculated to make man unhappy and disconsolate. Without the necessarys of life, Without even our daily bread and no prospects for the future. There in this wild land to lay him where the silence of his peaceful grave would only be broken by the savage yells of the natives seemed to come in bold relief before us. Discouraged, desolate & such frequent disappointments as had lately been my lot and no reason to expect any thing better in future could now only occupy my mind & the mind of my wife the bereaved mother We had now only one child a daughter left & that was born on the road & what was its fate was it to be laid by the way side also & we left utterly destitute & disconsolate

I have often heard people tell of loosing the darling object of their heart. I have often heard of people mourning as for the loss of an only son But never untill now did I fully feel and realize the keen & heart rending force of their words. I have once lost a companion for life and left without a bosom friend Left alone to lock sorrow and disappointment up in my own breast. Left to smile in the midst of the merry & happy but to smile only to hide and disguise the effects of an overflowing heart of woe. But not then did I feel the loss or mourn as for an only son. This last loss. This loss of my only son. This my hopes for comfort in my old age. This the darling object of my heart gone seemed to cap the climax of all my former misfortunes and seemed more than all else to leave me utterly hopeless. But I shall ceace to indulge in my feelings any longer

Suffice it to say that every attention and kindness was now proffered to me that I needed on the occasion. There was a good coffin made for him. After which we all moved on and buried him on a hill in the prairie about one mile from the Nodaway where there was the grave of an infant of Br John Smith and then pursued our journey leaving the two lovely innocents to slumber in peace in this solitary wild untill we should awake them in the morn of the resurrection We traveled four miles and encamped on a ridge in sight of one of the Pottawattamy villages. In the evening some of the brethren went to the next creek or river to see what the prospects were for crossing and found the bridge impassable and decided to build a new one This stream is called the Nishanabothany by the whites and Nickanabotany by the Indians and is a very large stream and now out of its banks and very deep and muddy.

Br Phinehas R. Wright came on to day from Pisgah He informed me that there were some officers of the United States Army at Pisgah with a requisition from the President of the United States, on us for 500 soldiers to march to Santa Fe against Mexico & from thence to California & there to be discharged and their arms given in at the expiration of one year. This officer's name was Jas Allen Capt of the First Dragoons He had issued a circular to the mormons making known the object of his visit

We were all very indignant at this requisition and only looked on it as a plot laid to bring trouble on us as a people. For in the event that we did not comply with the requisition we supposed they would now make a protest to denounce us as enemies to our country and if we did comply that they would then have 500 of our men in their power to be destroyed as they had done our leaders at Carthage. I confess that my feelings was uncommonly wrought up against them This was the universal feelings at Pisgah and Genl Rich sent me word by Br Wright to keep a sharp look out for him as he passed and see that he did not get any knowledge of the public arms which I had. For he supposed that he might be looking after them. Such was our feeling towards the President &c

This officer passed here today but I did not see him as I was encamped some distance from the road.

In the evening There was large numbers of Indians came into camp all friendly and seemed to understand perfectly well the nature of our move and also our ultimate union with them & our return to the lands of our inheritants &c &c.

Monday June the 29th 1846. To day all the men who possibly could leave their camps went down to work at the bridge I did not go but staid at home to fix up and to arrainge my affairs as they were now much out of order

Tuesday June the 30th 1846. To day I worked on the bridge. There was plenty of hands even more than could work to advantage. They had appointed a Foreman but all would not yield their oppinions to him and consequently there was much contention and confusion amongst them & but little done. They under took to build a Frame bridge and this evening failed to sink a bent in the deep water and abandoned it & thus lost all that had been done thus far

This morning Elder Parley P. Pratt came here accompanied by Solomon Hancock[43] on their way to Pisgah to try and forward the expidition to the Mountains and instructed us to push on with all possible speed that if we did not get to the Bluffs by the time that he returned it would be needful for us to go on and

---

43. Solomon and Levi Hancock, brothers, had been in the Mormon Church almost from the beginning. Solomon worked on the Kirtland Temple, came west with Zion's Camp, and then was selected to return to Kirtland that he might receive his endowments there. At the time of the Missouri troubles, the Hancock brothers were able to secrete and keep sixteen guns, which were later brought to Nauvoo.

At Far West the Hancock brothers were considered men of judgment and opposed to violence. The brothers wrote original songs and verses, played the flute and violin, and worked in lumber and shaped wood with their turning lathes. At Nauvoo they lived near the home of Joseph Smith, and he visited them so often that people generally recognized that they had the full confidence of the prophet.

That Solomon Hancock, now an older man, should accompany the United States recruiting officer and speak in favor of enlistment into the army was evidence that he had great influence among the people.

leave our families such was the necessity to push forward this expidition. The reason of which we could not imagine Neither did he as the sequel will soon prove.

As Elders Pratt & Hancock came here this morning they came to creek about one mile the other side of the indian village the bridge of which was also gone & our hand[s] now building it as well as this one. In an attempt to cross it by swimming his mule Br Pratt & the mule came very near being drownd. He floted to shore and was so much exhausted that he could not get out. After resting awhile he attempted it again and came near being drowned the second time. I believe he was finally assisted over by some indian boys, not however untill they were satisfied that they were "Good Mormonee" as they call us. He left Br Hancock & went on but he came on and followed as soon as he could. Br Pratt was in such a hurry that he would not wait an hour or so for Br Hancock such was the emergency of his mission.

Wednesday July the 1st 1846. To day all hands went to work at the bridge. Earley in the morning a lot of them met there before the rest and appointed a new Foreman and commenced work. But as soon as the rest came they were not satis-fied with him and so they had a new election and appointed a new one again this was Raymond Clark. He was more fortunate than the to others who preceeded him. For all hands went to work under him appearantly well satisfied. His plan was to rebuild the old bridge or in other words to build on the place where the old one was which was on a large raft or as some call it a drift on which the former bridge was built. He succeeded in uniting all the hands in his opinion so that they all went to work and about sun down finished it. This might have been done the first day had the matter been planed & executed as it was today by a competent foreman. At noon I went home and stayed there the rest of the day. On my way home I met a large company of hands coming to work on the bridge these were the men belonging to Henry W. Millers company which had just arrived and encamped Our encampment now was very large The hills were full of our tents & waggons and seemed to be nearley as large as the first camp when it started in February.

Thursday July 2nd 1846. We commenced moving again to day There was a general rush to cross the bridge. Every one seemed to be afraid that he could not get over before it would be gone. Which created a great deal of confusion and some feelings In fact the bridge looked as though it would not last long for as the water [rose] it put in something of a "bad fix"

The next bridge which was about one mile ahead and had also been finished yesterday came very near breaking down. But it was soon arrainged so that it was safe

There was large companies of Indians followed us today for several miles and in fact they thronged around us all the time we were building the bridge & at times would come in droves to the camp but they were very civil friendly & good natured and done none of us any injury while we were here.

They would amuse themselves sometimes by swimming in the creek in large numbers and sometimes at playing cards at which they seemed to be very dexterous. They appeared to be much interested at our opperations while at work which seemed to be a great novelty to them.

We travelled about 18 miles today and encamped in the prairie just after crossing a small deep stream. Here we found a good cool, clear spring of water.

Friday July the 3rd 1846. We started very earley & drove hard and my oxen give out after we had went about 12 miles & the company went on and left me. It was a point of timber after crossing a creek and a good place at which there was a beautiful spring that I had encamped Here I was left in a destitute situation For my provision had given out while at the Nodaway and we were driven to the necessaty of boiling corn to sustain life When we started to travel after finishing the bridge we prepared some to travel on which had now given out and left us with nothing for our supper untill we could boil more which could not be done tonight. I will here state that while with Br Billings, a man by the name of Henry Nepeker, who did not belong to the church kindly let me have the use of two of his cows which furnished us in milk but not as much as we needed He also in the mein time gave me a piece of bacon and lent me ten pounds of flour and was in fact very kind to me. I mention this because I tried to procure provision of the brethren who would not let me have it for the money neither lend it to me They knowing my situation.

We were now left without the use of the cows and entirely left destitute and what to do we knew not But a Br Daniel Wood and his company came up after a while & he let me have a peck of meal very reluctantly I also procured a few pounds of flour from another man which relieved us. this time & we felt again satisfied.

Before night this encampment was filled with a large camp for the brethren were coming in untill dark.

A short time before dark we saw a carrage and horsemen coming from towards the Bluffs & many supposed that it might be the United States officer & some one thing & some another But it proved to be President Brigham Young, Heber C. Kimball and Willard Richards of the Twelve and they were escorted by G. W. Langley James H. Glines Thomas Williams and Joseph S. Scofield

They were on their way to Pisgah & Garden Grove. I had a few minutes interview with President Young who briefly told me that they were going to comply with the requisitions of the President of the United States and furnish the 500 men demanded and that there was a good feeling existing between us and him & all was right & that they were going to Pisgah & Garden Grove to raise the men &c. Their presence seemed to give new life to all the camp who flocked around them and asking so many questions that they could not answer any of them But after a few words of comfort to us they went on.

Saturday July the 4th 1846. This morning I proceded on my journey slowly for my team was very weak and the weather hot & sultry. After traveling about six miles we came to another Creek at which there was a small grove.

This was called Cag-Creek [Keg Creek]. Here my oxen was about given out again. We turned here and rested and watered our cattle and remained untill five o'clock and then started again in the cool of the day We traveled about three miles and encamped in the prairie There was a hard storm & rain to night but we did not get wet.

Sunday July the 5th 1846. This morning I went on it being warm clear & pleasant. We did not go more than a mile before we came to some camps which were the outer camps of the main encampment although the Ferry across the Missouri was yet twelve miles. We did not go for [far] from this first part of the Grand encampment before I went on and left the teams to follow as fast as they could.

I went on in search of Elder Orson Hyde as he was the one now to consult in the absence of the president. I found him on a fine ridge which I called Hyde's ridge He was just starting to meeting. I made known to him my situation and the orders of Brigham to me and desired him to let me know what to do. He was entirely ignorant of what was wanted or required of me. He seemed to manifest a soft feeling for my situation and requested me to come & camp by him. He then went to meeting & I to meet my teams which were now not for behind. I accordingly encamped by him as he had requested my cattle being now worn down again.

After resting while I piched my tent and prepared to be as comfortable as I could for I expect to stay here some time

In the evening I went with my wife to see her mother who was about one mile down on the point of this ridge Our feeling on meeting was very tender without a word being said we all burst into tears in remembrance of the loss of my little son Hosea.

From Mother Taylor's I went, leaving my wife there to see Captain James Allen the United States officer and found him on another ridge neatly situated under an artificial bower near his tents with several men in attendance having the "Striped Star Spangled Banner" floating above them. He was a plain non assuming man without that proud over bearing strut and self concieted dignaty which some call an officer-like appearance. I came up and commenced a conversation with him. In a short time after which he at my request related in a short consise and intelligable manner, the circumstances of which led to and the famous battles fought on the 8th & 9th of May last on the Rio Grande near Metamoras between the United States & Mexico and which was the beginning of hostilities between the two nations.

The particulars of which I need not relate I was much pleased with his manner as a gentleman notwithstanding my predjudice against, not only him but also the goverment which he was sent here to represent From here I returned to Mother Taylors after my wife and went home

Monday July the 6th 1846. To day I went to the river to see Rockwood and others and try to find out what I had best do and moreover to learn what the President intended for me to do next as I had executed his last order to me. On my way thither I fell in company with Col. Scott. He was very friendly but did not seem to take any interest in my wellfare any way. I learned from him that he and Rockwood was still engaged in a "Punic War" with each other about their right and rank over one another and he came very near giving Rockwood a "brushing" as he said not long ago. I passed through the Indian village which consisted of some scattering houses and was mixed up with French & half breeds All not amounting to many. This was where they kept their trading houses & a large business no dout is carried on[44]

I found Rockwood at the Ferry. Br Lee had just started to Missouri to trade & I did not see him. Rockwood said he would help me and told me where to go and get meal without an order which would amount to begging on my part so I did not do it. I concluded that I would rather starve than live thus ignominously in the midst of the Saints He knew that the president intended to have me provided for but could not tell what to do for the present.

I crossed the river. The hill is uncommonly steep on the other side The landing was at the mouth of a deep ravine up which it was now contemplated to make a road as it would not then be a very steep hill to assend. I went with Rockwood O. Pratt. G. A. Smith and some others up this ravine to explore it in view of making this road It was heavy timbered and the wildness of its appearance was yet undisturbed. The hill very high on either side We were sometimes near being led off by ravines coming into the one contemplated for the road and it was truly a "wildering maze" more than a public road.

We traced it to its head and found it a good and practable rout for a road. It intersected the road I should think one mile from the river by way of the road but not more than half a mile up the ravine

---

44. This village was Point aux Poules, located on the east bank of the Missouri River opposite Bellevue. Peter A. Sarpey operated a ferry and trading post there for the American Fur Company. The Mormons used Sarpey's ferry until they could establish one of their own, fifteen miles upstream opposite Winter Quarters.

On my way home I fell in company with Father Harris & had a long talk with him, he advised me to enlist & go with the soldiers to Santa Fe as he said taking all the circumstances together. I then returned home again as I went not yet knowing what to do.

In the evening I saw & related the same to Br Hyde whereupon he advised me to go to Br Luther Bunnell and see if he would let me have something to subsist upon but it was like Rockwoods help for me to beg it so I did not go.

I was now left without recourse to look to or hope for I had to make my own arraingements to live or starve before the President returned

Tuesday July the 7th 1846. This morning I went to a mill on Musquto Creek about four miles from here. My object was to try and hire out there as a sawyer that I might make something to live on I intended to make a permanant arrainge- ment for work as the way was entirely hedged up for me to travail any further and this employment suited me. It was an uncommon rough road there. I did not get any work to do Neither was there much business going on

When I returned I was very sick and remained so all night so this last resort to obtain something to eat proved futile nor could I have done anything had I met with an oppertunity because of my health which seemed from all appearance to be on the wane.

Wednesday July the 8th 1846. I was engaged most of the day to day in over- hauling my goods to select such articles as I could do without and take them down to the settlements and try in that way to lay in some provisions Which was but a "furlorn hope" for my health would not admit of my going if the opportunity to sell was ever so good.

Thursday July the 9th 1846. Was unwell all day & was over-hauling my goods as before We had a fine cooling & refreshing shower this after noon.

Benjamin Jones came on to day from Pisgah. He informed me that my brother Allen was very sick while in the settlements as mentioned on the 4th of last June and that Br Anderson had taken him and his family to Garden Grove and left them there and gone back after his family.

Friday July 10th 1846. This was a rainy showery day. I was very sick, weak, and nervous all day and did not leave my tent

Saturday July the 11th 1846. I was some better to day & went to Br Jones but was very weak & nervous

A man came here today by the name of Kane.[45] He was from Washington. He said that we had nothing to fear and all was right between us and the

---

45. Thomas L. Kane was one of the most effective friends of the Mormon Church. He had visited Nauvoo in September 1846, immediately after the evacuation of the last Mormons and had been so impressed with the city, itself, and so repelled by the attitude of those who had driven them out, that he followed the camp of his own accord to assure the Mormons that no evil was intended by this call to furnish men for the Mexican War.

In a private council meeting held on August 7, following, Kane gave the leaders some sound advice which John D. Lee recorded thus:

Col Kane remarked that Ex-Governor of Mo our great enemy expects to be Execut- ing office of the upper California — yet I will endeavor with the help of my friends & yours to secure you a Territorial Government Independent & it would be to your advantage to draft a series of resolutions — in them remind the President of his promise to us & that you feel assured that his motives are purely for your good & in return for the high toned general & Philanthropic course that he has taken in our behalf will ever be his greatful Friends & the Friends of the Government Elder Richards asked Col Kane for his name & nativity. Thomas L. Kane fathers name Judge Kane corner of Locust & Schuykill 7th Street Philadelphia George F. Lehman esq Post Master Philadelphia. . . ." (Lee "Camp of the Saints" 87.)

Government &c   He was quite an intelligent man notwithstanding he was uncommonly small and feminine.

After some considerable conversation with some of the Twelve they went away to meet in council with him for he had some papers for us but more of him hereafter.

Sunday July the 12th 1846. Went to meeting today at Elder Taylor's camp Elder Wilford Woodruff[46] first spoke   He related his travels on his last mission to and from England whither he had been gone near two years.   It was very interesting.

He was followed by Elder P. P. Pratt who spoke against abominable practice of swearing which was so common amongst us and particular amongst the young men & boys   He then spoke at length in favor of sending off the 500 troops to Santa Fe and explained it to the satisfaction of most of the Saints   Indeed it needed considerable explaining for every one was about as much prejudiced as I was at first.

I went home and stoped at Jones on the way   When I got home I was just able to get around and was in tent all the rest of the day.

Monday July the 13th 1846. This was a rainy morning and the wind blew hard untill nine o'clock when it cleared off and was fair weather when I went to a meeting at Taylors camp again as previously given out yester   for the purpose of organizing the soldiers into companies.

There was a large meeting today. President Young and those with him having returned home again were present and all spoke on the policy of sending off the troops

There was four companies organized to day   The officers were at the request of the soldiers nominated by President Young & the Twelve

Jefferson Hunt[47] was elected captain of the first company.

Jesse D. Hunter captain of the Second

---

46. Wilford Woodruff was born in Farmington, Hartford County, Connecticut, on March 1, 1807. In his youth he had experience with running a flour mill and a sawmill. He was converted and baptized by Zera Pulsipher in 1833. The next year he went to Kirtland and in 1838 joined the western trek of the Kirtland Camp. He remained in Clay County (Missouri) in the home of Lyman Wight for a time and then devoted himself to missionary work in which he was very successful. Two of his companions were A. O. Smoot and Jonathan H. Hale. Due to his work as a missionary, Woodruff missed the persecutions of Missouri. In 1839 he moved to Quincy, Illinois, in the vicinity of Nauvoo. He spent the years 1840-41 in England on a mission; returned again to England in 1844 and arrived back in Nauvoo in 1846, just at the time the Saints were leaving Nauvoo. Because of his long absences he was not a part of much of the violence of this period, nor was he initiated into some of the practices. Woodruff had been ordained an apostle on April 26, 1839. He was to become president of the Mormon Church in 1889, and to be the one who issued the "Manifesto" abolishing the practice of polygamy in 1890.

47. Jefferson Hunt was born in Kentucky on January 20, 1802. While he was young his parents moved to Illinois. Here he was converted to Mormonism in 1834, and moved on west with the church to Clay County, Missouri. He left that state with the general expulsion of 1838. In Nauvoo, Hunt became a major in the Legion; in 1846 he enlisted in the Mormon Battalion where he was captain of Company "A," taking with him a family consisting of two wives and seven children. Upon his discharge from the Battalion he returned to Salt Lake Valley in October of 1847, but was immediately sent back to California to secure cuttings, seeds, and grain. Later he acted as guide to the company designated as the "Sand Walking Company" which, instead of following Captain Hunt's directions, took a cutoff and so gave Death Valley its name.
Hunt's family home was in Provo from 1849-51, when he went with Apostles Lyman and Rich to colonize San Bernardino, California. With the approach of Johnston's Army, he returned to Utah, settling first at Huntsville, which was named for him. He then moved to Cache Valley, and later to southern Idaho, where he died in 1879.

James Brown[48] captain of the third and Nelson Higgins[49] captain of the fourth

To day Br George A. Smith gave me an account of Col Kane the man from Washington spoken of before.

Col Kane & Elder Little from the East he said were the ones who brought about the order for the 500 mormon troops and that it was done as a special favor to us by the President & that they brought the dispaches to Col Kearney Commander of the West, who detailed Capt. James Allen to us to execute the same. This made the matter plain and I was well satisfied for I found that there was no trick in it

To day Peter the black boy left me.

This evening Elder O. Hyde who had moved over the river to the main camp there, came here to his camp and called a meeting and spoke at length to them on the law of adoption.[50] The first sermon I ever heard publickly. He desired all who felt willing to do so to give him a pledge to come into his kingdom when the ordinance could be attended to but wished all to select the man whom they chose &c

Tuesday July the 14th 1846. This morning earley I went to Taylor's camp to see President Young to learn what to do if I could or whether he intended to keep me any longer under his orders.

I saw him and had a long interview with him. He said that he wanted me to keep with him & as soon as General Charles C. Rich came he wanted a complete and thorough military organization effected but did not say on what principal but did not want anything done or said about it untill after the troops were gone as it would retard that movement to commence anything new. He enquired into & I related to him my situation and the suffering that I had passed through in executing his last order to me at Pisgah. At which he seemed to sympathise & said that he would assist me & for me not to go off peddling but might have my goods

---

48. James Brown was born in North Carolina in 1801. In 1838 he joined the Mormon Church and later moved to Nauvoo. When he entered the Mormon Battalion he was chosen captain of Company "C." He was sent with the sick detachment from Santa Fe to winter at Pueblo, Colorado, in 1846-47. From there he marched with his detachment to Fort Laramie and on to the Valley of the Great Salt Lake, where he arrived on July 29, 1847. A few days later he was sent to California to draw the pay due his company, and upon his return was one of the settlers of Ogden. He died September 30, 1863, as a result of an accident in a molasses mill.

49. Nelson Higgins was born in New York in 1806 and joined the Mormon Church in 1834. He had been a member of Zion's Camp in the march from Kirtland, and was in the difficulties of Missouri. He served as captain of Company "D" in the Mormon Battalion, taking with him on this trek his wife and eight children. On September 18, 1846, he was assigned to take the families who were along with the Battalion to Pueblo, Colorado, where they spent the winter. His group joined with that of James Brown and entered the Salt Lake Valley just five days behind Brigham Young and his pioneers. He died at Elsinore, Sevier County, Utah, on September 20, 1890, aged 82 years.

50. The "Law of Adoption" grew out of the concept of "kingdoms, principalities, and powers" in the "Celestial Worlds." Joseph Smith had sealed to himself a number of his most faithful followers, among them the first members of the Council of Fifty, to help to establish the Kingdom of God upon this earth and to share his exaltation hereafter.

Following that pattern, Brigham Young had adopted at least forty young men with their wives and families in a temple ceremony. Many of these added his name to their own and are often referred to by contemporaries as "A. P. Rockwood Young," or "George D. Grant Young," while others indicated the relationship by inserting a middle initial as "Adam Y. Empey" or "David Y. Candland." In the same way, John D. Lee had about twenty persons sealed to him and referred to them as "James Pace Lee," "Truman Gillett Lee," or "Samuel Gully Lee," etc.

Since some of the apostles had been away on missions, they had not heard of this plan, and so could not share the possible glory. Here Orson Hyde is definitely trying to secure some adopted children; later Heber C. Kimball explained that he had "lectioneered" with all his might for some. The whole plan became the subject of so much controversy that it was all dropped and the practice abandoned.

ready He borrowed 109 pounds of flour for me of Elder Woodruff and let me take it home with me and said if I could borrow any thing that I needed he would see it paid This was truly a favor for we were out & had borrowed flour for our living most of the time since we had been here My prospects for living seemed to brighten for he acted like a friend that was willing to help in time of need.

He called the place on which Taylor's camp was situated Chime Ridge because He lay on the chime of a barrel last night in a waggon

Wednesday July the 15th 1846. I went to Taylor's camp this morning & James Bird told me that he had procured 1900 pounds of bread stuff for me which he said was done by order of President Young to Elder Taylor. I forgot to mention yesterday that the President when enquiring into my circumstances was very particular to know how many I had in family & how many teamsters I would need which would in all be 8 upon which, he, it appears gave Br Taylor orders to procure me provisions for 8 persons for one year. This was very unexpected to me for he did not say any thing about it to me when I saw him yesterday.

There was a meeting at Br Taylor's camp in the evening to which I went & there saw Br Taylor who also informed me of the provision thus procured and seemed very anxious for me to take it away to night but I could not for I was not able to go home and then come back again so I staid to meeting

Elder Pratt taught the soldiers not to misuse their enemies when they fell into their hands neither to take or spoil their property but to remember that they were our fellow beings to whom the gospel is yet to be preached For them to set them a pattern of virtue & honesty &c While here I saw Br J. D. Hunter who had now come on. He told me how that he had located himself after I left him and had procured a crop of corn sufficient to do him and was in a fair way to do well when Brigham came to Pisgah and called on him to go in the army with the command of captain He also informed me that he had found my cows & that they would be brought on by his family who would soon follow him.

I hunted my cattle some to day which were strayed at this time

Thursday July the 16th 1846. This morning my horses were gone; having by some means got loosed. Went with my wife to Taylor's camp to take sacks to put in the meal & flour which Taylor & Bird had procured for me but did not get it because Br Taylor said that he had collected for Eight & learned that I had none at present but my family and wished to have it before the council but said he did not know but what Br Brigham understood it. I was very much dis- apointed for I was hardly able to go about so I returned home determined to see no more about for I did not believe that he wanted me to have it.

The troops were still preparing to go There was five companies organized in all and Daniel C. Davis[51] of Montrose Ioway was elected Captain of it

When I came home I was allmost give out and sick.

Friday July the 17th 1846. I was at home all day very sick and feeble There was a meeting at Taylors camp today at which there was a number of Bishops appointed to look to the families of the soldiers

---

51. Daniel Coon Davis was born on February 23, 1804, in New York. He had lived in Montrose on the Iowa side of the Mississippi River opposite Nauvoo. As captain of Company "E" of the Mormon Battalion, last to be mustered in, he had marched to California, accompanied by his wife and youngest son. His four other children were left behind with friends at Council Bluffs.

Upon his discharge from the Battalion, Davis re-enlisted and was placed in command of some one hundred men who also signed for an additional six months' service. He settled finally in Davis County, Utah, which was named in his honor. He died on June 1, 1850, at Fort Kearny, Nebraska, while on a journey east.

Saturday July the 18th 1846. Br Freeman found my horses to day & I rode out some to look for my oxen but was still weak and feeble.

Sunday July the 19th 1846. Hunted oxen some in the morning and then went to meeting at Taylors camp. Was with Capt Hunter. We saw Br Gillett who had been Col Scotts Clerk untill he came to Pisgah. They had fallen out and he seemed to be outrageously mad at Scott He told us that Scott was doing all that he could against Hunter and myself & that he had been teaching his company & predjudicing them against us all the way from Nauvoo and that he rejoiced at all the adversity which he could learn that we were in that he boasted that he was ahead of me now & would be to all eternity. that he was very mad at what Hunter & I said at Garden Grove about his two men going to work upon Brigham's orders his to the contrary notwithstanding, and many more reports of foul slander & scurrility such for instance as his holding keys independent of and equal to Brigham &c.[52] This was if true a mean principle in Scott for I had been his friend all the way & so had Hunter

Further he said that I had been & was yet trying to undermine him & get the Artilery away from him & to this end was leagued with Col Rockwood & that we were using all our power & influence to overthrow him &c &c

Taylor & Bird told me that all was right about my provision and for me to come and get it Went home & Hunted oxen & found one yoke

Monday July the 20th 1846. I got Br Buhunan to take my oxen which I had into his drove. Then went to Taylor's camp and there saw President Young again He wanted to know if I would organize a Cohort. I told if he would tell me on what principal he wanted I would He said that he was not quite ready for it yet but that he expected to stay here & some would go over the river that is those who chose to and those who stayed would assist in helping the poor from Nauvoo and else where. I went home and rested awhile and then with my one horse waggon back to Taylors camp to bring home the provisions which Taylor & Bird had procured for me. I there recieved of Bird which he had collected 6 dollars & 25 cents 5 bushels of meal, one of corn one of wheat. 12 pounds of flour & a small lot of bacon about 12 pounds and came home about dark

Tuesday July the 21st 1846. Dark, cloudy, rainy, Wrote some in my journal Went to Perkins Camp for flour that had been put in by that company to Bird but could not get it without an order for thus had Br Taylor ordered it. Hunted oxen some found one yoke

Wednesday July the 22nd 1846. Went to Taylors for the order for flour of Perkins and got it and came home sick and was laid up all day. In the afternoon it rained and blew very hard.

Thursday July the 23rd 1846. Went to Perkins camp after the flour before mentioned and got 275 pounds and then came home and went to Taylor's camp again for some corn and other thing which Bird said he would have for me but did not get any for the simple reason that those who had subscribed it were gone or concluded not to let it go. I will not neglect to state that those who thus subscribed for me did not know to what use it would be applied, but only give it liberally because it was needed by request of Elder Taylor. I did not recieve any more. which made it fall far short of the amount required by Brigham

---

52. John Scott's claim of "holding keys independent of and equal to Brigham," refers to the fact that he had been commissioned by Joseph Smith earlier than Brigham Young to be a member of the Council of Fifty, with the charge and responsibility to help establish the Kingdom of God upon the earth. All were acting under power from Joseph Smith.

Friday July the 24th 1846. Today I Hunted oxen on the creek & was at Taylors camp and got one yoke. I eat a lot of choke cherries today on account of their astringency for the disease of my bowells & they entirely cured me. I had been long troubled with diarhea which was like a consumption on the bowels & often proves fatal to those afficted with & this I thought was a very simple & cheap remedy.

Saturday July the 25th 1846. Hunters family came on today bringing my cows along & stoped at Taylors camp whither I went & got them & then Hunted oxen

We had the hardest wind to night that I have felt in a long time. It blew down my tent leavin all my meal & flour and most of my trunks exposed to the pelting rain We had hard work to hold on the waggon covers after it ceased I put them in the waggons.

Sunday July the 26th 1846. I was unwell today which was spent mostly by the family drying cloths & such thing as had been wet last night in the storm. My flour and meal was not injured much neither did anything get injuried any of consequence notwithstanding the amount of rain which fell on them

Monday July the 27th 1846. Hunted oxen some Passed by Taylor's camp and there saw Brigham again He spoke to me again about organizing a Cohort I now learned from him that he wanted the second Cohort of the Nauvoo Legion revived and that was what he wanted me to do

I also learned that he was going to stay over the river if not go on to Grand Island. He also told me to move over as soon as possible for he wanted me there

I now began to see what his designs were in relation to the military for he still intended to recognize the organization of the Nauvoo Legion which would of course cause me to take my place as the Brigadier General of the Second Cohort But how a cohort or a Brigade could be organized I could not tell for there was not men enough here now to make a regiment much less a Cohort

Tuesday July the 28th 1846. Went to the river to see what the chance was for encamping & crossing over for I now determined to go and leave the lost oxen if I did not chance to find them Had a storm & tent blew down again

Wednesday July 29th 1846. Hunted my oxen to day on the praire as I had heard that some stray oxen were out there but did not find them. While out saw Gillett & spoke to him to act as my clerk in the Legion in the event that I should need one. In the after noon I went in the timber & found one more yoke of my oxen. I now had but one yoke gone & determined to leave them

Thursday July 30th 1846. This morning I started to cross the river leaving the oxen which were strayed I was the only male person to do all the business on the journey & had three waggons. We moved as follows I put two yoke of cattle on the large gun-waggon as it was much the heaviest and attached the little one horse waggon to it for the want of a harness. This I drove The next waggon was drawn by one yoke and was driven by my wife, who understood nothing about driving oxen, and one of the girls drove the two cows & one lead the horses. We crossed Musqueto Creek at the upper bridge as the lower one on the main road was gone or spoiled Here we stopped and took dinner and rested our cattle for they were even now given out although we had gone only about a mile

The weather was intensly warm & it seemed that we should all faint together with our teams After dinner and when our oxen seemed to be somewhat rested we started on

The road from here goes to Taylor's camp and just before it gets there passes a verry high steep ridge The top of which is no[t] level but immediately commences to descend as steep as ever. It is something dangerous to lock a waggon on it because if you go a few feet too far it will pitch down the hill if you stop a few feet soon soon you are not up the hill & consequently the cattle cannot finish the ascent. Before attempting to rise it however I had to leave one waggon & double the team. The first waggon went over without much difficulty.

In going up with the second the cattle came near fainting and would stop on the steepest places and pant as if it was their last but by much whiping and a great deal of abuse to them I got them to the top and also down. No accident happened but the cattle was entirely given out. I took off the yokes & turned them out. I was in the mien time taken with a sun pain in the head or as some call it "Sun Struck" which came near taking my life. I lay in the shade of the waggon for hours unable to do any thing. It caused a high fever to rise on me

Neither myself nor any of my family knew what was the matter with me. Had circumstances called for a little more exertion from me at this time there is no doubt but it would have proved fatal. Towards night it clouded up and turned cool which revived me & the oxen and we went on about three miles and camped at the big slough in the bottom prairie

Friday July the 31st 1846. I had new trouble this morning for my horses had gone back to the bluffs to Taylors & when I returned with them the oxen were gone however I got them and went on. It was a wet morning & when I came within three miles of the ferry the road was so muddy that the oxen could go no further. There was no pasture for the cattle between here and the river. I tried several to assist me to the river but in vain. But fortunately I found a man going to the river with two yoke of oxen and got the man to put one yoke on each of my waggons and thus I got to the river, stopping a short time at the village to trade for some articles which we needed. When I came to the Ferry I tied up the oxen and went over with the intention of going to the main camp to see Brigham to know what to do next but met him about half way coming to the Ferry in a carriage & Heber, Orson Pratt, & John D. Lee with him. I left my horse with Peter the black boy that was with me and returned with them as we went back They were agitating the subject to stay near where the main camp now is or go on to Grand Island which resulted in the decision to stay. When I returned back across the river I sent my mare over to Peter who was on the other side who said he would take care of them untill I came there. I done this because there was no feed here for them. Here I expected to stay all night and prepared accordingly For Cutler & Cahoon's companies were crossing and were about half over

But fortunately for me all of Cutler's part of the company having gone over Cahoon not wishing to break in on his company by sending one boat load over tonight gave me the liberty of crossing It was the last load for the day and so I unexpectedly got over It was at sun down. Br Conover and some more who had cattle there assisted me up the first steep rise out of the boat into the mouth of the ravine up which the road now ran where I staid all night & had to chain up my cattle to keep them from straying in this wild mountainous place notwithstanding they had not eat any thing since morning. other wise all was well.

Saturday August 1st 1846. The cattle looked uncommonly bad this morning. The road up the ravine was nothing but a deep clay mud and my team was not able to draw me up to the top of the hill. There was a large drove of oxen and other cattle swam over the river this morning belonging to Cahoon's company & perhaps some others I was in hopes that they would help me out of the ravin & then I could go on to the camp without further trouble But in this I was mistaken for about the time that his waggons began to cross his son William F Cahoon came to me and wanted me to crowd my waggons a little to one side in this narrow

defile and let them pass and done it in such a way that I plainly saw that he did
not intend to help me as was the custom in passing up this place

I told him that I could not but he insisted on me trying so I put my oxen
on and drew my waggons to a narrow place in the road where a single cow or
horse could not pass without climing on the steep hill side and there stoped nor
could my team go further for there was a deep mud hole just before me which
I could not pass

After a while the old man came up himself and wanted to know what my prospects were for getting out & seemed to be very anxious about it

I told him that there would be teams from the camp to assist me after awhile.
He wanted to know when. I told about nine or ten o'clock

His waggons by this time had been sent over untill the ravine was filled
from me to the river & he could wait no longer & seeing that I was in no hurry
for I told him that I was going to take my cattle to the prairie to eat some for they
were starving and by that time I thought the teams would be here whereupon he
immediately sent team sufficient to move me to a good comfortable place about
half way up the ravine where I could camp and left me and went to drawing his own
teams up This much to his credit when he had some thirty or forty yoke of cattle
doing nothing on the bank of the river. This was fairly squeezed or spunged out
of him and when he got his own private waggons up he put out to camp & left the
rest to get out the best way they could so said some of his company.

We here took breakfast and began to make arraingements to stay all day for
I intended to take the cattle to the prairie to graze for they were very hungry and
weak & I did not intend to work them any more till they had recruited themselves.

Before we got breakfast over Father John Tanner[53] came from the camp with
a team to assist those who needed it to get up the hill and he turned in and helped me
up and learning that I had the public arms he assisted me on to camp He manifested a great interest in heping me when he found that I had public property.
We had no no difficulty in going to the camp.

On our way thither we met Brigham and others going to the river he told
me to select a clean place as near the springs as I could get and encamp near him.

This was the most singular springs I ever saw. It came out of the ground
in a place where there was no hills only on the side of a common declivity and
affords watter sufficient for the whole camp. In fact there was a continual dipping
of watter out of it which did not seem to lessen the stream

The cattle looked uncommonly lank for it was in the afternoon before I came
into camp and they had "Fasted" for about thirty six hours and kept in a working
or toiling most of the time.

There was numerous hosts of Indians strolling about camp all the time They
were the Otos and Mohas or more properly the Omahas. and differed widely in
appearance from the Pottawattamies on the other side of the river. They were
not so well dressed. Instead of good blankets they were at best dressed in old

---

53. John Tanner was born August 15, 1778, in Rhode Island. At the time he met the
Mormon elders, Jared and Simeon Carter, Tanner was a very wealthy man and a loyal member
of the Baptist Church. He was converted and baptized along with his older children in 1831,
and from that time was known as "Father" John Tanner. He moved to Kirtland, where he
contributed generously to the building of the temple, and where finally he lost all that he had
in the Kirtland bank failure.

In 1839 Tanner was at Far West, and soon after the Battle of Crooked River was captured
by a mob who struck him over the head with a gun and held him prisoner. He moved to
Nauvoo in 1840, where he helped with the Nauvoo Temple, and where his sons were active and
ardent members. Two of them later joined the Mormon Battalion. At Winter Quarters Father
Tanner and his family took over the responsibility of herding the cattle for the camp. He came
to Utah in 1848 and settled near the mouth of Cottonwood Creek, Salt Lake County. He died
April 13, 1850.

blankets & some entirely in dressed skins in their pure wild native dress but they were uncommonly friendly & would sell green corn for bread & such articles as they wanted to eat

Br John D. Lee informed me that all those who had been slandering me and propesying against me were now being put to shame for my course had been entirely satisfactory to Brigham and proven to all people the sincerity and integrity of my motives and that it was Brighams intentions to restore me to responsible & honorable stations again & that he thought it best to let matters go as it has this summer in order to prove to those who were my enemies that I was a good man and true & that he never doubted it himself. This he said he told me for my encouragement.

Sunday & Monday August the 2nd & 3rd 1846. I lay in camp and nothing of any importance took place.

Tuesday August the 4th 1846. Today the camp commenced to move to the place where it was contemplated to winter The teams were rolling out all day. I was at home all day.

Wednesday August the 5th 1846. Brigham returned to this place this morning and tendered me the use of a span of horses and waggon to move on in which I of course accepted It was the team which George & Joseph Herring the Mohawk Indians had the use of. They had come to the conclusion to go back and winter among the Pottawattamies for one of them an old acquaintance had proferred to find them in provision this winter gratis and Brigham wanted me to move them to the Ferry and then have the use of the team to move in which I did I went over the river & traded some and came home and prepared to start

Thursday Augt 6th 1846. Started to move this morning. The weather was very hot and sultry we only went about six miles stopping two or three hours at noon to let the cattle breath We encamped on the top of the river bluff but near six miles off. It was a beautiful camping place and all those who had gone before had stoped here by the appearance of the ground. There was a good spring near by.

Friday August the 7th 1846. We traveled on to day and arrived in the main camp after traveling about six miles. I found the camp situated on the prairie in two divisions and located on two ridges forming a beautiful sight

I encamped below Brigham's division and out side the [spri]ng. Each Division formed a hollow square. There was plenty of good water near by.

Saturday August 8th 1846. Today saw the President again on the subject of the Cohort He seemed to be very anxious to have the military put in opperation and have the officers of the Legion to take their places as near as could be consistently; I afterwards saw John D. Lee who said that he would take his place as Major of the 5th Regt Nothing more of importance to day.

Sunday August 9th 1846. I went to a meeting with my wife. It was in the grove North of this camp at a place previously prepared in a thick cool shade. Woodruff, Clapp Farr and Lorenzo Young spoke in the fore noon. There had been previously to my coming hear an organization went into which was had before the people today and was as follows. There was what was called a Municipal High council consisting of 12 men appointed who were endowed with all the powers of a High council of the church & also the powers of common council of a municipality and hence all the powers both polititical and ecclesastical were centered in them who were to act under the jurisdiction of the Twelve of course. The Twelve also sat in & had a voice in said council whenever they saw proper.

The council was composed of Alpheus Cutler as President 2 Reynolds Cahoon 3 Daniel Russell 4 A. P. Rockwood 5 J. M. Grant 6 B. L. Clapp . . . .[54] 7 Winslow Farr 8 Thomas Grover 9 Samuel Russell 10 Ezra Chase 11 Alanson Eldridge 12 Cornelius P Lott.

Samuel Russell was appointed Secratary Horace S. Eldridge was appointed Marshall. This Place or Municipality was called Cutler's Park at the suggestion of President Young.

There was a letter read designed to be sent to President Polk stating our intentions for the future & that we intended to petition Congress for a Territorial Government as soon as we got to Calafornia. It also loudly demured to the idea afloat that it was contemplated by some of the goverment officers to have L. W. Boggs appointed Governer of Caliafornia It said that "Lilburn W. Boggs and peace & Mormondom never could dwell together."

President Young informed us that there would be a council house built in which the saints could enjoy themselves and improve in the blessing which we have recieved in the Temple and sing and pray and if some had a mind to shout he did not care anything about it

It was now intended to live in this timber in the winter or as soon as cool weather set in. I came home from the after noon meeting about dark after which I saw Brigham and Rockwood at a council and learned the order of his camp and was informed how to proceed in relation to the company affairs & the order of working &c &c.

Monday August 10th 1846. I hunted cattle today. Most of the men were engaged in cutting and drawing poles to fence in the camp.

Brighams' or the First division it was intended to move to the next ridge West because the square was too small to let in all that wanted to come into it

So in moving it to a new place it could be made large enough and the ground would be clean and more pleasant. To day the council met and appointed a guard of 24 men to keep the cattle out of the timber in order to save the pea vine which would make good pasturage after the grass was killed by the frost.

I was appointed one of the guard.

We met and were to be under the direction of the Marshall. Myself & Jonathan C. Wright were appointed Sergeants of the guard and were to be on duty six hours at a time relieving each other. This kept us on duty half of our time that is half the day and half in each 24 hours I came on duty the latter part of the night to night.

Tuesday August 11th 1846. We moved to the other ridge to day which occupied most of the day. When the new camp was formed again it presented a most beautiful large hollow square with pens for our cattle & horses on the outside. The mail by P P Pratt arrived here today from the soldiers with 5,000 in mony[55] all was well with them I went on guard again in the after part of the night

---

54. Benjamin L. Clapp was born August 19, 1814, in Alabama. He joined the Mormon Church before 1838, for he was one of the participants in the Battle of Crooked River. He was made one of the seven presidents of the Seventies following the death of Daniel S. Miles in October 1844. He came west with the general migration of 1848, but by 1859 he was excommunicated from the church and moved to California, where he died in 1860.

55. As Stout has indicated, Brigham Young could raise the required 500 men for the Mormon Battalion only by convincing them that they could best serve by going ahead at government expense and contributing part of their wages to the general good.

At Fort Leavenworth the men drew their arms, provisions, and camp equipage, and "On the 5th [August, 1846] the soldiers drew $42 each, as clothing money for the year. Most of the money was sent back by Elder Parley P. Pratt and others for the support of the families of the soldiers, and for the gathering of the poor from Nauvoo . . . . The paymaster was much

Wednesday August 12th 1846. I went on guard again this after noon The whole "Camp of Israel" was now Divided into two grand divisions that is Brighams Company the first and Heber's company the second division.

It was to day divided into sub divisions by order of the council and Brigham came around to day dividing it off and set me to making out a roll of one of these Sub divisions to be ready for organizing this evening which was done by a meeting called by the President and a Forman apointed to each sub-division who was to have the charge of all the men & boys in his sub division and all were to work under him & he be subject to the council. Thus all the force of the camp could easily be called into requisition by the council to advantage

I was in the Fourth sub-division in the First Grand division of the Camp of Israel and Welcome Chapman was appointed Foreman. There was ten sub-divisions in the First Grand Division.

Thursday August 13th 1846. Three sub-Divisions or working companies commenced opperations this morning I was appointed Clerk of this Sub-Division by the Foreman and "immediately entered upon the duties of my office" and was engaged at it most of the day I went a graping in the evening.

Friday August 14th 1846. I was sick all day and at home

Saturday August 15th 1846. To day there was a general Cattle hunt The cattle had wandered untill they were scattered through all the woods creeks and ravines for miles around So this hunt was ordered by the council & to be under the direction of President Cutler all hands were to turn out and did

It was divided into two divisions one under Br Daniel Russell who went to the West & one under Col Rockwood who went East. The men were thus scattered for miles each way and receded North some miles and at a given signal the sound of a bugle all hands were to shout and then march abreast driving all before them cattle horses & sheep into camp Thus clearing the country at one sweep

I went under Rockwood East and had command of a detachment of horse while out I found myself sick again and discouvered it to be symtoms of the ague & had to leave & come in before the main body geathered. In the evening I took some medicine to stop the ague but was too late for it to do any good.

Sunday August the 16th 1846. Went to meeting today with my wife. We rode in Br Sandfords waggon for I was unable to walk. Orson Pratt spoke on the necessity of due subordination That we only had such a law given as we could stand That is the best which we would recieve & so it had been with this camp. When the best way was pointed out and we recieved it not the next best would be tried and thus we were governed

Brigham spoke on the subject of the money sent here by the soldiers and said that it was best to send it to St Louis and buy such things as we needed at wholesale instead of buying them here at a double retail price He spoke against those who were not thus willing to submit to the best policy for the whole camp &c

I was very sick while at meeting and had a high fever. In the evening I had a very light chill which was followed by a high fever which threw me out of my senses some time in the night and put me in great pain during the whole night.

Monday August 17th 1846. I was some better today but did not leave home.

---

surprised to see every man able to sign his own name to the payroll, . . ." Jenson, *Historical Record*, VIII (August, 1889), 913.

For full details of the Mormon Battalion experience, see Daniel Tyler, *A Concise History of the Mormon Battalion in the Mexican War, 1846-1847* ([n.p.], 1881).

Tuesday August 18th 1846. This morning I recieved the following order or resolution from the Clerk of the Municipal High Council to wit:

"Omaha Nation

August 17th   1846)

)   Cutlers Park.

To Whom it may concern.

This is to certify that at a council held at W. Richards Tent, Col Hosea Stout was appointed, by the unanimous voice of said council to make out a roll of all the commissioned officers of the Legion that are in this place in regular grade; also a roll of all the able bodied men between the age of 18 & 45 and make report to this council

Alpheus Cutler Prest
Samuel Russell Clk."

This was intended merely for a commission or authority for me to act on the case and seemed to be putting the military affairs in a situation to be come at.

After recieving the above I commenced making out the report but was very weak and not able to do much.

About two o'clock I had another chill which was harder than the former & was followed by a higher fever and consequently more pain and was out of my senses again. This reduced me very fast & I had no reason to expect any thing but a hard spell of sickness

Wednesday, Thursday, Friday Saturday Sunday and Monday, August the 19th, 20th 21st 22nd 23rd and 24th. I was in my tent during all this time The weather part of the time was bad for a sick person On the 20th in the afternoon I had another harder chill than ever which was followed by a harder fever. I as usual out of my senses or as my wife said had just come to them for she said that I could speak better than ever I could I was talking all the while. This last turn was the worst I ever had and seemed to wear me out in a way that all knew that I could not stand long.

To wards evening and before I had farly come to myself President Young came in & laid hands on me and said that I should get well & that he would let me have any thing which I needed either in food or clothing and that he was my friend and would be to all eternity and particularly enjoined it on me to let him know what my wants were. When he first came I was still about half cradled & he said I should recover to which I replied that I knew all the time if he came I would get well. He sent Doctor Sprague to me in the morning who give some pills which broke the chills and I was gradually recovering afterwards and getting more easy But was now so reduced that I could but just walk another such chill or two would have finished me. My child had the chills. each time that I did and was also cured the same way.

Tuesday August the 25th 1846. I was engaged in making out the report of the Legion by calling on the Forman of the Sub-Divisions but was unable to walk around

Wednesday Augt 26th 1846. Was engaged in making out a report of the Legion & completed it in the First Division

Thursday August 27th 1846. Still making out that report as before

To day Lieutenant James Pace arrived here from the "Mormon Battalion", bearing an express to the Twelve informing them that Lieutenant Colonel James Allen the United States officer before refered to who came with the requisition for the 500 soldiers was dead. He died at Fort Levenworth and that the soldiers were on the march to Fort Bent on the head of the Arkansas river. The council was called on the subject and several letters read from Samuel Gulley & some from some of the officers at the Fort

There was a great itching among some of the United States officers, to succeed him. But as the Battalion had marched from the Fort they had no jurisdiction over them so the command fell on Captain Jefferson Hunt our own man. Our men did not know whether it would be good policy for him to take the command or not and to this end had they sent here for council which here decided for Captain Hunt to claim his privilege and take command of the Battalion.

Col Allen had proven himself a firm & unwavering friend to the mormon soldiers and had gained their confidence and good feelings and his death was much lamtented by all the officers. He always seemed to be proud of the idea of having the command of the "Mormon Battalion"

There was six chiefs of the Oto tribe here today who had come on some business and this evening there came about eighty of the Omaha's who also came on business It appeared that both these tribes claim the land which we are on and are now almost ready go to war about it

Both claim the right to treat with us in relation to the terms of our staying here. The Omahas were ordered to encamp on the ridge East of us as there was so many of them. But the Otos being so few were afraid to camp out of our square for fear that the Omahas would fall upon them

This evening I wrote a letter to send to Hunter by James Pace also sent word to him about Col Price[56] was there &c & wrote a letter to Mother Taylor & one to Allen Weeks

Friday August the 28th 1846. I finished my order of the Legion today and found that there were 332 privates and 70 commissioned & non-commissioned officers in the two Divisions of the camp It was afterwards handed into the council by Col Rockwood & accepted.

I learned today that Samuel Bent the President of Garden Grove & William Huntington President of Pisgah were dead.

I went this morning to the camp of the Omahas and saw them taking breakfast They were seated about in squads near the tent and the chiefs would divide out the food and send to them There was not the least noise or confusion among them but all seemed patient and satisfied with what was given him. The provision had been furnished by the brethren and consisted of allmost every variety. I left there and went home as I was now fatigued & worn down and felt like having the ague

But at 8 o'clock the Twelve & High Council met with them in council. The following is the minutes of said council. Present on the part of the Omahas Big Elk a man sixty two years of age his son (Standing Elk) a man about 32 years of age and Logan Fontenelle the interpreter, a half breed, a young man of a very penetrating look, and something of a schollar, a decandant of the Omaha nation on his mother's side aged about 24 years and about seventy chiefs and braves.

President Young asked if they were ready to do business and they answered in the affirmative. The President said that we were on our way to Calafornia and getting as far as Council Point, was over taken by a government officer calling for men to go as soldiers to Santa Fe &c and in consequence of parting with so many men were left destitute of hands for teamsters in consequence of which we would ask of you the privilege of stopping on your lands this winter or untill we can get ready to go on again. We want the privilege of cutting timber and grass sufficient for our use. We have the privilege of the government if we can bargain

---

56. Along with the Mormon Battalion there was a regiment of Missouri cavalry under command of Colonel Sterling Price. There were frictions between this unit and the Mormon group.

with you. We have also Mechanics of different kinds that can be of benefit to you in repairing guns &c and we want to establish a trading house, & if we do will they trade with us as they do others. Ask them if they are willing we should plant & sow this fall and next spring. We want them to understand that we are their friends and we want to live with them as such and have our cattle and persons safe. Tell them that we are acting under the advice of the government — We will establish schools if they want us to. One thing we would not forget to mention. We bought corn corn of the Otos which we afterwards learned belonged to the Omahas and then we stoped buying.

The Big Elk answered and said I am probably the oldest man in council and hope you will not take offence if I call you all sons. I am willing my self and be glad to have you stay if my Grandfather the President is willing and as the Otos pretend to own this land I would advise you to settle here without making a bargain with any

My sons, I like what you say very much and I have it in my heart. I am weak, and because I am weak am imposed upon; If I go to hunt one way I meet enemies, and if I turn the other way I meet enemies. I am hunted like the dog on the prairie. We are killed by families without provocation and imposed upon every way and have been for the last ten years. But I have held still because I was advised so to do by the government or I could have done as they have done & killed some too

But I have not done it. I have young men that I can lend if you want help to guard your cattle. If you make improvements I would be glad to have you go to Council Bluffs as that land is not in dispute and I intend to build a town there that we may have the benefit of your improvements after you have gone. There is some few Elk & deer at the Bluffs and as you are numerous I do not want you should kill them all off

There is a tribe above here that may come down and do some damage in stealing and killing our cattle. And the Otos look out for them.

And if I send young men to help you I will instruct them how to do. I want your protection and hope you will take pity on us and help us and fix our guns and as you have asked us to sign a writing you may write what has been said to day and we will sign it You may stay two years or untill we sell as we mean to sell and go away

President Young said that we have said all that we have to say at present and we would call on him in four days and have what has been said committed to writing and have the business done right. Big Elk said there was some stone three miles below the Old Garrison and some brick on the spot the ruins of the old buildings &c[57]

They also desired us to take their corn & keep it for them for fear other tribes would get it for them which was agreed to & also to help draw it for them But it was understood that we would have nothing to do with any difficulty between them and any other tribe and also as we had lost some cattle sheep & Horses if they would find them and bring them to us we would pay them for it

Their supper was then provided for them which was similar to their breakfast. There was some more said but this includes the substance

Saturday, Sunday, and Monday, August the 29th, 30th and 31st. I was weak and feeble but somewhat on the mend. I attempted to hunt my horses on

---

57. This was the site which was later known as "Summer Quarters" or "Brother Brigham's Farm." Here under the general direction of Isaac Morley, members of Brigham Young's adopted family raised corn during the summer of 1847 for the next year's emigration. John D. Lee and nine of his adopted sons cultivated a large field upon which they produced some 4,000 bushels of grain.

Sunday was too weak on Monday The Twelve & High council went up the river to visit the old garrison & vicinity to see what the prospect was for settling there

Tuesday, and Wednesday September the 1st and second. I was at home writing & cleaning up my guns and pistols.

The Twelve & High council came home to day and had decided not to settle up at the Bluffs for the want of timber. They did not like the situation any way except the stone & brick.

Thursday Sept 3rd 1846. I was about camp today and in the evening went to the council at D Russell and heard Orson Pratt make the report of his mission to the Otos and Omahas which was in substance as follows that he in company with those who were with him called and had an interview with the Otos but could not get any thing definite from them whether they were willing we should winter here or not as the main Chief was not present but they said that the land belonged to them for one mile above the old garrison and that they said that they would call in a day or two and let us know about it He left them and went to the Omahas and got the article signed by the chiefs This article was in substance what was talked over on the 28th

They said that they could not spare their young men unless we would sent them as many of ours to help them He then stated to them how we had been driven & how our Great Chief found a book and what was in it about them and because we believed it and practiced it we were driven they listened with breathless silence

They said that they were going to send a party of their young men against the Souix to be revenged on them for killing one of their chiefs and that they urged to come by here and give us a dance that their young warriaurs might enjoy themselves while they lived to which he tried to prevent but they seemed to be very anxious to come & This is not all that that was said but the particulars.

Friday September 4th 1846. Was at home reading a lot of news-papers got of Dr W. Richards In the evening I went to a council at Rockwoods but there being no business the council adjourned. While here I saw Br Wilford Woodruff who informed me of the conduct of some young men towards some young women. President Young had also previously given me charge to keep a sharp look out for them and that they had undertakin to get hold of them and some one informed them what was up

Elder Woodruff said that they and the girls had been out for fifteen nights in succession untill after two o'clock and that it was his wish & the wish of the President that I should take the matter in hand and see that they had a just punishment by whipping them and for me to take my own course and use my own judgement in executing the same I told him that I would see to it This was I believe the first step taken since we were in the wilderness to enforce obedience to the Law of God or to punish a trangressor for a breach of the same. The crimes of these men were adultery or having carnal communication with the girls which was well known to many and the legal punishment was death

Saturday Sept 5th 1846. I was busy in making preperation to execute the order of the President and Br Woodruff and to that end I saw and collected together Levi Stewart, S. A. Dunn, M. D. Hambleton John Lytle S. H. Earl and H. S. Eldridge the Marshall and we went to the timber towards the meeting ground where one of these men was chopping wood. For I had managed to have him sent there on purpose

When we came he suspected our business and was uncommonly excited He began to plead and wanted to see Br Woodruff or Brigham and tried every way to get to come into camp but it was all in vain. He had seen Woodruff & did not make satisfaction nor could he as Woodruff told him this side of hell for he told him that nothing short of fire & brimstone could cleanse them so when we came two of us having guns he never thought of anything else but to be killed forth with. This was what excited him so much   At length I told in a few words that we must execute our orders whereupon Br Stewart took out a rope which when he saw it he begged not to be tied saying that he would submit to whatever we put on him without being tied so we did not tie him but all started off to a proper place He was weeping & begging all the time.   At length he exclaimed that he did not want to be taken off and killed this way.   I then first discovered what he expected so I told him that he was not to be killed.   He then expected we were going to put the next worst punishment[58] on him so then I told him that we were only going to give him a severe whiping which seemed to allay his excitement although he protested to be innocent all the time. We took him to a good place and the Marshall gave him 18 hard lashes which striped him well but did not bring the blood after which we taught him the principles of the law and the just punishment for such crimes and what he need to expect if ever we had to visit him again now since we had declared to him the law of God.   His name was Daniel Barnum son of Job V. Barnum who was a good old man and subject to the law & the order of the kingdom of God and deprecated the conduct of his son but could not controll him

We then came home about Eleven o'clock and in the afternoon went to the woods again to get proper switches for the next who were to be punished and then returned again and went to council at Rockwoods but there was not much done I forgot to mention in the proper place that all those who were with me were of the "Old Police" but the Marshall and it was his duty to execute the law in this place for he was the only executive officer yet appointed here.

Sunday Septr 6th 1846. This morning a number of the Police and the Marshall went over into Heber camp and took Peletiah Brown another one of the young men who had been with young Barnum and took him into the woods and give him 18 stripes which brought the blood in two places. He also protested that he was innocent. He was considerably excited when we came but after reasoning with him a short time he consented to go and in fact he & Barnum both acted manly after we took them   He requested go alone with me and let the others follow for he was ashamed to be taken off in a croud before the people

He took his whipping tolerable well but all the time protested he was innocent. When the Marshall had given him near what he was to have he loudly exclaimed "O Br Eldridge if you will only stop I'll never touch another girl again while hell's afloat." He finished this sentence at the top of his voice. When we were through we all came home we had now but one more case to attend to and that was A. J. Clothier or as he was more known by Jack Clothier. When I came home I was very unwell and the long walk had tired me down and I staid at home untill in the evening when George W. Langley and some more brought Jack Clothier here. He said that when he took Jack his mother and all the family railed on them and called them mobbers and every evil thing against them that they could think of and finally sent for Father Cutler to have him interfere but when he came he said he had nothing to do with it and advised him to go. His mother followed him here railing all the time which made no small stir among the people who did not know what to think of it.

We took him out of camp and gave him 23 stripes putting on five for his mean conduct while in our hands. We then gave him a long lecture on the law

---

58. The second worst punishment was emasculation.

in the matter before us as we did the others. He did not act honorably as did the others but manifested a mean low, and grovelling spirit all the time

We then sent him home & after having a long conversation among ourselves about what was wisdom for us to do in furture & the course to pursue in order to meet the excitement we came home It was now late in the night.

Monday September 7th 1846. Went to see President Young after breakfast and reported what [had] been done which he said was all right and perfectly satisfactory on his part but said for me to use the utmost care to keep down any undue excitement from those who did not understand the Laws & ordinances of this kingdom

I then went with the Marshall over to Heber's camp as we had understood that there was many who were hard against us over there. So we went & got G. W. Langley & W. J. Earl and went round the camp saluting every one friendly that we met & passed off and in an hour or so it was reported that we were after some four or five more to whip and so great was the excitement that some even went in their waggons & was prepared to shoot in case we came

By this means we, as we anticipated, learned who their accomplices in crime were. For of course no one was scared who was not guilty or aiding & abetting those who were and in fact some were in this way detected whom I little would have supposed to be any way engaged in such things. I still kept on the look out all day with some of the police to see that all was going right and saw A. Lyman, W. Richards, W. Woodruff in the mein time and reported to them how matters were going. Brown & Barnum was acting very friendly and said they were going to do better.

Tuesday Sept 8th 1846. I undertook to hunt my mare today that had strayed but did not find here & had to come home and met Elder Woodruff on my way home. He freely expressed good feelings and gratitude to us for the way we had dealt with the boys and was entirely satisfied. We had a rain storm in the evening

Wednesday September 9th 1846. This was a dark rainy day & I was at home untill in the evening when I went to a council at Russells tent. There was a letter read from a brother in St Louis stating that Elders Hyde & Taylor passed through there on their way to England in good health & spirits.

President Young here recommended to leave our families here one or two years & fit out a company of men & go over to Bear river valley next spring and thus prepare a home for our women before we take them   &c

Thursday Sept. 10th 1846. Read a lot of news papers today & then took my gun & went a hunting in the timber expecting to find my mare but did not I came home. In the evening there was a storm from the West. The clouds rolled up white & circling rising in all directions seemed to be strangely crazed & whirling and at lenght a west storm of wind & rain which blew down my tent and many others and exposed my things to the storm again I had to leave the tent down all night.

Friday Sept 11th 1846. At home reading newspapers and was engaged in drying cloths all day and fixing tent &c

Saturday September 12th 1846. At home all day Went to a council at Rockwoods tent at 7 o'clock P. M. Here President Young spoke with great power and spirit and adverted to the spirit manifested by some in consequence of the whipping which those boys got by the Marshall & old Police. He sustained the whipping of them and gave them to understand what they might expect if the Law of God came and we were disobedient to its mandates. That he meant to wach and nip all such evils in the bud

President Alpheus Cutler also spoke and manifested the best feelings in regard to the executive department of the kingdom that I ever knew him to and seemed to have his eyes opened in the right way this time I came home at ten o'clock P. M.

Sunday Sept 13th 1846. Went to meeting. Elder Orson Pratt spoke first he spoke some on the organization of worlds & the planetary system

He said that we could distinctly see with a common spy glass in the constellation of Orion (in the Sword of Orion) unorganized matter enough to make many millions of worlds as large as the sun. Heber spoke next on the Law of God and what had been done to the boys and what would be done to the unruly and also how some hid in their waggons for fear of being whiped and was ready to shoot the first that came

He said that all such were equally guilty and had been with the boys and hence their fears &c.

President Young followed and spoke somewhat similar to what he said last night only vindicating the Marshal & Police in stronger terms & said that he would put the Law of God in force if people did not ceace their wicked whoredoms or in substance to that &c and said many other things of importance which shall not now relate.[59]

On my way home Br Heber told me that one Brother refused to give him his hand because he supposed he was one who gave council to have the boys whiped. But Heber told him that he had forgot that there was a High council to order such things so the man was satisfied thinking Heber had nothing to do with it. I came home and nothing more of importance took place

Monday & Tuesday Sept 14 & 15th 1846. Nothing took place till the 15th when ten or twelve waggons started to Nauvoo to move the poor families out here They went under the charge of O. M. Allen.

Brs Shirtliff & Houtz & four French & half breeds came in today from Millers camp & reported to the council that they were going to winter at the mouth of the Puncaw river or the Running water and all was well. They were after some goods for the winter and intended to pay for them in peltry & were going to hunt with the Punckaw Indians

The Running watter is about 200 miles above here & Miller is on the Missouri river

The council dispached messengers to the Pawnee village to bring down the families left there by Miller as he passed there

---

59. Brigham Young's sermons were the basis of several entries in contemporary journals. Writing under date of Sunday, September 13, 1846, Norton Jacob recorded:

Attended meeting at the stand . . . . Brother Heber spoke upon the fuss made by some persons about those boys being whipped. Some went and hid themselves saying that they would shoot any body who should undertake to whip them, which he regarded as a pretty sure sign of their guilt. The whipping had been done by order of the council and he would support his brethren in the course they had taken.

President Young spoke very severely upon the course taken by some in undertaking to stir up strife in the camp because some boys had been whipped. They having been neglected by their own fathers. He thought the marshall had not whipped them severe enough as they would hold their tongues, and besides some middle aged men were engaged in encouraging them in their course. If they wished thus to corrupt themselves, he wanted them to leave the camp of Israel and go away among the gentiles. But if they remained here they must observe order and decorum and he swore twice in the name of Israel's God that such vile conduct should not be allowed in this camp, for if they could not govern without, the law of God should be executed and that would make short work. (Norton Jacob, "The Life of Norton Jacob [1804-1852]" [typescript, Utah State Historical Society], 32-33.)

Wednesday & Thursday Sept 16th 17th 1846. On the 16th I was unwell most of the day and on the 17th was at home writing untill in the evening when I went to a council at S. Russells tent. Br J. M. Grant reported that he had been to see Mr. Sarpee who informed him that the United States Marshall from Missouri was coming here after the Twelve & that he would give us notice thereof as soon as he knew that he was coming &c. He also reported that he had learned that the Secratary of War had instructed Mr. Mitchell the United States agent for the Pottawattamies to have all the Mormons removed off of the Pottawattamy land by the first of April next.[60]

The council decided to remove to the river about three miles to winter instead of staying here as was at first contemplated as there was a beautiful place there for a city &c.

After the council was over Prest Young called a private council which consisted of the Twelve, Marshall & one or two more at which he invited me to stay the subject of which was to determine what to do in case the Marshall came from Missouri with a writ for the Twelve.

There was many things spoken of but no specific arraingement entered into more than an expression of our feelings on the subject & orders for me to send two spies down on the other side of the river to see if anything was up After which the President expressed his wish to have the Military put in opperation as soon as expedient &c I came home at 12 o'clock at night.

Friday September 18th 1846. I was very sick & stupid all day & found out that I hurt myself by writing which caused the sick head ache My child took a relapse & had another chill today.

Saturday Sept 19th 1846. To day the wind blew uncommonly hard from the South I had to take down my tent to keep it from blowing down and so did many others some tents which were not taken down were torn on the ridge pole into two and fell on the ground & many others badly injured & some waggon covers also were blown off. We were all unwell today. I rode out a little to hunt my mare but did not find her. At 7 o'clock I went to council at Rockwoods tent Soon after I went there President Young sent me for Br G. W. Langley and after Council he informed us that it was reported that 12 dragoon United States horses had been seen taken on an island on the other side of the river and there kept by 3 men. The horses were fully equiped and it was supposed to be for the purpose of kidnapping some of the Twelve The report seemed to be correct and created considerable excitement and agreed well with the report which Sarpee made to J. M. Grant that the United States Marshall was coming here with writs for the Twelve &c now from this report we had reason to believe that they designed to catch some out and thus run them off on those horses. This was the natural conclusion and the President wanted me to send Langley and some one else over the river to ascertain the certainty of these things and also see if there was any hiding places for troops over there and for them to go down the river some distance below the Indian settlements and look out the situation of the country and the banks & crossing places of the river on that side and also send out an exploring party to explore the river from the ferry to the mouth of the Platte and up that river to the Horn and get perfectly

60. The land on which the Mormons were camped on the Iowa side of the river belonged to the Pottawattamies.

On September 8, 1846, Alanson Eldredge, Alpheus Cutler, Albert P. Rockwood, Jedediah M. Grant, and Ezra Chase were appointed a committee to locate a site for Winter Quarters. On September 11 the place was selected and approved, and surveying began. This site later became Florence, Nebraska, the headquarters of Mormon migration west. It is now a suburb of Omaha. For the next few years it was known as Winter Quarters.

acquainted with all the Boat harbors crossing, hiding places and passes to this place so that we could have a knowledge of these things in case of an attact from Missouri or elsewhere Accordingly I made arraingements for Br Langley & Gilbert Belnap to go over the river as above mentioned & for Luman H. Calkins & John P. Thomas to explore on this side. The President then desired me to assist the Marshall in the discharge of his duty in camp and we adjourned & I came home at 2 o'c

Sunday September 20th 1846. I was in camp attending to Military affairs & sending off Brs Langley and Belnap as before mentioned last night and also in preparing to fit out the exploring expidition for this side of the river after which I went to meeting at the stand. Br Kimball spoke on the order of the beef market and the idea of making our winter quarters some two or three miles East and near the river as he thought it a better place &c and was followed by Brigham on the same subjects and to the same effects. It appeared that some dissatisfied persons has been grumbling at the order of the beef market and the matter was explained to the people and all seemed satisfied. Brigham said that he did not feel very religious now and those who did might preach for he would not at present I suppose that his feeling came because of the reports of the United States Marshall coming &c. while speaking on the subject he said that instead of praying for our enemies he would pray that our enemies & all dissenters might be sent to hell cross lots. I came home and went to a council at Russells tent in the evening.

Monday Septr 21st 1846. I was in and about home attending on my little child and Marinda as they were now both dangerously sick and also sent off Br Calkins & Thomas on their exploring expidition mentioned last Saturday evening. I was up untill a very late hour at night and had just laid down ere I was called up by Col Rockwood who was going round to every waggon calling up every body to arms saying that our enemies were upon us and for us to meet on the square armed and equiped for fight

This created an unusual excitement particularly among the sick & the women Some were ready to go into fits almost I armed quickly and repaired to Brigham's tent. The men geathering in the mean time on the square

From Brigham's I went with Rockwood to Heber's camp whither Brigham had gone to call them up When we had arrived there we found that he had given them the alarm & gone over to the third grand Division of the Camp so we put after him and on our way we overtook him & Dr W. Richards. He then sent us on & they went to C. P. Lotts' camp to notify them We went and alarmed the Third Grand Division and joined them again and we all returned to Brighams.

The men had orders to remain in their own places untill the firing of a gun and then to rally in their own Grand Division & be prepared for immediate action all the time

We then went to see Br Mikesell who brought in the news. He informed us that Mr Sarpee give him the intelligence last Friday that there was a large posse coming after the Twelve and Br Mikesell had not give the notice untill now. This was a great oversight in Br Miksell For by his neglect we might have been taken on supprise.

After the above had occured the people were told to retire to rest with their arms in their hands and tomorrow was appointed for a general meeting for the purpose of organizing the Millitary. We then went into a kind of private council at Rockwood's tent to consult on matters in case of an attact but not anything definite went into

Tuesday September 22nd 1846. Met this morning at 9 o'clock with a Council of officers to determine on the way and manner of organizing the military

It was determined there to have a Regimental organization and to have the officers of the Legion put in according to their rank as near as could be conveniently after which we went to the place of rendezvous which was between the three Grand Divisions of the Camp near the butchery and there waited a long time for the people to assemble. The Twelve were there

The organization was at length went into by Lieutenant General Young who took the lead in forming the Companies.

It was now determined by the vox populi on the motion of Heber C. Kimball to put all the old Captains of the Legion into office before electing new ones.

There was much said about the best way to organize the companies and was finally determined to have each company consist of 25 men including the officers and to be officers with a captain and one Lieutenant and two sergeants.

This was done because it was thought that small companies could be more easily managed than large ones and more necessary when we had so few men After the foregoing regulations were made the Lieutenant General proceeded to organize the companies by nominating the captains as made out in a report by me to the City Council as before mentioned and as they were accepted they were ordered out and their number of men with them untill all the old Captains were used up Then some other officers of the Legion. Lieutenant Colonels & Majors included who were not needed in their rank & station were put in command as captains also some who were not officers untill 16 companies were made out and filled up which comprehended all the men it being 400 on the ground

After the foregoing regulations were completed the line was formed which made quite an imposing and war like appearance. The Lieutenant General had a First Lieutenant elected to each company who were also of the old officers when any were in the company after which they were put in the command of their companies and the Captains called together and also the higher officers which were not yet assigned any place and had another council as to the nature of organizing or unto what to constitute the corps now formed

The result of which council was to have a Regimental organization There being 16 companies. They were organized into 4 Battalions of 4 companies each and officered as follows Col Stephen Markham being the ranking Col was elected to the command of the Regiment as Col I being next in rank was elected Lieutenant Col of the First Battalion which was Infantry & Col John Scott being next to me in rank was elected Major of the Second Batalion which was Artillery This used up all the Colonels of the line Lt Col Henry Herriman of the Legion was elected Major of the third Battalion which was Infantry. He had just been elected one of the Captains and was now promoted and Lt Col A. L. Tippetts elected captain in his place

Major John S. Gleason of the Legion was elected Major of the 4th Battalion which was also Infantry He had also been elected captain here & Isaac C Haight his Lieutenant elected captain in his place.

Col Markham then appointed Brigade Major John Bills to be his adjutant and Quarter Master J. B. Nobles Sergeant Major. They were both aids to the Brigadier General of the Second Cohort Nauvoo Legion.

Col Markham now formed the Square and we were then addressed By the Lieutenant General who said among many other things that he wanted Col Rockwood to continue as his aid and that he was a good man &c and would do as he was told and then stop &c and then said that he had not the least hesitancy in offering himself as General of all to controll and dictate all things in relation to the Military as well as every thing else &c all of which was voted by acclamation unanimously

Then after raising 4 yoke of oxen to take one of the cannon to Bishop Miller and ordering Colonel Markham to raise another company to be mounted men for exploring purposes &c we were dismissed.

Immediately after dismission the Col & field officers met and divided the companies into Battalions as follows. The First Battalion which was under me was composed of the Companies of Captains William M. Allred George W. Langley, Welcome Chapman & Jas W. Cummings.

The Second Battalion was the Artillery under John Scott Captains John Lytle, Norton Jacobs[61] Harrison Burgess & James M. Flack[62] The Third Battalion under Herriman of Alva L. Tippetts, J. M. Grant, Levi Ritter and Augustus Staffords' companies

After the foregoing regulations were done I came home and took dinner and then met met with the field officers & Captains at two o'clock at Col Markhams tent where our regulations of the companies were laid before the Captains which was satisfactory to them. We then had a drill muster for an hour or so I took the command by order of the Col After drilling a while I took them through the old Missouri Danite drill. This was new to most and very entertaining. also to them and more so because it was such a short & simple method of manouvering small companies.

I then returned home again & went to a council at Rockwoods tent at dark. While there I recieved orders from Col Markham for me to notify my Battalion not to fire a gun & to take the caps of and put leather on the tubes or take out the priming & put tow in the pan as the case may be which order I executed immediately except Captain Cummings Company. This precaution was to prevent accidents also the fireing a gun was now the signal of alarm

I then came home and nothing more of importance took place tonight.

---

61. Norton Jacob was born August 11, 1804, in Sheffield, Massachusetts. He was baptized into the Mormon Church by Zenos Gurley in March 1841, and moved to Nauvoo the next year. Here he was active as a lumberman, carpenter, and wagon builder. He also spent much time on the Nauvoo Temple, working under William Weeks, the architect.

Jacob came to Utah with the pioneer company of 1847, and then returned with Brigham Young to Winter Quarters to bring his family out in 1848. He settled first in Salt Lake City, where he was foreman over the carpenters and joiners on public works. He died in Glendale, Kane County, Utah, January 30, 1879.

62. James Madison Flake (sometimes spelled Flack) was born on a large plantation in Anson County, North Carolina, where he married Agnes Love; here their first child, William Jordan, was born on July 3, 1839. Three years later they moved to Mississippi, where they were converted to Mormonism.

Flake came to Nauvoo in 1843, and at once became active as a mounted guard. When in 1845 it was evident that the Mormons would have to move west, he returned to Mississippi and exchanged his holdings for wagons, mules, cattle, and money. Although he set his Negroes free, two insisted upon remaining in the family — Green Flake, a large, strong young man, and Liz, the family maid. James Flake sent the colored boy, Green, to drive his white-topped carriage for the use of Brigham Young in the 1847 trek, while he followed as captain of one hundred in the Amasa Lyman train.

In the fall of 1849, James Flake was called to go on the "Gold Mission" to California, and elected captain of the train. On June 15, 1850, he was thrown from a mule, kicked and instantly killed.

His wife, three children, and the colored maid, went with Amasa Lyman to San Bernardino. When they withdrew from there in 1858, Liz fell heir to the property. Green Flake was given land on the east bench near Cottonwood, some of which is still occupied by colored people.

James' son, William Jordan Flake, was the colonizer for whom Snowflake, Arizona, was named.

PART IV

September 23, 1846 to September 24, 1848

SEPTEMBER 23, 1846 TO SEPTEMBER 24, 1848

Part IV

This part of the diary covers the period from September 23, 1846, to September 24, 1848. The diary tells of experiences at Winter Quarters on the banks of the Missouri River through the winter of 1846-47, and the summer and winter following, during which time Hosea Stout was still in charge of the police force. In the spring of 1848, Stout joined the main migration to the Valley of the Great Salt Lake. Among the other diaries that parallel his during this journey are those of John Pulsipher and John D. Lee.

Wednesday September 23rd 1846. I was at home all day to day attending on the sick. Marinda was very sick with the Dropsy & cold on the lungs. The camp commenced to move to day to new location.

Thursday Sept 24th 1846. Foggy morning. Camp still moving I went down to the new location today to make a location for the 4th Sub-Division of the First Grand Division of the Camp of Israel I located a place near the centre of the city it consisted of one Block containing twenty lots.

The City for so it was laid out, was situated on a level flat on the second bluff from the river, and about 50 or 60 feet above the watter and was quite narrow at the North End of the city. The third Bluff comeing near to the river.

As you go south the river seems to retreat from this bluff leaving this flat or city ground wider as you go south. The city is one mile from South to North & bounded at each end by two brooks of good running water. The North brook is calculated to have a mill built on it with some 20 feet or more fall

When I first came into the place I saw Brigham who showed me the plan he had for the defence of the place and the three high points where he intended to put the artillery which would most effectually protect the whole place This was a most beautiful and delightful situation for a City & I was well pleased with this my first view of it

Today Col Markham sent an order to Col Scott for one of the cannon to be sent to Miller as before mentioned & Scott refused to give it up whereupon Markham called out a large number of men to take it by force and from all appearance a person would suppose that "war" would ensue but Br Heber came along and by his mediation & advice the matter was settled & the gun sent off without any blood being shed.[1]   Just as I was going home Rockwood told me to give word to Markham to cause the men who were taking the gun to Miller to become personally responsible for it before they took it away.   it was orders from the Lieutenant General which was done & I then went home which closed the business of today.

Friday Sept 25th 1846. This morning I moved down to the new City and arrainged my tents and waggons after which I went round to see what was going on.

While out, I saw Brigham who urged me to have out the company of rangers to explore the country so I went and saw Col Markham about it and after much ado and running Luman H. Calkins was appointed to raise the company & also to be Captain of the same

Col Markham left the matter of raising the company & appointing the Captain to me & I arrainged it as above and gave him orders to be off forthwith on an exploreing expedition   I also had to make arraingements to keep out a picket guard. At night I was so tired and worn down with fatigue that when I laid down to sleep the fever rose on me and I was out of my senses most of the night.

Saturday Septr the 26th 1846. To day was another unfortunate day to me. A day when the destroyer stalked forth triumphantly in my family and tore another one from our midst.   Marinda, who had been very sick for some time was taken worse last evening and delivered of a child (born dead). after which she seemed to have but little pain during the night

She did not seem to realize much pain all day although her looks had for some day indicated her approaching end.   She retained her senses perfectly well as long as she could hear or see and only seemed to drop to sleep with the exception of the death glare of her eyes.

She died about two o'clock p. m.   her death came by the dropsy as the doctor said & was from the beginning of such a complicated nature that it was incureable

She had ever been true & faithful to me from the first of our acquaintance & had rendered her self by her study true & subordinate habits, very near & dear to me which made this stroke of adversity more accutely felt by me & the rest of my family.

There is now only four of us left and whose turn will be next God only knows.[2]

Sunday Sept 27th 1846. The 4th Sub-Division finished moving down here today.

This morning Capt L. H. Calkins started out on an exploring expidition

About the middle of the after noon I went to Marindas burial

Recieved orders this evening from Markham to put out picket guard which I did The order came about one hour after dark.   After this I wrote a letter to Allen J. Stout.

---

1. Norton Jacob, writing under the same date, told this story in great detail. According to his account, Scott did not refuse to give up the gun; he only refused to let it go without a receipt. The suggestion that he sign a paper for the gun threw Markham into such a rage that he threatened to take it by force. When the agent, Jacob Houtz, offered to sign the receipt, the affair was settled.

2. The four who are left include himself, his wife Louisa and her daughter, and his wife Lucretia Fisher.

During the late summer and early fall there was much sickness among all the Mormon camps. Colonel Thomas L. Kane estimated that more than 600 people died before the cold weather brought relief from the swamp fevers. Of it he wrote: ". . . the few who were able to keep their feet went about among the tents and wagons with food and water, like nurses through the wards of an infirmary. Here at one time the digging [of graves] got behind: burials were slow and you might see women sit in the open tents keeping the flies off their dead children, sometimes after decomposition had set in." Roberts, *Comprehensive History*, III, 153.

Monday Sept 28th 1846. I was at home most of the day today regulating affairs after sickness. Markham ordered me to still keep up the pickett guard. No more to day.

Tuesday Sept 29th 1846. I was at home today very sick with a head ache.

Wednesday Sept. 30th 1846. Was at home today untill in the afternoon and then went over the river hunting with Joseph Herring who was here. It was in a large thick bottom land and thick set with pea & grape vines & good cottonwood timber. It over flows every spring

In the morning Br Chapman called all the men of this Sub-Division together to consult their feeling in relation to their working together any longer. In the evening we had another meeting. The result of their deliberations were to continue to work together although some were a little offish and seemed inclined to draw off and set up business for themselves.

Thursday Octr 1st 1846. I drew watter in the forenoon. at dark the Capt met at my tent & I instructed them to give me a roll of their companies &c & be in readiness for any emergency

Friday October 2nd 1846. I was about home today laid up with the sick head ache
At 7 o'clock in the evening I went to the meeting of the Council at Rockwood tent where it was decided to have the City divided of into wards & Bishops appointed over each ward and Orson Pratt, Wilford Woodruff and Amasa Lyman of the Twelve were appointed a committee [to] lay of[f] the city as above and appoint the Bishops The Bishops were to see to the poor and other duties pertaining to their office.

Saturday October 3 1846. To day I went up the river to the place where the Big-hurd was kept for some cattle about 6 miles up & it was over a ruff & a rugged road & through matted bottom land. The cattle were scattered over a number of miles and it took a large number of hands to drive them out. So it was a custom for all who wanted any of their cattle to go on Saturdays and drive all out which could be found and every man look out his own cattle more easily this way. Individually a man might not find his cattle in a week we got what we wanted and came home about dark.

The low-lands where the cottonwood tree grows was full of men & teams cutting & drawing logs to the river for houses

Sunday October the 4th 1846. Went to meeting. Orson Pratt spoke on the first principles of the Gospel, as there were some present who did not belong to the Church. He delivered an able discourse, after which there was some letters cried of which were from some of the brethren in the army

During intermission the committee appointed to lay of the City into wards and appoint Bishops over them came round on that business.

At 4 o'clock there was another meeting Here the vox populi was taken not to buy of any pedlars who came in here to trade but to let them go and sell to our committee, who were appointed to buy up all things which were bought in the place provided it is needed and can be had at a reasonable price if not to let them take it back again.

Monday, Tuesday, Wednesday, and Thursday October the 5th, 6th, 7th and 8th 1846. I was round and about home, sometimes sick & sometimes trying to work &c We had an officer drill one eve (the 6th)

Friday Octr 9th 1846. Went to hunt my mare on the prairie to day A. B. Hunter was along. We traveled over the hills & hollers all day to no purpose We found a little grove in the prairie which was full of walnuts I do not believe that any mormon had ever been in it before.

Saturday October the 10th 1846. I was in and about home to day & recieved the following order from Col Markam.

Omaha Nation   )   Lieut Col
Winter Quarters   (Hosea Stout
Regimental Orders)   You are hereby required and commanded to keep
October 10th 1846 (up a City Guard as follows to witt

Firstly The Guard must be put on duty at or before 8 o'clock in the evening and not released untill the people are generally up in the morning.

Secondly To keep on duty 4 men at a time, each man to remain on duty one half of the night.

Thirdly To post two men on the North and two on the South of the public or Council lot.

Fourthly Their duty shall be to guard the City against fires or any accident which may happen to occur to inturrupt the peace or destroy the property of the citizens.

Fifthly To make report hereof to me in writing when all the men under your command shall have done each one tour of duty noting the names of the persons who does duty & the time when it is done

John Bills   )   Stephen Markham
Adjutant   (Col

I went to order out the men in the first Company in my Battalion but the officers were gone so that no men could be raised out of that company as I was informed about dark so I called on Capt Chapman & he could raise none. It was now late at night In fact the men & officers were mostly gone up to the Big Hurd after cattle to send them to the rush bottoms to be wintered. After Chapman failed to raise the men I abandoned putting out a guard for tonight for now it was now too late to raise any more

Sunday October 11th 1846. This was a wet day. The Big Hurd came in today. The people driving them was uncommonly wet, cold and in a disagreeable "fix" The herd allmost filled the Town. All hands turned out to select their own cattle out of the Herd They had a disagreeable time of it. I was very unwell all day but turned a short time to look for my cattle and found three. Some were not brought in today.

To night Captain Allred made out the 8 men necessary for the guard tonight but it was "a tight squeeze"

Monday Octr 12th 1846. Was around & about home & found my mare which had been gone for some six weeks. In the evening put out the guard again.

Tuesday October 13th 1846. At home. had the sick head ache. Cold North wind blowing.

The prairie was on fire to the South today & burnt up some 6 or 7 stacks of hay. In the evening large numbers of men went & put the fire out Put out the guard as before.

Wednesday October the 14th 1846. Rainy damp morning. I went today to Mother Taylors on the other side of the river crossing at the new Ferry & from thence passed on to H. W. Miller's & thence to Mother Taylors which was about

6 miles over hills and ridges and down ravines & was an uncommon ruff road The whole distance from here is about 14 miles by way of the road

I found them all well and a number of my old neighbours from Nauvoo settled near to her all doing well but most of the men were gone bee hunting.

Thursday Oct 15th 1846. To day I went to look for the oxen which had strayed from me in the yoke while I was on this side of the river. I passed by Musketo Creek mill and on down and traveled over most of the old range & my old camping place but found them not. There is now many houses here

This country presented to me a dreary appearance and especially my old tenting ground on Hydes ridge. I passed down by Taylors camp which was now but a deserted point all dreary & lonesome.

From here I went to Council Point about 6 miles where I arrived just after dark & put up with George & Joseph Herring my two Mohawk friends. Lewis Dana was there also. We had a joyful and entertaining evening together nor was I ever better recieved & entertained by my white brethren. I had often entertained them but never been with them before.

Friday October 16th 1846. To day was a cold chilling day well set out with a hard North wind. Joseph & I went down to the Pottawattamie village. But there was not much going on because of the cold There was many large companies of Indians there waiting for their annual payment

The whites had made great preperations to trade with them but were like to be disappointed because the payment was not like to be made soon We came back again and I staid all night again.

Saturday October 17th 1846. I came home today. Joseph Herring came with me. I arrived here at one o'clock, uncommonly sick with the head ache. & went to bed.

I in the evening I was some better and went out to enquire about the guard Saw Capt Allred who informed me that he had not done any thing about seeing to the guard so I found that the City was unguarded entirely during my absence & today he had not even thought of it he said but was very sorry.

Sunday October 18th 1846. Went to meeting President Young spoke. He spoke on the subject of the Omahas killing our cattle. He advised us to geather and form a square so that we could keep them out of our midst and then if they came in and went either to killing our cattle or stealing our clothing blankets or any thing else for us to whip them also for us not to give them any thing to eat nor be sociable with them &c Their interpreter & teacher came in the mein time who recommended the same method He also advised not to sell our dogs as some were doing for the Indians were buying them to get them out of camp so that they could more easily pilfer from us.

At this meeting meeting the subject of the guard was agitated by some one on the stand and was proposed for the Bishops to each one guard his own ward, whereupon they were all called up and requested to state how many men would be necessary to guard each ward and they decided that it would take two which would require in one night, there being 13 wards 42 men, whereas it now only takes 8

After it was thus arrainged Prest Brigham Young objected and motioned to have the business of guarding left in the hands of Col Markham myself & the Marshall, which was carried. This left it where they found it.

In the evening I put out the guard again.

Monday Octr 19th 1846. To day the Sub-Division to which I belong was unceri-moniously broken up and every man for himself & so "my secratory-ship was brought to an end of course. Brigham sent about 100 head of cattle to the rushes today. The first drove sent off I was in & about home and in the evening put out the guard again

Tuesday Oct 20th 1846. Today was another general cattle hunt. & all hands turned out and brought in a large number. I took a long walk much farther than I had traveled since I have been sick.

There was much fire out in the prairie today to the South and some in order to save their hay put fire in the grass without any judgement & burnt up their own and others hay which would not have been injured but for themselves. There was seven stacks burnt I understood.

Tonight I put out the guard again. There was but 2 men to be raised the remainder not being present in consequence of their being after cattle which thus caused a disappointment & left the city mostly unguarded. This finished my Battalion so my tour of duty is out according to the order on the tenth instant.

Wednesday & Thursday October the 21st and 22nd 1846. I was at home trying to work at times but not able to do much Capt Charles Allen who went back at the Chariton came into town to see what the prospects were. His family was at the ferry He concluded to to back some where on the Nichanabotany and there settle.

Friday October 23rd 1846. There was today a meeting called at the stand at a half an hour by sun It was to send out on a general cattle hunt. There was a large turn out We went up the river & brought in a large number and among the rest all all my cattle which were gone on this side of the river came in. In the evening went to council at Rockwoods tent. and was appointed clerk of said Council on the nomination of Col Rockwood and immediately went into the duties of said office

Saturday Octr 24th 1846. Worked at home and at 7 o'clock in the evening went to Council again at Rockwood's tent. This evening the subject of the Bishops was taken up. They had been called to the council to give an account of their wards & to let the Council know how & in what situation the poor was in & whether they done their duty or not. They were nearly all present and all reported their wards in a good situation. & doing well.

President Young stated that he had a talk with the Omaha chief on the subject of their killing our cattle he said he could not govern his men & we had best picket in the town &c.

Sunday October 25th 1846. Went to meeting at the stand Heber spoke on the subject of economy & saving our rags and sending them down the river to buy flour with, and was followed by Brigham on the same subject. He also laid the subject of picketing in the City as mentioned at council last night. It was unanimously voted by the people to do it and Monday week was the time appointed to commence. It was also advised for those who had not built to put their houses on the line which would save so much picketing.

He also spoke on the nature of our journey & suffering and said that in ten years it would be one of the most interesting histories in the world &c

There was ten men appointed to gather up all the stray cattle on this side of the river and take them up to the rushes and winter them on the same terms that other cattle are wintered there. This is to keep the cattl from falling into the hands of the Omahas. These belong to the sick & others who cannot look for them. Just before meeting was dismissed Bishop Miller came to the stand He had come down with about 40 waggons and teams to go to the settlements to buy provisions.

He reported his camp in a most flourishing condition In good health and spirits. That they were were living in houses & were on the Running Water. That they had had four deaths which were adults & two Deaths of children. That there was plenty of rushes on the Running Water all along it up to its head and that there was not any thing to hinder from traveling to its head in the winter

That they were on the nearest and best rout to the pass in the mountains That it was a level road all the way to Fort Larame That James Emmett Joseph Holbrook and Jos Mathews were sent as a committee to look out a road to the pass and report in time to start in the spring.

That the Indians were extremely friendly & John Kay was gone with the Punckaws on their winter hunt as a gun smith.

I think President Young some what doubted his report for he said that he had felt all the time to pray for Miller's company That they might be delivered from the violence of the Indians and that he felt so yet.

At 5 o'clock I went to council at Daniel Cahoons[3] House The council adjourned from thence to Harrison Burgess so as to meet with Bp Miller & his men as they wanted some advice in what maner to pursue to procure their provisions &c to the best advantage. The Council proceeded forthwith to the place and Miller and some of his men were there.

They were advised not to go in to Missouri but to stop here and send their oxen to the rushes & let them recruit & Brigham would give his hands work and pay them more than they could get in the settlements in such things as they needed. In the mein time to send some men to buy up the things that they wanted in such a manner that the citizens would not know who they were and thus not raise the price of grain and for Miller not to go to Sarpee's as he would know what he was down for and there being many up from the settlements waiting for the payment of the Pottawattamis, the word would go out and they could not do as well by it. Brigham also told Miller that he wanted to have a long talk with him & find out his manner of Deal and living and for Miller to find out his and perhaps each might improve by the other all of which he agreed to do. He said many other thing which I need not now mention

President Young spoke on the subject of stockading the place. There was a committee appointed of the council to locate the line and a meeting to be called at sunrise in the morning to let the people know where to build so as to be on the line. came home about 9 o'c —

Monday Octr 26th 1846. The meeting was called as desided last night and the people notified where to build on the line. nothing more today.

Tuesday and Wednesday October the 27th and 28. Made arraingements and sent off my oxen & one waggon to the Des Moines for flour & us to recieve one fourth of the flour for the use of the waggon & team also made arraingements with John Bills to use my team in partnership to a good advantage. Nothing more of importance.

Thursday October the 29th 1846. Drew wood all day.

At 7 o'clock I went to council at Daniel Cahoon's house. There was not much up at this council very interesting except the case of Bishop Miller Some of his men was here to enquire into the reason why they could not be set over on credit

3. Daniel Stiles Cahoon, third of Reynolds Cahoon's five sons, was born April 7, 1822, at Harpersfield, Ohio. He was baptized in 1831, and with his father's family lived at Kirtland, Far West, and Nauvoo. Here he was a stonemason on the temple, a member of the band, and one of the Quorum of the Seventy. On July 27, 1843, he married Jane Amanda Spencer, and in 1846 at Winter Quarters he married her sister Martha. Each wife bore him eight children.

Cahoon came west in 1848, settled at South Cottonwood, Salt Lake County, where he worked at farming, stonecutting, and bricklaying. In 1877 he moved to Deseret, Millard County, Utah. He died there on November 13, 1903.

This brought up the subject & it appeared that Miller had run reckless as usual down to Mr Sarpee's contrary to the council refered to on Sunday night & had sent word back for his teams to come on without paying for their ferriage This was the testimony of W. Richards He also said that he had ran directly contrary to council in every particular.

After the council had adjourned Brigham appeared at the door and took up the subject. He had been without and heard all that was said He handled the case very ruff. He said that Miller & Emmett had a delusive spirit and any one that would follow them would go to hell &c That they would sacrifice this people to aggrandize themselves or to get power. That he was now trying to go and raise the price of grain which would be for us to pay after he was gone & that he would not clean up after him any longer. He said that they would yet apostatize. He said many more things on the subject but this will suffice at this time.

Friday and Saturday October the 30th and 31st 1846. I drew wood all day.

Sunday Nov 1st 1846. Went to meeting at the stand. Nothin particular took place. At 5 o'clock P. M. went to council at Daniel Cahoons house. But nothing of importance took place

Monday Nov 2nd 1846. At home all day sick till in the after noon & then worked at home. At dark the 4th Sub-Division met here to divide their hay & appointed 4 men to settle and divide to wit W. Chapman J. C. Wright C. Sandford and myself. They were to divide it according to the amount of labor done by each one while making hay.

Tuesday Nov 3rd 1846. Met with the men to divide the hay & settle affairs for the Sub-Division, which we did without any trouble was all day at it.

Wednesday Nov 4th 1846. Was unwell. Taking a violent cold, But went up in the grove west and cut some house logs which was the first work that I had done towards building me a house. When I came home I was quite give out.

Thursday Nov. 5th 1846. Cut and drew house logs today & got very wet & cold coming home.

About one hour after dark the Marshall came here after me to go and help take care of a man named Beers who had kicked his wife out of the tent and was in the habit of abusing his family and also wanted to drag them away against their will

We went & finding he had gone to bed we let the matter rest where it was till morning His wife going to Br Rogers to stay as she darst not go home.

Friday Nov. 6th 1846. This was a damp day. I was around home most of the time. Went with the Marshall to see Brigham relative to this Beers mentioned last night. He appointed this evening to call the council together to act on the subject and then went to see Br G. W. Harris, who had had to settle like difficulties with him while on the other side of the river. He said that he found him to be a mean, disagreeable, willfull incoragable man and regardless of peace and good order and the council and authorities of this church.

At 5 o'clock the Council met on the Point overlooking the North End of the City. There were present of the Twelve Brigham Young, H. C. Kimball Amasa Lyman. Orson Pratt Willard Richards and of the High Council A. Cutler R. Cahoon C. P. Lott, A. P. Rockwood Thomas Grover J. M. Grant and Bishop Whitney & myself and the Marshall making in all 15. William Clayton also.

It was proposed what to do with those who were in our midst whose bodies were tabernacles for devils that is rebelious wicked ungovernable men who are breeding a continual disturbance & exciting others to discontent &c

It was unanimously decided to have the Law of God put in force on them &c. There was much said and but one feeling on the subject

Saturday Nov 7th 1846. Drew logs for house, and was uncommonly bad with the sick headache in the afternoon & all night.

Sunday Nov. 8th 1846. Got up before day and in company with Major Bills, went and drew in a load of hay. then went to meeting

Joseph Young spoke on the necessity of prayer, liberality &c wanted the Seventies to meet &c and was followed by Heber on economy again and how to kneed up musty flour to make it good &c. then Brigham on the speculation of the sisters making willow baskets & selling for some thing to live on instead of selling their fine things.

Got a letter from A. J. Stout all well at Garden Grove yet.

In the after noon went to a meeting of the Presidents of seventies at Brighams new house.

The subject of the Seventies taking care of their own poor was taken up and agreed to & many other thing. We were advised by Brigham to set our Quorums in order. He also asked us to take hold and dig the mill race which was agreed to &c and at 5 o'clock met the council at Brighams tent. There was nothing done except of a local nature.

Monday Nov 9th 1846. Worked at my house all day. It was a damp warm day.

Tuesday Nov. 10th 1846. Worked at home all day, riving boards for house.

Wednesday Nov. 11th 1846. Damp day. At home unable to work at 7 o'clock went to council at Brighams house. Nothing done of importance. Heard from Nauvoo & Hancock County. Things were in a state of anarchy and confusion The mob even driving each other & plundering at their will. The Govenor talks of doing something

To day I recieved a written notice that I had been appointed by a meeting of the Seventies last night to "visit each house, tent or waggon in which dwells any of the Seventies or any of their families" in the Ward in which I live and ascertain their names, age, standing, quorum, and also the condition of themselves & families according to a form given me at the time and make a report next Friday at a meeting to be held, also to notify every abled bodied man to attend a "BEE" to dig the mill race which is to be done by the Seventies next Saturday &c.

The object is to look up and set in order the different quorums of Seventies &c as will be noticed as we go on.

Thursday Nov 12th 1846. Drew Logs and worked at my house After dark went round to look up the Seventies as noticed last night

Friday Nov 13th 1846. Worked at my house and filled out the order to look up the Seventies, and at dark went to the meeting of the same and give in the report which was accepted. It was there determined to set each Quorum in order & have them look to their poor.

Saturday Nov. 14th 1846. Worked at my house.

Sunday Nov. 15th 1846. Went to meeting Heard a letter from Elder Taylor in which it was stated that Sidneyism was entirely down & Strangism going down also He gave an account of several men who had followed them of & showed their present situation which was truly desolate as all will be who turn from the truth.[4] He was at New York just ready to sail for England

4. The contest between Sidney Rigdon and Brigham Young for leadership of the Mormon Church has already been noted. By April of 1845 Rigdon had started a church of his own, which he called "The Church of Christ." It was set up in much the same pattern as the

In the evening met the council at 6 o'clock. amongst other things the subject of guarding the City was taken up. Neither the council or Twelve were satisfied with the present arraingements as it did not effect anything for it is well known to all that there is not a guard kept up at all and moreover the Military officers will not persevere hard enough to keep up one and it always comes out a failure

President Young was most decidedly in favor of a regular Police guard being formed again some were against it but after he gave his views at length the council concured unanimously in his opinion and appointed a committee of three to make out a list of the men who were to compose the guard and make report tomorrow evening. The committee was composed of Brigham, Heber and myself.

After Council we proceeded to make out the list & took down 19 names & agreed to meet tomorrow morning to finish our report. I then came Home in the rain

Monday Nov. 16th 1846. Rainy day. I went to Brighams this morning & Heber not coming I & Brigham increased the list of the guard to 24 names. & I then came home & was there all day not very well

At 6 o'clock P. M. I went to the council. Brigham made the report of what we had done & I read over the list of the names of the guard which was accepted & the Committee not to be discharged untill the same was organized Brigham then gave them some instructions showing how to proceed which was agreed to on the part of the council. nothing more took place of importance to me

Tuesday, Wednesday & Thursday Nov. 17th 18th and 19th 1846. Was engaged at working at my house & drawing logs wood & hay

On Wednesday evening met the council at Rockwood's tent when the subject of the sheep herd was talked over at length & I left before council was out.

On Thursday evening I met the guard at Rockwoods tent as had been previously called together to be organized into a "Regular Standing Police" Guard, President Young & Kimball was there with myself as the committee spoken of before to organize them which was done & I was chosen Captain by the unanimous vote of all present.

The names of those present were as follows
1 Jonathan C. Wright.
2 Phineas H. Young[5]
3 Isaac C. Haight[6]

Mormon Church with twelve apostles and a standing high council. His center of activity was at first in Pittsburgh, Pennsylvania, but was later moved to Iowa.

James J. Strang had been in the Mormon Church only four months when Joseph Smith was killed. He had been trained as a lawyer and was converted in Wisconsin by Lyman Wight. Strang's claims to leadership of the Mormon Church came from a letter which he said he had received from Joseph Smith, written just before the martyrdom. He set up his headquarters at Vorree, Wisconsin (now called Spring Prairie, Walworth County). For a time both John C. Bennett and John E. Page were associated with him. Jones, *Vintonia*, V, 19, 13.

5. Phineas Howe Young, a brother of Brigham Young, was born February 16, 1799, in Hopkintown, Massachusetts. In 1832 he went to Pennsylvania to visit members of the Mormon Church and soon after was baptized. He filled several missions, participated in the troubles at Far West in 1838, and fled with the group after the Battle of Crooked River.

Phineas Young was one of the pioneer group of 1847. In Utah he held various positions in the church; in private life he was a printer, saddler, and mail contractor. He died October 10, 1879.

6. Isaac C. Haight was born in Windham, Green County, New York, on May 27, 1813. He was baptized into the Mormon Church on March 3, 1839, and was immediately made an elder and began preaching. Soon he was president of a branch of the church in Cayuga County, New York.

Haight came to Nauvoo in July 1843; in December 1843 he was made a member of the Old Police there. In this capacity he assisted in destroying the *Expositor* press. He did not

4 Peter W. Conover[7]

11 George D. Grant

5 William Kimball

12 Edmund Ellsworth

6 George W. Langley

13 Lyman Whitney

7 S. A. Dunn

14 Augustus Stafford

8 Jas W. Cummings.

15 Garrett W. Mikesell

9 Perrigreen Sessions[8]

16 Luman H. Calkins.

10 Elijah J. Sabin

The whole number chosen at this time was 25 not counting myself. The names of those who were absent were as follows

17 Ira Eldridge

21 Henry Herriman

18 Appleton M. Harmon[9]

22 Elias Gardner

19 Stephen Winchester jr

23 A. O. Smoot[10]

20 Alvah L. Tippitts

24 John D. Parker

25 Daniel Carns

---

leave Nauvoo until June 1, 1846, but overtook the company before they reached Winter Quarters. He followed the pioneer group west in the Pratt and Taylor company, arriving in the Salt Lake Valley in September of 1847. The next year he went out to meet the incoming immigration. In 1849 he went with the Parley P. Pratt exploring expedition to the south. From 1850-52 he filled a mission to England, bringing back 369 Saints with him.

In 1856 Isaac C. Haight was made president of the stake at Cedar City, Iron County, Utah, and served until 1859. In 1870 he was excommunicated for his "not restraining [John D.] Lee" in the massacre at the Mountain Meadows, but two years later was reinstated in the church. In 1872 he went into exile and remained so until his death, which came on September 8, 1886, at Thatcher, Arizona.

7. Peter Wilson Conover was born September 19, 1807, at Woodford, Kentucky. He joined the Mormons sometime before 1841, for that fall he went with a group to the pineries of Wisconsin to get out lumber for buildings in Nauvoo. In 1843 he was one of the first horsemen to come to the rescue of Joseph Smith after he was kidnapped at Dixon. He became one of the prophet's bodyguards.

Conover came to Utah with the Heber C. Kimball company, arriving in September 1848, and claimed to have harvested the first wheat in the territory. He moved the next year to Provo. Here he was put in charge of the Utah County Military District. In 1854 he accompanied Colonel E. J. Steptoe to Carson Valley; in 1858 he was one of the group sent to call the Nevada colonists home, a trip in which the whole company came close to dying of thirst. He died September 20, 1892, at Richfield, Utah.

8. Perrigrene Sessions, son of David and Patty Sessions, was born at Newry, Maine, June 15, 1814. At Far West he signed the covenant to help the poor leave the state; in Nauvoo he was bodyguard for both Joseph Smith and Brigham Young.

In 1845 Sessions operated a wagon shop in Nauvoo, helped to bridge the Elk Horn River, and hauled food during the Winter Quarters period to help the poor Saints. In 1847 he was guide for the Parley P. Pratt company to the valley, and during the first season, in spite of the crickets, raised 500 bushels of grain. Sessions later moved to Bountiful where he served as postmaster. He was also a miller and stockraiser.

9. Appleton Milo Harmon, son of Jesse P. Harmon was born at Conneaut, Pennsylvania, May 19, 1820. Later in Nauvoo he was a member of the police and a third lieutenant in the Nauvoo Legion. A machinist and skilled mechanic, he constructed the famous roadometer used by the pioneers to measure distances. He erected sawmills in the Salt Lake area, a furniture factory at Toquerville, and the cotton factory at Washington, in southern Utah. He was a blacksmith, contractor, and builder. Harmon's home was at Holden, Millard County, where he died February 27, 1877.

10. Abram (Abraham) O. Smoot, born February 17, 1815, in Kentucky, joined the Mormons on March 22, 1835. He worked on the Kirtland Temple, came with Henry G. Sherwood to Far West, Missouri, and joined the Danite Band. In 1839 Smoot left Far West, traveling with John L. Butler in the Emmett company, but later joined the body of the church at Winter Quarters.

In 1847 Smoot came west at the head of his own company. He was made a member of the first High Council in Salt Lake City. From 1856 to 1866 he acted as mayor of the city and later was mayor of Provo for fourteen years. He became president of a bank, a lumber yard, and the Provo Co-op Flour Mill. He promoted the Provo Woolen Mills and contributed to the Brigham Young University. He died March 6, 1895.

President Young gave us the necessary instructions and also said that our number will be perhaps increased to thirty-two

It appears by the foregoing organization that the system of the "Old Police" so much feared despised and beloved in Nauvoo is now revived on precisely the same plan and mostly the same men as there was which composed the old Police in Nauvoo & with the same Captain at their head those who dreaded us because of their wickedness there may well have the same fears now. For the same men and the same organization the same leader, the same circumstances to act on will naturally produce the same results.

After the foregoin regulations I proceeded to arrainge the guard to commence duty tomorrow evening & came home

Friday & Saturday Nov 20 & 21st '46. Was at home working at my house. and regulated the guard each evening under the Police regulations puting on six men at once and relieving at one o'clock making 12 men on guard each night.

Sunday Nov 22nd 1846. Went to meeting and staid awhile & heard a lot of letters called off They were from the army.

We learned that they had got to Santa Fe and were to start for Caliafornia when the messengers left for here[11] they were all in good health & spirits.

In the evening went to council & regulated the guard Nothing done at council of importance. Not police yet enough to do the duty wanting some seven or eight.

Monday Nov. the 23rd 1846. Drew a load of cotton-wood limbs for the horses. The bark of which is good food for them. If they have plenty of it they will not need more than half the amount of hay and corn and do as well.

This evening after regulating the guard as usual I went to the Council at H. S. Eldridges at Six o'clock. This council was convened more particularly for the purpose of ascertaining who among them were willing to do their duty & stand in their place and magnify their calling and take their portion of the burthen of the people off of the Twelve for this was their calling and duty & also to make some regulation about the disposition of Church property & find out what to dispose of and what not to &c.

President B. Young then taught & said that he did not study the revelations more than to get the spirit of the thing & he would look it up and when he varied from the written word we may say that he has lost the Spirit

He also taught the council to call the Bishops to an account and see that they also done their duty & for the council to lay plans to take care of the poor & see that the Bishops also did the same. and cause the poor to be put in a way to sustain themselves and not to make the rich hand out all they have. About the mill he said he had plans to pay every dollar of the expense of building it & it would do good for years & years to come to this people. Also that Major Harvey the Superintendant of indian affairs now contemplated building a fort at this place.

Also that this Council was not stationary & could not handle property of the Church only for present purposes that Bishops Whitney & Miller was the lawful Trustees in Trust for the church in all the world & Wm Clayton was the Clerk.

---

11. This refers to the return of John D. Lee and Howard Egan to Winter Quarters from Santa Fe where they had collected over $1,200 from the Mormon Battalion to assist in the general migration of the Saints. John D. Lee noted: "About 10 the council dissolved, when I paid Pres. Young $1277 in check Bat. money; $50 from Capt. and $16 I paid him, it being my 10th while absent." Charles Kelly, ed., *Journals of John D. Lee, 1846-47 and 1859* (Salt Lake City, 1938), 21. (Hereafter cited as Kelly, *Lee Journals.*)

Lee kept a daily account of the journey to Santa Fe. See John D. Lee, "Mormon Battalion Mission [August 30, 1846-November 20, 1846]" (typescript, Utah State Historical Society; original, L.D.S. Historian's Library).

That if we follow council it will not be long before we will have no poor among us and there would be thousands and tens of thousands to write, preach the gospel & build temples

Tuesday Nov. the 24th 1846. To day I was employed in moving into my little house now partly finished it being 12 feet square on the outside In the evening regulated the guard as usual.

Tonight myself and family had the pleasure of once more sleping in our own house for the first time since we left Nauvoo on the 9th day of last February, making nine months and fifteen days that we lived without a house. During which time we have undere went allmost every change of fortune that could be imagined. One half of my family so dear to me has been consigned to the silent grave & we who yet remain have often been brought to the verge of death   often in storms & rains have I stood to hold my tent from uncovering my sick family expecting every moment to see them exposed to the rain & wind which would have been certain death.   often have I lain and contemplated my own sickness & feeble situation, without any thing for myself and family to eat with death staring me in the face and could only contemplate what would become of them in case I was called away.

And worse yet how often have I behel[d] my family one by one yielding up the Ghost & bereaving me of every earthly prospect with the melancholy reflection that there was yet more soon to follow. How often in sorrow & anguish have I said in my heart. When shall my trials and tribulations end. But amid all these adverse changes, these heart wrending trials not once yet have I ever regreted that I set out to follow the council of the people of God & to obey the voice of the spirit to flee from the land of the Gentiles.

But to return home again. We did not enjoy much comifort tonight for my house was yet open Neither door nor windows   not even but few of the craks was yet stoped and a hard North wind blowing. We were exposed to it all & could not sleep but little tonight but lay shivering in the cold all night.

The only thing that was any satisfaction to us was that we were out of the tent for if we had been there in addition to our troubles & cold we would have been expecting the tent to blow down every moment and thus left to the "merciless blast" which to be delivered from was even a great satisfaction. This day was the first day that my only living child [daughter of Louisa Taylor] now 7 months & 2 days old ever was in a house, being born in the wild rude and unhabited prairies and remained so till now "a perfect child of nature. So much for my "New house or more properly speaking my little shanty

Wednesday Nov 25 1846. Today I sat most of the day shivering over the fire burning and freezeing in the house & a hard howling North wind blowing all day.

In the evening after regulating the guard I went to a council at Horace S. Eldridge house. This evening the Bishops was present having been previously notified to attend   It appeared that most of their wards were too big as it would take all their time if they did their duty whereupon President Young proposed to have the wards divided and the Bishops were appointed to do it and also to nominate other Bishops to be ordained for the additional Wards and make report to the next council.

When the city was first divided into Wards and Bishops put over them some were ordained who were of the Seventies & as the Bishopric belonged to the High Priest unless the person was a litteral decendant of Aaron President Young stated that those who had been appointed Bishops of the Seventies were not under any obligations to serve & if they retained their Bishopric they must go out of the Seventies & be in the High Priest's Quorum This was laid over to the next council meeting.

President Young moved that every able bodied man be taxed every tenth day to be devoted to geting wood and doing such other thing as is necessary for the poor and that it be paid in advance & that the Bishops divide the city into Wards tomorrow and notify the people to commence next day to work out this tithing which was agreed to by the council The men who did not work out his tithing is to pay an equivalent

Thursday Nov 26th 1846. The fore part of today was yet so cold and disagreeable that I did not attempt to work But in the after noon I done some work at daubing my hous which made it a little more comfortable

In the evening after arraiging the guard I went to the council meeting again at H. S. Eldridges. The Bishops made their reports which was not accepted but returned with instructions They not dividing the city properely as they divided some blocks whereas each Block should be included in the same Ward unless it would make two Wards. They had part of three Blocks in one Ward which would be hard to understand in history.

Four of the men who had been nominated for Bishops were then ordained to that office under the hands of President B. Young & R. Cahoon. Their names were Ephraim Badger, Luman H. Calkins, Willard Snow[12] Isaac Clark and Thomas Lang

After the above was attended to President Young requested of the Council that those Councillors who belong to the Quorum of Seventies might be released as they had other business to attend to which was granted

The names of those belonging to the Seventies were J. M. Grant, A. P. Rockwood B. L. Clapp and Samuel Russell. The three former were then released and Henry G. Sherwood, George W. Harris and Isaac Morley put in their place

Russell yet remained for further orders. There was also some charges brought against John Scott but did not amount to anything of importance. No more tonight

Friday Nov. 27th 1846. Today I finished mudding up my house which leaves it very comfortable. and in the evening regulated the guard as usual.

Saturday Nov 28th 1846. Today I was unwell again and did not do anything of any importance more than to regulate the guard again and about 9 o'clock went on patroll guard up and down and through the city.

Sunday Nov the 29th 1846. Went to meeting at the stand. Br Ezra T. Benson spoke on different subjects & related some of his travels to the East. He had just returned home from a mission whither he had been gone for some three or four months.

At 6 o'clock in the evening I went to council at H. S. Eldridges' house. The report of the Bishops was read and handed back for further improvements. The Bishops were required to have the people turn out and work on the mill race so as for one third of the city may work in a day for three days in succession. This is to complete the race before the ground freezes.

Addison Everett & Thomas Lang were then ordained Bishops under the hands of President B. Young & Heber C. Kimball.

---

12. Willard Snow, brother of Erastus Snow, was born May 6, 1811, in Vermont and was baptized into the Mormon Church in 1833. He moved to Kirtland, where he was made a member of the First Quorum of Seventy in 1835. He went through the Missouri troubles and in Nauvoo was active on public works.

Snow came to the Salt Lake Valley in late 1847. Here he was counselor to Daniel Spencer, was a member of the committee on the Perpetual Emigrating Fund, a magistrate, and an officer in the Nauvoo Legion. In May 1851 he was called on a mission to Scandinavia. His health failed and he died on August 25, 1852, en route from Denmark to England; he was buried at sea.

President Brigham Young made the report of the Police committee which was accepted and the committee discharged It was then voted that the police recieve 75 cents for every tour of duty they perform of half a night for their wages and that the Captain recieve 75 cents per day for his services. Horace S. Eldridge as Marshall was then appointed assessor and collector for the Police & a committee appointed to draft an assessment law for the council. I came home about 10.

Monday Nov. the 30th 1846. Drew a load of wood from the timber for Bills and was engaged in arrainging the guard the rest of the day.

Tuesday Decr the 1st 1846. Warm hard south wind all day I was around home untill time to arrainge the guard after which I was called to a council at H. S. Eldridges at 6 o'clock. This council was specially called to act on the case, of Br Beers & his wife as before mentioned on the 15th of Nov. last Nothing very particular was done. She & the children were to keep the property or as much as came by way of his wife which was 4.50 [$4.50] dollars but he was to be allowed the use of his tools to go to work here. They of course parted but were forbidden to marry again to any one else by president Young They both agreed to abide the council.

A committee of three consisting of Daniel Spencer Daniel Carn and myself were then appointed to value the property and all over 450 dollars was to be left to him and thus it is. No more tonight

Wednesday Decr 2nd 1846. (I was very unwell all day today & did not go out of my house untill in the after noon when I went round the city as is my custom and arrainged the [crossed out]) guard for the night. Was at home writing all day & arrainged the guard in the evening, & at 6 o'clock went to a council at Horace H. Eldridges.

This evening the committee to draft an assessment law reported the same which was accepted. It taxed all personal property over certain amounts specified in different articles but did not fix the per cent on the amount.

Thursday Decr 3rd 1846. I was very unwell all day today and did not go out of my house untill in the after noon when I went round the city as was custom and arrainged the guard for the night at 6 o'clock I went to a meeting of the seventies at Prest Z. Pulcifer's[13] House.

The subject of taking care of our own poor as before spoken of was taken up and as so many Bishops had been appointed lately the poor was left to them & we were to refere to our poor to them & only see that they were looked to

It was also spoken of but not yet entered into that we would join several Quorums together in order to have enough to form a meeting & thus do Quorum business with more dispach

Friday Decr 4th 1846. Went G. W. Mikesells today and purchased about 4 buffalo skins dressed. This is intended for an over coat & leggins &c to stem

---

13. Zera Pulsipher was born June 24, 1789, at Rockingham, Windham County, Vermont. He joined the Mormon Church in 1832, and at once went out as a missionary, one of his first converts being Wilford Woodruff. He moved to Kirtland in 1835. In 1838 he was made a member of the First Quorum of Seventy, and later was one of the first seven presidents over all the church.

Pulsipher traveled to Missouri in the Kirtland Camp, a wagon train of more than 500 Mormons. In 1848 he was captain of one hundred in Brigham Young's company; in 1851 he was a member of the first municipal council in the Salt Lake Valley. In 1861 Pulsipher and his sons were called to southern Utah to care for the church cattle herds. They settled in Hebron, near the present town of Enterprise. He died there on January 1, 1872.

the North wind in on guard. After this I went and attended to the guard as before and attended a council at six o'clock P. M. at W. Richards new house

There was much up tonight in Council about the wheat committee & other temporal affairs but nothing of interest to me but the appointment of J. C. Wright to the office of Assessor and collector for the police in the place of H. S. Eldridge who had gone to Missouri with a team instead of attending to the duty of his appointment which would have disappointed the police very materially had the police tax been delayed

The council also decided that the police should have some Church beef which will greatly relieve us as most of us have now to live on bread and water & as our regular duty.

Saturday Decr 5th 1846. Was at home and around the city making arraiging police matters as usual. Last night Br J. C. Wright & I. [Isaac] C. Haight each lost one of their children who had been sick They were of the police and on guard. Such is the adversity attending police duty

Sunday & Monday Decr 6th & 7th 1846. Was at home & uncommonly sick on Sunday on Monday killed a cow Regulated the guard each day as ever

Tuesday Decr 8th 1846. Was at home arraiged the guard as usual (made me a pair of Buffalo Skin moccasins)

Wednesday Decr 9th 1846. This morning about three o'clock I was called up by S. A. Dunn one of the police then on guard. He said that there was a difficulty amongst the Omahas camped North of town & some had been shot. & I was wanted at President Young's so I went there and called up some more of the police & some others as I went

When I got there I found his house crouded full of the Omahas who had fled there for shelter. One squaw had been shot through the arm which was shattered to atoms & an old indian picking out the little bones with his fingers. Her arm was cut off the next day by Dr. Cannon[14]

Old Big Head a chief was shot in the head arm & had his thumb shot off He was badly wounded some were missing and supposed to be dead.

The utmost confusion reighned with them and they appeared frightened badly. I here learned that they had been attacted by a party of the Iowas who came to their lodges at this dead hour of the night and fired upon them & then fled I in company with a party of the police and some others went with some of the indians to their Lodges to see if any thing more was done and to hunt for the missing

Their lodges were in a gore of blood but could not find any one. However after a long while one of the old Indians raised a howling yell & was answered not far off where we found the one we supposed to be dead He was at Charles Patten's he was very badly wounded a ball passing in near the left eye. The ball was started out of its socket I did not think he would live.

---

14. Dr. Cannon's identity has not been fully established, but Dr. Priddy Meeks verifies the fact of his existence. Writing of the work of the Society of Health, Meeks said: "Old Dr. Cannon, a poison doctor, and poisoned against the Mormons too, could get but little to do among the sick; said if we would give him all the surgery to do he would quit doctoring; so we did and he joined the Council of Health and proved a great benefit to us, being a man of much experience and intelligence. I learned considerable by helping him to dissect the dead." J. Cecil Alter, ed., "The Journal of Priddy Meeks," *Utah Historical Quarterly,* X (1942), 178.

Many of the early doctors of Utah belonged to a cult of "Thompsonian Doctors," who treated disease with mild herbs. They referred to those with medical training as "Poison Doctors," hence the term as applied to Dr. Cannon above.

We then went back and after seeing that all was put to rights came home & yet it was not day While at their Lodges we could hear the Iowas howling on the other side of the river.

About the middle of the forenoon I went up again to see how matters were going on I found the wounded indians located in a sod house where they had been put by order of President Young and doing as well as could be expected.

The rest of the Indians moved their lodges by President Young's house as they were afraid to stay any longer where they were least they should be attacted agan

I went and examined the Lodges and found that the assailants had shot through them and of course what had been done was by a random shot.

In the evening I regulated the guard as usual which was all that took place of any importance.

Thursday Decr 10th 1846. Today I made myself a pair of Leggins after the real rude Indian fashion which was of more real service against the "chilling blast" than I had before imagined and I confess that I am much taken with them. I attended to the guard as usual today.

About dark my brother came he and his father-in-law Miles Anderson had arrived at the ferry but did not cross & he came over to see us. He was in good health and spirits. But Anderson & family was yet quite sick, weak and feeble.

Friday December the 11th 1846. Nothing up today of any importance I was at home and regulated the guard in the evening & after dark went with the committee to value the property of W Beers as appointed before When we got there we found them living together in seeming friendship again as if nothing had happened between them They both admitted that the property would not cover the 450 dollars and hence it would all belong to his wife so we had him to reciept his tools and left it at that for the present.

Saturday Decr 12th 1846. At and about home all day. Regulated the guard as usual.

This evening word came down from the Omaha hunting party that they had been attacted by the Soui and the whole band killed off except one who made his escape & he thinks another made his escape naked but has not been heard of. It is supposed that about 50 or 60 has been killed.

The indians hear had just got the news and were making their Lemintations in all their camps They would weep and howl, cry, writhe and twist and make every gesture of sorrow that could be imagined They made such a noise that President Young had them stopt.

Sunday December the 13th 1846. Today Allen Moved over the river & came and went into my tent. I went to meeting at the stand. Nothing of importance to relate.

At six o'clock in the evening I met the council at W. Richards house President Brigham Young gave the council instructions and in fact reproved them & the Bishops quite sharply for their negligence in not attending to the duty of their office and for working on the Sabath &c, and ordered the following items of business to be attended to forthwith

That a map of the city be procured by the next session for the clerk of this council

That the Clerk keep a regular list of the Bishops of the different wards & the wards over which they act.

That the Bishops meet with the Council once a week to recieve instruction

That the Council watch over the Bishops with a fatherly care and see that they organize and watch over their respetive Wards and see that none suffer

That the Council instruct the Bishops to have meetings in their several Wards for the men women & children once a week also to instruct them to have schools in their Wards.

He stated that he wanted the Twelve, the Council, & Bishops to search this place as with a lighted candle in their hands and put down all iniquity &c

He had an uncommon portion of the Holy spirit resting down upon him. & was filled with the sublime views of rolling forth this great and mighty work and if the council and Bishops will abide his advice a great and good work will soon be done here

Monday Decr 14th 1846. Myself & Allen cut and drew wood for A. P. Rockwood today for corn. Regulated the guard in the evening

Tuesday Decr 15th 1846. Cut & drew wood as yesterday & regulated the guard in the evening and at six o'clock went to a council at W. Richards house This council was especially called for the benefit of the Bishops who were to make a report of their wards and show the situation that they were in but their reports were not accepted for want of form so they were returned & they instructed how to proceed It appears from President Young's teaching & the way he is bringing them to their duty that he is determined to have them do business right & not neglect their duty as has been the case too much in days gone by.

He also required of the Council & Bishops to see to getting an out fit for Br George & Joseph Herring the two Mohawks, which the council & Bishops agreed to do.

After the business of the council was over they requested President Young to give them some teaching and he said that unless this people humble themselves & quit their wickedness God would not give them much more teaching and they would continue to slide off & it would not be long before those who hold the Priesthood will be hunted by those who now call themselves saints

President Heber C Kimball also said that unless there was a reformation among us he was afraid that God would send a plague among us.

They both seemed to be well aware of the murmurings of some & the disposition of some to spread the Spirit of insubordination among the people & was also aware that there was danger of them some day trying to overthrow the present organization of the church and drive off the Twelve for said he "I want us to get up a reformation and have the Holy Ghost in our midst & not have the Twelve drove from our midst for if they were it would be the greatest curse that possibly can befall us" President Young said that all that had been said was true but all that will do as he says will be safe and all that will do their duty will be saved in the celestial kingdom. He said he did not care any thing about this people going over the Mountains for it matters not any thing about it But to do the thing that God requires at this moment even to night is what he is ready to do and trust in God for the event.

Wednesday Decr 16th 1846. Worked at home & some for Rockwood for corn & in the evening regulated the guard as usual. Jos. Herring staid all night here

Thursday Decr 17th 1846. Myself & Allen cut & drew wood today. Regulated the guard in the evening and at six o'clock went to a council at W. Richards House

There was many things talked over but not anything particularly relating to me. The Bishops made reports again but did not have them right yet so they were again instructed how to do business &c

A snow about an inch deep during the session of the council

Friday Decr the 18th 1846. This was a cold day and nothing done by me of importance but to regulate the guard as usual.

Saturday Decr 19th 1846. This morning I and some others went to the Omaha camp below the city about a mile to hunt for some stolen property but did not find it but they promised to hunt it up and send it up to the owner.

While there the interpreter Mr Logan Fontanell informed me that when he went up to the place where the Sioux slaughtered the Omahas the other day they found 73 men women & children slain & two had since died of their wounds one last night.

Nothing more of importance took place today. In the evening I regulated the guard. At late bed time Allen & myself went out on patroll guard and was out some two or 3 hours.

Sunday Decr 20th 1846. Went to meeting at the stand and heard President Young preach on the subject of the insubordination of some of the people & their stuborness, their murmurings & complaining refusing to pay tax and tithing and comply with the requirements of the Council also their stealing and all such matters. He told all such what they depend upon when we got far enough to keep them from running back to the gentiles and also what the law would be in such cases & also said that he was not going to have any more of their grumbling at hom and all those who did not intend to abide council had best flee to the gentiles again for all who were among us should both help support the poor and pay their tax whether they belonged to the church or not, or leave the camp.

Regulated the guard as before and at six o'clock went to Council at W. Richard's house Jonathan C. Wright made the return to the council of the assessment on the police tax. The entire amount of property in camp subject to taxation in the city or belonging to the citizens of this place was 101550 dollars The report was accepted and a committee appointed to fix the per centage to be levied on the amount assessed to cover the expense of the police.

The subject of the police was laid before the council by President Young in relation to so many of them either being absent or unwilling or unable to do duty for I could not now make out a guard without some standing every night.

The matter of raising more to supply the wants to fill up the guard was refered to the committee to select & organize the police to wit Brigham Heber and myself. To morrow was set apart by the Twelve, Council and Bishops to go work at the council house.

Monday Decr the 21st 1846. Was at home today. Nothing up particular. In the evening I regulated the guard and after dark went on patroll Guard awhile in company with my brother.

Tuesday Decr 22nd 1846. To day I worked most of the day at the council house and went on patroll guard alone untill nine o clock.

Wednesday Decr 23rd 1846. Worked on the Council house part of today and was round arrainging the guard also in the evening went on Patrol guard

Thursday December 24th 1846. Worked awhile on the council house was quite unwell with the sick head ache in the after part of the day. Regulate the guard as usual & at six o'clock went to a council at W. Richards

The Bishops finished their reports by which we find that there is now in the City 3483 inhabitants. 75 widows. 386 sick — 502 well men 117 sick men 138 absent men 814 waggons, 84½ Days tithing done 83¾ cords of wood drawn for tithing 561¼ day work done on the mill race. 145 horses-29 mules. 388½ yoke of oxen & 463 cows in camp. 53 and women whose husbands are in the army[15]

---

15. This census bears out the observation that nowhere, either in the Lee or Stout records, does the author give the number of women and children. The diarists list the men with

The committee to fix the rate per cent on the police tax reported that there be three fourths per cent per dollar levied on the amount assessed which was 101550 dollars which will make the amout of tax to come at $761.12 cents which will most likely fall short of the police fund

The collector was ordered to proceede forthwith to collecting & Orson Pratt appointed treasurer —

The committee to fill up the police last Council made their report which was accepted and the committee discharged

The total number of police now on the list was 33 and the names of those who have been enlisted since the organization are

1. John S. Gleason[16]
2. A. J. Stout
3. Zebide[e] Coltrin[17]
4. Graham Coultrin[18]
5. Welcome Chapman
6. Willard Snow &
7. Benjamin F Cummings[19]

Out of this number Perrigreen Sessions & John D. Parker declined to serve and William Kimball & George W. Langley had to quit in consequence of their ill health as standing guard would soon weare them out. This makes 4 men less in the police reducing the actual number to 29 including myself Out of this there is 5 who has never done duty as yet But there is now but 19 who at this time pretends to or on whom I can expect any service and with this small number I have had the good fortune to keep the peace of this place as yet and there has not to my knowledge been any dissatisfaction by any of the authorities nor fears least all was not right. I believe I can say that all seems to be well and quiet. The number of men on guard each night is ten that is five at once and relieved at one o'clock at night

President Young spoke in relation to some of the brethren who were vending ardent spirits in this camp and was thereby taking from many the means which they needed to buy their bread.

There was much said by different ones of the council The result of their deliberations were that all those who had ardent spirits in this place to sell should forthwith deliver the same to the Bishops of their ward who was to sell it and the neat proceeds after paying the owners for it should be applied to the poor and any one who should bring any into this place for sale without the consent of the council should forfeit the same to the use of the poor & the the Marshall was

---

care, usually also the boys over fourteen years of age; they give the number of horses, mules, oxen, cows, pigs, chickens, dogs and cats, but not the women.

In this case in a total population of 3,483 souls, the men are counted as 502 well, 117 sick, and 138 absent with the Battalion. A little simple arithmetic shows a total of 757 men as against 2,736 women and children.

16. John Streator Gleason, born January 13, 1819, in the State of New York, joined the Mormons in 1842, became a bodyguard for the prophet and a member of the Nauvoo Legion.

He came to Utah in 1847 and settled at Little Cottonwood, where he operated a sawmill. He moved to Centerville, Tooele, and Farmington, building mills and improving the community at each place. He died at Pleasant Grove, Utah, December 21, 1904.

17. Zebedee Coltrin, born September 7, 1804, in Ovid, New York, was a Mormon missionary in 1832 and a member of the Quorum of the Seventy in 1835. In 1841 he was a counselor to Almon W. Babbitt in Kirtland. He came to Utah in 1847 with the pioneer group, settled finally at Spanish Fork, where he died July 20, 1887.

18. Graham Coltrin is not identified except that his name is listed with that of Zebedee Coltrin on April 10, 1843, as a member of a group called on missions. The two men might have been brothers.

19. Benjamin F. Cummings, born March 3, 1821, at Farmington, Maine, came to Nauvoo in 1840. In 1844 he was made a Seventy. Both his parents died at Winter Quarters during the winter of 1846, and he came west in 1847 with the Daniel Spencer company. A carpenter and millwright, he worked on the first mill in the valley. He also played in the band and led the Tabernacle Choir. His later years were devoted to temple work.

JANUARY 1847 221

authorized to seize on all such as did. The ferry-man was also forbid to take any across the river only as above provided.

The proceedings of the Council was put to the Bishops who who were present & also a large congregation which was unanimously concured in by them.

Friday Decr 25 1846. This of course is Christmas & is a fine clear warm day. A man can be comfortable without his coat while walking the streets. I was about the city as usual looking to peace safety & well being of the same according to the duty of my office as a Police officer

Saturday Decr 26th 1846. Was working with Allen at his house which was adjoining my own & the same size   regulated the guard as usual and went on patrol guard till about ten o'clock.

Sunday Decr 27th 1846. Went to meeting at the stand with my wife. Elder Orson Pratt spoke in relation to our journey in the Spring. Advising to send out a pioneer company to get to the head waters of the Running Water by the time grass comes or before and be ready to go over the Black Hills & put in a crop of corn somewhere on this side of the mountains near the head of the Yellow Stone.[20] He was followed by Woodruff & Benson approving of his views on the subject.

In the evening I went to a council at W. Richards   There was not any thing done of importance

Monday Decr 28th 1846. Today I was engaged some at work at my brother's house and also in looking to police duty. In the evening had a police meeting at my house to take into consideration best way to arrainge our accounts to draw our pay as the collection on the police tax was now coming in. After meeting I went on patroll guard an hour or so

Tuesday Decr 29th 1846. There was a light snow fell today   I was at home most of the time and also around on business as usual. I issued orders to the Treasurer O. Pratt for the amount of 20 per cent on the amount due each police-man as it was understood by us to draw that amount on our dues first.

Wednesday Decr 30th 1846. So I went and entered the police orders, issued yesterday, in the treasurey and had each policemans tax applied on his order and arrainged the residue so that it could be collected by the proper policeman on demand. After that I was around as usual and at dark had a police meeting at H. S. Eldridge's They there approved of my course in regard to the orders and also unanimously voted to pay the tax due the police from Prest B. Young which was 15 dollars as a token of respect due him from us & as a prophet & leader to this people. After this I came home and then went on patrol guard untill about Eleven o'clock.

Thursday Decr 31st 1846. This was a cold windy day. I was at home almost of the day, and was very unwell. I only went out in Town long enough to regulate the guard   There was a council this evening but I was not able to go to it.

Friday January 1. 1847. New Year's day and cold and windy at that   all peace and good order.

I have not heard a gun fire on this occasion neither this evening or this morning except three rounds of artillery in the morning. I attended to business as was usual. (no more for today [crossed out])

---

20. Their talk of making a way station somewhere "near the head of the Yellow Stone" only points up their indecision, their lack of knowledge and definite plan.

(**Saturday Jan 2nd 1847.** Quite sick all day with a head ache   Very little up. I attended to police duty as usual. [crossed out])

This being the beginning of another year and our sojourn in Winter Quarters perhaps is about half out I thought I would give you a synopsis of the "face of affairs".

The brethren have mostly got into their houses.

The city is divided into 22 wards & has a Bishop over each ward.   They seem to be doing their duty better than I ever knew the Bishops to do before. The poor are uncommonly well seen & attended to

The police Tax are being collected and the people are appearantly willing to pay the same though some have fled because of the police tax and are trying to raise an excitement against us in Missouri & all who have left here contrary to council as far as I can learn have had bad luck & they are truly "cursed"

The most opposition we have in Missouri is in consequence of the Stories of the dissenters   otherwise the Missourians are very friendly. Pork can be bought from two to four cents a pound.   Corn from 40 to 50 cents a bushel.   Wheat from 31 to 40 or 50 cents a bushel. and other things in proportion.   I have seen potatoes sell at a dollar per bushel here. Had not the Saints been here the Missourians could not have sold anything for previous to our coming they had no market for their produce.

The Seventies Quorum have established a factory to manufacturing willow baskets and are now employing some 20 or 30 hands to good advantage and have made quite a number of baskets   This gives employment to those who have no other means of supporting themselves by their labor.

Doctor Willard Richards has a house with 8 sides and covered with dirt. & forms an oval and is called by the names of the Octagon, potato heap, apple heap, coal pit, round house, The doctors den

I might have said that some here have great objections to police.

The mill will be in opperation in next month.

There are now arraingements being made to send off three hundred pioneers before winter breaks who will proceed to the head of the running watter and sustain their teams on the rushes as they will travail up the river. and wait there till grass rises & then proceed to the foot of the mountains near the head of the Yellow Stone where they will put in a crop.

The Twelve contemplate & are now raising companies that is each is raising a company who will follow after the pioneers when grass rises here with as many persons as can subsist on the crop put on by the pioneers

There is peace in this place and the Saints seem willing to abide council notwithstanding some dissent and escape & find fault with every move that is made for even now the transgressor in Zion begins to tremble.

I have heard of no report of adultery in this place since the affair last fall or summer with the three young men. spoken of at the time so effectual was the lessen give then on that subject.

The war between the United States and Mexico appears to be continued and there is yet no signs of its termination which creates great dissatisfation in the States.   Elders Hyde & Taylor both arrived in saftey in England

Our herds and flocks are wintering well on the rushes & are thriving well   The weather has been thus far uncommonly favorable but the wind often changing had no snow to interfear with any business yet & every body seem to be industerously & usefully employed

The Council decided to have this place stockaded or Picketed in to keep out the Omahas.   There are a great number of houses on the line, but it does not yet look like a fortified place as the line is not half filled.

The place hase the appearance of a log, town some dirt ruffs & a number of caves or "dug outs" made in the banks sometimes called "Dens" & such like names.

The town would be hard to set on fire & burnt down for there are so many "dirt toped & dirt houses[21]

We are not now troubled much with the indians, who at this time are away from here [¼ page blank]

Saturday January 2nd 1847. I was quite unwell all day with a sick head ache There is very little up in town I attended to police duty as usual

Sunday Jan. 3rd 1847. Was at home all day; only went out to attend to police duty. At six in the evening I went to a council at W. Richard's house There was nothing up of any general importance which need to be related here.

Monday January 4th 1847. This morning I went to Dr Richard's to get the minutes of the council of last Friday night as I was then unable to attend council While there President Young spoke to me to go in his company in the Spring which I agreed to.

While there I also learned that Elders Hyde & Taylor while on their way to England came very near being wrecked. They saw three vessels wrecked in the midst of the Ocean & they saved half of those in one vessel another ship taking in the rest.

I issued orders again to the Treasurer for 87 dollars for the police & regulated guard as usual.

Tuesday January 5th 1847. This morning I went to O. Pratts the Treasurer of the police tax to file in the orders of the which I issued yesterday & also took up some provisions in pay to myself & got an order on the store for a small amount These things greatly relieved me for I was in want very much.

I spent the remainder of the day, after taking my wife to the store, in notifying the police to go and get their pay. And regulated the guard as usual.

This evening there fell a cold snow with the wind hard blowing from the North howling through the city & spreading a lonely gloom on all nature which I seldom feel This is the first snow that realy deserves the name which has fell this year.

Wednesday Jan. 6, 1847. This was the coldest day that we have had this year and seems to scorch everything which comes in contact with the cold North wind. We were very uncomfortable all day in despite of our best fires and passed of the day to the best advantage to be comfortable

I went out in the evening & regulated the guard and returned and did not leave any more

Thursday Jan 7th 1847. Towards day the howling North wind, which had not yet ceased to blow, began to howl with renewed strength and filled our little Shanty full of its cold and piercing breath. The weather had increased in coldness & when morning light came I found one of those intolerable cold clear days that bids the most industerous to cease his labours & keep within

There was no stiring only by those who were either out of wood or hay or compelled by some means to meet the "chilling blast."

I was in doors all day untill I went out in the evening to regulate the guard and at six o'clock I went to a council at W. Richard's house. There was nothing

---

21. Nowhere does Hosea indicate the general suffering for food that other writers emphasize. John Pulsipher spent most of the winter on the road to and from the Missouri settlements obtaining provisions, and still there was never enough. John D. Lee always kept some of his adopted sons "out," several working for food and others hauling it in. He himself made several trips. The death count at Winter Quarters during the next few months was more than 600.

done of any particular importance. The wind this evening turned to the South where it blew all night.

Friday Jan 8th. 1847. Clear cold windy day. The wind changing to the North West. I was at home till time to regulate the guard in the evening after which I was at home. Joseph Herring was here all day. He was entirely dissatisfied with the Twelve and swore he would take Br. Willford Woodruff's life neither would he go on with us in the Spring but intended to take the team, which was now being raised for him to go after his people with, and leave us and never come back He said also that his brother George was of the same mind that he was. He was about half drunk & spoke what was in his heart. So it appears that all the trouble & expense laid out in them will prove futile because they have not integrity and stability enough be done well by when it is entirely gratis on our part. He staid all night.

Saturday Jany 9th 1847. Still cold all day. The weather was one degree colder than it had been this year. it being 9 degrees below zero. Herring was here all day drunk & still breathing out his corrupt mind & dissatisfied feelings against the policy of the Twelve. I was at home all day untill I went out to regulate the guard. While out I chanced to meet President Young and I gave him a hint of what was in the heart of the Herrings and agreed to see him further about this evening accordingly I & my brother went about dark to his house & saw him. Br Heber & J. D. Grant was there We related his sayings to them & gave our feelings about him and apprized them fully of what might be expected of him. After this Brigham & Heber went with us, (or we with them) to see Br Woodruff & let him also know what was in the heart of Herring who intended to take his life. When we came to Br Woodruffs, we found the house full so the President invited him to take a walk which he immediately consented to and we all set out & went to Br E. T. Benson's (& gave them a long [crossed out]) & there had an agreeable visit but there not being a convenient opportunity nothing was said abut the subject of Herring. We went away & Brigham gave him a hint of what was intended against him. Presidents Young & Kimball then went home and I related the particulars to Br Woodruff after which we came home. but had not been here long before Br Isaac C Haight one of the police then on duty, came to my house with Herring who he found had got into a scrape with Br Blazzard & was trying to dirk him & he brought him away, to me after swearing that he would revenge himself on those he was mad at he at length wanted to go to Brighams to get a Bowie knife to kill Br Blazzard.

He wanted me to go with him as he said I was his friend. I of course went and took Br Haight with me for we did not like to let him go alone while he was breathing out his threats against the brethren On our way we met with Br James W. Cummings who was on guard & I requested him also to go along which he did.

He stoped at Br James Hendrix's on the way, while we waited in the street From there we went on and he broke off abruptly and went into Br E. T. Bensons. They were going to bed but he detained them perhaps an hour

He then breathed out his feelings about Br Woodruff & the Twelve as I had related and thus became a witness against himself for he also declared that he would not go with us

From here we went to Brighams it being now about Eleven o'clock at night Brigham had not yet laid down. Herring gave him to understand that he could not lead us to the wilderness neither did he know how to deal with Indians &c

Brigham readily percieved his spirit and I was glad that it had happened for it confirmed all that I had said. After staying there about an hour, we came away & he staid at my house till day. The police however watched him till he laid down

Sunday January 10th 1847. Herring left here this after noon I was at home most of the day. About sun down I went out to regulate the guard and from thence to the Council at Willard Richard's house

At this council there were but five of the original Council present and the question arose whether they could do any business without 7 being present & then filling up the Council to Twelve and in case of there not being 7 of the original Council present whether they could fill up. It was decided by the president that they could not and so of course nothing more could be done and then came the the Question.

The councillors all give their opinions which all differed somewhat but all nearly thought that they could not act. Some however thought otherwise. The council called upon President Willard Richards & the rest of the 12 present to give their opinions.

President Richards said that I would ask two Questions, the first one is was Kirtland a Stake of Zion (answered it was) In the Doctrine and Covenants a law there established a High Council for the Stake. I have now a book that I learnt my letters from & it is as good now as then

The Second Question is this. Is this a Stake of Zion (answer no) now here is the spelling book again (like) the Doctrine & Covenants. I value it as high as any one else. There are three Councils mentioned there and another which was a Travling Council.

Is this a Stake of Zion or are we not Sir, a travelling council & can not we try any case we please.

In Nauvoo there was a City council to regulate trade &c If there was only two or three present of that Council; they went to work to fill it up (This was mentioned as a precedent)

Here if the council is not full, we can call in a dozen High Priests and if they are not to be had we could call in a dozen Elders &c. & fill up the council. Suppose there is Eleven left. do they go on [?] no, They fill up. If only 8 dont they fill up & is not a law made by them valid [?] certainly. If there is only six of the councillors present and they make a law can the six other councillors undo that law. Suppose eleven men go to Missouri and only one left & the salvation of Israel at stake and that one goes to work and fills up the council and does the business would it not be right

There was a time when I was the only acting president of the Church present. Suppose they had all fallen on that fatal day but me. If I could have found eleven High Priests worthy of the station I should have ordained them before the sun set behind yonder hill

It has been said that one of the 12 can not act here as a councillor I say I can act any where God will place me. but if there is a place that any of the 12 can not act & you will point it out to me I will thank you. so that I can keep in my place.

Where is the room for contention in this Council. If men are sick or necessarily detained other men can act for them. If a man will not attend to his place but neglects it for half a dozen times & does not give a reasonable excuse cut him off and put another man in his place that will act. This is my private feelings"

He was followed by George A. Smith who said "I have precisely the same views that President Richards has. If President Harris was here by himself, he has a right to go to work and fill up the Council. If a councillor is negligent and does not attend and I attend as a visitor, I can be appointed to act in his place. If you will take the Twelve for a pattern I will give it to you. If there are only 2 of them present and there is business to be done. They go to work and do it

If the junior member of this council comes here and all the rest are absent. Shall he stay here week after week? no But as President Richards said if all the rest of his councillors were killed we have a right to appoint others

The Doctrine & Covenants says there must be 7 of the council present to do business and does it not also say there must be three Presidents & if you go by that where is your three Presidents. I attended the very first High Council in Kirtlant at its organization If you are going back to Kirtland for precedents I want to see your three presidents. But I do not believe in having Twelve men called together for every little thing. I say are not the Twelve all Presidents, all Apostles but you seldom hear more than one or two speak and all the rest say: Amen. I want to know who ever heard of a Municipal High Council in Kirtland to try a few barrels of whiskey. They had a Council to try Spiritual things and it may be that barrels of whiskey are spiritual things

If there is only one member of the High Council present, he has a right to try cases — cut off — & make whiskey laws. Suppose some secret plott cuts off Eleven of the Twelve Apostles & leaves only the junior member, is he to set down and cry O! I can not act bcause there is not 7 of us? no he is not.

After this the council proceeded to business as usual and among other things ordered the assessor of the police tax to proceed forthwith and assess the property of those in the Ward on the East side of the river for the police &c and inquired of me how police matters were arrainged &c.

After Council I went and reported to the President the feeling & my opinion of Herring as I considered him unsafe for I verily believe now that he intends to take the life of Br W. Woodruff.

We had a long conversation on the subject and he told me to keep a sharp look out for him and see that he did not committ any violence on any one. He also said that he was going to have a council of the Twelve tomorrow morning & invited me & the Marshall, who was with me, to come to it. We then came home.

Monday January the 11th 1847. This morning I went to the council of the Twelve, as mentioned last evening at Br Ezra T. Benson's house We were there untill nearley dark

The subject of [blank left here][22] wicked intentions were taken into consideration and all gave their opinions which was one and the same thing to wit: the law of God to be administered in righteousness.

Br Isaac Morley was present.

The utmost confidence & good feelings seemed to prevail with all present. & I enjoyed myself extreemly well. President Young spoke of the order which he contemplated going into for our journey in the spring but nothing I think is yet definite on the subject.

I was happy to learn & see for myself that the Twelve are now perfectly aware of the evil intentions of their enemies who are thick in our midst and of whom I have more than once expressed my concern least they should take some private advantage

After council I regulated the guard and went on patrol guard with the Marshall & Br D. Carn

Tuesday January 12th 1847. This fore noon Br Carns & myself went over the river to look at the situation of the country as to the places for our enemies to lurk & hide up or prepare to carry out any evil purposes against us. We went some three miles below. I do not think it very convenient for their purposes

---

22. In the handwritten original there is a half line blank at this point into which the name of Joseph Herring should have been written since he had been the subject of discussion during the pages preceding. That "the Law of the Lord should be administered in righteousness," meant that Herring should be disposed of before he took the life of one of the leaders.

The time and place were evidently to wait upon circumstance. Herring was not mentioned again for more than a year; on April 7, 1848, Stout noted the return of Joseph Herring to Winter Quarters, but did not mention his name again.

We came back in the afternoon and stoped at Br Pratts and found that the police orders were about filled up so I came home & issued orders again amounting to 80 dollars & filed them in after regulating the guard & then (came home went on patrol guard and wrote untill late. [crossed out])

Wednesday January 13th 1847. This morning I went with my wife to A. P. Rockwoods to trade out some orders got against him from the Police Treasury but he not having his goods put up we came home & I went to W. Richards' office and wrote the minutes of the last Council and then went to Whitney's store and traded some and came home.

Br Amasa Lyman Came home with me and took dinner I then went and regulated the guard

This fore noon I sent G. W. Langley down to the Point to see if anything was going on to our injury there I wrote untill late (this Evening [crossed out]) to night

Thursday Jan. 14th 1847. Went with my wife to Rockwoods & traded some this morning & came home & went up in town again While there President Young informed me that the Twelve were going to have a council at one at Br Heber's and invited me to attend, so I came home & prepared and went accordingly.

Here the subject of our removal in the Spring was taken up & the order adopted how we should go and sustain the poor in the mein time.

There were three companies to be raised & put under three Presidents who was to have the controll of the company. It was then to be organized under captains of tens &c as usual.

The word of the Lord was obtained at this council in relation to our removal & I will give it, which will show the order of things better than I can give it.

Winter Quarters Camp of Israel
January the 14th 1847

The word & will of the Lord concerning the camp of Israel in their journeyings to the West.

Let all the people of the Church of Jesus Christ of Latter Day Saints, and those who journey with them, be organized into companies, with a covenant and promise to keep all the Commandments & Statutes of the Lord our God: Let the Companies be organized with Captains of Hundreds, Captains of Fifties, and Captains of Tens, with a President & his two Councillors at their head, under the directions of the Twelve Apostles: and this shall be our covenant, that we will walk in all the ordinances of the Lord.

Let each Company provide themselves with all the Teams, waggons provisions, Clothing, and other necessaries for the journey, that they can.

When the Companies are organized, let them go to with their might, to prepare for those who are to tarry.

Let each company with their Captain and Presidents, decide how many can go next spring; then chose out a sufficient number of able bodied and expert men, to take teams, seeds, and Farming utensils, to go as pioneers, to prepare for putting in Spring crops.

Let each company bear an equal proportion, according to the dividend of their property, in taking the poor, the widow, the Fatherless, and the families of those who have gone into the army, that the cries of the widow & the Fatherless come not up into the ears of the Lord against this people.

Let each Company prepare houses, and fields for raising grain for those who are to remain behind this season. And this is the Will of the

Lord concerning his people; Let every man use all his influence and property, to remove this people to the place where the Lord shall locate a Stake of Zion; and if ye do this with a pure heart in all faithfulness, ye shall be blest, you shall be blest in your Flocks, and in your herds, and in your fields, and in your houses, & in your families.

Let my servents Ezra T. Benson and Erastus Snow organize a Company; and let my servants Orson Pratt and Wilford Woodruff organize a company; Also let my servants Amasa Lyman and George A. Smith organize a company; and appoint Presidents; and captains of hundreds, and of fifties, and of tens; and let my servants that have been appointed, go and teach this my will to the saints, that they may be ready to go to a land of Peace.

Go thy way and do as I have told you; and fear not thine enemies; for they shall not have power to stop my work. Thou shall be redeemed in mine own due time, and if any man shall seek to build up himself, and seeketh not my council, he shall have no power, and his folly shall be made manifest

Seek ye and keep all your pledges one with another; and covet not that which is thy neighbours.

Keep yourselves from evil to take the name of thy God in vain; for I am the Lord your God, even the God of your fathers, the God of Abraham, & of Isaac, and of Jacob. I am he who led the children of Israel out of the land of Egypt, and my arm is streched out in the last days to save my people Israel

Ceace to contend one with another, Ceace to Speak evil one of another Ceace drunkeness and let your words tend to edifying one another. If thou borrowest of thy neighbour, thou shalt restore that which thou hast borrowed; and if thou canst not repay then go straitway & tell thy neighbour, least he condemn thee.

If thou shalt find that which thy neighbour has lost, thou shalt make diligent search, till thou shalt deliver it to him again, Thou shalt be diligent in preserving what thou hast, that thou mayest be a wise steward; for it is the free gift of the Lord thy God, and thou art his steward.

If thou art merry, praise the Lord with singing, with music, with dancing, & with a prayer of praise & thanksgiving. If thou art sorrowful, call on the Lord thy God with supplication, that your souls may be joyful.

Fear not thine enemies, for they are in mine hands & I will do my pleasure with them.

My people must be tried in all things, that they may be prepared to recieve the glory that I have for them, even the glory that I have for them, even the glory of Zion, and he that will not bear chastisement is not worthy of my kingdom.

Let him that is ignorant, learn wisdom by humbling himself, & calling upon the Lord his God, that his eyes may be opened that he may see & his ears opened that he may hear; for my spirit is sent forth into the world to enlighten the humble & contrite, & to the condemnation of the ungodly.

Thy brethren have rejected you and your testimony, even the nation that has driven you out; and now cometh the day of their calamity, even the days of sorrow like a woman that is taken in travail; & their sorrow shall be great, unless they speedily repent, yea very speedily! for they killed the Prophett, & they that were sent unto them, and they have shed innocent blood, which crieth from the ground against them: Therefore marvel not at these things, for ye are not yet pure; thou canst not yet bear my glory, but thou shalt behold it if ye are faithful in keeping all my words that I have given you from the days of Adam to Abraham, from Abraham to Moses; from Moses to Jesus and the Apostles; and from Jesus and his apostles to Joseph Smith, whom I did call upon by mine Angels, my ministering servants; and by mine own voice out of the heavens to bring forth my work; which foundation he did lay, and was faithful, and I took him to myself. Many have marveled because of his death, but it was needful that he should seal his testimony with his blood, that he might be honored, and the wicked might be condemned.

Have I not delivered you from your enemies, only in that I have left a witness of my name? now, therefore, hearken, & ye my people of my church; and ye Elders listen together; you have recieved my kingdom, be diligent in keeping all my commandments, least jaudgements come upon you, & your faith fail you, & your enemies triumph over you.

So no more at present.

Amen and amen.[23]

Such was the "Word & Will" of the Lord at this time, which was to me a scource of much joy and gratification to be present on such an occasion and my feeling can be better felt than described for this will put to silence the wild bickering & and suggestions of those who are ever in the way & opposing the proper council. They will now have to come to this standard or come out in open rebelion to the Will of the Lord which will plainly manifest them to the people and then they can have no influence

The council was interupted before sun down & I came home & on my way home arrainged the guard.

Langley came back from the Point & found all well there.

Friday January 15th 1847. This was one of the most cold & disagreeable day ever met with The wind in the North beating a driving snow which almost entirely obstructed the sight. I was in doors all day, & very unwell, & only went out long enough to arrainge the guard.

Saturday January 16th 1847. At home reading untill noon and then, with Allen, went to Pratt and got some provisions.

At one o'clock I attended a special call of the High Council at H. S. Eldridges. It was called together by president B. Young. The object of which was to lay before the council, "The Word & Will of the Lord" for their approval or disapproval.

The council recieved it as a revelation with joy and gladness

I will just state that it is in the order of the Priest Hood to lay a revelation before all the authorities for their sanction before it is considered binding. In this case it was done & recieved as above After council I arrainged the guard and came home after which nothing more took place today.

Sunday January 17th 1847. I was very sick all day today and could not go out.

Jos F. Herring was here all day drunk & drinking. At Bed time he was dead drunk & I had to lay him down to bed as a dead man. He was in the same mood towards the Twelve & Br Woodruff as before.

The wind was in the South all day; but about Sun-set it turned to the North & came howling back & driving a snow before it colder than had been this year it

---

23. This is the only revelation which Brigham Young ever set down as such, the only one of his to be included in the Doctrine and Covenants, where it comprises Section 136.

being 16½ deg. below zero. I could not attend to the guard but had to send for the police & do the business at home. I was up with Herring till 12.

Monday January 18th 1847.[24] Cold as ever. North wind. I was at home till evening & then went and arrainged the guard and from thence went to the first meeting of Brigham's Company which met at the council house. There was not anything done except teaching. Prest Young simply told the company what they might depend upon if they went with him & give some items of the Law of God &c all very edifying.

Tuesday January 19th 1847. Went and wrote the minutes of the last two councils, at W. Richards as I did not keep the minutes myself The last council not being able to go.

Allen was taken very sick last night. I was about as usual & arrainged the guard as usual

Wednesday January 20th 1847. Was at home all day only going to Br Pratts for some meat & tallow and arrainging the guard.

Thursday January 21st 1847. I was uncommonly sick to day & lame in the hip some what rheumatic. Could not go out & had to send for one of the Police to fix the guard.

Friday January 22nd 1847. There was a strong south wind all day We had to let down the tent, or it would have blown to pieces. It was the strongest S. wind which has been since I have been here, but at 8 o'clock P.M. it turned to North again cold as ever.

Allen had a chill today. I was weak but could go out To day I issued an order on the Treasurer for 45- dollars & 40 cents in cash for the police It was a draw of ten per cent on the total sum of their services up to this time

I drew 5. dollars & 80 cents & it was truly a "lift" to me. fixed guard as usual. Bills came home with my team today

Saturday January 23rd 1847. Today Allen moved into his house I was around as usual and went out and regulated the guard as usual.

Sunday January 24th 1847. Today my wife Louisa went to see her mother a distance of 8 miles. I was at home most of the time & "fixed" guard and at six met the Council at the Council House At this council it was decided to have all the powder in the City delivered up to me for safe keeping least it might be accidentally "blown up" and destroy the lives of some one &c but after much "talk" on the subject afterwards the vote was recinded.

Monday January 25th 1847. This was a dull dark cloudy day, trying to snow, A drove of some one or two hundred hogs came in today. I was around as usual & arrainged the guard as before. In the evening I went to the meeting of Brighams Company at the council house.

The company was organized by appointin. the following officer to wit Isaac Morley President, & John Young[25] & Reynolds Cahoon Councillors. This constituted the Presidency of the Company according to the "Word & Will of the Lord".

---

24. On this day, January 18, 1847, Joseph Herring, the Indian, was excommunicated from the Mormon Church by action of the Twelve Apostles. Brigham Young, "Manuscript History" (L.D.S. Historian's Library).

25. John Young, Brigham Young's eldest brother, was born May 22, 1791, at Hopkinton, Massachusetts. As a member of the Methodist Church he had already been trained for the ministry when he was converted to Mormonism in the fall of 1833.

He came west with the pioneer company and at the first organization of a stake in the Salt Lake Valley was made second counselor to Father John Smith, C. C. Rich being second

There was then four Captains of hundreds appointed to wit: 1 Daniel Spencer, 2 Edward Hunter, 3 Jeddediah M. Grant, 4 & Willard Snow.

There was then eight Captains of fifties: to wit: 1 Jacob Gates,[26] 2 Erastus Snow, 3 Benjm Brown, 4 James W. Cummings 5 Ira Eldridge 6 Benjm L. Clapp 7 Joseph M. Nobles, and James Bird

The captains of tens were not appointed but refered to the several hundreds & fifties

There was then instructions given to the officers how to proceede & the future plans of opperations explained but I will speak of these things as they come along. I then came home.

Tuesday January 26th 1847. This morining at ten o'clock I went to the meeting of Heber's company at the council house, which met for the purpose of organizing as Brighams did last night. It was organized as follows to wit Alpheus Cutler was appointed President & Winslow Farr & Daniel Russell[27] councillors. Henry Herriman, Isaac Higbee and Shadrach Roundy were appointed Captains of hundreds and John Pack, George B. Wallace,[28] Levi E. Riter, Milo Andrus,[29] Alvah L. Tippitts, and Harrison L Burgess were appointed Captains of fifties

The organization, as in Brigham's company, stoped here and was left for the several Captains of hundreds & fifties to complete in their several departments.

Br. Heber proposed to the brethren present to build a house for Br G. Miller in case he would come here & take his place as Bishop with Bishop Whitney, which was agreed to on the part of the people.

This put me in mind of what Br Brigham said when speaking about Miller's stubbornness and insubordination. He said that there was some men who had to be coaxed along with a lump of sugar to keep them from running off to the Gentiles & bringing persecution on us: But He said they would yet deny the faith & he would be glad how soon, for he would not coax much longer &c.

I regulated the guard as usual & was at home at dark.

---

counselor. John Young was later ordained a patriarch in the church. He was a farmer by occupation and died April 27, 1870.

26. Jacob Gates was born May 9, 1811, in Vermont and was baptized a Mormon on June 18, 1833. The next year he moved to Missouri and there shared the persecutions of the time. In 1838 he was made one of the first presidents of the Seventies, in which capacity he was still serving in 1884.

Gates filled several missions. In 1861 he managed the European immigration at Florence, Nebraska. In 1862 he was called to St. George, Utah, where he worked as a carpenter and joiner on the tabernacle and temple and was active in the church. He died in Provo on April 11, 1892.

27. Daniel Russell was born January 18, 1799, in New York State. He came to Utah in the fall of 1848 and settled at the mouth of Millcreek, Salt Lake County, near the homes of John Neff and Charles Crisman. He drew one of the first lots in the Seventeenth Ward. The first fruit in the area came from his orchard.

28. George Benjamin Wallace was born February 16, 1817, in New Hampshire. He was living in Boston, employed in the lumber business, when he was converted to Mormonism. He arrived in Nauvoo soon after the death of Joseph Smith. For some time he was undertaker and sexton there.

Wallace came to Utah in the A. O. Smoot company of 1847. Because his home was one of the largest in the Salt Lake Valley during the first years, meetings of various kinds were often held there. As a builder, contractor, and nurseryman, he was influential in many fields. He died January 31, 1900.

29. Milo Andrus was born March 6, 1814, at Pleasant Valley, New York, and was baptized into the Mormon Church on March 12, 1832. In 1834 he was a member of Zion's Camp. At Nauvoo he was a member of the police and an officer in the Legion; in 1844 he was made one of the presidents of the Quorum of the Seventy.

Andrus came to Utah in 1850, bringing an immigrant company with him. In 1856 he was bishop in the Cottonwood Ward in Salt Lake County and later was ordained to the office of patriarch. He died on June 19, 1893, at Oxford, Idaho.

Wednesday January 27th 1847. This morning I issued orders for the police, on the Treasurer Br W. Woodruff who acted now in the place of Br Orson Pratt, who is gone to Garden Grove. After that I was around as usual regulated the guard and came home & staid. The Seventies are holding a ball in the Council house & are enjoying themselves first rate

Thursday January 28th 1847. This morning there was a fine white, soft, warm, snow which had fallen last night, accompanied by a south wind. The snow continued to fall untill near 12. The wind was mild and no way uncomfortable. It was truly a beautiful morning.

I went down to Br Woodruff's to transact some business for the Police and then went around town & at one came home again. & arrainged the guard as usual in the evening. At six I went to the Council at the Council house. There was nothing done of interest.

Friday January 29th 1847. This was a fine clear warm day. No wind hardly. The snow soft. A man could take comfort in life. Every thing seemed to smile. I was around as usual attended the meeting of the officers of Brighams Company & was placed in J. M. Grants hundred. Arrainged the guard as usual

Saturday January 30th 1847. This morning I got up at one o'clock and went on guard with the Marshall. We went to W. Woodruff's and the policeman who was to have been there the latter part of the night failing to come, we stood guard there till day light.

We had suspected for some time that this policeman did not attend to his duty, for some of the others had often reported that he was not to be found on duty for four nights in succession, (when on this post). We now knew for ourselves that he was delinquent and that too at a post where he was to protect one of the Twelve, whose life he well knew was threatened by Jos F. Herring. After day light we came home & after breakfast, we went & reported the matter to President Young & he advised us to deal with him & if he did not abide what we done to bring it before the Council.

The remaining part of the day I spent as usual regulating the guard in the mein time.

At dark the Marshall & the delinquent policeman, spoken of met at my house & we sat on his case. He confessed to the delinquency somewhat as had been reported to us but notwithstanding he plad innocence & ignorance & thought with all that he was a first rate fellow. We, however, dealt with him different from what he expected, for he thought that a confession & a promise to do better & at the same time saying that he was the best kind of a fellow, would be a sufficient attonement on his part for leaving Br W. Woodruff unprotected & at the same time draw pay for not being there.

We told him that he must be droped from the police, and all his wages not paid, be forfeited, which was the lightest decision which we could give & if he could not abide that he could have it investigated before the Council and abide their decision be that better or worse.

He however agreed to abide ours

The arrearages on his pay was 19.75 which we considered a sufficient penalty withal to be afflicted on this case. His name I shall with hold for I do not wish him further injured if he does well & is true herafter.[30]

---

30. So great was the loyalty of these policemen to each other that Hosea Stout would not reveal the name of an offender, either here or later. On March 5 Stout recorded another case of neglect of duty, and in a meeting of the police on March 13, when another policeman was being tried, Hosea had said that "When we could not stand it any longer to cut him off — behind the ears — according to the law of God in such cases."

Sunday January 31st 1847. Today was one of the most mild and beautiful days in all nature, being very warm, clear, pleasant, The cattle could be seen strolling around town, & seemed to be enjoying life with some degree of comfort after their long chill. The West wind was mildly floating in the air giving life and animation to everything while all nature seemed to smile

I was mostly at home but sometimes would take a walk around town to enjoy the beautiful day I arrainged the guard as usual Met the Council at six as usual. Nothing done there of importance Some Omahas came in and put up in Council house & I detailed a guard to watch them.

Monday February the 1st 1847. This was a beautiful morning like yesterday morning I went down & around through Town and learned in the mein time that the Omahas who were here last night were looking for some articles which some one had taken from the bodies of their friends, who had been slain some time since by the Souix. I learned also that Arza Adams and H. W. Miller had taken a waggon load of buffalo robes leggins Lodges &c from them, thus robbing the dead which if it is true is a just cause of resentment on the part of the Omahas & I learn also that they were determined on revenge for this most sacralagious insult to their dead friends.

I reported the same to Dr W. Richards that he might have due notice of the affair. I was notified to appear at W. Richards at six o'clock this evening which I did after arrainging the guard. The subject of robbing the Omahas was taken up and decided to send a letter by a special messenger to the men concerned for them to restore the things taken to the place whence they took them & make satisfaction to the Omahas as soon as possible.

Another letter was to be sent to Maj'r Miller & the Omaha interpreter informing them of the action of the council on the subject & let them know the feelings here & also that the men who did it does not live in this place.

After the business was done a variety of subjects was taken up and talked over & we spent an agreeable evening untill about ten o'clock when we broke up & came home.

The wind had changed to the south this after noon & there was now a driving snow falling fast from the North. I came home and went out again on patroll guard untill twelve o'clock at night.

Tuesday February 2nd 1847. Cold windy morning but clear I was in doors untill noon I have just procured the field notes of the commanding officer of Nauvoo at the time of the Battles last June, and for the satisfaction of the reader will here give them an insersion

June 10th A large body of the mob with five pieces of artillery marched toward Nauvoo, from Carthage, & made a show of entering Nauvoo at the Point called the Carthage road but being resolutely met when within two miles of the City, they returned and encamped for the night, having fired several canon shott without effect.

11th Earley in the morning, the mob abandoned their Camping ground and moved their whole forces about one and a half miles further North, to what is called the New Laharp road

They were here met by a little band of thirty men, in ambush, commanded by by Capt William Anderson & was called the "Spartan Band being mostly armed with 15 shooters, who fired upon them and retreated a short distance & fired again thus retreating & firing, holding them at bay.

Since William Clayton later reported that Hosea had threatened to take his life after the Twelve were gone (Clayton, *Journal,* 73-74) there is a possibility that it was he who was the delinquent policeman to whom reference was made.

They were coming in with flying colors appearantly without any obstructions except from the 30 men when suddently, when only one & a quarter miles from the Temple, our home made cannon (of steam boat shafts) opened upon them under the command of Captain Hiram Gates, manned by William I Green & William Summerville.

The effect was electric. They halted in their tracks and after exchanging a few shots, retreted over the brow of a commanding emenence, and camped for the night

12th After negotiations had passed at about 12 o'clock the mob commenced deploying to the left taking advantage of cornfields to mask their movements, with 4 pieces of artillery and about 800 men — and showed a determination to take the City by storm at all hazzards.

We had to oppose them about 200 men, 130 of whom were in line — the rest were stationed elsewhere and 5 pieces of steam boat shafts — only 3 of which were in the action and one of them disabled after the third shot.

The mob came up to within rifle shot of our little band of men when a sharp action commenced, which lasted one hour & forty minutes, when the mob retreated on a full run, then rallied for 15 minutes; but retreated again, to their former camping ground. Hundreds of shots had been fired on both sides — our loss was three killed and two wounded on this day & but one more wounded in all the days fighting. Thus were the mob repulsed for the third time

13th This evening about eight o'clock all four of our field pieces went down & approached their camp and opened upon them — after firing a few rounds without recieving any answer from them, we returned to the City — This day the "Spartan Band" and some sharp shooters from Captain Gaits Company harrassed their wings and watering places

14th A few cannon shott were exchanged. The "Spartan Band" & sharp shooters continued as the day before — with some loss to the enemy every day.

15th As on the fourteenth

16th The enemy deployed as on the 12th and were met by the "Spartan Band" and 3rd Company of infantry commanded by Captain Gaits & his two pieces of cannon. Rifles & Musket shots flew thick — and the cannon shots were rapidly exchanged — and the mob retreated for the fourth time; finding our fortifications, which we had been constantly throwing up, were too strong for them. A committee of 100 citizens of Quincy now interfered a truce was proclaimed and finally a treaty entered into.

17th Mob entered and Mormons commenced leaving.

The above was the field note of Col Clifford[31] as taken by Cimon C. Bolton who is one of the brethern

I regulated the guard as usual & went out in the evening with the intention of staying on guard but not being well I came home & went earley to bed.

---

31. Colonel William E. Clifford was president of the trustees of the City of Nauvoo; and although not a Mormon, he commanded the defense of the city. He also led a company who went to release some of the brethren who had been kidnapped and held. He wrote an account of the battle and described the pathetic condition of the last of the Mormons who were forced to leave, walking from their homes to the banks of the river with only such possessions as they could carry. Here they were forced to wait for ferriage across and then for wagons to come back from the camps ahead.

Wednesday February 3rd 1847. Today I was quite unwell, but was around some I regulated the guard The wind is blowing hard from the south with a clear skye. No more today. Recd an order to collect the public arms.

Thursday Feb. 4th 1847. Today I was quite unwell was around as before. regulated the guard The following in a copy of the order I recieved from Col Markham.

Omaha Nation) February 3rd 1847
Winter Quarters (
) Col Stout you are hereby required and commanded to collect in, and take charge of all the public arms and accoutrements in this place, that are now in your possession; and if any persons having any such public arms and accoutrements in their possession, shall refuse to deliver up the same: you will report the same to me forthwith.

Stephen Markham Col

I proceeded today to execute the above order by ascertaining where the public arms were.

Met the council this evening as usual at the Council house The subject of the beef committee was taken up an the complaint of Father John Smith who was not satisfied with some things about it. The thing was talked out of "countenance" and finally Prest Brigham Young moved to have the whole matter laid over till the first resurrection & them burn the papers the day before

Friday February 5th 1847. This morning I sent Allen over with my team after my wife. He met her about half way here. One of her brothers was bringing her home

Today I was engaged in looking up the public arms & arrainged the guard in the evening

Saturday February 6th 1847. Today I was engaged in geathering up the public arms as before and arrainged the guard. The weather has been fine for a day or two. Today I took down my tent & was now entirely dwelling in my house

It will be just one year on the 12th of this month since I first errected my tent on the shores of the Mississippi river and have not been in a situation to live with out it untill today & even now we are prepareing to move on again.

Sunday Feb 7th 1847. This was a very fine pleasant day. I took a long walk up the river with my wife among the high bluffs and frightful precipices which was a fine relief to my mind after being so much hemmed up all winter we crossed the river on the ice & came down on the bottom & had an agreeable walk. I regulated the guard & met the council as usual Gen Rich came in today from Pisgah. Came home at ten

Monday February the 8th 1847. Today was [s]pent as usual. Regulating the guard &c was out awhile in the fore part of the night on guard.

Tuesday February the 9th 1847. Today was spent as yesterday and nothing going on of importance. The Bishops have a dance today and tomorrow in the Council house.

Wednesday Feb the 10th 1847. Spent about as yesterday. Very cold

Thursday Feb. 11th 1847. Spent as yesterday. and notified the Police to meet at J. W. Cumming to make arraingements for a dance if they wanted one. Which they concluded to have & appointed 3 managers for the same to wit Hosea Stout Horace S. Eldrige & Daniel Carn. We held our meeting till about 11 o'clock P.M. & had good enjoyment. I came home & went on guard till about 12 & came home.

Friday Feb 12th 1847. Around as usual today. regulated the guard as before
Today I learned and reported to Brigham that "Tom Brown[32] was threatning the lives of the 12
Orson Pratt came back home today. I went on guard also after leaving the Twelve.

Saturday Feb. 13th 1847. Sent my horses to Iowa by John Bills. Was around as usual. Regulated the guard as before. Went on guard in the night

Sunday Feb. 14th 1847. This morning the High Council met at the Council house at sun rise to hold a kind of "Class Meeting" at which they expressed their feelings & fellowship one towards another. It lasted untill about ten when it adjourned for public meeting in the house & I came home and was around all day it being very pleasant and warm. In the evening I regulated the guard and met the High Council at six at usual. Here the subject of the police was taken up by myself & a long debate ensued which resulted in good for us, for it was understood by the council for us to do our duty & they sustain us in it & stop the noise of the boys in the streets if we had to use the lash &c It was the first time that the Council had investigated our case After Council a lot of Indians came in and staid all night. I came home and then went out on guard untill Twelve o'clock at night

Monday Feb 15th 1847. At home untill noon and then went to a meeting of the police at one
We met and had an old fashioned "Police meeting" and of course felt well. I came home & in the evening went on guard awhile.

Tuesday February 16th 1847. Today I was around as usual & arrainged the guard. President Young has called together all his family & adopted children to have a feast and dance today & tomorrow, at which he will teach the true principles of family goverment. I went on guard in eve

Wednesday Feb 17th 1847. Went to a meeting of the first hundred of Brighams Company, which met to determine how many would go west in the Spring
They unanimously decided that all should go. I came home about Eleven o'clock very sick & was around in the afternoon and arrainged the guard & at dark went to a trial between G. W. Langley & Hathaway in case of debt. It was before Bishop Nobles' court. I then came home

Thursday Feb. 18th 1847. Around as usual nothing up particular. Regulated guard as usual. Wrote some at my earley Biography.

Friday Feb. 19th 1847. Last night a hard crusty sleety snow fell about one inch thick. North wind I was around as usual today and went on guard awhile about 9 o'clock.

---

32. Tom Brown was the outlaw who had reportedly killed the man for whose death William and Stephen Hodge were hanged. Edward Bonney wrote at some length in his *Banditti of the Prairies* of Brown's feats of open robbery. Bonney was the sheriff who after several years brought three others to justice and had them hanged, but Tom Brown had eluded him.
This is the only mention by Stout of his being among the Mormons until after the pioneer group was on its way. On April 19, 1847, Norton Jacob wrote: "Here Porter Rockwell, Redden, Little, Thomas Brown and another young man overtook us, having left Winter Quarters yesterday morning." Jacob and Jacob, *Norton Jacob*, 35.
On the same day Erastus Snow noted that: ". . . while Baiteing our teams . . . O. P. Rockwell and Elder J. C. Little and the notorious Tom Brown came up with us; . . ." Erastus Snow, "Journals of Erastus Snow, November, 1818-February 1857" (8 vols., typescript, Utah State Historical Society), IV, 113.
Both Howard Egan and William Clayton tell of the arrival of this group and mention Tom Brown often as one of the company of hunters and guards against the Indians.

Saturday Feb. 20th 1847. To day was the most snowy day we have had this winter. It was hurled full force with a hard wind from the sides of the North where old Lucifer sits, falling fast and bids fair to be a deep one. I was around town about as usual. The travelling was very uncomfortable.

Sunday Feb. 21st 1847. This morning the snow had blown and drifted untill it was near half way to the top of my door & I could scarcly get it opened & had to throw away the snow to make roads before I could get around It was decidedly one of the deepest snows that has fallen for some years & is still blowing and drifting all day, the air still full as in a snow storm

Those who are caught out in a large prairie are in a bad snap for the deep ravines will be filled level full & impassable But little stir this morning Went to council as usual nothing of importance up however

Monday Feby. 22nd 1847. Was around today about as usual heard of nothing particular transpiring Was on guard a short time in the eve.

Tuesday Feb. 23rd 1847. Hard South wind blowing this morn.

Today there is a large feast made by the Bishops for those who are poor and have been unable to partake in the jolifications of the city hitherto.

The wind somehow backed round from the south to the South East and then commenced its opperation in good earnest untill late in the night. Every thing went off about as usual today. I was on guard a short time in the fore part of the evening.

Wednesday February 24th 1847. The South East wind had produced another snow which was falling fast this morning While the wind backed round to N.E. Snow continued till near noon after which we had a fine day

This afternoon I called the police together & had a little sport at the expense of Br I. C. Haight & a time of good enjoyment among ourselves. & then arrainged the guard and came home & went on guard untill Eleven o'clock at night.

Thursday Feb. 25th 1847. Went around preparing for a police ball and at dark went on guard and staid till midnight.

Friday February 26th 1847. Cold, stormy & snowing most all day. Was in the house most of the day. Went on guard in the evening till ten.

Saturday February 27th 1847. Today I was engaged some in preparing for the police ball which was to come off next Tuesday.

Went to the Council House, and attended a meeting of the officers of Brigham's Company which had met to make preperations to send off the pioneers about the 15th of March Here, after the business of the meeting was over, President Young spoke of the manner that the parties had been managed, and proposed for those who had been, not to go any more, as the house would soon be needed for something else. This, of course broke up the arraingements of the police for they had mostly been to some of the parties and Here the matter rested for the present. This veto came on the police at the time when all had just made all the necessary preparations for the party.

I came home and was around as usual and prepared the guard and at dark went out on guard untill about nine o'clock

Sunday February 28th 1847. This morning there was to be a private meeting of the high Council at sun rise. About 9 o'clock I went & found only three members present so we staid awhile and come away home

In the afternoon I went to the Council house to a meeting at which Elder Henry G. Sherwood spoke after that I was around as usual At six went to a

High Council as usual   There was not much done of interest except some remarks of President Young which I will give in short   It is in relation to a spell of sickness he had had lately.

He spoke as follows.

"Another subject which I wanted to speak of is this.

On Wednesday morning I was taken ill and it has been asked if I had a vision I was taken so suddenly sick. just as I was getting out of my bed that I could not go out.   I tried to return to the bed again, but could not even get back

As to how I felt, No one can tell how I felt, untill he dies and goes through the vail and when he does that he can then tell how I felt

All that I know, is what my wife told me about it since.   She said that I said, I had been where Joseph & Hyrum was.

And again that I said, it is hard coming to life again.

But I know that I went to the world of spirits; but what I saw I know not, for the vision went away from me, as a dream which you loose when you awake.

The next day I had a dreem.

I dreamed that I saw Joseph sitting in a room, in the South West corner, near a bright window.

He sat in a chair, with his feet, both on the lower round.

I took him by the hand and kissed him on both cheeks, and wanted to know, why we could not be together, as we once was.

He said that it was all right, that we should not be together yet.

We must be seperated for a season.

I said it was hard to be seperated from him.

He said, it was all right and putting his feet down on the floor.

Now all you who know, how he looks, when he used to give council, know all about, how he looked then

I told him that the Latter Day Saints was very anxious to know about the law of adoption, and the sealing powers &c and desired word of council from him.

Joseph said; do you be sure and tell the people one thing.

Do you be sure and tell the brethren that it is all important for them to keep the spirit of the Lord, To keep the quiet spirit of Jesus, and he explained how the spirit of the Lord reflected on the spirit of man and set him to pondering on any subject, and also explained how to know the spirit of the Lord from the spirit of the enemy.

He said the mind of man must be open to recieve all spirits, in order to be prepared, to recieve the spirit of the Lord; otherwise it might be barred so as not to recieve the spirit of the Lord, which always brings peace and makes one happy and takes away every other spirit.   When the small still voice speaks always recieve it, and if the people will do these things, when they come up to the father, all will be as in the beginning, and every person stand as at the first.

I saw how we were organized before we took tabernacles and every man will be restored to that which he had then, and all will be satisfied.   After this I turned away & saw Joseph was in the edge of the light; but where I had to go was as midnight darkness.

He said I must go back, so I went back in the darkness.

I want you all to remember my dream for I it is a vision of God and was reveated through the spirit of Joseph".[33]

---

33. This dream or "vision" of Brigham Young's is remarkable in that it is so out of key with his own speeches. That the "Spirit of Joseph" should ignore his question about the "Law of Adoption," a problem which at the time seemed vital and one about which Brigham Young had asked specifically, seems unusual. One might have expected also maledictions against their

After council was over I came home but had not been home but a few minutes before I was sent for to be at Dr. Richards' office. I went & took the Marshall along as he was also wanted. The Twelve were in council there and it appeared that they had been talking over the matter of the police party, which the President had "knocked into pie" last Saturday

They had just learned the order contemplated for our party which was to have only the Twelve, police & Band present, which would not croud the house; but be a comfortable and an agreeable party. So when I came, Brigham said that the Question was before the house, for me to decide which was for the Police to have their party & have the Twelve there or for the Twelve to make a party and invite the police. I told him I was ready for either or both sides of the Question and also stated, that since his remarks on Saturday we had concluded to abandon the idea of a party and all turn out on the day and work on the mill dam. But they all seemed anxious for a party so we agreed to have one as before contemplated on next Tuesday-and so we arrainged accordingly. I then came home at mid night.

Monday March 1st 1847. Today I spent in notifying the police about the new arraingements of our party and other duties of the police which I have to attend to daily.

Tuesday March 2nd 1847. Was at home untill one o'clock and then went with my wife to the council house to our police party. It was an uncomly beautiful clear warm and pleasant day

We had the Police, Twelve & Band present, and enjoyed ourselves uncommonly will by dancing, talking, eating sweet cakes &c, and some little preaching and about had the old Police dance called "President Marks' return to mormonism" which I may describe some time. I preached a loud sermon on real Mormonism

About Eleven o'clock P. M. my wife not being very well came home, and I returned to the party again and tarried three o'clock A. M. when we broke up. and we all came home It is almost unnecessary to say that the Twelve seemed to enjoy themselves well.

Wednesday March 3rd 1847. To day I was uncommonly sick with the headache and could not set up long enough to dress my self & had to send Allen to arrainge the guard.

Thursday March 4th 1847. This morning I was very weak & feeble but able to go about and was engaged in looking up the public arms and colected some and in the evening went on guard awhile although still very weak.

Friday March 5th 1847. The day was cold & dark & ground hard froze I was around as usual and also wrote some in my Biographical history. I in the evening I went on guard and found one of the guard absent and in fact he had been reported absent more or less all winter I could never find him at his post, but he was sure to be at a party or a dancing school every time. Now I thought it time to report him so I went to Richards' office and finding the President there, waited till he went away and told him how it had been He was aware that all was not right so he went with me to the man's house and we there learned that he was at Br P. H. Young's to a party so we went and found him.

---

enemies and promises as to the future of the "Kingdom" about which Joseph himself had been so militant in his lifetime and for which the Mormons were now sacrificing so much.

Instead to tell them that "it is all important for them to keep the spirit of the Lord, To keep the quiet spirit of Jesus," would almost sound as a rebuke of some of their earlier policies. See "Journal History," February 23, 1847.

The day had turned warm in the after noon and the streets as a flood of mud and water and very disagreeable traveling

When we came in we were invited to join in the dance out Brigham said we had not time that he was returning for home from a council and found me, hunting some police which I could not find & he thought we would come up there and see if we could not find some here on duty & then give some more sarcastic slants at the delinquent policeman but all in a good humor.

We stoped a short time till they danced one reel and then we took a French Four and came away. He saw how matters were & gave me advice how to proceed in the case and then went home at 11 o'clock and I watched the policeman untill his tour of duty was out

He staid at the party untill it broke up & came home and staid in his house a while and came out a few minutes and went back and never appeared till one and then only to go and call up his relief and then I came home

I had now proof positive in his case and intended to deal with him. No more tonight.

Saturday March 6th 1847. This morning I went and saw Br Brigham and reported to him how matters went with the Policeman after he left me to which he only replied "You will then tyle[34] accordingly" So I went and notified the police to meet a 6 o'clock this evening at Jas W. Cummings for the purpose of trying the above case.

I also attended a pioneer meeting while there Bishop Miller sent in word for more help on the mill dam as the water was rising by the melting snow and was like to brake it so all hands turned out to the dam & I to see about the police meeting. We met and had his case up. He admitted most of the accusations to be true. He done well on an average during the trial His case was well handled by the Quorum and the merits of his case plainly made manifest

He was what might be called "whipped and cleared" for he was repremanded sharp as is customary among police in such cases, but all in the best of feelings and after the investigation was over all was well satisfied with him and if he will profit by what has passed he will do well if not he had best leave the police before he is disgraced. We broke up at 12.

Sunday March 7th 1847. Cold North Wind I was at home and only went out once a short time untill I went to arrainge the guard and to go to council which met as usual but adjourned immediately for the want of business. A large number of Omahas here again.

Monday March 8th 1847. Verry cold today I was at home journalizing in the forenoon. Arrainged the guard as usual

Tuesday March 9th 1847. At home most of the day. Went to a company of the ten which I belong to at Br Chapman's, then to H. C. Kimballs Company meeting at the C. house met to arrainge the pioneers

Wednesday March 10th 1847. Sick head ache today. Filled in another order for the police amounting to 130 dollars. Went around as usual. On guard at dark & staid till about Eleven o'c

---

34. The word "tyle" appears often in the John D. Lee diaries in connection with the Masonic rites and also the approaches to the Mormon Temple. The dictionary gives it as a Masonic word meaning "To protect from intrusion; to bind or swear to secrecy."

The officers of the Nauvoo Legion lodge of Masons named "Samuel Rolf, Tyler." Lee noted that ". . . the door of the outer court which I found tyled within by an officer," and at another time, "I and the Tyler kept the inner court," and still another, "Brother H.C.K. the Tyler at the door of the outer court."

In each case the word refers to a guard. Here it seems to refer to a questioning or cross examination.

Thursday March 11th 1847. Around as usual. Today Wm Meeks, one of the Captains of the guard came to see me. He was the last of the Captains who staid with me last spring and went with his company to Missouri to work from Locus Creek and was true and faithful to me to the last. I arrainged the guard as usual & went on guard untill Eleven o'c

Friday March 12th 1847. Fine day. Around as usual. Nothing particular took place. Went on guard a short time in eve. Twelve had a ball at council house in the evening which lasted till three or four o'clock

Saturday March 13th 1847. Dull cloudy weather North wind drizzling snow flying. General turn out to the mill dam.
    Today Capts A. McRae, Meeks & Langley were here most of the day. I was around as usual but nothing particular took place
    At dark I went to a meeting of the seventies at the Council house. Here J. P. Packer was up before them for a charge of stealing a brace of six shooters by getting them with a forged order. Some was for cutting him off. Some for keeping him on trial awhile and so on. I spoke quite lengthy on the subject and was for keeping him in fellowship as I could fellowship any man that could be suffered to live amongst us and when we could not stand it any longer to cut him off -behind the ears- according to the law of God in such cases. I came home about twelve o'clock at night.

Sunday March 14th 1847. Got up late this morning. William Meeks was here last night. M. D. Hambleton and G. W. Langley came here in the morning and staid all day and in the evening I arrainged the guard and went to council Nothing up of interest to me.

Monday March the 15th 1847. Up late. Cold day but clear. I was around as usual. The pioneers met today to begin to organize to be off
    At six o'clock this evening there was a Council held of the Twelve, most of High Council & the captains of 100's & 50's of the two Emegrating divisions of the Camp of Israel, at the Council house
    Here many questions were proposed and decided as the best policy for this people to pursue after the Twelve & pioneers are gone among the rest it was decided to keep up the police under its present organization & that they be sustained by taxation as heretofore. Also that the main camp which moves on in the summer be organized into a military body with Genl C. C. Rich at their head John Scott to be continued in his office & for me to have charge of the guard on the journey.
    This place is to be controlled by the High Council & the Presidency of the two divisions No one is to start in the camp without 300 bbs of bread stuff to each individual in his family [¼ page blank]

Tuesday March 16th 1847. At home untill about noon & was then around as usual. To night the guard could not be made out without enlisting another man. I went on guard a short time in the evening.

Wednesday March 17th 1847. Today there was a general turn out to work on the mill dam. I was around as usual. Made out the guard to knight. Went to a council at the Council house. It consisted of the officers of the emegrating companies. I came home about ten after being on guard awhile.

Thursday March 18th 1847. General turn out on the dam. Very warm clear day. South wind. I and Allen & G. W. Langley went up the river hunting & trying our guns and back at one o'clock. and I went around town again to visit the mill dam &c. Went on guard a short time at night. About eleven o'clock Carns & Langley came to my house with a large jug of whiskey which the B had hid out to glut their brutish appetites with, acting at the same time with as much contempt as they could towards the guard who were close by and they so they concluded to retaliate by taking it to themselves.

The [blank] had a party at the council house

Friday March 19th 1847. Dark, cloudy, foggy, warm, morning which may be followed by a general thaw & break up in the river. I & Allen went a hunting 4 or 5 miles down the river and home about 3 o'c. and then went to arrainge the guard and after dark awhile I went to a meeting at the council house. Prest Young, Kimball and Benson spoke and was followed by W. W. Major & Case. I came home at eleven.

Saturday March 20th 1847. The weather this morning was cold and windy having turned to the North yester evening and was howling all night as in the middle of winter. We had a clear sky to day notwithstanding. I was around as usual. Today the mill started and promises well. It runs beautifully grand and does a good business. I arrainged the guard as usual.

Sunday March 21st 1847. Warm south wind. There was a public meeting at the stand today. Brigham spoke on the necessity of keeping the spirit of the Lord and related his vision.

Went to the Council at six. Horace S. Eldrige, the Marshall, was put in assessor and collector of the residue of the police tax in the place of Br J. C. Wright and the subject of the police spoken of but not to the purpose. After council I staid with the guard till about 12 and then came home.

Monday March the 22nd 1847. Cold North wind and a handsome driving snow which is falling fast this morning I was at home untill one o'clock and then went to a meeting of the officers of the two Emegrating companies.

Here President Young gave notice that it was his intention & also of the 12 to proceede on the great Basin without stoping if they can, with only two pioneers to a waggon and that he intended to locate a Stake of Zion and this fall come back after his family also for only small families to go in the summer &c. also decided to move the houses West of Second Main Street and there form a line of Stockade with houses & bring up the south line to my house which is one block North and to commence the same this day one week. I went from there and regulated the guard and came home and staid.

Tuesday March 23rd 1847. At home and around town all day   Was unwell & hardly able to go about Went on guard and was out till 11 o'c

President Young called his family[35] together this evening to take into consideration the best way proceed in business & emegration

---

35. John D. Lee, at this time Brigham Young's private secretary, kept detailed minutes of this meeting. He named first the members of the "family" who were present, listing them in the order of their "adoption." Alphabetically arranged, they were:

Angel, Solomon	Earl, Sylvester H.	Lyttle, John
Angel, T. O.	Ellsworth, Edmond	Major, Wm.
Atwood, Millen	Empy, Wm.	Morly, Isaac
Brown, Benj.	Everett, Addison	Pierce, Robert
Busbee, Jas.	Free, A. P.	Rockwood, A. P.
Carns, Daniel	Grant, G. D.	Sanders, Moses M.
Chace, Isaac	Grant, George D.	Scofield, Jos. S.
Cook, Phinehas	Grover, Thos.	Shumway, Chas.
Davis, David	Gully, Samuel	Sprague, Samuel L.
Dayton, Hyrum	Hanks, Sidney A.	Weeks, Wm.
Decker, Chas.	Hutchinson, Jacob F.	Wilder, Jacob
Dun, S. A.	Kesler, Frederick	Wooley, Edward [Edwin?] D.
Dusette, E. P.	Lee, J. D.	

Wednesday March 24th 1847. Was around as usual. Nothing up more than common. Went on guard in the evening. Council House full of Omahas again Hard to keep up the guard

Thursday March 25th 1847. Last night two of Br G. A. Smith's horses were stolen by the Indians. Cold North wind all day. Was around all day as usual.

At six o'clock there was a special session of the High Council called at Joseph Busby's the object of which was to take into consideration the mill. It was decided that President Young be authorized to do as he sees proper with the disposition of it. That they were perfectly satisfied with him so far about the mill President Young stated that he had sold it for 2,600 dollars to Br Neff[36] It would clear the expense of building it. Council broke up about 9. and I came home.

Friday March 26th 1847. Clear fine warm day. South wind At Eleven o'clock today there was a public meeting called at the stand for the purpose of transacting business before the Twelve and pioneers go away and to lay the Acts and resolves of the different councils from time to time before the people for their approval or disapproval that there might not be any grumbling after the Twelve were gone, at what was done.

The first business was a vote to stockade in this place by houses as before mentioned which was carried unanimously.

The subject of killing the Indians was next taken up. It was thought best if any one did kill any, for their depredations, to give the offender up to them

At half past 12 meeting adjourned for one hour, after which the congregation came together again. The afternoon was mostly spent in teaching by Brigham & Heber. Brigham spoke particular in relation to what would follow when the Twelve were gone, that men would rise up and complain that the Twelve were not right & that they themselves we[re] the ones to lead and govern the people,

---

Brigham Young told the group that a part of them must stay and farm in order to provide food for the next year's mass emigration. He ordered them to work the land near Old Fort Calhoon, the site which was later to be called "Summer Quarters," or "Brother Brigham's Farm." Fifteen members were named to stay under Isaac Morley as general manager and John D. Lee as foreman. Later, others were added to the group. Kelly, *Lee Journals,* 132-33.

36. John Neff, born September 19, 1794, in Pennsylvania, was a wealthy man when he joined the Mormon Church. After his baptism in 1842 he made a trip to Nauvoo to meet Joseph Smith. He returned to Pennsylvania to sell his holdings. He gave the prophet some financial assistance, and contributed toward outfitting the ship *Brooklyn.*

Neff arrived in Nauvoo in late 1846, just as the last Mormons were being driven from the city, and moved on to Winter Quarters. During the winter of sickness and privation he learned of polygamy and became critical. On March 6, 1847, John D. Lee wrote that:

The old man but a few days [ago] stated that his money should not go to support the whores of the 12 when he was asked to loan a few hundred dollars to assist in building the mill. Refused by making the above remarks, when he had probably by him $10,000. Pres. B. Young told him that he should feel the hand of the Lord upon him and his family for his hard and foolish sayings and immediately sickness made inroads into his family. He remembering the prediction, became alarmed and sent for those men whom he once called whoremasters to pray the Lord that His hand might be stayed. (Kelly, *Lee Journals,* 108.)

On March 24, Lee reported that Brigham Young ". . . took with him Bro. H. C. Kimble, N. K. Whitney, A. P. Rockwood and visited old Bro. John Neff. Contracted the mill in part to him, rec'd on $2500." *Ibid.,* 131.

Neff followed the pioneer group to Utah in 1847, arriving in October. In early 1848 he set up the first flour mill in the Salt Lake Valley at the mouth of Millcreek. It is said that when flour was selling for a dollar a pound, Neff would accept only six cents but would sell only to the poor.

and that he knew who it was &c and plainly pointed out some who were now trying to raise up a party to themselves. The meeting lasted untill near sun set, after which I arrainged the guard and had to put out a patrol guard on the out side to the South & West of the city to keep off the Indians who were lurking about to steal horses and cattle at night. after the guard arraingements were done I came home at half past nine o'clock.

Saturday March 27th 1847. Went Early this morning with Allen, about a mile south of town & drew a load of hay home, and was then about town as usual but nothing was up particular.

Today was a beautiful clear warm still day and plasant as summer I was very unwell today and weak and nervous and went to bed at dark.

Sunday March the 28th 1847. The weather still beautiful clear & warm like summer.

There was meeting today at the stand In the forenoon the Twelve spoke to the congregation & the afternoon different ones spoke; but nothing of very particular importance was discussed except warning the people against those who may rise up and try to lead off parties

This every one who spoke I believe was one thing which they bore with the greatest wait on their minds.

I was very feeble today In the evening I went to the Council as usual but there was not anything up of importance.

Monday March the 29th 1847. Weather as yesterday. This morning the pioneers met again to make arraingements to be off. I was around as usual Hard times to keep up the guard for I can not get but two out at once as so many of the police are sick absent or preparing to go with the pioneers & tonight only one at a time could be got out at once.

Tuesday March 30th 1847. Clear & cold hard N.W. wind Around as usual. times calm, arrainged the guard only one out at once. Went to a concert this evening. William McCairey the Indian musician[37] performed. I came home about eleven

Wednesday March 31st 1847. Fine clear day I & Allen went a hunting in the timber and deep ravines North of town but did not kill any game. Came home at 12 and was around as usual and at dark went to a council of the officers of the emegrating companys they were making arraingements to put in Spring crops. Came home about 9½ o'c

---

37. Regarding William McCairey, the Indian, John D. Lee wrote:
Feb. 27, '47 . . . Messengers . . . reported that the Pres. was engaged in listening at the sweet sounds of a flute and other instruments of music by a half-blooded Indian, Mr. McGarry, musicioner . . . Mr. McGarry seems to be willing to go according to counsel and that he may be a useful man after he has acquired a experimental knowledge. His skill on the flute cannot be surpassed by any musician that I have ever heard, therefore use the man with respect. May 7, 1847 . . . Geo Miller and a part of the Puncah camp are going on to join Lyman Wight and McGarry the Indian prophet . . . . (*Ibid.*, 100, 103, 162.)
The spelling "McGarry" by Lee and "McCairey" by Stout would indicate that they were speaking of the same man. An entry by Lorenzo Brown supports the "Prophet" role of the visitor. Under date of Sunday, April 25, 1847, Brown wrote: "There has been in camp this winter a half breed Indian negro who styled himself as a prophet the ancient of days whose hair was as wool &c &c. He has induced some to follow him across the river to Mosquito Creek. He has since left his company taken his wife and gone south to his own tribe in consequence of a sermon preached by Elder Orso[n] Hyde against his doctrine." Lorenzo Brown, "The Journal of Lorenzo Brown, 1823-1900" (2 vols., typescript, Brigham Young University), I, 32.

Thursday April 1st 1847. Clear and warm. no wind in the morning but it rose high in the North West in the fore noon. Went a hunting & digging (hartachokes)[38] until near noon and then went and prepared for caching fish.

At seven o'clock P.M. there was a special council called at H. S. Eldrige's. It was to investigate a case wherein a Brother Rodney Badger[39] had stolen a horse from Missouri, He frankly confessed it which was all the proof the council had. However after a long time spent in speaking on the subject it was decided that he take two more good judicious men along with him and return the horse & make satisfaction to the (innocent holly unoffending) Missourian and pay all expenses and damage. I was glad that the Twelve could yet act on the case came home at 9½ o'clock P.M.

Friday April the 2nd 1847. Beautiful clear warm day S. wind Moving houses commenced today to form the line of stockade.

I wrote the most part of my leasure time today and was around as usual In the evening I went to Dr Richard's office on business. Bishop Miller was there.

He had met the Twelve there to relate to them his plans in relation to going to the south. He wanted to go and settle between the Rio Grande and the Neuses river and make a treaty with Mexico & have them give us the land &c But this was in dispute now between the United States & Mexico and was the great thoroughfare for both armies.

A very few words from different ones on the subject caused him to confess the impractibility of his plans[40] (I thought it a pretty "dry job")

While I was there I recieved a letter from Jos Herring the indian He was at Fort Leavenworth and manifested about the same spirit as when he left here. He said George was gone south He wanted me to attend the great indian council this summer at the Salt Plains and still says I am the only one who can do any thing among the indians.

From the council I came home about Eleven o'clock.

---

38. This is the Jerusalem artichoke, a large perennial sunflower, the tuber of which is succulent and edible. Almost every diarist of this period speaks of the suffering and death from malnutrition and the value of this root in curing the scurvy. Typical is the account of John Pulsipher: ". . . when the warm weather came the sick began to recover, they could get vegetables — which consisted of Pig weeds for greens and wild roots like potatoes ½ inch in Diameter — very good. Yet the flesh would rot and drop off from some to the bones. What the number that died I couldn't tell for certain, but it far exceeded anything that I ever witnessed before . . . ." John Pulsipher, "Diaries [1838-1891]" (2 vols., typescript, Utah State Historical Society), I, 13.

39. Rodney Badger was born February 4, 1823, at Waterford, Vermont. He joined the Mormon Church in 1839 and came to Nauvoo in 1840, where he became captain of a company in the "life guards" of the Nauvoo Legion. He was one of the pioneer company of 1847, his wife following later in the season in the J. M. Grant company.

In Utah, Badger became sheriff in Salt Lake County and was a lieutenant in the territorial militia. He was drowned on April 29, 1853, in Weber River as he was trying to rescue an immigrant family whose wagon had capsized.

40. For more than a year now the tensions between Bishop George Miller and President Brigham Young had become more pronounced. Miller had always moved ahead in the advance group, and while it was wonderful for the mass who followed to cross streams on bridges that he had built and roads that he had improved, he must not get too far away to accept counsel.

With a group of sixty-two wagons, ten of which were under the direction of Anson Call, Miller had set up his advance camp at the junction of the Running Water and the Missouri River. Though he himself came back to Winter Quarters at the request of Brigham Young, he did not want the whole camp to retrace the 134 miles.

Miller's account of his reasons for leaving the camp, walking back to Winter Quarters, and his final decision to withdraw from the direction of Brigham Young are given in Mills, "De Tal Palo Tal Astilla," *Annual Publication . . . Southern California*, X, 110-11.

Saturday April 3rd 1847. Around as usual and wrighting. Regulated the guard. Hard to keep up the police. Can get but two out at once. Dark Damp-like evening Like for an East rain. No more tonight

Sunday April 4th 1847. Dark, Damp, Warm, Pleasant. N E Wind. Meeting today at the stand but no particular circumstances transpired I passed of the day as usual. Was at the meeting. Arrainged the guard. "Hard Sledding" Went to Council as usual. The subject of stockading the town was here put on the Bishops who were to work under the supervision of the Presidencies of the two grand divisions of the Emegration. This was done because the Bishops could call out the men more readily than the captains of hundreds & fifties. President Young proposed to hire some 8 or 10 good men to go and raise a crop for the Omahas to keep them away from here in the fall. I think this is a good idea. I came home at about 9 o'clock P.M.

Had quite a rain in the night which is the first since I have been in my house, which is not far short of five months.

Monday April 5th 1847. This was a dark wet gloomy day. Hard South West wind and a beating rain accompanied by thunder and lightning.

About noon the wind turned to the North West and the rain ceased. Towards evening it blew hard from the North. I was around as usual & arrainged the guard all is well.

Tuesday April 6th 1847. Clear Cool morning Wind still north Today was a special conference which commenced at ten o'clock.

The first business was to try the standing of the different authorities as was customary at conferences. The Twelve was passed before the conference and recieved unanimously except Lyman Wight, whose case was not handled.

The first Presidents of the Seventies were next unanimously recieved Then the High Council except Samuel Russel, who was dropt because he was one of the Seventies and Phineas Richards put in his place. Bishop Whitney was then recieved again and a vote of thanks for what he has done (a sarcasm)

President Young spoke at some length very edifying and after making some arraingements to fit out some of the pioneers, the conference adjourned sine die. I spent the remainder of the day about as usual.

Wednesday April 7th 1847. Today most of the Pioneers started and some of the Twelve & Prest Young. Some however had gone previously. I was around as usual. Nothing up of importance. To night there was no police out.

Thursday April 8th 1847. Today more of the pioneers started. Elder Parley P. Pratt arrived from England in good health. I was employed as usual. No police out to night.

Friday April the 9th 1847. Clear fine warm day. Most of the Twelve back in town I was around as usual.

Saturday April the 10th 1847. Clear, fine, warm day. I was around as usual.

This evening there was a police meeting at my house. It was to find out the feeling of the police about doing [?] now the Twelve were gone for we had not recieved more than half our pay for what we had done and there was no provisions made to pay us any thing more, and it appeared that we were like to have to do duty all summer for nothing

It is time also for us to know what we have to depend on in relation to our agriculturial pursuts for we will have to make some arraingements for a crop. We concluded that it would be best have the matter brought up by the council tomorrow evening and have a definite decision for us to depend upon. We broke up about 9½ o'clock P. M.

Sunday April 11th 1847. Clear warm and still weather Meeting at the stand. P. P Pratt spoke and related an interesting history of his travels to and from England. No meeting in the after noon. No council. I was around as usual.

Monday April 12th 1847. Beautiful day. Traded my shot gun for a fine highly finished rifle Around as usual and in the evening notified the council to meet at S. Russell's house. It was to take the subject of the police into consideration.

It was decided to keep up the police and have another tax levied to pay them. It was to be levied on the same principals as the other tax was. I came home about Eleven o'clock at night. Twelve came back today

Tuesday April 13th 1847. Fine day. Hunting my cow most of the day. Not very well. Arrainged the guard as usual. Some more life to the guard under the idea of another tax for them. "Good" Elder John Taylor[41] arrived this evening from England in good health

Wednesday April 14th 1847. Dark & Cloudy looks like fixing to rain but did not. wind turned to the North. Today the Twelve except Taylor & Parley made their final start to the mountains. I was around as usual & attended to the guard and stood guard till one.

Thursday April 15th 1847. Today clear warm beautiful day. I went over about 8 miles to see about a yoke of my oxen which had been in the stray herd on that side all winter. They strayed from me while I was on Hyde's Ridge in July last & I never saw them till today & now only one which was at my mother-in-laws (E. Taylor) I found them all well & preparing to put in crops.

Friday April 16th 1847. Apearance of rain. I came home today & found all well only my cow missing. I arrainged the guard tonight as usual and had a long hunt for cow till in the night

Saturday April 17th 1847. Clear & very cold & windy. I spent the fore noon & home and in town. Saw some who had been to the pioneer camp & returned & it appears they are about 75 miles now.

In the after noon I hunted for my cow. Had a long walk to no purpose Thought I saw some Omahas driving away some of our cattle.

Came back and arrainged the guard, & had to put out two men who had never before been called on to do police duty.

Sunday April 18th 1847. Cold windy day I was at home At six o'clock I went to council at the council house. The first business done was to read an Epistle from the Twelve who were gone with the pioneers which reads as follows viz:

"The Council of the Twelve Apostles, to the brethren at Winter Quarters and especially to such as shall hereafter arrive at that place. Greeting.

Beloved brethren

We have now completed the organization of the pioneer company, of which we are members, and whom we are about to lead to the mountains, or over the mountains, as we shall be councilled by our Leader in search of a resting place for ourselves, our families, and all who desire

---

41. John Taylor had been editor of the publications at Nauvoo which helped to shape public opinion; he had been very impetuous and outspoken to the leaders of the opposition; he was not above enjoying a convivial drink with the police. Perhaps a more important reason for the "good" title can be found in the following: "But before making the final start, President Young and the Twelve once more returned to Winter Quarters to greet Elder John Taylor, who had just arrived from Europe, bringing with him over $2,000 in gold for the Church." Jenson, *Historical Record*, VIII (August, 1889), 938.

to follow us and work Righteousness; and by doing this, we prove to you and all the world that we do not wish to be a whit behing [*sic*] the first of you, in leaving wife, children, friends, rest or any of the enjoyments of social life; and that we are willing to take a full share of troubles, trials losses & crosses, hardships and fatigues, weariness & watchings, for the Kingdom of Heaven's sake; and we feel to say come calm or strife, turmoil, or peace, life or death; in the name of Israel's God we mean to conquer or die trying; We mean to open up the way for the salvation of the honest in heart from all nations, or sacrafice every [thing] in our stewardship, and if we fail in the attempt; having done all we could, Our Father will not leave his flock without a Shepherd.

In connection with the pioneer Company, we have organized all in your place and vicinity who wish to join the Emegration, into companies of tens, fifties and hundreds, in two divisions, with a President and two councillors to each division with the sanction of their respective companies, and having called the Presidents, Councillors and Captains of hundreds together, have advised with them and decided that all the High Council that is necessary to be left at Winter Quarters; after the present council shall have left, will be the President and captains of Emegration Companies. And where the present Presidents of Divisions and captains shall remove they will leave others similarly organized, with the approval of the brethren, or those who thus enter into the organization.

The brethren now organized, have heard the word and will of the Lord on which this organization is founded, and have given their hearty assent unto it, and any hesitating in carrying out their pledges or acting in concert with their Presidency, as they well [know] will be at the loss of a glory that they can never regain therefore, we say that these instructions generally are more especially to such as shall hereafter arrive at your place; so that they may recieve the principles and instructions that those have had, who have been with us the past winter.

The business of the Saints at Winter Quarters from this time is to journey West, untill further instructions; and while some will have the means to go forward at the springing of grass, others will have to stop and raise some grain to carry with them; and while some will come here prepared, others will have to stop and prepare for their journey; and in either case all preperation and organization is for journeying and not for a permanent location at Winter Quarters, and if any refractory member should mak their appearance, the Bishops will see that justice is done them and let no iniquity have place in your midst.

It is the privilege of the brethren who remain, or arrive hereafter, to decide, but the Council urgently recommends to them to remove the lesser houses, on to the line, of Winter Quarters, or on the borders of the most populated blocks, so as to defend themselves, by houses, pickets, ditches, &c against the Indians, so that your women & children may not be insulted and abused, and their tables robbed, while they are drawing water, or gathering the fruits of their gardens, or attending to any domestic duties in your absence.

Let the brethren labor unitedly, in making fields, fencing, planting, harvesting &c, all under the direction of their respective Captains of Tens, & fifties, — over whom will be the supervision of their Captains of hundreds and Presidents, who will allot to each family all the ground they need or can till, for a garden, *in the city of Winter Quarters* or its immediate vicinity — so that all may share equally in the comforts and luxuries of the table.

The Idler shall not eat the bread of the laborer, therefore let a record be kept, by the Captains of each ten, or his clerk, how each man employs his time, from day to day; and let the same be reported weekly to the clerk of the division or Presidency of the organization; and let one tenth of the avails of each man's labor be appropriated for the benefit of the poor and sick, under the direction of the Bishops, attending to the council of the Presidency; for the poor ye have always with you & the sick often; and he who administers to them, serveth the Lord.

Your crops, and cattle will be exposed to the aggressions of the Omahas, and other Indians, and we say to you, *take care of them*, learn to watch as well as pray, for the farther you go West, the more you will be exposed, and if the saints can not watch them safely here, what will they do when they get where civilization or half civilization is unknown. Make good fences around your corn fields, and locate families near sufficient to watch and keep them safe, and let the emegrants be dilligent and careful to plow, plant, and fence all they possibly can before they start on their journey.

We advise the brethren to keep up a police of their most effective men at Winter Quarters as we have done, for in an hour ye think not, evil may be upon you; and pay them for their services, so that they will not be obliged to neglect your safety, for a loaf of bread, to satisfy their hunger or that of their families.

It is highly important in this dispensation that every brother learns his duty, and acts accordingly, in doing which every one who can, will pay their herdsmen in money, flour, grain, &c. as they shall need, for their comfort, or to prosecute their journey, & not compel them to urge payment of the sisters whose husbands are in the army, the widows, and poor, and let the herdsmen be dilligent in striving to deliver all the cattle &c. entrusted to their charge, at the proper time, to those who are *emegrating West*, & such of those, as can not pay down, agree upon the cattle you shall mark as your own to be held in security, to be paid for or delivered to you at a future day.

It is our wish and council that the Emegration Company now formed, shall follow the pioneers as soon as the grass is sufficient to support the teams, and the Presidents and captains will examine & know that every soul that goes in said company is provided with from 3 to 500 pounds of bread stuff or a year and a half, and as much more as he can get, for we know not whether we can raise corn this summer, as we anticipated at the place of Location.

Let the first Emegration company take with them as many of the sisters whose husbands are in the army, as can fit themselves out, or can be conveniently fitted out.

It is wisdom that all the men in the Emegration Company shall be organized into a military body, under their respective Captains of Tens, 50s and hundreds with Charles C. Rich as their Commander-in-Chief, who will see that every man is properly armed, and ready to meet any savage encounter at a moments warning, taking care that caps and priming of all fire locks are secured so as to admit of no accidents; that John Scott Superintendend the artillery under C. C. Rich — Horace S. Eldrige be Marshall, Hosea Stout Captain of the Guard on the journey & that the guard to watch during the night and sleep as they have need during the day.

The first Company will carry the Temple bell with the fixtures for hanging at a moments notice, which will be rung at day light or a proper

time, and call all who are able to arise to prayers, after which ringing
of bell & breakfast, or ringing of bell and departure in fifteen minutes to
secure the cool of the day till breakfast time &c as the bell may be needed
— particularly in the night season if the Indians are hovering around
to let them know you are at your duty, and if any man acts disorderly,
punish him severely.

Whenever a Company of 75 men, who do not belong to the present
organization Company. shall be organized so as to carry out the principals of the Word & Will of the Lord and these instructions, according
to the pattern, with or without families, and provisions enough to sustain
each soul 18 months, they may come on till the 1st of July, but in all cases,
the brethren must run their own risk for food and not depend on the
pioneers, or any company, in advance for support in the least, either for
their teams, themselves or families, for we are credibly informed that
more than thirty souls of the Oregon Emegrants, perished in the mountains the last season, with hunger; and 100 bushels of corn can esier
be raised near Winter Quarters, than 50 bushels at the foot of the
mountains.

If a man of the first Emegration Company, who is going to stop,
at your place for the time being, should so far forget his covenant in
the Temple, and his more recent obligations, and agreements as to retain
his waggon or team, from the necessityes of the journey: it will be the
duty of the President to instruct the captains to take the same and apply
it where necessity requires, and thus compel the owner to do what he has
previously agreed to, for as some were compelled to *come in,* in ancient
days, others must be compelled to *remain* in in latter days and men who
are taken at their word have no reason to find fault.

                                    For the council
                                    Brigham Young Prest
Willard Richards Clerk
        Pioneer Camp of Israel — Platte river. About 50 miles from Winter
Quarters April 16th 1847.

After the above Epistle was read and accepted the council took up the subject
of the Omahas who were at this time committing unheard of depredations, by
driving off our cattle. They will lay around in the grass and groves untill an
oppertunity offers and then sally forth and drive all the cattle in their power,
even some times they will rush in among the herds, when there is no men present
and attempt to drive them off before our eyes or they will appear on horse back
and run all the cattle that stray off, away The amount of cattle killed by them
the past winter & spring is incredible

The object of the council was now send a committee to the Big Elk, the chief
& enquire the reason of such conduct.

After which the council took up the police subject again when the Treasurers
books were delivered into my hands as clerk of the council. I came home about
ten o'clock

Monday April 19th 1847. This morning I went to take my mare to Greens Taylors, who had agreed to take care of her and also as many of my oxen as I
brought to him. Br Bills had returned with my mare. She was dead poor &
had not been treated well, I think. I found the people all well & preparing their
farms. In the after noon I came home again & crossed the river about very tired

I had not been home but a few moments before the Marshall notified me
that there was a special meeting of the council at Br Saml Russell's at which I
was wanted I went accordingly. It had been called to take immediate action on
the matter of the Omahas killing our cattle for they were getting worse every day.

Much was said after which a committee was appointed to go and have an interview with Big Elk on the subject where upon President Alpheus Cutler Daniel Spencer, C. P. Lott and W. W. Phelps were apointed to go and complain of our grievances.

The feeling of the Council & also of Elders Taylor and Pratt were indignant at the conduct of the Omahas and the prevailing sentiment was to stop them if it had to be by harsher means.

I came home about ten o'clock.

Tuesday April 20th 1847. This morning earley there was a meeting at the stand of the Bishops Council & Parly & Taylor to take into consideration the best way to herd the cattle secure from the aggression of the Omahas. It was decided for the Bishop of each ward to form the cattle in his ward into a herd & appoint a captain over those who are with the herd, all to be well armed with guns &c to defend the cattle against them

I was ordered to take ten men on horse back and reconoitre the country and see if there were any Omahas lying in their hiding places and if so to scourge them severely.

The Bishop were also ordered to ascertain how many cattle had been killed by the Omahas and make report to the committee appointed last night, so that it might be brought before the agent and Big Elk.

After the meeting I proceeded to raise the company & went about ten o'clock & reconoitred to the South of town an the large flat plains & bottom land, untill about three o'clock & then came home, not finding any Omahas. We were armed with horse whips &c to give them a severe flogging in case we found. I was very sick with the head ache when I came home.

To day I appointed William Miller in the police as the guard was rundown so low that I could not get along without more help. It was the same Miller that was taken to Carthage for Brigham (on the [Blank] 18th [crossed out])

This afternoon I was around as usual after dinner

Late in the night I was awaked by Br Thos Clark saying that a large boddy of Indians were in town, that they had divided into two divisions and went in I immediately got up and had the police call up men enough to watch them. We padroled town for some hours but found none although there were some seen but not as many as Br Clark supposed to be.

Wednesday April 21st 1847. Like for rain this morning. I took my seed wheat to mill so pushed was I for bread stuff I was around as usual. The committee went to the Omaha village today as before mentioned In the evening we had a rain

Thursday April 22nd 1847. (Clear fine warm day, good breeze. [crossed out]) Clear cold morning North wind but turned out to be a fine day. I was around as usual.

At dark there was another council tonight at the Council house at which the committee to visit the Omahas, made their report. They had seen both the agent Mr Miller and the Omaha Chifs all of whom manifested plain enough that they were all consenting to the killing of our cattle and were putting up their young men to do it

They had a long talk and seemed willing to stop them in case we would draw two hundred dollars worth of corn from Mo which Miller had bought there for them. I came home after council at ten o'clock.

Friday April 23rd 1847. Clear fine warm day with a good cool breeze. I & Allen went a hunting & killed some birds

Today weighed my baby which weighed 19 pounds I weighed all my children this day one year ago she weighed then 8 pounds and the others O! where are they now!! hush Hunted for my cow, arrainged guard, as usual.

Saturday April 24th 1847. Clear fine warm day. I was around as usual & writing.

There was a council at the Council House at 7 o'clock which met to confer with the Otto chief Capt Caw, who came here to have an interview with us He said he was well satisfied and wanted us to stay here as long as we wanted to   He did not care how long for he believed we were his friends & would do him good.

He claimed this land and said the Omahas had no right to it.   Neither did he want us to pay them anything for being on it. He did not require us to pay him any thing unless we could as well as not   If we could he would be glad to have us draw him some corn from Mo if not it would be just as well.

He manifested hard feelings towards the Omahas   said they had killed our cattle and that he had not permited any of his men to molest any thing we had, and many more things said he all as a friend. He manifested a good spirit

After council they came home with me and staid all night.   They behaved very [well] nor did they seem any way inclined to take anything. I believe they are far above the Omahas and in fact I think he told the truth.

Sunday April 25th 1847. Clear fine warm day. This morning I took the old Chief Capt Caw to Br Cutlers to breakfast the other two took breakfast with Br D. Spencer all being agreed the last evening.

The council met this morning about 8 to give them an answer about the corn. They told him when the agent came home they would conclude their arrainge-ments & that they felt willing to help them & then expressed their good feelings towards them &c   which seemed perfectly to satisfy them.   They then wanted some few presents & Br Taylor gave them some calicos & I & Br Spencer gave them a small sack of crackers They went away now satisfied.

At eleven o'clock there was a meeting at the stand.   Elder Taylor spoke, relat-ing his travels to and from England & spok very emphatically about the manners & customs of the Missourians.   Two of whom were then on the stand.

The Council met at six o'clock & agreed to levy ¾ per cent on the present assessment of the police tax which was all of importance done.

Monday April the 26th 1847. This morning I & the Marshal rode to Belview to take a letter to Mr Miller the agent.

We got there about noon & the agent not being at home left it with his clerk, who seemed well pleased as to the policy we were taking with the Indians. We were well recieved & Sister Groesbeck who was there give us our dinners.

While there we were informed that four Omaha womens went out near to the big spring where we first camped after crossing the river, to get some corn and while there were attacted by some souix we we afterwards learned they were, who killed two and wounded one more of the women.   They fled to the village and gave the alarm whereupon about 150 Omahas & ottoes started after them on horse back and over took & killed seven, who they found in a deep ravin.   There were two Omahas killed in the conflict one by an otto through mistake.

While on our way home we saw the party in the prairie returning We came home about   had good pleasant ride after being so close all winter Belview is on this side of the river just below the lower ferry where I crossed last Augt

After I came home I had to go and arrainge the guard for the night & was out till ten o'clock

Tuesday April 27th 1847. This morning I & the Marshal went to the ferry & told Br Higbee the ferry-man not to take any one over who had not paid his tax, for there were now great numbers going off through disafection[42] & we took this plan to secure their portion of supporting the police. Some paid it willingly while others mad[e] bitter complaints. I was around as usual & wrote considerable In the evening it was like for rain.

Wednesday April 28th 1847. Clear & cool. there was a little rain last night. I was around as usual Went to Walter Gardners wedding a while in the evening

Thursday April 29th 1847. Clear Cool Still day. There was a meeting at the stand for the purpose of letting out the land in the South of town in lots of 5 and ten acres each to the highest bidder in making fence The avrage proportion of fence is one rod to the acre and the land nearer town being more desirable is let out to the one who will make the most fence pr acre.

It sold at from two to four rods per acre There was lots taken I believe to make 1200 rods of fence.

I came home from the "Land sales" and wrote awhile & went around the town as usual arranged the guard. Had a wind and rain storm in the evening.

Friday April 30th 1847. Clear & cool dark and drizzly in the evening Some of Sarpy's team came in from Pawnee village with peltry arrainged the guard as usual no more of importance up late watching dissenters teams

Saturday May 1st 1847. Cold North wind James W. Cummings & I went to see Allen & Green Taylor today to engage them to take care of some cattle & horses which may be detained, belonging to the dissenters who are going away They agreed to attend to it.

We came home about dark.

Sunday May 2nd 1847. Went to meeting at the stand Parley spoke on keeping our cattle & being ready for the journey and wanted the Company who were going to be ready to leave the Horne organized for the Mountains on the first day of June W. W. Phelps informed us that Genl Hardin, who came to Nauvoo with the Gov. troop to hunt dead men &c in the fall of 1845 was killed in a batle in Mexico, between Genl Taylor & Santa Anna. This is joy to me

I attended a council at six o'clock at the Council House. I had Br Robt Campbell appointed to act as clerk of the council in my place for a while as I was likely to be otherwise engaged for a time.

Monday May 3rd 1847. Clear & cold hard frost in night. around as usual and wrote considerable. arrainged the guard as usual.

Tuesday May the 4th 1847. Clear & cold. Today I took Elisha H. Groves into the police & was around usual went up the river hunting Can get but one police on at a time.

Wednesday May the 5th 1847. Clear & cold with an uncommon hard South wind blowing with the dust flying in clouds making it very uncomfortable traveling I was around as usual & wrote considerable today.

Thursday May 6th 1847. Wind as yesterday. Dark rainy day very disagreeable weather. Wrote most of the day, arrainged guard

Friday May 7th 1847. Dull cloudy weather North wind Omahas made another breach on the cattl driving off some seven or 8 oxen. About 20 men went in

---

42. Regarding the number of people who left the church at this time, John D. Lee wrote: ". . . the ferry is thronged continually with waggons to cross, that the scattering has become so general that bro J Taylor and P P Pratt put a vetoe on any teams crossing without a certificate from Pres. I. Morley to show his approval." Kelly, *Lee Journals,* 162.

pursuit brought in some of the beef. Went around as usual & took Wilber J. Earl into the police

The police is running very low hard to keep up a guard. The spirits of the people is dull about their own protection and safty & seem unwilling to do anything to keep up the guard.

About ten o'clock at night I got word that Omahas were on the bottom near town. Called on the Bishops to raise men to guard the South of town against their approach.

Saturday May the 8th 1847. Fine pleasant day but rather cool Nothing of interest going on. I was around as usual. One guard out at a time weak work.

Sunday May the 9th 1847. Clear & cool rather unfavorable for gardening.

This morning Br. Titus Billings & family move into one of my houses to live awhile. They were in company with me while journying from Mt Pisgah to the Bluffs and were uncommonly kind, benevolent & attentive to me, at that time when I was so much worn out with sickness poverty and distress

Meeting at the stand as usual. Parley spoke in the fore-noon on the subject of the stupidity of the people in observing the council & instructions of the Twelve & their heedlessness about their cattle in exposing them to the Omahas also in not working according to the instructions of the Epistle of the Twelve &c & touched very plainly on the dullness of the people, about as it exhisted. Said there was more to be said and requested a general attendance in the after noon. He also disabused some reports current that he gave council different from Brighams policy &c

In the after noon both Parley & Taylor spoke at length on the same things after which several votes were put all carried unanimously, viz: to obey council, To work in union & not individually, to finish the stockading & none go West till all stockade was done To sustain the poor & in short to work according to the pattern. Council was given to herd the cattle more closely & secure them against the Omahas and a company of ten tough Rangers to be raised to guard the out skirts of the Herds to prevent Omaha depredations. When I was voted capt of the same & to raise the men who were to be well mounted & armed so as to defend ourselves against them if necessary & whip them if caught in mischief.

Ten different individuals then were called for to volunteer to pay the Rangers each to pay one man.

The names of those who volunteered to pay the Rangers were

1 P. P. Pratt	6 Alpheus Cutler
2 Danl Russel	7 Jos Young.
3 John Taylor	8 Isaac Morley
4 David Boss	9 G. D. Grant
5 Danl Spencer	10 John Neff.

I came home from meeting and was engaged in raising the Company of Rangers, as we were to be out earley in the morning. I came home about 9 o'clock

Monday May the 10th 1847. It was all hurry and bustle to be off this morning. We started at 9 in the morning mounted & took a circuit to the North through the hills & breaks hunting for the lurking places of the Indians untill we got out on the prairie & then took the dividing ridge & went south turning our horses out occasionally to graze while we watched for Indians untill we were about six or 7 miles below town S. W. or S. near a grove & while turning our horses at, a large number of Indians were discovered coming towards town & some still in their rear

Supposing them to be Omahas going to the flat to drive cattle from thence I sent two men to notify the herdsmen there to drive in their herds, while we stayed on the hill to watch them least they should go around on the ridge & drive cattle from thence.

After they had mostly gone to the flat we also went on a force march to intersect them & met them just as we came to the flat

They were Ottos. There were some 40 accompanyed by their head chiefs in all 4. One could talk English & he told me who they were & I was satisfied that they would do no harm.

In a few moments the whole company came up. Capt Caw was along who knew me He was very glad to see me They all seemed to want to shake hands with me. I suppose he told who I was. The whole bottom was full of cattle, at this time all in a tumult running & driving dust flying to get to town so I sent a man to tell them to stop while we all turned out our horses to graze with they Ottoes for they had horses. after grazing a while we came into town about three o'clock & they went to the council house & put up for the night A church ox was given to them for their supper.

Jim & his brother, the war chief came home with me & took dinner. Capt Caw went with Br Major who took his likeness, which amused the rest very much when they saw it. They would laugh & say "Capt Caw."

They came to pay us a visit & see further about having their corn drawn for them. I spent the day in attending to business for them & arrainging the guard untill about 11 o'clock at night

Tuesday May 11th 1847. This morning when I got up I found Capt Caw & 3 more chiefs standing in my yard waiting for me to get up. I invited them in They informed me that they wanted two more beeves one for breakfast & one to take home them. I went & made report of the same to Parley & Cutler Their request was granted & I spent a long time in making preperations to get the cattle for them These he took breakfast with me & while they were eating five more came and stood around the door & Jim invited them in to eat as soon as he was done

While here Capt Caw made a long speech to me stating his good feelings for us and his willingness for us to stay on his land deprecating at the same time, the rascalty Omaha's &c.

The guard went down about six miles, which was below the place where we met them yesterday & there waited until the Indians came on.

They were engaged in dressing their beef to take home with them.

They came on not long after we arrived & we all went on together about two miles further & we turned North along the dividing and took our post on guard

This company of Indians went down to the Omaha Village & I sent word by them to let them know that we were out with a guard and were prepared to meet them in case they attempted to force our cattle away.

Wednesday Thursday, Friday, Saturday, Sunday and Monday the 12th 13th, 14th 15th 16th and 17th of May. I was out with the guard as usual, during which time nothing very different took place from day to day.

We enjoyed ourselves very well & had good times. We appointed Br J. C. Wright our justice of the peace before whom all were to be tried for any default or accident. If any one had bad luck he was fine for it If any one had any too good luck he was fined or if he did not come in time to go out with us he was fined If he was ignorant he was fined

My horse threw me off one day when I was trying to cach one that had got loose & I was allowed a pint for my good intentions and endeavors to catch the horse and fined a quart for having the bad luck of being thrown off while doing it This was our custom while the guard lasted

We posted ourselves on the dividing ridge along which the road ran which we moved here on last summer & we could guard the whole frontier of the cattle range. Some times we scattered out & some times we kept together

We had orders to keep the herds off of the large flat S. of town where the farm was to be We notified the herdsmen of the same several evenings to no purpose &

had finally to whip several before they would keep away. It was wanted to reserve this bottom for pasture for the oxen when plowing.

We had several good rains during this time & the grass grew finely while the plows were going in an incouraging manner.

Tuesday May the 18th 1847. This morning there were but for of the guard appeard for duty & in fact they had been running down for several days as they had but poor encouragement for their [service] and some had concluded not to come out unless they were assured of being remunerated according to the promise.

We were too weak handed to guard alone in saftey for the cattle so we rode around to the different ones in authority & notified them of the situation of affairs and desired to know what to do but none could give us any satisfaction on the subject so I dismissed the company with orders to hold themselves in readiness at any time in case they were called on to come out.

I intended to let the guard run down untill the authorities would rise up and help to bear it off & make some arraingements that could be depended on.

After this I took my gun & went out a hunting & as I passed by Elder John Taylor's he enquired about the guard & the reasons I was not out & I informed him & he wanted to to call out the company again & he would go. I done so & we all went out & spent the day very agreeably.

Wednesday, Thursday, Friday and Saturday, May the 19th 20th 21st & 22nd 1847. We were out as usual & had from 6 to 9 men each day

Sunday May 23rd 1847. Went out as usual dark morning In the evening we were informed that the subject of the guard was taken up at the meeting & one dollar per day allowed us for our services & some new arraingements spoken of about our pay.

In the evening I attended to the council & there the subject of the guarding was again taken up & left for the Bishop to arrainge amongst themselves to raise the pay for the guard out of the people for services done after today.

Monday May the 24th 1847. Very dark rainy morning. Alonson Ripley was taken into the guard this morning.

Br Nephi paid me ten dollars in gold on my two weeks guarding. cold North wind. Drizzly day Had ten men to day. A steam Boat came up today with a large lot of goods for this place belonging to Mr Beach & Wooley. Anna Jones came home on the Boat from Camden Mo

Tuesday May 25th 1847. Cool morning. Went out with ten men. To day a number of Omahas came up to bring up a number of horses which they had stolen from our people from time to time. We met them about six miles below here near where we met the ottos. We stoped them for Br Parley P. Pratt had forbidden us to let them come in because they had been so treacherous that he had determined not to have any thing more to do with them. We informed them of the determination which chagrined them very much & they contended hard for their right to go in but we told them that we could not violate our orders.

After some debate on the subject however & their declaring their determination to live in peace with us, we consented to let young Elk & two more of his chiefs go in and take in the horses and recieve the pay for them which the owners had promised them previously & also have an interview with parley & others which might explain matters better for them than it now presented itself for we now occupied a hostile attitude towards each other & the Omahas considered us at war with each other at present.

They took six chiefs & braves instead of three & we went in the others agreed to remain there till we come back They brought in six horses

When we came in I went to see Parley and reported to him what had been done and also told him that my reasons for admitting them in was because they had come to make offers of peace & to present the good desires & wishes of old Elk to us & enter into more friendly relations, then had hither to exhisted between us

He would not see them nor give me any satisfaction about them nor tell me what to do but said to tell them that our chiefs were mad & did not want to see them not have any thing to do with them that we were able to keep peace & take care of ourselves but if the local authorities had a mind to do anything they might do as they pleased & abruptly left me

I went then to see Br John Taylor who when he found out what Parly said took the same position thoug in a mild & friendly way & refered me to Br Lott & Father John Smith Br Lott chanced to pass by at the time & I reported to him who also said he had nothing to do with it to which I said rather in anger that neither had I & if they authorities had nothing to do in it I would go away & leave them in the streets where they had been standing all this time. All this was in hearing of Br Taylor I was going to leave & go on guard & Lott went & saw Father Smith while the Brethren were paying them for their horses.

They decided for Lott to go with me down to the other Indians & he & I to hear their report as it could not be maid only in the presence of all of them.

The Indians delivered up their horses & recieved their pay and we all started back and joined the others who had been very impatient while we were gone & tryed once to force the line but the guard stood firm and prevented them

We formed ourselves into a regular council. The Omahas on one side & Br Lott myself & the guard on the other other when the "talk" commenced by Young Elk who stated that he was now ready to hear any thing we had to say. Br Lott replied very angrily that we had said heretofore all we had to say & they would not live up to their agreements & if they had nothing to say it was no use talking &c

After several pases like that on both sides, Young Elk still waiting for us to lead out the talk commenced with very hostile & what I considered unreasonable feelings from Br Lott

Elk keep down his feeling admirably well and cooly related how he had been sent in by his father to bring in our horses & enter into a better understanding of peace & had been stoped on the praire like wild beasts & not even admitted a hearing & how it wounded his feeling to have to be guarded into town & leave his braves under guard to offer peace to us & deliver up stolen property & give their pledge that no more should be stolen & also how he had to contend with his own peple before he could get them to give up the horses & now he was not well recieved but said let all that pass & we would be at peace from this time & we might now know that what he said would be done on their part

He spoke very sharp at this ill treatment & laid it to our chiefs & said that if the "Big Red headed" chief (Brigham) was here it would not be so but he would have taken them in & fed them & spoke friendly

Said he did not expect to be stoped this way but he expected for his chiefs & braves to have seen the wives & children of our chiefs saying they would not have hurt them He often remarked that he wished the "Big Red headed" chief would come home & stay here & then we would always be at peace.

At another time he said they would not have stoped the meanest of our men from coming into their village much less our head chiefs and braves I thought his remark apt and just & so thought the whole company.

Br Lott's wrath abated & he talked reasonable in a short time & we all verily believed they were sincere in their words.

(Elk rebuked the authorities for their ill treatment towards him whi [crossed out])

After the above was over they wanted a definite answer from us & presents to take to his father which we could not give but agreed to take his words to our chief (Br Cutler) when he come from Missouri & then let them know his answer & what he would do and they went on not any too well satisfied and we started home about six o'clock.

Wednesday & Thursday May 25 & 26, [26 & 27] '47. Went out as usual with 8 & 9 men weather as usual warm South rain.

Got news that Genl Scott had defeated Santa Anna in a pitched battle at Cerro Gordo & taken his carraige & wooden leg and entirely broke up his army.

Friday May 28th 1847. Staid at home Sent out 8 men O. M. Allen Capt.

Saturday May 29th 1847. North wind. Went over river in the morning came back & went out on guard. Cloudy day

This evening I recieved a waggon load of fish for the guard and police sufficient for them all of P. Richards and was engaged in distribeting them out untill eleven o'clock. Had a hard warm still rain all night.

Sunday May 30th 1847. Cloudy drizzly day. Staid in sent out the company. Hyde & Parley spoke on morals. Parley spoke quite hard about us admitting in the Omahas

Today had a large lot of beef to deal out for the police & guard. I[t] was procured by the Marshall.

This evening council met at Br Morley's shop had a case against John Richards for refusing to deliver up a brace of public pistols.

Monday May 31st 1847. Went out with 8 men but nothing up of importance. rained some in the evening.

Tuesday June 1st 1847. To day I & G. W. Langley went to Bel-vue to report Prest A. Cutler's wishes to young Elk as agreed on the 24 inst

We found him in Town & he was pleased with what was said for Cutler recieved his offers as in good faith & had sent accordingly & proposed for them to send for the presents wanted before. Young Elk declined coming now as he was going to start tomorrow with a war party against one Band of the Pawnees but said he would come when he returned home again. We came home and on our way killed a Badger an animal much resembling a Raccoon but heavier & shorter legged slow to run & very strong

I[t] recieved one shot in the vitals & two in the head before it was killed from a six shooter

Wednesday June 2nd 1847. Went out on guard with 6 men

Thursday June 3rd 1847. Went out with six men. Four Indians came in today bringing a letter from Elk stating that he had given out going against the Pawnees & desired to know when it would suit us for him to come in also for some of our young men to meet them at the lower creek and attend them in.

I came in to see what their business was & sent G. G. Potter out in my place

This evening there was a police meeting called by the Marshall, at Br Morley's Shop which proved to be for the purpose of inducing the police to reduce their wages to 50 cents per tour of duty. He & W. Snow was hard up for it but all the rest against it

The Marshall lead out untill finally he accused the police of not doing their duty & also said that I did not do service for my pay & that I did not attend to the guarding of the city as I ought. (It was plain that "there was something rotten in Denmark".

I followed him & severely handled him & Br Snow for what they were about & told the Marshall that he was attending to that which was none of his business and in future to let my & the police's business alone.

While at this in high & a spirited tone Brs Morley & Harris came in & I then told them what was up & the reason of our warmth which was not any thing like a difficulty or hard feeling but plain speaking.

While I was explaining this Prests O. Hyde P. P. Pratt and John Taylor also came in so I stoped saying I had been catched twice

Elder Taylor replied to go on and not stop for them. I told him it was nothing but a police meeting and not interesting to them.

"Never mind says he we are police men too".

Says I. "I hope you will all conform to the rules of the police then". "Certainly" says Taylor "Bring on the jug" says I at which they were presented with a large jug of whiskey.

This was such an unexpected turn that it was only answered by a peal of laughter & they all paid due respect to the jug no more was said about our subject.

After drinking says Parley "I have traveled these streets all times of the night & never before have I saw a police man but now I know where to find them here-after" alluding to the jug

"Parley" says I "do you not know that some things in this kingdom are only spiritually diserned & so with the police". He give it up and Hyde pronounced the joke on Parley Their business was to find out what had become of some property that was missing on the other side of the river supposed to have been stolen & they thought we knew where it was.

Hyde also said there had been two horses taken with the pioneers from a man at the Point & he had paid for them.

He was going in to stop all stealing & hunt up all missing property &c and demanded of us in the name of the Lord to know where it was but not knowing we could not tell the Marshall however gave him a clue to some I think

It was two o'clock a. m. when I came home.

Friday June 4th 1847. Went out with 8 men as usual

Saturday June 5th 1847. To day the Omahas were to come in & I was ordered to meet them six miles below as they had requested in their letter They came about ten or 11 o'clock a. m. about 80 in number comprising all of what they call their chiefs and braves.

We recieved them as usual formed on horse back according to the Danite system of horsemanship and consequently I was in the center of the line

The chiefs were told who I was by those who knew me to be a war chief or captain & they all came to shake hands with me first.

I left some most of the company there to keep a look out & took 3 or four in with me & accompanied the Indians into town They came to the South point of the first ridge West of the city and encamped. Here they had a commanding view of the town & the town had also a commandin view of the Omahas.

There was a council held with them towards evening wherein all thing mentioned & promised by Young Elk was fully confirmed by "Old Elk" and all present and the best of feeling seemed to exhist between us.

Some beef was given them for their supper.

I was up until 11 o'clock P. M. arrainging the guard which now to be stronger than common because of the Indians. Old & Young Elk & Harvey took dinner with me

Sunday June 6th 1847. After the Omahas had took breakfast they commenced to scatter home I attended them 6 miles & all passed off well and we was on guard all day.

Monday June 7th 1847. Sent out 7 men & staid in to settle up the police account with the Marshal & to see about my going on with the company west as captain of the guard

I was round town to day & collected some police tax from some movers who was going on west as the Marshal was sick and could not be out.

Tuesday June 8th 1847. Went out as usual & had only 4 men today. Cloudy day & a hard S. wind & W. rain at dark.

Wednesday June 9th 1847. Staid in today. The mill dam was gone this morning.

A meeting was called to appoint the time for the company to start from the Horn and for those who had their grinding to divide with those who had not in consequence of the mill stopping for the dam breaking had made a great disappointment to many and caused a great stir.

Thursday June the 10th 1847. Sent out 5 men on guard & I staid in town as there was some business for me to attend to. The publick arms had by the order of the council been ordered into the hands of Prest Cutler and the waggon for Genl Rich to move in West.

I endeavored to find out today what was to be done about the guard for the journey & me going for as yet I could learn nothing accordingly I went to Genl Rich Elder Taylor, Prest Cutler & Morley & Bishop Whitney & could not learn anything about it nor as much as get any of them to talk on the subject to any satisfaction but to refere me to the other. Morley refered me to Rich & he to Taylor, who requested me not to trouble him about it for he said he had never considered it before, and refered me to Cutler & he said he had no time to talk & Whitney knew nothing about it. Thus I was sent around all day and learned nothing & so seeing that there was no arraingement for either me me or a guard on the journey I now give up the idea of going & bought a house of Br A. O. Smoot which was more spacious & comfortable than the one I now occupied. It is situated on [blank] street

Friday June 11th 1847. Sent out 5 men & I went over the river for my mare at P. G. Taylors. She was in fine order. I came home at dark.

Saturday June 12th 1847. Went out on guard with 5 men.

Elder Taylor & a large number started today West.

Sunday June 13th 1847. Went out with 5 men again.

Attended the council in the evening An order was passed to keep all cattle out of the corn field & I was instructed to keep or see it executed. All catle or Horses that were in the field the owner was to pay one dollar each & 25 on sheep The subject of the guard was taken up and an order passed allowing Prest Cutler & myself to keep as many men on guard as we thought proper.

We also heard from the pioneers. They were at the head of Grand Island on the 4th of May and all well.

Monday June 14th 1847. Sent out 5 men, two to drive cattle in from the corn field and three on guard.

I moved in the forenoon to the house which I bought of Smoot, which was much more comfortable than the one I now live in.

There was a large drove of cattle brought in from the corn this day which caused an unaccountable murmuring by some who owned them showing plainly that they were willingly ignorant of their cattle being on the corn

The stray pen was full tonight & we had to guard it to keep the cattle from being taken away without paying the forfeiture of the law. I was out untill eleven o'clock.

Tuesday June 15th 1847. I staid in town today & sent out 7 men. Four for guard and 2 to drive cattle off the corn as on yesterday.

This evening an Express was sent to me from the camp for me to come forthwith and go on as captain of the guard

It was as follows.

> "South West bank of Elk Horn river.
> Indian Territory.
> Tuesday 15th June 1847.

To

Captain Hosea Stout,

The Council here has made the following vote which is here copied. Motioned by Parley P. Pratt & Seconded by John Taylor that Hosea Stout be sent to mount his horse and come on immediately to act in his appointment as Captain of the Guard. Voted unanimously, and we will sustain him as a people both temporally & spiritually. This vote was made at a public meeting this morning, and we expect to see Hosea in conformity with this, at this place in 24 hours from the time he gets this notice.
>   P. P. Pratt.
>   John Taylor
>
> Rob Campbell
> Clerk"

The above speaks for itself As before observed I had tried to find out what to do about going and none would notice me and now after Rich had given me a written certificate showing that I was ready to go if means & men were furnished & all the authorities had refused to do any thing about a guard, I was now cited to mount my horse & leave home as a runaway & leave my family without any means for their subsistance or provisions for myself only their blank promise to "sustain me as a people" which was weak indeed and go & take my place as captain of the guard. What guard when not one man had been enlisted or one dime appropriated for it This looked like oppressive nonsense to me & excited my feeling to the highest pitch I felt insulted abused & neglected in the first place and now more so & I did not intend to comply but least I had wrong feeling I postponed my decision untill morning.

Wednesday June 16th 1847. This morning I sent word to the camp that I could not go and did not think it was a fair thing to ask it of me as I had been neglected so long and thus my expidition West was brought to a close I staid town today to enlist more men in the picket guard Sent out four men on guard

Heard much said about the requisition of the camp for me to go which made considerable excitement but mostly in my favor.

Thursday, Friday & Saturday June 17th 18th & 19th 1847. Went out on guard as usual with from 6 to 8 men   rainy wether mostly.

Sunday June 20th 1847. Went out with 6 men.

At meeting today Hyde preached his celebrated bogus sermon, denouncing all bogus makers, counterfeiters thieves &c & commanding all such & all who knew of any such to come forth with and tell him & also absolved them from all former acts and covenants to keep secrets.

This made quite a stir & caused some to "confess their sins"[43]

I attended the council in the evening. This was a lively time we had one or two trials about cattle taken from the corn fields S. C. Bolton for one

When I came to the council they were rasping away about my not going on west some casting implications about for me it &c.

President Morley seemed to sencure me, the hardest but wound up by saying that perhaps I had reasons for doing as I did but he would not (do it for [crossed out]) have done it for kingdoms.

He also at the Elk Horne instituted the inquiry what I had been about as if he did not know & also here said he did not know why.

I obtained leave of the council to speak & let off my feeling uncommonly plain denouncing the course that had been taken with me by the authorities & held up the way they had departed from Brigham's instructions to the gaze of all present and denied Morleys position of not knoing what I had been at as he and every body here knew very well. No pretended to say anything against me when I was through & so I stood justified The matter was then talked over & Hyde proposed to me, to take 10 men as a guard and overtake the camp yet to which I agreed but after many proposals Hyde finally decided for me to stay here as I was need here & let them do with out who neglected me.

Monday June the 21st 1847. Sent 4 men out on guard today and I staid to enquire into some cases of disorder reported to me by Elder Hyde, which however, did not amount to anything of importance in the sequel.

The main camp has all started on to the West & all the brethren who had gone to the Horne has returned.

I was out untill 11 o'clock P. M.

Tuesday June the 22nd 1847. Went out on guard with 4 men There was a council in the evening to which I was notified to appear It was to consider upon a letter just recieved from Elder Hyde stating that there was to be a demand made by Mitchel, the Pottewattamie Agent, upon the Omahas for the man who shot Wetherbee[44] & that 100 men would be raised at the Point to cross over to Bel-vue on next Thursday morning and desired 50 men to be raised here and put under my command and met them at 9 o'clock A. M. with the intention of making war on the Omahas in case they did not give up the murder and also the one who killed the man found dead on the Horn by our people

---

43. Most writers of the Mississippi Valley frontier mention the counterfeiting activities that were carried on. Some accused the Mormons of being involved, both at Far West and at Nauvoo.

The unpublished diary of John D. Lee for 1846 makes several references to members of the company who had been engaged in counterfeiting or "Bogus making." Entries of April 5 and 7 report Brigham Young's violent condemnation of such persons. On August 1 he wrote that ". . . the description of another villian was taken who passed off counterfeit money . . . ." Lee, "Camp of the Saints," 31, 33, 83.

Another point of view is given by William Hall: "At Garden Grove . . . we buried two bogus presses, which I carried in my own wagon, with a barrel of rosin and materials belonging thereto, amounting in weight to one thousand pounds." Hall, *Abominations of Mormonism Exposed*, 81.

44. From the reports of visitors to his farm at Summer Quarters, John D. Lee learned details of this incident:

About 5 Bro Dunn, Martin returned from W. Q. Reported that the mill was clear. Co. Started and one of the brethren was shot through the hip [by] an Indian supposed to be of the Sioux while on his way to the Horn. Pres Morley also reported that a party of Sioux had taken 2 horses and 2 head of catle from Bro Kimble's farm 2 days since. Since writing the above I have been informed that Bros. Fransis Weatherbee and Lampson were together when a party of 3 Indians, evidently Omahas, naked armed with guns, attacked them, cocked their guns. The two men without guns sprang at them and seized 2 of their guns, the 3rd Indian stepped off about 15 feet and when he saw that our brethren were using them up, shot Bro. Weatherbee as above stated. At the fire of the gun they all ran for life. (Kelly, *Lee Journals*, 179.)

The letter also stated that the expedition would be lead by Mr Mitchel in person.

The council decided to fulfill the requisition and ordered me to proceede forthwith to raise the company which I did by calling on all present who were willing to volunteer which many did and appointed sun rise in the morning to meet to report our situation.

Wednesday June 23rd 1847. Met at sun rise to here the report to the company and found that it was going to be a hard matter to raise horses for some would neither go themselves nor lend their horses so I saw the ferry man, Br Higbee and had him not to cross any horses over the river untill we were gone & sent men to press all the horses in town or have the owners go along with them. By this opperation we soon brought many horses to bear on the expedition.

Also sent several men over the river & to the upper farms on this side for men & horses. There was several pressed and brought over in a short time. Sent 6 men on guard today.

At 5 o'clock the company met again as previously understood to report after being buisly engaged all day in raising horses & men and found that we had thirty horses only could now be depended upon —

Thursday June 24th 1847. Started at sun rise for Bel-vue The company was small at first. Men however were falling in or over taking us for miles.

When we had gone about half way we stopped to organize the company which we did by appointing Jesse P. Harmon & Alexander McRae Lieutenants and dividing the the company into two platoons over which each officer commanded Harmon taking the first & McRae the second platoon I then selected Thomas Rich,[45] Daniel Carns, William Meeks Jas W. Cummings, Luman H. Calkins, and George D. Grant as picket guard and also sent them on ahead with orders to go into Belvue and report our arrival and tell Mitchel that we were at his service and only wanted his written orders.

This precaution was necessary because we knew he was only the Pottawattamie agent and had no authority on this side of the river among the Omahas. And not only so we knew him also to be a most infamous rascal and an inveterate enemy to us.

It would have therefore been very easy for him to played the game to engage us in a war with the Omahas and leave us in the difficulty. But suspecting him we determined not to act without the most positive & plain orders. Moreover in case he led us into an engagement and did not mentain his position or attempted to desert or betray us we would have put him to death instanter

Our company here amounted to 53 men and we had two baggage waggons along. Thus arrainged and organized we proceeded onward and stoped on the last high ground in the prairie before going to Belvue while the picket or vanguard aforesaid went on to learn the news After remaining here some time with a strong guard out & taking some refreshments in the mein time, and no return from those who had gone in; we all went to the Cold Spring where the Big camp was when I first came over the river last August. Here we quenched our thirst and regaled & refreshed ourselves well. This place looked now deserted, desolate, and lonesome & the Spring almost entirely filled up but the watter clear & pure as ever. After this we went back when we met our van guard who reported that Mitchel came

45. Thomas R. Rich was born November 29, 1817, in Floyd County, Indiana. A brother of Charles C. Rich, he was married to Henrietta Peck, a sister of Hosea's first wife. The two men were together at the Battle of Crooked River.

Thomas Rich was a member of Joseph Smith's bodyguard. He came to Utah in Joseph Young's company of 1850 and settled in Richville, Morgan County. He died on January 26, 1884, in Porterville, Morgan County, Utah.

over while they were there accompanied by Br Hyde The people in Belvue did not yet know anything of this move nor had mitchel done anything towards raising the 100 men spoken of by Br Hyde's letter to the Council and had just come over when they had come in town. They informed him that I was on the prairie and was ready for service & only waited for his written orders This seemed to confuse him considerable He confessed that he had no authority on this side of the river and only acted by verbal request of Majr Miller who was the Omaha agent and was absent.

He stated that the man found on the Horn was a Pawnee and had it been his own son as he at first suspected he would have raised the Pottewattimies & went against the Omahas. He seemed now to think that it was only an act of accommodation in him to come over for us and offered to go with us for the man that shot Wetherbee as a mere favor. They told him that it was a Government case and if he did not want us in that capacity we would return home again. so this expedition was but the resuld of folly & ignorance. The Omahas were now gone on their hunt.

When we come to the creek six miles below Winter Quarters we stopped to bait & watter our horses and Harvey Green in an attempt to light his pipe, set his powder on fire and blew up. His horn was full of powder & he had been cautioned several time to stop it but he heeded no one He was badly hurt but recovered in a few days.

We came home about sun set and at dark Myself Carns & Cummings went to see & relate our expedition to Presidents A. Cutler & Morley. They thought very little of the course which had been taken to call out this company and viewed Mitchel in a very unfavorable light. We were together untill about 12 o'clock P. M.

Friday June 25th 1847. Went out on Guard to day with 8 men. Nothing of importance.

Saturday June 26th 1847. Went out with 8 men again.

Had a hard rain at 3 o'clock & a police meeting at my old house just before dark to consult on the best way for the police to meet what was called Hyde's Bogus policy We generally thought best to be still & not take sides.

Sunday June 27th 1847. Went out with seven men and came in and went to Council in the evening. John H. Blazzard was tried today for wrestling an ox out of the possession of the guard which had been taken out of the corn field and threatning to fight for it. He was fined 2 dollars which was the first man fined by the High Council. It was put at two dollars not as a precedent in such cases but to prove or show that men should be fined for rebelion.

Isaac Allred from Garden Grove came to my house today which was the first time I had seen him since I left there.

Monday June 28th 1847. Sent out six men today and staid in to see to and attend Company business.

Tuesday June 29th 1847. Went on guard with six men Very hot day.

Wednesday June 30th 1847. Staid in today. Sent out 4 men. Sent 3 men viz W. Chapman O. M. Allen & L. H. Calkins to Belvue for some horses which had been stolen from our people by the Omahas & had been recovered & brought back by Logan Fontanell their interpreter. They came back in the evening with seven horses.

Thursday July 1st 1847. Went out at sun rise into the corn field after some horses and catle which had been turned into the field by their owners & brought in several Went on guard with 5 men today.

Friday July 2nd 1847. Today 22 head of Daniel Russell cattle were brot in off of the corn Went out with 4 men and came in at 2 o'clock and went out again

Saturday July 3rd 1847. Went out with 5 men. In the evening had a police meeting to consult how to divid the goods taken for the tax on Beech and Eddy's store amounting to some 46 dollars. It was decided to divide by per cent as was our custon It amounted to 12 cents on the dollar of our dues.

Sunday July 4th 1847. Staid in today & sent out five men on guard. Went to meeting at the stand. W. W. Major preached It rained in the after noon.
    Went to Council in the evening. The case of the Marshall against John Richards, for refusing to deliver up a pair of Public pistols upon Genl Rich's order was had and he being very contrary was very near being cut off the church before he complied.

Monday July 5th 1847. Staid in. Sent out 7 men. Today the police drew their portion of good taken for Beech & Eddy's tax.
    The Picket guard met this evening to adjudicate on the case of Daniel Russell's cattle 22 head which had been taken in the corn field and he rather than to pay the 100 [$1.00] pr head appealed to the council & they refered it to us to settle, so we left it to his own conscience & magnanimity to say what was just as he was one of the council and helped make the law. He decided to pay 10 bushels of corn & 10 of Buck wheat which we accepted.

Tuesday July 6th 1847. Went out on guard to day with 5 men. Elder Hyde sent us some beef today which he had had caused to be donated for the use of the guard, from the other side of the river.

Wednesday July 7th 1847. Went out to day with six men.
    This evening Danl Russell came to me & said that he had consulted with several of the council & laid the same before President Cutler & they had decided that there was no need of the Picket Guard and that he was sent to notify me of the same and therefore we were suspended in our opperations. I was very sick this evening with the head ache.

Thursday July 8th 1847. This morning before I notified the guard that they were suspended I went to see President Cutler for I suspected the truth of D. Russell's report It did not breath the proper spirit to me. and moreover seemed very impolitic. President Cutler said that he had sent him to me, but not to stop the Guard for he was not in favor of it and also that we were shamefully abused and mistreated & could not blame us if we did not serve any longer neither did he like such a way of doing business without the Council being in session & proposed to me to keep the guard in rediness untill Sunday and not have the horses disposed of and he would have the subject up at the next council and adjusted then & so I notified the guard accordingly.
    I was around town today & now relieved from the burthen of the Picket guard.
    This was one of the hottest days I ever saw But in the evening the wind came from the North accompanied by torrents of rain which ran like rivulets down the streets. It bursted in to my house in torrents and filled it up in a few moments untill I had to throw the watter out by the bucket full untill we were all completely drenched. This I believe was the hardest rain this season.
    To day Anna Jones my sister came here to live as her and her husband Ben Jones had parted for some of the dissatisfaction between them.

Friday July 9th 1847. To day I was around in town & at home wrighting in my journal

Saturday July 10th 1847. To day the two Grand Divisions of the camp of Israel was reorganized & filled up after the late emegration West. My child was now very sick & I was up most all night.

Sunday July 11th 1847. Meeting at the stand. O. Hyde spoke on religion & religious subjects.

The council met in the evening. Blazzards case up again & council decided to have an execution taken out from the Clerk of the council in all such cases & property taken when men would not comply with the law without.

The subject of the Picket guard was had up today as was before spoken of by President Cutler It seemed news to most of the Councillors & I could not but wonder who Daniel Russell had been consulting with as he had said on the subject for surely it seemed now to be the first time any of them had considered it & all with one consent declared in favor of keeping the guard out and gave me orders accordingly.

Monday & Tuesday 12th & 13th July 1847. Staid at home. Sent 6 men each day on guard Intensley hot. I had a stable built. My child is very sick and seems to be running down & not much hopes of its recovery.

Wednesday July 14th 1847. Staid in. Sent out 5 men on guard. Daniel H. Wells Esqr came in today from Nauvoo. This is a thing I did not expect for had not hitherto had much confidence in him, but all seems well now with him.

To day I learned that the Commanchee Indians are making war on the United States Sante Fe trains & determined to do all the mischief they can

Thursday July the 15th 1847. Staid in. Sent out 5 men again Was very unwell. Issued an order on the police treasury today amounting to Seventy two dollars

Friday July 16th 1847. Sent out 6 men and staid in Filed in the police order today My child is worse.

Saturday July 17th 1847. Staid at home. Sent out 6 men

Sunday July 18th 1847. Went to a council called by Elder Orson Hyde at 8 o'clock for the purpose of considering the case of Gardon Grove, as there were reports of stealing and other like charges against that place & Hyde was sanguine against them and was for cutting them all off wholesale. The subject was quite warmly debated Some doubted the legality of cutting them off without any specific charges against them & both parties face to face. But Hyde & some others were for smooth work.

They were cut off however by a majority of those present Some were against it There were I believe but six present of the Council & two against it which made quite weak work.

There was several cases of theft up and talked over but not any thing of importance done.

I came home & went to meeting at the stand Isaac Morley spoke & I came home and went to Council in the evening. C. Drown[46] was had up for stealing and honorably acquited. Jas Clayton had up and repremanded & acquited for firing

---

46. This is Charles M. Drown who with his wife, Sarah Tarbell, and his son, David Tarbell Drown, was living in western New York in 1837. He remained behind the general migration from Nauvoo and during the summer of 1846, was caught and cruelly mistreated by the mob as he attempted to harvest his crops. His activities after he arrived in Utah and his murder are discussed in Volume II.

pistols on the Sabbath. The case of Bills vs. Cox up, also Lees case vs. Berry[47] but none of importance

Monday July 19th 1847. Went out with five men. My oxen and waggon came home today. One yoke was dead   Stewart was willing to do right by me

Tuesday July 20th 1847. Went out with 4 men. We went out to Cutlers Park and rode down the papa-awe & found where the Indians had killed some cattle about six miles below there   It was late work

Wednesday July 21 — 1847. Sent out 6 men & staid at home to settle with Br Stewart who was willing to give me all he possessed; to pay me for the yoke of cattle which had died but I did [not] exact anything of him as it appeared that he had done the best he could while he was gone

Thursday, Friday, Saturday July the 22nd 23rd & 24th 1847. Was on guard, found goose berries. North and West.

Sunday July the 25th 1847. Staid in. Sent out 5 men around town. A steam Boat landed today   Went to Council in the evening
   Heard letters read from Hyde containg covenants which he desired to have the people [of] Garden Grove enter into before they could be restored to fellowship. The Council objected to them as unreasonable.
   These covenants required them to swear under the most bitter curses and imprecations & damnation to themselves to all eternity that they had not stolen or knew any one who had nor would not since they left the Mississipi river & that they would inform on all who they knew who had or did &c   Let this suffice that it was totally vetoed by the Council
   This Evening after Council there was a trial between Br D. H. Wells Esq & a Br Young for a span of mules which the latter claimed as his & Wells now had the case was laid over   Wells had bought them in Nauvoo.

Monday Tuesday July 26 & 27. Went out with 4 men on guard

Wednesday July 28th 1847. Sent 4 men out on guard & staid in to attend to a case wherein some young men were suspected of stealing a conoe from Br Lyman one of the fishermen. We ascertained that they had & hid it down the river some two or three miles & intended to go off at night. The council met on the case and adjourned the trial for further evidence.

Thursday July 29th 1847. Sent 5 men on guard and staid in
   Stewart had his trial with Dayton to who had took Stewart's wife & ran through with his property while he was gone back after provisions last winter He had also reported that Stewart had apostetized and sold my team & many more things. He proved to be a most consumate and contemptible scroundal. I was out on guard till eleven o'clock at night

Friday July 30th 1847. Sent out 4 men on guard & staid in
   The council met to try the case of the young men stealing the canoe but they had ran away & of course no trial and as there was no other business before the council the subject of the police came up and the council wanted us to make some reports which we were not willing to do because our evedence was only as the evedence of another man & in cases of adultery the chance would be against a single policeman if he reported. It was however decided that a policemans testi-

47. John D. Lee and James Berry, father of Lee's wife, Martha, were contending about a horse. Lee wrote of the trial in detail, concluding that the Council decided ". . . that Bro. J. D. Lee had acted in all good faith . . . that the loss of the horse was an unavoidable circumstance . . . ." He and Berry reached an amicable agreement. Kelly, *Lee Journals*, 192.

mony should be taken in preference to any one else & we would be safe in making all reports This council resulted in much good as may be learned hearafter

Saturday July 31st 1847. Sent 4 men on guard and staid in. Settled with Dayton for stewart.

Sunday August 1st 1847. Staid in today. Blessed infants at meeting. Council in the evening Scotts case. Bills case &c up today. Rainy.

Monday August 2nd 1847. Sent 4 men on guard & I staid in Cloudy day.

Tuesday August 3rd 1847. Staid at home & sent 4 on guard Warm still rain last night. around town as usual.

Some of the soldiers returned today from the Battalion viz Pugmire, Whiting[48] &c —

Wednesday Augt 4th 1847. Today was a council to take the Garden Grove case up again President Fulmer, D. McArthur L. A. Shirtliff & Hunt had come here and had not heard that they had been cut off at Garden Grove But learning it just before they got here they came to the council and demanded a trial which was granted & they was able to show plainly that they had not transgressed any law but had on the contrary done all they could for the wellfare of that place and also that they had been opposed by evil designing men who had reported lies about them & fully satisfied the council of their inocence and good intentions. The result of which was that the Branch of the Church at Garden Grove was reinstated in full fellowship

President Fulmer made an able appeal to the council & the spirit of God rested down upon him. I was at the council most all day.

Thursday Augt 5th 1847. Sent out 5 men on guard & staid at home.

Louisa, now my only child, who had been sick for a long time died today which seemed to complete the dark curtain which has been drawn over me since I left Nauvoo. My family then consisted of 8 members & now but two.[49] Five of whom has died & now I am left childless but I shall not dwell on this painful subject.

Friday Aug 6th 1847. Sent 4 men out on Guard & staid in to attend to the burial of my child.

Saturday Aug 7th 1847. Sent 5 men out on guard & staid in. This morning Henry Phelps son of W. W. Phelps attempted to wrest their horse out of the stray pen & I gave him a severe caining & broke a good fancy hickry cain given me by

48. Jonathan Pugmire of Company "E" and the Whiting brothers, Almon and Edmond, of Company "D," were among the sick who were sent under Captain James Brown to winter at Pueblo, Colorado. There were eighty soldiers in this group besides an unlisted number of women and children. They set out on October 18, 1846. About a month later fifty-five more men were sent to the same winter camp under Lieutenant W. W. Willis.

On the 24th of May 1847, all the survivors set out, presumably to California via Fort Laramie. While in that vicinity: "On the afternoon of the 11th of June, while on Pole Creek, . . . they were met by Elder Amasa Lyman, who was accompanied by Brothers Thomas Woolsey, Roswell Stevens, and John H. Tippetts, from Winter Quarters, bringing letters from the families and friends of the soldiers, as well as counsel from Brigham Young . . . ." Tyler, *History of the Mormon Battalion*, 198.

Most of the Battalion group followed west and arrived in the Valley of the Great Salt Lake a few days behind Brigham Young and the pioneer group, but these boys evidently returned to their families at Winter Quarters instead. Their names are not listed in any of the official records.

49. Stout's first wife, Surmantha Peck, had died in Lee County, Iowa; Louisa Taylor's first child was buried in Nauvoo. His loss on the journey included all three of Louisa's remaining children and Marinda Bennett and her baby. Since his family is now "only two," it would seem that Lucretia Fisher had left him. Her name does not appear in the record from the time they crossed the Mississippi River.

Br Stewart, all to pieces He ran through the lot and cried so loud that he excited the whole neighbourhood which caused much to be said for & against us a police. Henry was a young about grown & needed all he got for his imprudence for he was a rebllious person and had threatened us on former occasions if we did not do as he wanted. I reported the affair to Presidents Cutler & Harris who approved of it & thought it would do him good. I was around as usual and on guard till one o'clock at night.

Sunday Aug 8th 1847. Sent out 5 men on guard & staid in. Went to meeting and in the evening went to the Council. The subject of sheep Bulls and dogs running at large in Town & especially at night was taken up and arraingements made to have it stoped. reported the affair of Henry Phelps which was sanctioned

Monday Aug 9th 1847. Sent 4 men out on guard & staid in & was around town as usual.

Tuesday Augt 10th 1847. Hard to get a sufficient number for the guard today. Sent out Robt Campbell & John McRae. Still rain falling
I staid at home to trace up some complaints against Brs Blazzard & Cuthburt but it all amounted to nothing.

Wednesday Aug 11th 1847. Went out on guard with 4 men Had three & a half tons of hay brought to me today

Thursday Aug 12th 1847. Sent 4 men out on guard & I staid in. Meeks found 4 stray oxen today which had been lost by the company going West. *More hay come in today*

Friday Augt 13th 1847. Sent 4 men on guard and staid in. Lewis Dana came here today He says the Comanchees have attacted the United States trains on their way to Santa Fe.

Saturday Augt 14th 1847. Sent 4 men out on guard and staid in. William Meeks & Harvy Green had a suit today before Bishop Clark about their garden fence.

Sunday Aug 15th 1847. Sent out 5 men on guard & staid in. Went to Meeting at the stand. Preaching on different subject & the Sacrament.
Went to Council at 5 o'clock Stray pen cases discussed. Law against so much hay in town & committee to look after fires appointed &c. I was on guard till 12 o'clock at night.

Monday Aug 16th 1847. Staid in & sent out 5 men on guard. I was engaged all day in drying my hay which had got wet also in stacking it. Hard rain in the evening.

Tuesday Aug 17th 1847. Went out on guard. 5 men out I with 2 others went about 10 miles North today.

Wednesday Aug 18th 1847. Went out on guard with 6 men Came in at noon to stack hay & in the evening went out on guard on the bottom as the cattle were committing depredations on the corn there.

Thursday Aug 19th 1847. Went out on guard with 6 men I come in before night and felt some like having the ague.

Friday Aug 20th 1847. Went out on guard with 6 men and came in as yesterday.

Saturday Augt 21st 1847. Sent 7 men on guard and staid in Was very unwell. Very weak & nervous all day.

Sunday Aug 22nd 1847. Went on guard with six men. The brethren 2½ miles above town at Punckaw agreed to bear their proportion of picket guard tax to day as they were equally guarded by us as the people of Winter Quarters

Monday Aug 23rd 1847. Went on guard with 7 men. Came in at noon went to see President Harris about establishing a police at Brigham's Farm[50] as they had sent a petition to me to that effect   It was refered to the Council.

Tuesday Aug 24th 1847. Went out on guard today.   Put out 6 men in the after noon. Ripley Brought in several head of cattle from the bottom today.

Wednesday Aug 25th 1847. This morning I went to Brighams Farm to see about the policy of establishing a police at that place to guard them against the depredations of the Indians.   They had previously sent a petition to me to that effect.

I arrived at the Farm about noon.   It is in a low hemed in place and its looks is most desolate, sickly & gloomy   I found a majority of the place sick & in a most suffering condition.   Some whole families not able to help each other and worse than all they were quarreling and contending with each other in a most disgraceful manner

There had been some melons stolen just a day or two before I came & it was rumored by some that I had come to execute the law on those who were guilty which created an unusual excitement in the place but it was all kept from my knowledge untill the next morning.   It was a sad thing to see a camp of the Saints thus quarreling and trying to put each other down and more so when they were overwhelmed with sickness & death.

They all, when they learned my business, tryed to justify themselves to me and condemn their opponents, as though I was a judge, instead of an executor of the law.   I heard each one in their turn apart from the rest but did not give my opinion.

They had fine and extensive crops of corn beans cabbage melons &c and had they been at peace with each other, would have been in a fair way to do well. In the evening I had the people together and had the subject of the police before them   They unanimously desired me to establish it on the same plan, rules, and regulations as at winter quarters to be subject to me.   They also nominated those whom they wanted to act as police and for William Pace to be sergeant of the guard subject to my orders. This was done without any difficulty or feeling.

After the foregoing regulations were entered into the matter was then refered to the Council for their approval or disapproval before entering on the duties thereof   I staid there all night.   We had a rain in the night.

Thursday Aug 26th 1847. Came home today where I arrived at two o'clock P. M.

Today we heard that a party of the Souix were coming down against the Omahas & we prepared to guard against their depredations as it was expected that they would try to steal our horses if an opportunity occured.

Friday Aug 27th 1847. Sent 6 men out on guard and went and reported to President Morley, how things were at the Farm & how I had arrainged matters relative to the police

I also sent Earl and Glines up to the Farm to notify them of the approach of the souix. then went out on guard.   Had a dance till 10 at my house.

Saturday Aug 28th 1847. Went out on guard today with 8 men

Sunday Aug 29th 1847. Went out on guard with 6 men and I come in at three and went to the Council. The subject of the Police at Brigham's farm was dis-

---

50. Brother Brigham's Farm or Summer Quarters was situated about eighteen miles from Winter Quarters. Isaac Morley was assigned to oversee the place while John D. Lee was manager with a group of Brigham Young's other adopted sons to assist. (See footnote 35 in Volume I, Part 4.) Lee's diaries through the summer of 1847 and the spring of 1848 show the difficulties of this undertaking and also the amount of corn that was produced here. His estimate of 4,000 bushels would seem to be quite accurate.

The adopted sons of Heber C. Kimball operated another farm, also for the purpose of providing food for the mass migration. Complete records of the activities there have not yet been found.

cussed today and refered to President Morley & myself to act in the case as we deemed proper.

The subject of the Souix was had before the council also but nothing definite done.

A Steam Boat landed today. Hard rain in the evening.

Monday Aug 30th 1847. Sent 7 men out on guard & staid in to prepare to go to Brigham's Farm tomorrow.

Tuesday Augt 31st 1847. Sent 7 men on guard & I & William Meeks went to the Farm to set the police in order. Affairs were about as usual. We staid all night. I was very unwell to night.

Wednesday Sept 1st 1847. I was very sick this morning We started home about 11 o'clock I went in a one horse waggon & brought home a load of mellons & other garden sauce given us by the brethren there We arrived at home about 4 o'clock in the evening & found all well. I was around town some after I came home

Thursday Sep 2nd 1847. Sent 6 men out on guard This morning Councillor Phineas Eichards came to me & wanted an ox arrested belonging to Henry Boly for damages done by him in his garden & I sent Meeks & Gardner who took the ox but were followed by Boly & his son who attempted rescue the ox by violence, which caused quite an uproar in the Town. When they came in a violent menacing way, Gardner and Meeks drew a pistol and presented it to them and notified them to stand back and if anything was wrong to go to the Council.

The pistol stoped them & Young Boley swore he would shoot them for it.

The ox was brought to the stray pen & the report to me whereupon a charge was laid in against young Boly before Bishop Calkins for threatning to shoot & myself & Gardner & Meeks sent to arrest him. He had gone to the prairie for hay & we over took him about 4 miles below here. He uterly refused to come back till night at first but at last did come. & the trial was put off till 7 o'clock P. M. & he released till then by the Bishop & we prepared for trial in the mean time

At 7 o'clock we went to the trial and after a full investigation & a long and an interresting speach from the Bishop the charge was declared to be sustained & Boly fined five dollars. Boly manifested a very bad spirit after the trial. We had a hard rain during the trial which lasted till about Eleven o'clock.

Friday Sept 3rd 1847. Sent 6 men out on guard & I staid at home and issued an order on the police treasurey amounting to 93 dollars.

Today Hyrum Gates commenced a butchery on Main Street cloce to the stray pen.

Saturday Sep 4th 1847. Went out on guard to with 4 men. I & Groves rode all day in the forks of the Creek and came home by B. L. Clapps cornfield. We were hunting for indian sign.

Sunday Sept 5th 1847. This morning a calf belonging to Jesse McCauslin was in the stray pen & he refused to redeem it and abused the law and the police & so we killed it and divided out to the police and applied it on their wages. This was done to caution others from doing as he did which was not uncommon

At meeting today I was told B. L. Clapp one of the first Presidents of the Seventies on the stand spoke very preducidial of the police & guard and the killing of the calf and inflamed the minds of the disaffected to a high rate against us

President Joseph Young's also was by some construed in the same light.

Joseph Taylor my brother in law having returned from California came to see me. He came home with Genl Carney [Kearney] as one of his guards.[51] The Genl chose his guards all from among the Mormons as the most faithful

Went out on guard with 7 men   I & W. Meeks went south on the bottom and came home at 3 o'clock in the evening and attended the Council

Monday Sept 6th 1847. Sent out 7 men & I went in the forenoon to report to Prest Harris the killing of McCauslin's calf and gave my reasons for so doing. In the after noon I went out on guard.

To day 8 head of J. M. Flakes cattle were taken off the corn & 6 of A. J. Cox making a heavy bill of cost on them which they settled honorably   cox settled with Elias Gardner on a cash debt due tomorrow

I speak of it to the honor of those two men

Tuesday Sept 7th 1847. Dark rainy day & North wind   Went out on guard with 6 men and came in and staid in the after noon at home.

Wednesday Sept 8th 1847. Went out on guard with 4 men & I with W. Meeks went South and geathered a fine lot of good plumbs.   Had a hard rain at three previous to which we came home.

This evening I recieved a line from Brigham's Farm stating that the Indians had made a decent on that place and stolen all the horses and mules up there the night before whereupon I went to see President Morley on the subject who advised me to send two policemen up there to regulate the affairs which were in a deplorable situation.   I came home at 10 o'c.

Thursday Sept 9th 1847. This morning I sent Calkins and Cummings to the Farm to regulate them as mentioned yesterday.

Went on guard with 7 men   Went south as yester   with Meeks.   This evening Lee came here from the [farm] in gloomy feeling for the Loss of Horses

Friday Sept 10th 1847. Went out on guard with 5 men   I came home at one and was around town as usual.

Saturday Sept 11th 1847. Went out on guard with 4 men   I & Meeks went South about noon   Saw a smoke rise on the North whereupon we came home and found that the Indians were discovered and quite an excitement raised in the city about it.   Some Indians were reported to have been seen a mile or so up Mill Creek.   We raised a company of horse & foot and went in pursuit of them up Mill Creek & in passing through Benson's & Clapp's field in the West grove found the tracks of Indians but saw none   They made a decent on the Punckaw camp and took several of their horses; but they were soon retaken by the brethren one horse belonging to a Sister Garner whose husband was in the army was taken today. Her boy was herding with him some two miles N. W. beyond the prescribed limits and thus lost the horse

We had much difficulty in procuring horses after we reported the need of them immediately to pursue the Indians.   The brethren were not willing in many instances to let their horses go or to go themselves which subjected us to many inconveniences and greatly endangered the place

I confess that I was both mortified and chagrined at the penurious disposition of the people and after doubling the police guard for the night went to see

---

51. Another of General Stephen W. Kearney's guards was Nathaniel V. Jones. His diary gives details of the return trip: "May 10 [1847] . . . Today there was an order issued to have three men detailed from each company to go to the States as an escort for him. I was detailed as one of the number." He continues with an account of each day's travel, his descriptions of the deserted camps of the Donner party being most vivid. J. Cecil Alter, ed., "The Journal of Nathaniel V. Jones, with the Mormon Battalion," *Utah Historical Quarterly*, IV (January, 1931), 1-25.

President Harris on the subject after which with Elias Gardner we called in Pres Morley & Counr Cox to Harris' house and consulted on the subject and concluded to have a council at 8 o'clock in the morning on the subject after which I came home at 12 o'clock at night.

Sunday Sept 12th 1847. Council met this morning at 8 as before agreed upon and took up the subject of the police in general and the tardiness of the people to heed an alarm and many other inconveniences & finally agreed to have Counciller Cox preach on the subject at meeting which he did in an able manner and plainly showed the situation which we were placed in and the corruption and evil persons which we have to contend with also the dangers &c we run for the public good.

The Spirit rested down upon all and all the council & many others bore testimony to what he taught. It had a most salutary effect upon the whole congregation for after meeting every body seemed mild affable and well pleased and willing to do anything in their power for the police & guard. The good effects was plainly manifested for weeks afterwards; whereas, after the discourse of Prest Clapp last Sabbath which was construed to be against us and the administration of the law, the bad effects was felt all last week & a continual dissatisfaction was brooding through the town followed by quarrelling with the police & guard sometimes coming near to blows. How great a fire a little matter kindleth

If all the authorities and men of influence would only uphold the law & its officers as they at first agree to do there would not be half the trouble and perplexity there is with disaffected ones nor need for half as many guards & police and consequently only half the expense.

W. L. Cutler had a trial this morning before the Seventies for whipping a boy.

J. D. Lee came from Brigham's Farm says saw no indians there

Monday Sept 13th 1847. Bishop Whitney reported that his boys saw Indians South yesterday & I & Meeks went on the search of them today but no sign, false report. There was 8 men out on guard to day. We had a hard ride through the brush and over the ridges for nothing. A double guard still out at night yet. .

Tuesday Sept 14th 1847. Went out on guard with 5 men I with Gardner & Glines went West for several miles as the prairie was still on fire in that direction and in all probability the Souix were out there yet. The trail which they made when they attacted the punckaw camp was yet plain

This evening I heard that the Souix attacted the Otoes & Omahas while down this time & killed some 30 in all.

I still keep out a double guard of nights.

Wednesday Sept 15th 1847. Went out on guard today with 4 men & in company with E. Gardner and Earl went to Heber's farm. On our way there we met Calkins returning from Brigham's farm

Levi North was going up there and saw Calkins and supposed he was an Indian turned and ran back while Calkins taking him for one of the guard who was trying [to] play some prank on him put spurs in pursuit which frightened North almost out of his senses & on his retreat gave the alarm to some of Brighams boys who knew who it was We came up just in time to enjoy the scenery which created a good laugh at North's expense.

We went on to Hebers farm which is located in a deep hollow and is a narrow hemmed in place and in no way inviting to me

We found many sick and the place rather in a languishing condition but the crop looked well. Our arrival created an excitement here also for some who were on the bottom mowing saw us at a long distance supposed we were Indians and ran into camp "badly plagued"

We took dinner at Br Henry Herriman's and returned home at 4 o'clock just in time to save our selves from a hard rain which came suddenly up in fact rains would so suddenly come that we were often caught out and get wet.

Thursday Sep 16th 1847. Went out on guard with 4 men. Went on the Bottom South come in at noon and after dinner went out again

Friday Sep 17th 1847. Went out on guard with 5 men yesterday we found Counciller D. Russell's horse pastured in the head lands of the corn field which was not allowed as such privilege would lead to destroying the crops. We had before spoke to him about the practice and he promised to stop his boys from going there any more but it appeared that he did not so Elias Gardner by my order took the horse and brought him away with the intention of putting him in the stray pen as he had violated the law on that subject however he put him in his stable over night and early this morning while Gardner was gone from home Russells boy came and stole the horse and took him home and Gardner while on his way home was insulted by the boy and called a (damned) thief whereupon Gardner took after him and ran him into his father's house and there related what his boy had said which his boy acknowledged to be correct

Russell only told him that it was wrong but justified his boy in taking the horse and also threatned Gardner's life if he should attempt to take the horse when he was present. They had a few sharp words on the subject and parted.

Upon the affair being reported to me I reported it to Presidt Harris and afterwards to Prest Cutler as I thought it time to have an understanding on these subjects when the members of the council would threaten us while in the execution of their own laws and particular instructions as he had often done this sumer These Presidents manifested a proper Spirit as I thought on the subject and agreed to have an investigation before the council. unwell to day, feeble.

Saturday Sept 18th 1847. Went out on guard with 4 men and came in at noon sick and kept my bed all the after noon Was weak and feeble all night. I had to send for Glines and have him to post the guard to night as I could not be out

Sunday Sept 19th 1847. Still weak and feeble all day. Sent 2 men on guard.

Orson Hyde spork on the stand but I could not attend.

In the evening I attended the council. Daniel Russell was appointed take charge of the sheep.

Monday Sept. 20th 1847. Sent 5 men out on guard. I was week and feeble all day.

This evening at 4 o'clock the council met to here our report bout Dan Russell & other matter,

We first reported the affair of killing McCauslin's calf and then several other things which had taken place which had created more or less excitement. This was done in order for the council to hear both sides of the case.

We then commenced on Russell's case and he flatly denied the most essential points of the case and said that he could prove his assertions by his family & some others who were present.

The council was detained till near dark when Gardner, growing impatient as his contradicting him at last stated that he had lied and that this was not only the first nor the second but the third or the fourth lie that Russell had told and he could prove it, To which Russell only replied that what he said was pretty steep

President Harris then arose and said that one of their number had here been charged with lieing and he moved for an adjournment to morrow at 2 o'clock and then have Gardner prove his assertions or acquit Russell of any sencure which was agreed to.

Tuesday Sept 21 1847. Sent out 3 men on guard. I was still weak and feeble
We met the Council at 2 o'clock and proceeded to the case of Gardner and Russell which occupied all the after noon untill dark Russell brought forward some of his family as witnesses in his favor but they all proved what Gardner had said to be true even his son who took the horse was a good witness in Gardner's favor So he mantained his ascersions and the council decided accordingly after which he offered to prove him in another lie if called for
While in council 14 head of J. H. Blazards cattle were put in the stray pen and he gave an old cow to pay the bill the cow was valued to be worth only 5 dollars, and Allen Stout took her.

Wednesday Sept 22nd 1847. Sent 6 men out on guard and staid at home.
L. H. Calkins & his wife came here today on a visit & Father Burton came also drunk. He had lately lost his wife and it appeared that he was both drowning trouble and hunting another wife at any rate the women had a tedious day with him.
Today reports from Brigham's Farm says that Lee & Keneda [Charles Kennedy] had a fight about their stray pen opperations up there & Lee came off victorious for he badly worsted Keneda & did not get hurt himself.

Thursday 23rd 1847 Sept. Sent 4 men out on guard and staid in & went to see President Harris for council.

Friday Sep 24th 1847. Cold bousterous day in the fore part of the day. Sent out 6 men on guard & I staid in. Turned out fine day

Saturday Sep 25th 1847. Sent 6 men out on guard & I staid at home. At 2 o'clock The council met again on Daniel Russells case. It appeared that he had went to President Harris for council & he told him how to confess humbly and then with dray[w] from the council as the best means to save his credit which he agreed to do but today when he was called on to do it he partly confessed but did not say anything about withdrawing from the council and so President Harris manifested his dissatisfaction at what Russell had said and signafied that it was not in conformity to his previous council whereupon the council called upon him to declare to them what his council was which he did and an on being closely pressed he also declared him unqualified to sit in council as he had lost his privy members & was an eunech.
This threw a new shade on the case and the council hardly knew what to do. The cas was argued considerably on both sides but no decision given and so that matter rested for the present. But Russell said not one word on that subject and afterwards we went on with our reports on his case untill time to adjourn

Sunday Sept 26th 1847. Sent 5 men on guard but I was weak and feeble yet and could only be out a little.
To day 8 dragoons came into town with Rufus Pack as they stated to get a stolen horse that his brother John Pack had stolen and they were going to make him accountable for his brothers deeds who was now with the pioneers. We doubted their errand and also Rufus Pack integrity but have not learned any thing to the contrary as yet.

Monday Sept 27th 1847. Went out on guard today with 4 men and at 2 o'clock I came home and Allen went out in my place. To night Bishop Joseph Knights had a Ball for the the benefit of the poor

Tuesday Sept 28th 1847. Sent 9 men out on guard and I staid in. At two o'clock the Council and police met again to prosecute the investigation of D. Russells case. He had and yed does deny every assertion which we make and puts us to the proof of it which we have done to the perfect satisfaction of all present

To day matters assumed quite a different attitude and he again put us to prove some unbecoming things between him and a Sister Hart which we proved by her & his own wife & family which greatly served to render both him & her perfectly rediculous in the opinion of all present.

The subject of making some kind of a draw on the brethren residing on the East side of the river to assist the people here to pay the debt due the police was introduced to day in the Council by myself which was favorably recieved and laid over for further investigation after which the council adjourned to meet again on Russells case as we were not yet done with him.

Wednesday Sept 29th 1847. Went out on guard today with 7 men I went south in company with Meeks & Calkins. While down some ten miles towards Belvue we discovered a smoke rise to the North and judging it to be Indians we hurried home and there learned that they had made their appearance in that quarter and also had made their appearance to the West and one in the South field & he stole Lorenzo Johnsons horse and ran him some five miles and Johnson after him who met the horse returning badly frightened with a buffalo robe tied on him with a lasso & a pair of moccasins and I believe a pair of leggins. How the horse got away from the indian is not known.

Some others made an attact near the old camp ground at Cutlers Park on some small boys there & stole 2 horses one belonging to Bro T Burdic and the other to Br Blodget a young man. They were discovered by the brethren who were mowing in all directions, near about the same time which created an unusual excitement and the news soon reached town that some two or three herds were wholy taken & several horses

Col Scott came in from the N.W. stating that they in large numbers had attacted their herds & also burnt his hay and with it one waggon and all his camping & cooking utensils & bedding, a 15 shooting rifle and several other articles

His report created still a greater excitement. W. L. Cutler had already gone in pursuit with several men on horseback and many on foot had gone when I came in. So upon Scotts report we raised another company of horse and pursued also.

Scott stated that he saw two companies of Indians close in on & surround Glines & Ripley of the guard while they were trying to rescue some cattle and no doubt but they were gone He reported some alarming stories

We of course pushed on and soon met glines & Ripley and they declared that they saw no two companies & also some others who were along differed widely from Scott about the whole matter

We however pursued and went near to where his hay was burnt and as far as he thought necessary and could see no hear any thing so we fired off some of our pistols which gave us no information as to their whereabouts and came home about 9 o'clock Scott hay was what made the smoke we saw in the first place About ten o'clock Cutler also returned who saw nor heard anything

Thursday Sept 30th 1847. Went out on guard with 7 men I went North west with 3 or 4 of the guard. While out on the prairie some four or five miles I discovered a smoke to the South towards Belvue whereupon we directed our course in that way for about 4 miles when the guard in that direction gave us the alarm of indians

We also saw some one whom we supposed to be an indian and as before agreed with prest Cutler in such cases sent in L. H. Calkins to give him notice of what we saw and we proceeded still South for 4 or 5 miles further and waited untill Cutler came with a company of ten or twelve men so we joined them and proceeded towards Belvue several miles & found that the smoke was still a long ways off perhaps near the otto village at the mouth of the platte.

The company went home & I went West among the hills with 2 of the guard in search of indian sign but found none so we came home very late in the evening. It was a very hot day and we had altogether the hardest days ride to day that we had this summer I believe

The excitement was great in town to day and in fact the appearance was that the indians were in the immediate neighbourhood.

Friday October 1st 1847. Went out on guard with 3 men I & Meeks went to the North It was an unusual hot day We saw sign of Indians. We came in earley Had a guard meeting at my House to settle a question between Gardner & Calkins but did not come to a trial.

Saturday October 2nd 1847. Sent 5 men out on guard and staid in Saw President about Col Scotts report about seeing so many Indians last Wednesday. He did not believe that he saw any and in fact it was reported by all the guard that those whom he saw were the guard & his hay was set on fire by his own fire. It was the prevailing opinion that he was unusually excited and reported accordingly.

At 2 o'clock P. M. the High Council met again for the fifth time to act upon the case of D. Russell & the police.

This tedious investigation was brought to a close to day the police sustained every charge alleged to him which he also acknowledged before the trial was over. He manifested a stubborn willfull Spirit throughout the whole trial and denied every charge untill it was proven & then admitted it.

The Council decided that he should confess to the police and make them ample satisfaction for all he had done.

His confession consisted simply in saying that he was a young member in the church & did not wish to do any wrong &c. & justifying himself for all he had done.

Whereupon Councillor Harris asked leave to confess for him which was granted and also sanctioned by Russell.

Father Harris then arose and in a most humble and feeling manner confessed that he had wilfully lied to injure the police & had lied to hide it in the trial & also that all that had been alleged against him was true and that he had been willfull during the whole trial &c He made quite a long confession all very humble & asked the police to forgive him.

The police accepted the confession of Father Harris after it was sanctioned by Russell who agreed that it was true & such as he wished to make. It was decidedly the best confession I ever heard considering the practice of the confessor

After the case was settled between Russell & the police the council took up the matter as pertained to his being a Councillor. They considered that he was unworthy longer to have a place among them & accordingly droped him from the council. The council then adjourned.

Sunday Oct. 3rd 1847. Sent 6 men out on guard and staid in and went to meeting P. H. Young & some 3 more men returned home from the West & stated to the meeting that the pioneers had found a location in the Valey and laid out a city & had built about 40 rods of "adobie" wall around it and every thing was doing well there. J. D. Lee & others had a trial today before the Council

Monday Octr 4th 1847. Lees trial continued today[52] Sent 5 men out on guard. At nine o'clock some of the guard & also several men heard what they supposed to

52. John D. Lee's trial grew out of the fight with Charles Kennedy which Stout reported on September 22. This was the culmination of months of friction — differences as to the division of the farm land, trouble over stray-pen operations, perhaps even competition for the affections of Lee's youngest wife, Emoline Woolsey, who, against her husband's counsel, had gone to Winter Quarters with Kennedy. The court was called to settle the problems of the fight but listened also to the complaints of others of the Summer Quarters settlement. The decision

be the sound of artillery out in the direction of the Elk Horn and the majority of the people thinking that perhaps it might be the 12 and pioneers returning & gave that as a signal of their approach to us, sent me out there with a company of men on horse back to see about it   We arived there about 10 o'clock at night but found nothing

Tuesday Oct 5th 1847. The Horn is about 9 rods wide and can be forded in many places but it is too deep at the crossing   It is a good & comfortable place to encamp with plenty of timber & convenient to water stock.   The stream is not miry in many places.   We started home earley & went on to the Bluffs and there took a good view of the Horn & platte bottoms or plains all then in full bloom which lay before us in a beautifull leavel as far as we could see with good spy glasses It was altogether the best and most splendid view I ever had of a praire country.

This wide & boundless plain as it apeared lay beneath us decorated with flowers of every color and semed as the garden of nature & is a perfect contrast to the whole tract of land from there to Winter Quarters which lies like the rolling waves of a troubled ocean while the streams will always bog animals when they get into them which is but seldom that they can so deep & inaccessable are their waters to approach.

We now started for home where we arrived at 1 o'clock P. M.

I attended the council & Had the subject up for procuring means for the police from the brethren on the other side of the river.   This matter had been before Br Hyde & he approved of it.

Wednesday Oct 6th 1847. Sent 3 men out on guard & A. Ripley to Belvue to ascertain what was going on there as we had some reason to suppose that something was going on not altogether right.

In the evening when he came home he reported that there were troop marched from Fort Kearney to Grand Island and we were not certain as to their intentions towards us so the council thought best to send me with a company of men to meet the pioneers and put them on their guard and also assist them in case they need us.

Accordingly I went to preparing & Langley was sent over the river with an order from Bp Whitney for as many horses as were needed for that purpose Thus passed today.

Thursday Oct. 7th 1847. Was engaged all day in prepareing to start.   Langley returned with only 2 horses.   There was one or two councils on the subject   the unanimous feeling of them all was for me to go in all speed

I put the affair of the guard into Allen Stouts hand during my absence. He now confined with a hard attact of the chill fever.

Friday Oct. 8th 1847. Today about ten o'clock we all started on our journey West. The company consisted of sixteen men 12 horsemen & 2 waggons with 2 men to each waggon.

The following are the names of of the company with numbers of rounds of shot each one had in case we were attacted

---

was that Lee was wrong and that he should confess and apologize to Kennedy and to the group in general. They also decreed that any of his wives or adopted sons who cared to leave him would be free to do so. Lee made a token confession but later had a rehearing before Brigham Young.

1	Hosea Stout	21		9	W. Martindale	1
2	G. D. Grant	11		10	W. Huntington[53]	8
3	G. G. Potter	1			L. H. Calkins	9
4	G. W. Langley	3		12	J. W. Cummings	15
5	W. Kimball	21			S. S. Thornton	1
6	Jacob Frazier	1		14	L. Nickerson[54]	6
7	W. J. Earl	6		15	J. H. Glines	1
8	W. Meeks	3		16	C. Whiting	3

which made one hundred & Eleven rounds which would enabled us to make a good defence if occasion had required.

We arrived at the Horn at dark or a little after and encamped near the ferry in the timber

We kept up a vigalant guard all the way on this journey   all things went off well to night.

Saturday Oct. 9th 1847. All was well this morning.

Sent 3 men up the Horn to look for a ford as we understood that there was one some where up there   They returned in about and hour & reported that we could ford the river so we all started at 9 o'clock & found a beautiful patch of plumbs just at the ford where we all refreshed ourselves with what we wanted & left Bushels yet on the trees.

We crossed without any difficulty only the water came into the waggon beds a little.   After crossing we had to cut a road through thick willows and other bushes about a quarter of a mile which we did with axes knives & swords in a short time & was on the move in one hour from the time we left our place of encampment.

We traveled on a level bottom for 12 miles and encamped on the Platte at the Liberty pole which stood on a high mound on the Banks of the Platte.

The Bed of the Platte is as large as the Bed of the Missouri & was at this time almost dry at the place we came to it.   The current ran on the other side of an island & to us it presented but a large plain of white sand. The water of the platte is of a white milky coulor and is very pleasant to drink   It is seldom more than 2 or 3 feet deep The current often changes.

The Bed of the river is but a Bed of quick sand in which animals easily Bog and drown especially if they stand long in it in which case they settle down and are fast in the sand

We now had the best of weather being warm and dry

53. William D. Huntington was a member of a well-known family in Mormon history, the third of five sons. His two sisters, Zina and Prescinda, were both sealed to Joseph Smith and later became wives of Brigham Young and Heber C. Kimball, respectively.

Born February 28, 1818, in Watertown, New York, Huntington joined the church along with his parents and the older members of the family in 1835. At Kirtland they lost all their wealth when the bank failed, so they came in poverty to Far West and after a year moved on to Nauvoo.

At Nauvoo, Huntington was a member of the Nauvoo band and of the select group who appeared on special occasions. He left Nauvoo with the first group in 1846 but did not get to Utah until 1849. At this time he had a wife but no children. They settled in Springville, Utah, where William Huntington was active in dramatics and music. In 1853 he was called to the Elk Mountain Mission near the present city of Moab, Utah, where for a time he lived at peace with the Indians and raised successful crops. Huntington Ward in Emery County was named for him.

54. Levi Stillman Nickerson was born April 2, 1814, in Pennsylvania and baptized in June of 1833 by Amasa Lyman. In Kirtland he was a member of the School of the Prophets; in the spring of 1834 he joined the group called Zion's Camp in their trek to Missouri.

Nickerson was active in the Missouri troubles and remained in Nauvoo until the evacuation, participating in the final battle. He came to Utah in 1850. He died in 1852 while en route to England, whence he had been called on a mission, leaving a family of six children.

Sunday Oct. 10th 1847. Beautiful fine cool morn but smoky. Started at seven o'clock & traveled 13¼ miles up the river & nooned where the road joins the river & went on in an hour twelve miles and encamped on Shell Creek a beautiful swift stream 12 feet wide & three deep We saw one or two wolves to day for the first time on this journey. The day was cool and windy but ceased to blow towards night To night we commenced to attend our prayers night & morning which we strictly attended to the rest of our journey West.

Monday Oct. 11th 1847. Fine clear morning. all well We started at half past eight & traveled twelve miles and nooned where the road joins the river & over the same level sand prairie

This after noon was not so pleasant for it commenced to rain smartley while we were here although we went on our road was over sandy ridges for some five miles when we turned off to the river and put up for the night which was most disagreeablely cold and rainy. We now found we had not prepared ourselves with Bedding enough. We were all wet and cold all night but by keeping a good fire we did not suffer extreemly.

Tuesday Oct 12th 1847. We were all most uncomfortably situated this morning. Wet cold & hungry High wind & cold weather

We started at 9 o'clock & went to the Looking Glass about 15 miles at noon & then proceeded to the Beaver river about 9 miles further over similar roads. The road all along the Platte is near the same being level with now & then low sandy ridges to cross which is heavy on teams

Beaver river is 25 feet wide & two deep steep banks & not miry a most beautiful stream & a good place for large camps.

At dark the wind ceased & we had pleasant weather again.

Wednesday Oct 13th 1847. High wind rose in the night but pleasant at sun rise. Started at 9 and traveled 6 miles to the old Pawnee Station on Plumb Creek which is now in ruins except 2 or three houses There is some cornfields here about one mile further is the new Station — Several Houses & a fort partly finished Here was a large quantity of goverment property But all was in ruins by the hands of the Souix who had latly destroyed everything which was of much value. Not far from here towards the river is the ruins of an old village which was destroyed by the Souix on the same day that Joseph & Hyrum Smith were slain

The Souix ordered the Missionaries away this summer & have forbid the whites raising any more corn North of the Platte for the Pawnees one mile further we crossed Ash Creek and one & half miles further we came to the Loup Fork which is in all respects similar to the Main Platte. This is at another old Pawnee village. There is several of their Houses & some fences yet standing The land here is very rich.

One & a half miles further we came to Cedar Creek 8 rods wide and 2 feet deep a very pretty & sandy Bedded stream.

The land here is changeable. Now we travelled on level prairie and green grass then turn short to the Platte & over deep ravines & High level lands. untill we came to another old Pawnee village which was now entirely destroyed when we decended down a steep hill and crossed another stream & there encamped. We traveled today about 24 miles. We saw the first Deer & Atelope to day

On this Bottom is the remains of old corn fields & dirt fences & is I suppose an old Missionary station. We killed some geese & chickens today. Cold windy & disagreeable today. Very cold night & a hard white frost

Thursday Oct 14th 1847. Clear fine morning but cold & frosty. We started at 9 o'clock & only went about one mile when W. Meeks & L. Nickerson each killed a fine deer which detained us about one hour in dressing them. They came very seasonable for we needed them

We then traveled on six miles to the Upper Ford of the Loup Fork. Just before we came to the Ford we saw a red flag waving a little above ground and not knowing what it ment we proceeded cautiously up to it & found a late indian encampment and why they left the flag I never learned

While drawing near the ford we discovered a white man on the other side of the river which was soon followed by a long train of waggons which we soon knew to be   brethren   so we drew up in order & fired a Salute to them which gave them to know who we were   We then went on & met in the platte. Our meeting of course was joyful for we now got to hear from the Valley.[55]

This was but a portion of the pioneers who had been sent ahead with the ox teams to lay up Buffalo meat for the company who were to follow in a short time.

But insted of doing so they proceeded on & were now out of the Buffalo county leaving those who were to follow to shift for themselves. They informed us that the President and in fact all those who were behind were attacted by the Souix & robbed of some Eighty horses.

They sent on for this company to stop but they did not

They also said that we would meet them in 40 miles unless they had gone back to the Valley after loosing their animals. Thus deserting them all in this time of trouble. Those who bore the rule in this contemptable act of leaving the the Twelve & so many of our Bretheren robbed of their Horses in the Black Hills were John Pack & William Clayton[56] with some more to back them up. The main body of this camp were true and faithful Saints and viewed this treacherous act in its true light.

This is their own story and you may immagine our feeling of joy, anger & supprise on meeting them and recieving this intelligence. We all came back & encamped togeather to night. & I sent back to President Cutler a report verbal by Pack who promised to deliver it but did not.

We borrowed several buffalo robes of the Pioneers which added to what we had made us comfortable of nights

They said the United States troops were about Grand island which caused our suspicions increase that some trickery was afoot & we sent back word accordingly

This company of the pioneers were all in good health & spirits

Friday Oct 15th 1847. Fine clear morning. We all rested well after our addition to our bedding

We started earley and crossed the river which was quite miry in the quick sand our waggon horses bogged and some had to go into the watter to get them out

---

55. This could have been the group who had come on ahead, of whom William Clayton wrote on September 17: "This morning Thomas Brown, Ezra Beckstead, Matthew Welch, Benjamin Roberts, David Perkins and William Bird started . . . in consequence of having no bread." Clayton, *Journal*, 363.

Clayton gives the names of the company which returned to Winter Quarters to spend the winter 1847-48. While these men all left at about the same time, they arrived in small groups, some several days behind the leaders, others two or three weeks. *Ibid.*, 348-49.

56. William Clayton in his journal defended his action in coming on ahead of the church authorities. They had left the Valley of the Great Salt Lake on August 17, seven groups of ten men each, some of them returning members of the Mormon Battalion. Clayton traveled under John Pack with Return Jackson Redden as captain. There was trouble and contention in the group and a short supply of food. On Tuesday, September 14, 1847, Clayton wrote: "In consequence of some things which have passed and some which at present exist, I have concluded to go on as fast as circumstances will permit to Winter Quarters and I intend to start tomorrow. Some have opposed it, but not with good grace. However, I have no fears that the council will censure me when they know the cause. If they do, I will bear the censure in preference to what I now bear."

He later wrote with great bitterness of the actions of some of the group. *Ibid.*, 362.

We were all over safe at 9 o'clock   Jack Redding who was with the pioneers turned back with us as a pilot   We now traveled on over a leve[l] Bottom for five miles when we came to the Blufs through which we passed for thirteen miles.

It is a barren country of sand hills or a continual succession of Mounds through which we had to pass.   The day was very warm & still together with the heat of the sand, made it very unpleasant traveling to prairie Creek.   12 feet wide & 1½ feet deep   Low Banks and some miry where we arrived at three o clock and encamped Here was plenty of grass but no wood.

To night was the most sad and gloomy time which we had.   Not knowing where the Twelve and those with them were or what had become of them. Perhap they were broke down, & robbed of all their animals and now near Larimie coming slow afoot.   Distressed & nearly exhausted. We sat pondering over these things Some of our own company were sick. While in this melencholy mood Bishop Calkins took me out aside and said that he felt like he wanted to speak in toungs which he said was an uncommon thing for him   and if it was right & any one here who could interpret he would be glad to speak.

I spoke to the company about who all were anxious to hear him.   Saying if there was any intelligence for us in toungs there would be an interpretation also.

He spoke some time vehemently.   Levi Nickerson only understood enough to know that it was relative to our situation and those we were in pursuit of & that all was well.

Bishop Calkins then gave us the interpretation which in substance was that our mission was of God, whose eyes & the eyes of angels were over us for our good.

That the Lord had turned away our enemies from us & we had not been seen

For us to press on & be faithfull and our eyes should see those who we sought and we all should return to our homes in peace.

We all felt the force of what was said & agreed to try and do better if we could & press on untill we met them if we had to go to the valley.

This was a very singular circumstance for there was not one of us who was given to enthusiastic notions of this sort which is so common with some brethren But now we all felt an assureance that we would realize what had been spoken.

Saturday Oct. 16th 1847. Cold North wind. All well.   Started at 8 o'clock and went to Wood River 12 miles 12 feet wide and one deep. A most beautiful stream. Here we met S. H. Goddard & Kellogg who had come on in advance of the company trying to take over the ox teams.   Goddard was lying by the road side fast asleep & was waked by my hollowing to the company to Halt, badly frightened supposing it was Pawnees.   Kellogg was on Grand island hunting and saw us coming.   They starving almost   We turned out our horses & took dinner. They said we would meet some more today   But the main company was perhaps several days behind yet.   We felt well satisfied now for we learned that they were on the move but slowly & that they had recovered most of their horses from the souix.   We only staid here about an hour and then pushed on to meet A. Lyman & some more who Goddard said was hard by.   They turning back with us.   Our company now amounted to nineteen.

We traveled 14 miles and stopped on the main Platte and baited our horses on a good bed of rushes in the thick timber and got our suppers, and not thinking it a safe place to guard ourselves against the Indians we went about one mile out in the prairie where we staid all night.

Sunday Oct 17th 1847. All was well this morning. Cold south wind. Went back to the Platte to get our breakfasts & bait our horses on the rushes

Started at 9 o'clock and traveled a few miles & discovered a buffalo on the level plain.   Four of us pursuid him   Had a fine race.   None of us knew anything the quaities of one & supposing it to be very fat we fired on him & killed him but when Br Potter & Glines came up they told us he was too poor to be eat which we did not believe untill we opened him. After satisfying our courosity with him we went on a few miles further & saw another. This we soon found to be worse than the other so we satisfied our curiosity by running him and seeing his manouvers which was very interesting to us & then we let him go & we pushed on our journey, & came to a dog village a thing so much said & wrote about. As I had heard we found them on their posts looking for whatever might come to injure them & giving notice to the rest by a sharp bark & running from borough to borough in a few moments the entire village was apprized of our approach

The village was miles in extent and consists of thousands of these little republicans. Here we found the owl & rattle snake boroughed with them These villages is very common after this.

We saw drove of antelope today. We traveled on till 2 o'clock P. M. and turned to the river to bait & refresh staid one hour & went on untill sundown and encamped at the mouth of a large ravine on the river our animals was very tired tonight having traveled 25 miles today. Cold North wind all night. slept in the high grass in the ravine to shield them from the wind.

Monday Oct 18th 1847. All was well only we were all very cold and disagreeable. We started about ten o'clock & very soon come in contact with another Buffalo which we pursued & had a long race through a Dog village which is very dangerous to horses on account of the numerous holes in the ground This village is 5 or 6 miles long & very wide

Very soon after we left our buffalo chace and returned to the road we discovered some body on ahead which soon proved to be the pioneers who were strung along the road some on foot & some a Horse back for three or four miles

We formed in line at open distance with our two waggons in the centre and met them making a formadable appearance at a distance. We marched fast passing many who did not know us untill we met the Twelve when we halted & every man ran to greet his friends.

It is useless for me to attempt to describe this meeting. The whole of us was in a perfect extacy of joy & gladness. They were worn down with fatigue and hunger with many an anxious thought on home and the welfare of their families & the church. Many of their animals had to be lifted up every time they laid down.

As for us we had only one feeling now. All our anxiety & care was gone. In the midst of our brethren all our care and responsibility was gone we gave ourselves up to the enjoyment of meeting & being with them. All was well & we had only to tell them that we was ready to assist them to any thing we had.

The President said it was more joy more satisfaction to meet us than a company of angels for they heard from their families & we from the valley.

After our meeting was over we all went on with them & encamped within one mile of the place we staid last night.

About dark Thos Woolsey came in from those who were on a buffalo hunt & reported that he saw 500 Pawnee Lodges erected on Grand island and that he thought the hunters were in great danger from them. Whereupon President Young sent me with five other men to give them notice & tell them to hasten to the Company. Accordingly we set out about dark & went to Buffalo Creek & put up for the night It was now 11 o'clock. Here we staid without much grass for our horses and no water untill morning. We traveled about fifteen miles tonight.

Tuesday Oct 19th 1847. Fine pleasant morning but cold. Baited our horses till seven and went on in pursuit of the hunters whom we found after travelling some twelve miles, about ten o'clock near the Bluffs.

They had already killed all the Buffalos they wanted or at least as many as they could draw home and was now on their way to camp having gone about half a mile when they discovered us afar off. We saw them at about the same time & made towards them full speed. They not knowing what to think of us, not expecting to meet us, they naturally supposed us to be indians and prepared for battle which we saw and thereby knew them to be whites for went through the evolations of the whites and not indians.

We took this advantage of them and charged on them who kept in excellent order for an onset. But as we drew near they recognized us to be whites which still was the more strange to them. They kept good order untill we got within a few rods of them when Amasa Lyman recognising me broke ranks & ran to me calling me by name which broke the charm all now knew me & several of the rest.

Insted of a battle we had another meeting such as we had yesterday and such as is not to be realized only by friends under the same circumstances. several of the brethren went back with us to the place which they camped last night, while the rest went on with the waggon to the main camp.

We there took breakfast, which was served by Elder Wilford Woodruff in pure Mountaineer style, consisting of roasted buffalo ribs.

This I believe was the first pure hunters meal I ever eat. It is supprising how much we could eat at one single meal. Whilest we were very hungry we would eat the meat almost raw which had a good relish.

After breakfast was over we travelled being now about 20 miles from the main camp. We walked & rode alternately with those who had no horses. We travelled hard all day stopping a short time to dine. and arrived in camp about an hour after dark and found all well.

Several had went over the river today to kill some buffalo which were in sight & some of my company killed a fat cow which bountifully supplied us home.

We were about all over done when we arrived in camp & I was very sick with the head ache

The whiskey which we had brought along as well as everything else was given over to the order of the President, who treated us when we came in It came welcome to the pioneers.

Wednesday Oct 20th 1847. Cloudy cold disagreeable morning. I felt well. Travelled. Had orders to search a waggon this morning which had stolen money about it.

Four men travelled with this waggon. The money stolen belonged to Br Kelogg whom we met on Wood river. When he came back with us, he found his box opened and ten dollars in gold had been taken. He reported the same to the president who immediately gave me the orders to search them who belonged to the waggon & make dilligent search & find the money if I had to tear all their clothes to strings & tear up & destroy all they had & burn their good waggon & and harness to ashes & sift the ashes but what I found it & if I had to go to that extreemity let the man's bones who did the deed bleach on the prairie & for me to wait till the camp started and stop the waggons and make the search after the rest of the company had gone on. Accordingly I laid it before the company all who were ready to assist me

The camp started & Bishop Calkins ordered the waggon out of the line and halted them when we all came up formed a circle around them and I in a very few words informed them the object of the search telling them at the same time what the consequences were in cas we had to search to extremity.

They all protested their innocence declaring they were ready to be searched

I put them all under guard forbidding them to handle anything about their persons least it might be sliped away. several proceeded on to over haul the goods &c in the waggon but without any kind of a prospect of finding it

It Being very cold I set another set to search their persons but before the first man was searched G. D. Grant in looking over William Buckhannan's knapsack found the two pieces in one of his pantaloons pock[et] while he was looking on & not two minutes before said a man must be a damned fool to suppose he would put money in there.

Seeing the money was found he said that it was his own & forbid us taking it, Grant gave it to me however & I kept it of course the search now stoped & we began to pack up in a hurry for we were all very cold & the camp was now a long way ahead.

Just as we were through we saw Prest Richards & Benson coming back to us. I met them & reported the state of affairs who said that they had been sent back by Prest Young to tell us not to burn up anything in case we did not find the money but to come on & not detain the camp & we could look to it hereafter. I gave the money to Richards & told him to give it to the President.

We now all being ready to start formed a circle again and took a good pull at a large canteen of whiskey Buckhannan impudently wishing us success in the discharge of our duty as he drank

We all now hastened on This day terminated in a wet disagreeable day

We traveled about 25 miles and camped on the platte in the rushes where we supped on the night of the 16th inst. We arrived here at ten at night all very tired.

Thursday Oct 21st 1847. Let out our horses to the rushes very earley. They were very hungry, having been closely carralled all night. G. W. Langley & W. J. Earl were both very sick & had been for several days also were some more of my company but all else was well

We travelled today to the mouth of Wood river and camped in a dry branch of the platte to shield us from the wind which was very cold and disagreable travelling today

Friday Oct 22nd 1847. Clear & cold Hard frost and freeze. Started at 9 and went to prairie creek at 2 o'clock and stoped for the night.

Saturday Oct 23rd 1847. We were up at 4 o'clock The aurora shone most magnificiently this morning.

We started at sunrise & to the upper ford of the Loup and attempted to cross but the wind being very high caused the quick sand to be more loose, we bogged our animals and abandoned the idea and camped on the banks.

Sunday Oct 24th 1847. The wind was still very high. We attempted again to cross but bogged as on yesterday. backed out and went about a mile down the river and stoped for the night again. Cold Cloudy windy day.

Monday Oct 25th 1847. Handsome snow this morning Still cloudy but turned warm as the sun rose.

Several went out in the river in search I among the rest where we waded for a long time and finally located a crossing at the old ford and proceeded on our journey & stopped at the upper Old Pawnee village where we staid all night. To night the President sent Amasa Lyman & 6 men on to Winter Quarters to give notice of our coming.

Tuesday Oct 26th 1847. Started earley. Cold & cloudy I & W. Meeks rode on ahead today to look for some corn or any other vegitables which we might glean on the missionary farms. Several bushels were geathered. We staid at the old station all night

Wednesday Oct. 27th 1847. Went on. Crossed Beaver river at half past Eleven & the Looking Glass at half past one and encamped just above Sarpy's old trading house This is near the mouth of the Loup Fork.

Thursday Oct 28th 1847. Fine morning. South wind. Went to Shell Creek & staid all night. Here we found the Company with the ox teams had burnt the prairie and almost entirely destroyed our feed.

Friday Oct 29th 1847. Started at daylight and went two miles and turned out our horse in cottonwood timber where there was good feed and then travelled on to the liberty pole where all came before dark. We found rushes on a small island in the river Have 3 days South wind.

Saturday Oct. 30th 1847. Clear & warm — wind still South Went to the Horne & crossed at the Ford and went to the old road put up in the timber. Here we were met by Cutler Whitney & some 14 teams a large company of brethren who brought several loads of corn provisions groceries victuals cooked Whiskey & in short all that we needed. A very large supply was sent to my company by my wife & some others sufficient I suppose to do us two weeks.

We had a most joyful meeting and a very happy time Many of the pioneers had subsisted on buffalo meat entirely for months and when this supply came they hardly knew when to quit eating. It was a perfect feast & I enjoyed myself uncommonly well & we wer up till late.

Sunday Oct 31st 1847. North wind & cold day. All felt uncommonly well and joyful. We started at 9 o'clock and drove very hard untill we arrived at mill creek two miles above Winter Quarters stoping a short time at the papea. The company was strung along for miles according to the speed of their teams or the anxiety of their drivers

We were however formed at mill creek and waited untill all came up, when we were formally dismissed by the President with the blessings of God. He said that our coming enabled them to come home at least five days sooner. I went from there home and found all well

Monday Nov 1st 1847. I was engaged all day today in arrainging and distributing the articles of the company which were left in the two waggons at my house.

Tuesday & Wednesday Nov 2 & 3 1847. At and around home repairing & seting lots &c in order

Thursday Nov. 4th 1847. Went with my wife to see her mother on Little Pigeon Creek some 8 miles East. all was well there

Friday Nov 5th 1847. Swaped yoke of oxen here for a fine young horse & come home. cold rainy night.

Sat Nov. 6th 1847. Cold rainy windy day. at home most all day.

In driving some cattle to the stray pen we were opposed by C. Patten & others the result was quite a knock down.

Sunday Nov 7th 1847. Cold day. At home mostly. Went to council in the evening Charles W. Patten had prefered a charge against myself and Allen J. Stout for the yesterdays affair just as if he had been assailed by us when at the same time he had made an attack on Allen to rescue some cattle from him which he was driving to the stray pen The trial was however laid over for the present.

The subject of the pay for the police was had up and move made by some of the police to have a new Collector which caused the subject to be agitated with considerable spirit as some of the Council were very sanguine in favor of Eldrege and the police as sanguine against him. The subject was then laid over till tomorrow evening

Monday Nov 8th 1847. Snowy morning. Went around town considerable. The Omahas passed through today going North Wm Kimball recovered a horse from them which they had stolen.

The council met at H. S. Eldrege's to act on the case of a collector again but the police still objecting to Horace, there was nothing done except to adjourn till to morrow at 8 A. M. While at council I recieved orders from the Council of the Twelve to drive out & keep out all the indians which were all the time infesting this place & I being busy at this time sent L. H. Calkins to execute the same.

The Omahas as they passed through here would linger around town begging & stealing all they could get They were very troublesome

Tuesday Nov 9th 1847. Went to the Council at ten. Elias Gardner was appointed Collector & Assessor pro tem for the police with orders to proceed forth to assess and Collect another tax. Council then adjourned one hour and met accordingly when general matters were taken up and discussed at large.

The subject of Hydes policy the past season then the subject of vacating Winter Quarters & settling the East side of the river &c discussed & finally agreed to as the Government was unwilling for us to remain here any longer.

Wed. Nov. 10th 1847. Went to another Council at the Council House. Had up a variety of subjects That of vacating this place was had again & agreed to again. The President spoke at length on the subjects of the Merchants stating over the many articles we would need. The merchants Mudge & Woolley were present & agreed to supply us with all we needed

Adjourne an hour and met accordingly.

A report was heard from the Oneida Indians who were very friendly to us and desired us to furnish them with all their machanicks Farmers School teachers missionaries &c as they had the right to choose all whom the Goverment employed for them & we were their choice &c Much was said on the subject & Prest A. Cutler[57] who was well acquainted with them was appointed to take charge of the whole affair.

Thursd Nov 11th 1847. At and around home & around the City. In the evening had a police meeting at the Council House to decide who should have a cow that was in the possession of the police. It fell by lot to E. H. Groves. Also to decide how to dispose of taxes on the stores It was decided to divide it amongst us by percent on our dues. The collecor had now got his business in a forward state. The stores were all willing to pay their taxes honorably.

Friday Nov 12th 1847. Dark Cloudy damp Day. At home mostly settling up the police & picket guard accounts. Issued an order on our dues to Nov 1st amounting to 122 dollars & one on stores 15.75. This was on Smith & Donald Store.

Sat. Nov 13th 1847. Took up our store orders today

---

57. Alpheus Cutler, by this time called "Father Cutler," had been prominent in the Mormon Church since 1838. As captain of Joseph Smith's bodyguard and as a member of the Council of Fifty he was given other responsible positions. He was one of the small group present in the early morning of April 26, 1839, which dedicated the site and laid a cornerstone for the proposed temple at Far West. The conference at Nauvoo on October 6, 1840, voted to proceed with the work on the Far West temple. Cutler was placed in charge with Reynolds Cahoon and Elias Higbee to keep the books. Higbee died on June 8, 1843, but the other two men pushed the work to completion and participated in the dedication on May 24, 1845.

The settlement here was named Cutler's Park in his honor. He believed in the United Order and tried to enforce it there. He also opposed the move to the West. Cutler set up his own church in Iowa and in the 1860's moved north into Minnesota. His group did baptisms for the dead. Jones, *Vintonia*, V, 34.

Sund Nov. 14th 1847. Went to meeting at the stand The Twelve spoke about the valley Said it was a good place to serve the Lord in and that was what we wanted &c

The subject of vacating this place was laid before the people and agreed to.

Went to the Council. My case & C. W. Pattens was brought up again. We settled it.

President Young spoke against the present practice of dancing. Mingling with all manner of people in the dance. The control of dancing was left to the Bishops as they were the judges & had the over sight of their wards and for them to always be present at all such parties in their wards.

Mond Nov 15th 1847. Worked at home all day.

Tuesd Nov. 16th 1847. Not well this morning. Br Murdoc who was engaged with Patten in the affray the other day with the police came to me this morning and demanded satisfaction for several blows he recieved from me but not being satisfied went away to prefer a charge against me Attended a council at 2 o'clock P. M.

Wed & Thurs Nov. 17th 1847. At home writing & working most of the time.

Friday Nov 19th 1847. Hard South Wind. Mostly at home was not well. Some Omahas & ottoes came in at dark. B. Youngs Co met to prepare to emegrate again.

Sat Nov. 20th 1847. At home & around as usual Went to Council. Twelve acting on sending off Elders to preach. Mostly High Priests L. H. Calkins. J. C. Wright, E. H. Groves & J. W. Cummings were appointed from among the police

A short time after dark we had a report that there was a dance at L. N. Scovils that was unlawful there being no Bishop present L. H. Calkins went in and notified them to disperse which they did. Some of them had not yet learned the law.

Sund Nov 21st 1847. This morning at 8 o'clock my trial with Murdoc was to come off before Bishop Clark who was very much predjudiced against me for as soon as he read the charge he declared what I had done to be a most outragious act act and that I was entirely wrong

When It came to a trial he utterly refused to hear the most important of my testimony saying it was not necessary,

When It came to the decision his two councillors differed with him thinking that As we were attacted by him while in the discharge of our duty we had a right to defend ourselves as we did and that Murdoc was the one for them to decide against and not me.

However he persisted in his opinion and decided that I should make a confession to Murdoc which if I did now he would then give the rest of his opinion and then demanded if I would do it. I insisted on having all at once

He after a long time said I would in addition pay three dollars fine To which I entirely refused to do and told him I would appeal to the Council, who I knew would sustain me as I had only carried out their orders.

Thus ended this trial. I then went to meeting. Then home.

At 2 o'clock P. M. the Council met when my case came up We had a long trial. Several on the opposite side swore to positive lies. The most absurd was John L Butler who swore that he was more than forty rods off and heard me beat Murdoc with a large club & he could hear the licks distinctly which sounded like beating an old dry Buffalo skin. When in reality he was only struck across the arm and he was not disabled so that he could not raise his arm above his head. I make mention of this perjury because I want to remember it against him I can never view him in any other light than a corrupt perjured villian.

The others who sowre [swore] wrong I believe did it more through predjudiced and excited feelings than a desire to sware a lie as did Butler.

After this trial was over President Young desired to see the Council & police together alone. The house being cleared he told us that the council did right in sustaing me in what I had done & for us to mantain the law for the day we gave back or srunk we would be ran under foot. The subject of the picket guard was then taken up and agreed to be stopped only when the Indians were troublesome and then occasionally to appear out on horse back but to not let it be known that we were stoped Council then adjourned it now being late at night

Monday Nov 22nd 1847. At common business for me. L. H. Calkins prefered a charge against W. W. Phelps for refusing to pay a debt he owed to the stray pen or he rather sued him for it.

Tuesday Nov 23rd 1847. Phelps came to terms and wanted to settle which Calkins consented by him paying & agreeing to acknowledge to the council that he had lied to get round paying.

Wed Nov 24th 1847. N. W. wind. Cold. at home mostly. In the evening went to a meeting of the Seventies. The object of which was to select a number of them to send on a mission

Thurs Nov. 25th 1847. N. W. wind. Cold. Snow flying At home settling with the picket guard

Friday Nov. 26th 1847. S. wind. At home most of the day. One or two Lodges of Omahas had settled in the field South on the first creek & I[,] W. Meeks & T. Rich went down & ordered them away about sun set. They forthwith departed.

At dark Brighams Company met at the Council House The President raked down very hard on the conduct of Parley & Taylor last Spring while they were here.

Sat Nov 27th 1847. Fine clear warm day. Went with Meeks & Rich to the South to look for Omahas.

Found some in the willows in the Big Bend of the river. We returned at three o'clock. The police worked for the president today.

Sund Nov. 28th 1847. Went to council at ten. Today Phelps was to acknowledge to the council that he had lied to Calkins, which he did most scientiffically and so very easey that it seemed a pleasure and not a cross.[58]

The council forgave him He thanked them and told them that he would try & do them as good a turn some time. I could not help but admire how good & ready he was at a confession which was in consequence of his practice at that business Prest Young then spoke in favor of our possition.

Mond Nov. 29th 1847. At and around home & in town. The Omahas are passing down again today. They often pass to & fro killing cattle as they if they get an opportunity. Sent out some picket guards in the evening to watch their movements.

Tues Nov. 30th 1847. Went to a council today which had been called to investigate the cases of H. B. Jacobs & W. N. Phelps while they were East on a mission

It appeared that Phelps had while East Last summer got some new ideas into some three young women & they had consented to become his wives & he got Jacobs to marry them to him in St Louis and he lived with them as such all the way to this place After a long and tedious hearing of the matter which was altogether their own admissions, President Young decided that Phelps had committed addultery every time that he had lain with one of them & that Jacobs should be silenced for the part he had taken in marrying them.

---

58. Stout here refers to the fact that Phelps had been excommunicated from and reinstated into the Mormon Church at least twice before: in 1838 at Far West and in 1846, as recorded in this volume, and would be again on December 9 following this entry.

phelps had the privilege granted to him of being baptized again as his deeds did natturally cut him off from the Church.   adjd at 2 o'cl Not well in the evening.

Wed. Dec 1st. at home not well.

Thurs Frid 2nd & 3rd Dec 1847. At home rectifying the tax books which are in a "perfect state of confusion."

Sat Dec 4th 1847. At the tax books yet   Omahas are now passing up again this evening.

Sund Dec 5th 1847. Went to council   Nothing of any importance up today Major the painter took a pull at me for my likeness today Big Elk & some 8 or 10 more here again.

Mond Dec 6th 1847. Rectifying the tax books today *W. Meeks & J. Scott had a trial this evening before Bp Clark   Meeks V.S. Scott for stray pen account & gained it Scott appealed.   Trial ended both sides had warm feeling when it was over

Tuesd Dec 7th 1847. Rectifying tax books yet.
*Meeks V. S. Scott was this evening & not yesterday.

Wed Dec 8th 1847. Tax Booking yet. Went around town saw some Councillors about police affairs.

Thursda Dec 9th 1847. Warm morning.   Heavey damp snow falling fast in the fore noon.   I went over the river to attach some property in the hands of Simpson Emmett Son of James Emmett to satisfy a demand against him for property taken away from one Coons, while he was in the wilderness with Emmett.   Coons becoming dissatisfied was not willing to stay with them any longer so he was striped of all he had and sent away with his wife & children bare.   Simpson Emmett had a cow belonging to Coons or one taken away from him at that time.   I siezed on a horse & cart and some other articles of small value and brought them over to Winter Quarters

There was a Council today at which W. W. Phelps was formally cut off from the Church & John D. Lee's case up   Most of his wives & adopted children were dissatisfied with him & I believe it was so managed to let all go free who chose when 2 wives & almost all of his adopted children stept out.[59]

Friday Decr 10th 1847. Finished rectifying the police books which was a tedious job.   Settling diverse police & guard accounts.

Elias Gardner the police Collector set or deputized A. J. Stout to finish the collecting for the police. Major took another pull at my likeness again today.

Sat Dec 11th 1847. Atending to the police affairs.   Sixteen of our Brethren who went in the army returned today from the valley.[60]

---

59. Brigham Young reviewed the case of John D. Lee and sustained the earlier ruling that his wives and adopted children who wished to, might be free of him. Two of Lee's young wives, Nancy Bean and Louisa Free, were already estranged and were later given bills-of-divorcement. Two others left briefly but returned, so that Lee now had eight faithful wives, two of whom would die before they reached the West.

Four of Lee's adopted sons accepted their freedom at once; others continued with friendly relations but without any constraint. This action was really a death blow to the whole system of *Adoption*, already a bone-of-contention among the Mormon leaders. Once in the valley, no one honored it, so that its very existence is now largely forgotten.

60. When William Clayton and others organized to return to Winter Quarters, there were in the group thirty-two Mormon Battalion boys. Since each company traveled at its own speed, they arrived at different times: Clayton and his group on October 20, this group of sixteen on December 10, and Daniel Tyler and his companions not until December 17. They, too, suffered from cold and hunger. Tyler, *History of the Mormon Battalion*, 321-24.

They had an uncommon hard time. Suffered extreemly with cold and hunger, Was detained ten days at the Loup fork by floating ice. They report more on the way. All was well in the valley.

Sund. Decr 12th 1847. Went to Council. Scott & Meeks case up. I acted as defendant in this case here in Meeks place. We had a long trial which lasted nearley all day. We gained however & the Council sustained the police in every particular. The Twelve were also present who also sustained us. Emmetts case was also up too about the property taken & I believe laid over

Mond Dec 13th 1847. Council met at ten for police purposes but done nothing afterwards was around as usual.

Tues, Wed, & Thursd — 14th — 15th — & 16th, 1847. at home as usual. Wrote to T. S. Edwards on the 14th Very sick on 16th.

Friday Dec 17th 1847. At home. Some 20 more of the brethren came in from the valley today. Jos Thorn had also moved back with his family He got dissatisfied

Sat Dec 18th 1847. At home. Allen Taylor & wife came here on a visit.

Sund Dec 19th 1847. Went to Council not much up adjd at 12 o'clock Met again for police. Agreed to turn our tithing for the poor's tax Called up some stray pen poleticks &c. &c.
Lot more of Omahas & Many came in the evening. Hard N. W. wind this evening O! how it blows.

Mond Dec 20th 1847. Clear Cold day around as usual.

Tues Decr 21st 1847. Not well. Looking into Gentile dancing poleticks which were gaining ground reported it to the Twelve. Resolved to stop it. Milo Andrus had a trial today for living with a woman unlawfully

Wed Dec 22nd 1847. Went with a number of the police to search one Mr Long who boarded at D. Russells He was strongly suspicioned to be a spy & also taking notes & reporting all he could glean against us to Fort Kearney & many other such things When we came we found him ready & waiting for us. having been previously notified of our coming by Phineas H. Young as we soon learned. We however made dilligent search & found nothing wrong He treated us most impudently civil & seemed to be perfectly independant.
Immediately after the search I went to the Council of the Twelve yet in session and reported the thing to the President. Telling him that phineas had done. This I done in the presence of Phineas who did not utter a word or attempt to deny it.
We considered his conduct a piece of bass perfidity.
Being admitted in the Council of the Twelve at the time the order was given to me He took that advantage of it and thus betrayed what was going on.
The ballance of the day I was engaged in putting a stop to some of our folks going to a Millitary Ball to be held at the Point on Christmas evening.
In the evening E. T. Benson one of the Twelve was at my house till ten at night. He was very much dissatisfied with phineas for what he had done for he said he informed Long of what he had said about him, which gave his enemies the advantage over him when he was away from home but now phineas denies the whole affair.

Thurs Dec 23rd 1847. At home most of the day preparing to go to Conference

Friday Dec 24th 1847. Went to the General Conference at Millers Point, in company with Zera Pulcifer. Conference was held in a very large log House called the

Tabernacle. The day was mostly spent in preparing for business.

O. Pratt spoke at length on the policy of electing a First President. That God had saw proper to govern the Church by the Twelve since the death of Joseph the Prophet and that he could govern it by whatever authority he saw proper even by teachers and deacons. There was a time when this Church was governed by the Lesser Priesthood But now the Lord had manifested by his Spirit that it was best to appoint a First Presidency again that the organization of the Church might be perfected and the Twelve have a chance to spread abroad again to the Nations &c. His discourse was very interresting and was recieved with breathless silence. The Spirit rested down upon the whole congregation.

In the evening President Young requested me to take some three or four more of the police and go down to "Point au pool" to watch the moves of the officers and other persons at the Millatary Ball held at that place.

Accordingly I took Elias Gardner, L. N. Scovil and Luman H. Calkins. Got a span of horses and waggon of Daniel Miller and started just before dark We arrived at the Point earley in the evening about 7 miles

We were well recieved by all who knew us. Were taken in, had our suppers in the best of style. It was soon whispered around amongst the whole company who we were and our business was naturley known by some. All seemed to pay due regard to us. We were invited to partake in all their dancing & drinking always giving us the opportunity to dance oftener than any one else. We passed off the night very agreeably. Took breakfast paid one dollar each for our trouble & came back to conference earley the next morning.

Before the Ladies the officers were very civil as long as they were sober enough; but in the Barroom they were exceeding vulgar.

Saturd Dec 25 1847. We found all well at conference. In the forenoon the officers of the church were passed the ordeal as is usual.

One King was taken up today for stealing a blanket and had before the Council made pay four fold.

At noon went to Silas Richards,[61] the place where the Twelve boarded and took dinner & then reported the circumstances of the Ball last night.

This after noon the High Priests, Elders Teachers & Deacons Quorums were set in order & officers appointed to preside where there were any vacancies. Many of the Brethren marveled at our going to the Ball when it had been so strictley put down by the Twelve yesterday. They did not even suspect that we had been sent.

In the after noon went home with Allen Taylor & staid all night. Had a very cold ride It was seven miles.

Sund Dec 26th 1847. Went very earley to see Mother Taylor's and took breakfast. Allen & I then went back to Conference. Elder Applebee[62] spoke on the

61. Silas Richards was born December 18, 1807, in Highland County, Ohio. He joined the Mormon Church in 1840 but did not sell his farm and come to Nauvoo until 1844, arriving just after the death of the prophet. He worked on the temple and came west with the exodus to Winter Quarters where he remained until 1849, a member of the High Council and a counselor to Bishop Daniel Miller at the new town of Kanesville, Iowa.

Richards was captain of his emigrating company. He settled at Little Cottonwood in Salt Lake County where he was bishop from 1851 to 1864. He was called to Utah's Dixie (Washington County), but instead sent B. F. Pendleton to manage his affairs there by clearing his lots, putting up warehouses, setting out trees, and planting vineyards. Richards died March 17, 1884.

62. William I. Appleby, millwright, school teacher, and justice of the peace, lived at Ricklestown, New Jersey. In 1842 he was serving as a Mormon missionary in Delaware. In 1847 he was in Philadelphia raising money to buy a printing press and here had just returned in company with W. W. Phelps and Henry Bailey Jacobs.

In Utah, Appleby was made a regent of the University of Deseret in 1850; he served as legal counsel; and in 1857 he was clerk of the supreme court in Salt Lake City. Further activities will be noted in Volume II.

situation and policy of the Nations. His discourse was lengthy & very interesting to all present for our means of information at this time was very limited He is a beautiful & easy speaker.

In the afternoon Prest H. C. Kimball spoke against the Saints going to Gentile Balls and gentiles themselves and was followed by Prest E. T. Benson, after which I came home. Prest Young sent for several of his folks to come to the Ball tomorrow to be there.

Mond Dec 27th 1847. Sent off those to the Ball at the Tabernacle whom Prest Young & others had sent for but was not well & so I staid at home.

Mr Tull one of the Kearney officers was here today to engage more Ladies to go to another Ball at the Point on New Year's

Tues Dec 28th 1847. Heard from conference. The First Presidency are unanimously appointed to wit B. Young. H. C. Kimball and W. Richards.[63]

The Best of feeling prevailed and the Spirit rested down on the Congregation to an uncommon degree.

I was yet unwell but better than yesterday.

Went to a trial, before Bp Isaac Clark between C. Chapman & one Robinson. I believe the Prest & others came home to day from the conference.

Wed Dec 29th 1847. Very warm thawy day. The Church waggon which was executed by Gardner to satisfy the judgement against Scott was sold to day to Prest B. Young and the parties to whom the money was coming made a present of the same to the Prest immediately on the reciept thereof who blessed them & took it and appropriated it to the poor.

Went to Council. Heard Father Cutler's report of his mission which was as good or better than we could expect A great prospect of much good resulting from the works there. Had a police meeting in the evening at W. E. Cox shop, Police agreed to divide the night in three tours of duty. The case of Baalam's crown argued V. S. J. Bills.

Thurs Dec 30th 1847. Earley this morning I learned by Calkins that last evening while at the police meeting Mr Long had stolen his oldest step daughter & they had eloped to parts unknown. He was very much excited & wanted me to raise the police & pursue, but where to was the "Hard Question"

He however went to see the President on the subject who on learning that she was anxious to go said let her go which ended the matter now We soon learned that they had fled to Fort Kearney.

E. Gardner the police collector & my-self went to day to the Punka camp to settle the taxes there, and came home & fitted T. Rich & A. Ripley out to go to Belvue to see how matters and things were there in relation to us.

Friday Dec 31st 1847. Warm & clear comfortable to go without a coat. Rich & Ripley went to Belvue. I was employed in writing police orders &c.

Clouded up Hard wind North Blew Hard very cold evening. The year is past and gone! What is our fate for the next?

Saturday January 1 1848. Clear & pleasant day. The police were out on what we called a police spree.

---

63. Up to this time Brigham Young had been acting president of the Mormon Church, representing the Quorum of Twelve Apostles. His official acceptance here gave him more power in the management of the over-all policies of the church and in the direction of the mass move of the next year.

There were some persons in this place who were trying to set up a gambling table and to find out how the matter stood several of us went into a drinking spree with some who were concerned in it. They soon got high enough to develop their plans and thus we learned all about it

At dark the police met at the Council House with their wives and friends & had an agreeable party till Twelve at night. Police commenced on guard by 3 tours pr night.

Sund Jan 2nd 1848. Clear & pleasant weather. Went to Council at ten. Decided not to attend to temporal cases any more on Sunday. Several cases laid over. After Council I was around town the rest of the day.

Mond Jany 3rd 1848. N. wind. very cold day. Mostly at home writing. Police met at dark at Cox Shop Hoaxed Martindale for waring the Crown of Baalam.

Tuesd Jany 4th 1848. Today was a busy day for the police & Bishops.

Whiskey was at this time sold by a large number of brethren contrary to law which ordained that it should only be sold by the Bishops

The consequence was drunkenness was very prevelent and at some places they became very noisey. A complaint was made to the council by Bp. Whitney of the same whereupon the Council decided (Sund last) that the police & Bishops do their duty. Which was tantemount to saying put the law in force Bishops Carns & Knight made a move at it this morning & called on the police to back them up. They first demanded McCauslins whiskey. He gave it up without any difficulty, which the Bishops paid for — after that they demanded several others who gave it up manly in all such cases it was paid for out of the sales of the same. Alonzo Jones closed his doors against the Bishops who broke open his door & took his barrel of whiskey. also one Ferris refused to deliver up his which was taken. We then went to the redoubtable John Pack who also kept a barrel & the Bishops made known their Business telling him at the same time that they would pay him for it

He was very independant & saucy. He told them they had no right to it. He knew the law as well as they. He did not thank them to come to his Home to teach him the law &c.

Such is a specimen of his treatment to the Bishops who bore his slang a long while endeavoring to pursuade him to yield to the demands of the law not resist them or he would most surley loose his whiskey. He remained obstinate and dared them to touch it

They at last called on me to "lay hand on it which I did & the Spirit came". for the barrel was nearly full.

We now all decamped while he was pouring out a tirade of abuse & slang. We took 5 barrels today. The 3 latter was forfeited as they would not yield neither in that case would the Bishops pay. We were busy untill ten o'clock P. M.

Wed Jan 5th 1848. Went to H. Council at ten The case of Emmett came up (Coons V. S. Emmett).

The council Had a long trial Emmett called on John L. Butler and others of like stamp & was proving very plainly what solemn covenants all had made while with Jas Emmett, that if they did not abide with them & stay together they should forfeit all they possessed & many more such things when President Young demanded of the Council to first decide who & on what conditions could mak a covenant to bind people togeather as it appeared Emmett had done.

The council soon confessed their entire ignorance on the subject and desired the president to give the information.

He said that no man had a right to make a covenant to bind men together. That God only had that right and by his commandment to the person holding the keys of revelation could any man legally make a covenant & all covenants otherwise made were null & of no effect.

This of course up set all Butlers Hobbies while he was endeavoring so hard to make it appear that Emmett was a very good honest man.

After some time the proposition was made that all such property belonging to any of Emmetts company in dispute be Church property which was decided.

Several persons present who were contending about their property gave up their titles to the church Coons got some of his back & kept it not willing to yield to the decision.

Thurs Jan 6th 1848. At home wrighting most all day   Settling police till near 11 o'c P.M.

Friday Jan 7th 1848. Went to Council at ten. No business of importance. Occupied my time as usual.

Sat Jan. 8th 1848. Around as usual. At dark heard President Polk message read. It was very long.

Sund Jan 9th 1848. Was occupied today mostly in consulting with Prest Harris and some of the police on the best policy to be used to make a draw on the Brethren on the East side of the river to have them assist in paying the police

Mond Jan. 10th 1848. Was engaged in preparing to send some of the police over the river to collect means for the police. Prest Young assisted us by sending a petition. I will here insert the petition entire as it will more plainly show our situation also the situation of Winter Quarters, to wit:

To The Municipal High Council of Council Point, and all the Councils, authorities, branches, and members of the Church of Jesus Christ of Latter Day Saints on the Eastern banks of Missouri, or upon the Pottawottamie lands.

Camp of Israel   )   Greeting,
                   (
Winter Quarters   )   Beloved Brethren

The Councils of this place in their deliberations for the welfare of Israel, have concluded to lay before you, by way of petition, a laconic statement of their situation, and respectfully invite your attention to the same.

It is well known to many of you, the circumstances under which the great body of the Church located here; the many inconveniences & privations we have suffered through being huddled together in such large numbers, having the great majority of the poor, and the destitute thrown on our hands — the many families of our brethren to take care of (who for the temporal salvation of this people enlisted in the Battalion and went to California) — the publi burthens consequent upon our peculiar situation; also, the large amount of able bodies and expert men drawn from this Camp to be Pioneers, in search of a home for all the Saints, and who raised no crops at this point, — likewise the large Spring Company of emegrants who were fitted out from here and which embraced about all who had any means in their possession; and the many heavy losses we have sustained through Indian depredations, and destruction of our cattle; all these things have contributed largely to to the impoverishment of this Camp, and to render us in a measurably dependant and helpless condition, insomuch that at the present time, one of our Bishops has 301 individuals dependent on him for their daily bread; and those who have farmed it here are forced to leave this place, (in the spring [crossed out]) and must either go on to the mountains or recross the Missouri and begin anew.

Taking all these things into consideration — and having a public burthen on our shoulders of about 800 dollars, which we are unable to discharge, due to the police; a body of men who have never as yet in this church had an equivalent for their services — we deem it necessary to deputize a committee of their number viz: Elisha H. Groves, Luman H. Calkins, and Elias Gardner to visit your branches, and lay before the Brethren their situation, and the matters concerning the police which is needful for the people to know, and and recieve such donations as the Brethren may be disposed to give, either in teams, waggons, horses, cows, clothing of all kinds, for men, women, and children, & produce of all kinds, and who will keep an accurate [account] of whatever is given to them.

The Brethren in making this petition to you, realize that the comparatively advantageous circumstances which surrounds you, will warrant you in being liberal and benevolent, and while it will be taking a burthen off the brethren here it will only be equalizing the load, so that we may be one in all things, and it is fondly anticipated that you will shew by your hearty and liberal response to this petition that you are willing to bear equal burthens with us & sacrafice for the Gospels sake.

Hoping that this Petition will be recieved by you with that attention and exertion the case requires.

We are, &c.

Brigham Young
Heber C. Kimball
N. K. Whitney
Willard Richards
Orson Pratt
Geo A. Smith
Wilford Woodruff
Geo W. Harris
Jas Whitehead
    Clerk for the High Council.

Tues. Jan 11th 1848. Cold day. Mostly at home. at dark went to settle a Debt between E. Warner & T. Tanner.

Prest Young wants the police to put the public guns in order.

Wed Jan 12th 1848. Around home all day. amen

Thurs Jan. 13th 1848. Today Mr Long who had ran away with Calkins daughter returned accompanied by 4 soldiers they were in search of one Saml Smith a deserter

He came to me and wanted the help of the police saying they would give any price.

Smith had been here & crossed to the East side of the river just before they came. We watched for him till mid-night.

They agreed to employ 4 of us to go tomorrow to go in search of him with 4 of them for they were afraid to go with us only in case there was as many of them for what reason I know not.

Frid Jan 14th 1848. I & 3 more of the Police viz E. Gardner G. D. Grant and W. J. Earl. Started at sun rise with four of the soldiers in search of Smith the deserter. We crossed the river and proceeded up the river to Knowlton settlement and gaining no information of him we separated & I & two of the soldiers went across the bluffs to Little Pidgeon & took dinner at mother Taylors. We could get no trace of him. So we started back home.

The rest of the company went along the bottom and got track of him in McLellands settlement where he had staid all night & borrowed a gun. From here they discovered him on a hill at a great distance. Whereupon the proceeded towards him. He hid but they soon scared him up and took him and had started home with him when we passed by there & recieved the intelligence. So we hurried on and over took them and all went in together about sunset one hour.

Mr Long now that he found he was in no danger about stealing Calkins girl, had began to boast about what he had done. That he could outwit even the police &c

We concluded to give him a round on the subject of outwitting tonight. So several of the police geathered in W. Cox shop near to Calkins where Mr Long was & we sent Wm Miller into Calkins to get a pint of whiskey as an excuse but to arrest Long. He went in got the whiskey & started and as it happened Long came out with him. Not proceeding for Miller took hold of him saying "You are my prisoner. We entend to learn you what it is to kidnap young girls in this place as you have done you now have got to atone for it now before you leave this place". This spoken in an austerere and commanding tone had the desired effect. It scared Long almost to death He trembled like a leaf in the wind.

He was detained in Main Street while the North wind swept furiously over, untill he nearley froze. Gardner wanted him to go to a stock yard near by but he would not as he expected to have his throat cut & that was only to get him to one side for that purpose

At length he was taken into Cox Shop where we were assured at the same time that his time had come He need not expect to have friends to help him now. The atonement must be made. He must go before the Council & stand his trial but pretending to have some sympathy for him they undertook to plead with me not to report him if he would do anything fair.

After a long consultation in which all agreed that they would not divulge any thing that had passed we agreed to let him go in case he would pay four gallons of whiskey which amounted to 3.75 He gave Calkins orders to let us have it & he would pay it

After all this was over & the bargain fairley made we then ran upon him without mercy to suppose that we cared anything about a man marrying a girl whenever they could agree themselves. That we only wanted to let him know that we could outwit him. He was badly plagued & confessed that he did expect to die. We were bamboosing him around in this way till midnight.

Sat Jan 15th 1848. This morning we went to recieve our pay of the soldiers for our services but they were so very mean & penurious about paying us after so largely boasting that fifty dollars was nothing if only they could get the man that we told them that rather than take so mean & penurious a price we would not have any thing. Daniel Russell also used his influence for us not to be honorably paid as Mr Long told us.

After we were through with this soldier affair, I went to the office & reported their proceedings to the president also the way we handled Mr Long.

Here signed a petition to Washington for a post office at the Tabernacle.

Peresident Young went to the Tabernacle today to a feast called the Jubelee.

About dark a house was burned belonging to one of the Cutlers. Loss considerable

Sund. Jan 16th 1848. Mostly at home. Occasionally around. Several police here at times

Mond Jan. 17th 1848. Mostly at home today around town some.

At dark broke up a party at D Russels which was got up contrary to orders. After that the fiddlers went to Carns & then to Gardners and played for us, while we had a dance till Twelve

Tuesd Jan 18th 1848. Went to the Jubilee today. The Souix agent and General officers from Fort Kerney came there as spectators and were invited to partake in the dance. Come home in the evening; Several of the police & myself went to the South Line of the City to Break up a dancing party but finding Bp Clark there we said nothing.

Wed Jan 19th 1848. Went to the Jubilee again by the upper ferry. We arrived there at Eleven o'clock a.m. and staid till in the evening We came home about two hours after dark and then went out on guard with E. Gardner & Carns till eleven o'clock P. M. Saw and had an interview with Prest Harris about the seditious feeling of some in this place. He thinks it ought to be put down.

Thurs Jan 20th 1848. Engaged with E. Gardner and D Carns on the subject of the seditious feeling prevalent. We had repeatedly made mention of it to different ones of the Council desiring that would call a private council and hear our report but they seemed very easy and unconcerned which made us feel the responsibility the more on us. So today we were around & saw several of the Council who were as usual very easy. Very naturally supposing that we would see to it. Still we could not get a hearing. About dark I went to the Council house to a meeting of the High Priests and finding no one there except some of the Council, Clerk & some of the Bishops I Began about the spirits which were at work &c untill I grew very warm & spoke very long & loud untill they were fairley wakened to look into the subject and appointed tomorrow at 9 o'clock a.m to give the police a hearing for I said many thing that was hard for them to believe. From here I went to notify Prest Harris of the Council tomorrow who was well pleased with the arraingements.

This evening before dark a child belonging to Br Klingingsmith[64] had her clothes to catch on fire and nearly burnt her to death.

Frid Jan 21st 1848. This morning the Council & police met as agreed last evening at 9 o'clock. I was called upon to give a relation of things as they existed in & about this place.

I was all the fore-noon at my report when we adjourned for dinner and met again when I finished my report & was followed by several of the police who

---

64. Philip Klingensmith (sometimes written Philip K. Smith) was born in Pennsylvania in 1816. A blacksmith by trade, he was one of the leaders in the colonization of Manti, Sanpete County, Utah, where the 1850 census listed him as having a wife, Hannah, and four children. In 1853 he was an alderman and bishop of Cedar City. That year he took a train of thirty wagons to Salt Lake City to haul south a hundred and fifty immigrants who had come through the Perpetual Emigrating Fund.

Klingensmith was a participant in the massacre at the Mountain Meadows in which a company from Missouri and Arkansas was wiped out, except for eighteen young children. Klingensmith was responsible for placing these in Mormon homes. The burden of guilt for the massacre finally became more than he could bear, so in April 1871 he wrote out a confession for his part in it. He testified at the first trial of John D. Lee at Beaver, Utah, but was not summoned to appear at the second. The *Salt Lake Tribune* of August 4, 1881, quoted from the *Pioche Record* (Nevada) a report that Klingensmith had been found dead in a prospector's hole in Sonora, Mexico, evidently murdered. The implication was that he had been pursued by persons unknown and killed as a traitor.

also testified that my statements were all correct

I assure you that we unfolded a black budget to the astonishment of the Council who did not even suspect how matters were going

I do not wish to say any thing about the state of affairs as it is not very essential to the reader.

After the reports of the police were made the Council decided that we had not sounded a needless alarm. Also that a charge should be prefered by me against E. D. Woolley[65] as a beginning to put down some of the iniquity reported

The charge I prefered was for using seditious and unbecoming language against the Council and authorities of this place

The Council seemed determined to put a stop the course of things. After Council I went to see & have an interview with Prest Harris then came home about 9 o'clock and issued an order on Smith & Donalld Store for their tax

Sat Jan 22nd 1848. Went to Council again which was mostly spent in reading & correcting the minutes of yesterday's council.

The Twelve & A. W. Babbit[66] then came in. Council continued all day. Babbitt made a long report about the Committee Ship It was not very satisfactory

Brigham repramanded him once quite sharpley & he flew off in a tangent and tried to resign his office & Trustee &c

Drew another order on a store for taxes amounting to 15-00. Then went to the office to see about sending the police Committee off tomorrow.

Sund. Jan 23rd 1848. Several police here today. Whitehead the Clerk came here to read & correct the minutes of Frid last afterwards was around

Today Groves Calkins and Gardner the police committee started over the river to fill their mission. Prest Young wants the police to put the public arms in order.

Mond Jan 24th 1848. Today the Council met at ten a.m. on Woolley's case we had a long [session] which nearley all day. The case had created much excitement & the house was crouded.

The charge was fully and abundantly sustained. President Harris decided that he should be fined one hundred dollars which was followed by a general pause in which President Young proposed to me to withdraw the charge which I did after a long speech on the object and duty of a police & the reasons for bringing it up &c Presidents Young & Kimball also spoke on the subject

This trial was the cause of much good as the people were enlightened on the object & intention of a police. The dark cloud of dissatisfied and murmuring feeling was for the time being dispelled.

---

65. Edwin Dilworth Woolley was born June 28, 1807, in Pennsylvania, the son of a wealthy farmer. At the age of twenty-five he was orphaned, the eldest child of a family of seven. He accepted the responsibility of his younger sisters and brothers and helped them all get an education.

He was converted to Mormonism in 1837 and converted in turn Edward Hunter, later the presiding bishop of the church. Woolley sold his property in the East and brought the family to Nauvoo, where he became established in the mercantile business. He was prosperous enough to contribute generously to the church and to give the prophet $500 at one time to pay his lawyer's fees and secure his release from jail.

Woolley came to Utah in the Brigham Young company of 1848. Here he was a member of the territorial legislature and of the High Council, a bishop of the Salt Lake Thirteenth Ward after 1853, and later acted as superintendent of Brigham Young's private business.

66. Almon W. Babbitt had been active in the Mormon Church since its earliest times: a member of the Zion's Camp trek of 1834 and presiding officer in the Kirtland Stake in 1841. At the time of the exodus from Nauvoo he was one of three trustees to remain and manage the sale of church properties and the fitting out of families for the journey. His companions were Joseph L. Heywood and John S. Fullmer. Stout has already spoken disparagingly of Babbitt. Further note will be taken of his activities in Volume II.

Tues Jan 25th 1848. Today the police commenced to clean & put in order the public arms which I assure you was a laborious & tedious job. The Council House looked more like a gun smith establishment than anything else.

Last night J. P. Harmons pork house was entered and considerable pork taken out which Langley by strategem found out was done by Bushrod W. Wilson. He was had up before Bp H. Peck and made to pay four fold & restore the pork taken E. Gardner returned today with some corn the avails of their preaching.

Wed Jan. 26th 1848. Police are occupied at cleaning &c the guns yet.

Commenced to exchange corn with those who are going over the river to live for their corn here which saves transportation both ways We collected most of our corn in this way.

We had Langley tried tonight at Woolly store for not holding the truth sacred as we called it & fined Woolly one gallon all in fun

Thurs Jan 27th 1848. At the guns yet which will be continued untill completed.

Went to the Church ox mill now in progress in the North part of town. I do not think much of the plan.

Frid Jan 28th 1848. Today J. H. Blazzard came to Bp Carns & myself & said that he did not wish to have any more hard feelings towards us refering to the 180 and 186th page also stated that had learned something better and then give his hand in friendship telling us at the same time that Br B. Covey was practising a wicked and abominable thing of which we shall speak hereafter more fully and wanted us to look to it [page numbers are Hosea's references to original diary]

I went and reported the same to Prest Young who wanted the matter looked into. I was up till eleven o'clock at night.

Sat Jan. 29th 1848. Around as usual Council at ten Traples V.S. S. Wixom for stealing his daughter. But Wixom was too smart for he had been sealed to her Nothing more special up.

Sund Jan. 30th 1848. North Wind first sleeting & then turned to a driving snow. It had been very pleasant since the Jubilee. But now very cold It was altogether the coldest & most disagreeable today that we have had this year.

At 2 o'clock Elizabeth,[67] wife of my brother Allen died. (of child bed) She had been lingering for some time. She left him with three small children the youngest only a few days old.

Mond Jan 31st 1848. Mild clear weather. S. W. Wind. preparing for Elizabeth's burial Blazzards reports still more unfavorable against Covey which I reported to Prest Young.

Feb. 1st 1848. Today Elizabeth was buried and at dark H. C. Kimball preached her funeral at Allen's house. After meeting D. Carns and wife came home with us and visited untill 9 o'clock P. M.

---

67. Allen J. Stout tells how he courted Elizabeth Anderson, daughter of Miles Anderson, and in spite of the opposition of her parents, married her on July 17, 1843. The ceremony was performed at the home of James Pace, a neighbor, and the young couple left immediately for the pineries of Wisconsin where about a hundred men under the direction of George Miller and Lyman Wight were getting out lumber for the Nauvoo Temple.

After two years Elizabeth's parents forgave her and welcomed her family to their home. For some time Allen J. Stout and his father-in-law worked together to secure means with which to join the exodus. His arrival at Winter Quarters and setting up his home adjoining that of Hosea have been told in this record.

Elizabeth's health had been poor. On December 10, 1847, Allen called in Dr. Bernhisel who "gave her some medicine, bled her, and put a 'Spanish Fly' blister on her back, and she seemed to get better." On January 25 following she gave birth to a daughter; the child lived. Allen J. Stout, "Journal," 19.

Wed Feb. 2nd 1848. Engaged with police matters & B. Coveys case It is now plainly manifest that he is guilty of seducing two girls not over twelve years of age which was reported to the president.

Had a police meeting at Cox Shop at dark on the subject of the publick arms. Decided for each policeman to put in order five guns. They also agreed to allow Allen 50 cents pr day for keeping the stray pen to Nov and 25 cents to Jan.

Thurs Feb. 3rd 1848. Around as usual. The police committee have all returned having near one hundred dollars in goods clothing and money. I was engaged with them till late at night.

Those who were in the battle of Nauvoo in the fall of 1846, had a party today styled "The Defenders of Nauvoo at C. C. Bolton's[68] house. They had a high time some being very high. Cold N. wind in evening.

Frid Feb. 4th 1848. Sick head ache & weak all day Cold N. Wind.

Police met at the Council House this morning to divide the goods &c brot over by the comittee. In this divide which was by pr cent on our dues as usual I had a cow to fall to me. We were engaged untill one o'c

Sat Feb. 5th 1848. Around as usual & at one o'clock went to Council John Pack had prefered a charge against Bp Carns for taking his whiskey which after much ado and argument it was laid aside as he had went according to law

I here spoke in favor of sustaining the law and bore down on those who sold spiriteous liquors very hard.

In the evening I & several of the police met at E. Gardners with H. S. Eldrege to settle or rather explain to him the reason that the police did not want him for a Collector, which was done I believe to the satisfaction of all parties. I came home about Eleven o'clock P. M.

Sunday Feb. 6th 1848. I was around town today President Isaac Morley desired me to assist him in putting in order, his Emmegration Co. which I undertook.

Today I was presented by Pres Joseph Young with a charge against me by John Pack for abuse &c in the speech I made in the Council last Sat in the case of the whiskey when at the same time Prest H. Kimball was present and the Presiding officer & did not call him to order but being compldetely repulsed there he flew to the Seventies to gratify his disapointed feelings.

Monday Feb. 7th 1848. Made some preperations to meet Packs charge which I could easily & safely meet.

Tues Feb. 8th 1848. Occupied mostly at distributing some goods sent to the police by the committee over the river. Met the officers of the first Division today at Cox Shop Done but little business.

Wed Feb. 9th 1848. Occupied at the guns, the Emmegration, & Company, Packs case Lot of Omahas come in. Put one more man out on guard to night.

Thurs Feb. 10th 1848. Earley this morning John Pack came to me desiring to drop the suit against me & to let our difficulties and liquor all go by the Board

---

68. This is evidently Curtis E. Bolton who was active at the battle of Nauvoo. Born July 19, 1812, in Philadelphia, he was serving on a mission in Little Falls, New Jersey, on September 4, 1842. He came west with the 1848 emigration; in 1853 he was president of the French and German Mission.

On May 10, 1873, Bolton spent the night with John D. Lee and his family at Lonely Dell on the Colorado River on his way with a colonizing group into Arizona. This was a drought year, so that the colonization attempt failed. The people all returned across the river in a few weeks. Bolton died at Marysvale, Piute County, Utah, on December 6, 1890.

which I agreed to for I told Prest Young what I would prove & he advised him to drop it.

Frid Feb. 11th 1848. Today L. H. Calkins came home from his mission on the East side of the river having ended his mission. Today the Omahas were sent away.

Sat Feb 12th 1848. Council met at ten. private. Here a petition was presented by John Pack for pay for his whiskey which after much discussion, was burnt. This I believe, gave a finish to the idea of those who had lost their whiskey ever getting pay. Council was engaged at this till noon and adjd and met again but I did not go Was around as usual. After sunset the police concluded to have a party at the Ballroom, where they met & had an agreeable party till about Twelve. President Morley & some more good men attended and joined in the dance.

Sund Feb. 13th 1848. Clear fine warm morning. Went and made Prest Harris a visit who gave me a useful lesson and what constitutes good manners. Attended Council. No special business. Meeting at the stand Heber spoke on diverse subjects. Came home. Went around town. The Ferry Boat started today. I had the Head Ache

Mond Feb. 14th 1848. Rained last night. Warm day. South wind. Muddy roads.

Today E. H. Groves returned home from his mission to the Branches on the East side of the river to raise funds for the police. Calkins & Gardner both having previously returned. This ended their mission

The total amount subscribed by the brethren in the different branches for the police was 385 dollars and 53 cents. and the total amount collected and actually realized by the police was 378 dollars and 82 cents. only wanting 8 dollars 91 cents of being all collected.

This amount paid in corn Beans; potatoes, turnips, cabbage, buckwheat pork, Butter &c also in clothing to considerable amount. was an advantage to the police greater than any one could immagine who did not know their wants.

My proportion as divided by per cent on my dues amounted to about 65 dollars and had it not been for this assistance I could not have made my out fit to come West. It was from this fund that I procured means to hire a waggon to come in the want of which alone would have stoped me.

Tues Feb. 15th 1848. Went to a meetings of the 70's J. P. Harmon was had up for selling whiskey on the E side of the river but nothing of any importance came of the trial as he had done no particular wrong.

Wed Feb 16th 1848. Occupied in distributing corn to the police. Procured another cow of Lott on picket guard tax.

Thurs Feb. 17th 1848. Settled Meeks picket guard tax he was unwilling to come to a settlement. Recd a paper from the City of Washington today pr mail

Frid Feb. 18th 1848. Rained last night & wet morning. Wind S. E. then it cleared off. Around town as usual. Unwell today.

Sat Feb. 19th 1848. Occupied at exchanging corn. for the police. Went to Council Trial Langley V.S. Dayton. D. Russel had an unlawful dance to night & several of the police went to stop it, but Bp. Clark was there & so it ended

Sund. Feb. 20th 1848. Dark Day. Sister Anna came here today. Around as usual. Police wanted to work the road over the river through the willows General turnout of the brethren wanted

Mond Feb. 21st 1848. Not well all day. Exchanging corn for the police. Police meeting this evening. They all agreed to go to work on the road Next Wednesday as requested yesterday.

Tues Feb. 22nd 1848. Cold N. wind. Distributed 3 more loads of corn to the police

Wed Feb. 23rd 1848. The weather was so cold today that we did not go over the river to work the road throug the willows neither does it need it now as the deep mud there is froze to a good road.

One J. M. Stroder put up a Store & his clerk Br Bartlett wet his flag today as it is so called by treating the customers He was partly forced into it as he was unwilling to do it. Around as usual.

Thurs Feb 24th 1848. Was around to enlist more help to clean guns as the police were getting tired of their job, as well they might.

Today we got up the idea of making up a party and all who would put a gun in good order might come. They finding everything. This work was committed to E. Gardner & R. Stevens. Such was the dancing fever that they soon had as many at work as the police could superintend.

Frid Feb. 25th 1848. Mild pleasant weather. Busy time at the guns. There was enough cleaned to day for two parties, one for the adults & one for the Boys. The adults had their party tonight. So much good come out of the dancing fever. All went off well and satisfactory.

Satur Feb. 26th 1848. Last evening Daniel Russel had a party, which was the first one, of the many he has had this winter, that was in order.

Council met at ten. Benj Jones case was had up today. prefered by himself for living with Rosanna Cox unlawfully. After some inquiries of Allen & myself on the subject & the reasons which had parted him & our sister Anna He being very penetent it was decided to forgive him and for Prest Young to seal him & Rosanna, leaving him and Anna to settle their own difficulties, which they did

The Boys ball came of to night many came who did not clean any guns and intruded on the boys but were named out and ordered off by Geo D Grant and the Boys rights mantained

There were 27 guns cleaned today on the dancing order. I was around on guard late with E. Gardner tonight.

Sund Feb 27th 1848. Fine clear warm morning. Around all day Gardner Thos Rich Carns & Calkins and in the evening had a police meeting at the Council house. Here W. P. McIntire was taken into the Police. Decided to have only two tours of duty each night & have more police out at once.

Mond Feb 28th 1848. Around as usual today. Went over the river to see a waggon, but finally got one of Br Phippin for 15 dollars hire to move West in & to send it back this fall &c Not well.

Eighteen guns were danced out today. It goes well.

Tues Feb 29th 1848. Leap year day good for girls. Cold N. wind. Ferry Boat about stopped. Around at Common business.

March 1st 1848. Wed. Very cold N. E. Wind. Ferry stoped. Occupied at police accounts. Officers from Mo after Kay & Eli Nicherson did not find them. Snowing fast at dark.

Thurs March 2nd 1848. Deep snow & snowing this morning. Very cold N. Wind. Very cold. Only out to put out the guard.

Frid March 3rd 1848. Very cold. Snow flying. Finished the guns today.

The total number of guns put in order by the police &c were about 80. Another store put up by Bideman & Mulholland. Preparing for another Boys dance on gun cleaning today. up late.

Sat March 4th 1848. Very cold N. Wind. No council for want of Councillors attending. Boys party came of again tonight. all went off well this time.

Sund. March 5th 1848. Hard S. Wind. At home sick Head ache. Distributed a lot of Beans & Buckwheat today.

Police meeting this evening to decid how much we ought to have for fixing the guns. which was arranged as follows; For those who worked by the day in taking to pieces & putting together guns 1.00 dollar per day. For cleaning a gun 1.00 dollar For cleaning one Doz Bayonets 1 00 dollar

C. C. Pendleton[69] the gun smith who superintended the whole 1 dollar 50 cents and allowed me for my trouble 15 dollars Bishop Whitney was to give us credit for it on our tithing The sum total was over 100 dollars.

Mond March 6th 1848. The police had a cash and goods dividend today amounting to 28 cents on the dollar of their dues. The goods were the taxes on Bidemans & Mulholland & Smith & Donalds Stores. Had much business today. up late.

Tues March 7th 1848. Bideman & Mulholland wet their flag today. Had a lively time there. Occupied as usual afterwards.

Wed March 8th 1848. Went to search Saml Savary hous for stolen goods &c. Found corn but no goods stolen

This evening Mother Calkins mother of L. H. Calkins and Br Fisher were married Both over seventy but peart & lively. She left her former husband because he followed off Wm Chubby[70] the Negro prophet before noticed.

Thurs March 9th 1848. Snowing this morning. At home & around as usual.

Frid March 10th 1848. Occupied as usual The Bishops and police met to night at the Council House, by mutual agreement to interchange their views of the Laws and regulations of the place, which lasted till Eleven o'clock.

Sat March 11th 1848. Today Benjm Covey's case, as has been spoken of before, was brot before the Council for trial for unlawfully sleeping with a girl less than Twelve years of age. It appeared that two girls about the same age lived with him both of whom he had thus defiled, which was abundantly proven.

He was cut off from the church with this understanding, that his wives and children were under no more obligations to him Much was said that I need not relate.

This evening or after noon rather a trial between Jack Redding and J. M. Strodes, the owner of a store in this place for a debt due Redding on a contract for drawing good for Strodes came before Bp Carns Court Strode lived at the Point & when supeoned only threatned the place with Fort Kearney in case we done anything. He however sent on his witnessess and an aterney or agent to attend

---

69. Calvin Crane Pendleton was born August 25, 1811, in Hope, Maine. He had a good education for his time, graduating from the Eclectic Medical College at Worthington, Ohio. He was baptized into the Mormon Church June 10, 1838, and came to Nauvoo in 1840. A skilled mechanic in both wood and iron, he built wagons, repaired guns, and helped on buildings.

Pendleton's theory and practice of medicine differed sharply from that of his contemporary, Priddy Meeks, an herb doctor. Although Pendleton did compound pills and use poultices, he emphasized proper diet, temperance in eating, and ample rest in helping "Nature" effect cures. He condemned calomel, purgatives, emetics, and bleeding. He was effective in setting broken bones.

Pendleton was called to Parowan in 1852. Here he lived the remainder of his life, busy at the forge or lathe, treating patients, writing records and letters. He died April 21, 1873.

70. This would seem to be a nickname for the William McCairey of whom Hosea and others spoke just a year earlier. No other Negro prophet has been found.

the trial accompanied by a. scurrilious letter denouncing our rights to try the case as a farce.

When the case was opened the Atterney protested the Bishops right to try it but said he was instructed in case the trial went to make the best defence he could.

The Bishop of course went on with the suit which after a long trial was given in favor of Redding. This produced a general grunting among those who were not well disposed towards us as a people. All the half hearted mormons joined in this crusade of fault finding as is common in all such cases. But more of this hereafter.

Sund March 12th 1848. Abut in the fore noon & in the after noon took the sick head ache. Was out of my senses & could not detail the guard. Sick all night

Mond. March 13th 1848. Mostly at home still very sick One Tremain as he called him self who had married Roswel Steven's daughter & who was afterwards found to be a consumate thief. Had been tried found guilty & whiped & the tabernacle not long since He came over on this side & was taken up by the police & tried before Carns as He thought. He expected to be immediately killed & begged for his life which we told him would be spared in case he would go away and never more be heard of in this mormons territory this he gladly done & away he went

Tues March 14th 1848. Quite well again. around and at a Council at which was read a letter from O. Hyde & others on the other side of the river, written in great excitement least all should be immediately used up, for us here to deliver up Jack Redding & several others whom they only suspected, as thieves & for the police for God's sake to come over and help them as they had helped to pay the police.

All this flare up was only about a few vague reports of some one stealing and a whiskey Barrel broke open & its contents poured out by some good persons about the Tabernacle and the grog seller was making a fuss about.

Prest Young & those present only wrote to Br Hyde that if he would take a good smell of the old whiskey barrel to still his nerves & a little mountain opium & then be calm he thought it would all pass over. After this council I was around with the Present [President] some during which time he was at Mr Strodes Store whe[n] the objections to Strodes trial was thrown in his face in the same contemptable manner that now daily & hourly discussed. Threats of the United States troops & all such like was hinted at. I confess it was as much as I could do to hold my peace or keep my hands off from them The President kept very calm but his feeling were very warm & but little said by him then.

There was as much dissension now as ever I saw in Nauvoo or at any other period of the Church history.

Wed March 15th 1848. Sick all day. Today Strodes was sold or taken at the retail prices sufficient to satisfy the judgement in favor of Jack Redding Jack had employed me to act as his atterney in the case for which he now gave me 24 yards of calico.

Thurs March 16th 1848. Warm S. Wind. Sold some tools for corn. Was around with the police.

Frid March 17th 1848. Today was rather an unfavorable day for me. This faultfinding spirit was now raging to a great extent & Strodes Store was now all the time filled with those dissatisfied persons who were all the time railing at the authorities & upholding the course which Strode had taken towards us and in fact deprecating every thing that was right and righteous untill I had become sick & tired of it & so was every good man. Yet I had not come out against them so pointedly but what they supposed I had friendly feelings for them. This morning I stoped in at the store where several of these persons & two of the police were argueing the case of Strode warmly. Upon entering the store I resolved to let them know my opinion which I soon had an opportunity to do, whereupon several were mad (i.e.) S. C. Dalton Bartlett & Isaac Hill and after a volley of abuse & low scurrilious insults from Hill Dalton & Bartlett wanted me to explain myself which I did partly to which they said I was right but Hill continued his abusive language towards me. I claimed to be heard thro but he continued. I had resolved to put a stop to the course things were taking at the risk of my life & being highly inflamed or rather enraged at the mean course of Hill I "Lit upon him" determined to stop or kill him. We had a short scuffle when I got him across the counter and had him secured choked untill he could not breath intending to hold on peaceably as I was but was parted by John Lyttle which put an end to the matter now

After this "flare up" was over the police came together & we told Dalton & those who wer concerned that we would put an end to their course or end their lives. After this I never heard another murmur out of any of them.

In the afternoon I recieved a note citing myself W. J. Earl & John Bills to appear before Jos Young & the First presidency of the Seventies this evening at earley candle light to answer charges against us by I. Hill for assault and battery, for profane swearing & other unchristianlike conduct.

We had the privilege to have it tried before the Council.

I forgot to mention that Earl & Bills were the two policemen in the store.

We met for trial and there not being Presidents present sufficient for a quorum it was turned over to the Council who were assembled also. In the trial S. C. Dalton swore to a most positive and wilful lie as was proven on the spot in saying I used profane language.

President Young gave us all a first rate dressing out after which the Council decided that we should stop all further difficulties &c which we did

This was a final end to all further Strodeism & so far all was well. I was never sorry for what I done & I now know that good came out of it

Sat March 18th 1848. Went in company with Allen Stout down the river to the Big Bend hunting & come home unwell. Had to go to bed In the evening Meeks came & wanted a police meeting called which I told him to do at evening when we all met Him & J. W. Cummings had long been disaffected and now they supposed that the police could be made to lay all that had been said yesterday by by the President to my charge & thus impeach my conduct as a captain. In fact they at length come out in plain words to that effect which only exposed their concoction to the police without in the least affecting their good feelings towards me. It is true the police felt bad at the chastizement of the President but never a moment blamed me for it. They came off very much lessened in the estimation of the rest with out my saying a word to put them down.

Sund March 19th 1848. To day was more auspicious to me than the two preceding ones for my wife was safely delivered of a fine daughter at half past three o'clock in the evening weighing   lbs. I was at home all day Rained all night.

Mond March 20th 1848. Dark cloudy day. Home mostly all day.

Tues March 21st 1848. Cold, Dark, Damp, Cloudy day. Mostly at home. around some

Wed March 22nd 1848. Mostly at home exchanging corn. Mother Taylor came here on a visit (to see the Baby).

Thurs March 23rd 1848. President Young & Kimball came home today. I had sent Gardner after them as circumstances were suspicious. Out on guard for the want of more police.

Frid March 24 1848. Went to a council today Sidney Roberts was there. He was sent by the Whigs of Iowa to enlist the mormons on their side.[71] Their offers were accepted & for final acceptation it was refered to the authorities on the East side of the river No doubt but they will go the whig ticket next august. Lewis Dana is here. All is well with his tribe.

Sat March 25th 1848. Cold N. wind. Mostly at home. Council met today and passed the following law. "On motion of President B. Young it was unanimously voted that the Captain of the Police be authorized to call upon as many Brethren to volunteer free of expense as he needs out of each Ward to stand guard for one month to come to entirely prevent the Indians from coming into Winter Quarters at nights; also that no one trade with the Indians. If they do they are liable to a fine of one dollar and forfeit the article they have traded for"

After recieving a copy of this law I forthwith went to the executing the same which was a great task I assure you as men were full of excuses & not willing to stand guard.

Sund March 26th 1848. Fine day. Meeting at the stand. W. E. Cox spoke on the law passed yesterdy relative to guarding whenever I called on them Had out five men at once now

Mond March 27th 1848. Very sick & at home today.

Tues March 28th 1848. Cold N. Wind. Not well & mostly at home all day.

Wed March 29th 1848. Fine warm day. I & T. Rich went over to see Phippins waggon which I paid him 14.00 for the use of to go West in. come home at dark.

Thurs March 30th 1848. Ten Pawnees here now. N wind Today Prest Young requested the police to go with him to Conference on the 6th of April as there is some threats of the soldiers. & he intends to stand his ground

Went to fixing for Conference The Pawnees are very troublesome. Like for rain.

Frid March 31st 1848. At home fixing waggons preparatory for moving. A large company of the Pawnees which are in town had a very animated dance before Bidemans & Mulhollands store tonight.

Sat Apl 1st 1848. The Pawnees left today. Council met advise the Brethren to settle on the North of the Pottawattie tract to anticipated company from Ohio who were going to settle there.

Before Council rose a large Company about 80 pawnees from Bel-vue came in town with a letter from their agent desiring us to gave them some provision They had been there to enquire of Miller the cause why so many of their tribe had been so inhumanly massacred at Fort Mann Some of them were good looking men. They put up in a school house and were very troublesome.

---

71. Sidney Roberts carried with him a letter from John M. Coleman of the state executive committee, which was intended to conciliate the Mormons and elicit their support. In March 1848 a post office was established at Kanesville, Iowa, with Evan M. Greene as postmaster; and Pottawattamie County was organized with the following officers: Isaac Clark, probate judge; George Coulson, Andrew H. Perkins, and David D. Yearsley, county commissioners; Thomas Burdick, county clerk; Evan M. Greene, recorder and treasurer; John D. Parker, sheriff; James Sloan, district clerk; Jacob G. Bigler, William Snow, Levi Bracken, and Jonathan C. Wright, magistrates.

The church organization was presided over by Orson Hyde, George A. Smith, and Ezra T. Benson. Jenson, *Historical Record*, VIII (August, 1889), 900.

Sund Apl 2nd 1848. Hard South Wind all day. Today a fire broke out in Gates hay the South wind blew furiously the fire. Had it blown any other direction the town would have been been burnt to ashes before the people could have escaped for the dry hay was scattered over town so that the fire could communicate with all the stock yards in a few moments. It was an awful sight to see this fire in our situation. In the evening the people turned out and covered up the fire after it had burnt down some what and a guard was put over it to keep it from kindling in which case if the wind should change the town might be consumed. The confusion of the people on this occasion was great.

This evening Elder Hyde came here on the hot search of Tremain who was spoken of on the 13th inst. and Wm Bird, who we knew nothing about. But as for Tremain we told him he was "banished" from our Territory.

Mond Apl 3rd 1848. Wind North. Bp Laing [Thomas Lang?] came this morning to report the supposed whereabouts of Bird & Tremain It appears that after Tremain left here he was taken up some where near Fort Kearney for some of his stealing but had escaped. Hyde took breakfast with me. Pawnees here yet.

Tues Apl 4th 1848. Sick all day. W. Woodruff & wife made us a visit this evening till bed time. Preparing to go to Conference in waggons. T. R. Barlow, one of the first police of Nauvoo was here this evening. He had lost both his eyes by blowing in a well & was entirely blind.

Wed Apl 5th 1848. Fine day. Began to lay up flour for our move West.

Thurs Apl 6th 1848. Today went to Conference with a large company of the Police We went in two waggons.

We were well armed and prepared to meet those threats that were hove out against the Presidency. We arrived at the Tabernacle at Eleven a.m. & found the Brethren there awake to the same thing & were glad to see us come while here we kept close guard & a sharp look out. But no opposition manifested itself.

After meeting was out several of the police & myself were around with Prests Young Kimball & Hyde untill near mid night when they put up at a Br Kimballs & we went to Daniel Millers where several of the police were & staid till morning.

Miller treated us very kindly and entertained some seven or eight during our stay at Conference. I had the head ache all day.

Frid Apl 7th 1848. At Conference. Jos F. Herring the Mohawk came here part drunk I took him out and had talk with him & found him as full of his bad and evil feeling as he was when he left here.[72]

---

72. That Joseph Herring, the Indian, was under condemnation has already been noted. Hosea Stout makes no mention of Herring's fate, but William Hickman tells a story which seems to apply here: "One half-breed Indian from some of the tribes south, well educated, had been to Nauvoo, joined the Church, gone home and had come to Council Bluffs to see Brigham Young. Brigham had made him very mad, and he was swearing vengeance. He said he was well acquainted with the tribes west, and would be out ahead of him, collect them together, and scalp Brigham Young before he reached Fort Laramie — that he would have a war dance over his scalp in less than three months. Brigham Young's boys had got after him, but could not catch him, and he came on our side of the river. I found him, used him up, and scalped him . . . ." Hickman, *Brigham's Destroying Angel*, 46-47.

An affidavit published February 7, 1849, in the first issue of the *Frontier Guardian* may have reference to this incident: "State of Iowa Pottawattamie County Personally appeared before me, J. G. Bigler, a Justice of the Peace in and for said County on this the fifth day of February 1849, William A. Hickman . . . saith That whereas certain reports have been put into circulation . . . I do hereby solemnly declare that Mr. Hyde never induced me to commit violence on the person of any man, either white or red. Neither has he ever tried, by day or night, in public or private, to persuade me to injure any person, neither did I ever do anything of the kind at his instance. Signed William A. Hickman"

This is clearly an admission of having done injury, but at the instigation of someone other than Orson Hyde or upon his own responsibility.

After conference was adjd Prest Young & Kimball came home accompanied by E. Gardner and myself leaving the rest police of the police there yet awhile We arrived at home at dark.

Sat Apl 8th 1848. Around & not very well.

Sund Apl 9th 1848. Was going to Conference with the Prest but did not. S. Wind. T. Reid took my horses today to trade for oxen for me. Some Puneka Indians came in town today.

Mond Apl 10th 1848. At home. Sold my carpenter tools today for a Seven Shooting rifle. Was fixing my waggons

Tues Apl 11th 1848. At home fixing to go West. Another lot of Pawnees come.
Three men arrived here today from the Valley.[73] The news from there was good.

Wed Apl 12th 1848. At home fixg waggons. Pawnees here yet.

Thurs Apl. 13th 1848. At home as yesterday. Pawnees danced before Bidemans Store.

Frid Apl 14th 1848. Snow squall from North. More Pawnees come from Belvue They are very troublesome causing the Brethren to closley guard the city.

Sat Apl 15th 1848. Working at the waggons. Today I heard that John Gheen[74] in a scrape at Point-au-Pool, has shot Br Condit dead. River is rising. Up late.

Sund Apl 16th 1848. Warm Clear day. Went over the river to Thomas Rich's. Saw Round lake which is a pretty clear lake in the woods about two miles below the ferry. I was there mostly all day.

Mond Apl 17th 1848. At home. Cold drizzly day. Cold storm & wind from the N. in the eve.

Tues Apl 18th 1848. Occupied at home as usual.

Wed Apl 19th 1848. Occupied as usual at home. S. Wind but Cool Hard to get a guard. No police out but Arnold tonight The citizen guard runs low as so many are moving on the E. side of the river.

---

73. The Robert Bliss diary records that "Today 12th [January, 1848] a company starts for Winter Quarters."
   The "Journal History" of the church notes that: "Wednesday, May 3, 1848. Captain Gardner, accompanied by Samuel Lewis, Alva Calkins, William Garner, Ami Jackman, David Stewart, Robert S. Bliss, and Abner Blackman [Blackburn?] arrived at Winter Quarters from the Valley, bringing many letters." The three men who arrived on April 11 must have either come express or had been dispatched earlier. See J. Cecil Alter, ed., "The Journal of Robert S. Bliss, . . ." *Utah Historical Quarterly,* IV (1931), 128.

74. John D. Lee's unpublished diary of the exodus from Nauvoo, "Camp of the Saints," on March 8, 1846, states that ". . . 2 4 horse waggons & teams were sent back to Lick Creek encampment for Bro Turley's and Gheen's families . . ." On December 1, 1846, Lee indicates that Gheen has been doing some trading for him, and on March 17 following he himself stayed overnight at the Gheen home. Heber C. Kimball married two of Gheen's sisters.
   With regard to the incident here, Lee gives the full story, omitting only the name of John Gheen, as writers were apt to do when their friends were in trouble. He wrote: "Summer Quarters Sund April 16 . . . Reported that Bro Lilace W. Condit was shot through the heart by [_____] who had before forbid him passing through his garden 3 times & just before a Mob cross through to Taunt him. He raised his piece but it missed fire. As soon as the Horrid Deed was done the man whose hands were stained with Blood was most shockingly beat by the Spectators & then bound in chains." Cleland and Brooks, *A Mormon Chronicle,* I, 19-20.
   Further details of the activities of this man appear in Volume II.

Thurs Apl 20th 1848. Calkins came here to day & says that Mr Long, his son in-law has been baptized.

This evening I changed my plan of guarding as the citizens were moving over the river I adopted the plan of calling on those who are going West to guard. The town I divided into Beats & appointed a policeman to each Beat to detail a guard which relieved me as I could not attend to it all now in my hurry of business.

Frid Apl 21st 1848. To day Hyde sent a letter to Mulholland & Bideman stating what reports were. in circulation about them &c. which they said hurt their feelings very much. I was around with them most of the hearing their remarks.

Sat Apl 22nd 1848. Rained & sun shine mixed. At dark was at council. Br Newberry was sealed to Z. Pulcifur's sister. The Prest thinks it best to have out a Picket guard.

Sund Apl 23rd 1848. Very Cold North wind all day. Very sick head ache.

Mon Apl 24th 1848. Occupied in arrainging my loading P. Pedigrew's mule stole last night. Hard to get out a guard.

Tues Apl 25th 1848. Clear & cold. Loading. W. Richards ox shot by the Omahas Enlisting more guard but slow. The Prest sickish

Wed Apl 26th 1848. Went out on Picket guard to day. Jos Holbrook had seven head of his cattle stolen last night. We went South 6 miles and divided I with part of the company to the river bottoms & G. D. Grant with the rest to the West in the prairie where he found one of the Omahas with some of the Beef of Holbrooks cattle. He was asleep When he came to the Indian the Spirit rested upon Br Grant & he spoke to the Omaha in his native tounge to the astonishment of all present for they all knew a few words in the Omaha toungue & knew he spoke by the Spirit to the understanding of the Omaha After he was done speaking Grant took his horse & meat and his arms and brought them in. To night there was one man on guard on every Street running East & West in in all 18 men 9 at once. I came home at one o'clock with the sick head ache.

Thurs Apl 27th 1848. Cloudy wet Day. Occupied at my loading. Sent out the Picket guard but staid in. Another large Company of Pawnees come in today Guard as last night.

Frid Apl 28th 1848. Cloudy. N. wind. At home. Swarms of Pawnees all over town very anoying. Loading.

Sat Apl 29th 1848. Still occupied at my Loading &c

Sund Apl 30th 1848. Went to meeting at the stand E. Snow spoke on the Success of his mission East to ask aid of the people to remove the poor Saints West & was followed by E. T. Benson on the same subject To day the citizens were called to volunteer to guard the place & to be subject to my call.

This evening A. J. Stout was married to a girl named Amanda Malvina Fisk whose father died of colera in the Zion Camp in the year of 1834.

Mond May 1st 1848. [W]Arm Cloudy sprinkly & sultry. Meeting at ten to arrainge for our move West. & a picket guard of twenty men, ten of whom to be out each thus going out every other day. & placed under my control,

Tues May 2nd 1848. Sent out picket guard only 8 men made their appearance. Commenced loading my house hold goods.

Wed May 3rd 1848. Sent out seven men only. Warm & sultry. Eight men arrived from the Valley. News good. Slept in my waggon to night.

Thurs May 4th 1848. Occupied as usual.

Frid May 5th 1848. Went to Thos Rich's to day

Sat May 6th 1848. Writing mostly. Guard out rained some. Omahas dressed in American cloths stole an ox out of A Call[75] Herd.

Sund May 7th 1848. Meeting at the stand Subject of the picket guard up. Appointed two Captains who were to raise ten men each & go out on guard one day alternately The Guard to be men who were not busily engaged in preparing to go West. William L. Cutler and Harrison Burges were the two Captains.

To day a large company of the Ottoes came in with Capt Caw their chief with a line from miller the agent demanding their pay for our living on their land Mad out a double guard tonight.

Mond May 8th 1848. Settling police afc.

Tues May 9th 1848. Occupied as usual. This evening the Mandan [a river boat] arrived with many emegrants and a large amount of freight for this place which was what was detaining the Comp from going West.

Wed May 10th 1848. Rained some & was Boisterous N. Wind. Helped Br Stewart with his good &c to my house from the Boat. The town was all hurry and bustle to day in drawing goods &c from the Boat.

Thurs May 11th 1848. Occupied in Loading. Allen J. Stout moved over the river to day.

Frid May 12th 1848. Occupied as usual. The town is now full of goods On guard with D. Carns till 2 o'clock a.m. The ferry is now running all night transporting brethren both ways.

Sat May 13th 1848. Around town. Laid in my Sugar Some teams started some 3 or 4 miles West today where a camp is to be formed & where there will be plenty of grass for the cattle.

Sund May 14th 1848. Meeting at the stand. Near the last of the meeting Pres Young reproving the two Captains of the Picket guard for not being out earlier in the morning &c He also spoke of this land and Missouri from which we had been driven & cursed it to all who should live on it except for the Saints.

Monday May 15th 1848. Rained very hard last night. Dr Barnhisels two horses were stolen last night by two Pawnees who were around yesterday but he recovered hem by following them across the Platte at the mouth finding them asleep.

This is the first real hard rain we have had this year. Had sick head ache all day.

Tues May 16th 1848. Fine warm day. Got my oxen from T. Riches. Mudge refuses to pay his police tax. Laid up my coffee: 67 pounds

---

75. Anson Call was one of the great frontiersmen of Mormondom. Born May 13, 1810, at Thatcher, Vermont, he was baptized on May 21, 1834. Joseph Smith once predicted that Call would come to the Rocky Mountains and help to establish many settlements there.

That prophecy was literally fulfilled. Call came to Utah in 1848 and in 1849 was made bishop in Bountiful, Utah. In December of 1850 he went with the first company to establish Parowan, Utah; the next year he was in charge of the company which founded Fillmore, Utah. He later moved to the Bear River in Box Elder County, Utah.

In 1864 he was sent to build a large warehouse on the Colorado River at what was hoped would become a shipping port. Call's Landing was a monument to mistaken judgment until it was covered by the waters of Lake Mead. Anson Call returned to Bountiful where he was again made bishop in 1874 and served until 1877. He died August 31, 1890.

Wed May 17th 1848. Finished arrainging my loads and traded in the Store for my out fit and started on our journy to the Far West about two o'clock

I moved in two waggons which were arrainged as follows To one waggon was two yoke of oxen & one yoke of cows which were driven by Samuel Carns who engaged to drive a team & for me to board him & draw 400 pounds.

The other waggon had one yoke of oxen which I drove. This waggon I slept in.

The whole amount of my loading was 3,267 pounds weight. We proceeded on without any difficulty only having to double up the main hill after leavin town from the Summit of which we took our last long view of the town and the civilized world east of the Rocky Mountains.

We arrived in Camp about 3 miles from town in good time & turned our cattle out to bait on most excellent grass. There was a very large company here already The night was clear & pleasant with a full moon to cheer us.

Thurs May 18th 1848. All well. Baited our cattle again Lay up today while many waggons were continually coming into camp

Frid May 19th 1848. Warm clear & pleasant. Lay up Waggons continually coming in

Lorenzo Snow with the Pisgah company passed by today for the Papea where he was to build a new bridge somewhere above the old one. Some one or two also left this camp & went on Prest Young came into camp but returned again.

Sat. May 20th 1848. Very warm and clear. Lay up. Many waggons came into camp & many went on from camp. Rained very hard to night.

Sund May 21 1848. Fine warm day. Lay up again. Prest Young & Kimball came in to day intending to move on tomorrow.

Last night Mudge had 2 barrels of Molasses 1 of mackerel and one hogshead of sugar stolen —

Monday May 22nd 1848. Rained hard last night. Dark morning. We started about ten. The roads being lined with teams as far as we could see.

We traveled on untill about 4 o'clock when it commenced to rain & we turned out awhile two miles this side of the papea. The rain ceasing we went on to the papea where we found a large company assembled.

The Bridge was finished this evening and several of us crossed on it the first who went over But in consequence of the hard rains the crossing was extremely bad. This Bridge is about one mile above the old one We had another hard rain tonight.

Tues May 23rd 1848. Uncommon wet morning & still raining.

Teams were now crossing but the mud was deep & they had hard work. About noon it cleared off with a North wind drying the roads very fast.

Wed May 24th 1848. Cloudy morning. The crossing being much better the whole camp crossed this morning and we all moved on to the Horn where we arrived at two o'clock. This new rout is considerable nearer than the old one from the Papea to the Horn.

This evening there was a very large camp on the Horn and all was in motion. The raft was commenced to be repaired.

Thurs May 25th 1848. There was many at work this morning at the raft but in some confusion to avoid which a committee of three were appointed to superintend the whole business of crossing and directing the camp in relation to locating after crossing.

The committee were Daniel Carns, Chancy G. Webb[76] and myself. The raft was done at noon and 26 waggons crossed today which were located in the form of a hollow square for the main camp.

Frid May 26th 1848. This morning I crossed over immediately after breakfast.

There were 93 waggons crossed this day, A child of Br John Neph's[77] was drowned today.

Sat May 27th 1848. Hard S. wind all day. Went hunting. Prest Young and many more teams arrived at the Horne.

Sund May 28th 1848. Hard rain last night. The ground on which I was encamped is covered in watter. The Horn is rising. good day but cloudy. President Young crossed.

Monday May 29th 1848. Superintended the fixing the bridge on which the waggons lands off the raft which was now floating by the Horn rising. Stood guard the first tour tonight.

Tues May 30th 1848. Very sick head ache this morning which lasted all day. Pres Young formed his line one mile North of the main camp. D. Carns & I made him a visit untill bed time.

Wed May 31st 1848. Cold morning. Several of us went this morning to meet E. Gardner & others of the police who were coming We met them about three miles from the Horn. Over 100 waggons crossed this morning day.

Thurs June 1st 1848. This morning there was a hog & dog found dead which I suppose were put to death for some midnight sin.

Lorenzo Snow with the Pisgah Co started on today. Prest Kimball came to the Horn.

Prest Young organized his company this evening into two hundred (the first was [crossed out]) Allen Taylor Capt first & Daniel Carns & John Harvey Capt

---

76. Chauncey G. Webb will probably be best remembered as the father of Ann Eliza, the wife who gave Brigham Young so much trouble. He was born in 1812 in New York, and trained to be a carriage- and wagon-maker.

In 1833 Webb's parents joined the Mormon Church. He was also baptized and went with them to Kirtland where he opened a small wagon factory. Here he met and later married Eliza Churchill, a school teacher. He lost so heavily in the bank failure at Kirtland that he moved west to Missouri in 1837 and settled at Adam-Ondi-Ahman. When the Mormons were expelled from that state, Webb crossed the river and set up shop at Payson, Illinois, moving later to Nauvoo. Here he built a fine home and did a lively business during the years 1842-46, the demand for wagons and carriages for the move west being very great.

Just before the exodus he took a plural wife, Elizabeth Lydia Taft, who was to bear him eleven children. He came on to Utah in 1848 as one of the most prosperous and best equipped of the company. Again he set himself up to manufacture wagons and buggies, and after he was well established took three additional wives.

In 1875, soon after his daughter Ann Eliza had filed her suit for divorce from Brigham Young, Webb was excommunicated from the church but was later restored to membership. In Webb's later years he had several interviews with Wilhelm *Ritter* von Wymetal (Dr. W. Wyl, pseudonym) which were included in Wyl's book, *Mormon Portraits, Joseph Smith, the Prophet, His Family and Friends* . . . (Salt Lake City, 1886).

77. Regarding this incident, John Pulsipher wrote in his diary: "While we were here our joyful camps were suddenly changed to *mourning* by the Death of Charley Beer, Step-son of Bro John Neff a lively little Boy who accidently *fell* into the River & was drowned. We all turned out & searched 'til the body was found. A coffin was made by Geo. Alger & others out of a solid log of wood like a trough & lid, Hewn & smoothed up nice. The child was buried near the liberty Pole 27 of May 1848 . . . ." Pulsipher, "Diaries," 18.

50. The Second William G. Perkins Capt & Eliazer Miller & John D. Lee Capt 50. I was organized in Carns fifty

Sister Taylor wife of J. Taylor from Batavia N. Y. this spring died today of measles & was buried by Jacob Weatherbee's grave where some 4 or 5 were buried while we were here.

Friday June 2nd 1848. Prest Kimball crossed today. At 4 o'clock all the waggons on the other side of the river were crossed.

Capt Lee has had hard work to raise his 50. The people do not like to go with him. Zera Pulcifer starts today with his Company.

I was in the 4th Company of Carns 50 which were mostly police. We appointed A. L. Fulmer for our Captain of ten.

Today Elders Hyde & Woodruff accompanied by several more & some of the merchants from Winter Quarters made us a visit W. Woodruff took super with me when I spent an agreeable hour I stood guard till half past twelve.

Sat June 3rd 1848. Our 50 started this morning at 7 o'clock but did not go more than two miles before we put up for a hard rain. We camped here.

Sund June 4th 1848. Today we lay up because of wet weather.

Monday June 5th 1848. Started earley. The line of waggons was very long. Our ten in front where we travelled all the way.

To day Sister Groves who was very weak having been sick, fell out of her waggon which ran over her breast & leg which it broke & came near killing her

We put up for the night at the Liberty poll on the Platte at half past 3 o'clock.

Tues June 6th 1848. Fine day. Started in good time. Went 13¼ miles and stoped where the road joins the river

A meeting was called at dark to arrainge the order of traveling I was appointed Capt of the guard. We were to start at 7 a.m. and turn our cattle out to feed at half past three.

Wed June 7th, 1848. Hard S. wind all night, in the morning dark heavy clouds to the North like for rain. We went 12 miles to Shell Creek by noon & stoped for the night I stood guard the first tour. Rainy night.

Thurs June 8th, 1848. Cloudy disagreeable drizzling day untill noon. Lay up. Made out the guard roll today.

Friday June 9th, 1848. Travelled 12¾ miles to and stoped at Long Lak. Here was an abundance of Sweet flag or calemus a large quantity of which was geathered.

To day Oliver Duncan one of Prest Youngs Boys fell off the wagon toungue & the waggon ran over his leg & Broke it.

This evening I detailed the guard which was an uncommon long job where the carral encloses about ten or fifteen acres. It is all I can do after we stop untill dark.

Sat. June 10th 1848. Moved 18 miles. Stoped one or two miles this side of Looking Glass

Sund June 11th 1848. Lay up. Had a little meeting.

Journal of one year and 9 months wantin twelve days.

Mond June 12th 1848. Moved on. Crossed Beaver river at noon and encamped at the old Pawnee Station on Plumb cree[k] 14 miles. We heard from the advance Company today. Two Companies of which had crossed the Loup Fork.

Tues June 13th 1848. Passed the new station part of which is burnt down since last fall; all else looked about as it did last fall.

We crossed Cedar Creek at noon & went to the Upper pawnee village having travelled 16½ miles to day. It was late before all the teams came in to night. I was very sick with the head ache and was unable to detail the guard but left it to the two Captains of Fifties.

Wed June 14th 1848. Started earley & went to the Loup Ford at noon and carraled for the night. The advance Companies are nearley all over. one of Danl Miller's waggons Bogged in the quick sand.

Thurs June 15th 1848. Earley this morning a large number of teams were sent over from the other side of the river to assist us over. We were over by noon and encamped about one mile below the Ford. I got very wet. In the evening it rained very hard in which I had to detail the guard.

To day we heard from Kimballs Co who were at cedar Creek. After we left the Horn the Omaha made an attact on their cattle & horses. In trying to rescue them Br Ricks[78] & Egan were badly wounded. They in return wounded & perhaps killed some of them.

Frid June 16th 1848. Wet morning. Carns Company had carrelled wrong end to and this morning we changed ends. John Kays child died today. Heber's company came to the Ford today about two or three o'clock. Rainy afternoon and night. Very unpleasant weather.

Sat. June 17th 1848. This morning another large company of teams went over to assist Heber's company over. I returned about one or two to camp. Wet in the evening.

Sund June 18th 1848. Dark heavey clouds. Raining some. Had a meeting to day at Heber's camp. Jehu Cox's child was killed by a waggon running over it, between Cedar Creek & the Loup Fork Ford.

Lorenzo Snow & Zera Pulcifer's Cos encamped in the sand nobs but they had watter because of the heavy rains. Saml Meechan came to board with me today.

---

78. Thomas E. Ricks was just twenty years old at this time. John D. Lee reported on June 15, 1848, that George D. Grant had arrived with word that ". . . they had a batle on the Horn with the Indians in which 4 Indians were killed & two of the Brethr[en] wounded, Namely, Howard Egan & Bro Ricks." In his entry for the next day, Lee gave full details: Egan was shot in the wrist, and Ricks was struck in the back with a ball and two buckshot. Cleland and Brooks, *A Mormon Chronicle*, I, 39-40. See also the account in Egan, *Pioneering the West*, 140.

Thomas Edwin Ricks was born July 28, 1828, in Trigg County, Kentucky. He was baptized on February 14, 1845, and came to Nauvoo shortly after with his parents. He worked on the Nauvoo Temple until the exodus when he went as a teamster for Charles C. Rich as far as Council Bluffs. After receiving the wound mentioned here he was bedfast for more than a month.

Ricks' family located on North Millcreek in Salt Lake County. In 1849 he was sent back with an ox team to help in the migration; in the fall of that year, he went with the Parley P. Pratt exploring expedition to southern Utah. In 1856 he was sent with a company under William Bringhurst to the Las Vegas, Nevada, area to mine lead. Upon his return he went out to help bring in the ill-fated Martin handcart company.

In 1858 the family settled in Logan, and in 1882 Thomas E. Ricks was sent north to colonize the upper Snake River country in Idaho. He laid out the town of Rexburg and was prominent in the economic life of the whole area, establishing the first gristmill, the first sawmill, the first ferry across the Snake River, and the first store. Ricks College was named for him. For many years he was president of the Frémont Stake. He died September 28, 1901.

Monday June 19th 1848. We moved on today The ground soft & unpleasant travelling. The day was very hot. One ox of John Alger melted and died.

After a hard days tug over the sand nobs & soft ground between we arrived at prairie creek one hour after night but many teams did not get through and had to lay out in the prairie all night.

Tues June 20th 1848. Teams were coming into camp all night. We went on to Wood river where we arrived late.

Wed June 21st 1848. We had rather scant allowance of grass for our animals this morning We moved on to the place where the road runs to the river 14 miles.

Thurs June 22nd 1848. Drizzling day. Went on about 18 miles and carrelled on the high dry prairie some three miles from the River. Had to use the Bois de vache or Buffalo chips for fuel which were damp which made rather an unfavorable impression on our women relative to being entirely confined to them before we get to our journey's end.

Frid June 23rd 1848. Cool morning. Hard times for Breakfast because of our fuel. We traveled to Elm Creek 18 miles This is about the head of Grand Island and a few miles beyond the place I met the pioneers last fall Increased the guard.

Sat June 24th 1848. Cool morning. Moved about 10 miles, encamped in the prairie by a slough of clear watter using Buffalo chips for fuel again with better success as they are dryer.

To night W. J. Norten was tried for being found asleep on guard last night.

Sund June 25th 1848. Moved to the main Platte today 6 miles which is about 244 miles from Winter Quarters. Here we overtook the advance companies. We encamped away from the river & had to dig about two and half feet for water. There was a meeting today.

Mr Devlin a man who was spoken of while we lay up at Chariton ford was now lurking around and was now gone back to grand Island where the U. S. Soldiers were at work.
[Following entry crossed out]

Mond June 26th 1848. Lay up. Like for rain. Hebers company came up and stoped a mile or so above us Some stray mules were discovered and taken by A. Williams & others today on the other side of the river.

Tues June 27th 1848. Lay up. Hebers Co came today and stoped one mile or so above us. Some stray mules were discovered and taken by Alexr Williams & others on the other side of the river today.

Meeting at dark to Appoint men to hunt and kill Buffalo for the camp instead of men leaving their teams to run after them. Seth Dodge was tried tonight for being found asleep on guard.

Wed June 28th 1848. Moved on to day & corelled on Ptah Lake about 14 miles. All the Companies are in sight to night.

Thurs June 29th 1848. Moved on today about 14 or 16 miles camped on the river Banks higher than common. Large herds of Buffalo were seen all day on the other side of the river & a few were killed but not brought into camp. We now have occasionally sandy ridges to cross which is very hard on teams other wise the road is as usual.

Frid June 30th 1848. Moved on about 16 miles and encamped at the cold Springs (the most beautiful Springs here.) Oour road was over sandy bluffs which came up to the river. We are now fairley into the Buffalo range Swarms & herds of which are in sight all the time The range looks like an old pasture field the grass all fed off close.

The hunting fever seized on the brethren and they, regardless of the previous arraingements, to let hunters kill our meet often ran and left their teams pursuing & shooting at the buffalo all day. Many were killed & left out, & but few brought into camp.

Tonight about dark a skunk made us a visit Locating himself under my waggons. We endeavored to drive it away without exciting it but knowing the Power it held over us seemed perfectly tame while we had only to deal mildly with it. At length it went under Judge Phelps waggon & laid down in his harness where we were obliged to let it be in peace.

Saturday July 1st 1848. Went on. Had a Buffalo fight in the river. Saw 1000's of Buffalo today which moved as black clouds in the prairie. It is a sight not to be described & only to be realized by the sight

The people ran reckless and regardless to every principal of good order after them. Shooting them down and leaving them on the ground.

The President reproved the people for the course they had taken in running after the Buffalo and said he would have nothing more to do with it but every man might do as he pleased as they would not abide their own arraingements in hunting

It was long after dark before I could get the guard made out because the men were out after the buffalo.

How like a permanent location is the carral, formed every time alike. What a monotonous solitary feeling to go around every night in search of the guard

Sunday July 2nd 1848. Lay up 302 miles from W. Quarters. on the Platte. Many hunters out & some did not come in to night.

Monday July 3rd 1848. Went on about 18 miles and stoped after crossing the North Bluff Fork 6 rods wide & shallow.

Tues July 4th 1848. Moved on and again stoped on the Platte bottom.

To day is our Nation's annaversary or birth day of her liberty while we are fleeing exiles from her tyrranny & oppression.

Verry sick to night & all day.

Wed July 5th 1848. Hard on teams today passing over sandy bluffs. H. Gates upset one of his waggons on one but did not [injure] any body. The grass is still pastured very close by the buffalo looking like old pastured fields.

We encamped on Goose Creek 344 miles on our journey.

Thurs July 6th 1848. Nooned at the Cedar bluffs & went on 4 or 5 miles & encamped T. B. Foot & J. Ivie was courtmartialed tonight for being asleep or not on duty.

Friday July 7th 1848. Nooned near camp creek Passed wolf creek & then high sandy ridges and encamped on the West side.

Sat July 8th 1848. Went on and nooned at the Lone tree a well know land mark In the afternoon went to ash hollow and carraled for Sunday.

Opposite to us was a company of traders and Mormon Apostates who were returning to the States with their families[79]

---

79. The most detailed account yet found of this group of apostates was written by John D. Lee:

The general clerk of said company learned from 2 of their co., John Fields & David Stidham, That a co of 16 souls or gizards with 7 waggons, 12 oxen, 1 cow, 4 mules

Sund July 9th 1848. Lay up being about 380 miles on our journey. I was so sick with the head ache today that I kept my bed and could not detail the guard.

Monday July 10th 1848. I was some better but weak. Passed Sand Hill creek creek & stoped in the Prairie

Tues July 11th 1848. Moved on & stoped near Crab Creek It was ten o'clock before all came into camp. A few brethren met us to day from the Valley

Wed July 12th 1848. Moved on Passed Cobble hill from the top of which Chimney Rock is to be seen to the West

To night we put up opposite to ancient Bluff Ruins where we met some waggons which had come to meet us from the Valley[80]

Here was a large company of Sioux very friendly and altogether the best looking and neatest Indians I ever saw Proud spirited & seemed to disdain to beg & the men would seldom condescend to trade in small articles like moccasins but would have their Squaws do it. Had a meeting to night and agreed to lay up to morrow.

Thurs July 13th 1848. Lay up. Much trading with the Indians by the people. Hebers company came up. Tonight we had about the hardest rain I ever saw. It is peculiar to this country that there is now dews as in the States

Frid July 14th 1848. Today we moved on & some also who had come from the Valley & some from our company went back to the Bluffs with some teams, among those who went back was S. Meecham who had boarded with me.

Saturday July 15th 1848. Moved on and stopped opposite to Chimney Rock. Had to dig some 6 or 7 feet for water being about two miles from the river. We are now entirely out of the buffalo range.

& 3 poneys, became dissatisfied with the country themselves & Neighbours & left the valley on the 18th of May '48. Wm. Weeks & J. Fields left on the 8th, went up into the Mountains but could not cross on account of the snow drifts till about the 20th. (Names of the Heads of Families) John Fields, 7 in Family; Wm. Sears, 2 in Family, David Stidham, 3 in family; Wm. Weeks, 3 do. & 2 single men (SS) Loved Meeks & Benj. McBride. . . . They also Said that fear Seased hold of Wm. Weeks, from the fact that he had made way with Team & a waggon that had been left in his care by Pres. B. Y., having a mule Team rushed ahead to get out of the way before Pres. B. Y. should meet him, which he did by turning up the ash Hollow, it being the only Place where he could [turn?] off, on account of the Bluffs & shape of the country. All but Weeks seemed willing to & anxious to see the Pres. B. Y." (Cleland and Brooks, *A Mormon Chronicle*, I, 52-53.)

80. Writing under date of July 11, 1848, after giving a detailed description of the country and the streams, John D. Lee noted: "About 10 evening Some 4 Brethren from the vally came into Camp (SS) George Bean, Rufus Allen, Jas. Castro & Boice. Reported that about 20 waggons had reached Snou's [sic] co. from the vally Subject to Pres. B. Y.'s council & that whirlwind Band of Sioux were camped near Capt. Snou's co. on the opposite side of the River."

That the immigrants kept in touch with the Saints in the valley and received messages from them is shown by entries in the diaries of John D. Lee. On July 16 he wrote: "2ndly we want to Send 3 men to the valley with a mail. I have furnished a horse & a pack mule & fitted out John Green to go, & Bro. Kimble has fitted out Ben J. Rolf. Now an other man & Horse is wanted. Whereupon Cyrenan Taylor volunteered his Servises with his Horse."

The leaders in the valley had not waited for this word, but had dispatched mail carriers. On July 20 Lee wrote: "About 10 met an express from the vally to the Camp at Head Quarters carred by O. P. Rockwell, Horace Alexander, Lewis Robinson & [Scofield]. They brought firstrate news from the Land that the crops were promising."

Lee evidently did not know the name of the fourth messenger, but the next day learned it, for about noon he wrote: ". . . L. Robinson, Alexander, & Quincy Scofield, Messengers, returned [from visiting the rear emigration]. Q. Scofield rather concluded to drive Teams to the vally for Capt. Perkins, the other 2 with O. P. Rockwell to go to the vally." *Ibid.*, 55, 58, 63-64.

Sund July 16th 1848. Lay up and had a meeting at which the companies were divided Brighams into 4. Bishop Carns taking on[e] in which I of course fell as I belonged to it before.

Monday July 17th 1848. All moved on. Hebers company crossed over the platte this morning. We encamped nearley opposite to Scotts bluffs making rather a diminutive appearance now as Carn's company only consisted of two tens Fulmer's and Call's. It was here decided that I should continue Capt of the guard We had a hard rain in the evening.

Tues July 18th 1848. We traveled on and put up in a very large wet bottom of good grass We turned of to the river some 2 miles & stoped on the river banks This bottom was wet and strongly impregnated with alkali.

Wed July 19th 1848. Went on and nooned at a creek 200 yards south of the road on good grass and then travelled some 5 or 6 miles & turned south and put up where there was plenty of grass & timber While the Bishop went on further & stoped in the prairie This is the first timber on the N. side of the platte for the last 200 miles

Thurs July 20th 1848. To day we went to Raw Hide Creek having the heaviest sandy road we had since we started and no grass of any importance. To night we had no guard out for the first time after this we do not guard any more.

Friday July 21st 1848. This morning we recieved word from The President that he was crossing the river about two miles below us & desired us also to cross there as it was the best place. Accordingly we took the back track through the deep loose sand and crossed over & taking the Oregon road two or three miles all encamped together in a small bottom without much grass.

Larimie Peak has been in sight for the last three days. The Platte above here looses its wide shallow watters and is a narrow deep swift running stream of good water.

Sat July 22nd 1848. Went on a few miles and baited our cattle & proceeded on over a hilly & barren, land crossing Larimie Fork a deep swift handsome stream, & in a short distance we came to old Fort Larimie which is now in ruins The new Fort is two miles above on the Laramie Fork.[81]

After looking around the old Fort awhile to satisfy our curiosity we went on over barren & desolate looking bottoms some five miles and encamped on the river turning our cattle over on the other side for grass which was tolerable good. Sister Fulmer was delivered of a child to night.

Sund July 23rd 1848. Went on 4 or 5 miles to give room for the President & again turned our cattle across for grass.

Here was very high Buttes of marley lime stone. Several of us went to the top and enjoyed ourselves by rolling huge stone & dead sedar trees down their perpendicular side of some 2 or 300 feet.

---

81. Laramie was named for Jacques La Ramie, a French Canadian trapper who built a cabin near the junction of the Laramie and North Platte rivers in 1818. He was killed by Indians in 1822. In 1834 William L. Sublette began a fort on the Laramie River and left a part of his company behind to complete it. The place was named Fort Williams, perhaps to combine the names of William L. Sublette, William Anderson, and William Patton, all of whom were members of the expedition.

In 1835 it was sold to Milton Sublette, James Bridger, and Thomas Fitzpatrick, who soon sold it again to the American Fur Company. In 1836 the new owners moved up the river and built a larger fort of adobe which became Fort Laramie. In 1849 it was purchased by the U. S. government and became an important military post and a strategic point for all western travel. See Edgar M. Ledyard, "American Posts," *Utah Historical Quarterly*, III (April, 1930), 61-63. See also Roberts, *Comprehensive History*, III, 224-25.

Monday July 24th 1848. Moved 17½ miles today to Dead Timber creek where we found plenty of grass & water. We went over some very high Ridges of the Black Hills and passed one warm spring.

Tues July 25th 1848. We only moved about half a mile today to a small ravine which came out of the hills in which there was plenty of grass & watter where we recruited our cattle

Cap Call went on and did not any more travel with us. Had an evening rain.

Wed July 26th 1848. Moved on to Horse Creek 14 miles & 565 miles on our journey. Today we had high & steep ridges to cross. Here we met several of the brethren from the Valley on their way home They were mostly those of the Battalion.[82] All the companies were here togeather now & all turned out their cattle in the timber to run at large.

Thurs July 27th. Very rainy, boggy & cattle all out at random. All the camps lay up because of the hard rains and soft roads.

Friday July 28th 1848. Hard rain & hail in the night. We all made a general drive and brought in all the cattle at once and went on assending a hill ¾ of mile up where we had a fine view of the surrounding country & now about opposite to Larimie Peak which is to the left towering above the clouds.

We travelled 4¾ miles and stoped on a small creek where there is but little watter but good grass. Heber came in sight while we were on the hill. & Brigham passed one mile beyond us to night.

This evening we saw and had a hard chace after a buffalo for several miles but could not get near to it before dark.

The country to the left is very mountainous.

Sat July 29th 1848. Cattle look well this morning Went on over high hills 13 miles to the La Bonte which is a disagreeable looking stream of redish water and no grass. We had a very bad day being cold windy and cloudy.

Sunday July 30th 1848. Hard Frost last night and poor feed Went on today over the most barren & hilly road we have yet met with on our journey. Traveled 18½ miles to the A La Prele river where we found some grass but by no means plenty for the immense number of cattle which is now on it.

Monday July 31st 1848. Lay up. Some cattle strayed for the Platte but were recovered. Went with D. Carns hunting up the river. Passed an arch of stone which streched entirely across the river and over hung by very high hills of red sand stone.

The arch was more than 20 ft high. Passing up the stream we found that it broke through the high mountain in a rough & rugged current. There were fresh sign of Bear. We ascended a very high Peak from the top of which we discovered a very large grizzly bear on the edge of the watter & fired 4 rounds at him but only wounded him He made his escape by climbing the opposite hill From here we assended the next peak which was the highest in this vecinity from

---

82. This is the company known as Sam Brannan's mail express:

Among those of the Battalion who remained in California until 1848, were William Hawk, his son Nathan Hawk, Silas Harris, Sanford Jacobs, [Richard] Slater and another whose name is forgotten, who, together with four men who were not Latter-day Saints, were employed by Samuel Brannan to carry private mail from California eastward to emigrants journeying to California and Oregon, also to Salt Lake and Council Bluffs. They left San Francisco on the 1st of April, 1848, and passed Sutter's Fort on the 15th. . . . They were twenty-three days in traveling about forty miles. On reaching Salt Lake, Silas Harris remained there, and the others continued on." (Tyler, *History of the Mormon Battalion*, 341-42.)

which we could see to a great distance up this stream and found it wound its way along an appearently level plain untill it came to this mountain through which it seemed to force its way. Decending from this lofty Peak we came home when I found my wife sick and unable to set up for a moment with a verry severe attact of the mountain fever.

Tues Aug 1st 1848. Went on 8½ miles to the Fourche Boise River and encamped. Road some better today. Here we found plenty of grass about one mile up the river.

To night I had to be cook. My wife was worse with the fever.

Wed Aug 2nd 1848. I got breakfast this morning. Cattle look well. Wife yet very sick Went on. Passed Deer Creek, a beautiful place, and stoped 4 or 5 miles beyond turning our cattle over the Platte for grass. An uncommon hard wind storm arose in the evening and lasted an hour or so.

Thurs Aug. 3rd 1848. We had went only about 2 miles when one of my oxen took the blind staggers and died in a short time. Detained about an hour with him we went on to Crooked Mudy Creek & putting one of Carns oxen in my team went on several miles and put up again sending our catle over the river.

Frid Aug. 4th 1848. Went on to the Upper Ford of the North Fork and encamped. Here were several from the Valley who had come to meet us & had been also ferrying the Oregon Emegrants over the Platte.[83] There was good grass here when we first came. but the immense herds of all the camp soon consumed it all and left our cattle in a suffering condition.

Saturday Aug 5th 1848. Lay up as there had to be much reparing & also dispose of the waggons & teams which were from the Valley Prest Young proposed to assist me to another ox as my team was now broken.

This evening it was arrainged with me & Bp Carns for him to take his flour & Saml go with him which would lighten my load near 500 lbs in all and him go on as all were who were ready leaving more room & grass for our cattle who had yet to tarry.

Sunday Aug 6th 1848. This morning Carns and what few of his company were left with him went on & I & Josiah Arnold concluded to travil together and as my loading was considerably lightened for me to go with one yoke to each waggon & as his team was wore out for him to work my odd animal so as to release his partly and his boy Orson to drive one of my waggons & for us to travel no faster than our teams were able to go and try & make to the Sweet Water by the time President Young should get there. After which we went to let the Prest know that we would not now expect any assistance from him as he was scarce of teams.

We then returned & started on crossing the river at three trips and had hard drawing then. We then went on two miles & turned off to the river South & put up with Carn on a high bluff and turned our cattle over the river on good grass.

---

83. When the 1847 pioneers crossed the Platte River at this point in June, the water was so high that they were ferried over with difficulty. Since so many other westbound emigrants were on the road, Brigham Young detailed nine men to stay here, build a good boat, and operate a ferry. The group consisted of Thomas Grover, John S. Higbee, William A. Empey, Appleton M. Harmon, Edmund Ellsworth, Luke Johnson, Francis M. Pomeroy, James Davenport, and Benjamin Stewart. "The Mormon Ferry on the North Platte: The Journal of William A. Empey, May 7-August 4, 1847," edited by Dale L. Morgan, *Annals of Wyoming*, XXI (July-October, 1949), 111-67, gives details of this venture. For several years thereafter ferrymen were assigned to operate the ferry here during high water.

Now on August 4, the river was low enough that wagons forded it, though some said they had to prop the wagon boxes up on blocks to keep the contents from getting wet.

Monday Aug 7th 1848. Went on today our cattle done well last night. We went to Mineral Spring 10½ miles. I was very sick head ache today.

Tues Aug 8th 1848. Our cattle fared badly last night We had turned them out there being plenty of grass dow the stream and upon going down we found the whole land covered with a strong incrustation of saleratus & the water almost entirely alkali My two best oxen and one cow appeared as if they would not live an hour and every appearance indicated that I would be left without a team. This was the case with many more After giving the cattle some thing to work off the poison[84] we went on passing by a stray spring & lake of alkali. one of Arnold oxen was in the same fix.

We went about 14 miles today and my animals recovered.

Wed Aug 9th 1848. Our cattle fared badly last night for we only turned them out on a small patch of grass close around us their only chance and at dark tied them up to keep them from running away which they attempted to do. We went on two miles to the Willow Springs where there was tolerable good grass & turned out to bait them awhile and went on assending a very high hill from the top of which we had a fine view of the Sweet Water Mountains.

We had a rain this after noon which detained us awhile after which we went on makin about 13 miles today and had good grass for our cattle tonight which was the first good feed since we left the Platte on Monday morning.

In this vecinity the sage grows about 8 or ten feet high & some six inches in diameter, the largest I saw on the road.

Thurs Aug 10th 1848. Went on and encamped close by the West Side of Rock Independence. making 14 miles today & passing over very sandy and barren land also passed over the immense fields or lakes of saleratus where we laid in our stock of this article. Large lakes of which lay like fields of snow crusted sometimes six inches deep over the ground.

We were now on the banks of the Sweet Water where there was already many camps & plenty of grass.

This evening President Young came up. Better prospects were now before us. The Sweet Water Valley abounds in the best of grass It is almost marvelous how Br Arnold ever reached this place with our loads as we did over the worst road on the whole journey and such poor feed, but our cattle seemed to be in tolerable order and our hopes now brightened.

Friday Aug. 11th 1848. Lay up and explored Rock Independence from the sumit of which we had a commanding view of a large scope of country & a beautiful view of the extensive saleratus lakes like the new fallen snow.

We then went to a lake and geathered another lot of the best kind of saleratus.

Saturday Aug 12th 1848. Our catle having recruited we went on ten or 12 miles passing near by the Devils Gate a most singular curiosity where the river seems to break through perpendicular rocks 400 feet high. Curiosities are here too numerous for me to attempt to describe them. The Sweet Water Valley is now a most beautiful looking meadow and excellent grazing place and camps are now to be seen all along as we travel.

---

84. John D. Lee, writing on July 18, 1848, said: ". . . horses . . . supposed to be Poisoned by drinking the water that arrises from Salt Peter & Alkily. . . . One of Capt J D Lees & Perkins is also sick . . . [and were treated] by drenching him with ¼ of a lb of gun Powder same of salt and sweet milk enough to dilute it, then put down 1½ lb salt Pork."

For snake bites they were to "mix the spirits of Turpentine & Tobacco, wash the wound, and "Pray for the recovry of the Beast & start her on." Cleland and Brooks, *A Mormon Chronicle,* I, 51, 60.

Sunday Aug 13th 1848. Here I met with another very sad misfortune again. On going out to look for my cattle I found one of my oxen dead. He had manifested signs of not being well last evening when I turned him out. Every prospect now seemed to bid fair for me to make but slow headway

Meeting today. Prest Young wishes to go on so as to send back for those who can not help themselves Today the North wind blew uncommonly cold.

Monday Aug 14th 1848. This morning I obtained an odd ox from A. L. Fulmer as one of his had also died here & he obtained another yoke & thus I got unexpected help so as to travel just as I did, in slow time with Br Arnold So we went on 13 miles over a very heavy sandy road most of the way & stoped after dark on the Sweet Water.

Several cattle give out to day & were left dead by the road side.

Tues Aug 15th 1848. Slowly traveled on again 11¾ miles over deep sand part of the way having some times to rest the oxen evey few rods and again put up on the river having good grass.

Wed Aug 16th 1848. Went on crossing the Sweet Water three times making 9¾ miles & put up on the river again grass rather poor I traveled in Brighams ranks today.

Thursday Augt 17th 1848. Today we went 16½ miles I went mostly before and again stoped on the River having plenty of good grass. The express met us today from the Valley giving us the joyful information that a large number of teams and waggons were on the way to meet us.

Friday Aug 18th 1848. Went on ten miles. good grass Roads about as usual.

Saturday Aug 19th 1848. Went on over very high rough rocky ridges which was hard on men & teams Went 13¼ miles & encamped in a deep creek, a branch of the Sweet Water

To day I was taken with the Mountain Fever & suffered extreemly all night.

Sunday Aug 20th 1848. Our cattle fared poorley. I was unable to get up & very sick. Went on 7 miles to the Sweet Water & put up. My wife driving the team & me not able to raise up in my bed

Here the President concluded to send back the teams as there was an abundance of grass to enable us to lay up awhile

Monday Aug. 21 1848. I was yet very sick & suffering extremley.

Preperations were making to fit out those who were to go back & also reparing the waggons, unloading &c which gave very much of a business like appearance to the camp.

Tuesday Aug 22nd 1848. This morning I was able to get out of my bed but very weak

Some brethren came to day from Bridger & Smith's with Mackeson &c to trade to day. To the North is Mountain Peaks (the Wind river) to be seen covered with snow. They are I believe the Wind Mountains

Wednesday Aug 23rd 1848. Could walk around again. Frost & ice now every clear night.

Thurs Aug 24th 1848. Around. But weak

Friday Aug 25th 1848. Heard from Kimball's company to day. They were travelling very slowly. having to stop & send back for some waggons. He had lost many of his oxen.

Our cattle also had died at the rate of ten in one day since we came to this place

It is intended to send back & help up Hebers company.

Saturday Aug. 26th 1848. Several teams and waggons were sent for Heber to day.

A large drove of cattle took the back track & were pursued and over taken and put in the yoke at Hebers camp and worked back. Some of my oxen were among the rest. Wrote a letter to send back to A. J. Stout.

Sunday Aug. 27th 1848. Moved to a convenient place, out of the Carral, to unload one of my waggons preparitory to sending it back President Young went back to meet Heber to day.

Monday Aug 28th 1848. Herded cattle in the forenoon. More teams were sent back for Heber Lorenzo Young & several came in from the Valley & more on the way.

Tuesday Aug 29th 1848. Cattle which had died became so offensive that they had to be buried today

Wednesday Aug 30th 1848. Hunted my oxen in the fore-noon In the after noon 45 waggons and teams arrived from the Valley

Thursday Aug 31st 1848. President Young was taken sick today with something I suppose to be the Mountain Fever. Loading and distributing teams had now commenced.

The Presidency of the First Division or of Brighams Company to wit Isaac Morley, R. Cahoon & W. W. Major were set to alloting to each who needed the teams which were to assist them

Friday September 1st 1848. I went out to herd before breakfast and came in about ten during which time it had been raining smartly.

To day a waggon and two yoke of oxen had been set apart for me and Br E. H. Groves as we both had about enough to load it well. The team belonged to Bishop A. Hoagland & was driven by his son Peter.

We soon loaded up and started again on our journey. From here to the summit of the south pass the land is smartly rising (9¾ miles) so that it is difficult to know when you have gained the summit.

Just about the time we had fairley assended to the summitt we were met by a violent wind & snow storm soon turning into a still rain as it grew dark. We just had time to see the first ravine which conveyed the waters to the west before dark set in so that we had to decend to the Pacific Springs after dark traveling in a mild rain

We turned our cattle out in the dark not knowing where the range was. We had a disagreeable time of it for the wind arose from the North and blew cold all night.

Saturday Spr 2nd 1848. Very cold rainy morning & our cattle scattered and some not to be found. This was the situation with all those who were here & men were to be seen running to & fro in search of their teams.

We geathered up our teams at last and went on two miles to good grass and put up again during which time it was raining & blowing very cold.

Sunday Sept 3rd 1848. Went on 9 miles to day to Dry Sandy The water which is Brackish was now rendered by the late rains very good & our cattle done very well.

We met a few more teams from the Valley today. Snow Mountains rose very high to the North as we went on.

Monday Sept 4th 1848. Went on 13¾ miles to the Litle Sandy   Had plenty of grass & done well.

Tuesday Sep. 5th 1848. Went on 8¼ miles to Big Sandy & our cattle done tolerable well again.

Wednesday Sep. 6th 1848. Went on 17 miles to day and again put up on the Big Sandy.

Clear warm and pleasant but the Snow Mountains are still in view   These are the Wind river Mountains and Fremont's Peak.

Our cattle did not do very well for grass. Brighams Company passed us to day.

Thursday Sep. 7th 1848. Went on to Green River and crossed over.   It is a swift bold & rocky stream   We staid all night here & had plenty of grass.

Friday Sep 8th 1848. Only went 5 miles down the river & again put up.   Hebers company passed this evening

Saturday Spet 9th 1848. Went on over a hilly & Barren country 15½ miles and encamped on Blacks Fork   good grass for our animals.

Sunday Sep 10th 1848. Went on 12 or 13 miles and again put up on Black Fork. Had tolerable grass

Monday Sep 11th 1848. Went on and again put up on Blacks Fork 8¼ miles before we came to Fort Bridger.   Had a rain in the night.

Tuesday Sep 12th 1848. Arrived at Fort Bridger about noon   Brighams Company was there. We traveled about 9 miles further and put up where we had plenty of good grass. Rained in the evening & night.

Wednesday Sep 13th 1848. Moved on passing down a very steep hill in the morning which was rendered dangerous by the late rain.

To day we passed a curious copperas Spring & to night encamped on the top of the dividing ridge between the waters of Green River and Bear river 7700 feet above the level of the sea.

Clear & cold but good grass. We met several returning to the States to day

Sep 14th 1848. Thursday. This morning we arose earley and found that it was snowing rapidly & so we hurried on to decend out of the clouds & made our decent down a very steep hill for near two miles   our teams litterally slid down but the road was good.

We overtook Brighams Company at Sulphur Creek & then turned out and Baited our cattle awhile and then went to Bear river where we put up for the night. Weather now warm & pleasant.

Friday Sep 15th 1848. Went to Echo Creek 16¾ miles to day. Had good grass.

Saturday Sep 16th 1848. Travelled down this Creek 14 miles   It has many very bad crossings   We over took Bishop Carns to night   who had been detained by the sickness of his wife who was drawing her last breath when we came and died about sun set.

Sunday Sept 17th 1848. Went to the Weber & crossed over to day.   One of Hoaglunds oxen was dead this morning which left us very weak for teams.   Our road was uncommonly bad to day having to cross the creek many times.

We over took Br Arnold to night & nearley all the camp who had waited here for the President to come.

This evening the President passed on some three miles and encamped in a small branch up which he had to ascend the next Mountain.

Monday Spt 18th 1848. All started this this morning The Prest ahead. The road was crouded for miles having to waite for hours at bad crossings We arrived on Kanyon Creek 10 miles tonight & had to turn our cattle on the hills for grass. Many were camped here.

Tuesday Sep 19th 1848. We travelled up Kanyon Creek 10 miles crossing it 13 times This road was very hard on cattle.

Leaving the Creek we commenced ascending another high mountain & traveled up a Cannon about two miles & stoped having no grass & had to turn our cattl near a mile & a half down where they ascended to the top of the mountain and had tolerable grass.

Wednesday Sept 20th 1848. Five of our oxen was not to be found this morning. With the rest got my & Hoaglunds waggons to the top of the mountain. Stormy Rainy night.

Thursday Sep 21st 1848. Rainy disagreeable morning & I was growing very tired of my "Exalted Station".

After breakfast we went in search of our lost cattle which we found after a long hunt through high wet weeds & watery ground meanwhile our other cattle had got a good feed of grass.

We then brought Br Groves to the top of the mountain which is the highest one we had to ascend on this journey.[85] Here we had a view of the south part of the Valley & like old Moses could "View the landscape o'er" while many hills and bad roads yet intervened. Teams had been passing all the time we had been here.

At noon we commenced our decent which was very steep and down which Groves broke his waggon toungue out whereupon I took the animals & went on 6 miles to get grass leaving him to go back after in morn.

Friday Sep 22nd 1848. This morning while we were geathering up our oxen to go back after Br Groves we were agreeably disappointed to see him drive up having fixed in his waggon toungue again & borrowed some oxen of those who were coming on as it was down hill all the way & thus came on so we all traveled on again and crossing another mountain we at last came to Little Kanyon Creek the last one we had to cross which was a bad road having to cross it about 18 times over bad places and at night encamped at the mouth of the Cannon 5 miles from the City and turned our cattle agan on the mountains for feed waited with impatience for morning which would terminate our journey.

---

85. This was the top of Big Mountain, from which immigrants got their first view of the Valley of the Great Salt Lake. Other diarists have also described the valley as it first appeared to them.

   Aside from the Forts, there was but one house in the whole valley. The forts were built on a square covering about 10 acres each and adjoining each other. Three completed and the fourth was in process of building and nearly finished. The east side of the old fort which the pioneers built was of logs; the remainder was of adobe or as they are commonly called "do-by" . . . which are a large species of brick baked or dried in the sun; they are quite hard and have been known to last near 200 years. On the north, south, east and west was a large gate to each fort. The outside wall of the fort was the outside wall of the houses. Thus properly, the forts were formed by the joining of houses, and windows were regular bilt portholes. (Oliver B. Huntington, Journal, 43.)

John Pulsipher gives a few more details:

   We arrived in Salt Lake City on the 22 of Sept . . . . The city at this time consisted of 2 blocks 40 rods square & a half block 40 by 20 rods., all joining. These blocks were inclosed by joining houses in the form of a fort. These forts were built by the People that came last year, while their numbers were small they built so they could defend themselves against Indians in case of need. Besides these forts there was a small saw mill & a corn cracker for a grist mill & a small house by each mill, which was the amount of the building in this country at the time of our arrival. (Pulsipher, "Diaries," 25.)

I was very sick all day with the head ache which made this a tedious day for me.

Saturday Sep 23rd 1848. Dark heavy clouds overhung the mountains & Valley this morning We started earley & was overtaken by a hard rain & wind which extended over the valley. Our road was smartly desending all the way to the City. But we could not enjoy the view of the place because of the dark rain.

We passed through the Forts & encamped on the west side where there were hundreds of waggons already encamped and after driving my cattle out to grass, took a reconnoisance of the place.

The rain had now ceased & I saw that the mountain top were covered with fresh snow which fell while it rained here. All the houses built were in the Forts of which there were 3 adjoining each other and half mile long by 40 rods about. Here the entire people lived but a few scattered about.

Sunday Sep 24th 1848. Went to meeting which was held under a large Bowery[86] where a very large congregation of Saints met. Here I had the satisfaction to meet many of my old friends who had gone on last year & also of those who had been in the Batalion

President Young spoke commending the people here for their industry and his good feeling & joy in being able to come here in safety That this is the place he had seen before he came here & it was the place for the Saints to geather.

The afternoon was resolved into a conference meeting & decided to have a general conference on the Sixth of October next. Also to remove the mills & other works on city Creek as it fouled the water which would have to be used by the people for cooking and other purposes Also to live in a Compact and not scatter abroad.

Presidents Young & Kimball were appointed a committee to set apart to each one their lots both in the City & also for farming all thing went off well & with a good Spirit.

Warm fine day but rained in the evening.

Temple Block ten acres.

Lat N. Side 40° 45' 44" Long. " " 111° 26' 34"

Altitude 4,300 feet. Variation 15° 47' 23" East. From Winter Quarters as pr W. Claytons Roadometer, 1031 miles. I was 130 day on the road.

Thus ends this long and tedious journey from the land of our enemies. & I feel free and happy that I have escaped from their midst. But there is many a desolate & sandy plain to cross. Many a ruged sage bed to break through. Many a hill and hollow to tug over & Many a mountain & Cañon to pass. and many frosty nights to endure in mid-summer.

---

86. While all the 1847 group were working toward the erection of homes or the planting of crops, "the battalion contributed to the community service by erecting a bowery 40 x 28 feet under which to hold religious worship on the ensuing Sabbath day. . . ." Roberts, *Comprehensive History*, III, 285. For many years this outdoor meeting place served during the warm weather.

ON THE MORMON FRONTIER

The Diary of Hosea Stout
1844–1889

HOSEA STOUT

1810-1889

From a photograph, about 1885

ON THE
MORMON FRONTIER

Volume Two
1848–1889

EDITED BY

JUANITA BROOKS

UNIVERSITY OF UTAH PRESS
UTAH STATE HISTORICAL SOCIETY
Salt Lake City

ON THE MORMON FRONTIER

Contents

PART I

September 25, 1848 to August 27, 1852

SEPTEMBER 25, 1848 TO AUGUST 27, 1852

Part I

This part of the diary covers the period from September 25, 1848, to August 27, 1852. It tells of Hosea Stout's preparations for the first winter in Utah — securing fuel and building shelter. Stout went on an expedition against the Indians, served in the legislature, and defended men in court. His record gives details of resolutions and laws made in the territorial legislature, in which Stout was an active and effective member.

Monday Sep 25th 1848. Hunted my cattle this morning to the North West. The land here is swampy and rich soil.

This evening I move into the North Fort and encamped near to Genl Rich taking my wagon bed off so as to get the use of my waggon to draw wood on.

Tuesday Sep 26th 1848. To day was occupied in arrainging my loads &c.

Wednesday 27th 1848. Went and got a load of wood from the Red Butte Cañon which takes all day. From the high Bench lands near the Mountains you can see the broad blue waters of the Salt Lake.

Thursday Sep 28th 1848. Went after another load of wood Elder A. Pratt[1] returned to day from the Society islands where he had been five years having been sent by the Prophet Joseph.

Friday Sep 29th 1848. Went earley after another load of wood & returned to the Cañon and staid all night with the intention of making two lods tomorrow. Br W. Chapman was with me.

Saturday Sep 30th 1848. We were up earley & came home with our wood but learned at the same time that one load was sufficient for one day & did not go back but went to a meeting of the High Council.

---

1. Addison Pratt, born February 21, 1802, at Winchester, New Hampshire, had been called on a mission to the Pacific Islands by Joseph Smith in 1843. At the end of one year, he was sent again by Brigham Young, this time to take his family. In 1852 the French government ordered the missionaries home, so the Pratts returned to California, stopping first in San Francisco and then moving to San Bernardino. At the time of the Mormon War, Mrs. Pratt and her two younger daughters returned to Utah, but Addison and their two married girls remained in California. He died in Anaheim, California, October 14, 1872.

The "Journal of Louisa Barnes Pratt," published by the Daughters of Utah Pioneers in *Heart Throbs of the West*, VIII (1947), gives an illuminating account of the family.

A petition was presented requesting leave to cut all the timber both green & dry within 30 miles of this place and bring it in this winter which after some opposition passed. It had hitherto been unlawful to cut any green timber. Also decided to pay tithing. A plan to form in a Big Field also commenced. After Council I went to the "Land office" and had my city Lot set off to me which was in the North East of the City, which was
    Block 73, Lot 4.[2]

Sunday Oct 1st 1848. Very unwell today. Went to meeting. Addison Pratt spoke giving a relation of his mission to the Society isles which was very interesting. He has done a good work there. He was followed by Elder Kimball In the after noon President Young addressed the Soldiers & related to them the reasons why they were sent in the army. After he spoke Capt Hunt spoke at length contradicting some things that had been said aginst the Battalion

Monday Oct 2nd 1848. Not well. Went and got another load of wood and deposited it on my Lot.

Tuesday Oct 3rd 1848. Brought in another load of wood Last night there was frost which killed considerable corn and other vegitables.

Wednesday Oct 4th 1848. Another load of wood. Rained some A few of Amasa Lymans Company came in today. Wet night.

Thursday Oct. 5th 1848. Wet and cold day. We had to retreat into C. C. Rich house to warm. After the rain ceased I was around and went up city Creek to the mills.

Friday October 6th 1848. Hard Frost last night & cold day Conference met and adjourned till Sunday. Some of the soldiers came in from Caliafornia.[3] The soldiers had a large feast to day in the Bowery.

Saturday Oct. 7th 1848. Went for wood again.

Sunday Oct. 8th 1848. Conference met. The authorities passed the usual ordeal. Father John Smith appointed Patriarch of the whole Church & C. C. Rich Prest of this place & John Young & Erastus Snow his councillors
    The Prest then spoke against [Horace] Gibbs & [Andrew] Cahoon speculations in goods. D. Pedigrew A. L. Fulmer E. Gardner & myself &c were appointed to take up all loose cattle and put into a stray pen the owners to pay 50 cents for each animal put in which was for our pay for doing the same This was done because cattle were let run at large often breaking into and destroying the grain & other

---

2. The lot which Hosea Stout drew was on Second East just off South Temple Street. The site is presently occupied (1964) by the Freed Motor Company in Salt Lake City.

3. This group of Mormon Battalion men were among those who had re-enlisted and had been at Sutter's Mill when gold was discovered there. They left on July 2, 1848, and on July 10 organized, naming Jonathan Holmes, president, and Samuel Thompson, captain: "The company numbered about 37 individuals, all told, with 16 wagons and two small Russian cannon, which they had purchased before leaving Sutter's, one a four, the other a six-pounder. The cost of these was $400 . . . . In addition to the outfit already named, they subsequently obtained about one hundred and fifty head of horses and mules, with about the same number of horned stock, consisting of work oxen, cows and calves . . . ." Daniel Tyler, *A Concise History of the Mormon Battalion in the Mexican War, 1846-47* ([n.p.], 1881), 336-37.

The group had no road and no guide, but explored as they went. Within a few days travel, they found the remains of three of their comrades, David Browett, Henderson Cox, and Daniel Allen, who had tried to get to the Valley of the Great Salt Lake, but had been killed by Indians. The road marked out by this group became the highway over which thousands of emigrants would make their way during the following years. These men also brought the first gold dust into Salt Lake City.

eatables and every thing that could be had been said to prevent it & this kind of a force put was then adopted to preserve the grain This very much resembled the Winter Quarters regulations.

My temporal arraingements were now very much altered & I now had to abandon for the time being the idea of building on my lot as I was about to do.

Monday Oct 9th 1848. Occupied all day in driving up cattle we drove near 70 head today which were found in the fields. Amasa Lyman Came in this evening

Tuesday Oct 10th 1848. Occupied as on yesterday.

Wednesday Oct. 11th 1848. Occupied as above. In the last evening 3 young men, Marshall Hunt, son of Capt J. Hunt William Boren and Jesse Earl brought in 10 horses which they had loosed and brought here for the purpose of getting pay for bringing in. This morning the owners came protesting they had been loosed & we gave them up & after cross questioning the men who brought them in we made them confess it & also had them go and acknowledge the same to President Rich & upon their promise to do better let them go.

I then went with Elias Gardner to the Jordan cow hunting. The Jordain is a beautiful stream running from the Utah to the Salt Lake.

Thursday Oct 12th 1848. More of Amasa's company came today Stray penning as usual.

Friday & Sat Oct 13th & 14th 1848. Around the fields & Adobe yards driving up cattle &c as usual.

Sunday Oct 15th 1848. Stray penning as usual and at Conference. A. Pratt spoke in relation to his mission, giving us a specimen of the Tihitian Language which was very interresting to us all.

In the afternoon Andrew Cahoon spoke endeavoring to show that he did not intend to gull & take advantage of his brethren as the President had spoken of last sunday. His sermon was a succession of repetitions for about an hour none of which anyone that I heard say anything about believed one word that he said except that he said he was a "chip out of the old Block" I. E. like his father which every one believed. to be true

Monday Oct. 16th 1848. Stray penning as usual. The five acre Lots of farming land being now surveyed were disposed of by casting lots for them. I drew one beautifuly situated on Block   Lot[4]

Tuesday Oct 17th 1848. Stray Penning as ever. Another lot of Amasa Lymans Company came in today, the most of them went down South on the Cottonwood. Rainey afternoon & uncomfortable for those who are out without houses.

Wednesday Oct. 18th 1848. Stray Penning yet. Jesse Turpin & J. T. Packer each [took] some cattle unlawfully from the possession of the stray pen keepers today for which charges were prefered against them.

Thursday Oct. 19th 1848. Still Stray Penning. Tonight Packer was tried before Bishop Lewis for taking oxen unlawfully yesterday & fined five dollars.

Friday Oct 20th. Occupied at the Stray pen operations

Saturday Oct. 21st 1848. Stray Penning yet. Capt Hunt whose oxen were taken out of the field today, when he came for them swelled very largely denouncing the

---

4. The exact location of Hosea Stout's farm has not yet been found.

law & swore he would send some of us to eternity if we put any of his cattle in again &c A charge was also prefered against

Sunday Oct 22nd 1848. Stray penning and at meeting of conference. The laws was repealed and the Judges were to decide according to the justice of the case only being bound by what was right & not law.[5]

Mond Tues & Wed Oct 23 24 & 25 — 1848. Stray Penning as usual though not well. Have snow & rain some.

Wednesday Oct 26th 1848. Wet & rainy. Have pity on the housless Stray penning & at dark met at Bp Lewis to attend the trial V. S. Turpin & Hunt. Turpin settled & Hunt not present. Come home in the rain.

Friday Oct 27th 1848. While driving up cattle to day riding a mule it fell down with me in the level road and badly hurt one of my legs which laid me up.

Saturday Oct. 28th 1848. Not able to drive but attended to the pen. Council tried Br Shepherd for robbing a store in Missouri but did not sustain anything against him

Sunday Oct 29th 1848. Occupied as usual and at meeting B. Young spoke against persons who scatter off from the main body & denounced those who were trying to locate a farm on the other side of Jordin. He said that all such were opperating against the will of God & if they did not cease he would grant to them their desires & let them go to hell &c. In the evening the Eleventh Quorum of Seventies met but few attended No business was transacted.

Monday & Tues Oct 30 & 31, 1848. Driving cattle out of the fields. John Robinson raised a scrape about his cows being taken up who also had a charge prefered against him The 31st Hunts trial came on again but he settled it

Wednesday Nov 1st 1848. Moved into a house which I bought of E. Gardner for 40 dollars. It is in the Middle Fort and 4 doors North of the West gate. Worked hard today. The house is about 14 by 18 ft & is plenty of room for me.

Thursday Nov. 2nd 1848. Busied today at "Setting my house in order" Snow on the mountains.

Frid & Sat Nov 3 & 4 1848. Stray penning as usual

Sunday Nov 5th 1848. Went to meeting. Heber spoke & Father Kempton & was followed by President Young

Mon Tues & Wed Nov. 6, 7 & 8 1848. Stray penning as usual. Cattle destroys an abundance of corn

Thurs & Frid Nov. 9 & 10th 1848. Stray penning as usual. and also lay a temporary floor in my house

Sat. Nov 11th 1848. Stray penning. This evening President Young informed E. Gardner that the Council met today and concluded to stop the stray pen laws

---

5. At the conference of October 8, the rule had been adopted that the four officers were authorized to "take up all loose cattle and put into a stray pen the owners to pay 50 cents for each animal put in which was for our pay for doing the same." In the weeks following so many cattle had been brought in that the rule was modified and the "judges were to decide according to the justice of the case only being bound by what was right & not law." Evidently the fine was to be decided in part by the damage done by the stray animal.

and also had imposed a fine of 25 dollars on any one of the Council who divulged the same as they wished to let the force of the law do all the good possible after it was repealed.

Sunday Nov. 12th 1848. Damp rainy morning & I was mostly at home to day.

Monday Nov 13th 1848. Occupied at preparing to work in the Cañons, drawing out wood & timber.

Tues Nov. 14th 1848. Went & brought a load of wood from the Red Buttee.

Wednesday Nov 15th 1848. Around trying to buy some hay. John Scott came on today.

Thursday Nov 16th 1848. at home (Drew some hay which I bought about two miles to the south. [crossed out])

Friday Nov 17th 1848. Drew some hay which I had bought about two miles south.

Saturday Nov 18th 1848. Went to the North Cañon near 12 miles and brought a load of wood,[6] passing several warm & one hot spring on the way. The water is sulpher & considerably salt It was a very hard days work.

Sunday Nov 19th 1848. Went to meeting Taylor & Amasa spoke against thieves and those who take advantage in deal called gouguers.

Monday Nov 20th 1848. Went to North Cañon for wood & returned West of the warm Sprin Lake which is a better road arrived at home after dark.

Tues Nov. 21st 1848. Working at home all day.

Wednesday Nov 22nd 1848. Went after a load of wood Rained most of the time. Arrived home at dark My wife had been very sick to day.

Thursday Nov 23rd 1848. At home. Snowing on the Mountains & Cloudy dark day here.

Friday Nov 24th 1848. Around home doing nothing

Saturday Nov 25th 1848. Went after another load of wood

Sunday Nov 26th 1848. Went to meeting J. Taylor & J. M. Grant spoke on the subject of our being good and godly. President Young said that they were about raising a company to explore this country under the direction of Amasa Lyman. That when men were wanted they would be called on and they would be expected to obey and that it was not the way for men to volunteer &c
He said he wanted the council house to done as soon as possible

Monday Nov 27th 1848. Went to work on the Stone Quarry 7 miles East. in company with Bishop Lewis.

Tues & Wed Nov 28 & 29 1848. Worked on Stone Quarry as before.

Thursday Nov 30th 1848. Worked on Quarry till noon & came home being very sick.
To day a company came in from the bluffs bringing the mail, & among them was John Gheen who was in prison when we left for shooting Br Conditt at Point

---

6. North Canyon is in the vicinity of the present town of Bountiful, Utah.

au Pool. He had been discharged because of an error in the writ. They met Allen Taylor & C. at the Horn & Egan &c at Larimie all well.

Friday Dec 1st 1848. Cloudy day. Went to the office. There were a large number of letters in the office from the States.
Worked at home in the afternoon. Rained some in the evening & night

Saturday Dec 2nd. Worked on Quarry.

Sunday Dec 3rd 1848. Fine pleasant morning. Went to meeting which was occupied by the Clerk reading news from the States untill 3 o'clock. The minutes of the Conference on 6th of Oct at the Bluffs were read which shows all things to be in a moust prosperous & flourishing situation. Crops of all kinds had yielded an abundance & a general state of good health prevailed among the saints and amongst them since we left they had universal peace & good order.
In a letter from George A. Smith we learn that on the 4th of July last the people of Nauvoo borrowed a cannon from Carthage to celebrate the day & that night it left & was only tracked to the river where no doubt it passed through the cerimonies of immersion & he thought it would be wending its way west in search of new adventures. Also that the renowned Mobecratic Editor Thomas C. Sharp was now a ferryman at Warsaw. Also that there were now five Candidates out for the Presidency and among the rest was Martin Van Buren who came out at the head of a new party cald the "Free Soil" party or Barn Burners" which is composed of all the apostate poleticians of both parties, abolitionists &c and that he was likely to run a good poll to be elected. Their motto is to Burn the Barn and drive the rats out &c"
Matty will well grace their head.[7]
Also that Pottewattamie County was organized and at the Election they went the Whig ticket which greatly engrage the democrats who said that Hyde had been bribed by the Whigs & both Hyde & the Whigs denies it. That Ebenezer C. Richerson while returning from the election held at the Raccoon Fork stole an old mare & was followed overtaken & shot through the body the horse retaken & he left supposed to be mortally wounded but had recovered.
A Proclamation was read from Lyman Wight & Bishop George Miller, Calling on all the people to geather to them on the Rio Colorado about 75 miles from Austin Texas. It is a long document & contains some foul insinuations against the Twelve. It breaths a dishonest, low, and mean, Spirit and was recieved as such by the saints both here & at the Bluffs
Oliver Cowdery, David Whitmore & W. E. McLelland were trying to raise up the kingdom again. also William Smith. But the "Sound of their grinding is low" They are all waiting for the Twelve & Presidncy to fall.[8]

---

7. This important entry tells much of conditions at Kanesville, Iowa, the Mormon headquarters. "Matty" is evidently a nickname used in derision of Martin Van Buren.

8. This notation is interesting in view of the fluctuating reputation of Oliver Cowdery among the Mormons, especially concerning the fact that between 1872 and 1884, more than twenty years after his death, there were published stories and affidavits tending to show that he died a faithful member of the church. Many of these were published by Andrew Jenson in his [Church of Jesus Christ of Latter-day Saints] *Historical Record*, VI (January, 1887), 196-203.
George A. Smith's letter here, reporting that on October 6, "Oliver Cowdery, David Whitmore & W. E. McLelland were trying to raise up the Kingdom again . . . ." is contradicted by one dated October 31, 1848, also written by George A. Smith, which said that: ". . . Brother Reuben Miller and Bro. Baxter made a full confession that they had been mired in Strangism, and wished to be received into full fellowship by the Saints . . . . Peter Haws and the 'Pagan Prophet' having returned from Texas reported very unfavorably of Lyman Wight's prospects, . . . Oliver Cowdery who had just arrived from Wisconsin with his family, on being invited, addressed the meeting." *The Latter-day Saints' Millennial Star*, XI (Liverpool, 1856), 14.

After the news was read the case of Lyman [Wight] was taken up and he & all who were with him were cut off from the church as the Saints at the Bluffs also done at the conference.

In the evening I went to the Council. Savage & Snedeker had a case up. & Br Lawson tried to get a rehearing on a case against him for killing a cow but could not. The president explained the object of the exploring expidition now being raise. which was to look out a good place to locate a settlement on the gulf & California & a road from thence to this place. Hard snow this evening.

Monday Dec 4th 1848. Worked at home. Cold day.

Tues Decr 5th 1848. Extremly cold & clear. Went to the office and first heard of the move to petition to the Gov for a Terl Govt here.

Wednesday Decr 6th 1848. Cold as ever. I with others went in search of stone cole in the mountains over the warm Spring and was gone all day.

Thursday Decr 7th 1848. Cold as ever. At home and at the office

Friday Decr 8th 1848. Went alone to explore the mountain ridge immediately South of Emmegration Cañon and followed the ridge almost to the summit when the snow became too deep for traveling when I come down & arrived at home about sunset. Clear warm day but cold night.

Saturday Decr 9th 1848. Started to go back the ridge again but it was too cold & so I returned and went to the office and read.

Sunday Decr 10th 1848. Tolerable warm but snowed hard in the after noon. At home untill evening & went to the latter part of the Council

It was decided here to reduce the price of beef to 2½ cents pr pound on foot and sell it out at 3 and 3½ pr pound. This was not to be a law but all present agreed to do it themselves & use their influence to have others do so too. Signing a petition for a Terl Govt was also circulating. Also passed a law granting a bounty of one dollar each on wolf skins and for J. M. Grant to recieve them.

Another letter in the same issue of *The Millennial Star*, page 43, also contains word of the confession of Oliver Cowdery. Signed by Wilford Woodruff and dated Cambridge Port, U. S. A., December 26, 1848, it says: "Dear Brother Pratt: I received a letter from Elder Hyde, saying that Oliver Cowdery had come to the Bluffs with his family; had made satisfaction to the Church, who had voted to receive him into the Church by baptism; and Elder Hyde was expected to baptize him the next day. He was assisting Elder Hyde to put the press in operation for printing, expecting to send forth the Frontier Guardian soon . . . . I was truly glad to hear he had returned to the fold."

Yet on December 11, 1848, Orson Hyde himself wrote directly to Orson Pratt in England and made no mention either of the confession or the baptism. The *Frontier Guardian* (Kanesville, Iowa) made its appearance on February 7, but made no mention of the Cowdery visit, confession, or baptism. Nor did it record his death some fifteen months later though it normally printed death notices.

On June 15, 1850, the *Deseret News* (Salt Lake City), on a back page and without any striking headline did record the death: "We are informed that Oliver Cowdery, Esq., died at Richmond, Ray County, Missouri on the 3rd day of March last, of consumption."

All of these contemporary facts seem to nullify the later stories of Cowdery's reconciliation. The picture is all the more clouded by the appearance in Utah in 1857 of a purported "Confession of Oliver Overstreet," which began with the statement that "I personated Oliver Cowdery at Council Bluffs, Iowa on the 21st of October, 1848, in a conference at which Bro. Orson Hyde presided," and continued with the story of how he was persuaded to do this by Reuben Miller, who "insisted that I resembled Cowdery so much in form and features . . . that I could easily personate him without danger of being caught and exposed." "A Confession of Oliver Overstreet [October 21, 1848]" (typescript, Utah State Historical Society). See also, William Woodward, "Reminiscences of Elder Orson Hyde," *The Juvenile Instructor*, XXXV (March 15, 1900), 192.

Monday Decr 11th 1848. Warm & mild but a deep snow & now clear. Reading at the office in the fore noon & then at home.

Tuesday Dec 12th 1848. Tremendious snow storm in the fore noon. At home all day.

Wednesday, Dec 13th 1848. At home and at the office where I first saw our new gold coin which is perfectly plain only has the price 10 dollars 50 cents on it.[9]

Thursday Decr 14th 1848. Hard S. Wind all day. At home.

Friday Decr 15th 1848. At home all day.

Sat & Sund Decr 16 & 17th 1848. Hard S. Wind which nearly dried the snow without wetting the ground much. Mostly at home.

Monday Decr 18th 1848. A Beautiful clear snow fell last night two inches deep but still & pleasant all day. At home.

Tues, Wed, Thurs, Frid, Sat, Dec. 19, 20, 21, 22, and 23, 1848. During this time the weather was about one thing only snowin some, but mild. I was mostly at some times at Chrismans [Crismans] Mill, in the office &c

Sunday Decr 24th 1848. At home. Snowed to day. I learned today that John Pack and J. d. Lee had lead out to see who should kill the most crows & other noxious vermin each to choose 100 men and the party who killed the least number, counting the first of Feb next was to pay for a dinner for both parties &c I also learned that I was chosen on Lee's side but I declined to accept the office not feeling very war-like at this time.[10]

Monday Dec 25th 1848. At home. Weather as usual. The young people have a most happy Christmas as some four or five Couple are daily led to the alter of Hymen about this time.

Tues & Wed Decr 26 & 27th 1848. Everything goes about as usual. I am mostly at home trying to do without coffee which goes very hard.

---

9. Mention has been made of the gold dust brought in by the Mormon Battalion members. The waste which attended its handling prompted the leaders to coin it. This began on December 10. . . . Brigham Young, John Taylor, and John Kay worked out the inscription . . . . On the one side the phrase "Holiness to the Lord" would encircle the emblem of the Priesthood, which was a three-point Phrygian crown over the All-seeing eye of Jehovah. On the other side, the words "Pure gold" and the denomination would encircle clasped hands, the emblem of friendship. The stamps for the coin were engraved by Robert Campbell . . . . This effort at coinage, however, proved a failure. The crucibles were broken for all the dies by December 22, 1848. (Leonard J. Arrington, "Coin and Currency in Early Utah," *Utah Historical Quarterly,* XX [January, 1952], 56-76.)

10. At a meeting of the Council of Fifty (YTFIF) held at the house of Heber C. Kimball: The wasters and destroyers was taken into consideration, to wit, the wolves, wildcats, catamounts, Pole cats, minks, Bear, Panthers, Eagles, Hawks, owls, crow or Ravens & magpies, which are verry numerous & not only troublesome but destructive. $1000s of dollars worth of grain & stock have already been destroyed by those Wasters, & to check their career it was thought best to have a Hunt. Accordingly Pres. B. Young nominated J. D. Lee & John Pack captains to carry on a war of extermination against the above-named wasters and destroyers. (Robert G. Cleland and Juanita Brooks, eds., *A Mormon Chronicle: The Diaries of John D. Lee, 1848-1876* [2 vols., San Marino, 1955], I, 82.)

The two captains along with the recorder, Thomas Bullock, met at the home of John D. Lee on Saturday, December 23, to agree upon rules and to choose up sides. Each bird or animal was assigned a certain number of points, from one point for a raven to fifty for a bear or panther. The contest opened on Christmas Day.

Thursday Dec 28th 1848. Meeting called this morning for the purpose of consulting the practibility of issuing Bills of credit or notes to answer for curiency for the time being as the gold dust cannot be coined for the want of crusibles at present.

The gold dust to be deposited with the President & no more than the amount to be issued in bills. which plan was agreed upon.

Friday Decr 29th 1848. Good pleasant weather. Went to the office awhile The Clerks were writing off the Bills & the President signing them

I suppose that we here, are like our brethren at the Bluff Whigs with this advantage that we have got not only over them but also the Whigs in the States We have now got a National Band [Bank] and they cannot establish one because the Demecratic Presidents always vetoes it.

Saturday Decr 30th 1848. Warm weather yet. Went to Council. One Powell was had up for abusing Amasa & Porter while geathering up the strays animals & afterwars two different lots of boys were had up for firing gund on Christmast eve & for "Shivereeing"[11] a few weddings about the same time. They were all dismissed by the Council after giving them some good instructions.

Sunday Decr 31st 1848. At home and around in the Cany swamps South. Good weather. Farewell 1848, for in thy reign I have escaped from the land of my nativity from oppression & misrule where I could not enjoy the liberty of conscience.

Monday January 1st 1849. At and around home mostly. South wind. Warm & thawing.

Tuesday Jany 2nd 1849. Today the "National Bank commenced its opperations & those who had gold dust were depositing it in the Bank at a rapid rate. It seems to take well among the people. I was there awhile & today recieved 25-00 of it for a rifle. Thawing day.

Wednesday January 3rd 1848[9]. Down among the cain swamps awhile. Very warm and pleasant while the sun shone afterwards very cold.

Thursday Jan 4th 1849. At home mostly. In the evening went to the Council a short time, trial Tubbs V.S. Stains.[12]

Friday Jan 5th 1849. Mostly at home. Worked some for Lewis

---

11. "Shivareeing" is a colloquialism for the French, *charivari*, a mock serenade of discordant noises made with kettles, tin horns, etc. It was common to so serenade newly married couples as a request for refreshments of cake and wine.

12. William Tubbs had joined the Mormon Battalion in Company "B" and was one who had been sent with the sick to Pueblo, Colorado. From a later entry here (February 2, 1849) it would seem that he had brought liquor into the city for sale.

William C. Staines has been referred to as a "wine and spirits merchant" by Beadle and other contemporaries; while John Hyde, Jr., in his *Mormonism, Its Leaders and Designs* (New York, 1857), on page 44, gives in some detail the relationship of Brigham Young to the liquor trade with W. C. Staines, one of Brigham's adopted sons, handling the product.

William Carter Staines was born September 26, 1818, at Hingham Ferries, Northamptonshire, England. An accident at the age of thirteen injured his spine and cause a deformity from which he did not recover. He joined the Mormon Church in 1843, went on the exodus with the family of George Miller, but broke away and came west to Utah Valley in September 1847.

An expert gardener, Staines worked for a time for Brigham Young raising fruit and grapes. He built the first really fine home in Salt Lake City, the one in which Colonel Kane was entertained and Governor Cummings lived — the house which was to become known as the Devereaux House.

In 1863 he was appointed to manage the Mormon emigration at the New York office, a position which he held until his death on August 3, 1881. Though he had two wives, he left no posterity.

Sat Jan 6th 1849. New snow this morning. At home In the evening went to a prayer meeting at Br Benson's.

Sunday Jany 7th 1849. At home. Snowing again.

Monday Jan 8th 1849. At home. Had sick headache.

Tues & Wed. Jan. 9th & 10th 1849. At home. Hard south wind & thawing very fast.

Thursday Jan 11th 1849. This morning the wind still blew hard from the South. the mountain sides & places in the valley begins to look black being now bare of snow & we begin to feel like having a respite from this long & tedious snow storm but in this we were disappointed for about nine the wind changed to the N. W. & was followed by a hard snow storm which lasted untill about dark, depositing a new snow six inches deep which entirely blasted our hopeful idea of soon sowing wheat and other things which we were so very anxious to be doing. I was at home all day.

Friday Jany 12th 1849. Mostly at home and around the Fort some Mild weather today.

Sat & Sund Jan 13th & 14th 1849. Weather about as usual. I am still around & about home doing no work

Mond & Tues Jan 15th & 16th 1849. Mostly at home.

Wed & Thurs Jany 18 1849. Weather about as usual & I around home

Frid. & Sat Jan 19th & 20th 1849. Weather as usual & me also. On the 20th attended Bishop Lewis Court as witness & clerk in a case between Sherwood & [Samuel] Eweng. case of debt.

Sund & Mond Jany 21 & 22 1849. Weather some little milder & me still around home doing but little.

Tuesday January 23rd 1849. Cloudy & warm. Snow wet & thawing very like for rain at dark. S. wind. At home and at the office to day.

Wednesday Jany 24th 1849. This morning we have another snow which is fast falling & very wet, which ceased about ten & the day was warm, the snow fast melting. I was at home writing.

Thursday Jany 25th 1849. Fine warm day & thawing smartley I was at home as usual.

Friday Jany 26th 1849. Warm Thawin day. I went with T. Lewis to the Cañon to try to cut cedar posts but the snow being too deep on the mountans we could not ascend & so came home.

Sat & Sund Jany 27 & 28 1849. Warm & thawing. At home with the sick head ache all this time.

Monday Jany 29th 1849. Clear warm day & thawing. At home & at the mill for lumber &c.

Tuesday & Wednesday Jany 30 & 31 1849. Hunted up my oxen & at home. Thawing.

Thurs February 1st 1849. Attended a call made to hunt for a man who was lost namened Wm Crockett He was deranged & had been now lost for the last 48 hours.

We made diligent serch in almost every direction but did not find anything of him.

Friday Feb. 2nd 1849. Cold clear day. At and around home Pixtons house which had a lot of hay on it caught fire.

This evening assisted Genl Rich to arrest Wm Tubbs who had brought whiskey here to sell & took it away from him. He is to be tried for that & other misconduct tomorrow.

Sat Feb. 3rd 1849. Cold Clear day Mostly at home. In the evening attended the trial of Tubbs for speaking against the Authorities of this place &c. He was disfelloshiped and took an appeal. Trial before Bishop Lewis

Sunday Feb. 4th 1849. Cold day. Went to meeting on the warm side of the Fort wall. President B. Young spoke giving us general instructions & advice. He said that none should leave here & carry off the gold & silver &c without he pleases to let them that they can not get away unless he sees fit & those who go away contrary to council he will confiscate their property, for he is Boss &c.

He also said that we need not to be afraid of starving for there is plenty of provisions for all and proposed for the people to appoint a committee to go around and make an estimate of all the provisions here & let those who have a surplus impart to those who have not & he will do the same Also as there are many who have beef to sell and will not take paper money he told the butchers to go & kill fat cattle any how and pay the owners a fair price for it. That his cattle might be killed first & then the rest could not murmur.

That the Elders had, many of them, acted like they had entirely kicked out of the harness & were now running perfectly free but they would yet fine that they were not only in the traces but a man had hold of the lines who knew how to controll them &c

In respect to dancing he perfectly forbid having any more this season. How soon we forget God now we are delivered from our enemies and how many now are trying to take the advantage of his brother in the price of grain &c who had been driven and mobbed & had prayed to be delivered and brought here which we would not do if we were back in the midst of our enemies but would thank God for a crust of bread and rejoice with our brethren.

He also reprovd the people for their wild career in dancing this winter &c

That there was a difference in being in the Kingdom of God on this earth & being in the Church of J. C. of L. D. S.[13] That in the kingdom of God on the earth all men had a right to, & would be protected in his religion be that what it would and no man would be allowed to molest or abuse or redicule any one on account of his religion or manner of worship &c He spoke at consideral length although it was a cold day & this is but a faint sketch of what he said which was recieved with cheerfulness by most of the congregation but all those who were disaffected or did intend to leave were not well pleased with his discourse.

Monday Feb. 5th 1849. Cold day being 10° below zero, the coldest day this winter. I was at home laid up with the sick head ache and did not go out all day. This was as sick a spell as I evere had with a few exceptions

To day Bishop Vance came around taking the amount of provisions in conformity to the advice of the president yesterday.

Tuesday Feb. 6th 1849. Very cold and heavy frost flying all day like snow. I was around some & up to the office once but weak yet.

---

13. President Young's discussion of the difference between the Kingdom of God on the earth and the Church of Jesus Christ of Latter-day Saints is very significant. The Council of Fifty (YTFIF) in its secret operations constituted the machinery of the "Kingdom" while the Twelve Apostles with the lesser priesthood groups made up the officials of the church. A few men belonged to both groups.

There is again beef in the market to be had for paper money so salutary was the sermon of the president on sunday on that subject. The market had stoped for several days because men would not sell for anything but gold dust or coined money.

Wed & Thurs Feb. 7th & 8th 1849. Around the Fort & at home. Dull times. The weather is moderating some.

Friday Feb. 9th 1849. Clear warm day. Thawed smartley Went to Neph's mill about Seven S. E. on Mill creek. It is a good mill & Now grinds about 12 bushels per hour.

Sat. Feb 10th 1849. Went to the office & a short time at Council. and at home not very well.

Sunday Feb. 11th 1849. Fine pleasant day. Clear. Meeting as on last Sabbath. President Young spoke similar to his discourse last Sabbath only did [not] repremand quite so severe. His discourse was cheering. He was followed by P. P. Prat. The amount of Bread Stuff in the Valley as made out by the Comt last week was announced at ¾ lb. to each person with a small fraction over. In the evening I attended the High Priest's meeting. Here the Prest taught again. He said among other things that he was going to work & to morrow the Quorum of the Twelve would be filled up and that the Twelve should set in order the other Quorums. That the reins should now be tightened up &c.

I can not Pass over one thing which took place here. Prest Amasa Lyman, has been very sick & had so far recovered that he was here but his lungs being so disordered that he could not speak above his breath the President & several Elders laid hands on him. The President being mouth commanded the disease to be rebuked & pronounced the blessing of health to rest upon him that he should arise and speak to our edification to night which he did for in a few moments he arose and addressed for about half an hour. This took place in presence of a large congregation all who can bear testimony of the same.

Monday Feb 12th 1849. Went to Porters Mill[14] for Lumber & was around as usual.

Tues Feb 13th 1849. Assisted to remove the public arms to another house. They are in a bad condition. At & about home the rest of the day.

The Councils were in Session yesterday & to day, which has resulted in filling up the Quorum of the Twelve by appointing C. C. Rich, Erastus Snow, Lorenzo Snow & Franklin D. Richards to fill the vacancies occasioned by the election of the First Presidency & also to fill Lyman Wights place

John Young was appointed President of the High Priests Quorum & G. B. Wallace & Reynolds Cahoon to be his councillors.

Daniel Spencer was appointed President of the Stake and David Fulmer & Willard Snow Councillors to him.

The Council will be continued untill a complete organization is effected & all matters made strait.

Wednesday Feb 14th 1849. Went in Company with T. Lewis to the mountain to cut cedar wood. The snow on the mountain was soft & thawing but the benchland in the Valley dry & hard Strange to me for the snow to melt on the mountains sooner than in the Valley. Warm day. Thawed mud in the Fort.

---

14. Sanford Porter, a lumberman and sawyer, erected a sawmill at Millcreek, Salt Lake County, before he moved to Centerville, Davis County, Utah.

Thursday Feb. 15th 1849. Snowing some. Warm & Cloudy. At home all day, The Council has reorganized the High Council as follows by appointing Isaac Morley H. G. Sherwood, W. W. Major J Vance Ira Eldrege Titus Billings, Eleazer Miller Levi Jackman, E. H. Groves, S. Roundy, E. D. Woolley and Phineas Richards. Isaac Morley President of Council. and also dividing the City into 19 Wards each ward to contain 9 blocks that is three blocks square and appointing a Bishop over each ward.

Friday Feb. 16th 1849. Went in company with Bishop Lewis to the mountains and explored between the Red Butte & Emegration Cañons on the mountains. The clouds rested on them so that we could not do much

Saturday Feb. 17th 1849. Cool & clear. Thawing some. At home.

Sunday Feb. 18th 1849. Cold in the morning, but warm in the after noon. Some thin clouds & thawing faster than usual.
Meeting & usual Elder J. Taylor spoke & the laws & the organizations of the different Quorums published to the people. A law is passed to erect a bathing house at the warm springs.

Monday Feb. 19th 1849. At home. Only went to Chrismans Mill.[15]
The day was very clear and warm particularly in the afternoon & the snow melted fast. It was warm as summer nearley The ground is flooded with water. Warm evening.

Tues & Wed Feb 20 & 21. 1849. Warm & thawing very fast S. wind At home doing nothing as usual.

Thurs & Frid Feb. 22. & 23. 1849. Very warm & pleasant S. wind. Snow melting very fast. I am at home not very well.

Saturday Feb. 24th 1849. Dark Cloudy day & S. wind very warm At home doing nothing as usual.

Sunday Feb. 25th 1849. Warm S. wind & Cloudy. Went to meeting as usual at ten o'c Several ordinances were read which were passed yesterday by the Legislative Council and one in particular was an ordinance appointing H. S. Eldrege Marshall. another inflicting a fine of 25 dollars each on five young men named, Elias Pearsons, B. Brackenbery, John F Murdoc Jesse Earl & Frazier for unbecoming & demoralizing conduct.
They got up a party on the Cottonwood at Fraziers Mothers & they each selected their lady and marched there Spanish fashion with the Lady on before & they behind Staid all night & came home the same way. This and some more calculations of a worse nature still was the cause of their being fined.[16] The subject was spoken of by A. Lyman & E. Snow, who also spoke at lenght against all such proceedings & the introduction of other savage Spanish customs also against going to the gold minds, after which W. W. Phelps spoke & moved that those be cut off from the church who were fined as above, which was carried unanimously.

---

15. This refers to the small chopping mill, the first in the Salt Lake Valley, which was built by Charles Crisman. Crisman, born December 25, 1807, in Kentucky, had come to Utah in the J. M. Grant company of 1847. The first high council permitted him to increase his toll from one-sixteenth to one-tenth of wheat ground.

16. Writing of this same incident, John D. Lee said: "5thly, reported that 6 of the souldier Boys cut a Spanish Rusty by riding into the Fort with a young Lady sitting in the saddle before, & the man behind with his arms arround the woman. One of the men was sawing on the violin. This they called the Spanish manners or Politeness. Voted by the council that they all be cut off from the church & fined 25 dollars each & that the marshal collect their fine fourth with . . . ." Cleland and Brooks, *A Mormon Chronicle*, I, 96.

President Young then spoke to the same purpose a short time.

Daniel Spencer was appointed historian of Valley or of this Stake of Zion.

Monday Feb. 26th 1849. Worked on the Council House which was recommenced today. S wind in the morning & in the after-noon N. wind & cold. Rained some.

Tues Feb. 27th 1849. At home all day. Warm snow falling all day & melting.

Wednesday Feb. 28th 1849. Snow some two inches deep & now clear & cool. Thawed some yet a cool day. Went to the office & to Porters mill.

This evening was called on to go with an expedition to the Utah Valley against some Indians who had been stealing a lot of horses from Brigham's herd and began to prepare to start tomorrow

Thursday March 1st 1849. This morning a large drove of horses were driven in from the North by the order of President Daniel Spencer for the use of the expedition to the Utah Valley. In this case the Law imposing a fine of 25 dollars, for driving a horse from his range without leave from his owner was suspended by the President because the emergency of the case was such that the oweners could not be seen in time   There was about 100 horses drove in & taken out yet only thirty one men could be raised with horses to go.

The rest of the horses fit for service were taken out by their owners or some one interested under the pretence of going & then did not, which left the company minus 19 men as 50 men were ordered out.

The company went out under the command of Col John Scott, whose orders were simply to take such measures as would put a final end to their depredations in future.[17]

We started about noon and traveled to the Second Cottonwood where we encamped for the night on a blanket of deep snow which we overlaid with coarse willow brush.

The night was very cold & the wind penetrating under our bed through the brush rendered our situation very uncomfortable. The grass was also very poor which made the situation of our horses about as unpleasant as our own. About 9 at night Br La Fayette Grainger overtook us with word that the horses were not stolen & that he had sent back B Furgerson to report the same to President Spencer.

About midnight we recieved a letter from Spencer stating that as the horses were not stolen that we need not spend any more time in search of them but to proceed with the Indians for killing cattle as had been before directed so that the nature of our expedition was not in the least changed.

Our company being 19 men less than was required the Col raised some volunteers in these settlements which augmented our numbers to 35 men

Friday March the 2nd 1849. We were all glad to see the approach of day & were up earley. being driven up by the cold and immediately proceeded on to the Dry Cotton Wood where we put up for our breakfast & to pasture our horses which were now very hungry   There was however plenty of good grass here.

After refreshing ourselves & animals we traveled on to Orr & West's Herd on Willow Creek where we again put up. Here we were again disappointed for there

---

17. This is the most detailed account of this Indian expedition yet found. The beef that was killed belonged to Parley P. Pratt, who was later reimbursed for it from the public fund.

It was suggested that the authorities were dissatisfied with Scott's execution of his orders because he shed so much blood. In the light of their orders for the expedition following and the number of Indians, including women and children, who were killed, the opposite was undoubtedly true. Peter Gottfredson, ed., *A History of Indian Depredations in Utah* (Salt Lake City, 1919), 26.

was several of the men in the Company who had come without any meat as Br Shirtliff had agreed to accompany us to this place & here kill a beef for us which he had in this herd & had failed to come so the Col after consulting the Company on the subject concluded to kill the beef for the use of the expedition rathan [rather than] fail for the want of the necessary provisions.

The company unanimously agreed to sustain him in this thing and all bear an equal proportion in paying for the beef if required but at the same time agreed to ask the Legislative Council to make those pay for it who had drew horses for the purpose of going with us & failed & thus left us to do business with a company so small that it would in all probability might cause us to be attacted by the Indians. We looked upon them as desertors.

The beef was killed & as some of our animals were not fit for the service required the Col by the approval of the Company took a sufficient number of horses & mules out of the Herd to fit out the Company.

Thus suspending the law as did president Spencer & for the same reason to wit that the expedition should not fail while means were in our reach to carry it on.

All things being thus arrainged we again travelled on several miles and encamped on the Jordan under some cedar Hills where we had the best of grass & a good camping place where we rested well all night.

While at the Herd we learned that the stolen horses had returned to Brigham's Herd by one of his boys who came to inform us of the same.

The Jordan at the place of our encampment runs through a deep Cañon — has a narrow deep channel & swift current. being very different in all respects after it comes into the valley.

Saturday March 3rd 1849. Cold Cloudy morning which soon commenced to snow with a North Wind which continued to fall at intervals all day. We took an earley breakfast & travelled on to the Utah Valley. But before we started we were divided into two Companies the first under my own & the second under Alexr William's command the better to divide and scoure the country as we did not know where the Indians were located.

After we came into the Utah Valley the company under Williams was sent to reconortre the country up the Jordin & so on to the Lake while the company under me was sent directly South through the Valley to Dry Creek & thence down that creek searching in the thick brush along it, while the Col with some. six men travelled between the two companies the better to be prepared to give directions if necessary.

We travelled thus untill we all met some two miles from the Utah Lake on Dry Creek and finding nothing of the Indians we travelled on S. E. over a level prairie which was quite boggy untill we came to American Creek and travelling up it some three miles encamped for the night. We were now all very tired and cold. No sign could yet be found of the Indians.

Sunday March 4th 1849. This morning we had in addition to our usual amount of bedclothes a blanket of snow some two inches deep; But the morning was pleasant All seemed refreshed except my-self being afflicted with a severe attact of the sick head ache & scarcely able to set up It was in great pain & distress that I could traval.

We had an earley start and traveled South to the Provo, a fine large stream & well timbered on the valley. This is a beautiful farming country.

Here we found the Utahs, who were friendly who had been notified of our reproach by D. B. Huntington & B. Ward, who had been sent on earley this morning for that purpose. They recieved us friendly but were much excited being evidently afraid of us.

After spending an hour or so with them & learning what we could respecting those we were in pursuit of & also explaining the object of our visit we traveled on Little Chief accompanied us about three miles up the Provo where we encamped for the night The Little Chief then returned home promising to send his sons this evening to pilot us to the camp of those we were in the pursuit of who came accordingly about one hour after dark. They were in favor of attacting them to night least some one might be friendly enough to give them word. They declared that if we did go to night that they would go themselves.

We all concluded to go forthwith according to their plan & so we was soon on the move again, travelling up the provo The night was clear & a bright moon shone beautifully as we travelled along.

After following up the Provo to the foot of the mountains we ascended the high bench lands travelling North several miles when the Indians thought we had best leave our animals in a cedar grove on the mountain side and a detachment go on foot to make the attact. Accordingly the Col chose out ten men with one of the Indians and was soon on our march again leaving the animals &c here.

We travelled some six miles over the spurs of the mountains high above the bench land & found their fires in the first creek North of the Provo.

It was deemed best by the party now to fall back some distance and send for the rest of the company to join us.

Accordingly two men were sent back for them while we kindled small fires to keep from freezing. About two hours before day the rear came up.

Our Indian pilot, when he saw the fires of those we sought, his heart failed & he wished to go back saying he did not want to see them die but at the same time desired us to kill them. He was willing to stay when he learned that we would not require him to fight.

All things being ready now we only waited the dawn of day to attact them.

Monday March 5th 1849. At the dawn of day our company was divided into 4 parties the better to surround the camp of Indians. I first started with a party to close in on the farthest side of them to prevent them from escaping to the mountains while another party under A. Williams marched into the mouth of the Cañon to keep them from escaping in that direction. Judson Stoddard with a few horsemen formed below on the creek to be ready to pursue them in case they attempted to escape into the valley while the fourth party under D. B. Huntington marched directly to their camp.

They discovered us about the time we had fairley surrounded them while it was yet twilight & attempted to escape in several different directions but found themselves surrounded whereupon they commenced a long & loud speech which I afterwards learned only consisted in telling us to go away or they would fire upon us while our interpreters also told them that we desired to see them and wished them to come out.

The Utah who was along with us also tried to persuade them to come out but all to no purpose.

Some time was spent in this way while they steadily refused to give up threatning all the time to fire upon us if we did not leave & when finding we were determined to have them they gave the war hoop & fired 3 guns upon. We also now fired in return. The battle now commenced in good earnest and in a few moments one of the Indians was killed and several wounded.

They soon took shelter in the creek which had perpendicular banks about 4 feet high thickly set with willow which so completely shielded them that we could not see them only when they raised up to shoot at us. We were about two hours engaged with them.

They fought with the most determined resolution to die rather than yield as they could often be heard to encourage each other.

Sometimes they would connence to sing as if they were gambling as a token of defiance to us. some 5 or 6 times during the engagement we ceased firing and both our interperters & the Utah tryed to pursuade them to come out also to send out their women & children that they might be spared if they would not yield but all to no effect.

Some of the Squaws were at length found couch in the water under the thick brush & were induced to come out. They were in a most deplorable situation. Having been in the water about an hour & a half, they were nearley froze. We kindled up a fire for them which rendered them more comfortable.

By sending these back we soon prevailed on the rest to come out also and soon 13 women & children came out, among the rest a lad about sixteen gave up. He had fought manfully during the engagement.

Two of the women were wounded on the head with stones which we had thrown into the brush to ascertain where they were hid. Soon after they gave up we succeeded in killing two more men leaving only one more who immediately broke through the brush and tryed to escape to the Utah who was on the hill looking on. He was killed however before he ran far

Thus ended the battle without one of our men even being hurt although they shot hundreds of arrows at us sometimes at only a few yards distance.

Our men were perfectly calm and deliberate all the time and did not fire at random as is so common on such occasions There was no time during the whole engagement when the men could not be easily controled so much so that the wants of the prisoners were attended as well as circumstances would admit

As soon as they gave up they asked leave to start immediately to the city and insisted on it not being willing to go to the their tribe.

This little band had seperated themselves from the rest because they were determined to live by stealing from the whites while the rest were friendly and would not suffer it. They had for some time been very insolent and some of them had even shot at some of the whites. I suppose that the women were afraid of the Utahs.

We found 13 beef hides in their camp some of them were recognized.

We now returned to our camp where we found Little chief and several Indians. He said we had done right although he felt like he could cry when he saw what a bad end these men had come to by their dishonesty. He also said we did wrong in not killing the lad for he would kill a white man yet for revenge.

After taking a little breakfast & feeding & giving some presents to the Indians started for home. The Col and a few men went by the battle ground to leave some word with the squaws but found they had fled and took three of their dead up the Cañon.

We all now marched for home & baited our horses & took dinner at our former encampment on American Creek after which we proceeded to Orr & Wests' Herd and staid all night

Tuesday March 6th 1849. We started for home in good time this morning & on our way we took Curtis Purbelo a prisoner who we learned had been pursuading some indians to kill our cattle but nothing was done with him. after we came in to the City.

We arrived in the City about 2 o'clock P. M. and were all discharged by the Col after he had given an account of our expedition to a large company who had geathered together when we came in. Amen.

Wednesday March 7th 1849. Was around home & went to a meeting of the 13 Ward which I belonged to It was there agreed in order to save labor that the Ward be fenced in to one field.

Thursday March 8th 1849. Not well all day. Cloudy and cold Hard snow storm in the evening and night.

Friday March 9th 1849. We have a new snow this morning about three inches deep. At home all day. Quite snowy.

Saturday March 10th 1849. Weather as usual snowy. At home.

Sunday March 11th 1849. S. wind & cloudy & then snowed and quite disagreeable & muddy. At home. The 13 women & children which we left after Indian fight has arrived here prefering to abide with us it seems rathur than to live with the Utahs on the Provo.

Monday March 12th 1849. Today was our first political election which commenced at 10 o'clock a. m. A large assemblage of men convened when many subjects were discussed and among the rest was the subject of Ira E West who had been tried by the H. C. & cut off from the church & fined 100 dollars for lying, stealing & swindling &c and afterward had attempted to run away & was now in chains.

He was here offered for sale to any one who would pay his debts & take him untill he could work it out. No one however took him & awhile the prospect was fair for him to loose his head.[18] His brother C. West took him at last, I believe

The day was snowy squalls & cold & unpleasant & muddy. There was 655 votes polled for the following offices to wit

Brigham Young for Govonor   H. S. Eldrege, Marshal.
Willard Richards for Secratary   D. H. Wells, Aterney General.
H. C. Kimball Chief Justice   N. K. Whitney Treasurer
N. K. Whitney) associate   A. Carrington assessor & collector
John Taylor   ) justices.   Jos L. Haywood Supervisor Roads.[19]

The folling named persons were chosen justices of the Peace who were also the Bishops of the several Wards I believe

---

18. In his minutes of the Council of Fifty (YTFIF) meeting held on March 3 and 4, 1849, Lee gives background for this entry. Following are excerpts:

The forenoon was Spent in deliberating upon the case of Ira E. West, Thomas Byres, & others . . . . Some taul Speeches were made relative to the duties and Powers of this council . . . . Then can the members of this council suffer their sympathy to arrise to the extant that mercy will Rob Justice of its claims, Suffering infernals, thieves, Murderers, Whoremongers & every other wicked curse to, through mercy to live amoung us, adding sin to sin, crime to crime, corrupting the morals of the People . . . .

Pres B. Young Said to the Marshal, take Ira E. West & Thomas Byres into custody & put them in chains & on the day of the Election, there offer them for Sale to the highest Bidder. (Cleland and Brooks, *A Mormon Chronicle*, I, 98-99.)

This is rather difficult to understand since no specific offense is named. In the initial move from Nauvoo, Ira E. West was a captain of ten.

19. Joseph L. Heywood was born August 1, 1815, at Grafton, Massachusetts. He early became engaged in the mercantile business, which he followed after his conversion to Mormonism in 1842. He managed a store for Joseph Smith. In Nauvoo, Heywood was also a bishop and, with Almon W. Babbitt and John S. Fullmer, was left to manage the affairs of the church when Brigham Young and the other leaders left in 1846. He remained until the spring of 1848 when he caught up with the mass migration of Winter Quarters and went west with it, arriving in Utah in October of that year.

In 1849 Heywood was appointed postmaster at Salt Lake City. He made several trips to Washington, D. C., in the interest of the church, cooperating with Dr. Bernhisel. In 1851 he was made United States marshal, serving until 1855. During this same period he founded the town of Nephi, Utah. In 1861 he was called to the Cotton Mission and settled in the town of Washington, Utah, where he lived for only two years, moving from there to Harmony, Utah, in 1863. In 1872 he moved to Panguitch, Utah, where he lived the remainder of his life.

David Fairbanks	1st Ward	Daniel Carns	11th Ward
John Lowery	2nd Ward	Ben Covey	12th Ward
Chrisr Williams	3rd Ward	Ed Hunter	13th Ward
Ben Brown	4th Ward	John Murdock	14th Ward
Thomas W. Winter	5th Ward[20]	A. O. Smoot	15th Ward
Wm Hickenlooper	6th Ward	Isaac Higbee	16th Ward
Wm G. Perkins	7th Ward	J. L. Haywood	17th Ward
Addison Everett	8th Ward	N. K. Whitney	18th Ward
Seth Taft	9th Ward	Jas Hendrix	19th Ward
David Pedigrew	10th Ward		

Also the following other precincts had Justice of the Peace elected. North Cotton Wood — Joseph L. Robinson

[¼ page left blank]

Tuesday March 13th 1849. Cold & sually snows makes up the variety of weather yet, while the mountain sides & valley are again covered with snow as in the winter. I was at home and around as usual now days.

Wed Thurs & Frid March 14 15 & 16th 1849. Weather continued as usual with a little rain & much mud. Bad walking. I am still lying on my oars. Almost ready to take the "Blues" & not very well How long shall we yet wait for weather fit to work in?

Saturday March 17th 1849. Fine clear & warm day. The snow melted fast & the mud dried making the roads quite comfortable.

I & Blackwell explored the mountains immediatley over looking the Hot & Warm Springs North of the city. We went to the highest Peaks which were deeply covered with snow yet Found timber in the small Cañons but could not find means to get them out so deep are they in the hollows. We came home about two o'clock P. M. very tired.

Sunday March 18th 1849. The weather had the appearance of being foul this morning but the day proved to be tolerable good except a hard South wind.

There was a meeting as usual. C. C. Rich spoke & was followed by John Taylor who in the course of his remarks deprecated the practice of swearing & called on all who would agree to flog any one whom they heard to swear to raise their hands whereupon many did while many did not vote either way. I suppose they rightly considered that it would be rather a fast way of getting into business. This was my feelings.

I was quite unwell all day.

Monday March 19th 1849. pleasant weather in the fore part of the day then N. wind & snowed. I went on the Mountain immediately over the Hot Spring North of the city.

---

20. No bishop was appointed over the Fifth Ward in Salt Lake County at this time since there were only a few families living in the area — from Second West and Sixth South streets to the Jordan River on the west and the city limits on the south. The first bishop was Thomas W. Winter, who was ordained to the office on April 11, 1853. Born November 20, 1812, in England, Winter joined the Mormon Church in 1844 but did not arrive in Salt Lake City until 1850. He was a bridge builder. He died in Salt Lake City, August 11, 1882.

On the list of bishops as given here, Jenson's *Historical Record*, VI (August, 1887), on page 318 gives John Lytle as the bishop of the Eleventh Ward, as does Edward W. Tullidge, *History of Salt Lake City* (Salt Lake City, 1886), 57. In the same list Tullidge names Nathaniel V. Jones as bishop of the Fifteenth Ward and Shadrach Roundy of the Sixteenth. In each case the bishop named here served only a short time, Isaac Higbee being called to Provo in less than two months.

Tuesday March 20th 1849. Ground covered with snow & cold weather I was at home all day preparing to to the Cañon to work tomorrow.

Wed Thurs & Frid March 21 22 & 23 1849. Went after a load of wood to the Dry-Cotton-Wood-Creek and returned home at two o'clock & went after another load to Mill Creek & camp at the mouth of the Cañon.

Sat. March 24th 1849. Succeeded in getting a load of wood & came home leaving my oxen and waggon & turned my oxen on the grass till next Monday.

Sunday March 25th 1849. pleasant day.   Meeting near the C. House where a stand has been erected. Prest Young spoke V. S those who were going to California for gold Dust &c followed by P. P. Pratt on the due Subordination to the keys of the priesthood, & Heber on working on the C. House tomorrow &c

Monday, Tuesday & Wednesday March 26th 27 & 28th 1849. Drawing wood from the Red Butte & camped out.   Made 3 loads.

Thursday March 29th 1849. At home.   Fine Pleasant weather for the last 6 or 7 days.   Good for crops. People very busy.   Snow melting fast on the mountains.

Friday & Saturday March 30 & 31 1849. At home.   Worked some on Ward fence   Warm & clear.   Pleasant as summer.

Sunday April 1st 1849. Warm & pleasant but windy. Went to meeting. H. C. Kimball spoke.

Monday April 2nd 1849. Occupied in building my lot fence

Tuesday April 3rd 1849. Worked for the Council House.

Wed & Thurs April 4 & 5 1849. Worked for T. B. Foote who is building a Bridge across Cañon creek. This is the first carpenter work that I have done since the death of Joseph   Had rain on Wednesday & on Thursday morning a snow two inches deep & snowed hard all the afternoon.   Very uncomfortable working.

Friday April 6th 1849. Another snow this morning. I am quite sick to day.
    Today is our General Conference   But few met & adjourned till tomorrow at ten o'clock. This is the 19th anniversary of the Church of Christ.

Saturday April 7th 1849. Hard East wind.   Conference met   A. Lyman, H. C. Kimball & John Taylor spoke after which Conference adjd till tomorrow at ten o'clock.

Sunday April 8th 1849. Cold squalls & disagreeable for our Conference which met at ten but no particular business done only to pass the different authorities before the people as usual, all of whom were unanimously recieved.

Monday April 9th 1849. Plowed and planted some in my City Lot.   Rained some today.

Tues Wed Thurs. Frid & Sat April the 10-11. 12. 13. & 14 1849. Worked for T. B. Foote at the Bridge across Big Cañon.   On Friday the mail started to California under A. Lyman.   on Thursday [Apr. 12] a party of Wanship Band attacted the Utahs on the provo & some were wounded on both sides but none killed as I have heard. On Saturday the Mail started to the States under Allen Compton.

Sunday April 15th 1849. Fine warm day.   Went to meeting.   R. Cahoon, L. Snow, & John Young spoke. Had the sick head ache.

Monday April 16th 1849. Went to mill & worked some in the garden.

Tuesday April 17th 1849. Went to Pulcifer's mill on Cañon Creek. It is a very tempory concern, grinding only about two bushel per hour.

Wednesday April 18th 1849. Built my 5 acre fence & at home.

Thurs & Friday April 19 & 20 1849. Worked for Foote on the Bridge again. On Friday morning the Little Chief with some 15 men passed by here on his way to attact Wanship to recover his horses which they had taken in the fight last week. Little Chief was accompanied by another chief who lived on the Spanish Fork.

Saturday April 21 1849. Worked in the garden.

Sunday April 22nd 1849. Went to meeting. John Taylor spoke in the fore-noon & President Young in the after-noon. He gave out next Saturday to be set apart in the after noon to organize the Nauvoo Legion as the indians were acting suspiciously. Next Wednesday to be for fasting & prayer. For the Sacrament to be observed &c.

Mond Tues Wed & Thurs Aprl 23, 24, 25, & 26-1849. Worked in the garden.

Friday April 27th 1849. Done nothing except to hunt oxen

Saturday April 28th 1849. This morning I understand that the Party of Indians who passed here on the 20th inst. under the Little Chief attacted Wanship's party somewhere on Ogdon's Fork and killed some (& amongst the rest the lad which we took prisoner in the Utah Valley on the 5th of March. [crossed out]) They also killed some 40 horses and took the rest The Little Chief and one of his men were also killed.

To day the Legion was organized according to the appointment last Sunday. There was two Regiment formed one of horse & one foot constituting the First & Second Cohorts.

Daniel H. Wells Major General.	Willard Snow Major 1 B. 1 R. 1 C.
J. M. Grant Brigr Gen First Cohort	Ira Eldrege do 2 B. 1 R. 1 C.
H. S. Eldredge do do Second Do.	A. Lytle - do 1 B 2 R. 2 C.
John S. Fulmer Col 1st R. 1st C.	H. Herriman - do 2 B. 2 R. 2 C.
John Scott Col 1st R. 2 C.	

There was Companies orgainized. I fell into 2 C. 2 B. 1 R. 1 C. Benjm F. Johnson Capt Having the honor of being first Lieut my-self. This is rising some in the world. Because when the Legion was' organized in 1840 I held the office of Second Leut whereas I am now promoted a little.

One circumstance took place today which I never saw before John Pack & John D. Lee were each put in nomination for Majors by regular authority & both most contemptestously hissed down. When any person is thus duly nominated I never before knew the people to reject it But on this occasion it appears that they are both a perfect stink in every body's nose The reasons of which is not needful to relate.[21]

To day about two o'clock P. M. Alvin Horr, one of the Presidents of the Eleventh Quorum to which I belong, died of Dropsey. He had been afflicted a long time & came here from the bluffs for his health leaving his family

Sunday April 29th 1849. Went to meeting. Lorenzo Young spoke in the fore noon followed by H. C. Kimball the after noon was taken up by exhortations by different ones.

21. John D. Lee and John Pack had fallen into a dispute over the scalp hunt they had conducted since Christmas previous. It was originally set to last until the first of February. On that day when the count was taken, John Pack's side had won, but the Council of Fifty voted to extend the hunt for another month. At the end of that time, John D. Lee's side was ahead. Neither man would give the promised dinner, nor would they compromise and share the expense. Cleland and Brooks, *A Mormon Chronicle*, I, 82-85, 100.

Mond & Tues April 30 & May 1st 1849. Went to the North Cañon for a load of Timber for Foote for a Bridge across City Creek

Wednesday May 2nd 1849. Worked on the garden in the fore noon   In the after noon had a gentle rain which well wattered the crops.

Thursday May 3rd 1849. Plowed in the garden.   Cool day.

Friday May 4th 1849. Went to North Cañon for a load of Timber for Foote. Came home about mid-night. Cool night   frost.

Saturday May 5th 1849. Had a company drill.   This is the first time ever I took the command of Cavelry. Our Capt was sick.

Sunday May 6th 1849. Went to meeting.   H. G. Sherwood spoke followed by Prest Young in the forenoon The Prest prophesied that we would have an abundant crop this year. Also that this was the only place on earth for the saints to geather & if we were driven from here there would be no place for us.[22]

Mon. Tues. Wed. Thurs & Frid May the 7th 8th 9th 10th & 11th 1849. Worked at gardening on my lot

Saturday May the 12th 1849. Worked for Foote on City Creek Bridge.

Sunday May 13th 1849. Went to meeting Heard a letter read from Fort Bridger about an indian killed.   Brigham thinks they want to get us into difficulty with the Indians.

Monday. worked on City Creek Bridge again.   Tuesday went to the North Cañon to draw down a house I bought of Treples.[23] Rained this evening.

Wednesday. came home with a load   Cold windy Day   Had the sick head ache Thursday drew down another & Friday another load.

Saturday May 19th 1849. Attended officer drill this forenoon   Cool cloudy day & windy.   Drilled in the afternoon.   Very cold & windy.

Sunday May 20th 1849. Cold cloudy and rainy somewhat. Prest Young preached some in the after-noon & proposes to build a tabernacle on the present meeting ground large enough to accommodate the entire congregation.   Rainy eve.

Monday May 21st 1849. Worked on the garden in the forenoon & sick in the after noon.

Tuesday May 22nd 1849. Went to the North Cañon for a load of Logs again. Cold & windy in the after noon rained hard & blew from the North.   I got thoroughly wet & when I came was chilled numb   Snowed hard in the evening.

Wednesday May 23rd 1849. Snowed very hard all the fore noon   then mild & pleasant. Snow deep on the mountains.

Thurs & Friday May 24 & 25-1849. Worked for Foote on City Crick Bridge.

Saturday. 26th. Very sick all day   Today was our Company training But I could not go.   being sick

---

22. Brigham Young's suggestion that they might be driven from this place seems significant since they had so recently arrived and were so isolated.

23. This is evidently George Bentley Teeples. Born March 17, 1803, at Rochester, New York, he had joined the Mormon Church in 1843. He came west in the Heber C. Kimball company of 1848. His eldest son, William R., became a pioneer to Arizona.

Sunday May 27th 1849. Wife & I went to meeting. W. Snow preached & Prest Young made the application to his sermon which was to fence the field immediately

Monday 28. Went to N. Cañon for logs. Tuesday went for wood. Wednesday went to Pulcifers mill. Thursday 31st raised my house on my lot.

Friday June 1st. Worked some on my house but was sick & came home.

Saturday June 2nd. Company drill in the fore noon & Legion drill in the after noon. We were kept out till dark This is the first time our field and General officers took command.

Sunday. Went to porters mill to meeting & home & then with wife to lot & home Dr Sprague & wife came on a visit in the evening.

Monday June 4th 1849. Worked on my house Tuesday & Wednesday worked for Foote on the lower Bridge on Cañon Creek Thursday 7th worked on my house

Friday 8th. worked on my house.

Saturday 9th. Worked on my house some.

Sunday 10th. Went to meeting. John Lowry spoke lowly. The prest reproved 17th ward for not fencing &c a donation for Caleb Baldwin was made

Monday 11th. Moved on my lot. My house is 14 by 16 feet square 2 doors one window Not mudded but pleasant.

Tuesday 12th 1849. Rained last night Cloudy & cold. Not well & lay up

Wednesday 13th. Clear & cool worked at home. Caleb Baldwin for whom a contribution was made for on Sunday is dead. He is the first Elder I ever heard speak in Missouri & was in prison with Joseph & Hyrum &c in 1837 & 8.

Thursday 14th. Went with Ephraim Green to the Dry Cotton Wood to prospect for gold dust as there is every symptom there. We did not find any as there is no solid substance for it to rest on

Friday 15th. Came home at dark & brought a load of logs

Saturday June 16th 1849. Worked at home

Sunday 17th. Went to meeting awhile. Not well all day and at dark very sick

Monday 18th. Daubed the house.

Tuesday 19th. Worked at home.

Wednesday. Worked at home.

Thursday 21st. Went to the North Canon and go a load of wood & logs.

Friday 22nd. Worked at home.

Saturday 23rd. Today men were coming in from the states bound for the gold minds, on horse back & in waggons. They were coming in all day. Some came in a few days ago. Went to the High Council in the evening. The trial of P. Sessions was ended after some three or four settings. The charge sustained against him. He had been guilty of taking advantage of the people in the sale of his corn &c. and is now to make restitution to all he has injured.

Sunday June 24th 1849. Went to visit the Emegrants Camp Saw many. They are trading off their waggons. Harness & surplus clothings &c cheaper than State prices taking in exchange Horses mules saddles pack saddles &c at very high prices.[24]

Went to meeting P. P. Pratt spoke In the afternoon L Snow both gospel sermons intended for the use of the Emegrants.

Monday. worked on water ditch

Tues. 26th. at home and at the Emegrants camp who are still coming in selling out and going on to the Gold regions.

Wed & Thurs. 27 & 28. Worked for T. B. Foot on Bridge across Big Cañon creek

Friday 29th 1849. At home and once to the emegrants Camp To day was an officer drill but I did not drill. Looked on some.

Sat 30. At home and around in town some.

Sunday July 1st 1849. Went to meeting as usual. Emegrants are coming in as usual This evening A. W. Babbitt came in from the States bringing the United State mail and on appointment for Jos L. Haywood post master.

This evening Wm Bird was tried before Bishops Smoot Perkins & Hickenlooper for stealing a pair of boots from one of the emegrants and found guilty. Condemned to pay him four fold return the boots pay the man & officers for their trouble and fined 50 dollars to be applied on the roads.

Mond 2nd. Around town.

Tues Wed Thurs Frid & Sat. Worked at framing a Barn on the Church farm. The first one built in the Valley.

Sunday July 8th 1849. Went to meeting. Prest Young gave an excellent discourse on the nature of Gold politicks, religion &c showing the tendency which all these things were now leading the world &c

Mond Tues Wed Thurs 9. 10. 11 & 12th. Worked on the barn again.

Frid 13th. at home because my wife was sick.

Saturday 14th. To day was a general muster But few met & they adjourned the muster to work on the Tabernacle or shade for the meeting ground

Majr John Bills was at my house nearley all Day We turned our training into a Spree.

Sunday 15th. Went to meeting.

Mond 16. Tues 17 Wed 18th. Worked on the Barn again.

Thurs 19. came home this morning & was around home all day.

Friday 20th. At home.

Saturday & Sunday 21 & 22. Worked at harvesting for J. D. Grant on the Church Farm.

Monday July 23rd 1849. Worked to day for Grant harvesting on the Temple Lot.

To day a very large company of men were working on the Bowery preparetory for the Feast & grand celebration tomorrow. A Liberty pole was erected 100 feet high about dark amid the fire of Artillery.

---

24. One of the most frequently told stories of Mormondom is of this prediction that states' goods could soon be purchased cheaper in Salt Lake City than in New York; yet even with the full cooperation of the Church of Jesus Christ of Latter-day Saints Historian's Library, we have been unable to pinpoint the date or the exact wording.

Tuesday July 24th 1849. The people was awakened earley this morning by the fire of artillery soon after they began to geather to the Bowery.

There was a numerous host both of emegrants & well as brethren. each ward had prepared a table to themselves and a very large dinner for strangers & all was prepared & enjoyed to day it being the first celebration of the kind ever held here. Many speaches were made by different ones in the course of the day.[25]

Wed & Thurs July 25 & 26. Worked for Grant again harvesting on the Church farm.

Frid & Sat 27 & 28th. At home & trading for coffee &c of the emegrants.

Sund July 29th. Mail came in by H. Egan. I got a letter from States. President Young spoke putting down the Street Grog. Sellers &c In the after-noon Moses Martin spoke on the Gospel.

Mond & Tues 30 & 31. Worked for John Taylor harvesting & came home Tues night

Wed & Thurs. Aug 1 & 2. Worked for Taylor again.

Frid & Sat 3 & 4th. At home & Went home home with John Bills on Sat night to look at some land on the Cotton Wood Farm which I Bought of Langley 10 acres & a small house for 20 dol

Sund 5th. Came home. Went to meeting. P. Pratt spoke followed by several others.

Mond Aug 6th 1849. At home. Emegrants arrived here direct from Santa Fe across the mountains.

Tues Aug 7th. Went 8 miles North to hunt cow. Egan's Co came

Wed 8th. at home.

Thurs. 9th. At home. Mr. Pomroy came in with a train of 34 waggons loaded with goods & groceries. He started for the mines but fell short His waggons had 4 or 5 yoke of oxen each.

Frid 10th. At home.

Sat. 11th. At home and trading some

The council to day appointed a committee to notify Mr Pomeroy to pack up his goods & leave here as "he had found us in peace to leave us so". This was because he was said to be one who had assisted to drive us from Missouri. He demanded a hearing which was granted.

---

25. Lorenzo Brown gives a colorful account of this day's activities:
    The people were awakened at an early hour by cannon Bells & the beating of Drums At 7½ A. M. the people assembled at the stand Shortly after the first Presidency were escorted to the stand by 24 Bishops each bearing a flag 24 young men carrying in their left hand a sword sheathed & in their right the constitution of the U S 24 young ladies in white carrying the Bible and Book of Mormon 24 old men carrying flags all headed by the Brass Band after which the congregation were entertained by singing from the 24 young men & 24 young Ladies the 24 old men a number of speeches from different ones until dinner which I never saw equalled After dinner Toasts were given One by P P Pratt Deseret (which is the name of the Territory) Youngest member of the family. May she be a comfort to the old lady in her declining years By J. M. Grant: Martin Van Buren & all mobocrats may they be winked at by blind men kicked cross lots by cripples nibbled to death by ducks & carried to Hell through the keyhole by Bumble Bees, etc. etc. . . . (Lorenzo Brown, "The Journal of Lorenzo Brown, 1823-1900" [2 vols., typescript, Brigham Young University], I, 56.)

Sund 12th. Went to meeting in the fore noon and at 4 o'clock Mr Pomroys trial came off   He was tried before the people.

Some 5 or six of our people came forward and testified that they knew Mr Pomroy in Missouri during the time of our difficulties and that he was our warm friend and had to send off his family & property to keep them from mob violence such was the antipathy against him because he took such an active part in our favor.

Suffice it to say he was honorably acquitted.

Mond 13th. Went to frame a building on Mill Creek for H. Gibbs with 2 hands & nothing being ready returned home an hour after dark.

Tues & Wed 14 & 15th. at home

Thurs & Frid. At home. Anna Jones came in Friday.

Sat. Aug. 18th. Rainy for several days.

Sund Aug 19th 1849. Went to meeting. P. P. Pratt preached the law of tithing which he said was to pay the tenth day also the tenth of our increase of grain &c of our herds fowls &c &c speculations &c which was confirmed by H. C. Kimball & others also for the tithing to be paid up by next oct conference at one dollar per tithing day in cash

In the after noon J. M. Grant spoke saying we would never be driven from here unless it was for our transgressions for this was the voice of the spirit &c

Mond & Tues 20 & 21 1849. At home and around town

Wed 22nd. Went in Company with E Lee up the Red Butte Cañnon took sick in the night and came home the next day very sick with something like the Mountain Fever. High fever and out of my senses all night.

Frid Aug. 24th 1849. At home weak & nervous. A. Company of U. S. Topographical Engeneers came in today to survey the Lakes & Rivers in the Valley[26]

Sat Aug 25th. Weak yet. Went to see the U. S. Topographical Engeneers, and at home.

Sunday 26th 1849. Went to meet John Taylor spoke told howe he was convinced of the truth of Mormonism & B. Young in the after-noon.

Mond 27. Went home with John Bills & stoped all night

Tues 28. Explored the head of Dry cotton-wood & the Base of the mountain with J. Bills.

Wed. 29th. Explored Second Cotton Wood Cañnon alone and went and stayed all night with William Mathews.

Thurs. 30th. Came home by Neffs mill & got 50 lbs flour

Frid 31 Aug. 1849. Went to Red Butte and got a Load of wood

Sat. Sept 1st 1849. At home all day.

---

26. Word of Captain Howard Stansbury's expedition had reached Utah ahead of him. On this day his wagons arrived in charge of Lieutenant J. W. Gunnison; Stansbury himself remained for a short time at Fort Bridger. His assigned task was to survey routes to and from the Valley of the Great Salt Lake and to make a complete study of the lake itself. See Howard Stansbury, *Explorations and Survey of the Valley of the Great Salt Lake of Utah* . . . (Philadelphia, 1852). See also, Dale L. Morgan, *The Great Salt Lake* (Indianapolis, 1947).

Sund. 2. Went to meeting

Mond 3rd. Went to the Red Butte for wood & Broke my waggon & came home sick Had a hard days work.

Tues & Wed 4 & 5. Laid up with a lame back by hard lifting yester-day.

Thurs Frid & Sat 6, 7 & 8th. Worked at home commenced annother house.

Sund 9th. Went to meeting Rev Mr Crow preached German Presbyterian. Prest Young spoke about raising a fund to be applied for removing the poor to this place also to make a settlement south on tithing &c. in the afternoon J. M. Grant spoke on the fund for the poor.
W. Snow L. Snow J. S. Fulmer F. D. Richards & J. D. Lee was appointed a committee to collect the money for this fund as the people may donate and J. M. Grant is to carry it to the States to be laid out to remove the poor. Rained to day

August 10 to 15. that is six days this week I worked on the Council House.

Sunday 16th. At home all day.
Worked 5 day this week on the Council House. on Thursday the mail came in from the states. on Saturday was sick Gully's company is coming in

Sunday Sep 23rd 1849. Wife & I went to meeting. President Young spoke. Rebuked the people for their high prices on grain &c. and the mechanics on wages &c and also on tithing &c.

Mond 24th Tues 25. Wed 26 Thurs 27 and Frid 28th. Worked on the C. H.

Sat 29th. At home and went with my wife to the store & traded some 23 dollars.

Sund 30th. Went to meeting Levi W. Hancock spoke.

Mond Oct 1 - Tues 2 Wed 3 Thurs 4 Frid 5. Worked on the Council House Thurs was a wet day worked half that day.

Sat & Sund oct 6 & 7th. Was a General Conference. Elders were appointed to go to Itally Sweeden, Denmark France England & the Society isles.

Monday Oct 8th 1849. Worked till noon on the C. H. Not well in the after noon

Tues 9th. Worked on the C. H.

Wed. Worked on the C. H.

Thurs. Worked till noon on do

Frid 12th. Worked on the C. H.

Sat 13th. Worked on the C. H.

Sund 14th. At home all day.

Mond 15th. Worked on the C. H.

Tues 16th. At home. Mother Taylor & family came from the States.

Wed 17th. Worked on C. H.

Thurs 18th. Worked on the C. H.

Frid & Sat. Worked on Do

Sund 21st. Worked at home on my house. Mond Sickish at home

Tues 23rd. Worked on the C. H.

(Wed 24th. Sick around town [crossed out])

Wed 24. Worked on C. H.

Thurs 25. Sick around town

Frid & Sat 26 & 27. Worked on C. H.

Sund 28. Benson & G. A. Smith came in to day. Went to meeting. Big field commenced over Jordan.

Mond 29 Tues 30 Wed 31 & Thurs Nov. 1 Frid 2nd 1849. Worked on the Council House.

Sat Nov. 3rd. Sick went around to the stores and at home. Cold damp weather.

Sunday 4th. At home all day. rainy.

Mond 5. Worked in the after-noon on the C. House.

Tues 6. Wed 7. Thurs 8 Frid 9 and Sat. 10th. Worked on the C. H.

Sund 11th. Went to meeting in the fore noon and in the after noon went with my wife over the Jordan Bridge.

Mond 12 Tues 13 Wed 14. Worked on the Council house.

Thurs 15. Wet day. Fuddled around home and town A small train came in from the States with goods & mail.

Frid 16th Sat 17th. Worked on the C. H. Sat was wet day.

Sund 18th. Went to meeting in the fore-noon. Parley's Co. was preparing to go South.

Mond 19 Tues 20 Wed 21 Thurs Frid & Sat. worked on C. H. Had a fine snow Thurs morn & Sat evening

Sund 25. Rainy day. at home.

Mond 26. Moved our work into the Bowery. Snowy day.

Tues 27. Rainy. Worked on C. H. ¾ of a day.

Wed 28 Thurs 29 Frid 30. Worked on the C. House.

Saturday Decr 1st 1849. At home very sick all day. another Company came in from the States. They left their waggons a few miles beyond the Weber & their cattle over the second mountain and wallowed through the snow sometimes over their hips and came in to day. pleasant weather

Sund Dec 2nd. Cloudy. at home to day.

Mond. & Tues 3 & 4 1849. Worked on the C. House.

On Tues Evening I recieved a notification to meet the House of Representatives on Sat next I being a member of that Body. By what process I became a Representative I know not.[27]

---

27. Hosea Stout had evidently been selected by the YTFIF for this position. Public elections were not held in Utah before 1870; instead, the men for office were selected by the YTFIF and their names submitted to the people for approval. When asked specifically as to the political

Wed 5 Thurs 6 & Frid 7. Worked on the C. House.

Sat 8th. At ten o'clock a.m. I attended the Legislature & commenced acting as a member of the same.
The inhabitants of the Valley are now organized into a provisional State Government with a Govenor Lieut Gov. & other necessary state offices. A Senate of 15 members & House of Representatives of 30 members.

Sunday Decr 9th 1849. At home mostly but around some. Very Cold day.

Mond. 10th. Worked on the C. H. Mother Taylor & family moved away. Very Cold.

Tues 11th Wed 12th Thurs 13th and Frid 14th. Worked on the C. House. Thawing some

Sat 15th. Worked at home. A deep snow fell last night and snowed till near noon.

Sunday 16th. At home all day

Mond 17. Tues 18 Wed 19. Thurs 20 Frid 21. (Very hard South wind)

Sat 22. Worked on the C. House Very warm & thawing for 2 days

Sunday 23rd. Very warm & pleasant. I was at home.

Mond 24th Tues 25 Wed 26 Thurs 27 Frid 28 Sat 29. Worked on the Council House Weather warm.

Sund 30. At home only went in the S of town awhile.

Monday Decr 31st 1849. Worked on the Council House & thus ended the year. the weather is clear and pleasant Worker is going on well.

Tuesday January 1st 1850. Worked on the C. House.

Wed 2 Thurs 3 Frid 4. Worked on the C. House

Sat. January 5th 1850. Met with Legislature which went into joint Session. Committees were appointed as follows one to draft a Law regulating the Judiciary. One a Revenue Law, or Ways & Means one on Claims. Myself Col Rockwood & J. S. Stratton comprised this committee
The country as far as settled was divided into eloctorial destricts or precincts. Also a committee to draft a law concerning elections.
Legislature adjd till next Tues at ten a.m.

Sunday 6th. At home mostly but around town some.

Mond 7th. Worked on the C. H.

Tues Jan 8th. Met with the Legislature Heard a letter from the Utah Valley. The Indians a again committing depredations on the whites by stealing cattle Horses &c One Indian has been killed by the whites for attempting to shoot a man for attempting to take a shirt from him which the Indian had stolen This was reported to the Legislature

---

activities of the Council of Fifty, a member wrote: ". . . and I will say that this council . . . did continue . . . and become the legislature of the state of Deseret." Benjamin F. Johnson in a letter to George S. Gibbs, October 1903 (typescript, Utah State Historical Society; original, Brigham Young University). See also Dale L. Morgan, *The State of Deseret, Utah Historical Quarterly,* VIII (1940), 67-239.

The Legislature went into Joint session and took up the report of the committee on the Judiciary but did not finish the Bill to day.

Wed Jan 9th 1850. Met with the Legislature at ten a.m. The act reported by the Committee on the Judiciary was passed today & some joint resolutions passed concerning the non-attendance of its members fining any member who is not present at the calling of the roll fifty cents and one dollar if not present in half an hour & two dollars if not present in one hour thereafter.

Adjd till tomorrow at ten a.m.

Thurs Jan 10th 1850. Met with the Legislature again at ten a.m.

Frid & Sat 11 & 12th Jan 1850. Worked on the C. House.

Sunday Jan 13th 1850. At home mostly.

Mond 14th. Met with the L. again.

Tues Jan 15th 1850. Met with the Legislature again   An act to take out the Jourdain west was passed &c   adjd to 28th inst

Wed & Thurs. Worked at C. House

Frid & Sat. At home Snowing.

Sunday 20th 1850. The snow storm seems to be over The snow is now much deeper than it has been since I have been in the Valley.

Mond & Tues & Wed. at home   mostly at the tithing office some

Thurs Jan 24th. To day the wind blows uncommonly hard from the S.   driving the snow before it and through every crevice of the house makes it a very uncomfortable day   Prest Young has a party to which I had an invitation but was detained on account of the weather.   This is the most disagreeable day I have seen in the Valley.

Friday Jan 25th 1850. Weather calm but my house well supplied with snow which took all the fore noon to regulate   the weather is now clear & warm like a summer day except the mountains of snow which lies over the Valley   The greatest contrast in the weather is yesterday & to day.

Sat. 26th. Worked at the C. House

Sund 27th. Wife & I went to meeting to B. Y.'s house.

Mond 28. Attended the Legislature

Tues 29. Attended the Legislature.   To day D. H. Wells was appointed Judge of the Supreme Court of the State & Daniel & Orson Spencer associate Judges William Crosby presiding Judge & A. H. Perkins & James Hendrix associate Judges of G. S. L. County Daniel Carns Presiding Judge Isaac Higbee & William Miller associate Judges of Utah County   Isaac Clark presiding Judge & Daniel Birch & D. C. Davis Associate Judges of Weber County.   Also several other officers appointed.   Besides several County limits prescribid &c.

Wed 30th. Worked on the C. House

Thurs 31 Frid 1 Sat 2nd 1850. Worked on the C. House.   On Friday was sick   worked only half day.

Sunday Feb. 3th 1850. Clear pleasant day. At home.

Monday Feb 4th. Went to the Legislature. An expedition is now fitting out to go against the Utahs in Utah Valley for killing cattle, stealing horses &c also for shooting at our people. G. D. Grant started to day with one Company & Col Scott was ordered to raise another and join him as soon as possible.

But instead of doing so he came to the Legislature with his Adjutant and there both spent the after-noon without doing anything. About sun set he requested a hearing and commenced a series of implications against the Majr Genl & Gov under the head of misunderstanding.

After he was through the Gov gave him his mind roughly showing him that he was wilfully neglecting his duty, &c which ended by Scott giveing up his papers and withdrawing from the expedition.[28] No more at present.

---

28. From the time he took over direction of the Mormon Church, Brigham Young had resented the independent attitude of John Scott. Several times earlier Scott had taken a stand against the appointees of the leader and justified himself; and since he was an efficient officer and a loyal member, he had retained his position.

The difficulty here seems to have stemmed from several sources. His Special Orders No. 3 from the major general's office to him as colonel ordered Scott to raise a company of fifty men to carry on a campaign against the Indians of Utah County and concluded with the sentence: "You are also expected to operate in connection with Captain George D. Grant in carrying out this order." Orders, Utah Territorial Militia Records (Military Records Section, Utah State Archives).

In executing this order, Grant was permitted to take men from Scott's company as well as his own and was sent ahead, leaving Scott to follow with whatever additional men he would be able to raise. As a colonel, he felt that General Wells had insulted him by thus sending a captain ahead of him.

Of more importance perhaps, though not appearing in the record, was the order marked "Private Instructions to Col. John Scott," which gave him to understand that "attendant circumstances" would justify the killing of women also.

Special Orders No. 3
Head Quarters Nauvoo Legion
Major's Generals Office
G.S.L. City Jany 31st 1850

Col. John Scott

You are hereby ordered to raise forthwith a Company of fifty efficient men, and see they are provided with horses, arms, and ammunition, and rations sufficient for twenty days, and proceed with said Company to Fort Utah, in the Utah Valley with as little delay as possible, There to cooperate with the inhabitants of said valley in quilling and staying the operations of all hostile Indians, and otherwise act, as the circumstances may require exterminating such, as do not separate themselves from· their hostile clans, and sue for peace. You will march from Great Salt Lake City, as early as next monday morning, and make full report of all your proceedings under this order on your return, and keep my office apprised of intervining operations, should circumstances require: You are also expected to operate in connection with Capt. George D. Grant in carrying out this order.

Daniel H Wells
Major General
Nauvoo Legion

Private Instructions

To Col John Scott

Sir in carrying out the above order you will keep in exercise every principle of humanity, compatible with the Laws of War, and see no violence is permitted to women and Children, unless the same shall be demanded by attendant circumstances— The Utah Indians have been notified repeatedly of the consequences that would ensue to them, if they did not cease to molest the white Inhabitants and their Herds You will therefore proceed against them, without further apprisal or notice, and execute your orders.—

Daniel H Wells
Major General
Nauvoo Legion

Orders, Utah Territorial Militia Records (Military Records Section, Utah State Archives). In this instance Scott acted true to form by stating his position openly before his peers in the legislature and handing in his papers.

Tues 5th 1850. Worked on the C. House

Wed Feb 6th 1850. Worked on the C. H till noon Was sick. Went to the Fort.

Thurs Feb 7th 1850. At home till noon. Benj & Anna Jones met here before Prest Young to have their difficulties adjusted as they have come to the sober conclusion to seperate after being married 17 years. Was arrainged accordingly
In the afternoon worked on C. H.

Frid & Sat 8 & 9. Worked on the C. House.
Sat morning an express came in from Utah bearing the news that they had a battle yester after noon 4 men wounded The number of indians not known. The indians were in a deep ravine & could not be hurt with artillery The names of those who were wounded were Saml Carn, Alexr Stephens, Alfred Miles and James Orr, who was wounded by his own gun discharging accidentally.

Sunday Feb. 10th 1850. At home. Another express came in today from Utah The Brethren had another battle yesterday. Joseph Higbee was killed and Alexr Williams A. L. Fulmer Nowland[29] wounded
What impression has been made on the Indians is not known. Genl Wells has gone to the seat of war.

Monday Feb 11th. Worked on C. H. An express from Uth states no more fighting.

Tues 12th. Met with the Legislature. The Election Law passed to day also a grant to Company to Ferry across the Green river in two places. Wells Davis & myself comt for military law
An Express came in this morning. The Indians have fled from their thicket. Nine have been found dead on the ground and signs of many more being killed or wounded.
Genl Wells has laid the Utah under Marshal law & brought those who refused to do duty to submit to order and all things are going on well and preperations are being made to pursue the indians.

Wed Thurs Frid & Sat 16. worked on the Council House.
Friday morning an express came from Utah bearing intelligence of one or two more fights in which 14 Indians were killed and none of our men hurt and the squaws and children taken.
Most of the other Indians have fled to the mountians

Sunday Feb. 17th 1850. At home all day Mond worked on the C. House

Tues Feb 19th. Met with the Legislature Nothing of importance done. To day Gen Wells and most of the soldiers returned from their campaign to the Utah bring some 26 women & children prisoners & 13 horses The women & children were distributed among the people who were willing to take & educate and civilize them and the Horses are going to be given to some of the friendly Indians.[30]

---

29. This was Jabez Nowlin who had been a first corporal in Company "C" of the Mormon Battalion. He was sent with the sick detachment to Pueblo, Colorado, and returned with them to Salt Lake Valley.
In this expedition Nowlin was in charge of the foot soldiers and was slightly wounded in the nose. In 1853 as a colonel he led an expedition against the Indians near Manti, Utah. He is not to be confused with Lieutenant Howland of the Mounted Rifles of the Stansbury command, who also participated in this action.

30. Gottfredson in *Indian Depredations*, 28-35, gives full details of this encounter and justifies the killing because of Indian resistance. Tullidge in *History of Salt Lake City*, 66-69, quotes the Stansbury report, which considers the action as necessary to eradicate a nuisance. William A. Hickman in *Brigham's Destroying Angel*, . . . (New York, 1872), 56-70, pictures it as an

One company are left at Utah to guard or take those indians who fled to the canon near Fort Utah.

Wed Thurs Frid & Sat 23rd. Worked on the C. House.

Had a beautiful snow on Saturday morning about 3 inches deep. (A smart [crossed out]) Shock of an earthquake was felt this week

Sund Feb 24 1850. at home

Monday 25. Worked on the C. House part of the day and in the evening met with the Committee to draft the Military law.

Tues 26. Met with the Legislature No particular business was transacted.

Wed 27th. Met with the Legislature again. In the fore noon I was appointed States Atterney by the Joint vote of both houses. In the after noon the military law was passed

Very snowy day. The mail from San-Pete arrived. Walker approved of the war against the Utah Indians

Thurs Feb 28th 1850. Met with the Legislature again The fore noon was mostly spent in passing a bill providing for a University for the State which provided for a Chancellor 12 Regents & Treasurer to be appointed by the Legislature which was done also 5000 dollars voted out of the Treasurey to commence it.

The after noon was [s]pent in adjusting the pay for provisions ammunition &c and horses killed in the Utah war After which the Criminal Code was taken up & about half the after noon spent in discussing the first section defining wilful murder & did not pass it so the matter was laid over till tomorrow to be taken up again. This bill is likely to occupy considerable time before it is passed.

Friday March 1st 1850. Met with the Legislature again The criminal Code was again taken up and the whole fore noon spent in debating the first section & offering amendments but did not pass it.

The after noon business was mostly occupied in debating the 27th Section on "Unlawful Sexuel intercourse" which finally passed the Second reading. Some alterations were made in the appointments of the Regents of the University in consequence of the absence of some who were appointed yesterday.

Among others who were put in their place I was apointed one. Some other bills were introduced and passed the first reading and laid over till tomorrow.

Saturday March 2nd 1850. Met with the Legislature A bill providing for County recorders & one for survey Genl one to establish an arsenal and be ready for Indian depredations were passed besides some other business.

Sunday 3rd 1850. at home all day.

Monday 4th. Worked at C. H.

Tues 5th. Not well. Instituted a suit against Robt Porter & Peter Lish for tresspassing on the property of Lewis Vasques.[31]

---

action taken in much the same spirit as the "hunts" to do away with predatory animals. All agree that at least forty men and women were killed and that some children were taken prisoners.

31. Pierre Louis Vasquez was born in St. Louis, Missouri, on October 3, 1798, the youngest of twelve children. From his letters and the fact that he spoke both French and Spanish fluently, it would seem that he had a fair education. He early became associated with the mountain men whose names have made history during the fur trading era and followed this life on the frontier for more than thirty years.

Wed 6th. Worked on C. H.

Thursday March 7th 1850. At home in the fore-noon. Had Company visiting to day.

This after noon I attended a Court martial detailed by the Maj Genl to try Col John Scott for refusing to obey the orders of the Maj Genl to raise 50 and means to go against the Indians and for using abusive & unbecoming language calculated to discourage the men enrolled.

I was appointed Special Judge Advocate.

Scott acted very stubborn & abusive throughout the whole trial. The charge was clearly sustained and he was cashiered by the Court.[32]

Frid 8th. Worked at the C. H. till noon then went to attend to the suit against Porter and Lish.

Sat. 9th. Attended the trial against Porter & Lish before W Snow Esqr in favor of Lewis Vasques. There was nothing proven against them & they were acquitted.

This is the first suit I have prosecuted under my appointment as States Attorney.

In the after noon I also prosecuted another Suit H. S. Eldrege V.S Mr Long for killing an ox which did not belong to him. This case was sustained & Long had to pay 30 dollars. I was very sick all day.

Sunday March 10th 1850. At home all day.

Monday 11th 1850. Went to the Council House to work as usual but found that the price of labor had so arrainged that I would be allowed only 1.75 per day so I brought away my tools & came home as I did not think I could afford to work at that price considering the relative prices of every other thing.

Tues & Wed 12 & 13. Worked at home mostly

In 1842 Vasquez and Jim Bridger went into a partnership and built Fort Bridger near the Green River crossing, a relationship which was cordial until Bridger left in 1853. In 1848 Vasquez married a woman from Kentucky. Her maiden name was Lane, and she had one or two children by a previous marriage. In 1849 Vasquez opened a store in Salt Lake City; in 1855 he sold his claim to Fort Bridger to the Mormons. Daniel Mackintosh Papers (originals, Utah State Historical Society).

Soon after this Vasquez returned to Missouri, living for a time in a brick house on Hickory Street, St. Louis. Later he bought a home in Westport, Missouri, and had a farm less than two miles from the one owned by Jim Bridger, so that the two men continued to associate with each other in their declining years. Vasquez died in September 1868 and was buried in Kansas City.

32. Since Scott had already handed in his papers, this court-martial was only to make the dismissal final. The full account is found in the records of the Utah Territorial Militia (Military Records Section, Utah State Archives).

Scott was cited for "Disobedience to Orders and Unofficulike [sic] Conduct" with "Specification In this that Col. John Scott of the 1st Regt to Cohort Nauvoo Legion refused to obey the order of the Major Genral Comdy as recorded in Special Orders No 3 of the 31st of Jany for the Expedition against the Indians also made use of language publicly calculated to discourage the men enrolled for the Expedition against the Indians and other wise rendering an injury to the Service."

To these charges and specifications the prisoner pleaded "not Guilty."

The original minutes of the trial leave blank places for the personnel of the court but give the testimony in some detail. Almost two pages are devoted to the testimony of John Scott and his reasons for refusing to follow behind the expedition when as the commanding officer he should have been leading it. He also confessed to making a vulgar remark, "shit-arse and flat-out failure," but insisted that it was made only in the presence of his adjutant. The revised and carefully written minutes for the record have abbreviated the first testimony and stated that "The evidence on the part of the prosecution being closed, and *no* testimony on the part of the prisoner," (italics ed.) the court pronounced sentence. *Ibid.*

It would seem that the situation was built up to force Scott out of the military. He did not leave the church, however, but filled a mission to Ireland from 1854 to 1857.

Thurs 14th. At home. deep snow this morning & snowy day but melting

Frid & Sat 15 & 16th. Snowy weather continues and cold I was at home mostly but could not work much.

Sunday March 17th 1850. Pleasant clear day. I was at home

Mon & Tues 18 & 19 - March. Worked at home. Pleasant weather

Wednesday 20th March - 1850. At home snowy day at earley candle light I met with the Regents of the University but no particular business was done. came home at Eleven o'clock P. M.

Thurs. 21. At home all day Very clear day and warm.

Friday 22nd. At home all day

Saturday March 23rd 1850. To day was an officer drill Andrew Lytle was also elected Col to fill the vacancy of John Scott, cashiered.
I presented a resignation of my office as first Leiut to the Majr Genl but he did not accept it.[33]

Sunday March 24th 1850. Cloudy damp day — I was at home all day. C. [Charles] Shumway & some 8 or 10 more has arrived from San Pete. He states that they have lost 100 head of cattle and the snow yet very deep They had to come out on snow shoes. There was but 15 lbs of bred stuff to each individual when they left and no meat.
They have come for provisions. Walker the Indian Chief has been baptized and wants to go and preach to the Utahs.

Mond & Tues 25 & 26. At home and around the about the office. Very wet weather

Wednesday 27th 1850. at home. Met with the Regents at dark No particular business done Not being well I came home earley

Thursday March 28th. At home but not being well did not work.

Frid 29. Met with the Legislature. A law was passed prohibiting the selling any guns & ammunition to the Indians.
The remainder of P. P Pratts exploring company came in[34]

Sat. 30th. Rainy all forenoon Company musters to day.

Sund March 31st 1850. At home mostly. Around some assisted to bury Br T. Turley's wife.

---

33. Hosea Stout evidently submitted his resignation from the military because Andrew Lytle had been promoted over him to the office of colonel to take Scott's place in the military. From this time on Stout's interest seems to be in the legal rather than the military field.

34. Parley P. Pratt had been appointed to go on an exploring expedition south to study the land for the site of possible settlements and for a road toward the sea. He took fifty men in twelve wagons and one carriage with many extra horses, an odometer to measure distance, one brass field piece, and many small arms. The official personnel under Pratt were W. W. Phelps, topographic engineer; David Fullmer, counselor; and John Brown, captain; with captains of ten, Isaac C. Haight, Joseph Matthews, Joseph Horne, Ephraim Green, and Josiah Arnold. Robert Campbell was clerk and historian.
The group explored the Sevier River area and followed also the route paralleling the present U. S. Highway 91 as far south as Parowan, Utah, with their wagons. From that point they went horseback to the rim of the basin south, everywhere keeping careful record of distances, flora, fauna, and general geologic formations. Their reports formed the basis for future settlements.

Monday 1st April 1850. Rainy day till noon. I was engaged in a suit between Ivie & Hanks on the part of Ivie in matter of debt appealed from this Justice to the County Court.

Tues 2 Apl 1850. Spent the fore noon attending to legal business and in the after noon worked for G. D. Grant.

Wednesday 3rd Apl 1850. Worked for G. D. Grant in the fornoon. In the after-noon attended to legal business.

At dark met with the Regents of the University. It was decided that each one of the Board & Chancellor write a proclamation to be sent abroad, also two petitions were read & accepted and ordered to be printed &.

Thursday 4th Apl 1850. At 10 o'clock a. m. attended a trial before Bishop Whitney which had been appealed from Bishops Murdoc & Hickenlooper Jas Ivy against Ebenezer Hanks Appealed by Hanks.

I was council to Ivy. & sustained the former decision & costs to be paid by Hanks.

Friday 5th Apl 1850. In the fore-noon attended to legal business in criminal cases now pending.

In the after noon I attended as council for Jas Ivy another Vs Hanks which had also been appealed by Hanks as above to the County Court In this case I gained 14.50 more than the former judgment in favor of Ivy & Hanks to pay the costs.

Between 11 & 12 o'clock at night my wife was delivered of a son weighing 9¾ lbs and all well

This was better luck than success in legal buisness.

Saturday 6 Apl 1850. Attended Conference

Sund 7 Apl. Attended Conference

Monday 8th Apl 1850. Very Rainy day. Attended a suit before Aaron Farr Esqr wherein the State of Deseret was plff [plaintiff] and Joel & Rawson Harvey Deft [defendant] wherein Defts had opperated against the Utah Expedition against the Indians & abused the officers sent to press horses & ran one horse off so that it could not be had in the service after it was pressed I was council on the part of the State. The Defts were fined fifty dollars & costs amounting in all to about 75 dollars.

At dark met with the Board of Regents. Two or three circulars were read and adopted.

Tues 9 Apl 1850. Attended to legal business in the fore noon and around home gardening &c the rest of the day.

Wednesday 10th Apl 1850. Occupied at home gardening Mechanicks had a meeting at 5 o'clock P. M. for the purpose of regulating the price of wages &c.

Thursday 11th Apl 1850. At home gardening most of the day Regents met this evening at 5 o'clock P. M. Several circulars was read and approved.

Friday, April 12th 1850. Went to the Fort then home mostly all day. Very sick.

Saturday 13th April 1850. Attended to some Legal business and at home. In the evening attended an officer drill of a few officers who met to practice on the steps & manuel.

Sunday 14th Apl 1850. Went to meeting in the fore-noon. Heber, Geo A. & B. Y. spoke. In the after noon P. P. Pratt preached G. W. Langley & Father Tanner's funerals

Monday 15th Apl 1850. Attended a trial before Esq Farr at 8 o'clock. The State against Wm Kelley who was charged for conversion & Trover.[35] He was fined 18 dollars and costs. At home the rest of the day   Not well.

Tues 16th Apl 1850. Very unwell with cold. Attending to legal business in favor of the State. Stormy windy day.

The trains for the States and Eastern ferries started to day. Large companies are also going now to the Gold mines I do not believe that they can cross the mountains yet for many days.

Wed. 17th Apl 1850. fine snow. At home and around the tithing office & attending to legal business. At 5 o'clock P. M. met with the Regents of the University but there was not mebers enough to form a quorum. I was very weak & feeble to day.

Thurs 18th Apl 1850. At home working & gardening.

Friday 19th Apl 1850. At home working.   Gardening

Saturday 20th Apl 1850. Met the Supreme Court at the tithing office for the trial of Cimon Lance for assault & Battery but the case was refered to Esqr. Farr, whither we immediately repaired and had the case tried.   Lance was fined 75 dollars and costs 90 in all also to pay Scott 25 dol for unrendered services as he had been sold on crime[36] to him &c.

Sunday 21 Apl 1850. Stormy cold weather for several days past. I was at home all day nearly.

Monday 22nd Apl 1850. Attended a trial Dan Jones Vs E. Williams in matter of debt as council for Jones. The trial was adjourned till to morrow   I was uncommonly sick all day

Tues 23d Apl 1850. At home working till noon   In the after-noon attended to Jones trial before Esqr Farr obtained a Judgement in favor of Jones amounting to 239.17. This debt is due Br Jones from Williams for assistance in helping him from Wales.

Wednesday 24 Apl 1850. Working at home and around town and at Capt Stansberry's &c. He is at law with his Doctor.[37]

Thurs 25th Apl 1850. Raining and snowing all day.

---

35. This phrase, usually written "trover and conversion," appears often in these pages. It comes from the old French law as an action of trespass against one who found goods and would not restore them to the owner; hence it became an action to recover the value of goods wrongfully converted. It is often used in the recovery of horses and cattle. The term "conversion" later carried the connotation of changing the brand on an animal.

36. The fact that Lance ". . . had been sold on crime to him" seems to infer that Scott had paid a penalty or fine which Lance was to have repaid by labor. It was common practice to hire prisoners out for their board and a small sum to be paid to the state.

37. Stansbury hired as his geologist a physician lately from England, Dr. James Blake, who was to be responsible for making the scientific collections and keeping the geological notes. Dr. Blake had accompanied Lieutenant Howland on the second Mormon expedition against the Indians of Utah County.

Differences arose between Stansbury and Blake which caused the doctor to leave without notice, taking with him most of his specimens and leaving a note saying that he did this to secure his pay. Stansbury took his problems to Brigham Young, who advised him to secure a search warrant and regain his property. This he did. Justice Farr had ruled that when Blake made his final report at St. Louis he could claim his pay. Stansbury returned the report as wholly inadequate, so Blake brought him into the court on a suit to collect $1,436 for services rendered. The court ruled in favor of Stansbury. Morgan, *The Great Salt Lake*, 238-39.

Friday 26th Apl 1850. Rained & snowed till noon. Worked at home in the afternoon

Saturday 27th Apl 1850. Fine pleasant clear day. Worked at home gardening.

Sunday 28th 1850 Apl. Fine pleasant day. Very sick. At home and at meeting.

Monday 29th Apl 1850. Attended a sale of cattle at the Stray Pound in the morning. Sold high Pat Souette was arrested & tried & nepoed[38] to day. He escaped over the mountains with some others in the Utah war & came back & was trying to way lay & kill all the whites he could catch alone. One man had been killed coming from San Pete here lately.

Tuesday 30th Apl 1850. Worked at home. Moved old Dobie house timbers home. Warm and pleasant weather

Wednesday 1st May 1850. Warm & cloudy with hard south wind.

Thursday 2nd May 1850. Worked at home   Went down to Anna's   Hard winds.

Friday 3rd May 1850. Quite cool. Quite unwell. Around the office & at home.

Saturday 4th May 1850. Worked at home all day.

Sunday 5th May 1850. Went to meeting & at home.

Monday 6. Worked at home.

Tues 7th. Worked at home

Wednesday 8th. Worked at home

---

38. The *exact* meaning of the word "nepo" is not known. Since it is "open" spelled backwards, there is a conjecture that it might refer to a practice of disemboweling a murdered man, filling the abdominal cavity with rocks, and throwing the body into a stream or lake. A reference to the word is found in Edward Bonney, *The Banditti of the Prairies* . . . (Chicago, [190?]), 214. "*Eston C. Cropper sworn.*—'I have been keeper of the prisoners. Have overheard a great deal of conversation amongst them. They said Bonney would be "nepoed," which I understand to be their usual phrase for killed. They used the expression "*nepo*" seven or eight times. A good deal of their talk was blind, and I could not understand it.' "

In this case the young Indian was killed, but the disposition of the body is not learned. A letter in the "Journal History" (Church of Jesus Christ of Latter-day Saints Historian's Library), April 28, 1850, verifies this:

In the evening an express arrived from Fort Utah, bearing a letter of which the following is a copy:

                                                    Utah County, April 28, 1850
Daniel H. Wells, Esqu.
Sir: I understand that Patsovett is in your city, or was last Monday. He and his brother have been killing cattle since the war with the Indians and threaten to kill every white man that he can. We have been searching for him to kill him, but have not found him yet. But we found his brother and have killed him. We wish you would search for him, and, if he can be found in your valley, to kill him before he can do any more mischief.

                                                    Isaac Higbee, P. W. Conover
Further, Stout's statement that the young Indian was "arrested & tried and nepoed" is explained by an entry made in the John W. Gunnison Journals of the Stansbury Survey in the National Archives. Gunnison had come in from the lake survey on business and was in Great Salt Lake City most of the last week of April. On this same date — April 29 — he wrote: "Patsowits one of the Utah Indians has been discovered lurking about here. He is accused of killing an emigrant near Sanpete last week & has been driven from Utah 5 p.m.-a company is pointed out near Mill Creek who are to shoot & bury him. He strove manfully against being bound in the council house — but no earthly mercy is shewn." Entry of April 29, 1850, John W. Gunnison, "Notes & Journal Summer of 1850 in Salt Lake Valley, Field Survey Data of the Survey of Great Salt Lake by Captain Howard Stansbury, 1849-1850" (National Archives, Washington, D.C.), RG 77.

Thurs 9th. Worked at home

Friday 10th. Worked at home Had a fine refreshing rain last night good for gardens

Saturday 11th 1850. Woked at home Gardening some.

Sund 12. Went to meeting. The Persident reproved the People for not paying tithing & grumbling &c and the Welch & others who had been helped from England & else where & were not willing to pay those who helped them.

Monday & Tuesday 13 & 14. Worked at home Gardening &c.

Wednesday 15. Went to North Cotton Wood 17 miles with E. T. Benson. I have 2½ acres of wheat sowed here which looks well. I have taken up 30 acres of land here which I expect to improve for a farm. The country here appears to me to be better adapted for farming than any place I have seen in the Valley.
    My wifes mother & family live in this Settlement.

Thurs 16th 1850. Spent to day in looking at my lands wheat and viewing the country.

Friday 17th. Came home in company with Thos S. Smith[39]

Saturday 18th. Attended officer drill to day.

Sund 19 May 1850. At home & around town & at meeting. good rain last night.

Monday 20th May 1850. Very unwell to day. Brigham Heber & a large company of others started to Utah to meet the Indians relative to making a genl treaty with them & to trade with them. A large number of Indians have assembled there for the purpose.

Tuesday 21 May 1850. At home and attending to legal business for Miles Miller &c

Wednesday 22 May 1850. At home all day Very sick Hard south wind all day.

Thurs 23 Frid 24, 1850. At home. Gardening but not very well.

Saturday 25th May 1850. To day was a general company drill I attended in the fore noon and in the afternoon attended a trial before Esqr Farr, Lorenzo Perry Vs A. D L. Buckland in debt of 70 dollars 50 cents. I was council on the Part of Perry who sustained his afc & Buckland "Forked up"
    After this trial was over Buckland was taken for assault & Battery on said Perry. in this case I appeared on the part of the state Buckland was fined

Sunday May 26th 1850. Went to meeting to day. Tolerable rainy day & cold.

Monday 27th May 1850. Engaged some in legal business To day a few men came in from the States. They left Fort Kearney on 6th Apl more are expected in soon & some 300 went by Fort Hall.

---

39. Thomas Sasson Smith was born April 3, 1818, in New York. He was baptized June 15, 1844. He came west with the 1848 emigration, bringing his mother, Abigail Demont Smith, his wife, Polly Clark Smith, and a daughter who was born at Council Bluffs.
    In 1850 he went south with the colonists of the Iron Mission. The record lists him as thirty-two years old, a Seventy. Because of the winter weather, Smith left his family at home in Davis County, Utah, but returned for them later. In 1856 and through 1862, he is mentioned as living at Johnson's Fort or Summit between Cedar City and Parowan, Utah.
    In 1864 he was called to raise cotton in the Muddy Valley and was the first settler to arrive on the site of St. Thomas, Nevada, which was named for him. By 1870 the colonists were advised to leave the area because of the exorbitant taxes imposed by the State of Nevada.
    Smith returned to Farmington, Utah, where he lived until 1884, when he moved to Wilford, Idaho. He served as bishop there until 1887 and died July 1, 1890.

Tuesday 28th 1850. Went to Allen Taylors at the mouth of Mill Creek Kanyon then with D. H. Wells who was with me to the mill up the Canon about 8 miles and came home about dark

Wednesday 29th May 1850. Worked at home. Most all day.

Thursday 30th May 1850. Attending to Legal business Sally Murdoc V.S. S. O Holmes in matter of debt.

Friday 31st May 1850. At home mostly to day Irrigating.

Saturday June 1st 1850. Rained some. I was around home and about town.

Sunday June 2nd 1850. Went to meeting. Dan Jones[40] spoke At 6 o'clock P. M. Elders meeting had a case decided by the people which I had been employed to recover a horse which had been sold as a stray. & was claimed by Miles Miller. The horse was recovered. This method was adopted to save the time, expense & hard feelings of a long and tedious lawsuit

President Young recommended this method & for brethren to try their difficulties first in the church and not go to law untill a man will not abide the decision of the church tribunals

I also made a short address recommending the same measures.

Monday 3rd June 1850. The weather is tolerable cold & cloudy not good for crops I was around home mostly

The emegrants are still coming and numerous hosts expected to pass through here this season.

Tues 4th. Worked at home.

Wed. 5th. Worked at home.

At six o'clock P. M. the Regents of the University met at the Bowery. A committy was appointed to survey the lands selected for the University & locate the building &c for the different departments of the institution D. H. Wells D. Spencer H. Stout were said committee.

Thurs 6. Worked at home.

Friday 7th. Not well but around to Emegrants camps —

Sat 8th. Engaged in a suit Sally Murdock Vs. S. O. Homes in action of debt. Settled by Homes confessing Judgement for $100 before A. F. Farr Esqr. This evening Thos Williams & a large company of Emegrants came in from the States bringing the U. S. Mail to this place. among those who came was William Hibbard of Nauvoo. (See my journal of the January 9th 1846.

Sunday June 9th 1850. Went to meeting with my wife at the Bowery. L. W. Hancock, N. K. Whitney & E. T. Benson spoke in the fore noon Benson raked down Dr Blake late of the U. S. Topographical Engineers for his practic of medicine in

---

40. Dan Jones was born August 4, 1811, at Flintshire, Wales. He received a college education and then emigrated to the United States in 1840. Here he became the owner and captain of a little river steamer on the Mississippi known as the *Maid of Iowa.*

In 1843 Jones met Joseph Smith and soon thereafter joined the Mormon Church. In 1845 he went on a mission to Wales where he baptized some 2,000 people in four years. He returned, bringing with him a company of emigrants, in August 1849. Soon after this he went with the Parley P. Pratt exploring expedition to the south and in 1851 was sent to colonize Sanpete County.

After only a year there Jones was sent on a second mission to Wales from which he returned in 1856, bringing with him 703 persons. They sailed on the *Samuel Curling.*

In 1857 he began operating a boat, the *Timely Gull* on the Great Salt Lake. He died January 3, 1862, at Provo, Utah.

this place. In the after-noon the Sacrament was taken and exhortation by John Young & W. Snow. Elders meeting at six o'clock P. M.

Monday June 10th 1850. This morning I was applied to by one Kenicoot an emegrant as council to conduct a suit V.S Francis Drake & others, Emegrants who had established a raft ferry across the Weber & had sunk said Plff waggon and lost it together with all his entire out fit even to his wearing clothes but they had insured them safe over & would not pay him so he had appealed to the law, as above I went with plff to Esqr Farr and took out an attachment for all their goods & effects.

In the after noon came to trial. Both parties were much excited & very turbulent. Trial continued till dark. Judgement postponed till tomorrow.

Tuesday June 11th 1850. Went to Esqr Farrs to learn the decision which was $75 & costs in our favor Spent the day in trying settle the concern without much success as they talked of an appeal on the part of the Defence.

In the evening the Deft learning that several more suits were likely to come against them for others who had suffered in like manner, concluded to pay up and be off.

Wednesday June 12th 1850. At home and at the office & Livingistons store; not being very well

Thursday June 13th 1850. At home working some. Not well to day

Friday June 14th 1850. At home to day gardening. Raining showery day & windy

Saturday June 15th 1850. Worked at home To day the "Deseret News a weekly paper was first issued.

Sunday June 16th 1850. Went to meeting to day. At 4 o'clock there was a trial before the High Council against several of the Utah people relative to a dissatisfaction which arose with the Committee sent there to trade with the Indians about 2 weeks since. They were "whipped & cleared"

Monday & Tues 17 & 18 1850. Worked at home & read, frosty

Wednesday 19th 1850. June. Worked at home. At six P. M. met with the regents of the University.

Thursday 20th June 1850. Sick to day but around town some.

Friday June 21st 1850. Attending to legal business. one case Hibbard vs. Heth in assault & also same v.s. Heth & Francisco in debt.

Another case Steckleman v.s. Staenmitz & Cliner in Trover and conversion, all emegrants The last case was tried at dark before Esqr Snow ended about one o'clock P. M. I was council on the part of the plff.

Sat. June 22nd 1850. Attending to legal business all day. The cases of Hibbard vs Heth & Francisco came of at 9 a.m. The deft did not appear but took the Golden Slope in the night Judgement was rendered against them & Heth fined ten dollars and an officer sent after them.

Sunday June 23rd 1850. Attended meeting to day.

Monday 24th June 1850. Attending to legal business.

Tuesday June 25th 1850. Attended court to day before Esq W. Snow. State vs E. C. Dougherty Leach & Watts complainants. Mr Dougherty was arrested for leaving a man named Willard sick on the road to perish but upon testimony it was found that the report was not correct and he was honorably acquited.

Wednesday. June 26th 1850. Attended Court to day had 2 cases both times on the part of the plff. first case Larkin Price vs Ben F. Grewell 2nd Joseph Lamb vs Almon Fowler George D. Fowler Alonson Fowler Edwin Ray. Both cases was for a settlement and division of property among emegrants the parties wishing to seperate.

Thursday June 27th 1850. Attended Court as before Two suits Wm Burnham vs Caleb Bucknam & Moody Kimball Benj Phillips, Peter Woodin, & Abner Smith vs Joseph Davis all of Ia In the former case I defended the plff & the latter the Deft Both cases was a dispute & seperation between emegrants. People are beginning to harvest wheat, and eat peas.

Friday June 28th 1850. Attended Court as before. Two cases Marshal McIntire vs Jos Davis of Indiana. & Elijah Woodruff vs Benjm Gale of Indiana. Defended the Deft in the first and plf in last.

Disputes are arising among the emegrants as may be seen above while they appeal to law for a redress of grievances & division of property which is not very interisting to relate

Saturday June 29th 1850. Feel very much worn out having been so closely engaged in law for the last few days Was around the office to day

Sunday June 30th 1850. Went to meeting to day.

Monday July 1st 1850. Attended Court before Esqr Snow Dr Jas Blake vs Howard Stansbery of the U.S. T. Eneneer in demand $1436.00 - I defended plff Non-suited as he had previously obtained a judgment before Esqr Farr for what was due him. Spent the rest of the day about the office & Bowry which we now have for Courts.

Tuesday July 2nd 1850. Attended Court before Esqr Farr Dr Blake vs Capt Stansbery on a capas to show cause why he should not pay the judgement above refered to. Non-suited again.

In the after noon attended before Esqr Snow. State on the Complaint of Dan Jones vs Wm. C. Grant (Emegrant) for shooting Compt horse. Sustained

Wednesday July 3rd 1850. Attended Court before Esqr Farr 2 cases State vs Simeon Howd & also State vs Mr. Jacob F. Secrist In tresspass on the Big field by turning Emegrants horses in &c Sustained.

Thu July 4th 1850. Glorious day of American Independance. We had a Genl parade, while the Legislature met at ten a.m. about one the troops assembled in the Bowry three cheers to the Gov and others while the Band played several airs then an addreess from the Gov. Legislature then met granted several petitions and passed a law exempting iron leather groceries medicines &c from taxation

At 6 p.m. a Genl Concert at the Bowry croded [crowded] house all well entertained wife & I attended retired to rest about eleven p.m.

Friday July 5th 1850. Took in several boarders at 5 dols pr week. Attended Court before Esqr Z. Snow.[41] Two cases. I was council on the part of the Plff

---

41. Zerubbabel Snow was an elder brother of Erastus Snow, one of a family of seven sons and two daughters, all of whom joined the Mormon Church. He was born March 29, 1809, in St. Johnsburg Township, Vermont.

In 1834 Snow went west as commissary general of Zion's Camp but returned to Kirtland in the fall. Here he taught school. In 1839 he was admitted to the bar and continued to practice

in both cases. The first case Francis L Wood vs Barney Hicks in demand of $50.00 on failure to take deft to Gold mines. Case sustained. (of Ill)

The second Case Harlow Burch vs Andrew Sears, Danford Hingston & E. W. Walton of Ill This case was for a division of property in a joint Stock Company of gold diggers Case sustained. H. G. Sherwood Council on the part of the defence.

Saturday July 6th 1850. C. P. Lott died last night of a long illness. He has been a member of this church nearly from its rise. He was commander of the Horse in Far-West at the time of the surrender in which corps I served.

Attended Court to day before Esqrs Snow & Farr. S. Howd & F. Woodward vs Norman A. Bartlett for selling him a horse which he had previously sold to others. I was on part of the plffs charge not sustained

The second case before Snow Henry Alfred vs Abner & James Pearsons for stealling four horses from him on the Sweet Water. I was on the part of the plff & judge Phelps on the part of Deft — Charge partly sustained Defts pay the costs.

Sunday July 7th 1850. Very unwell to day. Went to meeting but did not stay long so I came home and went to bed attended Elders meeting at 6 P. M.

Monday July 8th 1850. Went to the old fork and attended court before Sqr Snow in the after noon Robert A. Wrisley v.s Ellis Lud for failure to take him to gold mines. The matter was compromised without a trial In the evening had up a lot of emegrants horses taken out of the Big Field & made them pay for the officers fees

Tuesday July 9th 1850. Attended Court before Esqr Snow. Had Br Campbell up for taking emegrants horses in the Big field made him pay costs and fined some.

Attended to some more Big field cases which however did not amount to anything of consequence.

Wednesday July 10th 1850. Around town & in the evening attended to legal business but did not have any trials.

Thursday July 11th 1850. Very sick to day. In the evening attended a suit before Esqr Snow Dr Blake vs Boley which was settled without a trial.

Friday July 12th 1850. Leisure day to day no business of any importance

Saturday July 13th 1850. Attended Court before Esqr Farr. State vs Joseph Phillipson complaint of Mathias Weaver for assault & Battery on his person which happened at Green river ferry both parties were fined Phillips 10 dols & Weaver 5 as both agreed to the attact & the costs were to be paid in proportion the fine.

Mr. Phillips & two of his brothers are on their way to the mines. They are the sons of Mr Joseph Phillips of Putnam County, Ill with whom I lived and raised a crop in the summer of 1833. While there in the fall Mr Joseph Phillips died while those his children were small boys They are now men grown & called on me as an old acquaintance but unfortunately I had to prosecute a suit vs one of them.

About 5 o'clock had another suit before Farr State vs I Chace & about 6 another State vs N. Bullen for tresspassing in the big field by allowing emegrants

with success for eleven years, handling civil cases, land disputes, and other litigations.

In 1850 Snow applied for and received the federal appointment as district judge in Utah. He was not reappointed at the end of his term so he set up a store in Salt Lake City. In 1856 he was called on a mission to Australia where he served until 1859. He was then made a judge in Cedar County, Utah. In 1862 he was probate judge in Utah County; in 1865 he became city and county attorney in Salt Lake.

In the difficulties with Judge James B. McKean, Snow represented the church and helped to win the celebrated *Englebrecht Case.*

to pasture their horse there   Chase was fined 15 dols & costs in all $29 and Bullen $10. & costs in all $20.

Sunday 14th. Attended meeting   Saml Richards E. T. Benson & Pres Young preached. Emegrants are coming in thicker and faster.

Monday July 15th 1850. Attended Court before Esqr Snow at nine a. m.   Wm H. Davis vs Dr Martin of Mo The case was compromised by labouring till one p. m.

In the afternoon had another trial before Snow   De haven & Gay vs Robt Martin of Mo which trial was adjourned till Sat for the want of witnesses Also had a suit before Esqr Farr Richard White vs Matthias Weaver for a horse which he claimed which was in the possession of Weaver   The horse was proven and willingly delivered up by the Deft

Tues July 16th 1850. Very unwell all day and at Sqr Farrs court but no legal busness   Alanson Ripley arrived here from the States & perhaps will go to the gold mines.   He says emegrants are not half done coming yet this season

Wednesday July 17th 1850. Attended Court before W. Snow Esqr   Wm Hutchison vs William Collier & others for a division of property & settlement.   I was council on the part of the Plff Sustained the suit.   Emegrants trial as usual.

At one o'clock P. M. attended court before Farr Esqr John Benenfeldt [Reuenfeldt] vs Jas H. Moore   In debt   I was on the part of Plff   demand not sustained Emegrants also.

At 5 o'clock P. M. another trial before Farr.   State vs A. Butterfield & some 8 or 10 more In tresspass.   Their cattle breaking in a field west of Jordain.   I was on the part of the State Charges sustained & recovered   the damages and costs of suit.

Thursday July 18th 1850. Very unwell today.   Settled up the State case of last night   Had another case State vs Wm McClure Emigrant for breach of the peace. He was fined three dollars & costs in all seven dollars

Friday July 19th 1850. Attended court before Farr   E. Gardner vs a Lot of emegrants.   damage in Tresspass   Case compromised.

Immediately after had a State case vs Wm Hamilton for abusing & trying to take a mule from an officer after it had been attached. He was fined five dollars and costs in all 14 dollars

In the afternoon was around the Bowry awhile Had shower very refreshing to-day.

Saturday July 20th 1850. Attended Court before Esqr Farr Jas Furgerson [Ferguson] Shiriff and G. D. Grant vs M. Pike & Strother in attachment   I was on the part of the Plff This case was as follows.

In the case of Davis vs Martin on the 15th inst wherein the case was compromised & Martin agreed to take Davis to the Mines in California Mr Martin instead of complying with the terms of compromise went on leaving the Shiriff accountable for costs & damage whereupon the shiriff & Grant pursued and overtook him 30 miles beyond Brownsville Weber County and was prevented from bringing him back by Strother & his train of about 60 passengers

The officers returned and attached the property of the train of McPike which was still here as the property of Strother & McPike to be made accountable for the interference of Strother & his train for costs and damages. The trial came of about ten a.m. and after a long trial it was decided that the property of McPike's train could not be made accountable for Strothers train on the point that McPike & Strother had dissolved partnership at or near fort Larimie   otherwise the property would have been held answerable to the costs & damages in the cases against Martin because Strother & his train shielded him from the just demands of the law.

Sunday July 21st 1850. Went to meeting. President Young preached on the redemption of man In the afternoon a Methodist preached.

Monday July 22nd 1850. Attended Court Before Esqr Farr First case at 9 a. m. State vs Wm Maykin upon the complaint of J. C. Dill for stealing two of his horses in Echo creek Cañon. The Defendand was convicted & sentenced to 2 years hard labor.

At 4 o'clock P. M. attended another suit W. W. Phelps vs Martin Eastwood for Trover & Conversion by taking his horse off his range and using him I was council on part of Plff. Deft fine costs of suit $11.

At 6 o'clock another on the part of Deft John G. Scott vs Sylvester Crank for Division of property. Case compromised.

Tuesday July 23rd 1850. Attended to Legal business &c. This evening the Large Carriage made for the Band first was used. I had the honor of a ride the first time she ran. This carriage is drawn by 14 horses and is 9 feet wide & 29 feet long with a suitable flag waving and is altogether a beautiful and magnificent sight. Altogether surpasses any thing of the kind I ever saw.[42]

Wed July 24th 1850. [Remainder of page is blank]

Thursday July 25th 1850. Attended Court at the Bowry before Esqr Snow. G. W. Tippetts vs Geo Spencer Cornelius Jones Edgar Harris & David Carrick

In attachment for the recovery of property. The parties are from Indiana Plff. is taking them to the mines while they attempted to take his outfit & help themselves. I was on the part of the Plff Plff recovered his property

At 2 o'c p. m attended another suit before Esqr Farr. Benj Griffin vs James Blair for breach of contract The parties are from Ohio. I was on the part of the plff.

The trial was adjourned till tomorrow at 9 o'c a.m. (I was verry sick all day and out of my head at night [crossed out])

Friday July 26th 1850. Attended Court as before. previous case tried Plff had no cause of action This evening I was very sick and at night was out of my senses.

Saturday July 27th 1850. Went to the Store and bought a coat & pair of pants. At one o'c p. m. went to Court before W. Snow Esqr. State vs James Fitzpatrick & Clark L. Hawley for grand Larceny by taking a cow & ox from near Green river ferry. It did not appear that they actually stole the animals but supposed them to be strays, which the court decided they should give up & they were acquited.

Had another suit State vs John Y Green for not delivering up the horse in his possession to J. C. Dill which was one of the horses stolen by Wm Maykin as tried on the 22nd inst. Green refused to diliver up the horse whereupon the court decided that he pay Mr Dill 100 dollars for the horse & fifty dollars damage and also fined him fifty more for contempt of court & costs of suit.

Sunday July 28th 1850. Went to meeting a while. Came home & went to bed worn out with Lawing the past week & was now quite sick. In the evening I felt considerable better.

Monday July 29. Attended Court before Esqr Snow at the Bowry at 9 o'c a. m Fitzpatrick & Hawley vs D. S. King & Albert Steadman for Breach of contract in not taking to the mine from here as pr agreement. &c I was on the part of Plff. W. W. Phelps for Deft

I sustained the suit and got a judgement for plffs of 96 dols The plff in this case are the ones had last Sat for Larceny No dout the deft in this case

---

42. The description here would give a special meaning to the colloquialism, "to climb a band-wagon." Here Stout has left an entire page empty, evidently intending to write in the details of the celebration. Stansbury noted that he and his party had a prominent position in the parade. Stansbury, *Explorations*, 217.

who were the Complainants then & were paid for taking the plffs to mines intended to criminate them & get rid of taking them to the mines as pr agreement. but failed.

At 4 o'c p. m. had another case before Snow on the part of the plff   Albert Mann vs John B. Woodruff for refusing to take him to the mines as pr bargain having had his pay from plf for same recovered 25 dollars & costs apportioned

Tuesday 30th 1850. At Court before Esqr Snow at 9 o'c a. m. at the bowry & on the part of plff J. D. Plott vs E. G. Langstone Noah Harrison and C. W. Martin for division of property as usual with Emegrants. Sustained the division & costs apportioned.

In the evening had another investigation relative to the property of a Deseased emegrant which was in the hands of J. B. Woodruff which appearing to be all right was left so.

Wednesday 31 July. Went to the Bath House to bathe. this house is now well prepared for the accommodations of persons who wish to enjoy the pleasure of the warm bath.

This morning I sold Wm Maykin the State prisoner to Col T. C. Wiley for the term of one yeare for the sum of 100 dollars he being to all expense & trouble and at his own risk payin 50 dollars pr advance.[43]

Occupied the rest of the day in settling up past law suits.

Thursday 1st Aug 1850. Settling up the case of J. Green and other legal matters. Was very unwell & feeble all day.

Friday Aug 2nd 1850. Attended Court before Esqr Farr at seven a. m.   Estill vs Barton in demand of 145 dollars.

Estill not appearing I had the Deft released being on his side   Estill then came and commenced a new suit which came off at 2 o'clock P. M.

Estill was taking Barton to the mine & he deserted Estill at the Pacific Springs and not having paid all his passage he sued for his demand of 145 dollars the ballance due for his passage to the mines.

Court decided that Deft pay the demand (or be requ [crossed out]) due for passage to this place which was 45 dollars & costs or go with plff to mines & pay the ballance of entire passage amounting to 145 dollars & costs

Mr Estill after obtaining his judgement delivered the Deft to the constable to work out the costs as he had no money, and then he was to be put in the service of Sister Charles C Rich to work out for her the judgement of 45 dollars this he gave to sister Rich

Saturday Aug 3rd 1850. At and around the Council house and at home all day.

---

43. Here is a clear case of a man's labor being sold to pay his fine. The problem of punishment of offenders was a major one. During the first short period, the law provided that they should be whipped "not to exceed thirty-nine lashes" for such offenses as disorderly conduct, disturbing the peace, stealing, house-breaking, robbing, or the malicious destruction of property.

The public whippings were administered at a post on which a bell had been hung October 25 for calling the people together and which was variously called the Bell Post or the Liberty Post. John Nebeker wrote in some detail of his first experience in administering the whipping law. The prisoner had been sentenced to a fine of ten dollars or a whipping of ten lashes. He chose the whipping but refused to be tied because the law did not specifically so state. Next he refused to be stripped, but in this he was overruled.

"The penalty for stealing in cases generally, in cases where people would promise to do better, was to make proper confessions and restore fourfold, if persons upon whom the theft was committed required it." Morgan, *State of Deseret, U. H. Q.,* VIII, 74.

But whipping was never well accepted by any — the offender, the executor, or the spectators; and in the absence of any jail, officers resorted to the ball and chain and to selling the services of prisoners to those who would pay the fines, as in the case of Ira E. West, already noted.

Sunday Aug 4th 1850. Wife & I went to meeting in the fore noon & in the after noon went alone.

Monday Aug 5th 1850. Around the Council House today. At 4 o'c P. M. had a suit before Esqr Snow. John C. Fleming vs Wm Riddle & others as usual this was a quarrel with a company about the division of property. I was on the part of the Deft & Jas McCabe on the part of the plff.

Court decided to divide the property according to the amount put in at Kains-ville The case was the end of a quarrelling journey of a small company from the States to this place.

Tuesday Aug 6th 1850. Around town some today & at home occasionally. Several brethren & men from the States came in from California a few days since.

Wednesday Aug 7th 1850. Around town as usual to day not doing any particu-lar business Had a rain in the evening.

Thursday Aug 8th 1850. Worked some today.

Friday 9th. at home & around

Saturday 10th. at home and around Not well for several days past.

Sunday Aug 11th 1850. Went to meeting and at home Rev. Mr Langworthy[44] preached in the fore-noon. He is I believe a Universalian preacher. P. P. Pratt spoke in the after-noon. Had a hard rain tonight

Monday Aug 12th 1850. Worked some in the morning. Had several cases for Legal advice & one case compromised before Snow. Thaddeus Fallstick & wife vs Absolem Woodward. At 4 o'clock P. M. State vs Rev. Alvin Mussett of Mo for forcibly taking his cattle from Ben Thomas after they had been empounded for breaking into his grain in the welsh settlement & threatning to shoot &c. He was fine ten dollars & costs & to pay for the grain destroyed. He is a perfect specimen of the Missouri ministry.

Tuesday Aug 13th 1850. Wife & I in company with A. L. Fulmer & wife went to the warm Spring Bath House then took a Buggy ride all together over Jordain and traded some with the Emegrants encamped there After all this was around the Council house &c the rest of the day.

Wednesday Aug 14th 1850. Around as usual to day. At 5 o'clock P. M. had a suit before Esqr Farr. State vs Mathias Keller a Jew for selling sugar which had been fouled by the excreement of a man dying with something like the Cholera had ran on it & had been thrown away by the owners & geathered up by Deft and sold for 25 cents pr lb. He was fined 50 dollars & costs.

Thursday Aug 15th 1850. Around as usual had some legal business

---

44. The Reverand Mr. Franklin Langworthy had been in Salt Lake City for more than a week before he spoke to the congregation. He had shared in the activities of the Fourth of July and wrote a description of the parade with the band and Brigham Young leading, followed by the various groups. He was not impressed with the speeches, however. "They said many hard things against the government and people of the United States, . . . [making] free use of insulting language against Uncle Sam . . . . They had a tall liberty pole from which waved the flag of Deseret. The flag was thirty feet wide and eighty feet long. [Probably an error here of trans-lation of numbers. A flag three by eight feet would be more likely.] A gale arose, and down came the flag, trailing in the dust. This little accident was a matter of joy to most of the emigrants." Franklin Langworthy, *Scenery Of The Plains, Mountains, and Mines: A Diary Kept Upon The Overland Route To California By Way Of The Great Salt Lake,* . . . (Ogdensburgh, New York, 1855), 74-95.

Friday Aug 16th 1850. Had a suit before Esqr Farr Thos Geagan vs Ambrose T. Chappel for Breach of contract for not taking him to California I was on the part of the plff and recovered a judgement in favor of plf. of $163.75 cents Was occupied all day in that and other legal business.

Saturday Aug 17th 1850. Attended to legal business The passenger Train of Glenn & Co which arrived here on sunday last had entirely split up and commenced suit against the proprietors for failing to take them to the mines as stipulated. The whole Train is in the utmost confusion while some are running off with part of the Stock &c while I was employed as council on the part of the proprietors and W. W. Phelps on the part of the passengers.

After much ado the matter was brought to bear by bringing up the entire case on its merits before Judge Wells, Esqrs Farr & Snow and finally adjusted except two single suits which had previously been commenced Thus far the matter was done to the satisfaction of both parties while the other matters were adjourned till next Monday.

Sunday Aug 18th 1850. To day I was very unwell and at home most of the day.

Monday Aug 19th 1850. To day the case of Glenns Co. was brought up as pr adjt an I was very busily engaged all day the different unadjusted cases were settled but yet the whole matter was not disposed of.

Tuesday Aug 20th 1850. Was engaged in legal business of different kinds but no suit was on hand to day.

Wednesday Aug 21st 1850. Still engaged in Legal business Bullard vs Tolton in debt on part of Tolton. Bullard endeavered to hire me to prove untrue to my client which resulted in Bullard withdrawing the suit paying cost. Tolton running away as he commenced by trying to corrupt me I only gave him "trick for trick. at his cost & was still true to my client. My wife is very sick & under the care of Doc Williams.

Thursday Aug 22nd 1850. To day I was still engaged in the case of Glen's Co. which is mostly settled up & the passengers gone except a few who are still in diffi-culty. The court sent an officer up to the Co. quarters to bring down some attached property on last Monday evening

The result of which was the officer was insulted & abused and the property retained The officer returned made complaint of the same whereupon three more officers were sent after the offenders along with the insulted officer, who arrested and brought them & all the rest of the property of the train to the City to answer to the same.

This possee of officers met with a similar reception as the first but as there was four of them they brought them down & the property with them. They were prosecuted in the name of the State for this breach of the peace.

The names of those prosecuted were Mrssrs (?) Lathrop one of the proprietors of the Train. Coll Holloway Burns and Duncan the last one was acquitted while the others were fine as follows. Lathrop 50. Cole 75 Holloway 100 and Burne 75 dollars and Costs of suit. They manifested a hostile spirit in the main and H. even laughed the court in contempt at first but they all appeared very pious after the decision of the Court.

Friday Aug 23rd 1850. Not much doing today but I was around about as usual.

Saturday. Around as yesterday.

Sunday Aug 25th 1850. Went to meeting. In the evening all those who could speak the German Language fluently were called for by the Twelve to ascertain how many & who of them could go on a mission to Germany. This matter will finally be adjusted at Genl Conference.

Monday Aug 26th 1850. Little rain again. Capt Stansbury of the U. S. Topographical Engeneers started back to the States to day having completed the survey of the G. S Lake Mr Holliday goods came in to day[45] I was around as usual but not much business up.

Tuesday Aug 27th 1850. Attended the sale of Bullards cattle. He sold 3 yoke and put off selling because they did not bring enough.

In the after noon went with H. C. Haight [46] to Blooming Grove 20 miles North. Went the lower road this is a beautiful country Blooming Grove is the most delightful situation I have seen in the Valley. From here I came to N. Cotton Wood and staid all night at mother Taylors

Wednesday Aug 28th 1850. Went to look at my land this morning, find it to be fine for farming & contemplate to have more surveyed.

Came home about three o'c brought down my oxen to trade for horses which I did with G. D. Grant for a span of horses giving 50 dollars to boot.

Thursday Aug 29th 1850. Knocking around town to day not bringing much to pass. any way.

Friday Aug 30th 1850. Around as usual, not much up This evening Milo Andrus and a company of about 50 waggons of saints arrived here all in good spirits it seems. Capt Andrus waggon bore a large flag with Holiness to the Lord inscribed on it. This is the first Co of Saints that has come in this year although several families have arrived previously. Some came in near six weeks ago.

Sat. Aug 31st 1850. Rained some to day Had some Legal business with with Bullard and around as usual & traded in store Legislature met no quorum.

Sunday Sep 1st 1850. Went to meeting & riding around

Monday Sep 2nd 1850. Around as usual & riding about at dark Had a case before County Court's special Term appeal from Esquire W. Snow. Daniel Baker vs Truman Gilbert in Debt. $25. Appeal by Gilbert. I was on the part of the plff

---

45. Of these early merchants in Utah, Edward W. Tullidge says:

In the year 1849 . . . two years after the entrance of the Pioneers, the first regular stock of goods for the Utah market was brought in by Livingston & Kinkead. Their stock was valued at about $20,000. They opened up in John Pack's adobe house in the Seventeenth ward . . . near where is now built the Seventeenth Ward Schoolhouse . . . .

The following year, 1850, Holliday & Warner appeared, who constituted the second firm in the commercial history of our Territory. William H. Hooper came in Salt Lake in charge of their business. They opened up in a little adobe building which had been erected for a school house on President Young's block, east of Eagle Gate . . . .

John & Enoch Reese were the third firm . . . and they built the second store on Main Street . . . . J. M. Horner & Co was the fourth firm, . . . succeeded by Hooper & Williams. Livingston, Kinkead & Co., changed to Livingston & Bell. Their commercial mart was the Old Constitution Building, which was the first merchant store in Utah . . . ."
(Tullidge, *History of Salt Lake City*, 379.)

46. Hector Caleb Haight was born January 17, 1810, at Windham, New York. He was baptized in 1845 by Isaac C. Haight and came to Utah on September 22, 1847, with the Daniel Spencer company. From 1855 to 1858 he was on a mission to Scandinavia, serving as president during the last year.

During the Utah War he was captain of the infantry in the Utah County division. His family home was at Farmington, Utah, where he was a successful farmer and stock raiser and also ran a hotel. He served as sheriff, assessor, and collector of Davis County, Utah. He died June 26, 1879.

W Richards & E. T. Benson on the part of Gilbert. The case was adjourned till tomorrow at

Tuesday Sep 3rd 1850. Was engaged in the above case all day. Joseph Taylor & Saml Driggs arrived today from the Bluffs with their families all in good health & spirits.

Wednesday Sep 4th 1850. Trial Continued but was brought to a close about 2 or three o'clock P. M. Decided against Baker.

Thursday Sept 5th 1850. Around with W. Snow in the fore noon. In the afternoon at 2 o'c the Legislature met Granted a privilege to Gardner & others on the Jordain.

The Regents also met and O. Hyde sworn in to office as a Regent.

Frid Sep 6th 1850. General Conference all day.

Sat Sep 7th 1850. Conference again G. A. Smith spoke took a regular old text.

At two Hyde delivered an address to the Regents at Conference on the Subject of Education

The Emegrating poor fund was then brought up and a large amount of money donated for that purpose. Many present subscribed 100 dollars each.

Sunday Sep 8th 1850. Conference Continued Prest B. Young spoke on the Law of tithing and Parley P. Pratt against the use of Tobacco &c.

Monday Sept 9th 1850. Pleasant Green Taylor moved North to day. Elder Orson Hyde took dinner here to day. He agrees to assist Allen J. Stout here &c

Tues Sep 10th 1850. To day the U. S. mail arrived bearing the news that Prest Z. Taylor was dead and Fillmore had appointed a new Cabinet He died 9th July.

A mail also arrived from California. Times there dull a monthly mail is established from the States to this place. Gold is growing scarce in the mines.

Wednesday Sept 11th 1850. To day the Legislature met at 2 o'clock P. M. A Charter for the Emegrating Poor fund was brout in and refered to a Comt and instructions to Our Delegates in Congress read and accepted.

Thursday Sept 12th 1850. Went to mother Taylors to hunt land for my-self & my brothers-in Law who have lately come on Staid all night

Friday Sept 13th 1850. Came home but found no suitable land. It is astonishing how the people are takeing up land now in all parts.

Saturday Sept 14th 1850. Legislature met at two P. M. Passed a Charter organizing the "Perpetual Emegrating Fund for the Poor" for which see the Charter.

Sunday Sept 15th 1850. Went to meeting. Officers were elected for the Poor Fund as pr ordinance of yesterday.

Monday Sept 16th 1850. Attended Justice Court W. Snow Esqr State vs D. Vaughan for Addultery. He was bound over to Court in a bond of 100 dollars.

Tues 17. Wed 18 & Thurs 19. Worked at home all day (building shop. [crossed out]) A company of troops were called out to go against the Snake Indians in Weber Co U. V. Stewart killed a Chief and they killed a white man

Friday Sept 20th 1850. Regents in Session all day G. A. Smith E. T. Benson & my self were appointed to preside over the schools North of the city &c

Sat Sep 21 1850. At home and around town

Sunday Sept. 22 1850. Went to meeting   Troops came home.   All peace again

Monday Sep 23 1850. Bp N. K Whitney died to day   Around preparing for the County Court   Wife sick

Tues 24. employed as ante

Wed 25. Raised my Shop

Thurs 26. Not well & around

Frid 27. Worked at Shop

Sat. 28th Sep 1850. General Company drill Regents met at two P. M. Legion officers at 4 P. M. I was appointed Quarter-master in Col Fulmer's Regt Nauvoo Legion Pro. tem. Wife very sick yet.

Sunday Sept 29th 1850. At home all day my wife being very sick.

Monday Sept 30th 1850. Trading in the Stores at Reese's & at Kinkeades &c crouded times there.

Tuesday Oct 1st 1850. Trading yet   Stores still crouded   We are decieved by the merchants about the quality of groceries which they were to bring.   Not a Sufficient supply.

Wednesday Oct 2nd 1850. Worked some and around &c

Thurs Oct 3 - 1850. Instituted a suit for Foot vs Vaughan[47] in damage $10000 in the County Court & had him arrested & held in custody for adultery with his wife which occupied most of the day

Friday Oct 4th 1850. Worked at home all day.

Saturday Oct 5th 1850. Legislature met at 9 and organized a county North of the Hot Springs & South of Weber to be called Davis County in honor of Capt D. C. Davis. also passed some grants to shingle machines &c.
   At 2 the Regents and transacted some business of small importance and at 4 the Legion officers met to agree on the days parade.   The troops returned from the North report that the Indians have killed a Company of Emegrants towards Fort Hall and took the women & children prisoners

Sunday Oct 6th 1850. Went to meeting awhile.   The preaching was principally against the high prices of the merchants

Monday Oct 7th 1850. This is the annual session of the County Court   which met to day & organized a Grand & pettit jury but no business
   The case of Dr Vaughan had been stopped by the Gov. So I spent to day.

---

47. Of Doctor J. M. Vaughan, little information has been found except that he carried the following advertisement in the *Deseret News* for July 13, 1850:
J. M. VAUGHN, M. D. Physician and Occulist, well known in the States as a successful practitioner, having located in G.S.L. City for the practice of his profession in its various branches, will be promptly attended to any call with which he may be favored.
Though a graduate of the Old School, Dr. V. is wedded to no sect, or system of medicine, but is ever ready to avail himself of all the lights that shine upon the Healing Art in its present highly improved condition.
Particular attention paid at all times to surgery, and diseases of the eye. All necessary operations performed upon the most complex organs of the body.
Office at the house of Timothy B. Foote, Block 138, near the Bath House.
It would seem that this case was dropped and that Vaughan moved into Sanpete County. There is much evidence that medical doctors were generally in ill repute in Utah at that time.

Tues Oct 8th 1850. Worked some but not much

Wed Oct. 9th 1850. Rainy day. Windy Cold. Snow on the mountains Worked some & prepared for General Training

Thurs Oct 10th 1850. General parade but the Legion did not get ready to march untill one o'clock P. M. When we were marched about 6 mile up the Jordan where we encamped but did not go through any evolutions after dark I sat on a Court Martial for the trial of Isaac Thomas for Disobeying orders on the *shoshones* He was fined ten dollars & sentenced to 2 extra tours of duty & to be repremanded by the Col

Friday Oct 11th 1850. Lay up in Camp untill in the after noon when the Gov & others came out & passed in review after which the Legion passed in review twice & were dismissed for the night. The officers were up till one o'c regailing over sardines & oyesters &c.

Sat Oct 12th 1850. Lay up till noon & after a few manouvers came into the City & formed on the Temple Block & were addressed by the Gov & dismissed by the officers. & all went home

Sunday Oct 13th 1850. Went to meeting to day in the evening met the Seventies The order of business was to raise $1000 to pay for Prest Jos Young a house

Monday Oct 14th 1850. Geathering up the garden vegitables to day

Tuesday Oct 15th 1850. Worked as yesterday. The U. S. Mail came in to day

Wednesday Oct. 16th 1850. Worked as before. We learn that the Congress has passed an act to organize this state into a Territory called Utah[48]

Frid & Sat Oct 18 & 19. Around home working a little.

Sunday Oct 20 1850. At home all day. My wife is dangerously ill

Monday Oct 21th. at home all day Wife very sick.

Tuesday Oct 22 1850. Wife very sick. at home nearly all day. To day I resigned my commission as first Lieutenant in B. F. Johnson's Company of Cavelry in the Nauvoo Legion

Wed. Thurs & Frid. 23-24 25. At & about home taking care of my wife. Ward meeting on 24th in relation to schools. Agreed to levy a tax to build a School House &c

Sat Oct. 26. At home all day.

Sund 27. At home and meeting A company is about to be made up to settle Little Salt Lake

Monday Oct 28th 1850. At home mostly to day.

Tues Oct 29th 1850. Went north to hunt a cow

---

48. On April 5, 1849, Dr. John M. Bernhisel had left for Washington, D. C., bearing the memorial asking that Congress establish a territorial government. The petition was twenty-two feet long and bore 2,270 signatures. The area which was to be included in this new Territory of Deseret included a great intermountain empire embracing Utah, Nevada, much of Arizona, and parts of Wyoming, Colorado, and New Mexico, southern California, and a narrow strip extending into Oregon and Idaho, following the natural boundaries of river and mountain. Stout's comment that the territory be called *Utah* carries a note of disappointment.

Wed Oct 30th 1850. At home to day. Several cases of stealing has lately happened and a company has gone out last night to take up some horse thieves who are on their way to California by the south route

Thurs 31 Frid 1 Sat 2 Nov. At home all the time nearley Stormy weather & snow

Sunday Nov 3rd 1850. Regents met at J. M. Grants and appointed Appleby to be Librairian & done some other buisness in relation to the Parent School raining & snowing to day.

Monday Nov 4th 1850. To day the annual Term of the Supreme Court met & adjourned having no business before them. In the after-noon I attended a case State vs Henry Meyer on Complaint of Ben Rist for petit Larceney before Esqr Farr Charge sustained Fine 25 dollars & costs. Stormy day yet.

Tuesday Nov. 5th 1850. Clear fine day. Attended a trial to day before Esqr W. Snow. On the part of the State H. G. Sherwood on part of Deft. State vs John Ryon on Complaint of Jas Brown For assault & Battery. Deft fined 50 dollars & costs $85 in all.

Wednesday Nov 6. 1850. (Went North to [crossed out]) At & around home to day.

Thurs 7th 1850. Went North Cow-hunting.

Frid & Sat 8 & 9. at home.

Sunday Nov. 10th 1850. Cold Cloudy day. At home in fore-noon then went to meeting. In the evening went to meeting of the Seventies at the Bowry.

Monday. At home & met with the Regents in the evening

Tues 12. Worked at home & puddled in the law some

Wed 13th 1850 Nov. Worked at home and attended attended two Lawsuits before Esqr Farr State vs W. H. H. Davis Trover and conversion Fine five dollars and costs
     The other case was W. H. H. Davis vs V. Gargus for the recovery of property which he claimed as heir to his uncle who was dead This case was non-suited. I was on the part of the Deft.

Thurs Frid & Sat 14, 15, 16. Worked at home

Sunday Nov 17th 1850. Cold day. Went to meeting Wife went to her mothers on a visit.

Mond Nov. 18th 1850. Worked at home in the fore noon. Attended a law case in the after noon. State vs John Galvin & Matthew Rice for assault on Jos Eggbert, before Esqr Farr Rich was acquitted and Galvin fined five dollars & costs. in all Eighteen dollars

Tuesday Nov 19th 1850. Worked at home House daubing The U. S. mail came in to day bring papers which contain the act of congress, orgainizing this country into the Territory of Utah, with a Gov. Secratary, Attorney, marshall & 3 Judges &c &c &c &c &c

Wed. Thurs & Frid 20-21. 22. Worked at home most of the time. Very warm weather.

Sat Nov. 23rd 1850. To day was an officer drill but a poor turn out. Attended a law suit before Esqr W. Snow. James P. Parks vs Benj. Hawkins in debt Demand

$101. Seth Blair attorney on the part of Hawkins   Judgement in favor of **Parks** of $71.

Sunday Nov 24th 1850. Went to meeting.   President B. Young preached on the principals of the Gospel.   Attended the Seventies.   Joseph Young called for help.

Monday 25th. Attended to settling up some Legal business to day.

Tues 26th. Worked at home

Wed 27. Went to Mother-in Laws to see my wife:

Thurs Frid 28 & 29. Staid there visiting   snowy weather & warm.

Sat. 30th. Warm rainy day and night.   Came home to day.

Sunday Decr 1st 1850. Went to meeting.   C. C. Rich and G. A. Smith spoke.

Monday Dec. 2nd 1850. To day the Legislature met in its Second annual Session at the State House and proceeded to the Election of its officers J. M. Grant was Elected Speaker of the House and James Furgerson Clerk.   The House then adjourned till one o'clock p. m.   The afternoon was spent appointing the several standing Committees and recieving petitions.   Allen Taylor & family stayed here last night on his way North where he was moving.

Tues. 3rd Decr. Attended the L. again.   A bill was passed orgain   the country around Little Salt Lake into a County called Iron County and G. A. Smith choses Chief Justice of the same
Several other bills were passed granting Kanyons to certain individuals City Creek K was granted to Prest B. Young for 500 dollars

Wednesday Dec 4th 1850. Attended the L. again   Passed several bill granting Kanyons to certain individuals also one chartering a Stage Co.[49] Levied a tax of 2 per cent. C. C. Rich & W. Woodruff were by the Gov apointed in the Senate in place of Whitney & Lott decd and Blair, Snoot, & Wright in place of Height Stratton & Davis the two last Decd [deceased]

Thurs 5th 1850 Decr. Attended the L. again   Petition for Rail Road. which was refered to Comt on Roads.
Dixon appeared and took his seat as reporter.
Some other bills and other mscellaneous business was done and the L. adjd till the first Monday in January next at ten a. m.

Frid & Sat. Decr 6th & 7th 1850. Worked at home making window

Sunday Decr 8th 1850. Went to meeting.   The company is *rolling* out for Iron County   They will cerainly have a cold trip and good *sledding.*[50]

---

49. It seems that the officials were very busy dividing the natural resources up among themselves, but there was also the idea of "stewardship" or operating for the general benefit. For example, men were often given the responsibility of building roads to their mills or bridges and maintaining them. It was also understood that when the operator had received back his investment the bridge should become public property.

50. For a day by day account of this winter journey to Iron County see Gustive O. Larson, ed., "Journal of the Iron County Mission, John D. Lee, Clerk December 10, 1850-March 1, 1851," *Utah Historical Quarterly*, XX (April, July, October, 1952), 109-34, 253-82, 353-83. This journal gives a vivid picture of the hardships which attended this colonizing venture.
Another very interesting account was kept by Henry Lunt, "History of Colonization of Parowan, Iron County, December 5, 1850-August 5, 1851" (typescript, Brigham Young University).

Mond & Tues 9 & 10th 1850. Worked at home and attending to some legal business &c wife came home

Wed 11th Decr 1850. At home untill noon then attended a suit before Esqr Snow James Cobern vs Thos Dean for threatning his life & driveing him from his home in the North Cañon. The witnesses did not swear according to the expectation of the Plff. Yet the Esqr decided that the deft pay the cost but did not fine him any There is evidently wrong among them & perhaps they darst commence on each other I was on part of Plff

Thursday Decr 12th 1850. At home in the fore noon then attended a lawsuit before Esqr Snow. Perry Miller vs David, John & Enos Curtis in debt Demand 534.52 I was on the part of the Plff. The Esqr decided no cause of action. The parties are in a perfect snarl.

Frid Dec 13th 1850. Worked at home to day The weather is now warm and pleasant. Mild as autumn.

Saturday Decr 14th 1850. I was very sick to day with the head ache. At 4 o'c attended a Law suit before Esqr Snow. Graham Coultrim vs Henry Standish in debt for 30 dollars I was on the part of the Deft William Snow on the part of the Plff.
Court rendered a judgement in favor of the plff of 25 dollars & costs apportioned between them.

Sunday Decr 15th 1850. Cloudy & warm with a wet snow falling. I feel very poorly to day. At home all day.

Monday Decr 16th 1850. Around home and the Council House At 4 o'clock P. M. attended a suit before Esqr Snow. Ferdinand Wilkie vs William Chapman In debt 15 dollars. Deft did not appear. I was on the part of the plff. Judgement vs Deft for the demand
Met with the Committee on Criminal Code at Daniel Spencers at dark. It seems to be an arduous task to make a Criminal Code which will pass the Legislature.

Tues Dec 17th 1850. Warm Cloudy & snowing. Worked at home to day.

Wed & Thurs 18. 19th 1850. Worked at home. On Wed morning had a fine snow. Then warm and pleasant weather.

Friday Decr 20th 1850. Worked at home to day & sick

Sat 21. At home to day. In the evening met with the Committee on Civil Laws at D. Spencers. Weather Cold but pleasant.

Sunday Decr 22nd 1850. Went to meeting at the Bowry. Cold cloudy weather.

Monday Decr 23rd 1850. At home to day. In the evening met with the Committee on Criminal Code at the tithing office. Snowing fast to night.

Tuesday Decr 24th 1850. Strolling around town in the fore-noon. In the afternoon worked at home. The boys are hailing Chrismas with shouts and firing guns this evening, also a few sky rockets & other such like things

Wednesday Decr 25th 1850. This is a fine clear cold day some snow on the ground but very pleasant under foot. The roads being bare & smoothe
The people are taking their Chrismas very pleasant with the exception that Rees' Store was broken in last night and robbed. Mostly of wine as I learn. I was around town to day enjoying the times by looking on

Thursday Decr 26th 1850. The people are slowly working off their Christmas spree. I was around town some & working at home & attending to some legal business.

Friday Dec 27th 1850. At home working and around town. In the eve attended an Exhibition at the Bowry

There was a variety of Dramaticks, Farces, Songs, dances, music &c after which a grand display of fireworks of sky Rockets &c. all together it was a tolerably good time

Saturday Dec 28th 1850. Around town and working at home.

Sunday Decr 29th 1850. Went to meeting. I was around attending to some Legal affairs which is expected to come of to morrow. —

Monday Decr 30th 1850. Attended Court before W. Snow State vs Henry Shenk and Phillip George Two German Emegrants who stopped here and joined the Church & married and set up a butchery. They were taken up for stealing an ox and attempting to steal another.

Shenk confessed the charge and also that they had stolen 2 more oxen. The Court fined them one hundred dollars each and costs and pay the owner of the oxen Thos Chappel 100 dollars for his ox and damages. I do not think the affair is over yet.

Tuesday 31st 1850 Decr. At home to day but around some Those who broke open the tithing office & a jeweler's shop some time since were arrested & 2 of the party convicted before Esqr Snow to day. perhaps more anon.

Wednesday Jan 1st 1851. Went to Esq Snow's He gave his sentence on those who were tried before him yesterday which was that they be held to answer for the same before the County court.

In the after-noon I attended another case against Phillip George & Henry Shenk on the complaint of John Quail and Joseph Wright each one of the complainants had recognized that they had killed an ox for them one found his ox's hide & the other the Head which was acknowledged by Henry & George admitted they were killed by them They were bound over to the County Court.

Thus passed New Years day with me.

Thursday Jan 2nd 1851. I was sick to day but about The County Court meets tomorrow & I am preparing for it

Friday Jan 3rd 1851. The County Court met at 9 o'c a. m. The Grand jury found several bills against different individuals while be noticed as they come to trial before the Court

Saturday Jan 4th 1851. Attended County Court to day The cases of Henry Shenk as principal and Phillip George as accessary before & after the fact in a charge for Larceny was taken up. I was on the part of the State and (Albert [crossed out]) R. C. Petty on the part of the defence

The trial lasted from 9 a. m till dark when it was submitted to the jury who had orders from the Court to report a virdict at 8 a. m on next Monday morning to which time the Court adjd Henry Shenk plead guilty to the charge & Phillip George not guilty. This is the first indictment ever submitted to a jury in the State of Deseret & also the first one I ever drew up to be presented to a court.

Sunday January 5th 1851. Went to meeting Parley preached & was followed by A. Lyman on his mission to Lower California I spent the after-noon at home

Monday January 6th 1851. Attended the County Court at 8 o'c a. m. The Jury gave in their virdict against Phillip George declaring him guilty after which the Court adjd till one o'c. P. M. and the Legislature went into session Several bills were passed in relation to County Courts &c At one o'c P. M. the Court met again and took up the case of Love & Kelly for Burglary & Larceny. Kelly was acquitted & the jury did not give in the verdict of Love

At dark met with the Judges of the Court & others The judges came was consulting on the decision to be given on Shenk & George which will be given in to morrow morning at 9 o'clock.

Tuesday January 7th 51. Attended court again The court sentenced Henry Shenk & Phillip George to 2 years hard labor each with a ball and chain with the priviledge of redeeming themselves by pay in lieu two hundred dollars each.

The jury's virdict of State vs Love was then read & he found guilty. The court sentenced him to 2 years hard labor with the priviledge of redemption by paying two hundred dollars. He gave security for one month in which time he expects to make arraingements to redeem him-self. In the after noon another suit came of. The State vs O. H. Speed for addultery & fornication R. C. Petty on part of Deft

The case was submitted to the jury and Court adjd

Wednesday 8th January 51. Attended County Court at 9 a. m. The jury in the Case of State vs O. H. Speed returned a virdict of guilty. Court then went into the trial of Shenk & George on another Indictment for Stealing ox belonging to John Quail, which occupied the day. But however before submitting the case to the jury another Indictment against them for stealing an ox belong to Joseph Wright was also submitted to the same jury by mutual consent of the parties concerned being sustained by the same evidences & under the same circumstances. The cases are now in the hands of the jury to be reported to morrow at 9 o'c This has been a snowy day. Snow some 6 or 8 inches deep

Thursday 9th January 1851. Attended Court at 9 o'clock Court sentenced O. H. Speed to 100 dollars fine or one years hard labor with the ball and chain He was afterwards bailed out by 10 of the brethren through sympathy.

The jury on the case of Shenk & George returned a verdict of guilty on both Indictments & the Court sentenced them to 5 years hard labor with a ball and chain each. This was on the 2 Indictments.

Henry Shenk was bailed out by Sheriff Furgerson & 2 others but George remains in custady only Petty stands surety for him untill Next Monday week. These proceeding took up the day & the Court adjournd till Next Monday Week.

The Legislature has been in Session all this week & this evening adjd till next Tuesday. They have done considerable buisiness but not being present cannot say what it is only they have granted this city a Charter predicated upon the old Nauvoo Charter.

The prospect for Legisla & judicial bisness is good

I met with the Committee on Military affairs at dark to draft a law more effectually to organize the Legion

Friday 10th January 1851. At home with sick head ache. Thawing to day.

Saturday 11th Jan 1851. Sleeting & Thawing morning Attended the first session & organization of the City Council.[51] Mayor J. M. Grant delivered an excellent

---

51. The officers appointed at this time included: Jedediah M. Grant, mayor; Nathaniel H. Felt, William Snow, Jesse P. Harmon, and Nathaniel V. Jones, aldermen; Lewis Robinson, Robert Pierce, Zera Pulsipher, William G. Perkins, Jeter Clinton, Enoch Reese, Harrison Burgess, Samuel W. Richards, and Vincent Shurtliff, councillors; Robert Campbell, recorder; Elam Luddington, marshal, assessor, and collector; Leonard W. Hardy, captain of the city police. Tullidge, *History of Salt Lake City*, 78.

inaugeral address The council proceeded to chose its necessary officers. The Gov and several other State officers were present.

Sunday January 12th 1851. Went to meeting. Prest B Young spoke against swearing & other profane and such like immorral practices. People voted to put it down.

At dark attended Seventies meeting which was preparitory to a two days meeting to be holden next Saturday and Sunday at the Bowry.

Monday January 13th 1851. Attended the City Council. They adopted the rules governing the City Council of Nauvoo in toto —

Tuesday 14th January 1851. Attended the Legislature. The fore noon was spent in recieving petitions & discussing the school tax of the 14th Ward

The after noon on the Criminal Code & passed from the 5th to the 16th section on the second reading. Quite sick today.

Wednesday 15th 1851. Attended the Legislature. The first business was to recieve petitions & reports of Committees then passed a few short ordinances on Cañons &c after which the Criminal Code was taken up and some ten or 15 sections passed.

The criminal Law takes more time & calls forth more debate & difference of opinion than anything ever brought up.

Thursday 16th Jan 1851. Attended the Legislature. An ordinance organizing Courts of probate was passed then the Criminal Code was taken up & finally passed its third reading.

Friday 17th January 1851. Attended the Legislature again The militia law was passed & some other business done.

Grant & Furgerson broke up two small distillerys to day

Legislature adjourned till the 4th day of February.

Saturday 18th January 1851. To day was an officer drill and also a general Seventies meeting to to reorganize & set in order the different Quorums which is to be a two day meetin. I was sick to day but was around at meeting some.

Sunday 19th January 1851. Warm pleasant day. Went to Seventies meeting. Prest B. Young proposed & put to vote the idea of commencing the Temple next season which was unanimously carried.

In the after noon went to meeting again. Some 6 or 8 of the *Winter Saints* and their wives were cut off from the Church. Winter saints are those Emegrants who stop here, join the Church & marry wives and go to the mines in the Spring &c

Randolph Alexander was cut off from the Seventies for contempt of council & not paying a just debt. I was glad to see an action taken on the Course that many were too freely falling into in mingling with Gentiles and partaking of their spirit.

Monday 20th Jan. 1851. Attended County Court. The fore noon was spent in settling up the case of Phillip George's property. The after noon The case of State vs Josep Alvard & William Sterit for Riot. Sterit was acquitted & Alvard was sentenced to six months hard labor with ball & chain. The Grand jury has found bills against several others which will be noticed in their place as they are brought up.

Tuesday 21 Jan 1851. Attended Court. Case of State vs Ashton In Larceny came off found guilty. Sentenced to pay ten dollars for wood stolen & fined forty dollars. Jas McCabe council for Ashton

Then State vs W. Loomis In Larceny. McCabe his council. Adjourned before it was through with the testimony

Wednesday 22nd Janr 1851. Attended Court. The forenoon was spent in the Case of Loomis when it was submitted to the jury The after noon the case of State vs John Brown In Larceny for stealing wheat from A. O. Smoot. The jury soon brought in a verdict of guilty and he was fined fifty dollars or on failure to pay to six months hard labor with ball and chain.

Thursday 23rd January 1851. Attended Court. The first case was State vs Washington Loomis in Larceny for stealing a pair of pants. James McCabe was his council Defendant plead not guilty. This trial lasted till about two o'c P. M. when it was submitted to the jury and court adjourned 1 hour This trial was caried with great heat & I made a very animated plea against the low chicanery of the opposite attorney

The after noon was spent in instructions in part by President Willard Richards to the Court & officers thereof in the grand jury room on the subject of the spirits manifested during the trial in the fore noon and salutary advice as to the proper mode of conducting Courts &c

I shall not attempt to describe the spirit and powers of darkness which was admitted and finally obtained the ascendency in this Court.

Suffice it to say that I learned a lesson on the subject of the power and influence of spirits according to the lenity which may be granted them which I hope never to forget and is a warning never to admit a foul spirit where the Holy spirit should rule and direct either the affairs of State or Church.

Friday 24th January 1851. Attended Court. The court first read the virdicts against Loomis In Both suits virdicts the jurys was that he was guilty

I would here remark that the jury on the first Indictment hung untill this morning. Such was the powerful effect of the court submiting to an evil spirit being introduced into Court which I need not here say much about.

Another case now came up State vs George Love for willful and corrupt purjury. The jury returned a verdict of guilty after being absent a few minutes

The case of A. J. Kelly and William Walker came up for Riot. Plead not guilty R. C. Petty was their Council This is the same Riot in which Alvord was convicted. The case was soon traversed & submited to the jury.

The case of State vs this same William Walker for Larceny in stealing wood from I. N. Spaulding came up. William Snow his council and after a short trial was submitted to the jury.

The case of State vs T. W. Ashton & William Stirrit came up. In Larceny for stealing wood from Spaulding. James McCabe their council. They were accquitted without submiting the case to the jury.

Next came the case of State vs A. J. Kelly & Oliver Johnson In Larceny for stealing wood from Spaulding. R. C. Petty their council this case was traversed and submited to the jury & court adjourned. till tomorrow

Those five persons last tried for stealing spauldings wood were all brought up in one Indictment, together with two others who were not present.

Saturday 25 January 1851. Attended Court again at 8 a. m The Court proceeded to declare and pass sentence to the verdicts of the several cases submited to the jurys yester. as follows.

State vs Wm Walker in Larceny on the wood. Not guilty.

State vs Kelley & Walker in Riot Virdict agains Kelly guilty and he was sentenced to ten years hard labor with the ball & chain

Walker as accessary. Guilty and fined 28 dollars.

State vs Love in Purjury. Guilty and he sentenced to five years hard labor with the ball and chain.

State vs Kelly & Johnson in Larceny on the wood. Kelly not guilty & Johnson guilty of stealing one stick and fined 22 dollars.

State vs W. Loomis in both Indictments. Guilty & he sentenced to two years hard labor ball chain[52]

Two other cases are on the Docket but the parties not being ready they were laid over untill the regular Term in March and the Court adjourned sine die

Thus ended the Special Term of the County Court which has lasted 12 days. The sum total of the Rendition of judgements are as follows 33 years & 6 months hard labor, with ball and chain and 240 dollars fine in favor of the State and ten dollars damage in favor of Teeples. Such is the progress in crime in this onece peaceful valley.

To day was a general Co. prade, and a tolerable good turn out. The weather is fine & clear

Sunday 26th January 1851. Went to meeting a short time & came home and was around some after wards I feel quite worn out after the last weeks lawing

In the evening attended a meeting of the Presidents of the Quorums of Seventies at the State house for the purpose of reorganizing and filling vacancies in the Quorums which has not been done since we left Nauvoo. There was I think fifty nine vacances in the presidents of Quorums by death and apostacy.

Monday 27th January 1851. Around settling up some business. To day Capt J. Hunt & a company came in from Ca by South route via Iron County & reports that G. A. Smith has arrived there and organized the County and Elected Hunt Representative to the Assembly He brought papers from the States which show that President Brigham Young has been appointed Governor of Utah and Broughton Davis Harris of Vermont Secratay Joseph Buffington of Pa Chief Justice of the Supreme Court and Perry E. Brochus and Zerubabel Snow Associate Justices.[53] Joseph L Haywood Marshal Seth M. Blair Attorney General

The after noon I spent with the committee appointed by the County Court to set apart so much of the property of the wife of Phillip George as she possessed when she married him, which amounted to 530 dollars as pr valuation of said committee The residue of the property goes to pay costs and judgement of Esq Snow on the 30th Decr last.

The weather is uncomfortably warm, & clear Thawing fast and mud deep especially on the low lands.

Tuesday 28th 1851 January. This morning quite a company went out with the Band to meet the governor B. Young[54] & others who were gone to Weber County Davis & the settlements North to preach visit & organize the County of Davis.

The went to congratulate him on the news of his appointment of Gov. by the President of the U. S. They returned about and were recieved here by the firing of artillery and the shouts of a large concourse of citizens and a display of fire

52. Writing under the same date, Lorenzo Brown commented: "This morning three culprits had their sentence George Love 7 years hard labor with ball & chain He had 2 years on him before A young man named Kelly 10 years for rioting & Loomis two years for stealing. Loomis is an interesting young man to all appearance & seemed to [be?] much moved by his irons The others appeared hardened & appeared quite diverted at the idea of wearing ornaments." Lorenzo Brown, "Journal," I, 67.

53. It is rather strange that the actions of Washington, D. C., should reach Utah first via California. The act had passed Congress on September 9, 1850. Hosea Stout's list given here is correct as to the appointments, but Buffington refused his commission and Lemuel G. Brandebury took his place.

54. Of this occasion Wilford Woodruff wrote: "When the news came, President Young was about fifteen miles north of the city. The leaders and a band went out to meet him; and upon his arrival in the city, he was welcomed by a salute of ten guns. Matthias F. Cowley, *Wilford Woodruff, . . . History of His Life and Labors, as Recorded in His Daily Journals* (Salt Lake City, 1909), 344.

works at Messrs Kinkead & Levingston's Store. The whole scene was joyful peaceable and quiet The Gov when he was escorted home delivered a short address to the people assembled.

I spent the day at home and around the Council house Weather fine clear & warm

Wednesday 29th January 1851. Around Council House and at home. High Council met to try the proprietors of Red Butte It was thrown open.

Thursday 30th 1851. At home and the Council House Not well. Warm day in the evening met with the City Council a short time. Anna went to McBrides to live awhile.

Friday 31st 1851. Worked at home some to day Weather is fine clear & warm About the Council House some

Saturday February 1st 1851. Worked very to day at home. but was around the State House some

Sunday 2nd February 1851. Went to meeting. Fine day. Thomas Bateman a very ordinary ignorant Englishman spoke by permission of Prest B. Young, in the behalf of Elijah the Prophet, who he said was in our midst but he would not tell who the prophet was. only we might find it out as he had done.[55]

This prophet is issueing numerous revelations to the saints and threatning us with terrible judgements if we do not reform yet he seems to acknowledge the presidency and other authorities. It is similar to all the pretenders who have continually been poping up in the church ever since its commencement.

Bishop Carns Came to my house and spent the evening till about ten in social chat.

Monday 3rd February 1851.[56] Worked at home in the for noon and was at the State house in the after noon. Met with the Regents at two. Some business was transacted in Relation to fencin the University ground &c.

Tues 4th February 1851. Attended the Legislature at 10. After several small bills & petitions were recieved &c a bill Incorperating the Church of J. C. L. D. S. was passed, constituting it a Body corporate & poletic.

This I consider a matter of the most vital importance to all the Saints.[57] (See the Bill)

After the L. adjourned the Board of Regents met and agreed to continue the Parent School but to discontinue the present teacher Mr Collins and put the school under the immediate tuition and direction of the Chancellor O. Spencer who could employ assistant — teachers &c —

Wednesday 5th Feb 1851. Several petitions & bills were presented to the Legislature to day and was either passed or refered to Committees. I was allowed five

---

55. Woodruff also noted this incident: ". . . on February 2nd, a pretender arose who styled himself Elijah, and a Mr. Bateman spoke for about nine minutes in his behalf. The new Elijah, however, received no encouragement." *Ibid.*

56. On this day Brigham Young took the oath of office before Daniel H. Wells, chief justice of the State of Deseret. The government officers did not arrive until the next summer.

57. Hosea was right in declaring that this act was vital: "The provision that the church should keep a registry of marriages, births, and deaths free for the inspection of all members, and for their benefit, is highly significant, since such records were not required by the counties until 1888. Still another interesting provision is that by which the church was empowered to solemnize marriage compatible with the revelations of Jesus Christ; the concept of polygamy, not yet avowed by the church, seems here considered." Morgan, *State of Deseret, U.H.Q.*, VIII, 109.

dollars for each person convicted at the Special Term of the County Court. Total 85 dols Several members of the two Houses resigned and others were appointed in their place. House adjd about three p. m.

I met the board of officers for the poor fund at 6 o'c P. M.

Thurs 6th Feb 1851. Met at ten with Legislature Four City Charters were passed to day similar to the charter for this City to wit. For Ogden in Weber County. For Provo in Utah County. For Manti in San Pete County. F Sedar in Iron County. Some other business was commenced but not finished.

Friday 7 Feb 1851. Attended the Legislature Spent the fore-noon in passing a law in relation to Estrays and Estray Pounds. The after noon was spent in trying to pass a bill on pasturage and cattle running at large but only got one section through the Second reading & Adjd till Monday at 10.

I attended an Exebition in the evening at the bowry a short time.

Saturday 8th February 1851. To day was Seventies Conference I was there & attended to some other affairs

Sunday 9 February 1851. Attended Seventies Conference again. The subject of the University was taken up & spoke of by Prest B Young. Attended afternoon meeting. The Seventies are now organizing the Quorums and filling up vacancies in the Presidents of the different Quorums.

Monday 10 February 1851. Attended the Legislature at ten. The fore-noon was spent in discussing the claims of the Court and juries at the last Special Term The Gov went against the practice of any one having any thing for their services either in church or state[58] In the after noon I attended a suit before Esq Snow. William Doyle vs Patrick H Fane In debt 75 dollars & damage 100 dollars

This was a debt claimed for sirvises in driving a team from the States here and damage for failure to take Plff to Ca

Court decided no cause of action There had been a previous settlement. R. C. Petty was council for and James McCabe and myself for the defendant.

This evening the Legislature adjourned till Monday the 24th instant.

Tues 11th Feb. 1851. Around town making preperations for County Court of March Term. Another Company has come in from Ca pr south route. News from Iron Co is people better satisfied as they become better acquainted with the Country.

Wednesday 12 February 1851. The weather this morning is dark & heavy & bids fair for storm. I was around City transacting some of my own business paying my tax &c.

My State & school tax for this year amounts to 18 dollars 36 cts on 435 dollars of assessed property, which is about $4\frac{1}{4}$ per cent which with $1\frac{1}{2}$ pr cent Road tax & $\frac{1}{2}$ pr ct City tax now levied make the whole tax for this year $6\frac{1}{4}$ pr cent (Quite tall!!)

This afternoon is very windy & snowy, which has fallen about 5 or 6 inches deep I think

Thursday 13th Feb 1851. Still very stormy & snowy. Cold winter again. I was at home writing to day & met with the Seventies at dark to organize the quorums.

Friday 14th 1851 February. Still & cold cloudy weather Not doing much now days.

---

58. The Mormon Church has always been opposed to its members being paid for service of any kind rendered the church. Furthermore, a law was enacted which placed restrictions on payment of lawyers' fees.

Saturday 15th February 1851. Last evening Charles Shumway and M. D. Hambleton came in from San-Pete They bring news that M. D. Hambleton on last Sunday killed Dr. J. M. Vaughan for similar conduct with Mrs. H. as took place with Dr & Foots wife last summer.[59]

Hamilton will have a trial on the case befor the Supreme Court soon I suppose, when more will be heard about the matter. I spent the day about the City and at home not however doing much business.

Sunday 16th Feby 1851. Went to meeting. President B. Young preach Sister Nobles (wife of J. B. Noble) funeral. In the afternoon Jos Young preach a gospel sermon.

The weather is pleasant again and the snow is going off.

Monday 17th February 1851. Worked at home to day. Attended the City Council at dark A petition was presented for a charter to construct a Rail Road from the city to Red Butte Canon and other parts of the mountain South of that point for the purpose of bringing stone and other materials in to the City.

Tuesday 18th February 1851. I was sick to day with Head ache. done nothing. Went to see Major painting Parley's family group which looked splendid It consisted of 7 wives & children[60]

Wednesday 19th Feb. 1851. Snow fell last night some two or three inches deep accompanied by considerable wind. Worked at home to day. The snow nearley all went off around town in the course of the day.

Thursday 20th Feb. 1851. Worked a little to day but was around considerable looking out for thieves. The Emegrants are commencing to move off. Several of our people are now out after them which I expect will result in quite a number of emegrants being arrested & brought back for trial. The appearance now is that we will have an uncommon full docket at the next term of Court in March.

---

59. Since Foote did not sustain the charge of immorality against Dr. Vaughan and since Hambleton had only a private hearing, the actual guilt of the doctor was not established. Whether it was for anything that he actually did or fear of what he might do will always be an open question.

Madison D. Hambleton was born November 2, 1811, at Hamburg, Erie County, New York. He joined the Mormon Church in 1842 and with his wife, Chelnicio, and two daughters moved to Nauvoo where he became a member of the Quorum of the Seventy and of the guard.

Hambleton came west in 1847 as clerk in the Daniel Spencer company. In 1852 he established the small village of Pleasant Creek, later named Mount Pleasant, Utah. His permanent home was at Manti, Utah. He served as sheriff of Sanpete County from 1867 until his death on May 29, 1869.

60. This painting has not been located nor has it ever been reproduced so far as can be learned. It was hanging on the wall of the Pratt home in Salt Lake City in February 1853, and was described by Mrs. Benjamin G. Ferris. She had spent the evening there in company with her husband and Eliza R. Snow. Pratt did have seven wives who bore him children, though on this occasion only five were present. ". . . as we got up to go . . . I turned to the wall to look at a garish-looking daub, intended to represent human beings. Parley immediately came up with the light, and said it was a family group, and proceeded to point out that such a figure was such a mother, then present in the room, . . . thus going through the whole collection. His own burly figure was in the midst and could be distinguished without the aid of the dutchman's expedient." Mrs. B. G. Ferris, *The Mormons At Home, With Some Incidents of Travel From Missouri to California, 1852-1856* (New York, 1856), 170.

Another interesting account is found in the "Reminiscences of Mary Lois Walker Morris." "During the latter part of the winter of 1854 and in the spring, my husband [John T. Morris] was engaged in making portraits. He made life size bust pictures of Apostles Parley P. Pratt and George A. Smith. Also a three quarter portrait of Patriarch John Smith . . . . He also painted a family group of about twenty persons for Apostle Parley P. Pratt and another family group for Edmond Ellsworth" (typescript, Mrs. Glynn S. Bennion, Salt Lake City.)

Numbers of emegrants are endeavoring to run awy in debt while others are stealing their fit out for the mines.

Friday Feb. 21st 1851. Attended a court of examination before Alderman J. P Harmon which was to elicit evidence preparitory to the County Court   one Cherry & John Freeman was brought up to take their depositions

Cherry after many objections gave his testimony but Freeman utterly refused whereupon The Court fined him twenty dollars for contempt of court & ordered him to be confined to ball and chain & fed on bred & watter untill the fine was paid & he would testify.   Stormy evening.

Saturday Feb 22nd 1851. Verry stormy day.   North wind & driving snow   The worst snow storm that we have had this year   I was at home to day.

Sunday 23 Feb. 1851. Went to meeting.   Sherwood, Murdock & A. Lyman preached their farewell sermon previous to their going on a mission to Lower Cali- afornia & else where.[61]   President B. Young then spoke on the subject of their mis- sion &c & mentioned about McCabe going to report us to Washington &c In the afternoon Woodruff & E. T. Benson spoke.   Fine day & clear

Monday 24th Feb 1851. Attended the Legislature to day. Several bills were presented and laid on the table and one or two passed.   One bill passed to encourage the starting a wollen factory.   Legislature adjd to the 4th Sat in March.

Tuesday 25th Feb 1851. Another snow last night 3 in —

To day I was occupied in Law Court of inquiry befor W. Snow Esqr prepari- tory for Court.

Part of the troops which went West after thieves came in this evening

Wednesday 26th Feb 1851. Attended Court of inquiry again before Esq Snow & then befor Alderman Harmon.   Several persons were brought up and among the rest was Harvey Whitlock an old Mormon spoken to in Book of Doctrine & Covenants & who apostatized about 1833 but now is here on his way to Ca and supposed to be accessary with Turner & others.[62]

In the Evening met several brethren in a prayer meeting at the upper room in Council House   The Endowment is commenced there & this was a meeting after the order of the Priesthood

The weather is snowy & clear alternately but not very cold.

Thursday 27th February/51. Attended court of enquiry again before Harman alderman   This morning Maj Grant & his company came in from the West   they did not find out what had become of Willis cattle.

---

61. Amasa Lyman and his company left from Payson, Utah, on March 24, 1851, and arrived at their destination in June. They purchased the San Bernardino ranch of 100,000 acres for $77,500 and at once began to open up vast tracts for grain, alfalfa, orchards, and vineyards and to establish lumber mills, flour mills, and other industries. By 1857 they had a prosperous com- munity but left it all with the approach of Johnston's Army and the threatened Utah War. For a full story of this enterprise see George William Beattie and Helen Pruitt Beattie, *Heritage of The Valley, San Bernardino's First Century* (Oakland, 1951), 170-311.

62. This company of immigrants had been forced to winter in the Salt Lake Valley and were now ready to move on west. Their camp was in the Tooele area; some had been employed to work on E. T. Benson's mill. Hosea's chief interest seems to be this Whitlock, though, as was shown five days earlier, he had in custody W. M. Cherry and John Freeman.

Letters in the Military Records Section of the Utah State Archives show clearly the objec- tives of the expedition. Sent by horse express from "Head Quarters White Indian Expedition, February 21, 1851," the members of the expedition had as their objective the capture of Whitlock, Turner, and other white men. From this record it is not clear what disposition was made of these men, except that on March 9 following, Jack Freeman was allowed to escape.

Friday 28th 1851 February. Around some but not much up to day. Worked some at home Fine day and thawed some.

Saturday 1st March 1851. Worked at home & was around some Have no news from the out posts who are after the thieves

Sunday 2nd March 1851. Went to meeting. No news from the out posts. Lorenz Young in attempting to run by the guard at the Jordan bridge got shot through the arm and was badly wounded but no bones broken

Monday 3rd March 1851. Attended the March Term of the County Court. No business done today except the grand jury commenced & all adjd to to morrow —

Tues 4th March 1851. Attended Court No business only before the grand jury in the fore noon. The after noon was spent by the Court in transacting the County business and then adjd leaving the Grand Jury in session with orders to finish the business before them and adjourn when ever they deemed it necessary.

Wednesday 5th March 1851. Attended the grand jury. Had up several Witnesses which elicited still more light in the Turner affair At 7 o'clock P. M. attended the prayer meeting at the Endowment room as on last Wednesday evening

Thursday 6th March 1851. Attended the grand jury to day.

Friday 7th March 1851. Attended the grand jury to day, which adjourned at noon till next Monday at 9 o'c A. M.
 The Grand Jury has found Indictments agains Turner & six others for Conspiracy to steal an out fit &c for the mines & against the two Cherrys for killing an ox which they stole & agains W. M. Cherry for threatning to kill G. D. Grant & W H Kimball.
 The grand jury has been in session for six days.

Saturday 8th March 1851. At Seventies Conference to day O. P. Rockwell brought Turner in

Sunday 9th March 1851. At meeting to day (70's Conference) Jack Freeman escaped from the officer to day. He was indicted by the G. jury with Turner & others.

Monday 10th March 1851. Met with the grand jury & as there was no business, they adjd till the next term of court. In the after noon worked at home.

Tuesday 11th March 1851. Worked at home to day and at dark attended a trial. City vs Chester G Stamps befor Alderman J. P. Harmon, for slander &c he was fined _____ dollars & costs

Wednesday 12th March 1851. Worked at home to day. In the evening at the pray circle at the Endowment room.
 The U. S. mail via Fort Bridger, came in bringing a very large mail & a number of official documents from Washington The news I have not learned. The mail was snow bound 4 weeks at the South Pass. I believe this was the December mail

Thursday 13th March 1851. Worked at home today. Was at the Post office awhile. The present mail is the largest that has ever come into the Valley.

Friday & Saturday 14 & 15th March 1851. Worked at home (amen)

Sunday 16th March 1851. Went with my wife to meeting W. I. Applebee preached on the first principals of the gospel In the after noon W. W. Phelps preached.

Monday 17th March 1851. The Supreme Court met to day   Special Term for the Trial of Madison D. Hambleton for shooting Dr J. M. Vaughan for the alleged crime of seducing his wife in San Pete   I was council on the part of the State & Gov Young spoke on the part of Hambleton.

The Gov did not take up as Council for the Deft but spoke on the case. Hambleton did deliberately shoot Vaughan on one Sabbath at meeting or just as the meeting was dismissed.   His seduction & illicit conversation with Mrs Hambleton was sufficiently proven insomuch that I was well satisfied of his justification as well as all who were present and plead to the case to that effect   He was acquitted by the Court and also by the Voice of the people present.[63]

The court was not a trial but a Court of inquiry.

The Gov and several others went today to Utah to visit Rich & Lymans Co who are geathering there to move to Lower Caliafornia

Tuesday 18th March 1851. Worked at home

Wed 19th. Worked at home.   Hard South wind to day and rainy & snowy night Attended the prayer circle at the Endwment room this evening.

Thursday 20th March 1851. Worked at home to day.   This morning there was a snow about 3 or 4 inches deep but otherwise pleasant weather

Friday 21st March 1851. Worked at home to day.   Some squally snows but warm.

Saturday 22 March 1851. Legislature met.   No quorum and adjourned till 5th Apl 10 a. m. after which I was around town   officer Drill also —

We learn that Hanks is on the Bear River with the mail of January.   He has been to Larimie since Christmas.

Sunday 23 March 1851. Went to meeting.   Br Kempton told his experience & W. Woodruff preach.   In the after noon Bp Pedigrew & E. T. Benson preached.

Monday 24th March 1851. Worked at home. to day. Hanks came in to day with the mail from Larimie.   This is the January mail from the States & it brings papers from St Louis to Jan the 10th

Tuesday. 25th March 1851. Worked at home windy day   about dark hard snow storm and N. W. wind very bad.

Wednesday 26th 1851. March. Cold storm is over & a Drifted snow   Worked some.   At 7 P. M. attend   the prayer meeting at Council H

Thursday 27 March 1851. Worked at home to day.

Friday 28 1851. (At home all day but not able to work much. [crossed out])

Worked at home.   In the evening the Legislature met at the State to recieve the Gov message and transact some business preparetory to the Territorial government and adjd till Sat the 5th Apl next.[64]

I then attended the City Council   Ther   was a trial also before the Municipal Court between B T. Mitchel & McEll

---

63. This was clearly not an open court case but a justification before a small group in a "court of inquiry." The fact that the governor justified the act cleared Hambleton.

64. On this date the General Assembly of the State of Deseret met to dissolve that government and to accept status as the Territory of Utah. A part of the resolution was that they should proceed at once to build the necessary buildings and that "We appoint an architect to draft designs and a committee of One to superintend the erection of said buildings." These were to have been erected on Union Square, west and north of the temple block, the site of present West High School. Plans were changed, and the first seat of government was located at the geographical center of Utah Territory, Fillmore, Utah. Final closing was not until April 5, 1851.

Saturday 29th 1851. At home in the Fore noon at work. General Training to day.

Sunday 30th March 1851. Went to meeting. J. C. Wright, H. C. Kimball, David Fulmer, and Danl Spencer preached.

March 31st Monday. 1851. Very stormy night last night & snow this morning. Squally day Worked very little to day

Tuesday 1st April 1851. Worked at home to day.

Wednesday 2nd April 1851. Worked at home to day. Attend the prayer meeting again but there was not a quorum present.
The Feb. mail came in this evening from the States.

Thursday 3rd April 1851. Worked at home to day —

Friday 4th April 1851. Worked at home to day.

Saturday 5th 1851. April. Legislature met at ten A. M. Several bills were passed & about 4 o'cl adjourned sine die which ends the Legislative Goverment of Deseret for the Legislature is now dissolved & I suppose that my office as Attorney General of the State is likewise ended with the State government The government of Utah will succeed.

Sunday 6th April 1851. To day the Church is 21 years old. General Conferance would have commenced to day but the weather was too wet & cold.

Monday 7th April 1851. Attended Confencerence. The usual business was transacted and some other items. In the evening the City Election went off —

Tuesday 8th April. Worked at home. Wed. Worked at home Thurs. Worked at home. Frid Worked at home. Sat Worked at home.

Sunday 13th April 1851. Went to meeting as usual to day

Mond. 14. Worked at home.

Tuesday 15th. Worked at home.

Wed 16th. Worked at hom — Attended the prayer circle at 7 o'clock P. M.

Thurs 17. Worked at home plowing garden to day.

Friday 18. plowing & gardening

Sat 19. Cold windy day. I attended the High Council to day

Sunday 20th. Cold rainy. At home all day.

Monday 21st 1851. Worked at home. Packard had a sale of his goods to day, but did not sell many for the want of bidders

Tuesd 22nd. Worked at home

Wednesday 23. Worked at home Went to the prayer circle but it was a failure. Last night a man named Custer was killed by the Indians in Toolie Valley. They had been taken prisoners by the whites & attempting to break away they were pursued by the whites & Custer was shot. The Indians were taken but permitted to keep their arms. A party is going out to night to Toolie against the Indians.

Thursday 24th Apl 1851. Woked at home. to day.

Frid. 25th. Worked at home

Sat 26th. Worked at home. To day was an officer drill

Sunday 27th. Went to meeting W. Snow & D. Fulmer preached in the after noon W. J. Appleby & Wm Snow preached.

Mond 28th. Worked at home. News has arrived that the troops in Toolie have killed five of the Indians which were taken when Custer was killed.[65]

Tues 29th. Woked at home

Wed. 30th. Worked at home and attended to some legal business.

Thurs May 1. 1851. Worked at home. The Ladies are out "in shoals & nation" geathering may flours.

Frid. Worked at home

Sat. worked at home.

Sunday 4th. Went to meeting

Monday. worked at home.

Tues 6th. Woked at home. Hardest wind to day since I have lived here.

Wednesday 7th May. Worked at home To day a train of 5 or 6 waggons loaded with bacon and sugar with some dry goods came in from Fort Larimie. This evening I attended the "prayer circle"

Thurs 8th. Worked at home.

Friday 9th. Had a hard rain last night & very dark and heavy this morning and raining some Went North in the after noon rained all the time. Stayed all night at Mother Taylors. Snowed hard about dark.

Saturday 10th May 1851. Wet & snowy this morning House leaked all night and anow very wet day. I went to Joseph Taylors 8 miles North. My Brother-in-laws have made a splendid Farms here on the high bench lands & got in good crops. Stayed there all night all the houses are leaking all night Very rainy weather.

Sunday. 11th. Still rainy. Went with Joseph for wood took a fine rain while out. The neighbours are all well damped with the. Dirt roofs will not answer. Stayed all night with S. Driggs

Monday 12. Came home Took breakfast with Mother Taylor got home abot noon all well. Very rainy after again

Tuesday 13th May 1851. Around town. The Brewry and at home. Rained today. This has been the longest storm & the most rain that I have seen this time of the year in the Valley.

---

65. Dale L. Morgan, in his "Historical Sketch of Tooele County" in the WPA, Historical Records Survey, *Inventory of the County Archives of Utah No. 23, Tooele County* (Ogden, Utah, 1939), says that: "Some capital has been made by Mormon critics of the only recorded Indian killings during this time, of L. D. Curtis and C. Custer, both emigrants, and contention being that at least the latter of these killings was actually by Mormon desperadoes rather than by Indians." See page 18.

The military records list but one, and that combined the intials of the first with the surname of the second: "Lorenzo D. Custer born in New York, killed by Indians April 22, 1851, buried in the Salt Lake City cemetery." (Military Records Section, Utah State Archives.)

Mormon writers tell the story much as it is given here, adding that Custer's body was brought in for burial and that on a later expedition "the Indians were sacrificed to the natural instincts of self defense" by the party under O. P. Rockwell. Gottfredson, *Indian Depredations*, 38-39. See also Edward W. Tullidge, *Tullidges Histories . . .* (2 vols., Salt Lake City, 1889), II, 83.

Wednesday 14th 1851. May. Around as yesterday. The weather seems more settled.

Thursday 15th May 1851. Worked on the roads to day. I understand that the Indians are troublesome in Toolie Valley again.

Friday 16th. Done nothing only around Town.

Saturday 17th May, 1851. Around as yesterday. To day a come and two teams 8 mules each came in From Fort Hall some left Oregon April 1st They were loaded with tobacco tea &c and are going soon to the States. They say a gold mine has been found on Klamet river between Oregon & Ca

Sunday 18th May 1851. Had a very hard rain last night which continued untill noon to day This is the hardest rain spell we have in a long time.

There was a meeting at the Council House to take in consideration the propriety of building a tabernacle which was agreed to and done by donation There was about 700 doll. subscribed It is contemplated to send subscriptions to all the branches in the State to solicit donations for the purpose.

Monday 19th 1851 May. Around as before. Cloudy & cold weather with some rain

Tuesday 20th. Around town again

Wednesday 21st. Around again. Met the prayer circle in the evening Had a good meeting

Thursday 22nd May 1851. Around town doing nothing of importance only waiting for the mail to come in from the States, which has been due 2 months. I do not know how to make a calculation for the summer untill I learn the news & prospects from the States

Friday 23rd May 1851. Rained & hailed some to day. I was occupied as usual now days.

Saturday 24th May 1851. Went with S. M. Blair to to Neff's mill to day.

The U. S mail came in to day from the East, and report that a train of goods are close by and will be in soon. President B. Young's Company came in from Iron County to day.[66] They were met by a troop of cavelry & the Band who escorted them home where they were recieved by the firing of artilery.

Sunday 25 May 1851. Went to meeting. Prest B. Young gave a relation of his visit to Iron County & the country. Reports many beautiful vallies and fine prospects of farming all doing well. Coal and other minerals has been found in abundance. The news from the States are dull as yet.

Monday & Tuesday 26th 27th 1851. Around town hunting and reading the news from the States which is dull as well as the times here.

---

66. This trip was reported in great detail in the *Deseret News* for June 28, 1851. The company left Salt Lake City April 22 and organized with seventeen officers, of whom Thomas Bullock was clerk. They visited briefly the Utah Valley settlements, stopped at Manti in Sevier Valley and organized the town, and proceeded to Parowan. Here they remained a full week, took the census, organized the town with William H. Dame as mayor; Richard Harrison, Tarleton Lewis, John D. Lee, and Matthew Carruthers, aldermen; Andrew A. Love, Joel H. Johnson, William A. Morse, William Leany, Priddy Meeks, Elijah Newman, Robert Wiley, John A. Wolfe, and John Dolten (Dalton?) as councillors.

At Parowan they were met and escorted into town by a body of horsemen to the salute of cannon, the raising of the flag, and the cheers of the citizens. The clerk wrote a careful description of the country en route.

Wednesday 28th May 1851. Spent the time as usual. The U. S. mail came in to day 26 days from the states and report a great number of emegrants on their way here on both sides of the platte. Some will be in in a few days.

Thurs & Frid 29 & 30 May. Doing nothing but reading the news which however was very Dry & uninteresting.

Saturday 31 May 1851. General parade to day. Nothing more of importance going on. Farewell Sweet May

Sunday 1st June 1851. Wife & I went to meeting. Prest B. Young preached on domestic Econemy.

Monday & Tuesday 2 & 3 June. Doing nothing as usual now days. Walker & his men are here[67]

Wednesday 4th June 1851. Worked at home some little attended pray circle this eveing

Thurs 5 June 1851. Woked a little. Phelps & Childes train of goods of 12 wagons 10 mules each came in to day. The first Ca U. S. mail came this evening

Friday 6th June 1851. Worked at home some today.

Saturday 7th June 1851. Worked at home some to day.

Sunday 8th June 1851. Went to meeting. President Young preached

Monday 9th June 1851. Worked at home to day.

Tuesd 10th June 1851. Went with my wife to her mothers on a visit.

Wed 11 June 1851. Went to Joseph Taylors & sold him my horses for a small farm, intending to make another effort to go to farming. how will it come out?

Thurs & Frid 12 & 13 1851. Still continuing our visit but came home on Friday

Saturday 14th June 1851. At home and around town some

Sunday 15th June 1851. Went to meeting today

Monday 16. At home at work. Tues 17. At home at work. Wednesday 18. At home strolling around some at dark attended the prayer circle

Thurs 19. Not well Strolling around town. Friday 20th. Around as usual.

Sat 21st. At home. Sunday 22nd. Went to meeting President Young gave the drunkards a scoring.

Mond & Tuesd 23 & 24. Worked in garden. Wed 25. Worked in garden attended prayer circle in the evening. Thursd 26th. Worked at home Friday 27th. Worked at home. The company which went to Toolie against the Indians came in to day after having killed Eleven but did not get any of our men hurt.[68] They had a very hard trip. Large party at the Bath House

Saturday 28th 1851 June. Officer drill to day I was around the city in different parts — did not work much.

---

67. This refers of course to the Indian Chief Walker (Walkara) and his band.
68. See footnote 65 preceeding.

Sunday 29th June 1851. Went to meeting to day. The mail came in from the States last night.

South Carolinia Convention decided that it is right & best for them to cecede from the Union.

Monday 30th June 1851. Worked some & read the news from the States.

Tuesday 1st July 1851. Occupied as on yesterday.

Wednesday 2nd July. Worked at dark attended prayer circle

Thurs 3rd. Worked in garden

Friday 4th July 1851. Worked at garden all day. A very large party with the Govr most of the officers &c have gone to Salt Lake to celebrate the Nationall Independence It is a windy day they will have dust in their eyes like politicians

Sat July 5th 1851. Worked at home to day.

Sunday 6th July. Went to meeting

Monday 7th. Worked at home

Tues 8th. Woked at home

Wed 9th. Not well around town (attended prayer circle as usual [crossed out]) Th 10. Around as usual Friday 11th. Around as usual Wrote some in the post office

Saturday 12. Around as usual Wrote in the post office some

Sunday 13. Went to meeting as usual Had a fine good rain which wet our gardens thoroughly which is some thing rare this time of year

Monday 14 July. Around town but unable to work with a lame back

Tues 15. Laid up but around as yesterday Wed 16 Around as before attended prayer circle in the eve

Thurs & [17]. Around as before Still lame back.

Friday July 18th 1851. Around as before Lame yet

Saturday July 19th 1851. Still Lame. To day the Hon A W. Babbit, Dr Barnhisel, Judges Z Snow, Secratary Harris, H. R. Day & [Stephen B.] Rose[69] Indian Sub agents and several others came in after tedious hard trip Large preperations are making for the celebration of the 24th

Sund 20th. Went to meeting

Mond 21. Very sick to day. Yet around town.

Monday 21st July 1851. Lame yet

Tuesd 22. Irrigating toay

Wed. 23rd. Irrigating to day.

---

69. "The first officer to arrive from the east was Lemuel G. Brandebury, appointed when Buffington refused his commission. Brandebury appeared June 7, followed July 19 by Zerubabbel Snow, Broughton D. Harris, two Indian sub-agents, Stephen B. Rose and Henry R. Day, and Bernhisel and Babbitt." Morgan, *State of Deseret, U. H. Q.,* VIII, 131.

Thurs 24th. To day the anniversary of the pioneers were held commencing at 8 a.m. I was with the D. U. Regents. It was altogether the greatest celebration ever held here.

Friday July 25th 1851. Not well to day but was around town some little.

Saturday July 26th 1851. Unwell to day. A County Convention was held to nominate officers for the coming election, which I shall not speak of now I was put in nomination for a candidate for the House of Representatives for G. S. L. County.

Sunday 27th. Went to meeting. Duncan M. Arthur & wife made me a visit to day

Monday 28th. Worked at home Tues 29th. Worked at home Wed 30. Worked at home attended prayer circle in the evening Thursday 31. Worked at home

Friday 1 Aug. 1851. Worked at home Sick O!

Saturday 2 Aug. To day all hands turned out from the city & country to work on and dig out the cellar for the Tabernacle I was thare

Sunday. Went to meeting

Monday 4th Aug 1851. To day is the General Election for State & County officers was held. The following officers were elected to the Legislature for this County to wit for Councillors H. C. Kimball, W. Richards, D. H. Wells J. M. Grant, E. T. Benson, O. Spencer. Representatives W. Woodruff, D. Fullmer D. Spencer W. Snow, W W. Phelps A. P. Rockwood N. H. Felt, E D. Woolley, P. Richards Jos Young H. G. Sherwood, B. C. Johnson and Hosea Stout

Tuesday 5th Aug 1851. Worked at home to day.

Wed. 6th. Woked at home

Thurs 7th. Worked at home

Frid 8th. Worked at home

Sat 9th. Wife not well did not work any to day.

Sund 10. Went to meeting A. W. Babbitt spoke today.

Monday. 11th. Worked at home

Tuesd 12. Worked at home

Wed 13th. Worked at home

Thurs 14th. Worked at home

Frid 15th. Worked at home

Sat 16th. Worked at home

Sund 17th. At home rained

Monday 18th. Worked at home O Hyde & Judge Broccus ame in to day The Pawnees robbed them on the head of the Horne[70]

---

70. The "Journal History" for Friday, July 11, 1851, records that: "Elder Orson Hyde and six others, including Judge Perry E. Brocchus, all enroute for G.S.L. City, were assailed by about 300 Pawnee Indians near a branch of the Loup Fork, and robbed of clothing, arms

Tues 19th. Worked at home

Wed 20th. Worked at home

Thurs - 21. Worked at home

Frid 22. Worked at home

Sat 23. Worked at home

Sund 24th. Went to meeting Hyde preached

Monday 25th. Worked at home

Tues 26th. Worked at home

Wed 27th. Worked at home

Thurs 28th. Worked at home

Friday 29th Aug 1851. Worked at home   Frost on the flats last night bit quite hard

Sat 30th. Muster day. I did not work much, around

Sunday 31st. Went to meeting Was very unwell. G. W. Oman & several other brethren came in from the States   The first arrived of our people with families this year

Monday 1st Sept 1851. Worked at home

Tues 2nd. Worked at home

Wed 3. Not well — do

Thurs. Worked at home The last fine days has been attended with an uncommon hard wind from the south.

Frid 5th. Worked at do

Sat 6th. Worked at home   People are coming to Conference in large numbers.

Sunday 7th. Conference very large congregation.

Mond 8th. Conference. Judge Brocchus made a speach in defence of the Goverment and condeming this people Prest B Young replied warmly[71]

Tues 9th Sept 1851. Conference yet 2 presiding travelling Bishops appointed. Voted to keep the word of Wisdom & to cut all off from the Church who do not & pay not their tithin.   Brethren are coming in from the States.

Wed 10th. Conference adjourned today at one

Thursday 11th. Worked at home

Friday 12. Worked at home

Sat. 13. Worked at home

---

and equipments, provisions, etc. to the amount of from seven to ten hundred dollars. The party were stripped of personal appearel, Judge Brocchus being left with nothing but his drawers, and even these were demanded."

71. This public exchange between Judge Brocchus and Brigham Young is mentioned by many writers. It opened the conflict which resulted in the return of federal appointees to Washington, D. C.

Sunday 14th. Went to meeting —

Monday 15th. Worked at home

Tues 16th. Worked at home

Wed 17th. Worked at home My wife was delivered of a son about 4 o'c A. M

Thurs Sep 18th 1851. Worked at home.

Frid 19th. Worked at home

Sat 20th. Worked some & was around town awhile

Sunday 21. Went to meeting to day. I learned to day that Howard Egan, who has returned forom the gold mines lately, and upon learning that his wife had been seduced or in other word had had a child willingly by James M. Monroe during his absence. Said Monroe had also gone to the States for goods for Reese and was now on his return here, whereupon Egan went and met him near Cach Cave and after talking the matter over sometime Egan drew a pistol and shot him dead which makes the second man who has been deliberately shot dead for the same offence in less than one year in the Territory.[72]
What will be the end of this last affair I do not now know.

Monday 22nd 1851 Sept. The Legislature of the Territory of Utah met to day for the first time and proceeded to elect the different officers pro tem and organize for business but did not do any thing else. Tomorrow I expect that the organization will be completed.

Tuesday Sept. 23 - 1851. Met with the Legislature The fore noon was spent in organizing the house. W. W Phelps was elected Speaker of the house

Albert Carrington Chief Clerk	Rodney Badger Messenger
James Cragun Sergeant at arms.	David Pettigrew Chaplain
John L. Smith doorkeeper	Henry E Phelps Fireman

After transacting some other of miner importance the house adjourned till 2 o'c But previous however the speaker apointed several committees.
I was apointed on the committee on Military afairs. and on the committee on the committe on claims and on the committee on Counties and destricts, on the committee on public printing _____
At two o'clock the house was called to order by the speaker whereupon the severall officers of the house were sworn into office, after which the two houses went into Joint Session when the Govenor delivered his message.
The two houses voted to have 1500 copies printed after which they adjourned till to-morrow at ten o'clock
A committee had been appointed to wait on the Judges of the Supreme court and secratary of the Territory to meet with the two houses to hear the Gov. message but they all excused themselves but Snow

Wednesday Sept. 24th 1851. At ten the Legislature met and appointed John Oakley to the office of assistant Clerk. Several acts and Resolutions were then passed The Speaker then declared several committees I was appointed on the committee on publick printing, also on a select committee to draw up rules for the house

72. The Egan-Monroe killing was mentioned by many diarists. Monroe, the schoolteacher at Nauvoo, whose record has been mentioned, was evidently a close friend of the Egan family, living at least part of the time in their home.
Egan had married two other wives and was away a great deal on official assignments. It was the child of Monroe and Mrs. Egan who preserved and copied the records of James M. Monroe and who also prepared the diaries of Egan for publication.

Legislature adjd till 2, and met accordingly passed some resolutions and about 4 o'clock the (Assembly [crossed out]) both houses met in joint Session, and passed an act commanding the U.S. Marshall to take into his possession the seal, press, papers monies & in the hands of the Secretary of the Territory which belong to the Territory for the reason that he refuses to act in his office and refuses to disburse any money to defray the incidental of the Legislature[73] — The Legislature then adjourned till to morrow at ten o'clock a. m. In the evening I met with the prayer circle but there was not a quorum present

Thursday Sept 25th 1851. Legislature met at ten a.m. and the House of R spent the fore noon in discussing the propriety or impropriety of adopting Rules for the govt of the same.

A large train came in today from Garden Grove.

At two o'clock P. M the L. met as pr adj't — A L. Fulmer was appointed assistant door keeper and A. P. Richards Second messenger Several resolutions were then passed.

A document was sent to the house from the Council directed to W. Richards & W W Phelps Esqrs by the Secretary in aswer to demand made on him by the Assembly for 500 dollars to defray the incidental expenses of the Legislature He does not admit that the Legislature is a legal body and gave his [reasons] why which I deem entirely too futile to mention the document was taken as an insult by the House He of course refuses to disburse any money for the use of the Assembly After hearing this document read the house adjournd as usual

Sept 26th 1851 Friday. At ten o'clock the house met as pr adjournment.

Accounts were hand in from several counties for pay for (several [crossed out]) services rendered at the last election.

A committee was appointed to take into consideration so much of the Gov message as relates to the U. S. Judges & Secratary intending to absent themselves from the Territory. I was on that committee. The house spent the after [noon] without transacting any very important business

This evening we had a splendid warm rain

Sept 27th 1851. Saturday. To day is a general training & a fine day after the warm rain last night which makes all things look fresh & beautiful

At ten o'clock the Legislature met as pr adjournment. The Special committee to draft rules for the house reported 21 rules for the govt of the same which was taken up and passed W Woodruff, E. D. Woolley & H. Stout was appointed a furnishing committee to supply the house with the necessaries of the house The house then adjd till 2 Rainy afternoon

A Joint Resolution legalizing the acts of the provisional government so far as they do not conflict with the organic act was passed

A bill was passed the House to locate the seat of Government at Parvin Valley and for the Legislature to meet there the 1st day of January next.[74] Adj'd till Monday at ten o'c a. m The Supreme courd decided that the Secratay was not accountable to any one here

---

73. The trouble stemmed from the fact that Brigham Young had taken the oath of office months before the other officers arrived; he had the census taken and called the legislature into session. The new secretary of the territory, Broughten D. Harris, insisted that the legislature could not be legally called without his signature and seal; hence, since they were not duly authorized, legislators should receive no pay for their services. To express their disapproval, the three federal officers decided to leave and did so on September 28, 1851.

74. The decision of the legislature to continue their government at Fillmore was an attempt to show their independence of the national appointees. The group continued to carry on its regular business without the presence of the secretary of the territory or the two judges, as the next week's activities show.

Sunday Sept 28th 1851. Went to meeting. Gov Young said that he had made friends the U. S. officers which were returning to the States and Brocchus apoligized for insulting the conference.

Many of the brethren came in to day from the States

Monday Sept 29th 1851. Legislature met at ten Several Bills were passed in the forenoon In the after-noon several accounts and bills of miner importance were presented, & some passed.

One bill, authorizing Judge Z. Snow to hold courts in the districts which were vacated by the two judges which left for the States was passed.

The house adj'd till to morrow at ten a. m.

Sept 30th 1851. Tuesday. House met as pr adjt Several bills were passed in the fore noon In the after noon several bills were passed.

A memorial was presented praying the President of the U. S. to fill the vacancies occasioned by the judes and Secratay of the Territory leaving to be filled by citizens of this place.

A Resolution authorizing the Chancellor & Board of Regents to appoint a Commissioner of common schools with a salery of not mre than $1000.

A bill on the Library was passed.

A Resolution to appoint a joint committee to revise the Laws of Deseret passed the House

A Bill granting James Brown the right to Erect toll bridges across Weber & Ogden.

W Woodruff H. Stout & B F Johnson were appointed a committee on Territorial expenditures. House adj'd till ten to morrow

Wed Oct 1st 1851. Legislature met at ten a. m. Several bills were passed to do which I shall not notice here. H. Stout D. Fulmer and P. Richards were appointed a committee to revise & clasify the Laws of Deseret as pr Resolution to act During the recess of the Assembly and to act jointly with a Comittee of two from the Council

This evening the Assembly adjourned till the first Monday in January 1852.

My Brother arrived here to (last [crossed out]) night with his family from the Bluff in tolerable health. Rainy weathr

Thursday Oct 2nd 1851. Worked some to day but was around town most of the time with my brother

Friday Oct 3rd 1851. Worked at home to day.

Saturday Oct 4th 1851. Worked at home to day. The brethren are coming in from the Bluff now in great numbers. O. Pratt came in this evening.[75]

Sunday Oct 5th 1851. Went to meeting awhile in the fore noon Conference commences again to day The Bowry will not hold the people to day. Attended meeting in the after noon —

Monday Oct 6th 1851. Conference continues. Worked some & attended C.

Tues Oct 7th 1851. Worked Rained to day Three days general parade & cold weather

Wednesday October 8th 1851. Rainy blustering day. Attended the District court in the fore noon. Z. Snow presiding. I was admitted to the Bar to day and

---

75. Orson Pratt had been in charge of the L. D. S. mission in England where he edited and published *The Millennial Star.*

sworn into office, a Councillor and attorney at law and solicitor in chauncery, by Judge Snow upon a motion of S. M. Blair

George A. Smith & W. W. Phelps were admitted to the Bar yesterday upon the same motion

Court was adjourned till friday at ten a. m. Several suits are pending at this time.

Thursday October 9th 1851. Worked at home to day. The California mail came in accompanied by a company of brethren from the mines Moses Leonard and _____ Smith was killed by the Indians on the road near Mary's River

Friday Oct 10th 1851. Attended Court to day. There was but one case came off —

Saturday Oct 11th 1851. Attended court and worked at home some

Sunday Oct 12th 1851. Went to meeting to day.

Monday Oct 13th 1851. Attended court and worked at home to day.

Tuesday Oct 14th 1851. Attended Court and worked at home to day.

Wednesday Oct. 15th 1851. Attended Court and worked some at home to day & in the evening attended prayer circle at the Council House

Thursday Oct. 16th 1851. Attended court and worked at home some to day.

Friday October 17th 1851. Attended Court to day. The trial of Howard Egan for the murder of James Monroe came up. Seth M. Blair was prosecuting attorney on the part of the U. S. and W. W. Phelps and G. A. Smith attornies on the part of Egan. The Indictment was found by the grand jury of the U. S. for the first Judicial destrict of the Territory of Utah.

From the Evidence it appears that while Egan was gone to the mines, Monroe seduced his wife by whom she had a bastard child. Monroe had gone to the East for goods when Egan returned, who upon learning the facts in the case, went to meet Monroe who was on his return to this place with a train of goods for Sirs Reese and near Bear River.

Egan met him some ten miles this side and camly saluting each other both appearantly friendly went some 100 yards from the carrall and appeared to talk peaceably some time when Egan drew a pistol and shot him in the face on the right side of the nose just below the eye. Monroe fell dead on the spot when Egan mounted his horse, rode to the company. told his name, made a short speech, said what he did he done in the name of the Lord. that Monroe had seduced his wife, ruined his family, and destroyed his peace on earth for ever and that they would find him in this place and then blessed them and hoped that they would have a safe journey to the city and rode off informing those he overtook on the road what he had done. This is in short the evidence of the case. after which Blair made his first plea and was followed by Phelps who used the Bible History, Homer, Virgil besides a large pile of law books & precidents to show that Egan was justified in his act when the court adjourned till tomorrow at ten a. m.

Saturday Oct 18th 1851. Attended court at ten a. m. The case of U. S. Vs Egan came up as pr adjt George A. Smith first made his plea. He justified Egan for what he had done said it was the duty of the nearest kin to a female who was seduced to take the life of the seducer He made an able plea & was followed by the prosecuting attorney when the jury retired and was absent about 15 minutes when they returned with a virdict of not guilty as found in the Indictment whereupon the court discharged Egan.[76]

76. The account of the trial of Howard Egan for the murder of James Monroe appears in the *Deseret News* of November 15, 1851, with the concluding note that it should "prove a sufficient

This is like to be a precident for any one who has his wife, sister, or daughter seduced to take the law into his own hands and slay the seducer & I expect it will go still farther but of that at the time

In the afternoon two more Indictments were brought up against others one was quashed and the prosecuting attorney entered a nolle prosequi on the other two. The court then adj'd after administring the oath of naturalization to James Furgerson & admiting him as a member of the Bar.[77]

Sunday October 19th 1851. Attended meeting in the fore noon. In the after noon was visiting & being visited by John Kay.

Monday Oct 20th 1851. At home working to day.

Tuesday Oct 21st 1851. Not well. Took dinner with S. M. Blair. Did not work any.

Wednesday Oct 22nd 1851. Worked at home today. Attended prayer circle to night. The Gov. & Judge Snow & other gone to San Pete to hold court.

Thursday October 23rd 1851. Worked at home to day.

Friday Oct 24th 1851. Worked at home to day. T. S. Williams Train of goods came in to day. All well.

Saturday October 25th 1851. Worked at home to day.

Sunday October 26th 1851. Went to meeting

Monday Oct 27th 1851. Worked at home to day

Tuesday Oct 28th 1851. Worked at home

Wednesday October 29th 1851. Worked at home to day.

(Thursday-O [crossed out]**)** attended prayer circle at dark —

Thurs. October 30th 1851. Worked at home and was around Williams Store[78] trading some little.

---

warning to all unchaste reprobates, that they are not wanted in our community . . . . It may be the means of saving some from a similar fate."

77. James Ferguson was born in Belfast, Ireland, February 28, 1828. He was converted and came to Nauvoo in time to share the problems of the exodus. At the age of eighteen, he joined the Mormon Battalion, serving in Company "A" under Jefferson Hunt. Tullidge in his *History of Salt Lake City* wrote of Ferguson in glowing terms as "Soldier, lawyer, actor, and orator," as "handsome, dashing, eloquent." As an officer during these early years he was one of the "B'hoys," active in all the expeditions.

In 1854 Ferguson filled a mission to his native land, returning in 1856. During the Mormon War he was adjutant general of the Utah Militia under Daniel H. Wells. He was one to welcome Captain Van Vliet, Schuyler Colfax, and other notables. He played the dramatic lead in the theater and was the co-founder of the paper, the *Mountaineer* (Salt Lake City). Ferguson died August 30, 1863, in Salt Lake City of dropsy.

78. Thomas S. Williams appears so often in this record that it seems appropriate here to summarize his background: "He was a Mormon young man of much promise in Nauvoo before the exodus . . . he was a member of the famous Mormon Battalion . . . one of the company of J. M. Horner & Co., which was afterwards changed to Hooper & Williams, and he built the third store on Main Street, on the side now occupied by the Deseret National Bank. Tullidge, *History of Salt Lake City*, 380.

Of his activities during the Mormon Battalion trek: "Sgt. Thomas S. Williams . . . had some of the sick in his wagon. Officer Smith drew his sword and threatened to run Williams through if he attempted to allow any more sick to ride in his wagon without permission. Williams braced himself, grasped the small end of his load whip and told him if he dared to make one move to strike he would level him to the ground; that the team and wagon were his private property and he would haul whom he pleased." Tyler, *Mormon Battalion*, 144-45.

Friday October 31st 1851. Worked at home today.

Saturday Nov. 1st 1851. Worked at home and traded some at Williams Store again.

Sunday Nov 2nd 1851. At home all day. William L. Cutler one of the Presidents of the Eleventh Quorum of seventies died this morning.

Monday Nov. 3rd 1851. Worked at home to day.

Tuesday Nov 4th 1851. Worked at home to day.

Wednesday Nov 5th 1851. Worked at home and traded some at T. S. Williams Store

Thursday Nov 6th 1851. Worked at home to day

Friday 7th Nov 1851. Quite sick to day but worked some & was at the stores awhile.

Saturday Nov 8th 1851. Raned some to day, worked at home

Sunday Nov 9th. At home all day.

Monday Nov 10th 1851. Rained moderately all last night and to day, but was not verry cold or windy Snowed some — I worked in my shop moderately steady

Tuesday Nov 11th 1851. Worked at home some little

Wednesday Nov 12th 1851. Worked at home and at dark met with the prayer circle

Thursday Nov 13th 1851. Worked for J. B. Nobles to day.

Friday Nov 14th 1851. Rained all night last night Worked at home

Saturday. Election to day & I was there

Sunday November 16th 1851. At home all day. Rained and snowed this evening but warm —

Monday Nov 17th 1851. Not well, was at home, worked some & was around the store some

Tuesday Nov 18th 1851. Rainy. Worked at home to day.

Wednesday Nov 19th. Clear day in the after noon — Worked at home Crouted[79] to night for the first time in the Valley.

At this time and for some years following, Williams was a loyal and active member of the church. The "Journal History" of the church under the date of September 2, 1852, reproduced a letter from Williams written from Sacramento, California, on that date. After explaining that he is established in the butchering business there and has started several slaughterhouses and meat markets, Williams writes: ". . . am in a fine way to make an immense percentage on my cattle . . . and I flatter myself that when I return I shall have enough to fully satisfy my greedy appetite, so that I can return to my peaceful home in the mountains and devote my time and influence to the up-building and rolling forth of the cause and Kingdom of God, for my eye is still Zionward, and my interest, my purpose and in short my whole heart and soul is still with the people of God . . . ."

These exerpts are especially interesting in the light of later developments.

79. Stout has evidently raised enough cabbage this season to make a keg of sauerkraut.

Thurs. Nov 20th. Worked for A P. Rockwood. Friday 21th. Worked for ditto again. Saturday 22th. Worked for ditto again

Sunday Nov 23rd 1851. At home to day but was at the Council House a short time. pleasant after noon.

Monday Nov. 24th 1851. Cloudy and warm to day. Worked for A. P. Rockwood.

Tuesday Nov. 25th 1851. Worked home. "dug taters" Warm & rainy

Wednesday Nov. 26th 1851. Worked at home to day. at prayer circle

Thursday Nov 27 1851. Worked at home to day.

Friday Nov 28th 1851. Worked very little to day & went down in town awhile.

Saturday Nov 29th 1851. Training day I was not well but was around in town some

Sunday. Nov 30th 1851. At home at in town & reading news papers late from the States Not well today

Monday Decr 1st 1851. Worked at home all day.

Tuesday Decr 2nd 1851. Worked at home to day. This evening met at the State house with the members of the bar & other gentlemen and Judge Snow to take into consideration the propriety of establishing a law School under the direcition of Judge Snow who tenders his sirvis as a teacher gratis for the benefit of all those who wish to inter into the Study of Law. After an agreeable time spent in Social conversation & politicks the Judge gave us a short lecture on the nature and origin of goverment & law, after which it was agreed to establish the school and meet next Tuesday evening at the same place

Wednesday Decr 3rd 1851. Worked at home some & was at the stores awhile preparing means as one of the furnishing committee for the House of Representatives preparitory to me meeting of the same on first of January next.

Thursday Decr 4th 1851. Worked at home some

Friday Dec 5th 1851. Worked at home

Saturday Decr 6th 1851. Wife & I had our Daguerreotype likeness taken to day, by M. Cannon[80] Snowy day

Sunday Decr 7th 1851. Around town. No meeting in consequence of the Bowery being torn down. Fine clear day.

Monday Decr 8th 1851. Very sick to day Could not work, but was around town some little.

---

80. Marsena Cannon, the first photographer in Utah, was born August 3, 1812, in Rochester, New York, and came to Utah in 1849. The first issue of the *Deseret News* (June 15, 1850) carried his advertisement for taking pictures, adding "Having had nine years of practice in the Art, principally in Boston, Mass., I fancy I can suit the most discriminating taste," and added as references Wilford Woodruff of the Twelve, W. W. Phelps, Heywood & Woolly, E. Whipple, and A. Badlam.

In the *Deseret News* of December 10, 1850, Cannon notes that "timber, wheat, wood, & store pay taken in exchange for likenesses. Cash and gold dust not refused . . . . A fine toned melodian for sale now."

In 1861 Marsena Cannon was called to the Dixie Mission but returned after a year and set up his business in connection with C. R. Savage. The original taken here is owned by Mr. LaFayette Lee, Salt Lake City.

Tuesday Decr 9th 1851. Worked at home to day. In the evening attended the Law school at the State House again.

Wednesday Decr 10th 1851. Around town till noon then worked the rest of the day & attended prayer circle in the evening

Thursday Decr 11th 1851. Worked and strolled around town to alternately.

Friday Decr 12th 1851. Around town & working at times

Saturday Decr 13th. Working &c Very dark & low clouds hang over the valley for several days past which indicate a general snow storm soon

Sunday Decr 14th 1851. At home and around the Town

Monday 15th 1851. Worked at home some and then strolling Dark heavy weather yet

Tuesday Decr 16th 1851. Strolling around again.

Wed the 17th. Spent the day as ante and at dark attended the Law School again

Thursday Dec 18th 1851. Day spent as before. The dark heavey cloud of Fog which over hung the Valley for some ten days disappeared about sun set leaving a very clear sky.

Friday Decr 19th 1851. Dull Heavy, foggy weathure again. Worked some. (Hung a grind stone [crossed out]) Attended a phonetic lecture by G. D. Watt at dark.

Saturday Decr 20th 1851. Hung a grind stone. done nothing more but stroll. Attended Law School at dark

Sunday Decr 21 1851. Snowed all day but still & tolerable warm. I was at home all day

Monday Decr 22nd 1851. Around the Stores & at home This evening a South wind arose

Tuesday 23rd Dec 1851. At homes & around as ante The weather is warm and a S. Wind still blowing and the snow gone by night

Wednesday 24th 1851. At home & around as usual S. wind & very warm and muddy Attended the Law School at dark
     The little boys are urshuring in Chrismas with fire works, squibs firing guns & yelling in crouds of hundreds around the Stores

Thursday Dec 25th 1851. Wife & I went to a dinner & quilting at Allen Stout's. I then went up in town to see the opperations of Chrismas which was carried very largely by the boys serenading in the streets to the great anoyance of the police whose duty it was to keep the peace
     Balls & parties of Different kinds were going on almost throughout the Valley and seems to be enjoying the times exceeding well

Friday Dec 26th 1851. Doing nothing except going around town and at home

Sat Decr 27th 1851. Around town as before & at home

Sund 28th 1851. At home & around town Snowed this afternoon very hard About sunset started North 12 miles, with W. B. Simmons who had come after me to manage a suit for him before Bp Brownell wherein Judson Stodard had prefered charges against him We arrived at his house 2 hours after dark. Weather cold.

Monday Decr 29th 1851. At one o'clock the trial commenced at Br Rixs It was an action of Debt and also to test the title of some land which both claimed. The case was divided & the land title tried first. It took till sunset to traverse the evidence when the court adjd for supper and met again then the parties came to geather & compromised the difficulties and all was amicably settled without a decision of the Bishops court.

Tuesday 30th Dec 1851. Came home about noon. The U. S. Destrict Court is now in sission to try 8 Mexicans who has been arrested for trading with the Indians without license I attended court in the after noon.

Wednesday 31st 1851 Decr. Attended Court to day. The case of the first Mixican, Pedro Leon was traversed & submited to the jury about dark. Attended the Law School at dark again.

Thursday 1st January 1852. A Happy New-Year and all well excep the poor Mexicans for the jury returned a verdict against Pedro Leon[81] this morning finding him indebted to the U. S. in the penal sum of five hundred dollars for introducing goods into the Indian country & trading with the indians
   An action of Libel will follow which will most likely result in a forfeiture of their goods also will each Mexican I expect be tried under the same penal Statute which Pedro has been.

January 2nd 1852 Friday. Attended Cout to day Another Mexican tried to day but he was not found indebted to the U. S.
   In the evening some 8 or 9 of the old police & others met at Egan's to take in consideration the propriety of having an old police party including other old veterans of "days gone by, but upon counting up the numbers it was found that no house would hold them so the Idea was Dropped for the present or untill we could have more room. I came home at 11 o'c

Saturday January 3rd 1852. Attended court again. The prosecuting Attorney upon the last Mexican being acquitted entered a *nolle proseque* on the other six so far as the penal Statute is conserned and the court adj'd till Monday next. Wet squally day.

Sunday Jan 4th 1852. At home all day. Warm & clear

Monday. Jan 5th 1852. To day I attended the Legislature which met at ten o'clock a. m. The day was spent in organizing and in the after noon the two houses met in joint session and recieved the Gov message and then adj'd to ten a. m. to morrow.

Tuesday Jan 6th 1852. Attended the Legislature The (The for noon was spent in [crossed out]) House adjd for a dance at 11 o'c

Wed Jan 7th 1852. Met with the Legislature The fore noon was spent in reading the Gov message and refering the same to the appropriate Committees.

---

81. When the Mormons arrived in Utah, they found the Indian slave trade firmly established; but usually it had been Chief Walker and his band that had preyed upon the weaker groups of the south and stolen their children.
   Pedro Leon held a license signed by James S. Calhoun, superintendent of Indian affairs in the Territory of New Mexico, dated Santa Fe, August 14, 1851, but Brigham Young declared that it did not authorize trade with the Indians in Utah. In an extended article Judge Zerubbabbel Snow defended Young's position and justified his sentence that Pedro Leon should leave the prisoners and return home. The article is included in the "Journal History" of the Mormon Church for February 10, 1852.

In the after noon I presented a bill creating the office of Treasurer & Auditor of public accounts and prescribing their duty, which was read the first time and refered to the committee on ordinances after which some business as to the different Committes going into business was acted on

Thursday January 8th 1852. To day the two houses went into joint session on the subject of Home manufacturies, Orson Pratt in the Chair.

Friday January 9th 1852. Joint session again   David Evans in the Chair. The subject was refered to a Select Comittee.

Discussed several proppositions to pay the Legislative expenses &c

This evening I performed the matrimonial cerimony between Benjn Allen & Adeline Butterfield.

Saturday January 10th 1852. Met with the Legislature   Spent the fore noon in the H of R. in passing one Resolution on the library and a Bill creating an auditor of Public accounts & Treasurer   In the after I was with a committee drafting a law organizing a Board of Code Commissioners.

Sunday January 11th 1852. Went to meeting at the Council House President Young preached. The rest of the day I was at home. Very unwell all day and last night.

Monday January 12th 1852. Legislature met at 9 o'clock A. M.   A. P. Rockwood presented a petition to appropriate 100 dollars on the State road between the Hot & Warm Springs. Jas Brown[82] gave notice of a Bill he intended introduce for an appropriation on the State or Territorial road in Weber County and afterwards by leave presented it which was laid on the table

Petition of Thomas Moore[83] for license to establish a ferry on Green River which was refered to a select Committee

In the after noon J. Grimshaw was elected reporter of the H. R. Chas Shumway reported a bill on the library which was read the first time and partly the second and discussed at considerable length and refered back. House adjourned.

Tuesday 13th January 1852. Legislature met at 9 o clock   C. Shumway presented a Petition for a new County refered to Committee on Counties

A. P. Rockwood presented a bill on the judiciary which was after wards passed. I presented a bill on Code Commissioners which was afterwards passed

---

82. James Brown, born September 30, 1801, in Rowan County, North Carolina, had taught school and served as sheriff before he joined the Mormon Church in 1838. He brought his wife and family to Nauvoo where she died, leaving eight children. In 1846 Brown joined the Mormon Battalion and at Santa Fe was placed in charge of the sick detachment which was sent to winter at Pueblo, Colorado. In 1847 he went to California and collected the back pay for the members of his group. With it he purchased the Miles M. Goodyear holdings at Ogden. Brown established his family in the Ogden area where he made roads and built bridges over Weber River.

In 1852 he served on a mission to British Guiana, traveling in the same group with Stout. He died in Ogden, Utah, September 30, 1863, as the result of an accident.

83. The Green River needed a commercial ferry most of the season for it was swift, wide, and deep as attested to by the first company of Mormon pioneers who crossed it: "June 30, 1847, the company arrived at the crossing of the Green River. The water was very high, one hundred and eighty yards wide, with a very rapid current. Two rafts were made and each was rigged with a rudder and oars. The wagons were safely crossed without taking out any of their contents. The animals were made to swim over. James Amasa Little, "Biography of Lorenzo Dow Young," *Utah Historical Quarterly*, XIV (1946), 93.

Thomas Moor had come to Utah in the A. O. Smoot company of 1847. He was at that time forty-six years old and had a wife and five children. It would seem that at this time Moor was already operating a ferry on Green River and was only asking legal sanction for it. On January 14 his request was granted.

H. G. Sherwood presented a petition to extend the State or Territorial road north to Box Elder. refered to Comt

Message from the Council for the House to concur in a Resolution fixing the enacting clause to all bills &c which was warmly discussed amended and passed & refered back which the (House [crossed out]) council refused to concur in whereupon a joint Committee was appointed from the two Houses who compromised the difference. A Bill from the Council appropriating 1000 dollars on the State road between the Hot & Warm Spring. Several other bills &c came up and I withdrew on a Committee.

Wednesday 14th January 1852. Legislature met at 9 o'clock. The bill creating the office of Code Commissioners as corrected by the joint committee last evening, was presented by A. P. Rockwood, read & accepted read the first time and passed read & passed the second time, read the third time and passed engrossed and sent to the Council for concurrance

Resolution to petition Congress to appropriate for a road from Fort Hall to San Diego via Salt Lake City & Iron County and refered to a Committee. Bill read making an appropriation to extend the Territorial road north of Ogden river & south of Weber river presented by Jas Brown which was read three times passed and sent up to the Council.

Bill appropriating 1000 dollars to improve the road leading to Davis County sent in from the Council read discussed at length and refered to the Committee on Roads & Bridges to confer with the same Committee from the Council.

Report of the joint Committee on Home manufacturies presented by Joseph Young refered to a joint session at 2 o'clock P M After noon I presented a resolution to purchase the first and second volumes of the "Deseret News" for the Territorial Library — passed A Bill granted Thomas Moore the prvilege of Establishing ferries on Green River. read three times & passed

At 2 o clock the two Houses met in joint on the subject of Home manufactories and other business W. Richards in the Chair.

The Committee reported rules for the government of both houses (was [crossed out]) which was to be governed by the Holy Ghost &c which was moved to be laid on the table without a record being made of the report.

A Resolution to require either house on the presentation of a bill to give notice of the same being before the House. which was refered to the joint Committee on rules.

A resolution for enacting clause for Bills was previously offered by O. Spencer of the Council and read once and passed.

Report of the joint Committee on Home manufactorys read this fore noon was read the first time and passed. read the second time discussed amended — and passed read the third time discussed upon its merits untill sun set when the Governor spoke on the subject and the resolutions was passed — In the evening met with the Committee on Militia It was decided there to provide by law for a Lieutenant General of the Nauvoo Legion of the Militia of the Territory of Utah, and other important alterations in the present military establishment.

Thursday 15 January 1852. Legislature met at 9 o'clock Mr Evans presented a petition for a portion of the waters of American Fork to be taken to dry creek for the use of irrigation which was refered to on Cannoñs and publick domain

Mr Groves presented a petition in relation to a record of brands in Iron County, which was refered to the Committee on Laws and ordinances

Mr Groves presented a bill organizing an exploring Company which was laid on the table to be taken up in its order.

Messages from the Council first the Ressolution to procure the the Deseret [News] for the Library was concured in.

Council also sent back the act on Code Commissioners asking concurrence in some slight amendments which they had made all of which the House concured in.

Mr John Brown presented a bill on revinue which was accepted and laid on the table to come up in its order.

Mr Groves' bill on exploring Company was taken up and on its second reading was refered back to the Committee with instruction.

Brown's bill on revinue was called up read the first time and laid on the table.

Resolution by Mr Groves to appropriate the territorial tax of Iron County for 1852 to the people of Iron County for exploring Iron County debated and withdrawn. Adjourned till ½ past one

Message from the Council refering the bill, to authorize Thomas Moore to establish ferries across Green River, back for concurrence on additional Section which was concurred in by the House.

Auditor's report read after which the Adjutant General's report was read Adjourned till 9 o'clock a. m.

(Dillie gave in notice to [crossed out]) bring in a bill creating County Treasurer.

Friday 16th January 1852. Mr Dillie gave notice to bring a bill on County Treasurer Mr Rockwod reported from the Committee on Judiciary which was adopted, and a special committee to bring in a bill on the subject of irrigation & other purposes.

The Bill appropriating 300 dollars for Territorial road in Weber County was refered back from the Council which was laid on the Table.

Committees reported progress

Bill from Brownell for fines assessed to be appropriated to the respictive counties which was refered to the Committee on Roads & Bridges Afternoon. Mr Brownell obtained leave of absence till Monday.

Missillaneous discussions and the House adjourned. Met with the Judiciary and attended a Masonic school in the evening.

Saturday 17th January 1852. Legislature met at ten. House went into secret session on the subject of the Laws heretofore passed Creating Code Commissioners & granting the ferries on Green River[84] which had been refered back by the Gov. for amendments which were confered in

Petition of S. Moore & others for charter an Agricultural &c society refered to proper Comt

A. P. Rockwood from judiciary reported a bill on the board of County Commissioners. which was laid on the table to come up in its order

Mr Dillie a bill creating the office of treasurer, accepted, laid on the table to come up in its order

Mr Roberry a bill extending a territorial road to black rock some distance into Toolie County, accepted, laid on the table to come up in its order

The bill judiciary presented this morning was taken up on motion to refer the bill back Mr Woolley presented a bill on the same subject which was read and accepted refered back to the Select Committee with the bill by Rockwood for consolidation. House adjourned for dinner ½ past one House met. A long debate on order came on the first business.

A Petition by Felt from W. Clayton on marks & Brands for relief of Recorder of marks & brands laid on table.

---

84. This "secret session" would seem to indicate that the governor had modified or reversed the decision to grant Thomas Moor the ferry on Green River.

A Bill read from the Council for the relief of the recorder read the first time and passed laid over to come up in its order on Monday next. Adjd till Monday at ten A. M.

Sunday 18th January 1852. Went to meeting at the Representative Hall and at home in the after noon

Monday 19th January 1852. Legislature met at ten a. m. Minutes read and accepted. Mr Jos Young presented a petition for a ferry across Bear river in Weber County. accepted laid on the table to come up in its order

Mr Groves presented a petition for a library in Iron County. read, accepted and laid on the table to come up in its order.

Mr Rockwood presented a petition of T. Bullock praying for remuneration for taking the census of Utah Territory. read with accompanying documents & recieved & laid on the table to come up in its order

Mr Groves presented a bill organizing an exploring in the Territory of Utah accepted laid on the table to come up in its order.

Mr Woolley reported a report of a bill from a special committee of a bill creating a County Commissioners Court in each County[85] an describing the duties thereof read and recieved and laid on the table to come up in its order

Mr Woolley presented an act in relation to public Domain. read and accepted. Laid on the table to come up after recieving the report of the Committee on public domain.

Bill on the table in relation to marks & brands read on the second reading & passed. read the third time and passed

A Bill creating the office of County Treasurer which was on the table. refered to the committee on laws and ordinances with Dillie added. Mr Woolley moved to recind the vote not recieved

Took up the act for the continuation of Territorial road west from Salt Lake City into Toolie County, withdrawn by Mr Roberry.

Mr Young's petition for ferry over Bear River of this morning was refered to committee road & Bridges

Pettition for Library in Iron County. (came up [crossed out]) Parowan City for a city Library. Mr Groves with drew the petition.

Adjourned till two P. M. House met at two P. M.   D. Spencer in the chair.

Petition for the relief of T. Bullock read and refered to the committee on Claims.

---

85. When finally adopted this bill placed the general management of county business in the hands of a court consisting of a probate judge and three selectmen who jointly possessed the power and authority of county commissioners of today.

   The County Court exercised jurisdiction over the conservation and disposition of timber resources, water privileges and the distribution of water for mill, community, and irrigation purposes, the districting of the county for road, precinct, school and other purposes, the levying and collection of the county taxes, and the submission to the people of ways and means of meeting extraordinary expenditures for public buildings, roads and bridges. This administrative body under a judicial name, in fulfillment of its numerous duties, was required by the law that created it, Feb. 4, 1852, to hold sessions beginning in March and September, and oftener if the public business warranted. Selectmen had separate duties imposed on them, namely the care of the poor, the orphans and the insane, and the Probate Judge had independent functions to perform . . . . Sheriffs and constables were conservators of the peace, while justices of the peace, assessors and collectors, treasurers, and lesser functionaries supplied the services indicated by their titles. (Andrew Love Neff, *History of Utah, 1847 to 1869*, ed., Leland Hargrave Creer [Salt Lake City, 1940], 200.)

   Exclusive of charter cities, of which there were now but twelve, these county courts exercised complete jurisdiction over unincorporated towns and villages, a fact which largely shaped the history of the area.

The act presented by Mr Groves organizing an exploring Company was taken up and on the Second reading was refered back to the committee from whence it came.

Message from the council refering back the act creating the office of Territorial Treasurer and Auditor of Public Accounts. for concurrence in amendments thereto, which passed as amended

The Bill in relation to County Commissioners was next taken up & read the first time and passed on the second reading the bill was laid on the table to come up in its order to morrow morning, when the House adjournd In the evening I met with a committee to prepare an act in relation to County Commissioners which had been refered back. This evening and in the night had a hard snow storm but without wind

Tuesday 20th January 1852. Legislature met at ten a.m Petition by Mr Brimhall presented a petition for a charter for Cedar City read and laid on the Table to come up in its order

Mr Sherwood presented an act to incorporate Uab County. Laid on the table to come up in its order

Mr Felt presented an act creating the office of County Treasurer which had been refered yesterday, Laid on the table to come up in its order

Mr Rockwood an act granting Joseph Yound et al. the right to ferry on Bear River in Weber County, Laid on the table to come up in its order

Mr Richards reported an act in relation to Cañnons and public domain. Laid on the table to come up in its order

The act in relation to County Commissioners, which was refered to the committee on its second reading last evening was taken up on its second reading.

After passing the 6th Section the rules of the House were suspended to hear a message from the Council which was an act in relation to minors which was read and recieved and laid on the table to come up in its order when the Co. Commissioners act taken up again, and on the 8th Sec was refered back to report at ½ past one when the house adjd

After noon. Mr Spencer in the chair took up the last business on the 8th Sec the bill on the 22nd sec was recommitted.

Message from the Council. An act in relation to master and apprentice was read & laid on the table to come up in its order Also an act in relation to guardian & ward, read and accepted Laid on the table to come up in its order.

The petition to incorporate Cedar City was referd to Comt on Laws & Ord. The report for Uab Co was taken up refered back House adjourned —

Wednesday 21st January 1852. Petition of John Robinson & others presented by Rockwood which was recieved Laid on the Table to come up in its order. Woolley again reported the act in relation to C. Commissioners as refered last evening. recieved Laid on the table to come up in its order.

Mr John Brow[n] reported an act in relation to revenue. accepted. Laid on the table to come up in its order

Mr Sherwood reported again the act organizing Uab County accepted & laid on the table to come up in its order Mr Stout reported an act creating a Probate Court &c read and accepted and the rules of the house suspended to pass the bill. read the first time and passed. read the second third time and passed with one amendment.

Messages from the Council. read and laid on the table to come up in their order

The act on Co Commissioners was taken up on the second reading at the 22nd Second. House adjourned at the 30th Sec for dinner.

House met at two and proceeded to the same bill, which was finally passed the Second reading after which it was read the third time and amended again in a few places and spiritedly debated passed.

An act creating a County Treasurer was taken up and read the first time and passed recommitted on the second reading of the first section.

An act granting the ferry across Bear river in Weber Co to Joseph Young & others for two years. read and passed the first time.

House adjourned till 9 o'clock a. m to morrow Met with the Committee on Militia at Rockwoods in the eve.

Thursday 22nd January 1852. House met at 9 o'clock A. M. minutes read corrected & accepted

Stoker give notice that he would introduce a bill on execution & sale of property tomorrow morning

The bill granting Jos Young et al. the Bear river ferry was read amended and passed the second time read the third tiime and refered back

The act on Cannons & public domain read the first passed read the second time. by sections and each section was stricken out.

An act for the protection of the Settlers on public domain, read the first time and passed. refered back on the second reading

An act concerning master and apprentice from the council, read the first time & passed and laid on the table to come up in its order. An act in relation to select men from the council read first time and passed. Laid on the table to come up in its order

An act in relation to minors from the Council. read the first time and Laid on the table to come up in its order.

Aa act in relation to guardians from the Council. read the first time and passed Laid on the table to come up in its order.

Memmorial of Pulcifer praying relief for farmers West of Jordain refered to the committee on Ways and Means.

An act in relation to revenue read the first time and passed. Laid on the table to come up in its order.

An act organizing Uab County passed the first reading Laid on the table to come up in its order

An act granting watters on Mill Creke exclusively to W. Richards Laid on the table indefinitely House adjourned till 2 o'c

Mr Felt reported the bill creating the office of County Treasury and an act incorporating Cedar City. Both Laid on the table to come up in its order

An act granting the waters on Mill Creek to W Richards was taken up on its second reading. debated at length and laid on the table.

Special committee to draft an act in relation to surveying. The committee were Sherwood, Woolley, & Rockwood House adjourned till ten a. m. tomorrow

Friday 23rd January 1852. House met at ten a. m. Minutes read. amended and accepted

Committee reported the Bear river ferry bill again by A. P. Rockwood, read and accepted. Laid on the table to come up in its order

Mr Rockwood reported a bill from the committee on roads and bridges in relation to the appropriation of certain fines on (said [crossed out]) roads. read & accepted and Laid on the table

Mr Rockwood on Comt on Roads and bridges in relation to act No. 12 Council file. read, accepted Laid on the table to come up in its order.

The bill organizing Uab County on its second reading (rules [crossed out]) Mr Johnson reported a bill creating a County called Summitt County to be considered in conjunction with the above. which was lost. and the Uab bill was taken up. & passed the county seat located at the city of Nephi.

The bill for Summit County was then taken up. House adjourned till two o'clock P. M.

House met as pr adjt passed the bill creating Summitt County the third reading

An act incorporating Cedar City Iron County. Rules suspended and the bill was passed.

An act for Bear river ferry was taken up again. rules of the house suspended & the bill passed. House adjourned till ten a. m. tomorrow —

Saturday 24th January 1852. House met at ten a. m. Minutes read and accepted. Mr Miller presented a remonstrance from the people of American Fork Utah County against a petition of David Evans & others for taking out the waters of American Fork to Dry creek. read and accepted refered to the Committee on Cannons and public domain.

An act appropriating fines to the Countys which was read the first time & passed and laid on the table to come up in its order

An act appropriating 150 dollars to be laid out on roads in the North of G. S. L. County read the first time and passed which was as a non-concurrence on the bill from the Council of 1000 dollars read the second & third times and passed House took a recess to read the News.

Message from the Council reporting the non-concurrence on the act creating the county of Summitt.

A bill from Mr Brownell setting a price on trade & labor and officers services of all kinds accepted & laid on the table to come up in its order.

An act appropriating 3,000 dol for taking out the waters of the river Jordain. on the West side Rules of the House suspended and proceeded to the first reading of the bill which passed. on the second reading House adjourned till ten a. m. next Monday.

Sunday 25th January 1852. At home all day to day.

Monday 26th January 1852. House met at ten a. m. Mr Young presented an act incorporating an Agricultural, Horticultural, Mechanical and Manufacturing association, read and recieved, rules of the House suspended to pass the bill read the first time and accepted read the second time and passed amended by striking out the last section. read the third time and and before the question was put to passed the bill a long discussion ensued and the House adjourned for dinner.

After noon the former bill was taken up again and debated some two hours and refered back to the committee with Felt & Stout added

Message from the Council The act appropriating 150 dollar on the North State road was read and concurred in.

The bill appropriating 3000 doll for taking the water out of the West side of Jordain was taken up on its second reading read second & third time and passed.

The bill regulating the prices of all manner of property & things and County & Territorial officers read the first time and passed. Bill read (third [crossed out]) second time and striken out by sections. House adjourned till 9½ tomorrow

Tuesday 27th January 1852. House met at 9½ a. m. Petition of B. W Elliot & others praying for appropriating the fines of military affairs to the University for a military school which was refered to committee on Militia an act taken on its second reading to appropriating fines to County House voted non-concurrence.

Message from the Council with 3 bills from the House consolidated into one by council and sent to the House for concurrence. it contains 45 sections. read and accepted voted the bill be the first order in the after noon adjourned till 1½ past twelve.

House met ½ past one. took up the former business Bill read the first time & passed at the 22 section House adj'd

Wednesday 28th January 1852. House met ½ past 9 o'c a. m. Mr Groves presented a report of a bill creating an exploring expidition or Company. accepted and laid on the table to come up in its order

Mr Rockwood reported a bill incorporating an (company [crossed out]) Agricultural Horticultural, Mechanical & Manufactural society for the purpose of rewarding premiums on the best specimens of the above branches recieved laid on the table to come up in its order.

Message on the table bill granting Richards the control of watters of Mill Creek which has been previously befor the house laid on the table to come up in its order.

The act on Judiciary up yesterday was taken up at the 22nd Sec. passed (section [crossed out]) reading and amended. House adjourned. Half passed one House met took up the same bill on motion to add a new section. the House adjourned. In the evening met with the prayer circle.

Thursday 29th January 1852. House met ½ past 9. a. m. Mr Brown pressented a memmorial to Congress for an appropriation to 60.000 dollars for a Territorial from Fort Hall to the suthren Extremity of the Territory Laid on the table to come up in its order. Two notices to brig bills.

Mr Young presented a bill to improve Emmegration Cannion to be continued to East Cannon Creek over the second Mountain. Recieved and laid on the table to come up in its order.

Messages from the Council read not concured in the bill to appropriate 3000 dollars to take out the waters on the west side of Jordain

Also an act in relation to Justices of the peace. which was read and laid on the table to come up in its order

Took up the business of yesterday on the third reading long debate and adjourned for dinner.

Met at ½ passed one James Brown in the chair Debated the bill till 4 o'clock on the third reading and the bill was lost

Message from the Council up an act to appropriating 2.000 dollars on the Cotton wood Canal read and accepted, read the first time and rules suspended and passed. read second time and passed passed the third reading the litte

Friday 30th January 1852. House met at ten a. m. Minutes read and accepted.

A bill to watter Ódgdon City and appropriating 1200 dollars for that purpose Laid on the table to come up in its order.

An act to incorporate the City of Lehi in Utah County by Mr Evans. laid on the table to come up in its order Message from the Council with a resolution in relation to the organic act which was read and passed.

Message from the council to meet in joint session forthwith, which was agreed to Joint Session convened and Houses went into secret secion.

The Gov presented some communications from the East relative to the goverment officers returning to the States last fall The papers are loud for and against the Governor of Utah but they have not heard our side of the story yet The Gov then addressed the Houses after which the Houses adjourned

Houses met at two again. Moved and carried to appoint a joint committee on judiciary which was for the standing committees of both Houses to be that committee

Sherwood made missellaneous remards [remarks] for the entertainments of the Houses. untill further busines.

About ½ past two the Regents held a session in the Council Chamber. The Secratary made a report of the fiscal and other affairs of the university which was read and accepted.

A Petition of D. S. Thomas for relief in loss by weighing & measuring provisions to the hands of the fence for the University read and accepted. then relief granted. and refered to the Building committee to adjoust the same.

Discourse from Judge Z. Snow

Phelps & Appleby appointed a committee to select certain school Books from the Library to be sold for the use of the university. The joint session of the Legislature met in the Representative Hall at 6 o'clock

memmorial to congress for a Territorial road from the North settlements south by Fillmore City &c and asking 60,000 dollars for the same. also one from the citizens for the same object and asking for the same amount, both of which were adopted.

Preamble & resolutions in relation to State House read the first time and passed E. D. Woolley, appointed a committee to purchase the Council House Voted for both Houses to sit in joint session during the remainder of the present term

Memmorial to Congress for 60-000 dollars to be appropiated for a prison.

Resolution for the pay of members & contingent expenses of the Territory be drawn on the tithing office. Long debate. ensued withdrawn.

Resolution on the State House came up on the third reading and passed. Adjourned till six o'clock P. M.

Resolved ourselves into a council of elders on the subject of our per dium allowance   adjourned about 11 o'c P. M

Saturday 31st January 1852. The two Houses met in joint session at ten o'clock a. m. O. Spencer, O Pratt, David Fullmer was appointed a committee to draft a memmorial to Congress for an appropriation to pay the Code Commissioners.

The Bill on the Judiciary which was lost on its third reading in the house on the 29th inst. was again taken up to be reconsidred. was taken up by Sections. Houses adjourned at noon for dinner

Houses met at ½ past one P. M. The committee to draft the memmorial for pay for the Code Comrs was read and adopted.

Houses then proceeded to the business of the fore-noon on the 11th Section of the bill. passed the 2nd reading & read the third time by its title and passed The bill in relation to Selectmen called up. read passed

Report of the Commissioners to locate the seat of Government was read and adopted.

Bill of expenses for locating the site for Fillmore city the seat of Goverment read amounted to 1544. dollars — adopted.[86]

The Bill in relation to Master & apprentices taken up read and passed

The Bill creating the office of County Treasurer read three times and passed Adjourned till six o'clock P. M.

Met at 6 o'clock P. M. The bill in relation to minors read and passed

The Bill in relation to Guardians read and and accepted three times

Mr Woolley made the report in relation to the purchase of the State House. for 18,500 dollars about The purchase was completed

An act to incorporate the City of Lehi in Utah County read and passed.

Memmorial read to Congress praying for a mail rout South via Iron County to San Deigo. read & adopted.

Voted one almanac for each *member & officer of both Houses* Houses adjourned till ten on Monday next.

---

86. A good account of the settlement of Fillmore, Utah, is that of Everett L. Cooley's, "Report of an Expedition to Locate Utah's First Capitol," *Utah Historical Quarterly*, XXIII (October, 1955), 329-38.

February the First 1852. Sunday. Went to meeting at the State house. In the afternoon was at home

Monday 2nd Feb. 1852. The two houses met in joint session at ten o'clock A. M. Rules dispensed with to take up the unfinished business on the table[87]

An act in relation to the Writ of Habeas Corpus read three times and passed

An act organizing the exploring Comp from the House taken up. and read refered to a special which were orson pratt, H G. Sherwood & N. H. Felt. Pratt was relived & G. A. Smith appointed.

An act in relation to Fees. read the first time and refered to the committee on Judiciarey.

An act to incorporate the Agricultural &c society for rewarding premiums read and rejected.

A committee to be appointed on the part of the House to act with the committee of the council on appropriation. O Pratt W. Woodruff and G. Brimhall

The Bill granting W. Richards the controll of the waters of Mill creek taken up read the first time and passed and also passed the third reading.

Act granting the waters of Mill Creek taken just below Neffs mill to Brigham Young. Passed. Houses adjourned for dinner. —

2 o'clock Houses met as pr adj't Bill for the improvement of Emmegration Canñon to the Second mountain and errecting a toll gate. read three times and passed.

An act in relation to service read three times and passed

An act in relation to Justice of the peace read three times & past Adjourned till ½ past 9 tomorrow

Tuesday 3rd February 1852. Two houses met at ½ past 9 a. m. voted to have all the claims vs this Legislature be brought forthwith before this house.

I went into the committee on appropriations. While I was on the committee a bill to take one third of the waters of American Fork to Dry creek . . . Houses adj'd for dinner.

½ past one Houses met again & Took up the revenue bill. read three times and passed with some few exceptions.

Fee Bill regulating the fees for certain officers therein named. read the first time and passed. debated at length on the first Section of the Second reading and the Houses adjourned till ten o'clock a.m. tomorrow —

in the evening went in company with my wife to a party at A. J. Stouts where we stayed till about mid-night.

Wednesday 4th Feb. 1852. Houses met at ten a. m — an Act in relation to attorneys read and refered to a committee on laws and ordinances and I & was G. A. Smith & James Brown added to the committee.

A proclamation by the Gov. for the calling a special session of the Legislature immediately after the close of the Present Session The Legislature voted adj tomorrow evening till the 16th inst.

An act in relation to the Militia taken upon its second reading read one section and rules suspended and the Bill passed

The Fee Bill then came up again. refered back to the Com from whence it came Adj'd for dinner and met at 2

An act creating the office of Marks and Brands in different Cotys Laid on the table to come up in order

---

87. The laws which were finally passed at this session are preserved in the volume, *Acts, Resolutions and Memorials . . . Territory of Utah, From 1851 to 1870 . . .* (Salt Lake City, 1870). (Hereafter cited as *Laws of Utah*, with the date.)

An act in relations to Elections read three times and passed Adjourned till ten tomorrow Attended prayer circle in the eve

Thursday 5th February 1852. Two Houses met at ten a. m. Report of a committee in relation to the Woollen factory and appropriating 2000 dollars for the same

An act to incorporate Utah City in Utah County. read

An act incorporating Cedar City read and passed finnally. Mr Rockwood offered an adenda to the Judiciary read and passed by its first reading.

An act in relation to apportionment of the Representation of the territory read and passed.

An act incorporating Fillmore City Millard County read three times and passed.

Orson pratt votes vs all acts prohibiting the right of Negroes the privileges of voting.

An act came up again to incorporating the city of Utah. read & debated at lenght and the Houses adj'd for dinner

Two o'clock met again. An act in relation to the library presented by O. Spencer read and accepted, read the first time and passed read the second time and passed read and passed the third

I met with the committee on appropriations & while there the Legislature appointed the Judges of probate, after which the legislature adjourned till the 16th instant Leaving the committee on claims to adjust the claims against the next setting.

Friday 6th February 1852. Merely loafing to day.

Saturday 7th February 1852. At the State house and at home attending to to the appropriation bill and in the evening attended a Masonic school

Sunday 8th February 1852. Went to meeting awhile & at home Elias Gardner &c at my house

Monday 9th February 1852. Attending to the appropriation bill today.

Tuesday 10th February 1852. Attending to appropriation bill to day.

Wednesday 11th February 1852. Attended to the appropriation bill to day and in the evening attended the prayer circle at the C. House

Thursday 12th February 1852. At Court partly & worked a little and attended some little to the appropriation bill.

Friday 13th February 1852. Attend court & was assigned to assist S. M. Blair to the prosecution in a case the Territory vs Capt Wales in an indictment for stealing cattle and altering the Brand. At 12 the court adj'd at the close of the testimony & Blair did not make his appearance in the afternoon & the case was submitted to the jury without any pleas The jury returned a verdict of Not guilty. G. A. Smith & W. Picket was on the part of the Defence.

Saturday 14th February 1852. Attended the High Council to day. case up Mr Kite & wife parted. Traded with Williams some.

Sunday 15th February 1852. Went to meeting Very fine day Remarkably warm weather this winter. dry. mostly clear and pleasant. Sometimes foggy but now days like Spring.

Monday 16th February 1852. Legislature met in joint session at ten a. m. Voted to set apart next Thursday for fasting and prayer.

An act on Marks & Brands read the first time and passed. recommitted to committee on second reading.

An act locating the County Seat of Davis County by A. L. Lamereaux read first time and laid on the table   on second reading.

An act appropriating 2,000 dollars for the use of the Woollen factory on the jordan river read the first time and passed   Houses adjourned till two & met accordingly.

Took up the previous business. Bill passed after long debate

The appropriation Bill was then took read and passed — House adjourned till ten a. m tomorrow morning

Tuesday 17th February 1852. Legislature met at ten a. m.   Stout presented an act continuing the officers appointed by the governor, in force till filled in due course of law. read three times and passed.

The act locating the County Seat of Davis County on North Cotton wood creek. read and passed.

An act incorporating Utah City, Utah County.   read and withdrew on the first reading

Some accounts presented and accepted and the House adjourned for dinner and met at two —

Accounts brought in for pay of members officers and contingent expenses to the Deseret Legislature and auditor &c refered to a Select comittee consisting of Smith, O. Spencer Woolley Stout Rockwood. —

An act authorizing O Pratt to organizing a Topographical & exploring company taken up on first reading and rejected. — Recess for ten minutes —

Houses went into secret session on the subject of attorney. The House adjourned till ten a m tomorrow

Wednesday 18th February 1852. Legislature met at ten a. m.   Minutes read & accepted.   An act in relation to surveyors laid on the Table to come up in its order.

Resolution for a committee to be appointed to inquire into the situation of the Bath House.   passed & Wells Woolley D. Spencer said committee. Some accounts read and allowed

An act in relation to Marks and Brands.

An act in relation to attorneys presented by Stout read the first time and passed. passed the second and third reading. Adjourned for dinner and met at two P. M. Several acts were anounced as approved by the Gov —

An act in relation to decent of property.   read and accepted & laid on the table to come up in its order.

The Bill appropriating the delinquent taxes in Iron County for opening coal Creek Cannon. was called up by G. S. Smith.   Largely debated, amended, and passed.

On motion of Wells ordered to have 500 copies of the Bill on Militia printed for distribution

An act in relation to surveyors   refered back

The first session of the Legislature closed having completed the forty days to meet to morrow at ten a. m commencing a Special Session according to the proclamation of the Govornor   The first day of said session to be spent in fasting and prayer.

Thursday 19 February 1852. Special secion of the Legislature met at ten o'clock a.m. and went into committee of the whole for fasting and pray.   After opening by pray & singing by the Chaplain of the house committee was appointed to wait on the govornor to meet with us to give instruction & teaching Speach by Orson Pratt followed by the governor on the duty of Legislators. to be humble & enjoy the Spirit of God and act as Elders of Israel &c.

The Gov. recommended a law authorizing the Probate Courts to grant Divorce.

President Kimball next spoke and was followed by Prest W Richards Prest D. Spencer then spoke in relation to the duty of Legislatures — At ½ past twelve adj'd till two. and met accordingly.

Singing and praying and then exhorting by L. W. Hancock, G. S. Smith O. Spencer, W W Phelps, E. H. Groves, D. Fulmer, President B. Young Adjourned to meet tomorrow morning at ten o'clock.

At dark met in the State house with several persons to set up a Micrascope and experimented on small objects which worked well magnifying 1400 times.

Friday 20th February 1852. Houses met as pr adjournment Resolution by self to continue the previous organization which was passed.

Bill to appoint certain officers untill the opperation of the Election Law laid on the table to come up in its order pr Jas Brown.

Bill in relation to Divorce. Laid on the table for its order.

Resolution by Rockwood to appoint certain officers by Judge of Probate. Laid on the table for its order

Bill in relation to teams meeting in the road by Rockwood Laid on the table as ante

Bill in relation to Marks & Brands again taken up and debated some hour & a half and refered back again with an addition to the committee which Wells as Chairman of sd Comt

Bill in relation of decent of property — read the first time & passed finally.

Bill authorizing probate Court to appoint certain officers &c & passed Adjourned for dinner & met at two P. M.

Bill in relation to Bills of Divorce read three times and passed[88]

Bill in relation to passing of teams in the High Way read three times and passed —[89]

Bill in relation to joint enclosure and division fences &c &c Laid on the table and the House adj'd till ten tomorrow —

---

88. The law in relation to bills of divorce provides that "the court of Probate in the county where the plaintiff resides shall have the jurisdiction in all cases of divorce and alimony, and distribution of property connected therewith . . . ." Grounds for divorce must be submitted in writing, and causes include impotence of either husband or wife, adultery, habitual drunkenness, and in summary "when it shall be made to appear to the satisfaction and conviction of the court that the parties cannot live together in peace and union together, and that their welfare requires a separation."

It concludes with the ". . . duty of the courts of probate in their respective counties, to punish by fine or imprisonment, or both, at their discretion, any person or persons who shall stir up unwarrantable litigation between husband and wife, or seek to bring about a separation between them." *Laws of Utah, 1852*, pp. 49-50.

89. Custom and usage greatly modified the rules of the road. Under the law as here enacted *An ACT regulating the passing and meeting of teams on the public highways.*

Sec. 1.—Be it enacted by the Governor and Legislative Assembly of the Territory of Utah: That whenever it is necessary for a fast traveling team to pass a slower one, it shall be the duty of the teamster of the slow team to give the other a convenient opportunity to do so, if it can be done without endangering his own.

Sec. 2.—Whenever teams of any kind meet, each shall turn to the right, so as to give the other half of the traveled part of the road, whenever it can be done with safety.

Sec. 3.—Any person neglecting to conform to the provisions of this act shall be liable to pay all damage accruing therefrom, and be fined not exceeding one hundred dollars. (*Ibid.*, 86.)

Later it was considered a challenge for one team to try to pass another, and usually resulted in a wild race. A loaded team always had the right of way, but it was a matter of courtesy to pull off and stop to permit a faster team to pass.

Saturday 21 Feb 1852. Houses met at ten as pr adjt   Minutes read and excepted — Houses adjourned till Monday at 9 o'clock a. m   for the purpose of enabling the Committees to prepare reports.

Spent the after part of the day on the Criminal law.   Children very sick tonight

Sunday 22nd Feb 1852. Went to meeting to day   U S. mail came in to day —

Monday 23rd Feb. 1852. Legislature met at 9 a. m.   Spent the for noon in hearing the news & Prest message.

Met at two P. M. An act in relation to joint enclosures passed.

An additional section to the act of Decidents by Fulmer and passed Adjourned till tomorrow at 9 o'clock a. m.

Tuesday 24th Feb 1852. Destrict Court met at ten   Grand jury sworn & I was appointed Prosecutor for the time being.   Grand jury commenced inquiring into case of ox stealing and adjourned till two o'clock. Legislatur   also met as pr adjt

I met at ½ past 11 a. m. Bill on Marks & Brands before the Houses and finnally passed. and ordered to be inserted 4 times in the Deseret News.

In the after noon met with the grand jury on the previous business and Adj'd till two tomorrow at 4 o'c P. M.   Met with the Legislature Subject up the exploring Company Bill and on motion it was rejected   House adjourned till tomorrow at ten o'clock a. m.

Wednesday 25 February 1852. Legislature met at ten a. m. Bill by Sherwood in relation to surveying & surveying. Laid on the table to come up in its order and immediately taken up and passed with a fee bill to the same appended thereto.

Bill by Smith appropriating 100 dollars to Bridge Chicken Creek in Uab County — accepted read and passed.

Bill in relation to counties refered to a special Committee Wells, Rockwood, J. Fulmer Pratt Sherwood, Smith, afterwards Wells was excused.

The subject of the Bath house called up some talk of selling it to the Church or some body else.

Motion of Wells for committee on civil Code. Jas Brown, Dillie, Groves Evan, A Johnson, appointed Adjourned till tomorrow at 9 o'c to morrow at 9 o'clock

In the afternoon met with the grand jury, found a bill vs S. P. Davis for Larceny. In the evening met with the prayer circle.   Heber was present and taught us till 11 o'c

Thursday 26th Feb 1852. Met with the Court on the case of Davis read the indictment he partly acknowledged the charge and the court adjd till two. I then met with the Legislature.

Resolution by Rockwood to inquire why the Attorney Genl has not discharged his duty in the Territory &c was before the house.

An act in relation to Counties and defining the boundries. read the first time and passed — passed the final & the Legislature adjourned till two o'c —

At two met with the court on the case of Davis as prosecutor.   Case confessed jury rendered verdict of guilty without leaving their seats.   Court's sentence was was one dollar fine 5 years imprisonment at hard labor   Amt stolen one hundred and ten dollars[90]

At three met with the Legislature   Bill in relation to the unlawful assembling of Indians in the vicinity of the settlements - was before the Legislature & passed.

Stout presented a bill in relation to improve the watter course for common use.   Laid on the table

---

90. S. P. Davis has not yet been identified. The punishment seems so out of line with the offense — five years imprisonment at hard labor for a value of $110—that there must have been some other reason.

An act in relation to the practice before the courts in civil cases. read three times and passed -

An act in relation to attachments and Capias[91] read three times & passed. Adjourned till tomorrow at ten

Friday 27th February 1852. Legislature met at ten a. m. Pettition of O. P. Rockwell & E Neff for Cannon privilege — Leave granted to withdraw.[92]

An act in relation to Supervisors of Roads. Laid on the table to come up in its order

Dillie presented an act in relation to writs of replevin. Laid on the table to come up in its order.

One section on Lawful interest by Browning.

Resolutions for an Hospittal in Great Salt Lake City by for sick travellers Laid on the table

Resolution appointing or electing prosecuting attornys in each county laid on the table

Resolution to elect Recorder of Marks & Brands Laid on the table.

An act in relation to waters in common use. Laid on the table indefinately

An act in relation to Tresspass and damage by Jas Brown read and passed Adjourned for dinner and met at two P. M.

An act in relation to Marshalls and Attorneys by Stout Laid on the table to come up in its order

An act in relation to marriage by A. Johnson. Laid on the table to come up in its order.

An Act authorizing Forman of Grand jury to andminister oath to witnesses &c Laid on the table to come up in its order

An act in relation to indian prisoners by Wells. Laid on the table to come up in its order.

An act in relation to manufacturing associations. Laid on the table to come up in its order.

Memmorial to Congress for the privilege to form a State Goverment Laid on the table come up in order. Immediately taken up for its passage read debated and recommitted -

An act in relation to Constables read amended and passed

An act in relation to Marshalls & attornys read debated and the house adjourned till ten a. m to morrow.

Saturday Feb 28th 1852. Legislature met at ten a. m Memmorial to Congress by Smith for privilege to form a state government.[93] Read and adopted.

An act in relation to weights & measures Laid on the table to come up in its order.

An act in relation notaries public Laid on the table to come up in its order.

An act in relation to ejectment Laid on the table to come up in its order

---

91. *Capias* is a legal term from the Latin *Thou mayst take;* therefore it signifies a writ of process commanding the officer to take the body of the person named in it—in other words, to arrest him.

92. By action of the Salt Lake County Court, O. P. Rockwell and Franklin Neff were assigned "Neff Canyon" to take out timber and permit others to do so at twenty-five cents a load. But Rockwell and Neff were to build and maintain the road. "Road Book, Salt Lake County [1852-1916]" (Utah State Archives).

93. This was one of a succession of memorials to Congress. The first, sent in April of 1849 had 2,270 signatures and was twenty-two feet long. This one asked Congress to authorize a constitutional convention. "Congress rarely paid any attention to memorials from Utah, and its appropriations for the territory invariably were niggardly." Morgan, *State of Deseret, U. H. Q.,* VIII, 133, fn. 151.

An act authorizing the selectmen to act as coroners. withdrawn

An act in relation to distillerys Laid on the table to come in order

Act in relation disturbing religious meeting Laid on table —

Act vs profanity &c Laid on the table to come up in order

O. Spencer read a memmorial to congress to pay for the expenses of the provisional Government of Deseret.

Bill in relation to Marshalls & Attorneys again taken up. on the second reading amended and passed - Wells in the chair.

An act in relation to common schools. Laid on the table to come up in its order. (read and rejected [crossed out])

An act in relation to supervisors of roads &c read & rejected Adjourned for dinner and met at two. Not having a quorum a long discussion ensued.

An act in relation to replevin. read amended and refered —

Bill in relation to interest read and rejected.

Memmorial to congress for an appropriation to build an Hospital read and adopted

W Clayton elected recorder of Marks and Brands and Auditor of Public accounts and W J. Appleby Treasurer.

2000 copies of the Laws were ordered to be printed immediately and a committee two to superintend & prepare the same & Orson Pratt & James Brown said committee.

Memmorial to Congress for privilege to form a state government was again read and recieved

An act in relation to marriage. Laid aside to take up business of more consequence.

Bill authorizing Forman of Grand Jurors to administer oath to witnesses read and passed.

Bill in relation to Indian slaves and children passed[94] Adjourned till 9 a. m Monday. Vote recinded.

Bill in relation to home manufactories read withdrawn

An act to regulate weights & measures refered back again.

Bill in relation to Notaries public read three times and passed Adjourned till Monday at ten a. m.

Sunday 29th February 1852. Went to meeting to day In the after-noon Orson Pratt spoke He said that the first living body with flesh and bones that was. ever created or rather formed on this earth was *Man* but the spirits of beasts were formed before the spirits of man.

Monday 1st March 1852. Minutes read amended & accepted

Act in relation to writs of Ejectment. refered back on the third reading

Act in relation to distilling refered back after near two hours debate, or to a special committee Felt, Rockwood, Johnson Adjourned for dinner and met at ½ past one.

act in relation to weights & measure Laid on the table to come up in its order

Act repealing the 11 Sec of the act incorporating the University of Deseret Laid on the table to come up in its order.

---

94. Brigham Young's message encouraged the purchase of Indian children by the Mormon people, charging them to educate these children and teach them the gospel. He insisted that ". . . it is essentially purchasing them into freedom instead of slavery."

The law provided that when any person purchased such a child, he should go before the probate judge and make out an indenture that the apprenticeship should not exceed twenty years; that the master should send his ward to school at least three months of each year between the ages of seven and sixteen; that the apprentice should be clothed in a comfortable and becoming manner, according to his master's condition in life. *Laws of Utah, 1852*, pp. 91-92.

Act in relation to disturbing the peace on Sunday and passed.

Act in relation to profanity and drunkeness & cruel treatment to domestic animals read and passed.

Act in relation to common schools read and refered back again

Act in relation to the time of the meeting of Legislative Assembly read and passed

Act in relation to weights & measures refered to Stout for correction

Act to repeal the 11th Sec of the act incorporating the University of the State of Deseret read & passed

Act in relation to common schools read amended & passed.

Motion of Jas Brown to elect the Marshalls & attorneys, adopted   Governor nominated James Furgerson for Attorney General & elected. and H. S. Eldrige Marshall A. L. Siler District attorney for Second District and James Lewis do for third District

Memmorial to Congress for an appropriation to build an Hospital read and adopted.

Orson Pratt H. Stout D. A. Fulmer appointed said committee to draft the above memmorial. Adjourned till tomorrow at ten a. m.

The members then took into consideration the propriety of having a Legislation Ball. which was decided to be held at the State house on next Thursday at one P. M. & Edward Hunter chosen to furnish the supper and music and a committee was appointed to manage the concern.

Tuesday 2 March 1852. Met at ten roll called and recess for ten minutes Criminal Code presented by Wells. read and accepted then taken up by sections read to the 32nd section and the bill was passed Legislature adjourned for dinner and met at ½ past two P. M.

Motion to have the minutes of the two houses published in the "Deseret News" adopted.

Bill granting Jas Brown the wright to errect a toll bridge across Ogden & Weber rivers passed.

Act in relation to writs of replevin read three times, amended and passed

Resolution requesting the Secratary of the Territory to call on the Secratary of the Treasury of the United States for a set of weights and measures as established by Congress to be kept for the use of the Territory adopted

Resolution appropriating five hundred dollars to the Surveyor General for services due from the appointment to office to the first of Augt 1851. adopted.

Resolution extending the Territorial road north to Bear river adopted

Act in relation to writ of Ejectment read amended and refered back Adjourned till ten tomorrow a. m.

Went into meeting of citizens W Richards in the chair the object was ascertain whether we should bring more than one lady at the Legislative Ball or any of the previous officers of the assembly Judge Snow Esqr Blair and Marshall Haywood U. S officers were invited to the ball

Wednesday 3rd March 1852. Legislature met at ten a. m.   Committee appointed to memmorialize for a railway from the States via Salt Lake to Sandeigo. One for a teligraph for same

Resolution to distribute the Mitia Laws passed

Criminal Code taken up again on the 60th section the former part having been passed yesterday. passed having 123 sections

Act in relation to writs of Ejectment read a.. d passed

Act in relation to fees (rejected [crossed out])

Memmorial to Congress for National road from Counc:. Bluffs via Salt Lake South pass to Sacramento adopted Another for a rail road most eloquently written, adopted.

Memorial to congress for a weekly mail from States to the place. read and adopted

Memmorial to congress for a teleigraph from the States via Salt Lake City to Western coast adopted —

Memmorial to Congress for some of the Topographicll Engineers to continue the Survey of Capt Stansbury in this Territory — read and adopted.

Resolution to recind the Resolution to publish the laws and journals of the two houses in the "deseret news" passed

Motion to publish 1000 copies of the Laws in addition to the former 2000 ordered with drawn and also to publish 500 copies of the journals were then ordered to be printed

Memorial to Congress to extend the annual session of the Legislature to ninety days. read and adopted.

(Memmorial to [crossed out]) Act in relation to vagrants read and withdrawn

Appropriation Bill for Deseret Govt passed

Memmorial to congress to pay the expenses of the Indians Wars. read and adopted.

Passed a Liquor Bill

Memmorial to congress to appropriate for the use of the schools read adopted

Memmorial to Congress for pay for this Special Session read and adopted.

Memmorial to congress to to authorize the Supertendent of indian affairs to purchase the indian titles to land. read and adopted.

executive Session arose without doing any business Adjourned till ten Friday at ten a. m.

Thursday 4th March 1852. At one o'clock P. M. wife & I went to the Legislative Ball at the State House. This was altogether the best party that has been in the Valley as was frequently remarked by different ones. There was some 65 men and over 100 women. The supper consisted of the best to be produced in this place & plenty for all. The spirit of the people was calm interesting and lovely. I never saw so large a company before all of whom I believed at the time enjoyed pleasure unmingled with any feelings to mar their social enjoyment as on this occasion. The party continued till two o'clock in the morning.

Friday 5th March 1852. Legislature met at ten a. m Petition to incorporate the City of Nephi in Juab County refered to B. F. Johnson & Hosea Stout

Fee bill again discussed & withdrawn.

Resolution allowing H. S. Eldrige the assessor & collector 1000 dollars for his services for last year and W. Clayton was allowed 400 dollars for his services as auditor of public accounts Adjourned for dinner and met at two p. m.

Memmorial to Congress for the Land laws or Laws similar to be extended over this Territory read and adopted.[95]

Memmorial to congress to have the southern boundry line of this Territory established read and adopted.

Bill introduced by Judge Snow making certain intermeddling between citizens of different states criminal read discussed and laid on the table

Executive session and elected the folliwing to the office of Notary public C

G. W. Pitkin for Weber County   Robert Campbell for G. S. L. County
Jas Leithead for Davis County   Peter Maun[96] for Toolie County

---

95. This points up the fact that although some local surveys had been made, the Mormons were essentially squatters on public land.

96. This is Peter Maughan, who was born May 7, 1811, at Breckenridge (Milton), in the parish of Farley, county of Cumberland, England. He joined the Mormon Church in 1838 and came to America in 1841 with Brigham Young and other returning missionaries. That year

Isaac Higbee for Utah County
Zimri H Baxter[97] for Juab
A L. Siler for San pete County

C. Holbrook[98] for Millard and
James Lewis for Iron County

Bill in relation to conveying real estate Laid on table

Act to incorporate Nephi City Juab County read and refered back

Memmorial to congress for an appropriation for the relief of the post mastr of G. S. L. County & for a distributing post office & mail agent &c in Salt Lake County read and adopted. Legislature adjourned till to morrow at ten a. m.

Saturday 6th March 1852. Legislature met at ten a.m. Resolution to extend the Territorial road south through the big field south of this city that is survey it

Act in relation to the conveyance of real estate read and refered back to the committee again

Act to prevent officers from recieving fees by James Brown which was added to the fee bill of yesterday which withdrawn

Act in relation to conveying real estate introduced by Sherwood. read three times and passed

Resolution to elect 12 select men in each county as arbritartors. passed. Adjourned for dinner & met at two P. M.

Bill in relation to road tax & supervisors of road. read three times and passed.

An act incorporating the City of Nephi Juab County. read and accepted. read and passed.

William Snow was appointed Code Commissioner in the place of William Pickett resigned.

Memmorial to the Post Master General praying for a distributing post office in Salt Lake City and a mail agent read and adopted. Adjourned sine die.

Sunday 7th March 1852. At home to day most of the time A very hard south wind has been blowing almost incessantly during this month. and this evening commenced storming

Monday 8th March 1852. Around town attending to some legal business. Snow this morning & hard North wind last night Warm still clear day snow melting all off

Tuesday 9th March 1852. Hard south wind again. I am attending to legal business to day.

Wednesday 10th March 1852. Attending to Legal business to day Snowed very hard in the evening

Thursday 11th March 1852. Deep snow this morning and snow squalls to day. Attended Destrict Court before Judge Snow. T. S. Williams vs J G. Peoples in

Maughan's wife (Ruth Harrison) died, leaving him with a family of six children. In 1842 he married Mary Ann Weston Davis, another English woman. They came to Utah in 1850.

Maughan settled first in Tooele Valley where he was county clerk and assessor in 1851. In 1856 he moved into Cache Valley where he was presiding bishop and president of the stake. He died on August 24, 1871, in Logan, Utah.

97. Zimri H. Baxter was born February 14, 1807, in Maine. He came to Utah in December of 1849 and settled at Big Cottonwood, Salt Lake County. In 1851 he moved to Nephi, Juab County, where he built a flour mill and a nail factory. A contractor, carpenter, joiner, and millwright, he was responsible for building the tabernacle at Nephi in 1871. He served as the captain of the "Silver Grays," a group of older men who had been in the Nauvoo Legion. He died December 10, 1887.

98. Chandler Holbrook, born September 16, 1807, in England, joined the Mormon Church early. He was a member of Zion's Camp in 1834 and was active during the troubles at Far West in 1838 and 1839. He came west with the 1848 emigration and moved south to Fillmore, Utah, at its founding.

case of debt of some 900 dollars in assumpsit[99] Which came up on attachment W. W. Phelps, S. M. Blair, Culver, W. Pickett & myself were attorneys on the part of the plff. and G. A. Smith and Slayton on the part of the Defence

Only two witneses were examined to day and the court adjourned till 9 tomorrow.

I was also retained on a case pending against Lefering who paid me fifty dollars retaner in advance. in a case wherein he is sued on an attachment by H Cook in action of debt for $338.80 or thereabouts.

Friday 12th 1852 March. Engaged to day in the Suit Williams v. Peoples as yesterday

Saturday 13th March 1852. Engaged in Court to day also. A case of Certori[100] brought up from the mayors Court of Provo City Utah County. Lucius N. Scovil plantiff in error v J Neale Deft The Judgement of the court below was reversed In this case before the Court below Scovil had sued out a Replevin to recovor and ox from the defendant but upon trial the court Mr Ames the Mayor reversed the parties making Mr Scovil the defendant who lost the case as far as the verdict of a jury is concerned but the court had not rendered judgement on the verdict.

The Court above ordered a new trial in this place and remanded the ox to the possession of Scovil untill the determination of the suit. The case of Williams v Peoples occupied the most part of the day and the case is not yet submitted to the jury. The debates grew very animated at times and disorderly

One thing transpired to day which I never before in a Court of Justice to be said by a Judge while on the Bench Mr Slayton in questioning Mr Sutherland a witness sarcasticly said that he was one of these (easy or [crossed out]) willing kind of witnesses whereupon Mr Culver objected on the ground that Slayton was impeaching the witness whereupon the judge ordered Mr Culver to stop and said that he (Sutherland) was a willing kind of a witness.

Now the prerogative assumed by the court to join in with the sarcastic and insulting insinuations of the bar which are to apt to be practiced in court in dispite of the judge is a thing to me totally unheard of and preposterous. Not only so it is only the province of the jury to decide the validaty of evidence and theirs only at a proper time The thing only proved to me a biased and a corrupt heart in the breast of the court.

Sunday 14th 1852 March. At home mostly to day but was at the Council House awhile.

Monday 15th March 1852. Attended Court and Engaged in the case of Williams v. Peoples yet The case was submitted to the jury and about half of the plas made to the jury The Court put Mr Culver under arresst to day which was occasioned by a misunderstanding between him & Slayton But he was released this evening by the Court on the petition of Mr Pickett Very hard North wind and driving snow to day and snowing at bed time.

Tuesday 16th March 1852. Engaged at Court in the case of Williams V Peoples The case was submitted to the jury at five P. M. and the verdict perhaps will be brought in to morow morning. This makes five days that the Court has been engaged in this case.

Wednesday 17th March 1852. The jury on the Case of Williams v. Peoples has not this morning made out their verdict. They were up all night.

---

99. *Assumpsit* denotes an action on contract to recover damages for a breach of contract.

100. A case of *Certiorari* is a writ from a superior court to call up for review the records of an inferior court or a body acting in a quasi-judicial capacity. Stout explains the case in question.

About noon they came to an agreement. The court met at two P. M to hear the verdict.

They had rendered 139 dollars and some cents in favor of Williams leaving out a certain number of accounts on both sides pertaining to some liquors brought on by Peoples & Williams from Kainsville on the ground that it was a partnership concern and did not belong to a book account.

This liquor partnership is strictly a Chancery case but both parties have concluded to submit it to the High Council for their decision and save the expense of a suit in chancery.

I attended the prayer circle at the council House at seven o'clok P. M good weather again.

Thursday 18th March. 1852. Attending to legal affairs in the fore noon. In the after noon engaged in the case of Cook v. Liffering on a motion to dissolve the attachment vs Liffiring

Slayton council on the part of the plff & myself Pickett Culver and Blair for Defence.

Friday 19th March 1852. Engaged at Court winding up the case of Williams v. Peoples In the after noon most of the time was taken up in discussion The judge confessed that he was and had been prejudiced against Williams in the suit and was determined to put his foot on him in the trial if he could judicially and quite an altercation took place on the subject which is too disgraceful & contemptible to notice

Saturday 20th March 1852. Yet at law the judge rendered judgement in the case of Williams v Peoples and ruled to divide the costs between the parties

The case of Cook v. Leffering came up and the attachment was on the previous motion of the 13th inst. dissolved. Spent the after noon at the Library and around town

Sunday 21st March 1852. Took a general stroll over town and came back and went to meeting & so spent the day

Monday 22nd March 1852. The High Council met to day to determine the partnership transactions of the case of Williams V. Peoples which was not determined by the jury on the 17th inst Council adjourned at five to meet tomorrow on the same case. The Case which was taken by certori Scovil v. Neal is agreed to come before the High Council also.

Tuesday 23rd March 1852. The High Council have been all day engaged in the case of Peoples and Williams and had not come to a decision at sun hour high.

To day I commenced preparing the laws for the press in the place of the printing committee which was appointed by the Legislature which will occupy some 20 or 30 days I expect.

Wednesday 24th March 1852. Engaged in preparing the laws for press & writing the marginal Notes. The High Council, on the case of Williams V. Peoples rendered a judgement in favor of Williams of 423 dollars and 83 cents. Peoples was dissatisfied with their judgement and told them that it was no better than robery.

Thursday 25th March 1852. Engaged in writing marginal notes to the law. To day a party went out to meet the eastern mail The California mail came in to day. The first mail from the West since Oct The mail carriers are probably killed by the indians

Friday 26th March 1852. Engaged in writing marginal notes for the law. The Eastern mail came in to day.

Saturday 27th March 1852. Attended the High Council The case of Scovil & Neal about the ox affair which had been refered there from the court, as before mentioned, was tried. I was appointed to take the place of Parry No 12 and appointed one of the Speakers on the part of Scovil who was deft. The trial occupied all day. Scovil gained the ox.

Sunday 28th March 1852. At home all day, being sick with the headache. Cold East wind

Monday 29th March 1852. Engaged in writing marginal notes to the laws today —

Tuesday 30th March 1852. Engaged in writing marginal notes to the laws to day.

Wednesday 31st March 1852. Engaged in writing marginal notes to the laws to day Mr Levingston and others left this place to day for the States The mail will leave tomorrow The snow is very deep in the mountains.

Thursday 1st April 1852. Engaged in writing marginal notes for the law to day.

Friday 2nd April 1852. Engaged in writing marginal notes to the law to day.

Saturday 3rd April 1852. The mail came in to day from the East briging the mail for two months. Reports of the mail are that Gov Young is removed & Gen Doniphan of Mo appointed in his place.
There was a very large mail I have not learned the other news

Sunday 4th April 1852. I was quite unwell to but went to meeting in the fore noon — Mary Taylor, wife of Joseph Taylor died to day about noon

Monday 5th April 1852. Engaged in writing marginal notes for the laws to day

Tuesday 6th April 1852. General Conference met at ten at the new Tabernacle[101] a new building just finished for the purpose of Divine worship on the Temple Block. It is 123 feet long by 63 feet wide and is beautifully arched on the in side The stand is on the west side in the centre with doors leading out of the building from the stand into a vestry.
The floor is built on an ascending floor rising from the stand in each direction to accommodate every one in the house with a view of the Speaker. It holds about 2500 persons.
In the fore noon the Tabernacle was dedicated by prayer by Prest W. Richards. In the after noon I could not get in such was the croud of persons at conference
The Seventies had a meeting at dark at the Tabernacle, on the subject of building the 70's hall but there was not much done

Wednesday 7th April 1852. Conference met at ten the officers of the Church were presented as usual and recieved with the exception of B. L. Clapp who was objected to and his case was laid over
After the officers of the Church had been presented & recieved President Young was presented as Gov of Deseret & H C. Kimball Lt Gov which carried
This was done only for amusement. In the after noon I could not get in to the Tabernacle. This evening there was a meeting of the male members at the Tabernacle

---

101. The "New Tabernacle" in which they met on April 6, 1852, was started in May of 1851. It stood until 1879, when it was torn down to make room for the present Assembly Hall. Stout's description of it is excellent.

Thursday 8th April 1852. Attended Conference in the fore noon which was devoted to the subject of education & Orson Spencer, Z. Snow W. W. Phelps and President B. Young spoke on the subject. In the after noon I could not get in the Tabernacle.

This evening there was a General meeting of the Seventies who met in Quorums for the purpose of filling vacancies and ordaining Seventies.

Friday 9th April 1852. Stormy morning. attended conference House much crouded, did not stay in the House long after noon was not in because of the croud -

Another meeting this evening. President B. Young taught that Adam was the father of Jesus and the only God to us.[102] That he came to this world in a resurected body &c more hereafter

Saturday 10th April 1852. Attended Conference but did not stay in much of the time because of the croud. had to give way to the ladies. Carrington spoke on the subject of Doctors & their practice.

The Origon mail came in to day. They found the remains of Capt Wooward, who was supposed to have been killed by the Indians with the California mail last fall and they picked up some few letters which were laying around him.[103]

Attended a night meeting but there was not much said or done at it.

Sunday 11th April 1852. President Kimball preached to day Spoke against brethren taking the wives of dead brethren and having them seald to them for eternity and divers other subjects He said we never should be again brought under the Gentile yoke. Bishop Hunter was ordained Head Bishop and chose presidents B. Young & Kimble Councillors which was accepted. Seth Taft A Hoagland, D. Pettigrew, D. Fulmer, D. Spencer, were appointed travelling Bishops.[104]

In the after noon I staid at home and my wife went to meeting In the evening went to meeting J. C. Wright preached. Conference closed this after noon

Monday 12th April 1852. Attended a lawsuit before Esqr. A. F. Farr. J. G. Peeples v- Jos Worthen in debt 10 dollars T. S. Williams & myself Council for Williams. Peeples was non-suited on the plea of Jurisdiction as Taft lived in another County. Writing marginal notes for the law the rest of the day

Tuesday 13th April 1852. Writing marginal notes for the laws to day. John Kay and others gave Harvey Morse 39 hard lashes (to day [crossed out]) last night for frequently attempting to rape two little girls not six years old. He had materially injured the girls.

---

102. This speech on the "Adam-God" theory gave rise to much later discussion, some of which continued into the 1920's. It is not now accepted as L. D. S. Church doctrine.

103. The full name of Mr. Woodard, the California mail contractor, has not yet been found. The only man who spells his name "Woodard" is George Woodard, a member of Brigham Young's 1847 pioneers.

A note on the fate of Woodard is found in a letter from Lorin Farr to Governor Brigham Young, dated April 10, 1852, and filed in the "Journal History" of the church under that date: "Sir: I have taken this opportunity to inform you that Mr. Johnson, the mail carrier, has returned from his trip out after his things which he left this side of Goose Creek Mountains . . . . They found about 70 miles this side of Goose Creek Mountain where Mr. Woodard, the mail contractor, had died or perished. Mr. Johnson found a part of the mail that he had, also his watch and some of his clothing . . . ."

104. Since much of the tithing was paid "in kind,"—grain, produce, cattle, fruit, molasses, etc.—the traveling bishops collected from the scattered wards and brought the contributions into the general storehouse for distribution among the poor. Sometimes they hauled out items to localities where there were shortages.

Wednesday 14th April 1852. Engaged to day in the governors reading and examining the laws preparetory to their going to the press. The Governor W Richards, D. H. Wells, A. Carrington were also present.

Thursday 15th April 1852. Wrighting marginal notes and examining the law to day.

Friday 16th April 1852. Engaged writing marginal notes to and examining the laws. To day I have completed this work for the laws and commenced on the Resolutions.

Saturday 17th April 1852. Engaged in writing marginal notes to the resolutions to day.

Sunday 18th April 1852. Went to meeting The Tabernacle was full to day which makes about 2,500 people for a common congregation President B. Young preached in the for noon & Heber in the after noon

Monday 19th April. Engaged in writing the laws & resolutions for the press.

Tuesday 20th April 1852. Engaged in preparing resolutions & memmorials for the press. I was appointed Clerk of the Board of Code Commissioners to day

Wednesday 21st April 1852. Engaged as yester day. Gen Rich and some 15 other arrived to day from Caliafornia by the south rout all well. Rainy eve

Thursday 22nd April 1852. Engaged as yesterday. Commenced the index for the law today Govornor Young and a large Company started south on an exploring expedition to. [the south] Stormy evening

Friday 23 April 1852. A good snow this morning Engaged as yesterday.

Saturday 24th April 1852. Engaged as yester day. Stormy & snow — squally to day

Sunday 25th April 1852. Wife & I went to meeting to day Gen Rich gave an account of his mission.

Monday 26th April 1852. Engaged in preparing memmorials for the press. To day the we have completed the laws, Resolutions and memmorials for the press. The minutes of the two Houses and joint sessions are yet to be prepared.

Tuesday 27th April 1852. Engaged to day on printing affairs Last night Joseph Worthen was shot while lying in bed with his wife and children.[105] The ball entered his hip just above the joint fracturing the bone the ball lodged in the opposite groin He is not expected to live.

Wednesday 28th April 1852. Engaged as usual. Mr. James Keel and Willis Morse were arrested to day and brought before Elias Smith Probate Judge, for an examination on the charge of shooting Jos Worthen. They were acquited.

Stormy evening again This evening attended the prayer circle. I have unavoidably been prevented from attending pray circle for some three weeks.

Thursday 29th April 1852. Verry stormy this morning. Engaged at the printing as before I learn that Joseph Worthen has died of the wound he recieved on Monday night. No trace of the assassin yet

---

105. A biography of Joseph Worthen has not been found. At Nauvoo in January 1845, he was one of the twelve officers of the Mercantile Institution; he operated a store in Nauvoo; in 1846 he was one of six men appointed to secure provender and food for the exiled Saints.

There is no account of Worthen's death or of this shooting in the *Deseret News* of either May 1 or May 15 following or in any of the church records.

Friday 30th April 1852. Engaged in reding proof sheets of the law The Eastern mail came in to day. News from the States Oregon The excitement is still great for and against us Very stormy bousterous night

Saturday 1st May 1852. Engaged in hearing and reading the news from the States. Very hard wind to day from the South, which turned to the north and was followed by a sivere snow storm which covered the ground The weather was very cold at dark. Singular May day this

Sunday 2nd May 1852. Went to meeting in the fore noon In the after noon attended quorum meeting at Br Amy's.

Monday 3rd May 1852. Engaged in preparing the Journals of the Legislative assembly for the press.

Tuesday 4th May 1852. Engaged in reading proof sheets & indexing the law to day. Cold, cloudy, windy, snowy.

Wednesday 5th May 1852. Engaged in indexing the law & reading journals for the press. In the evening attended the prayer circle.

Thursday 6th May 1852. The weather appears to be settled and perhaps Spring may yet come

Friday 7th May 1852. Engaged in reading proof sheets and indexing the law to day

Saturday 8th May 1852. Engaged in indxing the law

Sunday 9th May 1852. Went to meeting in the fore noon C. C. Rich preached. Attended quorum meeting at one at Br Amy's took one or two members into the quorum

Monday 10th May 1852. Engage in indexing the law and preparing the journals for the press.

Tuesday 11th May 1852. Engaged in reading proof sheet of law and examing journals of Legislature for press

Wednesday 12 May 1852. Engaged in reading proof sheet and indexing the law Attended prayer circle in the evening.

Thursday 13th May 1852. Engaged in indexing and reading the journals to day Had a fine rain this evening

Friday 14th May 1852. Hard rains this fore noon. Engaged as usual to day — Hard rains in the afternoon.

Saturday 15th May 1852. Wet rainy muddy morning this engaged in examing the journals today

Sunday 16th May 1852. read proof sheet to this fore noon Went to meeting in the after noon. Weather very fine to day —

Monday 17th May 1852. Engaged as usual in the fore noon In the after noon attend the City Council, having been appointed a member thereof and just entered on the duties of my office An ordinance providing for the building of a tempary Hospital at the mouth Emmegration Cañon was passed and Dr Jerter Clinton[106]

---

106. Jeter Clinton came to Utah in 1850. On January 9, 1851, he was made a member of the first city council, a position to which he was reappointed in April following. During the 1860's he was a druggist and doctor in the city, always prominent in public affairs.

appointed to take charge of the same. This is on the Quarantine law to prevent the introduction of disease into the city by emmegration.

Tuesday 18th May 1852. engaged at indexing the law and reading the Journals to day.

Wednesday 19 May 1852. Reading Journals to day. To day the Clerks completed the Journals of the Legislature for the press. There is also 164 pages of the laws come out of press.

Thursday 20th May 1852. Engaged as usual this fore noon after noon went with wife visiting to Mrs Patridges.

Friday 21 May 1852. Engaged in indexing the law. President Young and Company returned home to day having went no further south than Coal Creek Iron County. All were well.

Saturday 22nd May 1852. Training day. I was not engaged at any particular business to day

Sunday 23 May 1852. Went to meeting. Very full house president Young preached in the fore-noon. In the after-noon I was not there but a short time Very warm day.

Monday 24th May 1852. A company of Indians came to the State house from Fort Hall to see Gov Young Engaged in reading proof sheets &c

Tuesday 25th May 1852. Reading proofs and indexing today

Wednesday 26 May 1852. Engaged in examing the laws of the U. S Attended prayer circle this evening. Messrs Kinkead, Cogswell and Packard merchants, arrived this evening from the States, having left the frontier on the. Reading proof to day some.

Thursday 27th May 1852. Done but little to day not being well, but attend to the printing affairs of the law —

Friday 28th May 1852. Attended to the printing &c of law The Eastern mail came in to day. Wet, having been under water several times. The news from the East is good.

(Saturday 29 May 1850[2]. Went to meeting. C. C. Rich preached & was followed by Prest B. Young who still condemns thes who went to San Barnadeno In the afternoon wife & I went [crossed out])

Saturday 29th May 1852. Engaged as usual at the law.

Sunday 30th May, 1852. Went to meeting to day C C. Rich preached & was followed by Prest B. Young. after noon attended with wife.

Monday 31st May 1852. To day was writting and copying documents to send to Washington by the morrow mail.

Tuesday 1 June 1852. reading proof sheet of law to day.

Wednesday 2 June 1852. Indexing the law to day attended prayer circle at sun set.

In 1869 Clinton opened a pleasure resort on the south shore of Great Salt Lake called "Lake Point." By 1874 he had replaced his first building with an impressive stone house known as the "Clinton House." This became the stopping place for the overland stages to 1893.

Thursday & Friday 3 & 4 June. Attended to the indexing yet

Saturday 5th June 1852. Indexing still. O tedious! This evening the committee of arangements at the State house preparitory to the 4 of July. I was one of the committee, and was among several others appointed to deliver an oration on the occasion.

Sunday 6th June 1852. Attended church but was very unwell

Monday 7 June 1852. reading proof to day, in the evening the Committee of arraingements for the 4th of July.

Tuesday 8 June 1852. Reading proof and indexing Committee meet this evening

Wednesday 9th June 1852. Writing index to day. Emmagration commenced to roll in to day.

Thursday 10 June 1852. Fine little shower to this morning. Indexing to day —

Friday 11 June 1852. Indexing to day —

Saturday 12th June 1852. Indexing to day the law as usual.

Sunday 13th June 1852. Went to meeting but was so unwell that I could not enjoy myself.

Monday 14th June 1852. proof reading to day and indexing Emmegrants roll in now

Tuesday 15th June 1852. Indexing and proof reading. City council met last night and agreed to apply city revenue on Streets and appointed M Phelps street commisioner

Wednesday 16th June 1852. Indexing to day. attended prayer circle at sun set —

Thursday 17th June 1852. Indexing to day. Completed the index for the law to day. Mr Holladay with 10 waggons and a drove of horses arrived from the States this evening.

Friday 18th June 1852. to day examing manuscripts for the press. The golden pilgrims are now rolling into the valley quite plenty

Saturday 19th June 1852. Reading proof to and other things as usual.

Sunday 20th June 1852. Not well to and was at home mostly

Monday 21st June 1852. proof reading to day

Tuesday 22 June 1852. Engaged in the library to day searching church History.

Wednesday 23rd June 1852. Engaged as yesterday. This evening the hardest rain fell that I ever knew since I have been in the valley. The ground on the highland was completely flooded Mr H. B. Clawsons house fell down and the family narrowly escaped. The cellar filled with water and the foundation gave way. The water also ran into the door of the vestry of the Tabernacle and filled the stand with water other building were badly flooded.

Thursday 24 June 1852. Engaged as usual to day The "Gold enemegrants" are still rolling in.

Friday 25 June 1852. Engaged as usual. Proof reading

Saturday 26 June 1852. Engaged in a law suit to day. between two Emegrants.

Benjamin McColey vs Lewis Lafontain in attachment on failure of contract to take him and wife to Caliafornia from Michigan.

Debt and damage 879 dollars, before Elias Smith Judge of Probate S. M. Blair Esqr council for plff and G. A. Smith and myself for the defence. The trial occupied most of the day.

The Court decided that the defendant pay the plaintiff one hundred and thirty dollars and cost of suit.

Sunday 27th June 1852. Went to meeting awhile but then went to the office to read some late papers which had just come from the States by which we learn that President Fillmore has sustained Gov Young in all things against the Judges & Secratary & appointed W. Richards Secratary of the Territory, & Orson Hyde associate Justice of the Supreme Court in the place of Perry C. Brocchus. Brandebery's place has not been filled as we learn yet.

Monday 28th June 1852. Engaged in preparing the journals of the House of Representatives for the press. This evening had another suit between two Emegrants. on breach of contract. The case come up on attachment before Elias Smith Judge of Probate. Debt 125 and damage 100 dollars Jacob Hancoop vs J. H. Woods S. M. Blair on the part of plff & myself on the part of the defence The case was adjourned till to morrow at 7 o'clock A. M

Tuesday 29th June 1852. Case called up and investigated   judgement against deft of 41.66. and cost divided

This evening attended a suit before Esquire William Snow in an action of debt on attachment demand 100 dollars. Edward Kusel vs Francis J. Dyer and Sydney J. Cowel I was on the part of the plaintiff. Judgement against Deft of 50 dollars and cost divided between them The trial lasted from dark until almost daylight.

Wednesday 30th June 1852. Engaged in legal affairs to day and on suit came up which was compromised. Royal Barney vs some Pilgrims. Attended prayer circle this evening at dark

Thursday 1 July 1852. Attended a suit this fore noon before E Smith, Judge of Probate Robert Rutledge vs John Mains debt 65 dollars and damage 100 for failure to take him to California from Kainsville Iowa I was council for plff.

Friday 2 July 1852. Attended suit before Judge Smith. Charlotte Lisgo vs John Mains for damage for non performance of contract to take her to California from Larimie I was on part of Plantiff Judgement in favor of Plff. for 100 dollars and costs.

Saturday 3rd July 1852. This fore noon I was in council in the Gov. office on the subject of the fourth of July hearing the Speaches of Thomas Bullock & James Furgerson Esqrs for the furth celebration. The other speaker was not present with their speach.

Hon A. W. Babbitt came in this morning from the States. he states that the cholera is raging hard on the road and that about one thousand persons had died on the road

Several suits are now going on in the probate Court against Bridger and Vasques for selling horses to the Emegrants with out vending the brand.[107] The cases has been refered to arbritrators who render tolerable liberal damages agains the defts on the cases.

---

107. To "vend the brand" on an animal is to be sure that it is the brand of the seller; otherwise there is no guarantee that the horse was not stolen.

Sunday. Went to meeting about as usual to day

Monday July 5th 1852. This morning the citizens of this city were awakened by the roar of artillery at break of day followed by a Serenade from two Bands of music to hail the birth day of our national liberty and at half past seven I went to the Tabernacle to meet the Committee of arraingements preparitory to forming the Gov escort after which according to a previous invitation from his excellency the Gov I repaired to his house at half past 8 o'clock to join his suit to be escorted to the Tabernacle where the ceremonis of our celebration would commence

When the escort arrived The 31 veterans, then the "Mormon Battalion" The escorted pay and Gov forming betwen them while the Minute company of Horse were in the rear the escort proceeded with proper cerimonies to the Tabernacle under the continual roar of cannon. After which the meeting was opened by prayer and the order of the celebration commenced which consisted of alternate speaches, songs, airs, toasts &c.

I read the Declaration of Independence, immediately after the opening prayer.

Had a short adjournment for dinner. The day past off well and all seemed to enjoy themselves well. About four the assembly dispersed. Had some legal business for Thomas Moor to attend to about dark. So well was Mr Lely [Lehy?] satisfied with the compromising manifested that he gave me 5 dollars in the presence of Br Moor although I was Moor's attorney vs him

Tuesday 6th July 1852. To day I was engaged in settling the case of Thomas Moor with the Emegrants for charging them unlawful ferriage on Green River. He has been prosecuted by the Atty General on the part of the people for a misdemeanor and brought here for trial. The Emegrants now claim the amount overcharged to be paid back or on failure to do so to sue him. He is refunding the overcharged ferriage.

He had his trial before the Probate Court to day. James Furgerson the Attorney General on the part of the prosecution & I was on the part of the defence The case was submitted by the parties while the defendant admitted the charge The Judge defered giving judgement till to morrow morning.

This evening about dark had a suit before Esqr William Snow Joseph Schach vs _____ Powell in an action of damage for assault and battery. I was council on the part of the plaintiff

The party plead not guilty to the charge but on investigation the court sentenced the defendant to pay twenty dollars damage and costs. Rainy night.

Wednesday 7th July 1852. Sick to day and in the after-noon keep my bed done no business of consequence

Thursday 8th July 1852. The book binder on whom we depend for binding the laws have disappointed us and I was engaged to day in trying get the law binding started as they are much needed The laws were all printed last Saturday.

Friday 9th July 1852. looking to the book binding which seemed to go slowly.

Saturday 10th July 1852. Around to day doing little or nothing This evening had a suit before Esq William Snow. Michael Considine vs Martin Coragan for settlement I was on the part of the plaintiff and James Furgerson on the part of the defence. Court gave judgement in favor of the plaintiff for thirty four dollars and costs.

Sunday 11 July 1852. Went to meeting to day but did not stay long.

Monday 12th July 1852. Emegrants are still coming in to the city faster than ever. To day the first "Bloomer" made her appearance (in the [crossed out])

flaunting through the streets puzzling the causual observer to properly determine the sex.[108]

Two of the law books were bound to day.

Tuesday 13th July 1852. Engaged to day in planting suits for golden pilgrams, in the probate Court Rain and hail to day quite hard. After noon rain very hard.

Wednesday 14th July 1852. At ten o'clock this morning had a suit before E. Smith Judge of Probate Edward Buckwell vs Samuel Brown and William K. Davis. In attachment for debt of 30 dollars for part of passage money from Zainsville Ohio to Calafornia and for services on the road one hundred dollars and for damage on contract for faling to take him to California as pr agreement for 100 dollars more I was on the part of the plff and James Furgerson on the part of the defence Court rendered judgement for plaintiff for twenty five dollars and costs paid by defendent. There is more cases pending. Attended prayer circle at sun set

Thursday 15th July 1852. At 8 o'clock a. m had a suit before E. Smith Probate Judge. Phebe Jane Emmerson vs John do in Replevin for 3 yoke of oxen waggon and loading. I was on the part of the plaintiff. The deft did not appear. Jugement by default in favor of plff, who paid the cost as deft had nothing

Immediately after which had another suit before same. People vs Frederic Schaller and Phillip Watler on a charge for larceny for stealing two mules from George Hegebacke. I was on part of defence & James Furgerson on prosecution Court the parties plead guilty and claimed mercy. Court sentenced them to one years hard labor each and to wear a ball and chain

Then another before same George Hegebocke vs the above for damage for stealing the above mules. Judgement of court vs the two, of 56 dollars each.

Friday 16th July 1852. Attended Court awhile and then was reading proof of the Legislative journal To day was a wet rainy day but not much wind.

Saturday 17th July 1852. District Court in session. Attended to some suits now pending.

Sunday 18th 1852 July. Not well to day was around & at meeting and home

Monday 19 July 1852. Engaged in law affairs but had no suits to day Attended City council at 7 P. M. subject of police was the topic voted to suspend the issue of city scrip.

Tuesday 20th July 1852. This fore noon I took the manuscript of the Council Journals to the printer. The House Journal being about all in type. At two p. m. went to Judge Snow's and took dinner with a few members of the bar who he had invited for a social repast We had a good dinner served by his lady and a bottle of gin and enjoyed ourselves very agreeably untill about five P. M.

Wednesday 21 July 1852. preparing the Journals of the joint session for the press.

Thursday 22nd July 1852. Reading the proof of the third form of the journal which completes the journal of the House and some few pages of the Council.

Friday 23 July 1852. Attended discrict Court to day which is now in session

Saturday 24 July 1852. To day was the celebration of the arrival of the Pioneers in this valley, which opened at sun rise by the firing of three rounds of artillery

---

108. Named for Mrs. Amelia Bloomer, who adopted them, this costume consists of very full pants or trousers gathered to a wide band just below the knee. As Stout indicated, this is the first woman so clothed to come to Salt Lake City.

and followed by music by the brass bands serenading the streets on horse back.

At 8 o'clock the escort met at the tabernacle in the following order. Star Spangled banner Marshalls. Marshall music Pioneers with banner and implements indicating the part they took in exploring out the valley

Next the public Hand[s] with banner and appropriate implements.

Clerks & printers. Baner

Then Chancellor and regents of the University of Deseret (in this corps I marched) with banner.

Then 24 aged (mothers [crossed out]) fathers with banner.

24 aged mothers. banner

Capt Ballo's Band

24 young men in uniform & banner.

24 young ladies in uniform with banner

24 boys in uniform. banner

24 girls in uniform, banner

Capt Pitts Brass band

24 warriors in uniform and banners.

Then came the escorted party consisting of the President & his councillors.

The twelve who were here and some others who he had invited

The rear guard consisting of the Bishops.

When the Escort left the house of President Young the flag was unfurled on the liberty pole under a salute of 24 guns well "ramed home"[109]

When the congregation was seated in the Tabernacle the services commenced by music then song of thanksgiving then prayer, "pioneer song" oration by G. A. Smith, music by Ballo's band when speaches songs and music and solos were introduced in proper order untill in the after noon when the congregation dismissed.

The day was "suffocatinglly" warm and cut short the performances, yet all enjoyed themselves well.

Sunday 25th July 1852. Went to meeting but was not well

Monday 26. July 1852. Attended District Court. a case came up which I had to do with but was compromise

Tuesday 27th July 1852. Attended District Court a case has been pending Scott V Lucas & Levan Blair for Plff & A. W. Babbitt for Deft I was called to the deft to day This evening a misunderstanding betwen the Court and Babbitt occurred and the court ordered him under arrest which created considerable excitement.[110]

Wednesday 28th July 1852. Attend D. C. to day again the affair of Court v Babbitt came up and was settled. Babbitt accusing the court of giving the first insult which was not denied. The court and suits pending were adjourned till Saturday at 10 o'clock a.m.

Thursday 29th July 1852. Mail came in last evening from States and California Very sick to day & weather very hot and sultry.

Friday 30th July 1852. Reading the proof of the Council Journal to day wether hot 114°.

Saturday 31 July 1852. District Court & County Court sitting to day I was attending them had a hard rain in the after-noon but no wind.

---

109. Their cannons are evidently muzzle-loaders, and so make a louder sound when the packing is well rammed in.

110. Nothing definite has been found on the nature of this disagreement, but it is significant in that it shows the disfavor which is growing toward Babbitt.

Sunday Aug 1 - 1852. Went to meeting A. W. Babbitt spoke followed by Prest B. Young in the fore noon

At 5 o'clock p. m. Alfred Smith preached a sermon Gladenitism He believes that F. G. Bishop is Jesus Christ in the *flesh* Smith and all who acknowledged Gladenism were cut of from the church.[111]

Monday 2nd Aug. 1852. To day Mr Cogswell's train of goods came in this morning. Wrote a letter to Hon. Isaiah Morris of Ohio To day the General election came of. The names of the candidates for the Legislature for this County were as follows. For Councillor to fill the place of Edward Hunter resigned. Franklin D. Richards for Representatives J. M. Grant W W Phelps, A P. Rockwood N. H. Felt E. D. Woolley, W Woodruff, H. Stout, D. Spencer, John Brown, N. V. Jones,[112] J. W. Cummings, J. C. Wright. I have not heard from the other precincts, but as there is no opposing candidates to my knowledge I presume they were all elected. There was only 150 votes poled in the city.

Tuesday Aug 3 1852. To day preparing the Gov proclamations &c as an appendix for the Journals of the Legislature now in course of Publication.

The code Commissioners to day organized for business and appointed Elias Smith Charman and myself clerk.

Wednesday Aug 4 1852. C. C met to day and obtained the Library room for the seat of Operations. Attended prayer circle at sun set.

Thursday Aug 5 - 1852. Engaged with the Code Commission and Legal affairs. Had a compromised case to day Lewis Dubois and others vs John M. Montgomery emegrants

Friday Aug 6th 1852. To day engaged as yesterday and finished the case of Dubois and others vs Montgomery Compromised and the parties all satisfied.

Saturday Aug 7 1852. Clerking for the Code Commissioners in preparing a Code of practice. Not well to day.

Sunday 8 Aug 1852. Went to meeting. President B. Young on the vision given to Joseph and Sidney. After noon at home.

Monday 9th Aug 1852. Engaged at the C. Commission affair attending to legal affairs. Jane Eliza Davis vs P H. Ellsworth compromised

Tuesday 10th Aug 1852. Attended a law suit befor Probate Court. The People vs. P. H. Ellsworth for resisting officer. fined $100 & costs of 55.25 in the afternoon

111. The Gladdenites were a group of Mormon dissenters but evidently not important enough to merit notice in Brigham Henry Roberts, *A Comprehensive History of the Church of Jesus Christ of Latter-day Saints* (6 vols., Salt Lake City, 1930), Orson F. Whitney's writings, or other official documents. They took their name from Gladden Bishop, who had been a member since the days of Joseph Smith. Hubert H. Bancroft, *History of Utah, 1540-1887* (San Francisco, 1891), 643.

112. Nathaniel V. Jones appears often in these pages. He was born October 13, 1822, at Brighton, New York; was baptized into the Mormon Church in 1842; and the next year came to Nauvoo. In 1846 he joined the Mormon Battalion, leaving behind his wife and two children. At his discharge he was appointed a guard to escort Colonel John C. Frémont back to the states.

In 1849 Jones brought his family west. In 1851 he was made a city alderman and soon after was appointed bishop of the Fifteenth Ward, Salt Lake County. He filled many missions of various kinds for the church, both before and after the one to which he is here called. In 1856 he was sent to the Las Vegas area to get out lead for bullets; during the "Mormon War" he was acting colonel in charge of activities in Echo Canyon. In 1861 he was sent to the southern part of the state to help with the production of iron. Jones died February 15, 1863, at the age of forty, as a result of overwork and exposure.

had another Martha Wood and Mrs Jones vs S. D. White in (all) the (these [crossed out]) last cases I was on the part of the plaintiff.

Wednesday 11th August 1852. Settling up the above cases. in the after noon had another suit W. H. South v. Francis Kenyon befor Judge E. Smith I was on part of Plff Furgerson for defence. Court adjourned the decisions till morning

Thursday 12 Aug 1852. Court decided for deft. No cause of action. Applied on old partnership Had another suit before same Edward Carrol v F. & C Kenyon in attachment I for Plff Furgerson for deft Judget for Plff 18.00 & costs. Took out Bill of exception in the case of South v. Kenyon.

Friday 13th Aug 1852. In the Library reading the most part of to day. Elder John S. Higby came in to day from a mission to buy land and the brethren are beginning to come in with their families from the Bluffs.

Saturday 14th Aug 1852. District Court to day, had some business before it of small importance. At two o'clock attended the city council which is trying to obtain reports from the different departments but the prospect to get any is dull.

Sunday 15 Aug 1852. At home till noon then went to meeting with wife. O. Pratt was preaching on the subject of our being begotten Sons of God &c

Monday 16th Aug. 1852. Code commissioners sat again to day and commenced writing a Code of practice for the Courts of law and Equity. I of course acting as their clerk today.

Tuesday 17 Aug. 1852. Engaged clerking for the C. Commisrs

Wednesday 18 Aug 1852. E[n]gaged as yesterday. Today a company came from Tous in New Mexico with a drove of 3,000 sheep A few days since another drove of 5,000 sheep passed through here from the same place. They are going to California with them. This evening attended prayer circle.

Thursday 19 Aug. 1852. Engaged with the code Commission Annother drove of sheep passed to day

Friday 20th Aug 1852. Engaged to day in the library alone Elders Taylor, Benson, Richards, Grant and others came in this evening from their missions.

Saturday 21. Aug. 1852. Cool day, but clear very like fall. To day a large company of Snake indians made their first visit to this place They are about making a treaty of peace with walker the Ute Chief. I was engaged with the Code Commissioners to day.

Sunday 22 Aug 1852. Wife went to visit her mother I went to meeting. Elders G. B. Wallace Franklin D. Richards, John Taylor and E. T. Benson, all who had just returned from missions, preached.

Monday 23. Aug 1852. Writing for Code Commissioners to day.

Tuesday 24th Aug 1852. Engaged with the Code Commissioners to day but was very unwell.

Wednesday 25th Aug 1852. Engaged with the code Commissioners
    Recieved fifty six dollars to day from the U. S. Goverment for Jos. L. Haywood, U. S. Marshall for serving in the District Court last february for prosocuting in the case of the people vs Wales and also in case of do vs Davis. The Govt has paid all the expenses of said Court for last winter.

Thursday 26 Aug 1852. Clerking for Code Commissioners

Friday 27 Aug 1852. The Eastern mail has come in but no news as I can learn of any importance yet except the death of Henry Clay of Kentucky and Gov Calhoon of New Mexico Not well to day I did nothing at the law. Wife came home.

PART II

August 28, 1852 to December 31, 1853

AUGUST 28, 1852 TO DECEMBER 31, 1853

Part II

This part of the diary covers the period from August 28, 1852, to December 31, 1853. Hosea Stout was called, with a number of others, to fill a mission for the Mormon Church, his assignment being to China. His preparations, his overland journey to San Diego, and his voyage by ship to San Francisco are all detailed. Among others who kept diaries of this part of the journey was Amos Milton Musser, who traveled with Stout.

Stout secured funds for his passage, made the long boat trip, tried to preach his gospel to uninterested people, and returned home to find his wife and baby dead and his other children living with his mother-in-law.

This part of the diary ends with his adjustment into life in Utah again.

Saturday August 28, 1852. To day was the Special Conference held for the pur- pose of sending Elders abroad. There was about 80 or 90 chosen to day to go forth to different parts of the world[1] I need not relate the particulars of all the different missions. Myself, James Lewis Walter Thompson and Chapman Duncán were chosen to go to China

The brethren who were chosen all manifest a good spirit & seem to have the spirit of their Calling. I feel well pleased with the mission allotted to me and feel in the name of my master to full it to the honor and glory of God.

Sunday 29 Aug 1852. Attended Conference to day. Orson Pratt preached to day on the subject of Polygamy or plurality of wives as believed and practiced by the Latter day Saints.

In the after noon the Revelation on that subject given to Joseph on the 12th of July 1843 was publicly read for the first time to the great joy of the Saints who have looked forward so long and so anxiously for the time to come when we could

---

1. The Mormons believed that they must preach the gospel to "every nation, kindred, tongue, and people," and then the end would come. This, the most extensive undertaking they had yet tried, was generally disappointing. For a summary with details of missions and men involved, see Roberts, *Comprehensive History*, IV, 68-76.

publickly declare the true and greatest principles of our holy religion and the great things which God has for his people to do in this dispensation[2]

I feel that the work of the Lord will rool forth with a renewed impetus. The nations of the earth will be wakened up to an investigation of the truth of the gospel and the nation that has driven us out of their midst so unjustly and unlawfully will have to again investigate our principals and thousands among them will yet be brought to and understanding of the truth by virtue of this revelation

Immediately after Conference adjourned the missionaries met at the Council house to make arraingements preparitory to their departure The eastern mission will leave first and then arraingements for those going west will be made.

Monday 30 Aug 1852. Attending to some 8 or 9 law suits now pending in the probate Court. Also preparing to start on my mission to China.

Tuesday 31 Aug 1852. Engaged in lawing to day in a suit before Judge Smith wherein A. L. Whedon was plff and J. W. and O. Shaw was deft. in debt I was on the part of the plff and Furgurson for deft. Plff obtained a judgement for thirty five dollars. This evening went with my wife and Eliza Lyman to a party made by Br J. M. Gammel for those who were going on missions. We had a good oyster supper and enjoyed ourselves extreemly well till about mid night.

Wednesday 1 Sept 1852. Around preparing for my mission and also prayer circle at sun set.

Thursday 2nd Sept 1852. Around as yesterday. At two met with the city council John Van Cott, N. V. Jones and myself resigned our seats in the council as we were going on missions.

Friday 3 Sept 1852. To day my wife and youngest child was very sick. My wife was unable to set up most of the day and I was attending to them

To day Smoots' company of Saints came in.[3] They were met and escorted by the president & Band. They are bringing in the *Bones* of Elders Burton and Barnes who died on a mission to England.[4]

Saturday 4 Sept 1852. Engaged in preparing some law suits to day. In the afternoon suit commenced. M. H. Bisly v. H. L. Hawley damage on breach of contract to take to C Judgement 33.33 and costs apportioned. I for Plff Furgerson for deft two other cases then compromised Wm Johnson & Thos Smith v same for same we were until 9 o'clock P. M before it was all settled.

---

2. The law of "Celestial Marriage" had been revealed to a few select friends of Joseph Smith as early as 1839 and was given orally to some of the Twelve Apostles in 1842, but it was not written and formally presented until July 12, 1843. Even then it was publicly denied, even among the Mormon congregation, many in Nauvoo not learning of it until after the exodus. Some converts came all the way to the Salt Lake Valley before they knew of its practice.

Hosea expressed the general sentiment of many of the church membership. For the next fifty years the Mormons preached and practiced plurality of wives proudly and defiantly.

3. This was the first company to come under the Perpetual Emigrating Fund. Under the direction of Abram O. Smoot, they had chartered a ship at Liverpool and traveled in thirty-one wagons from Iowa and brought to Utah people who otherwise could not have left England. This in itself was enough to bring out the Mormon leaders, Pitt's Band, and a group of relatives and friends; but the fact that they were also carrying the remains of two elders who had died abroad made it a public occasion.

4. Elder William Burton died at Edinburgh, Scotland, on March 17, 1851. Elder Lorenzo D. Barnes died at Bradford, England, December 20, 1842, the first Mormon elder to succumb on foreign soil. Born in 1812, he had joined the church in 1832, been a member of Zion's Camp and of the High Council at Far West, and was active in Nauvoo. Memorial services were held for him in that city with Joseph Smith preaching the funeral sermon.

Sunday 5 Sept 1852. Wife and youngest child very sick. Went to meeting but the Tabernacle was so crouded that I did not stay in.

Monday 6 Sept 1852. Around town to day not doing much

Tuesday 7 Sept 1852. Around as yesterday. In the evening had a law-suit before Judge Smith. Samuel Backus vs Michael King in debt demand fifty dollars. The trial was laid over till tomorrow at ten o'clock in the morning

Wednesday 8th Sept 1852. Attended to the lawsuit of yesterday judgement for plff. 10 dollars. in the after noon another suit before same. The people vs John Hously on the complaint of Andrew Hooper (for a [crossed out]) on the part of a minor Boy which Hously has, charging him with abusing the boy. the court decided the boy should be given up I was on the part of the people and took the boy home with me to night. His name is Henry Allen a fine peart lad about Eleven years old

Thurs & Friday 9 & 10 Sept 1852. Around town settling up my small affairs preparitory to my leaving.

Saturday 11th Sept. 1852. To day the brethren who were appointed to go on Missions met at the Tabernacle to recieve their blessings and to be set apart on their missions The roll of all those who are going East was called and nearley all reported themselves ready to start next Monday. After which they adj'd for dinner and met at two o'clock. The Twelve proceeded to bless and set apart the High Priests and the Presidents of the Seventies viz Jos Young A. P. Rockwood and J. M. Grant to Bless and set apart the Seventies and thus passed the after noon.

Sunday 12th Sept 1852. The Seventies met at the Council House to recieve their blessings who did not yesterday. Then went to meeting. Elder O. Pratt preached the funeral sermon of Brs Barns and Burton who died in England whose bones were brought here a few days ago.
  In the after J. M. Grant and others spoke against the distillerys and grog shops tipling shops &c also against some paper money now in the city being put in circulation &c &c

Monday 13th Sept 1852. This fore noon wrote a petition for Divorce before Elias Smith Judge of Probate. Elizabeth Mount vs Joseph Mount, after which attended a suit before same. Adeoline Bush vs Richard Bush in divorce. petition allowed. Afternoon spent in settling up my affairs. The brethren are preparing to go East on their missions.

Tuesday 14th Sept 1852. Like for rain to day, The brethrern are "rolling out" to day on their Eastern mission while I am trying to fit out for mine West

Wednesday 15th Sept 1852. Brethren still "rolling out" Rainy eve Spent the day as yesterday. Attended prayer circle at sun set, after which attended the Theatre an hour or so.

Thursday 16th Sept 1852. Around to day as before.

Friday 17th Sept 1852. Around to day as before.

Saturday 18th Sept 1852. Around to day as before

Sunday 19 Sept 1852. Wife & I went to meeting in the fore noon. Elder Sherwood preached his farewell sermon before he starts to move to Lower California In the after noon went to meeting

Monday 20th Sept 1852. Preparing and trading around for my out fit West.

Tuesday 21 Sept. 1852. Engaged as yesterday.

Wednesday 22 Sept 1852. Engaged as yesterday and in the evening attended a Law Suit before Esqr William Snow Samual Cooley vs William Westwood in debt 82 dollars   I was for deft and Peter Van Valkenburgh for plff   we were up till mid night.   Judgement vs Deft $22.25. cents.

Thursday 23rd Sept 1852. Arrainging my Goverment claims for sale. (and reading proof of the journal of the Legislature. [crossed out])

Friday 24 Sept 1852. Reading proof of journal of the Legislature.

Saturday 25 Sept 1852. Went to Allen J. Stouts to day. Around the City.

Sunday 26th Sept 1852. Went to meeting J. M. Grant and John Taylor preached. In the after noon I was over hauling my things and preparing to start on my mission.

Monday 27th Sept 1852. The Eastern mail came in last night but the news I have not learned yet   I am to over hauling and preparing as yesterday.

Tuesday 28th Sept 1852. Making arraingements to go on my mission. This evening I effected a trade with Messrs Levingston & Kinkead for my Goverment claim of 580 dollars for preparing the laws and journals of the last Legislature for printing and am to take goods for it.

This with 42 dollars which I traded with them some time since in all amounting to Six hundred and twenty two dollars in all is "material aid" just as I am going on a mission for which I feel unusually greatful to my Heavenly Father for and feel encouraged to press on to the accomplishing of every duty enjoined on me by the priesthood untill I shall have finished my probation on this earth.

Wednesday 29 Sept 1852. Winding up my affairs quite fast to day   The prospects for my leaving and leaving my family in good circumstances are coming out better than my sanguine expectation.   This evening I read another proof sheets of the Journal of the Legislature

Thursday 30th Sept 1852. To day I paid up all my back tithing amounting to one hundred and ten dollars.

Then contracted with Br D. H. Wells, Superintendent of the Public Works to build me a house 18 feet square with a good cellar under it.   The house to be one story high.   I paid him in advance three hundred and forty dollars towards it and shall if no disappointment happens pay about one hundred more before I leave.

Very unexpectedly did I find myself able to procure the building of a comfortable house for my family before going on a long mission. Otherwise they would have had to remained in the old log ones   which will neither screen them from wind snow, or rain   This I esteem a special act of providence for when I was first set apart to this mission I did not know how I could procure a scanty outfit without selling my farm or other things which would leave my family very destitute.   This evening another rain storm commenced

Friday 1st Oct 1852. rainy day but not much wind.   The snow lies on the Mountains almost to their base.   I was not well to day and did not transact much business, only traded some little in the store.

Saturday 2nd October 1852. This morning 4 hands came from the public works and commenced to dig my cellar.

Attend a law suit before William Snow Esqr at one P. M.   Robert Willson John vs B. Dushamps in debt 85 dollars   The trial was adjourned for want of evidence.

Sunday 3rd Oct 1852. Went to meeting as usual at The Tabernacle.

Monday Oct 4th 1852. Got my horse to day which I need for traveling. To day my brother-in-law Joseph Taylor brought from my farm a load of wheat. He and his brothers William and Levi had the kindness to thrash and clean all my crop of wheat gratis as I was going on a mission. This was a great accommodation to me for I was too busy here to do any thing with it myself May they be rewarded an hundred fold for this kind act

Tuesday Oct 5th 1852. Doing but little to day. Wet eveing

Wednesday 6th Oct 1852. Today the Semi-annual Conference commenced at the Tabernacle at ten a. m. Elder J. D. Ross preached the first discourse on the House of Israel and was followed by O. Hyde and J. M. Grant when conference adjourned till two o'clock P. M. In the after noon I did not stay in the Tabernacle the House was too warm & unhealthy so I came home. Had and over stock of company & my wife & youngest child being quite out of health made things go rather hard and unpleasant.

Thursday 7th Oct 1852. Went to Conference but the Tabernacle was so crouded I did not stay there The Seventies had a meeting at Tabernacle at dark to take into consideration the Seventies Hall I attended nothing was done.

Friday 8th Oct 1852. Attended Conference in the fore noon. Prest B. Young spoke In the after noon did not go. Not well. My youngest child unwell. Myself unwell. We are much crouded and not much to eat

Saturday 9th Oct 1852. This morning I am badly afflicted with sore throat and child dangerous Staid at home company all left to day.
  We are all about used up and eat out. Conference has been a hard tug on us this time.[5]

Sunday 10th Oct 1852. Went to Conference to day but the congregation was so crouded that I did not stay, not being very well There was hundreds more than could get in the Tabernacle. G. A. Smith preached to a large congregation out doors. Conference adjourned to day. The missionarys met at the Council House and those who live south recieved their blessings.

Monday 11th Oct 1852. To day I sold my carpenter tools for sixty five dollars & paid the same over to the public works towards paying for my house.
  Attended prayer circle this evening.

Tuesday 12th Oct. 1852. Arraing and settling up my affairs Went to Allen Stouts. His oldest son is very sick and so is all my children. Went to see Abram Palmer who has just come in from the States one of the "old police" He almost blind

Wednesday 13th Oct 1852. Went to mill to day but did not get my grinding.
  This evening I assigned the rest of my government claims to D. H Wells a mounting to Seven Hundred and seven dollars. He is to collect them for me and pay the same over to my wife the the medium of the church.

Thursday 14th Oct 1852. Went to mill to day and got part of my grinding and then in the evening sold twenty dollars of my books to the Church towards paying for the building my house This amounts to 425 dollars that I have paid towards building the house.

---

5. The custom of families coming in to conference from the outlying settlements and staying with relatives often proved to be a real hardship on the host family, as Hosea here indicates.

Friday 15th Oct 1852. Very unwell to day and did not much   My children is very sick yet all three of them.[6]

It seems that the destroyer is determined to use up my family on the eve of my leaving.

Saturday 16th Oct 1852. To day the Elders who are going on the Western missions met at the Council House to recieve their Blessings.   But before I met with them I went and with several others were baptized by Bp A. Hoagland.   Henry Allen the boy who lives with me was also baptized   He was bound to me this week.[7]   I recieved my blessing under the hands of Elder Wilford Woodruff one of the Twelve Apostles, which was as follows

Br Hosea in the name of Jesus Christ of Nazareth, and by virtue of the Holy priesthood confered upon us, we lay our hands upon thy head and set the apart unto the mission whereunto thou art called by the revelations of Jesus Christ through the Servants of God.   And we bless thee with the blessings of Abraham Isaac & Jacob, and with the spirit and power of thy mission

We ask God the Eternal Father to grant unto thee, the Comforter, that it may be poured out upon thee, to be a light to thy feet and a lamp to thy path that thou may be clothed with light, and filled with joy, that that the spirit and power of God may rest upon thee more fully than it ever has been in all the days of thy life

Let thy heart be comforted, for the Lord thy God shall make thee as a flaming sword in his hand, thy toungue shall be loosed, and thy voice shall be as the voice of the angels of God, thou shalt have power to go forth to that nation, whose bars have been strong, and who have been secluded from all nations under heaven in the generations that have past and gone.

The Lord has opened a way for thy foot steps to go among that people, and thou shalt do a great work there, thy words shall be as the words of the angels of God unto them, and they shall recive them, and thousands shall be brought into the kingdom of God through thy instrumentality.

Thou shalt have power to command the elements and they shall obey thee, Thou shalt have power to perform mighty miricles, and cast out divils heal the sick, and cause the blind to see, the lame to (walk [crossed out]) leap as an hart; for when thou shalt command in the name of the Lord thy commands shall be obeyed, because the eyes of thy heavenly father shall watch over thee for good, and the Holy Ghost shall accompany thee to perform all that thy heart desires, therefore be comforted. Though the nation and people may be shrouded in darkness, and the prospects before thee gloomy yet it shall be light, and thy feet shall walk the land whereunto thou art sent, and the angels of God shall prepare the way before thee.   Thou shalt find funds, and in a singular manner. and that people shall recieve the gospel, and be geathered unto Zion, because of the mighty power of the most High God.   Many shall also recieve the Holy Priesthood, for much of the seed of Abraham is among that people.

Go thy way trusting in the Lord, and thou shalt return again to thy family and friends with honor and glory upon thy head, and the time thou hast

6. The three children are Elizabeth Ann, born March 19, 1848; Hosea, Jr., born April 5, 1850 (it was customary to name a second son after the father if the first had died); and Eli Harvey born September 17, 1851.

7. Henry Allen became a member of the Stout family at this time and remained with them until 1861. For Hosea's responsibility toward him, see footnote 94, Volume II, Part 1.

employed in passed days in treasuring up knowledge of Countries and laws, shall be of use unto thee, even a great advantage, and the Lord. shall give thee power to obtain a knowledge of their langauge so as to have access to them, and ordain men who shall assist the in spreading the gospel through that mighty nation. We seal these blessings upon thy head and say it is one of the most important missions that was ever given to any who have yet gone to the nations of the earth, and thou shalt have power to honor it. When snares are set for thy feet thou shalt have power to escape them, and be like Nephi and Alma who over came their enemies and every obsticle through their faith and the power of God. This shall be thy lot therefore go forth and and all shall be right with thee

We seal these blessings upon thy head and seal thee up to eternal life, and say no power shall take thy crown, and God shall give thee all thy heart desires. We ask our heavenly Father to acknowledge these blessings and seal them upon thee, and we will ascribe all honor and power, and glory to God and the Lamb now and for ever Amen.

Taken by George D. Watt

Reporter'

The day was spent in blessing the missionaries

Sunday 17th Oct 1852. Went to meeting to day at the Tabernacle. In the after noon I was called to the stand to preach which I did for a short time and bore my testimony to the truth of the work of God in the Last Days My son Hosea is now very sick and badly afflicted with canker and a high fever. It seems that the Destroyer is seeking to thwart the purposes of God by afflicting my family but I feel to say in the name of the Lord Jesus Christ that the power of the destroyer shall be rebuked in my family that my children shall be healed and their lives and the life of my wife held precious before the Lord. That they shall be prospered and protected from all evil even untill I return from my mission because I know that it is the will of my heavenly father for it to be so. Which may God seal in the heavens. **Amen.**

My other two children are better.

Monday 18th Oct 1852. Today I traded for another Horse which I think will answer my purpose and am now ready to start on my mission as soon as my horse is shod. which will be tomorrow

Tuesday 19th Oct. 1852. To day I have got my business all wound up to my perfect Satisfaction. I have been prospered beyond my most sanguine expectations in all things since I was appointed to go on a mission to China & I feel that the hand of the Lord is upon me for good notwithstanding the sickness and affliction of my children. I feel the assuranc that they will recover and my family be prospered while I am gone. I feel to dedicate my family, my self and my all to the God of Israel invoking his blessings upon them for it will be verily so. I have been enabled to leave my family well provided for in good and clothing besides some Eighty dollars worth of wood on good and responsible men and forty dollars in beef and pork or wood at the option of my wife as well as one hundred and twenty dollars in cash besides a good comfortable house now in progress of building for all of which I feel that the Lord has blessed me with, in a most singular manner.

Besides all this I have deposited with Br Daniel H. Wells, claims on the goverment amounting to seven hundred and seven dollars, which if he succeeds in collecting will amply sustain my family for a long time, yet, independent of all these recourses I have not the least doubt but my family will be well provided for and do well, for I leave them in the hands of the Lord and commend them to his mercy and guardian care which will ever be extended over them and shield them from all harm.

To day the stone commenced to be drawn for the cellar wall of my house

Wednesday Oct. 20th 1852. This is the day which we expect to start on our mission I am going with Brs Chauncey W. West,[8] Richard Balentine[9] and William Fortheringham[10] and are all going in one Waggon with four animals attached to it We expect to start about ten o'clock a. m. and go to Dry Creek in Utah County to day

[A double entry appears for this day because the second entry marks the beginning of Hosea's China Mission diary.]

Wednesday 20th October 1852. About one o clock p. m. all things being ready the waggon drove up to my house and my travelling companions viz Chauncey W. West, Richard Balentine and William Fotheringham, when my luggage was soon loaded into our waggon and after taking the parting hand with my wife and children commending them to the tender mercies of God I bid adieu not only to them but to all the Saints in the peaceful city of Salt Lake and took my departure to a nation whose language manners and customs I knew not.

My brother Allen & Thomas Bullock accompanied us some three miles on our way when we bid them farewell they returned & we proceeded on our journey 12 miles & Staid all night with Charles Terry who furnished us with all the feed for our animals which we needed & for our selves a good supper.

Thursday 21 Oct. 1852. Travelled on this morning 12 miles to Joel Terry's, who regaled us with what Beer we could drink.

At noon we found ourselves on the point of the Utah mountain where we took our last look at Great Salt Lake City. A light cloudy fog rested on it, in which we could see President Brigham Young's House, like Solomon's Temple in the midst of the glory of God.[11]

Here we bid a last adieu to the peaceful city and again commended our families to the tender mercies of God, and proceeded on our way, arriving at Lehi City we put up at Bishop David Evans, who was awaiting our arrival, to feed our animals

---

8. The entire company was divided with four men to a wagon to camp and prepare their food together. Hosea's messmates became men of some distinction. Chauncey W. West, born February 6, 1827, in Erie County, Pennsylvania, came to Nauvoo in 1844 where at the age of seventeen he was made a Seventy. He arrived in the Valley of the Great Salt Lake in late.1847 and was among the first to move to Provo. Here he joined the Parley P. Pratt exploring expedition to the south. He was twenty-five years old at the time of this mission.

After he returned, West settled at Ogden where he became a leader in business enterprises— promoting roads, canals, and sawmills. He also owned a store, a hotel, a tannery, a livery stable, a blacksmith shop, and a meat market. With Ezra T. Benson and Lorin Farr, West took contracts for the construction of the transcontinental railroad. The competition and trouble with competing companies impaired his health, and he died in San Francisco on January 9, 1870.

9. Richard Ballantine (also Ballantyne), the eldest of the three, was born August 26, 1817, in Scotland. In his boyhood he learned the bakers' trade but abandoned it upon coming to America. In Nauvoo he was manager and bookkeeper of the Coach and Carriage Association. He also worked in the printing establishment with John Taylor.

Ballantine came to Utah in the Brigham Young company of 1848, and in 1849 he organized the first Sunday schools in the church. After this mission he brought home a company of emigrants in 1855. In 1860 he moved to Ogden and for many years prospered greatly but lost most of his fortune in the depression of 1893. He died in Ogden, November 8, 1898.

10. William Fotheringham, like Chauncey W. West, was a younger man and like Ballantine, was Scottish. Born April 5, 1826, in Scotland, he was baptized in 1847 and arrived in Utah in 1849. He was an early settler in Lehi, arriving there in 1850. He died February 27, 1913, in Milford, Beaver County, Utah.

11. That President Young's house did look imposing is shown by the comments of a visitor of this same fall: "What a singular spectacle! We beheld what seemed a thickly-settled neighborhood, apparently about a mile distant from us, composed of low, lead-colored dwellings, with a single white building occupying a prominent position . . . ." Ferris, *Mormons At Home*, 93.

on good oats and ourselves with the best he had. Here we put up, but I went on to Br Bell's and took dinner and paid a visit to my aged mother-in-law- Mary Bennett, who I had not seen for some seven years. We had an agreeable visit for about two hours after which we travelled on some 4 miles and put up for the night with Robinson, who treated us with the hospitality becoming a saint of God.

Friday 22 Oct 1852. Travelled on this morning some 14 miles to provo city. putting up with Oliver Stratton and took dinner and fed our animals, after which we proceeded on the Peeteetneet and put up at Charles Shumway's about two hours after dark. After supper I went and staid all night with A. J. Stewart. Here we met with some ten or twelve of our brethren, who had started before us with whom we expect to travel the rest of the way to Calafornia. Here we were all kindly recieved and entertained as we have been previously

Saturday 23 Oct 1852. Good weather this morning. Got an earley start and went 6 miles to Summitt Creek. Here we found a few more of our missionary brethren The train of waggons now make quite an imposing appearance. Travelling on ten miles we came to Willow Creek where we fed our animals with Br Wolfe who was standing in the road with a Sheaf of wheat under his arm waiting for us to come as he said for our animals to eat his grain for he had more than he knew what to do with.

After partaking of Br Wolfe's hospitality to our full desire we proceeded on ten miles to Salt Creek. We put up with Bishop G. W. Bradley and the rest of the company among the saints all of whom were kindly treated by all.

This evening we held a meeting at the School House We nearley all spoke our feelings and had a good meeting, speaking in the name of the Lord and prophecying. Here we over took the advance of those who had gone before us, & nearly all the missionaries are now together.

After meeting it was agreed to tarry over Sabbath and give those in our rear an opportunity to over take us, wishing to pass from here to Fillmore in a body.

Sunday 24th Oct. 1852. Meeting at ten a. m. which was well attended Elder James Brown first spoke, followed by others of the missions, all of whom was filled with the Spirit and power of God predicting that the spirit and power of God would attend us on our missions. The way would be opened before us and mens hearts would be soften to administer to our wants when ever we would need it &c also that success would attend our word. and many would obey the gospel.

At intermission myself & W McBride took dinner with Thomas Tranter. The good feelings and liberality of the Saints here seem unbounded, all seem to vie with each other in administering to our wants & the wants of our animals

At one P. M. Had another meeting. Elder Wm Hyde[12] spoke, followed by several others with the same spirit and power as before after which the Elders held a meeting to take into consideration the subject of organizing ourselves so as to pass the Indian country in safety; whereupon the folling persons were chosen to the following offices viz.

---

12. William Hyde, for whom Hyde Park in Cache County was later named, was born September 11, 1818, in York, Livingston County, New York, the son of a well-to-do farmer and wool-carder. He joined the Mormons on April 7, 1834, and came to Kirtland in 1836; he went on to Far West, Missouri, in 1838 and to the site of Nauvoo in 1839. Hyde filled several missions for the church during this early period and in 1846 joined the Mormon Battalion under Jesse W. Hunter, arriving in the Salt Lake Valley on September 22, 1849.

Hyde was one of this missionary group called to Australia where he remained for more than a year and returned in March 1854 with a company of sixty-three Saints. In 1860 he moved into Cache Valley where he set up a wool-carding machine, a grist mill, and a store. He was made the first bishop of the Hyde Park Ward and probate judge of Cache County; he held both offices until his death on March 2, 1874.

Hosea Stout Capt
Nathaniel V. Jones Chaplain
Burr Frost [13] Seargeant of the guard
Amos M. Musser[14] Clerk.

This evening those in our rear came up I recieved a letter from William Stout of San Bernardino enquiring as to our relationship.

All the missionaries are now present except Brs Lewis & Duncan who are in Parowan waiting for us to come by, when they will join us

Monday 25 Oct 1852. This morning we bid adieu to the good people of Salt Creek and proceeded on our way 25 miles to Sevier River encamping on its banks. Rainy evening or drizzling mist Mounted guard to night for the first time since we started. I stood the first tour.

Tuesday 26 Oct 1852. Wet and muddy Heavy drizzling mist. Travelled three miles down the river and crossed, all safe over, Overtook a train of Emegrants and some saints on their way to Calafornia. Travelled 14 miles and baited on the mountain side after which we travelled on to Cedar Creek 25 m to day Here we encamped on good feed.

Wednesday 27 Oct 1852. Clear cold morning, all well. Went on 9 miles to Fillmore City.

Here the Saints took us, fed ourselves & animals and treated us with the same warm feelings of hospitality that we have met with since we left home. Visited the site for the State House which is partly built. It is on a beautiful elevation & will most likely be ready for the Legislature in one year from this time

I and some others took our dinner with President Anson Call In the evening we held a meeting at which I first spoke and was followed by James Lawson N. V. Jones & W McBride.

Thursday 28 Oct 1852. Clear & cool morning. This morning attended to a lawsuit before the Probate Court of Millard County Territory vs Halyard for resisting officer for which he gave me a cow which I sold to A. Call for 20 dollars which I took in corn for the company. Br Call then gave me five dollars.

We then proceeded over a rough road for 12 miles encamping on Corn Creek

Friday 29 Oct 1852. Travelled on about 20 miles to cove Creek Rainy sleightly & Roads heavey.

Saturday 30 Oct 1852. This morning we met William H. Kimball on his return from Iron County by whom I sent five dollars to my wife Travelled to Bever Creek 30 miles.

Sunday 31 Oct 1852. We had no grass for our animals last night and our feed is nearley gone. Started at sun rise and went some 8 miles and baited our animals on a mountain top after which we proceeded to Red Creek [Paragonah] 27 miles to day

---

13. Burr Frost, born March 8, 1815, in Connecticut, was a well-known blacksmith. He had come to Utah with the 1847 pioneers, and in 1850 accompanied the group to Parowan, returning to Salt Lake City in 1851. After this mission he spent most of his time in Salt Lake City where he died March 16, 1878.

14. Amos Milton Musser kept a daily record of this trip which closely parallels that of Stout. Born May 20, 1830, in Pennsylvania, Musser had arrived in Utah in 1849 and had been employed as a clerk in the Tithing Office. After his return from this mission, he became a clerk for Brigham Young, then traveling bishop from 1858 to 1876. His later years were spent in the Historian's Office. He died September 24, 1909. For a more complete account of Musser's life, see Karl Brooks, "Amos Milton Musser" (Master's thesis, Brigham Young University, 1962).

Here we found a small settlement of Saints seven families, as few as there was they rejoiced in the priviledge of entertaining us over night and would not consent for us to go any farther.

Here I found job & Charles Hall who came with me in the guard when we left Nauvoo in the Spring of 1846. They were then only mere boys, but now are married and doing well.

Their goodness and kindness to me and my family then, in the days of my deepest affliction, as well as their devotedness to the cause of God, can never be forgotten by me while the feelings of gratitude burns in my bosom. I took supper with Job.

Monday 1 Nov. 1852. This morning after taking breakfast here we proceeded on to Parowan City where we found President George A. Smith and nearley all the people of the place waiting our arrival who recieved us under the American flag which proudly floated over us while we carralled under it.

After sending our animals out to graze we scattered among the people and had Homes Had a meeting in the evening at which the missionaries occupied mostly.

Tuesday 2 Nov 1852. This morning the missionaries met at the School house to take into consideration our furture movements G. A. Smith was present who proposed that the temporary organization at Salt Creek be continued The clerk then made out the Statistics of the company as follows.

> 38 missionaries Elders
> 3 other men
> 1 woman & 1 child[15]
> 15 waggons
> 46 Horses and mules.

After which we were engaged in procuring our horse feed and arrainging our affairs for our journey untill 2 o'clock, when we assembled at the Tabernacle with the brethren and sisters of the place to enjoy a party got up expressly for ourselves. We had joyful time dancing, relieved occasionally by singing untill mid-night

Wednesday 3 Nov 1852. To day we put up our horse feed and other necessaries for our journey which the Saints here freely donated to us. Snowy day.

Thursday 4 Nov 1852. To day was a regular fast day for the people of Parowan. All met and spent the day preachin & praying

In the evening G. S. Smith delivered a lecture to the missionaries relative to our duty while abroad among the several Nations. Sent one letter to Prest B. Young and one to my wife.[16]

Friday 5 Nov 1852. This morning we took the parting hand with the saints of Parowan and proceeded on our journey to Cole Creek 18 miles, where we were recieved by President Heny Lunt and the authorities of the place, with the same spirit of good feelings and kindness, that we have met with since we left our homes. They came in flocks to meet us and bid us welcome to their homes and our animals to their grain. Took supper with Sister Easton, after which we held a meeting at the School House, where the saints came to hear from us. I delivered an address for about one hour and was followed by several other Elders.

---

15. The "3 other men, 1 woman & 1 child," joined the company only as far as the settlement at Coal Creek, Cedar City, Iron County, Utah.

16. The letter to his wife summarizes the trip thus far and expresses his love and concern for her. The original is owned by Mr. Lafayette Lee of Salt Lake City. A copy, dated November 7, 1852, is part of the volume of miscellaneous writings of Hosea Stout at the Utah State Historical Society.

Saturday 6 Nov. 1852. Clear pleasant weather again. This morning, went with several of the Elders and brethren of the place to see the Iron Works just commenced here, which promises fair soon to produce Iron sufficient for the demands of the people of Utah. We then paid a strolling visit to the beautiful Site for the future location of Cedar City, the beautiful situation of which I need not describe.

At half past two P. M. met again at the School House for worship, singing and dancing which was continued untill 12 A. M.

Sunday 7 Nov. 1852. Held another meeting which was occupied by the missionaries In the after noon Prest G. A. Smith was there & James Lewis and Chapman Duncan[17] also came which now constitutes all the missionaries who are now alltogether. In the evening G. A. Smith delivered an address Specially for the missionaries, in which discourse he delivered the following prophecy which however is only an extract of what he said viz: Speaking of the Missionary Elders present.

"Every people to whom they preach, their words shall (kindle [crossed out]) tingle in their ears, every language they shall engage to learn, they shall learn it, and shall learn it quicker than any one who has learned it hitherto. — and they shall, many of them, be called to stand before the kings and princes of the earth, and shall bear that testimony to them which will bring to pass the saying that kings shall be their nursing fathers and Queens their nursing mothers, In th name of Israel's God — amen.

After meeting I sent a letter to "Deseret News"

A tribute of praise is due the Saints of this place, for their hospitality to us, most of whom were strangers to me, yet I was recieved with that tenderness and affection which a mother would manifest for the return of a long absent son.

Monday 8 Nov 1852. To day about noon we took the parting hand with the good saints here and proceeded on our journey. Here we left the borders of Saints in Utah and launched forth into the Deserts and mountains and now feel that we have left our homes

Encamped at Iron Springs 9 miles, where we found a company of Emegrants of some 20 waggons.

Tuesday 9 Nov. 1852. Travelled 24 miles to Pynte [Pinto] Creek. Windy night & poor grass & only on the high mountain tops

Wednesday 10th Nov 1852. Travelled 9 miles to a creek on the Summit of the Basin rim, baited & dinnered & went on passing over the rim decended over hills & ravines rapidly to Santa Clara 12 miles. The mountains are lowering to wards the South and the climate sensibly warmer

Thursday 11 Nov 1852. Travelled down the Santa Clara in a deep Cañon. Road rough, sandy & heavy for our teams. Weather warm as summer Baited a short

---

17. Since these two men are to be Hosea Stout's companions traveling with him for months, and since he nowhere makes any comment about them, it would seem appropriate to introduce them here. James Lewis was born January 12, 1814, at Gorham, Maine, and was baptized into the Mormon Church at Keokuk, Iowa, in 1842. He went to Nauvoo that year and the next was sent on a mission to the Eastern States. He came to Utah in 1849, bringing with him a wife not yet eighteen years old and two young children. In 1850 they were sent with the first group to Parowan. At this time he set out for China leaving his wife with three children and another to be born within a month. Eventually she bore him fourteen children, twelve of whom grew to maturity.

After Lewis' return, he was sent to southern Utah, the Cotton Mission, in 1861; later he taught school in Panaca, Nevada; in 1871 he moved to Kanab, Utah. In 1882 he was called to go to San Juan County, Utah, but after a few years returned to Kanab where he died.

Chapman Duncan was born July 1, 1812, at Bath, New Hampshire, and came to Utah in 1848. He left two wives, each with one child, when he went on this mission. He too lived on the frontier all his life. He died in Loa, Utah, December 22, 1900.

time at noon and encamped at Camp Springs which on a mountain top   26 miles to day.   Two Piutes camp this evening who after being disarmed staid all night and were civil & we fed them well.

Friday 12 Nov. 1852. Earley start.   Up hill for six miles & heavy road, warm & sultry.   We found a kind of mountain Plumb which is in great abundance & a most excellent fruit where we treated ourselves abundantly.   Passed over a high mountain, decending a Cañon baited a short time, and travelled to Rio Virgin 26 miles to day Hard drive.

An old green Dutch Doctor who has been trying to keep up with us, was left behind his Horses gave out and two passengers of his Dutch too, cut out leaving him & overtook us at dark, begging to be allowed to stay in the company.   Doctor Dutch would not leave his team though given out choosing rather to risk the Indian hospitality than leave his given-out team.

Saturday 13 Nov 1852. Sultry weather.   Heavy sandy road nooned & went on only 12 miles Stopped in the timber at good feed

Sunday 14 Nov 1852. Lay up to rest our animals   Held meeting & then went on some five miles road as usual.

Monday 15 Nov. This morning N. V. Jones is very sick.   Animals well filled and look well, Road as usual still going down Rio Virgin which we cross 16 miles Sultry weather.

10 Piutes in camp to night whom we disarmed   They are rather ill mannerly.

Tuesday 16 Nov. 1852. Leaving the Rio Virgin, now comes the tug, to ascend the mountan which is very high and steep having to ascend at a place where we had to assist our animals up with ropes for they could not pull but little some places it took 20 men to pull a waggon up which however we accomplished by noon having the last waggon up but our men and teams were nearly exhausted

Br Jones is getting weaker & now is very low   We now proceeded on to Muddy about 20 miles over an unusual rough road & warm day. We came to Muddy one hour after dark, go[o]d feed.

Wednesday 17 Nov. 1852. Went 3 miles up the Muddy & baited and took in water to cross the 50 mile desert.

Indians in large numbers geathered around our company.   One stole a lasso and was detected in an attempt to steel a pair of boots & Burr Frost gave him a decent whaling, after which we drove them off not allowing them in camp any more.   But they posted themselves on the hills and commenced hallowing to us, Narra Wap, Narra Wap (Swap, Swap) Shaking their articles of trade at us, to which we paid no attention   .

The Indians on the Rio Virgin & Muddy are the most low and contemptible I ever saw and show the most degraded & dishonest disposition.   They are worse than the Otoes & Omahas & I believe they are more treacherous and fickle.   About 12 we left, rough road for 12 miles & baited at sun set after which we went on untill ten at night when we encamped being about 30 miles in the desert.

Thursday 18 Nov 1852. Started very earley and arrived at Los Vagus 52 miles from Muddy about 4 P. M.   This is the first stream, since we left the basin which, I have seen that could be used for irrigation, or where the Soil would produce any thing for the use of civilized man.   Here we found the wild cabbage, evidently the original of the tame; also grapes vines in abundance presenting the appearance of an old dilapidated vinyard.

The grape vines, the luxuriant soil in the extensive valley, all conspire to make this a most desirable spot for man to be,   Like the oasis of Arabia the weary traveller can here set down in calm repose & rest himself, after passing the parched desert. But there is no timber, neither water sufficient to sustain a settlement sufficiently large to secure against Indian depredations. N. V. Jones is yet very weak & sick and feeble. He has some complaint on his lungs, and will most likely not be able to travel only in his wagon while we are going to San Bernardino.

Friday 19 Nov 1852. Last night was a rainy night, all well, Good feed in abundance Did not start till late in the morning.

There is now Snow on the distant mountain tops but warm here. We only went five miles to day in consequence of Br Jones' health and encamped at the head of Los Vagus which is formed of a boiling Spring of pure water about blood heat. This Spring is some 20 feet in diamiter, of a circular form, the water about 2 feet deep, the bottom quick sand, boiling and heaving up like thick boiling soup, as the water forces its way through it. Held prayer circle & meeting & again prayers, for Br Jones after which he was better Hard rain again to night.

Saturday 20 Nov. 1852. Cold morning went 17 miles encamped at Cottonwood Springs. rough up hill road. Had the tooth ache and was so nervous that I had to ride in the waggon this after noon and about ten p m. had it drawn.

Sunday 21 Nov 1852. Clear & cold. Earley Start. Jones is better, & my jaw very sore. Went only ten miles up hill and encamped at mountain Springs High in the mountains & in the regions of snow.

The atmosphere was like Utah. To the N. W. lay high mountains covered with snow & timber Here the mountains are covered with cedar Cold windy night. Held a meeting about 9 P. M.

Monday 22 Nov. 1852. About day light commenced raining and snowing very hard accompanied by hard wind. Started earley. good decending road travelled fast. Snow blowing in our faces & when we started was 4 inches deep. Went 20 miles to Stump Springs fed, watered and went on 8 miles and encamped on a desert There was no snow in this valley.

Tuesday 23 Nov 1852. Went on to resting Springs, fed & baited warm weather then went on to Amagoshe or Saleratus Creek 7 miles. Here we overtook H. G. Sherwood's company en route to San Bernardino, all well, also met Amasa Lyman & C. C. Rich and several others from San Bernardino en route to Utah with whom were Elder B. F. Grouard[18] from the Society Islands where he has been on a mission for 9 years, also Elder John Murdoc from a mission to Australia also going to Utah, all well

Thus three three companies of Saints met togother, in the most desolate, dry, mountainous and picturesque place which I have met with in all the mountains.

The night is very cold and windy. All three of the companies have agreed to lay up tomorrow to exchange letters & pay each other a Short visit.

Wednesday 24 Nov 1852. Very cold and windy all else well. Spent the day very agreeably with our friends and writing letters to our friends at home

---

18. Benjamin Franklin Grouard was born January 4, 1819, at Portsmouth, New Hampshire. Early in life he went to sea and had visited many parts of the world before he joined the Mormons. With Addison Pratt, another sailor Noah Rogers, and Knowlton F. Hanks, Grouard was sent by Joseph Smith to open up a mission in the Pacific Islands. They left Nauvoo in October 1843.

Hanks died less than a month after they set sail and was buried at sea. Rogers returned after one month's service; Pratt remained four years, but Grouard married a native wife and remained nine years. At this time he was en route to make his report to headquarters. He returned to San Bernardino with the next company back and remained in California the rest of his life, leaving the Mormon Church to become a member of a spiritualist group. He died in the Santa Ana Valley March 19, 1894.

In the after noon had a meeting preaching by A Lyman, C. C. Rich, J. Murdock, H. G. Sherwood and in the evening another, preaching by A. Lyman & Rich and T. R. Leonard Some of the animals are nearley killed by drinking Alkali

Thursday 25 Nov 1852. All three of the companies are briskly preparing to start. We started earley & went 14 miles to Salt Springs dined & fed our animals having heavy sandy up hill road. Here in the mountains we found a gold mine where the Mexicans have been digging & from appearance have done well Here is only brackish water so we had to depend on the water which we had taken in to cross the desert of 62 miles.

From hence we proceeded some 12 miles on the desert and encamped, some of our animals being very nearly given out, while those which had been alkalied were rolling and lying on the ground as though they would die

Part of Sherwood's company passed in the night & part about day light.

Friday 26 Nov 1852. Earley start & good road. Travelled fast. Soon passed the advance of Sherwood's company. This was the hardest days drive we have had. My mare allmost gave out. Sent some of the strongest teams ahead to find water and grass. The road in the after noon was rough and heavy. We all however arrived at Bitter Springs soon after dark where we had good water and plenty of grass 62 miles from Amagoshe. Sherwood's company commenced to come in about 9 P. M.

Saturday 27 Nov 1852. Our animals are well recruited and look well and seem to be able to cross the next desert of 30 miles. First 12 miles up hill and heavy road. We baited and fed the first eight miles while some teams which were more able were sent on to look for grass & water. Warm sultry day.

Had another hard days drive which was worse than yesterday. It was 11 in the evening before I got to camp. Many of the animals are given out and two teams did not come in. The men are also tired and fatigued more so than I have seen on the journey.

Sunday 28 Nov 1852. Warm & pleasant like summer plenty of timber, grass & water, grapes vines & grapes dried on the vine in abundance

Here on the Mohave a beautiful country bursted to our view, when the light of day came to our assistance which forms a beautiful contrast with the surrounding mountains, timberless, dry & rocky.

We again lay up to recruit our teams and send back for the rear Held a meeting at two p. m during which time the rear came up, all well enough, but nearley worn out both men and animals after regailing a short time and feeding our last grain to our animals we went on ten miles and again had good feed & water. Met 2 men from San Bernardino who were hunting up discarded animals.

Monday 29 Nov 1852. Started late & travelled very slowly going only 8 miles because our animals are very weak Encamped at good feed and water where both men and animals could rest from the fatigues which had nearly worn us out.

Held a meeting in the evening.

Tuesday 30 Nov 1852. Animals & men seem refreshed and in good spirits. Road heavy in the forenoon. The snow capped Sierra Nevada hove in sight this morning, beyond which we fondly hope to enjoy rest and repose a short time with our brethren and friends.

Stopped to bait & dine after 15 miles travel in a beautiful cottonwood grove but the water was about 1 mile from camp so we went some ten miles and encamped for the night with little grass.

Wednesday 1 Dec 1852. Slowly travelled 12 miles and encamped having only tolerable feed our animals worn down. Here the road leaves the Mohave.

To day I suffered more and was worse worn out and tired than since I have been on my journey. It was only noon when we arrived but in consequence of Br Jones feeble situation as well as the rest of the company we concluded to stay all night.

This singular stream the Mohave, in some places barren & dry, in others the water rises, while the valley is well timbered, would afford favorable facilities for scattering settlements to all appearance.

Thursday 2 Dec 1852. Started at sun rise. Up hill, road not very good. Weak teams. Dull music. whack, whack, gee up, whack, whack, roll on, trot a little, walk a little, "The sound of the grinding is low" More than half the Company is out of provisions & horses failing and has to be taken out of the teams. Bait our teams awhile then roll on My mare is given out and has to be "beaten along"

At last and with much ado we gained the Summitt of Cahoon pass at 4 P. M. when we straggled along down Cahoon Cannon 8 miles we encamped. Three teams and some with loose animals did not come in Men & animals are now completely used up and I am sick.

Friday 3 Dec 1852. Earley this morning some of those in the rear came up, after which we proceeded on down the Kanyon Untill noon when we baited and dined for the last, eating up all the provisions of the whole company or nearley so, during which time all those in the rear came

Since coming out of the Cannon the weather is very different, warm & mellow the wind like the zephyrs of summer, sweet and exhilerating, the face of the country presents the appearance of all in the States, contrasting the green herbage just springing to life, showing that autumn & winter is past. Happy country with no winter.

We now started again from our last short rest, arriving at San Bernardino at Sun set, where we were recieved by the Saints who came together to recieve us & offer their fire sides and tables to us for our homes while we tarry here.

Now we felt again the comforts of home in a small degree and again rejoiced with our friends again rested from the fatigues of our journey.

San Bernardino was purchased from som Mexicans (Lugo) by Lyman & Rich in 1851 for 785.00 dollars.[19] There has only one crop been raised of 1800 acres which yielded abundantly. Eevery one has plenty, while the products of the earth bear a good price in cash; nothing appears to hinder the Saints here from soon becoming rich.

I and several more took supper with my old acquaintance John Harris and slept at our waggons which were carralled together The people had only temporary small houses were not well prepared to give us lodging.

Saturday 4 Dec. 1852. Spent this day very agreeably visiting my old acquaintences. Here I also became acquainted with William Stout mentioned Oct 24 last. We found by tracing our lineage that we sprang from the same father & mother who settled in New Jersey. This evening moved my lodging to his house. He recieved me not only as a kinsman but as a Saint.

Sunday 5 Dec 1852. Attended meeting to day. Elder James Brown preached in the fore noon & myself in the after noon. At Earley candle light Elders W. Hyde, B. F. Johnson, N. V. Jones of the missionaries & Bishop Crosby preached. The meetings were well attended and all enjoyed the spirit of truth.

---

19. Stout has his decimal in the wrong place. Amasa M. Lyman and Charles C. Rich had purchased the San Bernardino Ranch for $77,500. It was said to contain 80,000 acres of "good" land in addition to some that was not tillable. The first colony of Mormons numbered 437 men, women, and children, traveling in 150 wagons, with 588 oxen, 336 cows, 21 young stock, 107 horses, and 52 mules. Beattie and Beattie, *Heritage of The Valley*, 183-84, 171.

Monday 6 Dec 1852. Visiting with my friends, visited the new grist mill which is doing well.

This evening went in company with B. F. Johnson and staid all night with our old friend Justice Morse.

Tuesday 7 Dec 1852. Spent the day among my old acquaintences   Meeting in the Evening   Elders J Lewis E. Thomas & P. Dowdle preached

Wednesday 8 Dec 1852. Wrote a letter to Elder Williams Camp, now in Tennessee.   attended meeting in the evening which was for transacting the local business of the place in relation to the market.

Thursday 9 Dec 1852. Spent the day as before & selling out our teams   meeting in the evening Elders Badlam, C. W. West, H. G. Sherwood & Bp. Crosby preached Sherwoods' company arrived to day.

Friday 10 Dec 1852. Wrote a letter to W. E. Horner St Joseph Mo and in the evening paid a visit to Bp Crosby & staid all night.

Saturday 11 Dec 1852. Writing in the fore noon.   In the after noon paid a visit to Brs Simmons & Stewart's & took dinner in company with 7 other of the missionaries Meeting at dark Elders Farnham, Tanner, Mc Bride & Capt Hunt preached.

Sunday 12 Dec 1852. Very sick to day yet was able to be around and went to meeting   Elders N. V. Jones & J. Brown preached on the subject of baptism.   At intermission some 60 or 70 persons were re-baptised and a few baptised into the church.   In the after noon I was unable to attend but a short time

Monday 13 Dec 1852.   To day I was very sick and unable to attend to any business. Visited Theodore Turley an old friend a short time after which had to take my bed the rest of the day

Tuesday 14 Dec 1852. Elders Brown & Thomas started for their destinations, British Guianna South America

Wrote a letter to Hon. Isaiah Morris of Ohio.   Staid all night with Bp Crosby. Hard rain to night.

Wednesday 15 Dec 1852. The missionaries having mostly sold out and are preparing to start for San Francisco except the China mission.

Thursday 16 Dec 1852. This morning Br Gilbert Summe[20] gave me 50 dollars to aid me on my mission, saying he had considered the importance thereof & desired to bear a part of the burthen.

This evening went to a party at Gilbert Hunt's which he had made expressly for his father's enjoyment, who being a member of the Legislature, was going to Vallejo to meet that body in a few days.   We kept the "fiddle & the bow" in operation till 5 a. m to good advantage.

Friday 17 Dec 1852. This fore noon the Elders bound for the Sandwick, Island, Australia, Siam, & Calcutta missions, left for San Francisco   The China mission remaining.   after which paid Justice Morse a visit.   Some five families of Saints arrived here from San Jose Cal.

Saturday 18 Dec 1852. Hunting my mare.   Not very well.

---

20. This is evidently Gilbert Summe, born August 22, 1802, who was one of the 1847 pioneers. In 1865 he was called to the Muddy Mission (in present Nevada) to raise cotton. He died June 13, 1867, at Harmony, Utah.

Sunday 19 Dec 1852. Meeting. Bishop Crosby preached on the policy to be pursued in settling San Bernardino. Evening meeting to appoint teachers. Rainy day & Rainy night.

Monday 20 Dec 1852. Pleasant weather again. Writing to day. A Company arrived from Salt Lake having left on the first of Nov. Met Lyman & Rich on the Rio Virgin Dec 1. all well. Horace Clark says my family was well when he left

Tuesday 21 Dec 1852. Rain & heavy thunder. Nathan T. Thomas gave a tittle to a Claim which he owns in the gold mines worth 150 dollars, to assist my mission which I have hopes may be of benefit to assist me to gain access to the Chinese.

Wednesday 22 Dec 1852. Rained all day while I lay in doors.

Thursday 23 Dec 1852. Rainy weather yet. Br David Frederick me 5 dollars. While this rainy weather continues we are laying up in the post office, where we enjoy ourselves well, in reading, writing &c

Friday 24 Dec 1852. Weather unsettled but not raining Hiram H. Blackwell gave me three dollars
   In the afternoon, William Stout the School teacher, gave a party to his scholars, to which we were invited, and spent the after-noon very agreeably.
   San Bernardino sounds like a battle field, The boys are celebrating Chrismas

Saturday 25 Dec 1852. This morning all is life and enjoyment By way of Christmas gift B David Frederick gave me a pair of boots worth seven Dollars.

Sunday 26 Dec 1852. Raining again. Meeting C. Duncan preached & in the after-noon I preached
   About ten at night the brethren who took the missionaries to San Pedro, returned, bringing with them William Perkins and wife. on his return from Sandwick Islands, also. Addison Pratt & family returned from Society Islands.
   They report that the missionaries procured a passage on the brig Fremont for $17.50 each, whereas they expected to pay $55 each, saving thereby for 36 of them the sum of $1350.

Monday 27 Dec 1852. Clear weather. Hunting my mare. We went and staid all night with John Holladay.

Tuesday 28 Dec 1852. Hunting mare again. Rainy, David Seeley gave me five dollars, Chapman & I took Supper with John Hughes.

Wednesday 29 Dec 1852. William Mathews gave us one dollar each. Hunted mare. We took supper with Thomas Bingham

Thursday 30 Dec 1852. Hunted mare to day and attended prayer meeting at night.

Friday 31 Dec 1852. Farewell to the old year. Hunted mare

Saturday 1 Jan 1853. Preparing to start for San Francisco on Monday next

Sunday 2 Jan. 1853. Meeting. James Lewis & H. G. Sherwood spoke in the fore-noon & in the afternoon C. Duncan & myself spoke. There was a collection made to day for our mission and $55.45. raised

Monday 3 Jan. 1853. Preparing to leave. Washington Cook gave me five dollars and Andrew Lytle the same. Charles Burk a vest, & William Stout $20. About ten we took leave of San Bernardino. Br John Goodwin drew our trunks & other luggage. Some 15 teams started for San Pedro but we left all behind except 3 waggons, travelling 30 miles.

Tuesday 4 Jan. 1852 [3]. Travelled 30 miles. Fine country, numerous herds of cattle scattered over the plains and mountains.

Wednesday 5 Jan 1853. Four miles brought us to Pueblo de Los Angelos. Here I found my old friend Capt Jesse D. Hunter[21] who lives here but I had but a few moments to spend with him

From here we proceeded on encamping within 4 miles of San Pedro. Now for the first time in my life, the roaring Surges of the ocean saluted my ear like the distant sound of a coming storm.

Thursday 6 Jan 1853. Soon we found ourselves on the shores of the Pacific Ocean, but owing to a heavy fog, could not enjoy the sight of its broad bosom, so we had to content ourselves with beholding the mild Surges breaking on the shore, while the tide was ebbing

The Steamer had not yet arrived. We found some 8 or ten persons at San Pedro waiting for a passage, a company of whom had rented a small brick house, with an adobie foundation and no floor, for one dollar a day where we also took lodging, by paying our ratio while waiting with all immaginable impatience for some opportunity to leave the loathsome, lousy and miserable excuse, for convenience which San Pedro affords to strangers

The brethren who came with us started back to feed to await for the rear. Br John Goodwin gave J. Lewis 4 dollars Thos Tomkins 15 dollars.

Friday 7 Jan 1853. This morning the Steamer Sea Bird came in and left at three for San Deigo. She brought the San Francisco mail for Salt Lake pr South route, expecting to meet the December mail from Salt Lake here. They informed me that the Nov. mail was blocked with snow in Carson Valley.

Saturday 8 Jan. 1853. Steamer Ohio arrived this morning. Some 3 or 4 Mormons on board. Five Waggons which left San Bernardino when we did came in evening. Rainy day.

Sunday 9th Jan 1853. This morning or just at 12 at night the Sea Bird returned from San Deigo, when we were aroused from our slumbers & took our things to the beach and there waited till day light in the mud and drizzling rain before we went on board. I was very sick all this time and would have had to kept my bed if haply I had been fortunate to have had one The Boat did not however leave till noon when we put to sea under good headway.

We took Cabin passage for $55 each. Saw several whales spouting at a distance yet had not a sight of them. I had to go to Bunk at 4 being sick. Br Jas Lewis soon became seasick

Monday 10 Jan 1853. This morning I found we were at Santa Barbara 90 miles from San Pedro where the boat anchored at midnight, & lying up till noon, we put to sea again, having head wind and rough sea until midnight

Tuesday 11 Jan 1853. At San Louis Obispo this morning 80 miles from Santa Barbara again laying up till 3 p. m. put to sea with rough sea & head winds all night.

Wednesday 12 Jan 1853. Sun rise brought us to the ancient famed Monterey, having a tolerable port, backed by a small town, not equal to its ancient fame. At 12 noon we left arriving in the Bay of San Francisco at mid night.

---

21. Hunter had been appointed Indian agent for southern California. See footnote 9, Volume I, Part 1.

Thursday 13 Jan 1853. At day break we went ashore at the City of San Francisco putting up at a Hotel we took breakfast. Soon after we found the Elders who sailed on the brig Fremont, who had arrived a few days previous, and had rented a House for $12.50 pr week — where we also repaired Had a meeting here at ten. President Morris Q. S. Sparks also James Brown returning missionary from the Society Islands were present. Previous arraingements had been made to call on the good people of this place to contribute means to help bear off the missions and to this end papers were made out and Elders chosen to visit different parts of the city to solicit the means.

Recieved a letter from Elder James Brown from San Deigo & one from Hon. J. M. Barnhisel

Spent the rest of the day looking around the city. Another meeting in the evening.

Friday 14 Jan 1853. Around the city purchasing some clothing and making what preperations I can for my out fit for China.

The Elders who visited the good citizens of this city only collected about 14 dollars. Br T. S. Wiliam paid us a visit this evening and donated 500 dollars[22] for the missions

Saturday 15 Jan 1853. The Elders had similar Success today as yesterday. Became partially acquainted with some Chinese who are affable and friendly, also a man who promises to assist me to some chinese books if to be procured. Mr Benjn Holladay visited us this evening and promises to assist in helping us off as well as to use his influence with capitalists & ship owners for our benefit.

Sunday 16 Jan 1853. Very warm day. Took a stroll with Elder McBride on the hill, having a beautiful view of the city, the Harbor, and Shipping, after which we paid Mr Holladay a visit and then visited some Jews.

It is a remarkable fact that the Jews seem to be more believing & friendly towards our religion than any other peple here, manifesting, the same in many cases by presents and donations to the missionaries & otherwise favoring us in trading. Held an evening meeting at "our House".

Monday 17 Jan 1853. Strolling around the city viewing the wonderful State of society. The Stores, the groceries churches, gambling houses, Houses of ill fame, Hotels, Hawkers, brokers, Bankers Law offices and innumerable other establishments all mingled and all mixed & inter mixed with every degree of compound, as though all classes and grades of society were of one heart and mind & in full fellowship with each other and all trades, professions, misteries and occupations were equally honerable.

Paid Mr Holladay another visit this evening. He had as yet done nothing for us. Saw George S. Colemear jr for the first time for seven years. This evening.

Tuesday 18 Jan 1853. paid a visit to Sister Hollenback with McBride, and took dinner.

Wednesday 19 Jan 1853. Visited a Chinaman named Achick who peaks good English who proposes all the information he can give me after which spent the day in viewing the wonderful compound of San Francisco, and writing my journal. Afflicted with a severe cold.

Thursday 20 Jan 1853. Paid a visit to Br Knowles & took tea. Elder William Hyde returned from San Jose accompanied by Br John M. Horner who lives there and is

---

22. This generous contribution from Thomas S. Williams is evidence of his loyalty to the church up to this time.

doing an extensive business In the evening went with Horner & staid all night on his steam boat. Very sick to day.

Friday 21 Jan 1853. Sick yet. Meeting at ten to take into consideration the amount of means neecssary to fit out the different missions which in all amounts to 6250 dollars which will mostly be paid by Brs John M. Horner[23] & Q. S. Sparks.[24] Held an evening meeting Q. S. Sparks preached a powerful sermon after which I went home with him and staid all night.

Saturday 22 Jan 1853. Returned to the city at ten. Recieved my passport from Washington from Hon J. M. Barnhisel Utah Delegate to congress Several others but not all recieved theirs

Sunday 23 Jan 1853. Meeting at Q. S. Spark's who preached to a mixed congregation of Saints & Sinners then returned to our lodgings

Monday 24 Jan 1853. Looking out for our passage to Hong Kong which I partially engaged.

Tuesday 25 Jan 1853. This morning went on Board the Bark Graf Van Hogendorf, Holland. Van Hees Capt. made a conditional contract for our passage for 128 dollars each.

The Capt & crew are Hollanders and extreemly pious, upon my telling them that we were preachers they were very anxious for us to go.

In the evening visited Mr Holladay who kindly forgave me a note of $36 which I owed him, upon presenting him the money, promising to yet do more for the missions

This evening the China Mission moved to a house furnished us gratis by F. Cheney Several of the Elders returned from the County, not having good success in collecting means for the missions

Wednesday 26 Jan 1853. Very sick The Australian Mission shipped on the Bark Pacefic and the Sandwick mission on the Huntress.

Three more of the Elders returned from the country with poor success. Wrote a letter to my wife. Elder J. Brown left for San Bernardino on the Sea Bird taking letters and papers to our wives and friends at Salt Lake.

Thursday 27 Jan 1853. Writing. Rainy day. Prayer meeting this evening

---

23. John M. Horner was a member who had come with Sam Brannan in the ship *Brooklyn* and was doing a thriving business in San Francisco. Soon after this, Horner moved to Salt Lake City where he was listed as "J. M. Horner & Co., capital $200,000 . . ." in 1854, the first named on the list of businesses in the city. Neff, *History of Utah,* 337, fn. 1.

In describing the business growth of Salt Lake City, Tullidge wrote: ". . . J. M. Horner & Co., was the fourth firm, and they did business in the building occupied by the *Deseret News* Co. This firm continued in business but a short time and was succeeded by that of Hooper & Williams . . . ." Tullidge, *History of Salt Lake City,* 379.

The *Deseret News* of December 23, 1857, spoke of the "late firms of J. M. Horner & Co., Hooper & Williams, and W. H. Cooper" as being willing to accept payment in cattle, grain, hay, hides, and pork so it would seem that Horner left the territory early.

24. Quartus S. Sparks came to California with his wife and one child on the ship, *Brooklyn.* He had previously filled a mission in 1843 for the church in New Jersey and in 1844 was working as a missionary in Connecticut. He was listed as an attorney.

Several persons have mentioned Sparks as active and fervent in the church. Louisa Barnes Pratt wrote on August 1, 1852, that, "After the departure of Bro. Pratt, Brother Quartus Sparks presided over the branch [in San Francisco]. He was an eloquent speaker, had been a traveling elder . . . ." Pratt, "Journal of Louisa Barnes Pratt," *Heart Throbs of the West,* VIII, 296.

Sparks moved to San Bernardino where he remained for the rest of his life, but there he apostatized from the church and became very bitter. Two of his pamphlets were *Mormonism Exposed* and *Priestcraft in Danger.*

Friday 28 Jan 1853. Rainy. Purchased some books. The Calcutta & siam Missions shipped on the Monsoon (& sailed to day [crossed out]) all the missionaries are now on board except the China Mission

Saturday 29 Jan 1853. Calcutta Mission sailed to day. Staid all night with Q. S. Sparks.

Sunday 30 Jan 1853. Meeting Quartus S. Sparks preached. came to the city and evening meeting at Sister Evans W. O. Clark present says his faith is yet good but he is rather wild.

Monday 31 Jan 1853. Doing nothing of importance.

Tuesday 1 Feb. 1853. Went with, Br Sparks, on board the Huntress to pay a last visit to the Elders of the Sandwick Mission who sail today Then visited the Australian mission who also sail to day.

Wednesday 2 Feb 1853. C. Duncan crossed the Bay to San Jose and J Lewis (& myself [crossed out]) went to Sparks, & I home to writing

Thursday 3 Feb 1853. Prominaded the Bay coast with Lewis and Sparks then visited H. Kimball & took supper. evening prayer meeting at widow Evan's.

Friday 4 Feb 1853. Writing to day.

Saturday 5 Feb. 1853. Eastern mail came in but no news of importance to us.

Sunday 6 Feb 1853. Meeting at wd Evans at dark spent the day around the city with Br Faulke.

Monday 7 Feb 1853. Spent most of the day on the warves & in the evening myself and Jas Lewis went home with Q. S. Sparks

Tuesday 8 Feb. 1853. Returned home in the morning & spent the day there

Wednesday 9 Feb. 1853. This morning Chapman Duncan returned from San Jose. Prayer meeting in the evening at Widow Lincoln's.

Thursday 10 Feb 1853. We were preparing for raising our means and other necessaries for sailing.

Friday 11 Feb 1853. Around on the warfs and looking at the vessels bound for Honk Kong with a view to suit ourselves in obtaining our passage.

Saturday 12 Feb 1853. Not quite suited yet but expect to sail on the 20th on the Bark "Invincible". Staid all night with Hollenbeck.

Sunday 13 Feb 1853. John Clawson sent us 25 dollars this morning. Spent the day at our Lodgings, Studdying Chinese & attended a meeting of the Chinese where two american Missionaries preached to them in their own toungue. At dark had a prayer meeting at Wid Lincoln's

Monday 14 Feb 1853. Made a permanent contract with Capt Augustus Myers of the Bark Invincible for our passage to Hong Kong for 160 dollars each Widow Corwin gave us five dollars.

Tuesday 15 Feb 1853. Recieved 400 dollars from Q. S. Sparks of the money raised for our mission. Spent the day as usual & the evening at Wid Lincoln's

Wednesday 16 Feb 1853. Went to Br Sparks at staid all night

Thursday 17 Feb 1853. Came home in the morning. Br Sparks sold his House and Lots in San Francisco for 9,000 dollars. Spent the day with him & at our Lodging and writing. Br Sparks expects to move to Great Salt Lake Utah

Friday 18 Feb 1853. Br C. Duncan & myself went home with Br Sparks and staid all night.

Saturday 19 Feb 1853. Returned to the city this morning and on going to the Consignees' office found that the Bark Invincible on which we had engaged and paid part of our passage to Hong-Kong, had been condemned as not sea-worthy. This was a great disappointment to us, for we expected to have sailed on Monday next. There is now no vessel in port bound to Hong Kong which we know of, on which we can obtain a passage. The Eastern mail came in this morning but no news for us.

Sunday 20 Feb 1853. This morning we explored the wharfs but could find only two which were not however going under two weeks. At 2 o'clock a large Company of saints repaired to North Beach to witness the baptism of three men who had come forward to renew their covenants after which Had a meeting at dark at Wid Evan's where they were confirmed.

Monday 21 Feb. 1853. Hunting an opportunity to obtain a passage hardly knowing what to do next. Attended the theatre to night.

Tuesday 22 Feb 1853. San Francisco is celebrating Washington's birthday The Firemen are marching in procession beautifully uniformed. Each company is preeceeded by a Band of music, while the rear is brought up by a company of cavalry. The Salt Lake mail arrived to day bringing the Deseret News up to Dec 25 reporting all well in Utah as a general thing yet bearing the tidings of the death of Charles Heber oldest son of my brother Allen Br Jas Lewis recieved letters from his wife but myself and Duncan recieved nothing. Why I have not recieved any intelligence from neither my family or friends I know not.

Wednesday 23 Feb 1853. Drew back the money which we advanced on our passage on the Invincible and now have to seek a passage on some other vessel. In the evening prayer meeting at Wd Evans.'

Thursday 24 Feb 1853. Raining and muddy again. While we are reading the Deseret News & otherwise killing time.

Friday 25 Feb. 1853. Raining & More muddy. At our lodging most of the day. The fact is the streets & side walks are so muddy & disagreeable & filthy that a man must have urgent business before he can prevail upon himself to walk out in rainy weather. This evening Br Orin Smith paid us a visit and paid our way to attend the American Theatre which we attended till nearly midnight where we were well entertained. Last Monday night Br Cyrus Iray I forgot to state also paid my way to the same Theatre.

Saturday 26 Feb 1853. This morning I closed my letters to my wife and two to T Bullock at Salt Lake. Elder Lewis engaged our passage to Hong Kong on the Bark Hoorn Capt Bonten for 80 dollars each which makes the third time we have had our passage engaged whether as before this will fall through I do not know but it is certainly a favorable oppertunity for us to procure our passage so very cheap. This evening we visited Wid Lincoln again who gave each of us a pair of Shoes.

Sunday 27 Feb 1853. Sister Evans gave me a fine pocket hdkf. Spent the day till 4 P. M. at widow Lincolns where a small company of Saints had assembled to enjoy themselves after which myself & Br Sparks went to the African church to hear the sable minister hold forth his hopes In the evening had a prayer meeting at Wid Evans'

Monday 28 Feb 1853. This morning we went to the Bark which we had engaged and found that it suited us. unwell to day and at home.

Tuesday 1 March 1853. To day I recieved two letters from my brother which had bein sent to J. M. Horner which was the reason I did not get any by the mail. They bear the pleasing intelligence that I had a son born on 30 Dec and all well. My children had been sick but were all well first January. My brother also had a son born on _____ all well   Everything is going on as well as could be expected

Wednesday 2 March 1853. This morning we paid our passage to Hong Kong on the Dutch Bark "John Van Hoorn". Capt Bonten for 80 dollars each for cabin passage We finding our bedding and Liquors.

Saw Roswell Stephens who gave us ten dollars.

Wrote a letter to Allen J. Stout & sent it by John Clawson to Utah by the North route. & one to H. G. Sherwood at San Bernardino to send by Q. S. Sparks. prayer meeting & ordained Z Cheeney an Elder.

Thursday 3 March 1853. We all three went out to pay our last visit to Br Sparks and returned about noon when Br Duncan & myself visited an ex missionary from China, who discouraged us as to our going on our mission without the means of support for he does not believe that we can depend on the Lord for our support there althoug he admits that is the way we are commanded to go, while we held that we should trust in God &c after we discussed our religious principals awhile in good feelings & parted. He does not understand our faith & the principals of our religion. but holds to presbyterian doctrine. Spent the evening with Br Barton Morey.

Friday 4 March 1853. To day we saw our Capt who informed us that he would not sail untill Monday the 7th instant. This evening the good sisters made a supper and had a social party for us at which nearly all of the Saints in this neighborhood were present where we spent the evening very agreeably.

Saturday 5 March 1853. To day I was very sick yet Elder Duncan & myself visited a Sister Corwin

Sunday 6th March 1853. Spent the day with the Saints in social chit chat and reading spiritual manifestations Evening pray meeting at wid Evan's. Everle paid ten

Monday 7 March 1853. This morning we saw the Capt who said we would sail to morrow. Made up a package of articles presented (by [crossed out]) me by Sisters Evans, Corwin & King for my family to be taken to them by Br Sparks. Wrote a letter to my wife by Sparks. Attended the American Theatre this evening with a small party of brethren & sisters where we we enjoyed ourselves untill twelve very agreeably

Tuesday 8th March 1853. Very busy this morning preparing to sail and about 11 o'clock A. M. took the parting hand with the saints here and went on board of the Jan Van Hoorn Capt Bouton

We were kindly administered to by the Saints in this place who furnished us all the sea stores we needed nearly They have a good spirit and the blessings of God will surely attend them (for their faith and faithfulness. [crossed out])

We are well supplied with an abundance of sea stores Liquors &c such as we need after going on board the vessel droped out into the stream and anchored for the night.

Wednesday 9 March 1853. About noon the pilot came on board and all (things [crossed out]) hands commenced to prepare for sailing against a head wind which blew hard from the mouth of the Harbor and consequently had to tack forward and back like a dancing master untill we zizaged our way out to sea. We however soon got out and headed West, South, West, with a good stiff breeze and tolerable rough sea

Soon after we got to sea and before the pilot left, I had to retire to my bunk quite sea sick where I staid till morning

There are 60 chinese passengers stowed away in mid ships and one cabin passenger Mr Nash, besides ourselves. The crew consists of 16 men officers & boys included.

Thursday 10 March 1853. Good breeze yet. I feel very quarmish yet & Mrs Lewis & Nash no better than myself while Duncan is well. As for the chinese poor fellows they are stowed away in their dens like so many sick pigs. In the after noon saw a vessel to the S making out. We are sailing to the same point yet. The weather is cloudy. Sailing at some 4 or 5 miles an hour ·

Friday 11 March 1853. Some better yet quarmish. At noon 320 miles out. Chinese laying in yet only 2 or 3 of them out on deck. Sailing W.S.W. yet at 4 or 5 miles an hour.

Saturday 12 March 1853. Course W.S.W. yet. Smoother sea and lighter wind. Chinese lying in yet. We all feel quite peart now. Weather cloudy
In the after noon the wind nearley ceased to blow. The ocean became smoothe so that no white caps appeared. Nothing but the smoothe heaving billows came sleepily & lazily along, tilting and rocking the vessel, flapping her sails, sporting at our anxiety to go ahead.
How beautiful is the calm Ocean now, like hills and dales ever rising, ever disappearing, Her ever changing heaving bosom, like the never ceasing hopes and fears of the human heart. Sporting at all our attempt to allay them About sun set the wind ceased and the vessel stopped while we had patiently to contemplate her soft repose.

Sunday 13 March 1853. Good luck to my first sea Sunday. This morning we were favored with a stiff breeze which however sent us (S.S.E. [crossed out]) W.N.W. untill noon when the ship tacked S.S.E and sailed finely all night, yet out of our course.

Monday 14 March, 1853. Still on the same course at about 7 or 8 knots Rather cool weather. We were favored with a visit by a school of porpoises this morning. Wind changed to a gale in the evening

Tuesday 15 March 1853. Cool stiff breeeze 8 to 10 knots course W.S.W. occasionally bearing more to the North Sea rather too rough and we on the sick list again O! how the ship careens.

Wednesday 16 March 1853. Sailing W. by S. under 8 or 9 knot breeze Fine times now sea not so rough and we not so sick

Thurs 17. Course W. by S. warm & pleasant fine evening shower. Passed an Island 60 miles to the North of us to day about noon.

Friday 18 March 1853. Not well, Head ache. Warm pleasant weather, good breeze and sailing in the same direction.
It is the custom to take observations at noon and determine the Latitude & Longitude at which time they ascertain the number of miles they have sailed in the last previous 24 hours from which I shall state the daily distance which was to day 204 miles.

Saturday 19 March 1853. Reading a novel all the fore noon. At noon changed the course to W.N.W. hazy weather & like for rain soon.

Sunday 20 March 1853. Very weak & nervous. Spent the day reading the life of Sir William Wallace Sailing 8 knots, good weather

Monday 21 March 1853. Cloudy. Quite well again. Sailing same direction yet Sailed 216 Miles. Rained in the evening. I am very tired

Tuesday 22 March 1853. Some better weather, brisker breeze & rougher sea, rained at noon, squally in the after noon. Passed 20 miles to the North of the Sandwick Islands at at ten o'clock at night

Wednesday 23 March 1853. Milder wind and sea. at noon we were 25 miles south of Bird Island. Calm a few hours in the after noon then rain and storm in the night. Sailed 215 miles

Thursday 24 March 1853. Sailed W. by N. till noon making 117 miles and calm at noon when a sudden squall took us aback running the vessell backwards like a baulky horse untill I began to think she would soon come on to her haunches. She was however soon set right and a calm followed The night was squally and rainy.

Friday 25 March 1853. Sailing S.S.E. slowly making 51 miles. Saw a whaler off to south.

Saturday 26 March 1853. Verry calm. changed at 8 a. m to N.W. making 61 miles.
    I am very weak and feeble and am trying to dispense with tea & coffee. Saw a Bark to south to day.

Sunday 27 March 1853. Sailing W. bearing slowly to N. W. Low wind 25 miles to day. Clear fine weather. I am weak and feeble.

Monday 28 March 1853. Good breeze and good headway. Sailing W. Made 102 miles I feel quite well to day

Tuesday 29 March 1853. Changed course to W. by N with a very rough high sea creening, tilting & sailing fast. Made 190 miles hazy weather. Made a song, "Mountain Home."

Wednesday 30 March 1853. Sailing W. by S. brisk wind Made 184 miles. Drank no tea or coffee.

Thursday 31 March 1853. Sailing W. Cloudy dark day raining in the after noon. No observation to day could be taken wind very hard from S at dark.

Friday 1 April 1853. Feel very weak and nervous with head ache this morning but better in the evening. Becalmed to day Made 99 miles in two days.

Saturday 2 April 1853. Sailing W. with rougher & higher sea than we have had. Made 180 miles. are now 60 miles past half way to Hong Kong at noon

Sunday 3 April 1853. Course same Breeze better making 271¼ miles This is 5¼ miles farther than ever this vessel (ever [crossed out]) sailed before in 24 hours

Monday 4 April 1853. Breeze & course the same making 240 miles.

Tuesday 5 April 1853. Course same breeze some lighter making 213 miles

Wednesday 6 April 1853. Course W. breeze very light making 198 miles

Thursday 7 April 1853. Course W. breeze very light, making 146 miles.

Friday 8 April 1853. Course W. light breeze making 158 miles

Saturday 9 April 1853. Course & breeze the same making 178 miles.

Sunday 10 April 1853. Course and breeze the same making 140 miles. This morning there was quite a row between the chinese and second mate which created considerable excitement which however soon passed off

Monday 11 April 1853. Course and breeze the same making 178 miles The thermometer stands at about 80° now days.

Tuesday 12 April 1853. Very calm. Sea smooth, going about 2 knots 116 miles

Wednesday 13 April 1853. This morning we were in sight of a group of 4 island the first (Asomption) lay about 6 miles to the south is some 2000 feet high cloud capped & shaped like a pyramid or sugar loaf. It seemed to be entirely composed of rock.

The other three lay to the North some 6 or 8 miles and formed a triangular group in the center of which appears to be a tolerable safe harbor, some of these had grass and shrubery on but seem to be mostly composed of rock The name of this group is Uracas

It was truly a relief to the eyes to see land whis is the first time since the ninth of March. These islands belong to the Ladrone groupe. Course and breeze the same making 126 miles

Thursday 14 April 1853. Course same breeze brisker making 176 miles.

Friday 15 April 1853. Course same, breeze very light, making 136 miles —

Saturday 16 April 1853. Course and breeze the same making 154 miles.

Sunday 17 April 1853. Course W Breeze same making 146 miles.

Monday 18 April 1853. Course W. Breeze same making 144 miles.

Tuesday 19 April 1853. Last night was a rainy night but pleasant Course W. Breeze very light making 146 miles

Wednesday 20 April 1853. Course W. breeze very light making 102 miles.

Thursday 21 April 1853. Course W. breeze brisker, making 147 miles.

Friday 22 April 1853. This morning at day light we were just entering the Formosa Channel. To the South lay the Bashee Islands Some five or six of them were in sight. The wind was south, the vessel sailing 9 or ten knots Course West

Shortly after passing those islands we espied an English Bark to the south making East. Sailed 192 miles. At noon we were 30 miles south of Formosa point and just entering the Chinese Sea. We could not see Formosa for fog. In the evening Course W.N.W.

Saturday 23 April 1853. This morning the Ocean sleeps. The rolling swells have disappeared and nought but smiling eddies dimple over the wide expanse as though all nature was at rest. The broad blue ocean & the the blue vault of heaven face each other in majestic silence while our vessel sleeps. With a warm south breeze playing just perceptibly among her sails, she rests like the smiling infant in her sleeping mother's arms.

Now while nature (nature [crossed out]) sleeps let me reflect, let me contemplate the past and think on the future. Now my wife & my little ones, dance playfully before my imagination. Now the scenes of home reveal themselves.

Now the saints in peaceful Utah roll by, busy in their different avocations. Now their fervent prayers ascend on high in my behalf. The kingdom of God rolls to all nations. Millions shout hosanna to hear the glad tidings. and they geather to geather to that land which is my home, as doves to their windows, while the wicked howl and prepare themselves for the doom which awaits them & I again rejoice in the blessed association and society of "home kindred and friends" in the fastnesses of Utah's mountains, amid the fat vallies of Ephraim, where the prayers of faithful millions will continually ascend to our Father in heaven to bless and geather Israel. Now let me close the vision for O the future opens too wide. ....?

Sailed only 82 miles and at noon changed course to South, half East. The calm continued. This afternoon an old chinaman died who had been sick all the voyage.

Sunday 24 April 1853. Very calm this morning Course W. Sailed 62 miles

Monday 25 April 1853. Tolerable good breeze. Course W. Sailed 78 miles. Had some sport to day to relieve the dull hours. Fired 2 cannon & Mr Nash shot two hawkes which lit on the yards. Saw a vessel to South headed E.

Tuesday 26 April 1853. Light breeze going at 5 knots Course W. Sailed 77 miles This afternoon saw 14 Chinese junks at one sight, besides another which appeared in the evening Soundings at 25 fathoms & mud bottom

Wednesday 27 April 1853. This morning we saw 12 more China junks also an American Bark which was sailing East there is land in sight from South to North in places while we are still westward bound. Sounding at 18 fathoms

Now the junks appear in fleets bespotting the face of the sea not to be numbered any more.

Now comes the opposition in two chian boats who came to us bantering to pilot us in to Harbor We had a fine sail throug the group of Islands in the midst of which Hong Kong was situated and arrived in harbor at three p. m. where we had a fine view of the shipping and the city of Victoria which is situated on the side hill A description of Hong Kong and the city of Victoria I must defer until I have more time.

We had scarcely dropped anchor before the deck was covered with chinees men and women as well as *professional* whites who were seeking for an opportunity to make a drive on the *Green Horns*. While the china men were seeking employment and the women also were soliciting our washing patronage, while others came forward to bargain off their *professional* sex to the crew and all whom it concerned at the lowest possible rates, which seemed on board to range at about one dollar each The custom far exceeding the patronage even at that (rates [crossed out]) reduced rates, and I was informed by those who said they knew by experience, that in the city such services could be procured for from ten to twenty cents. We staid on board.

Thursday 28 April 1853. This morning Elder Duncan and myself went ashore and spent the fore-noon in reconoitering the city. We became acquainted with Mr Emeny a ship chandler who gave us all the information he could and offered us one of his rooms after which we went on board again and after dinner and wine, packed up our traps and came to our newly acquired lodgings which Mr Emeny furnished with the necessary furniture Here we rested and felt like we had at least a tempory home. Mr Nash also puts up with us. Here we rested well baring the musquetoes which prayed upon us all night most unsparing, which brought to my recollection bright rememberance of "olden times" on the low lands of Illinois and Missouri rivers. We also board with Mr. Emeny.

Friday 29 April 1853. To day we occupied in purchasing some clothing more adapted to the warm climate and also in learning what we could about the situation of affairs here but as yet we have not obtained any information of any consequence. Elder J. Lewis and myself visited the American Consul Mr Anthon and appointed tomorrow at ten a. m to have an interview with him.

Saturday alias Sunday 1 May 1853. Here I am compelled to enter two days in one There is 9 hours difference in the time here and at great Salt Lake. The time here is computed by East Longitude while in the U.S. it is computed by West Longitude hence the difference So that Saturday here is accounted sunday.

Elder Lewis & myself visited the Consul this morning, who recieved us kindly and proffered to give us all the information he could.

Monday 2 May 1853. This morning Duncan & myself visited the Rev. Mr Johnson, Babtist missionary. He recieved us friendly, giving us the information we desired but no way inclined to enter on the subject of religion. I do not think he will take any (inter [crossed out]) interest for or against us.

Tuesday 3 May 1853. Thus far we have been delligently seeking for a place to locate ourselves and find some one who will be willing to hear the message we have to this nation but as yet we find none. The cheapest possible chance for board that we can yet find is about thirty dollars each per month. Still we feel to press on and not be discouraged yet certainly we have come to the darkest hour. This evening we made ourselves acquainted with one of the soldiers who promised to (giv [crossed out]) procure access to the soldiers and also saw a Mr Dudell who would let us have a room to hold forth in How these things will come out I do not know but I most earnestly pray that it may prove an effectual opening to establish the gospel in this place.

Wednesday 4 May 1853. This morning Elder Duncan and myself visited Mr Dudell again, to whom we explained the nature of our mission. How and in what manner we carried the gospel to the nations. How the gospel was spreading in every part of the world. All this was news to him but he said he would give all sects a fair chance and offered us a suit of rooms gratis for at least some three months.

He said he would like to here our doctrine of which we promised to inform him. We then started to see the proferred house being guided by a *Cooley* who led us some two miles out of the city in the hot sun which nearley over came us before we came back. I then went to see the House which was close by which will suit us well provided we can make other arraingements suit accordingly.

This after noon we went to see the soldiers train. They went through a variety of marches, counter-marches, wheelings, echelons, firing &c all of which was done in good order and decipline,

Thursday 5 May 1853. To day we moved to our new location the "Canton Bazaar" where we have and excellent suit of rooms the gratuitious benevolence of Mr Dudell, who is now acting the part of a most excelent friend and benefactor. Here we are comfortably situated in the third stories of the "Bazaar" on the south side of which however we can step off on the ground It is very cool & airy. We have employed a chinese servant at six dollars & fifty cents per month, who does all the duties of cook market man & chamber maid

Such is the force of custom here that it is far cheaper to employ one than to do without for we can not purchase in the markets if you do you will be cheated in both weight and measure & shaved in your change.

Now we have to go through the cerimony of purching some household furniture. Here we can have room to hold forth to a respectible congregation provided they will turn out and also entertain in private conversation all those who will give us audience

We feel that the Lord has thus opened our way to obtain a home where we can offer our prayers to God according to the order & plan of his holy priesthood. Previous to our moving here we settled with Mr Emeny who charged us 15 dollars for the five days we were with him which was however very cheap in comparison to the prices at the hotels which is ten dollars a week each. American money is discounted at about ten percent. In changing a fifty dollar slug I got 44 dollars for it which is a fair price in the market Then the coolie will shave all he can & the seller cheat all he can. Taking all things togeather it is the best place to get rid of money I ever was in. Sanfrancisco is behind the times

Friday 6 May 1853. Spent the fore part of the day in the house the weather being so warm and the air so oppressive that it is dangerous to expose ourselves to the sun In the evening we had a meeting. The first too which has been held in this dark and benighted land since the dispensation of the gospel has been revealed in the last days. In the tower room in the "Bazaar" is a place of worship occupied by five methodist (who nightly meet [crossed out]) soldiers who meet nightly there to mutually build each other up in their faith. Br Lewis went down to see them telling them we were preachers They were glad to see us and invited us to attend their meeting and preach to them, as their minister was gone to canton. We went. Br Lewis preached, echoing the first sounds of the glad tidings of Salvation and gospel light to this land of Spiritual darkness, after which I devoted a few moments to exhortation. They were truly rejoiced. Their Class Leader dismissed meeting by pray and a good Mormon prayer it was too He thanked God that we had been sent by his Holly spirit to visit this dark and benighted land. To comfort those who mourn, and bring many to the knowledge of the truth. That his spirit might be a guid to our feet and that the Lord would work mightily throug us &c to all of which we responded a hearty amen for it was all the very things we were sent to do and were praying daily and hourly for the same things ourselves.

They arrainged with us to have another meeting on sunday evening at 6 p. m. to which they would invite their friends while we also would induce as many as we could to come and hear for themselves and we earnestly pray our Father in Heaven who has sent us here to be with us, that this may be an effectual opening to plant the standard of gospel truth in this place amen

Saturday 7 May 1853. Kept in doors nearly all day but went out and conversed with a few on the subject of our mission.

Sunday 8 May 1853. Went out into the city only once and preached to one or two individuals a short time. At six p. m. we had a meeting according to previous arraingements. There was only six soldiers and one citizen Elder Duncan preache and quite boldly declared our principals, and by the way, gave the Sects a tolerabley Severe turn. Whether or not our methodist friends could see that their religion was declared false, I do not know, but when one of them dismissed meeting, he prayed most fervently for our success, telling the Lord we had been guided by his Spirit here to lead the heathen into gospel light.

Monday 9 May 1853. To day I attended an auction and purchased some articles of household furniture. In the after noon two of our Methodist soldier friends came to reason on the Scriptures. They were very reasonable and gave great attention to what was said and towards the last they did not dispute any thing that was said but acknowledged that our doctrine was perfectly fair and reasonable and borrowed the book of Mormon, promising to read it with a prayerful heart. Brs Duncan & Lewis met with & prayed with them in their prayer meeting, where they continued to pray for our success.

Tuesday 10 May 1853. purchased a few more articles for house keeping and are now pretty well fixed for keeping bacherlor's hall; a thing the most repugnant of all others to our faith and feelings.

Wednesday 11 May 1853. Trying to day to find some one that I can preach to when it is cool enough to be out, and writing letters

This evening we were visited (this evening [crossed out]) by two Chinamen one of them a Taylor in this place

The other had been raised under the fostering care of the London missionary society, having just returned from an eight years residence in England, where he acquired a good English education, talking fluently and intelligently & a most devoted Christian, well versed in the scriptures, having a complete knoweldge of the missionary system of reconciling all sects and parties in love and unity, and construing the Scriptures acordingly

We taught them the difference between their system of religion and ours, and the necessity of having lawful authority as well as the gift and power of the Holy ghost to lead them into all truth, which if they would had [heed?] the Lord would bless them, and pour out his spirit on them, while the gospel would thereby take root and grow in the hearts of their benighted country men. They promised to come again and see us further on the subject.

Thursday 12 May 1853. This day has passed of and we have done nothing only try to do and can't. This evening there was pleasant hard rain with thunder and lightening

Friday 13 May 1853. Visited the acting Editor of the "China Mail" by whom I was recieved with more cordial friendship than any one since I have been here. He lent me some papers & gave me some others and offered to publish any notice of our meetings which we might want and recommends us to lecture on the "green" because we will have more hearers and proposes not only to attend but will give us all the information we need which he can This evening our methodist brethren invited us to meet with them in their evening exercises Br Lewis & myself attend.

Saturday 14 May 1853. Took a notice to the pring office (China Mail) to advertise that we would lecture on the parade ground on Monday next at 5 o'clock P. M. afterwards busied in arainging our marketing so as to be shaved as little as possible Rainy after noon.

Sunday 15 May 1853. This morning Br Lewis is quite sick with a diarrhea and we all staid at home all day. I wrote a letter to Prest B. Young and directed it to Joseph Cain.

Monday 16 May 1853. To day we were anticipating preparing for our meeting at five p. m. but a very hard rain storm came just at five and prevented it. At the same time I was taken with a very severe chill, followed by a high fever which lasted all night I was very sick

Tuesday 17 May 1853. This morning put notice, in two different papers that we would hold forth, on the parade ground to morrow at 5 p. m., the weather permitting, if not, on the following evening. Rainy after-noon again.

Wednesday 18 May 1853. Spent this day around the city forming acquaintences as hitherto and reading the news.

At five p. m. our meeting came off, on the parade ground, according to, previous advertizement in the papers. There were about 100 citizens and as many soldiers present. Elder Lewis spoke on the first principals of the gospel, showing also the difference between our religion and the sects of the day. He delivered a powerful discourse, handling the sects quite uncerimoniously. The congregation paid good attention & after meeting desired to hear more. We accordingly appointed next Friday at 5 p. m. for another lecture. There was considerable interest which seemed to be manifested on the occasion and we feel that the ice of superstition is broken and a good work will follow.

Thursday 19 May 1853. Went to see Mr Dudell & Dixon, Editors who offer to do our advertising gratis & use their influence to continue our lecturs to the people

I am also informed that the effect of Elder Lewis sermon was good as many are anxious to hear more, and are desireous to obtain the reading of our books. Some 4 or 5 Editors were present last evening and paid good attention so that I feel that the leven is fairly in, and we feel encouraged.

Wrote a letter to my wife.

Friday 20 May 1853. Spent the day in & through town as is my custom At 5 p. m. we held another meeting on the parade ground. Elder Duncan preached. There was some thirty citizens & part of the time some two hundred soldiers present. They paid good attention and made some inquiries after meeting. yet it is amusing to see how very nice and reserved they are, acting with an assumed modest bashfulness like the false modesty of a tickelish flaunting coquette wanting to talk and not be seen.

Saturday 21 May 1853. Went to see Mr Dixon, who showed me this morning paper (Friend of china) containing three lengthy bursts against "Mormonism" The first in substance was the stale and discarded account of the celebrated fugutives U. S officers. The second was a fresh *estampede* from the "N. Y. Tribune" who had worked himself up into a strange state of excitement least the Mormons should overthrow the U. S. Government by the dangerous & as he says, the newly developed doctrine of Patriarchal Matrmiony, and loudly calling on the U. S to look out and take immediate measures to put a stop to our successfull career which is taking deep root in the four quarters of the world.

The third is from a Religious paper (Advocate & Reflector) which quotes from O Pratts paper at Washington (The Seer) showing the *modus operandi* of a *"Mormon second marriage"* He is also awfully alarmed and denounces us most unmeasuredly but produces no argument to expose our errors.

All these taken together with our exertions on the parade ground, we hope may stir some one at least to become interested to investigate our religion

Mr Dixon also made a present to us of a ticket to attend the Theatre this evening. Attended the Theatre at 8 p. m with C. Duncan while there a singular circumstance occured a few Persians some of whom was present at our last lecture, were there. One of them came to me and introducing himself, enquired when we would have another lecture I informed him it would be next Monday. He then spoke to the rest of his country men in their own language after which he said to me that he was telling them that we were the men who lectured and that we believed in having more than one wife and they desired to know more about it. We never had mentioned the subject but it has been humbuged to day through this city in consequence of what came out in the papers as above and to day the Persians has been informed on the subject by those who are opposed to us which has had the effect to make them believe we are correct.

We were not very well entertained at the Theatre The actors are certainly inexpurenced and spoke too low and indistinct & the audience very noisy.

Sunday 22 May 1853. At home nearley all day but around town once or twice No opportunity to do any thing in relation to religious affairs.

Monday 23 May 1853. This morning I took the "book of Mormon" accompanied by a note to the office of the Hong "Kong Register" and left it for the perusal of Mr W. F. Bevan the Editor. Requesting in the note the perusal of the same and also informing him that I would be pleased to have an interview with him on the subject of our religion at any time & place which would suit him. After this I was called in while passing Mr Franke's where I had a conversation on our religion. He promised to attend our meeting to day and invited me to call again and he would here more

Coming home I found that Mr Bevan had responded to my request for an interview and desired me to set the time which I did in a note to be tomorrow at two P. M.

Our meeting was prevented this evening in consequence of rain. Two of our methodist brethren came in this evening to make some further inquiries & they seem quite reasonable having read the "Book of Mormon" they find no fault but question its authenticity.

Tuesday 24 May 1853. Rained all this forenoon and we staid at home. At 2 p m paid the contemplated visit to Mr Bevan, who recieved me friendly and conversed very freely on religion. He denies the necessity either of any priest hood, organization, officers The power of the Holy Ghost or revelation being in the Churches or among men. Nor does he admit the materiality of God or Spirit, but seems perfectly willing to let every one have their own way.

Wednesday 25 May 1853. Arrainged to have advertisements inserted in "Dixon's Recorder" and the "Advertiser" that we would hold forth again on Friday evening at 5 and on every Tuesday & Friday afterwards the weather permitting, if not on the succeeding evenings.

In the after-noon went to the library and read the English & American papers Times go quite dull now we have to use our best judgement to obtain even a priva- ledge to preach in the parade ground and it is a harder job to get a hearing from a private individual   Rains very hard to night. -

Thursday 26 May 1853. We learn from the last news from the North that the Patriots have taken Amoy on the 18th instant, after a bloodless opposition by the Mandarins and "powers that were".   The patriots treated the citizens & foreigners with respect and kindness, abstaining from plunder & abuse and put a guard over the foreigners for their protection, admitting them to pass into their camp and have an interview with the "Rebel Chief" who showed every mark of respect & gave every assurance of his friendly intentions to them that could be expected.

It is expected that Canton will be taken next.

Reading "New York Weekly Herald" to day. Took a long walk with Br Duncan, to the S. E. and ascended a peak, taking a full view of the shipping & harbor.

Friday 27 May 1853. Had an interview with Mr Drinker who desires to peruse the "Book of Mormon" He says he personally acquainted with Joseph Smith in his early life.   That his grand father was owner of the "Hill Cumorah" when the plates for the "Book of Mormon" was taken from the ground.   He is very friendly and willing for us to succeed.   Gives the Missionaries a bad name. says they are idle, lazy, luxurious.   We were again prevented having our meeting this evening in consequence of rain.

Saturday 28 May 1853. Rainy bad morning.   Took a "Book of Mormon to Mr Drinker this morning and spent some time in conversation with him and some others. Rains very hard all day accompanied by heavey thunder.

Sunday 29 May 1853. We all staid at home untill evening when I visited Dr Leister a short time from hence took a long walk down the Harbor in company with Mr Wheeler.

Monday 30th May 1853. Around among the people.   In the after noon took a tour up the mountain and upper parts of the City

Tuesday 31 May 1853. This morning's No of the "Hongkong register" has a long article showing the necessity of having the "Mormonites" indicted for Blasphemy, and set to "picking oakum and kept on bread and water" but the Editor replies that his prescriptions "savours too much of the dark ages & days of thumbkings" and recommends for the people to let us alone.   I confess I admire the Editor's judge- ment.   When the Devil begins to rage and howl, it surely betokens that the Lord has a work to do.   Therefore we feel encouraged in opposition. At five P. M. we held another meeting at the parade ground.   Elder Lewis preached, showing the difference between our system of religion and the "popular religions of the day", which he done most effectually.

There was perhaps about twenty citizens and thirty soldiers present, all who paid good attention, but did not ask any questions, after meeting so we do not know what impression was made on them.

Wednesday 1 June 1853. Reading in the Library, not having had an opportunity to converse with the first individual today on religious subjects.   Indeed the people seem to be continually more inaccessible showing a pre disposition not to investigate and learn for themselves the principals of truth of the gospel.

Thursday 2 June 1853. To day passed off about as yesterday with me. Raining

Friday 3 June 1853. Rainy disagreeable day. This makes very dull times for us, being compelled to preach in the streets as the only way to obtain access to the people and then have our appointments so often disappointed by rain, nevertheless the Lord controlls our mission and we feel to exercise patience and rely on Him to open the way for the gospel in this land.

This evening at five the rain ceased and we went to our appointment on the parade ground but not the first individual made his appearance.

Saturday 4 June 1853. Reading in the Library part of the day At five we went to the parade ground to our appointment but not one individual attended this time, so it appears that our chance for preaching seems to be dull.

Sunday 5 June 1853. We all staid at home to day. Br Chapman has been quite sick for several days and I am now laboring under the influence of a bad cold.

Monday 6 June 1853. Verry unwell yet was able to go aboard of the "Rose of Sharon"

Tuesday 7 June 1853. Very sick and had to stay in the house. At five p. m. Lewis & Duncan went to the parade ground appointment, but no one attended. We feel that we have done all that God or man can require of us in this place. We have preached publickly and privately as long as any one would hear and often tried when no one would hear.

Wednesday 8 June 1853. Yet very unwell and confined to the house all day.

Thursday 9 June 1853. To day I begin to feel very much recovered from the effects of my cold and am able to go out. We have decided that our labours in this place be discontinued With all the faith and prayer that we were master of, we have dilligently taught both publickly & privately every one to whom we could in any way obtain access, the truths of the gospel and continued our labors as long as we could obtain audience from even one individual, and we find that no one will give heed to what we say, neither does any one manifest any opposition or interest but treats us with the utmost civility, conversing freely on all subjects except the pure principals of the gospel When we approach that they have universally in the most polite possible manner declined by saying that they did not wish to hear any thing on that subject for they are willing to extend the mantle of charity over all christian believers and ourselves among the rest, not doubting but we were good men and all would be right with all. And thus it is this day we do not know of one person in this place to whome we can bear our testimony of the things of god or warn to flee the wrath to come. And as to our staying here to learn the chinese language without one friend or one possible rescourse to us appears totally impractable and Paul-like we can truly say that the spirit speaketh expressly, that we preach the gospel no more in Asia for the present. This being the only port which now is safe, for foreigners, because of the rebelion in china we have no place to fall back on but California, whither we have concluded to sail the first opportunity and there await the orders of the First Presidency, and the dictates of the Holy Spirit to yet learn by what means the Lord will open, to introduce the gospel successfully in this benighted land.

We feel satisfied that our mission to this place will result in good, for we have obtained a knowledge of the times, circumstances, and situation of both the people & country which we never could have known & appreciated, had we not come and learned for ourselves, which will be of future binefit so that we are satisfied and yet feel encouraged to press on and fulfill our mission as the Lord may open the way.

Went again on board the "Rose of Sharron" a magnificent English Ship, bound for San Francisco in about ten days, and engaged a *Semi* Cabin passage for fifty dollars each, we furnishing our own board.

Friday 10 June 1853. Last night there was a burglarous attempt made by some persons, to us unknown to rob us of what little we have, but they only succeeded in taking a garment, shirt, & pants of mine which I had left unthoughtedly in an outer room So we have concluded "to take due notice thereof and govern ourselves accordingly" by keeping guard while we tarry here.

Paid Mr Dixon a visit again. He wishes to exchange papers with the "Deseret News"

Saturday 11 June 1853. Dark and rainy all day, with thunder & lightening, and as a matter of course we staid at home.

Sunday 12 June 1853. We all staid at home to day. Weather more pleasant.

Monday 13 June 1853. Occupied in procuring our provisions and out fit preparitory to sailing for San Francisco —

Tuesday 14 June 1853. Making preperations to sail and expect to go on board on Thursday or Friday next.

Wednesday 15 June 1853. Still preparing for Sailing as anticipated.

Thursday 16 June 1853. Went on board again to see the Captain and appointed next Monday to ship for Sailing on Wednesday.

Friday 17 June 1853. Reading in the Library and around the City & home.

Saturday 18 June 1853. This morning went on board the "Rose of Sharon" and paid our passage to San Francisco which is fifty dollars each, we finding our own provisions. The money was discounted ten per cent which is in reality fifty-five dollars each.

After returning I paid Mr Dixon & Lemon my last visit. They gave me a file of the "China Mail" and desired me to write to them and they would send me the papers when they had my address.

Witnessed a chinese funeral, which singularly different from any thing of the kind I ever before have seen. The corpse was born by "coolies" and was preceeded by a band of musick playing some kind of airs totally unknown to me. The sound all taken together reminded me some of a fidler play *back* of the *bridge* One stringed instruments, gongs, and a kind of a Squealing claronet constituted the musical instruments. The musicians were dressed in red while the processions bore tables of flower pots meats, cakes, flowers, a roast pig, and the like while others bore banners on which were suspended lanterns, ribbons and many such things, all *fixed up,* and ornamented in the most fantastical manner, blending the civilized & savage custom and was all things taken together a very interesting sight.

This after-noon paid my last visit to Mr Bevans. He was remarkably friendly and affable spent some two hours. He gave me a file of his papers & promised to forward others on to me. Requests me to give any of our Elders who may come here a letter of introduction to him & wished to pay us a visit before we sail which we appointed to-morrow evening.

Sunday 19 June 1853. To day we all staid at home expecting Mr Bevan's farewell visit, instead of which he substituted a polite note apologising for not being able to come, being *indisposed* but he sent the file of the "Hong Kong Register" and also the "Overland Register & price current" Br Lewis & myself then took our last stroll down the Bay.

Monday 20 June 1853. This morning Br Duncan and myself purchased our provisions and took it on board, viz 75 lbs bread 30 lbs sugar, 50 catties[25] Irish potatoes, 50 sweet do, 40 catties pork 50 Doz Eggs, 50 catties rice, 15 catties dried fish, 5 catties tea. and in the after noon we went on board. Hard rains to night.

Tuesday 21 June 1853. This morning Br Duncan and myself went on shore a short time after which we all staid on board. Every thing is hurry & bustle to day The chines passengers are coming on board Rainy day and the mates storming and all trying to be off in the morning.

Wednesday 22 June 1853. This morning every thing is still in an uproar Chinamen are crouding on board, and the crew are preparing to sail and about ten a. m. we were under way going out of the Harbor to the West. We doubled the island of Hong Kong about dark and set sail due East with a good breeze

While making out the captain rope-ended a boy and the mate chained a sailor to the mizzen for an assault on himself and the destruction of two of his shirts. (Capt name, was Thompson)

There are on board 37 chinamen and two Doctors and two cooks & 49 china women, who are going to California under charge to opperate professionally for those who will most likely get all the proffits. Some of them are very free to converse on their (golden [crossed out]) anticipations of future enjoyments and the golden harvest, which awaits them

There are also two cabin one deck passengers Mr Hill & Schaffer and a crew of 20 whites and 28 (Maylays [crossed out]) Lascars,[26] not including the officers, cabin boys &c.

Thursday 23 June 1853. Sailing East, with a good breeze all well only the chinese emptying their stomachs, over board.

Friday 24 June 1853. Sailing E. ½ S. very hard breeze and squally, sea rough. Saw a ship to s. in fore noon & one N in the after noon, making towards Hong Kong.

Saturday 25 June 1853. Course E by S light breeze We are now just off to the S. of Formosa which is in sight 60 miles to the N. and about the same distance and a little S is the Bashee islands in sight so we must be just entering Formosa Channel at 6 o'c p. m.

Sunday 26 June 1853. This morning we are in a dead calm and not yet passed the islands but continue to tumble on the smooth waves till near noon when a breeze came & we sailed N by W. some two or three hours making almost direct to Formosa which now is in fair view, when coming to some (ref [crossed out]) reefs ahead, tacked to S. E. by S under a good breeze are now making towards the same islands we (was [crossed out]) had ahead last night.

To day we dined with the Captain, who gave us a standing invitation to dine with him every sunday and a most excellent dinner we had.

We passed the head of the Bashee goupe about dark having a good breeze and sailed fast all night.

Monday 27 June 1853. This morning we are fairly out of the white looking Chinese Sea and sailing with a good wind over the blue waves of the pacific.

Tuesday 28 June 1853. light wind & slow sailing Course E. N. by N.

Wednesday 29 June 1853. good breeze last night. Sailing brisk but quite calm to day Course N. E. ½ E.

---

25. *Catties* refers to a unit of weight in eastern countries, which varies from one land to another. In China, a *Cattie* is one and one-third pound.

26. Lascars are East Indian native sailors.

Thursday 30 June 1853. This morning when I awoke we were in a fine squall and had a good breeze all day.

Friday 1 July 1853. This morning we were sailing by the side of Loo Choo island which was to the North perhaps 30 miles but in plain view, we afterwards passed several others smaller ones in the course of the day. They all appear to not have any timber on them. Our course is N. N. E. and at times still more N. Still have a good brisk breeze. In the evening the wind having changed, we steered almost N. barely passing an island which lay to the "Lee bow" with another island ahead. The wind East bearing N. at dark we could discover fire in many places on the island which we suppose to be Japanese fishing boats.

Saturday 2 July 1853. This morning I found the ship had tacked to a little south of East at 4 o'clock and lay to the same position to the islands as in the evening only farther South, but was again tacking to her former course when I arose and now made directly to the center of the island ahead, which I learned was Harbor island about 25 miles long, laying from N. W. to S. E. Soon however she tacked again to the lee-ward of Harbor island to the W. N. W. as she could not beat round to the east in the winds Eye under some two days While Sailing thus, to break the monotony, kill (dull [crossed out]) dull care, and dispell "enui" the captain with *malice prepense* and without the fear of God before [a fore thought] his eyes, but instigated &c had an inocent goose hung by the hind legs and hoisted to the main top yard, when he took a gun in his hands and wilfully, deliberately, pointing in the direction of the said goose, with the said gun, pulled trigger causing the fire to ignite &c causing instant death to the said goose &c against the peace and dignaty of the whole aqutic tribe &c[27] After the above "*Fowl-tastrophe* (had [crossed out]) had happened the vessel bore to the E gradually while we were endeavouring to round Harbor island (which we find consists of a groupe of several considerable islands), and before the morning had come born to the East.

Sunday 3 July 1853. Spent the day reading and dind with the captain Course N. N. E.

Monday 4 July 1853. Spent the day reading. Course as yesterday. We are now in about "Lat 30" and just of the East of the South of Japan which is now in plain view.

Tuesday 5 July 1853. Calm wind & changing out course occasionally from N. N. E. to East, while I am reading.

Wednesday 6 July 1853. Calm as ever Course East while I am deeply pouring over novels to kill time.

Thursday 7 July 1853. Calm breeze. Course East sailing at some 5 knots

Friday 8 July 1853. Breeze some better Course the same.

Saturday 9 July 1853. Brisk breeze. & Course still East.

Sunday 10 July 1853. Brisk breezee & course East. We dined with the captain to day, most sumptuously

Monday 11 July 1853. Still Sailing East with a good breeze & all well.

Tuesday 12 July 1853. Dark and rainy this fore noon, good weather in the afternoon, wind & course about the same.

---

27. Here Stout adopts a legal jargon, evidently in a lighter vein, although it is clear that he did not enjoy the sport of the captain.

Wednesday 13 July 1853. Rainy with changable winds last night, but today Calm and pleasant. Course N. E by E half N. Sailing about three or four knots.

Thursday 14 July 1853. Hard breeze from the S. E. Sea quite rough & white caps beginning to rise. We had a mess of excellent fish for dinner which had been caught to day, called Albercaw which was a good treat to our apetites. This evening the course is bending to the N. E. gradually.

Friday 15 July 1853. Course N. E. by N sailing brisk Cool S. E. wind

To day our potatoes & Eggs are are all gone, more than one half of them have Spoiled & consequently leaves us short of provisions as we now have only bread, rice, sugar & tea, & a little pork

Saturday 16 July 1853. Course & wind about the same. Cool weather. Reading novels to kill time.

Sunday 17 July 1853. Course & wind about the same. Cool weather Dined with the Captain. Three Fin Backed whales passed spouting just under the Bow.

Monday 18 July 1853. Very calm to day but course the same. Several large fish in sight. The Captain, Lewis & some others succeeded in harpooning a large nondescript fish, which they at first took for a shark, but proved to be a species entirely unknown to any present. It had no tail after harpooning & shooting it twice it got away and thus disappointed our curiosity.

Tuesday 19 July 1853. Very calm. Course the same. Dined to day on Albratross soup presented to us by the Captain From the appearance as well as the *olfactory* reports of the bird I certainly never would have thought of eating it, but notwithstanding those forbiding symtoms the meat and soup was excellent although I confess that it was very materially aided by a goodly portion of fresh mutton which was cooked with it.

The albatross follow the ship and are easily killed and Captain Thompson seems to be remarkably fond of this kind of *Marine* poaching which is (in fact [crossed out]) no little amusement heightened by the fact that he is not subjecting himself thereby to the *pains* and *penalties* of the game laws which his own country impose to bar this innocent amusement

Wednesday 20 July 1853. Course N. E mostly to day. I had a fair view of a whale which came close alongside and blowed several times. The ship was then hove to for the Captain to go gunning awhile after which the ship tacked to the south. Wind East.

Thursday 21 July 1853. Sailing fast to south After noon tacked again to N. E. by N. Hard East wind.

Friday 22 July 1853. Last night the ship hauled to about E. N. E by N. and is sailing very fairly. all else as usual.

Saturday 23 July 1853. Reading very busy. Course N. E. light winds.

Sunday 24 July 1853. Reading. Reading! good breeze. Course N. E by E.

Monday 25 July 1853. This morning ship tacked south. In the after noon saw a regular *naval* Engagement between a whale & a thrasher. The thrasher would raise itself some ten or 15 feet out of the water and precipitate itself upon the whale with a tremendous thrash, which made the whale flounder exceedingly. This was repeated several times in plain view & am told that a Sword fish always accompanies a thrasher keeping under the whale thrusting him in the belly to keep him on top of the water and thus they continue untill the whale is killed.[28]

---

28. Stout's description of the battle between the thrasher and the whale and also his story of the efforts of the Chinese courtesans to propitiate the wind gods are so vivid and illuminating that one might wish he had written in more detail of the sea experiences.

About 4 p. m tacked again to the former course.

Tuesday 26 July 1853. Course & wind same only the ship sometimes bears near south. The obstinate wind keeping us off our course so long we are growing some what impatient in so much that a considerable congregation of the Chinese *Courtesan* ladies assembled on deck and solemnly invoked or as they say *Chin Josh* to change the wind, by burning josh sticks & perferating and casting josh paper to the wind, while one of them sat on the Deck, resting her face on her knees, fidgeting and twitching seemed to act as medium while the others were anxiously enquiring in an under tone of her the news from joshs. which was as near as I could learn, that the wind woud change favorably in two days and we would arive at California in two weeks

I do not know that I have given a full description of this *Chin Josh* neither do I understand the principal which they act on only they say that *josh* comes from the Sky and tells the medium the things enquired for.

Wednesday 27 July 1853. Very calm to day, but fortunately towards evening the obstinate East Wind which had so long kept us too far north had now changed nearly West & the ship squared her yards & headed E half South So that the Chinese prediction of Josh's favor was duly fulfilled to the great joy of all

Thursday 28 July 1853. Cloudy damp and chilling weather Course same & wind increasing.

Friday 29 July 1853. Wind is still increasing & course the same Ship in sight to the West.

Saturday 30 July 1853. Badly afflicted with cold & kept my bunk almost the whole day.

Sunday 31 July 1853. Day passed about as usual. Not well.

Monday 1 Aug 1853. Well as ever again. Course still E by S Cloudy, drizzling cool weather. Saling 8 knots

Tuesday 2 Aug 1853. Course same. Wind brisk. Weather cloudy

Wednesday 3 Aug 1853. Very calm. Course same 3 knots.

Thursday 4 Aug 1853. Almost entirely calm so that the ship will not obey the helm, so the Capt went gunning.

Friday 5 Aug 1853. Sailed briskly S. E all night & in the morning tacked to E N. E. Stiff S. E. wind & rain.

Saturday 6 Aug 1853. The wind increaced last night so that the sails had to be reefed. Sea very rough. this morning and still raining

Sunday 7 Aug 1853. Course & wind the same all as usual

Monday 8 Aug 1853. Course E by N. Sailing about 8 knots.

Tuesday 9 Aug 1853. Course same & calmer weather.

Wednesday 10 Aug 1853. Weather so calm that the ship will not obey the helm.

Thursday 11 Aug 1853. Breeze increasing. Course same

Friday 12 Aug 1853. This morning we overtook the ship John N. Gosler which left Hong Kong 27 May by which we by the politeness of Mr Nash had forwarded our letters & Dispaches home. They were all well and in good heart. We however soon left them far astern with a 8 or 9 knot breeze.

Saturday 13 Aug 1853. Calmed again and our anticipations of speedily arriving on the shores of the "Home of the free" are lulled with the breeze again

Sunday 14 Aug 1853. Light wind &, we flickering from E. S. E. to N. N. E very slowly

Monday 15 Aug 1853. High wind from the E. & we tacking some times from south some times to the North.

Tuesday 16 Aug 1853. Sailing at from 6 to 8 knots from E. N. E to E.

Wednesday 17 Aug 1853. Sailing about as yesterday. About 4 p. m. a Bark to the N. bearing N. W.

Thursday 18 Aug 1853. Cloudy, cool and drizzling Course same about dark tacked to W. N. W.

Friday 19 Aug 1853. Sailed briskly all night and met the John N. Gosler this morning after which we again took the other tack to E by N. and are now sailing parallen to and near the Gosler

Saturday 20 Aug 1853. Sailing as yesterday only in the evening the wind hauled three points West.

Sunday 21 Aug 1853. Sailing still N. E Strong breeze & sea rough Course still bearing to the N. The bright color of the water begins to indicate our proximity to the land which sensibly increases our anxiety to terminate our tedius voyage

Monday 22 Aug 1853. This morning the wind nearly ceased to blow and we proceeded at about 2 knots untill one o'clock when land was dicovered to the North which proved to be the Farrallones islands. at dark we cast anchor in 17 fathoms and staid all night 8 miles from Harbor

Tuesday 23 Aug 1853. The pilot came one board this morning at five. We lay at anchor untill three p. m when we again set sail at about 2 knots. and arrived in port about ten at night

Tuesday 23 Aug 1853. Here I have to count time by West Longitude and consequently have to Have two days of the same date Earley this morning I went ashore, leaving Brs Lewis & Duncan on Board, and went to visit the Saints in this place finding them all well and rejoiced to see our return but the joy and satisfaction which I expected to be a happy partaker of in their society was only heighten to be overcast in sorrow & deep mourning. Too happy in the anticipation of at last hearing from my wife and children, the last news from whom had left my wife in such critical circumstances had only increased my anxiety to hear how she was now, (which [crossed out]) But my anxiety and better hopes was now doomed to be blasted by the inconsoleable intelligence of her death and the death of her child.

Baffled & disappointed in our hopes & wishes relative to our mission & so soon return I gladly looked forward for consolation in the intelligence from home & a word of comfort from her who was always so ready to console me in the hour of deep distress by proving her self the good angel to administer the balm to the disconsolate

Why attempt to pen grief, disappointment & sorrow totally unuterable; why write the anguish which rends the heart? When the companion of our toils, the partaker of our sorrows, grief, anguish, and despondencies of this mortal life is so rudely torn from our bosom, carrying her last tender offspring with her, while we are absent and in blissful ignorance, of the ravages of the destroyer why should we attempt to depict the feeling which such sad news brings to the heart as this morning beclouds my hopes when I learned that Louisa was no more

Let those who have drank of this bitter cup respond to my feelings and drop a tear of compassionate sympaty with me in this hour of my deepest mourning

That blissful sorrow of soothing the last agonies of her death and recieving her last (death breathed [crossed out]) departing benedictions and farewell as her immortal (puts on immortality part [crossed out]) Spirit drops the mortal coil. Ye a more those dear pledges which God had given us to recieve them in my arms with her dying blessings on them, but alas this was denied me.

Bereft of her and not knowing how or where my children are with no one who can appreciate my feeling now for who who can sympathise with me now only the disconsolate, let me not forget from whence comfort & consolation comes

She died on the 11th day of January last the child died on the 9th day of the same month.

We spent the day in bring our traps from the ship & put up with Br Barton Morey.

Wednesday 24 Aug 1853. This morning we held a council and decided that I should return to the Valley with the letters and papers which we brought from Hong Kong and make report of our doings and the situation of affairs in China, to the President, and learn his will in relation to our furture course, Meanwhile Brs Lewis & Duncan will remain here and act as the Lord opens the way, after which we set about preparing to accomplish what we had decided

Thursday 25 Aug 1853. To day I spent around the city with Br H. Green.[29] In the evening a large party of saints met at Br B. Moreys for social chat among whom was Br J. M. Horner & also C. W. Wandle[30] returning missionary from Australia.

While here we tried the experiment of *Spirit Rappings* which was duly responded to and several communications passed the principal of which I do not understand I was declared a negative medium but more of this when I know more for I am sure a novice

Friday 26 Aug 1853. This day Elder Cyrus Canfield came here He & Elder Wade have been appointed to join us in our mission & had come thus far & meeting us thus returning are left in the same uncertainty that we are not knowing what to do. He brought two letters one from S. M. Blair of May 3 & one from Allen both bearing the sad news of my wife's death Allens letter dated April 11. States

---

29. Harvey (Hervey) Green was born December 4, 1806, in New York. He came to Utah in the Heber C. Kimball company of September 1848, and was one of the first to draw land in what became the Seventeenth Ward in Salt Lake County. He went with the group to settle San Bernardino and returned with them to Salt Lake City in 1858. Here he made his permanent home.

30. Charles W. Wandell was born April 12, 1819, at Courtland, New York. He joined the Mormon Church in 1837 and proceeded at once to do missionary work in his home state. At one time he presided over forty-eight elders in that area.

Wandell came to Nauvoo where he was a steamboat officer on the Mississippi River. In 1846 upon the rise of the Strangite movement, Wandell wrote an article purporting to be a revelation of God to J. J. Strang. This was read in public, but so many in the audience accepted it as genuine that Wandell confessed that it was a trick.

Soon after this he came by boat to San Francisco where he was associated with Sam Brannan and Parley P. Pratt. In July 1851 he was called to assist John Murdock on a mission to Australia and the two set sail on September 8, 1851, on the bark *Petrel.* In Australia they published a periodical called *Zion's Watchman* and pursued their proselyting with such success that on April 6, 1853, "A small company of Saints in charge of Elder Charles W. Wandell and bound for America sailed from Sidney, Australia, per ship *Envelope.*"

Wandell remained in California until the fall of 1857 when he accompanied a group of Saints to Utah. He stopped in Beaver where he taught school for several years. From there he moved to Corinne, Utah, and in the early 1870's ran a series of articles in the *Utah Reporter* under the name of "Argus," accusing Brigham Young of being accessory to the Mountain Meadows massacre and to other murders in the state.

In 1872 Wandell joined the Reorganized Church of Jesus Christ of Latter Day Saints and went as a missionary for them to Australia. He died there on March 4, 1875.

that he lives in my house & has charge of my children & property and is doing all he can for their comfort & sending Elizabeth to school, all else he says is doing well.

Saturday 27 Aug 1853. To day I was at Br Morey's mostly all day

Sunday 28 Aug 1853. This morning Elder Wade, G. D. Grant E. D Woolley and T. S. Williams and several other Brethren from different parts came here to a meeting at Br Moreys Elders Woolley & Green & Everleth spoke. After meeting was over several of the brethren & sisters assisted to means to go home Brs Everleth & Davids gave fifteen dollars, Sister Lincoln Twelve, Br F. Cheney fifty, Sister Corwin four Sister Mory two fifty, Sister King a bundle of goods. In the evening took my luggage on board the (schooner [crossed out]) Brig Fremont intending to sail tomorrow for San Pedro. This is the same (schooner [crossed out]) Brig on which the missionaries sailed from San Pedro to this place last winter. The officers favor our people generally charging less then they do any other people Br Harvey Green & son Ammon are also going Br Harvey procured my passage for fifteen dollars cabin passage when the usual price is twenty five dollars. We went and staid all night again with Br Morey

Monday 29 Aug 1853. By mistake I have recorded my going on Board on Sunday which should have been on Monday which was the day which I was occupied in procuring my passage &c

Tuesday 30 Aug 1853. This morning earley we went to the vessel which soon left the wharf I took the parting hand with Elders Lewis & Duncan. They to tarry here while I go home and larn what is the thing which we shall do next. I feel very lonesome now I have parted with the companions whom I have been so closely associated with so long and under such peculiar circumstances. At two p. m. we were fairly under way having to beat out of Harbor but before night we were out of sight and sailing under a good breeze

Wednesday 31 Aug 1853. This morning we were beautifully becalmed but the wind rose with the sun and we were soon under good headway so that before night we were sailing some ten knots with very rough sea

Thursday 1 Sept 1853. Calm again this morning but another breeze arose with good sailing untill evening when we were again becalmed & the vessel hove to untill morning

Friday 2 Sept 1853. Becalmed again and tilting on the waves, the vessel bearly manageable by the helm. A light breeze however soon arose and we arrived at Santa Barbara about noon where a considerable portion of the freight had to be discharged
    The Schooner "Laura Bevans" arrived here an hour before ourselves & the Steamer "Goliah" was here & just leaving for San Francisco as we arrived. Nearley all the passengers went ashore except Brs Green and myself.

Saturday 3 Sept 1853. Still at anchor & the crew discharging Br H. Green and myself went ashore this forenoon & spent some two hours, exploring the Scatered situation of this ancient place.
    We found nothing to attract our attention and but a slim excuse for a city. We came back about two and went on board again. The day is very warm.

Sunday 4 Sept 1853. About ten a. m. we set sail again. The Laura Bevans also started about 15 minutes ahead of us. We had a good light breeze which died away gradually so that towards night we were going only about two knots. just after dark one of the Pacific Mail Steamers passed us going to San Francisco

Monday 5 Sept 1853. Going two knots yet with the Laura close bye The breeze gradually arose and we arrived at San Pedro about 6 p. m but did not go ashore

Tuesday 6 Sept 1853. Went ashore at nine, leaving Ammon on board to attend to some freight which the capt could not or would not deliver untill his own convienience was served So Harvey & myself took stage for Los Angelos pay seven dollars each passage and arrived there at three putting up with Capt Jessed D. Hunter and spent the day eating pears & greaps of (the [crossed out]) which there is a great abundance.

Wednesday 7 Sept 1853. To day is a great day in California The general election when all hopeful lads are undergoing the ordeal of the ballot box which is to determine their future exhaltation or hopeless demolition of their sanguine anticipations

The people are all life, and doing their best for their especial favorites, all worked off well however for there was but one man (Spanierd) shot during the whole day

Thursday 8 Sept 1853. The weather is intensely warm & I stired only enough to procure what grapes I wanted to eat.

Friday 9 Sept 1853. To day we have an opportunity of going to San Barnidino with Br William Mathews who has come here with a load of flour, accordingly in the afternoon we left Los Angelos and traveled some twelve miles to Monte

Saturday 10 Sept 1853. Traveled to San Jose to day under a very hot Sun, and put with an old Spaniard, where we staid all night

Sunday 11 Sept 1853. Started earley arriving at San Barnideno at 4 p. m. Here I find the saints all well & in a prosperous situation some of their crops however have failed yet the settlement abounds with plenty. Here I can once more rest from the fatigues & anxieties of traveling feeling myself at home Here I put up with William Mathews who desires me to make his House my home while here

Monday 12 Sept 1853. Spent the day visiting & staid all night with Br John Holladay. He like myself has been called to mourn the loss of the darling object of his heart in the person of his youngest daughter.

Tuesday 13 Sept 1853. Spent the day visiting again in company with my old San Francisco friend Br Q. S. Sparks

Wed. 14 Thurs 15. Frid 16, Sat 17, Sept. Visiting around amongst my old friends.

Sunday 18 Sept 1853. Attended meeting. Spoke a short time giving a short account of our mission to China.

Monday 19. Visiting Had a meeting at dark preparitory to our starting to the Valley There was only 14 names presented & the time of starting not to be untill after the conference on the 6 next month.

Tuesday 20 Sept 1853. visiting around the fort as usual.

Wednesday 21 Sept 1853. Started in the afternoon with Br C. C. Rich to Mill Creek Cannon passing by old San Bernardino Here is a beautiful country which has some good farms & a vinyard in a high state of cultivation. It was not untill an hour after dark that we arrived at his saw mill about 20 miles from where we started

Thursday 22 Sept 1853. This morning we breakfasted on Speckled trout with which these mountain streams abound. Lyman & Rich has a most excellent saw mill here which would clear perhaps 50 dollars pr day if well attended to but there is not any thing of consequence doing there

We arrived at home about one p. m   I was almost worn out riding in the oppressive hot sun

Friday 23 Sept 1853. To day was entirely dedicated to visiting among my old acquainteances.

Saturday 24 Sept 1853. This is a day of joy and rejoicing to the young people of this place. The last day of school which terminates with a dance & old and young become equal in actions & feeling For my part I feel quite blythe & boyish The "Fantastic toe" was tipped till ten at night when all retired peaceble & happy

Sunday 25 Sept. Attended church Elders Lyman & Rich preached good meeting. all well.

Monday 26 Sept 1853. Visiting away very leasurely.

Tues 27. Wed 28. Thurs 29 Friday 30 Sept '53. Visiting as usual. The prospects for going to the Valley seem dull. Such is the unceartinty and dubious situation of the Indians that those who wish to go do not know what to depend upon & there is a probability of the entire party failing to go

Saturday 1 Oct 1853. Went with Br H. Green to visit Br T. Tomkins

Sunday 2 Oct 1853. Meeting. Elder H. Green & A. Lyman preached At early candle light attended a wedding where Daniel Harris & Lydia Harris (no kin) committed matrimony (and we [crossed out])

Monday 3 Oct 1853. Engaged in legal business to day for one Don Jose Maria Valdez in case of Ejectment for which he gave me 25 dollars which really in my situation was very acceptable

Tuesday 4 Oct 1853. To day Prests Lyman & Rich Br Wandle, from San Francisco, Green & myself took a general buggy ride over the country & looking at the newly laid off city. At Dark attended the High Council to take in to consideration the price of city lots

Wednesday 5 Oct 1853. Had another law suit. Louis Robidoux compt vs. Diego Labarra for driving off his calves & killing his calves cows & beeves, court before John Brown J. P. The complaint had neither Tittle, Court, nor venue & was consequently quashed. I was on the part of the defence. & am to recieve as fee a horse (& saddle & rigging [crossed out]) (If I am lucky enough to ever get it)

Thursday 6 Oct 1853. General conference at eleven. Business was to accept the officers of the church in the usual manner & preaching by Amasa, Charles & Br Green & adjd till tom-orrow at ten.

Friday 7 Oct 1853. Attended Conference Elder C. W. Wandle preached on the *sure* fulfilment of prophecy then my-self on the subject of *"auld lang sine"* after which A. Lyman versus The use of tobacco & the Boys *Bronco* riding on Sundays.

Saturday 8 Oct. 1853. Attended conference Q. S. Sparks preached then C. C. Rich making a financial report of the Ranch accounts &c adjd an hour, met A. Lyman Continued the Ranch sermon.

Sunday 9 Oct 1853. Attended Conference Elders C. C. Rich & A. Pratt, Lyman, preached. Afternoon Wandle, Crosby, Seeley, Lyman & Rich preached after which there was a subscription taken up for the "Poor Fund amounting to [Blank]

Monday 10 Oct 1853. Very much afflicted with cold.

Tues 11. & Wed 12 Oct 1853. Doing nothing. Very unwell.

Thurs & Frid 14 Oct 1853. General turn out to work on mill race

Saturday 15 Oct 1853. Attended a general party to day where old & young mingled in the dance untill ten in the evening. All seemed to enjoy themselves extreemly well
News from Salt Lake says the indians have killed two whites & still hostile. Salt Lake being walled in

Sunday 16 Oct 1853. Attended meeting Elder Rich, Lyman & Grouard preached. In the evening the company, which anticipated going to Salt Lake met to conclude what to do & determined that it was impractible for so small a company to travel considering the present hostile demonstrations of the Indians & that we would wait a more favorable opportunity

Monday 17 Oct 1853. Circuit Court to day only one case on docket Prudhommce vs Valdez. I was admitted to the bar.

Tuesday 18 Oct 1853. Attended Court in fore noon C. adjd In the after-noon went and staid all night with Br Thos Thompkins.

Wednesday 19 Oct 1853. Spent the day around as usual and staid all night with Henry Boyle, who made me a present of a Six shooting revolving rifle. Mr Louis a jew pedler made me a present also of beautiful southern dirk to serve me as an aid in travelling to Utah.

Thursday 20 Oct 1853. To day completes one year since I left home where I was surrounded by all the endearing ties of an affectionate wife, whose ashes now lies mouldering in the dust and my children lonely orphans, my home, with all its kindred ties, no more. I feel a disconsolate blank, my tears dries in their fountain & I groan without a response for only those in like affliction can appreciate the heart felt anguish that burns in his bosom who has had, torn from him the dearest object of his heart the solace of all his cares, the repository of (his [crossed out]) all his joy and sorrow, another self, the wife of his bosom. True I am surrounded by friends who care for me but Home, & family only can make happiness in this world.

Friday 21 Oct 1853. Went in Company with Robt Clift to Louis Robedoux to see to some legal matters wherein there will most likely proceed some tolerable heavy lawsuits We returned home about dark. I was very tired mule riding

Saturday 22 Oct 1853. Feel very bad to day from yesterday's ride staid all night with Justice Morse

Sunday 23 Oct 1853. Attended meeting to day. Elder Grourard preached followed by Elder Lyman.

Monday Oct 24 1853. Hunting cows today. Very tiresome

Tuesday 25 Oct 1853. The Salt Lake mail arrived to day 24 days out by which I recieved a letter from President B. Young, directed to Hong Kong. In the evening Elder James Lewis arrived here from San Francisco in good health.

Wednesday 26 Oct 1853. This evening we had another meeting to take into consideration going to Utah at which we concluded to go and start on Monday next as those who come with the mail report the Indians friendly from here to Cole Creek

Thursday 27 Oct 1853. Trading for an out fit to go to Utah

Friday 28 Oct 1853. Occupied as yester-day.

Saturday 29 Oct 1853. Occupied as yester-day.

Sunday 30 Oct 1853. Went to meeting. Elder James Lewis first preached followed by myself A. Lyman & C. C. Rich then the Sacrament & a contribution to fit out Elders A. Pratt & Grouar to the Society isles on a mission. Wrote letter to Duncan

Monday 31 Oct 1853. preparing to start tomorrow. The Brethren are very kind in furnishing me with the necessary out fit.

Tuesday Nov 1 1853. Preparing to start to day but got disappointed   Went & staid all night with Br Tompkins.

Wednesday 2 Nov 1853. We were again disappointed about starting   James Lewis bought another wagon to put one span of mules on for him & me & I think we will now soon be off.

Thursday Nov 3 1853. To day we made out to start and went up the Cajon Cannon to the narrows some 15 miles from San Bernardino. Brs Albert Tanner and Montgomery E. Button accompanied us to assist us up the Cajon Pass   All the rest of the company is ahead but Ira S. Miles & wife.

Friday Nov 4th 1853. Started earley, met a few men from Salt Lake, and arrove at the foot of the Pass at 2 p. m.   Those in advance had just got their waggons up and came back to help us   The day was very warm and we almost exhausted ourselves and animals before we reached the summit   I for one gave out and had to throw myself down on the ground and gasp for breath unable to stand.   But we were safely up by 4 and started for the Mohave 20 miles down the good decending road driving very fast.   We arrived in camp some two hours after dark perfectly *used up* and threw ourselves on the ground to rest turning our animals out to take care of themselves   Here we found the encampment of the Pacific Rail Road surveyors who was looking out the most feasable pass over the Sierra Nevada for the Rail Road on the Southren Rout.

Saturday 5 Nov 1853. This morning the animals except four had taken French leave going in two bands. After some fretting and chafing by Hiett two parties of two each started in pursuit returning about noon with all while another party started back on the road after some provisions which the pack animals had distributed last night in our double quick march from the pass.   They also returned after dark having found the lost provisions &c.

This evening the company was organized by choosing me captain.   The company consists of twelve men viz

1 Hosea Stout	7 Evert Osser
2 John Kimball	8 Hiram Curtis
3 James Lewis	9 David Hall
4 Elisha Hiett	10 F. M. Perkins
5 Harvey Green	11 Samuel Reed
6 Washington Cook	12 Madison Cook

To night, not being so tired an consequently more prudent we kept out a guard.

Sunday 6 Nov 1853. Rolled on this morning leaving Cook & Perkins to wait here for Miles, while we would go on some fifteen miles to good feed and wait for them.   We encamped at the same beautiful grove Cotton wood in which we nooned on the 30th Nov last. Feed was excellent clover.

Shortly after we encamped Cook & Perkins overtook us accompanied by Mr John C. Leonard who had started with David Hall and was followed Sheriff Clift arrested at the top of Cajon pass & taken back as an escaped prisonor from San Deigo but not being the individual he was of course released and followed on & is going through which makes our Company thirteen.   Leonard brought the word that Miles had taken sick in the Cajon Cannon & had returned back so we are now ready to *go ahead* at last.

Monday 7 Nov 1853. Travelled only fifteen miles and encamped at one p. m.

Tuesday 8 Nov 1853. Travelled to lower camping on the Mohave 10 miles put up at one p. m. all well.

Wednesday 9 Nov 1853. Travelled to Bitter Springs thiry miles Hard drive Poor feed. Animals and men tired. But we had the first picking here this year.

Thursday 10 Nov 1853. To day we have the Big Desert to cross, fifty two miles, accordingly we started earley, and travelling some 8 or ten miles we met the advance of this fall's emmagration. A large train scattered almost entirely across the desert, which consisted of waggons & teams, droves of cattle & horses Some of the animals were giving out while men came straggling along carrying their bedding on their backs, trying to get their given out animals along There were several thousand head of animals[31]

We had hard drive arriving at Salt Springs near nine p. m but it was near Eleven before Green & Cook came into camp.

Here we had nothing but Salt grass & salt water for our animals which only increased their thirst and has a tendency to weaken them Most of the animals were kept tied up all night to keep them from leaving This is the hardest part of the road on animals

Friday 11 Nov. 1853. Started before Sun rise arriving at Maragoshie Springs at Noon. Kimball broke the fore axle of his waggon to day

Here we met another large train with Horses sheep and cattle amounting to five or six thousand who were recruiting before passing the desert

Saturday 12 Nov 1853. Rested this fore noon on good feed.

Here Green and Cook found their teams were inadiquate to draw their heavy waggon, some of their animals being nearly given already, while none of the company had strength of team to assist them, they concluded to return back. Br Cook sending his sone Madison with us who had to pack,

After the above arraingements were made we went on to resting Springs where we found another large camp with droves of animals

Sunday 13 Nov 1853. Travelled on to Stump Springs 21 m. meeting another large drove of sheep and cattle Finding no grass we rested an hour took supper and went on 15 miles and tied up for the night with out grass or water, men & animals fatigued.

Monday 14 Nov 1853. Started at three a. m. arriving at Mountain Springs at Sun rise. Here the grass and water is off the road and has not been found by the

---

31. There was heavy traffic over this road during 1853. An excellent source is found in the "Diary of Dr. Thomas Flint, California to Maine and Return, 1851-1855," edited by Waldemar Westergaard in *Annual Publications Historical Society of Southern California*, XII (1923) Part III, 53-127. Flint gives a detailed account of the towns en route and the other companies on the road. At Parowan, Utah, he wrote on page 108: "Monday 17th [October 1853]: Had some blacksmithing done by a Mr. Whitney, originally from Maine . . . . Five wagons of Mormons going out for California, joined us here, requested the privilege of travelling with us. Their stock very troublesome at night but not one of the men would go out to look after them at night— it was said for fear of the 'Destroying Angels.' "

Flint and his company had started with "1800 sheep, 11 yoke of oxen, 2 cows, 4 horses, 2 wagons, complete camping outfit, 4 men 3 dogs and ourselves." At Salt Lake City and environs he purchased 400 more sheep and additional oxen.

Traveling ahead of him was the Hollister train, and following close in his wake the McAlister train and the McClanahan train. The Frazier train and the White train were mentioned as overtaking or passing his en route.

emmagration this year so that we had plenty for our animals, leaving at one p. m we went to Cottonwood Springs, 10. m. having poor feed.

Tuesday 15 Nov. 1853. Met two or three companies of emmigrating Mormons on their way to California mostly English from Cole Creek settlement.

They had become disaffected because of martial law being declared in Utah during the Indian difficulties there

Considering themselves oppressed when called on to defend their families and effects from the knife of the savage they have denied their faith and are now cursing those principals in which they have formerly rejoiced so much, in and are going to mingle again with the wicked & join hands with the ungodly, who are kindred spirits now with themselves.

We encamped on the Los Vagus flat on the borders of the desert

Wednesday 16 Nov 1853. Started this morning at one, travelling about 20 miles by sun rise, meeting some three or four trains driving sheep & cattle pretty well worn down, We arrived at the Muddy at eight and camped on good feed We find our teams are beginning to fail.

Thursday 17 Nov 1853. Animals done well yet we lay up all day to recruit them One year ago to day I encamped on the Muddy on my outward journey. More camp of emmagrants here.

Friday 18 Nov 1853. Travelled to Rio Virgin and encamped three miles up it Annother camp of emmagrants.

Saturday 19 Nov 1853. Good days drive encamping in the same Musquet Grove where we stayed 13 Nov last year. Met another train with sheep and cattle.

Sunday 20 Nov 1853. Travelled to last camping on the Rio Virgin some ten or 15 miles

Monday 21 Nov 1853. Travelled to Mountain Springs near thirty miles. Tolerable feed Hiram Curtis was shot by an Indian in the breast, with an arrow, from the mountain side, but fortunately was not injured, the arrow being nearly spent. Leonard fired at the Indian but without effect, which happened all well for the men were becoming very careless & neglectful while this had the effect to put us on our guard more, for it convinced them that the Indians were more hoslite than we expected to find them here

Tuesday 22 Nov 1853. Travelled up the Santa Clara, followed by a large number of saucy Indians We did not allow them to come near us. In avoiding a steep hill we we came into an Indian Cornfield, the corn being geathered but plenty of excellent bunch grass & fodder we camped at 2 p. m.

Wednesday 23 Nov 1853. Started earley. Met Mr Kinkead and a train He was carrying the mail. We camped on the Rim of the Bason. Very cold to night. Snow in sight for the first time.

Thursday 24 Nov 1853. Travelled 35 miles to Iron Springs Several friendly Indians came to us to day saying they are mormons.

Friday 25 Nov 1853. Started at three in the morning arriving at Cole Creek (Cedar City) for breakfast Here we found Erastus Snow and F. D. Richards of the Twelve. All peace and prosperity among the saints here

After stoping here an hour Hiett & my self rode post & double quick to parowan, part of the company coming on behind us. Here Elder Lewis met his wife & family all well and rejoicing to meet him once more. How different will be my return home.

While here I staid with Bishop Tarleton Lewis The company here disbanded as several stop here

Saturday 26 Nov 1853. Visiting my old friends.

Sunday 27 Nov 1853. At meeting James Lewis spoke followed by my self & Prest J. C. L. Smith Attended prayer circle then evening meeting Snow & Richard came and preached to the congregation.

Monday 28 Nov 1853. To day we prepared to start for Salt Lake. Several of the company went on 15 miles to the springs, while Snow, Richards (and [crossed out]) myself & several others tarried till tomorrow for the purpose of enjoying a party this evening, which we kept up warmly till 2 o'clock.

Tuesday 29 Nov 1853. Started this morning Our company consists of those who came through with me who does not stop here and the Hon. C. C. Pendleton Representative from Iron County and his guard through the Indian Country going to meet with the Legislature

Col Little detailed me as one of the guard so that I could draw pay This is killing two Birds with one stone I put my luggage in John Griffins waggon which had no cover

We went to the Springs and finding the advance had left we struck for Beaver River. But some five miles before we got there our waggon shed one of the fore wheels, which caused three of us to be left behind.

Here our selves and effects were now exposed to the tender mercies of the Indians which were lurking about here. It was now dark and not knowing what to do sat down to reflect awhile. The result of which was that we would *cache* some of our trunks & *traps,* take the Horses, arms, ammunition & such other things as we could carry and go to camp. We did so, proceeding on very Scripturely "heavy laden" & werry too arrived in camp safe & tired when Capt Carter sent back for the waggon and loading which arrived before day

Wednesday 30 Nov. 1853. This morning William Leaney's horses were gone which detained till noon during which time Griffin pached [patched] up his waggon so as to be barely moveable while I had to put my luggage in Henry Nebeker's carriage which already had Snow Richard & a young Lady Miss Gaddis *on Board* with their luggage making his load very heavy while I had to walk most of the way, riding however occasionally when the road was good

We arrived at Pine Creek at dark

Thursday 1 Decr 1853. Drove fast arriving at Fillmore at dark, while the company was left behind some seven miles I staid with Henry Standage

Friday 2 Decr 1853. Feel much refreshed this morning after the kind treatment & good bed which I had last night.

Fillmore looks different from its appearance last year being in complete fort form with an adobie wall in a considerable state of completion Here we made some different arrangements as to my self Several persons joind us here Hon James McGaw and guard from this county went with us any trunk, bedding &c was taken by different ones, lighting Nebiker's Carriage so that I could ride more. We started at noon leaving about half our former company who wished to travel slow.

We encamped near the summit of the Sevier Mountain without any water only for ourselves.

Saturday 3 Decr 1853. Started earley there being only three waggons & some eight of us, crossed the Sevier breakfasted, went to Salt Creek at dark. I staid with T. B. Foote.

Sunday 4 Dec 1853. Had a meeting this morning at 9 o'c in the school house, preaching by Erastus Snow, followed by myself and F. D. Richards, after which we again proceeded on our journey about noon, arriving at Payson at dark I put up with Chas Shumway. There were two meetings called to night at one of which Elders Snow & Richards preached and myself & Elder James McGaw at the other.

Monday 5 Dec 1853. Here Henry Nebiker & his carriage stopped, he having arrived at home I of course had distribute my luggage with the remaining teams & drove to Springville Dined with Br Bird's then *Rolled* on to Provo City Here I found Elder George A. Smith with whom I tarried all night. well entertained with his agreeable social *yarnings*.

Tuesday 6 Dec 1853. George A. was intending to go to Great Salt Lake City, but it appears that before he can start it is necessary for him to join Marshal Kinsman & Sarah Snow daughter of James C. Snow, in the Holy bands of matrimony, which he did about noon. I accompanied him where fared well on the *Bridal repast* Joy to their bright prospects for they were a promising looking couple While Elder Smith was *Launching* the above chosen two into a State connubial bliss & we all were engaged in dispaching the *preperations* those of our company who were behind us, arrove and went on, leaving me & George A to follow with A. J. Stewart who took us in his carriage to the next settlement (Springville) putting up with my old friend and fellow policeman Duncan McArthur.

Wednesday 7 Dec 1853. Started at early dawn Breakfasting with Leonard A. Herrington at American creek, where Stewart returned home leaving us to our luck for the next team which might come by. This was however by mutual concent of us all We however did not wait long before we had an opportunity going on with William Seeley, when we again set out to Dry creek where George A. stopped while I went on with Seeley to Little-cotton wood & staid with J. C. Wright I forgot to state that while at American Creek I had the satisfaction to witness the triumph of Mormonism over the traditions of our fathers for George A. sealed Arza Adams to an old maid aged 48 as withered and forbidding as 4 Doz. years of celibacy might natturally be supposed to indicate. She joyfully took his hand and consented to be part of himself as number two. Thus entering into a respectible state of matrimony under auspicious circumstances when nothing except the privileges of Mormonism would have permitted

Thursday 8 Dec 1853. This fore noon I arrived at home or what more properly might be said where once was my home.

Here, not 14 months since was concentrated all my earthly happiness. Here, the confiding Louisa, the dearest object of my heart, the solace in all my troubles and my inocent prattling children, was left, in the most perfect enjoyment of earthly bliss. To them I fled as a refuge from trouble & disappointment & how often I have rejoiced that I was thus blessed with that most essential ingredient for man's comfort, a true, faithful & confiding wife, and obedient lovely children They *were* here then, Here *then* was my own *ocean* of affection & love I left them by the command of the Lord to preach the gospel in foreign lands & returned but not to them.

Louisa was no more, the scource of my happiness was beneath the cold sod while the very geniuse of desolation & loneliness seemed to brood over the scenes of by gone happiness.

What did I find? Even my brother had removed into the country & not the first vistage of former associations moved on the desolate place.

A family of English saints, total stranger to me resided here and could give no account of neither family or friends.

I gazed upon the sad wreck of all my hopes in silence while my heart sank within me & those around could not refrain from mingling their tears with mine for a few moments when we all hastily with drew from a place so full of sad reccollections as my *HOME*.

From hence I hastily ran around through the city distributing some letters & then saw president Young delivered my report & took passage in a carriage with

Anson Call, travelling some ten miles north to my brothers who I found well   Here I staid all night

Friday 9 Dec 1853. This morning my brother took me to Mother Taylor's where my children were whom I found well & were well taken care of but if I felt disconsolate before If I felt overwhelmed in sorrow, If grief had dried up the fountain of my tears when I came home how can I attempt to describe my emotions when I embraced those three dear pledges which Louisa had left me of her love and fidelity They were living evidences of the uncertainty of man's best & surest earthly hopes.

But let me indulge no more in the sad thoughts which burn my brain and rend the vital cords of my heart.

Saturday 10 Decr 1853. Staid here with my children all day.

Sunday Dec 11 1853. Returned to the city and staid with Alex McRae.

Monday 12 Dec 1853. The Legislature convened to day Spent the day arrainging my affairs which I found to be in a very scattered condition

Tuesday 13 Dec 1853. Attended the Legislature to hear the govornor's message delivered, after which I spent the day as yesterday.

Wednesday 14 Decr 1853. This morning early I visited Louisa grave, by the side of which rests my son who I never saw and my brother's Charles Heber.   Here I must not indulge my feelings in attempting to describe them   How calmly, sadly, happily, seemed to rest her ashes.   How quiet seemed that heart which once beat for me so warmly   Her smiling countenance, but all now rests in death's embrace while I remain as a blank on earth, a monument of disappointed hopes.

I have followed three wives to their graves and beheld the (silent [crossed out]) earth enclose seven of my own children yet I had hopes of better days but now hope vanished & I must give myself up to inconsolable sorrow

After my sad visit I returned to the city and went over Jordan to the Welch Settlement[32] to attend a law suit for deft Loker in an action for Damages before Esqr Benion.   Thos Butterfield, et. al. vs. Paul Loker   Suit withdrawn and I came back at dark

Thursday 15 Dec 1853. Attended to having house finished which needed some work before it is ready to occupy

Friday 16 Dec 1853. Occupied as yesterday

Saturday 17 Dec 1853. Occupied as yesterday.   At early candle light attended the meeting of the Regents of the University at the council house

They are endevoring to get up a new and simpler alphabet on the Phonetic principal so far as sound is concerned   Their object is so to shape the letters that they will answer for both writing and printing and take up as little room as possible. To do this and mentain the necessary dissimelarity of letters is no easy task but I think they will succeed.

Sunday 18 Dec 1853. Attended meeting at Tabernacle.

Monday 19 Dec 1853. Choring at my house.   Attended the Legislative Council called to deliver a lecture on China & the Chinese which I did.

Tuesday 20 Dec 1853. Doing nothing in particular to day, only went to see J. P Harmon in the evening & he was not at home

---

32. "In the fall of 1849 a company of Welsh Saints, under the direction of Reese Williams, located what was known as the Welsh settlement, on a spot now embraced in the late Feramorz Little's farm in Granger Ward, but the farming proving unsuccessful, the settlement was subsequently broken up." Jenson, *Historical Record,* VI (December, 1887), 286.

Wednesday 21 Dec 1853. Busy to day as yesterday & attended the Theatre in the evening. Was well entertained till ten The performances came off well.

Thursday 22 Dec 1853. My sister Anna came and helped me clean up my new house preparitory to me seting up a Bachelor's Hall which however will be done only in a very limited sence of the word.

Friday 23 Dec 1853. Dodging among my friends to kill time & keep down more serious reflections

In the afternoon went into the Representative's Hall when I was again called on to deliver a lecture on the Celestial Empire which I did

Saturday 24 Dec 1853. Dodging around as before

Sunday 25 Dec 1853. Attended meeting at the Tabernacle in the fore noon, was called and preached on the subject of my late China mission after which took Chrismas dinner with O. D. Hovey. Then rode in David Session carriage north to see my brother & staid with Thomas Rich.

Monday 26 Dec 1853. Had a partial settlement with Allen, the Substance of which is that the most valuable part of my property is [gone] & no use in looking after it, afterwards walked to Jonathan Smiths took dinner & jogged on to Mother's, found my children well.

Tuesday 27 Dec 1853. Packing up some of my house hold goods to take home & visiting.

Wednesday 28 Dec 1853. Went to Jonathan Smith's then back again   attended meeting Charles Dalton preached Very snowy disagreeable evening & some 8 or nine of us staid with Mother Taylor.

Thursday 29 Dec 1853. Allen Taylor came home with me and brought a load of my household traps   Met with the Regents at the governor's office to take into further consideration the New Alphabet which however has been adopted and is now only acted upon by way of improvement

This evening I learned that I have been elected again to the Regency by the Legislature.

Friday 30 Dec 1853. Adjusting my house hold affairs. Took a walk & then a Sardine Supper at Secratary Babbitts office after which staid alone in my new house as the first lesson to my meditated Bachelorship, which leaves any thing but a favorable impression. It rathar has however a tendency to impress on my mind that Scripture which says that "it is not good for man to be alone"

Saturday 31 Dec 1853. Solatary & alone I arose this morning and commenced the solemn cerimony of getting up my breakfast. This to me was a serious undertaking but however I was relieved for my sister came & finished the job a thing which I was wholy incompetent to do for myself   Preparing for a grand Pic nic on Monday given by the Govornor to be at the Theatre.

PART III

January 1, 1854 to June 30, 1857

JANUARY 1, 1854 TO JUNE 30, 1857

Part III

This part of the diary covers the period from January 1, 1854, to June 30, 1857. During these years Hosea Stout served a short term mission as an officer of the newly created Green River County in present-day Wyoming. He returned to take up the practice of law. In writing of various court cases, Stout showed clearly the conflict between the local lawyers and the federal appointees. These conflicts were partly responsible for some of the officials deserting their posts to return to Washington, D. C. Their actions led finally to the sending of an army to Utah to put down a reported rebellion.

Sunday January 1 1854. At home, my Sister helping me set my house in order.

Monday 2 Jan 1854. Attended the Presidents social pic nic party at the Theatre at 2 p. m. where we had Dancing singing and preaching till three in the morning The most quiet and peaceable Spirit prevailed I ever witnessed on such an occasion

Tuesday 3 January 1854. Attended U. S. District Court at State House Hon Leonidus Shafer[1] presiding I was appointed on the grand jury and appointed foreman

Wednesday 4 Jan. 1854. Attended Grand Jury.

Thursday 5 Jan 1854. Attended Grand Jury again and at dark met with the Regents.

Friday 6 Jan 1854. Attended Grand Jury We all dined with S. M Blair where I staid all night

Saturday 7 Jan 1854. Attended Grand Jury all of whom dined with Col Little at the Bath House In the evening attended the Theatre was well entertained

Sunday 8 January 1854. At home in the fore noon & attended meeting in the afternoon J. M. Grant preached on the subject of the conversion of the Lamanites

---

1. Judge Leonidas Shaver had arrived in Utah in October of 1852 while Stout was on his mission. A Virginian and an affable bachelor, Judge Shaver had up to this time maintained cordial relations with President Brigham Young and the Mormons in general. Although there is no account of a definite or violent break, there is evidence of a growing coolness. At the time of Shaver's death in June of 1855, there were many expressions of sorrow and a public demonstration of honor.

Monday 9 Jan 1854. Attended the Grand Jury again.

This evening about dark a change took place in my fortune which will most likely effect my furture life. I was married to Mrs Aseneth Gheen widow of the Late William Gheen. She has had three children two of whom are dead and one living she is a daughter now nearly eleven years of age.

Mrs Gheen was born Nov. 12th 1823 in the State of Indiana Fayette County She is daughter of Henry and Agnes Harmon. Elder Jonathan C. Wright officiated as minister on the occasion. She lives in the seventh ward of this City

Tuesday 10 Jan 1854. Attended the Grand Jury again. To day we were discharged. We have found three indictments one against William May[2] for murder one against Henry C. Ross for challenging another to a duel & one against _____ for offering to act as his second or friend.

Wednesday 11 Janu 1854. Took my new wife and daughter to see House where we expect to move in a few days.

Thursday 12 Jan 1854. Wet snow falling to day. Attended Court a short time and met with the Regents in the evening.

Friday 13 Jan 1854. Warm South wind blowing all day, melting the fine snow which fell last night Attended the Legislature part of to day.

Saturday 14 January 1854. Warm South wind blowing. Snow melting. Roads full of water. Took my wife & her daughter North today Wind changed to North accompanied by a severe snow storm. To avoid which we turned in at Thos Rich's and staid all night. My Brother's youngest Son Hosea is very sick with the chill fever

Sunday 15 Jan 1854. Bro Rich took us to Mother Taylor's where we arrived in the after noon finding my children all well, and very glad that I had got them a new mother who they were very fond of. Her daughter and mine very soon became much attached to each other, and evry appearance bids fair to work well in my family arraingements thus far.

Monday 16 Jan 1854. Snow squalls continued while we spent the day visiting at Isaac Allred's

Tuesday 17 Jan 1854. To day we were packing up my trap preparitory to bringing my children home In the evening myself & wife went & staid all night with Saml Driggs.

Wednesday 18 Jan 1854. To day Levi Taylor brought myself & whole family to Thomas Rich's except Henry Allen who will stay with Jos Taylor to go to school this winter.

Thursday 19 Jan 1854. Cold time to be from home with an entire family. Thomas rigged up a covered waggon in which we stowed the little ones and came to the city where we arrived about Sunset cold enough but otherwise well enough.

Friday 20 Jan 1854. Preparing to move to my house. Coldest night last this winter.

Legislature adjd to day having completed its 40 days session including Sundays Holy Days &c according to Congressional rules.

Saturday 21 Jan 1854. Very cold day. I am doing nothing

---

2. On June 8, 1853, William May had been convicted of murder in the first degree and sentenced to be executed on January 13, 1854. Just one day before the sentence was to have been carried out, Brigham Young issued a reprieve ordering a stay of execution which is found in the Utah Territorial Executive Papers, 1850-1855 (Utah State Archives).

Sunday 22 Jan 1854. Went to meeting in the forenoon to hear Elder Woodruff preach & in the after-noon wife & I went visiting to Bp W. G. Perkins'

Monday 23 Jan 1854. Moved to my house to day

Tuesday 24 Jan 1854. Adjusting matters at home to day

Wednesday 25 Jan 1854. Snowed again last night a little. To day Joseph Taylor came here bringing the sad news that Samuel D. Driggs was dead and that Allen Taylor would be here with his corpse in an hour or so which accordingly was the case when we went to the burial and returned about dark.

When I was north a week since he was well and hearty but took sick the day I left and died last Monday night   He was attacted with what was supposed to be an inflamation of the lungs.   45 grains of calomel was given him without producing an opperation   He died with the calomel in him   He leaves a wife & 5 children to mourn his loss.

Thursday Jan 26, 1854. Warm Clear day but not thawing much   attending on President Willard Richards who is dagerously ill.

Friday & Saturday 27th & 28th 1854. At home writing letters to San Bernardino Cal to my friends there.   The weather is slowly moderating.   President Richards is reported to be failing. Sat with the High Council on Saturday trial C. D. Harlin vs Loren Babbitt. Neither party was satisfied with the Decision of the Council.

Sunday 29 January 1854. At home till in the evening went visit

Monday 30th Jan 1854. At home choring to day —

Tuesday 31 Jan 1854. At home choring (of course)

Wednesday 1 Feb 1854. At home choring as usual. Yester there was a general mass meeting at the Tabernacle to express the views of the Territory in regard to the pacific Rail Road & to memorialize Congress on the most practable rout for the same which would bring the road down Provo Cañon in Utah County. Speeches were made by Hon. A. W. Babbitt & Col Furgerson to gether with the two Brass Bands & a Song by Miss E. R. Snow[3] made the meeting a very interesting one This is the first *Real* move made in Utah on the subject

Thursday & Friday 2 & 3 Feb 1854. Working at home most of the time

Saturday 4 Feb 1854. Attended suit Hezekiah Duffin against Anthony Lovett Anthony in debt and damage for 262.50 before Probate Court Elias Smith Judge J. Furgerson on part of plff & S. M. Blair & myself for Deft   Court rendered Judgement against the Defendant for Eighty Sevend dollars and fifty cents.

---

3. Eliza Roxey Snow was born January 21, 1804, in Becket, Berkshire County, Massachusetts, a sister of Lorenzo Snow. She was well-educated and was skilled in needlework, straw braiding, and bonnet and hat making. At an early age she began to write poetry, some of which appeared in print and brought her into contact with the leading literary minds of her area.

In 1835 she joined the Mormon Church, moved to Kirtland, Ohio, and set up a school for young ladies.   Much enamored with Joseph Smith, she turned her complete legacy to him for the building of the Kirtland Temple. On June 29, 1842, Eliza R. Snow was sealed to Joseph Smith as a plural wife. When the first Relief Society was organized, she was appointed the first secretary.

All her life she wrote songs, some of which are still sung. During the trials of the exodus, she wrote verse of courage and cheer, and spent much of her time among the sick.

In 1849 Eliza Snow was married to Brigham Young; in 1866 she was made general president of the Relief Society in which capacity she traveled throughout the wards of the church. She always proudly told that she had been a wife to Joseph Smith and always proclaimed the divinity of plural marriage. She died December 5, 1887.

Sunday 5 February 1854. Went to meeting in the afternoon. President Brigham Young preached

A general thaw seems to be setting in.

Monday 6 Feb 1854. At Blairs & at home. Snow is melting very fast. The ground is all afloat.

Tues 7 Wed 8 Thurs 9 Feb 1854. At home mostly choring. Some tines out through town

Friday 10 Feb 1854. Working at home

Saturday 11 Feb 1854. The southern Mail came in last evening from which I recieved letters one from W McBride, Sandwick Isles He has been very unhealthy while there and is yet very feeble otherwise the work of the gospel is progressing rapidly. One from Henry G. Boyle San Bernardino anouncing the death of his wife & considerable sickness there, Hiram Clark had cut his own throat and died.[4] Several others had died since I left there

I also learn from the San Deigo Herald that Lower California had declared its independance. One Col William Walker President They were recruiting and fighting Sharply how this *filerbustering* will be met by Santa Anna time must show There is however no doubt but they will give him trouble yet if they get fairly to going This is modern progress to use up, absorb or other wise exterminate the mexicans The present american enterprise unchecked will surely doom poor Mexico

The magnificent Steamer "Winfield Scott" which ran from Sanfrancisco to panama has been lost.

The war between Russia & Turkey has actually commenced and four battles fought The Turks successful every time. Success to them

The Chinese rebelion progressing another battle at Amoy, rebels ahead. They have invested Shanghae (all well enough then).

A letter from Br James Lewis says he has moved to Cedar City & has took charge of the Iron works for Snow & Richards.

Sunday 12 Feb 1854. Went to meeting in the fore noon Snow Storm. did not go in in after noon

Mond 13 Tues 14 Wed 15 Feb 1854. At home most of the time choring reading &c Badly troubled with an influenza cough.

Thurs & Frid 17 Feb. 54. Around home and the city not able to do any thing even if I had a disposition in consequence of a severe bad cold.

Saturday 18 Feb 1854. Very feeble to day. Attended a law-suit John Braden v.s. R. E. Pettitt in debt demand 158.50, before Elias Smith Judge of Probate I was

---

4. Hiram Clark had a long history of service in the church. Born September 22, 1895, in Rutland County, Vermont, he joined the Mormons early. He was one who signed the open letter to Oliver Cowdery and others ordering them to leave Far West "forthwith."

As a high priest, Clark was sent on a mission to Europe with Parley P. Pratt in 1839; on his return he brought 235 converts to Nauvoo. In 1844 he was sent again, this time with Wilford Woodruff, and again brought Saints with him on his return.

Clark left Nauvoo with the 1846 evacuation but did not get to Utah until 1849. The roll shows that he brought with him his wife and two teen-age sons. In 1850 he was sent to California as one of the "gold mission"; and from thence in the fall of the year, he was ordered to go on to Hawaii and preside over a group of nine missionaries. Some differences developed among the elders in the field as to whether or not they should proselyte among the natives, as a result of which Clark left his post and returned to San Bernardino. Here he faced the stigma of having failed to carry out his assignment.

The full story of Clark's suicide was published in the *Deseret News* from a letter signed by Amasa Lyman and Charles C. Rich dated January 10. This was reprinted in *The Millennial Star*, XVI, 363.

on the Defence & Hartley[5] a gentile stranger for plaintiff. Court rendered Judgement against Deft for 93.50 and costs of suit.

Sunday 19 Feb 1854. At home to day not being able to leave safely, being badly indisposed.

Mond 20 Tues 21 Wed 22 Feb 1854. At home mostly being afflicted with a bad cold

Thursday 23 Friday 24 Feb 1854. At home very sick particularly on the 24 Something like a bad cold and some symtoms of ague seem to be my complaint now.

Saturday 25 Feb 1854. some better to day but quite weak   Attended Probate Court wherein Elder O Hyde & Jas Furgurson were militant   Hyde as attorny for Ben Hawkins had sued Jim for over 200 dollars for board of some prisoners taken there by Furgerson as Shiriff   in his plea he bore down on Jim very hard which was returned by Jim at least five to one on the Elders devoted head

I felt, and so did numbers present express themselves, that Elder Hyde has most shamefully condescended beneath the dignaty of an Apostle to stoop, as he does here before all Israel and play the small intrigueing pettifogger in our lower courts making him self often the butt of ridicule & low abuse.   The saints feell justly indignant at his course   I left court when the case was submitted to the jury & sincerely hope I may never again see such condescension in our Courts (again [crossed out]) by one of our Apostles[6]

Sunday 26 Feb 1854. severe driving snow from the N. most all day while I in doors & most of the time confined to my bed hardly knowing if I am growing worse or better.

Monday 27 Feb 1854. Eastern mail came in to day I am just able to be about.

) closed letter to
(McBride

Tuesday 28 Feb 1854. Just able to be around my lungs are very sore from hard coughing

Wednesday 1 March 1854. western mail came in via San Bernardino   Not learned the news more than the chinese rebals had taken Shanghae & filibustering was still prosperous in Lower Calafornia. Very boisterous weather

Thursday 2 March 1854. Made arraingements to take a herd ground and enter into the herding business in copartnership with R. C. Petty & William W. Taylor The Herd ground to be located at the mouth of Bingham Canon, East of the West Mountain in this county   We filed Bonds for 20.000 dollars as a preparitory work for commencing the herding business according to law after this we will obtain a licence also an order from the Co Court to have the Herd ground surveyed & located. This secures to us the premises & right to Herd for one year   When to obtain the

---

5. This man, "Hartley a gentile stranger" who won the case over Stout, is Jesse T. Hartley. Of him, Mrs. Mary Ettie V. Smith wrote: "About the time referred to in the last chapter, Jesse T. Hartley came to Salt Lake City. He was a man of education and intelligence, and a lawyer by profession. I never knew where he was from, but he was a Gentile when he came, and soon after married a Mormon girl by the name of Bullock, which involved a *profession*, at least, of Mormonism. It was afterwards supposed by some that his aim was to learn the mysteries of the church, in order to make an expose of them afterwards . . . . Hartley was a fine speaker and a man calculated to make friends. . . ." Mary Ettie V. Smith, *Fifteen Years Among the Mormons*, . . . (New York, 1858), 308.

6. Since the summer of 1847 Stout was critical of Orson Hyde and lost no opportunity to write disparagingly of him, though not always with his present candor.

the same premises & prviledges (an other [crossed out]) again we have to commence
the same cerimony & go it "de novo"

Friday 3 March 1854. Feel much better to day & hope I may soon be well again.
Col Freemont and a party came to Iron County a few days since nearly [starved]
to death & frozen They had suffered & endured great hardships, some of his men
have died.[7] He is exploring the Central rout for the pacific Rail Road and is very
sanguine that it will be located on his line of exploration He was destitue provisions
&c and made large purchases in Parowan giving drafts on a House in San Francisco.
This I believe is Col Benton's favorite Route

Saturday 4 March 1854. Commenced taking medicine to day to cure my cough
which seems to have some bad symtoms, bordering on consumtive & spitting blood
off the lungs What the real nature & reason of this severe cough & forbidding symtoms are I do not know, but it is very weakening & reduces my flesh very fast —

Sunday 5 March 1854. Snowed all last night & continues to day melting some
however. Snow now is quite deep again. We seem to have an uncommon portion
of snow this winter and now rather inclines to run into the spring I am closely
housed to day.

Monday 6 March 1854. Still snowing & wet disagreeable weather Attended County
Court a short time in the fore-noon
      Cough no better very weak yet not able to do any work that exercises

Tuesday 7 March 1854. Attending County Court to day

Wednesday 8 March 1854. Attended County Court again & wrote a letter to
David D. Jones at San Bernardino Cal

Thursday 9 March 1854. Attended County Court again still trying to secure our
statutory claims to our Herd ground which the Court after dallying four days have
laid over till next term which will then make our object in Herding uncertain untill
then hence I shall give up any further idea of Herding as before then I must be in
some other channel of business.
      Attended another meeting of the Regents to again consult on the new alphabet
and see the new type for the same.

Friday 10 March 1854. Started North this morning taking passage in T. S. Smith
& H. W. Miller's waggon and staid all night with Jonathan Smith.

Saturday 11 March 1854. Went to Mother Taylor's to day.
      This morning about 8 o'clock we have to record the death of President Willard
Richards after a protracted illness.

Sunday 12 March 1854. Staid all day in doors — Stormy

Monday 13 March 1854. Came back as far as my brothers and staid with Thomas
Rich.

---

      7. The *Deseret News* for March 16 following published an account, taken from a letter from
John C. L. Smith:
            On the 6th of February the man on the lookout at Parowan reported a company,
      supposed to be Indians, coming into the valley, twenty miles distant from Parowan, about
      eleven o'clock on the morning of the 7th Colonel John C. Fremont, with nine white men
      and twelve Deleware Indians, arrived in Parowan in a state of starvation; one of his
      men had fallen dead from his horse the day previous, and several more must inevitably
      have shared his fate had they not had succor that day . . . .
            Although Colonel Fremont was considered by the people an enemy to the Saints,
      and had no money, he was kindly treated and supplied on credit with provisions for
      himself and men . . . and went on his way rejoicing on the 20th of February.
      (Reprinted in *Millennial Star*, XVI, 362.)

Tuesday 14 March 54. Staid here all day and with John D. Parker.

Wednesday 15 March 54. Came home to day   Allen & Rich coming with me.

Thursday 16 March 1854. Doing nothing to day but attended a meeting of the Regents at night.

Friday 17 March 1854. Occuped as yesterday & attended another meeting of the Regents at night. The subject before the board is the new alphabet.

Saturday 18 March 1854. To day my wife moved down to here house while. I stay here for the time being with my children

My sister Anna comes here to keep house for me (and [crossed out]) a few days untill I have an opportunity to send my children up to their grand mother's. The arraingements in all this, is for me to go to Green River this Summer,[8] Mother Taylor take of the children, and my wife & her daughter live in her house   Thus almost entirely disbanding my family again   What next I know not. except that total uncertainty alone lies in the future.

Sunday 19 March 1854. Attended meeting Heber preached in the fore noon and Brigham in the after noon

Monday 20 Mar 1854. The Eastern mail came in to day.

The Turks & Russians have had a very hard naval engagement near the Harbor of sinope in which the Russians were victorious   Turks lost 13 out of 14 vessels and the Russians lost 7 out of 24 vessels

Tuesday 21 March 1854. Sent my children to their grand mother's to day, by Joseph Taylor, where they will stay this summer

Wednesday 22 March 1854. Overhauling to day preparitory to going to green River this summer

Thursday 23 March 1854. overhauling as yesterday.

Friday 24 March 1854. overhauling as yesterday attended the meeting of the Regents at dark   The subject was the new alphabet which was printed and presented to the Board to night.   It is anticipated to send by F. D. Richards to England for type &c also to introduce it there & use it hereafter in our correspondence also to immediately introduce it into our schools here.   It is termed the Deseret alphabet[9] and is as follows [At this point in the diary, Hosea's rendition of the alphabet appears. See page following for the Deseret alphabet version of the Book of Mormon.] this is quite awkwardly executed as it the first time I ever attempted to write any of the characters. & only inserted them to have some kind of a Specimen in my journal.

Saturday 25 March 1854. Overhauling as yesterday.

Sunday 26 March 1854. attended meeting awhile.

---

8. Since a mission was supposed to last at least two years, a man who did not complete his assignment in one area was often assigned to another. The Green River colonization program was hopeless from the first, and Hosea leaves no doubt as to his own feeling regarding it.

9. The Deseret alphabet was an attempt to simplify the writing of the English language. It was evidently designed to help European converts and to set up a common medium of communication. George D. Watt was chiefly responsible for working out the system, which contained thirty-eight phonetic characters. An article in the *Deseret News* for January 19 preceding praised the undertaking and reported that preliminary instruction would begin at once.

Difficulties of getting this new type cast delayed any effective action until 1857, when a firm in St. Louis was hired to cast it. Although two readers, the Book of Mormon, and excerpts from the Bible were printed, the system never came into general use.

Long Sounds.				Letter.	Name.	Sound.
Letter.	Name.	sound.		ꓶ	p	
ə	e	as in	eat.	ꓭ	b	
Ɛ	a	"	ate.	ꓖ	t	
ə	ah	"	art.	ꓷ	d	
Ɵ	aw	"	aught.	C	che	as in cheese.
O	o	"	oat.	Ꮆ	g	
Ø	oo	"	ooze.	ꓳ	k	
				ꓳ	ga	as in gate.
Short Sounds of the above.				P	f	
†		as in	it.	ꓯ	v	
		"	et.	L	eth	as in thigh.
		"	at.	Ɣ	the	" thy.
		"	ot.	ꕄ	s	
Γ		"	ut.	Ꮾ	z	
q		"	book.	D	esh	as in flesh.
ᴧ	i	as in	ice.	ꙅ	zhe	" vision.
Ɛ	ow	"	owl.	ꝙ	ur	" burn.
ɯ	woo			ι	l	
Y	ye			ꓛ	m	
ʔ	h			ꓵ	n	
				Ɯ	eng. as in length.	

[Deseret Alphabet title page text]

NEW YORK:
PUBLISHED FOR THE DESERET UNIVERSITY
BY RUSSELL BROS.
1869.

Monday 27 March 1854. Overhauling as yesterday.

Tuesday 28 March 1854. overhauling as yesterday.

Wednesday 29 March 1854. Went North and staid all night with Jonathan Smith

Thursday 30 March 1854. Went to Mother Taylor's and found my children all well   Staid all night Stormy & snowing to day

Several of the missionarys passed here to day to England viz F. D. Richards W H Kimball, G. D. Grant E. Ellsworth J. A. Little Jos A Young (son of Prest) Wm Young &c and Judge Reed & others.

Friday 31 March 1854. How long affliction, Bad luck, and trouble is to attend I do not know

Just being on the eve of going to green River I came here to see my children for the last time before starting but only found that fickle fortune was yet tampering with me after I vainly supposed I had made permenently arraingements for this summer at least, Mother Taylor has concluded not to take care of my children. My wife not willing too either.   The President wants the use of my house this season & here I am left thus unexpectedly disappointed in all my previous arraingements.   My children thrown on my hands without a mother's care, while I am totally unprepared to take care of them   Without money or provisions for them or even enough to take with me to Green River. What next I know not neither do I know what to do.

I settled with Mother Taylor for the time she had my children which in all is seven months or 210 days   She charged me seven dollars per week or one dollar pr day 210 dollars. For which I paid her by selling my farm to her for 180 dollars and paid the rest part in cash and the residue in wheat from last year's crop which she already had used.

It is impossible for me to describe my feelings when contemplating the sad dilema I am placed in at this time when dark clouds of more misfortune & sorrow hang heavily over my head yet. & I can not see one bright ray of future happiness (in the furture [crossed out]) not possibly devine when prosperity will smile on me & my little ones or when I can peacibly enjoy their society without fore seeing coming disappointment and trouble.

Hope on Hope ever is a good adage & perhaps it would be well for me to practice on it now. After all this I started home came to my brothers then went to J. D. Parker's and staid all night.

Saturday 1 April 1854. Came home afoot & tired   the mails had come in I re-cieved 2 letters one from san Bernardino one from Cedar from James Lewis & answered them immediately and thus closes to day.

Sunday 2 Apl 1854. Attended Meeting. P P Pratt delivered an address in reply to a scurrilious report published in the Missouri Democrat acusing the Mormons of the murder of Capt Gunnison and his party. He was followed by several others Did not attend after noon Service

Monday 3 April 1854. Doing nothing of importance only reading the news of the day.

Tuesday 4 April 1854. Occupied about as yesterday. I see a specimen of glass said to be manufactured in this place.

Monday evening the Regents met at the Theatre and exhibited the Deseret alphabet to the Public which was well recieved.

Wednesday 5 Apl 1854. Occupied as usual doing nothing

Thursday 6 April 1854. To day the general Conference commenced   President B. Young opened the Conference Stated some of the business to be transacted was to choose a man to fill the vacancies occasioned by the death of President Willard Richards also that it was contemplated to establish stakes and geathering places for the Saints one in Ohio, one in Missouri, one in the Territory of Nabraska, and one at San Jose, Calafornia and also send missionaries to Oregon. This opens a wide field of labor. He was followed by Elder H. C. Kimball. In the after noon Elder O. Hyde preached followed G. A. Smith & some others. In the evening another meeting preaching by several Elders The day was very disagreeable and windy and rain in the evening which continued all night.

Friday 7 April, 1854. Attended Conference Jedediah M. Grant was chosen to fill the vacancy of President Willard Richards Decd as second Councillor to President Young and George A. Smith chosen Church Historian which office was also filled by President W. Richards

Twenty three Elders were appointed to foreign missions.

A specimen of one ream of paper was exhibited to the public which was manu-factured in this place[10]

---

10. That the Mormons early tried to manufacture their own paper is shown by an advertise-ment in the *Deseret News* for November 30, 1850: "Save your rags, everybody in Deseret save your rags; old wagon covers, tents, quilts, shirts, &c., are wanted for paper. The most efficient measures are in progress to put a paper mill in operation the coming season . . . and all your rags will be wanted. . . ."

In the after noon the report of the Perpetual Emmegration Fund was read also the report of the tithing office and Eleven more missionaries were appointed

The President then proposed a more close system of account as he termed which was to form a Common Stock association and all who entered into it to deed their property to the church and enter into something of a patriarchal arraingements in business & labor which the Conferince voted to adopt The peculiaralities of this organization was not fully explained

Last evening Allen Taylor brought my children home.

Saturday 8 April 1854. Conference yet. President Young spoke on the subject of of the association spoken of yesterday which is not Common Stock but to deed up all our property to the Church and then the Bishop set off our inheritance, paying our tithing and dealing with each other as we do at present This is only after the true order of Zion.[11]

Meeting was held out doors in the after noon. P. P. Pratt continued the subject of the fore noon after which several Elders were sent to different missions, among the Rest O. Spencer to Cincinnatti to be associated with O Pratt, E. Snow to Saint Louis & P. P. Pratt to San Jose Cal. Evening meeting of the Seventies to ascertain the number of vacancies in the Presidencies of the different quorums.

Sunday 9 April 1854. Conference yet, held out doors preaching by L. Snow on the subject of deeding our property to the church Two more Elders were sent on foreign missions and Father John Murdoc appointed patriarch. In the after noon I was not present much of the time but the same subject was continued and lectures were delivered against girls marrying gentiles & winter Saints & one Mr Hartley cut off from the Church who had been appointed a mission to Texas. He is said to be a runaway horse thief from oregon came here & married joined the church & had sent up his name to get his endowment.[12]

Conference adjourned till the 27th of June next The day Joseph & Hyrum was martyred in 1844.

We have had an unusual good Conference. Peace Harmony & the Spirit of God prevailed.

Another plea appeared in the *Deseret News* on January 12 preceding this conference: "His EXCELLENCY the Governor, having granted the use of the northeast corner of the Public Work shop for manufacturing paper, we the undersigned, solicit the citizens of Utah Territory to send all kinds of rags and waste paper of all descriptions, to the Tithing Office immediately, as we are anxious to be in operation so as to have a sheet of home made paper ready for presentation at the April Conference. Thomas Hollis Thomas Howard"

This was only a sporadic production. As late as July 12, 1861, the Mormons were still struggling to make paper. On that date Elias Smith wrote: "Friday 12.—By invitation of President Young I went with him in his carriage to see the Paper mill put in motion in company with bro Carrington Calder & Ellerbeck. Prests Kimball & Wells & F. Kesler in another carriage also went to witness the making of the first sheet of paper but from some cause the mill did not operate as well as anticipated . . ." A. R. Mortensen, ed., "Elias Smith, Journal of a Pioneer Editor," *Utah Historical Quarterly,* XXI (January, 1953), 258-59. Even with this imported mill, publication of the *Deseret News* was sometimes delayed for lack of paper.

11. This new law was called "The Law of Consecration" and was preached throughout the Mormon Church during the next two years. Although many of the faithful did comply and fill out the necessary forms to deed their property to the church, it was not generally adopted. This was a supreme test of faith and loyalty for the deed included not only land, improvements, livestock, and home, but furniture, clothing, and personal effects. All, in short, was deeded to Brigham Young, his heirs and assignees forever. So far as can be determined, few of these, if any, were literally carried out.

12. Of the public rebuke reported here, Mrs. Mary Ettie V. Smith wrote: ". . . the Prophet rose at once . . . and said, 'This man, Hartly, is guilty of heresy. He has been writing to his friends in Oregon against the church and has attempted to expose us to the world, and he should be sent to hell cross lots.'" Smith, *Among the Mormons,* 309.

Monday 10 April 1854. attending to some legal business. give my name to enter into the general association.   Attended Quorum meeting at dark at Stringhams to regulate the list of members and found eight vacancies in the list of members.

Tuesday 11 Apl 1854. Attending to legal busines to day Met again with the Regents at the Theatre as at last meeting.

Wednesday 12 Apl 1854. Occupied as yesterday   Squally & rain

Thursday 13 April 1854. Attending to legal business before the Probate court.

Friday 14 April 1854. Attended Suit before Probate Court Elias Smith Judge. The People vs Wm Robinson on indictment for unlawfully branding cattle not his own I was on the part of the prosecution (The prosecuting atty Mr Furguson having dodged his duty) and S. M. Blair for the defence   The jury rendered a verdict against the deft for fine of 40 dollars and ten dollars damage to the owners of the cattle, and costs of suit.   The Deft to be kept in confinement till all the demands are paid.

   In the after noon another suit Paul Loker v. Matthew Gaunt in Replevin & damage 75 dollars

   Before same Court.   Myself for plff & Blair for Deft.   no jury.   Court sustained the Replevin & rendered judgement against deft for ten dollars and Costs of suit.

Satur Sund 15 & 16 Apl 1854. doing nothing only trying to fix for Green River

Monday 17 April 1854. Trying to procure my outfit for Green River making slow headway. attended Quorum meeting

Tuesday & Wed 18 & 19 Apl 54. Trying to fix for Green River mission

Thurs 20 April 1854. occupied as yesterday

Friday 21 Apil 1854. Went to my brother's north

Saturday 22 Apil 1854. Rained nearley all day making rather a wet visit for me.

Sunday 23 April 1854. Came home about noon very tired walking in the mud.

Monday 24 Apil 1854. Rainy morning.   Attended suit before Probate Court Elias Smith judge. Keller vs Jesse Earl John McDounald, Hopkin C. Pender & others for an assault & a variety of offences the whole of which taken together might possibly constitute a general Row   I was on the part of the defence.   The plff failed to make out a case   Cause dismissed.

Tuesday 25 Apl 1854. preparing to go to Green River.

Wednesday 26 Apl 1854. Engaged in a law suit before Probate Court Elias Smith Judge   H. B. Taylor vs Charles, Henry & F Woodward   In assault and personal injury.   Damage $1000. Myself & J. C. Little was on the part of the plaintiff & S. M. Blair & Jas Furgerson on the part of the defence.   It appeared that the Woodwards & Taylor & others had got themselves into a Free fight at a party on the 20th inst in which Taylor's right arm was dislocated and he severely beaten.   The Woodwards also were considerably beaten   Taylor sues for 1000 dollars damage   There was quite an excitement on the occasion.   Each party & friends viewed the matter favorable to their own side.

Thursday 27 Apl 1854. This morning at 9 o'clock the Court met to render judgement in the above case and adjudged fifty dollars damage and costs of suit against the defendants.

Friday 28 April 1854. Attended probate Court E. Smith Judge Cyrus H. Wheelock v. Thomas Heap in Replevin.   I was on the part of the plaintiff Case decided in favor of the plaintiff

Saturday 29 April 1854. General training to day, attended as a spectator

Sunday 30 April 1854. Attended meeting to day but the Tabernacle was too much crouded to gain admittance. Weather still appears unsettled & hazy.

Monday 1 May 1854. This morning all was hurry and bustle with me. The company which was going to Green River[13] was ready to start and to go with them was my only chance for a passage when at the same time I was as yet totally unprepared, having been disappointed in collecting any means from my creditors My family was without that necessary "Staff of life" Bread and otherwise not very well provided for. So after trying every expedint I could at length obtained 60 pounds of flour of Dustin Amy at 8 dollars per hundred and on a credit till the first day of July. This was a great acommodation at this particular time

The Eastern mail came in this morning but I had not time obtain any news or papers. About noon I started for Green River G. W. Boyd hauling my provision and luggage. I took Henry Allen along with me and left my children with Anna We crossed over the first mountain & encamped on the creek changing my loading in the mean time into W. A. Hickman's waggon

Tuesday 2 May 1854. Started earley arriving on the top of the Big mountain about noon Here we had much difficulty in decending down the East side The snow being very deep and wet our animals "Bogged" as well as waggons and with much labor & difficulty to both man and beast we at last succeeded in decending so far down the mountain as to be out of the snow which was succeeded by deep mud & gulches making the road very bad and to cap the climax Hickman's waggon tounge was carelessly broken about half way down the mountain and we compelled to camp while the rest of the train passed on some three miles down East Cañon

Being now left to our sober reflections we set about making a new tounge which we nearly completed by late bed time.

Wednesday 3 May 1854. After completing our repairs we traveled on quite cherily to East Kayon Creek where a new misfortune befel us by our careless driver John Flack ran the off wheels of the waggon into the bank while crossing the creek and in the deep water and in endeavoring to draw out the end of the unwieldy fur tounge brok off leaving in a new difficulty which was however soon *patched up* & we were again under way. and again at the second crossing had another job of *waggon tounge patch work* after which we got along with out any more trouble notwithstanding the water was high arriving at noon at leaving of East Kanyon and Baited & went overtaking the train in a short time when we all went to Weber & camped. This evening Elder Hyde informed the company that Mr J_____ Hartley who did not make his appearance to day with us had most likely had some dishonest intentions by his leaving & wished the guard to renew their diligence least their horses might be stolen.[14]

---

13. Green River was important to the Mormons as an area through which all emigration must pass, with two rivers, which for much of the season, had to be ferried. When the first company of Utah pioneers arrived at the crossing of the Green on June 30, 1847, "The water was very high, one hundred and eighty yards wide, with a very rapid current. Two rafts were made and each was rigged with a rudder and oars. The wagons were safely crossed without taking out any of their contents. The animals were made to swim over." Little, "Biography of Lorenzo Dow Young," *U.H.Q.*, XIV, 93. The 1848 immigration arrived later in the season and found the river about two and a half feet deep with a gravelly bottom, making a good ford.

As soon as Brigham Young was appointed governor of the territory in 1851, he made moves to get control of the ferries, which to that time had been operated at the upper crossing by Jim Bridger and his partner, Louis Vasquez. The story of the struggle for power in this area is highly controversial. See J. Cecil Alter, *James Bridger, Trapper, Frontiersman, Scout and Guide* . . . . (Salt Lake City, 1925), 244-64.

14. The story of what happened to J. Hartley is more fully told by Hickman:

When we had got across what was known as the Big Mountain and into East Canon, some three or four miles, one Mr. Hartley came to us from Provo City. This Hartley was a young lawyer who had come to Salt Lake from Oregon the Fall before,

Thursday 4 May 1854. Forded the Weber without any accident or trouble befalling us although the water was tolerable high.

Here Mr Busby & Dewey stopped to errect a ferry. The company assisting them to put the rope across the river when we went and encamped some four miles up Echo Kanyon

Friday 5 May 1854. Met an express from Green River who anounced the death of Major E. A. Bedell[15] indian agent at Green River   all went well to day and we encamped in the little cannon beyond yellow Creek   However Hickman's waggon had the misfortune to have the axle broke just as we encamped & had to leave it.

Saturday 6 May 1854. Hard rain Squalls occasionally all day.   Forded Bear River easily and encamped at Soda Spring   Cold windy time.

Sunday 7 May 1854. Snow squalls & cold west wind   Baited at Bridger and proceed on to fort Supply where we arrived at dark.   This is the most forbidding and godforsaken place I have ever seen for an attempt to be made for a settlement & judging from the altitude I have no hesitancy in predicting that it will yet prove a total failure but the brethren here have done a great deal of labor.[16]

---

and had married a Miss Bullock, of Provo, a respectable lady of a good family.   But word had come to Salt Lake . . . that he had been engaged in some counterfeiting affair. He was a fine looking, intelligent young man. . . . But previous to this, at the April Conference, Brigham Young, before the congregation gave him a tremendous blowing up, calling him all sorts of bad names, and saying he ought to have his throat cut, which made him feel very bad.   He declared he was not guilty of the charges. (Hickman, *Brigham's Destroying Angel*, 96-97.)

Hickman goes on to tell of the decision to do away with this man and says that he himself fired the fatal shot as they rode alone back to meet his wagon, which had been delayed. Hartley's body fell into a deep, swift canyon stream and his horse went back to camp. "When supper was over Orson Hyde called all the camp together, and said he wanted a strong guard on that night, for that fellow that had come to us in the forenoon had left the Company; he was a bad man, and it was his opinion that he intended stealing horses that night." *Ibid.*, 98.

15. During the troubles in Illinois, E. A. Bedell lived near Nauvoo and was so friendly to the Mormons that they trusted him and Daniel H. Wells to represent them at a truce meeting with the local citizens.   In October 1845 Bedell accompanied George Miller to the office of Governor Ford to present the message from the Mormon leaders.   When Bedell was assigned to this post the people of Utah felt that they had a friend, but his death cut his term to only one year.

16. Because of the importance of this area during the next years, it seems appropriate to include here a brief history.   The first Mormon settlement at Fort Supply was begun in 1852 when Dimick B. Huntington and his brother, William D., were sent to found a colony.   They selected a site about twelve miles southwest of Fort Bridger and set to work to build houses and a stockade and to clear the land.

Their younger brother, Oliver B., who arrived in Salt Lake City on October 2, 1852 wrote: "At Green River I found Dimick who was the foreman of a company sent out there by the President of the Church to build a bridge over Green River and form a settlement.   Between there and the City I met William and a small company going out to join them at the River. This company and settlement was broken up by the Indians and mountaineers and forced to return to the city . . . ." Oliver B. Huntington, Journal 1842-1900 (3 vols., typescript, Utah State Historical Society), 81.

That the colonizing here had been considered seriously by the church leaders is shown by the following excerpts, taken from letters in the "Journal History" of the church, signed by Brigham Young:

Aug. 30, 1852

To the Brethren who are emigrating to the valleys of the mountains
Greetings:

We send by our beloved brethren Dimick B. Huntington and his brother William, Elijah Ward and Brigham H. Young this our letter containing our wishes pertaining to making a settlement on Green River.   It has long been our cherished object to have a good permanent settlement located and established at that point . . . . [He gives encouragement for all who will stop en route to the valley].

. . . it is not our wish to oppress the brethren, but wish those who remain to do

Monday 8 May 1854. Cold squally day while I was visiting my old friend whose residences present the pitiable and *anti mormon* appearances of *Bachelor's Halls.*

Tuesday 9 May 1854. Judge Appleby organized the County of Green River by appoing Robert Alexander Clerk of Probate Court, W. A. Hickman Sheriff also assessor and Collector as well as prosecuting attorney.

He also appointed the other requisite County officers, after which Isaac Bullock, James Brown, Elijah Ward and James Davis were appointed to go to the Shoshonei Indians to assure them of our good wishes and feelings towards them also to allay the predjudice which some unprincipaled mountaineers had raised against us   after the council was over we celebrated the inauguration of the newly appointed officers in the usual way.[17]

Elder Hyde held a meeting in the evening.   In the discourse he recommended the marrying of squaws in the most positive and strong terms and particularly the immediately taking Mary an old haggard mummy looking one who had been here all winter   He was very eloquent on the occasion all of which was generally understood to be squinting at M. M. Sanders who already seemed to have some inklings that way and was well pleased with fair opportunity thus to safely commit himself so he readily bit at the bait and the courtship commenced immediately after meeting by interpreters for he could not talk with her   She wanted time to consider he being a stranger & she dont like him much any how.   The affair created an unusual amount of fun & jokes among the *disinterested*

Wednesday 10 May 1854. About noon to day the proxied courtship between Sanders & Mary the Shoshone (the flower of the desert as Elder Hyde called her) was brought to close and they both were launched into a State of matrimony by Elder Hyde who acted the Parson   The cerimony being performed over by the interpreter James Bullock   our joy now was full & the fun loving corps enjoyed the

---

so of their own free will and choice . . . . Consider these things, brethren, and let your judgment and the spirit of wisdom dictate you . . . .

As the season advanced, there were developments which made him change his mind, for on October 14 he wrote:

To William D. Huntington, Brigham H. Young and others at Green River

Dear Brethren: I wrote you on the 4th inst., per Indian Simons [Ben Simons] to return .rom that place and for all of you to come away and bring your effects with you to this city and leave not one behind. Owing to the uncertainty of your getting the letter f.om that source, I now write you by Bro. Hutchinson . . . .

During the month of August 1853, Daniel H. Wells sent a posse of fifty minutemen under Major James Ferguson with orders to bring in Jim Bridger, Elisha Ryan, and any others carrying on trade with the Indians at Green River on the accusation that they were supplying them with arms and ammunition with which to fight the Mormons. The first orders, "Special Orders No 2 Instructions to Major Fergusen Commdg Battalion Minute Men" from D. H. Wells, were issued August 20 and were to the effect that "you will raise from your Command 50 Men fully Equipped for service with rations for Ninety days and proceed East wardly . . . and arrest any and all persons engaged in furnishing Indians with Guns and Ammunition."

On August 24 was issued "Special Order to Lieut Col Wm H. Kimball" to the effect that he should take "thirty Men Mounted and fully Armed and Equiped with the necessary luggage wagons teams etc . . . and with as little delay as possible join Major Jas Ferguson now enroute for Green River Via of Fort Bridger. . . ."

They arrived to find that Jim Bridger had been warned of their approach and had gone into hiding. According to instructions, they took possession of the fort and confiscated such contraband as "powder Lead cofee Liquor, Guns, etc." Correspondence is found in the Utah Territorial Militia Records (Military Records Section, Utah State Archives).

A second attempt to colonize the Green River area came in 1853, when at the October conference thirty-nine men were called to go under the leadership of John Nebeker and fifty-three under Isaac Bullock, the whole proceeding to be directed by Orson Hyde. James S. Brown in his *Giant of the Lord, The Life of a Pioneer* (Salt Lake City, 1960), gives a detailed account of this undertaking.

17. Though the legislature had officially organized Green River County on March 3, 1852, this was the first time the full personnel of officers was set up to do business.

time to the best possible advantage. Elder Hyde, John Leonard, Ute Perkins & John Fawcett left about noon for Great Salt Lake City

Thursday 11 May 1854. Weather continues sharp cold and windy frost & ice in the night and snow squalls in in the day time. Captain Hawley arrived this evening meeting Hyde & co at sulpher Creek. They were undoubtedly under forced march In fact Elder Hyde seems to [have] an invincible repugnance to Fort Supply.

Friday 12 May 1854. Some six waggons started to Green River ferry to day having to face a Severe snow squall on the road and camped half mile below Bridger Sanders came with us to Bridger to purchase some goods for "Flower of the desert," which however we afterwards learned she would not accept and even refused to have any thing to do with him The matrimonial alliance thus entered into has proved a signal failure

Saturday 13 May 1854. Encamped to night on Black's Fork some 26 miles to day. Cool day but good weather while the *eternal* black cloud Snow squalls were yet hanging over Fort Supply

Sunday 14 May 1854. Crossed Ham's Fork which we had to ferry in Hawley's Skiff Here we found Mr Shockley's waggon loaded with alcahal and other things This we all knew what to do with so after helping ourselves we took his waggon on with us some 4 or 5 miles and camped soon after which Shockley & Russell came after their wagon, both very glad that we had brought it along for with Hawley's skiff they could not have crossed Ham's fork. Bullock & company also came and put up with us on their way to the Shoshonees so all was well now & plenty of good company.

Monday 15 May 1854. Rained & snowed in the night which continued part of the day making the road *exceedingly inconvenient* But however we arrived at Russell's Baiting with Batise at twelve Here at Russell's is where Huntington & Co. commenced a Settlement in 1852 which was wisely abandoned afterwards.

Tuesday 16 May 1854. Foggy morning we moved two miles (to the mo [crossed out]) down the River to the Mormon Crossing of Green River Ferry and ferried our traps & waggon across in Hawley's skiff Here was three log buildings in which we took possession of shielding us only a little from the Storms for they were in a bad condition After crossing over we had plenty to do drying our clothes & bedding for this day. Nearly all the mountaineers came to day to pay us our first visit

Wednesday 17 May 1854. Clear & cool mornings. Another mountaineer visit & dull time for those not interested in our visitors company

Thursday 18 May 1854. I am doing positively worse than nothing Mr Hawley put his rope across the river and Joseph Busby[18] came from (Bear Riv [crossed out]) Weber ferry to commence suit against Bridger[19] & Lewis in a matter pertaining to Ham's fork ferry last year wherein all three were partners.

---

18. Joseph Busby had been in charge of this ferry the year before.

19. James Bridger had not returned since his escape the summer before. One of the best known of all the mountain men, he was born March 7, 1804, at Richmond, Virginia. In 1812 his family moved to St. Louis, then the center of western exploration. At the age of thirteen he was apprenticed to a blacksmith; at fifteen he was orphaned, and his sister and he were cared for by an aunt.

When Bridger was eighteen he joined the company of General William H. Ashley and from that time on lived on the frontier. In 1842 he and Louis Vasquez built Fort Bridger, his headquarters until 1853. He married in succession three Indian women, each of whom left him at least one child.

Bridger came west with Johnston's Army, but did not get control of his property, the Mormon Church having purchased it from Vasquez. Bridger died July 17, 1881, near Little Santa Fe, Missouri.

Friday 19 May 1854. Attending legal business Joseph Busby vs James Bridger & Suece Louis. A large company of Bannack indians crossed the river to day In the after noon 21 of the missionary brethren crossed en route for the States   Benj L. Clapp Captain of the company

Saturday 20 May 1854. The missionaries lay up to day making the time pass very pleasantly in their society which formed an agreeable contrast to the society of this section of country.

Sunday 21 May 1854. The missionaries *rolled on* leaving *as we were.*

Monday 22 May 1854. Mail for Salt Lake passed to day who report a large emmigration this year and also Col Connell's train of 6 waggons arrived

Tuesday 23 May 1854. Lounging around with nothing to do and so lazy that life is almost a drug

Wednesday 24 May 1854. G. W. Boyd the constable started for Bridger and Mr Sanders with a train of 6 or 8 waggons arrived and a drove of horses.

Thursday 25 May 1854. Wrote to [Dustin] Amy.   Hard rain and all wet and I am mad.

Friday 26 May 1854. All mud & saleratus   mixed   Rain again and River rising

Saturday 27 May 1854. Cloudy & muddy.   Hickman & Hawley started their teams to Hams Fork with a boat to start a ferry at that point.

Sunday 28 May 1854. River rising & over West bank Boyd returned bringing letters to some but none for me, from Fort Supply   The Mountaineers as usual throng in here to day drinking swearing & gambling.

Monday 29 May 1854. Law suit before Judge Appleby.   John H. Bigler vs F. M. Russel administrator of the estate of same   M. Caldwell deced[20] in Replevin for the recovery of a mare Hickman was council for plaintiff & myself for Defence Judgement no cause of action & coust [cost?] apportioned equally.

The day was wound up in hard drinking & gambling meantime we had a cold wind from the West followed by a severe snow storm

Tuesday 30 May 1854. Squalls & hard wind, cold and uncomfortable while we are all shivering around in these miserable old log huts and suel & Winters are quite sick & I have took up my boarding with Hawley.   He has returned from Ham's Fork having started the ferry there

Wednesday 31 May 1854. Clear & pleasant weather again giving us a chance to sun ourselves which we were very much inclined to do.

Thursday 1 June 1854. Bullock, Brown, Ward & Davis came here this evening on their return from their mission to Shoshonees.   They report the indians somewhat ill disposed but some were friendly & expect some of them here in a few days.   Two more trains crossed and emmigration seems to be fairly commenced.

---

20. Samuel M. Caldwell was a mountain man who lived in the Fort Bridger area. He is mentioned several times in the 1853 military correspondence as a man of some influence and much property. His death is told by James S. Brown, one of the Mormon missionaries: "About this time [January, 1854], Louis Tromley, a Frenchman, stabbed Samuel Caliwell [*sic*]. The affair took place near Fort Bridger. Callwell was said to be at the head of the gang of desperadoes who plied their vocation from Bridger to Green River, and back on the emigrant route to Laramie; he was a large, trim built man, about six feet six inches tall, and very daring. But after a bowie knife was plunged into his vitals he did not survive long, dying in about twenty-four hours from the time he received the fatal wound. Tromley was one of Callwell's band, and made his escape." Brown, *Giant of the Lord,* 326.

Friday 2 June 1854. Shivering in the cold blast again.

Saturday 3 June 1854. The case of Busby v. Lewis & Bridger came up to day and was adjourned by plff for want of a material witness.

Sunday 4 June 1854. Cold again. Gammell & others came from Salt Lake bringing me a letter from Isaac Allred now in England but no word from home. My friends seem to forget me it would seem.

Monday 5 June 1854. Suit before Judge Appleby, people by Isaac Packer Complainant vs Josiah Reynolds on Examination for Petty Larceny. W. A Hickman Prosecuting Atty. for people & myself on the part of Defence. Judgement no cause of action & suit dismissed at cost of Compt

Blazzard and others arrived to day from the City of Great Salt Lake.

Tuesday 6 June 1854. Suit of Busby V. Bridger & Lewis came up to day at ten a. m. I was on the part of the plaintiff & Hickman for Defence

This was an interesting trial which terminated in a judgement against the defendants for 540 dollars & about 75 dollars cost. An appeal was called for by Plff. which was however was waived afterwards and Mr Bovee who was an agent for Bridger & Mr Hawley give bonds for the payment of judgement and costs in ten days.

The day was wound up according to custom by fiddling, drinking & gambling in Earl's & McDonald's grocery and finally about 11 o'clock in the night wound up by two of the party's having a knock down The fact is our place is improving fast. Earl & McDonald has a grocery and gambling table both well patronized every law day Hawley another grocery & Blazzard a Brewry, so when Emmegration & law gets in full blow every body can be accommodated

Wednesday 7 June 1854. Dull day now with all those who spent such a merry night laying on on Counters Benches & the ground asleep or taking the "Seber Second Thought" untill the after noon when drinking & gambling broke out afresh which resulted in a magnificent fight between Russell & McDonald for which the Judge fined them ten dollars each.

Thursday 8 June 1854. Cold Cloudy weather again Emmegrants are coming and crossing

Friday 9 June 1854. The Judge and officers of court are busily engaged repairing to miserable old log house which we occupy for a Court house. Vasques & Stringfellow arrived bringing the report that Mr James Bridger was left by them very sick & not expected to live. He was some where on the Missouri river.

Saturday 10 June 1854. Br William D. Huntington is very sick and I am sleightly afflicted with cold.

Sunday 11 June 1854. Feel very *dumpish* to day. Huntington is some better. Weather warm & still.

Benjamin Hawley returned from Salt Lake bringing Hickman's & McDonald's wives. Hitherto only two women, Hawley's wife & daughter-in-law were the only women who graced our society. This in a company of some twenty Mormons seems to be verging into a state little short of *Modern* Christanity but since we have been blessed with two more female arrivals the aspect of our society seems to brighten.

Monday 12 June 1854. Nothing special occured except one man drowned at Kinney's ferry, and the appraisment of Mr Caldwell's Estate

Tuesday 13 June 1854. A company of some ten waggons crossed from Salt Lake bound East Some were Gladdenites and some were mormons who were tired of their religion and all were very desirous of leaving the territory of *Mormonism.*

Wednesday 14 June 1854. Russell & Shockley had a suit in Replevin which ended in a nights gambling.

Thursday 15 June 1854. Mr Elisha Ryan[21] with some seven Shoshonee Indians arrived here, There is several lodges of shoshonee's been encamped here sevral days. In the after noon we had a regular talk with Ryan, as chief, and his braves He said he was sent by the Head Chief to learn what our intententions were. Whether we intended to take their land & if so whether peaceably or not. What was the feelings of the General Goverment & also Governor Young and the mormons, towards them. That they did not want their timber cut or have houses built on their land nor have settlements established. That if we did not and were friendly all was well for they desired to live in peace with all men but at the same time they would not allow any infringement on their lands.

That they had given Green River to him the said Ryan and those mountaineers who had married shoshonee wives. They complained bitterly about the general goverment neglecting them in never making a treaty with them and not sending men to trade for their skins and furs &c Ryan said he had been robbed of his last bottom dollar (refering to the suit against him last year) That he considered this land his own and no one had a right to keep a ferry here but himself and those who had married shoshonee wives. He said he [had] nothing against the mormons as a people but had againts those individuals who robbed him last year, and many such things spake he.

The rope broke yesterday but done no damage. A pack train from California and could not be ferried. Rainy after noon.

Friday 16 June 1854. Clear & cold with sharp N. W. winds. Another talk with Ryan and his braves He claims all the ferrys on Green River in the most positive terms, denying the right of the Legislature of Utah to grant a legal charter without the consent of the shoshonees who own the land. He does not quite threaten hostilities but at the same time says he will have it and seems to want us to understand that he he has the power to redress his own grievances, and offers to arbitrate his claim by referring his right & the right of the ferry company to Chief of the Indian Beureau at Washington which Hawley agrees to do on the part of the company.

The conditions of this I will not relate. He agrees to have another meeting and grand talk in about fifteen days.

The rope being fixed the ferrying has commenced again

Saturday 17 June 1854. Ryan on the part of those who claim Green River on the one part & Jones, Russells, and Hawley on the part of the company entered into bonds of 50.000 dollars to abide the result of the arbritration and Ryan gives bond to the same amount to keep the Indians peaceable in the mean time.

Sent letters home by A. Hale.

---

21. Elisha Ryan had been arrested the year before. A letter dated Fort Bridger, August 28, 1853, addressed to Brigham Young and signed by James Ferguson reads: "I send in charge of Lieut Ephr. Hanks, Lt. Walker, Wm A. Hickman, & Rufus Stoddard the prisoner Elisha Ryan charged with resistance to the Territorial Marshal in the service of the process from the U S Dist. Court."

An answering letter from Daniel H. Wells dated August 31, 1853, admits that "I am a little astonished at Ryan Escape . . . ." Correspondence in the Utah Territorial Militia Records (Military Record Section, Utah State Archives). William A. Hickman writes an interesting version of this episode in his *Brigham's Destroying Angel*, 92.

James S. Brown also has much to say about this man, whom he designates as L. B. Ryan, "We had also learned that L. B. Ryan, successor to Samuel Callwell as chief of the organized band of desperadoes, was at that time beating up and organizing a war party to carry on his nefarious work of robbery, and that he had sworn vengeance on the first Mormons he met." Brown, *Giant of the Lord*, 338.

Sunday 18 June 1854. W. D. Huntington having partially recovered from his sickness started home by whom I sent 48 dollars to Dustin Amy to pay for the flour which he had credited me with previous to my leaving home.

Mr Jones train of goods arrived some ten waggons bound for Salt Lake.

The *plot thickens* and a considerable excitement   Mr F. M. Russell came this morning complaining that Ryan had broke his treaty or arbritration and had attempted to take forcible possession for the ferry at Kinney and had made an attempt to cut the rope   Judge Appleby issued a writ for him but while this was going on Mr Shockley came express reporting that Ryan being joined by eight other mountaineers had actually taken possession of the ferry and was crossing Emmegrants and taking their money.   The writ was however given to Mr Hickman the sheriff who with a *possee* of six men besides Russell & Shockley started after Ryan.   The excitement quite well got up now. When the sheriff arrived at Kinney's he found *Ryan in a sound drunken sleep.*

Ryan was drunk when he took the ferry so after occupying untill the sober second thought returned he gave up the ferry & money he had taken & fell quietly asleep.

Circumstances being thus & Ryan agreeing to behave in future those on the part of the ferry concluded to drop the matter and the excitement ended without smoke And thus ended the Sabbath day on Green River.

Monday 19 June 1854. Extreemly cold & windy   Mr Charles Levingston arrived in advance of his train of goods.

Tuesday 20 June 1854. Dull times but better weather & a few pilgrams come and went.

Wednesday 21 June 1854. Ryan & company executed the affrsaid bonds   John Cooper & family passed en route for Cal   New rope put up.

Thursday 22 June 1854. New rope broke the fastenings.   Gilbert's train of 26 waggons of goods for Salt Lake crossed and other trains & herds of cattle also.

Friday 23 June 1854. Warm summer weather   Wrote to Br J. L Haywood. Sokoper a Shoshonee Chief came. Another big talk.   He don't want his timber cut or his land settled but says his heart is good towards us.

Saturday 24 June 1854. Mail from the States.   Levi Stewart & others along as passengers.   suit before Judge Appleby   Joseph S. Tondrow V. John M. Russell in damage three hundred dollars in assault and Battery.   Hickman was council for plff & myself for Deft   The court decided no cause of action & laid costs on plff.

The fact is Tondrow had taken up a quarrel in which he was not concerned and Russell gave him a sound drubbing with an ox goad for which the court decided he was justified. (Meddlers take warning.)

Sunday 25 June 1854. Consulting my Horiscope with Mr Sanderson the astroliger.

Monday 26 June 1854. Working up my Hiriscope to correct some mistakes in the reconing.   Not being satisfied that it was properly corrected I shall not state the results for I am naturally skeptical about such matters

Judge Appleby & several others went to Kinney's to the sale of the property of the Estate of Caldwell.

Tuesday 27 June 1854. River rising and every thing else dull.

Wednesday 28 June 1854. Moniseur Vasques sr and also Levingston & Co's train of goods for salt Lake arrived under the charge of Mr Patterson   also Joseph Thompson & several others from Salt Lake bringing me a letter from Allen.   My family were all well.

Thursday 29 June 1854. All dull only Shiriff & *posse* went to Kinney's to arrest a man.

Friday 30 June 1854. Wash-a-keek the Head chief of the Shoshonees and another Indian came He was not here long before he became intoxicated when he acted very bad but when sober he professed to be all very good He left mad creating considerable excitement.

Saturday 1 July 1854. Hawley moved two waggon loads over the river & *cached* his liquor for fear the indians might come & get drunk and thereby create a difficulty. Several left for home among the rest I went in John Mott's waggon.[22] There was two waggons & six men We went to *Batise's* eight miles and staid all night.

Sunday 2 July 1854. Travelled on some ten miles after crossing Ham's Fork which is now fordable taking the road North of Blacks Fork We passed Mr Patterson's train He had a man drowned this morning in an attempt to swim Blacks Fork. We camped together to night.

Monday 3 July 1854. Nooned to day near Fort Bridger and travelled on some ten miles having good camping.

Tuesday 4 July 1854. Early start & travelld lively and nooned at Bear river, passing several emmegrants waggons and travelled on to yellow Creek

Wednesday 5 July 1854. We made another good drive to day passing several trains & encamped at the mouth of Echo Cañnon. The Horses were considerably fatigued this evening.

Thursday 6 July 1854. Went to Weber which we found barely fordable But we crossed on the boat. Here I paid Joseph Busby 283 dollars and 55 cents of the collected for him of Bridger & suice. Travelling on we encamped in East Kanyon We met several on their way to Fort Supply. We had the waggon to come uncoupled in Kanyon Creek and wet our loading

Friday 7 July 1854. Earley start crossed the Big mountain with out any trouble only hard pulling and walking, nooned and went on arriving at home before night finding my family well. Aseneth as I had expected had obtained a Divorce and all was well.

Saturday 8 July 1854. Attended probate Court in a case of the people vs Warren Smith. A. Carrington Atty Genl for people & J. C. Little and my self for defendant The trial had been partly carried on yesterday but to day it was adjourned till Monday next for lack of evidence. Took dinner at U. S. Hotel.

Sunday 9 July 1854. Went to meeting Prest B. Young spoke vs thieves & thievery, Law and Lewyers &c Took supper at the Bath House again

Monday 10 July 1854. Case of people vs Smith which occupied most of the day which after it was submitted to the Court, the case of people vs Nephi & Jos Loveless was called up attorneys same as above. part of the evidence was heard and court adjd

Tuesday 11 July 1854. Closed the testimony of the Leoveless case & court again adjourned.

Wednesday 12 July 1854. Case of Joshua Davis vs Thomas S. Johnson was called up. In attachment for breach of contract Phelps for plff & my self for Defence

---

22. Stout gives no indication that he was officially released from this mission. He seemed to feel that he could clear himself with Brigham Young.

This was a most insignificant thing to come before court judgement against defendant for sixty dollars & costs

The Court proceeded then to render judgement against W. Smith & Loveless Smith was found guilty of Larceny and fined 100 dollars and costs which was about 100 more.

The two Loveless were also found guilty and fined each 50 dollars & costs.

Thursday 13 July 1854. aiding Warren Smith to procure bail for fine assessed against him yesterday

Friday & Sat 14 & 15 July 1854. Doing but little to day. The weather is oppressively warm & sultry.

Sunday 16 July 1854. attended meeting to day.

Monday 17 July 1854. Writing for my Quorum.

Tuesday 18 July 1854. attended Court but done no business Court adjourned till Friday.

(Wednesday 19 July 1854. [crossed out])

(Tuesday 1. [crossed out])
In the evening had a suit before William Snow Esquire. George Seaman v. Thomas Clarkson In debt 36 dollars & 44 dollars in damage for assault & Battery. I was on the part of plff. & Carrington for Defendant.

Judgement against Deft for 36 dollars debt & 30 dollars damage for assault besides costs of suit.

Wed 19. Transacting some legal business for Henry G. Sherwood.

Thursday 20 July 1854. Case before William Snow Esquire John Robinson William Bracken, James Bracken, vs Thomas Clarkson In debt Demand thirty dollars. I was on the part of plff Judgement for demand & costs.

Friday 21 July 1854. Case before Judge Smith Loren H. Roundy v. H. C. Branch agent for C. A. & E. H. Perry In Replevin which was decided in favor of the plaintiff. I was on the part of Defence.

Another suit Before same. Abraham Peck v.s. McMichan & McConnell in debt demand $449.62 cents I was on the part of the plaintiff & J. C. Little for Defence. Court is to give judgement tomorrow also another case before same Thomas Burke vs James McGrath I was on the part of the plff who is a bound boy to Defendant who sues for relief from abuse. Court decided that the boy be released.

Saturday 22 July 1854. Court rendered judgement in the case Peck vs McMichan & McConnell in favor of Peck for 440 dollars 62 cents.

Sunday 23 July 1854. Visited Louisa's grave this fore noon & returned home and there remained all day.

Monday 24 July 1854. The seventh anneversary of the first arrival of the pioneers in the Valley of Great Salt Lake was duly celebrated to day in great pomp and splendor. The programme was too long, for me to remember (but the trains [crossed out]) which was mostly constituted of small girls & boys &c The day was extreemly hot & thousands there could not get into the Tabernacle

Tuesday 25 July 1854. Engaged in Court all day in case of Sherwood vs Abrams.

Wednesday 26 July 1854. Engaged in the above case again which was finally referred to the High Council for adjustment.

Thursday 27 July 1854. case before William Snow Esqr Hickman vs Danl Patterson Demand 30 dollars. Hon? A. W. Babbitt[23] & myself was on the part of the Defence. Decided no cause of action.

another case befor same ____ Jett vs Dr ____ Alexandre Damage in assault & battery 100 dollars case adjd for want of plaintiff's witesses I was on the part of plff & Babitt & Little for Defence.

Friday 28 July 1854. Engaged in case of Jutt v Alexandre again case adjourned again. Case before Gibbs Esq F Pullin v.s. R Knight demand 30 dollars on part plaintiff case adjourned.

Saturday 29 July 1854. The case of Sherwood v. Abrams came off before the High Council and decision will be given tomorrow morning. I compromised the case of Jett vs Alexandre recieving 20 dollars damage for the assault.

Sunday 30 July 1854. Went to meeting & heard Lorenzo D. Young who was followed by president B. Young.

The case of Sherwood vs Abrams was decided this morning by the High Council, who rendered judgement in favor of Sherwood for one hundred & 97 dollars and for Sherwood, to pay the cost which had acrued before the Probate Court. This evening we were refreshed with a cool shower & hard wind

Monday 31 July 1854. Suit before Horace Gibbs Esquire. John H. Shirley v. John Bradley in damage in refusing to take him to California for one hundred dollars. I was on the part of the plff & A. W. Babbitt for Deft Jury case. Judgement for plaintiff for sixty dollars & costs in all 94 dollars

The case of Pullin v. Knight was refered to the Bishop & decided against plff.

The rest of this week was spent mostly in reading the news papers which came in to day and sunday was spent at church & home.

Monday 7 Aug 1854. To day was the general Election for Territorial, County & precinct officers which resulted the election of the following persons to wit. for Councillors to fill vacancis which exhist by death & resignation

    Albert Carrington
    Orson Pratt
    Wilford Woodruff

For Representative

Jedediah M. Grant	Edwin D. Woolley
Samuel W. Richards	Hosea Stout,
A. P. Rockwood	James W. Cummings
Horace S. Eldredge.	W. W. Phelps
Lorenzo Snow	John L. Smith[24]

There was some little opposition to Mr Rockwood who did not seem to "take" well[25] Stephen was run against him & got 83 votes otherwise the Election went off calm as usuel.

---

23. The "Hon? A. W. Babbitt" is another of Stout's derogatory references to this man. He uses this device occasionally in reference to others also.

24. John Lyman Smith was born November 17, 1828, at Pottsdam, New York, the son of John Smith and Clarissa Lyman. He was baptized in 1836 and came to Utah in 1847. He took part in some of the Indian wars and filled two missions to Europe. He died February 24, 1898, in St. George, Utah.

25. That Albert P. Rockwood, for years Brigham Young's most trusted assistant, should have received eighty-three negative votes on a slate where all other candidates received unanimous approval would indicate that there was strong feeling against him.

Of this election John Hyde, Jr., then an apostate from the church, wrote: ". . . Among other nominations for representative for Salt Lake County, one was A. P. Rockwood. He was very much disliked; and a few men got up an opposition ticket, substituting the name of Stephen H. Hales instead of this Rockwood . . . . A small body of voters were brought and Hales

The county & precinct officers I shall not say anything about.

Thursday 10 Aug 1854. Had a suit before Esq Gibbs William J. Coil v.s William Lowry In damage for assault Demand one hundred dollars. A. Carrington for plaintiff and myself for Defence After the parties appeared the matter was compromised by the Defendant paying the cost.

Monday 14 August 1854. There has been an Examination going on before the Probate court since friday last against H. B. Taylor for assertions made on the road East and in this place to one Mr Rayney stating that E. T. Benson & others were out there to rob, plunder & kill certain emmegrants That a plot had been laid to rob Mr Childs & kill him and that it was very common to kill strangers & take their cattle and other property and many other such things. Taylor at first denied the charge in toto but afterwards confessed it. Sunday he was cut off from the church & to day the examination was brought to a close and Taylor was acquitted from the fact there was no law made & provided against any thing charged to him

The emmegrants who had heard Taylor's reports were very much excited and alarmed for their safety.

Tuesday 15 Aug 1854. The Southren mail via San Bernardino. arrived to day. They had an attact from the Indians at resting [Resting Springs] in which 3 indians were wounded & one of the whites, one mule & one of the mail sacks were lost but otherwise they had no difficulty. Elder William Hyde returned with them from his mission to Australia whither he went when I went to china two years ago. He done a good work while there and brought a company of saints from thence to San Bernardino. He returns with very poor health.

Sunday 20 Aug 1854. Attended meeting in the forenoon Prest B. Young spoke at some length He proposed rather a new feature in religious duties one of which was to have Saturday for a day of rest & preparation & sunday for sacrament meetings &c He also proposed to have a law passed at next conference to cut off all who leave the territory with out Council also all who go out on the roads trading with Emmegrants & such like *land Sharking*

Monday 21 Aug 1854. This morning Brigham H. Young son of phineas H. went down into his well to bring out a Bucket & by some means the stone give away and the wall fell in onto him covering him up some twenty feet deep There was a great excitement about it He was taken out after removing the stone & dirt which covered him and was fortunately not badly injured althoug he was much exhausted.

Tuesday 22 Aug 1854. Hon Judge Kinney Chief Justice of the Supreme Court of the Territory of Utah, & Mr Jos Holman District Attorney also Hon? G. P. Stiles[26] who might be called a *Judicial Cadet* for he came here in expecting *to be* appointed Associate Justice, have arrived to to day and several others.

Wednesday 23 Aug 1854. The District Court was called to day on petition for special session for the trial of two Indians for the murder of two boys in Cedar

obtained a majority . . . and was therefore legally elected . . . . Hales was accordingly sent for by Brigham, who gave him a severe reprimand for *daring* to allow his name to be used as an opponent of 'the Church nomination,' . . . compelled Hales to resign the election, while Rockwood had the seat . . . and the per diem." Hyde, *Mormonism: Its Leaders and Designs*, 189.

26. Here again Stout uses the "Hon? G. P. Stiles" to register his disapproval. George Stiles was nominally a member of the Mormon Church. In 1844 with Babbitt and others he had advised Joseph Smith to destroy the *Nauvoo Expositor* press.

For a time Stiles and Stout associated in apparent friendliness but they later clashed so sharply that Stiles accused Stout of intimidating him in his own court. Stout recorded the excommunication on December 22, 1856, and the departure of Stiles on the following April 15, "with nearly all the gentile and apostate Scurf in this community . . . ."

Valley. William & Warren Weeks Sons of Allen Weeks on the instant. The grand
jury was called and organized

Thursday 24 Aug 1854. Court met to day but done no business grand jury still
in session.

Saturday 25 Aug 1854. To day the grand jury presented the indictment against
the two Indians (Long hair & Antelope for Murder Hon A W Babbitt & myself were
assigned their council. Mr Holman prosecuting Court adjd till Monday Thomas
S. Williams & S. W. Richards arrived at home to day.

Monday 28 August 1854. Court met at ten a. m. The trial of the two indians Long
hair & Antelope was brought up. Mr Holeman Esqr U. S. District attorney prossecuting & Babbitt & myself Defending the prisoners. Filed a motion to quash the indictment which was over-ruled Then Plea to the jurisdiction of the Court to try the
Indians filed & pleaded and Court adjourned.

This evening about five o'clock I married Ether Knight to Jane Terry at the
residence of C. C. Rich

Tuesday 29 Aug 1854. Court met at ten a. m. The pla to the jurisdiction by the
defence was overruled. Council for the Defence excepted to the rulings in both
cases. In the after noon Babbitt objected to the Court being held in the State House
and the Court adjourned till to morrow at ten after instructin the marshal to procure
a house to hold Court.

Wednesday 30 Aug. Court met at ten at Blair's Hall The witnesses in the case
of the U. S. vs the Indians being called up a difficulty arose bettween Mr Babbitt
& Judge shaver as to how the *voir dire* of the witnesses, they being indians should
be taken, which caused Mr Babbitt to abandon the defence & Col J. C. Little Esqr
was assigned in his place In the after noon the evidence on the part of the
prosecution was heard

Thursday 31 August 1854. This fore noon the testimony on both sides was
closed. It appears in short as follows that Allen Weeks living in Cedar Valley
Utah County sent his two sons William F. & Warren D Weeks on the 8th inst. to
the kanyon for a load of poles with an ox team. The Indians a small band of ten
or twelve *Gosh Utes* who had seperated from the tribe & would not make peace with
the whites untill some of their friends & relations were revenged or a recompense
given which had been killed & Salt Creek Juab County last year, had concluded after
waiting 12 moon for a recompense and recieving none, to reveng their death on some
of the whites & accordingly the lay in wait in the mouth of a kanyon to which the
inhabitants of Cedar Valley were accustomed to go for wood and poles and br Allen
Weeks two sons happened to be the two unfortunate ones who first came alon &
were slain & their bodies mutilated & scalped by the indians.

They not coming home at night a search commenced earley next morning when
they were found

The two prisoners Long Hair and Antelope were taken & brought here by some
friendly Indians. The Chief and several other indians were accessary to the same
murderous deed.

The evidence was plain & positive both from an eye witness & their own confessions, without the first paliating circumstance on which to hang even a pretended
plea of defence In the after noon the pleas of the attorneys were made and Court
adjourned till 7 P. m when the virdict of the jury was given of "Guilty as charged"

Friday 1 September 1854. Court met at ten and pronounced the sentence of death
by haingin on the "said Long Hair & Antelope Indians as aforsaid" which hanging
was to take place on the fifteenth instant

Thus ended the first trial which has ever been held in this Territory where an Indian was arraigned as a prisoner.[27]

The U. S. Eastern Mail came in las evening & part of this morning with some 25 hundred pounds of mail matter.

Friday 8 Sept 1854. probate Court met to try a Replevin Brown vs Bell which was compromised I was on part of plff

Monday 11 Sept 1854. Suit to day before Probate Court James McGouth vs Charles G McLure in an action of damage for five hundred dollars for personal injuries This case has been several days going on & Saturday came up and some points were argued & finally this morning I appeared as Counsel for plaintiff and Stiles & Holeman for defence.

The counsel for the defence filed three motions first to require the plaintiff to give Bonds for costs & damage, second to the jurisdiction of the court. Second to dissolve the attachment all of which were argued at *full* length. The court over-ruled the first two motions but sustained the third & dissolved the attachment.

They next (filed a motion [crossed out]) plead a misnomer which was over-ruled after which they answered & then moved an adjournment for want of evidence which was granted till next Monday.

This has been a very exciting case The plaintiff is a poor ignorant Paddy and the Deft a prominent man attached to the service of U. S. troops who have recently arrived und command of Col Steptoe

An attempt was made to crush the proceedings by bribery & otherwise but not succeeding they have now undertook to take advantage of the papers which however has failed.

To day the merchantile firm of "J. M. Horner & Co." opened their store to day in the room formerly occupied as the tithing store, offering good much cheaper than other merchants This has created quite an excitement among the merchants & I am told that they are reducing the price of their good & even say they will under sell Horner & co. This is the first competition ever got up among the merchants in this place.

Tuesday 12 Sept 1854. The probate Court for settling the Estate of S. M. Caldwell, met

Friday 15 Sept 1854. To day the 2 indians Longhair & Antelope were executed, according to the sentence of the Court on the first instant.

They were hung some two miles below the Jordain bridge on the other side of the river. There was not a very large company of spectators present from the fact that the place of their execution was kept secret untill the procession started with the two Indians. Col Steptoe & a company of the U. S. Dragoons by request of the Marshal were present.

Nothing of importance took place on the occasion more than is common This is the first execution ever had in the Territory of Utah

Saturday 16 Sept 1854. Lawing again before probate Jos A. Thompson v.s. Geo. W. Parrish in debt 80 dollars. I was for Plff & G. P. Stiles for Defence. The case was adjd for evidence & then compromised by Deft confessing judgement & costs

Wednesday 20 Sept 1854. The cas of James McGouth vs Charles G. McLure came off to day by the jury's virdict being declared awarding 15 dollars damage to platff and he pay his own witness. This case occupied the Court all day yesterday

The fact is the probate Court is in session every day & the probability it will continue many days yet for there is a number of suits yet before the Court.

---

27. Here Stout admits that the young Indian who was "nepoed" on April 27, 1850, did not have a public trial but was condemned by a military group. See Vol. I, Part 1, footnote 38.

Thursday 21 Sept 1854. The case of J. H. Jones & Co v.s. W. J. Hawley[28] came off to day in the fore noon   The Court gave judgement against Hawley for 901.11 cents   Little & Holman was attorneys for Plff & Babbitt, Stiles & myself for Deft   There had been several motions Demures filed during the trial   all of which had been over-ruled and now an appeal to the District Court by the Defendant.

In the after noon the Case of John Stiles vs Ben S. Jones for assault & personal injury demand 300 dollars.   G. P. Stiles (son of Plff) for Plff & myself for defence   Jones in a quarrel had struck father Stiles on the jaw & broke the jaw bone.   Court gave judgement vs defendant for 154 dollars   A large company of Texian Saints arrived to day. & more Saints are expected all most every day.

A Company of some 40 shoshonees passed through here yester eve on their way South to attact the utahs in retaliation for stealing some of their horses.   The recent disagreeable and hostile feeling of some of the Utahs made the people wish them sucess.

Saturday 23 Sept 1854. The case of William J. Hawley & Co. v.s. Estate of Caldwell after a two days trial was brought to a close before Probate. Stiles & myself was on part of Plff & Babbitt & Holman for deft.   Demand some 2,100 $ Court rendered judgement for no cause of action

Another case before Esqr Gibbs on Replevin Joseph Tomblinson vs Chas Woodward.   J. C. Little for Plff & myself for deft   Court rendered judgement for the delivery of the waggon & ten dollars damage. —

The Band of shoshonees who passed here on the 20 returned.   They fell upon a Band (Sqush Head's) and took seven scalps as I learn. & wounded Sqush Head

This evening Br Williams Camp arrived at home all well, having been gone on a mission with his wife & two children for two years.

Tuesday 26 Sept 1854. probate Court still in session every day   The case of Joseph A. Thompson vs Estate of S. M. Caldwell was finished up and submitted to the court.   Demand $768.   Myself & Stiles Council for Plff & Babbitt & Holman for deft   Court rendered judgement rendered no cause of action.

Wednesday 27 Sept 1854. Case of Joseph A. Thompson vs F. M. Russell came up Stiles & myself for Plff & Babbitt & Holman for deft   case dismissed

Thursday 28 Sept 1854. Eastern mail came in to day.   The report of some 25 or 30 officers & soldiers being killed by the indians at Larimie is confirmed.

Sunday Oct 1st 1854. Several companies of saints have arrived from the States. Elder Daniel Carn came in with a company to day.   He has been absent on a mission three years.

Tuesday Oct 3rd 1854. Suit before probate.   C. R. & S. S. Barnes vs. John Probasco   In debt demand 122 dollars 50 Babbitt & Holman for Plffs & myself for Deft. This was a singular suit & has not a parralel in the jurisprudence of this Territory.[29]

The Defendant in this case sued & obtained a judgement of 100 dollars against the plffs in this case before Esqr W. Critchlow of Weber Co. which judgement & costs were duly paid in all amounting to the demand of $122.50

The defendants in that suit then comes from Weber County, crosses Davis county & commences suit against the said plff. for the judgement and costs recovered against

---

28. W. J. Hawley, was a captain in the Nauvoo Legion whose permanent home was in Battle Creek (Pleasant Grove), Utah County. He had been operating the ferry on the Green River, and along with Joseph A. Thompson and others was suing for a part of the estate of Samuel M. Caldwell.

29. This case and the one immediately following point up the frictions which developed between the probate courts and the district courts in Utah. The first was controlled by the Mormon Church, the second dominated by the Gentile appointees of the federal government.

him before Esquire Critchlow of Weber County. Thus disdaining the law of appeal within said County & sues direct for the judgement & cost in the probate of another county for moneys had and recieved and as obtained wrongfully & only under pretence of law, yet strange to say the judge, with the docket of Esqr Critchlow's docket before him and the matter of the trial and judgement lawfully plead in bar, rendered judgment against the Defendant for $122.50 being the whole judgement and costs in the previous trial. A more anomilous a more illegal, a more unjust decision of a court I do not think I ever witnesed.

Wednesday 4 Oct 1854. Suit before probate C. R. & S. S. Barnes vs. Saml Demoss. In debt. Demand 110.55. Babbitt & Holman for Plffs & myself for defence. This case was brought for the recovery of a judgement & cost before Esq. Critchlow and is exactly parallell to the preceeding one & decided accordingly.

The Saints are coming in for the Country to Conference in large numbers.

(Friday [crossed out]**) Sunday 8th Oct 1854.** General Conference commenced on friday last & continued untill this evening. Horace S. Eldredge was chosen to fill the vacancy of J. M. Grant in the first presidency of the seventies. There was no elders sent on missions at this conference, a thing some what unusual. There was more people at conference than common all who enjoyed themselves exceeding well.

Friday 20 October 1854. The last four days I have been engaged in a very exciting lawsuit which arose it is true from a very trifling circumstance

R. T. Burton Deputy U. S. Marshal served a writ of Replevin on Twitchel for the recovery of eleven head of horses claimed as the property of Widow Isabel Brooks. After serving the writ the Marshal left the horses in the yard of B. Hawkins & in his care some two or three hours after he came for them. Twitch had taken possession of 4 of the horses selling two of them to Levi Abram a mean & contempible Jew who had put them in his stable & refused to deliver them up to Burton on demand Burton called on W. A. Hickman to assist to recover the horses which had to be done by force. A considerable altercation ensued. The Jew posted to the probate Judge complained that Hickman had drawn a knife also a club on him with intent as he said to take his life.

The Judge E. Smith naturally chagrined that the process had issued from the District Court insted of his own granted a process to arrest Hickman which was done on Monday. Hickman having every reason & indication before him, that the Probate Judge would not do justice, sued out a writ of Habeas Corpus from the District Court which was granted pending which the probate Court called him to trial, refusing to let him have time to go before judge Shaver to swear to his petition, called on him to plead "guilty or not guilty" to the charge and again refused to let him have a few moments to consult council before he plead. During this time the papers had been completed & the writ of Habeas Corpus ready by a stratagen Hickman was got out of the Court room & swore to his petition & returned, a few minutes after the writ of Habeas Corpus was served on A. Cunning the officer having the prisoner in charge. At this the Judge in high dudgeon & in a state of great mental excitement declared the prisoner not to be in charge of the officer but in charge of the said Probate Court and untill a writ was directed thereto the prisoner could not go (an entirely new idea to me) However to waive any point of controversy between Courts & wink at ignorance Judge Shaver Directed the writ to E. Smith Judge of probate after which the prisoner was forthcoming. The most intense excitement ensued while the report was industerously spread that the District was endeavoring to run over & devour the probate Court. than which nothing could be more untrue

The only object which Mr Hickman had was to be delivered from a court which he verily believed had already pre-judged him an if not had no right to call him to account for his doings by order of another & higher court. The case was adjourned till Tuesday. When it [w]as called up, the excitement increasing. Mr Babbitt &

myself appearing for Hickman & Little & Carrington for the defence of the redoubtable, highly chagrined & insulted Court of probate (now turned *Bum bailiff* or a
sort of Judicial *Calaboose* to put and retain prisoners in if I may say so speak)
Thus prepared the trial commenced which ended to day about noon The course
taken by opposite council will not bear comment & therefore I shall pass it over.

Judge Shver discharged Mr Hickman for several reasons among which were
illegality on the face of the papers, another was that the Probate Court had no right
to interfear with or call officers of his court to account for actions done in compliance
to an order from his court. And further from the evidence he had been guilty of no
crime. He also frorbid any Court to meddle or trouble him further on the subject

Monday 23 October 1854. Yester went North with Pleasant Green Taylor to pay
my old mother-in-law a visit & returned to day in company with Eebr Brown & In
the after-noon attended a case of investigation before District Judge Shaver wherein
one Sullivan alias Sarpee is charged with Embezzling one James Simonds property[30]
cause adjourned till tomorrow at ten a. m.

Tuesday 24 Oct 1854. Case of people vs. Sullivan on investigation closed this
morning & he bound under 1000$ to appear at next term of District Court. Babbitt
& myself was on part of prosecution.

Another train of J. M. Horner & Co's goods came in this fore noon.

Monday 6 Nov 1854. Case to day before probate Court Philander Bell appellor
vs. Bradford Leonard appellee from H. Gibbs Esqr Babbitt & myself for plff
& J. C. Little for defence Council for plff moved to dismiss the case on the grounds
that Gibbs had been succeeded in his office by J. Hendrix Esq when the case was
tried before him which was abundantly proven.

The court will give judgement on the motion on the 8th inst Council for
defence claimed that the court could not decide on the question whether Gibbs was
justice or not only on a writ of Quo Warranto. Case was however dismissed

Tuesday 7 Nov 1854. To day I started to parowan Iron County to attend the Nov.
Term of the U. S third Judicial District Court. I went in company with Judge Geo
P. Stiles & Marshal Jos L Haywood and a guard in all to consist of some 20 men.
I went in the capacity of both guard and U. S. Deputy District attorney. There
was only six of us left here the remainder of the guard to be made out at provo
under the direction of Alex Williams Deputy Marshall

We left here about noon and staid all night at Dry Creek with Rawlins

Wednesday 8 Nov 1854. Went to Battle Creek Utah County and dined with Capt
Hawley & thence to provo Stopping with A. Williams There was a party here to night
at Harlow Redfields, which soon terminated in a drunken "Row" & a Knock down
or two when the Bishop ordered 'em *home*

Thursday 9 Nov 1854. About noon we started for Payson and staid all night
Here we completed our arraingements for the trip which consisted of one baggage
waggon, two carriages one buggy & some nine horsemen I rode in Henry Nebeker's
carriage in company with Judge stiles & Marshal Haywood. Government paying the
expense of the Horse feed boarding for the men which was fifty per meal and horse
fee proportionably liberal

Friday 10 Nov 1854. Went to Nephi, (Salt Creek) I put up at Haywoods. Here
W. Meeks & Richd Bentley joined the guard.

---

30. This case of "one Sullivan alias Sarpee" continues until December 16 and ends with
Sullivan's being fined $500 and confined to the penitentiary for one year. James Simonds was
a trader on the Green River.

Saturday 11 Nov 1854. Travelled to the Sevier and encamped by the new bridge just finished across it by Mr T. B. Foot. The night was clear & very cold. Here we had a meeting & prayers & by Haywood Stiles Williams, Stout & others after which some went to bed some on guard some endeavouring to keep warm by the fire while others taking times more easy amused themselves by playing cards

Sunday 12 Nov 1854. Arrived at Fillmore about sun set. I H Scovil putting up with Elias Bassett. & lay up on monday to lay in provision & horse feed.

Tuesday 14 Nov 1854. Encamped on Cove Creek where the night was spent about as on the Sevier.

Wednesday 15 Nov. Encamped on Beaver to night. We saw a few Indians to night who were very friendly

Thursday 16th Nov '54. Arrived in Parowan this evening where we was joyfully recieved by our old friends. & acquaintances.

Parowan is in a flourishing condition the city was is nearly finished while other improvements have been going on. A new grist mill is nearly ready to go into opperation in side the wall. Walker & his band a camped near by professing to be very friendly.

Friday 17 Nov 1854. Spent to day visiting as also saturday and attended a party at Br Daltons in the evening where we *operated* untill about midnight, enjoying ourselves to a very good advantage.

Sunday 19 Nov 1854. Attended meeting, preaching by Haywood, E. H. Groves I. C Hait [Haight], Judge Stiles Williams & my self which was wound up by Prest J. C. L. Smith[31]

Monday 20 Nov 1854. District Court commenced at 10 o'clock a. m Court held five days during which time the grand jury were enquiring in to the nature of some tradings with the Indians by some Mexicans but testimony could not be elicited sufficient to obtain an indictment

To night there was a party given on the occasion of our being present & a large company met where we waited on two o'clock in the morning with the most extreem pleasure.

Another party came off on Thurs (Friday [crossed out]) night with similar results For me I can say I enjoyed my self well while I know a good Spirit prevailed among the people

Thus ended our Court tour & visit to parowan. The Court adjourning without having a suit at law to disturb the peace or drain the pockets of the good people here. On Friday the 17 Elder C. C. Rich from San Barnardino. Elder George Q. Cannon returning missionary from Sandick Islands, whither he has been laboring some five years, and several others arrived here all good health.

The[y] left on Saturday for Salt Lake.

Friday 24 Nov 1854. This morning the Court adjourned and our party started for home encamping on the Beaver again where we over took a number of ox teams bound for Salt Lake market, loaded with produce. Saturday night encamped on

---

31. The presiding officer at Parowan at this time was John Calvin Lazelle Smith, of whom both residents and visitors spoke in the highest terms. Born September 8, 1821, in New Salem, Massachusetts, he joined the Mormon Church in 1841 and came to Nauvoo in 1843. Here he married Sarah Fish, who came with him to Utah in 1848. In 1851 he was called to Parowan to preside over the settlement and the next year was made president of all the southern colonies.

In 1855 the stake was divided, and Isaac C. Haight was made president of the wards at Cedar City and vicinity while Smith remained in charge at Parowan. He died December 30, 1855, of heart disease.

Cove Creek again & reached Fillmore the next evening meeting Dr Andrus[32] & Cyrus Canfield and others on their way to Cal on Corn Creek.

Monday 27 Nov 1854. The State house at Fillmore is now being built   The wall is now to the tops of the windows second story above the basement.

The good citizens here are in high hopes of having the Legislature meet here another year.

We left this morning encamping in round prairie   Here a large camp was again formed by travellers going both ways & happening to meet at dark thus forming a good visiting party to spend the evening with & drink tea.

Tuesday evening. we arrived at Salt Creek. & Wednesday evening at payson   Thursday evening at Provo   Here we again lay up on Friday for the most exquisite & ostensible object of having a party on Friday night at Harlow Redfields where we tiped the fantastic toe till three a. m & retired all well satisfied

Saturday 2 Dec. 54. Left Provo & dined at american Fork staid all night on Willow Creek arrived at home about Eleven a. m the next Day, finding my family all well & doing well in my absence.

Mond. 4 Dec 1854. This morning a beautiful snow some four inches deep covered the ground so that our arrival at home seems to have been very opportunely.

The District Court commenced its December Term to day which has continued all the week.   The grand jury has found a bill vs Sullivan who was bound over on the 24 Oct. last

No civil business will be attended to untill the criminal business is disposed of.   The[re] is much both civil & criminal business likely to come before this Term.   More than has ever been before one Term of Court in the Territory before.

Thursday 7 Dec 1854. Met with the Board of Regents at the New tithing office this evening to take into consideration the Common schools.

Spent the week settling the guard pay & accounts with Marshall Haywood. My services & guard amounted to 108 dollars or four dollars per day & boarded & fees milages & services as Deputy U. S. District Attorney was   dollars in all amounting to   dollars Sunday I attended Church.   C. C. Rich, W. Woodruff & E. T. Benson preached.

11 Dec 1854. This morning at ten o'clock the Legislative assembly of the Territory of Utah assembled in the Council House and proceeded to organize   After being duly sworn by Secratary Babbitt by Electing Hon J. M. Grant Speaker of House of Representatives, Thomas Bullock Chief Clerk, Leo Hawkins assistant Clerk, Robt T. Burton Seargt-at-arms, George Q. Cannon Messenger John Stiles Door keeper, Alba Sherman Foreman & Rev. Daniel Carn Chaplain after which the usual Stationary was distributed to the members, and the committees from either branch of the Legislative assembly passed when the House adjourned till 2 o'clock p. m to recieve the govorners message.   The Rules of the former session were adopted with some little amendments.

At 2 p.m. House assembled again when the two Houses met in joint session in the Representatives Hall   The Chief Justice of the supreme Court and the two associate Justices District Attorney & Col Steptoe Capt Ingalls of the U. S. Army, also

---

32. This is Dr. Woodville M. Andrews, who accompanied the William H. Kimball contingent south on an expedition from July 22 to August 24 to drive back the surplus cattle. Immediately after, he was sent on the Green River expedition of August 27, 1853. His name appears on the roll of the Nauvoo Legion for 1855 as surgeon general.

Andrews remained in San Bernardino, where he became estranged from the church and later a bitter critic and opponent. Beattie and Beattie, *Heritage of The Valley* gives the details of his later activities.

present. after which the Governor appeared and delivered his message which was read by Mr William Clayton Esqr after which on motion of Mr Benson ordered that 5000 copies of the Message be printed for the use of the Assembly & for distribution joint session adjourned

That 100 copies of names of the members of the assembly and the names of the committees be printed for the use of the two Houses &c

That Joseph Cain be public printer and several other motions carried, House adjourned till tomorrow at ten a. m. Attended the District Court which is now holden at Union House. The case of J. S. vs Sullivan was up for consideration

Tuesday 12 Dec 1854. House met at ten a. m.

Speaker delivered an address acknowelgement for the trust reposed in him by the House in electing him speaker He then declared the names of the different committees.

On Motion Mr Phelps the various portions of the gov's message was refered to the appropriate committees During which time the Secratary was distributing the laws and journals of the previous sessions of the Legislature among the members. House adjd till tomorrow at 11 A. M. after which I attended the Court. The indictment against Sullivan was quashed for want of certainty & for double meaning.

Paid br. C C. Rich this evening

Wednesday 13 Dec 1854. House met at ten as pr adjt Petition of 100 from San Pete County for appropriation to work Salt Creek Kanyon refered to committee A variety of motions offered and notices to bring in bills.

Committee of Indians affairs Reported Resolutions which was accepted to come up in its order.

afternoon Bill in relation to County Surveyors laid over to come up in its order

Bill to extend the charter of James Brown for a bridge across Weber & Ogdon rivers for five years laid on the table to come up in its order.

Bill in relation to County surveyors taken up & refered to committee on Judiciary

Bill to extend the charter to Jas Brown for a bridge across Weber & Ogden rivers for five years was taken up & passed the first reading and refered to Committee on Roads Bridges & Ferries.

Bill in relation to Indians taken up read the first time and refered back to committee for amendment.

Minutes read & accepted. Adjd till ten to morrow.

Thursday 14 Dec 1854. House met at ten a. m. as pr adjt several motions of minor importance were put & passed when the House adjourned till two p. m. afternoon. Rockwood moved to call on Lt Genl Wells report the condition of the Military school

Committee on Roads Bridges and Ferries to whom was was refered the petition for an appropriation to work the road in Salt Creek Kanyon reported adversely to the petition.

The same reported bill to extend the charter for bridge across Weber and Ogden rivers which repealed the charter and introduced a new bill which was recieved & laid on the table to come up in its order

Mr Dame Resolution in relation to the Iron Works, Laid on the Table to come up in its order

Mr. T. S. Williams requested and obtained leave to speak in relation to certain claims which he had paid to officers of the Legislature in the year 1851 & 2 amounting to 1131 dollars asking the Legislature to reimburse him for the same which was answered by the gov. objecting to the claim[33]

---

33. This might well have been the beginning of Thomas S. Williams' break with Brigham Young. His early zeal for the cause and his generous contributions to the missionaries have already been noted. His claim for reimbursement was not honored.

Mr Cummings reported Resolution in relation to Code Commissioners. **Recieved** & laid on table to come up in its order

Weber & Ogden Bridge bill called up read the first time & passed on the second reading refered back.

Resolution by S. W. Richards for Librarians Report.

Resolutions in relation to Iron Works read & passed first reading and refered to the committee on Trade Agriculture & Manufactures

minutes read & accepted Adjd till

Friday 15 Dec 1854. Summoned before the U. S grand jury during which time the Legislature adjourned till next monday at 10 a. m.

The trial of Sullivan was brought to a close this evening and he found guilty & fined in the sum of 580 dollars and ordered to be kept in the penetentiary untill it was paid.

Saturday 16 Dec 1854. attended Court. Sullivan was sentenced to the penetentiary for one year in addition to his fine of 580 dollars   Court adjourned till Monday at 11 o'c

Met with the Regents in the evening   Subject the New Alphabet which is now becoming a subject of interest in the primary schools in the Territory

Sunday 17 Dec 1854. Attended meeting to hear President J. M. Grant preach a very interesting discourse on the first principals of the gospel

Monday 18 Dec 1854. House met at ten a. m Librarians Report recieved read & refered back to the Librarian for more full particulars.

A petition of T. S. Williams praying for a reimbursement of the sum of $1131 read & refered to comte on Claims

Bill in relation to common schools presented by Mr Green?

Comte on Indian affairs asked leave to bring in a bill tomorrow on the construction of Forts &c

Mr Snow from the committee on the Judiciary reported the bill in relation to county Surveyors. Laid on Table.

Mr Benson reported a bill to appropriate 1000 dollars to fix the warm Spring Mud Hole. Laid on the Table

Bill in relation to Deseret Iron Compy read the first time & laid over till the 8th day of January.

Mr Browns Weber & Ogden Bridge bill taken up read the first time & passed

Bill appropriating 15 dollars to John Stiles ex door keeper passed its three readings

Act attaching a portion of Davis to G. S. L. County taken up read & (to committee on Counties [crossed out]) passed its first & second readings & refered to C. on Engrossing

Bill appropriating 1000 dollars to repair the warm Spring mud Hole read first time & passed & (refered to [crossed out]) laid over till 9th January. Adjd till 2. p. m.

Mr Greene reported Bill for establishing & promotion of common schools refered to comte on Education.

Message from gov. recommending the election of a warden for the penetentiary refered to C. on Elections

Bill in relation to County surveyors read the first time & passed.

Mr Stout presented Bill in relation to search warrants refered to the C. on Judiciary & Wright & Cumming added to said committee.

Mr James Brown sen's Weber & Ogden Bridge bill taken up on second reading and amended & passed & refered to C. on Engrossing. Adjourned till tomorrow

Tuesday 19 Dec 1854. Attended District Court. this fore noon.   2 cases went by default.   Capt W. J. Hawley is indicted for selling liquor to the Indians after noon The bill attaching a portion of Davis county to G. S L County read and (refered to committee on Counties [crossed out]) passed its third reading & sent to the Council

Mr Benson from the Committee on Indian Affairs reported a bill for the construction, repairs & preservations of Fortifications recieved and ordered to be printed for the use of the House

Mr Loveland presented a bill to lessen the boundaries of Ogden recieved and refered to the C. on Incorporations

Mr Stout moved that the Council be invited to meet the House in joint session at 2 p m. to morrow to elect a Warden of the penetentiary & other officers. Council concurred.

Committee on Engrossing & printing reported an act in relation to Surveyors & surveying which was taken up on its third reading and lost. adjourned

Wednesday 20 Dec 1854. attended District Court in the case of C. Woodward appallant vs J. B. Tomblinson Appellee from Gibbs Justice Court. Court Decided for Appellee on the grounds that there was no appeal from a Justice of the peace to the District Court.

After noon met the Legislature in joint Session on the subject of electing a warden for the penetentiary & filling orther vacancies in Territorial offices when the following vacancies were filled. Elias Smith was re-elected one of the Code Commissioners. Albert Carrington Attorney General. Andrew Love District Attorney for the Second Judicial District

Jonathan Browning Probate Judge of Weber County, Isaac Bullock probate Judge of Green River County. William Critchlow Notary Public of Weber County. John Eager Notary Public of San Pete Co- Isaac Bullock of Green River County. Ira Eldredge Territorial Road Commissioner

A Resolution to create the office of Warden of the Penetentiary passed and Daniel Carn elected Warden.

A Resolution to appoint a committee to draft a memmorial the President and Senate of the United States for the re-appointment of Brigham Young gov. of Utah passed & Albert Carrington, Hosea Stout John L. Smith, S. W. Richards and W. W. Phelps said committee Adjourned till tomorrow at 10. a. m.

Thursday Dec 21 1854. Committee appointed to draft an act for Rules & Regulations of the Penetentiary. and J. W. Cummings, Hosea Stout & Loren Farr said committee.

Act for the Construction of repairs & preservation of Fortifications taken up and passed its first reading and laid over to be taken up on its second reading to morrow at ten a. m.

Committee to report a memorial to the president & one to the senate of the U. S. and adopted adjourned till tomorrow at 10 a. m. & the two Houses met in their respective rooms forthwith.

A Bill for an Appropriation on the Terrial Roads reported & laid over untill January 12th adjd till 2. p.m.

Mr Brown reported an act granting John S. Wright & others the right to erect a toll Bridge across East Weber River and refered back to the committee.

Mr Brown reported an act to locate a Territorial Road between provo City & South Pass in Green River. Recieved.

Mr Carling presented a Resolution to examine the Rivers in the Territory of Utah which after some remarks was with drawn

House adjourned till to morrow at ten a. m to meet in joint session.

Friday 22 Dec 1854. Two Houses met in joint Session at ten a. m

Mr Cummings moved that the "Act for the construction, Repairs, and preservation of Fortifications in the Territory of Utah be refered to the Joint Committee on Judiciary which was carried and Mr Benson and Mr Wright were added to said Committee.

Some discussion then took place on the subject of making Jordan Bridge a toll Bridge

On motion of G. A. Smith it was refered to the joint Committee on Icorporations

The Assembly adjourned till Tuesday 26th at ten a. m to meet in Joint Session

Attended Court to day which adjd till Tuesday next

Saturday 23rd Decr 1854. Attended Court to day which adjd till Tuesday next

This evening a considerable *melee* happened at the Theatre between a policeman (Thos Hall) and a soldier in which quite a number of soldiers participated and about as many on our side It commenced immediately after the curtain droped.

The soldier who began it was put in the lock-up. Several attempts were made by soldiers to rescue him which however proved unseccesful and several of them were knocked down but no material injury was done to either side[34]

Monday 25 Dec 1854. This is a merry chrismas here warm pleasant & cloudy day. Drunken soldiers were seen strolling the streets at an earley hour who seemed be hunting a fight to gratify the appetite which was created last saturday at the Theatre. After a small knock down with a few soldiers & our people which only served to warm the citizen blod, a large number had assembled in the streets on both sides when a general out break ensued which soon resulted an a *regular melee* In a few moments the soldiers give ground a short distance leaving two of their number on the ground whether dead or not as yet I do not know

Both sides rallied again with sticks clubs & stones the work going on briskly when the soldiers introduced their guns fired some five rounds not hitting any one however at which a large number of sitizens ran home to arm. Every thing bid fair to have a general engagement. The U. S. officers present done every thing in their power to stop the soldiers and The city Marshal meantime rallied the police to restrain and disperse the now enfurriated citizens which was hapily done before many had arrived with arms otherwise it must have proved a serious day to many engaged in it.

The soldiers were immediately but in barracks (and [crossed out]) the remainder of the day. Hopkins Pender, E. Everett & Brigham Young Jr were some hurt but not seriously

Tuesday 26 Dec 1854. Joint session met pursuant to adjt

Councilor Pratt from the joint Com. on Education reported "An Act in relation to common Schools" which was recieved & 50 copies ordered to be printed for the use of the Assembly.

Some other committees reported progress & asked time.

Councilor Harrington from the joint committee on Incorporations reported "An act in relation to Jordan Bridge in G. S. L. City, recieved

Councillor G. A. Smith moved that the joint Committee on Incorporations be instructed to bring in a Bill for "A general Incorporation Acts for Towns & Cities" and report the same at their earliest convenience which was carried

Joint Session then adjourned till tomorrow at ten a. m.

Attended Court a Short time when Court adjd till tomorrow at Eleven a. m

---

34. Lieutenant Colonel Edward Jenner Steptoe had been sent to the Salt Lake Valley with a party of 300 soldiers and men to examine the feasibility of constructing a road from Salt Lake City to California. In addition to his assignment to mark out and survey the road, he was to investigate the Gunnison massacre.

Steptoe did so well that President Franklin Pierce offered him the position of governor at the expiration of Brigham Young's term. When the time came, however, Steptoe joined with the other government officials and the prominent men of the church in signing a petition asking that Brigham Young be reappointed. This was done.

The riots described here are mentioned by John Pulsipher, Lorenzo Brown, and other diarists.

This evening I attended a complimentary party given the Honor of Col Steptoe & officers and the citizens of Great Salt Lake City by Kinney Green & Co[35] at the Union Hotel on Union Square.

The judges of the supreme Court (except Shaver) governor Young the presidency of the church, the 12 Col Steptoe & officers together with a large number of citizens & resident strangers were present forming a large assembly. Every attention was given by Judge Kinney & others for our comfort and entertainment

The Ball room was tastily ornimented with cedar boughs inter spersed with wreaths of artificial flowers The only objection exhisting was that the room was too small for the company although a spacious Ball room. The company though composed of Jews & gentiles or in other words saints & sinners enjoyed themselves extreemly well Judge Kinny though a stiff Presbyterian who never had as he said graced a Ball room in his life could not refrain from dancing with a Spirit and will becoming the occasion & bids fair to make a *fantastical* adept shortly

About mid night we took supper an excellent one too & returned to the dance continuing the *fanatasticks* till about three in the morning when all returned home well satisfied.

Wednesday 27 Dec 1854. Joint Session met at ten a. m. Mr Brown presented "An Act to appropriate $1000 for the Territorial Road Commissioner" read and recieved and passed its three readings

"An Act transferring the right to Jordan Bridge to G. S. L. City" was taken up passed its first & second readings. Title amended & passed

"An Act relating to Common Schools was then taken up on its first reading & passed and laid over to be the Special order of the day tomorrow at ten a.m.

Mr Benson presented "A Resolution to encourage Home Manufactures & raising grain" which was recieved and refered to joint Committee on Argiculture Trade and Manufactures" Joint session adjourned till to morrow at ten a. m. and the two House to meet in their respective Houses. this after-noon

House met at 2 P. M.

"An Act to locate a Territorial Road between provo and the South Pass" read and refered back to committee on Roads & Bridges & Ferries." Mr Richards "An Act to amend the charters of G. S. L. City, Provo, Ogden, Manti, and Parowan which was read & laid on the Table to come up in its order.

Message from the Council "Your Bill entitled 'An Act granting unto James Brown Sen. the right to errect Toll Bridges across Weber & Ogden Rivers' has been adopted with some amendments" which were concurred in. When the House adjourned to meet in joint session tomorrow at ten a. m.

I was subpoenad to appear at the District Court as witness in the case of United States vs W. J. Hawley.

Thursday 28 Dec 1854. The Secratary of the Territory was requested to furnish a Stove, by which the Hall could be kept of an equal temperature.

"An act relating to common schools" was taken up on its second reading and passed with some amendments and long and teadious debates in which I took a decided part against the Bill after all the Bill passed its final reading

On motion of Mr Benson the Bill appropriating $1.000 to the Territorial Road Commissioner which had previously passed, was taken up for a reconsideration & laid on the table and the Commissioner requested to furnish this Assembly with a condensed report of the services he has rendered the Territory.

Joint session adjourned to meet in their respective Halls to morrow at ten a. m.

Friday 29 Dec 1854. House met at ten a. m.

on motion of L. Snow Mr H. Stout was called to the Chair.

---

35. Judge Kinney was in business in Salt Lake City and entertained this group as an act of good fellowship. Stout makes a point of the fact that Judge Shaver absented himself.

Mr Brown, Chairman of the Committee on Roads, Bridges, and Ferries, reported "A Bill to locate a Territorial Road from Utah Valley to Black's Fork, in Green River County, and to make an appropriation to the Territorial Road Commissioner" which was recieved & laid on Table.

The Bill entitled "An Act to amend the Charters of Great Salt Lake, Provo, Ogden, Manti, & Parowan Cities" was taken up on its first reading & refered to the Committee on Incorporations

The Speaker having arrived took the Chair.

The Bill to locate road from Utah Valley to Black's Fork &c was taken up on its first reading when the further consideration thereof was postponed till the 11th of January. Speaker giving the casting vote

The speaker giving the casting vote. House adjourned till Wednesday next ten a. m.

This evening at 6 I attended a social party at Br Lorenzo Snow's He has a Hall splendidly fitted up for the purpose of social entertainment where his friends assemble about once a week.

The Evening from 6 to 10 is spent in music, public speaking songs, Essays & the like in all well calculated to elevate the mind & promote a high toned feeling in society.

Monday 1 January 1855. Hard South wind blowing all day & very dusty & disagreeable.

To prevent the recurrence of such scenes as transpired on Chrismas in the streets a large number of police were stationed along the streets and the soldiers kept in barracks mostly

At 2 p. m a party, got up by the govornor & Legislative Assembly to the Honor of Judge Kinney and associates & Col Steptoe & his officers, assembled at the Theatre where every preperation had been made to recieve them.

Great pains & care had been taken to procure & prepare the best the Land could produce or afford to have the best dinner & supper ever got up in the Territory which without doubt was the case.

The bassment story which is used for an Eating room was beautifully ornamented with furr boughs in which was interspersersped a variety of artificial flowers of different kinds and varied hues as well as flags representing the flags of all nations The whole scenery presented at one view a most beautiful forest with vines & flowers in full verdue & bloom together with the different national flags all taken together seemed to indicate that we were at a feast of nations

The Table was no less romantic and beautiful with three changes of Dishes. The first course was oyster & ox tail Soup. The second course Roast Beef, Roast Bear, do veal, do Mutton, do chicken do Turkey, Boned Turkey, Hares, Beuf ala Mode, Rolle Eau de, Boiled chicken, Fricasseed chicken, Boiled Mutton, Fried Steaks, Fried Turkey, Fried Cutlets, Stewed Lobsters.

Vegetables

Potatoes, Turnips, parsnips, slaw, Fritters, Cabbage.

Third Course

Pastry.

Pound Cake, Washington Cake, Ladies' Cakes, Pain-au-Ris, Charlotte Rushe, Transparent, Damson Pies, Raspberry Pies, Mince Pies, Cherry Pies, Peach Balls, Deseret Pudding, Royal Favorite, Custard Pudding, Blanc Mange, Omelets, Fancy Mange, Ice Cream, Water Melons, green.

The above is a correct account of the Bill of fare at which all seemed to honor by their individed attention and solicitude to devour to their utmost limits of their several Corporations many of whose proved to be entirely too small for the preperations and appetites. Dinner came off at 8 p.m. and supper at 12 at night. Between Dinner and supper the Ice Cream was passed bountifully among the party.

The time was mostly spent in cotillions with some waltzing singing, speaking &c &c

Making altogether a very agreeable evening entertainment. until about two when the party dismissed and went home amid a very heavy snow storm which was now falling fast and driving severely in our faces

Wednesday 2 Jan 1855. Snow some 8 or 10 inches deep and snowing all day. Weather otherwise moderately warm   Little stiring & I feel very dumpish

Thursday 3 Jan 1855. House met at ten a. m.   Message from the Council that they have decided to refer the "Act to attach a portion of Weber County to Davis; also to attach a portion of Davis to G. S. L. County to a select Committee to consist of the Members of the Council & House from Davis & Weber Counties provided the House concur therein   House concurred.

Mr Foot presented a Petition from J. G. Bigler & 88 others to extend the Eastern Boundary of Juab County recieved & refered to the committee on Counties.

Mr Foot presented an account for grading the Road on the South side of the Sevier River Said account was recieved and refered to the comte on claims

Mr Dann presented a Petition from John Steele & 6 others praying for compensation as witnesses before the U. S. D. Court which was recieved and refered to the Comte on Claims. adjd for Dinner

2 p. m   Met again Report from Col H. B. Clawson on the situation recieved & ordered to be printed with the journal

Mr Woolly Chairman of the Committee on Claims reported That the sum of ninety-eight dollars be allowed Hon T. B. Foot for grading &c the south side of the sevier River bank on the Road leading from G. S. L. City to San Bernardino Cal recieved and refered to Comte on appropriations

Mr L. Snow Chairman of the Committee on Judiciary reported "an Act in relation to Search Warrants" recieved, read the first time & passed, and 50 copies ordered to be printed

Mr Stout presented account for guarding the Poll Books of election from Iron County to the Seat of Governments in 1853 also an account for guarding Members of the Legislative Assembly from Iron County to the Seat of governt in 1853. recieved & refered to the Committee on Claims   House adjourned till 10 A. M. to morrow —

Thursday 4 Jan 1855. House met at ten a. m. Mr Wright moved — That the Council be requested to meet the House in joint session at 2 p. m. to take into consideration "An Act for the construction, repairs & preservation, of fortifications, carried and notification sent accordingly

Mr J. L. Smith pursuant to notice presented "An Act in relation to Dogs, and for the prevention of cruety to animals recieved & refered to Committee on Judiciary. The Speaker giving the casting vote, and Mr Rockwood added to the Committee.

Message from the Council not concurring in the motion for a joint session on the grounds that the Act on Fortifications &c was not prepared by the Committee.

Mr Smith Moved the Bill "In relation to the Deseret Iron Works" be made the Special order of the day at 2. P. M. carried   House adjourned till 2 p.

2 P. M. House met according to adjt   Message from the Council anouncing the Resolution assigning the U. S. Judges to the several Districts asking the concurrence of the House, which was laid on the Table to come up in its order, carried by 10 votes 9 negatives & 5 not voting.

"A Bill in relation to the Deseret Iron Company" was taken up on its second reading. A very animated discusion ensued for and against the Bill pending which the House adjourned till tomorrow at ten in the morning.

At six p. m. met with the Joint Committee to whom was refered the Act in relation to Fortifications &c.   The Bill was prepared to report

This was a windy boisterous day south wind. snow drifting and after dark a Severe Snow Storm from the North The Snow is now some twelve inches deep and is drifted in Huge banks, making travelling very difficult.

Friday Jan 5 - 1855. House met at ten a. m. The "Bill in relation to the Deseret Iron Company" was resumed. The first section was read & Mr Stout moved That the section be amended by substituting "one Share in the place of "two shares" & $2422 in the place of $4844 motion carried.

Mr Benson moved that the Section be amended by inserting the words "Loan" in place of Subscribe. carried

On motion of Mr Stout The Bill was referred to the Committee on appropriations

The above Bill elicited more animated discussion than any previous subject this sission Adjourned till 2 p. m.

2 p. m House met Message from the Council that they have passed the accompanying "Resolution relating to Green River County" asking the concurrence of the House, also requesting the House to meet the Council in joint session at ten a. m. Resolution was concurred in and the House concurred with the Council to meet in joint session.

Mr Woolley Chairman of the Committee on Claims to whom was referred the Petition of John Steele & six others, witnesses, subpoenad in the case of "United States vs Jerome Owens"[36] from Iron County to Salt Lake County, praying for an appropriation to them as compensation for services rendered in the above case as witness

also the account of Barnabas Carter and nine others, for guard service to the Legislative Assembly the members from Iron County for 1853 & 4. Also the account of William Leany & three others for guarding poll Books of Elections from Iron County to seat of Government for the year 1853.

Reported adversely to all the aforesaid petitions & accounts, which was recieved.

Mr Eldrege presented "An Account for services rendered as Territorial Marshal in 1852, in the U. S. District Court recieved and refered to Committee on Claims

Mr Wright Chairman of the Comte on Incorporations reported "An Act to amend City Charters" recieved

Mr Woolley Chairman of the Comte on Counties reported "An Act defining the boundary line between Juab & San Pete Counties" Recieved & Laid on Table.

Report of the Librarian was presented, read, recieved, and refered to the Committee on Appropriations

Mr L. Snow Chairman of the Committee on Judiciary, presented the following report, "The Committee on Judiciary to whom was referred, "An Act in relation to Dogs, & cruelty to animals" report unfavorably & beg to be discharged from further duties on that subject" Report was recieved.

The "Resolution assigning the U. S. Judges, to the several Judicial Districts" was taken up & concurred in.

---

36. The request here of John Steele and six others for expenses incurred in the case of Jerome Owens was long overdue. Jerome Owens had been held for murder on January 2, 1852, tried in Parowan, and then given a change of venue. He appeared in the court in Salt Lake City before Judge Zerubbabel Snow where he was given a trial by jury. On October 11, 1852, Owens was convicted and sentenced to be put to death on the fourth Wednesday of February following.

On December 16, 1852, because of "his tender age, the uncertainty of human testimony, and the fact that he was convicted by circumstantial evidence only," Brigham Young issued a full and complete pardon and directed that Owens be discharged from the custody of the sheriff, Horace S. Eldredge. See Utah Territorial Executive Record Book "A" (Utah State Archives), 15.

Since the legislature "reported adversely" to all the aforesaid accounts, it would seem that none of the people involved would be reimbursed.

"An Act to amend City Charters" was taken up, read the first time and passed Whereupon it was taken up on its second reading and after several amendments passed its second reading. Passed its third reading by its title House adjourned till to morrow at ten a. m to meet in joint Session.

Saturday 6 January 1855. The two Houses met in joint Session at 10 a. m. Councillor Pratt, from the joint Committee to compile the Laws, reported "An Act relating to the U. S. Courts" read & recieved & laid on Table

Councilor G. A. Smith of the Committee to whom was refered "An Act for the construction, repairs, and preservation of fortifications," reported as a substitute "An act concerning Fortifications" which was read and recieved after which it was read the first time and passed

Then taken up for the second reading and was after several amendments passed after which it passed its third reading by its Title.

Mr Greene was added to the Committee on the penetentiary

Mr Councilor Carrington moved That the vote of Dec 20th 1854, electing a Probate Judge and Notary Public for Green River County be recinded, carried

"Act in relation to the U. S. Courts was taken on its second reading and laid on the Table indefinately

The Committee to compile the laws were Honorably discharged and G. S. Smith appointed in their place adjourned till monday at 10. a. m.

Monday 8 January 1855. Two Houses met at 10. a. m. on Motion of Mr J. L. Smith "An Act in relation to search Warrants" was taken up read the first time, & on Motion of Mr Benson that the Bill do not pass its first reading & that no further Legislation be had on the subject during this session Carried after a long debate 16 in the affirmative & 15 in the negative Adjd till 2 p m and met accordingly.

The Report of Ira Eldredge Territorial Road Commissioner was presented & referred to the Committee Revenue.

Councilor Harrington Chairman of the joint committee on Incorporations, reported on the subject of a general Incorporation act, that it was unnecessary to legislate thereon Report Recieved & comte discharged.

Councilor G. A. Smith the Committee appointed to compile and arrange the laws, presened a schedule of acts, resolutions & memorials, amended, repealed and obsolete, or superseded; and also those acts, resolutions, and memorials, proposed to remain, and constitute the new Book of laws. the Report was recieved· & 50 copies ordered to be printed.

Councilor T. S. Smith, chairman of the select Committee to define the boundaries line of between Weber & Davis Counties, reported that the Committee had met several times, but could not agree.

Councilor T. S. Smith asked and obtained leave to present forthwith, "An Act to attach a portion of Weber County to Davis County. said Bill passed its three readings & passed after several amendments and long debates.

The Committee to prepare for the Legislative Ball on the first inst made their final report of the expenses of the same which was just 26 dollars each member & officer of the two Houses. The Report was recieved & the Committee discharged with a vote of thanks

Joint session adjourned to meet in their respective Houses to morrow morning at ten.

Tuesday 9 Jan 1855. Mr Rockwood, Chairman of the Committee on Counties, to whom was referred the Resolution from the Council, attaching Green River County to G. S. L. County, reported as a substitute, "An Act attaching Green River County to Great Salt Lake County also a "Resolution, repealing a resolution relating to the Representation of Green River & Great Salt Lake County, Approved Jan. 19 1854.[37] Report was recieved

"Resolution appropriating $1,000 on the North Territorial Road, in G. S. L. County was taken up & after some amendments passed its first & second readings and refered to Engrossing Comte

On Motion of Mr Brown the Council was invited to meet the House in joint session on Thursday next at ten a. m. to take into consideration "the claim of T. S. Williams' also a "Bill for the government of the Penetentiary"

Mr Wright from the Committee on claims to whom was referred the accounts of H. S. Eldredge for $75 for services rendered as Territorial Marshal in the first Judicial District Court at its July Term 1852 wherein the people were vs O. H. Cogwell et. al. beg leave to report adversely", recieved "An Act defining the boundary line between Juab San pete Counties was taken up read the first and second times & passed and referred to the Engrossing Comt

"An Act attaching Green River County," was taken up and on Motion of Mr Rockwood The subject matter contained in this, & the Council Bill on the same subject, was referred to the Committee on Judiciary.

"A Bill to locate a Territorial Road from Utah Valley to Black's Fork, in Green River County, and making appropriation to the Territorial Road Commissioner" was taken up on its second reading, amended & passed and referred to the Engrossing Committee.

Message from the Council concurring with the request of the House to meet in joint Session on Thursday next at 10 a. m adjourned till 10 a. m

Wednesday 10 Jan. 1855. House met at 10 a. m.

Mr Dame, Chairman of the committee on Elections (wish [crossed out]) presented the following Report:-

Your Committee on Elections wish to offer an amendments to the 8th Sec. of "An Act regulating Elections," approved January 3rd 1853" by adding the words "Election for County and precinct officers & the names of persons voted for" after the word "person" on the fifth line of said section" which was recieved.

on Motion of Mr J. L. Smith The Committee on Petitions & memorials were instructed to draft a memorials to Congress for a further appropriations to finish the Territorial House at Fillmore City.

Mr Brown Chairman of the Committee on Roads, Bridges, and Ferries to whom was referred the Bill granting John S. Wright and others the right to errect a Toll Bridge over East Weber River, reported unnecessary to take further action thereon which was recieved.

Mr Stout moved that the Secratary of the Territory be requested to inform the House, whether application has been made to the Secratary of the U. S. to furnish this Territory with a full set of standard Weights and Measures as established by Congress, in conformity to a "Resolution approved March 3rd 1852". Second and carried, —

Message from the Council. "The accompanying 'Resolution Specifying the times of holding U. S. Courts in the several Judicial Districts,' has this day been adopted by the Council and is now respectfully submitted for your concurrence" on Motion of Mr Phelps, concurred in.

Report of D. H. Wells in relation to the Military school which was recieved.

Two P. M. Message from the Council. "The accompanying Bill 'An Act relating to the duties of County Surveyors', has this day passed the Council, and is now

---

37. The act "attaching Green River County to Salt Lake County" would make it possible to handle all cases in the Mormon courts and to dissolve the county organization at Fort Bridger and Fort Supply before they fell to the Gentiles. It was later "laid on the Table indefinitely."

respectfully submitted for your concurrence" On Motion of Mr Stout The Bill was recieved and laid on the Table.

Also, "The accompanying Bill, 'An Act in relation to the Delinquent taxes, of San Pete County has this day passed by the Council &c" on Motion of Mr Rockwood The Bill was laid on the Table.

Mr Richards, Chairman of the Committee on Engrossing, reported back "An Act altering and defining the boundaries line between Juabe and san Pete Counties" also "An Act to locate a Territorial Road from Utah Valley to Black's Fork, in Green River County" also "A Resolution Appropriating money for re-locating and construction of a road from the Bath House in G. S. L. City to its northern boundary" Last Bill then passed its third reading.

"An Act to locate a Territorial Road from Utah Valley to Black's Fork in Green River County, and making an appropriation for the Territorial Road Commissioner" was taken up on its third reading and passed with some amendments.

"A Resolution appropriating money for locating and construction of a Road from the Bath House in G. S. L. City to its northern boundary" was taken up on its third reading and passed & title amended.

Mr L. Snow, Chairman of the Committee on Judiciary, reported "An Act in relation to Green River County" as a substitute to Mr Rockwood's Act, and the Resolution sent by the Council to the House for concurrence, which was read, and, on Motion of Mr Stout was laid on the Table indefinitely.

The oldes Bill being called for "An Act relating to the duties of County surveyors" was taken up & passed its first reading and passed and on its second reading was referred to Committee on Counties.

"An Act in relation to the delinquent taxes of San Pete County" was taken up and read and passed. after several amendments.

The following letter from Mr Secratary Babbitt:-

Sir I have recieved your note of this date, and in answer have to report that this is the first intimation I have had of this matter, I (have [crossed out]) will make the necessary application to the Secratary of the U. S." for a full set of Standard Weights and Measures as established by Congress, &c' at earliest convenience, and make report to you, the reply when recieved."

House adjourned till tomorrow at ten a. m. to meet in joint Sission.

This evening at 6 met with the Committee on appropriations to take into consideration the appropriation to the "Deseret Iron Company"

Thursday 11 January 1855. The two Houses met in joint session at ten a. m.

The "Memorial of Thos S. Williams and the Resolution appropriating money to Thomas S. Williams for money advanced by him to officers of the general assembly in the Session of 1851 & 2" were taken up and on Motion of Mr Stout Passed its first reading on Motion of Mr Eldredge passed its second reading

on Motion of Mr Brown the Resolution was read the Third time, pending which an animated & spirited debate ensued which continued till sunset without dinner Mr Williams had leave to speak. Bill was lost on the final vote

The following communication was recieved from his Excellency the Govornor, under date of Jan. 10-

"I beg herewith to return to the Assembly 'An Act granting James Brown, sen. of Ogden City, the right to erect Toll Bridges across Weber & Odgen Rivers, in Weber County,' which would meet my approval if it were inserted in the proper place in said Bill, that the said Brown shall make good roads across the flats, and that when the bridge becomes Territorial property he shall be paid the value of said roads at the time, as appraised by the Commissioner; also, that the Bridge shall be constructed of the best red pine, where it now reads, in 3rd section 'must be of good material.' " which was concurred in.[38]

Mr Cummings, Chairman of the Committee on the Penetentiary reported "An Act in relation to the Penetentiary" recieved & 50 copies ordered to be printed.

On Motion of Mr Stout the Bill was laid over to be the special order of the day next Monday. Joint sessioned till to morrow morning at 10.

Friday 12 Jan 1855. Joint session met at ten a. m according to adjournment.

Councilor Woodruff Chairman of the Joint Committee on Revenue, presented the following, "The Joint Committee to whom was referred the 'Resolution to grant Ira Eldredge $1000 also the Report of sd Eldredge Road Commissioner Report 'A Resolution in relation to delinquent Taxes' and 'A Resolution appropriating money to the Territorial Road Commissioner" recieved & laid on the Table.

Councilor Farr presented "An Act appropriating $500 to J. W. Fox" which was recieved.

Report of the special Committee to compile the Laws was taken up Recieved & referred to the Joint Committee on Judiciary.

"Resolution in relation to delinquent Taxes" taken up and passed its first & second readings and referred to the Committee on Revenue.

"Resolution appropriating money to Territorial Road Commissioner was taken up and passed. after some amendments.

2 P. M. Act appropriating 500 dollars to J. W. Fox" read the first time and passed and referred to Committee on Claims

Councilor Wells presented "Resolution concerning Marks & Brands' recieved the first, second & third time & passed.

Councilor Wells presented "An Act incorporating Cotton Wood Canal Company" recieved read the first, second and third times & passed. Joint session then adjd till next Monday at ten a. m.

Went to meeting on Sunday.

Monday 15 January 1855. Two Houses met in Joint Session at ten A. M.

"An Act in relation to the Penetentiary" was taken up read the first time & passed and on the second reading was amended several times & passed after, which it passed its third reading.

An invitation from the Committee of the Dramatic Soiree was presented by Mr Cummings tendering to the Legislative assembly a free ticket to the Theatre on next Thursday eve in compliment to Ball & super to them on the 2nd January.

2 P. M. Councilor Woodruff, chairman of the joint Committee on Revenue, reported back "Resolution in relation to certain delinquent Taxes, read first, second, & third times & passed.

Mr Benson represented a petition of Peter Maughn & 33 others praying for the Incorporation of the City of E. T. recieved & referred to committee on Incorporation

Mr Benson presented,"An Act locating the County seat of Toole Co. Read three times & passed.

Mr Richards presented a Petition from the Chancellor & Board of Regents from the university of Deseret for an an appropriation of $1500 for the Establishing a High school in great Salt Lake City recieved & refered to Committee Appropriations.

On Motion of Mr Rockwood the Committee on Claims were instructed to enquire if anything is due to the university of the State of Deseret on appropriations already made.

---

38. The letter from Brigham Young stipulating that the bridges across the Weber and Ogden rivers should include good access roads, that they be constructed of specified materials, and that eventually they become the property of the territory was characteristic of the demands made upon those who asked for franchises of this kind.

Mr Dame moved that the Committee on Petitions & Memorials be in structed to report a memorial to Congress for 50.000 dolls for Military Road, from Fillmore parowan; Cedar & Harmony to the Head of navigation on the Colerado. carried.

Mr J. L. Smith moved same for memorial for 25.000 dolls for Military Road from G. S. L. City to Eastern boundary of Col Carried

Joint session adjourned. Joint session having adjourned the House proceeded to business.

Message from the Council that they had concurred the "Act to amend the charters of G. S. L. Ogden provo, Manti & parowan Cities

"A Bill to make Apropriations on the Territorial Roads" was taken up and while under consideration the House adjourned

Tuesday 16 Jan 1855. House met at ten a. m. Message from the Council that they had concurred in "An Act in relation to the Delinquent Territorial Taxes of San Pete County

Also Act altering & defining the boundary line between Juab & San Pete Counties.

"Bill to make Appropriations on the Territorial Roads" was resumed on its second reading and was lost by striking out the Sections.

Mr Benson Chairman of the Committee on Appropriations reported an appropriation of 98 dolls for T. B. Foote which was recieved & passed

Mr Benson of Committee on Appropriations to whom was referred the Report of Librarian reported inexpedient to further Legislate thereon.

Mr Phelps moved That a Special Committee be appointed to examine into the state of the Library. carried. The speaker appointed Messrs Cummings & Richards said Comte

Mr Benson presented "Resolution in relation to 'Deseret Iron Works," read three times & passed

Mr Dame presented account of G. A. Smith, & others for hire of guards to L. Assembly, in 1854 & 5. Recieved & referred to committee on Claims, who reported favorably & referred to Committee on Appropriations

'Sirs J. L. Smith, Grover, and Brown appointed Committee to examine the laws relating to Estrays &c.

2 P. M. Message from the Council that they had not concurred in "An Act to locate a Territorial Road from Utah Valey to Black's Fork &c also that they amended "Resolution in relation to Territorial Road in G. S. L. City which the house concurred in said amendments.

Also "The Council respectfully invite the Hon. Speaker and Members of the House of Representatives to meet them in Joint Session, in their Chamber, to morrow, at 10. A. M.

House concurred in the above

Mr Phelps from the Committee on Petitions & Memorials presented, "A Memorial to the Congress for 15.000 dolls for the completion of the Penetentiary recieved & adopted Adjourned till to morrow at ten a. m to meet the Council in joint session.

Wednesday 17 Jan 1855. Two houses met in joint session in the Council Chamber at ten a. m. — Councilor Thos S. Smith, on behalf of the Committee on Petitions presented "Memorials to Congress for a Military Road from Cedar City south to Harmony, thence south Easterly to the Head of Navigation on the Colerado" which was read & adopted.

T. S. Smith from same Committee presented "Memorial, to congress for further appropriation for a Military Road from G. S. L. City south through Provo, Fillmore, Parown, & Cedar Cities, to the Eastern boundary of Cal on Motion of Mr Farr.

The vote to adopt the first Memorial was re-considered and recinded & the Two Memorials were referred back to the Committee, with instructions to bring in a Memorial for a Road calling for an appropriation large enough to meet the demands.

Councilor Harrington, from the Joint Committee on Incorporations to whom was referred the Petition to Incorporate E. T. City in Toole Co reported "An Act to incorporate E. T. City, Toole County" Bill was read the first, second, and third times & passed.

O. Pratt from the Joint Committee on Appropriations, to whom was referred the Petition of the Chancelor & Board of Regents of the "University of the State of Deseret", asking for an appropriations of $1500 for the immediate establishment of a "High School" in G. S. L. City, reported unfavorably, in consequence of the numerous appropriations already made & unpaid, and the impoverished State of the Treasury. Report was recieved and the Committee discharged.

Bill of Adjutant Genl H. B. Clawson of $575 for services, rent, desks, &c being presented & refered to comte on Claims.

Councilor Carrington, on behalf of the Code Commissioners, reported "An Act concerning Transfer of Land Claims, & other property, which was read, recieved & read the first second and third times & passed without amendment

Councilor G. A. Smith presented Presented of J. & E. Reese & Co. for making Roads & erecting Bridges on Carson River Kanyon, Carson Valley, & for recieving toll &c" referred to Committee on Roads, Bridges & Ferries.

D. H. Wells from the Joint Committee on Judiciary, reported "An Act in relation to the compilation & revision of the Laws and Resolutions in force, their publication & distribution", with the Constitution of the U. S. organic Act of Utah & constitution of Deseret which was read three times amended & passed.

on Motion of Mr Stout. The Declaration of Independence and the "Articles of Confederation were ordered to be printed with the present compilation of Laws.

Two P. M. Councilor Johnson from Committee on Claims, to whom was referred the Adjutant General's Report reported with same with, 'An Act appropriating Monies to the Adjutant. General and others" which was read first second and third times & passed

Mr Cummings of the special Committee to whom was referred the Report of Librarian & also the Report of the standing Committee of the House on Appropriations thereon, report "They have examined said reports and numbered the books now in the Library, and those booked to individuals, & by comparing the number with the catalogue, learn that there are but few volumes missing or unaccounted for, & your committee are informed that other individuals, than the Librarian have had access to Library under circumstances which he could not control, because of which he does not feel responsible for any deficiency of Books or Papers, belonging to said Library

Report of committee was recieved & the Assembly, expressed their entire Satisfaction with the passed services of the Librarian

Librarian was instructed to procure a sufficient lock to Library door, whereby he can keep the property of Library secure under his own charge

Adjourned till ten A. m to morrow to meet in joint Session.

Thursday 18 January 1855. Two Houses met in Joint Session at ten a. m. By permission of the Assembly Hon. A. W. Babbitt read his instructions from Hon Elish Whittlesey, Comptroller of the U. S. Treasury, in regard to Utah Library, & remarked on the Resolution passed the Assembly last evening. He stated, that should the Library be put under his charge agreeable to the instructions of the Comptroller, he should feel himself authorized to allow the Librarian a salary of 400 dollars a year

on Motion of Mr McArthur The committee on Incorporations were instructed to bring in a bill to incorporate Pleasant Grove City Utah County

"An Act pertaining to the duties of County surveyors & Recorder" recieved read the first second (time [crossed out]) and (third [crossed out]) and passed and referred to the Committee on judiciary.

An Act granting to Orson Hyde, J. & E. Reese the right to errect Bridges across Carson River, & make Roads in Carson Valley" referred back.

D. H. Wells reported An "Act in relation to taxes" recieved and read three times & passed

D. H. Wells reported "An Act in Relation to County Recorders & the acknowledgement of Instrument of Weighting recieved, read the first, second & third times & passed.

Two P.M. "Resolution in relation to the "Deseret Iron Works" Recieved, read the first, second and third times and passed.

Appropriation of 98 dollars to T. B. Foote passed

Memorial to Congress read & adopted

"An Act granting orson Hyde &c " was reported again recieved read three times amended & passed.

A. Johnson Presented "An Act to incorporate the Provo Kanyon Road Company" Recieved, read three times & passed.

"An Act to incorporate Big Kanyon Road Company" Read the first, second and third time & passed,

"Resolution appropriating money to be paid out on the Territorial Road in Weber County.' Recieved, read three times & passed

"An Act to encourage the raising of flax, Hemp, and Tame Sun Flower seed" Recieved read three times and passed

Act granting Miles & Franklin Weaver a Herd ground in Utah County, recieved Read three times & passed.

"Act pertaining to duty of County Surveyors" Recieved, read three times & passed.

An Act appropriating money for Educational Purposes" Recieved Read three times & passed.

Act to incorporate the Weber Kanyon Road Company" Recieved Read three times & passed. Adjourned till tomorrow at ten A. M.

At six P. M. the Members of the Legislative Assembly with their families met at the Theatre. pursuant to an invitation from the officers of said association tendered to the members *gratis* The House was well filled subject "Leap Year" or the Women's Priviledge" which was very entertaining & the performance was well executed.

Friday 19 Jan 1855. Two Houses met in joint Session at ten A. M. Councilor T. S. Smith, Chairman of Committee on Petitions, reported Memorial to Congress for appropriation for a Military Road from G. S. L. City, south, through Provo, Fillmore, Parowan, and Cedar Cities to the eastern boundary of California which on motion of Mr Phelps was adopted.

Mr Phelps from Committee on Petitions from the House reported "Memorial to Congress for $25,000 to complete the South wing of the State House at Fillmore city" which was read & adopted.

Petition from David Canfield, & 4 others for the appropriation of $500 as compensation for rebuilding the Provo Bridge was and allowed,

Mr Green Presented "Resolution for Educational Purposes in Provo City" which on Motion of Mr Grover was laid on the Table indefinitely

Hon Orson Hyde having been nominated by the Govornor, on Motion of Mr Grant was unanimously elected Probate Judge of Carson County, with instructions to organize said County s[p]eedily.

Mr Aurelius Miner having been nominated by the govornor on Motion of Mr Grant was unanimously elected Notarie Public of Carson County.

On Motion of G. A. Smith The Committee on Judiciary were instructed to report an amendment to the Judiciary

Act making Carson County a Judicial District, and to attach Iron & Washington Counties to the second Judicial District."

Two P. M. Mr McArthur from Committee on Incorporations reported "An Act to Incorporate Pleasant Grove City" which was read the first, second and third times & passed.

Mr S. W. Richards presented "An Act granting Heber C. Kimball, Jedediah M. Grant, Samuel Snyder and their associates, the right of ground for Herding" which was read the first, second and third times & passed

Mr Harrington, from the Committee on Incorporations "reported "Resolution to extend the Jurisdiction of the Municipal Aurthority of the City of Payson" which was recieved and read the first, second, and third times and passed.

Mr Benson from the Committee on Appropriations, reported "General Appropriation Bill" which was read 3 times & passed.

Mr Benson presented, "Resolution Appropriating monies to "Deseret News office" which was recieved, read three times & passed.

On Motion of Mr J. L. Smith, The "Resolution specifying the time of holding U. S. Courts in the several Judicial Districts "passed the 10th inst. was called up for reconsideration, and On Motion of Mr Stout was refered to Committee on Judiciary.

Councillor Carrington on behalf of said Committee reported back said Resolution with amendments, which were agreed to.

"An Act to amend an Act relating to the U. S. Courts" Approved January 12, 1854, was then taken up, read three times and passed.

On Motion of Mr Cummings, the Resolution passed on the 4 instant, "Assigning the U. S. Judges to the several Judicial Districts" was taken up for re-consideration and readopted without amendment.

Mr Green presented Petition of John Berry & 56 others praying for an "Act Incorporating" The Upper Settlement of Spanish Fork Utah County", which was read & on Motion of Mr Grant. The prayer of the petitioners were granted, and the Members from Utah County appointed a Special Committee to draft a charter similar to Pleasant Grove Charter, excepting the boundaries and Name, with instructions to embrace in said Charter the boundaries named in said Petition.

(Mr Cummings reported "Resolution electing the officers of the Utah Penetentiary" which was read three times & passed.

Councilor Carrington presented "Resolution apportioning a Representative to Carson County" which was read three times & passed. [preceding lines crossed out])

Mr Green, Presented The following "Resolution in honor of the Memory of the Late Willard Richards: —

Resolved, by the Govornor & Legislative Assembly of the Territory of Utah,- That we hold in grateful remembrance the Honorable Willard Richards, President of the Council for the Winter of 1853-4. The friend and asso: ciate of the Prophet & Patriarch in peace, and shall we say 'their companion in assassination'? 'yes!

We have in remembrance his chering influence in times of trouble and peril — the sweet associations of his instructions to the Saints, and wisdom in Legislation: — he whose constituents comprised the world, and who legislated for the redemtion of Israel" which was read and on Motion of Mr Stout was unanimously adopted.

Mr Green presented, "Resolution for convening the Legislative Assembly and concerning the Library" which was read & on Motion of Mr J. L. Smith was adopted.

Mr A. Carrington Presented "Resolution in relation to the Utah Library", which was read an on Motion of Mr Dame unanimously adopted.

Mr J. L. Smith presented "Resolution defining the boundaries of Alpine City" which was read and on Motion of G. A. Smith was unanimously adopted.

On Motion of G. A. Smith, The members from Utah County were appointed a Special Committee to draft a Charter for Alpine City, similar to the Pleasant Grove Charter, excepting the boundaries and name.

Mr Grant presented the following "Resolved, by the Govornor & Legislative Assembly of the Territory of Utah, that we return to the Hon. A. W. Babbitt, our sincere thanks, for his kind, accommodating and gentlemanly treatment towards us during this session of the Legislative Assembly" which was unanimously adopted.[39]

On Motion of Mr Stout, A vote of thanks were unanimously tendered to President H. C. Kimball. and J. M. Grant, for the able, wise, and kind manner in which they have discharged the onerous duties devolving upon them during this session of the Legislative Assembly.

On Motion of Mr Phelps, the Legislative Assembly adjourned, to meet in the State House, in Fillmore City, on the second Monday in December next, at ten o'clock A. M.

Immediately after the adjournment the Hon. Secratary A. W. Babbitt, spread, in the large Council Chamber, a plentiful, and tasteful cold collation in which many distinguished invited guests participated.

Appropriate and happy remarks were made by His Excellency, the Govornor, Secratary Babbitt, Chief Justice Kinney, Associate Justice Stiles, Orson Hyde, and others.

Many felicitous, and appropriate sentiments, toasts and anecdotes, enlivened the union & hilarity of the passing hours untill about ten p. m. when the numerous Company seperated, without a discord having occurred during the Session, or a jar to mar the harmony of its closing scene.

Yesterday evening Mr John Y. Green returned from Bridger with the Eastern mail & reported that the hostile attitude of the Indians were such that it was unsafe to for white men to travel He also brought the intelligence that Mr Elisha Ryan had been shot by a spaniard at Bridger and died in a few minutes. He having also shot the Spaniard wounding him badly but not mortally. It will be remembered that said Ryan is the man who made so much trouble & excitement at Green River Ferry in June last.

Saturday 20 January 1855. Attended the District Court which adjourned to day after holding its session regularly since the 4th day of Decr last being 47 days.

The Grand Jury continued in session during the whole time & to reported that they still had plenty & important business before them, nevertheless Judge Shaver discharged them, at the same time commending their deligence and perseverance in the discharge of their duty.

After Court adjourned it was decided to get up a Judiciary Party on the 23 inst

Sunday 21 January 1855. Quorum meeting at my house at dusk Present 5 presidents & 2 members

Monday evening. attended a lecture on grammar by O. Hyde

Tuesday 23 Jan 1855. This evening at 4, the judiciary Party came off at the "Union House" There were only about 50 gents present & some 70 ladies

The Judges of the Supreme Court & practicing attorneys Gov. Col Steptoe The Twelve and some few invited guests also the First Presidency composed said Company. Party opened by prayer by Elder Hyde & a speech by Judge Shaver. The dancing then commenced & was briskly kept up till 12 when supper was ready and well patronized about 3 a. m the party broke up.

The party had much cause of regret that the feeble state of the Gov's health prevented him from being there otherwise all enjoyed themselves extreemly well.

Mr James M. Gammell returning from a trading tour some 600 miles S. E reports that a small party of Whites have been killed by the Indians near the Devil's Gate. as he learns from the Indians.

---

39. The resolution that "we return to the Hon. A. W. Babbitt, our sincere thanks, for his kind, accommodating and gentlemanly treatment towards us during this session of the Legislative Assembly" was a happy conclusion, perhaps with the knowledge that Babbitt was preparing to entertain them all at dinner.

Saturday 27 Jan 1855. The southern mail came in   Elder Pratt is very spiritedly debating the Question whether Gov Young should be reappointed or not   which naturally brings in the subject of Poligamy.

He is in San Francisco & surrounding town.   There is much excitement for & against, but nothing hostile.

Sunday 28 Jan 1855. Attend my ward meeting at dusk   C. C. Rich preached on "What it is to be saved"

Monday 29 January 1855. Supreme Court met at 11. a. m   On Motion of A. W. Babbitt and J. Holeman. Orson Hyde and myself were admitted to plead at the bar of said Court.

This evening attended Seventies meeting at the New Hall. where the setting the different Quorums to rights seems to be the order of business.

Sunday 4 Feb 1855. Supreme Court was in session every day last week but done but little business except adopt rules and admit persons to the bar who never read, study or even looked into a law book.

This even the Eleventh Quorum met at my house.   One man was taken in to the Quorum & three members cut off.

Monday 5 Feb 1855. Attended Supreme Court.

About 9 o'clock p. m the Eastern mail came in,   Dr Garland Hurt[40] of Kentucky Indian agent for Utah also arrived They report the Indians as being friendly on the route and no particular danger in travelling.

News has arrived that Walker the Great Utah Chief[41] died on the 29 Jan at the Meadow Creek some six miles beyond Fillmore, and that the Utahs had killed 2 *piede* squaws & 2 *piede* children and some 12 or 15 of Walkers Horses and intended to kill 2 Pauvans & 3 mormons.   This is done on the death of a great chief as a sacrifice I understand.

Tuesday 6 Feb 1855. Suit before W. Snow Esqr. J. M. Gammell vs J. H. Blazzard in Replevin   I was council for Plff.   Judgement for Plff.

Supreme Court Still in Session.

Thursday 8 Feb 1855. Supreme Court in session. The point being made to the Court whether the Common Law was in force in this Territory or not, a law of the Legislature to the contrary   The Court ruled that it was, which settles a point which has been a vexed question in our Courts since the organization of the Territory.

---

40. Garland Hurt, a doctor from Kentucky, was educated and respectable. His theory of dealing with the Indians was much like that of Brigham Young — that they should be placed on farms, provided with tools and clothes, and trained to raise crops and care for cattle.

Hurt soon became suspicious of the Mormon missionaries to the Indians and wrote in protest of their activities. He left the territory in late September 1857. His reports to Washington, D. C., were partly responsible for sending the United States Army to Utah.

41. David Lewis, who was with Chief Walker just the day before his death, wrote a detailed account to Brigham Young. This was entered in the "Journal History" on January 29, 1855:

I arrived at Fillmore on the 28th inst., and started next morning for Walker's lodge, and met the Utahs coming with Walker and supporting him on a horse. He held out his hand and shook hands, and seemed glad to see me . . . . I showed him the letter you sent to him and gave him all the articles you sent to him. He seemed greatly pleased with them, and wanted me to come next morning to Meadow Creek, and read the letter to him.

On the next morning, before day, the Pauvans came running into the Fort and said that Walker was dead, and the Utahs were mad; that they had killed two squaws and two Piede children . . . . About eighteen of our people went out in the morning, and found that the Utahs had killed two Squaws, Piede prisoners, and two Piede children, and about twelve or fifteen of Walker's best horses . . . . They had buried Walker with the letter, and all the articles you sent him . . . .

Saturday 10 Feb. 1855. To day the Supreme Court adjourned *sine die* having been in session 14 days, and disposed of 3 casses which had been appealed, from the D. Court, and one of said cases orginated in the Probate Court.

Sunday 18 Feb 1855. Quorum meeting at my house at Earley candle light. A respectable number present and four new members admitted to fill vacancies

Monday 19 Feb 1855. Met with C. C. Rich J. P. Harmon D Carn and A. L. Fulmer to make out the History of the company who went to Ottowa in 1843 in June to rescue Joseph, the Prophet when he was taken at Dixon Ill

Tuesday 20 Feb 1855. Met as last night & completed the History of that Expedition as well as our memories would serve us. To day is very cold with a strong east wind blowing

Sunday 25 Feb 1855. Weather the past week has been squally. windy snowy & sunshine
Attended meeting W. Woodruff & H. C. Kimball preached giving the gentiles & Mormon Evil doers a rathar cool reception There is now much hard feelings (between [crossed out]) with the gentile part of our community towards the authorities of the church because they have come out boldly and proclamed against their inequity.

Monday 26 Feb 1855. The High Council met to day to adjuts the differences between John Ostler & Widow Eliza Knight The case was Sarah Green an aged woman & Mother of Eliza Knight died in November last when Mrs Knight took out letters of administration on her estate before E. Smith Judge of Probate in Great Salt Lake County. John Ostler claimed the Estate by will from Widow Greene and presented said will for probate which was of course contested by Mrs Knight as administrators and heir of said Estate.
A long and animated suit ensued before the Court of Probate in which the Court decided the will to be invalid whereupon Ostler appealed to the District Court. Mr Babbitt & Phelps was attorneys for Ostler & J. C. Little for Mrs Knight administratrix
Pending the appeal she advertized the property for sale whereupon Ostler enjoined the same from the District Court & the parties were cited to appear at Ogden Court (Term) to answer said injunction.
Some time previous however I was employed on the part of the admrx as council
Thus situated the Estate amounting to some $1500 was in a fair way to be *Eat* up in *Law* when the whole matter was submitted to the High Council who were to settle the same as arbitrators according to law To be heard by themselves or council. The parties entering into bonds & the award to be entered on the docket of the probate court & a decree of the same.
The High Council met on last Saturday heard the bonds read and objected to acting only as a High Council in the Church & not as referees and that on the conditions that the parties give up the Bonds and agree to submit to their decision as saints should do, which all parties (Lawyers & all) agreed to do. Such being the case the Council heard & examined the whole affair to day and decided as did the Probate Court the will to be invalid & the heirs to have the property.
There was much feeling manifested and the Council seemed to think false swearing to sustain the will but all in vain.
The case of course was taken out of the (Probate [crossed out]) Court the Estate paying the cost which had accrued in relation to the injunction & Bonds for refereeing amounting to 28 dollars
How much better it would be if saints would always adjust their differences before the proper tribunals of the Church free of costs and in humility & the Spirit of the Lord than to go before the courts of law which so often involves fortunes

to the stubborn will of man, engendering an evil spirit & irreconcilable enmity & hatred towards each other which is seldom cured.

Wednesday 29 Feb 1855. Southern mail came in last night bring me one letter from my old friend Robt Clift which I answered to day. The General news I have not heard

Friday 2 March 1855. Brs William Field & John Binns two thick-headed English having a law suit pending in the probate Court involving some 1200 dollars. I spent the day having them to settle which they finally did thereby saving a round bill of cost to one party.

Sunday 4 March 1855. Quorum meeting this evening at my house. Admitted two members into the Quorum, Joseph Dudley & Elihu H. Hiatt

    Br Hiatt is a distant relation of mine and is the only relation I have in the Valley except my brother & sister & familys & mine That is belonging to the Church

Monday 5 March 1855. Went to Ogden City Weber County to day in the mail stage to attend the March Term of the District Court which commences to day & arrived there about 6 p. M.

    I do not like the appearance of the City of Ogden which is so far as improved on very low land (on the [crossed out]) between the rivers Weber & Ogden I staid all night with Bishop Browning. Rainy after noon.

Tuesday 6 March 1855. Court met to day two cases were disposed of. Rainy day and Ogden streets mudy, nasty and almost impassable. Went to Bingham's Fort at noon and staid all night with Green Taylor Here I see John Taylor my wifes oldest brother who left Nauvoo in 1844 in Lyman Wight's Company and left Wight in Texas & arrived in the valley last summer.

Wednesday 7 March 1855. Attended Court again, but had nothing to do. Rainy yet & Weber & Ogden on the rise.

    Put up with my old friend Capt. James Brown who made me a present of a pattern for a (suit of [crossed out]) coat, vest, pantaloons, with the trimmings worth perhaps 40 dollars Besides refusing to accepting any remuneration for my board while I attended Court.

Thursday 8 March 1855. To day the case of United States vs. Henry Rau for secreting deserted soldiers came up. The defendant plead not guilty and no money to pay council so the Court assigned me to be council for him.

    Mr Babbitt after declining to act wrung in for ten dollars, after I had discovered the law on which he was indicted was repealed the prisonor of course was discharged on a motion to quash.

Friday 9 March 1855. Court adjourned to day & we started home at one p. m and came to Judson T. Stoddard's and put up. Rainy after-noon

Saturday March 10 1855. Came home about Eleven a. m. Raining all forenoon.

Monday 12 March 1855. Engaged settling a difficulty between John Binns & Wm Field on a running account of some $1200 which was affected after much difficulty

Wednesday 14 March 1855. I have bid for carrying the mail on 4 different routes to day Route No 12806 From Salt Lake City to Mountainville 25 miles.

    My Bid was $1300 the estimated expense of carrying mail $955 Route 12807. From Salt Lake City to Cedar Valley 45 miles

    Bid for $1700 — expense $1360 Route 12808 From Tooele City to Grantsville 12 miles.

Bid for $525. Expense $150 Route 12809 From Nephi to Cedar City 180 miles Bid for $7000 expense $3880 —

The profits arising on the 4 routes as per Bids & estimated cost of carrying the mail will be $4170.

Thos S. Williams goes in partnership with me in the whole concern and should the Bids be accepted at the department he will furnish the means for carrying the mail and I will attend to the business here & divide the profits & losses. 1 Sept next is the time to commence the mail.

Sunday 18 March 1855. Quorum meeting at my house this evening.

Wednesday 21 March 1855. Suit before probate Court Martin Fahy vs Ben D. Barnes in debt $88 I was on the part of defence case was dismissed on a plea to the jurisdiction.

Thursday 22 March 1855. Mr Rankin & Luent Livingston of the U. S. army complained of Brigham Young Jr Heber P. Kimball Lott Huntington & Stephen Moore before the Mayor Grant, for riding voilently by them & bowing, while they were riding the streets with some Ladies &c

The trial lasted all the afternoon & was lost because there was no law against it.

Friday 23 March 1855. Suit before probate Court Martin Fahy vs Ben D. Barnes as on 21 March Judge vs Barnes for 88 dollars & costs I was for deft & Little for plff defendant took an appeal to the District Court.

Sunday 25 March 1855. Went to Tooele Valley to day with P. K. Dodson to settle some business for I & J. M. Hockaday,[42] with Howard Coray who owes them some $1500 and staid with Henry Michall [Michael?]

Monday 26 March 1855. This morning we travelld on some ten miles to E. T. City, which is located some seven months Since in a beautiful valley just after passing the point of the West mountain The city is in a flourishing condition and bids fair to become a delightsome place

In passing the point of the mountain the road runs near the shores of the Lake which was now very ruff in consequence of high winds & large swells running and lashing the shores having all the appearance of a sea coast.

To the North there is no land visible. The horizon dipping into the lake covered with white caps was a most beautiful sight

We put up with Br Coray and transacted our business with him which was to take a mortgague on his house & lot in E. T. to Hockaday for $1474 due Oct 1st next we then returned home where we arrived at eight in the eve.

During our absence from home the southren mail arrived at the Special Term of Court called to try the Indians who murdered Capt Gunnison had adjourned and the Judge (Kinney) and other officers returned home having discharged 3 and

---

42. John M. Hockaday was a Virginian who had had some experience in the West. It was he who had surveyed the land surrounding Fort Bridger in 1852, which Jim Bridger had recorded to secure his claim.

In the summer of 1854 John and Isaac Hockaday, evidently a relative, advertised a monthly passenger service from St. Louis to Salt Lake City to run in connection with W. M. F. Magraw's mail route. He set up a store in Salt Lake City, also.

In 1857 Hockaday was named U. S. attorney for Utah and came west with the army, joining Magraw at Camp Scott. The next year (1858) he was awarded a mail contract for $190,000 to run a weekly service. (The highest price previous to this was $23,000 for a monthly mail.) His partner, William Liggitt, withdrew from the company after the Indians attacked one of their stations, killed the keeper, and took the supplies and animals. Hockaday sold his contract to Jones, Russell & Company, a subsidiary of Russell, Majors & Waddell. See William P. MacKinnon, "The Buchanan Spoils System And The Utah Expedition: Careers of W. M. F. Magraw and John M. Hockaday," *Utah Historical Quarterly*, XXXI (Spring, 1963), 127-50.

sentenced 3 more indians to the penetentiary for three years each for murder in the Second Degree.

The further particulars of this court and its *etceteras* I may speak of again but now pass it. The court was held at Nephi in Juab County.

Sunday 1 April 1855. Quorum meeting in the Evening The time of meeting was changed to meet the first & third sundays of each month at 12 noon at my house.

Monday 2 Apl 1855. Several Lawsuits to day Three vs some Norwegians who owed the Perpual Emmigrating Fund & were trying to leave for Cal without paying. 2. case settled & judgement vs the other also case Geo B. Simpson vs Recides & McGraw.[43] Babbitt for plff. & self for deft Demured which was overruled & 2 motions over ruled.

Wednesday 3 Apl 1855. Suit of Simpson vs Resides & McGraw up again which was finally adjourned till 10 May next.

Wednesday 4 Apl 1855. The U. S. troops left the City to day for Rush Valley Tooele where they are expected to remain some one or two months.

April 5 1855. Br Hiatt & wife & children came here to stay through Conference.

Friday April 6 1855. General Conference to day which lasted till Sunday evening. The usual amount of business was done and one hundred and fifty four Elders appointed to different missions but mostly to the indian tribes

The Consecration law was agreed to be entered into Conference was numerously attended

Monday 9 April 1855. Appointed attorney to collect the perpetual Emmigrating Fund debts of all those who are about to leave the Territory without paying and commenced several suits immediately

There are a number who when they are brought from the old Country here on the avails of this Fund endeavor to leave without paying, forgetting the kind aid recieved to bring them from bondage to this land of liberty

Saturday 14 Apl 1855. Lawsuit before Probate. C. A. & E. H. Perry vs Abel Lamb in debt $314. Babbitt for plff & myself for deft. Judgement confessed.

Monday 16 Apl 1855. Suit before same. Kinney Green & Co. vs Lamb in debt $530. Hon J. F. Kinney for plff & myself for deft Judgt confessed.

Thursday 19 Apl 1855. District Court met today in special session there being much business both civil & criminal accumulating which needs attending to. A grand jury was called & the case of C. A & E. H. Perry vs Trustees of the 14th Ward to test the legality of the city ordinance in relation to school tax

Friday 20 April 1855. Assisted A. Carrington the Attorney General to draw an indictment against Capt Rufus Ingalls[44] of the U. S. A. for abducting a female minor child and am employed to assist in the prosecution although I have had three applications to defend Capt Ingalls with a handsome fee annexed.

---

43. W. M. F. (William Miller Finney) Magraw was a business associate of John M. Hockaday. In March 1854, Magraw was awarded a four-year federal contract to carry the mail monthly on a round-trip service from Independence, Missouri, to Salt Lake City. John E. Reeside withdrew in November following an Indian attack, and John M. Hockaday became his second partner. The service was so unsatisfactory that the contract was annulled on August 18, 1856. Both Magraw and Hockaday "displayed a remarkable affinity for strong drink and violence." Magraw died April 7, 1864, in his forty-seventh year. *Ibid.*

44. Captain Rufus Ingalls was one of Steptoe's command who later wrote violent criticisms of the Mormons.

Saturday 21 April 1855. This evening A. W. Babbitt came to me from Capt Ingalls again to induce me to join in his defence offering me five hundred dollars but my mind is made up to defend our own rights on preference to plan for money

Had a suit before Probate Court. Ezra Thompson vs Abel Lamb in debt demand $147.17 I was on the part of the defence.

Monday 23 Apl 1855. The case of the people vs Capt Ingalls was called up in the District Court A. W. Babbitt for the defence, who met the indictment by a motion to Quash as he always does, which motion was argued & submitted, and Court adjd

Tuesday 24 Apl 1855. Case of Ingalls up again. The Court sustained the indictment with amendments. His right and authority to do which is about to raise a another question which I fear may prove a serious one to the Prosecution The amendment was with costs.

Wednesday 25 Apl 1855. Case of Ingalls up yet. Babbitt filed his exceptions to the ruling of the Court yesterday and defendant plead not guilty. then motion by prosecution for time to obtain a witness overruled & venire out for traverse Jury and the Court adjourned till 11 o'c to morrow morning.

Thursday 26 Apl 1855. Southern mail came in to day Case of Ingalls up again and the Attorney General withdrew the prosecution & the case was dismissed at the cost of the people The defendant had previously agreed to pay $100. cost which they did, to me immediately afterwards.

Sunday 6 May 1855. Quorum meeting at my house at noon 2 members recieved into the the Quorum in place of two ordained presidents

Tuesday 8 May 1855. The missionaries bound East started yesterday & to day. Some are going to Europe & some to the Cherokees.

The Govornor, accompanied by the rest of the first Presidency started south on their annual Tour among the settlements. They will probably go as far south as Harmony in Washington County.

Thursday 10 May 1855. The case of Simpson vs Reside and McGraw as commenced 2 April in the probate came to trial at ten a. m The court decided in favor of the plaintiff for 300 dollars and costs I immediately called for an appeal

Monday 14 May 1855. Suit before probate C A & E. H. Perry vs Andrew J. Stewart in debt Demand $616.93. Babbitt for plff & myself for Deft. Judgement vs Deft for demand Defendant appealed.

General C. C. Rich left today for San Bernardino Cal with several of the missionaries among the rest was George Q. Cannon and several other printers who are going to establish a press in San Francisco where it is contemplated to print the Book of *Mormon* in the *Haiawian* dialect. Elder Cannon while on his mission to Sandwich Islands translated the Book of Mormon into that dialect. Elder P. P. Pratt is expected also to Edit a paper there.

Tuesday 15 May 1855. To day Judge Stiles & Judge Hyde started for Carson Valley Marshal Haywood also goes with a guard of some 25 men, under pay at 4 dollars pr day for man & horse they being found I have my douts about govt paying the guard.

Sunday 20 May 1855. This after noon there was a light shower of rain which is the first rain that has fallen since about the first of April. The drough has been very severe while the grasshoppers cover the land destroying almost all green vegitation both on mountain & valley which presents a dreary prospects for our incoming crops. Whole fields of wheat are swept smooth & appear to be entirely used up yet the people seem to be in good spirits

Thursday 24 May 1855. Took stage this morning and went to Ogden where I arrived just before sun set putting up for the night with my good friend Capt Brown

Friday 25 May 1855. Went to Binghams Fort three miles north. Rainy weather now and to night had a refreshing shower which was so much needed

The grasshoppers are doing very much damage to the crops yet there are much wheat which looks well and bids fair for a good crop The people seem to be in good spirits fighting grasshoppers and planting & sowing where the crops are eaten up.

Saturday 26 May 1855. Returned to Ogden. Transacted some business for the Firm of I. [Isaac] & J. M. Hockerday, with Browning

Tuesday 29 May 1855. Took stage & came home recieving a cooling shower in the evening which put our gardens in good growing condition

Thursday 31 May 1855. Suit before Probate Mary R. Du Fresne vs Gale in debt 57 dollars I was on the part of the Defendant & Babbitt for Plff. case was dismissed

To day Judge Kinney started for the states. Genl Holman started a few days previous.

Their buisness evidently is to try to have governor Young removed and Judge appointed in his place while Genl Holman is to be appointed to be Chief Justice in his place or supersede Babbitt in the Secrataryship but Babbitt is intending to go also and oppose them at Washington which will result in the ranks of our enemies[45]

Saturday 2 June '55. Judge Kinney returned this Evening having proceeded to the Weber & the advance companies had left him The thoughts of the Indians & the waters of the Weber proved too much for his courage

Sunday 4 June 1855. Quorum meeting at my house —

Tuesday 5 June 1855. The Eastern mail arrived about sunset. Our Delegate to Congress The Hon. John M. Barnhisel came with the mail He was in good health & spirits

Wednesday 12 June 1855. To day C. Lamberts son & another boy went up Emme-gration Cañon for wood and by some means some of their oxen in sliding down the side of the mountain uncovered some stone coal which is supposed to be a good rich coal mine If this be true it will be truly fortunate to the good people of this city in respect to fuel

The Boys who unfortunately had their oxen to slide down the mountain, most fortunately slide on to a premium of $1000 which the Territory had offered for the discovery of coal adjacent to this city.

Monday 18 June 1855. To day Govornor Young accompanied by a large com-pany started North on an exploring expedition They took along scientific instru-ments with the intention of determining the Oregon line.

The coal mine found in Emmigration on the 12, turned out a Hoax

Monday 25 June 1855. The govornor and suit returned from their northern rout on the fore noon to day, having been gone seven days, during which tour the terri-

---

45. Stout here infers that Babbitt will unwittingly play into the hands of the enemies of the church. Furniss characterizes Babbitt thus: "The choice of emissary was an unhappy one, for Babbitt whose eccentric conduct later earned him the perilous disfavor of Brigham Young, succeeded only in drawing upon himself the dislike and ridicule of Whigs and Democrats in the Capitol." Norman F. Furniss, *The Mormon Conflict, 1850-1859* (New Haven, 1960), 7.

Both Bernhisel and Kane had written in criticism of Babbitt's conduct, while this year Steptoe, Kinney, and Garland Hurt advised that he be removed from office.

torial line between Utah Oregon was determined by Prof O. Pratt that is the 42° north where a stone was set up on the line & trenches dug on its crossing the fort Hall road

Thursday 28 June 1855. Caliafornia Mail came in but there is no news of importance except that the wheat crops at San Bernardino have been nearly all destroyed by rust.

Frid 29 June. This after noon the citizens of this city were suddenly called to mourn the loss of our esteemed friend Judge Leonidas Shaver who was found dead in his bed about one to day. An inquest was immediately summoned by the Mayor, who decided that he came to his end by a disease in the ear and brain.

Saturday 30 June 55. At ten this morning the members of the Judiciary & bar assembled at the Council House to express their sentiments & feelings in relation to the sudden death of Judge Shaver. Chief Justice J. D. Kinney was called to the chair & W. I. Appleby clerk whereupon a committee of three to wit A. W. Babbitt, Z. Snow, G. A. Smith were appointed to draft resolutions on behalf of the meeting which they reported in a short time which were accepted.

The remains of Judge Shaver were borne into the House meanwhile Judge Kinney then delivered an Eulogy upon the life of the diseased to a dense concourse of people who had no[w] assembled, after which J. M. Grant the Mayor offered a Resolution on behalf of the people of Utah one part of which was as follows, that we will hold his name in honorable remembrance in all time to come, and when the Archangel's trump shall give the signal to bring the Sleepers forth, those who hold the keys of *life and death* will not forget Judge Shaver." which were enthusiastically adopted.

Professor Orson Pratt then preached a funeral sermon on the diseased. Meeting adjourned by prayer by Gov Young when the funerall procession was formed. as follows at one P. M.

At 2 P. M. the procession started

1. Battalion of Life Guards
2. Nauvoo Brass band.
3. Hearse bearing corpse
4. Intamate friends.
5. Gov & suit, Kinney & Barnhisel
6. Judges secratary &c
7. Members of the Bar
8. Citizens

The occasion was a solemn one and called forth more heart felt grief & sympathy than has ever been manifested for any person not a mormon who ever died in our midst.[46]

Monday 2 July 1855. Lawing to day. George B Simpson vs Reside & McGraw &c in attachment issued from the District Court demand $8,340

The Marshall levied on the animals carriages &c belonging to the Mail service and which were just starting East this morning. I was on part of Deft and imme-

---

46. The honor accorded Judge Leonidas Shaver at his death seems proof of the esteem in which he was held and would discount the accusation later made by Judge W. W. Drummond that he had been given poisonous liquor.

Mrs. Mary Ettie V. Smith also advanced the theory of poisoning: "I knew Judge Shaver well, and recollect the circumstances of his death. He occupied a room in my brother Howard's house; and died there. There were a great many things connected with the trouble between him and the Prophet [Brigham Young], which I never understood, and I have good reason to believe, much more than has yet been disclosed . . . ."

She recounts an incident when Brigham Young came to the house to see the judge but found the door locked, the room dark and the blinds drawn, and assuming that he was out, Young talked loudly and freely when he heard Shaver get out of bed and knew that he had been overheard. "The difficulty between them increased after this, and one morning the judge was found dead . . . . He was unquestionably poisoned." Smith, *Among The Mormons*, 246-47. Mrs. Smith's book is bitterly anti-Mormon.

diately sued out an injunction from the same Court enjoined the proceeding & had the property released so that the mail started at five P. M.

Wednesday 4 July 1855. This was a great day in Utah   This morning at half past four I was awakened by the roar of artillery and the ringing of bells accompanied by the sound of several bands of music as if the Allies were singing Te Deum and celebrating the taking of Sebastapol which continued until six   All this had a tendency to arouse my patriotism and hastily leaving my bunk before the files had an oppertunity to anoy me I beheld City over shadowed with all sorts of banners, flags streamers while the *Star* spangled seemed to predominate.

Now I began to feel proud of my country so while I was thus congratulating myself on my happy stars for being born an American & particularly in old *Kentuck* I beheld the Nauvoo Legion assembling near the Council House (Horse & foot) as though they were determined to let the "rest of mankind" know how we valued liberty I felt my courage rise too and could in my very soul damn all secessionists and political carpers who seek to stake our free institutions and sacrafice our constitution at the shrine of corrupt ambition and party strife, "glorious government, free and equal *esto perpetua*" I breathead involuntaryly, but just then I remembered that not only my sweet self but all these were exiles.   Exiled.   American exiles But let all that pass now for this is the glorious fourth.

About half past 9 the Legion formed (as follows [crossed out]) and marched away to be reviewed by the govornor and half past 12 all was dismissed ½ past two when all hands met at the bowry to let off the patriotic steam in good stile by prayer, music, speaches, toasts, and the like untill accompanied and interspersed by the fire of artillery and waving of banners untill near sun set when we all went home free & happy and glad that the fourth was over

Friday 6 July 1855. Sanford Brannan & Co train of goods from Los Angelos Cal of some ten waggons came in to day bring a good lot of groceries among other things which was much needed here at this time

Saturday 7 July 1855. Lawsuit before probate for defendants.   George Gregory vs. John & Edward Morgan and Isaac Scott (son of Col John Scott) for assault which proved to be only a free jaw, the cost was consequently divided,

Monday 9 July 1855. Eastern Mail arrived bringing no news of importance only "Sebastapol is not taken and Brigham Young is still Govornor of Utah"

W. W. Drummond & lady came as passengers   The Judge is the successor of Judge Leonidas Shaver

Sunday 15 July 1855. Elder C. W. West and some other Elders arrived to day from missions.   Elder West left when I did in 1852 and has been to the East Indies.

Thursday 19 July 1855. This evening about dusk I was married to Miss [Alvira] Wilson[47] Daughter of Lewis D. and Nancy Ann Wilson

Miss Wilson was born in Green Township, Richland County, Ohio, on the 21st day of April A. D. 1834.   She has been raised in the Church of Jesus Christ of Latter Day saints.

President Brigham Young performed the Marriage cerimony.

Friday 20 July 1855. Law suit. Before probate. Hugh Hilton vs Wm J. Westwood on attachment.   In debt. demand $115   I was on part of plff & Babbitt for deft Court decided in favor of plff for a Judgement of some forty-dollars & costs

---

47. This marriage was to prove a happy one. Alvira bore her husband eleven children, eight of whom grew to maturity.

Tuesday 24 July 1855. This day was not celebrated in this City as usual but at Provo it was and while in the excitement of firing a cannon it was loaded with clay pounded hard which burst the cannon killing a young man named William Nixon

Friday July 1855. The U. S. Survey General for the Territory of Utah & son Mr Burr and several others came in to day from the East.

Saturday 28 July 1855. Elder William McBride having lately returned from Sandwick Islands paid me a visit with his wife & several others with Bp. W. G. & W. I. Perkins and ladies we passed a very agreeable day.

Thursday 2 Aug 1855. Took stage and went to Davis County. The annual Election coming on next Monday The good people of Davis had brought out their nominees for the Legislature.

Bishop John Stoker for the Council and Anson Call & Jesse Hobson for the House of Representative My business to Davis was to have one of the nominees to withdraw and John D. Parker put on the track in his place accordingly I called the Bishops and other leading men together and laid the matter before them The plan was adopted & A Call withdran & Parker put in his place all to the most perfect satisfaction of all parties[48] staid with my Brother all night

Friday 3 Aug 1855. The Eastern mail arrived last night I found on coming home. Elder S. M. Blair came as a passenger.

Saturday 4 August 1855. Law Suit before Probate Anthony F. Navarre vs S. S Brattleson in attachment Demand $120.80. Defendant is a non resident I was on the part of the Plff. Judgment for Plff for the demand

Monday 6 August 1855. To was the general Election throuout the Territory The following is the ticket for this County & there being no opposition they are no doubt all Elected

For Delegate to Congress.	Samuel W. Richards
John M. Barnhisel	Jesse C. Little
Councillors	Hosea Stout
Heber C. Kimball	Edwin D. Woolley
Daniel H. Wells	James W. Cummings
Albert Carrington	Phineas F. Young
Wilford Woodruff	William Snow
Representatives	Claudius V. Spencer
Jedediah M. Grant	Select-man
William W. Phelps	Samual Moore
Albert P. Rockwood	

There was only 227 votes poled in the city.

Tuesday 7 Aug 1855. Law suit before Probate Alfred Nethercott vs Jacob Noe In Ejectment & damage $28 I was on the part of the plff & A. W. Babbitt for defence The case went down on demurrer by defence after which the parties compromised

yesterday we enjoyed a fine refreshing shower which well irrigated our gardens It came from a cloud which hung as if suspended over the city the rain descending rapidly untill the ground was flooded. There was no rain either north or south of the city It seemed to be a special favor the benifit and refreshment of the alone.

---

48. Here is another good example of the politics in early Utah. That the authorities should name John D. Parker, a member of the Council of Fifty, to replace either of the other candidates, and that Anson Call should accept the decision with good grace speaks of the reality of the ghost government.

We have had no rain before this summer and our gardens were suffering & crops being cut off

Saturday 11 Aug 1855. Lawsuit before Probate Thomas Frazier vs Thomas Morris in Damage Demand $80   I was on the part of plff & A. Babbitt for Deft.   Court adjourned till Monday for arguments & Decision.

Monday 13 Aug 1855. Court rendered judgement in favor of the plaintiff for ten dollars & costs.

Wednesday 15 Aug 55. Suit before probate Hannah Hatch vs her husband Hatch for assault & Battery.   Mr Grow on part of plff & self for deft who was put under his own bond of 50 dollars to keep the peace for six months.

Thursday 16 Aug. Took stage and went to provo Utah County, to attend a lawsuit before the probate Court of said County to be had on Saturday.

Friday 17 Aug 1855. Visiting my old provo friends at their sugar making which they procure by washing the rich & abundant honey dew which settles on the cotton-wood leaves & boiling it down to sugar or molasses.   There has been some three thousand pounds already made in & about provo[49]

Saturday 18 Aug 1855. Attended the case of David Malcom vs Lewis Hatch before the Probate Court of Utah County in Replevin for a yoke of oxen Joseph A. Kelting was on the part of the plaintiff & myself on the part of the defence. Jury trial who brought in a virdict for plaintiff with costs

Sunday 19 Aug 1855. Came to Battle Creek & took breakfast with Capt Hawley and then came with him home and found my wife had gone on a visit to her fathers at Ogden

Monday 20 Aug. 1855. Lawsuit before Elias Smith Probate Judge.   Mark Earnshaw vs Daniel C. Patterson In Damage in assault and batttery.   Demand $300. J. C. Little & self for Plff & A W Babbitt for defence Jury Trial who rendered a virdict against the defendant for $150 and costs of suit.

Thursday 24 Aug 1855. The train of goods belonging to Gilbert & Garrish commenced arriving this evening. They will *hold forth* at the House formerly occupied by C. A & E. H. Perry

---

49. Stout's account of sugar-making at Provo is verified by articles in the *Deseret News* for July 31, 1855, and August 18, 1855.

In his *History of Provo* (privately printed, 1934), Marinus Jenson gives the following account:
  There appeared in August, 1855, on the leaves of the cotton-wood trees in Provo a hard, white, sacchrine substance, called by the settlers honey dew, from which sugar might be made. As sugar at that time was worth a dollar a pound, the settlers looked upon this (sugar manna) as a great blessing . . . . Families went into the river bottoms and established camps for the manufacture of sugar. Limbs of trees were cut and the honeydew was washed from the leaves in barrels of water which was then strained into large kettles hung on poles supported by stakes, and boiled. The product was a sweet, brown sugar. Between three and four thousand pounds of "manna-sugar" was obtained.
  Bishop Blackburn took 332 pounds of this sugar to the general tithing office in Salt Lake City. Of the amount, 210 pounds was distributed among the hands at work on the temple and other "public works" in Great Salt Lake City, who gratefully acknowledged its reciept from Provo, together with forty bushels of new potatoes, in a card of thanks published in the "Deseret News."
The diary of Bishop Elias Blackburn during this period is very brief with no mention of the sugar-making project. In a large leather-bound ledger copied at a later date, the following entry is written in the margin for the year 1855: "July 10 About this time a honey dew fell the Saints Paid of what they gethered tithing 332 lbs of Sugar I delivered it to Gen T. office delt to Temple hands." Elias H. Blackburn, "Elias Blackburn Journals and Papers" (original, Utah State Historical Society), 12.

Monday 3 Sept. 1855. Capt Hindleys company of saints arrived having some 60 waggons & some 5 or 6 returning missionaries also arrived a fine shower of rain to day & tomorrow another

Wednesday 5 Sept 1855. The first train of T. S. Williams & Co's goods arrived consisting of 26 waggons

Friday 7 Sept 1855. The second company of emmigration saints arrived Noah T. Guyman Capt

Tuesday 11 Sept 1855. Seth M. Blair's train of goods of 45 waggons including a few Saints from Texas He puts up his goods at Reese's old stand on East Temple Street

Sunday 16 Sept 1855. Went to Union Fort and then to Big cottonwood & attended meeting and dined with Charles Shumway & returned home about dark.

Thursday 20 Sept 1855. Suit before probate E. P. Thomas vs Kinney Green & Co. In Replevin Col J. C. Little attorey for plff and Myself & Col A W. Babbitt for Defts the defence demurred and the case was dismissed.

Also another suit before same Kinney Green & Co vs E. P. Thomas in Assumpsit Demand $81.14. The same attorneys as before Defence filed a set off. Jury trial virdict for Defendant of $31.50 plff appealed.

Tuesday 25 Sept 1855. Capt R. Balentine's Company of P. E. Fund saints arrived just at sun set all seemed to be in good order and condition.

Friday 28 Sept 1855. Elder Thurstin's Company of Saints arrived. all well to day — News arrived that the Indians attacted the brethren at the Elk mountain Mission and killed three to wit Wiseman Hunt, William Behunin and Edward Edwards. President A. N. Billings was wounded in the fore finger They abandoned the fort and took the Horses & left for Manti where they arrived on the 30th Sept The affair took place on the 22nd Sept[50]

Haywood & Stiles returned from the Carson Valley Mission having held the Court & organized the County and all well pleased.

Satur Oct 6 1855. General Conference held untill Monday evening the 8th inst. There were a larger concourse of people than at any previous conference My house was crouded and my wife & sister quite used up waiting on company. Ezra T. Benson Lorenzo Snow of the Twelve and Phineas H. Youn High Priest were appointed to Europe on missions to go in the spring —

Friday 12 Oct 1855. This morning Mr Secratary A. W. Babbitt's office was found to have been broken open last night The clerk of the Supreme & 1 District Court also kept his office in the same room. The Clerk kept his papers in a small tin box which usually sat on his desk at this time it was full of papapers which were the Complaints & other pleadings of suits pending in the District Court which were to

---

50. The Elk Mountain Mission to establish a settlement in the vicinity of the present town of Moab, Utah, was preceded by a company which had taken five wagon loads of provisions out and cached them. This was in 1854. In the spring of 1855 forty-one men with a "fit-out" of fifteen wagons, thirteen horses, sixty-five oxen, sixteen cows, two bulls, one calf, two pigs, twelve chickens, four dogs; and flour, wheat, oats, corn, potatoes, peas left Salt Lake City.

By mid-July the company had planted crops and built a stone fort and had converted and had baptized some of the Indians. During late September, in a series of sudden attacks, Indians killed three of their number and set fire to their haystacks and outbuildings. See *Utah, A Guide to the State* (New York, 1941), 426-27.

The official mission journal was kept by Oliver B. Huntington, and is on file at the L. D. S. Church Historian's Library.

be tried at the Special Term to be holden on the 15th inst   There were 39 cases then on Docket & all the papers in relation thereto were in the Box and the object of breaking into the secratary's office seems to have been to lift the box as that is all that was gone

This will *non plus* the Court & attornies. I had some eight or ten cases & Babbitt nearly all the rest and we have not a paper left only on the Docket on account that they *were* Babbitt's cases were mostly civil suits in debt on notes which notes were filed & also and gone.[51]   The taking of the box must prove to those sued a most excellent pain extractor these tight times

Saturday 13 Oct 1855. The having become troublesome at Fort Supply[52] & commenced killing cattle Major Burton with a company of the minute men started this morning to the relief of the people there & to protect the emmigration

Monday 15th Oct 1855. First Judicial District Court of the U. States met to day at the Council House Special Term   I was appointed Special District Attorney for the U. S and Jos A. Kelting for the Territory   The case of Simpson vs Curry, Elder, Reside & Mc Graw &c commenced on the 2 June last in attachment Demand 8340 dollars was called up and Simpson not being present the case was struck from the docket. I was on the part of Defts   at 4 p m the probate Court met Mrs Riley vs Thos Margrets & John Sheffield in debt 21.50 I was on the part of plff.

Also James Gammel vs John H. Blazzard in debt $368. I was for plff. & Almiren Grow for deft. Court rendered judgement for plff for the demand of $368 and costs.

Tuesday 16. Oct 1855. Attended District Court at ten after instructing the grand jury. The case of James Smith plff in Error vs William P. Goddard and William B. Pace defendants in Error, taken up from the Probate of Utah County. was called up

---

51. The theft of the official court papers is another evidence of the contempt in which the Mormons held the district courts, the government officers in general, and Almon W. Babbitt in particular. This disrespect shown the federal courts was one of the reasons cited for dispatching troops to Utah.

52. On the day preceding, Brigham Young had issued a proclamation to the effect that, "Whereas, reliable information has been received that the Shoshones and a portion of the Utah Indians have commenced hostilities against the whites at Green River and other Counties by killing Edward Edwards, Wm Behunin, and Wiseman Hunt, and are continuing to commit depredations upon the people by killing cattle, destroying grain &c . . . ." Utah Territorial Executive Record Book "A" (Utah State Archives), 113.

The military forces were to hold themselves in readiness to march in any direction. On the same day, Brigham Young ordered Major Robert T. Burton of the Life Guards to "forthwith raise twenty five men with horses and accoutrements, armed, and suitable equipage, with thirty days rations, and proceed without delay to Fort Bridger and Fort Supply . . . ."

The interesting thing here is the fact that the men who were killed were at the Elk Mountain Mission near the present site of Moab, while the army was sent in another direction entirely. They were to protect the immigration and render protection to the Mormons at Fort Bridger and Fort Supply. Specifically, the reason for their expedition was that: "We should very much regret a resort to the last alternative of leaving and abandoning those places and the foundation, however small, already laid at those posts. If therefore the places should be sufficiently fortified and replenished by the residents thereof returning, so that they may be able to maintain those locations, you will in that case return without them."

Burton wrote a report from Fort Supply on October 20 that he had carried out his orders and arrived at that point on October 16 after three days ride: "I met the Indian Agent Mr Armstrong about thirty miles from this place who advised me to return as he had settled all matters of difficulty existing between the whites and Indians in this country but this I could not do and carry out my instructions . . . ."

Burton then told of meeting with the Indian chiefs and of sending groups to ride over the country in search of stock. He reported that some of the emigrant trains en route could not make it in to the Valley without assistance. The incident serves to show the continued interest in this eastern approach to the Valley. See Utah Territorial Militia Records (Military Records Section, Utah State Archives).

and no one appearing on the part of the plff the case was stricken from the docket at the cost of the plff. Kelting, Babbitt & Stout attorneys for defts

Also the case of Williams Camp plaintiff in Error vs Alvin Green taken from Justice court called up. No one appeared on the part of the defence Stout & Babbitt for plff The case was argued and judgement below reversed.

Wednesday 17 Oct 1855. Attended Court again. The case of Louis P. Drextler vs George Goddard & B. Leonard came off I was on the part of plff. & A. W. Babbitt for deft action of Debt 2174.38 cents and interest 13.25 cents Judgement confessed. There was several other cases tried & passed off which I was not concerned in.

Thursday 18 Oct 1855. Attended District Court among other cases tried the case of Lewis Hatch vs. David Malcolm In appeal from the Probate Court of Utah County In Replevin was called up. Stout & Babbitt for the plff & J. A. Kelting for defence Hatch was deft in the Court below and Appealed The judgement of the court below was reversed.

Friday 19 Oct 1855. Attended District Court among other cases tried the case of Edward Barr agent for Curry Elder Reside & McGraw vs Geo B. Simpson In Injunction commenced on 2nd of July last came up and the deft not appearing the case went by default to his cost —

Also the case Reside & McGraw vs G. B. Simpson In appeal from the Probate of G. S. L. County came up and on motion of defenant council (was [crossed out]) the appeal was dismissed. for defect of the Bond In both cases I was for plff & A. W. Babbitt for defence.

Also the case of Thomas S. Williams vs Levi Abrams in an action of Debt $308 56/00 I was on part of the plff & Babbitt for the deft Jury rendered a virdict of no cause of action.

20 Oct 1855 Saturday. Attended District Court and among other business the case of A. J Stewart vs C. A. & E. H. Perry on appeal from the probate of G. S. L. County was taken up and Judget confessed. Myself for Plff & Babbitt for deft

at noon the court adjourned till Monday the 22 inst Engaged in the after noon writing indictments

Monday Oct 22 1855. Attended District court I had no case to come off to day. Court adjourned at noon & I was writing indictments in the after noon

Tuesday Oct 23 1855. Attended Court. The grand jury this morning presented two indictments one against George Holmes for trading with the Indians and one against Carlos Murry for the murder of an Indian.

The case of Hockaday Morris & Co vs Thomas S. Johnson for the Replevin of 30 Head of cattle also came up This was a verry excitable case

In the case of Earnshaw vs D C Patterson before in the Probate on the 20th Aug last for $150 and costs an execution was issued against D. C. Patterson to satisfy said judgement T. S. Johnson the Constable executed and sold 19 Head of fat oxen as the property of Patterson, which were afterwards claimed as belonging to Hockaday Morris & Co and as such were replevied but the writ was not served nor the cattle taken but Johnson appeared in Court and answered and the case was tried on the merits & the virdict of the jury was for the defendant "no cause of action" to which Babbitt on the part of the plff filed a motion for a new trial which was overruled. Myself Little & Hickman for deft.

Wednesday 24 Oct. District Court met and adjourned till tomorrow at 9 o'c A. M. I was then with the grand jury.

Thursday 25 Oct 1855. District Court again the case of Jos F Mason vs W. J. Hawley on note for one thousand and thirty Eight dollars came up W. A. Hickman for plff and Babbitt & Stout for defendant. Judgement confessed.

Friday 26 Oct 1855. District Court. case of the United States vs George Holmes indictment for trading with the Indians Babbitt for defendant. He moved to quash which was sustained & I excepted to the ruling of Court.

Suit before the probate Job Bray vs John Wardle in debt $75 — I was for plff. Judget for plff for 62 52½ cents.

Saturday 27 Oct 1855. District Court. Grand jury presented Indictment against Thomas Greenwood for Larceny which was tried in the afternoon I was Special Prosecutor and Babbitt assigned by the court for the defence. Jury's virdict of guilty of Pettitt Larceny and imprisonment for six months.

Monday 29 Oct 1855. This fore noon the court did not meet. We all attended the funeral W. J Appleby's Eldest daughter who very suddenly died President B. Young preached followed by J M. Grant and W. Woodruff

In the after noon court met Grand Jury presented two indictments. one against Joe a Spaniard for the murder of Elisha P. Ryan and one against Moroni Green for an assault with intent to kill Nathan Tanner. This after noon also I was excused by the court from acting as Territorial prosecutor as I have to start to Fillmore about next Monday.

Tuesday 30 Oct 1855. Attended Court at three p. m.

Wednesday 31 Oct 1855. Attended District Court at 3 p. m

Thursday 1 Nov 1855. Attended District Court again. The case of People vs Moroni Green was tried In indictment for assault with intent to kill. Second count with intent to inflict bodily injury. I was prosecuter & Babbitt for the defence Jury brought in a vidict on the second count and imprisonment for six months.

Friday 2 Nov 1855. District Court Babbitt for the defence in case of The people vs Green moved for arrest of judgement argued and overruled & Babbitt accepted which was allowed

Saturday 3 Nov 1855. D. Court case of People vs David Jones Larceny came up Carrington for plff & Babbitt & Myself for defence Jury's virdict guilty & fine 25 dollars.

The court adjourned sine Die having set 18 days, during this term there was cases on the docket cases in debt and went to trial and judgement cases dismissed and indictments in which 3 cases were tried & convicted & indictments quashed and Nolled & still on docket total number of cases on the docket and cases laid over to next term.

Monday 5 Nov 1855. Preparing to start for Fillmore to attend the Nov Term of the 2nd Judicial District Court on next Monday the 12th inst Expect to start this evening which I accordingly did about two o'clock p. m. in company A. Call Deputy U. S. Marshall who had Levi Abrams in custody, a prisoner, indicted for the murder of Too-ebe an Indian and is to be tried at Fillmore during the term of Court now pending. D. B. & C. A. Huntington[53] interpreters also in Company

We travelled some six or eight miles and after bogging a horse or two in an almost bottomless mud hole at the crossing of Mill Creek, on the State road put up for the night with James Gorden.

---

53. This is Clark Allen Huntington, son of Dimick B. Huntington and older brother of Lot Huntington. With their mother and two younger sisters these boys had gone on the Mormon Battalion trek along with their father. At the last crossing of the Arkansas, they were sent with the group to Pueblo, Colorado.

Wednesday 7 Nov 1855. Late start but we made out to reach Pleasant Grove by dark & put up with Bishop Hanson Walker without any occurrence, material befalling us.

Thursday 8 Nov 1855. Started earley and went to Provo Here Marshall Call ordered some 50 bushels of oats to Fillmore for the use of the Court and then proceeded on dining at Springville with W. D. Huntington thence to Payson puting up with Bishop Charles Hancock for the night

Friday 9 Nov 1855. Hence to Salt Creek where we all arrived safe and sound before dark putting up with Patriarch William Cazair. Here we met with Deputy Marshal W. M. Wall with a Posse in search of some Indians, who had been heretofore indicted for malicious mischief &c He had been in search of them for some days but found them not, so he concluded to accompany us to Fillmore

This evening Elders G. B. Wallace and several of the Home Missionaries who were here held a meeting Myself and Marshall Call first held forth to a crouded house followed by Elder Wallace and others.

Saturday 10 Nov 1855. Wet rainy disagreeable morning which left us pondering whether to go on or lay up, finally however about ten a. m. after laying in horse feed and engaging a load of wood for a camp fire we started and went to Chicken Creek Springs overtaking some others who were en route, as Jurors &c to Court where we all encamped, enjoying a luxurious oyster supper served up by Abrams the prisoner, meanwhile the load of wood arriving we fared extreemly well barring an occasional shower and gust of wind.

Sunday 11 Nov 1855. Earley start and fine travelling only roads rather heavy after the rains. Leaving Marshall Wall at the Sevier River to make farther search for the indicted Indians we proceeded on to Round prairie and dined & again forward without further trouble we arrived at Fillmore just after dark.

Here I found His Honor W. W. Drummond & lady all well and in good spirits patiently awaiting our arrival to Court which is to commence to morrow at ten a. m. I put up with Br Peter Robinson the Clerk of the Court

Sunday 12th Nov 1855. United States second District Court at ten a. m Hon W. W. Drummond preseding. Anson Call Deputy U. S. marshall in the absence of Joseph L. Haywood U. S. marshall.

I was sworn in as U. S. District Attorney pro tem and Joseph A. Kelting Territorial District Attorney pro tem The grand jury was organized John D. Lee Forman

In charging the grand jury the Judge took occasion to express his opinion of the Laws of Utah in relation to the powers and Jurisdiction of the probate Courts.[54]

He most emphatically declared that under the organic Act of the Territory of Utah the Legislature could not confer, civil and criminal jurisdiction by law on the probate Courts, or any powers whatsoever othan matters of Probate proper and that the judiciary act conferring these powers on the probates Courts, were not only contrary to, and inconsistent with the organic act; but an unwarranted strech of power, not only beyond, but amounting to an abnigation of all law

He also instructed the grand jury that if they found that any of the Probate Judges had exercised civil or criminal jurisdiction that it was their duty to indict not only the judges, but all jurors and officers who had acted under them.

Also that if they found any person of the secret order of the "Star Spangled Banner or Know Nothings" that it was their duty to indict all such as conspirators against and enemies of the federal government.

---

54. Judge Drummond's speech outlining the limitations of the probate courts explains some of the earlier frictions and some of the difficulties which developed later.

This evening Hon A. W. Babbitt arrived from Salt Lake City. He came as council in the defence of Levi Abrams.

Tuesday 13 Nov 1855. Court met at ten a. m. Case of the U. S. vs Abrams called up. Myself council on the part of the U. S. and A W. Babbitt for defence. Abrams plead not guilty, and Court adjourned.

Wed 14 Nov 1855. Court met at ten a. m. Case of Abrams called up. The parties joined issue and the day was spent in the examination of witnesses on the part of the prosecution.

Thursday 15 Nov 1855. Court met at ten a.m. Case of Abrams called up Several Indians were offered as witnesses on the part of the prosecution
The first was Parrah-Shont the Pah-vante war chief was introduced when on being questioned as to his belief in future rewards and punishments. He said that if he told the truth and done right in this life, he would go to a good warm Cañon in California, after death, where there were plenty of fat elk and good game Where there groves and grasses in eternal green, Where ran never failing streams of limpid and cool water; beneath the genial rays of a cloudless sun, in one eternal summer. Where he would live in peace and dwell in the society of the good and the brave and subsist on the choisest game and fattest elk.
But if he told a lie, he would go to a barren, dreary and frozen Cañon filled with eternal snows, where he would drag out a miserable exhistence, poor naked and bare foot without good bows and arrows, doomed to persue his lean game and poor Elk over the rugged and frozen steeps of this desolate and dreary Cañon forever in the society of the wicked, the cowardly and the mean
This was deemed quite orthodox by the court and his testimony allowed

Friday 16 Nov. 1855. To day the evidence on the part of the (defence [crossed out]) prosecution closed & the Evidence on the part of the defence was introduced which did not occupy much time. When the parties rested and the pleas commenced on the part of the prosecution by myself, followed by Mr Kelting & Babbitt for the defence, which was continued untill about 9 p. m. when court adjourned in the midst of Babbitts speech
Mr W. Meeks U. S. D. Marshall left for Weber County for witnesses about 11 o'clock a. m.
Josiah Call U. S. D. Marshall returned from Iron County with Enyos an Indian boy indicted for murder of Capt J. W. Gunnison and others

Saturday 17 Nov 1855. Court met at ten a.m. When Mr Babbitt wound up his plea to the jury and was followed by Mr John Bair Esq who joined with me in the prosecution His plea was lengthy & loud which however came to an end about three p. m. and was followed by a few remarks by myself when the attornies filed their instructions and the case was submitted to the jury, which they held under consideration till near ten p. m when they rendered a virdict of not guilty as charged.

Sunday 18 Nov 1855. Mr Babbitt & Abrams, left for Great Salt Lake City. As for myself I appropriated the day to the service in drawing indictments.

Monday 19 Nov 1855. Court met at ten a. m. The grand jury presented an Indictment against Samuel G. Baker for the murder of Isaac Whitehouse a dunb [dumb] boy. Also indictments against John F. Coffman & Joseph Holman for trading with the Indians.
Alexander Williams U. S. D. Marshall with a possee left for Parowan to arrest Mr S. G. Baker for murder. Judge Drummond attempted to have Enyos confess guilty of manslaughter and waive the trial of willful murder this the Indian would not do but said he was not guilty of either. The judge wished me to come into court without interpreters and introduce evidence to prove that he had confessed

guilty of being at the massacre of Capt Gunnison and party and assisting in the murder and then closing the evidence against him without allowing him the opportunity of proving his innocence or having the interpreters in court to give him any chance for his life. For the judge was determined to have him hung guilty or innocent This arraingement was not complied with.

This evening Mr Conger arrived with the Cal. mail.

Tuesday 20 Nov 1855. Court met at ten a. m. Case of U. S. vs Enyos called up. Bair and Kelting attornies for defence pead not guilty. Witness called only proved that Enyos had frequently said that he was present aiding at the masacre of Capt Gunnison & Company.

Court refused to allaw the defence to prove that Enyos was not there case argued and submitted to the Jury about 9 o'clock p. m.

Wednesday 21 Nov 1855. Court met to recieve the virdict of the Jury which was "Not guilty as charged

Thursday 22 Nov 1855. Court met but no business to day.

Friday 23 Nov 1855. Court met. Grand Jury presented Indictment against James Hart, John and Thomas Hildreth, Andrew Tippetts & Robert Lazenby for murder of Too-ebe an Indian on Meadow Creek This is the same Indian which Levi Abrams was indicted and tried for killing

The court adjourned and I wrote an Indictment against Naw-oo-guich et al. Indians for the murder of Capt Gunnison and party on the 26th Oct 1853

Snowing this evening at dark Robison and King gave an Oyster Supper and party to their boarders and friends this evening at which we eat oysters and danced and danced and eat oyster untill one a. m.

Saturday 24 Nov 1855. Court met at 7½ a. m. No business adjourned and I wrote Indictment against Charles an Indian for the murder of James W. Hunt at the Elk Mountains.

Alexr Williams U. S. D. M. returned from Parowan with Samuel G. Baker prisoner & his wife He being indicted for murder of Isaac White house a dumb boy Myself and Bair have engaged to defend him

Sunday 25 Nov 1855. Engaged investigating Baker's case.

Monday 26 Nov 1855. Court met at ten a. m. I commenced suit against Baker the prisoner and in favor of the perpetual Emmigrating Fund in the sum of $155.20.[55] Mr Bair atty for defence who confessed judgement for the amount of the demand & execution issued.

The Case of The People &c vs Saml G. Baker for murder was taken up Joseph A. Kelting Prosecutor & I & Bair on defence We moved to quash which was argued half a day Court Quashed first count and sustained the second Prisoner Plead not guilty. Jury empannelled and witnesses introduced occupying the rest of the day U. S. D. M. Alex Williams again started for Parowan to summons witnesses on the part of Baker's defence and to execute his property in favor of the P. E. F. Company

This evening Elder Amasa Lyman and a company arrived here from San Bernardino Cal on his way to Great Salt Lake City

Tuesday 27 Nov 1855. The trial of Baker occupied all day.

Wednesday 28th Nov 1855. The trial of Baker Continued The prosecution closed. The Judge took a very active part in the trial against the prisoner and today even took on himself the examination of the witnesses very unbecomingly.

---

55. It seems strange that Stout, defending Baker against a charge of murder, should first open suit against him for failure to pay his debt to the Perpetual Emigrating Fund and later show such compassion for his wife as being "poor and destitute."

Thursday 29 Nov 1855. The trial of Baker continued

Elder T. D. Brown[56] and a company of saints from Great Salt Lake arrived to day bringing me letters from home, all is well there

Friday 30 Nov 1855. The case of Baker was rested the pleas of council heard and the case submitted to the jury

The grand jury dismissed untill the second Monday in January next

Saturday 1 Decr 1855. Court met at nine a. m. and found the jury well hung, but at one p. m. they brought in a virdict of murder in the Second degree, & punishment 10 years in the penetentiary to which the council for the defence (at [crossed out]) claimed untill Monday to file a motion in arrest of judgement.

The traverse Jury was then dismissed untill the 2nd Monday in January next.

The time having drawn nigh when the court would close, we all like officers of hope, concluded to have a fashionable adjournment, so we ordered a good oyster supper, Brandy and cherry brandy to the tune of some ten or twelve bottles. All pitched in court, officers and bystanders and all got gloriously drunk, and went it till mid night.

William Meeks returned from Weber County without finding the witnesses he went after

Sunday 2 Decr 1855. Dull times to day only I was busy writing letters home.

Monday 3 Decr 1855. Court met at 9 a.m. and the motion in arrest of judgement having been waived the Court pronounced sentence on poor Baker and then adjourned — till the Second monday in January.

Meantime Baker was delivered into the hands of the shiriff to be sent to the Penetentiary at Great Salt Lake City.

Thus ended the First Session of the court of 21 days actual Sitting.

Mrs Baker now poor and destitute, (sentenced to ten [crossed out]) bereft of all she had on earth and her husband sentenced for ten years imprisonment, and herself in a peculiar condition and her fullness of times having expired was delivered of a son, whose name was called Douglass Drummond in token of his some day becoming a great man and a leading Democrat

How could it be otherwise (for [crossed out]) born under the heigh auspecies of a Democratic Court while the same day his father was sentenced to the peneten-

---

56. Thomas D. Brown had been sent south in April 1854 as secretary and historian of the Southern Indian Mission. In the statistical account of the group he gives the following details about himself: he was forty-six years old, married, the father of two children, one of the presidents of a Quorum of the Seventy in Salt Lake City, and had come on this journey with *no* wagon, horses or mules, flour, plows, axes, guns, ammunition, cows, bushels of corn or wheat, pistols, cattle, or "fixins." He did take his record book, pen and ink, and kept one of the most detailed and colorful accounts yet found of any Mormon colonizing activity. Thomas D. Brown, "Journal [of the Southern Indian Mission April 14, 1854-May 20, 1855]" (typescript, Utah State Historical Society).

Born in Stewarton, Ayrshire, Scotland, December 16, 1808, Brown had joined the Mormon Church on June 9, 1844. He was then a married man and father of two children. He remained in England as an active missionary for at least two years. In 1852 he was operating a store in Salt Lake City.

At this time Brown had visited briefly with his family in Salt Lake City, having arrived there on October 1, and was en route back to his mission in the south. One year later he was released. By 1860 he had become one of a group of dissenters. On May 20 of that year John D. Lee wrote: ". . . a conspiracy has been detected against Brigham Young, the Man of God. Jno Banks, T D Brown, Clayton, & Candland & others are implicated in the Clan, whose names will hereafter be made publick . . . ." Cleland and Brooks, *A Mormon Chronicle,* I, 255.

In 1870 Brown was affiliated with the Liberal party of Utah as one of their central committeemen. He continued to operate a mercantile establishment under the title of "T. D. Brown & Son."

tiary for ten long years by said Court and then the names of two such conspicuous Democrats as Senator Douglass and Judge Drummond placed upon his head.

Immediately afater the advent of the son the officer started with the father to his long 10 years home in prison

Tuesday 4 Dec 1855. Dull times to day now court is over & nothing to do but to wind up my writing. Dr Hurt Indian agent and a company arrived this evening with Indian presents

Wednesday 5 Dec. Writing all day.

Thursday 6 Dec 1855. Dr Hurt and a company went to Corn Creek to locate an Indian farm

Friday 7 Decr 1855. Gov Young and most of the members of the Legislative assembly arrived today. Recieved letters from home all is well, Saturday & Sunday doing nothing.

Dec 10th 1855. This morning at ten o'clock the Legislature met in the new State House which is however not entirely finished yet the upper room in which the House of Representatives meets is a spacious Hall   feet by   and well finished.

Mr Bullock the chief Clerk of the former House called the House to order and all the members answered to their names except W. A. Hickman of Green River County.

On motion of H. Stout, Jedediah M. Grant was elected Speaker of the House and Hon A. W. Babbitt administered the oath of office to (him [crossed out]) the members by Counties and Hon W. W. Drummond administered the oath to the Speaker

On Motion of E. T. Benson the following persons were elected to the following offices

Thomas Bullock of G. S. Lake County
Chief Clerk
Jonethan Grimshaw of do. assistant Clk
Alfred N. Billings of San Pete Seargent-at-arms
Jacob F. Hutchinson of G. S. L. Messenger
Chandler Holbrook of Millard
      Foreman   and
Rev. Joel H. Johnson of Iron County Chaplain

The speaker then tendered his thanks to the House for the confidence reposed in him in electing him speaker

A committee was then appointed to inform the Council that the House was organized and ready for business.

A committee from the Council then informed the House that the Council was organized and ready for business and that they meet in joint Session to morrow at 2 clock p. m to recieve the Govornor's Message.

Which was concurred in by House House adjd till one p. m. to morrow.

Tuesday 11 Dec 1855. Beautiful snow this morning & still snowing but warm. House met at one o'clock p. m Mr W. A. Hickman Repe from Green River appeared and took his seat

Rules of the former House recieved and 100 copies ordered to be printed on motion of Mr Phelps George Hales was unanimously elected Public Printer

The Freedom of the House be extended to His Excellency Brigham Young, Hon A. W. Babbitt, Secratary Hons J. F. Kinney, G. P. Stiles & W. W. Drummond, Judges of the supreme Court. Hon J. L. Haywood U. S. Marshal Hon R. T. King Probate Judge of Millard County and the Hons Amasa Lyman and Erastus Snow.

The sergeant at arms — was instructed by the Speaker to notify the Council that the House was ready to recieve them in joint session

In a short time the Hon President & members of the Council made their appearance and the two Houses went into joint Session. The Hon. H. C. Kimball president of the Council presiding

The joint committee appointed to wait on His Excellency were instructed to escort him to the Joint Session After which in a short time His Excellency was introduced and presented his annuel message which was read by Mr T. Bullock Chief Clerk of the House.

After which Councilor Wells moved That 1000 compies of the message be printed for the benefit of the Legislative Assembly, which was carried

On motion of Councillor Geo A. Smith a Joint Committee was appointed to take into consideration that part of the Gov message relating to the preliminary measures necessary for calling a convention to form a Constitution for a State Government, and that they be instructed to report thereon at an early day

Whereupon George A, Smith, D. H. Wells, & A Carrington were appointed on the part of the Council.

And W. W. Phelps, E. D Woolley, Hosea Stout, S. W. Richards, J. C. Little and Wm Snow on the part of the House.

On Motion 100 copies of the daily Journal of the two Houses be printed for the use of the members and officers To this Hon Secratary Babbitt objected Saying 20 numbers were sufficient & that the members could read them and pass them around &c.

To Mr Babbitts ungentlemanly interference the Governor replied very spiritedly and quite an altercation ensued.

The House voted that Mr Babbitt insulted them and also the freedom of the two Houses be withdrawn &c[57]

After the above had cooled down the joint session adjourned each House to meet in their seperate rooms to morrow at ten a. m.

Wednesday 12 Dec 1855. This morning Deputy Marshal W. M. Wall who came in some two days ago with Carlos Murry Indicted for murder and had him under guard, at Mr Robison's for some cause left unknown to the Judge and bent his course for Salt Lake

Legislature met at ten a. m The Speaker announced the standing Comts namely On Judiciary, Hosea Stout Jesse C. Little & Aaron Johnson. On Education W. W. Phelps, Hosea Stout & J. C. Wright.

Mr Stout presented a petition from Brigham Young & Thomas Rhoads praying for a grant for a Ranch & herd &c and also gave notice that he intended to introduce a bill on the subject which was carried when the rules were suspended and the bill presented as (H. F. No 1) which after much debate the bill was recieved als the petition and finally read the first time & passed and while undergoing the second reading a message from the Council announced that they had voted to have 100 copies of the names of the members, officers and standing Committees of both Houses printed for the benefit of both Houses

House adjourned till two p. m. This evening the Committee

Thursday 13 Dec 1855. Hon A. W. Babbitt left this morning for Great Salt Lake City.

House met at two p. m. Message from the Council that they had adjourned till Monday at ten a. m.

---

57. This open break between the governor and Secretary Babbitt seemed to confirm Stout's earlier sentiments. Since he had no longer "the freedom of the two Houses" with the legislature, Mr. Babbitt could only return to Salt Lake City.

The speaker called the attention of the House to the Govornor's message, and referred the various subjects therein to the appropriate Committees a part of which I shall record.

That portion relating to the laws of Utah to Committee on Judiciary.

2 That portion relating to the expense incurred by Hon Orson Hyde and others in determining the western boundary between Utah and California, and in locating Carson County to the Committee on Claims.

3 That portion in relation to peace and good will, to the entire House as a Committee of the on the State of the Union

4 And That most important part of the message relating to the admission of the Territory into the Union as a free and independent State, and our political affairs, be cheerfully submitted to the warm hearted Douglass Democrats, believing them competent to do the subject ample justice

The Bill No 1 An act granting a ranch &c was again taken up on its second reading and passed with amendments.

The Bill was then read the third time and passed and ordered to be engrossed and sent to the House for their Concurrence

Mr Haight presented a petition from William W. Willis and 154 others praying that the County Seat of Iron County may be removed from Parowan to Cedar City which was read, recieved and referred to the committee on Counties

Mr Cummings presented a petition from Silas Richards, Assessor and Collector of G. S. L. County praying for lenity to be exercised in relation to to the delinquent taxes of 1855 in that County which was read, recieved and referred to Committee on Revenue

Mr Haight presented a Resolution authorising B. Young to subscribe for two shares in the Deseret Iron Company &c which was read, recieved and referred to the Committee appropriations.

Mr Stout presented a Resolution appropriating money to defray the expenses of opening a road to the Coal banks in San Pete County which was read, recieved and referred to the Committee on Appropriations

The House then adjourned untill next Monday at ten A. M. with instructions for the Several Committees to prepare business for the House on Monday next

Friday 14 Dec 1855. Engaged to day in drafting a bill for taking the Census of this Territory. Weather warm but plnty of snow on the ground and rather sloppy.

Saturday 15 Dec 1855. Engaged with the Committee on the subject of an election for Delegates to form a Constitution

Sunday 16 Decr 1855. The Special weekly mail from Salt Creek to Fillmore arrived this morning bringing me two letters from home bearing the gladsome news that my family is well.

Mr William Meeks U. S. Deputy marshall with two others started south after Indian witnesses to attend Court vs. Carlos Murry at the January term of court.

also Josiah Call U. S Deputy Marshal Started for witness for the same to San Pete and Davis Counties.

Monday 17 Decr 1855. House met at ten a. m. Mr A. Johnson presented a petition from Urich Curtis and 122 others for the right to take one third of the water of Spanish Fork Creek for irrigating, which was read, recieved and referred to Committee on, agriculture &c.

Mr Rockwood presented petition from Joseph Young for a charter for a ferry over Bear River in Weber County & a toll bridge across the Malad which was read, recieved and referred to the Committee on Roads &c

Mr Hobson presented a petition from the inhabitants of Farmington Davis Co. for a city Charter signed by John L. Gleason & 29 others which was read, recieved and referred to the committee on Corporations.

Mr Hickman presented a petition from Luke Johnson, Samuel Benion & William A. Hickman for a grant of a Herd ground in Rush Valley Tooele Co which was read, recieved and referred to the committee on Herding

Mr Wright presented a petition from Brigham Young, Trustee in trust for a Herd ground in Cache Valley, which was read recieved and referred to the Committee on Herding.

Mr Bigler asked and obtained leave to to introduce a bill tomorrow at 11 a. m. to enlarge the boundaries of Nephi City

Mr Brown asked and obtained leave to bring in a bill to morrow at 10 a. m. for a ferry across Green River

Mr Haight Chairman of the Committee on Counties reported "An Act removing the County Seat of Iron County to Cedar City" which was read recieved and laid on the table to come up in its order

Mr J. C. Snow of Committee on Revenue to whom was referred the petition of Silas Richards &c. reported "An Act to amend an act prescribing the manner of assessing & collecting County and Territorial Taxes, which was read, recieved and laid on the table to come up in its order.

The Bill (H. F. No. 2) An Act removing the County seat of Iron County to Cedar City being called up for its first reading, was laid over till the first of January to give the people of parowan a chance to remonstrate.

Message from the council wishing to meet in joint Session which was concurred in whereupon the Council appeared and the two Houses met in joint session Whereupon Councillor G. A. Smith chairman of the joint committee to whom was referred that part of the gov's message relating to the preparatory steps for holding a convention reported "An Act providing for the Enumeration of the inhabitants", also "An Act for holding a convention &c which was read recieved and read the first second and third tines and passed without amendment

Mr Stout moved that 500 copies each of said acts be printed for the use of the two Houses and for distribution as soon as the same should become a law

Joint Session then adjourned the House to meet at 2 p.m.

House met at 2 p. m Mr J. C. Snow presented an account of Hon E. M Green for compiling the Laws of the last session amounting to $103 which was read recieved and referred to the committee on claims.

Mr Stout moved that said committee be instructed to enquire into and make report as to how and in what manner the said laws had been published and indexed carried

The oldest bill on the table being called for The Bill (H. F. No 3) An Act to amend an act entitled An Act prescribing the manner of assessing and collecting territorial & county taxes was taken up and read and referred back to the committee for re-consideration adjd to 10 tomorrow.

Tuesday 18 Decr 1855. Mr Brown reported that he was not prepared to present the bill of which he had given for this morning.

Mr P. H. Y presented a petition from his sweet self. A. P. Rockwood and Jessen [Jesse Hobson], for a grant of Fresh Spring water Island in Great Salt Lake, as a herd ground for twenty years which was read recieved and referred to the committee on Herding

Mr Reese presented an account of expenses incurred by Orson Hyde and others in determining the western boundary of the Territory and in organizing Carson County, which was read, recieved, and referred to the committee on Claims

Mr J. N. Smith reported a memorial to Congress for the establishment of a daily mail from Independence, via Great Salt Lake & Fillmore, to San Francisco which was read, recieved, and referred to the committee on memorials.

Mr Bigler according to notice reported a Bill (H. F. No. 5) An Act to enlarge the boundaries of the city of Nephi which was read, recieved and referred to the committee on Corporations

Mr J. C. Snow of the committee on Revenue reported again "An Act to amend an act entitled An act prescribing the manner of assessing and collecting County and territorial taxes which was read, & Mr Rockwood moved that the report be referred back with instructions to report a Resolution in accordance with the prayer of the petitioner Ayes 10 noes 11

Mr Stout moved That the committee be discharged from further duties on the subject carried Message from the council that the Bill (H F. No 1) An act granting a Ranch & Herd ground to B. Young and Thos Rhoads was concurred in by the Council with amendments and striking out the 4 section

House concurred in the ammendments.

Message from the Council enclosing Resolution appropriating money to Loan M. Green, Read recieved and referred to the committee on Claims Adjd till 2. p. m.

Joint Session met at 2 p. m. Mr Cummings of Committee on Herding reported An Act granting to Brigham Young Trustee &c Cache Valley for Herding & other purposes.

Mr Richards moved the Act be recieved and acted upon forthwith carried

The Bill was then read thru several times and passed

On motion of W. Snow the Bill (H. F. No 1) Act granting a ranch' & Herd ground unto Brigham Young & T. Rhoads was taken up for reconsideration and an amendment offered which was debated verry spiritedly for nearly all the after noon when the amendment was lost Ayes 17 noes 19. Adjourned till 10 a. m.

Wednesday 19 Decr 1855. Message from Council that "An Act granting unto Isaac Bullock and Lewis Robinson the right to errect ferries across Green River & to controll the same" had passed the Council asking the concurrence of the House Said Bill No 1 C. F. was read, and passed the first reading. On the second reading a debate arose which continued all the fore noon with much spirit on both sides. When it passed with the amendments adj'd till ten a. m. tomorrow.

Thursday 20 Decr 1855. House met at ten a. m. Mr Reese presented a communication from Orson Hyde on the subject of traders on the Roads who are acting very dishonestly, and suggesting legislative enactment to check or put a stop to the Evil which was read and referred to the committee on Judiciary.

Mr Woolley of Committee on claims presented a report and resolution appropriating money to Orson Hyde as Commissioner for services in establishing the line between Utah & California which was read recieved and laid on the table to come up in its order.

Mr Woolley of the Committee on Claims to whom was referred the Resolution of the Council appropriating money to E. M. Green for preparing and publishing the laws of former Legislature returned the same fully concurring which was recieved and concurred in

Mr Benson presented report on the petition of U Curtis & 122 others for one third of the waters of Spanish Fork &c with "An Act (H. F. No 6) granting the control of the waters of Spanish Fork in Utah Co. unto Aaron Johnson, William Miller, John Berry and their associates which was read recieved and laid on the table to come up in its order.

Mr Peacock of the Committee on Incorporations reported (H. F. No 5) An Act to enlarge the boundaries of Nephi City not expedient to legislate thereon which was recieved & Mr Bigler asked and obtained leave to withdraw said Bill.

Mr Parker gave notice that he intended on Tuesday next to report a bill for a herd in Davis County. Leave granted.

Mr Wright asked and obtained leave to report An Act (No 7 H. F.) creating and defining the boundaries of Box Elder County which was read recieved and laid on the table to come up in its order

Mr Wright asked and obtained leave to report An Act (H. F. No 8.) creating and defining the boundaries of Bear River County recieved and laid on the table to come up in its order.

Mr Peacock of Committee on Incorporations reported, on the petition of J. S. Gleason & 29 others for 'Incorporations' of Farming Davis Co reported (No 9 H. F.) An Act Incorporating Farmington City in Davis County, read recieved and laid on the table to come up in its order.

Mr J. C. Snow asked and obtained leave to report (No 10 H. F.) An Act granting to Elias Smith, Joseph Cain, Samuel W. Richards and their associates, the right of a herd ground in Juab County read and (laid on [crossed out]) referred to the Committee on Herding.

Resolution appropriating money to Orson Hyde was taken up read three several[58] times and passed.

Mr Stout moved that the Committee on Elections be instructed to inquire into the number and kind of offices which have to be filled by the joint vote of this Legislative Assembly. carried

Mr Rockwood moved that Committee on memorials be instructed to draft memorial to congress for appropriation to defray expenses of determining the boundaries of Utah carried and House adjd till 2 p. m.

2 P. M. The oldest Bill on the table being called for (H. F. No 6) An Act granting the control of waters from Spanish Fork in Utah County to A. Johnson, W. Miller and John Berry and their associates was taken up and read three siveral times and passed, after a long and spirited debate in which the House was nearly equally divided

Message from the Council that they *Did* not concur in the amendments passed by the House to "An Act granting unto Isaac Bullock and Lewis Robinson the right to errect ferries across Green River and to control the same.

Message from the Council inviting the House to meet them in joint session tomorrow at ten A. M. which was concurred in and the House adjourned accordingly.

Friday 21 Decr 1855. Two Houses met in joint session at ten a. m. Councillor D. H. Wells nominated Leonard W. Hardy, of Great Salt Lake City, for Census Agent to take the enumeration of the inhabitants of the Territory of Utah and he was unanimously elected

On motion of Councilr Farr, The Bill (C. F. No 1) entitled "An Aact granting unto Isaac Bullock and Lewis Robinson[59] the right to errect firries across Green River, and to control the same was taken up and referred to the committees of both Houses for their action.

Joint session then adjourned and the House proceeded to business.

Mr Benson presented a petition from John A. Ray, W. W. Phelps and John Eldredge for a ranch and Herd ground in Round Valley in Millard County, read recieved and referred to the committee on Herding

---

58. Stout has evidently been studying his law books and has the idea that the word *several* means *separate* or *complete*. For some reason he uses the phrase "three several times" to indicate that a bill has had its final, third reading.

59. The act granting Isaac Bullock and Lewis Robinson the right to erect ferries across Green River "and to control the same" gives legal recognition to what was already established. The Burton expedition of October preceding reported that they found Lewis Robinson in charge of Fort Bridger and Isaac Bullock of Fort Supply, both under "pres. James Brown."

Brown's account tells how, because of poor health, he left the area on December 14, 1855, and made his way alone through the snow to Ogden. "Having acquired a fourth interest in three ferries on Green River, I arranged with my three partners, Isaac Bullock, Louis Robinson, and W. Hickman, so that I did not have to go there, as my health was not very good . . . ." Brown, *Giant of the Lord*, 390.

Mr Reese asked and obtained leave to report "An Act to attach a portion of Weber and Desert Counties to Carson County read recieved and referred to the Committee on Counties

Mr Cummings from the committe on Herding reported back An Act granting to Elias Smith, Joseph Cain, and Samuel W. Richards, and those whom they may associate with them, the right of a herd ground in Juab County. report recieved and laid on the table to come up in its order

Mr Woolley asked and obtained leave to report "An Act providing for the appointment of a Supreme Court Reporter, read recieved and laid on the table to come up in its order.

Mr Wm Snow of the Committee on memorials reported the memorials to Congress to establish a daily mail from Independence, Mo to San Francisco Cal which was read and adopted.

The oldest Bill on the table being Called for (H. F. No 7) An act creating and defining the boundries of Box Elder County, was read and referred to the committee on Counties

The Bill (H. F. No 8.) An Act creating & defining the boundaries of Bear River County was read and referred to the Committee on Counties

The Bill (H. F. No. 9.) An act to incorporate the City of Farmington in Davis County was taken up in its order

On motion of Mr Stout said Bill was laid on the table till the second Monday in January next

The Bill (H. F. No 10) An Act granting to Elias Smith, Joseph Cain, and Samual W. Richards and those whom they may associate with them the right to a Herd ground &c came up in its order was read three several times and passed.

The Bill (H. F. No 13) An Act providing for the appointment of a Supreme Court Reporter came up in its order and was read the first time and laid on the table indefinately House then adjourned till tomorrow at ten a. m.

Saturday 22 Decr 1855. Stormy night last, and this morning there was a deep snow on the ground while my bed room had a Carpet of snow some two inches deep. and snow still falling fast

House met at ten a. m. Message from the Council that the Bill (C. F. No 1) an act granting I Bullock & L. Robinson the right to errect ferries &c had again passed the Council and asking the concurrence of the House

Mr Woolley moved that although said bill has come to the House through an unusual channel, as it properly was the duty of the chairman of the joint committee, to whom it was referred in joint session, yet we will waive all technicallities, and consider the bill as amended on its merits Carried

The Bill was read the first time and passed. and on its second reading was again amended and passed

The Bill then passed its third reading and again sent to the council for their concurrence

Mr Phelps moved that the Committee on memorials be instructed to bring in a memorial to Congress for an appropriation of $25-000 for the purpose of making a passable mail route from this City to Carson Valley where it will intersect the Cal road now making to Sacramento &c Carried

Mr Cummings of Committee on Herding reported sundry bills to wit.

The Bill (H. F. No 11) act granting to James Brown et. al. Ogden Valley for a herd ground which was read, recieved & passed its three several readings

Also (H. F. No 4) An Act granting unto Phineas H. Young et. al, Fremont's Island in Great Salt Lake for herding and other purposes read three several times and passed.

Also An Act (H. F. No 14) granting to Brigham Young, Wilford Woodruff, Luke Johnson James W. Cummings Samuel Benion, William A. Hickman, Jesse C.

Little and Claudius V. Spencer, Rush Valley for a herd ground and other purposes was read three several times and passed.

House adjourned till Monday at ten a. m.

Mail from Salt Lake came this evening with letters from Sweet Home.

Sunday 23 Decr 1855. Weather intensly cold, but clear. Writing letters home to day.

Monday 24 Decr 1855. House met at ten a. m. and no business being on the tables the House adjourned till ten a. m to morrow.

The California Mail arrived to day but not bringing news of any importance except the carrier was nearly frozen by travelling in the cold weather which is still growing colder.

Tuesday 25 Decr 1855. Cold Christmass but still times No guns firing no boys hooping No petty fandangos, No brilliant cotillion parties Every one minding his own business. and perhaps some few wife hunting or rather hunting the raw material House met at ten a. m.

Mr Benson presented a petition from Thos H. Clark sen and 50 others praying for the incorporation of Grant City, in Tooele County which was read, recieved and referred to the Committee on Incorporations

Mr Bigler according to notice reported "An Act granting unto the citizens of Nephi the right to a Herd ground which was read recieved and laid on the table to come up in its order.

Mr Wright Chairman of the Committee on Elections who was instructed to ascertain the number and kink of offices now vacant which have to be filled by the joint vote of the Legislative Assembly reported the same which report was read & recieved

Mr Parker asked and (recieved [crossed out]) obtained leave to introduce a bill tomorrow, granting a ranch and herd ground in Weber Valley Davis County.

The Bill (H. F. No 15) "An Act granting unto the citizens of Nephi the right to a herd ground" was taken up and read the first time and referred to to the Committee on Herding

Mr Stout asked and obtained leave to report "An Act granting unto Geo Peacock, John Price, John Reese, John Williams, and their associates, a herd ground in San Pete County" which was read and referred to the Committee on Herding

Mr Phelps moved that we invite the Council to meet the House in joint Session at 10 a. m on Wednesday the 2nd of January to fill all offices necessry to be filled by the joint vote of the Legislative Assembly carried

House adjourned till tomorrow at 10 a. m A party for all Fillmore was had at the State House in the evening which lasted till midnight which passed off verry agreeably. Representatives Hall is a fine spacious room for cotillions where 8 can be worked off at once

Wednesday 26 Decr 1855. House met at ten a. m. Message from the Council "Your wish for a joint session on Wednesday, 2nd proximo at ten a. m. is concurred by the Council"

The following Bills are also concurred in (H. F. No 14) An act granting unto Brigham Young Wilford Woodruff, Luke Johnson et. al. Rush Valley for a herd ground and other purposes.

Also (H. F. No 4 An act granting unto Phineas H. Young, Albert P. Rockwood and Jesse Hobson, Fremont's Island in Great Salt Lake for herding and other purposes.

Also (H. F. No 11) An Act granting unto James G. Browning et. al. Ogden Valley for a herd ground

Also (H. F. No 6 An Act granting unto Aaron Johnson William Miller, John Berry and their associates the rights of water from Spanish Fork river in Utah County.

Also your amendment to (C. F. No 1) An act granting to Isaac Bullock and Lewis Robinson the right to errect ferries across Green River and to control the same

Also the accompanying bill (No 3. C. F.) An act granting unto Ormus E. Bates, Orson Pratt sen, and their associates the right of ground for herding and other purposes" has this day passed the Council and is submitted for your concurrence."

The said bill was then read the first time and passed, and on the second reading reading was amended and passed and sent back to the council for their concurrence where the bill was finally lost.

(On motion [crossed out]) Mr Woolley presented a petition from himself Levi E. Riter and Vincent Shirtliff for the right of a herd ground in Utah County which was read recieved and (laid on [crossed out]) referred to the committee on herding.

Mr Johnson moved that there be a special committee appointed to act jointly with a like Committee from the Council for the purpose of drawing an approximate map of this Territory for the Benefit of the Legislative Assembly seconded and carried House then adjourned till ten a. m to morrow.

Thursday 27 Decr 1855. The weather has been very much moderated and is now very pleasant. House met at ten a. m.

Mr Peacock of Committee on Incorporations reported "An Act Incorporating Gra [Grantsville] City in Tooele County (H. F. No 17) which was read & laid on the table to come up in its order

Mr Haight of Committee on Counties reported, as a substitute for the Bill enlarging the boundaries of Carson County, said substitute (H. F. No 12, An Act to attach a portion of Weber & Desert County to Carson which was read, recieved and laid on the table to come up in its order

Mr Haight also reported on the two Bills creating and defining the boundaries of Box Elder & Bear River Counties, an amendment and recommending Bear river County to be changed to Malad read recieved and laid on the table to come up in its order

Mr Stout of Committy on judiciary reported on the communication of Orson Hyde, inexpedient to legislate thereon read recieved and Committee discharged from any further duty thereon

Mr Cummings of the Committee on Herding reported the following Bills granting a Herd Ground to T. J. Thurstin et. al. (H. F. No 18) also (H. F. No 19) granting to John Stoker et. al. a Herd ground. also (H. F. No 20) granting to George A Smith et. al. a Herd ground which said Bills were severally read and laid on the table to come up in their order.

Mr Rockwood presented a claim of Daniel Carn, of $931.66. for Services as Warden of the Penetentiary which was read and referred to the Committee on Claims.

The oldest Bill on the table being called for (H. F. No 17 "An act incorporating Grant City in Tooele County and was read the first time and referred back to the committee for redrafting.

The Bills (H. F. Nos 12 & 7 & 8 were taken up and referred to the Committee on Counties

Mr Phelps of the Committee on Education reported in expedient to legislate thereon, report was accepted

The Bill (H. F. No 18) An act granting unto Thos J. Thurstin, J. M. Grant et. al. a Herd ground and other purposes, in Weber Valley was taken up and read three several times and passed. The Bill (H. F. No 19) an act granting unto John Stoker, William Smith, John W. Hess and Abiah Wadsworth the North End of Weber Valley for a herd ground and other purposes which was read three several times and passed.

House adjourned till to morrow at ten a. m.

Friday 28 Decr 1855. High winds last night which was accompanied with snow which again filled my bed room and spread another blanket on my bed, but clear calm and pleasant in the morning.

(House met at ten A. M. [crossed out])

This evening Elder Erastus Snow with the rest of the Home missionaries, returned from Iron County (this [crossed out]) preparitory to holding a general Conference in this place to morrow and next day.

(Sunday & Sunday. [crossed out])

House met at ten a. m Message from the Council that the Bill (H. F. No 10) An act granting to Chas Smith, Joseph Cain and Samuel W. Richards and those whom they may associate with them, the right of a herd ground in Juab County, had been concurred in with ammendments which bill was laid on the table to come up in its order

Also that the Bill (No 5 C. F.) "An Act appropriating money for Educational purposes and defining certain duties of the Chancellor and Board of Regents of the University of the State of Deseret," had passed the Council, and is submitted for concurrence" which Bill was concurred in

Also that the Bill (No 4 C. F.) "An Act granting unto B. F. Johnson and Isaac Morley, the right of controling the district of Santa Quin or Summit Creek with its natural facilities, establishing a herd ground &c" had passed the Council as is submitted for concurrence," which Bill was concurred in.

Also that the Bill (No 8. C. F.) "An Act. granting and confirming unto the University of the State of Deseret, certain land claims therein had passed the Council, which Bill was concurred in

Mr Brown asked and obtained leave to introduce, "An Act granting to F. D. Richards Alexr Brown, Daniel Spencer & Wm Brown a herd ground (H. F. No 21) read recieved and referred to the Committee on Herding

Mr Woolley presented a petition from Gilbert Webb, W. H. Hooper,[60] T. S. Williams D. Candlin and others for a Herd ground in Lone Rock Valley, which was read, recieved and referred to the Committee on Herding

Mr Cummings moved that the petitioners for a Herd ground in Round Valley have leave to with draw their petition — carried,

The Bill (H. F. No 19 was taken up on its third reading and passed, Mr Cummings of the Committee on Herding reported "An Act (No 22 H F) granting to E. D. Woolley et. al. Lone valley for a Herd ground and other purpes, read recieved and laid on the table to come up in its order

Mr Rockwood presented a petition from Levi Abram, praying that his name may be changed to Abraham E. Levi read, and referred to the Committee on Petitions

60. William H. Hooper was born December 25, 1813, at Warwick Manor, Eastern Shore, Maryland. In 1832 he came west intending to set up in business at the Galena, Illinois, lead mines, but lost his money in the 1838 panic. From 1844 to 1849 he was engaged in river traffic on the Mississippi, coming to Salt Lake City in 1850 with Holliday & Warner, merchants. In 1852 Hooper joined the Mormon Church and married Mary Ann Knowlton, by whom he had nine children, three sons and six daughters.

In 1853, as a result of a successful business venture in California, he set up a mercantile business with John Reese; for a time he was affiliated with Thomas S. Williams. In 1855 Hooper was made a member of the legislature, and in that capacity was at this time petitioning for a herd ground. In 1857 he was appointed to fill the position of secretary of state in place of A. W. Babbitt, deceased, but relinquished the position to John Harnett, the government appointee. In 1859 he was sent to Washington, D. C., as a delegate to Congress, which position he held for several terms.

Hooper was one of the founders of Z. C. M. I. in 1869 and served as president of that institution from 1877 until his death on December 30, 1882. See Stanford Cazier, "The Life of William Henry Hooper, Merchant Statesman" (Master's thesis, University of Utah, 1956).

House sent message to the Council to meet in joint session to day at 2 p. m. which was agreed to by the Council.

The oldest Bill on the the table taken up (H. F. No 20) An Act granting to G. A. Smith et. al. a herd ground in Utah County was taken up and read the first time & passed   House adjourned till 2 p. m.

Two Houses met in joint session at 2 p. m. on Motion of Councilor (Farr [crossed out]) L. Snow, the Bill "An Act creating and defining the boundaries of Carson, Box Elder, and Malad counties was taken up read the first time and passed.

Joint session adjourned to Monday next 10½ a. m.

Saturday 29 Decr 1855. Conference to day but I did not attend

Sunday 30 Decr 1855. Cold day. The mail did not arrive till late this evening having been detained one day to our great disappointment.

Monday 31 Decr 1855. The Two Houses met in joint Session at ten ½ a. m. An Act creating and defining the boundaries of Carson, Box Elder, and Malad Counties was resumed on its second reading when said bill was referred to a Special Committee —

Councilor Carrington reported "An act to amend an act in relation to Marshals and attorneys was was read recieved and adopted.

An address was then read on Marriage and Morals in Utah, which was written by P. P. Pratt Chaplain of the Council, after which it was ordered to be published in the "Deseret News"

On motion of E. D. Woolley the thanks of the Assembly were tendered to Mr Pratt for his invaluable lecture on morality

Adjourned till 2 p. m. to the respective Houses.

House met accordingly. Message from the Council that the act (H. F. No 18) granting to Thomas J. Thurston et. al. Herd ground &c had been concurred with amendments, which said amendments were concurred in by the House

Mr Peacock of Comt on Corporations on (H. F. No 17) reported inexpedient to Legislate thereon which report was accepted.

Mr Cumming of Committee on Herding. on the Bills granting to George Peacock et. al. Herd ground in San Pete County, and Bill granting to the Citizens of Juab County a herd ground, reported inexpedient to legislate thereon

On Motion of Mr Woolley the Bill granting to citizens of Juab County a herd ground was referred back

Mr Benson presented a petition of W. W. Phelps & Hugh McKinney for a herd ground & Ranch north of Kamas prairie which was read recieved and referred to the Committee on herding.

Mr Benson presented a petition of Sidney Roberts et. al. for right of turning water out of Big Cottonwood to propel machinery for making paper, read and referred to committee on trade &c.

Mr W. Snow of the Committee on the petition of L Abram to have his name changed reported inexpedient to Legislate thereon which report was discussed and referred back —

Mr Johnson of the Committee on Roads &c reported (H. F. No 23) An Act granting to Brigham Young sen and Joseph Young sen the right to establish and control ferries on Bear River and Bridge on Malad read recieved and laid on the table to come up in its order.

The oldest bill on the table being called for (H. F. No 20) An Act granting to Geo A. Smith et. al. a herd ground in Utah County was taken up on its second reading and passed also passed its third reading

The Bill (H. F. No 10 "An Act granting to Elias Smith &c was taken up on the question of the concurrence with the amendments made by the Council and concurred in.

The Bill (H. F. No 22). An Act. granting to Edwin D. Woolly, Levi E. Riter, Vincent Shurtleff and Enoch Reese, Lone Rock Valley for a herd ground and other purposes was taken up and read three several times and passed.

The Bill (No 23 H. F.) An Act granting to B. Young sen & Jos Young sen &c was taken up & read three several times & passed.

House adjourned till Wednesday at 10 a. m to meet the Council in joint session.

Tuesday 1 January 1856. Hail the new year, but O the dull times in Fillmore City. My long tarry here is sinking me *ennui* and recalling vivid rememberance of "Sweet Home". Still we have good cold weather and plenty of snow. This evening there was a new year's ball at the State House to ball I did not attend choosing to spend my time in solitude and my own sober reflections. In fact my mind has been surfeited with a rush of business for the last two or three months

Wednesday 2 Jan 1856. The two Houses met in joint session at ten a. m. The special joint committee to whom was referred the Bill on counties reported "An Act in relation to counties which was read, recieved and passed its first reading The Bill was taken up on its second reading and passed with several amendments, adding several new counties and finally passed its third reading said Bill provides for the organization of some 8 new counties.

Mr Cumming presented a "Resolution in relation to the election of the Chancellor and Board of Regents and Treasurer of the University of the State of Deseret, which was read and duly passed.

The following officers were then elected by the joint vote of the House.

For Great Salt Lake County
Elias Smith Judge of Probate
W. W. Phelps Notarie Public

Weber County
Jonathan Browning Probate Judge
William Critchlow Notarie Public

Davis County
Joseph Holbrook Probate Judge
James Leithead Notarie Public

Tooele County
Peter Maughn Probate Judge
Eli B. Kelsey Notarie Public

Utah County
Dominicus Carter Probate Judge
Aaron Johnson Notarie Public

Juab County
George W. Bradley Probate Judge
Zimri H. Baxter Notary Public

San Pete County
George Peacock Probate Judge
John Eager Notarie Public

Millard County
Thomas R. King Probate Judge
William Felshaw Notary Public

Iron County
James Lewis Probate Judge
Calvin C. Pendleton Notarie public

Green River County
Isaac Bullock Probate Judge
Lewis Robinson Notarie Public

Carson County
Orson Hyde Probate Judge
Thomas Pitt Notarie Public

Cache County
Bryant Stringham Probate Judge
Andrew Moffitt Notary Public

Malad County
John P. Barnard Probate Judge
James Fradshaw Notarie Public

Box Elder County
Jonathan C. Wright Probate Judge
Samuel Smith Notarie Public

Washington County
John D. Lee Probate Judge
Charles W. Dalton Notarie Public

Beaver County.
Lorin Babbitt Judge of Probate
Ross R. Rogers Notarie Public

Cedar County
Allen Weeks Judge of Probate
Claiborne Thomas Notarie Public

Territorial Treasurer Daniel McIntosh
Auditor of Public accounts
James W. Cummings.

District Atty. 2nd Dist
Almirin Grow
Territorial Marshal Alex McRae
Road Commissioner Thos D. Brown
Surveyor Genl Jesse W. Fox
Librarian   William C. Stains
Code Commissioner William Snow
Atty Genl Albert Carrington
Recorder of Marks & Brands
   William Clayton
Chancellor of the University of
   Deseret Albert Carrington

The Election being over

Board of Regents
Daniel H. Wells
Orson Hyde
George A. Smith
Hosea Stout
W. W. Phelps
Lorenzo Snow
Willford Woodruff
Elias Smith
Samuel W. Richards
Parley P. Pratt
Orson Pratt
William Willis
David Fullmer Treasurer

The Bill H. F. No 2) An Act removing the County seat of Iron County to Cedar City was taken up to be considered in joint session and after some discussion

On Motion of Mr Cummings the bill was laid on the table indefinitely. When on Motion George A. Smith said bill was immediately taken up and the presentor had leave to withdraw said Bill.

Mr Rockwood presented An Act amending an ordinance creating a surveyor General's office &c which was read and finally passed.

Mr P. H. Young presented petition of sundry persons for Herd ground in Box Elder County recieved and referred to Committee on Herding

On Motion Mr Wright the subject of the Coal Bed in San Pete County was referred to the Committee on Corporations

This session lasted till about 4 p. m. without dinner or recess. so after the foregoing business was done the joint session adjourned to meet in their respective Houses tomorrow at *10 A. M.*

Thursday 3 January 1856. House met at ten. a. m.   Mr Woolley presented Resolution appropriating money to Danl Carn Warden of the penetentiary &c Read Recieved & laid on the table to come up in its order

Also Resolution appropriating money to James Otis Biglow &c Read Recieved and laid on the table to come up in its order

Message from the Council that the Act (H. F. No 23) granting to B. Young *sen* & Jos Young *sen* &c had passed the council with amendments. which were concurred in by the House.

Mr Little of committee on Military reported (H. F. No 24) An Act to provide for the further organization of the militia &c Recieved and 100 copies ordered to be printed.

Mr Parker asked and obtained leave to introduce An Act granting unto Heber C. Kimball, John D. Parker a ranch and herd ground Read, recieved and referred to committee on herding.

House adjourned to tomorrow 10 a. m.

Friday 4th January 1856. House met at ten a. m.   Message from the Council that the Bill (H. F. No 19) "An act granting to John Stoker, William Smith et. al. the north end of Weber Valley for a herd ground and other purposes" had passed the Council with amendments which amendments were negatived by the House ayes 10 noes 13.

Also Bill (H. F. No 22) "An act granting to E. D. Woolley et. al. Lone Rock Valley for a herd ground and other purposes" had passed the council with several amendments which several amendments were concurred in by the House.

Also Bill (H. F. No 20) An act granting to G. A. Smith et. al. a herd ground in Utah County had passed the Council with amendments which several amendments were concurred in by the House

Mr Cummings of Committee on Herding reported (H. F. No 26) An Act granting to W. H. Hooper et. al. a herd ground in Lone Rock Valley read recieved and laid on the table to come up in its order

Mr J N. Smith presented (H. F. No 27) An Act to amend an act entitled "An act in relation to County recorders, and the acknowledgement of instruments of writing which was read recieved and laid on the table to come up in its order

Mr Peacock presented (H. F. No 28) An to amend the charter of Manti City which was read and laid on the table to come up in its order

The Resolution appropriating money to Daniel Carn &c was taken up on its first reading when Woolley asked and obtained leave to withdraw it for further consideration

The Resolution appropriating money to James Otis Bigelow &c taken up and referred to the committee on appropriations to be put in the general appropriation Bill.

The Bill (H. F. No 26) An Act granting to W H Hooper et. al. &c was taken up and read three several times and passed.

The Bill (No 27 H. F) An Act to amend "An act &c was taken and referred to the committee on Judiciary.

The Bill (H. F. No 28) An Act amending the charter of Manti City for the first reading and was negatived

Mr Parker presented (H. F. No 29) An Act incorporating the Davis County Canal Company" which was read recieved and referred to the committee Corporations

The House then adjourned till tomorrow at ten a. m.

Saturday 5 Jan. 1856. House met at ten a. m. Mr Stout of committee on Judiciary reported back (H. F. No 27) An act to amend "An act in relation to County recorders, & the acknowledgement of instruments of writing and "An act pertaing to the duties of county surveyors, and recommended its passage which was recieved and laid on the table to come up in its order

Mr Peacock of committee on corporations reported "An Act (H. F. No 29) incorporating the Davis County Canal company" and recommended its passage which was read recieved and laid on the table to come up in its order

Mr Cummings on Herding reported (H F No 25) An Act granting a herd ground to H. C. Kimball & J. D. Parker and recommended its passage which was read recieved and laid on the tabl to come up in its order

The oldest Bill on the table being called for (H. F. No 27) was taken up on its first reading and on motion the Bill was negatived, and the presentor had leave to withdraw the Bill

Message from the Council requesting a joint session on Monday next at ten a. m which was concurred in.

Also that (H. F. No 26) An act granting to W. H. Hooper et al &c" had passed the Council with amendments which said amendments were concurred in.

The Bill (H. F. No 29) An act incorporating the Davis County canal Company was taken up and read three several times and passed.

Mr Woolley of claims reported back Resolution appropriating money to D. Carn &c which was read and referred to Committee on appropriations

Mr Rockwood moved that the Committee on Memmorials be instructed to memorialize Congress for an appropriation to defray the expenses of the Warden of the penetentiary. carried

The Bill (H. F. No 25) was taken up and read three several times and passed.

House then adjourned till Monday at ten a. m. to meet in joint session

This evening Mr Judge Kinney & Stiles T. S. Williams and a large company arrived from Salt Lake.[61]

The probate Court of this County called a special session of said Court & grand jury which found a Bill of indictment vs Judge W. W. Drummond and his Negro Cato for an assault on the Body of Levi Abrams with intent to kill. & the Hon. Judge & his servant was arrested about 9 P. M. thereon

Sunday 6 Jan 1856. Recieved last evening and this morning Eight letters from home and others all bearing good news. Weather warm clear and pleasant. Writing letters to my family

Monday 7 January 1856. This morning at half past Eight the probate Court met on the case of the People vs Drummond Mr Grow council on the part of the People and myself on the part of the Defence. Case adjourned till tomorrow at 9 a m

Joint session met at ten a. m. The Bill (H. F. No 19) "An act granting to John Stoker, Wm Smith, John W. Hess and Abijah Wardsworth the North end of Weber Valley for a herd ground as passed by the Council with amendments, and the Bill was read as passed the council and the bill (first [crossed out]) was finally amended and passed three several times

Mr Harrington of the Committee on Incorporations (Joint) reported "An Act to Incorporate the San Pete Coal Company" recieved and read three several times and passed with some few amendments.

Mr Pratt of Joint Committee on Education reported "An act adopting the Deseret Alphabet and Legalizing the laws of Utah, &c printed in the same" and also reported adversly which was recieved and the Bill laid on the table indefinitely

Mr Peacock presented Act Incorporating Farmington &c read debated and referred back adjourned to Wed ten a. m.

Supreme Court met in the Council chamber at ten a. m. Court appointed myself attorney for U. S. pro. tem.

The case of Moroni Green vs The people of the U. S. &c taken up on Writ of Error from the 1 Judl Dist was called up and Mr Green not appearing the forfeiture of his reconizance was taken at 3 p. m. Court met again Mr Judge W. W. Drummond left the Supreme Bench to present a petition to the court for a writ of Habeas Corpus to relieve His Honor & his servant Cato from imprisonment on indictment from the probate Court as aforsaid on the ground that the probate Court had no criminal jurisdiction which was allowed instanter by Ch Just Kinney as a Writ of right but objected to by Judge Stiles who wished to hold it under advisement when the court adjourned till to morrow

Tuesday 8 Jan 1856. This morning the case of People vs Judge Drummond and cato his servant came up before his Honor Chief Justice Kinny on Habus Corpus.

---

61. With the arrival of Chief Justice John F. Kinney, Associate Justice George P. Stiles, and the group of attendants, there opened two weeks of contest and controversy in the courts. Officials were humiliated, ridiculed, and intimidated, some of them almost at the mercy of mob action. Of the arrest of Judge Drummond and his negro, Cato, Hickman wrote:

I was then elected representative of the [Green River] County. The Territorial Legislature then met at Filmore, one hundred and fifty miles south of Salt Lake City. . . .

During the sitting of the Legislature, a Jew, by the name of Abrams, had a difficulty with him, in which Judge Drummond threatened to kill him. The other two Judges were holding a term of the Supreme Court, and I thought this a good chance to get even with him, so I got the Jew to swear out a writ, and had him arrested. The Jew got me to prosecute the case for him. I got another attorney to assist me, as I learned Drummond had employed two. [Stout lists the attorneys as himself, Kelting, and A. Miner for Judge Drummond and J. C. Little, Hickman, Thomas S. Williams, and Almerin Grow for the "people."] We went into the case, and in spite of all opposition, showed him up in his proper light. We went into his character and general course, which we made look bad enough. After working at this four days, we got the Jew to withdraw the prosecution by Drummond paying the costs. (Hickman, *Brigham's Destroying Angel*, 110-12.)

The petition of Judge Drummond befre the Supreme Court yesterday being abandoned as the two Judges Kinney & Stiles could not agree, Judge Drummond therefore applied to his Honor the Chief Justice who granted the writ and hence the case came up this morning.

Myself, Kelting & A. Miner councillors for his Honor & Cato and Little, Hickman T. S. Williams & Grow councillors for the defence.

Objections being made to Mr Grow as an Attorney at Law, He being suspended by Judge Kinney last October at Great Salt Lake but since elected Territorial District Attorney for the Second District, now came forward as such to defend the right of the probate Court, to exercise criminal jurisdiction. So the Question arose whether Mr Grow being suspended from practicing law, by the District Court and then by the joint Vote of the Legislative Assembly elected Territorial District Attorney had a right to act as such without being restored to practice by the Court suspending him, which Chief justice Kinney decided that he could not therefore Mr Grow had to withdraw.

The defence raised several objections to the papers in the case which afeter long debate was overruled.

When the merits of the case was finally reached in the afternoon and debated untill night when the court adjourned till tomorrow

This evening there was another party at the State House.

The Excitement created by the said Writ of Habeus Corpus testing as it would the civil and criminal jurisdiction of the probate Court, had to day attracted the entire attention of the community and Chief Justice Kinney Presiding in the case while Drummond with his negro Cato were plaintiffs and of course engaged also, leaving Judge Stiles unoccupied

The Supreme Judiciary of fair Utah was now in rather a novel situation which caused the day to pass off without the supreme Court meeting as per adjournment on yesterday.

Wednesday 9 January 1856. This morning the Supreme Court should have met at the State House but while the three Judges were wending their way thither, Judge Drummond still being under the aforesaid arrest and virtually in the hands of the officer was intercepted on the way by a *Possee* who informed him that they had orders not to suffer him to pass out of the fort and so stoped him

This entirely took the Judiciary aback. A parley ensued, the two other Judges remonstrated, The Possee were inexhorable. They would not let Judge Drummond go. So the place of the meeting of the Supreme Court was changed to Mr Kings House & the three Judges repaired there to undergo a still worse humiliation for then the Posse would not let Drummond sit on the Bench and again the wheels of Judicial proceedings were brought to a stand still and the Supreme Court was certainly in a "fix" and not knoing exactly what to do adjourned till next Friday

Now comes another tack in the history of the Judiciary. The time had now come to commence opperations on the Habeas Corpus Case, Drummond & his negro vs "The People" &c Chief Justice Kinney repaired to the school house to hear the closing aruguments for and against the Powers of the probate Courts as on that Question alone hung the lawful or unlawful imprisonment of His Hon. Judge Drummond & Cato. It now seemed that the death Knell of the probate Courts would inevitably be sounded, as Judge Kinney's known and avowed opinion was adversely to the powers of the Probate Courts, yet their time had not come for Judge Drummond on the meeting of Kinneys Court with drew the suit and thus the Probates lives.

This ended the affair of the Habeus Corpus & also ended the prosecution against Judge Drummond.

During the progress of the above very interesting and novel proceeding in the Judicial department the Legislative Assembly was doing business as though nothing was happening out side the Halls.

Joint session met at ten a. m.

Mr Peacock reported (H. F. No 9) An Act to incorporate the city of Farmington" that further action was inexpedient which was recieved and the Bill and petition withdrawn by the presentor.

The Bill (No 11 C. F.) An Act amending, confirming and legalizing 'An ordinance incorporating the Pertual Emigrating Fund Company" was taken up and read three several times and after some amendments passed.

The Bill (H. F. No 24) An Act to provide for the further organization of the militia" was taken from the file of the House, and made the order of the day for Friday next at ten a. m. in joint session.

Councillor Snow, of joint Committee on Herding reported as a substitute for the Bill (H. F. No 21) An Act granting a herd ground to J. C. Wright, E. H. Pierce, P. H. Young, Lo Farr, C. W. Hubbard, D. Spencer S. Smith, and J. D. Reese was read, recieved and read the first time & Lorenzo Snow was prefixed to the names in said Bill, and all the other names stricken out except Pierce & Hubbard after which the Bill passed its several readings and passed as amended

Councillor Harrington of the joint Committee on incorporations reported back Bill (H. F. No 29) An Act incorporating the Davis County Canal Company which was recieved and read three several times and passed.

Mr Cummings reported An Act granting to W. W. Phelps & H. McKinney a Herd ground which was recieved and read three several times and passed. Joint session adjourned till Friday at 10 a. m and the House to meet to morrow at 10 a. m.

This evening there was a mass meeting to take into consideration the expediency of establishing a daily express from Independence Mo via Utah to San Francisco Cal The prevailing feeling was favorable to such an enterprize

Thursday 10 January 1856. House met at ten a. m. Mr Rockwood presented a petition from Joseph A. Kelting for an appropriation of $152 for services as prosecuting attorney pro. tem. for the First and second districts which was read, recieved and referred to the committee on claims

Mr Rockwood presented (H. F. No 31) An Act pertaining to corporations and grants, which was read, recieved and referred to the committee on Judiciary

Mr Johnson presented Bill (H. F. No 32) An Act to provide for damage done by water, which was read, recieved, and referred to the committee Judiciary. House adjourned till Saturday.

Friday 11 January 1856. Joint Session met at ten a. m.

Bill (H. F. No 24) An Act to provide for the further orgainization of the militia was taken up in its order and read the first time and passed.

On the second reading of the bill after several amendments the Bill was referred to a special committee consisting of O. Pratt, S. W. Richards and C. Spencer.

Councillor Carrington presented "Resolution concerning furnishing a certified copy of court records and papers" which was read, recieved and read three several times and passed

Mr Hickman presented "An Act creating and defining the boundaries of Shambip County[62] which was read recieved and read three several times and passed

---

62. The name of Shambip County derives from a Goshute Indian term meaning "rush" or coarse, swamp grass. This county was cut from Tooele County and included chiefly the area known as Rush Valley. Its boundaries as defined here were "all that portion of Tooele County bounded on the south by Juab County; on the east by Cedar County to where it will strike a direct line running west on the summit of the dividing ridge between Tooele and Rush valleys; thence west to St Mary county; thence south along the line of said county to Juab County."

By 1860 the census numbered a population of 162 for Shambip County with farms worth, in all, $2,320, and livestock in the value of $8,200. Following the death of Luke Johnson in December 1861, the legislature, in an act approved January 17, 1862, required the administrator of his estate to deliver to the probate judge of Tooele County "the seal and all the books, records, documents, and other papers pertaining to the probate and county courts," but none seem to be extant. Historical Records Survey, *Inventory of . . . Tooele County,* 10.

Adjourned till 4 p. m and net accordingly

Mr Richards presented the report of the librarian, which was read and recieved and the accompanying claiming $216 was referred to the committee on appropriations

Mr Cummings presented "An Act granting to J. G. Bigler et. al. a herd ground in Juab Valley, which was read, recieved, and, read three several times, and passed.

Mr Woolley presented "An Act in relation to the Deseret Iron Works, which was read, recieved, and read three several times and passed.

Mr Woolley on Claims reported adversly to granting the petition of Joseph A. Kelting for an appropriation for services as prosecuting attorney pro tem Report was recieved and the petitioner had leave to withdraw his petition

A communication from S. M. Blair on the subject of manurfacturing oils was read and referred to the joint committees on trade &c

The subject of making a road from the South Pass to Carson Valley was referred to the Joint Committees on Incorporations.

On Motion of G. A. Smith the Committees on petitions were instructed to repor a memorial to Congress for an appropriation of lands for cities, towns &c Adjourned till to morrow at 10 a. m.

The Supreme Court also met at ten a. m. The case of "Green vs The people &c" was brought up. The forfeiture of Green's recognizance was set aside for cause shown Next came a motion by myself to dismiss on the grounds that the transcript of the record of the court below, being so contradictory and imperfect that the plff in Error had not brought up a case

This motion after being argued was overruled & the defence required to join in Error or else have the priviledge to perfect the plff's papers.

This of course I was not willing to do as to perfect the plff's papers was only to operate against my own interest so I gave notice accordingly, and also that I would defend the suit no farther, nor disgrace myself submitting to such unlawful and unjust rulings of court.

Chief Justice Kinney being sick was not on the bench.

I left and went to the Legislature and the Court adjourned.

Saturday 12th January 1856. Supreme Court met at ten a. m still on the Case of Greene, and Judge Kinney still sick I had left and met with the Legislature not intending to defend the case any farther, but Mr Carrington the Attorney General wishing to have the case defended requested me to attend with him as he did not understand its merits which I did. Mr Babbitt made his plea and the court adjourned till 4 p. m. when Mr Carrington replied followed by Mr (Carrington [crossed out]) Babbitt when Court adjourned till Monday to deliver the opinion of the Court.

William Meeks U. S. Deputy Marshal, returned from the Santa Clara with 3 Indian witnesses in the case of the U. S. vs C. Murry and Josiah Call also returned from the North with other witnesses in same case bringing also A. P. Chesley, W. M. Wall, and G. Parrish prisoners in ball and chain, arrested for contempt of Drummonds Court.

Mr Secratary Babbitt also arrived on the fifth instant a prisoner in charge of T. S. Williams for same offence.

A ten a. m. House met

petition of Eli Curtis and twenty others praying for memorial to Congress, for pay for sirvices rendered by them in Indian troubles in 1849, 51 & 3

The said petition was under consideration when the President and Council arrived and the two Houses went into joint session. when

Councillor Pratt of the Special Committee on military affairs appointed yesterday reported that said committee had revized the Bill entitled "An Act to provide for the further organization of the milia" which was recieved when

Mr Little from the committee on military affairs from whom the Bill emanated asked and obtained leave to with draw it

Mr Little on behalf of the chairman of the House on Judiciary, to whom was referred (H. F. No 32) An Act providing for damage done by water, reported to the joint session adversely to the passage of the Bill, which was recieved and the presentor had leave to withdraw it.

His Excellency having returned "An act granting a Herd ground to L. Snow, E. H. Pierce & C.W. Hubbard, suggesting that a few other names be added to the Bill

When the names of F. D. Richards, P. H. Young D. Spencer and J. Browning were added to the Bill and so passed.

The petition of Eli Curtis & 20 others &c was taken from the files of the House and referred to the Lieut Genl of the Nauvoo Legion to dispose of as he thinks proper.

The Joint Session then proceeded to elect on the nomination of the Govornor Luke Johnson probate Judge and George W. Hickman[63] Notary public of Shambip County.

Mr Woodruff moved That the Committee on memmorials be instructed to present a memorial to congress for an appropriation of $50,000 for the continuation of the Sate house at Fillmore which carried unanimously.

Joint session adjourned to Wednesday next at ten o'clock a. m.

Sunday 13th January 1856. To day I was busy with the prisoners, who were brought here under arrest.

Monday 14 January 1856. The Second Session of the District Court met to day as per adjournment.

The Grand and petty Jury were duly empannelled and instructed. and the Court adjourned till to morrow.

The Supreme Court also met and the opinion of the Court (below [crossed out]) given in the case of Green which was to affirm the Judgement of the Court below and to remit the cost of the suit against Green when he was again sentenced to the penetentiary for six months.

The prisoners arrested for contempt that is the Hon. A. W. Babbitt, William M. Wall, U. S. D. Marshall and George Parrish do, and A P. Chesley attorney at law sued out a writ of Habeas Corpus before Hon. Judge George P. Stiles, to be released from their arrest and the case was tried to day and all the prisoners released.

During the time of the above trial of the Habeas Corpus, His Honor Judge Drummond becoming uneasy, and doubting the result of his own doings, became anxious to set in judgement on the case of the prisoners he had caused to be arrested for contempt and brought from Salt Lake & Provo, called a private, side session of his own court. Present His Honor and clerk and myself, in a private room of the state house. Mr Wall was brought in before him and answered a few questions of littl importance whereupon the Court discharged him without costs.

Mr Wall then retired and Mr Parrish & Chesley were introduced in like manner and underwent the same process with the same result, when they all returned to Sites [Stiles] court and were again discharged on Habeas Corpus, which two discharges certainly made them free indeed

Tuesday 15 January 1856. District Court met to day. The case of Almerin Grow vs Chief Justice J. F Kinney for damages to the tune of $5,000 for suspending him from the bar at the District Court in Great Salt Lake last October, was called up Mr Grow council for himself and Myself and Hon. Chief Justice were council on the defence

---

63. George W. Hickman was a brother of William A. (Bill) Hickman. Other officers appointed later were George W. Burridge, William G. Russell, and Enos Stookey, selectmen; and John J. Childs, assessor and collector. Two years later, January 5, 1857, Luke Johnson was again justice of the peace with R. H. Porter, notary public.

We filed a motion to dismiss the case because the complaint did not set forth a sufficient cause of action which was argued and the case held under consideration by the court, and the court adjourned

In the Evening the Supreme Court met and John S. Fullmer and Benjamin F. Johnson were admitted to the Bar of said court as attornies and councillors at Law and solicitors in Chancery

This I believee wound up the career of the supreme court at Fillmore for this session.

About and a little before dark the grand Legislative Supper commenced It opened by a fierce attact upon oysters sardines, crackers and a variety of eets well got up and well served out This was Mr A. W. Babbitts the Sacratary's generosity.

After the usual cerimonies and diligence was bestowed on these table comforts the second part opened by a volley of discharge from about 190 champaigne bottles which strongly indicated that the Battle had become general.

Many a fine coat & vest bare marks of the heroism of their owners and a very many glad heart and pleasing face left the state House this evening

Wednesday 16 Jan 1856. District Court met and sustained the motion against Grow.

The case of U. S. vs Murry was laid over & and the witnesses held to recognizance and this session of said court adjourned

Assembly met in joint session at ten a. m.

A petition from E. W. Davis and 58 others praying that Congress may be memorialized for remuneration for them for services in the Indian expeditions which was referred to the (committee [crossed out]) to the Lieut Genl

G. A. Smith presented a petition from Albert Merril and 29 others praying that a [law] may be passed to prevent the distruction of Beavers and Otters between the months of April & September which was read recieved and referred to the committee agriculture, trade and manufacture.

Mr Harrington presented "An act to incorporate the Deseret Express and Road Company,[64] which was read recieved three several times and amended several times and finally passed

G. A. Smith repeported on the petition of A Merrill et. al. inexpedient to legislate thereon

Mr Peacock presented An Act granting to the San Pete Coal Company a Herd ground which was recieved and read three several times and so passed

Mr Benson presented an act granting to Frederic Kesler a herd ground which was recieved and read three several times amended and passed

Mr Cummings presented "Resolution concerning the further completion of the Penetentiary which was recieved and read three several times and so passed

Councillor Wells presented An Act incorporting the Deseret Agricultural and manufacturing Society which was recieved and read three several times and passed.

Mr Benson reported on the petition of Sidney Roberts, praying for the privilege of taking the water out of Big Cottonwood in Great Salt Lake County not expedient to legislate thereon and wish to be discharged from further duty on the subject which report was recieved and the committee discharged

G. A. Smith presented "An Act apportioning the representation of Utah which was read and recieved and read three several times and so passed

---

64. The Deseret Express and Road Company was assigned the responsibility of constructing a road from South Pass on the eastern border of the territory to Carson Valley on the western border. Mass meetings were held; the legislature memorialized Congress for $200,000 with which to construct the road and asked for daily mail. Since the appropriation was not granted the company came to naught. Leonard J. Arrington, *Great Basin Kingdom: An Economic History of the Latter-day Saints 1830-1900* (Cambridge, 1958), 164.

G. A. Smith presented Resolution defining the Judicial Districts for the United States Courts in the Territory of Utah which was recieved, and read three several times and passed.

G. A. Smith presented Resolution Specifying the times of holding the United States Courts in the several Judicial Districts in Utah which was recieved, and read three several times and so passed.

Mr Spencer moved that the Govornor be invited to nominate for the organization of the Deseret Agricultural and Manufacturing Society seconded and carried. Whereupon His Excellency mad[e] the following nominations which were severally confirmed by the Assembly.

Edward Hunter of G. S. L. City)	President
Jedediah M. Grant ")	Board of
Charles Oliphant ")	Directors
William C. Stains ")	
Seth M. Blair ")	
James Brown sen of Ogden City)	
Calvin C Pendleton "Parowan")	

Mr Woolley moved That all the members living north of Fillmore pay one dollar each for the benefit of the mail carrier between Nephi and Fillmore during the present Sitting of the Legislature seconded and carried and the said members "Forked over"

Mr Peacock presented "An act repealing an act concerning fortifications which was read and recieved and read the first time and passed and on the second reading Mr Peacock asked and objained leave to with draw said bill.

G. A. Smith presented "Resolution assigning the United States Judges to the several Judicial Districts which was read recieved and read three several times and passed. Adjourned to 4 p. m.

4 p. m. Joint session met. A. Carrington presented memorial to Congress for $50.000 to complete the State House, which was read, recieved and adopted.

Mr Carrington reported memorial to Congress for $200,000 for making a Road from Bridger's pass to the East line of Cal read recieved and adopted.

Mr Carrington reported memorial to Congress for $11.318 to defray expences of determining points of boundary of Utah which was read and adopted.

Mr Carrington reported "Memorial to Congress for the right of way for a telegraph from the Missouri river to the East line of Cal which was read recieved and adopted

A. Carrington reported "Memorial to Congress for grants of land for certain cities, towns &c in Utah which was read and adopted

A. Carrington reported "Memorial to Congress for establishment of a Daily mail from the Eastern States to California read & adopted.

O. Pratt reported, "General appropriation Bill" which was read, recieved and read three several times and passed.

Mr Rockwood reported the "Territorial appropriation Bill which was read recieved and read three several times and passed.

Mr Richards presented "Resolution relating to the publishing and distribution of the Laws and journals of the present session which was, read recieved and read three several times and so passed.

Joint session then adjourned till Friday morning at five o'clock.

Thursday 17 January 1856. Nothing of importance going on to day except every body settling up their accounts preparitory to starting tomorrow, and a farewell dance at the state House this evening.

Friday 18 January 1856. About day light this morning His Excellency and the members of the Legislature, after duly adjourning the Assembly, commenced rolling out for home, and I left about 9 a. m and travelled to the cedars between round

Valley and Sevier Where we passed a verry cold but still night around a large cedar fire, while on the next cedar Hill ahead about ten miles we could see a similar fire where the Gov and another large company was camped

Saturday 19 January 1856. Arrived at Salt Creek about 2 p. m and put up for the night. Weather very calm but cold.

Sunday 20 January 1856. Went to Payson dined with Pardon Webb and then went to springville and staid all night with Gideon Wood The company was now lengthened out from payson to dry Creek occasioned by the different speed of travel.

Monday 21 January 1856. Travelled to provo, stoped, a short time and went on arriving about sunset at Willow Creek and put up with Ebenezer Brown. Wind was very cold at the point of the Utah mountain.

Tuesday 22 January 1856. Arrived at home just after noon and found my family all well and living in peace.

Wednesday 23 January 1856. Resting to day, happy to be relieved from the cares which hung so heavy on my mind for several months past.

Thursday. to had the papers signed for the Pardon of Samuel G. Baker, and sent them to him by D. Carn the warden of the Penetentiary and on Friday Mr Baker came to my house, rejoicing that his term of ten years had expired so soon.[65]

Saturday 26 January 1856. Weather clear & cold. Mass Meeting to day at the Tabernacle on the subject of the Deseret Express & Road Company, where many large speeches were made to "Buncum" but every one seems to be in favor of such an enterprize.

Sunday, Monday January 27 & 28. At home writing and around time.

Tuesday 29 January 1856. Writing, still writing The Legislative party came of at the Social Hall this evening but I did not attend.

Wednesday 30th January 1856. Suit before probe Court. Almerin Grow vs Ch. Justice John F. Kinney in damages to the amount $5,000 for suspending him from practicing at the Bar as an attorney, this is the same which chief Justice Kinney was sued for in the District Court at Fillmore (on [crossed out]) (see Journal of 16 inst). Mr Grow was his own attorney & Myself & Hickman for the defence. The denfence filed motion to the Jurisdiction of the court to try him for his Judicial acts which motion was argued and sustained by the Court so the case went down to the cost of the plaintiff

Saturday 2 Feb 1856. Law suit before Probate Court Hon. E. Smith Judge, Joseph Chadwick against George W. Bradley in Assumpsit Demand 120 dollars, Self council for defendant, Judgement against the defendant for demand and costs

Sunday 3 Feb 1856. At home writing all day

Monday 4 Feb 1856. The adjourned term of the First District Court met at ten a. m The grand jury was called and organized and the cases called in their order and Court adjourned till ten a. m tomorrow

At dark I met with the Regents of the University in the Sealing Room on the Subject of publishing a First Reader for children in the "Deseret Alphabet. Willford Woodruff, Samuel W. Richards & George D. Watt were appointed a committee to

---

65. Record of the pardon of Samuel G. Baker is found in the Utah Territorial Executive Record Book "B" (Utah State Archives), 44.

prepare said First Reader and report to the Board of Regents. It is contemplated to prepare the book and sent the manuscript by Orson Pratt, to be printed in Liverpool next spring.

Tuesday 5 Feb 1856. District Court at ten a. m. The case of the United States against Carlos Murry for the murder of an Indian in Thousand Spring Valley was brought up. I was on the part of the United States and A. P. Chesley, W. A. Hickman, and Thomas S. Williams Council for the defendant.

Prisoner plead not guilty whereupon a jury was empannelled and the Court adjourned till three p. m.

In the afternoon the Evidence in the case was introduced on the part of the prosecution and the defence rested without introducing any evidence

The Evidence before the jury against Murry is very weak and I do not see how a jury cand find him guilty

Wed (Tuesday [crossed out]) 6 Feb 1856. Court met at ten a. m After several motions were argued the Case of Murry was called and submitted without argument to the jury who after recieving the charge from the court, retired and about three p. m brought in a virdict of not guilty

Several cases of debt were called up and dispensed with and the court adjourned till to morrow at ten o'clock a. m

Thursday 7 Feb 1856. Court met at ten a. m Several cases were called and laid over and the court adjourned till tomorrow at ten a. m.

At two p. m a Suit came up before the probate. Miner & Dennis Winn against Royal Cutler and Josiah Arnold for assault and Battery The case was withdrawn and taken before E. T. Benson & Wm Snow referees. It appears that Cutler & Arnold were levying upon & taking a waggon of Dennis to pay a Fort tax when the two Winns undertook to take it away and a row ensued in which the Winns came off second best The case was heard and the referees are to give their decision next Saturday.

Friday 8th Feb 1856. Court met at ten a. m Several motions, demurers, motions to admit to the bar ect & several cases on notes on which judgement was duly rendered.

When the case of E. A. McConnell against Goddard & Leonard came up Babbitt for plff & Snow & Egs for defts. demand $3496. debt interest and damges. judgement less than demand, the $1000 damages and interest 4 percent less than claimed

Saturday 9th Feb 1856. The case of Russell Jones & Co vs W. J. Hawley in assumpsit demand $719.65 was called up. Myself & J. C. Little for plff & A. W. Babbitt for deft Jury brought in verdict against the deft for the demand.

In the after noon the case of Kinney Green & Co vs. Elijah Thomas in assumpsit called up Judgt by default for the demand of $3040 and interest. Self & Z Snow for plff and Blair, Williams, Little, & Grow for deft who moved to set aside default Court adjourned till Monday.

This evening attended an oyster supper at Livingston Kinkead & Co. store This was the initiation fee of several new members admitted to the Bar, and lasted till after 12.

Sunday 10 Feb 1856. Quorum meeting to day at W. W. Rust shop.

Monday 11 Feb 1856. Court met at ten a. m. and the day was occupied in argueing Motions untill 4 p m when the case of Hockaday Morris & Co vs Thomas S. Johnson Constable of G. S. L. County Parties appeared. A jury called and Court adjourned till morning.

Regents met this evening again The committee is progressing with the first reader.

Tuesday 12 Feb 1856. Court met at ten a. m. The case of Hockaday, Morris & Co vs Johnson called up. The evidence on the part of the plff given and Court adjourned till 2 p. m.

2 p. m evidence on the defence rested and one plea on each side heard and court adjourned.

Wednesday 13 Feb 1856. Suit against T. S. Johnson continued. W. H. Hickman, John M. Hockaday and J. C. Little occupied the day in their pleas to the jury, and court adjourned. Mr Babbitt yet having to make the closing plea.

Thursday 14th Feb 1856. Court at ten a. m Mr Babitt made the closing to the jury & the case went to the jury who brought in a virdict of no cause of action two thirds of the jury concurring, Whereupon Mr A. W. Babbitt gave notice of a motion for a new trial

Friday 15 Feb 1856. Court met at ten a. m. Several motions were argued and some few cases continued over and court adjourned till Monday next to give place for Elections of Delegates to the state convention tomorrow

Saturday 16 Feb 1856. The conventional Election came of to day The candidates for this County are

Daniel H. Wells
J. M. Grant
A. Carrington
E. D. Woolley
A. W. Babbitt
William Bell.
Wm H. Hooper
T. S. Williams

P. P. Pratt.
S. W. Richards
Hon J. F. Kinney
Garland Hurt.
S. M Blair
Orson Pratt
J. C. Little
Geo P. Stiles

There was   votes polled in the County, but not much stir or excitement on the occasion.[66]

Monday 18 Feb 1856. District Court at ten a m. In the case of Hockaday, Morris and Co. vs. T. S. Johnson the motion for a new trial was argued till noon & the court granted a new trial and the case was continued till the next term court met in the after noon and adjourned after hearing a few motions argued.

Tuesday 19 Feb 1856. Court again. The case of T. S. Williams vs. B. Leonard in an action of Covenant to make deft give up a note came up Williams & Z. Snow for plff & self for deft. It took till noon to pass the jury & open the case and the after noon to examine a few witnessess and court adjourned.

Wednesday 20 Feb 1856. Court met at ten   Trial of Williams vs Leonard up and the day spent in examining evidence.

Thursday 21 Feb 1856. Court and Williams vs Leonard all day but fortunately I hoped that the Evidence is closed and only six long winded Lawyers pleas at the most can now be inflected on the jury, with as long a charge from the court to be followed by Attorneys asking special instructions ect ect —

Snow last night & mild warm slushy thawy day

Friday 22 Feb 1856. Court and Lawyers pleas all day & not closed yet by some 3 or 4 speaches The Presidint & council attended the Court to day to hear the long winded spouters

---

66. Since this was only a vote of approval of a group, many of whom were federal appointees and none of whom was opposed, there was no cause for any excitement.

Saturday 23 Feb 1856. Court met and the pleas to the jury were closed and the case went to the jury about five p. m. and just after mid night the jury returned a virdict for Williams one juror dissenting whereupon the defence moved for a new trial & an arrest of judgement.

Sunday 24 Feb 1856. Went to meeting President Young spoke against the corrupt practice in Courts and particularly in this last trial on the part of the plff.

A large number of names were called to different mission to Europe, to East Indies, to Salmon River, Oregon, to Green River, and to Los Vagos, My brother Allen was called to go to Los Vagos.

Monday 25 Feb 1856. Court met but done no business and adjourned till to morrow at ten a. m.

The Regents met at dark on the subject of the Deseret First Reader. The Committee is progressing finely on the subject To night the subject of accent was taken up for the first tine

President Young exhibited the Seer's stone with which The Prophet Joseph discovered the plates of the Book of Mormon,[67] to the Regents this evening

It is said to be a silecious granite dark color almost black with light colored stripes some what resembling petrified poplar or cotton wood bark It was about the size but not the shape of a hen's egg

Tuesday 26 Feb 1856. Snowing very fast this forenoon Court met at ten and adjourned till tomorrow at ten a. m

Wednesday 27 Feb 1856. Court met at ten. The case of Williams vs Leonard came up on a motion for a new trial which was argued and overruled by the court and excepted to by the defenants Council. To day the U. S. Grand Jury was discharged

Thursday 28 Feb 1856. Court met as usual to day and the first case on docket was Grow vs. A. W. Babbitt in an action of slander in damages to the tune of ten thousand dollars but the deft being drunk the case was continued untill two p. m. But then the Hon deft was so highly *halusinated* that the court deemed it wisdom to adjourn till to morrow. to give the parties a fair chance to to investigate their Characters if they had any. Wasn't this very kind in the Court.

Frid 29 Feb 1856. Court met and parties sober & went to trial and the jury found Hon A. W. Babbitt innocent of the slander alleged by Mr Grow Whether they found Grow with out a character to slander or that Babbitt did not slander I can not say, but Grow left court in heigh dudgeon when the Jury found "not guilty" and asked to have his name stricken from the list of attorneys (Lawyers Lawing each other for legal character)

Sold my per diem and fees to Judge Drummond for my services as United States District Attorney pro tem at Fillmore last court, in all amounting to $551.40 at a discount of fifty dollars on the whole amount and took in pay 39 voluns of Law books (new) and excellently bound in calf, at two hundred and Eighty dollars, also one hundred and fifteen dollars on the store, also twenty five dollars cash, and one double barrel shot gun and accoutrements at fifty dollars and saddle and bridle at thirty one dollars. The Hon Judge takes the account "without recource"

---

67. Stout was wrong here. The Prophet Joseph Smith maintained that he was directed to the plates of the Book of Mormon by a heavenly visitor who showed them to him in a vision. The seer stone had been found as Smith was digging a well for Clark Chase. He exhibited this stone December 27, 1841. *The Millennial Star*, XXVI, 119. See also Roberts, *Comprehensive History*, I, 129.

This stone should not be confused with the Urim and Thummim which were said to have been in the box along with the golden plates.

Saturday 1 March 1856. Court met. The cases of Jones & Co vs W. J. Hawley & also of John Kerr vs W. J. Hawley which had been continued was again opened for trial this term. and the traverse jury dismissed and Court adj'd till Monday. The Cal mail arrived but not much news more then the good people of Kansas were killing each other. on the quarrel for and against the "niggers"

Monday 3 March 1856. Court met and adjourned
  Commenced work to day and really hope I may continue faithful, in the business
  Attended the General meeting of the presidents of the Seventies at their Hall.

Tuesday 4 March 1856. Court met and adjourned & I worked all day.

Wednesday 5 March 1856. Court met and adjourned again worked the rest of this week at home

Monday 10 March 1856. Court met and adjourned till tomorrow. Regents met at dark to examine the report of the committee on the first reader.
  There is a geat scarcity of bread now in all the valleys and nearly every body are living on rations who are lucky enough to have any meal or flour.
  To day my family commenced on their allowance which is two pounds of flour and one pound of meal   for the whole family consisting of seven persons. This is a scant portion considering that we have so many comers amounting to more than one constant boarder. potatoes are also very scarce in fact there is none in market.

Tuesday 11 March 1856. District Court to day   The case of John Kerr v. W. J. Hawley in assumpsit was called up Demand $760.88 cents.   Babbitt for deft and Self & Little for plff.   Mr Babbitt made no defence.   Judget for plff for the demand.
  Also "Jones & Co." v. Hawley in assumpsit.   Demand $691.73 and interest Attorneys same as above judgt for plff for demand and interest at ten pr cent

Wednesday 12 March 56. Court again.   the case of Jenne vs Russell was taken from the court and arbitrated before Isaac Bullock.   H. S. Eldredge and W. P. Mc-Intire in which they rendered an award of 41 dollars and some cents in favor of Jenne.   W. A. Hickman was atty for plff and self for deft

Thursday 13 March 1856. Court met case of Hockaday vs Twitchel,   Hawkins & Abrams came up and defts confessed judgement for $114 60/100.   Myself for plff & Babbitt for defendant. this afternoon the Court not having any case on the docket adjourned sine die with this reserve that if any of the indians against whom there were indictments were brought in then the court would be called to try them

Saturday 15 March 1856. This morning we recieved the melancholy news that my wife's father L. D. Wilson was no more   He died very suddenly at Ogden on Tuesday last at 8 p. m. after an illness of about 16 hours with an attact of the Cholic.

Monday 17 March 1856. To day the Convention to form a constitution for Utah to be admitted as a state met.
  The "Star Spangled Banner" was hoisted on nearly all the stores and Council House,   Gov House & many other places while the day was celebrated by the firing of cannon nearby.
  I had to attend a Law before the Probate Court.   W. J. Hawley vs J. M. & F. M. Russell J. H. Jones & J. Kerr In an action of assumpsit for $4407.83. Babbitt for plff and myself for deft Kerr.   I moved for a continuence which was overruled then demurred & the court after argument held the matter under advisement till 9 o'clock to morrow a. m.

Friday 21 March 1856. The suit of Hawley v. Russell et. al. has continued every day this week the demurer was over as well as a plea in abatement.   I then filed an answer for Kerr pleading the general issue and a former settlement after which we went to trial which has occupied the last two days untill this evening about o'clock when the jury brought in a virdict of no cause of action Two jurors dissinting whereupon judgement was rendered against Hawley for the costs of suit

Tuesday 25 March 1856. The case of Hawley vs Russell et. al tried last friday has been before the court every day since on motion for new trial which was allowed to day on the second motion on the conditions that Hawley would pay the cost.

Thursday 27 March 1856. To day the State Convention adjourned sine die having completed the Constitution and electing Hon G. A. Smith and John Taylor as Delegates to take the constitution to Washington to assist J. M. Barnhisel to the admission of Deseret into the union as a free & independent State.

March 31 1856 Monday. To day I traded my claims on government to Judge Kinney for my services as United States District attorney protem for the special October term of his court, amounting to $135 also for fees & per diem for the last february term amounting to $180. He also pays me $50 for my claim to a District attorney's salery for the last year He takes the claims with out recourse and pays me down in good property. The total amount of these claims are $365

Thursday 3 April 1856. Southren mail came in to day from Cal News very dull The House of Rep in congress had not elected a speaker about the middle of Jan after Ballotting 117 times The war in Kanzas was still raging between the Anti & Pro Slavery parties whil the Territory was writhing under the administration of two govs one for each party. Thus it seems that there is really no peace only in Utah. How thees national and Territorial stifes will I know not.

Sunday 6 April 1856. General Conference commenced to day A Large concource of people present. The particulars I shall not give (See "Deseret News" on Monday a refreshing but cold rain which was much need the ground being parched and dry and vegitation put back every was beginning to show tokens of another dry season.

Saturday 12 April 1856. In the case of Williams vs Leonard in the District Court on 23 Feb. last the motion for a new trial being over ruled, was followed by a motion in arrest of Judgement which to be heard in chambers before Judge Stiles was argued yesterday and this evening the judge delivered himself of his ruling which was that judgement be arrested & each party pay his own cost and the plaintiff have the privilege to file a more specific state in his complaint to which I accepted for deft so far as paying the cost.

Suit before probate B. Leonard v. W. I. Appleby in debt 66$. Williams for plf & self for deft Judge held case under consideration (of ther [crossed out]) after parties were through

Monday 14 April 1856. We had a very welcome and refreshing shower last night which was renewed occasionally during the day.

I hear that Jacob Lance who was under an arrest in Lehi Utah County for an assault with an intent to commit a Rape? on a Danish woman, this morning while his guards were snoozing and he either asleep or nodding had his head split assunder by a woman supposed to be the injured one, who came in and split his head with an axe then gently retiring with out saying a word

Thursday 17 April 1856. Recieved a certificate of appointment of U. S. Deputy Marshall from Marshall Haywood[68]

---

68. Joseph Leland Heywood, born at Grafton, Worcester County, Massachusetts, August 1, 1815, had held many prominent positions in the Mormon Church. In Nauvoo he managed a store for Joseph Smith and was one of those left to sell the property at the exodus. He had represented the Saints in Washington, D. C., and had served as U. S. marshal since 1851.

Heywood led in the colonization of Nephi and went with Orson Hyde to form a settlement in Carson Valley, Nevada. He spent his later years in southern Utah.

It is not my intention to act as such but I recieve the office because Marshal Haywood is going to the City of Washington soon to be gone till fall & I shall have charge of his business during his absence more to prevent abuse and extravagance than any thing else

Sunday 20 April 1856. This evening another refreshing and sufficient shower fell which relieves the anxiety of many who greatly fear another dry season

Monday 21 April 1856. To day the missionaries are leaving for the States in large numbers Judge Kinney and family also goes to day Oour Delegate to Congress Hon G. A. Smith also leaves in the same Company and Marshall Haywood, and E. T. Benson O. Pratt to England.

I have commenced to build me another house joining on to the North End of my house which is to be 14 wide and to day had the foundation wall laid I intend to have it finished before winter sets in if possible

Sunday 27 April 1856. This morning about half past twelve o'clock my wife was delivered of a Son, fine, healthy, and fat, weighing nine and a half pounds. This makes the Eleventh child which has been born unto me, only four of whom are living. Surmantha had one (still born) Louisa had Eight, 3 of whom are living Marinda one (still born) and lastly Alvira one last night alive and well.

Monday 28 April 1856. Went to Farmington Davis Co to attend a law suit before the probate Court in an action of Divorce and alimony, wherein Sarah Jane Winter plff vs Jacob N. Winter Deft I was on the part of the plff & John Bear for deft Judge Holbrook deferred the Judgement till first of September next and appointed J. D. Parker & James Duncan Guardians ad litenn[69] who also were to take charge of the property of the parties untill a decision of court, &c.

Tuesday 29 Apl 1856. Rainy, windy, Snowy day & myself weather bound

Wednesday 30 Apl 1856. Came home to day wife and family doing well.

Friday 2 May 1856. Suit before probate I. S. Miles vs Gabrael Huntsman In assumpsit Demand 83 dollars. Myself for plff — J. C. Little for defendant. The case was compromised by Miles taking a note 3 months from date for 71$.

Cold, Cloudy, windy weather Like for rain, Like for Snow Like for hail and quite likely we shall have neither —

Tuesday 6 May 1856. Gov Young and a company started North to day to meet at the rendesvous of the Carson Valley missionaries and to be present at the launching of the Ferry Boats at the Bear River. They will be absent some two weeks

Saturday 10 May 1856. Refreshing rain to day which proves sufficient at present for the ground. The Eastern mail came in to day in the fore noon.

Saturday 17 May 1856. Judge Drummond and guard started for Carson Valley to accompanied by the Australian missionaries[70]

Hooper & Williams' train of goods came in to Day (some 27 wagons) from Bridger where the goods have been all winter arriving there too late last fall to cross the Wausach range

---

69. Stout here evidently means "Guardians ad libitum," or at his own wish or desire, as one wishes.

70. Judge Drummond did not reveal his plans but left ostensibly to hold court in Carson Valley, Nevada. Instead of returning to his post, he went on to California and east by boat via Panama, arriving in early 1857. His letter of resignation was dated March 30, 1857. From that time forth he worked against the Mormons.

Monday 19 May 1856. Filed a pitition and sued out an injunction John M. Russell et al vs W. J. Hawley to stay the proceedings of the probate Court of Utah County in the case of Hawlley vs Russell et al.

After obtaining the writ I served it on the party defendant, as a deputy mashall which is my first act in that capacity

Tuesday 20 May 1856. Went to W. Hickmans and staid all night coming home the next day in the afternoon.

Monday 2 June 1856. Eastern Mail left this morning. This evening there was an Indignation meeting held at the Council House against the conduct and practices of the mail agents, conductors &c which was adjourned till to morrow evening

Tuesday 3 June 1856. Indignation meeting this evening which was adjourned to Saturday the 14 instant at the Bowry.

Wednesday 4 June 1856. The Eastern mail came in this evening after being detained 3 or 4 days at the Weber and loosing one mail sack in the stream and 2 or 3 other sacks being unaccountably missing

Monday June 9 1856. A singular case before the Probate Court to day. one Robert Galispie had been put under bonds to appear to day before said Cout to answer for stealing a calf He appeared and there being as yet no indictment found and he being anxious to be disposed of requested the Court to judge him in an off hand and Summery manner. There were no witnesses present and he confesses that he did steal the calf but done it because he was starving

Whereupon the Court fined him ten dollars and costs besides for him to pay the owner Frank Pullin fifteen dollars for the calf.

Wednesday 18 June 1856. Law Suit before probate on an examination People vs William Camp et al. for kidnapping a Negro Dan. The case commenced Monday evening and lasted yesterday & to day till noon

It appears that Camp was the owner of Dan who had ran away and C. had went with three others to bring him back. The court acquitted them Carrington atty Genl for the people & Mr T. S. Williams & self for defts

There was a great excitement on on the occasion The question naturally involving more or Less the Slavery question and I was surprised to see those latent feeling aroused in our midst which are making so much disturbance in the states.[71]

Wednesday 25 June 1856. Probate Court called a grand jury to Enquire into a certain matter of stealing which has lately been brought Several men have been arrested and held to await the action of the grand jury. I attend the grand jury as prosecutor.

Thursday 26 June 1856. Attended with the grand jury to day who presented 3 indictments against Thomas Bird, wife & son for Larceny one indictment for stealing two guns one for Stealing a lot of whip lasshes one for stealing a pair of shoes.

In the evening after the grand jury was discharged I attended a suit for the defendant in an action of Replevin for the recovery of a Red Heifer. Charles White v Feremorz Little T. S. Williams for plff the case went down on demurrer at the plff's cost. The matter was then arbritrated before Judge Smith.

---

71. That Stout should uphold Camp in his property rights over the Negro is somewhat surprising in view of the attitude of many of the Mormons. The "latent feeling aroused in our midst" might be one reason why President Brigham Young later said so little regarding the issues that were shaking the rest of the nation.

Friday 27 June 1856. The case of the people v Bird on the indictment for stealing the shoes came up to day Mr T. S. Williams council for prisoner He made sevend different motions to quash the indictment all of which was overruuled In the after noon the case was tried and sustained and prisoner fined twenty and costs.

Saturday 28 June 1856. The case of the people v Bird on the Whip lash indictment came Councils as before, two motions to Quash and overruled The indictment sustained and the prisoner fined fifty dollars and costs.

The Eastern mail arrive this evening

Monday 30 June 1856. Engaged all day in the cases of people v Bird The resunt of which is that he is to pay the costs of the two preceeding cases against him amounting to near four hundred dollars including the two fines of seventy dollars and I am to enter a Nolle proseque in the case of the the other indictment, as he has no more property and any further prosecution would only be at the expense of the County.[72]

Thursday 3 July 1856. Building my new house again have the adobies laid up to the windows

Friday 4 July. 1856. Great day in town Banners out & a general parade and the day celebrated with a great deal of splendor and ceremony

Thursday & Friday 17 & 18 July 56. Building my house and have the adobies laid up to near the top of the door Frames and again stop for more adobies which time & perseverence I hope will yet procure

Saturday 19 July 1856. A company of mormon Emmigrants of five wagons from the southren states arrived here to day, the first this season.

Suit before Probate H. W. Larance v W. B. Simmons. T. S. Williams Council for Plff. Myself for defence. Action for damages. Judgement for plf for Eight dollars

Thurs 24 July 1856. Gov B. Young and a large party celebrates this day in Big Cotton Wood Kanyon.

Served an injunction on Ed Whipple Deputy Sheriff of Utah County who was going to serve a garnashee on L Robison and others and in favor of W. J. Hawley vs John M Russell et. al.

Tuesday 29 July 1856. Suit before Probate, George P. Stiles vs Thomas Bowman in an action of Assumpsit Demand 500 dollars with ten per cent secured by a mortgage which was also to be foreclosed This is the first case for the foreclosure of a mortgage in the Territory and what point may be raised I cannot tell in the total silence of the Statutes

Wednesday 30 July 1856. This morning the California mail arrived bringing news that the mormon dissenters at San Barnidino are making considerable opposition to the Church authorities in that place while their numbers are gradually increasing The[y] seem to be striving for the ascendency in politicks and openly denounce President C. C. Rich

Among the number are found Quartus S. Sparks who so nobly assisted my self and others at San Francisco when I was there on my way to China — Besides Dr W. M. Andrus and others some of whom are of long standing in the Church.

There is no doubt in my mind but the Saints if there is any there will be finally out numbered and have to leave San Barnardino. Suffice it to say that San Barnidino has been a refuge for nearly every foul and unclean spirit and disaffected hypocrite that has ever apostatized and left Utah and congregating there it is no wonder that there is like to be an outbreak.

---

72. The inference here is that legal proceedings will continue so long as the victim has property or money; after that, there is no point in prosecuting further.

The Eastern mail also came in just after dark after having laid up just long enough on the Road not to give time for the people to answer by the return mail. From some letters it appears that Babbit is at Washington & Haywood at Chicago the lates dates. But the whereabouts of Judge Kinney G. A. Smith & others I have not learned.

Thursday 31 July 1856. Suit before Probate the P. E. F Co vs. Martin Teasdall for 159 dollars judgt for plff —

Saturday 2 Aug 1856. The Eastern mail left to day about ten a. m under an escort of some 14 men commanded by Col Little City Marshal. The object of which escort was to see that they did not leave the city whooping and swearing as they did when they arrived There was intense excitement after the escort met in rear of the mail coaches and before they started as it was not known what the object was.

Monday 4 Aug 1856. To day is the General Election for Territorial and County officers
The candidates for the Legislature are as follows — for G. S. L. County — Parley P. Pratt, Councillor to fill the vacancy of Orson Pratt resigned —
For Representatives.

1	J. M. Grant.	6	Hosea Stout
2	W. W. Phelps.	7	J. C. Little
3.	H. B. Clawson.	8	S. W. Richards.
4.	J. W. Cummings	9	Alex McRae
5	A. P. Rockwood	10	Danl Spencer.
		11	Jos A. Young

The above were elected without a dissenting vote.
The Election passed off quietly But about dark an affair came off which caused considerable excitement, that was simply two young men, Emery Meecham & John Flack pitched aboard of one Joseph Troskieloskie with more zeal and ability than the poor Polander could endure and gave him a most unmerciful Horse whipping bruising & marring him very much
Troskieloskie is an employ'e of Mr Burr the surveyor general, for the United States How this affair will come out I do not know The law has been violated and the grieveance must be redressed —

Tuesday 5 Aug 1856. Suit before the probate to day W. M. Magraw ad vs Erastus Snow in assumpsit for $900 for carrying the mail from here to Independence Missouri. Myself & T. S. Williams for the (plff [crossed out]) Magraw the defendant (not plff as above) and J. C. Little for the plff Snow.
Jury brought a virdict for $630 in favor of Snow The deft. called for and obtained an appeal

Wednesday 13 Aug 1856. This Evening Elder P. C. C. Merrill after a three year's mission to England returned home in good health He comes in advance of a train of some sixty waggons of saints of whom he was captain, which is some sixty miles back and will be here in a day or so. Elder Jerter Clinton & Saml A. Woolly is in the train. This is the advance train of the Mormon Emmigration this season.

Friday 15 Aug 1856. This after noon there was a very hard shower of rain wetting the ground completely — This is the first rain whis has fell in this City this summer which continued in Showers the next day.

Monday & Tuesday 18 & 19 Aug. Working on the house which is raised to the Square —
On Tuesday evening had a suit before the probate Court Esther Fuller vs. William K. Parrish for the recovery of two Horses and Harness which she claimed

as being taken feloniously by him I was for plff. The horses proved to be hers and was adjudged accordingly with costs of suit. Very sick to day with the head ache.

Wednesday 20 Aug 1856. Levingston Kinkead & Co's large train of goods came in this after noon, from the East.

Thursday 28 Aug 1856. The Eastern mail came in this evening The news unimportant Prospect dull for Utah to be admitted into the union

Great excitement at Washington to see who will be next president. Dis-union rife. Kansas question warm

Sunday 31 Aug 1856. Awakened this morning at day light by the cry of the Public Blacksmith shop being on fire.[73] Rose quickly & started to assist in putting it out but the fire was extinguished before I got there it having done but little damage burning the ruff and destroying a bellows &c fire caught in the ruff from sparks from the forge as supposed.

Monday 8 Sept 1856. This evening Br Pullin finished laying up the adobies for my house —

Was engaged in a suit in the probate Court. A singular case. The People vs Luke Johnson and others on a charge for an assault & Battery on Robert C. Caldwell & wife in Shambip County. The case was commenced before the Probate of Tooele County on an examination, but Mr W. A. Hickman defendants Attorney So managed as to obtain a change of venue to this County

Here Hickman, Little & myself were defendants council and J. L. Stoddard & L. Gee for plff We filed a motion to dismiss on the grounds that Judge A. Lee of Tooele County was not qualified as Judge he having never given bonds according to law.

This motion was argued at great length by both sides When the Court dismissed the Case.

Tues. 9 Sept 1856. Suit before Probate Court Edwin Ruston et al. v. Simon Baker in an action of Tresspass & Damage Demand $290 Self Council for plffs and Col Little for Deft. Judgement of the court in favor of the plaintiff for seventeen dollars with cost of suit

Saturday 13 Sept 1856. This morning at ten the 3rd District Court met at the Council House Special Term for the trial of the suit between E. Snow vs. W M. F. Magraw Mail contractor &c appealed from the probate Court of 5th Aug last Demand $900 — J. C. Little Council for the plff — and T. S. Williams and myself for the defence. Jury trial

Case occupied all day and untill mid night when the jury brought in a virdict of $900 for plff. Defence moved for a new trial which is to be argued on Monday at two p. m. There was much warmth and feeling on this occasion with some of the parties

Monday 15 Sept 1856. The motion for a new trial followed by a motion in arrest of judgement was argued in the District Court in the case of Snow vs Magraw by

73. The "public works program" in Utah was organized in 1850 in an effort to provide work for needy immigrants and answer public needs. Skilled workers in the trades were classified and credited with their work, drawing pay from the tithing office:

Headquarters for the various types of work were established on the northeast corner of Temple Block. These included a carpenter shop, paint shop, stone-cutting shop, and blacksmith shop. A lime kiln was built at the entrance to one of the canyons . . . , and a public adobe yard was located not far away from Temple Square. These shops functioned not only in connection with public works but also did a sizeable business as well . . . the blacksmith shop, in addition to providing tools and materials for public works projects, shod horses, cast wheels, and fashioned many types of machinery and equipment. (Arrington, *Great Basin Kingdom,* 109-10.)

Col Little & myself. Both of which motions were overruled to which rulling the defence excepted. and Court adjourned *sine die.*

Friday 19 Sept 1856. Suit to day before Judge Stiles in chambers on Habeas Corpus Luke Johnson et al *ex parte* taken from the Probate of Tooelle County wherein three men were tried & condemned unlawfully. They were discharged before Stiles.

This morning about 2 o'clock W. Luffkins chair shop was discovered to be on fire and the flames bursting through the roof. The shop was a total loss and was a severe reverse to Luffkin It was well furnished. Had an excellent water power turning lathe & circular saws and well supplied with tools and at the time filled with newly finished firnature.

22 Sept 1856. Suit this Evening Robinson V Jo Davis for 50$ damages before E. Smith P. J. I was for plff & A. McRae for deft Judg't for plff — $28.

Friday 26 Sept 1856. To day the Hand Cart Company of saints arrived under the direction of E. Ellsworth & D. D. Mc Arthur The company was escorted in by Prest Young and a large concourse of Saints who met them in Emmigration Kanyon with a treat of melons, fruits vegtables The marched in good order & fine Spirits and seemed to be happy and in excellent health They have drawn their Carts from Iowa City a distance of 1300 miles. Thus men women & children young & old have been their own teams and performed this long journey far out travelling ox trains without incurring the expense for an outfit which would have taken them years of harder labor to procure than thus coming in Carts. This is a new and improved method of crossing the plains[74]

Monday 29 Sept 1856. Cal mail arrived bringing me two letters one from H. G. Boyle & one from Judge Drummond

The Cal news I have not yet learned, except that Los Angelos was almost in a state of Seige by the discontented Spaniards citizens.

Oct. 1 1856. Fair commences at the Deseret House where the Home Manufactured productions are exhibiting besides the products of the Earth works of art & science &c &c. which is to continue three days.

Saturday 4 Oct 1856. On the second inst Elder Bunker's Company of Hand Carts arrived

To day 12 Elders returned home from different missions. G. D. Grant F D Richards Furgerson Jos A Young &c among the number They bring news that the Cheyennes have killed several apostate mormons returning to the states, and attacted Mr A. W. Babbitt's Train of goods killed several of his teamsters and himself is missing and supposed to be killed.[75] Elder F. Little returned with them on learning the hostile appearane of the Indians

---

74. For firsthand accounts of the "new and improved method of crossing the plains," see LeRoy R. and Ann W. Hafen, *Handcarts to Zion: The Story of a Unique Western Migration, 1856-1860* (Glendale, 1960). This collection of diaries and journals pictures the labor and suffering of the handcart pioneers as one long torture.

75. This entry by Hosea Stout is very significant. Of these twelve individuals, nine were returning from bona fide proselyting missions.

Andrew Jenson, *Church Chronology, A Record of Important Events Pertaining to the Church of Jesus Christ of Latter-day Saints* (Salt Lake City, 1899), under the general heading for 1856 says that "Daniel Spencer acted as general superintendent of immigration on the borders, assisted by Geo. D. Grant, Wm. H. Kimball, James H. Hart, and others." James McGaw was in this case evidently one of the others. Clearly, the "mission" of these men was of a different order, being now to guard the company safely to Zion, after having protected the interests of the church on the road generally.

The apostate Mormons of whom Stout spoke were Thomas Margett, formerly president of the L.D.S. London Branch, his wife; and James Cowdy, and his wife and child. They had

Monday 6 Oct 1856. General Conference commenced to day which lasted two days. Congregation unusually large.

Thursday 9 Oct 1856. To day the peaceble citizens of this city were astonished by an unusual and singular breach of the peace cause by the willfully ignorant counsel of two lawyers T. S. Williams & Garland Hurt.[76]

Mr P. K Dotson wishing to set a hand at work in the Tannery of Hockaday & Taussig to which Taussig was not willing and refussed to admit him locked up his rooms.

Mr Dotson as agent of Hockaday called upon the two legal sages for advise They after due reflection advised him to break into the finishing room of the Tannery and set the hand watters to work which he did and Taussig forth with complained

---

been joined at Fort Laramie by a soldier who wished to travel with them for safety. A day or two's travel from the fort they were all murdered, the soldier returning to say that while they were encamped and he had gone out to bring in a deer, the Indians had attacked, killed, and scalped them all.

The fate of Almon W. Babbitt is clouded by such vague and differing reports that the truth is hard to determine. During the winter of 1878-79 the *Salt Lake Daily Herald* published in weekly installments the "Reminiscences" of John Jacques, who came to Utah with the Martin handcart company. From the issue of December 8, on the front page is the following entry:

> The company traveled on the day named [August 25, 1856] from Florence to Cutler's Park, two and a half miles, and camped, staid there the next day and night, and left the next morning. While there A. W. Babbitt, dressed in cordoroy pants, woolen overshirt, and felt hat, called as he was passing west. He seemed in high glee, his spirits elastic, almost mercurial. He had started with one carriage for Salt Lake City with the mail and a considerable amount of money. He was very confident that he could be in Salt Lake within fifteen days . . . .

Babbitt had started a train of four, ox-drawn wagons out ahead, expecting to pass it at Fort Kearney. Before the train reached that point, it was attacked by Indians. Two of the drivers were killed, and a third was wounded. With the help of W. H. Wharton of Kearney, Babbitt recovered most of his goods, secured other drivers, and got the wagons on their way again. This was on September 2nd.

Thomas Sutherland and Frank Rowland remained with Babbitt on his express west. Before they reached Fort Laramie, all three men were killed, their effects stolen, their animals driven away, and their buggy burned. Of this John Jacques wrote:

> On September 23 about six miles east of Bluff Creek and about seventy yeards to the left of the road, a little harness, two wheels, and the springs of a burnt carriage or buggy and a few other things were seen. These were supposed to be the relics of A. W. Babbitt's outfit . . . . Babbitt had left Kearney about the 2nd of September with Thomas Sutherland and a driver . . . .

Some questions naturally arise. Who first found the bodies of the murdered men? Indians would not bury them or otherwise dispose of them. The odor of decomposing human bodies so near the trail would certainly attract attention.

The returning missionaries had passed this point some ten days before Jacques, but their official report made no mention of the Babbitt murder. The report told of the earlier attack upon the Babbitt wagon train; it listed all the companies they met and those they passed, even giving a careful census of some; but it ignored this massacre entirely.

Investigations made by the officers at Fort Laramie and Fort Kearney named the Indians responsible for these murders and for others. See *Transactions of the Kansas State Historical Society, embracing the Fifth and Sixth Biennial Reports, 1886-1888* (Topeka, 1890), Vol. IV, 492-95.

Mrs. Julia Ann Babbitt, wife of Almon W., with her brother, Joel H. Johnson, made her own investigation, visiting both Fort Laramie and Fort Kearney and gathering information from every available source. In a letter written by her dated Crescent City, Iowa, July 11, 1857, she summarized her story. She concluded that "I have not a doubt that the murder was committed by Indians," and again "I have no shadow of suspicion that white men were implicated." See the *New York Herald*, July 25, 1857. This was reprinted in *The Mormon* (New York), for August 1, 1875. See also *Millennial Star*, XIX, 324.

76. This case, which occupies the court for the next ten days, is more interesting in its sequel. After the trials, the convictions, the sentences, Brigham Young issued a full pardon on February 17, to Peter K. Dotson, Thomas D. Pitt, Joseph P. Watters, and Thomas S. Williams in the amounts named here by Stout. See Utah Territorial Executive Record Book "B" (Utah State Archives), 52-54.

& Dotson, Watters & Pit were arrested and brought before Judge Smith examined and held to bail. Mr Williams boasting that all was done by his own counsel and order as an attorney at Law. Hickman & myself appeared on the part of the people & Williams & Hurt for defendants.

Friday 10 Oct 1856. This after noon at the Special request of T. S. Williams and Dotson et al. a grand jury was called to inquire to the breach of the peace mentioned yesterday which met and adjourned till to morrow at 9 a. m.

Saturday 11 Oct 1856. The grand jury closed its business by presenting an indictment vs Peter K. Dotson, Thomas D. Pitt Thomas S. Williams, and Joseph P. Watters for breaking open the finishing room of the Tannery charging them all in three Counts as principal and accessary before the fact, whereupon the grand jury was discharged and the persons indicted came forward and urged an immediate trial to day, treating the whole matter with the utmost contempt and openly insulting the Court in all its proceedings saying they were in a hurry to get to the penetentiary to save the expense of their board

The Court granted their request & had a pettit jury summoned immediately while the parties were urging to be arrained. When at their own request they were arrained and plead "not guilty" Mr Williams as attorney for himself and the rest of the prisoners assisted by Garland Hurt Indian agent. Thus arrayed & thus defended after the plea of not guilty and all at their own request those learned Councils came up with a demurrer which they argued at great length and was met by myself & W. A. Hickman on the part of the people We took the ground that after plea was too late to demur & by pleading they had waived the right to demur. Judge Smith sustained our position to which they excepted and then moved to quash which shared the fate of the demurer Williams then asked and obtained leave to have a Separate trial, which trial was carried on in a violent and turbulent manner on his part all through near midnight the case was after windy insulting & contemptuous pleas on the part of the defence, submitted to the jury, who retired and after a short time brought in a virdict against Williams of guilty as accessary before the fact and fine of five hundred dollars. Williams gave notice of an appeal.

Monday 13 Oct 1856. To day President B. Young, H. C. Kimball, J. M. Grant and D. H Wells and several others started to Bridger to make a visit to the Shoshone Indians and to see and visit the bretheren at Supply. And meet the immigration They expect to be absent some three weeks

Mr Pitt was next called up for trial Mr Hurt this morning came into court to ask leave of absence he having a faint reccollection of official buisiness elsewhere which leave of course was granted & he *vamoised* and A. Miner appeared in his place as council for defence with Williams

The fore noon was spent in argueing pleas. The case against lasted till late at night and was not submitted to the jury till after 12 o'clock and the jury not being likely to agree very soon court adjourned.

Tuesday 14 Oct 1856. The jury brought in a virdict vs. Pitt of Guilty as accessary before the fact and fine of three hundred dollars.

The Case of Dotson & Watters then was called up and both went on trial after the jury was empannelled and the attorneys opened the case court adjourned for dinner and met again Dotson asked to have the case adjourned till to morrow as Williams his senior Council could not be in court this evening he being drunk and vomiting not able to be out of bed so his case was adjourned till tomorrow

The Eleventh Quorum had a meeting at Prest Harmon's at which I attended this evening at dark.

Wednesday 15 Oct 1856. Case of Dotson & Watters called and tried without much difficulty jury found a virdict against both fined Dotson as accessary before the fact four hundred dollars and Watters as principal and fined two hundred dollars.

This evening about dark President and those with him returned to the city They had proceeded as far as East Kanyon when the President was taken violently and dangerously ill and to go to fort Supply was deemed unsafe and impractable He was some better when he arrived at home

Thursday 16 Oct 1856. Court met & the fore noon spent in argueing pleas, and in the case of Pitt the court granted a new trial on the ground that the jury dispersed after retiring to make up their virdict & before they had been discharged.

Attended ward meeting this evening. Mrs Camp, Robt Benham & wife were cut off from the church

Friday 17 Oct 1856. Finished Shingling my house.

Saturday 18 Oct 1856. The case of Pitt came up again for a new trial which lasted till ten in the evening when the case was submitted to the jury who soon Hung untill after midnight when they were discharged by the Court so the second trial fell through in his case.

A moderate rain about ten to night.

Monday 20 Oct 1856. Court met again overruled a motion for a new trial in the case of Dotson & Watters. The case of Pitt was adjourned till Tuesday 28 inst

Heavy weather like for snow

Saturday 25 Oct 1856. To day Mr C. R. Van Emman, agent for the American Bible society arrived with a large number of bibles of various sizes & stile and in various languages, designed both for sale and gift in this Territory

Tuesday 28 Oct 1856. The case of Pitt came off again for the third time to day which lasted all day and untill 9 p. m. When the jury, brought in a virdict against him for $300 fine.

Thus ends this prosecution in the Probate Court The whole amount of fine against the four is fourteen hundred dollars Mr Williams has maintained an insolent insulting overbearing and defiant course towards the Court officers & jurors throughout. the whole proceedings and still intends appealing to the District Court

Monday 3 Nov 1856. Third District court met at ten. Grand & petit juries empannelled and cases laid over till to morrow.

Tuesday 4 Nov 1856. D. Court agan time taken up in filing motions. Mr Pitt sued out injunction to stay proceeding in his case in the probate court.

O. P. Rockwell arrived this evening with Babbitts train of goods[77] & some of the Bibles so humanely and benevolently sent here by the Bible Society.

---

77. Stout's casual remark that "O. P. Rockwell arrived this evening with Babbitts train of goods" indicates that this was expected, though the missionary report had not mentioned it. It said only that:

On the 16th inst., . . . we camped with br O. P. Rockwell, who had 5 wagons and 11 yoke of oxen in charge, in addition to three families, viz., Grimshaw, Cook, and Barnes, whom he had turned back toward Laramie, deeming them too weak, to pass in safety. Br. Rockwell accompanied us to Fort Laramie, where we arrived on the morning of the 19th . . . . (Report signed by F. D. Richards and Daniel Spencer, Agents P. E. Fund. [*Deseret News,* October 22, 1856].)

The memoirs of Stephen Forsdick, a Mormon twenty-one years of age and a cook at Fort Laramie during the fall and winter of 1856-57, reported that O. P. Rockwell arrived there alone and was in the vicinity a short time before the Babbitt murder. (A typescript of this document is in the hands of Dr. LeRoy R. Hafen, Provo, Utah.)

That Rockwell was evidently en route to Fort Kearney is shown by an affidavit executed before W. I. Appleby, clerk of the United States Supreme Court of the Territory of Utah. Dated February 11, 1857, and stripped of its verbiage, it states that during the last days of August

Wed 5 Nov 1856. District Court. Time taken up in arguing motions.

Thursday 6 Nov 1856. This morning my sister Anna fell down the cellar steps & hurt herself very badly.

An Express came in this morning announcing that the first company of Hand carts were in Echo Kanyon doing as well as could be expected and that the snow fell one foot deep this side the Little mountain last night. What the depth of snow on the Big mountain was may be imagined, to be at least two feet, while the weather is still like for more snow and the poor thin clad Hand Cart company must have yet a very cold hard time before the get in.

District Court and the time taken up in arguing three applications for writs of certiorari, in the cases of people vs Williams, Dotson & Watters and Pitt from the Prob Ct

Friday 7 Nov 1856. District Court to day which was taken up in arguing motions The case of John M. Russell et. al. vs W. J. Hawley commenced 19 May last in an action on Injunction was submitted to the Court

Attended the Theological scociety this evening at the Theater

Saturday 8 Nov. 1856. District Court met to day and discharged the grand jury heard a motion or two and decreed the injunction in the case of Russell et al vs Hawley to be perpetual and then adjourned the Court untill the second Monday in February next.

Sunday 9 Nov. 1856. Smoot's Company and the Company of Hand Carts Came in this after noon There was some 100 waggons. They seemed to be in good heart.

Tuesday 11 Nov 1856. An express came in from Fort Bridger to the effect that C. N. Spencer & John Van Cott having been to the Sweet Water and hearing nothing of the last train of Hand Carts had returned and returning had caused all the teams which had gone on the road to help them in in all 77 teams which had arrived at Bridger and was now only waiting word from Prest Young

This news was very unexpected as the Hand Cart Company was in a suffering condition being beyond the South pass and destitute of clothing and provisions Immediately upon recieving the news the president sent W. H. Kimball, Joseph Simmons James Furgerson & myself as an express to go and turn the teams East again and for us to find where the Hand cart company was, according we started about Sun Set and went to John Killians about 5 miles up Emmigration Kanyon where we staid all night

Wednesday 12 Nov 1856. Started this morning and after crossing the Big mountain we met Van Cott coming home about 200 yards from the top of the Mountain Spencer having gone home in the night.

Van Cott justified himself for returning and abandoning the Hand Cart Company as he could get no information of them and had concluded they had returned to the states, or Stopt at Larimie, been killed by the Indians or other wise gone to

---

1856 (exact date not remembered), the Honorable A. W. Babbitt, then secretary of state for the Territory of Utah, employed Orrin P. Rockwell to freight or transport from Fort Kearney, Nebraska Territory, to Salt Lake City, Utah Territory, forty-three cases of books and stationery, weighing a total of 5,643 pounds at the rate of fourteen cents per pound. The said affiant had received from the A. W. Babbitt estate the sum of $790.02 as payment in full for these services. (Original in files of Utah State Historical Society; photostat in possession of editor.)

It is not likely that Rockwell set out from Salt Lake City to escort the Babbitt train in unless he were ordered to do so. The safe arrival of these wagons was important to the welfare of Zion.

Another interesting sidelight is from Thomas Bullock who, with a group headed East, met the missionaries "including F. D. Richards, W. H. Kimball, J. McGaw" near Independence Rock. They told Bullock of the murder of Babbitt and others by the Indians. (*Millennial Star,* XVIII, 811.)

It is interesting that of the twelve missionaries Bullock should name only these three, evidently his informants.

the devil and for him to have gone further was only to loose his team and starve to death himself & do no good after all and as for G. D. Grant and those with him who had gone to meet them they had probably stoped at Ft Larimie. So on these vague conclusions he had not only turned back but had caused all the rest of the teams to return and thus leave the poor suffering Hand carters to their fate.

Br Kimball repremanded him severely for his course and after hering the President's letter he turned back and went with us. when proceeding a but a little ways our Wagon tire broke and we had to leave it & put our loading in Van's waggon went on to within about 8 miles of Weber we met Jos A. Young and John Garr returning from the H. Cart Company which was left at the Devils Gate in a suffering condition and here we met another team which we turned back and camped some 3 miles further on with Smoots company & Gilbert & Gerrish's train of goods all oxen. Snow here some five or six inches deep

Saturday 15 Nov 1856. Arrived at Bridger about noon, staid four hours, took dinner had a beef killed and sent on to the company.

Here we learned to our suprise that the Ogden Company of some 15 or 20 waggons who after learning the whereabouts of the H. Carts some 4 days since were still tying up 15 miles below. We started on and arrived at the Ogden Company's camp at dark when they also started and we all went to Ham's Fork 30 miles from Bridger

Sunday 16 Nov 1856. Went on overtaking several ox teams and advised them to lay up at Green River untill further orders also some horse teams who proceeded with us. Camped at Big Sandy with several teams from Centerville and a large number of oxen from Fort Supply, all who were hurrying on to meet & relieve the H. Carts

Monday 17 Nov 1856. Camped on Little Sandy here we found one team loaded with provisions. Our train now began to look quite large being some 30 wagons

Tuesday 18 Nov 1856. The weather which had been clear and pleasant ever since I left home began to be cloudy and after noon comenced to snow and blow hard from the North. We overtook another team at Pacific Creek. When travelling on fastly we arrived at the Station on Sweat Water just before night, the rest of the teams coming in shortly afterward. Here we met the advance of the Hand Cart Company who informed us that the company would be here to night. Several teams were dispatched to meet them and help them in Soon they began to come in some in wagons, some on horses some on foot, while some. hed to be lead or carried on the backs of men.

This presented a sad sight to see men women & children thinly clad poor and worn out with hunger & fatigue trudging along in this dreary country facing a severe snow storm and the wind blowing hard in their face.

The wagons could not accommodate the half of those not able to walk. Many were sick and many frosted and some severely. G. D. Grant when he met them left a company of 20 men at the Devils Gate at an abandoned Station where he left a very great portion of the loading of the ox train besides wagons, Hand Carts, and worn out cattle and horses, with provisions to winter them. The snow storm increased all evening but the tents were reared and the poor sick saints hand many of them to be carried in.

Wednesday 19 Nov 1856. Still snowing this morning all hand stirring for a Start, With the addition of the teams which arrived last evening the entire company could be put in wagons as comfortably as the nature of the case would permit and travel at the rate of 25 miles a day. Some teams were sent back to the assistance of the ox train some Eight miles below. G. D. Grant & W H. Kimball tarried here to see and arrainge matters with the ox train while all the rest proceeded facing the drifting falling snow and encamped on a dry ravine some 20 miles having no water for men or animals to night Some time after night William & Geo. arrived leaving the ox train at Pacific Springs

This evening I went with Eph Hanks to visit and administer to the sick and had an opportunity of seeing the suffering and privations through which they had passed.[78] Some were merry and cheerfull some dull and stupid some sick some frosted & some lazy and mean but all seemed to be elated more or less with the idea of speedily arriving in the Valley.

Thursday 20 Nov 1856. This morning G. D. Grant, W. H. Kinball, G. W. Grant, H. P. Kimball and myself started for the City as an express meeting the Fort-Supply ox teams before we reached the Little Sandy who were going to the relief of the ox train & between the Little & Big Sandies met 3 good 4 horse teams who were also to help the ox train We took supper on our old camping on Big Sandy and travelled to Green River in the night and camped Late in the night Isaac Bullock & James Ivie over took us on their way to Fort Supply.

Friday 21 Nov. 1856. Travelled on to day quite Briskly, starting on the ox teams on Green River and meeting several teams from the City with feed and provisions going to the relief of the ox trains We dined at the first crossing of Black's above Ham's Fork and proceeded on to Bridger travelling some fifteen miles after dark when arriving there ourselves and animals were nearly over done with fatigue, hunger, and cold For myself I could scarsely stand alone or keep awake.

Saturday 22 Nov 1856. After arrainging matters here with some fresh animals we about noon started on facing a severe snow storm and wind and the coldest and most piercing weather we have had during our journey, and camped at Quaken Asp Grove on the mountain side seven miles before reaching Bear River

Sunday 23 Nov 1856. Travelling on we camped at the mouth of Echo Kanyon with some ten miles night travelling and Breaking the springs of one wagon and leaving it

Monday 24 Nov 1856. This morning George D. Grant & William H. Kimball went ahead on horse back intending to reach the city this evening as our animals were fast failing and one wagon broke and left here our loading now all in one wagon we could not travel fast The snow deepened as we travelled to day and travelling became harder

We encamped about one mile up the East side of the Big mountain the snow being here about Eighteen inches deep.

Tuesday 25 Nov 1856. This morning we commenced ascending the Big mountain on foot to save the team having six animals on the wagon still the ascent was very laborious for our team as well as our selves for the snow deepened as we ascended

Within two miles of the top we met Jos A. Young Brigham Young Jr F. Little and several more who had come to break the road over the mountain Their trail greatly relieved us The snow on the mountain being waist deep but now we passed over with out any difficulty and decended with out locking passing another company with oxen about half way down & another at the bottom who came to break the road.

---

78. Stout now "had an opportunity" of seeing the results of what he had earlier called a "new and improved method of emigration." Strangely, Ephraim Hanks makes no mention of Stout in his story of the handcart disaster. He says that he set out alone as the result of a prompting of the "Spirit" and was able to carry fresh buffalo meat to the rear companies. Hanks does name George D. Grant and William H. Kimball as helping with his administrations to the sick. Since the book was written in his later life, the omission is understandable. See Sidney Alvarus and Ephraim K. Hanks, *Scouting for the Mormons on the Great Frontier* (Salt Lake City, 1948).

We had heavy travelling over the Little mountain and down Killians Kanyon the snow being very deep untill we arrived in Emmigration Kanyon when it became less and in the valley there was none to speak of

We arrived at home about sun set finding all well with the exception that President Jedediah M. Grant was dangerously sick

(**Thursday** [crossed out]) **27.** C. H. Wheelock came in last night   reports that the company will cross the Weber this after noon   President Grant continues dangerously sick

Sunday 30 Nov 1856. The Hand cart companies arrived to day in the fore noon or rather the companies who went to the relief of the Hand Cart company brought them in wagons   The train of wagons was very large

These poor persons were sent to different parts of the Territory immediately to be taken care of untill they could support themselves.

Monday 1 Dec 1856. Had a compromised case which was pending before the probate Court Mary Ann Mogher v James Emalay in assumpsit wherein the plff claimed $317 against the deft for sundry articles &c furnished and for being seduced and made the mother of a fine son to her great damage now the boy was dead I was on the part of the deft but after great labor and pains induced them to settle by him paying her $117 and cost of suit

This evening about 20 minutes past 10 Jedediah M. Grant Second Counselor to President Brigham Young died at his residence after a short but severe illness

Thursday 4 Decr 1856. To day the funeral obsequies of President J. M. Grant took place The concourse of people was very large   As a Major General he was buried in the honors of war   As a Master Mason he was buried as such and above all as a Saint he lived, died and was buried as such.

This evening about dark Myself & J. W. Cummings started for Fillmore to the Legislature and staid all night at F. Little's some 4 miles out and the next day went to Provo city and staid with K Bullock

Saturday 6th Dec 1856. Being joined here by Isaac Bullock member from Green River Co. we went to Salt Creek and put up, procured another team, rigged up a slay & early next morning started on our way, the snow gradually deepning as we travelled and after crossing the Severe River it was so deep say 12 or 14 inches, that we had to travel in a walk, but taking our time and being dilligent we arrived at Fillmore at five in the morning.   The snow on Beaver Mountain was say two feet deep & very heavy travelling.   We passed all the members who had started before us

Monday 8 Dec 1856. At ten A. M the Legislature met and there not being a Quorum in either House adjourned till 2 p. m and met accordingly   Both houses organized temporarily. The Hon. Lorenzo Snow president pro tem of the Council & Myself speaker (pro-tem [crossed out]) of the House.   The officers were then elected and a Bill introduced changing the seat of Government from Fillmore to G. S. L. City and for this session to adjourn to meet at the Social Hall there on Thursday the 15 inst The Bill passed[79]   We then adj'd and commenced the cerimony of returning and

---

79. The official account book for the legislature shows for this year the regular mileage cost in relation to the distance traveled: the members nearest Fillmore in amounts as low as $18.00, those in the Salt Lake City area $48.00 each, and Enoch Reese from the Carson Valley in Nevada $258, with each legislator receiving the regular per diem of $120 for the term of the legislature.

In addition to this, thirteen men named as officers received another $120. Hosea Stout, speaker of the house, was one of these, and it would seem that these are the men who gathered at Fillmore and voted to adjourn and reassemble in Salt Lake City. A third list of twenty-four were given mileage of from $10.50 from American Fork to $48.00 from Fillmore. Incidental expenses included providing, cutting, and stacking wood; plastering, white-washing, and cleaning

at seven I was on my way home and arrived at Salt Creek at sun set the next day and staid all night.

Wednesday 10 Dec 1856. Having a fresh team here we started gaily on this morning being over taken by a snow storm which attended us all day we after missing our road between Payson & Spanish Fork arrived at Provo just about bed time

Thursday 11 Dec 1856. Fine day and deep snow We had to break our road in the snow to Battle Creek but tolerable good road but heavy afterwards we arrived at home about 8 in the evening all well thinking we had made a quick trip of 160 miles and back

Friday 12 Dec 1856. Snowing hard all day this snow storm extends all over the territory and is now very deep The members of the Legislature will, if the snowing continues have a merry time to meet here at the time of their adjournment.

Snowing continues Saturday & Sunday. Quite a large train arrived on Sunday of the relief train.

Monday 15 Decr 1856. All the teams which went out to help in the Emmigration came in to day bringing in the rest of the Saints The snow on the Big Mountain was some 14 ft deep yet the teams looked well and there was but few persons frosted

Thursday 1856. Today the Legislative assembly met at the Social Hall the House in the stage room and the Council in the room below.

The officers of the council as elected previously were Heber C Kimball Prest
> Leo Hawkins Secratary
> John T. Caine Asst do
> George D Grant Sergent at arms
> Saml L. Sprague Messenger
> Richd Harrison Foreman
> Cyrus H. Wheelock Chaplain

And the officers of the House were Hosea Stout Speaker
> James Furguson, Ch [chief] Clerk
> Jas H. Martineau Asst do
> Wm H. Kimball Sergeant-at-arms
> Brigham Young jr Messenger
> William Derr Foreman
> Jesse Haven Chaplain

After the House had met & proceed to business on Motion of Mr Cummings Messrs Spencer Cummings and Richards were appointed a committee to join a simalar Committee from the Council and inform His Excellency the Govornor that the assembly were prepared to recieve any communication he might have to make The committee returned and stated that His Excellency wished to meet the (joint session [crossed out]) assembly in joint session and that the Council were ready for the same

On Motion of Mr Reese the Council was notified that the House was ready for the same whereupon the Council appeared and the two Houses went into joint Session the President of the Council Presiding

His Excellency then presented his annual Message which was read and 500 copies ordered to be printed for the use of the assembly

On motion of Counr Carrington James Mc Knight was elected Public Printer.

On Motion of Mr Rockwood 100 copies of the daily minutes were ordered to be printed for the use of the assembly after which The Governor & Prest Kimball

---

the buildings; repairing furniture; and providing stoves, spittoons, stationery, shovel & tongs; etc.

The total expense of the legislature as of March 2, 1857, was $12,837.35. See records of the Utah Legislative Assembly, Account Book (Utah State Archives).

delivered Each a most excellent discourse on the true order of Legislation &c after which the Joint Session dissolved & the House adjd

2 P. M. The following appointments of Committies were then announced by the speaker

On judiciary J. C. Little and A. Johnson.

on Petitions Jas C. Snow J. C. Wright & J. W. Cummings.

On Claims H. B. Clawson, E Reese Jas Lewis.

On Militia J. C. Little A. P. Rockwood I. C. Haight H. B. Clawson

On Revenue Snow Richards and J. D. Parker

On Education W. W. Phelps S. W. Richards J. C Wright.

On Agriculture &c Peter Maughn Geo Peacock C. W. West J. A. Young

On Counties Haight I. Bullock J. G. Bigler

On Roads &c Johnson Grover self and Spencer.

On Indian affairs McRae N. W. Bartholemew & E Reese

On Herding Cummings Snow D. Spencer

On Engrossing Printing and the Library Richards Lewis J A. Young

On Corporations Peacock McRae and Bullock

On Appropriations Rockwood McRae & David Evans.

On Elections Wright, Evans, Snow and Phelps

On Public Works Parker, West, Haight & Bigler

The Secretary of the Territory was instructed to furnish each member & officer of the House with with a copy of the "Deseret News" for the current year.

adjourned till (Monday [crossed out]) tomorrow at ten a. m.

Friday 19 Decr 1856. House met at ten a. m. Mr Cummings presented H. D. No 1. An act granting to H. C. Kimball & William Mc'Bride a herd ground which was recieved and referred to Committee on Herding

Mr Rockwood presented Petition of L. D Young for a herd ground recieved & referred to Comt on herding.

On motion of Mr Rockwood the House adopted the rules of the former sessions of the Council which was to be governed by the dictates of the Holy Spirit

The Comt on herding reported Act No. 1. as above which was read the first time and laid on the table adjd till Monday

Saturday 20 Dec 1856. Special Election to fill the vacancy of J M. Grant Elder Orson Hyde was elected

Sunday 21 Dec 1856. Went to meeting Prest Kimball preached. Quorum meeting at noon at my house.

Monday 22 Dec 1856. House met at ten a. m. O. Hyde having been elected took his seat in the House to fill the place of Hon J. M. Grant.

Mr Rockwood presented "Resolution in relation to the late Hon J. M. Grant" which was read and referred to a select comte of Little Rockwood & Richards

On Motion of Rockwood "A select comte was appointed to bring in a bill defining the duty of County Courts & select men in the granting of Mill sites and distribution of waters" consisting of Rockwood Spencer Grover and Johnson

Act No 1 granting to H. C. Kimball &c was called up, & laid on the table untill called for by the presentor

Mr Peacock presented petition of David Evans for a herd ground, which was read and referred to Comte on herding.

The Speaker added Mr Hyde to the Committee on Judiciary

Mr Johnson presented Remonstrance from J. H. Glines & others to the petition of David Evans which was read and referred to the Comte on Herding

Mr Clawson presented Communication from William Clayton recorder of Marks and Brands which was read and referred to a special Comte consisting of Hyde Little and Phelps. Adjd till tomorrow

This evening attended the Seventies meeting at their Hall. Hon? George P. Stiles was tried for adultery found guilty & cut off from the Church root and Branch. Amen to the damnation of that wicked & corrupt Judge.

Several of the Twelve were present who advised all the First Presidents of the seventies except Joseph Young to resign their office and let men be put in their place who would magnify their calling and not stand at the head of all the 40 Quorums of Seventies and obstruct the work of the Lord and keep back the Spirit of God &c.[80]

All present responded to this with a hearty & heart thrilling Amen. Some of the Presents expressed a willingness to do so, which if the do I venture to predict that there will be more spirit power influence among the 70's than has ever been known for those presidents seem as dry branches in the House of Israel.

Tuesday 23 Decr 1856. House met at ten a. m. On motion of Mr Rockwood the committee on Elections was instructed to report all offices to be filled by the joint vote of this Legislative Assembly.

Mr Lewis Reported "An act (No 2. H. F.) providing for the relief of Stock or share-holders in manufacturing companies" which was read, recieved, and referred to the committee on revenue.

Mr Parker reported "An Act (No 3 H. F.) to incorporate the Weber Canyon Road Company" which was read, recieved and referred to the Committee on Roads &c

On Motion of Mr Richards The committee on Trade & manufactures was instructed to inquire into the expediency of reporting a bill encouraging domestic production and manufactures &c.

On motion of Mr Peacock a select committee was appointed to report a bill for the preventing the introduction of contagious diseases into inhabited portions of this Territory consisting of Peacock, Hyde, and Clawson. Adjd till Friday at ten a. m. when the House went into the Council Chamber where President H. C. Kimball was preaching with great power being filled with the Spirit of God.

Nearly all the members spoke all being filled with the spirit the meeting lasted till dark The power and testimony of the Elders of Israel exceeded any thing that I have seen in many a day It was truly a pentacost —

Thursday 25 Dec 1856. This is a happy christmas a warm fine snow falling all day and the streets filled with sleighs —

This evening a young woman by the name of Williams committed suicide by cutting her throat

Friday 26 Decr 1856. House met at ten a. m. An act (No 1. H. F.) granting unto H. C. Kimball and W. McBride a herd ground" was called up and read three times and passed

The Speaker referred the different portions of the Govornor's message to the appropriate committies

Mr Little, on behalf of the committee to whom was referred the subject reported the following. . Preamble and Resolutions in relation to the death of Hon J. M. Grant, Late Speaker of the House of Representatives.

Whereas it has pleased an All wise and over-ruling Providence to remove from this House, by the hand of death, Honorable J. M. Grant late member elect from G. S. L. County, who died at his residence in this City, at 20 minutes past 10 o'clock P. M. of the first instant

---

80. Although the church leaders were very pointed in their suggestions that all the older presidents of the Quorum of the Seventy resign and make room for new and more active men to take over, it would seem that none followed the counsel. At this time the seven presidents in the order of their appointment were: Joseph Young (1837), Levi W. Hancock (1837), Zera Pulsipher (1838), Henry Herriman (1838), Albert P. Rockwood (1845), Benjamin L. Clapp (1845), and Horace S. Eldredge (1854). Clapp was removed in 1859 and Pulsipher in 1862; all others died in the service.

Therefore Resolved That we deeply regret the loss of this valuable, man who so ably and satisfactorily, presided as Speaker of this House, during its last three sessions; a man whose presence cheered and gladdened the hearts of the wise, just and good in every department of life where he was known, and whose voice like the dew of Heaven upon the tender plant, animated with joy and inspired with hope immortal, every sorrowful and afflicted heart; and also like the resistless current of a mighty river, it swept down before it everything that dared to rise up to oppose the demands of justice, to rob virtue of her crown, innocence of its laruels or truth of its merits.

As a citizen, he was kind, sociable and familiar; as a public officer, fearless and efficient; as a husband affectionate and devoted; as a father tender and engaging.

Resolved further, that we cherish with undying memory his invaluable services on all occasions, and especially in times of adversity and peril; and most cordially do we extend our warmest sympathies to his interesting & afflicted family, who are bereft of a husband so kind and devoted and of a father so tender and affectionate; which report was recieved and adopted

On motion of Mr Cummings the committee on Judiciary where instructed to report a bill authorizing sheriffs to convey real estate &c.

Mr Parker reported H. C. N 4. "An Act to amend an Act incorporating the Davis County Canal Company approved Jan. 12 1856 which was recieved and read the first time and passed.

On its second reading Sec 1 was struck out and another inserted in its stead after which the bill was read the third time and passed

After some other business the the House adjourned till 10 a. m to morrow.

Saturday, Dec 27 1856. House met at ten a. m. Mr Snow from the Committee to whom was referred H. F. No 2 An Act providing for the relief of stock holders &c reported not expedient to Legislate thereon which report was accepted

Mr Johnson reported back H. F. No 3 An act to incorporate the Weber Kanyon Road Company with H F. No 5. An act to amend "An Act to incorporate the Weber Kanyon Road Company," Approved Jan. 19 1855 and H. F. No 6 An Act to amend 'An Act granting to John Stoker et. al. the North end of Weber valley for a herd ground and other purposes Approved Jan 8 1856 as a substitute which report was was accepted and the bills read the first time and passed and then referred back to the committee

Mr Maughn reported H. F. No 7 An Act to encourage the raising of cotton Indigo and Madder which was read and laid on the table to come up in its order

Mr Wright from the Comte on Elections reported the offices to be filled by joint vote of the Legislative Assembly which was accepted

Mr Cummings (reported [crossed out]) presented petition of Silas Richards and 42 others for the incorporation of Union City which was recieved and refered to the committee on incorporations

Mr Cummings presented Memorial of A. F. Navarre and 20 others for a Fishery to be granted to R. Weimer which was recieved and referred to a select comte consisting of Phelps Hyde and Richards

Mr Little presented Petition of John Stiles for remuneration for services as Door keeper in the House of Repve in the year 1854, which was recieved & referred to the Comte on Claims

Mr Little of comte on Judiciary reported H. F. No 8 "An Act authorizing conveyances by shiriffs and ollectors of taxes which was recieved and laid on the table to come up in its order and 50 copies ordered to be printed Adjourned till Monday at 10.

Monday 29 Decr 1856. House met at ten a. m

Mr Bullock presented a petition of S. M. Blair & others for herd ground which was recieved and referred to comte on herding

Mr Rockwood reported H. F. No 9 "An act concerning division fences" which was recieved and laid on the table to come up in its order Mr Johnson chairman of the committee on Roads &c reported back H. F. No. 5 An Act to amend an act to incorporate the Weber Kanyon Road Company approved Jan 19, 1856 which was recieved and laid on the table to come up in its order

Mr Johnson chairman of the comte on Roads &c also reported back H. F. No 6 An Act to amend an act granting to John Stoker and others the North end of Weber Valley for a herd ground and other purposes approved Jan 8 1855 which was recieved and laid on the table to come up in its order

H F. No 9 An act concerning division fences" was read the first time and 50 copies ordered to be printed and the bill laid over

H F. No 5 was taken up and read three times and passed

H. F. No 6 was taken up read 3 times amended & passed

On motion of J. A. Young the committee on appropriations was instructed to confer with a corresponding committee of the council on the expediency of compiling a general appropriation bill which motion was recieved adjd till tomorrow.

Tuesday Dec 30th 1856. House met at ten a. m   Mr Haight reported H. F. No 10 An act granting to Rufus C. Allen, Lorenzo W. Roundy, Amos Thornton, Richd Robinson and their associates a herd ground which was recieved and referred to the comte on Herding

Mr Phelps from the select comte to whom was referred reported H. F. No 11 An Act (authorizing [crossed out]) granting to Robert Weimer the right to establish a fishery on Jordain River which was recieved and laid on the table to come up in its order

H. F. No. 8 An act authorizing conveyances by shiriffs and collectors of taxes" was read the first time and passed and on its second reading was laid over till tomorrow

The Speaker added Cummings Phelps Richards & Rockwood to the Committee on Judiciary, with instructions to act with a like committee from the Council in compiling from the U. S. Statutes at large all laws applicable to this Territory

Adjourned till to morrow at ten a. m. and joint session met in committee of the *whole* on the state of the Reformation and passed an unanimous Resolution to repent of and forsake our sins and be rebaptized for their Remission and in conformity therewith   went to dinner then repaired to the *Font* filled it with water and some fifty-five were Baptized[81]   I was baptized by F. D. Richards one of the Twelve and confirmed under the hands of A. P. Rockwood & Thomas Grover

There was an unusual out poring of the spirit of God manifested in joint session on this occasion during the Preaching of Presidents B. Young & H. C. Kimball.

Last night the Law library of Judge Stiles & T. S. Williams was broken open and the books and papers thereof taken away. A privy near by was filled with books a few thousand shingles and laths added and the concern set on fire and consumed. *Sic transit Lex non Scripti*[82]

---

81. This is a natural outgrowth of the death of Jedediah M. Grant, who had been the most ardent in pressing for a general reformation throughout the church. The meeting two days before Christmas in which Stout said that "all being filled with the spirit the meeting lasted till dark   The power and testimony of the Elders of Israel exceeded any thing that I have seen in many a day   It was truly a pentacost," is a prelude to this baptismal ceremony at the close of the year.

82. As on October 12, 1855, when persons unknown broke into the office of Almon W. Babbitt and carried away all the official papers, now again some zealots looted the offices of Judge Stiles, lately excommunicated, and Thomas S. Williams, also out of favor with the church. Later these books were found and returned, the burning of the privy and some papers being only a trick to anger and deceive the judge. *Sic transit lex non Scripti*—"Thus passeth away the unwritten law."

Wednesday Dec 31 - 1856. House met at ten a. m. On Motion of Mr Little the Council was invited to meet the House in Joint Session to which the Council concurrid and the council made their appearance when on Motion of Mr Little H. F. No 8 "An act authorizing coveyance by sheriffs and collectors of taxes" which had been put upon its second reading in the House, was read the first time and passed and on its second reading was referred to joint committee on Judiciary.

H. F. No 9, An "Act concerning division fences" reported to the House, was read the first time and passed and on the second reading was referred to the joint Committee on Judiciary.

H. F. No 11 "An act granting unto Robert Weimer the right to establish a fishery on Jordan river" reported to the House was read the first time and laid on the table.

On Motion of D. H. Wells His Excellency the Govornor was respectfully requested to nominate the candidates to fill the vacancies by joint vote of the Legislative Assembly.[83]

On Motion of F. D. Richards the President appointed D. H. Wells, F. D. Richards, H. B. Clawson, J. W. Cummings, and J. C. Little a special committee with instructions to report on the Subject of the Fortification Act at an earley day.

Adjourned till Friday January 2

Thursday 1 Jan 1857. This is a happy New Year but the day dawned in the midst of a hard snow storm which continued till noon the snow falling some 8 inch

Went to the Globe saloon and took dinner with Prest H. C. Kimball when we went to the governor's office and spent most of the day listening to their teachings

Friday 2 Jan 1857. The two Houses met in joint session at ten a. m.

Mr Rockwood, from the Special committee to whom was referred reported J. S. F. No 1. "An Act defining the duties of county Courts & Select men in granting of Mill Sites, and distribution of irrigating waters" which was read and accepted and fifty copies ordered to be printed

H. F. No. 7. "An Act to encourage the raising of Cotton, Indigo and Madder" reported in the House, was read the first time and passed and read the Second and third times and passed.

Mr Evans reported J. S. F No. 2 "An act regulating the duties of the Territorial and County Surveyors in relation to Corporations" which after being debated at length was withdrawn and House adjourned till 5th inst at 10 a. m.

Saturday 3 Jan 1857. South wind all day melting the snow very fast.

Sunday 4 Jan 1857. This morning the snow was falling very fast and had been all night but broke away about ten a. m. having fallen some Eight inches deep.

Had a Quorum meeting at my house at 1 p. m.

Monday 5 Jan 1857. This morning at ten the two houses after meeting in their separate rooms came into joint Session

Mr Peacock chairman of the committee on incorporations reported unfavorably to granting the petition of Silas Richards and others asking for an incorporation for Union City which was recieved and the petition laid on the table indefinitely.

J. S. F. No 1 "An act further defining the duties of County courts &c was read three times and passed

A Report from G. D. Watt Secratary of the University of Deseret was read and placed on the minutes.

---

83. That "His Excellency the Govornor was respectfully requested to nominate the candidates to fill the vacancies" is evidence of his complete control of government functions.

Counr Wells presented a memorial to the President of the U. S. which was read & adopted

On Motion of Mr Stout the session went into Committee of the whole on the State of the Territory

At 1. p m. the committee arose and the Joint session resumed

The report of the committee on Elections was taken up and the following persons elected on the nomination of His Excellency the Govornor.

A. Carrington Chancellor of the University of Deseret.

Board of Regents

1	Willford Woodruff	7.	F. D. Richards
2	Hosea Stout	8	John T. Caine
3	Danl H. Wells	9	Robt L. Campbell
4	Saml W. Richards	10	Jos A. Young
5	William Willis	11	Leo Hawkins
6	Orson Hyde	12	W. W. Phelps.

Danl Spencer, Treasurer of Deseret University.

H. B. Clawson Territorial Treasurer

J. W. Cummings, Auditor of Public Accounts

Thomas D. Brown Territorial Road Commissioner

Alex McRae Territorial Marshal

Hosea Stout Attorney General

Jas Leithead Dist Atty 1st Dist

Jesse N. Smith do 2nd Dist

Jesse W. Fox Surveyor Genl

W. C. Stains Librarian

W. Clayton Recorder of Marks and Brands

Danl Cairn, Warden Penetentiary

W. Woodruff)
S. W. Richards) Inspectors of do.
A. P. Rockwood)

E. Smith P. Judge G. S. L. County
W. W. Phelps Notary Public do.

John D. Parker P. J. Davis Co.
J Leithead N. Public — do

C. W. West P. Judge Weber Co
W. Critchlow N. Public do

J. C. Wright P. Judge Box Elder Co
Saml Smith N. Public do

P. Maughn P. Judge Cache Co
G. Bryant N. Public do

I. Bullock P. Judge G River Co
L. Robinson N Public do

John P. Bernard P. J. Malad Co.
J. Frodsham N. Public do.

D. Carter P. Judge Utah Co.
A. Johnson N Public do

Allen Weeks P. Judge Cedar Co
J. H. Glines N. Public do

G. W. Bradley P. Judge Juab Co.
Z. H. Baxter N. Public do

G. Peacock P. Judge San Pete Co.
John Eager N. Public do

W. Felshaw Probate J. Millard Co
B. Robinson Notary Public do

P. T. Farnsworth P. Judge Beaver Co
John M. Davis N Public do

James Lewis P. Judge Iron Co
C. C. Pendleton N Public do

J. D. Lee P. Judge Washington Co
C. W. Dalton N. Public do

A Lee P. Judge Tooele County
L. Gee Notary Public do

L. Johnson, P. Judge Shambip Co.
R. H. Porter N. Public do

On Motion of Mr Rockwood The committee on Elections was instructed to bring in a bill creating the office of sealer of weights & Measures.

Councillor Wells of the Comte on Judiciary reported back H. F. No. 8. "An act authirizing conveyances by sheriffs and collectors of taxes" with J. S. F. No 3. An act to amend "An act regulating the mode of procedure in civil cases &c" approved Dec 30, 1852 as a substitute which was recieved and the bill substituted read three times & passed;

JANUARY 1857

Mr Little of the Comte on Judiciary Reported J. S. F. No 4 "An act for the foreclosure of mortgages which was recieved and 50 copies ordered to be printed. Adjourned till 10 tomorrow.

This morning President H. C. Kimball announced to the assembly that President Young had chosen and ordained Daniel H. Wells to be second Councillor to the First President of the Church

Tuesday 6 Jan 1857. Joint Session met at 10 a. m. An address upon the Subject of a righteous and form of government was delivered by the Chaplain of the.

Mr Stout presented J. S. F. No 5 "An act repealing certain laws therein named" which was read the first time & and referred to the Committee on incorporations.

Counr Woodruff of the Comte on Agriculture reported back H. F. No "An concerning division fences", which was read three times and passed.

Joint session then adjourned to meet at the "Globe Saloon" to take dinner to the honor and hospitality of Secratary W. H. Hooper whither we all repaired and all I believe recieved "a fullness" and met in joint session at 4 o'clock P. M.

Councilr Wells presented "Memorial to the President of the U. S. which was recieved and adopted.

On motion of D. H. Wells J. S. F. No 1. "An act defining the duties of County courts &c" was taken up for reconsideration and laid on the table indefinitely. J. S. F. No 4 "An act for the foreclosure of mortgages" was taken up and on its second reading was referred back to the committee

Councilr Wells presented "Territorial Road Commissioner's Annual Report" which was read recieved and referred to the Comte on Roads &c

On motion of Mr Stout the Election of William Clayton as Recorder of Marks & Brands was reconsidered and His Excellency the Gov. requested to nominate another candidate whereupon H. B. Clawson was nominated and Elected

Councilr Wells presented "Resolution in relation to the Recorder of Marks and Brands" which was read & adopted.

Adjd till 8th inst at 10. a. m.

Wednesday 7 Jan 1857. Southern mail arrived last night by which it appears that Buckhannan has quite certainly been Elected President by a handsome majority over Freemont & Fillmore both. Buck has 174 votes other two 117 [votes]

Thursday 8 Jan 1857. Joint session met at ten a. m.

Mr Cummings of Comte on Herding, reported J. S. F. 6 "An Act granting unto L. D. Young a herd ground" which was read three times and passed

Also reported J. S. F. No. 7. "An act granting unto S. M. Blair a herd ground in Rush Valley" which was read three several times and passed.

Also J. S. D. No. 8 An Act granting to Rufus C. Allen and others a herd ground in Iron and Washington Counties" which was read three times & passed

Also (J. S. F. No [crossed out]) reported on the petition of David Evans &c" and remonstrance thereto, inexpedient to legislate thereon which report was accepted

Mr Wright of the Comte on Elections reported J. S. D. No. 9 "An act creating the office of Sealer of Weights and measures &c" which was read and 50 copies ordered to be printed

Mr Spencer reported J. S. F. No. 10. "An act to amend An Act entittled 'An act regulating the mode of procedure in civil cases in the courts of the Territory of Utah" which was read and 50 copies ordered to be printed.

Mr Bullock reported J. S. F. No. 11. "An act granting to Lewis Robinson the right of certain lands for a herd ground, farming & other purposes in Green River Co" which was read three several times and passed.

Mr Little reported the "Report of Treasurer of Deseret Ag'l and Man'g Society which was referred to Comte on agriculture" &c.

Mr Peacock reported J. S. F. No. 12. "An act granting to W. S. Snow et. al. a herd ground in San Pete County" which was read and referred to Comte on Herding

Mr Phelps of the Comte on Education reported no Legislation needed thereon, which was recieved.

Mr Bigler presented a petion of G. W. Bradley et. al. for an appropriation of $1000 to make road in Salt Creek Kanyon referred to Comte on Roads &c"

S. W. Richards presented Report of Librarian which was referred to Comte on Library

Mr Little of Joint Comte on Judiciary reported J. S. F No 4. "An act for fore-closure of mortgages" amended which was read and laid on the table adjourned. the Eastern mail which went out the other day returned having only gone to the top of the Little Mountain & had one man frozen to death.

Friday 9 Jan 1857. Joint Session met at ten a. m. J. S. F. No. 9 "An creating the office of Sealer of Weights and Measures &c was read and referred to the joint Committee on Judiciary.

J. S. F. No. 10 "An act to amend an act entitled 'An act regulating the mode of procedure in civil cases &c was read three several times and passed.

Mr Woodruff of the Comte on Agriculture &c. reported on the report of the Treasurer of the Deseret Agricultural &c Society recommending the appropriation of $1000 therefor which was accepted

Mr Clawson presented J. S. F. No 13. "An act to attach Carson county to G. S. L. Co. which was read and referred to the joint committee on judiciary.

Mr S Richards presented J. S. F. No. 14 "An act granting to B. Young Sen and F. D. Richards the control of waters from Mill Creek in G. S. L. County" which was read three times and passed

Mr Daime of the Comte on Roads &c reported, on the Territorial R. Commission-er's report, *inexpedient to* legislate thereon

Mr Daime of same reported J. S. F. No 15. "An act appropriating for a Terri-torial Road in Juab County" which was read three times and passed.

Mr J. C. Snow presented a petition of A. Williams & others for bounty on wolf pelts, which was recieved and referred to committee on Revenue.

Mr Bullock presented J. S. F. No. 16 "An act to amend 'An act granting to Isaac Bullock & Lewis Robinson the right to errect ferries on G. River & control the same, which was read three times & passed.

The President instructed the Council Committee on Claims to act with the House Committee on Appropriations.

Mr Reese was added to the Committee on judiciary for the consideration of J. S. F. No. 13. Adjourned till 12th inst at 10 a. m

Sunday 11 Jan. 1857. I was very unwell all day and staid at home.

Quorum meeting at my House. 4 members were recieved into the Quorum viz Jesse Tye, Samuel Cusley, John Muir and Anthony F. Navarre.

Monday 12 Jan. 1857. Joint session met at 10 a. m. Mr Phelps presented "Resolu-tion creating the office of superintendent of Meteorological observations, and appro-priating money to pay for the same" which was read and adopted.

Mr Little presented, Petition of Orson Hyde for water privileges on Truckee River which was recieved & referred to the joint committee on Petitions

Mr Cummings of the Comte on Herding reported back J. S. F. No 12. "An act granting to W. S. Snow, J. Hatch, D. B. Funk & J. Lowry a herd ground in San Pete County" amended, which was read three several times and passed.

He also reported J. S. F. No 17. "An act granting a herd ground and making an appropriation for military purposes", which was recieved and read three several times and passed.

Councillor Wells from the Joint Comte on Military presented J. S. F. No 18. "An act to amend 'An to provide for the further organization of the Militia" ap-proved Feb 2, 1852, which was recieved and 50 copies ordered to be printed.

Count Wells of Comte on Judiciary reported back J. S. F. No 9 "An act creating the office of Sealer of Weights & Measures" which was read 2 & third times and passed.

He also reported back J. S. F. No. 13. "An act to attach Carson County to G. S. L. County" amended which was read three several times and passed.

Councillor Richards of the joint committee on Revenue Reported on the Petition of A. Williams and others that it was inexpedient to Legislate thereon which was recieved and the committee discharged from further duty thereon.

Mr Phelps presented J. S. F. No. 19 "An act to amend 'An act granting to W. W. Phelps & H. McKinney a herd ground," approved 12 Jan 1856" which was read three several times & passed. Adjourned till tomorrow 10 a. m

Tuesday 13 Jan 1857. Joint Session met at 10. a. m. J. S. F. No. 18 "An act to amend 'An act to provide for the further organization of the militia &c" approved 5 Feb 1852. was read the first time and laid over.

Mr. J. C. Snow presented Petition of Saml Simmons and others of Spanish Fork City praying for the extension of the city bounds &c, which was referred to the committee on Petetions

Mr A. Johnson presented Remonstrance to said Petition which was also referred to same Committee —

Councillor Wells ch of Co. on Judiciary reported in relation to compiling the U. S. Laws applicable to Utah recommending the revision and publication thereof to the Code commission and also reporting J. S. F. No 20. "An Act authorizing the compilation and publication of the U. S. Laws in force and applicable to the 'Territory of Utah" which was read three times and passed.

Mr. Lewis presented "The Deseret News office Bill for $223 which was read and referred to Comte on Claims.

Mr Hyde presented J. S. F. No 21 "An Act for the appropriation of money to defray the expenses of seals and blanks for Carson County" which was referred to the committee on Claims —

Mr. Peacock of the Select committee reported J. S. F. No 22 "An act in relation to Quarantine" which was read three times & passed.

Mr. J. C. Snow presented J. S. F. No. 23. "An Act granting a ranch and herd ground to G. W. Bean, E. Barney, and others" which was referred to Comte on Herding.

Mr. Little presented Petition from J. Haven for Free Schools which was referred to Join [Joint] Comte on Education.

Comr Wells presented Resolution authorizing the Auditor of Public afc to settl with the Recorder of Marks and Brands which was adopted

Mr Wheelock Chaplain of the council presented an address which was read. Adjourned.

Wednesday 14 Jan 1857. Last night Jarvis House was broken into and his family drove out, the House set on fire in two or three places and he beaten and drove off and hell played generally

Joint Session met at 10 a. m. Counr Woodruff of Comte on Claims reported, unfavorably to the passage of the act J. S. F. No 21. "An act for an appropriation of money to defray the Expenses of seals and blanks for Carson County" which was recieved.

Councilr Woodruff of the joint Comte on Education to whom was referred Petition of Jesse Haven for free Schools Reported no Legislation needed on the subject which was recieved

Councilr (Woodruff [crossed out]) Wells of Select Comte on Fortifications reported J. S. F No 24 "An Act to repeal 'An act concerning Fortifications which was read the three times and passed.

J. S. F No 18 An Act to amend 'An act for the further organization of the militia" Approved Feb 5 1852 was taken up on its Second reading & passed and on its 3rd reading was laid on the table indefinately.

Mr Farr of the Comte on Incorporations reported on the petition for Extension of the boundaries of Spanish Fork City and reported J. S. F. No 25. "An act granting unto John L. Butler and Aaron Johnson, the right of water from Spanish Fork river, in Utah County" which was read three times & passed.

Conr Wells of Comte on Military presented J. S. F. No 26 "An act for the organization of the militia of the Territory of Utah" which was read three several times and passed.

On motion of S. W. Richards His Excellency the Govornor, who was present, was requested to nominate three Code Commissioners, and one Sealer of Weights & Measures for the Territory of Utah whereupon His Excellency nominated

    Hosea Stout   )
    Jas W. Cummings)   Code Commissioners
    Saml W. Richards)
Nathan Davis. Sealer of Weights and Measures who were Elected unanimously

Councilr Wells presented Memorial of S. L. Sprague and others for an appropriation for an Infirmary, which was referred to Comte on appropriations Adjd till tomorrow at 10 A. M

Thursday 15 Jan 1857. Joint session met at 10 a. m. J. W. Cummings of Comte on Herding, reported back J. S. F. No 23. "An Act granting a ranch and herd ground to G. W. Bean E. Barney W. A. Follett P. Colton & J. Adams" with J. S. F No 27. "An act granting a ranch and herd ground unto J. C. Snow, James Adams, Chas Carroll, Geo. W. Bean E. Barney W. A. Follett & P. Colton as a substitute, which was read three several times & passed.

Mr Rockwood of the Comte on appropriations to whom was referred the Petition of S. L. Sprague and others for Infirmary reported that it was inexpedient to Legislate thereon which was recieved

Mr Rockwood presented Petition of D. Carn, Warden of Penetentiary asking for revision of Penitenteary laws which was referred to a select committee to wit Rockwood & Cummings

Councillor F. D. Richards moved that a select Comte be appointed to bring in a law for preparing laws for publication &c, and Cummings S. W. Richards & F. D. Richars were appointed

Mr S. W. Richards presented J. S. F. No. 28 "An act to amend "An act prescribing the terms of certain offices" ' which was recieved and read three several times & passed

Mr Rockwood of Comte on appropriations presented J. S. F. No 29 "General Appropriation Bill" and also the J. S. F. No 30 Territorial Appropriation Bill" both of which were read and referred back to the committee.

The "Resolution creating the office of Superintendent Meteorological oservations &c was returned from the Governor suggesting several amendments which were read and concurred in.

Councillor Farr presented J. S. F. No 31 "An act to incorporate Ogden Kanyon Road Company" which was withdrawn on its second reading.

Adjourned till 3 p. m. and several of us went to the "Globe Saloon" and dined, and met at 3 p. m.

Councillor Farr, of Comte on Incorporations reported J. S. F No. 32 "An Act to extend the incorporation of Spanish Fork City, which was read three several times and passed. Adjourned till tomorrow at 10

Friday 16 Jan 1857. Joint session met at ten a. m.

Mr Rockwood presented, "Resolution for convening the Legislative Assembly" which was recieved and adopted

Councilr Richards reported J. S. F. No 33. An act providing for the publication and distribution of the laws, Journals &c of the present Session" which was read three several times and passed.

Mr Rockwood from said Comte reported back J. S. F No 29 "Territorial Appropriation Bill" amended which was read three several times and passed.

Councillor Wells presented J. S. F. No 34. "An act concerning partnerships" which was read three several times and passed.

Councillor Harrington presented "Memorial to Congress, praying for the reimbursement to the Territory of funds expended on the Penitentiary, and asking that provision may be made hereafter by the general government for the support of that institution" which was recieved and referred back for revision.

Adjd to 3 p. m and a few of us went to the "Globe" to luxurate on oyster soup ect and met again at three pursuant to adjournment.

Mr Rockwood from that Comte reported back J. S. F. No. 30. General Appropriation Bill amended which was read three several times and passed.

Mr Cummings, of Comte on Memorials &c reported back memorial to Congress on Penitentiary &c amended which was read and adopted

Mr Cummings presented J. S. F. No 35. "An Act to amend 'an act in relation to the Judiciary," which was read three several times and passed'

On motion of Councillor Wells. The thanks of this Assembly were tendered to His Excellency the Govornor, for his numerous acts of kindness and beneficial suggestions to this Legislative Assembly.

On motion of Mr S. W. Richards, The thanks of this assembly were tendered to William H. Hooper Esqr, for the kind faithful and generous manner in which he has performed the duties of Secratary of the Territory to the present Legislative Assembly.

On motion of Councillor Woodruff, The thanks of this assembly were tendered to Hon. Heber C. Kimball, president of the Council, for the able, wise, and kind manner in which he has discharged the duties incumbent upon him.

On Motion of Mr Hyde, The thanks of the assembly were also tendered to Hon. Hosea Stout, for the wisdom and kindness manifested by him, while occupying the position of Speaker of the House of Representatives

The Legislative Assembly then adjourned *sine die*

Sunday 18 Jan 1857. Quorum meeting at my house at 2 p. m. 3 members to wit William Warwood, John Smith and John Goaslind were ordained and recieved into the Quorum

Snowing hard lately. The snow is now deper than I ever saw perhaps two & a half feet deep. Some houses & the Bowry broke down with the weight of snow.

Monday 19 Jan 1857. Mr Gerrish arrived to day from the States. he left the Eastern 13 Nov. The mail stopped at Platte Bridge to rig for packing

Marshal J. L. Haywood was with the mail. Mr Gerrish met Feramorz Little & Eph Hanks at Independence Rock on their way East with the mail.

I learn from Judge W. W. Phelps that the entire fall of snow in this city this year has been eight feet.

Wednesday 21 Jan. 1857. To day the Code Commissioners met and organised by choosing myself Chairman and John T. Cain[84] Secratary after which we pro-

---

84. John T. Caine was born January 8, 1829, near the town of Peel, Isle of Man. At the age of seventeen he came to America, finding work first in New York City. In 1847 he was baptized into the Mormon Church and the next year came west to St. Louis. Here he met and later married Margaret Nightingale, who bore him thirteen children and was to remain his only wife.

Caine arrived in Salt Lake City in 1852 where he taught school, became affiliated with the Deseret Dramatic Association, and was a clerk for Brigham Young. In 1854 he filled a mission to Hawaii and upon his return was employed again by President Young.

ceeded to the business of codifying the Laws of the United States applicable to Utah according to the law of the Legislature on that subject I also was occupied Thursday, Friday & Saturday at the same business

Sunday 25 Jan 1857. Quorum meeting at my house in after noon

Saturday 31 Jan 1857. Worked every day this week with the Code Commissioners preparin the Laws of the U. S. for publication as above spoken of —

Sunday 1 Feb 1857. Quorum meeting at my house quite a large attendance
The unusual deep snow which has laid on the ground so long has been dissolving fast for the last ten days while the weather has been warm and pleasant without wind so that the cattle will to all appearance now have a chance for their lives

Sunday 8 Feb 1857. Quorum meeting at my house W. A. Hickman and some 8 others started this morning with the Eastern mail
I have been Engaged Every day the last week with the Code Commission

Monday 9 Feb 1857. The adjourned Nov. Term of the District Court met this morning at ten.
The Judge ordered a traverse Jury of 24 men for the U. S. although the U. S. had no case in court

Tuesday 10 Feb 1857. Court met at ten a. m The Jury empannelled. Mr Minor moved to open the [case] of Hawley v Russel et al in Injunction which was over ruled
I filed a motion to change the venue in the case of Pitt v McRae in Injunction which was argued and held under advisement.
Messrs Little & Furgerson came into court to defend the case of Winters v. Parker et. al. and filed a motion for a change of venue on account of the partiality of the Judge for Winters & His attorneys Williams Miner Such was the manifest partiality of Judge Stiles for Williams & the hostility of them and their party to the Laws of Utah that We on the part of the Territory and the people were not willing to risk a case before him

Wednesday 11 Feb 1857. Court met at 11 a. m. The motion for a change of venue in the case of Pitt v McRae was with drawn also the motion for a change of venue in the case of Winter v Parker et. al. and a plea to the jurisdiction of the court was filed and argued by the defence
The points made were that the court sitting as it now was as a U. States Court had no jurisdiction to try cases arising under the laws of the Territory.

Thursday 12 Feb 1857. Court met at ten a.m. Court overruled the plea to the jurisdiction of the court but decided that while sitting as a U. S. Court it could not try Territorial cases and that the U. States Marshall could not execute the laws of Utah nor act in her courts and dismissed the U. S. Jury and Dotson the U. S. Marshall left the Court.

Caine's appointment here was the beginning of many years of public service. As a loyal Mormon he had the confidence of the people; as a monogamist and a realist he had the respect of the Gentile population. In 1870 he became Utah's fourth delegate to Congress and in 1872 a member of the Constitutional Convention.
"The Democratic convention for the nomination of State officers, in anticipation of the early admission of the State of Utah convened in Ogden, Sept. 5, 1895, when Hon. John T. Caine was almost unanimously nominated for the first governor of the State. . . . The Democratic State ticket, however, was defeated at the polls, and Bro. Caine shared the fate of his party." (Heber M. Wells was elected governor, serving from 1896-1905.) Andrew Jenson, *Latter-day Saint Biographical Encyclopedia* (4 vols., Salt Lake City, 1901-1936), I, 737-38. Caine died September 20, 1911.

Friday 13 Feb 1857. This morning when the Court met on reading the minutes of yesterday D. H. Burr U. S. Surveyor Genl found fault with the record and endeavored to have Judge Stiles record some of his collateral rulings on matters not in point on any cases in Court and demanded to know of the Court whether he held the laws of Utah to have the preference to the laws of U. S.

Mr Furgerson Replied to him calling him a cowardly cur who wished to attact our laws clandestinely but had not courage to do it openly & gave notice to the court that he should prefer charges against him at an earley day to have his name struck from the Bar as a man too mean and incopetent to plead law.

Mr Williams then presented an affidavit to the Court *in chambers* as he called it praying the Court to enjoin itsself as a court unauthorized by any law of the U. S. or Utah but that the Judge Clerk & Marshal were an assciation of men assuming Judicial powers & wished His Honor to bring their selves before themselves to be tried and brought to Justice for so doing.

To all this cold and debiberate contempt the Judge only overruled it as a matter of course but Mr Furguson and my self took it up & demanded his expulsion from the Bar for that & his incompetence to act as an attorney and gave notice that we would prefer charges against him also at an early day

Feelings were very high In fact this was a contest for the supremecy of our laws in our own courts over the unlawful usurpation and rulings of of the District Courts in continually rendering our laws nugatory by their decisions and palming the U. S.tates marshal & his deputies upon us to pack juries and serve our processes and making our own officers a mock & a bye word.[85]

Our making these points is what agitated Burr and excited the indignation of all the gentiles and enemies to Utah, and their hostility aroused ours while the Judge was willing to pander and vassalate to both parties and disgrace himself and our laws if he could only suit all and render justice to neither and secure to the gentiles their demands

At one time the feelings ran so high that several laid off their coats while two gentiles not wishing to take a hand in the contest left the Court. Little & Furguson filed a motion to Dismiss the case of Winters against Parker et. al. and Williams filed a motion to the jurisdiction of the Court in the same case.

The court then adjourned

Saturday 14 Feb 1857. Court met at ten a. m. William's motion to the jurisdiction was overruled

The motion to Dismiss in the case of Winters v Parker et. al. was argued at great length and sustained the case dismissed at the cost of the plaintiff. During the arguments on this motion T. S. Williams resigned his attorneyship. And Burr in the morning sent in his resignation.

These resignations were now taken up Mr Furguson presented his charges against them as he had given notice and objected to Burr resignation being accepted as he had only done so to escape the charges which he knew could easily be sustained

The Court ordered that he be expelled from the *Bar.*

Thus ended the contest not however untill one man Mr Watters who had been armed and sent into court to defend T. S. Williams was kicked out of Court and his pistols taken away.

The Court then abruptly adjourned leaving those cases of *Certiorari* which originated in the probate of G. S. L. Co. v. Williams, Dotson Pitt & Watters, not even calling them up.

---

85. The quarrels of this day and the next, resulting in the resignation of the government officials and the theft of the records, and the general Mormon attitude weighed heavily with the government officials and were an immediate cause of sending the army to Utah.

Sunday 15 Feb 1857. Quorum meeting at my house two Elders Aluis Toussig and Neriah T. Moore were recieved into the Quorum

Monday 16 Feb 1857. Williams, Dotson, Pitt & Watters are petitioning the Gov to remit the fines (in all 1400$) against them in the probate Court & which had by Certiorari been taken to District Court. Their fines were remitted

Tuesday 17 Feb 1857. To day took dinner with Br Toussig which dinner was given to the presidents of the Eleventh Quorum of Seventies which he joined last Sabbath. The Bishop of his ward & several more were there

The dinner was excellent & of great variety and all partook of it as though they appreciated its qualities an richness

Thursday 19 Feb 1857. This evening met with a committee to draft a new military law. The object which is trying to be obtained, seems to be to get up a military organization according to the good old Bible rule of Captains of 10's 100's &c and at the same time to correspond with U. S. tactics as such an organization is thought by some to be more efficient. The subject was only discussed and will be farther considered hereafter

The committee adjourned to meet this night week

Saturday 21 Feb 1857. Occupied every day this week Except Monday with the Code Commissioners.

Sunday 22 Feb 1857. Went to meeting at the Tabernacle The names of a number of Elders were called to go on different missions in the spring and a large number to accompany Prest B. Young to Salmon River in Oregon.

Quorum meeting at my house David Hilton was recieved into the Quorum & ordained under the Hands of Zera Pulsifer who was present.

Thursday 26 Feb 1857. Attended to the code Commissioning the three previous days.

To day attended the (endowm [crossed out]) endowment, attended military comte at dark

Friday 27 Feb 1857. Attended the endwment. My wife had her endwment and sealing to day. Saturday worked at home gardening.

Sunday 2 March 1857. Quorum meeting at my house

Wednesday 4 March 57. Worked Mon, Tues & Wed. at the Code Commissioning. This day the 13th Ward was rebaptised my wife and my daughter Elizabeth Ann was baptized.[86]

Saturday 7 March 1857. Worked Thursday, Friday & Sat. in the the Endowment House.

Sunday 8 March 1857. Quorum meeting at my house

Monday 9 March 1857. Rainy day and to night hard rain but warm and pleasant.

Saturday 14 March 1857. Worked Monday Tuesday & Wednesday in my garden and with the Code Commission and Thursday and Friday in the Endowment. and Saturday at home.

Sunday 15 March 1857. Quorum meeting at my house Ephraim Snider was recieved in the Quorum

---

86. This rebaptism of Stout and his wife, Alvira, was a rededication to the cause. The daughter, Elizabeth Ann, was now nearly nine years old, her first baptism evidently delayed by the absence of her father. Normally a child was baptized on or soon after the eighth birthday.

Monday 16 Tuesday 17 Wed 18. Worked with the Code commission and gardening.

Thursday 19 March 1857. Learned this morning that on last sunday evening that Gardner G. Potter, William Parrish and his son were killed at Springville.[87] The circumstances and how I have not learned.

Worked in the Endowment to day and the remainder of this week.

Sunday 22 March 1857. Quorum meeting as usual two members D. W. Perkins & John McIntosh were recieved into the Quorum.

Tuesday 24 March 1857. Worked at Code yesterday and today and to day completed all the laws of the U. S. to be published.

that is completed the compilation. The Eastern mail of Nov last arrived to day I[t] lay up all winter at the platt Bridge and at the Devils Gate Ex Marshal Haywood also returned from Washington with the mail.

Saturday 28 March 1857. Worked Wednesday at Code. and the rest of the week in the Endwment

Sunday 29 March 1857. Quorum meeting at my house Two members, John Moore and Thos W. Spiking were recieved into the Quorum

We were refreshed with a hard rain accompanied by hail which covered the ground about 2 p m.

Saturday 4 Apl 1857. Worked Monde with Code Comn and the rest of the week in the Endowment house

On Friday Evening the South mail came, news unimportant. The people are flocking in from all parts of the Ter & to Conference The city seems full of waggons teams and Saints The weather is dry, cool, clear

Sunday 5 April 1857. Went to meeting in the fore noon and preached a short discourse. Quorum meeting at my house at 2 p. m. four new members recieved in the Quorum. People geathering for conference My house over full.

Monday 6 April 1857. General Conference commenced to day There is a much larger congregation assembled at this conference than I ever saw before —

Thursday 9 April 1857. Conference closed to day at noon an uncommon lage number was called on different missions and there was a large concourse of people than I Ever saw before at a conference.

My house was overrun with people small and great. The weather was warm clear and pleasant but some what cool.

Sunday 12 April 1857. Quorum meeting at my house at 2 p. m. Two members to wit Ansil P. Harmon and Baldwin B. Watts were recieved into the Quorum.

Monday 13th April 1857. The apostates are preparing to leave while I am try to collect debts due from them to the Poor Fund and others.

---

87. Among the papers of Hosea Stout in the possession of Lafayette Lee are copies of the coroners' inquests held over the bodies of William R. Parrish; his son, Beetson (Beason) Parrish; and Gardner G. Potter, copied from the "Justice's Docket for Springville Precinct." The first, signed by John M. Stewart, acting-justice of the peace, lists the members of the jury as A. F. McDonald, M. N. Crandall, N. T. Guymon, William Smith, G. McKenzie, Philo Dibble, Uriah Curtis, S. P. Curtis, John Daley, Wilbur I. Earl, Joseph Bartholomew, and Thomas G. Sprague.

The second lists the property found on the bodies; the third is an account of the testimony of Abram Durfee and Orreh Parrish, who had escaped being killed. This last was listed as a copy of an original made by P. M. Westwood, clerk, and was endorsed "Report of Court of Inquiry, DURFEE & PARRISH."

Tuesd 14 April 1857. T. S. Williams' daughter Caroline Eloped to parts unknown last night He blames Prest H. C. Kimball and thinks David Kimball has got her[88] and threatens to kill President Kimball.

The police arrested Williams for Breach of the Peace He rages and raves like a mad man.

To night I was out nearly all night on guard.

Wednesday 15 Apl 1857. To day T. S. Williams Judge Stiles Genl Burr and P. K. Dotson with nearly all the gentile and apostate Scurf in this community left for the States

Thursday 16 Apl 1857. Settling with Matthew Gaunt for $2665 — due the Territory He sells his Woollen Factory to the Church for some 2000[89] — and is making every preperation and sacrafice to apostatize and leave.

The fire of the reformation is burning many out who flee from the Territory afraid of their lives This is scriptural. "The wicked flee when no man pursue and so with an apostate Mormon he always believes his life in danger and flees accordingly.

Sunday 19 April 1857. Quorum meeting again at my house at 2 p. m. John Carver and Joseph Crook was recieved into the Quorum.

Monday 20 April 1857. General training under the new law or in other words the Legion was called out to be organized under the new. There was new officers elected. George D. Grant was elected Major General and William H. Kimball Brigadier of the Horse and Franklin D. Richards Brigr Genl of the Infantry in the Great Salt Lake District The Lieutenant General had previously and since his re-election on the 6th April Appointed his staff. I recieved the appointment of Judge Advocate of the Nauvoo Legion in which capacity I came out to day. There was not a very general turn out, owing to the people not having sufficient notice.

---

88. At this time David Kimball was eighteen years old and Caroline Williams fourteen, so that her father felt justified in his protest. According to Dale L. Morgan:

> The young couple was determined not to be thwarted, even when Caroline's father placed trusted guards over her to watch her night and day. Just before the hour of departure, she seized upon an unguarded moment to dart out of the back door into a carriage that was waiting for her. Before the guards had fairly missed her, Solomon Kimball says:

> "she and her intended were hurled over to Judge Elias Smith's office and were made husband and wife for all time. They then jumped into the carriage, drawn by two fiery steeds, and accompanied by four mounted guards, composed of Joseph A. Young, Heber P. Kimball, Quince Knowlton, and Brigham Young, Jr., they made a dash for Antelope Island, reaching their destination in less than three hours." (Morgan, *The Great Salt Lake*, 265.)

The young groom, David Patten Kimball, was born August 23, 1839, in Nauvoo, Illinois, and came to Utah with his parents in 1848. He went to the rescue of the handcart companies in 1856 and was remembered by several diarists as one who for hours waded back and forth carrying children, women, and sick men across the streams, or with George D. Grant and Clark Allen Huntington formed a line in the water and passed them across from one bank to the other.

Little additional information is found regarding this marriage. David P. Kimball filled a mission to England in 1863-65. In 1877 he was president of the Bear River Stake. The next year he moved into Arizona. No other wife is listed, and Caroline Williams bore him only one child who lived, a son named Thatcher, born August 3, 1883, when the mother was forty years old. David P. Kimball died November 22, 1883, at St. David, Arizona.

89. Matthew Gaunt built the first woolen mill in Utah, and in 1851 added new machinery to his carding machine and expanded his factory on the Jordan River. By 1855 it was reported that he was producing $500 worth of cloth every week. His advertisement in the *Deseret News* for that year read: "Fulling, Dyeing &c done at Jordan Woolen Factory Wool taken to make into Cloth, Jeans, Flannel Satinette or Blankets on Shares or otherwise. Wool, Grease, Wheat, Flour, Pork &c., &c., taken in exchange for Cloth, Blankets, Linseys &c at the Jordan Woolen Factory Carding done on the usual terms by MATTHEW GAUNT."

In the evening had a suit before the Probate Court. Laura L. Smith v Thomas Keeler for 390 dollars Col Little for Plff.

While about half through the trial Court adjourned to partake a supper at the Globe given by the newly elected officers where all parties gained their case & then we finished the trial Judgement for plff for $235 —

Tues & Wed 21 & 22 Apl. Worked in the Endowment House. On Wed some 85 persons recieved their Endowments. this is the largest number ever recieved their Endowments at once in this city & I believe the largest number in this last dispensation

Thurs 23 Apl 1857. This morning the missionaries going East started from the Temple Block to cross the plains with Hand Carts.

The company consisted of some 74 men and 35 Hand Carts They all seemed to be in unusually good spirits They are bound for different parts of the U States, Canada and Europe.[90]

Friday 24 Apl 1857. This morning the First presidency started on their northern tour expecting to visit Salmon river mission and be gone some four & six weeks They were accompanied by perhaps 150 persons.

Saturday 25 Apl 1857. Very lonesome times now sance all the gentiles and apostates & missionaries mail carriers, besides the large number of good saints who have gone with the govornor on his northern tour.

This leaves me nothing to do or think of but hard work which I seem to perform tolerbably well.

Sunday 26 April 1857. To day I entered on my duties and water master again. The unusually dry spring requiring irrigation much eairlier than usual.

Quorum meeting at my House at two p. m.

Monday 27 April 1857. Law suit to day at 2 p. m. in the Probate Court Theodore Thorp v Evans P. Thomas in assumpsit for 592 50/100 $ & I was for Thomas Plff obtained Judgement for 442 50/100 and costs. Deft called for an appeal which was allowed

Friday 1 May 1857. To day was celebrated by the little schollars of the various ward sunday schools marching and perambulating the hills and Kanyons geathering May flowers and after all assembling at the music Hall were excorted by the Brass band to the Tabernacle where they were addressed by Elder W. Woodruff in a very appropriate manner.

I spent the week working in my garden

Sunday 3 May 1857. Quorum meeting at my house

Wed & Thurs 6 & 7. May. Hard south wind blowing dust flying, disagreeable to be out doors.

Friday 8 May 1857. This morning the ground in my garden was covered with frost & every thing seemed thouroughly frozen in the garden This I believe has been the severest frost that has ever been seen in the valley this time of the year. There has been much damage done to fruit.

Sunday 10 May 1857. Quorum meeting at my house to day.

This week has been cloudy cool and louring weather towards the last rainy and snowing occasionally squally like March weather The ground is well saturated and

---

90. This "Missionary Handcart Company" seemed to be Brigham Young's way of re-establishing the handcart as a mode of travel after the disaster of the winter before.

every indication of good times for farmers in case no frost nips their prospects — On Saturday the weather became fair

Sunday 17 May 1857. Quorum meeting at my house Weather very warm.

Monday 18 May 1857. Suit before Probate Dan Jones v. Lewis Jones in assumpsit Demand $100. I was for deft. The case was lost on demurrer on the ground that the same had been once sued for and tried before another court.

Some Rain this evening —

Wednesday 20 May 1857. Sit with Levi Jackman as arbitrators in a case betwen W. W. Phelps and Benn Sears. Award in favor of Phelps. Weather clear & warm.

Sunday 24 May 1857. Quorum meeting as usual The Quorum decided to meet here on the first Sabbath in each month in stead of Every Sabbath as heretofore.

Monday 25 May 1857. Last evening Howard Egan here bringing intelligence that His Excellency and those who went with him were on their return That he left them on the Head waters of the Malad on the 23rd All were well and getting along finely I attended the prayer circle this evening.

Tuesday 26 May 1857. This evening the Gov and company arrived here all in good health and spirits There is considerable stir & activity in the streets now manifested. Capt Smoot is fitting up a train for the stations betwen here and Laramie for the Carrying Co.[91] which gives the city a business like appearance He is taking out about 100 men besides a number of teams.

Friday 29 May 1857. The Eastern mail arrived to day being the first time since Nov. last The Hon. George A. Smith & J M. Barnhisel and Elder T. O Angel[92] came as passengers I spent the evening untill late in assisting to open the mail which was very large. The spirit of the people & rulers of the Nation seem to be hostile and surley towards the mormons, so much so that our Delegates did not even present our petition to be admitted as a state

The company of Hand Cart missionaries were at Devil's Gate the 10 May having been ten days traveling from Bridger They were doing well.

Sunday 31 May 1857. Went to meeting in the fore noon President Young gave a short account of his tour north.

Monday 1 June 1857. To day witnessed the humiliating spectacle of seeing W. Camp thrash his wife This is the first time in my life I ever beheld such a sight After dragging her three times by the hair of the head through the porch and finally on the ground down a flight of stone steps he struck and stamped her in the breast and again in an hour or so gave her another hair pulling and chocking & knocked down & choked another one of his wives & raised the surrounding neighborhood

---

91. The Carrying Company, commonly called the Y X (Young Express) Company, was designed to establish way stations approximately every hundred miles between Salt Lake City and Fort Laramie to provide food, lodging, equipment, and repair service to the western travelers. This would make it unnecessary for emigrants to carry a full supply for the trip, would insure shelter in bad weather, and would greatly diminish the hazards of the journey. It would make possible a fast passenger service for those who could afford to pay, insure regular mail service, and supply such items as tools or drugs at more reasonable rates. The idea was an excellent one, but was never brought to fruition because of the Utah War of the next year. For a detailed discussion, see Arrington, *Great Basin Kingdom*, 162-70.

92. When William Meeks left Nauvoo in February of 1846, Truman O. Angell was put in charge of completing the Nauvoo Temple. In Utah he was acting architect for the temples at St. George and Salt Lake City and also for the Salt Lake Tabernacle.

Angell was born June 5, 1810, at Providence, Rhode Island, and died October 16, 1887, in Salt Lake City.

by the screams and cries of the family & two *thrashed* women when the City Marshal came and arrested him took him before Alderman Raleigh who fined him 50 dollars and cost.

Commenced indexing the United States Laws now in press   six forms having come out.

Wednesday 3 June 1857. The Southern mail arrived News unimportant. Elder A Lyman came in with the mail   He left C. C. Rich at Coal Creek.

Friday 5 June 1857. Smart little hail storm to day. and fine rain on Saturday

Sunday 7 June 1857. Quorum meeting at my house Jacob K. Butterfield recieved into the Quorum.

Monday 8 June 1857. Warm rainy day.   The most refreshing gentle and thorough rain I have ever seen in the Valley.

Saturday 13 June 1857. Worked on the road to day and indexing the U. S. Laws this week.

Sunday 14 June 1857. Went to meeting at the Tabernacle at 8 a. m   The fore noon was taken up in reading to the congregation the different accounts against the mormons as came in last mail

It appears that there is now through out the U S. the most bitter, revengeful, and mobocratic feeling against us that has ever been manifested

Tuesday 23 June 1857. Eastern mail came in to day at 2 p m. All was peaceable on the road

The news paper writers were louder against the mormons than ever whether govt will take notice of the excitement or is not known.

Accounts are current in the papers that Elder Parley P. Pratt had been assassinated some eight miles from Van Buren Arkansas by one Hector H. McLean, that he was shot and lived some two hours[93]   The truth is not known

Wednesday 24 June 1857. W. A. Hickman and others came in from the states. He was six and a half days from Larimie   all still peace on the road.

Saturday 27 June 1857. General training in this city. The Lieutenant General and staff as well as all other field and staff officers came out on foot Several regimental officers were elected.

Monday 29 June 1857. Suit before the Probate Court E. D. Woolley v. James Sloan debt $307 with interest. I appeared for Plff.   case decieded for plff for debt and interest.

At 4 p m general meeting of the Gov & officers of the Legion at the Social Hall to take into consideration the policy of doing military duty entirely on foot only in cases of emergency, as more calculated in its nature to inure the youth to hardy and vigorous exercise and mountain services.   It took well & was adopted

---

93. Parley P. Pratt had been killed on May 13, 1857, and in spite of poor communication, the word spread quickly. Andrew Sproul, on the plains in charge of a herd of church cattle, wrote in his pocket diary on May 26, 1857, that "E Snow tells me that P P Pratt is in trouble and that McLean has got him prisoner also woman and children. God deliver him if this is true." On June 23, 1857, the "Journal History" of the church tells of Pratt's death, and Wilford Woodruff wrote in his diary: "Eastern mail arrived bringing the sad news of the assassination of Elder Parley P. Pratt who had been killed near Ft. Smith in Arkansas by a man named McLean." Note is made of this because B. H. Roberts and other Mormon writers have insisted that the facts were not known in southern Utah as late as September of 1857.

SALT LAKE CITY, ABOUT 1870 (FROM THE TOWER OF CITY HALL LOOKING NORTHEAST) The large home in the foreground, facing First South, is John W. Young's. The lumber yard on the corner of First South and Second East belonged to Feramorz Little. Across the street are stables of Wells Fargo Company. The two-story building immediately north of the stables is the home of Hosea Stout. It is further identified as the unpainted building directly over the rear portion of the St. Mary Magdalene Church.

UTAH TERRITORIAL MILITIA (THE NAUVOO LEGION)

*Hosea Stout was an officer in the Nauvoo Legion during the battle for Nauvoo,
in charge of the public arms across Iowa, and judge advocate in
Utah. He helped plan the defenses in the Utah War and was
a faithful scribe for many of the military actions of his day.*

PART IV

July 1, 1857 to December 25, 1859

JULY 1, 1857 TO DECEMBER 25, 1859

Part IV

This part of the diary covers the period from July 1, 1857, to December 25, 1859, with five short entries in 1860 and four in 1861.

It begins as Stout prepared for a celebration commemorating the arrival of the Saints in Utah. At the celebration in Big Cottonwood Canyon, it was announced that a federal army was marching to Utah. Through the next turbulent year and the ones following, Stout was active as an officer in the military and also as a lawyer defending Mormon interests in court, his account being one of the best available.

Wednesday July 1 1857. Writing to the Weston Argus and Mo Republican in answer to slanderous reports of Judge Drummond and others.

Thursday July 2 1857. Rained briskly nearly all this fore noon wetting the ground most thoroughly.

Saturday 4 July 1857. General training to day by way of celebrating the glorious Independance

Sunday 5 July 1857. Quorum meeting recieved two new members Thos Mantle & William Hill in to the Quorum to fill vacancy of Zora Thurstin & Ichabod Gifford

Saturday 12 July 1857. Indexing the Law and at work in my garden this week Times dull no news only a few emmigrants passing through here from Cal to States

Wednesday 22 July 1857. To day I started in company with a company of brethren from Ogden to Big Cotton wood Kanyon to celebrate the 24 July. People are geathering from all parts of the Ter for the same purpose We camped about one mile up the Kanyon while teams are passing us all night The Kanyon seemed full of men and teams.

Thursday 23 July 1857. We started about day light with out breakfast and proceeded on but soon found our way hedged up by the road being full of waggons & teams so proceed in on afoot about a mile I came to the gate at the first mill. Here preperations were making to number the persons teams & animals going up which resulted as follows 2587 persons, 464 carriages & waggons, 1028 horses and mules, 332 oxen & cows We arrived at the Lake about one p. m. A large number had already ariven, and teams continued to come all the evening The head of this Kanyon is a picturesque and romantic scenery The Kanyon is well set with heavy forests of timber from the base to the summet of the mountains A large opening in the vicinity of the Lake make a beautiful camping ground with an abundance of grass for animals plenty of trout in the lake & streams. There is some four saw mills in the Kanyons. The road is good but very much up hill and has been made at great expence

This evening passed off quietly as every body was weary. Still when evening came the dance commenced in three places which had been prepared for the purpose.[1]

Friday 24 July 1857. I was up earley this morning, in fact I froze out for the night was cold and frosty The sound of musick, and a few rounds from a howitzer soon had every one in motion. The people enjoyed themselves as suited them best the day was qu[i]et and every body seemed happy some military evelutions going on.

About noon A. O. Smoot Jud Stoddard, O P. Rockwell an Judge Smith came into camp Smoot & Stoddard were from the States in 20 day and they report that the Post office department has annulled Mr Kimball's contract to carry the mail so they had to come without it

They also report hostile feelings to wards us in the States Some talk of troops coming.

The evening was spent in singing and dancing which was kept up nearley all night I never went to sleep the night was cold and frosty.

---

1. This is one of many descriptions of the celebration of the Twenty-Fourth of July. The *Deseret News* for July 29 gave more detail of the programs.

Lorenzo Brown's account seems especially eloquent:

23 [July, 1857] Started early & drove 13 miles to the top of the kanyon by 3 p.m. Weather very hot & a great crowd of teams not less than 500 wagons

It is wonderful to see the quantity of timber the kanyon wide & filled with white & red pine, Fir, Quaken asp a portion of it very large size & immense quantities Enough to last for years There are 4 saw mills in operation & another nearly ready to operate

Evening dancing on 3 large flours [*sic*] made of plank for the purpose & all went off in good order

July 24, 1857 was awakened this morning by music from five different bands playing alternately This is the 10th Anniversary since the Pioneers entered the valley & Pres. Young has given about 2,000 invitations to all parts of the Territory to meet him here for recreation

Here is a small open prairie surrounded by lofty pines without underbrush & back of this again are seen the lofty summits of mountain ridges on whose Tops at different points floats conspicuously the flags of our nation, the self same banner that has been at different times unfurled by our enemies of Illinois & Missouri when they came in Martial array to drive the saints from their hard earned homes & peaceful firesides. In or near the center of this small prairie is a lake of 12 or 15 acres abounding with fish on whose glossy surface floats a boat of primitive construction laden at all hours with some party of both sexes whose joyful countenances are radiant with pleasure.

Within the recess of the wood, suspended by two lofty pines may be seen a swing of no ordinary dimension but suitable to carry 3 or 4 persons that have sufficient nerve to be carried thereby several yards upward & with astonishing velocity back & forward.

This added to the different amusements of walking in the shade of forest trees, dancing, feasting on the finest productions of the vallies served to while away the pleasant hours. While meeting continually the smiling face of some old & valued friend caused me to exclaim what can come nearer than this to perfect felicity

But in the midst of this joyful scene there comes a mounted messenger with news. Those happy faces benign with radiant joy now gather around but alas! a cloud comes o'er the spirit of their dreams. News, News of vital importance to citizens of Utah is quickly but quietly communicated. The mail that was expected was refused to be delivered by the Post Master at Independence & an army is actually advancing on Utah. For what purpose is enquirred by one & all as no one knows each countenance seems to resume its former cheerfulness the doubts & cares are thrown aside as a vain thing & the amusements & sports are continued with redoubled interest.

At a late hour all retired to rest after asking the blessing of the Supreme Ruler & thanking him for past favors & we sank into a tranquil & quiet repose. (Lorenzo Brown, "Journal," I, 283-84.)

Saturday 25 July 1857. Teams began to roll out at day break I started about sun rise and arrived at home at about one P. M very much worn out by hard travil, change of climate, want of sleep but all else well.

Monday 3 Aug 1857. General Election to day. The Hon John M. Barnhisel was elected Delegate to Congress. and for this county.

Heber C. Kimball	Hosea Stout[2]
Daniel H. Wells	Jesse C. Little
Albert Carrington	S. W. Richards
Franklin D. Richards	Daniel Spencer
Wilford Woodruff	Orson Hyde
Councilors.	Joseph A. Young
	Alexander McRae
W. W. Phelps	H. B. Clawson
J. W. Cummings	John Taylor
A. P. Rockwod	Representatives

The other candidates to the Legislature from other Counties I have not ascertained.

There was no opposing candidates but all went off peaceably and harmoniously as usual.

Friday 7 Aug 1857. John Taylor, & Erastus Snow of the Twelve, Bishop Andrew Cunningham, Elders H. W. Miller W. Martindale, G. J. Taylor, & Dustin Amy arrived, from their various missions. and report times very hostile towards the "Mormons" in the States They had no difficulty on the road.

Thursday 13 Aug 1857. A few horsemen[3] started East to protect the incoming Emmigration

Friday 14 Aug 1857. Some 50 more horsemen started to day. (Saturday 16 [crossed out]) They will be under the command of Cols R. T. Burton & J. W. Cummings

Sunday 16 Aug 1857. Levi Stewart & Isaac Bowman with several others came in having left Leavenworth on the 11th July, reporting our emmigration as being in a prospering condition The advance on Deer Creek on the 8th inst. The troop had not left the States when they left.

Monday 17 Aug 1857. Some 50 more men principally from Utah started East to day which is thought to be enough to protect our emmigration at present.

A Company arrived from Carson Valley & Cal about this time consisting of 31 men 10 women and 18 children under command of P. G. Sessions.

Thursday 20 Aug 1857. Elder William Walker came in to the city in advance of his train & reports peace on the road.

Tuesday 25 Aug 1857. Joseph Peck and others came in to day from Deer Creek He reports that he met our troop on Ham's Fork. They were going to move on towards the South Pass. He also reports that the goverment trains had lost a large

---

2. Hosea Stout was speaker of the House of Representatives during the previous session (1856-57).

3. No record has been found of the personnel of the "few horsemen" who started east on this date to investigate the approaching army. John Pulsipher at Fort Supply wrote in his diary on August 20 that "Bro Charles & a few minute men came as spies," and again on August 27, "Bro Charles came to see us right from the enemys camp where he and a company of others have been watching the movements of the troops." John Pulsipher, "Diaries [1838-1891]" (2 vols., typescript, Utah State Historical Society).

number of cattle and desertions of the soldiers were frequent. Sumner had not been heard of since he went after the Cheeyenes.

Thursday 27 Aug 1857. Acting as teacher to day

Monday 31 Aug 1857. The goods train of Stewart and Bowman of ten or twelve wagons came in to day

Tuesday 1 Sept 1857. Engaged in two suits to Camp v Allen and Twitchel v. Baker, both of which were refereed.

Wednesday 2 Sept 1857. Hard rain Earley this morning accompanied loud thunder and unusual vivid lightning. The lightning came down the chimney of Br Burnett in the tenth ward, killing his wife and badly injuring his child

Saturday 5 Sept 1857. This morning at just 15 minutes two my wife Alvira was delivered of a son weighing 9 lbs. We named him Brigham Hosea

John Murdoc came from the States and reports that Gen. Harney with all the infantry designed for Utah have been ordered to Kansas to help still the nerves of that turbulent Territory, leaving only about 1000 troops for Utah Their animals were in poor condition.

Col Sumner had had a brush with the Indians, burnt some 300 lodges, some two killed on each side.

Thomas B. Marsh the old apostate President of the Tuelve arrived this Evening. He apostatized in Missouri 19 years ago this fall in the time of our greatest troubles at Far West and with Orson Hyde and others went to Richmond Ray County mad affidavits against the Saints which was forwarded to the Govornor upon which he ordered out ten thousand troops (and [crossed out]) to accompany his exterminate the saints or drive them from the state The scenes of suffering and death which followed are sufficiently known and remembered to need no further comment.

Sunday 6 Sept 1857. President B. Young in his Sermon declared that the thred was cut between us and the U. S. and that the Almighty recognised us as a free and independent people and that no officer apointed by goverment (sent to [crossed out]) should come and rule over us from this time forth.[4]

T. B. Marsh appeared on the stand, was introduced by Prest Young to the congregation Marsh made a short speech presenting a sad spectacle of the effects of apostacy His head was entirely silvered over, He has been palsied on one side having to cripple along with a staff this with his aged emaciated countenance gives him the appearance of a very old man yet not but little more than one year older than Brigham & Heber both of whom look to be in the prime and bloom of life

His intellect presents a still more deplorable spacticle of apostate degeneracy which seems to be in the last stage of dotage

The congregation voted to recieve him into the Church

---

4. Sermons of Brigham Young during this period have been privately reported by many faithful members. The *Deseret News* for August 12, 1857, reported the one for the preceding Sunday as follows: "The time must come when there will be a separation between thy kingdom and the kingdom of this world . . . . I shall take it as a witness that God desires to cut the thread between us and the world when an army undertakes to make their appearance in this Territory to chastise me or to destroy my life . . . ."

A week later Jesse B. Martin wrote: "Sunday, Sept. 13, This morning I went to the tabernacle & there heard Brother Brigham speak, he told us that if we would assert our independence we should be a free people but if not in the name of Israel's God the kingdom should be rent from us." Jesse B. Martin, Diary (original, Henry E. Huntington Library, San Marino).

John Pulsipher, now home from Fort Supply, attended the October 6th and 7th conference and wrote: "Bro Brigham was firm, that if government does sustain this approaching hostile forse & will not let us have peace then the thread is cut that bound us to them & we will be free . . . ." Pulsipher, "Diaries."

After meeting I accompaned Prest B. Young and others into the Tabernacle to hear the Big Organ[5] whis had just been put up It is the largest I ever saw the music was most melodious.

At 2 p. m. attended a Quorum meeting at my house.

Tuesday 8 Sept 1857. Spent the fore noon with Br Best teaching

About noon Bryant Stringham & N. V. Jones arrived from Deer Creek bring Capt Stewart Van Vleit U. S. Assistant Quarter Master He comes in advance of the U. States troops to make preparations He was visited in the evening by Gov Young and others He puts up with W. H. Hooper.

In the after noon I was engaged in examining the Law in relation to Indian affairs as complaint had been made to Gov Young that Yates and Ely were trading good and liquors to the Indians on Green River[6] It is in contemplation to have them siezed as forfeited to the United States.

Wednesday 9 Sept 1857. At 9 a. m there was a meeting at the Social Hall to recieve Capt S. Van Vleit.[7] He was introduced by the Gov. to those present. He then presented a letter to Gov Young from Gen Harney requesting his assistince in providing for the troops now en route for Utah

He addressed Gov Young as President of the Mormons & and through to the Mormons not either recognizing Gov Young or any of the Saints as citizens of Utah or the U. S.

His instructions disclosed the fact that there is to be a station within 30 miles of G. S. L. City for the purpose of enforcing the *civil law* and that Utah is errected into a "Military (District [crossed out]) to be called the "Department of Utah" He met a cold reception altho treated very friendly.

I accompanied A. Carrington and others to his peach orchad in the evening where I had as many peaches as I could eat for the first time in the valley with priviledge of filling my pockets.

Friday 11 Sept 1857. The First Hand cart company of Saints arrived in charge of Israel Evans & Ben Ashby and Jesse B. Martin with the first waggon Co

Saturday 12 Sept 1857. Express from Col Cumming at Devils Gate of the 6th inst Bringing intilligence that the U. S. troops were about to leave Larimie for this place.

Sunday 13 Sept 1857. Went to meeting Elder John Taylor and Prest B. Young preached. President Young declared the policy he would pursue in case the United States did declare war against the Saints which I will not now pen

In the evening attenended with the Governor, presidency Twelve and others, an interview with Capt Van Vleit. The Gov most distinctly informed what would be the consequences in case of a war with the U. States and that he was at liberty to inform the President of the U. S. accordingly He professes to be our friend

5. This big organ was built by an Englishman, Joseph Ridges, in Australia, whither he had migrated and where he joined the Mormon Church. He dismantled the organ and brought it by sailing vessel to California in 1856 and thence by mule train to Utah. It was set up in the old Tabernacle and was first played for regular services on October 11, 1857. Hosea Stout evidently listened to a private concert. Theodore L. Cannon, "Temple Square: The Crossroads of the West," *Utah Historical Quarterly*, XXVII (July, 1959), 254.

6. Here Stout makes it clear that the Mormons contemplate seizing the goods of Yates and Ely if they can find a section in the law which will permit.

7. The visit of Captain Van Vliet has often been told. Brigham Young was defiant, threatening to keep the army out. He called upon Brother Dunbar to sing "Zion," one of the war songs of the period which boast that, "On the necks of thy foes thou shalt tread And their silver and gold As the Prophets foretold Shall be brought to adorne thy fair head." Van Vliet carried back a report to the effect that the Mormons would fight and were planning a full scale resistance.

Monday 14 Sept 1857. At 6 a. m Capt Van Vliet and J. M. Barnhisel started for Washington, The Capt to report the situation of affairs here in a military point of View and Barnhisel as our Deligate to Congress

In the evening attended a Council at the Historian office to take into consideration whether to declare Martial Law which was decided in the affirmative

Tuesday 15th Sept 1857. This after noon heavy rain and hail with hard South wind

Thurs & Friday 17 & 18 Sep. Worked for A. O. Smoot at carpenter work.

Saturday 19 Sept 1857. The company stationed at Deer Creek[8] and other places arrived to day, coming in advance of Uncles' troops, clearing the way

Jesse Earl and others came in on express from our troops He had been in the camp of the U. S. troops over night They were marching on very unconcerned and deliberate not dreaming of trouble but anticipating fine times here this winter while walking over our people, hanging up our rulers and prostituting our women, &c

Many of our troops were unwell for want of proper food but a large supply was sent to then to day.

Sunday 20 Sept 1857. The remainder of the (St Louis [crossed out]) Texas Company and part of the St Louis arrived to day

Friday 25 Sept 1857. This morning N. V. Jones arrived on express. He went out with Van Vliet untill he met the second regiment of U S troops.

Capt Van Vliet tried to dissuade the troops from coming into Utah but without effect, the first Regiment when they found they would be opposed raised the shout and threw up their hats & said they would have fun now the Mormons had spunk enough to fight. The second regiment were more calm and wanted neither to come in or fight The advance is now about Little Sandy

(The [crossed out]) Troops are now being sent out every day so that we may expect a merry time soon. I expect an attact will be made the first opportunity perhap by stampeding their animals.

I worked for Smoot all this week till noon to day

Saturday 26 Sept 1857. The Lieutenant General of the Legion having made a call on his staff to be ready to march with him tomorrow I have been engaged all day in preparing my self to to go to meet Uncle's troops. If nothing prevents we will start tomorrow & most likely before we return it will be determined whether a legalized goverment mob can force themselves on us against our will and contrary to all law or not. We go in the name and Strength of Israels God

Sunday 27 Sept 1857. About noon to day I started with Lieut Gen D. H. Wells and Staff.[9] The company consisted of 9 wagons and several horsemen We encamped in Killian's Kanyon and after prayers were addressed by the Lieut Genl on the necessity of taking good care of our animals and putting our trust in Israel's God for strength and deliverance from our enemies against whome we were now going and he was followed to the same effect by Elder John Taylor and George A Smith of the Tuelve.

Monday 28 Sept 1857. At day light Van Etten and Jesse Jones came into camp on express from the East said that the attempt of our troops to stampede our enemies

---

8. Deer Creek, Wyoming, was the Mormon camp about 100 miles west of Fort Laramie, the furthest Mormon frontier. It was to have been a station for the Mormon (YX) Express Company but was now abandoned as being too far away.

9. Stout's account through the next week is one of the most accurate and detailed of the military preparations of the Mormons.

animals had proved a failure the animals being tied down or Hobbled with iron hobbles. this happened at the Pacific Springs on Friday night last

We crossed the Big Mountain at noon, when Joseph A. Young and O. P. Rockwell were sent ahead on express to Col Burton. We encamped at Spring Creek 4 miles this side of Weber river.

Tuesday 29 Sept 1857. During the night an express came from the city and W. Henifer with another from Col Burton with news that the U. S. troops were within ten miles of Bridger and still on the march last evening and that Bridger was left & would most likely be burned

This news changed the plans of the Genl so leaving all the teams here except three and lighting them, with John Taylor, G. A. Smith Jas Furgerson, my-self, J. J. Stoddard, B. Stringham, H. B. Clawson, N. V. Jones, Stephen Taylor, B. Young jr J. Simmons, H. S. Beattie, he started on leaving the rest here in command of Col J. C. Little. Col Rockwood was left here in charge of the Commissary department. Here was established Spring Creek Station.

We dined at Cache Cave Station in charge of Cyrus Wheelock. Passing Capt Bannion's Co of horse just below this station

Here another arraingement was entered into to wit for Col N. V. Jones with my self, Beattie, Simmons, S. Taylor, & H. Margretts to go back down Echo and stop all the troops that might come on and put that Kanyon in a state for defense, and Gen Wells would go on with the rest, so we returned accordingly some twenty miles, and encamped.

Just after dark Majr Jos Taylor with 50 men from Ogden arrived and encamped.

Wednesday 30 Sept 1857. This morning after breakfast we all marched down to within 4 miles of the mouth of Echo Kanyon and at the second crossing of K. Creek and encamped. Located a Station Called "Echo Station" Here it is calculated to make a stand and meet the enemy if they come which however no one believes they will.

Here is the most formadable part of the Kany, being surmounted on the West by high perpendicular ledges of rock immediately over looking the road. While the East side is very high and difficult of ascent.

So after locating the encampment we took an exploration of the West side of the mountain or rathar Kanyon, and decided to errect batteries on the summit of the rocky crags.

Major Pugmire with 68 men, Major Sharp with 84 men both of G. S. L. City, and Major D. P. Curtis with 184 men of Davis Co. and Maj Munroe 75 men of Ogden all arrived (with [crossed out]) to day in all amounting to 411 men.

This evening about sun set and when a large number of men were on the high crags and among the Cedars a man by the name of Frederic Neilsen a dane and who had been a soldier & good marksman took a yager and deliberatily took aim at and shot William Simmons through the head. The ball entering his left temple and coming out at his right ear.

Simmons never spoke and only fell over and fell over and expired What was Strange they were both of one Co. and good friends & Nielson knew the distance was with in dead range. Nielson was put under arrest and the Body of Simmons sent home.

This morning an express passed going to Gen Wells bearing the news that Dr Hurt the Indian Agent had fled to the mountains with 300 Indians. He had been suspended by the Superintendant of Indian-affairs Gov Young and was fearful that he would be arrested for his mis deeds on the Indian farm in Utah Co. Some excitement was felt at first about this "Elopement" which soon passed off.

Thursday 1 Oct 1857. Last evening Major W. Maxwell with 64 men arrived from Payson. He reports that only 75 Indians left with Dr Hurt[10] and that some of them had come back saying that they only went to get some of his horses and other property

This fore noon Jos A. Young & J. W. Cummings passed to the City, express, 11 hours from Bridger and Report that the U. S. troops were 10 miles up Ham's Fork and were not coming towards Bridger as before reported and General Wells was at Bridger.

Several Families passed here to day from Fort Supply to the city who supposing the enemy were making a rush on them Burned the fort and left.[11]

At say 6 a. m. J. A. Thompson & R. R. Pettitt came express from the city to Gen Wells.

In the afternoon, Major W. S. S. Willis with 50 men arrived from Nephi Utah Co. (Horsemen) Shortly after Major Blair with 60 men arrived from G. S. L. City. Large numbers of teams with families from Supply passing this evening.

The Forces here are preparing the hills & crags to recieve the enemy in due form.

Friday 2 Oct 1857. Went to Spring Creek Station after my trunk &c.

Saturday 3 Oct 1857. Went with Major Taylor exploring the mountains West of Echo and followed a dividing ridge some six miles back on to the highest peek where I had a good view of the surrounding country The country is cut up into Kanyons in all concievable shaps and forms and totally impractable for horsemen and it would be a slow march to flank Echo on foot.

Shortly after I returned H. P. Kimball and John Smith Patriarch on express to the City

They say that the troops are yet on H. Fork and refuse to answer any inquiries from Gen Wells untill the Commanding officer arrives and *gives them orders to to march in.*

Sunday 4 Oct 1857. Exploring with Col Jones the mouth and hills of Echo and find the same not good for defence Returned and Explored above our Station and find it good and easy to be definded. An Express came in stating that Genl Wells has moved from Bridger to Cache Cave.

---

10. Of his leaving the state on October 24, 1857, Garland Hurt wrote from his camp on the Sweetwater in Wyoming to Colonel A. S. Johnston. He declared that his interpreter told him that, "it was understood all over the country that I was about leaving . . . and handed me a note from . . . Bishop of the Spanish Fork Settlement, stating that he had learned from various sources that I intended going out with the Indians in violation with the *Marshal law* now in force. He felt it his duty to inform me that I could not leave, that they were resolved to enforce the law at all hazards." Hurt's long letter leaves no doubt that he thought he would have been murdered had he remained in Utah. U. S., Bureau of Indian Affairs — Letters received by the Office of Indian Affairs, Utah Superintendency, 1849-1880 (originals, National Archives, Washington, D. C.; microfilm, Utah State Historical Society).

11. This was the final abandonment of Fort Supply after five years of frustration in a climate where there was frost every month. Jesse W. Crosby wrote the details of burning Fort Supply and Fort Bridger. He left Salt Lake City on September 25:

I went to Fort Supply with a small company to help take care of the crops and to make ready to burn everything if found necessary . . . . We took out our wagons, horses, etc. and at 12 o'clock noon set fire to the buildings at once, consisting of 100 or more good hewed houses, one saw mill, one grist mill, one threshing machine, and after going out of the fort, we did set fire to the stockade, grain stacks, etc. After looking a few minutes at the bonfire we had made, thence on by the light thereof.

I will mention that owners of property in several cases begged the privilege of setting fire to their own, which they freely did, thus destroying at once what they had labored for years to build, and that without a word. "The History and Journal of the Life and Travels of Jesse W. Crosby," *Annals of Wyoming*, XI (July, 1939), 147-219. (A typescript of this journal is at the Utah State Historical Society and the original is in the L. D. S. Church Historian's Library.)

Monday 5 Oct 1857. Major Taylor left with his command to join the forces who were acting upon the borders of our enemies

Col Jones left for Gen Wells' Quarters leaving me in command and returned in the evening and reports that Gen Wells has removed his quarters 4 miles below Cache Cave

Teams with families passing to the city from Supply yet.

Tuesday 6 Oct 1857. Learned last night that Capt Lott Smith had captured six waggons of our enemies and took the cattle in conformity to the orders to annoy and harrass our enemies and break them down but not to kill any of them and also that he since has taken and burned 52 more wagons on Green River and took the oxen. These wagons had some 5000 lbs lading of the most choice and costly suplies but he before burning them caused the teamsters to take out their own property & such suplies as they needed to furnish them to the States. The teamsters were glad the wagons were burned and they thus discharged and sent back

Gen Wells and Staff came here about noon to make us a visit and see what progress we were making in fortifications whith which he was well pleased By the General we learn that a large number of wagons and carriages had arrived in the enemies camp accompanied by 150 horsemen suposed to be the Commander (Harney or Johnson)

Myself & Preston Thomas were appointed by Gen Wells to make a Topographical reconoisance of road hence to the top of the Big Mountain & the side Kanyons leading into East Kanyon with a view to fortifying and putting East K. in a state of defence and make report of the same.

Wednesday 7 Oct 1857. Started at ten a. m on our recoinisance. Col Jones & Maj. Blair accompanying us some two miles below the mouth of Echo while we went to Spring Creek Station to fit up and staid all night. Fine rain in the night.

Thursday 8 Oct 1857. We set out this morning with the addition of Luke Johnson to our Co. and reconoirtered up East Kanyon up to the first Cotton wood grove and camped with J. D. Parker & several others. Warm and Rainy & clear & frosty night.

Friday 9 Oct 1857. Continued our reconoinsance to the Big Mountain and find many good places for defence some 8 side Kanyons on Either side mostly good as a place to take our enemies by suprise.

We returned to the 9 crossing of K. Creek and encamped. An Express says that Lott Smith has burned some 26 more waggons in all about 83, besides taking their cattle said to be about 700 head which are now on their way in. A drove of say 130 passed us today. The cattle looked well.

Saturday 10 Oct 1857. Arrived at Spring Creek Station, took dinner and reach Echo Station at Sun Set.

Sunday 11 Oct 1857. Like for a Storm this morning. 149 Head of the captured oxen passed, look well.

The Col (Jones) went to Signul height to display signal The signals can be seen from all the Batteries

Br Thomas & myself made out our Topographical report to Gen Wells.

149 head more of oxen passed, three teamsters, and one deserter from the enemy who were driving the oxen.

The deserter a long slab sided Dutchman reports that many of the soldiers would desert if they believed they would be well treated here, also that they were dissatisfied with their officers and that the officers were divided in their councils what to do.

Monday 12 Oct 1857. In the evening learned that M. Meecham & W. W. Stirritt who were sent to U. S. S. Camp with dispaches and "Deseret News" were well treated

The "Deseret News" had been sent by Gov Young as a spcial favor to the Commander Col Alexander, in the absence of any mail communication

They were heard to say after going into their tents and reading Gov Young's Letters and papers

"That's damned Cool"

Tuesday 13 Oct 1857. Accompanied Col Jones and others in an excurstion to examine Flank Kanyon and the preperations now ready to recieve our enimies, which are truly formadable, besides the natural advantages the batteries, many of them masked are capable of holding 1000 men who can pour a deadly fire upon their enemies while they are secreted and unseen

The deserter who passed here yester laughed with joy that he had the priviledge of passing here in peace for he said we could destroy the enemies' whole army here in a short time. Besides the hidden batteries high in the rocky crags there are three impassable ditches 12 feet wide and six or 7 deep filled by means of dams across the Creek which entirely obstructs the road and will keep our enemies exposed to a galling fire (if we ever get them there) There is no possibility of our being flanked

At Dark Col Burton with his command of 50 men arrived from Bridger. He has been out some six weeks. He brought one deserter also news that the enemy were moving up Ham's Fork at the rate of 5 to 8 miles a day. The 5th Infantry under Col Waite going before and the 10 Infantry under Col Alexander behind and their Baggage in the center which was flanked by *copious* guards on the Hills.

Wednesday 14 Oct 1857. Went on the mountains to try the signalls which worked well Recieved two letters from home my family had been down with the bad cough which is going the rounds (called *Horse distemper*) A number of families passing to day News that 700 head of cattle have been taken from the enemy again and that G. W. & T. J. Hickman who had gone into their enemies camp on private business were detained as prisoners, and orders were brought by Stephen Taylor for Maj Willis to march with his command to Bridger &c (His are Horsemen)

Thursday 15 Oct 1857. Cols Jones & Burton left in pursuit of a better range for our stock leaving me in charge at 11 a. m. Jos A. Young came express to the city Col Alexander expressed his willingness to treat but said he was perfectly able to carry out the President's order?[12]

Friday 16 Oct 1857. Lay up all quiet, and good natured A large lot of flour arrived

Saturday 17 Oct 1857. Mooved Camp one mile below the mouth of Echo and on the Weber bottom and called it Weber Station leaving a small force to see to the works here and *keep house.*

We were met at Weber Station by Col Pace (with [crossed out]) & Maj Thurber with about 300 foot.

O. P. Rockwell came in from the East at 11 P. M. with news that the enemy was yet on H's Fork Col Curtis & Maj Munroe's command left for home

Sunday 18 Oct 1857. Visit from Col Little. H. P. Kimball arrived with a party of Col Burton's command & news that Capt Lott Smith had been fired upon by the enemy. It appears that Lott and his company were met by Capt Marcy and a Company of Mule Horse men just at day light both parties met unexpectedly and halted the captains meeting in the centre they talked friendly a short time & Marcy

---

12. Here again Stout uses the question mark to show his own disbelief of what he has written. After his eloquent descriptions on the previous days of their effective fortifications, he feels certain that Colonel Alexander is mistaken when he says that "he was perfectly able to carry out the President's order." In effect, this question mark is a thumbing of the nose at the colonel or a daring, "You try it!"

declining a *twist* as Lott says they parted when Marcy's Co fired on Lott's unawares but no body was hurt.

Stormy and like for storm in the evening Some 700 head of the captured cattle passed to day being driven by teamsters who left the enemy. At dark W. A. Hickman came in with Mr Yates a prisoner.[13]

Monday 19 Oct 1857. Col Burton left with his command for the city   Weather better

News that Maj Jos Taylor and his adjutant William Stowell are taken prisoners by a party of the enemies Mule Cavalry. It appears that they rode into the enemies camp without ever looking to see who they were supposing them to be friends. the rest of his party escaped

Orders from Gen Wells to be ready to move at the shortest notice.

Tuesday 20 Oct 1857. Gen W. H. Kimball came on an Express that the Enemy had after march up H's Fork to the crossing of Sublett's road had now commenced to countermarch but for what reason does not appear but they say that they have an express from Col Johnson to meet him on G. R in 12 days. The snow is 12 in deep on H's F.

Wednesday 21 Oct 1857. Clear & Cold morning. An Express from Ogden that 300 men had marched to Cache Valley This was to head Uncle Sam who was expected to come in that way by his marching up H's Fork but since he has commenced a countermarching of course he has abandoned his northeren tour

------

13. Yates was murdered that night as he slept, a fact for which Stout was called to account six years later after the confession of Bill Hickman. See Hickman, *Brigham's Destroying Angel*, 122-27.

A contemporary account which establishes place and date is Lorenzo Brown's. On September 30, 1857, he wrote, "Drove four miles up Echo to the camp commanded by Col N. V. Jones where we expect to make a stand." On October 18 he noted: "Wm Hickman came in with a prisoner named Yates He has sold 3 or 400 lbs powder & some lead etc to the troops which he had promised to us." In that war climate, this would brand Yates as an enemy. Lorenzo Brown, "Journal," I, 290, 296.

Another account was given by Dan Jones: "This Yates was a personal friend of mine, a kind-hearted, liberal man of whom I had received many kindnesses . . . . I was camped with a small party about four miles west of the Weber valley and ten or twelve miles from Echo. One very cold morning about sunrise, Hickman and two others came to my camp. They seemed almost frozen . . . . Hickman asked me if I had any whiskey. I told him I had not. He then asked if I had coffee. I replied that we had. 'Then make us a good strong cup.' While the coffee was being made he took me outside and asked me if I knew Yates. I told him I did. 'Well, we have just buried him,' he said."

Jones went on to say that Brigham Young would never have ordered such a thing and that Hickman had simply murdered Yates for his money. See Daniel W. Jones, *Forty Years Among the Indians, A True Yet Thrilling Narrative of the Author's Experiences Among the Indians* (Salt Lake City, 1890), 129-30.

That some Mormons did confiscate Yates' property is shown in the diary of Newton Tuttle, at that time adjutant to Major John T. D. McAllister: "Sat 24 [October 18, 1857] . . . 7 teamsters have come in to camp from the enemy. Lewis Robinson got back from Green river he took 48 Horse & colts 36 pair of blankets &c that belonged to Yates . . ." Hamilton Gardner, ed., "A Territorial Militiaman in the Utah War, Journal of Newton Tuttle," *Utah Historicaal Quarterly*, XXII (October, 1954), 311.

Still another interesting sidelight comes from Albert Tracy, a member of the Johnston expedition. On April 10, 1860, as they were leaving the territory, he wrote: ". . . drew up for a change of teams at the identical adobie trading house of Yates. Yates! He has neither been seen by any of us since the day we purchased his powder . . . . The story of his horse ridden and his overcoat worn by Bill Hickman — 'Destroyer' — at Springville as told me by the woman . . . affords beyond doubt the key to his fate." J. Cecil Alter and Robert J. Dwyer, eds., *Journal of Captain Albert Tracy 1858-1860, Utah Historical Quarterly*, XIII (1945), 96-97. This confirms the story that Yates actually did sell his powder to the soldiers rather than to the Mormons, thus branding himself an enemy spy.

This evening I went in Company with J. Remington to General Wells Quarters where we arrived at midnight We had a cold toilsome trip I was worn up or down and had a severe head ache.

Thursday 22 Oct 1857. Returned to our Station leaving all well with the General

Friday 23 Oct 1857. Gen Wells and Staff arrived this evening and informs us that the Enemy is still Slowly marching down Ham's Fork yet & that they had left 13 mules 1 pony and 1 ox dead in their camp in one night such is the effect of the last cold spell on their weak poor animals and also that Maj Maxwell had captured one of their waggon masters and one cow and calf.

Saturday 24 Oct 1857. This morning Gen Wells had the entire correspondence between Gov Young and himself on the one part and Col Alexander of Uncle Sam on the other, read to the troops here which were long loud and interesting.

There was new orders entered into here Gen Wells and staff were going home, and Col Jones and myself (were to [crossed out]) with troops from Utah Co (300 men) were to march to East K. and commence putting it in a complete State of defence[14] the rest to remain here under command of Maj Pugmire

According to the above arraingements Gen Wells and Staff, Col Jones and myself with the 300 men from Utah Co. took up the line of march The Gen and Staff stopping for the night at Spring Creek Station while our command proceed to the head of Spring Creek where we camped enjoying a most lovely mild warm calm Summer rain during the night.

Sunday Oct 25 1857. We travelled on to day to the East Kanyon and camped below Cottonwood Grove and prepared to go to work on the Batteries &c Gen Wells passed us on the march leaving orders for me to come in home the first chance Maj W. S. Snow of San Pete Co with 50 men passed us here on his way to join the opperatives

In the after noon I met with a passage with Andrew Wilds and started for home encamping between the two mountains.

Monday 26 Oct 1857. Arrived at home at 11 a. m without breakfast. Family all well, garden green and no signs of frost notwithstanding the cold weather in the mountains and the cold at zero on Ham's fork.

Last night an express came in that the U. S. troops were yet on H's Fork laying up.

Wednesday 28 Oct 1857. Express again And lo! U. S. A. Laying up yet.

Friday 30 Oct 1857. Express Uncle Sams troops laying up yet "thar" Their mule-steers are flanking around some one company of whom fired on Capt Thos Abbott and ten men "never touched" Br McDonald (a Scot) came in with 7 teamsters, one deserter and 1 prisoner.

Sunday 1 Nov 1857. Quorum meeting at my house at 2 p. m.

Tuesday 3 Nov 1857. Another express came in. Moore cattle taken and a chase between the beligerents one of U. S. Capt thrown in the creek our boys fired on again but not touched though the balls came very close Cal mail came and six Cal prisoners taken at Box Elder supposed spies)[15]

---

14. The defenses built in East Canyon at that time are still clearly visible. They are located at the base of Big Mountain on hills overlooking Mormon Flat, where Little Emigration Canyon joins East Canyon.

15. These "six Cal prisoners taken at Box Elder supposed spies" are the Aiken party. They had left Sacramento early in May 1857, going east, joined a Mormon train from Carson Valley, and with them traveled into the Salt Lake Valley, entering ahead of the Mormon group. They

Saturday 7 Nov 1857. Capt J. F. D. McAlaster came in with one prisoner, one returning apostate mormon, who had deserted (a teamster) and one discharged teamster and 130 head of cattle and 33 mules & horses. Weather clear & cold snow 3 feet on Big Mount

Br Groesbeck arrived from the States and reports that he sold his train of Church goods at Platte Bridge to Rashan a french trader and also that Cols Johnson & Cook were on their way here with Gov. & civil officers for Utah, besides their commands of some 7 companies of dragoons

Sunday 8 Nov 1857. Express to day that Col Johnson the Commander of the U. S. Army for Utah had arrived and that Gen Wells who was now at Bridger had moved to Sulpher Creek The snow was ten inches at Bridger. Col Johnson was moving towards Bridger which was vacated & burned also Supply

We hear also that Col Johnson was much dissatisfied with Col Alexander for allowing the Mormons to take so many of their cattle and annoying them so much and declared that if he had been there it would not have been so but unfortunately for his gusto it so happened that Maj W. Snow just when he was letting off on poor Alexander was in the act with a party of our men of relieving them of the last beef oxen which they had that were in any kind of decent order 400 in number This brave Col now had the ill fortune to see his boasted courage vanish for he like Alexander had to quietly submit to it also about this time Maj Taylor made his escape from them and arrived safe in Gen Well's camp notwithstanding Col Johnson placed a guard of 25 men over him instead of 12 as heretofore

Monday 9 Nov 1857. In consequence of learning that Col Johnson with the U. S. A. were on their march towards Bridger 500 infentry and the same proportion from other counties about 1500 in all are now *enroute* for Echo Kanyon

The weather is very severe snowing in the Mountains & rain here. our brethren will have a cold time to cross the mountains the snow being 3 or 4 feet deep.

I am guarding the prisoners from Cal.

Tuesday 10 Nov 1857. Snowing hard & south wind.

Wednesday 11 Nov 1857. G. W. Hickman came in today having been discharged by the officers He reports them on Black's Fork where the snow is 2½ inches deep and weather cold and animals dying.

He was astonished when he arrived with our troops at what had been done and the number of cattle taken from our enemies for they had not let (them [crossed out]) him know any thing about it.

Tuesday 17 Nov 1857. Several brethren have been sent home badly but not dangerously frosted The cold in the mountains has for some days passd been intensly cold C. Wheelock came in express says that the enemy have moved 11 miles up Black's Fork in two days so weak are their teams.

Friday 20 Nov 1857. O. P. Rockwell with 3 or four others started with 4 of the prisoners, which we have been guarding for some days, South to escort them through the settlements to Cal via South route The other two are going to be permitted to go at large and remain till spring and the guard dismissed[16]

---

were arrested at Kaysville as spies, taken in to Salt Lake City and confined in a house at the corner of Main and First South streets where they were held for some time. Hickman, *Brigham's Destroying Angel*, 205-9.

16. According to Hickman, the four who started south were escorted as far as Nephi by Porter Rockwell, John Lot, _____ Miles, and one other. There, other local men joined the company, and at the first camp two of the number were killed. Two escaped to Nephi, but near Mona were shot while they were traveling back toward Salt Lake City. Hickman gives details of the disposal made of the two who were "permitted to go at large and remain till spring." *Ibid.*, 128-29. Evidence was produced in court in 1872.

Israil Ivins came express that the U. S. A. are at and above Bridger's ruins, the weather warm & clear.

Sunday 22 Nov 1857. Weather heavy with dark low fog which envelopes the valley.

An Express states that from the apparently increased number of horsemen it is supposed that there has been more arrivals in the enemies camp.

Saturday 28 Nov 1857. Weather continues dark, heavy, foggy. Ben Simons[17] bring news that the late cold weather has killed 500 mules and mules and cattle poor in our enimies camp.

Also that Col Cook and the Territorial officers for Utah had arrived at our enemies camp.

Sunday 29 Nov 1857. An Express arrived bring a letter and proclamation from (the Pretender) Gov A. Cumming which was read in the Tabernacle

He accuses Gov Young of all their misfortunes and losses and calls upon him to come out and own (it [crossed out]) or disavow it and denounces the good people of Utah with Gov Young at their head as traitors.

That the informal injust and illegal document sought to be palmed on us as a proclamation may not be forgotten I insert a copy, viz

"Green River County

Near Fort Bridger Utah Territory.

21 Nov. 1857.

To the people of Utah Territory.

On the 11th of July 1857 the President (*who*) appointed me to preside over the Executive department of the government of this Territory. I arrived at this point on the 19th of this month, and shall probably be detained some time in consequence of the loss of animals, during the recent snow storm. I will proceed at this point to make the preliminary arraingements for the *temporary* organization of the Territorial government. Many treasonable acts of violence having recently been committed by lawless individuals, supposed to have been commanded by the late Executive, Such persons are in a state of rebellion

Proceedings will be instituted against them in a court organized by Chief Justice Eckles held in this County which Court will supercede the necessity of appointing military Commissions for the trial of such offenders: It is my duty to enforce unconditional obedience to the Constitution, to the organic law of this Territory and to all other laws of congress, applicable to you. To enable me to effect this object I will, in the event of resistance rely first (on [crossed out]) upon a *Posse comititas* of the well disposed portion of the inhabitants of this Territory and will only resort to a military *posse* in case of necessity. I trust this necessity will not occur.

I come among you with no predjudices or enmities and by the exercise of a just and firm administration I hope to command your confidence.

Fredom of conscience, and the use of your own peculiar mode of serving God are sacred rights, the exercise (of [crossed out]) guaranteed by the Constitution, with which it is not the province of the government or the disposition of its representatives in this Territory to interfere.

In virtue of my authority as Commander-in-Chief of the militia of this Territory, I hereby command all armed bodiy of individuals, by whomsoever organized to disband, and return to their respective homes.

---

17. Ben Simons was a friendly Indian who for several years had carried messages for the Mormons.

CITY HALL

COUNTY COURT HOUSE

COUNCIL HOUSE

Both in his position as governmental officer and as a private lawyer, Hosea Stout's duties brought him into these three public buildings in Salt Lake City. All of them served as locations for governmental offices — — territorial, county, and city.

HOSEA STOUT HOME

This home was located on Second East just south of Brigham Street (South Temple). Hosea rushed to complete the house before he left for his China Mission in 1853. He returned to find strangers residing here, his wife and infant child dead, and his family scattered. A parking lot now occupies this site.

HOSEA STOUT'S COTTONWOOD HOME

After returning from St. George, Hosea spent his last years in this home at what is now Holladay Boulevard and Kentucky Ave.

ALVIRA WILSON STOUT, 1834-1910

Sixth wife of Hosea and mother of eleven of his children. She outlived her husband by twenty-one years.

The penalty of (disobeying [crossed out]) disobedience to this command will subject the offenders to the punishment due to traitors

A. Cumming

Govornor of Utah Territory.

Tuesday 1 Dec 1857. C. C. Rich returned home to day and reports that our forces are being sent in leaving only a small force at Echo to keep up a guard and look out for our enemie's movements.

Their animals are dying at rapid ratio

Thursday 3 Dec 1857. This morning I and my family commenced dispensing with the use of coffee & tea and what is more strange we feel no bad effects as yet. (9 o'clock p. m)

Saturday 5 Dec 1857. Gen Wells and Staff being expected this eve I accompanied the band and a large Company of others to meet and escort them. We proceeded some four miles and dispairing to meet them started back when we were soon overtaken by one of his party who had heard the drums and came ahead whereupon we halted a few moments when the Gen and about 100 horsemen came up and we all returned.

Monday 14 Decr 1857. Legislature met at ten a. m at the Social Hall and proceed to organize The council by electing Heber C. Kimball President and the House by electing John Taylor Speaker after which they adjourned till 10 tomorow.

Six or Eight teamsters came in reporting that Gov A. Cumming is very unpopular as are the military officers.

Tuesday 15 Dec 1857. Legislature met at ten in joint session & recieved the Gov's message, 1000 copies of which were ordered to be printed.

D. H. Wells, Orson Hyde, G. A. Smith J. W. Cumming & myself were appointed a committee to draft resolutions expressive of the feeling of this Assembly of the message and past course of Gov. B. Young

Wednesday 16 Dec 1857. Legislature met at ten. The speaker declared the list of the different committees. Speeches from W. H. Hooper, O. Hyde and the Speaker. I C. Haight member from Iron & Washington Countis exhibited a canister of good rifle powder made by Eleazer Edwards of Cedar City of valley materials.

Saturday 19 Dec 1857. Prosecuted a Suit before Probate Court "The people vs Chas Taylor & B. Dallow for selling putrid and unholesome meat.

Minor, Hickman & Stoddard attorney for defts The case sustained and defts fined twenty dollars each and costs.

Monday 21 Decr 1857. Legislature met at ten in joint session D. H. Wells presented the Resolutions expressive of the feeling of this assembly of the course & message of Gov B. Young which passed unanimously.

Mr Councillor Carrington presented an act attaching Green River Co. to G. S. Lake County which passed.

Tuesday 23 Dec 1857. Legislature met at ten. Petition of J. Roberry and others for a herd ground which was refered to the Comte on Herding.

A subscription was presented to the Legislature for the number of men well furnished, equiped, & mounted each member could furnish for the defense of Utah I signed one, some two & some as high as 6. Adjourned till first Monday in January.

Friday 25 Dec 1857. Attended a Court martial as Judge Advocate where John Redman & Isaac Rowley were tried for mal-conduct as guards over the U. S. prisoners.

The charges were sustained and they & the officer of the guard repremanded. Dined with a Company at Ben Dallows. Good dinner and plenty of whiskey.

Saturday 26 Dec 1857. The 3 prisoners taken some time ago from U. S. A. were sent back to day.

Friday 1 January 1858. New Year sets in quiet and peaceable every seem content several Balls and the Theatre are in high motion

The Spirit of peace and happiness which pervade every brest in the Territory is a perfect miricle.

Monday 4 Jan 1858. Legislature met at ten in joint session. Petition of J. Worthington and others for Herd groung in Ivenhoe Vally referred to Committee on Herding.

Librairian's report read & Referred.

Road Commissioners report read, referred.

D. H. Wells moved that the Gov be requested to lay before the assembly the correspondence between him and the U.S.A. with a view to their publication carried. Bill for the pay of Code Commissioner's presented referred to comte on claims. The Cal mail having arrived last night the news from the states were read. It appears that the new from here had reached them to the time Capt Van Vleitt left His report was in the N. Y. Herald and every paper was full of the news from Utah but what was strange there were no Editorial remards in any of them They seemed to be perfectly astonished not knowing what to say.

Preached at the Seventies meeting in the evening.

5 Jan 1858. Joint session the Govornor's Correspondence was read and highly approved and ordered to be printed in the "Deseret News"

Comte on Claims reported Code Comrs Bill allowed

Wednesday 6 Jan 1858. Light snow last night. Joint Session met at 10 a. m D. H. Wells presented Memorial to the President of the U. S. and to Congress which was adopted.

John Taylor's letter to Capt Marcy of the U. S. invading army read and ordered to be printed

Preamble & Resolutions by J. W Cumming read & referred to Comte on Territorial affairs.

A Loud long speech from Col Little full of *dunder* and *Blixum*

Friday 8 Jan 1858. Joint session met at ten a. m The Speaker announced that Prest H. C. Kimball was sick

Bill reported to extend the Corporate limits of the city of Payson pased once and referred to Comte on incorporations

Bill granting Herd ground in Tooele Valley to O, Pratt sr and others passed

Another granting one to Brigham Young sr in Ivenhoe Valley passed. Adjourned till Monday 11th next

Monday 11 Jan 1858. Joint Sessioin met at 10 a. m shortly after which President Kimball appeared waving his hat & shouting hurra!! to our great astonishment as we did not know that he had recovered from his late sickness so as to be able to go out doors

Petition to remove the County seat of Tooele Co from Richville to Tooele City, which was referred to the committee on Counties

Jos A. Young reported presented a memorial to the Prest of the U. S. which & adopted to be signed by the members and officers of both houses and the citizens generally.

Missillanious discussion about establishing a bank, mail routs, revenue, which was referred to the Comtes on Territories

Tuesday 12 Jan 1858. Joint session met at ten a. m. W Woodruff reported the returns of the Deseret Agricultural and Manufacturing Society which was referred to the committee on Agriculture Trade and Manufactures after which followed a long course of speeches on the subject of Home Manufactures.

Wednesday 13 Jan 1858. Joint Session met at ten a. m. An act amending the grant for a herd ground to S. M. Blair and others approved 14 Jan. 1857 was passed.

An Act granting Jos Young & Jacob Gates a herd ground in Parley's Kanyon was reported by Comte on Herding and referred back

Report of G. A. Smith and John Taylor Delegates to Congress to present our Constitution & was read approved and ordered to be printed in the "Deseret News".

The Committee on Elections reported the number and kind of offices to be filled by the joint vote of this assembly which was recieved and a vote taken that the Gov be requested to nominate those to be elected

The committee on Counties reported adversely to removing the County seat of Tooele County which was recieved. Adjourned till Friday next.

I have commenced having a well dug in my back yard.

Thursday 14 January 1858. Snowing this morning with the deepest snow on the ground that we have had this winter I was engaged making a well curb.

Friday 15 January 1858. Joint session met at ten. Being engaged finishing the well curb I was sent for by the Chaplain of the Council as he said to defend the lawyers as the joint session was electing the officers to be elected by them I went and found the Election over They had filled the several offices by electing nearley the same individuals. I was elected to the same offices as last year to wit Code Commissioner, Regent of the "University of Deseret" and Attorney General

The subject of a Bank was discussed.

An act concerning delinquent fortification taxes reported by D. H. Wells. Read three times & passed. Several acts relating to Herdgrounds was passed before I came. Adjourned till Monday.

Attended City Council in the evening.

Saturday 16 Jan 1858. To day my well was finished being 22 ft deep. The water is quite plenty. At one p. m. there was a mass meeting at the Tabernacle to memorialize Government &c and the citizens to express their views as to the course pursued by prest B. Young Three memorials one to Prest Buckhannan one to Congress and one to the Govt & people of the U. S. all couched in the plainest and most determined language declaring that they not only approve of Gov Youngs course but that they will not submit to their hellish outrages and tyrannacle oppression any longer.

The Tabernacle was crouded and every vote was unanimous.

Monday 18 Jan. 1858. Joint Session met at ten a. m. D. H. W from the Comte reported "An [act] to authorize Notaries Public to take and certify oaths, affirmations and acknowledgements in certain cases" recieved, passed first time and referred back

Also presented "Resolutions concerning Service ordered by courts" Read three times and passed

Also "An Act concerning appointees to office" Recieved, Read three times and passed.

Also "An Act to repeal Territorial taxes"[18]

Recieved, Read three times & passed.

Also "An Act to amend ordinance regulating the manufacturing (of ardent [crossed out]) and vending of ardent spirits Read three times & passed.

---

18. The abolition of territorial taxes has some interesting implications. The members of the legislature evidently felt that Gentile appointees should depend on federal appropriations with which to carry on their programs. They were unwilling that local funds go to support these officers. Public works would be supported by tithing.

Tuesday 19 Jan. 1858. Joint session meat at ten a. m. Mr Bullock of Committee on Incorporations reported "An act to establish the boundary line between Payson and Spanish Fork Cities Read three times and passed.

Adjourned till ten tomorrow

I worked at home the rest of the day.

Meeting at the Tabernacle at dark to take in consideration the subjects of a Bank &c It was decided to have a Church Bank Charter which was passed called the "Bank of Deseret"[19] President B. Young was elected President and H. C. Kimball, D. H. Wells and W. H. Hooper Directors The capital stock of said bank to be founded on a property basis and the Bills redeemable in live stock The people passed the act of incorporation with great enthusiasm and unanimity.

The Territorial tax being abolished all public works was to be done on labor tithing and under the control of the Bishops

A standing army was also to be raised of 1000 or 1100 men from levies from the different Wards and Counties.

The army thus raised were to be sustained by the Wards and Counties (thus [crossed out]) from whom they are raised

Elders O. Pratt E. T. Benson John Kay having returned from England via California to day were present and addressed the meeting

Wednesday 20 Jan 1858. Joint session met at ten a. m. Petition of E. Hunter et. al. for a Seed distributing office was recd and referred to Committee on Trade &c

Petition C. White & S. Lever (runn [crossed out]) for Black Rock Kanyon recd and referred to C. on Incorporations

Petition of C. White for Herd ground at Black Rock recd referred to C. on Herding.

A. P. Rockwood reported appropriation Bill referred back with O. Hyde J. W. Cummings & H. Stout added to comte

D. H Wells reported back back "Act concerning Notaries Public" Read three times amended and passed.

D. H. Wells reported the condition of finance and Department of War. Also list of the officers for the Standing army, ect. ect. ect.

Thursday 21 January 1858. Joint session met at ten a. m Warren Snow of Comte on Herding reported adversley to the petition of C White. accepted

Rockwood reported back the "General appropriation" recieved and passed. Comte on trade &c reported adversely on the petition of E. Hunter for a Seed distributing office accepted.

Friday 22 Jan 1858. Joint session met at ten a. m. Harrington reported memorial to Congress for mail recieved and adopted. A vote of thanks to gov Young, W. H. Hooper, H. C. Kimball & John Taylor as officers Thus ends the *Seventh* Session of Utah's Legislature what will be the Eghth and under what crcumstances?

Wednesday 3 February 1858. Commenced to make me a loom to day in conformity to the prevailing spirit to aid & promote home manufactures.

The Cal mail arrived to to day bringing the president's Message of 4 Decr 1857. He recommends 4 additional regiments to be raised to march against Utah which he declares to be in a state of rebellion. Many leading papers denounce his course towards Utah but the general feeling is bitter

---

19. Stout was one who referred to this effort as the "Bank of Deseret," but the name adopted was the "Deseret Currency Association." The capital stock consisted of church property, the notes redeemable in livestock. The Deseret Currency Association, therefore, represented an attempt to meet the need for currency and credit by using the one type of commodity which was generally available — " _stock. Arrington, *The Great Basin Kingdom*, 188-92, gives an excellent discussion of the .orking of this medium of exchange.

Thursday 4 February 1858. This evening Alvira was taken very sick we had to be up all night nearley.

Sunday 7 February 1858. Quorum meeting at my house. good attendance Alvira better, Elizabeth sick and baby too.

Sunday 14 February 1858. Alvira quite unwell yet Elizabeth, Henry and Baby quite unwell last week. Been working on the loom which is nearley finished. Looks like to weave well!! heh!!

Tuesday 16 Feb 1858. I attended a law suit to day, Peter W. Conover vs. Gilbert & Gerrish in assumpsit Demand $850 — Hickman & myself were Council for Plff and Furguson for defts The defence brought in a set off of $145.25/100. The judgement of court gave plff $13.65 Each party to pay their witnesses and defts pay the costs.

Saturday 20 February 1858. Yesterday and day before I was gardening. The ground was in good order. To day was wet and rainy, warm Spring rain

Sickness continues in my family. Alvira still confined to bed. Elizabeth nearly so. The baby sick and little Hosea quite unwell.

Monday 22 Feb. 1858. Yesterday was rainy and warm. Frost and light freeze this morning.

Little Hosea much worse, rest better I was taken with a stitch in my back this morning and am very lame Weather bodes more storm.

Tuesday 23 Feb 1858. Wife & children no better. Henry unwell. Snow last night some 3 in. deep. day warm pleasant, snow nearley all off the valley. I have to lay up with lame back.

Thursday 25 Feb. 1858. This evening Col Thos L. Kane[20] of Phila arrived here He left N. York in the Cal mail steamer on the 5 Jan He was quite out of health by hard travelling when he arrived. His business here is not made known yet.

Saturday 27 Feb 1858. This evening several persons disguised as Indians entered Henry Jones' house and dragged him out of bed with a whore and castrated him by a square & close amputation

Wednesday 3 March 1858. Myself and family are better and little Hosea is able to get out of bed and walk around a little.

Sunday 7 March 1858. Quorum meeting at my house at 2 p. m. Agreed to make a small donation for Prest Joseph Young such as butter, Eggs, groceries cheese ect ect.

Monday 8 March 1858. Col Kane accompanied by Egan, Rockwell, Hanks and several others of the "Be'hoys"[21] left for the United States' troops' Camp to go by the up Weber Route

---

20. Hosea Stout, who knew Thomas L. Kane well, made no reference to his traveling incognito as "Dr. Osborne." Kane, full of concern about what seemed impending bloodshed, had traveled by sea to California and hurried to Salt Lake City over the San Bernardino road, eager to have an interview with Brigham Young before real hostilities began. Public announcement of his arrival was made the Sunday following: "23 [February] 58 Preaching by A Lyman, O Hyde, F Little, H C Kimball & B Young who told of Doct Osborne who proved to be Col. Kane from Philadelphia 40 days since with dispatches from Washington & settle if possible the Utah difficulties." Lorenzo Brown, "Journal," I, 308.

21. The listing of Egan, Rockwell, Hanks, and others as "Be'hoys" sent to guard Colonel Kane suggests that the term was applied to a definite group of men. As early as 1853 Ferguson had referred to the "b'hoys" at the end of a letter; *Webster's Dictionary* lists it as meaning a "gang member, a rowdy." Hickman referred often to a group of "Brigham's boys." Tullidge listed all the officers of the Nauvoo Legion detailed for the Utah War with "O. P. Rockwell, Eph Hanks, and others" as special scouts. Tullidge, *History of Salt Lake City*, 168.

What the result of his mission will be I do not know of course.

A Report or rather an Express arrived to day from Salmon River fort that the Indians around there had become hostile and had attachd the brethren there killing two, Miller & McBride to young men and wounding some five others among the rest Thos S. Smith the President[22] besides driving off their cattle & horses. The Indians were headed and set on by white men

Wednesday 10 March 1858. A Report came in town that Ben Simonds and a large company of Indians had banded and was about to take possession of Echo Kanyon to favor the coming in of the United States troops whereupon 50 men were raised and sent to Echo

Friday 12 March 1858. Attended City Council this evening where I was appointed City Water Master

Sunday 14 March 1858. South wind for several day past which went down last night and was succeeded by a heavy snow storm which untill 12 to day The snow is some six inches deep and the wind in the North which will endanger the fruit trees which are now leaving and budding, gardens are also in fine order my radishes lettuce tongue grass, pease &c are up. The consequences of a severe cold storm would be seriously injurious

Thursday 18 March 1858. Attended a general Council at the Historians office of the first Presidency, Twelve, and officers of the Legion The object of which was to take into consideration the best plan of opperations to be adopted to counter act the purposes of our enemies, whether to attact them before they come near us or wait untill they come near, or whether it is yet best to fight at all only in unavoidable self defense or in case a large force is sent against us this spring whether to fight or burn our houses & destroy every thing in and around us and flee to the mountains & deserts &c &c &c[23]

It appears that the course pursued hitherto by Gov Young in baffelling the oppressive purposes of Prest Buckhannan has redounded to the honor of Gov Young and the Saints and equally to the disgrace of the President & his cabinet Mormonism is on the ascendancy and now what is the best policy to maintain that ascendancy. If we whip out and use up the few troops at Bridger will not the excitement and sympathy which is now raising in our favor in the states, be turned against us. Whereas if we only anoy and impede their progress while we "Burn up" and flee, the folly, and meanness of the President will be the more apparrant and he and his measures more unpopular &c This was about a fair statement of the subject matter in council There was no definite measures adopted many spoke on the subject and the council adjourned till 8th April at 2 p.m. at the Tabernacle.

Friday 19 March 1858. The Brethren who escorted Col Kane to Bridger came in this evening, bringing 9 mules "with lassos" After the Col had been in the enemies camp 5 days he came to our brethren who were in and around Muddy (for they did not go into camp with him) and made arraingements for them to come home

22. The Salmon River Mission was established in 1855 when twenty-seven men had been called with Thomas S. Smith as leader. They settled about 180 miles north of Salt Lake City in what is now Idaho. In the spring of 1857 Brigham Young and a large company visited the place where Thomas D. Brown was acting as engineer and clerk.

The two men who had been killed were George McBride and James Miller; their leader was wounded. The colony was now withdrawn and the town abandoned in accordance with the general church policy.

23. This report is eloquent of the problems which faced the Mormon leaders and of their sensitivity to public opinion throughout the nation. The notation made on February 22 preceding that the President of the United States in his message to Congress on December 4 had requested four additional regiments to be raised to march against Utah no doubt colored their decisions.

and meet him at quaken asp grove on Wednesday or Thursday next to escort him in here.

He said he was kept close had to pay six dollars pr day for board can not see his friends who are in camp and so forth but did not say what progress he was making as to what he went there for.[24]

Weather stormy yet which has continued since the 14th snowing but warm. dark low clouds full of snow.

Saturday 20 March 1858. Clear day snow melting fast weather looks settled.

Sunday 21 March 1858. Attended meeting at the Tabernacle which meeting was resolved into a special Conference for the transaction of business.

The subject matter was "fleeing to the" deserts and mountains. It was decided to send 500 families from this city immediately to be selected from among those who had never been driven from their homes and from that class to take the poorest and most helpless[25] This 500 was to be selected by the Bishops from the several wards

The plan of Emmigration being thus established in this city was to be an en-sample other citis wards and settlements throughout the Territory North more particularly The precise destination was not made known as yet.[26]

In the evening attended Ward meeting where the subject of Emmigration was taken up and names called for to Emmigrate The brethren seemed some what loth to volunteer for which reason I gave my name to go in the first Company although I did not come in that class who were called upon Hard snow storm from the west at dark.

Monday 22 March 1858. Capt Egan, Gen W. H. Kimball and several others started this morning to meet Col Kane at Quaken Asp Grove on Thursday according to previous appointment with him Warm pleasant day, snow melting

---

24. For a detailed account of the difficulties which Kane encountered, both with General Johnston and Governor Cumming, see Furniss, *The Mormon Conflict*, 176-82.

25. The decision to move the "poorest and most helpless" is rather hard to understand — unless the church provided their means of transportation, food, and shelter.

26. "The precise destination was not made known as yet," because it had not been decided upon.

On Monday, February 8, 1858, John D. Lee, just returned from Salt Lake City, wrote: "I Started South acording to my appointment to locate or Point out the location intended to be made by Pres. B. Young for a resting place for his famely & that of the 1st Presidency." For the next four days he rode around the Virgin River valleys accompanied by Joseph Horne, Jacob Hamblin, and others, but could find no spot that was very inviting.

On March 31 Lee received an express from Brigham Young with a "circular" and a private letter. This last closed with the sentence, "It is at present expected to make Headquarters at Parowan for a time when we arrive there."

Knowing the limitations of that area, they changed the plan again. On April 13, Lee wrote: "Spent the night at Pres. W. H. Dame, who had Just returned from G. S. L. c. with instructions from Pres. B. Young to raise a co. of from 60 to 70 men, 20 waggons with 4 mules to each wagon, 2 Teamsters & a Horseman, with seed, grain, tools, &c. to Penetrate the Desert in search for a resting place for the Saints. Said that he hoped the co. would find a Desert that would take them 8 days to cross, but was affraid that it would take them only 3 days to cross it. Conting this is the 4th attempt & if you can't find the Place, I will go myself when I get to Parowan . . ." Cleland and Brooks, *A Mormon Chronicle*, II, 149, 156, 158.

These orders were strictly carried out, in one of the most expensive and least fruitful of all the exploring experiments of Mormondom. Among the papers of William H. Dame is the day-by-day account of this journey into an unknown desert. At one place the spring was dry and the drivers had to dig holes into the gravel to where they could get water by the tablespoon, enough to fill a cup, then a bucket. They were twenty-four hours working shifts getting one bucketful of water for each horse.

They found an uninviting place, broke ground, planted a little seed to fill their assignment, and left. Ten years later one of the company returned to the site and recovered a small box of flour which had been cached.

Wednesday 24 March 1858. The Expidition which went west in search of Indians returned to day not succeeding in capturing any Indians or recovering any stock

Attended a Bishops meeting to night Subject our removal hence. It is in contemplation to send for all the teams south to assist us in moving We when moved will be distributed among the settlements south of this County and some new settle made one on Chicken Creek — South wind is blowing hard again & appearences bodes more falling weather

Sunday 28 March 1858. Gen W. H. Kimball returned to day. He met Kane at the place appointed & staid with him a day & a half but he returned to Bridger and appointed a future time for Gen Kimball to again meet him & accompany him in here

Teams are beginning to come and the people are moving south

Tuesday 30 March 1858. Attended Bishops meeting where arraingements were made to move the people at the rate of some 40 families a day

Wednesday 31 March 1858. 500 troops that is 400 foot and 100 Horse are being sent to Echo again to meet the emergency which may arise

Henry Allen marched this morning leaving to prepare and move without his aid.

Thursday 1 April 1858. Presidents Young, Kimball, & Wells and some of the 12 rolled out to day for Provo. Hard Sout wind like for rain.

Friday 2 April 1858. Cal mail arrived at dark, bringing the Eastern news to the 5th Feb. Parties rabid on the Kanzas question. Prest Buckhannan's recommendation to increase the army four regiments was brought up in the senate & lost by a vote of 4 to 1, The tide of feelings seemed to be turning in our favor.

Dr Barnhisel proposes to the President to send out Commissioners to arrainge and settle the terms with us and we sell out and go hence say to some island. heigh o!

Saturday 3 April 1858. This after noon Presidents Young, Kimball & Wells returned from Provo. Emmigration is now going on briskly to the south I anticipate starting next Monday.

Monday 5 April 1858. Teams are coming from the south in great numbers to move the people from this place. My wife is laid up with inflammatory rheumatism she is not able to walk.

Tuesday 6th April 1858. General Conference as well as General parade to day. President Brigham Youg spoke on the Emmigration South He said the order of Emmigration would be for those living in this city not to go beyond Utah County and the people of Ogden to stop here, and those N. of Ogden to stop in Ogden & thus keep compact and keep our arms always with us

when we have thus moved then go further according to the same order & so be prepared to defend ourselves. There was an exception made to this rule in cases where teams come from South of Utah County.

Wednesday 7 April 1858. Rained all all last night. Alvira is very sick with a kind of inflamatory rheumatism and had to be set up with all night.

This morning M. D. Hambleton came with a team and took about 1200 pounds of my "goods & effects" to Salt Creek Juab County, where I expect first to move.

Monday 12 April 1858. To day Col Kane accompanied by Gov A Cummings arrived here escorted from Davis Co by the Mayor, Alderman, Marshal and many other prominent citizens of this place.

Friday 16 April 1858. Alvira continues helpless with the inflamatory rheumatism Has to be set up with all night since the 5th

The people from Ogden are flocking in here and settling in the houses vacated by those who have moved to Utah co.

Saturday 17 April 1858. Another snow and rain storm which continued all day which most thoroughly saturated the ground. The garden is growing finely The peach trees, currants, and strawberries are in bloom. Aside from the pending exodus which seems to be our doom I am in a fair way to have the most excellent garden I ever had, but there seems to be no alternative but to leave our houses and fine gardens just as they begin to produce something for our enjoyment but such is the fate and always has been with those in every age who would dare to worship the true God

My wife continues helpless while Anna and me are worn out and nearly sick with sitting up every night

Monday 19 Apl 1858. This evening in company with Col J. C. Little and Gen J Furguson I made a visit to Gov A. Cumming and Col Thos L. Kane at W. C. Stains' residence[27] was introduced to them and scraped up an old acquaintance with Col Kane on the strength of seeing him at the Bluffs in 1846. Had an agreeable conversation with them on various subjects untill about 10 o'c. Gov Cuming declared it was his intentions to make favorable reports to government for us and do all he could to prevent a colission between *us* and the U. S. He expresses to be dissatisfied with the doings of Col Johnson and the troops at Bridger &c &c &c &c &c ahem! He was very much astonished to find that the Utah Library and the Court records were not burned as reported to government and wondered how such utterly false reports could be raised ect ect ect

We we very courteously recieved and treated by both them and left with an invitation to "call again when convenient"

Friday 23 April 1858. Attended a court martial at the council House at ten a. m Composed of the following officers to wit Brig. Gen F. D. Richards President Col J. W. Cummings, Col R. T. Burton Col H. Stout, Col J. D. Ross, Col N. V. Jones, Lt. Col H. S. Beatie Major J. F. D. McAlister & Maj H. Lawrance and also H. Stout Judge advocate. Convened for the trial of Private Rufus Allen for betrayal of orders &c and John Schenfeldt for disobedience of orders &c both plead guilty after much testimony was introduced to set forth the degree & nature of guilt which occupied all day without dinner.

Saturday 24 April 1858. Attended Court martial as yesterday on the same cases. Decision against Allen and Schenfeldt That they be reprimanded and dismissed from the Legion with disgrace and their arms &c be forfeited.

Sunday 25 April 1858. Attended meeting this fore noon Gov. A Cuming & Col Kane were there

Gov Cuming was introduced to the people by Gov. Young He declared that it was his purpose to do us all the good he could and be our friend and attempted to justify the government of the U. S. in sending troops to enforce officers upon us against our will &c

He requested to know the feelings of the people and was answered by Gilbert Clements who stated the objections which the *People* had against his being our Gov while backed up by an armed force. 'Send home youre troops said' Clements and then come among us as a friend &c After his reply an altercation ensued betwen the Gov & C. when John Taylor of the 12 made a short speech on the same subject

Clement's speech was enthusiastically cheered continually and when gov C. said that he would not hang as a rag on our garments against our will, the congregation

---

27. "The first mansion reared in Utah that could fairly claim the initial place under the classification of the 'beautiful homes of our city' was undoubtedly that of William C. Staines . . . ." Tullidge, "Biographies," *History of Salt Lake City,* 79. This later became the Devereaux House, but even at this early date was known for its luxury and was the place where visiting dignitaries were taken. Staines had two wives but no children.

cheered loudly giving him to see that the quicker he was *oph* the better would they be suited.

There was many personal sarcasms thrown at the gov & twice when he arose to speak he was most roundly *hissed* still He seemed to take all in good parts as he said to me after meeting "that we had had quite a discussion to day and all would soon be understood and work well yet. and really seemed to be very much encouraged by the proceedings as if he had been well recieved.

He also had read a notice or proclamation or as some called it a pronunciamento, while others insisted that it was a *Bull* at all events it gave notice that if there was any one in durance vile or kept here against their will to come to him & he would work their deliverance. and all who had any thing to complain of to call and see him or write to him or Fay Worthen sealed &c

This wonderful document seemed to me to be a cross between a *Pronunciamento* and a *Bull* It to signyfy that he was invested with most extraordinary powers to give every one both political and religious rights and privileges while at the same time it seemed to signify that he could forgive *sins*

He also appealed to the *Women* as he called them to back him up said that he depended on them for support and may such strange things.

Monday 26 April 1858. Attended Court martial to day. Quite a number of cases were tried for minor offences but none of grave importance.

Cout martial adjourned till Saturday at ten o'clock a. m.

Tuesday 27 April 1858. Went in company with J. Furgerson R. T. Burton & G. D. Grant to see & visit Gov. Cuming We had a lengthy conversation on the subject of those persons who are running to him dayly to lay before him their grievances He very frankly showed us the statements of all those who had come to him which he had taken in writing which he said was all that they said There was nothing in any of those statements which reflected sencure [censure] on the people or authorities here They mostly were in relation to their wanting to leave here besides some family dificulties &c

He also pledged himself that where statements were made against the community or people he would hold the same open for rebutting evidence as well as hold all such statements open to public inspection. He declared himself to be our friend and would not be in our midst any longer than he could be of use to us. He also read to us his correspondence with Col Johnson and also his report in part which he is preparing to send to government, which was vindicating Gov Young's character &c

Saturday 1 May 1858. Court martial met at ten a m and was dismissed sine die.

Monday May 3 1858. Suit before Probate Court J. B. Kimball v Theodore Thorp in assumpsit demand $655 I was on the part of the plff. Deft confessed judgement. The case came up by attachment and the property attached was clained by Albert Varney who undertook to Replevy it and had a suit in the after noon which went down for want of a Replevin Bond. W A. Hickman & John Bear Attorneys for plff & myself for deft Kimball.

Wednesday 5 May 1858. Hard rain last night and this morning Cal mail came in yesterday. News from W favorable to us. Congress has refused to grant a dollar or another man to president B. in addition to the regular forces & expenditure of the army to aid him in his tyrannical crusade against us.

This fore noon I sent Anna, Elizabeth and Eli with another load of my goods to Salt Creek by John Webster About two more loads will I think take all my effects & family

Friday 7 May 1858. Henry returned to day from his campaign to Echo where he has been since the 31 March. Severe East wind this morning and last night which blew down fences & unroofed a barn but weather clear &c

Monday 10 May 1858. Law Suit Before probate Court, John Gheen v. David J. C. Beck in an action of Damages for personal injury & destruction of property Myself & A. Miner Council for plff and Judson J. Stoddard for deft jury of six men. Beck did not appear & Stoddard after trying twice to have the suit dismissed for want of jurisdiction refused to answer so the jury was called to assess the extent of damages, still Stoddard continued the defence. Jury brought in a virdict of $1500. in favor of Gheen.

This suit was founded on a circumstance which happened in 1848 in Pottawattamie County Iowa. Beck and about 30 others under took to lay out a town site on land which was claimed and owned by Gheen and on which he resided. They threw down his fences &c he put them up They came and commence throwing down again He took his rifle in hand and went to putting up again warning them not to encroach on him any more or he would shoot them They crowded on him and he shot one man (Conditt) who fell dead The mob rushed upon Gheen and pell mell beat him untill they thought him dead. Gheen when found not to be dead was taken by them for murder and imprisoned but was subsequently acquitted This is a brief outline of the cause of action in this suit[28]

Elder S. W. Richards and two others arrived to day via Larimie some 37 days from Florence (old Winter Quarters) he left several Elders on the Sweet Water who with one waggon would soon be here

Thursday 13 May 1858. Dr J. Clinton, J. W. Wakely and the rest of the brethren whom S. W. Richards left on Sweet Water camin to day They passed through Col. Johnsons Camp and Wakeley was arrested and put under $5000 bonds to answer to a charge of murder which was sworn against him by one of the mountaineers

To day or yester Gov Cumming & col T. L. Kane left here for Col Johnson's Camp at Bridger Col Kane is en rout for home He is to be escorted by H. Egan and several of the brethren who will accompany him home

Gov Cumming intends to bring his wife here and accompany us in our emmigration as he says he will stick by us in our ups & downs.

(Friday 14 May 1858. [crossed out])

Sunday 23 May 1858. Sent off about 1100 pounds of my goods and effects to Salt Creek by Homer Brown for which I paid him Eight dollar cash. I have one more load which I shall try and send as soon as convenient

Times are dull we have hardly a neighbour in this vicinity. The people are moving rapidly and ere many days Great Salt Lake City will be deserted.

Monday 24 May 1858. Started at one p. m. with Jas Furguson & went to Provo where we arrived near sun set Two men are here trying to sell land in the little imaginary kingdom of Musgeto in Central America They meet with poor success. They offer us the land at ten cents per acre and agree to guarentee us an independant government & good title to the land &c all which is well known to be a perfect sham.

Tuesday 25 May 1858. Started at 2 p. m for home and about dusk met my wife and family encamped at Mill Creek on the state road in the mud and rain. Two brethren Davis & Wright of Salt Creek had come with teams for me & had thus started

---

28. The incident of the murder of Lilace Conditt by John Gheen was noted in Volume I, Part 4, footnote 74. That after ten years Gheen should be cleared and reimbursed for damages is an interesting commentary on frontier justice.

with remainder of my goods and effects. I stoped here and we slept in a cow shed very comfortably

Wednesday 26 May 1858. Started at day light. Weather lowry roads mudy We went to Springville and staid with Br M. Daily. rained all night

(**Friday.** lay up [crossed out]) **Thursday.** lay up.

(**Saturday.** [crossed out]) **Friday 28.** Wife went on and I returned to the city and staid will Allen at Battle Creek

Saturday 29 May 1858. Went to the city

Sunday 30 May 1858. Spent the day with two of the men of Musqueto & G. A. Smith and W Woodruff and others.

Monday 31 May 1858. Packed up 35 vols of Annals of Congress & 15 vols Howards Reports to take with me to Salt Creek

Thursday 3 June 1858. Started for Salt Creek and staid all night with Joseph Murdock at American Fork.

Friday 4 June 1858. Went to Springville and staid all night with my old friend Andrew Hamilton. There is about 1000 Indians here on their return from Col Johnson's Camp. They profess to not like the Americans but they are quite thievish and saucy

Saturday 5 June 1858. Went to payson staid with A L. Taussig. Learned that the Indians had killed three men and one woman in Salt Creek Kanyon.

Sunday 6 June 1858. Came to Salt Creek found my family well and in a little dirty house which will not hold near all my goods.

Tuesday 8 June 1858. Irrigating in the fore noon. Heard that Gov Cumming & the civil officers with two peace Commissioners have come to Salt Lake City bringing a proclaimation from Prest Buck — offering a free pardon to all mormons who will repent of past deeds and do better but by what right he does all this I do not know but the right story on the subject I have not learned.

Tuesday 15 June 1858. Left home to day for Provo and staid all night at Springville Rained some in the evening

Wednesday 16 June 1858. Went to Provo this morning Here I saw the Two peace Commissioners sent by Prest Buck to make peace on any terms which would save him from disgrace and his party from ruin. The Commissioners Rowell & Benjamin McCullouch Made a speech to the people at 5 p. m in the Bowery congratulating us on the happy event of peace being declared &c his Powell's speach was a miserable effort to eulogise Utah and Uncle Sam both and altogether was very shallow, & not much liked Hard rains to day.

Thursday 17 June 1858. Rainy day still. The peace Commissioners left for dry creek to day where they intend to make another speach

Friday 18 June 1858. This morning the eastern mail came to Provo which has been accumulating & kept in Col Johnson's camp where the letters have many of them been opened & some kept May [many] letters & papers have been en route more than one year. Staid all night at springville

Saturday 19 June 1858. Went to provo Rained all the after noon. no news of importance.

Sunday 20 June 1858. Went to meeting heard President Young preach and after started home and staid all night at Pond Town.

Monday 21 June 1858. Came home family all well

Tuesday 22 June 1858. Recieved letter from Chas Bullance Esqr of Peoria Ill which has been in the office & en route for 13 months.

Saturday 3 July 1858. Left home to day for Salt Lake City in Company with W. W. Stirritt & N. Stewart and went to Payson staid all night with Allen Weeks. Here the people were celebrating the 4th in advance one day by fiddleing and dancing

Sunday 4 July 1858. Came to Provo to day and staid with William Meeks. President Young and the authorities had removed hence to Great Salt Lake City and the roads were crouded with people who were following their example.

Monday 5 July 1858. Staid all night with Duncan McArthur at Battle Creek.

Tuesday 6 July 1858. Left at daylight and travelled to American Fork and breakfasted and went on afoot to the point of the mountain where I met the advance of Gen Johnson's Command who were marching to Cedar Valley   day very hot

At the Big Spring Thos Collister invited me to ride which I did to Cottonwood. Went on a foot and soon was in Br Cooley's Buggy and arrived at home in Great Salt Lake City   My garden looked very luxurious the mustard and weeds higher than the peach trees.   Peas ripe and the garden looked well

Wednesday 7 July 1858. Worked in garden pulling weeds. paid a visit to President Young.

Thursday 8 July 1858. Thos S. Williams arrived here from Mo Was introduced to Mr Hartnett Secratary of the Territory &c

Friday 9 July 1858. Severe Sick head ache.   Was introduced to Judge Eckles by Col Little   He is a very talkative man who has a great opinion of himself but with all I think very superficial and no friend to Utah and her people.

Tuesday (Saturday [crossed out]) 13 July 1858. Finished weeding my garden.

Wednesday 14 July 1858. With W. A. Hickman visited Judge Eckles .

Sunday 16 July 1858. Started about 4 p. m. for Salt Creek for my family with 2 four mule teams kindly furnished me by President Brigham Young gratis.   Jorome E. Remington & Danl Johnson in charge of the teams Camped on Dry Cottonwood

Monday 19 July 1858. Went to Payson staid with Toussig and next day about 4 p. m arrived Salt Creek and found that Alvira had started for home with a small load and three children and camped near Payson the same night I did but we missed each other.

Wednesday 21 July 1858. Loaded up and started for home, leaving Anna, Elizabeth & Henry and taking Hosea and Eli with me.   We took dinner with B. F. Johnson at Santa Quinn and staid all night at Payson again

Met Col Loring and his command *en route* for New Mexico, from Camp Floyd, with perhaps all told 4 or 500 men.

Thursday 22 July 1858. Left and travelled on finding Alvira & the children at Allen Stouts where learning I had gone down she stopped sending her loading ahead we took her *aboard* and went to American Fork and stopped with Bp Herrington

Friday 23 July 1858. Arived at home about one p. m. all well Day very dusty.

Sat. Sunday, Monday, Tuesday. Fixing up my books and puting the house in order Great deal of trouble Rained finely on Monday.

Thursday 29 July 1858. Budded 17 apricots in my peach trees Excellent quality. Stood guard at B. Y. till 2 o'c a. m.

Saturday 31 July 1858. Saw John Chapman one of my old school mates and Archd Johnson teacher in Stout's Grove Ill in 1829. He brought in the Cal mail

The Eastern mail to day with William Gilbert Merchant and Judge St Clair as passengers.

Monday 2 Aug 1858. To day was the General Election for County and Territorial officers.

The gentiles and some few apostates as I understand it got up an opposition ticket

The Regular Ticket was as follows: for Great Salt Lake County
Representatives
1 John Taylor. 2 Orson Hyde. 3 Danial Spencer 4 A. P. Rockwod, 5 Hosea Stout, J. W. Cummings 7 J. C. Little, 8 Jos A. Young, 9 H. B. Clawson 10 W. H. Hooper, 11 E. D. Woolley, 12 A. Mc Rae, 13 S. W. Richards.
Selectman
Nathaniel V. Jones
Co. Treasurer John G. Lynch.
Shiriff Robert T. Burton
Co Recorder
Leo Hawkins
Co Surveyor
Israel Ivins

The opposition ticket was *Orson Hyde,* 2 Abel Gilbert, 3 *John Taylor* 4 Jefferson Hunt 5 John W Powel 5 *Ed Hunter* 7 *James M. Levingston* 8 *S. M. Blair* 9 Thomas S. Williams 10 *Danl Spencer* 11 Albert G. Browne jr 12 W. I. McCormick for the Legislature.
Selectman *William H Hooper*
Shiriff John B. Kimball
County Recorder *Curtis E. Bolton*
Co   Treasurer   *Thos D. Brown &c*

The names underscored refused to run on the ticiket

The whole number of votes poled was about 1050 and 37 of these were for the opposition in the city, and 1250 in the county.

I was called upon to day to attend for the defendant in case before Judge Eckles. Case of Habeas Corpus to recover a minor girl by her father from her mother.

The circumstances were these a Mrs Polydore[29] in 1854 abducted here daughter then 8 years old from her father or from a school where her father had placed her in Lancaster Eng. and after much trouble succeed in evading the pursuit and seach made by the father brought her here

The mother returned and last winter met with John Hyde[30] an apostate Mormon at New Orleans where he learned the whole affair & informed Mr Polydore the father

---

29. Full information on the case of Henrietta Polydore is found in the U. S., State Department — Territorial Papers, Utah Series, April 30, 1853 to January 3, 1873 (originals, National Archives; microfilm, Utah State Historical Society).

30. John Hyde, Jr., had joined the Mormon Church and came to Utah in 1853, but became disaffected and apostatized. After he returned to the East, he wrote the book, *Mormonism, Its Leaders and Designs* in which he disclosed all of the endowment ceremony, accused the leaders of dealing in whiskey and of ordering undesirable people killed. He viewed this "Zion" as a barren, difficult land with little natural resources to support a large population. He especially resented the practice of polygamy.

who communicated the whole affair to Lord Napier British Minister at Washington requesting through him the aid of his government to recovor his daughter His Lordship requests the aid of our goverment by calling on Hon Lewis Cass Secratary of States. Cass Calls on Floyd Secratary of War, who orders Gen Johnson at the sacking of Great Salt Lake City to find and return her to her father Upon the peaceful termination of affairs in Utah Gen Johnson hands the matter over to Mr McCormick U. S. Dist Atty pro tem to be tried and settled by the civil authorities and thus arose the writ of Habeas Corpus

The trial lasted till Wednesday in the afternoon when the dughter Henrietta was awarded to her father and placed in custody of the U. S. Marshal to be sent by proper means & company to her father Mean time to still reside with her aunt aganst whom and S. W. Richards the writ was against.

Thursday 5 Aug 1858. Stood guard at B's till 12 o'c at night

Thursday 12 Aug 1858. Stood guard at B's again.

Sunday 17 Aug 1858. Col Rugles of the 5 infantry arrived in the city from the States with 350 recruits for his regiment.

Was invited by Judge Eckles to day to his room He gave me a letter from one Wm R Yancey to him stating that one John Beal had been castrated in Ogden lately for adultery with E. Lish's wife. He requested me to make the proper inquiry and ferrit the matter out and have the parties engaged in it brought to justice He also spoke of several other cases of larceny which he wanted hunted up and punished

Monday 23 Aug 1858. Judges Eckels and Sinclair left for Fillmore to meet at the seat of Government to appoint the "Times and places of holding the District Courts as provided by law of Congress that is they have saw proper in the abundance of their wisdom to decide that the seat of government is at Fillmore and not at Great Salt Lake City notwithstanding the act of the Legislature removing the seat of govt to this place.

These judges have set aside our law without any cause being brought before them or any one objecting to the Legislature being held here except those whose business it is to find fault every thing pertaining to ourselves.

They left here for Camp Floyd where they are to have an Escort of U. S. troops furnished them to protect them from danger and harm while passing through our settlements. Gen Johnson is to furnish them with an escort of 80 men officered besides an out fit of provisions and conveyances

Wednesday 25 Aug 1858. This morning Howard Egan and those with him who accompanied Col Kane to the States returned being 21 days on the road from the States They left Col Kane very sick and considered dangerously so

I have not learned what news he brought as to Utah affairs.

Thursday 26 Aug 1858. Last Evening Elizabeth came home from Salt Creek.

To day at one p. m there is to be a picnic party at Mill D. Big Cottonwood Cañon The invited guests were toling out early this morning so that they might be there in time as the distance is 20 miles.

Prest B. Young, H. C. Kimball D. H. Wells & some of their ladies, Gov Cuming & Lady with Hooper & Lady & myself went together, besides a large number of brethren & sisters attended. It was near sun set when I arrived there the party was encamped in a large dense forrest of tall timber in the midst of which was a large dancing room prepared sufficiently spacious for six cotillions Just before I arrived, an old grizzly bear & two cubs came into camp as it seemed to pay a friendly visit but she soon left wounded & one cub killed

The evening was spent in visiting & dancing.

Friday 27 Aug 1858. The day was spent in calmness & some little dancing which but few seemed to enjoy much Every one seemed to be content to pass their time conversation I took a long walk up the high timbered mountain.

Saturday 28 Aug 1858. All came home to day with out any accident or any unpleasant circumstance happening.

Tuesday 31 Aug 1858. Attended a suit before Mayor Smoot in which T. S. Williams was tried before the mayor for an assault & batterey on George D Grant on Friday last I was prossecuting & McCormack & Smith for deft. who was fined $100. and costs He gave notice of an appeal.

Wednesday 1 Sept 1858. This morning I accompanied my wife up City Creek Kanyon several miles hunting haws and found none We then took up a side Kanyon coming out on the top of the mountain and came home about 11 o'clock when I learned that two negros has been fighting and one killed the other.

Last night Nesbits house caught fire and burned up with nearley every thing he possessed.

This after noon there was another trial before Mayor Smoot between W. H. Hooper and John Pack for fighting both were fined $50-each and costs and afterwards George D. Grant was brought before the same for the fight with T. S. Williams on Friday last & fined $100 and costs and held in $100 bond to keep the peace one year.

Thursday 2 Sept 1858. The negro who survied the late fight was brought before J. Clinton Esq on examination this after noon and acquitted on self defence

Friday 3 Sept 1858. Suit before Squire Clinton at ten a. m J. R. Dye v Cromwell & Case on a charge of stealing 6 navy revolvers and a coat. T. S. Williams & Mc Cormack attys for plf and myself for deft who were acquitted.

Saturday 4 Sept 1858. This evening Judge Sinclair returned from Fillmore leaving Eckles at Camp Floyd.

They have appointed the District Courts to come off as follows at Farmington on the first Monday in September, at Great Salt Lake City the first Monday of October and at Fillmore the first Monday in November, but Judge Eckles will not hold his court at Farmington this fall. They do not inform us where they will hold them that is at what house neither the time of day. The matter is left very vague. Why Judge Eckles will not hold his court after his anxiety to bring offenders to justice is best known to himself it may bee because of glass houses.

Thursday 9 Sept 1858. This evening two men Rucker and Beal got into a fuss as is said about gambling affairs Beal shot Rucker through the body and recieved a shot in the face each recieved another wound. Rucker died immediately, the fate of Beal is not known but his wound is dangerous.

Some two Companies of U. S. troops passed this week through the city en route for the Humbolt River to protect the mail from indians, who are troublesome.

Monday 13 Sept 1858. Suit before Judge Sinclair. Almerin Grow vs A. M. Musser on Habeas Corpus to recover a child, daughter of Grow The case commenced on Saturday.

Grow claiming that his right to the child to Musser was relinquished under duress which M. denied & further set up that Grow was insane & otherwise incompetent to take care of himself or children.[31]

---

31. Amos Milton Musser, then a young man, married to his first wife only three months previous, wrote on April 17, 1858: "Almerin Grow has given me his daughter [now twelve years old] to raise. He has appointed me as her guardian. Prest Young has given him a mission 'go south and never return.' Though naturally smart he has become immeasurably insane, striking tokens of which are seen in his acts of extracting all his teeth, wearing his wife's clothing, etc." Brooks, "Amos Milton Musser," 71.

The court decided that the duress was not proven nor the insanity but that G. was not fit to take care of the child which he remanded to M. to be fully determined at the next Dist Court McCormack Atty for plf and self for deft.

Wednesday 15 Sept 1858. Judge Eckles Left for home to day with a small escort of U. S. troops and siveral apostates and friends He takes all with him Henrietta Polydore who is accompanied by her aunt Jane Mayer. He leave without an attempt to put the laws in force as he boasted he would.

Yesterday and to day have been engaged in sittling old and rancourous difficulties which exist between C. M. Drown and R. D Sweasey which had been effected if they will only stick to what they say now.

Thursday 16 Sept 1858. The city Council is about organizing a police force of 200 men and for this purpose the police recruits met in Prest B Youngs' Barn where 102 new police were sworn in to office and Andw Cunningham chosen Capt There was 11 deputy marshals Sworn in.

Two comets now appear in the Heavens one can be seen in the evening and one in the morning in the northern Hemisphere

Friday 17 Sept 1858. Suit this evening before Esqr Clinton Boly et. al. v Childs, that is 4 french men vs a wagon master, who had one of his company for his attorney Myself & Miner for plf. Judgement for plfs for $120 & costs.

Tuesday 21 Sept 1858. Suit before the Mayor John Gheen Compt vs F McNeil[32] for threatning his life T. S. Williams atty for deft & myself on part of the city Court decided that the deft be fined ten dollars and cost.

In the after noon another case City v John Gheen for threatning the life of McNeill Attorney for plf T. S. Williams & myself for Gheen who plad guilty and was fined ten dollars and costs.

McNeill was still held under arrest for threatning the life of David Candland.

Friday 24 Sept 1858. on Police duty to day. Suit before probate Jos Donahoe v. John Mitchel and J. M Guthrie for $140 Judgement for $125. was on part of the plaintiff —

Attended another Suit City v F. E. McNeill for threatning to Shoot D. Candland. Before Mayor I was prosecuting Deft plead guilty fined 50 dollars and imprisoned three months.[33] Stood guard all night.

Saturday 25 Sept 1858. Suit before Esq Clinton Wm Robinson vs Russell Major & Wardle for 37 dollars myself for plf & De Wolf for deft Judget for deft.

Sat on an arbitration with Br J Houtz to determine the ownership of a pony between C. Shumway & J. P. Rose. decide for Shumway

Monday 27 Sept 1858. 2 Suits to day against Russell Major & Wardle by Eli Roof & John McEwen I was on the part of plff & De Wolf for deft Judgement for the plfs. Clinton Esqr

Wednesday 29 Sept 1858. Last night I was called out of bed near mid-night to attend for the City. It appeared that McNeil had sued out a Habeas Corpus before

---

32. Frank McNeil had come West in the fall of 1857, was arrested as a spy, and was imprisoned. Upon his release he was involved in disputes with various Mormons in some of which both parties were fined for threatening the lives of opponents as here recorded. McNeil, who signed his name F. E. McNeil, sued Brigham Young, Daniel H. Wells, and others for false arrest, asking damages of $25,000; almost a year later he was killed by one Joe Rhodes. Hickman, *Brigham's Destroying Angel*, 141.

33. On this same date, Governor Alfred Cumming issued a pardon to McNeil, releasing him from the jail term if he would pay the fine. See Utah Territorial Executive Record Book "B" (Utah State Archives), 79.

Judge Sinclair I went to T. S. Williams Law office & found the parties there Williams and McCormick attorneys for the prisoner after some two hours humbugging the case was adjourned till ten next morning So at ten we met and continued untill about four McNeil had been pardoned by the gov on condition of paying the fine of 50 dollars and costs of 81 dollars The court decided that in the absence of and statute or city ordinance regulating the rate of fees there could be no costs taxed by a court The law allowing the courts to assess and tax the costs he said was entirely arbitrary and unlawful and so now it it established as he thinks that in Utah there can be no costs in any case.

Saturday 2 Oct 1858. Suit before H Gibbs B. Leonard v R. Gill on note at 60 pr cent I appeard for Gill and confessed judgt for 38 dollars.

In the evening suit before Clinton. People v. Peter Goodrich for Larceny party bound over.

On guard all night rainy all night.

Monday 4 Oct 1858. This morning attended a suit as prosecutor before J. Clinton, Esqr The people v Edward Davidson for Larceny Bound over.

At Eleven a. m District court met at the city Hall Judge Sinclair on the Bench The grand and pettit Jurors were called and adjourned untill the first Monday in November, which was followed by an address from the Judge to the Bar which was responded to by Blair Kirk Anderson[34] was admitted to the Bar & Court adjourned till ten tomorrow

Attended the State fair which commenced today in the social Hall.

Tuesday 5 Oct 1858. District Court met at ten a. m. minutes read and approved.

Order entered that the dockets and proceeding of the First District held at this place now in the possession of J. W. Cummings be handed over to the clerk of this court upon the service of said order on him & he be cited to appear at the adjourned session of said court to answer such questions as may be propounded to him by the court Court adjd till first Monday in Nov next

Very cold rainy day, but little wind.

Wednesday & Thursday. General council of the official members of the church in the Tabernacle.

Friday 8 Oct 1858. Suit before J. Clinton Esqr People v. A P Brookie for threatning H. C. Pender's life He was bound to keep the peace for one year 1000 dollars

This evening I was appointed a member of the city Council and took my seat. Rainy night.

---

34. Of Kirk Anderson, one author has written:
Nothing is known of Kirk Anderson's background and training. The earliest information available is that he was nominated for city attorney of St. Louis by the Whig Party in 1850 and elected by a big majority. In 1854 the St. Louis city directory listed Anderson as the local editor of the *Missouri Republican*. He remained with the newspaper during the next few years and took part in many of the railroad and river conventions to urge better transportation facilities. *The Western Journal of Commerce of Kansas City* noted that Anderson . . . had passed through the city on the boat *Skylark* enroute to Salt Lake City, where he planned to begin publication of a newspaper. (Eugene T. Wells, "Kirk Anderson's Trip to Utah, 1858," *Missouri Historical Society Bulletin*, XVIII [October, 1961], No. 1, pp. 3-19.)
Anderson published the story of his trip to Utah and his first impressions of Salt Lake City and Camp Floyd in the *Missouri Republican* in the form of letters written at important points en route.
On November 6, 1858, the first issue of *Kirk Anderson's Valley Tan* (Salt Lake City) appeared, and though he claimed that it was only an independent paper, the Mormons branded it a "scurrilous sheet." It became more and more anti-Mormon; by May of 1859 the editor returned east, the date of his departure withheld until he was safely away. The paper under the shortened title of the *Valley Tan* continued only until 1860.

Saturday 9 Oct 1858. Had an interview with Gov Cumming to day in company with President Wells, & Blair & Furguson relative to the seat of Government for Utah The Gov seems to hold that it should be at Fillmore & we that it should be here The subject is not decided yet. Attended the city Council this evening the subject of paying the police was discussed.

Tuesday 12 Oct 1858. Met with the city Council and from there went to Col Little's to partake of an Oyster supper prepared by the Col for the members of the council About 8 o'clock an attact was made by three men on Br William Cook Keeper of the Lock up in which was two prisoners, to release them and Br Cook was shot through the thigh breaking the bone one of the assailants was arrested.

Saturday 16 Oct 1858. Smart snow storm last night and snoing still this morning snow 3 or 4 inches deep. vegetation is yet green as spring and my peach treas and shrubry with their green leaves are prostrate with the load of snow.

The city Council was in session this evening and in waiting for the reception of David Broderick Senator from Cal to Congress who is expected by the next mail to be here on his way to Washington

The Council propose to tender the hospitality of the city to him but he has not arrived at ten P. M.

Sunday 17 Oct 1858. The city Council are still in waiting for Hon. D. Broderick who is not in hearing

Monday 18 Oct 1858. Senator Broderick has arrived and the Mayor A. O. Smoot has tendered to him the hospitality of the city with a suit of rooms at W. C. Stain's residence which he most cordially & thankfully excepted

Tuesday 19 Oct 1858. Went on Police duty to day.

R. T. Burton has returned from pursuing McDonald the man who shot police-man William Cook, but did not get any trace of his wheareabouts, but reports that Josiah Call & Samuel Brown[35] have been found murdered by the Indians on the summitt beyond Chicken Creek.

Last evening William Cook died of the wound he recieved

Wednesday 20 Oct 1858. This morning I resigned my office of Policeman in this city.

Friday 22 Oct 1858. The detachment of troops sent out on the Humbolt for the protection of the mail returned to day on their way to Camp Floyd

Sunday 24 Oct 1858. Last night an attact was made on the police and several Shots fired at them but none hit but Jacob Weiler who shot himself slightly in the calf of the leg One man was robbed (McGarry) of $150 —

Monday 25 Oct 1858. Suit before J. Clinton Esq Charles F McArty Compt vs Henry E. Phelps William W. Miller and Henry Spiers for robbing Compt of $160 odd last Sat. night They were bound over in $5,000 each There were three others engaged in the robbery not known names.

Wednesday 27 Oct 1858. Three Suits to day before Esqr Clinton one vs Thomas Truett for assault and Battery fined $25 — appealed. one vs. Francis Pullin and William Eads for fighting. P was acquitted and Eads Bound ovver. one vs. Moses Clark on the last Saturday's robbery ofc but he was acquitted.

Friday 29 Oct 1858. One man was shot at last night in the Empire House and grazed on the inside of the thigh.

---

35. Josiah Call and Samuel Brown had been killed on October 7 near Chicken Creek (Levan), Juab County. The *Deseret News* for November 3, 1858, gave a full account.

Saturday 30 Oct 1858. One Richd Jame private police for Russell Miller & Co shot a man through the thigh last night flesh wound The man came in the back yard of R. & M. premises. This morning a man shot another at Dry Creek 15 miles south of here at a grocery

To night learned that McDonald alias Cunningham had been killed by one Scotie who attempted to arrest him for the murder of Cook policeman.

Monday 1 Nov 1858. District cout met and adjourned till 15 inst to wait for the U. S. Dist Atty who is betwen here and Bridger *en route* here.

Thursday 4 Nov 1858. The Hon Judge John Cradlebaugh arrived to day. He lay on the top of Big mountain and frosted his fingers quite bad.

Friday 5 Nov 1858. Mr Alex Wilson U. S. Dist Attorney and Lady arrived to day in good health.

Tuesday 9 Nov 1858. Suit to day befor Probate Court. Russel Miller & Co vs. J Harvey in debt $3875 De Wolfe Atty for plf & myself for deft Judgement for plf for the amount.

Saturday & Sunday 14 Nov 1858. Engaged with A Wilson, in preparing cases for the District Court next monday.

Monday 15 Nov 1858. District court met at the city Hall and after calling the rolls of the Juries dismissed them untill next monday The court then excused several delinquent Jurors, &c

Wednesday 17 Nov 1858. To day I was served with a notice by P K Dotson U. S Marshall to appear next Monday at the District Court to show cause why my name should not be stricken from the roll of attorneys in said court on charges preferred by David H. Burr for preferring false slanderous and infamous charges against a member of the Bar of said court.

and for intimidating and threatning a judge of said court and causing him to adjourn his court &c which it seems I have to answer for but what attorney I preferred charges against & when or what judge or when I threatened &c I am not informed. James Furgurson and J. C. Little are joined with me in Burr's charges.

Saturday 20 Nov 1858. Sat with the High Council at the social Hall three cases were tried one appealed by Josiah Arnold from Bishop Harker's[36] Ward Arnold had been cut off but was here restored

The second case was an appeal from the same Bishop by Charles Drown who had been cut off from the church He was restored by baptism

The third case was an appeal from The Presiding Bishop Hunter's Court by Homer Duncan from a charge by the Bishop Harker & his ward ward for pasturing his cattle on the range of the people of said Ward and the Bishop's Court had decided that he should pay them Eighty-five dollars The council reversed the decision

Monday 22 Nov 1858. District Court met at ten a. m.

The grand jury was then sworn and charged. The charge was an extraordinary one The court reviewed the subject of treason and intersperced his charge with lengthy quotations from the constitution of the U S. followed by the presidents pardon of

36. Joseph Harker was the first settler west of the Jordan River in the Salt Lake Valley. When the West Jordan Ward was first organized in January 1852, Harker was made first counselor to John Robinson, bishop. "In May 1858 . . . William A. Hickman was chosen as Counselor to acting Bishop Harker." Jenson, *Historical Record*, VI (December, 1887), 343.

Both Arnold and Drown were here restored to fellowship over the action of the bishop and his council. About a year later both men were shot and killed at the same time at a house on Main Street, Salt Lake City.

6th April 1856 The whole drift of which seems to indicate that he wishes the grand jury to totally disregard the general pardon of the president and throw the whole transactions of last winter & fall open to Judicial investigation and reopen the breach so lately healed between Utah & the U. S.

This is followed by lengthy quotations on the subject of pardons Then follows some instructions on the laws of the United States with quotations therefrom and also from the criminal code of Utah

After this comes the subject of polygamy, the views of the court are couched in (the [crossed out]) extracts from Kent & Blackstone and asks the grand jury to find the fact whether polygamy exhists in Utah or not and report to him. that the world as well as the Legislature of Utah & Congress may know what to do about it but says the court has no power over it.

This evening Anna arrived from Salt Creek in Company with Br Artemus Millet & wife.

Tuesday 23 Nov 1858. Last night an attact was made on the police by a party issueing from the Store of Livingston & Kinkade. The police soon settled the affair by breaking in the heads of several of the assailants. A few shots were fired and one army Doctor wounded with a ball. Matters were then quiet

(**24 Nov 1858.** [crossed out]) Court met again but there was nothing of any importance done.

Wednesday 24 Nov 1858. Court met at 11 a. m. The grand jury was for the first time put in charge of the Marshall

Thursday 25 Nov 1858. I forgot to mention that on yesterday Anna[37] was married to Artemus Millet Started home with him to San Pete Co.

Court met at ten took a resess to meet at the social Hall at 2 p. m. where it will be held in future.

Friday 26 Nov 1858. Court met at ten a. m The Question as to the right of the Attorney & Marshall for the U. S. to prosecute & Execute the laws of Utah in preference to the Marshal & Attorney for Utah under her laws was to be argued this morning between the U. S. Dist Attorney & the Attorney Genl for Utah (ie) between Mr Wilson & myself.[38] The agreement between was that each should have the assistance of one attorney, and that Mr Smith should assist Mr Wilson and Mr Blair should assist me The debate was opened by Smith who spoke but a short time not bringing one or showing one authority or even refiring to the organic act of the Terretory He made a few blank & barefaced assersions and broke down.

Blair then commenced and before he had laid out the grounds of his arguments was taken sick & had to lay down on a bench and the court adjourn

The grand jury had previously been adjd to give the judge time to decide a question submitted to him by the Grand Jury.

At half past three Court met and adj'd on account of Mr Blair being sick.

Saturday 27 Nov 1858. Court met at Eleven and adjourned the Grand jury till Monday not being yet prepared to answer the question propounded to him by the grand jury

Mr Blair having eaten nearly a whole rooster for breakfast this morning appeared in court quite well and ready to crow, finished his speech and court adjourned till

37. Stout's sister, Anna, was married to Benjamin Jones, a widower with five children, in 1832 and had been granted a divorce by Brigham Young in February 1850. She had no children of her own.

38. Here begins the long contest for control of the courts in Utah, a struggle which was to continue throughout the territorial period.

half past three when I commenced my arguments which lasted untill candle lighting and court adj'd

Monday 29 Nov 1858. Court met at Eleven a. m. The Judge informed the grand jury that he had discharged his duty to them when he delivered his charge and as each officer of court had their seperate duty and responsibility he would turn them over to the U. S. District attorney who would also do his duty

The District Attorney then delivered an address to the grand jury which in nearly every particular conflicted with the charge of the Judge He expressly charged them that they had to observe and respect the Presidents pardon as well as the proclamation of the Gov Cummings

The Judge and Attorney were greatley confused when they were speaking They were pale and trembled while their voices faultered while they spoke showing that there was great conflict of feelings existing between them The District Attorney then entered upon last Saturdays debate which occupied all day in a dry uninteresting under tone without bringing any arguments in favor of his position.

Tuesday 30 Nov 1858. Court met at Eleven a. m. Grand jury was adjourned till next Monday week.

The charge or motion of Gen D. H. Burr to strike Furguson myself and Little from the roll of Attorneys was called up and after I had arose to argue a demurer to the motion Burr withdrew the charge against myself and Col J. C. Little which ended our career in the defence. Jas Furguson then asked time untill tomorrow to plead.

The court then adjourned till 11 tomorrow.

Wednesday 1 Decr 1858. Court met at Eleven a. m Case of Burr v Furgurson called deft demurred verbally. Court ordered plf to amend instanter But first defendant tendered his resignation which was refused The deft then asked the court to give judgement against *pro confesso* which was refused also. The deft asked time to plead which was granted till Friday at Eleven a. m to which time court adj'd

Thursday 2 Decr 1858. Cold East wind drifting the little snow on the ground like flour and penetrating evry crevice.

This morning Secratary John Hartnett started to Fillmore by way of Camp Floyd to meet with the Legislature, well knowing however that said Legislature intends adjourning to this place.

Yet he is taking the money and other needfuls to pay off and otherwise accommodate the legislature.

Superintendent Forney returned last night from his tour to San Pete Fillmore &c to visit the Indians.

Friday 3 Decr 1858. Court met at Eleven Case of Burr vs Furguson[39] to expel &c was called up Furguson demurred which was sustained and Burr ordered to make a new motion and the court adjourned till Monday

President Brigham Young attended court to the suprise and disappointment of his enemies who had vainly hopped he would not even if required by law which was designed by them and on his refusal to call on the U. S. troops and thus kick up a fuss and have a new cause for keeping the troops in this Territory

---

39. One account of the event is as follows: "In November 1858 Burr instituted proceedings to disbar James Ferguson on the grounds that he had slandered Judge George P. Stiles and had ultimately driven him from his bench . . . . When [Brigham] Young entered the courtroom he walked in with Kimball, Wells, Pratt, Smith, Taylor, Woodruff, and Richards clustered around him, their pistols and knives ready for service . . . . [in addition they] had distributed three hundred well-armed brethren about the room." Furniss, *The Mormon Conflict*, 213.

The severe East wind on the 1st & 2nd inst has done much damage. Br Lever was frozen to death coming from Camp Floyd to this city. And is feared many more have in different parts. but the weather is now more moderate still the ice nearly covers the streets and side walks & the watter is still spewing over them.

Monday 6 Decr 1858. Court met at Eleven a. m. Case of Burr v Ferguson called up on the new motion Court refused to entertain a demurer although the case greatly needed it.

On motion of Ferguson the case was put off till monday next for the want of evidence that is for the want of G. P. Stiles evidence whether the case will come off next Monday or not I can not tell.

Yesterday was hard south wind & to day north with snow & weather cold and bad.

Sunday 12 Decr 1858. The weather has been intensly cold for a few days past untill relieved by a strong damp south wind yesterday and last night which was followed by a mild snow of some two inches deep. and the weather to day is warm and pleasant

Monday 13 Decr 1858. At ten a. m. the Legislative Assembly met in the social Hall and proceeded to elect the officers and organize The House of Representatives Elected John Taylor Speaker

> Thomas Bullock Chief Clerk.
> Patrick Lynch Assistant Clerk
> George P. Billings Sergeant-at-arms.
> Heber John Richards Messenger
> Joseph Busby Forman.
> Joseph Young chaplain
>   The Council Elected
> [Five spaces blank]

The Legislature then adjourned to meet at Fillmore on the next Saturday at [blank] o'clock

I went from the Legislature to court at Eleven a. m The case of Burr vs Ferguson was called up and laid over till tomorrow on the grounds the the case was under process of being settled.

The court on its own motion called the attention of the grand jury to that part of the said charge which relates to frightening Judge Stiles and intimidating him &c after which the grand jury retired.

Nothing more was done in court only waiting on the grand jury the court taking some three recesses. Thus passed the first day.

Tuesday 14 Decr 1858. Court met at ten grand jury found a presentment against James Furguson for endeavoring to intimidate Judge Stiles at the Feb Term of Court 1856 and adjourned till to morrow at 11 o'clock a. m.

Wednesday 15 Decr 1858. Court met at Eleven a. m. The grand jury presented their indictment against (the [crossed out]) James Ferguson as before mentioned yesterday and court adjourned untill to morrow and the grand jury untill monday

Thursday 16 Decr 1858. Court met at Eleven a. m and discharged the pettit jury till Monday & no other buisiness appearing adjourned till Monday.

Monday 20 Decr 1851 [8]. Court met at Eleven a. m. Grand jury made a present ment against an Indian for killing a man in Rush Valley.

Case of U. S. vs J. Furgurson for intimindating Judge Stiles called up Furgurson had till to morrow to file his preliminary pleadings.

Tuesday 21 Dec 1858. Court met at eleven case of Furguson was called up and plea in abatement filed and laid over till to morrow to be argued whether it will be recieved or not.

The examination of Christensen for killing Dummy[40] which has been going on for several days (some Eight) closed and C was bound over.

Several members of the Legislature returned from Fillmore to meet next Monday.

Wednesday 22 Decr 1858. Court met at Eleven case of Ferguson called up and the plea in abatement with drawn & a motion to quash argued and over ruled and excepted to Furgurson then plead not guilty grand jury found several indictments against persons who had been bound over a [blank]

Court ruled on the question argued on the 27th and 29th instant. relative the rights of the Territorial Marshall and attorney

Court decided that the Legislature could not pass a law creating an officer to execute the laws passed by the Legislature but that the Attorney and Marshall appointed by the President for the United States were the officers designed by the Organic Act to execute the Laws of Utah.

Thursday 23 Decr 1858. Court met at Eleven. The grand jury presented another indictment against a horse thief and the court then adjourned untill next Monday week.

Friday 24 Decr 1858. Suit before Probate on appeal of Robinson McEwen & Roof's cases from Esq Clinton court of Sept 25 & 27 appeal dismissed —

Snowing this afternoon.

Saturday 25 Decr 1858. Merry Christmas to day. Everybody seems to be out slayriding excellent slays plying in every direction running races and yelling Town in a universal good natured drunk hollowing and yelling but noting particularly bad. wife and I went to Capt Jef Hunts to a party had in the evening.

All went of pleasantly & quietly.

Presidents message 15 days from Washington arrived this evening.

Monday 27 Decr 1858. The Legislative Assembly met at 10 a. m at the social Hall and are now ready for business.

William J. Osborn presented his certificate of election as a member in the House from Green River County.[41] The subject of his admission was referred to a committee consisting of C C. Rich, J. C. Snow, I. C. Haight, A. P. Rockwood, and H. Stout with instructions to report thereon at an earley day.

The speaker then proceeded to appoint the standing committees I was placed on the committee on the Judiciary and on Education.

---

40. The indictment against N. L. Christiansen (Christensen in Stout) for killing Dummy had received a great deal of publicity. On December 10, 1858, an editorial in the *Valley Tan* asked for information concerning the boy called "Dummy," who had been seen about the streets. The writer had missed him for more than two weeks now and would appreciate any information concerning him.

On December 17, 1858, in the *Valley Tan*, two letters appeared both unsigned. One rebuked the paper for raising the question and stated that it was "necessary for his salvation, and consequently his sudden transition from this to another world." The second letter evidently also written by a Mormon, stated "that Dummy had been killed up the canyon near Eph Hanks' cabin by a policeman from this city. The Policeman's name is _____ _____, and added that he himself did not believe, as some of the brethren do, that it may be necessary to kill a person in order to save his soul."

The *Valley Tan* for December 24, 1858, gave the result of an investigation. Andrew Bernard, commonly called "Dummy" because he was a deaf mute, had been caught in repeated thievings in the city, so was arrested. Some of the items he had stolen had been hidden up the canyon, and the policeman, N. L. Christiansen, took the young man up to recover them. He became so angry and violent that the policeman was forced to kill him in self-defense.

41. The original abstract of votes given at an election held in the county of Green River, Utah Territory, on Monday, the 2nd day of August, 1858, shows that "William J. Osborne received one hundred & thirty-five (135) votes for Representative in the Legislative Assembly," which was the highest vote given any candidate in this election. Elections, 1858; Utah Territorial Executive Papers (Utah State Archives).

The two houses then went into Joint Session had the Govornor's message read and 500 copies ordered to be printed and Elected Jas McNight public printer &c and dissolved and the house adjourned.

Tuesday 28 Decr 1858. House met at ten a. m. I presented a petition from sundry members of the Bar suggesting a code of practice to regulate the proceedings in civil cases, which was referred to the committee on judiciary

On motion of Mr Rockwood the Comte on Elections were instructed to take in to consideration the several electoral districts & if necessary bring in a bill on the subject

On Motion of Mr Stout the public printer furnish the assembly with 50 copies of the daily minutes

Mr Farnsworth presented the petition of A. Lyman & others for a Heard ground in Beaver Valley, which was referred to a seclect committee

Mr Farnsworth presented petition of A. Lyman & 112 others for a herd & mowing ground in Beaver Valley refered to same committee. Secratary Hartnett informally presented petition of John Gallagher and Wm Burch for Herd ground on Promontory Point N. W. of Ogdon City refered to same a Kirk Anderson Editor of the "Valley Tan" sent to the assembly a copy of His paper (to each member) containing the Pressidents message which was unanimously by both Houses acting seperately, sent back the said "Valley Tan" being declared a scurrilous sheet &c.

Kirk was present and left Shont Tobuck [Paiute: "Very Mad"] House then adjourned.

Wednesday 29 Dec 1858. House met at 10 a. m.

Mr Rockwood moved that the Committee on Counties be instructed to take into consideration the propriety of reorganizing Carson & Green River Counties and report a bill if need be &c carried

On motion of Mr Stout, the Com on elections were instructed to report the number and kind of officers to be filled by the joint vote of this assembly &c

Mr Cummings moved that John W. Snell be Elected assistant Messenger referred committee consisting of H. B. Clawson, H. Stout & E. D. Woolley & Wright to consult Mr Hartnett on the subject

Mr Rich chairman of the special committee reported (H. F. No 1) "An Act granting unto Amasa Lyman & others a herd ground in beaver valley" recieved and laid on the table

Mr Peacock presented a petition of B. L. Clapp and 167 others to incorporate Ephraim City Sanpete County which was recieved and laid on the table

Mr Rockwood called for the oldest bill on the table when the act granting to A. Lyman &c was read and laid over for the present

William H. Hooper presented his resignation as a member of this house which was accepted.[42]

The freedom and courtesy of the house was tendered to the gov and others

House file No 1 was again taken up and referred back to the committee The minutes were read & accepted & the House adjourned.

Thursday 30 Decr 1858. House met at ten a. m. Mr Stout chairman of the committee to wait on Mr Hartnett reported that they had waited on him who satisfied them that an assistant messenger might be elected without interfering in any way with the duties or pay of any other officer of the house, which report was accepted and John W Snell was elected assistant Messenger.

---

42. William H. Hooper, church-approved representative from Green River and Salt Lake counties, probably resigned his position with the state legislature because he knew he was in line for a higher office. Soon after this he was appointed Utah delegate to the Congress of the United States. He had just been released from the position of territorial secretary by the arrival of the federal appointee, John Hartnett.

Mr Haight presented the petition of the inhabitants of Washington County for the removal of the county seat from Harmony to the town of Washington referred to the committee on counties.

On motion of Mr Rockwood the committee on Revenue was instructed to ascertain from Charles Hopkins and others the reciepts and expenditures on the bridge over Jordan river near Lehi in Utah County as contemplated in an Act approved January 21, 1853.

Mr Rich chairman of the committee on the case of Hon W. J. Osborn as member from Green River County, presented the following report. Gentlemen.

Your committee to whom was referred the subject in controversy between the Hon Wm H Hooper and the Hon W. J. Osborn for admission to a seat in this house beg leave to make the following report.

That Mr Hooper had a large majority of votes, but having resigned his seat and Mr Osborn having recieved a certificate of election from the secratary, we therefore recommend that Mr Osborn be permited to take his seat as a member of this House in the place of W. H. Hooper, from Great Salt Lake and Green River Counties in accordance with the representation apportioned to said counties by law" which report was accepted. and on motion of

Mr Cummings William J. Osborn was accordingly qualified and took his seat.

Mr Rich chairman of the special committee presented "An Act granting to A. Lyman and others a Herd ground &c which was not recieved and the petition &c with drawn

Mr Rockwood presented the petition of Jos Young for the exclusive right to establish a ferry on Bear River North. Recieved and referred to the committee on Roads Bridges and Ferries

Mr Rich chairman of the Special committee reported (H. F. No 2) "An Act granting unto P. T. Farnsworth and others a Herd ground in Beaver Valley

Mr Stout moved that the report of the committee be not recieved and the petitioner have leave to withdraw his petition carried

Mr Rich chairman of the Special Committee reported unfavorable to granting the petition of John Gallagher & Wm Birch for a herd ground on Promontory Point &c recieved

The freedom and courtesy of the house be extended to Ex Gov. Young, O Pratt & E. T. Benson, A. O. Smoot, E. Smith & E Hunter[43]

On motion of Mr Rockwood the librarian was requested to make of the number & condition of the books in the library.

The Speaker appointed Isaac C. Haight Jacob G. Bigler Geo Peacock and Philo T. Farnsworth a committee on incorporations.

On motion of Mr Stout the petition of B. L. Clapp and others to incorporate Ephraim City, was referred to the committee on Incorporations.

On motion of Mr Osborn the Public printer be requested to print 100 copies of the list of the members & officers of the Council & House for the use of the Assembly & also a list of the Standing committees of each House. Adjourned till tomorrow.

Saturday 31 Decr 1858. House met at ten a. m. Mr Haight chairman of the committee on Incorporations reported on the petition of B. L. Clapp and others unfavorably to granting said petition recieved.

Mr Young chairman of the committee on Counties reported "An act changing the county seat of Washington County" read, accepted and laid on the table.

Mr Richards moved that the Auditor of Public Accounts be requested to furnish the House with a statement of the conditions of the revenue &c which was carried

43. These men, accorded the "freedom and courtesy of the house" though not official delegates, could sit through and participate in the discussions and help to make decisions. Pratt and Benson were apostles in the church; A. O. Smoot was mayor of Salt Lake City; Elias Smith was editor of the *Deseret News*; Edward Hunter was presiding bishop of the church.

and the report furnished by the auditor, which was read and on motion of Mr Hyde said report and the report of the Warden of the penetentiary and all necessary documents pertaining thereto was referred to the committee on Revenue with instructions to furnish the House with the necessary information on the subject

Message from Secratary Hartnett to wit.

"I Herewith hand you a copy of what purports to be the returns of an election held in Carson County on the 30th day of Oct 1858. In consequence of informality, I have declined giving Mr Clemons a certificate of membership in your honorable body.

I herewith furnish you with copies of all documents in my possession, relating to this subject, and will cheerfully furnish you any further information in my power

John Hartnett
Secratary, U. T.

which was referred to a Special committee for investigation H. B. Clawson, Daniel Spencer, & E. D. Woolley were appointed said committee

Message from the council.

S. W. Richards added to committee on Judiciary.

On motion of Mr Osborn Messrs Little Rockwood, & Cumming were appointed a committee on the Library.

Adjourned till Monday.

Saturday 1 January 1859. Hail 1859 which came in under favorable auspices The slighing is excellent and those who delight in that kind of exercise are making good use of their time. May they pass through the year as merrily as they have began all hands were merry many goodnaturedly drunk but no one seemed to be visious or bad tempered Weather clear & cold.

Sunday 2 January 1859. There was a meeting in the Tabernacle to day for the first time since last April. The order of meeting is materially changed. There is a petition passing through the center of the Tabernacle East & West The Ladies occupying the North End and the gents the South End[44] The Organ in the East side instead of the North End. The whole arraingements is pleasant and an improvement.

Elder Orson Pratt preached taking for his subject the authenticity of the Book of Mormon and the testimony which can be adduced in support of it as contrasted with the evidence which can be adduced in support of the Bible.

The subject very ably handled. and certainly there was more direct and certain evidence in favor of the authenticity of the Book of mormon than the Bible His discourse occupied two hours.

Monday 3 January 1859. House met at ten a. m. Mr Johnson of Comtee on Roads Bridges & Ferries reported (H. F. No 4) "An Act granting unto Joseph Young the right to Establish and control ferries on Bear River, also a Bridge on the Malad" which was recieved and laid on the table

Mr Rockwood that the Comtee on Education be instructed to take into consideration the subject of creating a revenue for the university, and to bring in a bill providing for carrying into effect the provisions of an act of congress entitled "An Act to Establish the office of Surveyor General of Utah & to grant lands for school and university purposes" Approved Feb 21 1855 carried.

---

44. The custom of having all the ladies sit on the north side of the aisle and all the men on the south side persisted, even in outlying settlements, for many years. Children sat on the front benches. Later, husbands were permitted to sit with their wives and children, and by common consent the back rows were reserved for courting couples.

On motion of Mr Rockwood the comtee on Counties was instructed to take into consideration and bring in a bill if expedient for incorporation of towns with such provisions as may be necessary to secure the pre-emption right extended in an act of congress entitled "An Act for the relief of citizens of towns, upon the lands of the U. S. under certain circumstances" approved May 23 1844. The oldest being called for (H. F. No 3) "An act changing the county seat of Washington County" was read and passed its first reading and laid on the table

(H. F. No 4)   An act granting to Jos Young &c was next read and passed its first reading.   Adjourned

Tuesday 4 Jan 1859. House met at ten a. m. Mr Rich chairman of the committee on Elections reported the number and kind of offices to be filled by the joint vote of the Assembly which was accepted and laid on the table

Mr Rockwood presented the report of the librarian showing that there is now in the library 3385 volums Books loaned 150 vols   In the hands of the bookbinders 20 vols total 3555 worn out & missing 72 volumes

Said report was referred to the Committee on Library

Mr Hyde chairman of the committee on Education reported (H. F. No 5) An Act to provide for the selection & location of two Townships of Land for the Establishment of a University recieved and laid on the table and 50 copies ordered to be printed

Mr Clawson Chairman of the committee to whom was referred the claim of Mr Clemons to a seat in this House from Carson County reported adversely to his claim which was accepted

The oldest bill being called for (H. F. No 3) "An Act changing the county Seat of Washington County," was read the second time and passed, and read the third time and passed, by its title (H. F. No 4) "An act granting to Jos Young &c" was taken up on its second reading

After several sections had passed the bill was referred back to the committee for amendment.

Notice from the council with two Bil (C. F No 1 & C. F. No 2) Both of which passed their first reading adj'd

District Court met to day and the grand jury ignored the Indictment against Christensen for killing Dummy, which created mutch excitement among the outsiders.

Wednesday 5 Jan 1859. House met at ten a m The speaker referred the different parts of the Gov message to the appropriate committees

Mr Johnson Chairman of the Comtee on Roads &c reported back (H. F. No 4. "An act granting to Jos Young &c amended, recieved and taken up on its Second reading & passed and sent to the comte on grossing.

Recieved from the Council (C. F. N 7) "An act attaching Shambip County to Tooele County" and (C. F. No 8) "An act in relation to Territorial Revenue" also "Memorial to congress for the donation of public lands to settlers" (C. F. No 7) was reat the first time & laid on the table to come up in its order so also (C. F. No 8)

The memorial to congress was read & adopted

(C. F. No 7) was taken up read the first time & passed and referred to the committee on counties.

C. F. No 8 was read three times & passed.

Mr Rockwood called for (H. F. No 5) "An act to provide for the selection and location of a quanty of land equal to two townships of land fo the establishment of a University" was read the first and passed and taken upon the Second reading & read amended and passed & also read the third time & referred to the engrossing committee adjourned.

Thursday 6 January 1859. House met at ten a. m.   Mr Young of the comte on Counties reported back "An act attaching Shambip Co to Tooele Co," amended which was read three times and passed.

House File No. 4 "An act granting to Joseph Young" &c was taken up on its third reading and passed.

"An act to provide for the selection and location of a quanty of land equal to two townships for the establishment of of a university" engrossed was taken up and read the third time & passed.

(C. F. No 1) An act apportioning the representation of Utah Territory" was read & referred to the Commte on Judiciary

(C. F. No 2) An act in relation to Carson St Mary & Humbolt Counties" was taken up and referred to same committee.

Mr Thomas presented a petition from David Evans & others of Lehi City, praying for an act for a Special Election for city officers. referred to the committee on incorporations

Mr Stout chairman of the committee on Judiciary reported "An act in relation to Code Commissioners recieved and laid on the table.

Mr Young chairman of the Committee on Counties reported "An act regulating the vending & bartering Spiriteous liquors recd & laid on the table & printed

Message from the Council that they had passed (H. F. N. 3) "An act changing the seat of Washington County with some few amendments, all of which were concurred in by the House. Adjourned

The grand jury was dismissed to day by the court after nearly coming to blows & pistols.

Friday 7 Jan 1859. House met at ten a. m.

Mr Haight, chairman of the Committee on Incorporations reported (H F No 8) "An act granting a Special Election in Lehi City" Utah County" recieved and read the first time and referred back.

Mr Peacock, of committee on Roads, Bridges & Ferries reported (H. F. No 9) "An act providing for the bridging of ditches or Sects leading across the high ways" recieved & read the first time & referred back.

Mr West, chairman of the committee on Revenue, reported the accounts and disbursment on Jordan Bridge near Lehi, which was referred back.

The oldest bill being called for (H F. No 6) "An act in relation to Code Commissioners" was taken up and read the first and second times and ordered to be engrossed.

(H. F. No 7) An act regulating the vending and bartering of spiriteous liquors" was taken up and read the first time & passed on the second reading amended in several places and passed and ordered to be engrossed.

Message from the council requesting a joint session on Monday next at 11½ a. m. for the Election of officers" to which the House concurred. Adjourned.

Saturday Jan 8 1859. House met at ten a. m. Message from the council with (the [crossed out]) "Memorial to congress for the preemption of irrigated lands which was recieved and adopted.

Mr osborn presented petition of Levis Robinson & Isaac Bullock for the exclusive right to run ferries on Green River for five years recieved and referred to the committee on Road Bridges & ferries.

Mr Haight chairman of the committee on Incorporations reported back 'H. F. No 8) "An act authorizing a Special election in Lehi city Utah" recieved and read the first & second times and passed and ordered to be engrossed.

Mr Richards chairman of Engrossing reported reported (H. F. No 6) "An act in relation to Code Commissioners" which was read the third time and passed. (H. F No 7) "An act regulating the vending and bartering of spiriteous liquors" engrossed was read the third time and passed.

Mr Young Chm of the Comte on Counties Reported (H. F 10) "An Act in relation to the entering of public lands" recieved and laid on the table to come up in its order.

Mr Stout Chm of Comte on Judiciary reported back on (C. F. No 2) "An Act in relation to Carson St Mary & Humbolt Counties" which was read the first & second times amended and passed. & read the third time & passed.

(H. F. No 8) "An act authorizing a special election in Lehi, Utah County" duly engrossed was read the third time & passed.

Message from the council with memorial to Congress for an Act authorizing the purchase of Indian lands in Utah, and locating the Indians on a Reserve" which was recieved and adopted

The oldest bill called for (H. F. No 10) "An Act in relation to the entering of Public lands" was read the first time & passed   adjourned.

Sunday 9 Jan 1859. Meeting at the Tabernacle   Orson Pratt preached on the Evidence of the Book of mormon

Monday 10 Jan 1859. House met at ten a. m. Mr Rockwood presented petition of J. A. Kelting praying for payment of a bill which was referred to committee on Claims

Mr Stout introduced a bill (H. F. No 11) "An act in relation to the manufactoring of Spirituous & malt Liquors" which was recieved and laid on the table.

Mr West Chm of Comte on Revenue reported back the Jordan Bridge affair as correct which was recieved and committee was discharged from further duty thereon

Mr Rockwood presented a resolution in relation to the purchase of the bridge over Jordan, in Utah County, recieved and referred to the committee on Roads Bridges & Ferries

A motion from the council proposing to adjourn the joint session untill Thursday at 11½ a. m. House concurred.

(H. F. No 11 "An act in relation to the manufactoring of spirituous and malt liquors" was read the first time & passed and 50 copies ordered to be printed. Adjourned.

The case of U. S. vs Jas Furguson was up in Court and witnesses commenced to give in their evidence last Saturday and finished to day and the case is set for argument tomorrow.

Tuesday 11 Jan 1859. House met at ten a. m. Mr Wright chairman of Committee on Counties reported not necessary to provide a Special revenue to build a central jail as recommended by his Excellency in his message said report was recieved and the committee discharged from further duty on that subject.

Mr Clawson moved that inasmuch as the Hall wherein the District Court is now held is insufficient in strength, & unsafe crouded as it will be during the argument of Ferguson's trial,[45] this House adjourn adjourn untill ten tomorrow, so as to accommodate his Hon Judge Sinclair with the use of this Hall to day carried and the house adjourned. and the Court convened and the argument was entered into by Wilson for the U. S. & Furguson for himself, and the case submitted to the jury & Court took several recesses

The jury after hanging untill about 8 o'clock p. m. brought in a virdict of "Not guilty" and Thus ends this miserable & vindictive farce concocted and got up by Burr under the sanction and promised aid and assistance of the court and his accompanying clique.

Wednesday 12 Jan 1859. House met at ten a. m Mr Johnson Chairman of the committee on Roads, bridges, & ferries reported (H. F. No 12) An act authorizing the Territorial Road Commissioner to negotiate with the proprietors of Jordan bridge near Lehi Utah County" recieved and read the first and second times and passed and ordered to be engrossed.

---

45. That the hall wherein the court was being held was "unsafe crouded as it will be during the argument of Ferguson's trial" shows the pressure of public opinion upon the jury.

Mr Rockwood moved that the commite on Incorporations be instructed to enquire into the propriety of incorporating the "Placerville, Humbolt and Salt Lake
Telegraph Company" and report by bill or otherwise, and that Mr Osborn be added
to said committee carried

Mr Richards moved that the committee on Counties be instructed to inquire
into the efficiency of the present existing laws reletive to town sites, and the recording of town plots, and if deemed necessary to report by bill authorizing the locating
of town sites within the meaning of "An act of Congress for the relief of the citizens
of towns upon the lands of the U. S." approved May 23, 1844 Carried

(H. F. No 10) An act in relation to the entering of public lands" was read the
first time and passed and referred back.

(H. F. No 11) An act in relation to the manufacturing of Spirituous and malt
liquors" was taken up and read the first time and passed and referred to a select
committee viz Stout, Hyde, Rich, Woolley & Wright

(H. F. No 12) An Act authorizing the Terrial Road Commissioner to negotiate
with the proprietors of the Jordan Bridge near Lehi Utah County" engrossed was
read the third time & passed

Mr Clawson chn of the Come on claims reported adversly to the claim of Joseph
A. Kelting recieved and the committee discharged from further duty thereon

The committee on R. B. & F reported (H. F No 13) "An Act granting to Isaac
Bullock and Lewis Robinson the right to errect ferries on Green River" recieved
and laid on the table to come up in its order

(H. F. No 7 "An act regulating the vending & bartering of spirituous" was returned not concurred in which together with (H. F. No 11) "An Act in relation to
the manufacturing of spirituous and malt Liquors" were referred to the Select Committee to whom was referred the said No 11.

(H. F. No 13) "An act granting to I Bullock &c was read the first time and
passed and read the second time and passed. adjourned

Thursday 13 Jan 1859. House met at ten a m Mr Johnson, chairman of the committee on R. B. & F reported back (H. F. No 9) "An act providing for the bridging
and ditches or sects leading across highways" amended recieved and laid on the table

Mr Osborn of the committee on Counties reported back (H. F No 10 "An Act
in relation to the entering of public lands" amended, recieved and laid on the table.

(H. F. No 13 "An act granting to Isaac Bullock &c" engrossed was read the third
time and passed.

Mr Stout, chairman of the committee on judiciary on the memorial of John
Hartnett asking the adoption of "Wells' Code of Missouri practice" reported adversly recieved and committee discharged thereon

The House went into Joint Session met and proceeded to elect the following
officers.

For Chancellor of University
Orson Pratt Sen

Regents for University
Daniel H. Wells
Orson Hyde
Jos A. Young
Robt L. Campbell
Gilbert Clements
William Eddington
Claudius V. Spencer
Isaac Bowman

Orson Pratt jr
Geo J. Taylor
S. W. Richards.
Isaac Grow

Treasurer of University
Thomas W. Ellebeck

Territorial Treasurer David O. Calder

Auditor Pub Accounts Wm Clayton

Territorial Marshal John Kay.

Attorney General Seth M. Blair
Surveyor General Jesse W. Fox
Librarian William C. Stains
Recorder of Marks & Brands   Wm Clayton
Inspectors of Penetentiary.
     Wilford Woodruff A. P. Rockwood Samuel W. Richards
Warden of Penetentiary Daniel Carn
Sealer Weights & measures   Nathan Davis

Washington County
Jas B. McCollough Probate Judge,
Geo Spencer Notarie Public

Iron County
James Lewis Probate Judge
James H. Martineau Notarie Public

Beaver County
Danl M. Thomas Probate Judge
Charles W. Wandle   Notary Public

Millard County
John A. Ray   Probate Judge
Thomas R. King Notary Public

Sanpete County
Gardner Snow Probate Judge
John Eager Notary Public

Juab County
Andrew Love Probate Judge
Madison D. Hambleton Notarie public

Cedar County
Zerubbabel Snow probate judge
Thomas Irwin Notarie Public

Utah County
Silas Smith Probate judge
L. N. Scovill Notarie Public

Great Salt Lake County
Elias Smith probate judge
Edward A. King Notarie Public

Davis County
Thomas S. Smith Probate Judge
James Leathead Notarie Public

Weber County
Aaron F. Farr Probate Judge
William Critchlow Notarie Public

Box Elder County
Samuel Smith Probate judge
John Burt Notarie Public

Tooele County
Ormus E. Bates Probate Judge
Lysander Gee, Notarie Public

Green River County
William A. Carter Probate Judge

Carson County

John S. Child, Probate Judge

John A. Thompson Notarie Public

Shambip County

Luke Johnson Probate Judge

Samuel Bennion Notarie Public

Joint session then adjourned to meet next Wednesday at 11 a. m and the House resumed its business

The oldest bill on the table being called for (H. F. No 9 "An act providing for the bridging of ditches or sects leading across highways, was read the first time & passed. On the second reading it was referred back and Mr Stout added to the Comte adjourned.

Snowed all day and nearly all night Snow some six inches deep.

Friday 14 Jan 1859. House met at ten a. m.

Mr Rich, chairman of the Come on Elections Reported (H. F. No 14) "An act in relation to the qualifications of officers" Recieved and read the first, & second times & passed

(H. F. No 10) An act in relation to the entering of public lands" was read the first and second times and passed.

Message from the council that the accompanying bill (C. F. No 11) "An act reorganizing Carson & Green River Counties, and attaching St Mary & Humbolt Counties" (as a substitute for (C. F. No 2) "An act in relation to Carson, St Mary, & Humbolt counties" amended by the House) has passed the Council and asking the concurrence of the House.

also that (H. F. No 8) "An act authorizing a special election in Lehi City" had been concurred in with amendments. which said last act was referred to the committee on Incorporations

On motion of Mr Osborn (C. F. No 11) "An act reorganizing Carson and green River Counties and attaching St Mary and Humbolt Counties was read three times amended and passed

Mr Henderson moved that the committee on R. B. & F. be instructed to confer with the Road Commissioner and learn whether the bridge as contemplated in an act, approved June 4 1853, granting Abijah Wadsworth and others the right of erecting a bridge across Weber river is now the property of the Territory, also the condition of said bridge, and report as soon as convenient. carried

Memorial from the Council, to congress for an appropriation to defray the expenses of suppressing Indian hostilities in Utah in 1853 & 6. On motion of Mr Clawson the House concurred

Mr Osborn presented a Resolution in relation to mail service, referred to the committee Petitions & Memorials.

Mr Haight, Chairman of the Committee on Incorporations reported back an act autherizing a special election in Lehi city amended by the council recieved and the amendments concurred in.

(H. F. No 14) "An act in relation to the qualification of officers", engrossed which was read the third time and passed.

On motion of Mr Stout the title of the bill was amended so as to read "An act specifying the time in which officers shall qualify and give bonds"

On motion of Mr Clawson, the Speaker appointed Rockwood, Cummings & Stout, a Special committee on Appropriations

Mr Stout chairman Chairman of the Special committee reported "An act regulating the manufacturing and sale of liquors" recieved and laid on the table to come up in its order and then taken up and read the first time & passed & 50 copies ordered to be printed

(H. F. No 10) "An act in relation to the entering of Public lands" engrossed was read the third time and passed.

Message from the council that "An act creating a special committee, prescribing their duties, and to provide for the payment of their services and their consequent necessary expenses" as a substitute for (H. F. No 6) "An act in relation to Code Commissioners" had passed the Council" which (Substituted bill was was read three times and passed with one amendment.

"Memorial" from the council" for the admission of the State of Deseret" to which the House concurred   adjourned.

Saturday 15 January 1859. House met at ten a. m. Mr Rockwood acting chairman on the Library made a report on the condition of Library & recommending an appropriation of $150 to defray the expenses of rebinding and incidenal expenses of the library.

Mr Johnson, chariman of Committee on R. B. & F. reported back (H. F. No 9) "An act providing for the bridging of ditches &c amended, accepted and laid on the table.

Mr Rockwood presented the account of the Code Commissioners which was referred to the committee on Claims.

Mr Haight chairman of the committee on Incorporations reported back (H. F. No 15) "An act to incorporate the Placerville, Humbolt & Salt Lake Telegraph Company" also (H. F. No 16) "An act changing the time of holding elections in Nephi City" recieved and laid on the table and the Act No 16 was read the first time & passed, Read the second time amended and passed Read the third time and passed.

Mr Spencer chairman of the Committee on Petitions & memorials reported back "Joint Resolution for the increase of mail service" which was read amended and adopted.

Mr Johnson Chairman of the committee on R. B. & F. reported on the motion of Mr Henderson in relation to the Bridge across the Weber River which report was recieved & committee discharged from further duty thereon.

(H. F. No 16) "An act changing the time of holding elections in Nephi City engrossed was read the third time & passed

(H. F. No 9) "An act providing for the bridging &c engrossed was read the first & second time and passed.   adjourned.

Monday Jan 17 1859. House met at ten a. m. Message from the council with (C. F. No 4) "An act concerning costs and fees of courts, & for other purposes" which was read the first time and passed and referred to the Committee on Judiciary.

Mr Wright presented a petition from County Court of G. S. L. County, recieved and referred to the committee on Revenue.

(H. F. No. 9) "An act providing for the bridging of ditches or sects leading across the high ways" engrossed was taken up read the third time and passed.

(H. F. No 17) "An act regulating the manufacturing and sale of liquors", being called for was read the first second and third times amended and passed.

Message from the council that (H. F. No 14) "An act Specifying the time in which officers shall qualify and give bonds" was not concurred in

Also that (C. F. No 9) "An act prescribing certain qualifications necessary to enable a person to be eligible to hold office, vote or serve as a juror" had passed the Council. Which was read three times and passed.

Message from the Gov. that

"An act autherizing a special election in Lehi City"

"An act creating a special committee (for codifying laws) &c"

"An act reorgainizing Carson &c

"An act granting to Isaac Bullock" &c had been approved.

Mr Clawson chairman of the Committe on Claims reported favorably on the claim of the code commissioners of 1857, which was recieved and referred to the committee on appropriations

(H. F. No 15) "An act to incorporate the Placerville, Humbolt and Salt Lake Telegraph Company" was the first time & passed adjourned.

Tuesday 18 Jan 1859. House met at ten a. m. (H. F. No 15) "An act to incorporate the Placerville" &c was taken read the second time and passed amended.

Mr West Chairman of the committee on Revenue reported (H. F. No 18) "An act amending an act prescribing the manner of assessing and collecting Territorial and County taxes" recieved (Laid on Table [crossed out]) & read the first and passed and referred back for amendment.

Mr Hyde chairman of the committee on Education reported (H. F. No 19) "An act to amend an ordinance, entitled an ordinance incorporating the University of the State of Deseret" recieved and read the first second & third times and passed.

(H. F. No 15) "An act to incorporate the Placerville" &c engrossed was read the third time and passed. Adjourned

Wednesday 19 Jan 1859. House met at ten a. m. Message from the council that (C. F. No 3) "An act defining the three judicial Districts for the Dist Courts in the T. of Utah" had passed the C.

Also that (H. F. No 17) "An act regulating the manufacturing and sale liquors" had been concurred in by the Council with amendments

Mr Farnsworth presented petition of 68 citizens of Beaver city praying for a city charter which was referred to the Comt on Incorp

Mr Stout presented the account of Thos Bullock and others for services rendered of $143 recieved, referred to comte on Claims.

Mr Stout presented petition of Joshua Terry & Joel Terry for water privilege recieved and referred to the Committee on (Claims [crossed out]) Agriculture Trade & manufactures.

Mr Rockwood presented an account from the "Deseret News office" for services rendered the Territory referred to the Committee on Claims.

Mr West chairman of the Committee on Revenue reported on the auditors report & the Warden's &c recieved and Comte discharged.

Message from the council that "An act changing the times of holding elections in different cities has passed the Council as a substitute for (H. F. No 16) "An act changing the time of holding elections in Nephi City which was not concurred in & the council requested to concur in (H. F No 16)

Message from the council that they had adjourned the joint session till 11½ a. m. to morrow the House concurred.

Message from the Council that (C. F. No 13) "An Act concerning Notarys Public for Great Salt Lake County" had passed the council which Bill was read three times and passed.

Mr West chairman of the Committee on Revenue reported (H. F. No 18) "An act amending an act prescribing the manner of assessing and collecting T. & Co. taxes, recieved and Read the second and third times and passed. Adj'd to 3 p. m and met according

Mr Hyde Chairman of the Committee on Agriculture Trade and Manufacture reported adversly to petition of J. & J Terry recieved

Message from the council that (H. F. No 5) "An to provide for the election and location of a quantity of land equal to two townships for the establishment of a University" amended had passed the council House concurred in said amendments.

Also that (C. F. No 14) had passed the council to which the House concurred

Also that (C. F. No 15) An act appropriating money to Deseret agricultural and manufacturing Society" had passed the council, to which the House concurred

Also that (H. F. No 19) "An act to amend an Ordinance" &c and "An act to providing for bridging of ditches &c were not concurred in.

Also that (H. F. No 15) "An act to incorporate the Placerville &c was concurred in

Message from the Council that (C. F. No 12) "An act defining who are exempt from serving on juries and prescribing the mode of procuring and pitit juries in District Courts and and for other purposes" had passed the Council.

Also that the council do not concur in (H. F. No 16) An act changing the time of holding elections in Nephi City" and asking the concurrence of the House in the "Act chinging the times of holding elections in certain cities" which was laid on the table

(C. F. No 12) "An act defining who are exempt from serving on juries" &c was read and laid on the table.

(H. F. No 17) "An act regulating the manufacturing and sale of liquors" was read as amended by the council & passed.

Mr Stout chairman of the committee on judiciary reported back the apportionment bill amended, the first time & passed the second reading amenended. and passed its third reading.

Mr Stout chairman of the committee on judiciary reported back (C. F. No 4) "An act concerning costs and fees of courts, & for other purposes" without amendment. recieved and read the second & third times & passed. (C. F. No 3) "An act defining the three judicial Districts for the U. S. Dist Ct in the Ter of Utah" was read three times and passed.

Mr Haight chairman of the committee on Incorporations reported adversly to the petitions of the citizens of Beaver for a city charter recieved adjourned

Thursday 20 Jan 1859. House met at ten a. m. Mr Snow presented petition of James McLelland and other citizens of Payson for aid from the Legislature to indemnify them for losses in herding &c recieved and referred to the committee on claims (Substitute for H. F. No 16) "An act changing the times of holding elections in certain cities" was read three times amended and passed

(C. F. No 12) "An act defining who are exempt from serving on Juries" &c was read three times and passed.

Message from the council that (Substitute for (H. F. No 16) Had been concurred in Assembly then went into joint session

Hosea Stout, George A. Smith and Seth M. Blair was elected a Special Committee of Revision to embody a code of laws for Utah

Peter Maughn Elected Probate Judge for Cache County Curtis E. Bolton Notarie Public for Great Salt Lake County.

The Election for two District Attornies was posponed. Joint session adjourned and the House resumed its session.

Mr Young presented a "Resolution ordering the Laws and journals of the present Session printed which was read twice and passed.

Message from the Council that (H. F. No 10) "An act in relation to the entering of public lands" had passed the council with amendments to which the House concurred in

Mr Clawson chairman of committee on claims reported favorably on the claim of Thomas Bullock and others for $143.

Message from the Council that (H. F. No 12) "An act authorizing the territorial Road Commissioner to negotiate with the proprietors of Jordan Bridge, near Lehi city" was not concurred in.

Also that (C. F. No 3) "An act defining the three judicial districts" & had been re concidered and amended which amendments (had been [crossed out]) was concurred in by the House

Message from the House that (C. F. No 17) "An act repealing an act granting unto Brigham Young and others, Rush Valley for a Herd ground and other purposes" which was read and laid on the table.

Mr Stout presented (H. F. No 20) "An act to amend an act in relation to marshals and attorneys, approved March 3 1852" which was read and recieved and read the first time and passed, read the second time and amended and passed and passed the third time by its title

"Resolution ordering the Laws and journals of the present session to be printed and published" engrossed was read and adopted adjourned till 4 p. m. and met accordingly.

Mr Rockwood, chairman of the committee on appropriations reported (H. F. No 21) "Territorial appropriation Bill" which was recieved and read three times and passed.

Mr Rock moved that the committee on Revenue be instructed to bring in a bill providing for the salary of the Adjutant General, Treasurer, and Auditor of Public Accounts and other officers not provided for

Mr Clawson, chairman of the committee on Claims reported adversly to the claims of James McLelland and others for losses in herding, recieved

Message from the Council that (H. F. No 18) "An Act amending an act prescribing the manner of assessing and collecting territorial and County taxes" had been concurred in by adding an additional section which amendment was concurred in by the House.

Message from the Council that (C. F. No 16) "General appropriation Bill" had passed the council which was read the first time and passed and referred to the committee on revenue

Message from the Council that "Resolution ordering the laws and journals of the present session printed and published" with several amendments, which amendments were concurred in by the House Adjourned till tomorrow at ten a. m

Thursday [Friday] 21 Jan 1859. House met at ten a. m. Mr West, chairman of the committee on Revenue, reported back (C. F. No 16" general appropriation Bill without amendment and read the second and third times & passed with one amendment.

Mr West chairman of the committee on Revenue reported (H. F. No 22) "An act establishing the salaries of certain officers" recieved and read three times and passed.

(C. F. No 17) "An act repealing an act granting to Brigham Young, Wilford Woodruff & other persons, Rush Valley for a herd ground & other purposes" was read and on motion of Mr Stout not concurred in.

Mr Hyde chairman of the committee on (Education [crossed out]) Trade and Manufactures &c reported inexpedient to Legislate on the subject of "Domestic Manufactures" adjourned till 2 p. m. and met accordingly

Message from the council that Messrs Kimball, Woodruff, & Farr have been appointed a special committee on the part of the council to confer with a similar committee on the part of the House on the subject of (C. F. No 17) "An act repealing an act granting to Brigham Young" &c

The speaker apponted Rich, Roberry and Haight said committee

Message also stated that the amendment to "General appropriation Bill" was not concurred in.

Also that (C. F. No 18) "An act prescribing the manner of challenging petit jurors had passed the council.

Message from the Council asking the House to concur in adjourning the joint Session to be at 2. p m to day untill 6 p. m. The House concurred therein. (C. F. No 18) was then read the first time and passed.

Message from the council that the following memorials had passed the Council to which the House concurred in. viz "Memorial for a daily mail" do to congress for the construction of of a national central Rail Road, via G. S. L. City"

"Memorial to defray the expenses of the Legislature for 1856-7 and 1857-8"

"Memorial to Congress for the construction of a magnetic Telegraph across the continent"

"Memorial to Congress for the election of Gov. and judges, Secratary and other Territorial officers by the people"

Also that (H. F. No 22) "An act establishing the salaries of certain Territorial officers" had been concurred in by the council.

Also that (H. F. No 21) "Territorial appropriation Bill" has been amended as per enclosed copy, which said amendments were concurred in by the House

Mr Osborn, presented (H. F. No 23) "An act to incorporate the Brown City Company" which was read and referred to the committee of Incorporations. (C. F. No 18) "An prescribing the manner of challenging petit jurors was taken up on its second reading and referred to the Committee on Judiciary adjourned till 6 p. m

House met at 6 p. m. Mr Stout chairman of the committee on Judiciary reported back (H. F. No 18) An act prescribing the manner of challenging pettit jurors" with amendments recieved and the bill read as amended and its three readings

Message from the council that "Memorial for a donation of Lands to cities towns and villages" was adopted by the council which was concurred in by the House.

Message from the council that (H. F. No 20) "An act to amend an act in relation to marshals and attorneys, approved March 3, 1852 had passed the Council with amendments On motion of Mr West the amendments were concurred in

Message from the Council that (C. F. No 6) An act assigning the Chief Justice and two associate Justice to their respective Districts had passed the Council which was read three times and passed.

"Memorial to Congress to defray the expenses of the Legislature of 1856-7 and 1857-8 was read and adopted

Message from the council that (C. F. No 17) "An act repealing an act granting unto Brigham Young" &c had been reconsidered & amended, which was read and concurred in

Mr Haight chairman of the Committee on Incorporations reported (H. F. No 23) "An act to incorporate Brown City Company" that said bill being presented at this late hour of the session, they deem it inexpedient to legislate thereon at this session.   recieved

Message from the Council that they had concurred in the amendments to (C. F. No 18)

Message from the Council that they had concurred in "Joint Resolution in relation to mail service" with several amendments which amendments were concurred in by the House.

Message from the council that they had reconsidered "An act defining the three Judicial districts for district courts in the Territory of Utah" and had added "This act to take effect and be in force from and after the first day of May 1859, to which the House concurred in

Message from the council that the council did not concur in the House amendments to (C. F. No 1 and that (C. F. No 19) "An act apportioning to certain Counties Representatives to the Legislative Assembly" had passed the Council as a substitute therefor which was read three times and passed.

The two houses then went into joint session

Jesse N. Smith was elected District attorney First or Southren District and W. H. Bloomfield District Attorney for the second or Carson District A very complimentary Resolution then passed in respect to Gov A. Cumming The Joint Session then dissolved.

Message from the Council that "An act concerning costs and fees of couts and for other purposes" had been reconsidered and amended, which amendments was concurred in by the House

Message from the council that "An Act defining who are exempt from serving on Juries" &c had been reconsidered and amended to which amendments the House concurred

Message from the council that (C. F. No 16) "General appropriation Bill" had been amended to which amendment the House concurred in.

Message from the Council that "Our table is clear, and we are about to adjourn. Have you any more business to present prior to said adjournment?" There being no business to present the council was notified accordingly.

Mr Rich presented "Resolution for convening the Legislative Assembly" which was adopted.

Mr Stout presented "Resolution in relation to notifying persons elected to office by joint vote of the assembly" which was adopted.

The Council notified the House that the two last named Resolutions had been concurred in.

The House adjourned to meet in the Social Hall in Great Salt Lake City, on Monday the 2nd Monday of December 1859 at 10 a. m.[46] It was now about three and a half o clock a. m

Saturday 22 January 1859. To day the members of the Legislature met again in joint session to learn what Secratary Hartnett intended to do in relation to paying the members their per diem He hesitates to pay only for *Sitting* days whereas the members claim the full forty or none The feelings are warm and some sharp sayings are the consequence.

We have kept up waiting for an answer untill near midnight and no answer.

Monday 24 Jan 1859. Went as a committee with C. C. Rich & T. W. Richards to wait on the Gov and Hartnett, in relation to our aforsaid per diem but did not learn any thing definate. The members are therefore going home without only drawing their mileage & intend to give Mr Hartnett time to take the "sober second thought" and so let him do as he pleases.

Thursday 27 Jan 1859. Hard south wind this morning which continued nearly all day but towards noon commenced snowing hard until night depositing some six inches snow.

Sunday 6 Feb 1859. The weather for the past week has been mild. The snow has been melting and the streets flooded with water The elements begin to appear like spring. The times are unusually calm. The Pike's Peak and the Gila gold mines are beginning to attract the attention of the trancient residents and companyies are being formed and talked of for the gold mines.

This evening commenced raining which continued all night so that in the morning the ground was flooded with water and still raining. The snow in the mean time was going very fast.

Thursday 10 Feb 1859. Hard south wind all day yesterday till about 8 p. m. ground afloat snow going very fast then wind to N. W. and snowing hard This morning snow some six inches deep followed by a fine warm day, thin clouds and snow melting fast.

Saturday 12 Feb 1859. Suit before Probate Court B. Leonard v. Thos J. Wheeler for $750 I was on part of the defendant the plf was non suited Weather fine, snow melting.

Monday 14th Feb 1859. Snowing hard this morning which continued untill about 8 a. m. leaving a mantle of snow on the valley about 8 inches thick The day was warm and pleasant

---

46. The work of the legislative period is so complicated that space will not permit a detailed study of the individual bills. The work of the territorial legislatures during these years would merit consideration as a topic for a master's thesis or perhaps even a doctoral dissertation.

Saturday 26 February 1859. For the last elevend day, that is since last Monday week I have been engaged in an arbitration in a case wherein Williams and Woodard are plaintiffs and Guthrie & Mitchell defendants The case was commenced in the District Court Woodard & Williams claimed that the defendants let them have their cattle 1300 head to herd. for some seven months at 80 cents per month per head while the defendants claim that they had been decieved by the fraudulent & false representations of the plaintiffs and hence the contract was null and void.

Williams and Woodward sued for $700 damages on the breach of the contract and the defendants denied this and set up a counter claim for over $5000 damages so that there was some $12000 difference Mr T. S. Williams & C. M. Smith were attornies for the plaintiff and Mr Willson & myself for the defendants.

The case not coming up in the District Court and both parties anxious to have it settled, they agreed to have left to arbitrators viz W. H. Hooper E. H. Terry and C. C. Branham

The case commenced Monday the 14th inst and last evening the arguments were closed & and the case submitted The arbitrators are to render their award on or before next Tuesday evening.

Today I had a suit before Probate Court Thomas J. Wheeler v Bradford Leonard in damages $166. This was in consequence of Leonard failing to obtain judgement v W. on the 12 inst in this court on an attachment I was council for Plf & Blair for defence Jury trial. verdict for plf for $50 and defendant gave notice of appeal.

The weather has for the last two weeks been mild and thawing fast and south wind and then a snow keeping the streets and roads continually wet and muddy.

Monday 28 Feb 1859. Snowing nearly all day. Snow damp and disagreeable. Snow about 6 inches deep.

Tuesday March 1 1859. The arbitrators in the case of Woodward & Co vs Guthrie and Mitchell rendered an award of $1114. dollars in favor of Woodward & Co The weather still appears unsettled The snow is nearly one foot deep in the valley.

Sunday 6 March 1859. Started to day, in company with Elder George A. Smith, Seth M. Blair, Attorney General John Kay Territorial Marshal, John V. Long Reporter to Provo to attend the U. S. District Court on the 8th inst. and went to Bishop Harrington's American Fork and staid all night.

Monday 7 March 1859. We all arrived at Provo about Eleven a. m. and (except George A. Smith) put up at Isaac Bullock's Hotel. In the evening the Hon John Cradlebaugh the judge & Gilbert & Brookie U. S. Deputy marshals also arrived accompanied by one company of U. S. Infantry under Capt Heth. The troops encamped at the west end and close too the Simenary in which the Court is to be held. The officers put up at Bullocks

This evening U. S. District Attorney Alexander Wilson & Lady arrived and put up with A. J. Stewart Bullock's Tavern was over crouded. The preperations were bad I slept very cold on a pallet.

Tuesday 8 March 1859. This morning the weather is fine pleasant & warm but cloudy. The ground generally in Provo Valley is bare and dry & roads good but in Great Salt Lake Valley the snow is deep and the roads muddy and bad travelling

Court met at ten[47] The Grand Jury was duly empannelled and Dr John Riggs appointed Foreman

47. Judge John Cradlebaugh's court in Provo has been the subject of much controversy, Mormon writers generally condemning his procedure and anti-Mormon writers defending him. There is a general summary of his experience in Utah printed in a pamphlet, *Utah and the Mormons: Speech of Hon. John Cradlebaugh, of Nevada, on the Admission of Utah as a State* (February 7, 1863). Also included in the pamphlet is an Appendix containing affidavits which Cradlebaugh secured relating to crimes committed in Utah.

The Judge then proceeded to charge the jury and in doing so he took occasion to display his venom and predjudice against the people of Utah & particularly the church authorities and the laws of the Territory.

He denounced the Probate Courts in the bitterst terms and impugned the motives of the Legislature, accused them of legislating for the purpuse of tramiling the District Court &c for the purpose of preventing the punishment of crimes and the like and then referred to every thing that had happened or been even falsly reported in the District for the last 3 or 4 years and charged the whole to the authorities of the church and in the plainest terms declared that he was now ready to do anything he could against both the church & people.

The whole charge was a tirade of crimination after which the grand jury was allowed to retire and court adjourned till the after noon.

In the after noon Judge Sinclair C. M. Smith T. S. Williams & a lot of military officers arrived

Court met in the afternoon and called in the Grand Jury and gave them another charge in relation to crimes committed at & about camp Floyd and explained why the troops were brought here

They were here at his request not to interfere with the citizens but to keep and take charge of prisoners and keep the peace and save the county expense.

To all this the Mayor remonstrated with the Judge & the shiriff informed him that he was ready and prepared to take charge of prisoners and discharge his duty in all other respects according to law, but this was all of no avail.

This evening Judge Sinclair as a sample to the people was beastly drunk. Snowing in the evening and night.

Wednesday 9 March 1859. There was no business done in court to day, but there was a knock down or so between the soldiers and citizens. The Judge has taken no steps to remove the troops who are very anoying Snowing again in the evening and afternoon

Thursday 10 March 1859. Court met at ten a. m. S. M. Blair presented his commission as attorney General and asked the court to decide whether he should prosecute for the Territory or not.

The court after some equivicating remarks decided that the U. S. District Attorney was the proper officer to prosecute cases arising under the laws of the Territory. Yet he said the Legislature had a right to create the office of Attorney General but did not tell what service that office could be to the Territory or what duty the Legislature had the right to assign to such office. I recieved the Deseret News this evening and find Elias Smith is now the Editor. A. Happy change.[48]

Friday 11 March 1859. Court met at ten a. m. I presented John Kay's commission of Territorial Marshall and asked the Court to have the same spread on the record that he might be recognized in his office

The Court allowed his commission to be spread on the record but refused to recognize him in his office.

In the after noon the Grand Jury came into Court and presented three indictments against Mose & Lookinglass two Indians for rape committed on an old Danish woman & her daughter about twelve years old at Spanish Fork last summer. Also one indictment against Morgan ignored, whereupon Morgan and another man in custody both brought from Camp Floyd were discharged. The court then gave the jury some instructions said they must regard the opinions and advice of the prosecuting attorney, and excused W. J. Earl from the jury because he said there were

---

48. Albert Carrington was the editor of the *Deseret News* preceding the appointment of Elias Smith.

charges against him, and then adjourned This evening George A. Smith went to Spanish Fork. Saturday evening Col J. C Little came here as minister plenapotentiary, extraordinary from gov. Cumming to the court and the rest of us to keep the peace and have every thing pass off coolly. The Mayor and city council is still remonstrating with the court for the removal of the troops out of the city There has been another knock down with the soldiers and citizens. Much excitement was manifested and several soldiers came to the rescue with their guns with fixed bayonets but did not attempt to use them. The excitement was promptly quelled by the city marshall ore there is no doubt but the affair would have terminated seriously.

It commenced by wrestling and one of the Provo boys proved the bully which caused the contest to turn into a fight.

Monday 14 March 1859. Court met at 10 a. m and after naturalizing a few foreigners adjourned till 4 p. m Petition came in to the judge from Spanish Fork to the Judge to have the troops removed from the court.

Court met at 4 p. m. and the grand jury came in and presented an indictment against John Cazier for running off Deserters.

Gov Cumming & Dr Forney arrived here this after noon.

Tuesday 15 March 1859. Court met at ten a. m. Mr Wilson wishing to be with the Grand Jury asked to have the case of Mose & Looking Glass adjourned till next Monday, which was done & court adjourned till two.

In the afternoon T. S. Williams objects to foreigners being naturalized who were in Echo Cañon to oppose the enterance of the U. S. troops and wants to make this a test question, which the Judge seems pleased with and desires a case in point to enable him to rule thereon and requested Williams to make the point. Mr Miner opposes it so the witness are closely questioned on the Echo affair but no point made

Wednesday 16 March 1859. Court met at ten a. m. I did not attend but was with Gov Cumming who wishes to take the best course to prevent a collision between the soldiers & citizens untill instructions can be recieved from Washington on the subject.

Thursday 17 March 1859. The court spent the after noon in naturalizing one Englishman The difficulty was whether he had been in Echo Cañon or not.

Thursday 18 March 1859. The court spent all its Judicial time today naturalizing another Englishman [Hosea makes a double entry for Thursday.]

Friday 18 March 1859. Court spent this fore noon in naturulizing Robinson on the Echo question (this [crossed out]) yesterday evening the court ordered subpoenas for 17 citizens of Springville to appear and testify before the grand jury, and by this means decoyed two men A. F. McDonald and Hamilton H. Carnes into court,[49] who came forward and were sworn and directed to go before the Grand jury, but immediately were arrested by virtue of a private bench warrant issued by the judge in chambers.

This was the intention with all the 17, but the rest many of whom were present, but not recognized by the Judge and officers took the hint and left and cannot now be found.

A posse now started for W. J. Earl A. Durfee and Jos Bartholemew at Springville but they learning also that foul play and treachery was the cue of the court, were not found by the *posse.*

---

49. Both A. F. McDonald and Hamilton H. Carnes had been accused of complicity in the murder of William R. Parish (also Parrish) and his son, Beason, and Gardner G. Potter two years earlier, March 18, 1857. Wilbur J. Earl, Abram (Abraham) Durfee, and Joseph Bartholomew had also been named as accessories. Cradlebaugh, *Utah and the Mormons,* 43ff.

George A. Smith started for the city this evening B. K. Bullock Mayor of Provo was also arrested this evening. All these arrests were for the murder of Potter and Parrishes, as alleged.

There was much feeling manifested by the citizens of Provo at this wanton piece of treachery and double dealing of the court The Police force of the city had to be doubled.

Saturday 19 March 1859. Wind in the North and snowing hard this morning & untill about noon.

The U. S. District Court with all its dignaty, dwindled down to that of a committing magistrate's court and while the Grand Jury was in session and enquiring into the same case now proceeded to examine into the cause of these arrests made so uncalled for by His Honor. The day was spent on the case of these prisoners and by their own evidence proved mayor Bullock to be perfectly innocent of the charge so disgracefully prefered against & was acquitted T. S. Williams joined with Mr Wilson in the prosecution and S. M. Blair & myself were attorneys for the defence

Sunday 20 March 1859. Went to Springville to day[50] accompanied by Blair, Kay & Long and were followed by P. K. Dotson and some 6 Or 10 of his deputies and others in quest of more men to subpoena and bring to court to be arrested. In the evening learned that some 80 more troops were coming from Camp Floyd. Their only business here in the first place as declared by the Judge at the opening of court was to take care of prisoners but now they are sending more without even a pretext for so doing

The fact is the marshall let, to the officers of the command of Capt Heth, the Jury room in the court house which was under the Grand Jury room where they could hear every thing said in the grand jury.

The whole affair shows a complete military espoinage and their pretences and reasons for bringing them here a farce They pretend that they brought the troop because there was no prisons and to save the county expense, when there was a good and sufficient jail in the very building in which the court was held and they had been repeatedly informed so and that the sheriff was ready to take charge of all persons according to law and the county would pay the expense

Monday 21 March 1859. Court met at nine a. m. and called in the Grand Jury before they were all assembled and delivered to them an abusive and slanderous harangue in which he accused them and the whole community of conspiring to not only commit crime but seeking to evade the law. He again took occasion to revert to the church and Territorial authorities in the most abusive manner and notwithstanding the jury informed him that they had business before them on which they were nearly ready to report they were discharged.

The case of U. S. against John Cazier was then called up. S. M. Blair & myself his attorneys This case occupied the rest of the day and about dark the jury brought in a virdict of "not guilty" and were discharged John Daly had been subpoenad to appear before the grand jury this morning and on his appearing was arrested and put into the guard tent as Carnes & McDonald had been

Tuesday 22 March 1859. Court met at ten a. m. and called in the Indian prisoners and two prisoners from camp Floyd which had been brought with the troops and against one an indictment had been found. He informed these prisoners that they

---

50. During this trip to Springville Hosea Stout secured copies of the pertinent documents relating to the murder of the Parishes and Potter. They include a copy of the "Coroner's Inquest," copied from the "Justice's Docket for Springville Presinct," "Property Found on the Bodies," and "Copy of Coroner's Inquest copied from a loose sheet of paper in the above named Docket." (Typewritten copies are in the Hosea Stout Miscellaneous Papers, Utah State Historical Society.)

were guilty of crimes for which they deserved to be punished, but as the community in which they were now in were guilty of worse crimes than they and would not punish each other he was going to discharge them which he did but retained the Indians to be taken to Camp Floyd and there discharged.

Severe wind & snow storm from the north

The rest of the day was spent in examining the three prisoners who had been so treacherously arrested

Marshal John Kay returned home today

Alfred Nethercott[51] was called as a witness to day and not testifying to suit T. S. Williams & the judge was arrested by a bench warrant previously prepared for him This makes 4 prsons arrested for the murder of Parrishes & Potter against who there is not the shadaw of evidence.

Wednesday 23 March. Blair and myself Left Bp. Blackburn's where we had been boarding since the 9th inst and went to Horace Roberts to board.

Court engaged in the examination of the prisoners as yesterday. The prosecution being nearly through court adjourned to give the attorneys an oppertunity to prepare to argue the question whether the defence shall have the privilige to introduce testimony or not to morrow

William Meeks started to the city this eve. Weather fine to day.

Thursday 24 March 1859. Court decided after argument that evidence could be introduced in criminal cases   The case of Nethercott was taken up also Daily this morning attorneys same.

This evening Marshall Kay returned from the city bringing me 6 or 8 papers.

Friday 25 March 1859. Court adjourned till tomorrow at 9. Carnes' & McDonald's wives came to see them but could not get admittance   Heard that A. Durfee & Joseph Bartholemew had gone to Great Salt Lake City and give themselves up to Secratary Hartnett claiming Gentile protection

Saturday 26 March 1859. Court met and adjourned and made an ineffectual attempt to get up something as to the killing of Jacob Lance in Lehi some two or three years ago   He was killed as is reported by a Danish woman whom he had ravished

Sunday 27 March 1859. Hard wind from the north and snowing   Marshall Dotson returned from the city with Durfee & Bartholemew who have now got the gentile protection they so much sought for.

Monday 28 March 1859. Dark cold day.   Hard wind from the North   Court met and adjourned without doing any business but the Judge and Williams are in secret caucus with Durfee & Bartholemew trying what can be elicited from them

Tuesday 29 March 1859. Court met again on the cases of Carnes et. al. and continued the examination   recieved an express this morning containing a proclamation of Gov A. Cumming in which he protests against the "armed neutrality" of the court. Says the troops were brought here with out his knowledge or consent and contrary to his instructions and most effectually exculpates himself from any blame and puts himself in a proper position before the public

---

51. An affidavit made out by one — Phillips — stated that he had been at a meeting in Provo where the speaker had much to say about apostates and persons desiring to leave the territory, and how they would be disposed of: "After the meeting Pres. Snow inquired if there was anybody going to Springville that day. A man by the name of Nethercot went up, and Snow handed him a letter, and told him he wanted it to be delivered to Bishop Johnson that day without fail, and remarked that dead men tell no tales. Nethercott took the letter. And further deponent saith not." Cradlebaugh, *Utah and the Mormons,* 60-61.

Major Paul's command of 8 companies of infantry and one Battery is now posted on the hill 2 or 3 miles north of Provo so as to be ready to bombard the town if it so please them to do so   They are in good range.

A company of 56 dragoons and several deputy marshalls started to Springville this morning and before day surrounded Bp Johnson's house expecting to arresting him but failed.

Wednesday 30 March 1859. Court met and adjourned for want of evidence for the defence, and agreed to let the case lie over untill Monday and give Blair & myself time to go to our homes; and upon this promise Blair & Lady went home.

Stormy, Squally, weather

Thursday 31 March 1859. Court met and adjourned till Monday, but kept the committing magistrate's side of the court open and examined Bartholemew who had however been examined in chambers so the court brought him into Court and read his testimony[52] and he merely assented to it   He has told a long and wonderfull story about Springville affairs, criminating the Bishop and some 15 or 20 others but keeping himself in the mean while perfectly innocent.

The evidence adduced shows on its face a one sided concern and is evidently a garbled statement got up and prepared by the court and his coadjutors for the purpose of criminating others a thing so much desired by them & openly avowed

Friday 1 April 1859. Court met and was engaged till three in the after noon examing Durfee[53] who like Bartholemew has turned states evidence and seeks to save his own neck by implicating others and criminates nearly the same persons as Bartholemew but is more specific and pointed.

After this two or three witnesses were introduced in defence of Nethercott and the court ordered the cases of all four of the prisoners to be argued against the express agreement made with the Judge before Blair left, not to move in the matter untill Monday and then allow us to introduce our evidence.

I remonstrated against his arguing the cases in Blairs absence but the prosecution & court persisted and Mr Wilson made his plea and I was called on to make mine but then I arose and called the judge to his promise in open court whereupon he gave me 24 hours to send for Blair from G. S. L. City and adjourned the court accordingly, and William Meeks went express for Blair I learn that Daniel Stanton has been arrested at and left at Camp Floyd as one of the persons engaged in the murder of the Parrishes & Potter

Saturday 2 April 1859. Cold clear weather   At about 3 p. m. the cases of the prisoners was called up and the arguments of counsel heard.

---

52. Joseph Bartholomew testified that he had attended a meeting at the home of Bishop Johnson about the first of March where there was discussion as to the Parrishes evident intention of leaving, and two men, Potter and Durfee, were assigned to watch them and learn of their plans. Bartholomew was assigned to guard the Parrish home for a time on the evening of the murder and then went with the wagon and a group to get the bodies. He said that he himself was suspect and that several attempts had been made to take his life. *Ibid.*, 48-51.

53. Abraham Durfee's confession was made of "his own free will and accord, and without being influenced by any promise of any kind, by any person whatever . . . now, this first day of April A. D. 1859, comes before Judge Cradlebaugh, and makes the following confession." He tells of meetings wherein the brethren had discussed the plans of the Parrishes for leaving and "The Bishop said there were some demands against them for debts they were owing . . . ." Durfee and Potter were assigned to watch and find out their intent. Durfee gave the story of the killing, but insisted that he himself was only trying to help the Parishes get away. Potter was evidently killed by mistake. Durfee named the people who were present at the two meetings, and said that the actual killing was done by William Bird. H. H. Carnes, A. F. McDonald, and John Daly were all named as having been members of the police at Springville and present at the meetings. *Ibid.*, 56-60.

Alfred Nethercott was acquitted and H. H. Carnes, A. F. McDonald, and John Daly committed all without the first shadow of testimony that could possibly be recieved as legal evidence, in a court of justice on a final trial. Durfee & Bartholemew were also committed Blair had not arrived & I was alone on the defence.

The court adjourned till Monday, and after court adjourned Williams commenced suit against Aaron Johnson Bishop of Springville for $500 and interest at ten per cent thereon for two years.

The suit was in favor of Mrs Parrish and commenced by attachment.

Sunday 3 April 1859. I went to Springville this fore noon to visit the wives of the prisoners and Mrs Johnson on the subject of the attachment against her husband's while there A. Williams Deputy Marshall came with the attachment and levied it on Johnson's flouring mill. It was the intention of Williams to have attached some 8 or 900 dollars worth of Johnsons horses and cattle and so get possession of his property not caring how the suit came out

This I suspected last evening and came forward and informed Williams & Dotson that I was Johnsons Attorney and that there could be no advantage taken of his absence for I was ready to answer any demands against him. This disconcerted their plans & so they slid off their plans by attaching his mill.

This evening took supper with L. N. Scovil who had got up the supper in honor of Judge Cradlebaugh and others.

Monday 4 April 1859. Court met and adjourned sine die this morning but previously the judge came to me and offered to release John Daly if I would enter into a recognisance for $1000 with him to appear at the next term of the District Court as a witness on the case of the other prisoners. I accepted the offer and Daly was released.

While this was going on the troops and court trappings were preparing to leave Major Paul with his whole command marched into town to recieve the prisoners and all marched off leaving the town of Provo once more to themselves I then left for home. Stoped to see my brother Allen he was well but his wife was bed sick I could stop but a few minutes and went on to Lehi and put up at Uncle Bells where I found Seth as per previous arraingements.

The troops encamped in the edge of the town to night

The judge went in quest of the Lance case here and tracked it hence to American Fork and there lost its track & I believe abandoned it for the present.

Tuesday 5 April 1859. The troops and the Judge started early this morning for Camp Floyd I saw the prisoners here, & Carnes & McDonald were in good spirits, better than usual. After the troops and followers were all safely over Jordan Seth with his Lady and myself started for home, dined at Silas Richards at Fort Union and arrived at home near sundown. My family all well

Thus ended this singular Court its object and aim needs no comment because that has been sufficiently declared by the judge from time to time during court.

Wednesday 6 April 1859. Spring weather now. Snow off the garden for the first time this winter General Conference commenced to day I did not attend having too much other business on my hands.

Thursday 7 April 1859. Attended Conference to day

Friday 8 April 1859. Visited Gov Cumming this fore noon He thinks there will be a warrant yet issued for President B. Young and if so believes it will be necessary for him to give himself up & that he will not be harmed I remonstrated. I know this will not do.

Sunday 10 April 1859. Snow some two inches deep fell last night and all went off to day. Weather squally all day.

Monday 11 April 1859. Bigger snow than ever this morning and still snowing fast. Squally day. Tuesday snowing by spirts all day and Wednesday morning snow six inched deep but weather mild & unsettled. Levi Stewart had several loads of goods to arrive from Cal. yesterday.

Sunday 17 April 1859. S. M. Blair left this morning for Camp Floyd for the purpose of getting McDonald and Carnes released from their imprisonment on a Habeas Corpus to be issued by Z. Snow Judge of Probate for Cedar County

Tuesday 19 April 1859. To day Blair returned from Camp Floyd Judge Snow not being at home he could not try the virtue of the Habeas Corpus.

Thursday 21 April 1859. Suit before Jeter Clinton Esqr "The people &c vs. Tom Coulbourn negro slave belonging to J. H. Johnson on examination for shooting Shep negro slave belonging to W. H. Hooper. The negros had got into a row about two wenches belonging to T. S. Williams and love and jealousy was the main cause of the fuss. Like their masters under such circumstances would probably would do they went to shooting each other. Shep is badly wounded and his life is precarious. Dist Attorney Wilson prosecuted and Blair and myself defended. Tom was held to bail for $1000 to appear at the next Dist Court.

Sunday 1 May 1859. We had a warm pleasant rain last night and to day untill about 8 p m. saturating the ground well.

Wednesday 4 May 1859. Raining this morning accompanied with snow which continued until noon then cool and pleasant, cloudy

Suit before Esqr Clinton. Perpetual Emmigrating Fund Co vs Hugh L. Briggs Demand 20 68/100 dollars. I was attorney for Plf and T. S. Williams for deft

This case arose on a promissory note given by Susanna Preston to the P. E. F. Co for her emmigration from England to this place & Briggs marreying her refused to pay her debt was sued, & called for a jury of 12 denying the liability of the Husband for the debts of the wife contracted before coveture Jury found a verdict for the plf & deft appealed

Thursday 5 May 1859. Suit before E. Smith Probate Judge Chas Crisman vs J. B Kimball & Co Demand 15,000 dollars. S. M. Blair atty for plf & A. Miner & self for deft. The case was called up to day Deft demurred to Complaint Demurer sustained and Plff givin till to morrow at 9 a. m. to amend complaint.

Saturday 7 May 1859. The suit between Crisman v J. B. Kimball & Co was brought to an issue to day & tried before a jury who gave a verdict of $6896.73 against the defendants, the amount which the defendants acknowledged to be due the plaintiff It was mid night when I came home.

Thursday 12 May 1859. To day the committee appointed by the Legislative Assembly to prepare and arrange a code of laws for the Territory met at G. A. Smith's and commenced their labors. and have rented a room in the Historian building for that purpose and chose George A. Smith for chairman. The other two are S. M. Blair & H. Stout and we have occupied friday and saturday following at the business of the committee.

Judge Sinclair has returned from Camp Floyd to this city again.

Wednesday 18 May 1859. Two men William Harris and Joseph Abbott were struck by lightning this after noon and Abbott was instantly killed and Harris seriously injoured but will recover.

News from San Pete County is that Isaac Allred my brother-in-law has been murdered by Thomas Ivie the particulars and (reason [crossed out]) circumstances which led to his murder I have not learned.[54]

---

54. Isaac Allred and Thomas Ivie were both good Mormons of long standing in the church, neighbors, and friends. They became involved in a quarrel over some sheep.

Friday 20 May 1859. Spent 4 days this week with the code committee. This morning I started to provo to attend an arbitration between Thomas J. Wheeler & Thomas Ross and arrived there just before night

Saturday prepared the bonds &c for the arbitration and sunday preached to the good people of Provo.

Monday 23 May 1859. Arbitration commenced. C. H. Wheelock, E. W. Whipple & Eli Whipple arbitrators Jos L. Thompson & W. Wall attorneys for Ross & myself for Wheeler. The arbitration lasted four days.

The difficulty arose in 1855. Wheeler & his fathers' family started for Cal and Ross sued out three attachments against them for fifty six dollars in all upon which G. W. Parrish as deputy shiriff pursued and attached some six hundred dollar's worth of property The Wheelers had no summons for trial The property was hid and the Wheeler's wer compelled to go on their journey without it Judgement was rendered against them & the property or a great portion of it sold to pay debts and cost. Ross recieved only twenty three dollars and no more because there was not property enough to pay any more The costs were extravigantly high so at the end of four days investigation both parties becoming satisfied that the wrong done to Wheeler did not rest altogether on Ross withdrew the arbitration and agreed to refer the whole matter to the High Council.

Saturday 28 May 1859. The High Council commenced this morning. The investigation showed that the entire property of the Wheelers that could be accounted for had been consumed in costs except the 23 dollars that Ross got. The charge before the Council was against Ross Isaac Higbee the then Judge of the probate Court & L. N. Scovil clerk The[y] could nor or dare not give any account of the property. A more glaring case of extortion embezzlement and malfeaseance in office I have never become acquainted with which was too fully proven.[55]

The council decided accordingly and that Ross, Higbee, & Scoil should pay to Wheeler one hundred dollars not as a compensation for his wrongs so much as a condemnation of their dishonest and unjust proceedings.

The Council closed on Sunday night.

Monday 30 May 1859. I started home & staid all night with Allen and came home the next day.

Sunday 5 June 1859. Spent four day with the code commission this last .week.

I watered my garden this morning for the first time this year. Dr J. M. Barnhisel our Delegate to Congress returned home on Tuesday the 1 He is in good health but looks care worne

Thursday 9 June 1859. Levingstons & Kinkead's train of goods arrived to day consisting of 38 waggons & 8 mules to each wagon. this is the first train this season from the East.

Monday 13 June 1859. This evening I was appointed by Council for the Seventies to take a short mission to the south part of this County to preach the necessity of the people saving their grain and provisions ere a famine which is near at hand comes upon us.

After coming home and retiring to bed I was called up by Col J. C. Little to go to Gov Cumming's office I went and was informed by the Gov. that a detachment of troops under command of Capt Bradford H. Anderson 2nd Dragoons U. S. Army had encamped with 174 horses & mules besides tents & wagons in John Van Cott's wheat field in the five acre lots and that Van Cott had waited on the captain to

---

55. Here Stout openly and vigorously condemns some of his own people for their unjust treatment of non-Mormons.

request his removal and the Captain had arrested him and that he learning these facts had sent secratary Hartnett to the captain with a request to have Van Cott released which was refused and he wanted me to apply for a writ of Habeas Corpus for the release of Van. I did so by petitioning Judge Sinclair who being called out of his bed after midnight issued the writ which was served by Marshal Dotson who brought Van Cott but Capt Anderson did not come so the Judge remanded him back with orders for Capt Anderson to make return of the writ and prisoner as the law diricts but the Capt turned Van Cott loose and failed to answer the writ. The damage to the wheat during the night was immense How all this wanted tresspass upon property so common by the United States army will come out I can not tell.[56]

I was engaged at the above business all night and till seven in the morning To day the probate Court commenced the June term of its sessions

Wednesday 15 June 1859. The grand jury of the Probate Court has found an indictment against Deloss Gibson[57] for the murder of James Johnson son of Luke Johnson.

I had a suit wherein Margaret Harrington was plf and Elizabeth Gordon deft In Ejectment I was on the part of Plf and T. S. Williams for deft virdict of the jury for the plf.

Thursday 16 June 1859. Chief Justice D. B. Eckles & son Mr A. Humphreys Indian agent in the place of Dr G. Hurt and others arrived here from the states

Sunday 19 June 1859. The Rev Mr Vox chaplain at Laramie Episcopalian held forth at the tabernacle to day in a doctrinal discourse.

Saturday 20 June 1859. I have been engaged in attending to the business of the Code commission & attending a few small suits for W. H. Hooper &c.

The arrival of goods trains are of so frequent occurrence that it is not now even spoken of.

This evening at six a meeting was held at the Historian office to nominate for the coming Election. H. S. Eldredge was nominated for a delegate to congress and also nomination for council & Representatives &c.

Hon J. M. Barnhisel was chosen Chairman of the meeting. The weather is most intensly warm

Monday 4 July 1859. Glorious fourth has again arrived and announced at day light by the firing of cannon followed by music and by a missellaneous discharge of small arms by all whose patriotism inclined so to do. The Stars and stripes floating from all the stores & houses of those who wished to show forth their devotion for their country.

Friday 8 July 1859. Last night my wife was delivered of a son weighing 8¾ pounds. This is my ninth son and fifth one now living and also my thirteenth child and the Sixth one now living that I have five boys and one girl living out of thirteen. We call this one's name [Alfred Lozene]

---

56. The action of the soldiers in turning their cattle into the grain fields shows also their contempt for Mormon property rights and helps to explain some of the vindictiveness shown toward immigrants generally.

57. No further mention is made of the case of Deloss Gibson in this record, but an entry in the diary of Lorenzo Brown may explain: "12 [August, 1859] . . . Last night Deloss Gibson under arrest for murder made his escape from the county jail while taking their supper . . . ." Lorenzo Brown, "Journal," I, 347.

Gibson's freedom lasted only a year. Elias Smith, writing on August 1, 1860, noted that "Deloss M. Gibson was brought before me on a writ of Habeas Corpus on Monday last and the matter postponed till today." Smith released him. On September 2, 1860, Gibson was brought into court for trial, was found guilty, and was sentenced to ten years labor in the penitentiary. Mortensen, "Elias Smith," *U.H.Q.*, XXI, 76.

This after noon there was a hard rain which lasted some hours and saturated the ground well.

Saturday 9 July 1859. This after noon David McKenzie[58] was arrested by Marshal Dotson on a warrant issued by Judge Eckels in Camp Floyd. McKinzie sent to see me on being arrested I went and mad[e] four or five different applications to have an interview but was denied the priviledge The marshall said he had orders from the Judge to let no one not even counsel speak to him only before the officers

Sunday 10 July 1859. This afternoon Mr Horace Greely Esqr Editor of the N. Y. Tribune arrived with the Eastern mail en route for Cal He Expects to spend a few days here.[59]

McDonald Karnes & Bartholemew who were committed to the tender mercies of a Camp Floyd Prison by Judge Cradlebaugh at Provo in March last have been sent back to Provo to be kept in the charge of the shiriff of Utah Co. but Durfee who was the only one who confessed himself guilty was turned loose in camp. So goes U. States' system of Justice

Thursday 13 July 1859. This evening I recieved a letter from David McKenzie[60]

---

58. David McKenzie was born in Edinburgh, Scotland, December 27, 1833. At the age of eleven he was apprenticed to an engraver for whom he worked seven years. On February 11, 1853, McKenzie was baptized into the Mormon Church and the next year came to Utah. On March 7, 1857, he was made a Seventy, and that fall he was a part of the military force in Echo Canyon. He was engaged to engrave the plates for the Deseret currency, and while thus engaged he lived with the family of Brigham Young in the Beehive House. On February 28, 1859, he married Mary Ann Crowther, and four months later was involved in the counterfeiting scandal recorded here.

Of this Lorenzo Brown wrote: "July 10, 1859 . . . David McKenzie one of our near neighbors & an engraver was arrested yesterday on charge of forgery or engraving a plate for U S drafts He was handcuffed and taken to Camp Floyd this morning Myron Brewer was arrested the day before at Camp detected in passing counterfeit drafts . . . ." Lorenzo Brown, "Journal," I, 345.

McKenzie was convicted and sentenced to a two-year prison term, at the end of which he became disbursing clerk at the tithing office. Later he became one of the most popular actors at the Salt Lake Theater. In 1868 McKenzie was made private secretary of Brigham Young; still later succeeded Horace K. Whitney in keeping the church books. He died March 10, 1912, in Salt Lake City.

59. Horace Greeley published his experiences on this journey in a book, about fifty pages of which were devoted to his impressions of Utah. He was not impressed with the fortifications which the Mormons had constructed in their campaign to hold out the government troops, calling them "childish affairs more suitable to the genius of the Chinese than of civilized warfare. I cannot believe that they would have stopped the Federal troops . . . for more than an hour." Horace Greeley, *An Overland Journey, From New York to San Francisco in the Summer of 1859* (New York, 1860), 224.

Greeley was pleased with the appearance of Salt Lake with its small adobe houses with a "neat and quiet look, its wide streets, the running water and the growing trees." He became eloquent over atmosphere so pure that distant mountains seemed near at hand. He visited with Brigham Young in the company of his friend, Dr. Bernhisel, and reported the discussion of doctrine and politics. Greeley's attendance at the Sunday service brought forth his condemnation of speeches unprepared and disorganized such as he had heard and of the total time wasted by an audience as a result of one such wasted half hour.

In conclusion, Greeley declared that the Mormons were not knaves or hypocrites, nor were they organized banditti: "Do I, then, discredit the tales of Mormon outrages and crime — of the murder of the Parrishes, the Mountain Meadows Massacre, etc. etc.? No, I do not. Some of these may have been fabricated by Gentile malice . . . but there is some basis of truth for the current Gentile conviction that the Mormons have robbed, maimed, and even killed people in this territory . . . but that Mormon witnesses, grand jurors, petit jurors, and magistrates determinedly screen the guilty. I deeply regret the necessity of believing this, but the facts are incontestable." *Ibid.*

60. The letter from David McKenzie is on file among the Hosea Stout Miscellaneous Papers. An excerpt follows:

Camp Floyd, July 13, 1859

The prosecution was conducted by a gentleman by the name of Thomson, I believe. Myron Brewer . . . testified that I engraved a copper plate, which he there identi-

He states that he has been committed to the district court at Nephi and that Brewer & Wallace turned States' evidence and were turned loose. [From this entry through July, the remaining dates are confused.]

Monday 26 July 1859. District Court met at 11 a. m. at Mr Hartnett's office and adjd till tomorrow at 11 for want of a proper Court house being procured.

Tuesday 26 July 1859. District Court met and adjourned to meet at the council House Thursday at 11

Thursday 28 July 1859. District Court at eleven which adjourned till four and empannelled the Grand Jury. Motions filed to Quash the array which were over-ruled.

Friday 30 July 1859. Court met at ten a. m No business only quashing one attachment and partly culling the Docket. There is some seventy five cases now on the docket.

Saturday 31 July 1859. District Court in session. The case of Hartnett v Wells was settled and with drawn

The grand jury presented an indictment vs Thorp for Burglary & Larceny and one vs Coulson (negro) for murder and adjourned till next Tuesday

Monday 1 Aug 1859. General election to day. The candidates were as follows

For Delegate to Congress
    William H. Hooper
For commissioners to locate University lands.
    Ira Eldredge
    Chester Loveland.
For Great Salt Lake County.
    For Legislative Council
    Daniel H. Wills
    Albert Carrington
    Orson Pratt Sen
    Franklin D Richards
    James Ferguson

For Representatives
John Taylor
Hosea Stout
David Candland
Hiram B Clawson
Joseph A. Young
Edwin D. Woolley
Seth M. Blair
A. P. Rockwood.
John Moody

The whole number of votes cast in this County were 1440 —

Tuesday 2 Aug 1859. The Court decided that the Probate Courts have no criminal jurisdiction

In the afternoon the Judge came into court very drunk.

---

fied; that John M. Wallace was in league with himself and me, and . . . spared no pains to liberate himself. Major Porter of the U. S. army and Col. Crossman of the same, testified that John M. Wallace sometime since revealed to them personally and by letter of the whole contemplated forgery (said letters were read in court), that the whole had been watched until it ripened so as to effectually entrap those concerned . . . .

I am not a far-seeing man but there is an evident intention on the part of some to inveigle Prest. Young in on this matter, if possible . . . he [Brewer] further asserted that I was employed only as a mechanic to do the engraving and printing and there ended with me . . . . (By the way, there are plates and paper here belonging to the Association. Cannot they be seen after? I am positively afraid of their being rendered useless, if they cannot be handled so as to avoid scratching.)

Young McKenzie refused to implicate Brigham Young or anyone else, but took his sentence of imprisonment for two years. His suggestion as to the Deseret currency plates was followed up, and Marshal Dotson was arrested for carrying them away and fined $2,600 for the fact that they were scratched and rendered useless. Upon his failure to pay the fine, Dotson's property in Salt Lake City was confiscated.

The People vs Thomas Colbourn (negro) was called up and 4 jurors were empannelled during the after noon. Colbourn was arraingned for the murder of Shep another negro Blair & myself defended.

Wednesday 3 Aug 1859. Case of Colbourn was taken up and the jury empannelled, and the evidence for the prosecution given except one negro who being absent the court waited several hours & learning that he had nost likely ran away or hid to evade giving evidence the court was quite put out and discharged the jury and remanded the prisoner without his consent.

Thurs. all day spent doing nothing

Friday 5 Aug 1859. Last night Franklin E. McNeil was shot just below and to the left of the naval by a man supposed to be Joe Rhodes.[61]

Case of People vs Theodore Thorp for Burglarry & Larceny was called up & Thorp plead guilty. Thorp had broke into Zacheus Cheney's house in Davis County and stolen some $1800 therefrom

In the after noon Lott Huntington was arrested and brought into Court on a charge for being accessary to the shooting of McNeil defended by Blair and myself.

Saturday 6 Aug 1859. McNeil died last night of his wound. Lott Huntington was discharged from his arreat There was not the shadow of evidince against him

The court sentenced Thorp to ten years at hard labor in the penetentiary and at noon adjourned untill Monday.

Monday 8 Aug 1859. Day spent in court in argueing motions calling the civil Docket and talk.

Tuesday 9 Aug 1859. No trials to day No nothing else but calling cases and dismissing a few.

Wednesday 10 Aug 1859. The case of Drown v. Hickman was taken up and tried by the court and in the The People v Henry Phelps and Henry Spears for robery of McArty called up Mr Willson Prosecutor being sick I prosecuted the case & Miner & Williams defended The Jury was partly empannelled and one witness being absent the court adjourned.

Thursday 11 Aug 1859. The People v. Phelps & Spears tried and submitted to the jury who were hung at mid night & the court adjourned.

Today a man by the name of Ralph Pike sergeant in the U. S. A. a man who was brought from Camp Floyd to be tried for an assault to kill Howard Spencer was shot in the street about noon in the presence of about one hundred men The man who shot him escaped.

Pike said it was Spencer shot him some time last winter at Rush Valley Sergeant Pike with some ten or twelve soldiers undertook to dirve Spencer from his possessions and on his refusing to go away Pike struck him over the head with a

61. According to Judge Sinclair, McNeil was killed on the night preceding his trial. Cradlebaugh, *Utah and the Mormons*, 23.

Hickman says that he and others were on the lookout for him, "among them one Joe Rhodes, not a Mormon, but a cut-throat and a thief, who had had some difficulty with McNeal, and was sworn to shoot him . . . . Rhodes followed him around the house and shot him in the alley. McNeal shot once at Rhodes but missed him . . . ." Hickman, *Brigham's Destroying Angel*, 141.

Elias Smith wrote in his journal on August 5, 1859: "A man named Mr. Neil was shot at the California house last night by someone unknown but supposed to be by a man named Rhodes who had had a quarrel with Mr Neil the night previous, and shot at him then but without effect[.]" Elias Smith, "Elias Smith's Journal, From Jany 1st 1859 to Aug 24th 1864" (typescript, Utah State Historical Society), 35.

gun and broke his skull near killing him   his head is not well yet   Perhaps it was Spencer who shot him in revenge.[62]

Friday 12 Aug 1859. The jury presented a sealed verdict in the case of Spears & Phelps verdict of Guilty & Phelps to the penetentiary and Spears two.

In the after noon motion by defendants Council to set aside the verdict for various irregularities in trying to prove which Miner & Williams proved that they had been eves dropping and peeping into the windows of the jury room for which the Court called them to appear at 10 tomorrow to show cause why they should not be dis-barred.

Saturday 13 Aug 1859. Williams and Miner were discharged from the rule against them to show cause why they should not be disbarred

The court quashed the indictment against Ralph Pike and adjourned till Monday.

Sunday 14 Aug 1859. Sergeant Pike died this morning of the wound he had recieved last Thursday.

Monday 15 Aug 1859. The court naturalized one Englishman & then adjourned for the day because of fatigue.

Tues 16 Aug 1859. To day there was nothing done in court but talk over business and adjourned to meet to morrow when his Honor announced that to morrow the civil docket would be called and business actually would commence which we look for?

Wednesday 17 Aug 1859. To day business has actually commenced in Court. The case of Miller v Williams in Replevin for the recovery of two negro girls.

After much palaver in which His Hon. seemed to be senior Council on the part of Miller the case went before a jury who brought in for the defendant whereupon the court not to be beat set aside the virdict

Thursday 18 Aug 1859. The court spent the forenoon doing nothing and late in the after noon the case of G. B. Smith vs T. & W. Wheeler came in assumpsit for 300 dollars Williams for plaintiff and myself for defts. The jury gave a verdict for defendants for 14 dollars on the set off in the case. Williams gave notice for a motion for a new trial.

Friday 19 Aug 1859. The motion of Mr Williams for a new trial in the case of Smith v Williams was overruled

Nothing more done in the fore noon and in the afternoon court adjourned till the 12th day Sept next

Saturday 27 Aug 1859. The history of the last ₁eek has been the history of a new system of business to me. On Sunday evening last myself Seth M. Blair & James Ferguson concieved the idea of publishing a news paper in this city to be an independent paper so far as religion and politicks are concerned. On Monday we made arraingements with the Editor of the "Deseret News" for the use of his press and type for the time being and also paper. On Tuesday we Employed J. S. Davis for forman and set the hands to work and on Saturday we issued 2400 copies of the paper and called it "the Mountaineer"[63] and distributed some 1000 which seemed

---

62. The killing of Sergeant Pike by Howard Spencer is told by both Mormon and anti-Mormon writers much as it is given here: "12 [August, 1859] Yesterday a U. S. A. Sergeant Pike was shot while standing in a crowd by some person unknown who deliberately made his escape although persued by a host & strange to say although seen by hundreds no one knew him and no two gave the same description of him." Lorenzo Brown, "Journal," I, 347.

63. The *Mountaineer*, the second independent newspaper to be published in Utah, was greeted with more warmth than the *Valley Tan* had received. On this date, Elias Smith, editor of the *Deseret News*, noted in his journal: "Saturday, 27 [August, 1859] . . . On my arrival I ascertained that a newspaper had [been] issued called the Mountaineer edited and published by Blair Ferguson & Stout. This I had anticipated as it was under way when I left home on Thursday in the evening."

to take well with all classes of the people. On sunday I was all day doing up and mailing the papers to diffirent. on Saturday evening Charles M. Drown was shot by some persons unknown. Josiah Arnold was also shot through the thigh It was done by a party of persons who came on them at a house on Main Street occupied by one Eddy a spiritualist.[64] Cause as yet unknown

This evening Saturday we gave the typos a supper at the "Globe" on the occasion of the issue of "The Mountaineer".

Monday 29 Aug 1859. All day in the office. Our office is the N. W. room of the council house. We have rented the lower room of the Council House & the N. W. room for $600 a year This evening James Brown 3rd arrived from the states with a large company of saints 69 waggons.

Friday 2 Sept 1859. Josiah Arnold who was shot last saturday through the thigh, died of the wound.

Monday 12 Sept 1859. District court met to day and adj'd for the want of a proper House. The marshall had not tried to get one. I did not attend. The Judge declared he would hold his court if he had to in the streets That's right Judge.

Wednesday 14 Sept 1859 [Tuesday, Sept 13]. The district Court met at the Social Hall to day and intends to do business this time. This morning I withdrew from my connexion with the Mountaineer. Leaving that paper in the hands of Ferguson & Blair

Wednesday 14 Sept 1859. District court found a permanent lodgement in the social Hall to day and proceeded to organize the grand jury by excusing Mr Bell Forman and appointing D. H. Wells in his. and delivering a short charge to them

Thursday 15 Sept 1859. The case of "The people v. Thos Colborn for killing shep. both negros was tried to day Mr Blair & myself defended him. he was sentenced to one year in the penetentiary & one hundred dollars fine for manslaughter.

---

64. Various reasons have been given for the shooting of Charles M. Drown and Josiah Arnold. According to Judge Sinclair: "A man by the name of Drown brought suit, upon a promissory note for $480, against the Danite captain, Bill Hickman. The case being submitted to the court, Drown obtained judgment." Sinclair accused Hickman and his band of committing the murder. Cradlebaugh, *Utah and the Mormons*, 23.

Stout's mention of the case, Hickman vs Drown, on August 10 would give some credence to this version. Hickman's account accuses Drown of stealing cattle and says that he .was one marked as a public menace. "But this Summer he commenced running to Camp Floyd and telling all the bad stories on the Mormons, he knew or could invent, so said." Hickman says that he was with the party celebrating the advent of the newspaper, the *Mountaineer,* and the murder was committed in his absence. Arnold's death was not intended. Hickman, *Brigham's Destroying Angel*, 133.

J. H. Beadle, who edited the Hickman book, gives another reason for the death of Drown: "According to the best testimony of the best men who were then members of the Mormon Church, it was not for stealing . . . that these men were killed, but for apostasy and spiritualism! . . . Drown and Arnold were spiritualists, and were holding a 'circle' — or seance — with one or two others, when the house was attacked — as testified to by a reliable man who was present." *Ibid.,* 209-10.

Note has already been made of the excommunication of Drown and Arnold by Bishop Harker and Hickman, and their restoration by the stake High Council, in November 1858.

On July 3, 1859, John Bennion, also a counselor to Bishop Harker, wrote: ". . . Elder Orson Hyde Preached a very good discourse said that spirituilism or medium? was the strong delusion sent by the Lord that they who rejected the truth might believe a lie & be damned . . . that they would bring evil on the servants of God it Should come on themselves . . . afternoon meeting Josiah Arnold was cut of[f] from the church for apostacy also C. N. Drownes he was present & opposed Eld Hyde showed much bitterness." John Bennion, "Journal [1855-1877]" (5 vols., original, Utah State Historical Society), II, 79.

William Marsden, who mentioned these men occasionally as neighbors, arrived in Salt Lake the morning after the shooting and visited the place. He spoke as though the wounded Arnold still lay on the floor unattended. "Journal and Diary of William Marsden," *Heart Throbs of the West*, XII (1951), 165.

Friday 16 Sept 1859. People v Yoads an Indian was tried to I appeared as prosecutor now in place of Wilson who is going to leave for home. Yoads was sentenced to one year in the penententiary for mule stealing

Saturday 17 Sept 1859. The people v J. Wade for mule stealing and the people v. M Clark for do were both tried and Wade sentenced to one year and Clark to three years to the penententiary.

This morning earley Thos H. Ferguson shot Alex Carpenter wilfuly and C. died at one at night.

Sunday 18 Sept 1859. To day is my forty-ninth birth day Was engaged in writing two indictment for murder one against Rodney D. Swazey for the murder of C. M. Drown and one against Thos H. Ferguson for the murder of Alex Carpenter.

Monday 19 Sept. Court met at ten and sentenced the four prisoners found guilty last week, to the penententiary and continued some other criminal cases.

Tuesday 20 Sept 1859. Court arraigned T. H. Furguson who plad not guilty case (continued till tomorrow Grand jury discharged [crossed out]) was called up and tried Mr T. S. Williams & W. A. Hickman attorneys for the defence & myself for the prosecution

The virdict of the jury was guilty of murder in the first degree. Rainy day.

Friday 23 Sept 1859. Mr Ferguson the prisoner was sentenced to be hanged on the 28th day of October next between 12 & 1 o'clock p. m.

The court then adjourned sine die

Monday 26 Sept 1859. This evening Col Stambaugh and suit arrived in the city in conformity to his appointment as surveyor Genl of Utah.

This evening also John Gheen was found with a ball hole through his head It is supposed that he committed suicide.[65]

Monday 3 Oct 1859. The State fair came on to day at the social Hall which lasted three days.[66] The exehibition is not so good as last year. The fruit is generally smaller yet there was fine Specimens of nearly all kinds of home productions.

Thursday 6 Oct 1859. The general Conference commenced to day which lasted till Sunday evening. The number of people present was unusually large & quiet. In fact there is not much trouble among us now.

Those who have been making the most noise is gone and going & we shall soon be left to ourselves if things keep the course they are going.

During conference the High Council of this place was dissolved by the general Conference.

Sunday 16 Oct 1859. Last night a man named James Vincent[67] was found dead by a ball passing through his head coming out at the fore head His murder is unknown

---

65. The suggestion that John Gheen had committed suicide was sheerest nonsense, yet that is the word that evidently was given out. George Laub wrote on this date in large letters, "John Geen Suiside John Geen Comited Suisids." Laub later (October 3, 1859) added "John Geen Committed Suiside by Shooting himself through the head he is said to have killed a man in Iowa some ten years ago." "Diary of George Laub, 1814-1880" (3 vols., typescript, Utah State Historical Society), II, 58-59.

66. This was the fourth annual state fair of the Deseret Agricultural and Manufacturing Society. These fairs were continued here, and local fairs were held in the various counties.

67. James Vincent has not yet been identified.

This evening a new High Council[68] was organized for this place by appointing the following named persons, to wit 1 William Eddington 2 James A. Little. Samuel W. Richards, 4 Edward Partridge, 5 Joseph W. Young, 6 Gilbert Clements, 7 John T. Caine, 8 Joseph Smith, 9 George Nebeker, 10 Franklin Woolley, 11 Claudius V. Spencer, and Orson Pratt jr. A majority of these are young men who have been raised in the church.

Saturday 22 Oct 1859. Last Thursday I went with H. S. Eldredge and several others to Salt Lake Island. The day before Presidency and several others went. It is about 21 miles to the place we encamped There is a house garden & orchad there. The Island is well set with grass and is excellent for grasing. It is about 4 miles from the mine shore to the Island. but now it is only about one mile that we had to go through watter which is about 4 inches deep but when the North wind blows the water rises some 3 or 4 feet on the beach. We had a pleasant visit and returned last evening.

Friday 28 Oct 1859. To day the melancholly duty to hang Thos H. Furguson for the murder of A. Carpenter. He was taken to the gallows about eleven a. m and about one p. m. hanged. There was not many spectators present. He had no confession But he reflected very hard on Judge Sinclair for not giving him a fair trial. but said he had been treated well by every one else in Utah only blaming the Gov for not commuting his sentence to imprisonment for life.

Tuesday 8 Nov 1859. Started this morning with R. Potter to Springville to attend to a suit pending in the probate Court in Utah County wherein he is sued by Levi Stewart & Bro We staid all night at American Fork. Here was a suit pending before S. Chipman Esq. The people vs Simon Lance for stabbing one W. A. Wood. I was feed by Lance and the examination came off in the evening. Lance was held to bail in $1000.

The next morning we proceeded on and took breakfast with with Allen. Amanda was not well. We arrived at Springville in the after noon & I staid all night with Bp. A. Johnson.

Thursday 10 Nov 1859. Attended Court at provo at 10 a m The suit against Potter was with drawn and we returned to Springville.

Friday 11 Nov 1859. Went to provo, and found that Stewart & Bro had commenced a suit against H. L. Craw & I Potter for $782.16. The defts confessed judget for $553.16 and in the meantime Craw commenced suit against I. & R. Potter for the same amount. Levi Stewart & Bro had sold goods to Craw & I Potter who had undertook to play the merchant, but on finding that bankruptcy was probable Craw sold out to I Potter who was to pay the debts of the firm after a short time Ransom Potter seeing that Isaac Potter his son was in a fair way to fail and he bing surety for him for $600 bought out Isaac so that the object of the last suit was an attempt

---

68. Members of the First High Council in the "Great Salt Lake City fort," who were sustained in the organization of the Stake of Zion the summer of 1847, were: Henry G. Sherwood, Thomas Grover, Levi Jackman, John Murdock, Daniel Spencer, Lewis Abbott, Ira Eldredge, Edson Whipple, Shadrach Roundy, John Vance, Willard Snow, and Abraham O. Smoot, with Albert Carrington as clerk.

New appointments and reorganization were effected thereafter at each general conference as members of the High Council moved to colonize other areas, were sent on missions, died, or for various reasons could not fulfill their duties in this organization. Finally, "At the General Conference held in G. S. L. City, Oct. 8, 1859, the High Council was, on motion, dissolved, because of its members being too scattered to attend to business." A few days later (October 16), a new High Council was organized. For a history of the stake presidency and the High Council in the Great Salt Lake Valley from 1847 until 1887, see Jenson, *Historical Record,* V (January, 1887), 276-81.

to Reach R. Potter who was a man of property. Stewarts wanted their pay and was trying to reach him but could not

This last suit was withdrawn and Ransom Potter gave his note to Stewart & Brother for half the amount recovered against Craw & Potter to be paid one year after date   Stewart & Bro. had the costs to pay in all three suits which amounted to near $100.

In not commencing his suits right he was very unfortunate (I went to pr I staid to nig [crossed out]) Sunday morning I started home and travelling nearly all night got there just before day

The weather had been stormy nearly all the time and hard rain on Thursday night & Friday morning.

Friday Dec 2 1859. The weather has at last cleared off after nearly one month cloudy and wet weather. I have been engaged in an arbitration in which A. O. Smoot is plf and Smith Amy & Fuller is defts about the payment of a note for $2527 which has been pending ever since Tuesday.

Saturday Dec 3rd 1859. attended a trial before the probate where Thomas J. Wheeler was brought up charged with stealing 16 horses and mules in Cedar County There was no evidence to prove the fact but he was remanded to that County for an examination into the case.

This case is said to be connected with with a large gang of horse thieves[69] who are infesting the Territory.

Sunday 4 Decr 1859. To day Emma Brown 3 years old and daughter of John & Levina had her left leg amputated just below the knee by Dr W. France,[70] at my house. Emma is a neice to my wife Alvira   The child has been afflicted with the canker and other complaints the result of which was her left foot mortified & the flesh seperated just above her ankle and hence the amputation.

Saturday 10 Decr 1859. Annother suit before the probate   Graham & Allen vs Herrick on Habeas Corpus. The plff had been tried and condemned by A. F Farr probate judge of Weber County for Larceny with indictment & jury & no other evidence but their own and were sent to the penetentiary one for one year and one for five years. Herrick the shirriff of Weber took them to the Warden who refused to recieve and the shiriff holding on to them they were brought before Judge Smith and discharged.

Monday 12 Decr 1859. To day the Legislative Assembly met in the social Hall and both Houses organized ready for business   I shall not as heretofore undertake

---

69. The large band of horse thieves which operated in the territory may refer to the group of whom John D. Lee wrote on November 12, 1859:

> Reports reached here that one Johnson had Stolen about 150 head of Government Mules. Had in his company Lot Huntington, Cub Johnson, Young Neiber & Chas Flake to assist him, all Mormon boys. One Webb, Jno King & Jno Hamilton with a small co in Persuit of them . . . . On Wed., Nov 16th, another Co. came in persuit of the same thieves. O. P. Rockwell, with the sheriff of Parowan at the head of the Co., came up with the party at Loss vagus . . . .
> Nov. 28 . . . About dark the Sherrif Razer & 10 of the Co. that had been in persuit of the thieves arrived & put up with me. Reported Rockwell back at the Clara, Had with them 4 Prisoners — namely, Huntington, Johnson, Neiber, & Flake. Cleland and Brooks, *A Mormon Chronicle*, I, 222-23.

Evidently the term "Mule merchants" used by a number of writers refer to these and similar activities.

70. Dr. William France was born at Kidderminster, England, July 15, 1814. He graduated from the University of Glasgow in 1841 and practiced for several years in Liverpool, England, where he served an apprenticeship under Dr. Parr, a well-known surgeon of that city.

Converted to Mormonism, France came to Salt Lake City in 1850 and set up a surgical practice; his operation on the three-year-old girl reported here was evidently successful. He died of pneumonia on March 20, 1860.

to give the proceedings daily but in brief remark that nothing unusual transpired

The code of laws prepared by the special committee consisting of 64 Chapters and 556 sections were disapproved.

Sunday the 25 Dec 59. This was as usual here a very happy Christmas with one exception a renconter ensued between W. A. Hickman Lott Huntington[71] which resulted in a shooting match six men being on the side of Hickman and Lott alone some 60 shots fired Hickman & Lott both wounded in the thigh   Hickman thought to be mortally The cause not known.

January 1 1860. New years day came and went without any body being killed. or any ill feeling being manifested

Thursday Jan 19 1860. To night Jos Rodes was killed by Jacen Luce. He was attempting to force himself into a house where Hickman was confined of his wound as above stated, and his enterance being disputed he turned on Luce and stabbed eleven times and died instantly.

Friday Jan 20 1860. The Legislature adjourned to day.   among other bills passed was one re-incorporating the City of Great Salt Lake.

Tuesday 7 Feb 1860. This afternoon a grand party came off at the Social Hall. commencing at 4 p. m Prest B. Young and councillors & the Twelve Gov Cumming and Col Stambaugh & Staff were present I and my wife attended Tickets $10 supper at Eleven p. m.   Dancing till 5 a. m. fine time this and is the Grand Ball of the "Season"

Saturday 3 March 1860. made a trip up City creek kanyon accompanied by wife and 2 sons for the purpose of getting Sarvice berry bushes to plant in my orchard The road was very muddy and we had a very unpleasant trip and came home about two p. m. loaded with the bushes and mud weary enough.

Friday 23 March 1860. The probate Court for G. S. L. County has been holding the march term of its court and the grand jury have found several indictments against several presons for Larceny six persons to wit C. Allen Huntington Moroni Clawson Truelove & Charles Manhard Isaac Neiber and Joseph Covey were indited for Stealing an ox belonging to Philander Bell and were tried this week commencing on Monday and ending last evening.   Miner & Little were attorneys for the People and James Furguson for the prisoners.   Huntington was found guilty and sentenced to one year in the penetentiary, Moroni Clawson do and Eighteen months, and R. Manhard to six months.   The other three were found not guilty.[72]

---

71. There is ample evidence that gangs were organized in Salt Lake City as in many other frontier communities. Hickman, up to this time in fellowship and favor with the church, headed one; Cub Johnson, the California gambler, headed the other and had in his employ several Mormon boys. The Christmas Day fight recorded here evidently grew out of the attempted theft of mules noted above. Hickman's account is from his own point of view, but the reader should know that Jason Luce was his brother-in-law.

For a time the killings follow a pattern: Joe Rhodes killed Frank McNeil; Jason Luce killed Joe Rhodes; Luce was later executed for another murder. A number of the gang were killed by Porter Rockwell in his capacity as sheriff.

72. Elias Smith had named this group on March 17 as having been brought into court in connection with some horse stealing. George Laub's account on March 19, 1860, of this day's court proceedings is a parallel: ". . . at this time there ware Some 7 or 8 of the young men who ware Reckless & theavish put in confindment to await their trial and on Wensday ware Three of them centenced to the Penetentiary for one year & Eighteen months. Albert [Allen] Huntington 12 months Moroni Closen & one of the manhart boys 18 months Joseph Covery & one of the Manhart Sons & ware not convicted[.]" Laub, "Diary," II, 70.

The boys were evidently not kept long in confinement, for on April 3 following Elias Smith wrote: "The prisoners Martin Wheeler C. A. Huntington Moroni Clawson Freelove Manhard

Monday 18 Feb 1861. This morning about ten o'clock my wife was delivered of another son weighing nine and one half pounds. We named him Allen.

Friday 29 March 1861. Abut this time I was taken sick with an attact of erysipelas in the head and more particularly in the eyes   I was dilerious some four week and have no recollection of the treatment I recieved afeter consciousness returned I was blind some two weeks and my hearing impaird but am now appearently as well as ever.

Friday 21 June 1861. Today my two oldest sons Hosea Jr and Eli Harvey were baptized in City creek by Bishop Edwin D. Woolley.

Saturday 30 June 1861. This evening I saw for the first time a comet in the region of the great Bear   It was just after sun set.   The tail extending S. E. and must have been more than 60° in length. and was exceedingly beautiful   This comet was I think larger and the tail longer than the comet of 1858.

Wednesday 10 July 1861. To day the first teligraph pole was errected in this city, connecting the East and the pacific states

Here the principal portion of the Hosea Stout diary ends. A brief part for 1869 is all that is known to exist of the later period of Hosea Stout's life. This small diary is in the Utah State Historical Society. The intervening period of his life has been pieced together from various sources.

---

and William Wesley Wheeler were released from the penitentiary on writs of Habeas Corpus issued by Judge Eckels returnable at Camp Floyd where he discharged them without ceremony or investigation[.]" Mortensen, "Elias Smith," *U.H.Q.,* XXI, 151.

PART V

The Year 1860 to March 2, 1889

THE YEAR 1860 TO MARCH 2, 1889

Part V

This part of the diary covers the period 1860 to March 2, 1889, but differs from the preceding parts due to the paucity of entries for certain years and no entries for the bulk of the period. No diary of Hosea's has been located for the years 1862-68. Of the year 1869, Hosea kept a rather condensed and unexciting journal. For the remainder of his years, 1870-89, no journal has been uncovered.

As with the earlier period, so with his last years, his life's history has been pieced together from various sources.

Hosea Stout's entries for 1860 and 1861 are so brief that it seems appropriate here to fill in items which indicate some of his activities for these years. From the journal of Elias Smith, we find the following:

Tuesday 24. — [April, 1860] . . . Rodney Swazey was brought in accused by an indictment of the Grand Jury of horse stealing . . . . H Stout Esqr appeared as his counsel and asked for a postponement of the trial till the June term on account of witnesses which was granted and he was required to give bail for his appearance in the sum of $1,000 or be committed to prison

Wednesday 17th. — [July, 1861] There was a caucus meeting at the Historians office in the evening at 6 o'clock at which I was present. Hon J. M. Bernhisel was nominated as a Delegate to Congress to be voted for at the election on the first Monday in August. Also D. H. Wells, W. Woodruff A. Carrington, D. Spencer, and F. D. Richards for councellors; and J. Taylor, H. B. Clawson, H. Stout, H. S. Eldredge, E. D. Woolley J. A. Young, J. V. Long, A. P. Rockwood and J. M. Moody for representatives in the Legislative Assembly next to be held in this Territory.

Thursday 25th. — [July, 1861] Having received an invitation from President B. Young, I went with him again to see the operations of the Paper Mill. President Wells was also along with part of his family in his own carriage also F. Kesler Hosea Stout and John D. Parker also with me, had seats in the carriage of the President.

Thursday 3rd. — [October, 1861] . . . The suit between Cummings & Jones and Howard & Bowring progressed slowly. A jury was called to try the case and a verdict rendered at about ten in the evening. On its rendition

H Stout Esqr. Counsel for plaintiffs gave notice that a motion to set aside the verdict would be filed on the meeting of the Court next morning.[1]

The years 1860 and 1861 were troublesome ones, full of problems with the army, the government officials, and gangs of local boys. The Civil War had cut off the supply of cotton from the South, so the Mormon leaders decided to colonize Utah's Dixie and produce their own. At the October conference the names of more than 300 heads of families were read off; their assignment was to settle permanently in the area set aside for the city of St. George.

This, the largest group yet sent out, consisted of men with various skills — farmers and craftsmen in all the building trades, and a sprinkling of teachers, musicians, lawyers, and clerks. Trained both as a carpenter and a lawyer, Hosea Stout was one called to go. No contemporary account of the journey has yet been found; but since in the comparatively short and temporary move south to Nephi in 1858 it had taken four wagon-loads to transport his goods, it might be expected that this move would require at least that many wagons if not more.

The Stout family at this time consisted of the three children of the deceased Louisa Taylor — Elizabeth Ann, thirteen; Hosea, Jr., eleven; and Eli Harvey, nine — in addition to the four little sons of Alvira, ranging in age from eight months to six years. The adopted son, Henry Allen, was also along. A permanent move would require not only food, clothing, and bedding, but furniture, tools, and the library of law books. For the journey Stout also must have had at least two large tents.

The call came on Sunday, October 6. On the 17th following, the "Journal History" of the church notes: "The President said it was his intention to have Hosea Stout, Horace S. Eldredge, and J. M. Moody to return this winter and fill their places in the Legislature." In the light of this announcement, Hosea might have argued that his wife and children should remain in the shelter of their home in the city for the winter and make the move in early spring. But that was not his way. For him a call was to be obeyed promptly.

So it was that Hosea Stout gave his farewell address in the Salt Lake Tabernacle on October 27 and arrived on Cottonwood Creek, Washington County (site of the ghost town of Harrisburg) on November 28. Loaded wagons and loose cows could scarcely make it in less time. Yet ten days later, on December 8, according to the record of Lorenzo Brown and the "Journal History," Hosea Stout spoke in the morning session in the Salt Lake Tabernacle! That means that he could have had only five days, or six at most, in which to set his family up for the winter. This would include clearing land, setting tents, arranging furniture, storing food and seeds, and hauling wood from the foothills several miles away.

The winter of 1861 is still referred to as the time of the "Big Flood," the only time in the history of the area when it rained for forty days. On Christmas Eve it began, and not until February did the skies clear. A woman with eight children, living on a dirt floor with a tent roof, would experience much inconvenience if not actual suffering.

On Monday, December 9, 1861, Hosea Stout was appointed one of a special committee to arrange the printing of the governor's message. Throughout the month he was active in legislative affairs, and when the session closed he remained to represent the southern part of the state at the constitutional convention, to which position he was elected in absentia by the people of Cedar City on January 7. Serving with Stout from that area were Silas S. Smith and Horace S. Eldredge. The convention closed on January 23, 1862.

On February 17, following, the "Journal History" reported that "Hosea Stout has been detained in this city by sickness since the close of the Legislature until

1. Mortensen, "Elias Smith," *U. H. Q., XXI*, 153-54, 260-61, 336.

today, when he started to the southern part of the Territory, where his family are." He was evidently delayed further, because two weeks later he had gone only as far as Nephi, Utah.

The "Journal History" on March 2, 1862, reported that in the town of Nephi "we were favored with short speeches from the following well-known gentlemen: Hon Hosea Stout, Timothy B. Foote, Esq., Dr. Matthew McCune and John Borrowman, Esq., [prosecuting attorney for this county] all in favor of sustaining the Constitution of the State of Deseret . . . ."

On April 6, 1862, the first city election was held in St. George. That evening the new mayor, Angus M. Cannon, met with his council. Among the items of business transacted was the appointment of James G. Bleak as city recorder and Hosea Stout, city attorney.[2]

On April 14 Stout was back in Salt Lake City as representative from Washington County. Four days later he was sworn in as attorney for the United States for a term of four years, his commission signed by President Abraham Lincoln. Dated March 6, 1862, it stated that "reposing special trust and confidence in the Integrity, Ability & LEARNING OF HOSEA STOUT, of Utah Territory, I HAVE NOMINATED, and, with the advice and consent of the Senate, DO APPOINT HIM Attorney of the United States, in and for said Territory . . . ."

His oath was taken before W. I. Appleby, clerk, U. S. Supreme Court for Utah Territory.[3]

That Hosea Stout should take the oath of office for this position and then move to St. George, away from all the duties of the office, with Aurelius Miner acting as his deputy for the entire term, has raised some controversy as to his integrity. It is clear that here as in all his activities, Stout placed his loyalty to the Mormon Church above all else; his obedience to the orders of Brigham Young was prompt and unquestioning. He had been called to Dixie and to Dixie he would go and there remain until he was released.

Hosea Stout received full pay for his office at the rate of $250 per annum, the total amount received being $977.50. A letter from Mr. W. Neil Franklin, acting chief, Diplomatic, Legal, and Fiscal Branch, National Archives and Records Service, dated January 11, 1963, gives full details and adds:

> There is evidence that Hosea Stout arranged to have at least some of the duties of the office performed by someone else. The records of the Department of Justice (letters received relating to accounts, Utah, NA Box 685 contain a letter from Aurelius Miner to the Secretary of the Interior, August 4, 1863), transmitting his accounts (totaling $325) for services as Deputy United States Attorney for Utah with which is enclosed a document signed by Hosea Stout on April 18, 1862, appointing Miner, under authority of a United States statute that he cited (section 14 of an act of August 16, 1856), as "deputy Attorney of the United States in and for the said Territory."
>
> An endorsement on Miner's letter of August 4, 1863, reads: "Substitution Sanctioned & the a/c ref. to First Auditor for examination and *adjustment*. Payt. to be made fr. Jud. fund to Aurelius Miner."

It seems clear that Hosea Stout did not at any time defend the interests of the United States in court. Diaries make no mention of him, and one letter from Judge Thomas J. Drake indicates that he did not. Dated "G. S. L. City, May 7, 1863," and addressed "To his Excellency, Governor Harding," the twelve-page account tells of a case wherein one Mrs. McMillian from England, after joining the Mormon Church and coming to Utah with her two daughters, Agnes and Margaret Lowry,

---

2. Albert E. Miller, *Immortal Pioneers* (St. George, 1946), 43.

3. A copy of this appointment is in the Miscellaneous Papers of Hosea Stout (Utah State Historical Society).

by a previous marriage, had left the elder girl, Agnes, in the care of a friend; and when she returned to get her, Mrs. McMillian found her married to Ward Pack, son of John Pack.

The mother, declaring that Agnes, not yet eighteen years old and hence a minor, should be released from the marriage and allowed to return to the East, took the case to court. The letter of the judge describing his inability to get action, concludes as follows:

> . . . soon after I got to the court Room Ward Pack and his counsel Mr. Miner who assumes in most cases to represent the Government as the appointee of Stout, the U. S. Atty for the Territory, appeared and Agnes attended by two females did also Marshall Gibbs as one having Special Authority . . . .
>
> It is unpleasant — it is painful to know that there is no competent and faithful U. S. Attorney here — and it is more painful to know that the U. S. Marshal now here has no care for the honor of the Government — his whole desire is to get money and to that desire he deems it prudent to play into the hands of the Mormons he is today the advocate and apologist of Mormon mores and not the friend and faithful servant of the General Government. Thus surrounded and destitute of any official support we can do nothing.
>
> With ardent hope for an improvement in our conditions
> I am most Respectfully yours
> Thomas J. Drake[4]

The activities of Hosea Stout during his four-year stay in southern Utah have been pieced together from contemporary sources. Following is a chronological account of all information found to date.

When he rejoined his family in late May or early June, the village of Harrisburg boasted ten families or a total population of forty-one souls. The only permanent home was that of Father Moses Harris. On June 12, 1862, officials of the church from St. George visited and organized a branch to be under the direction of Bishop Robert D. Covington of Washington Ward. The local officers named were James Lewis, presiding elder; Moses Harris and Hosea Stout, counselors.[5]

From July 14 to 26 following, Stout was again in Salt Lake City, a representative of Washington County. Here he served on both revenue and judiciary committees.

Although his family had lived in Harrisburg since their arrival the fall before, Stout himself spent little time there. His appointment in April to be city attorney at St. George would necessitate his moving. The Leeds Ward record noted that "On August 24, Hosea Stout had been called to live at St. George and Mosiah L. Hancock became a counselor in his stead."[6]

The activities of Hosea Stout are recorded by James G. Bleak, the official stake historian in St. George, the first mention of Stout being: "Sunday, Sept. 7, 1862. The morning meeting at St. George was occupied under the Presidency of Apostles Orson Pratt and Erastus Snow, in giving instructions relative to the Ordinance of laying on of hands to confer the Gift of the Holy Ghost on some 39 members who had been baptized the preceding Fast Day, [Thursday] 4th, by Apostle Orson Pratt.

4. U. S., State Department, Territorial Papers, Utah Series, April 30, 1853-January 3, 1873 (microfilm, Utah State Historical Society).

5. James G. Bleak, "Annals of the Southern Utah Mission [1847-1869]" (typescript, Brigham Young University), Book A, 95.

6. Marietta M. Mariger, *A Saga of Three Towns, Harrisburg, Leeds, and Silver Reef* (Panguitch, 1959), 7.

These baptized members were then confirmed by Presidents Pratt and Snow and Elders Gardner, Carter, Stout, and Bleak."[7]

During the eight months immediately following his arrival, Stout had evidently concentrated upon building a home. On February 8, 1863, Lorenzo Brown, now also moved to southern Utah, wrote: "Sunday at meeting Evening ward meeting at Hosea Stouts."[8] This would indicate that the home was finished and that it had a room in it large enough to accommodate the ward members.

On March 20, 1863, George A. Smith wrote a letter from Salt Lake City telling of difficulties with the government officials, who seemed determined to arrest Brigham Young, but with no suggestion that Stout come up and assume his duties as U.S. attorney: ". . . Marshal Gibbs has done me the honor to summon me as a juror to be in attendance on Monday next at the Federal Court Room in this City; a like honor has also been conferred upon Elias Smith, and six other attaches of the 'Deseret News,' also J. V. Long and T. Bullock in this office . . . . Hon John Cradlebaugh of Nevada, Ex-Judge of Utah . . . not being allowed time to deliver his effusion, was permitted to print a speech at Federal expense; a copy has been received; it is replete with the blackness of hatred; affidavits form the principal part of the matter, which closed up with a quotation from John Hyde, jun . . . ."[9] In all, this letter seems to be telling Stout that he is well off in southern Utah.

If Hosea held any high official position in the church during the first two years of his stay in southern Utah, it is not mentoned. On May 7, 1864, the record shows that "Elder Hosea Stout was chosen a member of the High Council to be the foreman thereof unless John Nebeker comes to reside in St. George." On May 14 "he was set apart by Erastus Snow as above ordered."[10]

At every semi-annual conference thereafter, Stout's name was read first on the list of high councilmen, and the congregation sustained him by vote of the uplifted hand, along with all the general and local authorities.

In this position Stout was sometimes asked to visit the outlying towns. "During the latter part of July [1864] President Snow and Hosea Stout, Walter E. Dodge, James G. Bleak, and David Cannon, also Jacob Hamblin and others visited the settlements on the upper Virgin."[11]

"March 4, 1866 Sunday . . . P M G. A. Smith gave a historical sermon on the church persecutions. He was followed by Hosea Stout . . . ."[12]

"May 13, 1866 Went up to the Bowery Brother H. Stout spoke on the corruption of the Government officials sent to Utah. Felt to curse them in the course they had pursued to us as a community, and I think he was right in his premise."[13]

Soon after his term as United States attorney had expired, Stout was given a formal release from his mission:

Great Salt Lake City
June 1st, 1866

Hosea Stout, Esq.,
St. George
Dear Brother

It is by the suggestion of President B. Young that I write to you to have you return with your family to this City with a view to practice Law for our people and the City. We need your services in this respect, and hope that

7. Bleak, "Southern Utah Mission," A, 101.

8. Lorenzo Brown, "Journal," II, 459.

9. A copy is in the Hosea Stout, Miscellaneous Notes 1829-1869 (typescript, Utah State Historical Society; original, Lafayette Lee, Salt Lake City), VIII, 149.

10. Bleak, "Southern Utah Mission," A, 143, 145.

11. *Ibid.*, 167.

12. Lorenzo Brown, "Journal," II, 530.

13. Charles L. Walker, "Journal of Charles L. Walker [1854-1899]" (12 vols., typescript, Utah State Historical Society), VII, 420.

it will be agreeable to your interests and meet with your favorable consideration.

Should you conclude to come please advise us by return or first mail how soon we may expect you.

> With kind regards,
> I remain
> Your brother
> DANIEL H. WELLS[14]

One additional item completes the record of Hosea Stout in St. George: "November 4, 1866 . . . As Elder Hosea Stout, Member and Foreman of the High Council of the Southern Mission has removed to Great Salt Lake, it was moved, seconded, and carried that he be honorably released."[15]

The four years in the southern part of the state had brought some changes in his family. His daughter, Elizabeth, at the age of seventeen, had been married as a plural wife to Isaiah Cox. She remained in St. George to raise her family in the adobe home which her father had built. Stout's wife, Alvira, had borne a fifth son and her first daughter, the latter arriving on June 5, just ahead of the letter-of-release from the mission.

Mid-summer would not be a good time to leave Dixie since the grain harvest would be on in July, the fruit and grapes at their best in August, and two cuttings of alfalfa due before fall. Family legend says that the Stout family arrived in Salt Lake City in late September — just before the October conference.

For the year 1867 little information has been found. The following, however, does seem very significant:

> January 25, 1867
> At 1 o'clock Brigham Young met with a Council of Elders at the City Hall. There were some 40 present. The following persons had not met in this Council before: Edward Hunter, Hosea Stout, Dr. Jeter Clinton, Abraham O. Smoot, John Sharp, Robert T. Burton, George J. Taylor, David P. Kimball, Parley P. Pratt, Jos. Rich and Chas. Kimball, Several of the Elders spoke.[16]

This list is interesting chiefly because, with one exception, the names all appear on the 1880 roll of the Council of Fifty. The one exception is George J. Taylor, who was replaced by his brother, William Whitaker Taylor.

References to Hosea Stout in 1868 include the following: the territorial appropriations bill allowed him $13.00 for services rendered; he was named district attorney at the regular term of court which opened the second Monday in March; he was also listed with the municipal authorities as city attorney.

On May 23, 1868, Stout took an important step in his life, when he had Sarah Cox Jones, sister of Isaiah Cox, sealed to him. Isaiah Cox had married Hosea's daughter, Elizabeth. Sarah was the widow of David Hadlock Jones, who had been killed by Indians on May 29, 1865. Sarah was the daughter of Sarah Pyle Cox and Jehu Cox, and was born February 28, 1832, at Greencastle, Indiana. No children from her first marriage are mentioned.

Sarah had no children by Hosea Stout but was to prove a kind and affectionate "auntie" to those of Alvira. Family legend says that Allen Edward, who was a sickly child, became her special care; in later life he always said that he had two mothers.

Hosea Stout was present at the meeting held at the city hall on October 15, 1868, which led to the organization of the Zion's Co-operative Mercantile Institution.

14. Stout, Miscellaneous Notes, 152.
15. Bleak, "Southern Utah Mission," A, 235.
16. Stout, Miscellaneous Notes, 256.

He was listed as "Judge Stout," and his name appears fourth on a list of fourteen. These fourteen named first did not include the presidency of the church who came into the meeting after it was in progress. ". . . the meeting adjourned until tomorrow morning [October 16] at 10 o'clock, to re-assemble at the City Hall, when all those who have subscribed for stock in the proposed Co-operative Association are requested to attend, that steps may be taken for properly organizing."[17]

Friday January 1, 1869. The advent of the year was announced by the ringing of the great bell at the city Hall The weather is warm and pleasant Some little snow on the ground The Rail Roads are approaching us with unprecedented rapidity Union Pacific is now completed so that the cars come about one third of the way down Echo Cañnon. Every thing morally, socially, politically, religiously through out this Territory seem to unusually quiet and peaceable.

Spent the day in my office attending winding up the arbritration case of Webb the Bankrupt[18] V Prest B. Young & Sharp and Young which had been pending since last June

The day passed off quietly and not drunks enough to pay the police for arresting them

Saturday 2. This morning finally settled the arbritration matters & paid the award of $794.49 to Webbs Assignees. Also getting up an application for a Pattent for Snow Plow for E L Erixzon. The weather keeps open and warm and cloudy

Sunday 3. Spent nearly all day in my office isted of going to church looking up the patent laws to see on what terms an alien could obtain a patent or if at all, which I think is very doubtful.

Monday 4. Spent most of the day in office on the subject of that Patent and am not satisfied yet if we can make it succeed to our liking.

The weather is fine clear & pleasant like spring warm & still remarkably so.

Tuesday 5. The weather and my occupation same as yesterday

Wednesday 6. Weather as yesterday only sone colder Engaged in the office as yesterday

Thursday 7. Fine warm Snow last night Some two inches deep. Engaged in the office as yesterday

Friday 8. Attended probate Court in the case of Pine V B. L. Adams & spent the whole day in determining the question whether Ben Lovern should be admitted to testify on the grounds of interest which question was at 8 o'clock P. M Submitted and held under advisement by the court till 10 a m tomorrow.

Saturday 9. Snowed some three inches more last night. Engaged all day in case of Pine V Adams and case submitted to the jury at dark with instructions for them to bring in a Sealed virdict Monday at 11 o' A. M.

Sunday 10. At home nearly all day. Alvira is badly afflicted with rheumatism in the hip

17. *Ibid.*, 257.

18. This Webb, the bankrupt, is Gilbert Webb, eldest brother of Ann Eliza, Brigham Young's wife who gave him so much trouble. As early as 1866, Gilbert had been engaged in freighting, having at that time a train of ten wagons and sixty mules as well as some ox team outfits. In an enterprise to get out telegraph poles he borrowed heavily, and when he could not meet his obligations, was forced into bankruptcy. William H. Hooper, Utah delegate in Washington, D.C., held some of the notes. Webb later moved into Arizona, where he was mayor of Pima for a term. He died in Colonia Juarez, Mexico, in 1923.

Hon W H. Hopper our delegate left for Washington

Monday 11. This morning at 11 A M the jury in the case of Pine V Adams brought in vidict of $800 and same against Adams. Miner gave notice of appeal.

The Legislature met at 10 a. m and proceed to organize the two houses and got ready for Gov message at 11 a m to morrow. I spent the day mostly in my office

Judge Drake Started for Provo this morning accompanied by by Judge Z Snow as prosecuting atty of Utah and C. H. Hempstead U. S. Dist Atty and also Ter Dep Marshal Richd McAllister who had in charge Chancery Millard charged with the murder of Mr H. P. Sroutt some where west of Lehi in Utah County, and west of Jordan

Tuesday 12. Spent the day in the office

At 11 A. M the Gov sent in his message to the Joint session of the Legislature Mr Secratary Higgins as acting Governor's message was a very good one, and I was well pleased with.

I presented to the chairman of the Committee on Judiciary of the Council "An act regulating Service of Process in certain cases This act is intended to provide for service on foreign Corporations and non residents who who do business & have property here as by the now existing laws they can not be brought into court.

Wednesday 13. In my office again to day and very busy now a days.

The trial of Millard before Judge Drake in Provo was had, found guilty of the murder of Swett and sentenced to be shot at Provo on the 29th instant

Thursday 14. To day occupied as yesterday

Friday 15. Snowing sleightly this morn. In the office nearly all day

Elder Ira Ames one of the oldest and best members of the church died at 8.25 a m at Wellsville

Laying of the track of the U. P. R R reached Echo

Saturday 16. Spent most of the day in the office and was out but very little

To day the Iron Horse arrived at Echo City at the mouth of Echo Cañon and within 40 miles of this place while the track layers are going ahead.

Sunday 17. At home all day with Alvira who is still suffering with inflammatory rheumatism and which keeps changing in her hips legs and feet. The pain and suffering is most excruciating.

Monday 18. At the office nearly all day

Tuesday 19. Engaged as yesterday Sent in a bill to appropriating _____ dollars to chief justice for extra duty as judge of the 3rd judicial District to the council.

Wednesday 20. Still Engaged in my office collecting.

Alvira's rheumatism is nearly cured so at least that she can now begin to walk

Thursday 21. Engaged in the office.

Augustus St. Clair died She was a lecturer Had come here and was taken sick and died before she could deliver a lecture

The U. P. track reached Slate Point 9 miles below Mouth of Echo.

Friday 22. Engaged in my office.

Saturday 23. Engaged as yesterday.

Sunday 24. Attended church in the fore noon Elder Marion Lyman preached.

In the afternoon attended a furnel meeting at 13th Ward Assembly rooms on the occasion of the funeral of a Miss St Clair who in company with her father were travelling

She was a lecturer on education &c. Arriving here she was taken sick and after an illness of eight weeks died yesterday. President B. Young preached her funeral sermon

Monday 25. Engaged in my office.

Tuesday 26. Engaged in my office

Wednesday 27. Engaged in my office
This evening I attended a party at the 13th Ward Assembly Rooms got up for the benefit of John H. Rumell for money paid by him for building the Hall

Thursday 28. Engaged in my office.
Hugh McCowan prosicuting Attorney for Tooele County entered on a course of Study of legal Study for a short time that he may be better prepared to discharge his duty, a thing very necessary in all our Counties

Friday 29. Engaged in my office.
About 11 o'clock Chancy Millard was duly executed by being shot in pursuance of the Judgement of Drake's Court He was shot by direction of the Shiriff of Utah County.
Elder Harman Cutter of West Jordan another faithful old Saint died.

Saturday 30. Engaged in my office

Sunday 31. At home all day

Monday February 1, 1869. Engaged in the office

Tuesday 2. Ditto

Wednesday 2. Engaged in my office
Elder Simeon Carter of Brigham City one of the first Elders died

Thursday 4. Engaged in my office and collecting some little for myself.

Friday 5. In the office

Saturday 6. In the office

Sunday 7. At home all day afflicted with erysipelas which seems to attack me whenever we have a change of weather.

Monday 8. In my office today. My health is some better to day
Commenced using Dr Burton's tobacco antedote said to cure and entirely eradicate all desire for Tobacco in a few days
I am trying the experiment and will either prove the antidote to be a nostrum or cure myself of the use of tobacco.

Tuesday 9. Office as usual. Warm Snow last night two or three inches deep. Notwithstanding the soft changeable weather my health is improving

Wednesday 10. In office as usual Weather very warm & muddy. All else quiet.

Thursday 11. In my office to day

Friday 12. In my office nearly all day.

Saturday 13. Snowed two or three inches last night but weather warm. Warm, thawing and muddy.
In my office nearly all day. Red letters and Laws of Cong of Hon H Hooper to day.

Sunday 14. At home and only attended prayer c and walked out a little

Monday 15. Wrote letters to Hon W. H. Hooper and several other persons In office to day.

Tuesday 16. Had a severe attack of the Cholera Morbus last night and am only just able to be in my office

Wednesday 17. In my office all day

Thursday 18. In office and in the evening attended theater.

Friday 19. At office nearly all day

Saturday 20. At office nearly all day.

Sunday 21. Staid at home and wrote letters to Judge Wilson & A. M. Stout a supposed relation at Washington D. C and also wrote to other friends
   A very cold drifting snow fell last night and the coldest weather we have had this winter

Monday 22. In my office all day.
   The Legislature of Embryo State of "Deseret met to day as is the custom after the adjournment of the Territorial Legislature.
   This is to keep alive the State organization of 1862 untill Congress shall pass an enabling act for the admission of Utah into the union.

Tuesday 23. In the office and in fact I have hardly been any where else during office hours, this winter

Wednesday 24. Weather is moderating again so that we can say we have had our three cold day in February. Engaged in my office again

Tuesday 25. The weather being more pleasant I was running around town considerably to and much less in my office and in the eveing went with Alvira to the Theatre as saw forcibly represented the "Grecian Bend."
   The Navajoes made a raid on Harrisburgh drove of 40 head of stock

Friday 26. At my office and shopping at Eldredge & Clauson.

Saturday 27. Quite busy in my office

Sunday 28. At home nearly all day The weather is fine and lovely

Monday 1 March 1869. At the office nearly all day.
   Zion's Wholesale Co-opperative institution commenced today.
   (United States Land office opened today.
   Elder G. Widerborg died
   The Indians made a raid in Round Valley and captured [crossed out])

Tuesday 2. In the office. There was a warm soft snow falling verry fast all day till about 3 o'clock when it cleared off and was very warm

Wednesday 3. In the office as usual

Thursday 4. In the office as usual
   The inaugural address of President U. S. Grant was transmitted here and printed and distributed at 4 o'clock P. M.
   This evening Judge gave an entertainment at his residence to the members of the Salt Lake City bar in honor of the inauguration of Grant to the Presidency, at which I attended until about 11 o'clock p. m.

Friday 5. In the office as usual

Saturday 6. do. and in the afternoon attended "School of the Prophets"

Sunday 7. attended meeting in the fore noon   In the after took a long pleasure walk with Alvira and Sarah[19]

Monday 8. The District court should have met to day but Judge Wilson not being here, the Gov. fixed the 26th April next as the time for beginning the said court.

The Rail Road cars having passed through the Snow drifts which have delayed them some three weeks and brought the mail and passengers to the terminus now near Ogden City about twelve stages filled with passengers arrived to day.

The Iron Horse reached Ogden in the afternoon to day, and it was a gay time there on the occasion.[20]

The U. S. Land office opened.[21]

Tuesday 9. Settled suits pending in the District Court against Wells Fargo & Co & in favor of McNight, Cloggy and Peterkin [f]or injuries recieved by Stage coach running against a wagon in which they were riding

Settled for two thousand dollars.

Also attend a suit befor Justice Clinton wherein Robert Caldwell was brought up for seduction.

Maj Hempstead & myself for deft who was held to Bail.

Wednesday 10. Attended to business around town and in my office.

Thursday 11. In my office but in the after went to west side of the 15th Ward to look at a lot which I may take in exchange for my place in St George

Friday 12. At my office mostly all day. Wrote several letters or began them

Saturday 13. At the office as usual. My boys are putting in the garden this week and planted peas &c

Sunday 14. Engaged in my office on pressing legal business

Monday 15. Raining and snowing mudy and unpleasant went to Court House business there put off The rest of the day in my office

Tuesday 16. Snowed all night Snow about 6 in deep this morning & still snowing a little.   In my office Afternoon warm & pleasant.

Wednesday 17. Rainy bad muddy weather Attended Probate Court to day and then in office as usual

Thursday 18. Weather muddy and lowring At my office mostly to day.

Friday 19. Rainy day. Began suit in Probate Court Marshall and Carter v William Showell. Rest of day in office

Saturday 20. Rainy, muddy   At office. Attended School[22] and was appointed in connection with J. C. Little and A Miner a committee to regulate and attend to the

---

19. This is the first time Stout has mentioned his wife, Sarah. The going for a walk with both of his wives would indicate that there was a friendly relationship between the two women.

20. The arrival of the train in Ogden would greatly change conditions in Utah. Not only the handcart companies but the long freight trains of oxen and mules were now displaced.

21. Soon after the Mormons arrived in the Valley of the Great Salt Lake, their leaders had the land surveyed and divided into uniform lots within the city and fields in the valley. From these the men highest in authority selected the ones they wanted; others drew numbers from a hat to designate their property. This plan was used in the outlying settlements, the bishop issuing deeds, and the men assuring their right to the land by helping with the community ditches and dams in proportion to their holdings. The coming of the railroad and the opening of a land office in 1869 made it necessary for each owner to have his holdings validated.

22. Under the Pacific Railroads Act, the railroads were given alternate sections of land along their right of way except where property rights were already vested in private citizens. This

tracing the old lines of the U. S. Survey of the Public lands preparitory to checking and filing homested and pre-emption claims and town sites &c taking it all in all it is a big job for the land matters in this Territory are in very confused condition

This evening the committee met in my office where it was arrainged that surveyor Genl Fox would commence immediately to retrace find and reestablish the lost corners of the U. S. Survey.

Sunday 21. This evening my wife's brother David H. Wilson Alvira's brother and Hannah Mariah Drake arrived for the purpose of getting maried. Wrote letters and did not attend church.

Monday 22. In my office perusing the land laws.   David and Mariah Drake were married

Tuesday 23. Engaged in office as yesterday

Wednesday 24. Engaged as yesterday.

Thursday 25. Engaged as yesterday My boys have been gardening since Tuesday.

Friday 26. Engaged as yesterday. Annother Cold rain Storm set in this morning from the N. W.

Saturday 27. Engaged as usual and in the after noon attended The School at the Tabernacle.

Indians made a raid in Round Vally captured 100 horses

Sunday 28. Spent the day at home with my family and writing letters.

Monday 29, 1869. In the office nearly all day.

Tuesday 30. There is an unusual heavy Snow raging with light wind from N. W. I think this is the heaviest Snow Storm, that has fall this winter and in consequence I kept colose to my office.

Wednesday 31. Stormy wet muddy and snowing

At Probate Court obtained Judgt against W Showell for $407.33 and in favor of Marshall & Carter

Thursday 1 April, 1869. Weather clear and fine.   Looks as if the storm was over. Laboring in my office.

Friday 2. Weather still fine and seems settled.   Am in office again.

Saturday 3. Storming again and very disagreeable

Hosea and Eli returned home this fore noon from St George whether they have been this last winter[23]

Sunday 4. At home nearly all day Attended P. circle at noon

Monday 5. At home and in my office. People are beginning to come to conference while the weather is also very favorable for them.

Snow Slide in Mill Creek. Killing three persons and injuring several others

---

meeting of the "School of the Prophets" was called to protect the rights of members who were on missions or otherwise absent or unable to protect their own. The members of the school were also to assist their brethren who did not know the procedures in laying claim to their lands. See "Journal History," March 20, 1869.

23. Hosea, Jr., and Eli had remained to live with their sister in the family home at St. George. Isaiah Cox evidently purchased it later, for Elizabeth continued to live in it until her family was grown.

Tuesday 6. Conference began   I attended   much good instruction was given and several Elders called on missions

Wednesday 7. Second day of conference as yesterday   Several more Elders called on Missions.

Thursday 8. Third and last day of conference   Several more Elders called on missions about fifty in all

Eli Bennett & wife and Allen Weeks son & daughter[24] Staid with me during conference.

Friday 9. Attended Probate Court and in my office at the land business

Saturday 10. In my office at Land business

Sunday 11. At home till afternoon then took a walk to West side of town.

Monday 12. In office engaged in Land business

Tuesday 13. As yesterday

Wednesday 14. Cold windy rainy weather. In office again
John V. Long found dead in the streets.[25]

Thursday 15. Cold windy hard from the South I office as usual.

President Young and a large company started to day on a tour South to Dixie

Friday 16. Hard South wind yet   occupied as usual

News has reached here that Elder F. B. Woolley was murdered some where toward the head of the Mohave about a mile from Denlap's Station supposed to be by Indians on the 21st march last[26]

The body after some day was found and taken to San Bernardino and enclosed in a zinc coffin to be sent home to St George, where it arrived this morning.

Saturday 17. South wind yet and like rain Engaged as usual.

Sunday 18. At home weather being bad.

---

24. These people were relatives of Stout's plural wife, Marinda Bennett, who died at Winter Quarters.

25. John V. Long was born September 28, 1826, in Wickersburg, Yorkshire, England. In 1852 he was acting as reporter for the general conference, and for the next fifteen years he traveled often with Brigham Young and his parties in visiting the various settlements. At the April conference of 1861, he was made a member of the High Council; at the April conference of 1866, he was dropped from that position, but with no reason given.

The 1860 *Salt Lake City Directory* lists him as "Long, John V., Attorney at law and Collector, 13 ward, 2 East between 1 and 2 South." Family legend says that he fell out of favor with President Young when the president asked him who he thought was the best speaker in the church, and he answered, "Orson Pratt." Long had also become too fond of liquor and wine and having attended so many private meetings and conferences, could not be trusted to be discreet in his talk. The *Deseret News* for April 14 reported that he was found lying face down in the ditch, the inference being that he had fallen in a drunken condition and drowned.

The obituary in the *Deseret News* for April 21 shows that he was not now considered a member of the church: "Funeral of J. V. Long Esq. — The funeral obsequies of this gentleman took place at his residence at 10 o'clock this morning. There was a large number of his friends present, who evinced deep sympathy for the bereaved family. The assembly was addressed by Elders W. S. Godbe, S. W. Richards, and Bishop E. D. Woolley. At half past eleven the procession left for the cemetery."

26. Franklin Benjamin Woolley was born June 11, 1834, at Rochester, Columbiana County, Ohio, and was killed by Indians on the Mojave Desert on March 20, 1869. His remains were disinterred and taken to St. George for burial. A full account of the murder, signed by Edwin D. Woolley, a brother, is in Bleak, "Southern Utah Mission," A, 291-94.

Monday 19. In my office and looking after Hooper's house vacated to day by A. Gilbert In the afternoon a man performed the feate of walking a tight rope across Main street and trapezing &c.

Tuesday 20. Cold and Snowy with N W wind Kept in the office closely to day

Wednesday 21. Ground covered with snow this morning and snowing briskly all day and myself keeping in my office

Thursday 22. (Cold and snow from N. W. & [crossed out]) Kept in office closely. Warm and cloudy snow. melting fast

Friday 23. (ground covered with Snow this morning and snow briskly all day which keep me close in office [crossed out])
Fine clear warm clear day Snow fast and streets drying very fast. Engaged as usual

Saturday 24. Fine weather   attended the School of P. spoke on the subject of Pre-emption and Homestead
Another performance on the tight rope and Trapez by Houne a Sorry affair not worth looking at.

Sunday 25. At home nearly all day but attended Circle.

Monday 26. To day commences the District Court and the Judge C. C. Wilson has not returned from Illinois and we are all anxiously looking for him He came at about 8 o'clock p. m and adjd Court till to morrow. and barely saved the term from a lapse.

Tuesday 27. Attended D. Court The day was spent in organizing the grand jury and naturalizing foreigners

Wednesday 28. Clear, Cold and hard E wind Eli commenced to work for Col J. C. Little to learn the Black Smith trade

Thursday 29. Court Settled the B L. Adams vs Pines to day by agreement

Friday 30. Court met called the Docket and adjd

Saturday 1 May, 1869. Very busy on land business all day

Sunday 2. At home and at office writing

Monday 3. Busy in & about my office To day two Penetentiary prisoners Cook & Watson attempted to disarm their keepers when out at work and escape were Shot and killed

Tuesday 4. Land, Land, Land business

Wednesday 5. District Court at ten I settled and struck from the docket the case of Gilbert & Hurd v Burt et. al. being the result of a compromise.
Nathaniel Riggs of Provo died

Thursday 6. District court again I had no case called to day. Like for rain Hosea Jr went to Kaysville to try and take up a piece of land & make him a farm.

Friday 7. Land Land business people are entering and Homesteading their Land very rapidly —

Saturday 8. Rainy at my office till noon then attended the School of the Prophets & Spoke on Pre emption and Homsteads and its incidents

Sunday 9. Went with Sarah to the first ward about 12 Blocks to look at a house which I have been talking of buying but do not like the place

Elder John Neff Sen of Mill Creek died.

Monday 10. At noon the last spike in the great Pacific Rail road is to be drove at the Promintory which is to be the finishing stroke to road All the principal Cities in the Union are in waiting for the tick of the wires announcing the fact when simultaneously the great event is to be duly celebrated

at just ½ past 12 noon the wires ticked the road finished and it was answered by firing cannon and we in common with the rest of the nation commenced celebrating.

Had a mass meeting and big and little speaches at the new Tabernacle and a good dinner at the city Hall, where I celebrated the occasion in a manner worthy of myself. The city was illuminated at night.

Tuesday 11. In my office Land Land yet. President Young and company arrived at home to day[27]

Wednesday 12. Land affairs as usual

Thursday 13. Still Land Land.

Friday 14. Attended District Court. Willie and Briggie are taken down with the measles

Saturday 15. District Court Engaged in the defence of three men charged with murder

Sunday 16. Engaged in preparing to plead tomorrow in the case of Branagan, Howard and Leviele the three men charged with the murder of Russel at Wausach and in the afternoon heard a Mr Allen methodest minister preach in the Tabernacle He professed to believe the doctrines of morminism as he had heard it to day.

Monday 17. All the rest of my children, Eli Lewis, Brigham, Alfred, Allen, William and Alvira are now down with the measles.

Engaged all day with Baskin arguing in demurrer to the indictment against Branagan et. al. which was overruled by the court.

The first sod was cut by President Young for the Utah central Rail Road at Ogden from whence it is to come to Salt Lake City[28]

Tuesday 18. Attended D. Court The case of Branagan et al the parties plead not guilty.

Wednesday 19. District Court. and I returned to the Land business. Hosea came home yesterday from Kaysville with the measles.

All my children are now down with the measles with the exception of Allan who has nearly recovered

Thursday 20. At District Court but no business coming on which I was conserned in came back to land matters

Friday 21. At Court but left having no business called up and was then at office at Land again

---

27. Brigham Young and his party had returned from a tour of the southern settlements and so missed both celebrations of the coming of the railroad, the one at Ogden earlier and the one at Promontory Summit the day before.

28. The Utah Central from Ogden to Salt Lake City was built by the Mormon Church under the direction of Brigham Young and was later extended to the Utah Southern. See Arrington, *Great Basin Kingdom*, 270-75.

Saturday 22. Beautiful rain last night My children seem to be recovering from the measles finely

Sunday 23. At home most of the day Eli & Briggie are much worse to day and to night while the symptoms of disease are bad Was up nearly all night attending to them

    Rained hard all night.

Monday 24. Wet drizzly day. Eli is better this morning but Briggie condition is criticle. Office business.

    The Register of the land office received notice that the Rail Road land is withdrawn from market.

Tuesday 25. Drizzilling day and some times raining hard.

    Tried the case People v Tasky for shooting Westlake. Baskin & myself for defence case went to the jury to report in morn

Wednesday 26. The Jury in Tasky's case brought in a virdict of two years imprisonment. The trial Branagan, Howard and Laville for murder of C. F. Russell commenced to day Baskin & myself for defence. Jury was empannilled and one witness examined.

Thursday 27. Case of Brannagan and others continued The evidence for the prosecution (continued [crossed out]) closed and the defence not having any witnesses closed also.

    Barnabas L. Adams died very suddenly in City Creek Cañnon where he with several others were at work. They were eating dinner he had just finished a hearty dinner and with some victuals unswallowed in his mouth fell over backwards and expired without a word or groan. He was one of the Presidents of the Eleventh Quorums of Seventies.

Friday 28. The case of B. and others was argued by council to day and at 6 p. m went to the Jury who returned a virdict of guilty of murder in the first degree

Saturday 29. At the office and otherwise attending to leagal and land business

    The weather begins to clear up and my children to amend

Sunday 30. Staid at hom and in the afternoon took a look as several different places. offered for sale in the city.

Monday 31. Distritc Court Motion in arrest of judgement argued in case of Peope v Branagan et. al.

Tuesday 1 June 1869. Court again adjd till Sat

Wednesday 2. In office Land land land

Thursday 3. At office as usual

Friday 4. At office business and land

Saturday 5. District Court the Court overruled the motion in arrest of Judgement in the case v Branagan, Howard & Lavelle and sentenced them to death by being shot on the 26th July next

    I was engaged in land entries the rest of the day.

Sunday 6. At home and writing letters and land land land

Monday 7. Engrossed in land matters Called on for counsel by Martin Taylor. Case seduction

Tuesday 8. Land as yester day.

For the last week have been getting Pre emption claims at the rate of about 15 or 20 through the Register's office each night after office hours for the small fee of 50 cents each   addition and Pre emption for myself the S. E. ¼ of S 33 T. 1 S. R 1 W

Wednesday 9. Was present at the presentation of Gen Hancock[29] and friends to President Young

Thursday 10. Had to keep at home tolerably close to day and done very little business

At 35 minutes past 9 o'clock P. M. Alvira presented me with her sixth son which weighed eight pounds and called his name Frank Henry Stout

Friday 11. Went over Jordan eight miles to see my land and was well pleased with it.
Left Hosea there to recieve a set house logs which I paid $100 for.
Elder Heman Hyde died

Saturday 12. At and about office to day

Sunday 13. Writing letters, attended Prayer circle and at home.

Monday 14. At Probate Court and office

Tuesday 15. At Probate Court and at office

Wednesday 16. At Probate Court and at office

Thursday 17. At office and home

Friday 18. At Probate Court & office
Hosea and Jonathan Smith went over Jordan to put up the house on my Pre empted land. It is of logs 14 x 16 feet.
The Pacific Circus opened to day in City Hall lot.

Saturday 19. At the office mostly Hosea and Jonathan returned having put the house up to the square

Sunday 20. Had a visit from my old friend T. B. Foote this morning and went to meeting to hear the Rev. Dr Todd of Massachusettes preach.

Monday 21. Engaged in office

Tuesday 22. Engaged in office

Wednesday 23. At office   Mrs Howard mother of Charles Howard now under sentence of death and who is in the city prison called and had an interview with her unfortunate son in my office.   It was a scene which I hope I may witness but seldom. She lives at Denver.

Thursday 24. At office.   Mrs Howard and her son there during the afternoon

Friday 25. Engaged in Land office. Hon W. H. Seward and his party was being showed around the city and at 3 p. m. took lunch at the city hall   at night went to

---

29. This is General Winfield Scott Hancock, who in 1880 was to run for President of the United States against James A. Garfield. Of his visit the *Deseret News* of June 16, 1869, said: "We were pleased this morning to meet Major-General W. S. Hancock in command of the department of the North West. He is accompanied by his staff . . . . General Hancock is now on his way to Montana, . . . but has left the direct line of travel for the purpose of visiting our world-renowned city.   He expresses himself as pleased with what he has seen . . . . The distinguished party called on Prest. Young this morning and had a very pleasant interview. They will remain in this city until Saturday next."

Theater to see Hartz perform his illusions.

The first company of emegrants pr Rail Road reached ogden

Saturday 26. At Land office most part of the day

Sunday 27. At home nearly all day

Monday 28. Opperating at land office for people from Cache County   Dun Custello's managare was paraded through town this fore noon and in the after noon was commenced the exhibition on the 8th ward Square

Tuesday 29. Engaged in land office put 8 through children went to circus to night

Wednesday 30. Went to Circus this after noon

Thursday. Engaged at land office all day

Friday 2 July, 1869. Engaged in land office.

Saturday 3. Engaged in land offices today.

Sunday 4. At home and at my office

Monday 5. The glorious fourth was duly celebrated today yester being Sunday.   The turn out was uncommonly large grand and pompous in the extreme

Tuesday 6. Engaged in land land land

Wednesday 7. Engaged in land business

Thursday 8. Engaged as yesterday

Friday 9. At just 8 this morning my little son Frank Henry died after an illness of four days gangreene having set in before his death   he was buried at 4 p. m.

Saturday 10. Engage in office as usual

A large company of political and merkantile men came in from Chicago and had audience with president Young, on commerce and politicks.[30]

The plotts of the United States survey for Township one South South and one east and Township one North and one East were filed in the Registers office to day which subjects the same to the right of Pre emption and homestead

Sunday 11. At home most of the day only went to Townsend House to see some of those politicians and merchants.

Monday 12. Supreme Cou't met at ten and adjourned till Wednesday.

An attempt was made to enter the warm Spring land in opposition to the right of the city to enter it.

Tuesday 13. The mayor of Salt Lake City entered by pre emption only four sections of the City plots and including the 80 acres filed on by Nelly Robinson[31] for the Warm Spring

---

30. These are evidently the men mentioned by Linn: "When in July, 1869, a delegation from Illinois that included Senator Trumbull, Governor Oglesby, Editor Medill of the *Chicago Tribune,* and many members of the Chicago Board of Trade, visited Salt Lake City, they were welcomed by and affiliated with the Gentile element."

A report of the interview between Senator Lyman Trumbull and Brigham Young is included. See William Alexander Linn, *The Story of the Mormons From the Date of their Origin to the Year 1901* (New York, 1923), 556.

31. Nellie Kay Robinson, christened Ellen Kay, was the third living ⟨ ⟩ ghter of John Kay, the well-known iron and silversmith who was a popular musician of Nauvoo and Salt Lake City. Her mother was Ellen Cockroft, the first wife. Her father had died September 27, 1864, en route

Wednesday 14. Supreme Court again met and the case of People V Branagan et al. appeal, called up for argument Z Snow & C. H. Hempstead for the people and N R Baskin J. W. Towner for deft I took no part in the argument. The day was occupied by Baskin.

Thursday 15. Fore noon occupied by Baskin and afternoon by Snow, in the Brannagan case

Tuesday 16. Fore noon occupied by Snow afternoon by Hempstead which closed argument for the people

Saturday 17. Whole day occupied by Towner who closed argument for defts
Saw and was introduced to two Sons of Joseph the Prophet Alexander and David Smith who have come here to preach the Doctrine that Joseph the son of the Prophet is his lawful Successor.[32]

Sunday 18. Attended Church the fore noon and P. Circle after noon at home

Monday 19. District court, but had no case called in which I was interrested, except a motion to set aside service in the case of Nounan v U.P.R R
Bought wagon from Watt Sleater and Ajax for 191.80 [$191.80] it being a retainer.

Tuesday 20. D. Court but none of my affairs came up; only ruling of court sustaining the service as argued yesterday

Wednesday 21. At my office and land office. Hosea and myself were vaccinated to day

Thursday 22. The Supreme Court ruled in the case of People V Brannagan et. al. Setting aside the judgement of the Dist Court and remanding the prisoners back to the Court below to be dealt with according to law. Ch Justice Wilson dissenting.

Friday 23. District Court again.

Saturday 24. The Glorious 24th was duly celebrated. The procession was too immence for me to describe but as usual all went off well

Sunday 25. At church in fore noon Elder Geo Nebeker of Sandwick Isles gave an acc of his labors followed by Elder J. H. Napela a native who spoke in his own langague

Monday 26. At office defended W. H. Moulding for Larceny &c He was committed

---

home from a mission to England, and was buried on the Plains some seven miles west of Little Laramie.

Mrs. Robinson's husband, Dr. J. King Robinson, had come to Utah as assistant surgeon of the California Volunteers and had decided to establish himself in Salt Lake City. He took up land around the Warm Springs to the north of the city and prepared to build a hospital there but met great local opposition in the form of acts of vandalism on his buildings. On October 22, 1866, he was called out near midnight ostensibly to set the broken leg of a friend, but was knocked down and shot dead at the corner of Main and Third South streets in Salt Lake City. None of his assailants were ever identified or brought to justice.

In this entry Stout says that the mayor of Salt Lake City has filed on the eighty acres which Mrs. Robinson's husband had claimed.

32. From the time of the death of Joseph Smith, his wife Emma had insisted that the leadership of the church should pass through the family. For a time both Sidney Rigdon and William Smith supported her in this claim. Many of the influential men of the church before the death of Joseph Smith — William Marks, John E. Page, and others — wandered for several years before they attempted to unify into a "Josephite" branch of the church.

A preliminary reorganization was held at Zarahelma, Wisconsin, in 1852, but the official beginnning of the Reorganized Church was on April 6, 1860, when Joseph Smith, III, was elected as president. David T. Jones, *Vintonia*, V (Vinton, Iowa, 1945), 27-31.

Tuesday 27. At office & District Court

Wednesday 28. At District Court Nounnan v U.P.R.Road motion to Strik out part of the complaint argued.

Bought Span gray horses of G. C. Riser for $225.00 cash.

Received telegram from my Daughter Elizabeth that her child was very sick.

Thursday 29. Busy in my office in chancery suit making out Interpleader in Executors of Estate of Horacks V B Young sen Trustee &c.

This evening Eli was vaccinated and Hosea's vaccination is rendering him unable to work

Friday 30. Attended Probate Court and attended to some little business before grand jury because Z. Snow the P. Atty was otherwise engaged.

Saturday 31. Dist Court Nounnan vs UP.RR. Plf had leave to amend. An unusually good rain this evening

Sunday 1. August, 1869. At home and writing letters Letter from my niece Lydia Griffin Her husband Charles at Coalville has the Small pox which is now somewhat prevelent there

Monday 2. Fixing wagon and team for hosea to draw poles, posts, and wood

Tuesday 3. Went to the Farm with 3 of my boys and Br I Ivins to survey and establish the corners which we did of the land.

Wednesday 4. At District Court Nounnan v UPRR. Plf had leave to amend

Thursday 5. Engaged in gitting up suits vs Nicholas Rumell and in favor of Prest B. Young., The P. E F Co and Trustee in Trust.

Friday 6. Engaged in the business of yesterday. Cloud burst in City Creek

Saturday 7. District Court again and Nounnan v Rail Road on demurrer argued and held under advisement.

Sunday 8. At meeting in fore noon and P C. and home afternoon.

Monday 9. Court over demurrer but allowed plf to amend this brings the R. road to answer.

Tuesday 10. Writing in my office

Wednesday 11. A Probate Court Case of Horracks will argued.

Thursday 12. Argueing case of Horracks will again.

Friday 13. Engaged writing in office.

Saturday 14. Office business

Sunday 15. Attended Church in forenoon at home rest of the day

Monday 16. Very busy in office

Tuesday 17. Very busy in my office

Wednesday 18. Verry busy in my office

Thursday 19. Verry busy in my office The finest and most copious rain this evening and night I have seen an years.

Water spout burst in American Fork Cañnon doing much damage.

Friday 20. Making digest of the Collection laws of Utah

Saturday 21. Examining and correct the proceedings of Utah Central Railroad Company.

Sunday 22. Attended church this morn
An unusual number of Senators and members of Congress present.[33]
Henry G. Boyle redurned missionary and G. Q. Cannon spoke
Was only at part of afternoon service   G A Smith spoke

Monday 23. At the C.P.R.R. business all day.

Tuesday 24. Engaged as yesterday.

Wednesday 25. Engaged as yesterday though I was very sick and had to quit work Another heavy rain last night.

Thursday 26. Engaged in my office My heath much improved

Friday 27. Engaged as yesterday.

Saturday 28. Engaged as yesterday

Sunday 29. Meeting fore noon and then P. C.   visited G D Watt eat peaches and made self sick

Monday 30. To sick to do business but was at D. Court then in bed, at office and bed again Spent restless night

Tuesday 31. Some better but weak at office and around some on business
Attended Theatre to hear hear George F. Train's second lecture here Very rich affair

Wednesday 1. September, 1869. At office and around again

---

33. The *Deseret News* for August 25, 1869, published the following account:
OUR DISTINGUISHED VISITORS. — Late on Saturday evening the joint Congressional Committee on Retrenchment, accompanied by a number of invited guests, reached this city in three special coaches. The members of Congress consist, on the part of the United States Senate, of Hon. James W. Patterson of New Hampshire, Hon. Carl Schurz of Missouri, Hon. Allen G. Thurman, of Ohio; on the part of the House of Representatives, Hon. M. Welker, of Ohio, Hon. J. R. Reading of Pennsylvania, Hon. Jacob Benton, of New Hampshire; also D. F. Murphy, Esq., Clerk of the Committee, and J. I. Christie, Esq., Sergeant-at-arms. The committee was accompanied by Hon A. G. Cattell, U. S. Senator of New Jersey, Hon. J. S. Morrill, U. S. Senator from Vermont and a number of ladies and gentlemen.
Yesterday the party attended the morning and afternoon services at the Tabernacle, and to-day they visited President Brigham Young, took a walk around his grounds . . . . Accompanied by a number of our leading citizens they also visited the Tabernacle, the Theatre, the City Hall and other places and objects of interest in our city . . . .
This afternoon they again started on their journey westward to San Francisco . . . .
In sharp contrast to the *Deseret News* report, which ends on a happy note of wishing well, is the one made by Tullidge. He indicates that after a pleasant meeting with President Young, the group joined the Gentiles of the area, and:
. . . their council on Utah affairs was held at the residence of Mr. J. R. Walker . . . . Over forty persons were present . . . . There was, they say, that day "the fullest and freest expression that had ever occurred in Utah," all of course with a strong, decided anti-Mormon animus and aim. "Everybody gave vent;" "war talk ran around;" Senator Trumbull related to the company that famous conversation between him and President Young, in which the latter had said to the effect that, if the Federal officers didn't behave themselves, he would have them ridden out of the city; and from this meeting the report of that conversation between Senator Trumbull and President Young ran throughout the United States; and gave to Vice-President Colfax the advantage to push General Grant almost to the verge of actual war against Mormon Utah. Such was the bearing of that counsel held at the house of Mr. J. R. Walker, over Utah affairs in July [sic], 1869. (Tullidge, *History of Salt Lake City*, 396-97.)

Thursday 2. Engaged in the office.

Friday 3. Engaged in the office. At 7 p.m. Elder Ezra T. Benson fell down deat at Ogden in an apoplectic fit as was Supposed   He was in his usual good health and spirits to the moment when he fell.

Saturday 4. Engaged in the office and running around on business untill noon and then attended the School.

Sunday 5. At meeting in for and after noon and P. Circle.

Monday 6. office and running after business transactions.

Tuesday 7. As yester day.

Wednesday 8. Last evening the city Council reduced my salary from sixteen hundred dollars per annum to twelve hundred whereupon I sent in my resignation as city attorney[34]

Thursday 9. Attended probate Court in two cases appealed from Aldermans Court for selling Spirituous liquor without lisence   Motion to reverse Judget [Judgement] in court below

Friday 10. Prbate Court refused to reverse the judgt case set for trial tomorrow at 9 a. m.
John Goddard Son of George was drowned in Jordan while bathing

Saturday 11. The two city cases came up on the merits in the Probate Court upon an agreed statement of facts and was argued.

Sunday 12. Not well taking cold, at home took night Sweat, better in morn

Monday 13. District Court Sept Term grand and pettit jurors called about 2/3 of each present Hoge v Hawley Quowarranto to see who is judge.
Probate Court in the 2 city cases ap overruled one and sustained the other.

Tuesday 14. Did not attend D Court but making arraingement consequent upon my resignation as City Attorney.   The City Council accepted of my resignation.

Wednesday 15. Moved my office and Library from the City Hall to my House

Thursday 16. District Court Judge decided in case of Hoge v Hawley that Hawley was Judge
was retained by Bates in two cases vs the U.P.R.R. Co in a sum of about $20,-000.00 each.

Friday 17. D Court The case of Nounnan &c v R R again up on motitan to strike part of Reply also a Demurrer to another part.   argued and submitted

Saturday 18. D Court again. no business. No grand jury yet not having a full panel in attendence.
Very rainy and cold wind. And by the way this same week day is my 59th birth day.

Sunday 19. At home all day.

Monday 20. D. Court again no quorum of G. Jury. Court overruled the motion to strike out and sustained the demurrer to Reply to defts answer in Nounnan &c v U. P. R R. Co.

---

34. Stout's persistent poor health for the week before might have been a contributing factor to his resignation as city attorney though his hurt pride at the large reduction in his salary was the real reason. This no doubt marked the beginning of the end of his public service.

Indians made a raid on Fairview San Pete County and drove of 18 horses

Tuesday 21. D. Court again 3 grand jurors lacking and C. adjd.

Wednesday 22. Grand Jury completed and went to business
Found bill vs Snellgrove for violation of Int. Rev law. for making and selling shoes and boots without license
First case under Rev laws.
Track laying on the Utah Central Rail Road.

Thursday 23. Grand jury found bill v Kilfoyle for murder of Frazier

Friday 24. D Court going on still

Saturday 25. D. Court going on.

Sunday 26. At home to day makeing use of Sunday to commence a Suit against Hussey Dalker & Co for $40,000 in favor of B. Y.

Monday 27. D Court again no trials yet

Tuesday 28. D. C. again as yesterday

Wednesday 29. D Court. Grand Jury found another bill against Brannagan Howard and Levelle, and were then discharged.

Thursday 30. People vs James Kilfoyle for the murder of Thos L. Frazier at Waunship was taken up. Hempstead Atty for deft. I am on the prosecution with Z Snow.
The witnesses were examined

Friday 1 October, 1869. The case of Kilfoyle was taken up and the testimony of all the witnesses taken and court adjd.
Sleight shock of an earthquak felt at Fillmore

Saturday 2. Killfoyle case ready for argument I should have made the opening plea on part of prosecution but did not. I was only able to attend Court and had to return home. Scarcely able to get there totally exhausted with diarhea of some four or five weeks standing

Sunday 3. At home all day too weak to travel around.

Monday 4. At home Sick Father Cox and his two wives and Benj Jones arrived to day and put up here for conference

Tuesday 5. Still very sick Isaiah and my daughter Elizabeth arrived to day from St George

Wednesday 6. Sick sicker The conference met which with my sickness and the croud of people who have come here makes it very disagreeable to me

Thursday 7. Conference and the croud yet My disease took a turn for the better to night

Friday 8. Conference still going on I am better and kept out of bed all day Albert Carrington was appointed an Apostle in place of Ezra T. Benson, deseased.

Saturday 9. Conference still in session
Isaiah and my daughter Father Cox and his folks & B. Jones all left for home
I am much better and went to the Post office in the eve but the trip was too much for me.

Bought of Milo Andrus a Small farm of about 13 acres in Holladay'sburgh 9 miles S. E of this City on which is a large peach and apple orchard and a house with five rooms[35]

Sunday 10. At home all day but very weak

This evening I sent a letter to Mayor Wells that all things considered I would hereby tender my services to Salt Lake City gratis It will be seen that I resigned my office as City Attorney on the 8th Sept

Hosea and Eli moved out to the farm which I bought yesterday of Andrus They expect to keep bachelor's Hall for the present while they work on the place.

Ex president Franklin Pierce died at Concord

Monday 11. This morning I was called on by the said City to act under my offer of gratuicious services in the cas of Elmer vs Harris a contested land claim before Register & receiver where I spent the day.

Tuesday 12. Closed the contested land case mentioned yesterday

Wednesday 13. The contested land case between the City and Nellie Robinson for the W half of S. W ¼ of Sec 25 North Range one West Commenced before the Register and receiver today Baskin & Hempstead for Nellie and A. Miner and myself for the city

Thursday 14. District Court the demurrer in the Nellie Robinson City case was argued

Friday 15. Court sustained the demurrer in the Nellie case and (plfs all [crossed out]) defts allowed to amend their answer.

The contested land case was also continued in the land office

The case of People vs Popper in the court was laid over to next term.

Saturday 16. The case of City v Nellie K Robinson in the land office was resumed to day.

Sunday 17. At home making out the argument in the case of Elmer v Cox & Harris in the land office.

Monday 18. The City vs Robinson in land office progressing to day

Tuesday 19. The testimony in the City v Robinson closed at noon

Wednesday 20. Went to the new bought farm at Holladaysburgh which I purchased of M Andrus and was well suited with it.

Thursday 21. Engaged in making the argument in the City — Robinson case

Friday 22. Engaged as yesterday

Saturday 23. Finished said argument attended School of P.[36]

---

35. This is the final Hosea Stout home, good pictures of which are extant. A part of the house still stands.

36. The School of the Prophets was first organized in Kirtland, Ohio, in February, 1833, ". . . in which institution of learning the Elders made good progress in the knowledge of God." Jenson, *Historical Record*, VII (January, 1888), 407.

At this time the school was concerned with spiritual and supernatural things, and ". . . many important and instructive meetings were held, in which the Saints were favored with great and glorious manifestations of the power of God. The gift of tongues was enjoyed by many of the Elders in a great measure, and the ordinance of the washing of feet, according to the practice recorded in the 13th chapter of St. John, was attended to by the Elders." *Ibid.*, V (May, 1886), 63-64.

The School of the Prophets was organized in Salt Lake City in December of 1867 and was composed of over 900 leading adult males, with branch "schools" established in all the major

Sunday 24. At home nearly all day

Monday 25. High Council to day Wm. S. Godbe and E. L. T. Harrison are up for apostacy and cut off from the church[37]

Tuesday 26. Went to Farming Wife & I visited Jonathan Smith. I was on some business for J. W Hess.

Wednesday 27. Came home again

Thursday 28. doing very little

Friday 29. (Came home again [crossed out])

Saturday 30. Bought another piece of land adjoining that which I bought of M Andrus on the south end and back of the road Three acres with some apple and peach trees on it.
Bought of A. Olesen but deeded to me by Milo Andrus.

Sunday 31. At home and at P. C at 12 o'c Indians raiders took horses from Kanarra Filing answer in Warm Spring case.
(Another old Saint John Woodland died aged 95 [crossed out])

Tuesday 2 November, 1869. As yesterday.

Wednesday 3. As yesterday

Thursday 4. Completed said answer

Friday 5. Reviewing Mr Baskins arguments in the Warm Spring case

Saturday 6. Wrote the closing argument in the contes land case of Salt Lake City v N. K Robinson

---

outlying settlements. Not a school in the usual sense, it served more as a forum or town meeting in which social and economic problems were discussed, policies adopted, and plans worked out for community betterment.

In the Salt Lake area it was concerned with the effects of the coming of the railroads and with the business of creating cooperative ventures. In smaller towns it determined prices and hours of working on the irrigation ditches, bridging ditches, graveling streets, hauling wood for the meeting houses, getting the community Christmas tree; in short, it discussed and planned community ventures. Arrington, *Great Basin Kingdom*, 245-51.

37. The excommunication of William S. Godbe and E. L. T. Harrison brought into the open differences that had been smoldering for some time. As early as May 20, 1860, John D. Lee had written: "A conspiracy has been detected against Brigham Young, the Man of God. Jno. Banks, T. D. Brown, Clayton & Candland & others are implicated in the Clan, whose names will hereafter be made publick." Cleland and Brooks, *A Mormon Chronicle*, I, 255.

The difficulties were essentially economic. From the time the people arrived in the valley, Brigham Young had encouraged a society based upon agriculture and manufacturing and had discouraged mining. Now with the coming of the railroad and with the opening of mines operated by non-Mormons, the question arose: "How far should Brigham Young or the church leaders control a man's economic life?"

Some of the most brilliant and articulate members of the church were members of this dissenting group who, in defiance of counsel, continued their mining and independent business investments.

The first issue of *The Utah Magazine* appeared on January 17, 1868. In it Elias L. T. Harrison, the editor, contended that Utah's economic future must depend largely upon its mineral resources. From that time until the excommunication here recorded, the group had been active, both through the press and public meetings, in setting forth their views.

Among those who joined with William S. Godbe and Elias L. T. Harrison were Eli B. Kelsey, Edward W. Tullidge, W. H. Shearman, Henry W. Lawrence, John Banks, and others, all of whom had been loyal and active members, effective missionaries, and leading citizens. Most of them had plural wives. Details of the controversy with biography and a statement from each man involved, are given in *Tullidge's Quarterly Magazine*, I (October, 1880), 14-86.

Sunday 7. Rainy and warm

Monday 8. Commenced correcting the Records &c of the Central Utah Rail Road company

Tuesday 9. ditto

Wednesday 10. As before

Thursday 11. do and raining

Friday 12. As before Still rainy

Saturday 13. do — do Utah Central R. Road is completed to Kaysville.

Sunday 14. Rainy and me doing nothing only staying at home

Monday 15. Went to Gardner's mill on the Jordan 16 miles away, to attend a law suit A D. Heat on V R Watson I went on the part of W. Case withdrawn
    Came home most of the way in a driving snow storm in my face.

Tuesday 16. Attending to business for R. Pixton. Leasing his storeroom

Wednesday 17. Raining all day At home

Thursday 18. Raining steadily all day.

Friday 19. ditto

Saturday 20. At school in after noon

Sunday 21. At home The first Excurtion train passed over the Utah Central[38]

Monday 22. District Court Judge Strickland presiding Could do nothing because the clerk had not made up the record of last Court

Tuesday 23. Same difficulty as yesterday

Wednesday 24. Same difficulty as yesterday and court adjourned till Monday

Thursday 25. Rainy snowy me doing but little business

Friday 26. Hard freeze last night and cleare this morning
    At and about home

Saturday 27. At and about home

Sunday 28. At home, Snowing brisk.

Monday 29. 3 inches Snow last night D. Court adj'd to Wednesday

Tuesday 30. D Court again adjd to 20th Dec

Wednesday 1 December, 1869. Weather better. running around business to day

Thursday 2. This Evening Joseph Hammond's wife and two daughters arrived from St. George.

Friday 3. Around on business

Saturday 4. Settling the land title between Barnaisel & Randall

---

38. The Utah Central Railroad extending from Ogden to Salt Lake City was constructed by local contributions and contractors. Later it was extended south as far as Nephi. Arrington, *Great Basin Kingdom*, 270-82.

Sunday 5. Staide at home Isaiah Cox came with Martha Cragun[39] This makes six persons and seven animals quartered on me. In all a crouded house and corral.

Monday 6. Isaiah was married to Martha to day
Utah Central permanantly finished to Farmington

Tuesday 7. Isaiah Started for home this morning.

Wednesday 8. Hammond wife and daughter left for home leaving Elizabeth here

Thursday 9. Eli came from the farm to day
business for R D Swazey

Friday 10. Business for McLelland in the land office

Saturday 11. Obtained a pardon for Aug. Tusky.

Sunday 12. At home all day.

Monday 13. Hosea Jr and Elizabeth Hammond was married
Bought another piece of Land from William Howard which adjoins the land I Bought of Andrus and paid $250.00 for it This little farm now contains about 18 acres and has about 90 apple trees on it
Indians drove off 100 head of horses from Parowan

Tuesday 14. Sarah and myself went with Hosea and his wife to duly install them in their home on the farm I bought of M. Andrus.

Wednesday 15. Was engaged with Hosea & Eli in raising a log stabl

Thursday 16. Came home again.

Friday 17. Around on business.

Saturday 18. At home mostly

Sunday 19. At home all day.

Monday 20. Attended D. Court but not much done

Tuesday 21. At home sick all day. Could not go out Neuralgia in the teeth and jaw.

Wednesday 22. Able to go out some on business

Thursday 23. Quite well collecting with considerable success.

Friday 24. At home Hosea and wife came here on a visit Preparing for Chrismas

Saturday 25. Kept Chrismas at home all day

Sunday 26. Kept myself at home being badly afflicted with Neuralgia in the teeth and face.

Monday 27. Am going out on business matters some little

Tuesday 28. Laid up all day with neuralgia

---

39. Isaiah Cox married first Henrietta Janes in 1856; he married Elizabeth Stout in 1865 and now Martha Cragun in 1869. The first wife bore him nine children; each of the other two bore eight. Martha wrote an autobiography in which she explained her reasons for entering plural marriage and told of the complications of life on the frontier under these conditions. She always spoke of the other wives with much affection, saying that they were "dearer far than sisters," and referred to Isaiah as "our" husband. Martha Cox, "Autobiography [1814-1932]" (typescript, Utah State Historical Society).

Wednesday 29. do

Thursday 30. Laid up all day feverish & scarcely able to set up.

Friday 31. Still laid up   had a tooth pulled which seems to relieve me some little

Saturday 1 January, 1870. I now commence my journal for the coming year in the last years blanks

With the close of this diary, we must again piece together the events of Hosea Stout's life from other sources. It would seem that he still carried on business as a lawyer and an adjuster of land claims.

Samuel W. Richards mentions him a number of times: "Sept 9, 1870 . . . I was all day in High Council, till 9 p.m.   Case, Bishop A. Cahoon vs H. Stout & Simeon Atwood."[40]

Richards, writing on page 386 of his diary says: "By request of Prest Wells & H. Stout I called upon Mrs. Tate at the Delmonica Hotel and enquired into the circumstances by which she was there and making application to G. B. Maxwell of the Register's office, for property from her divorced Husband to support her children . . . ."

Samuel W. Richards' other entries all have to do with land claims:

29 May [1871] Issued warrants for C. R. Taylor & J. H. Picknell, for taking water . . . . With Hosea [Stout] about land.

31 May [1871] . . . . Team came from farm with Hosea abt Orrs Claim.

June, Fri 9   Called on Prest. Wells abt Land.   Called by H. Stout abt it.

Thur 19 [October, 1871] Returned from farm.   Called to see Hosea Stout, A. Miner &c.   Just heard High Council Met but could not attend.   With Committee witnessed trial of the Fire Engine on Temple Block.

Oct 1871 Sat 28 . . . . About 5 P.M., D. H. Wells, Hosea Stout, & Wm Kimball were arrested by the U. S. Marshal and taken to Camp Douglas, on indictments for murder . . . ."[41]

Words of this arrest scattered far and wide, with writers from all parts of the state noting it. John D. Lee, now in Kanab, Utah, awaited word, since rumor had said that "all Hell seemed to boil over about Salt Lake City."

When Bishop Levi Stewart and Jacob Hamblin returned, Lee wrote: "Sat., Nov. 10th [11th], 1871 . . . . Reported that Pres. B. Young at St. Geo., Closely persued by officers & soldiers, only 6 hours ahead. Lawyer [Thomas] Fitch Notified Pres. B. Y. to make his escape or he would be arrested before Midnight. Then Fitch went to the city of Washington to lay our case before congress. Gen. D. H. Wells, H. Stout & W. H. Kimball arrested & in custody at camp Douglass. Wells was let out on Bail of $50,000, Jennings & Eldridge sureties . . . ."[42]

The *Salt Lake Herald* for October 29, 1871, reported: "The indictment charges Daniel H. Wells and Hosea Stout, among others with having on the 15th of Novem-

40. Samuel Whitney Richards, "Diary [1846-1886]" (3 vols., typescript, Brigham Young University), II, 359.

Andrew Cahoon, son of Reynolds Cahoon, had been a member of the Nauvoo band which played at the capstone ceremony at the temple; since 1854 he had been bishop of South Cottonwood Ward, to which the Union Ward was added in 1865. He served until he "apostatized and was discontinued as Bishop in 1872." Jenson, *Historical Record*, VI (December, 1887), 334.

Whether or not his leaving the church was connected with this dispute is a matter of conjecture. A family friend, U. G. Miller said, "I have a definite knowledge and am a living witness to the fact that Andrew Cahoon's differences were . . . of a personal nature with Brigham Young." Stella Cahoon Shurtleff and Brent F. Cahoon, *Reynolds Cahoon and his Stalwart Sons* (Salt Lake City, 1960), 133.

41. Richards, "Diary," 410, 412, 420, 421.

42. Cleland and Brooks, *A Mormon Chronicle*, II, 174.

ber, 1857, killed one Richard Yates at the mouth of Echo Canyon in Summit County. There is little doubt that Yates was killed, and it is generally conceded that the notorious Bill Hickman committed the crime." The fact that the date given, November 15, was nearly a month later than the actual date of October 18, 1857, greatly helped the case for Stout.

Hickman's account of his turning state's evidence, a fact which led to the arrests, said: "He [Deputy Marshal H. Gilson] conversed about many cases with which I was connected; and finally elected the case of Yates as the one on which we could with greatest safety rely for prosecuting Brigham Young. I then gave him a full statement of the case and the names of the witnesses that would make the circumstances complete."[43]

J. H. Beadle in editing Hickman's book added: "His [Yates'] remains have been disinterred from the spot named by Hickman, and the chain of evidence is complete. Hosea Stout, a Mormon lawyer of considerable prominence, who was arrested for complicity in this murder, and on Hickman's testimony, admits that Yates was killed *as a spy*; but insists that he was not present and had no knowledge of the transaction; that Yates was delivered to Hickman to be taken to the city, and neither he nor any other officer saw him again."[44]

The facts of the case, as accepted in Mormon circles, were stated by Tullidge: "The said Richard Yates, during the period of the 'Buchanan war,' was taken a prisoner as a spy. He fell into the hands of the notorious Hickman to guard; but it is thought that the murderer, knowing or believing that Yates had considerable money in his possession, at night murdered his victim to obtain it."[45]

In the National Archives, General Records of the Department of Justice, are selected documents from the appointment clerk relating to Utah judges, 1853-1903. The entry for January 31, 1872, deals with the attempts to get prisoners released on bail, Hosea Stout among them, and the judge's speech in refusing to grant the request.[46]

The prisoners were confined in the city hall, where they were allowed to have visitors. The "Journal History" of January 1, 1872, notes that: "Brothers Wilford Woodruff and John Henry Smith called at the City Hall to see Hosea Stout, Brother [John L.] Blythe, Brigham Y. Hampton and Wm Kimball."

On December 1, 1871, Samuel Richards had "Interviewed H. Stout and Wm Kimball at City Hall," and the next day ". . . took a copy of a letter from Land Commissioner abt Jones entry, saw Hosea Stout, how to proceed."

An interesting sidelight on the life of these men while imprisoned is given in the *Salt Lake Tribune* for March 23, 1872.

THE PRISONERS SHINDIG AT THE CITY HALL

. . . When I [Marshal John M. Neall] went as guard of the prisoners, my instructions were to let their friends see them at any and all times. Upon the evening of the dance, ladies with baskets upon their arms . . . came into the room prior to 8 o'clock and by 9 there may have been some 70 persons there assembled. A few moments afterwards they commenced dancing (I among the number) . . . .

Marshal Neall was protesting his discharge on the grounds that he had followed orders but found that he could not be reinstated.

The Mormon troubles of this parictular time had begun with the appointment of Judge James B. McKean, an appointee of Ulysses S. Grant in 1871.

---

43. Hickman, *Brigham's Destroying Angel*, 191-92.
44. *Ibid.*, 204-5.
45. Tullidge, *History of Salt Lake City*, 543-44.
46. (Microfilm, Utah State Historical Society; Series No. 1 of this film is not arranged in chronological order, so that the records of the courts for 1871 and 1872 cannot be more specifically cited.)

McKean was exemplary in his private life, a fine scholar, and a man of high principles. His principles, however, he was willing to sacrifice for the ends to be attained. He set aside the Territorial law governing selection of jurors by lot from the taxpayers' lists, and transferred selection to the U. S. marshal. With the handpicked grand jury thus obtained, he set about scuttling the Mormons. A Salt Lake City alderman and his officers were arraigned before McKean for destroying the stock of the Engelbrecht [sic] Liquor Store, which had violated the city license ordinance. A decision was rendered against the city, with damages in excess of $50,000. By one slender thread the whole Mormon resistance hung: damages above $50,000 could be appealed to the U. S. Supreme Court. Had McKean limited the amount to $49,999.99, the Mormons would have been utterly without recourse before the arbitrary dicta of his court. Carried to the Supreme Court, the decision in the Englebrecht case was unanimously overturned in 1873, and all indictments made by McKean's juries were ordered quashed.[47]

During all this stormy period much was written by both Mormons and non-Mormons. There seemed to be no middle ground, so that the claims of both sides must be considered if one is to come to any understanding of conditions.

After his release, Hosea Stout continued to practice law for a time, but family legend says that he was so beset with ill health that he retired from public life after the death of Brigham Young in 1877.[48] He lived at the home in Holladay, Salt Lake County, Utah, where he busied himself as he could with his books, garden, and the affairs of his family. His wife Sarah died on May 27, 1885. His own death came on March 2, 1889. His wife Alvira outlived him twenty-one years.

The *Deseret Weekly* (Salt Lake City) for March 9, 1889, summarized his life.

At 2:45 a.m., March 2nd, in Big Cottonwood Ward, Hosea Stout, Esq., who has figured prominently in the history of the Latter-day Saints for the past half century, passed from life, the immediate cause of his death being paralysis, with which he had been affected for the past four weeks. He was a native of Kentucky, having been born in Mercer County, September 1810, but migrated when very young to western New York and thence to Missouri, where he embraced the Gospel and from that time shared in the vicissitudes through which the Church passed. He served in the Black Hawk War, taught school in Illinois for a number of years, was intimately associated with the Prophet Joseph Smith for a number of years prior to his death, and for some time acted as his body guard, as well as being an officer of the Nauvoo Legion and chief of police. He came to Utah in 1848, and located in Salt Lake City. He was a member of the Utah Legislature for a number of sessions, also of the City Council, and practiced at the bar, when in the Territory from the time the first court was established here until a few years since, when his health became so impaired that he retired to his farm. He performed a mission to Hong Kong, China, in 1853, was also one of the early settlers of St. George in Southern Utah, where he remained about five years. He was a man of sterling integrity and excellent ability; has filled a long and useful life and leaves a large family — a wife, nine sons and two daughters, besides a large number of grandchildren to revere his memory and emulate his virtues.

47. *Utah, A Guide to the State*, 79.
48. His ill health is corroborated on page 281 in Jenson's *Historical Record*, VI (December, 1887), "At the special Stake conference, held in Salt Lake City, May 7th and 8th, 1887, Alternates Milando Pratt, Henry P. Richards, Jesse W. Fox, Elias Morris and James P. Freeze were sustained as members of the High Council, instead of Thomas E. Jeremy (to be ordained a Patriarch), John H. Rumel (dropped), Miner G. Atwood and Hosea Stout (excused because of failing health) . . . ."

Index

Goaslind, John, 620
Godbe, William S., 723 fn. 25; excommunicated, 735 fn. 37
Goddard, ..., 591
Goddard, George, 563, 732
Goddard, John, drowned, 732
Goddard, S. H., 282
Goddard, William P., 562
Goliah, ship, 490
Goodrich, Peter, 666
Goodwin, John, 466, 467
Goodyear, Miles M., 413 fn. 82
Gordon, Elizabeth, 697
Gordon (Gorden), James, 564
Governor, leg. on, 686
Graham, ..., 705
Grainger, LaFayette, 344
Grant, ..., mission, 445
Grant, George D., 13, 25, 30, 36, 46, 56, 99, 211, 254, 263, 284, 285, 296, 303, 310, 361, 361 fn. 28, 366, 374, 379, 388, 394, 490, 607, 607 fn. 78; adopted son B. Young, 178 fn. 50, 242 fn. 35; met returning pioneer co. (1847), 279; life threatened, 395; mission, 510, 601, 601 fn. 75; rescued handcart company, 606, 607, 625 fn. 88; sergeant-at-arms leg., 609; major gen. Nauvoo Legion, 625; visited Gov. Cumming, 658; fined, 664
Grant, Jedediah M., 136, 161, 194, 208, 214, 224, 232, 335, 337, 354, 355, 356, 357, 383, 387, 451, 452, 453, 503, 529, 534, 547, 548, 549, 553, 557, 564, 577, 603, 613 fn. 81; presided over Seventies, 3 fn. 1; pres. of Seventies, 93; bio. sketch, 93; issuing commissary for Fifty, 144; Cutler's Park municipal-high councilman, 185; committeeman to locate Winter Quarters site, 194 fn. 60; capt. Nauvoo Legion, 197; capt. of Hundred, 231; brig. gen. Nauvoo Legion, 351; 24th of July speech, 355 fn. 25; speaker House of Rep., 384, 532, 569; mayor S.L. City, 387 fn. 51; leg., 402, 444, 524, 559, 599; second councilor to B. Young, 511; board D.A.&M. Soc., 589; candidate for const. conv., 592; died, 608; leg. resolution on death of, 610, 611, 612
Grant, Ulysses S. (President), 720
Grant, William C., 372
Grantsville (Grant City), Utah, petition to incorporate, 576, 577
Great Salt Lake County, see Salt Lake County
Greeley, Horace, arrived S.L. City, 698; impressions of S.L. Valley and Mormons, 698 fn. 59
Green (Greene), ..., 534, 547, 548, 586, 587; leg. committee, 541
Green, Alvin, 563
Green, Ammon, 490
Green & Company, Kenney (Kinney), 537, 554, 561, 591
Green, E. M., 572, 573
Green, Ephraim, 112, 154; wife died, 160; prospected, 353; capt. of Ten Pratt Exped., 365 fn. 34
Green, Harvey, 264, 269, 490, 491, 492, 494, 495; bio. sketch, 489 fn. 29
Green, John, 318 fn. 80
Green, John Y., 375, 376, 549
Green, Moroni, 564, 573, 583
Green River, 325; leg. on, 362, 413, 414, 415 fn. 84, 572, 573, 574, 577, 617, 677, 679; description, 413 fn. 83, 514 fn. 13; controversy over, 441, 514 fn. 13, 520-21
Green River County, organized 516, 516 fn. 17; leg. on, 540, 541, 542, 542 fn. 37, 543, 649, 673, 681
Green, Sarah, 551
Green, William I., 234
Greene, Evan M., recorder, treasurer, postmaster Potawattamie Co., 307 fn. 71
Greenwood, Thomas, imprisoned, 564
Gregory, George, 558
Grewell, Ben F., 372
Griffin, Benjamin, 375
Griffin, Charles, 730
Griffin, Lydia, 730
Griffins, John, 497
Grimshaw, ..., family turned back to Fort Laramie, 604 fn. 77
Grimshaw, Jonathan, 413; assist. clerk S. L. Co., 569
Groesbeck, ..., 645

Groesbeck, ... (Sister), 252
Groesbeck, John, 145
Grouard, Benjamin Franklin, 493; mission, 462, 494; bio. sketch, 462 fn. 18
Grover, ..., leg. com., 545, 610
Grover, Thomas, 117 fn. 69, 271, 208, 613; high councilman, 9 fn. 18, 704 fn. 68; accident on Mississippi River, 114, 117 fn. 69; bio. sketch, 159 fn. 36; operated ferry Platte River, 321 fn. 83; Cutler's Park municipal-high councilman, 185; adopted son B. Young, 242 fn. 35
Groves, ... (Sister), accident, 314
Groves, Elisha H., 287, 288, 296, 299, 302, 324, 326, 414, 415, 416, 417, 420, 425, 531; guard, 253; high councilman, 343
Grow, Almirin, 560, 562, 583, 583 fn. 61, 584, 587, 588, 590, 593; dist. atty. 2nd District, 581; lawsuit to recover custody of child, 664, 664 fn. 31
Grow, Isaac, regent U. of Deseret, 679
Grub and Richie's Store, 59
Guardian and Ward, leg. on., 417, 418, 421
Gully, ..., co. arrived S. L. Valley, 357
Gully, Samuel, 23, 26, 32, 47, 54, 62, 90, 97, 124, 128, 130, 132, 135, 138, 188; contractor of Fifty, 145; adopted son J. D. Lee, 178 fn. 50; adopted son B. Young, 292 fn. 35
Gunnison, John W., 368 fn. 38; arrived S.L. City, 356, 356 fn. 26; see also Gunnison Massacre
Gunnison Massacre, Mormons accused of, 511; investigation ordered, 536 fn. 34; Indians tried for, 553, 554, 566, 567
Guthrie, J. M., 665, 688
Guthrie (Gurthrie), John T., 166
Guyman, N. T., bio. sketch, 123 fn. 1; capt. emigrating co., 561; Parrish murder investigation, 624 fn. 87

Habeas Corpus, leg. on, 422; tested civil and criminal jurisdiction of probate court, 584
Haight, Hector Caleb, 379; bio. sketch, 379 fn. 46
Haight, Isaac C., 224, 379, 379 fn. 46, 571, 572, 577, 613, 649, 672, 674, 677, 681, 682, 684, 685, 686; capt. Nauvoo Legion, 196; bio. sketch, 210-11 fn. 6; child died, 216; capt. of Ten Pratt Exped., 365 fn. 34; pres. Cedar City Wards, 531 fn. 31; leg. com., 610, 674
Hale, A., 520
Hale, Jonathan H., 17, 22, 65, 66, 82; bio. sketch, 10 fn. 20; military exped. (1845), 70 fn. 34
Hales, Charles, 155
Hales, George, clerk of Fifty, 144; public printer, 569
Hales, Stephen H., candidate on opposition ticket, 524; reprimanded by B. Young, 524 fn. 25
Hall, Charles, 459
Hall, David, 494
Hall, Job, 156, 158, 164, 459
Hall, Thomas, policeman fought with U.S. soldiers, 536
Hall, William, 105, 142, 143; bio. sketch, 101 fn. 56
Halyard, ..., 458
Hambleton (Hamilton), Madison D., 10, 11, 190, 241, 656; disaffected with Old Police, 95; killed Vaughn, 393; bio. sketch, 393 fn. 63; trial, 396, 396 fn. 63; notary public Juab Co., 680
Hamblin, Jacob, 655 fn. 26, 715, 738
Hamilton, ..., 70
Hamilton, Andrew, 660
Hamilton, Jonathan, 705 fn. 69
Hamilton, William, 374
Hammond, Joseph, 736
Hampton, Brigham Y., 739
Hancock, Charles, 565
Hancock County, Illinois, 209
Hancock, Levi W., 22, 23, 25, 51, 58, 72, 88, 357, 370, 425; pres. of Seventies, 3 fn. 1, 611 fn. 80; board Seventies Library and Institute Assoc., 12; bio. sketch, 12 fn. 24, 172 fn. 43; trustee Mechanical and Mercantile Assoc., 22, 48
Hancock, Mosiah L., 714 fn. 6
Hancock, Solomon, 173; bio. sketch, 172 fn. 43
Hancock, Winfield Scott (General), visited S.L. City, 727, 727 fn. 29

Hyde, William, 457, 464, 468; bio. sketch, 457
fn. 12; mission, 525

Incorporations, Committee on, *see* Legislative Committees
Independence Rock, 322
Indians, 170, 173, 223, 243, 276, 277, 289, 398, 398 fn. 65, 493, 566; Louis Dana, 35 fn. 65, 152, 158, 205, 269, 461; Joseph Herring, 245; protection against, 248, 249; Stansbury report concerning, 362 fn. 30; court trials, 368, 368 fn. 38, 526, 527, 566, 567, 689, 690, 703; hostilities, 381, 397, 398, 399, 549; leg. on, 363, 365, 426, 427, 428, 428 fn. 94, 430, 533, 678, 681; battle with, 400; slave trade, 412 fn. 81; Fort Supply abandoned because of, 515-16 fn. 16; Ben Simons, 516 fn. 16, 646, 646 fn. 17, 654; Bureau, 520; attacked Elk Mountain Mission, 561, 561 fn. 50; murdered, 564, 567; indicted for Gunnison massacre, 566, 567; implicated in murder of A. W. Babbitt, 601, 601-2 fn. 75; Committee on, *see* Legislative Committees; *see also* Bannock, Cherokee, Cheyenne, Commanche, Delaware, Memorials to Congress, Omaha, Oneida, Ottowa, Pawnee, Piute, Potawatomie, Punckaw, Shoshoni, Sioux, Snake, and Utah Indians
Ingalls, Rufus, 532; trial, 554, 555; capt. U. S. Army, 554 fn. 44
Invincible, ship, 470, 471
Iray, Cyrus, 471
Iron County, 384 fn. 50, 392, 419, 431; organized, 384, 390; B. Young visited, 399, 399 fn. 66; leg. on, 415, 416, 424, 547, 571, 572, 581
Irwin, Thomas, notary public Cedar Co., 680
Ivie, J., court martialed, 317
Ivie, James, 366, 607
Ivie, Thomas, murdered I. Allred, 695, 695 fn. 54
Ivins, ..., 38
Ivins, Israel, 646, 730; candidate for surveyor S. L. Co., 662

Jackman, Ami, arrived Winter Quarters (1848), 309 fn. 73
Jackman, Levi, 627; high councilman, 343, 704
Jacob, Norton, capt. Nauvoo Legion, 197; bio. sketch, 197 fn. 61
Jacob, Sanford, 320 fn. 82
Jacobs, Henry Baily, 141; pres. Seventies, 3; bio. sketch, 141-42 fn. 18; performed plural marriage, 289
Jacques, John, 602 fn. 75
Jame[s], Richard, 668
Jarvis, ..., beaten, 618
Jenne, ..., 594
Jennings & Eldridge, 738
Jennings, Ebenezer, 78 fn. 39, 79
Jenson, Marinus, 560 fn. 49
Jeremy, Thomas E., patriarch, 740 fn. 48
Jett, ..., 524
John N. Gosler, ship, 487, 488
John, Robert Wilson, 452
Johnson, ..., 435 fn. 103, 705 fn. 69; Baptist missionary, 476
Johnson, Aaron, 13, 21, 43, 427, 547, 570, 571, 618, 704; high councilman, 9 fn. 18; in charge of Garden Grove settlement, 161 fn. 39; leg. com., 426, 610; notary public Utah Co., 580, 615; granted control water of Spanish Fork River, 573, 574, 577, 619; Parrish murder investigation, 692 fn. 51, 693 fn. 52; bishop Springville, 694
Johnson, Archibald, 662
Johnson, Benjamin F., 24, 359-60 fn. 27, 382, 418, 428, 430, 464, 465, 546, 577, 579, 588, 612, 613, 661, 675, 676, 679, 682; capt. Nauvoo Legion, 351; leg., 402; leg. com., 406, 610; granted herd ground, 578
Johnson, Cub, 705 fn. 69
Johnson, Daniel, 661
Johnson, George D., 137 fn. 10
Johnson, J. H., 695
Johnson, James, murdered, 697
Johnson, Joel H., councilman Parowan City, 399 fn. 66; chaplain leg., 569
Johnson, Joel H., brother-in-law A. W. Babbitt, 602 fn. 75

Johnson, Lorenzo, 276
Johnson, Luke, 572, 575, 576, 641, 697; operated ferry Platte River, 321 fn. 83; died, 585 fn. 62; judge Shambip Co., 587, 615, 681; trial, 600, 601
Johnson, Lyman E., excommunicated, 15 fn. 32
Johnson, M., 107
Johnson, Oliver, 389
Johnson, Robert, 123, 166
Johnson, Thomas S., 151, 522, 563, 591, 592
Johnson, William, 450
Johnston (Johnson), Albert Sidney, 640 fn. 10, 641, 643, 643 fn. 13, 655 fn. 24, 657, 658, 659, 660, 661, 663; commander U.S. Army for Utah. 645
Johnston's Army, 394 fn. 61, 517 fn. 19; *see also* Utah War
Jones, ..., 24, 112, 131, 521, 711
Jones, ... (Mrs.), 445
Jones, Alonzo, 294
Jones & Company, 594
Jones, Anna Stout, 158, 256, 302, 303, 356, 391, 500, 509, 605, 657, 658; received endowments, 98; left husband, 265; divorced, 362; married, 669, 669 fn. 37
Jones, Ben S., 528
Jones, Benjamin, 6, 11, 17, 25, 29, 30, 35, 37, 44, 45, 46, 53, 92, 98, 103, 104, 107, 111, 121, 135, 146, 158, 159, 160, 164, 166, 167, 176, 177, 265, 733; supervisor of streets 3rd Ward Nauvoo, 19, 27; capt. of Fifty, 124; trial, 303; divorced, 362
Jones, Cornelius, 375
Jones, Daniel W., 367, 370, 372, 627; bio. sketch, 370 fn. 40; account of Yates murder, 643 fn. 13
Jones, David, 564
Jones, David D., 508
Jones, David Hadlock, killed, 716
Jones, Henry, castrated, 653
Jones, J. H., 528, 594
Jones, Jesse, 638
Jones, Lewis, 627
Jones, Nathaniel V., 458, 464, 465, 637, 638, 639, 640, 641, 642, 643 fn. 13, 644, 657; guard for Gen. S. W. Kearny, 272 fn. 51; bishop 15th Ward, 349 fn. 20; councilman S.L. City, 387 fn. 51; bio. sketch, 444 fn. 112; resigned S.L. City council, 450; chaplain missionary party, 458; ill, 461, 462; candidate selectman S.L. City, 662
Jones, Russell & Company, 520, 553 fn. 42, 591
Jones, Sarah Cox, *see* Stout, Sarah Cox Jones
Jordan River, 345, 358, 360; beauty of, 333; settling on, 334; leg. on, 380, 419, 420, 536, 537, 612, 613, 614, 674, 678, 679, 684
Josephites, 729 fn. 32
Juab (Uab) County, leg. on, 417, 418, 426, 431, 539, 540, 542, 543, 545
Judges, 586; leg. on, 686
Judiciary, leg. on, 420, 421, 423, 547, 589, 620, 686; Committee on, *see* Legislative Committees
July 4th, celebrations described, 372, 377 fn. 44 (1850); 401 (1851); 441 (1852); 558 (1855)
July 24th, celebrations described, 355, 355 fn. 25 (1849); 442, 443 (1852); 523 (1854); 634, 634 fn. 1 (1857)
Justice of Peace, leg. on, 420, 422

Kanarra, Utah, 735
Kane, Thomas L., 178, 339 fn. 12, 654, 655, 655 fn. 24, 656, 657; friend of the Mormons, 176, 176 fn. 45; criticized Babbitt's conduct, 556 fn. 45; arrived S. L. City, 653, 653 fn. 20; guards assigned to, 653, 653 fn. 21; left S. L. City for Fort Bridger and East, 659; ill, 663
Kanesville, Iowa, Mormon headquarters, 336 fn. 7
Kay, John, 21, 30, 36, 38, 39, 45, 46, 54, 56, 61, 65, 68, 70, 89, 207, 408, 435, 691, 692; musician, 55; child died, 315; mission, 652; terr. marshal, 679; attended court, 688; commission as marshal not recognized, 689; bio. sketch, 728 fn. 31
Kearney (Carney), Stephen W., commander U.S. Army in the West, 187; selected Mormons as his guards, 272 fn. 51

Lucas, Scott V., 443
Luce, Jason (Jacen), killed J. Rhodes, 706; executed, 706 fn. 71
Lud, Ellis, 373
Luddington, Elam, 109, 117; sergeant of guard Nauvoo Temple, 108; bio. sketch, 108 fn. 64; injured, 124; marshal, assessor and collector S.L. City, 387 fn. 51
Luffkin, ..., 601
Lundy, ..., 130
Lunt, Henry, 459
Lyman, Amasa M., 35, 46, 47, 50, 52, 54, 74, 108, 139, 192, 208, 227, 267, 268 fn. 48, 282, 284, 285, 339, 350, 386, 396, 462, 463, 466, 492, 493, 494, 506 fn. 4, 567, 569, 628, 653 fn. 20, 673, 674; bio. sketch, 4 fn. 3; trustee Seventies Library and Institute Assoc., 12; divided Winter Quarters into wards and appointed bishops, 203; organized co. for move West, 228; pioneer co. arrived S.L. City, 332, 333, 335; directed exploring co., 335; ill, 342; mission, 394, 394 fn. 61; purchased San Bernardino, 464 fn. 19; owned sawmill, 491
Lyman, Clarissa, 524 fn. 24
Lyman, Eliza, 450
Lyman, Marion, 718
Lynch, John G., candidate for selectman, 662
Lynch, Patrick, assist. clerk leg., 671
Lyon, W. P., 58
Lyon's Store, 36
Lytle, A., major Nauvoo Legion, 351
Lytle, Andrew, 10, 24, 54, 63, 90, 140, 466; disatisfaction with Old Police, 95; col. Nauvoo Legion, 365
Lytle (Lyttle, Little), John, 61, 89, 140, 190, 306; disatisfaction with Old Police, 95; capt. Nauvoo Legion, 197; adopted son B. Young, 242 fn. 35; bishop 11th Ward, 349 fn. 20; candidate for leg., 662

McAlister, ..., wagon train, 495 fn. 31
McAllister (McAlaster, McAlister), John T. D., 643, 645, 657
McAllister, Richard, deputy marshal, 718
McArthur, ..., 546, 547
McArthur, Daniel Duncan, 48, 52, 54, 63, 64, 80, 85, 88, 89, 104, 105, 106 108, 135, 143, 145, 268, 498, 661; capt. of Ten, 93; capt. of Fifty, 124, 128; handcart co. arrived S.L. Valley, 601
McArty, Charles F., 667, 700
McBride, ..., 391
McBride, Benjamin, apostate, 318-19 fn. 79
McBride, George, killed, 654, 654 fn. 22
McBride, William, 457, 458, 465, 468, 506, 507; mission, 559; granted herd ground, 610, 611
McCabe, James, 377, 388, 389, 392, 394
McCairey, William, Negro and/or Indian prophet, 244, 244 fn. 37, 304, 304 fn. 70; see also Chubby, William
McCauslin, Jesse, 27, 272, 342; relinquished alcohol, 294
McClanahan, ..., wagon train, 495 fn. 31
McClelland, James, 684, 685
McClure, William, 374
McColey, Benjamin, 440
McConnell, ..., 523
McConnell, E. A., 591
McCormick (McCormack), ..., 664, 666; U.S. dist. atty., 663
McCormick, W. I., opposition ticket for terr. election, 662
McCowan, Hugh, prosecuting atty. Tooele Co., 719
McCullough, Benjamin, 660
McCullough (McCollough), James P., judge Washington Co., 680
McCune, Mathew, 713
McDonald, ..., 519, 644; shot policeman, 667; killed, 668, 698
McDonald, A. F., Parrish murder investigation, 624 fn. 87, 690, 690 fn. 49, 691, 692, 693 fn. 53, 694, 695
McDonald, John, 513
McDougall, John A., Illinois atty. gen., 74 fn. 37, 80 fn. 42
McEll, ..., 396
McEwen, John, 665, 672

McGarry, ..., robbed, 667
McGaw, James, 497, 498; mission, 601 fn. 75, 605 fn. 77
McGouth, James, 527
McGrath, James, 523
McGraw, ..., 555, 557, 562, 563
McGraw, James, 87, 89
McIntire, Marshall, 372
McIntire, W. P., 594; policeman, 303
McIntosh, Daniel, terr. treas., 580
McIntosh, John, 624
McKean, James B., 372-73 fn. 41; judge Utah courts, 739; conflict with Mormons, 740
McKenzie, David, 698; bio. sketch, 698 fn. 58; Deseret Currency engraving plates, 698-99 fn. 60
McKenzie, G., Parrish murder investigation, 624 fn. 87
McKinney, Hugh, granted herd ground, 579, 585, 618
McKnight, James, public printer, 609, 673
McLean, ..., 93
McLean, Hector H., assassinated P. P. Pratt, 628, 628 fn. 9
McLelland, ..., 737
McLelland, James, 82, 88, 90
McLelland, W. E., controversy with church, 336, 336 fn. 8
McLelland, William C., 161, 297
McLure, Charles G., 527
McMichan, ..., 523
McMillian, Agnes, 713, 714
McMillian, Margaret Lowry, 713
McNeil, Franklin E., threatened J. Gheen, 665; bio. sketch, 665 fn. 32; shot, 700, 700 fn. 61
McNight, ..., 721
McPike, ..., 374
McRae, Alexander, 67, 69, 70, 71, 72, 73, 76, 77, 78, 79, 80, 81, 241, 499, 601, 610, 621; capt. Nauvoo Legion, 66; lieut. of co. on exped. against Indians, 263; terr. marshal, 581, 615; leg., 599, 635, 662
McRae, John, 269

Mackeson, ..., 323
Magraw, W. M. F., 553 fn. 42, 599; mail contractor, 600
Mail, leg. on, 421, 430, 431, 572, 575, 589, 650, 652, 681, 686; see also Memorials to Congress
Mains, John, 440
Major, William W., 242, 255, 265, 290, 324; artist, 25; bio. sketch, 25 fn. 52; adopted son B. Young, 242 fn. 35; high councilman, 343
Majors, and Waddell, Russell, 553 fn. 42, 665
Malad County, leg. on, 577, 579, 675
Malad River, leg. on, 571
Malcolm, David, 560, 563
Manhard, Charles, 706
Manhard, Truelove, 706
Manning, Peter (Negro), 168, 178, 182
Mansion House, 9, 26, 33, 34, 66
Manti, Utah, 362 fn. 29; charter granted, 392; organized, 399 fn. 66; leg. on, 537, 538, 545, 582
Mantle, Thomas, 633
Manufacturing, leg. on, 414, 427, 428, 537, 611, 651, 685
Marcy, Randolph B., capt. U.S. Army, 642, 643, 650
Margett, Thomas, apostate, 601 fn. 75
Margrets, Thomas, 562
Margretts, H., 639
Markham, Stephen, 27, 33, 39, 59, 63, 65, 71, 129, 137, 156 fn. 34, 197, 201, 202, 203, 205, 235; capt. pioneer group, 124; capt. of Fifty, 144; col. Winter Quarters military organization, 196; order regarding Winter Quarters City Guard issued by, 204
Marks and Brands, 610; leg. on, 414, 415, 416, 422, 423, 424, 425, 426, 427, 544; recorder, 428, 616; treas., 428
Marks, William, bio. sketch, 20-21 fn. 47; first counselor J. Smith, 154 fn. 32; joined Reorganized Church, 729 fn. 32
Marriage, leg. on., 427, 428
Marsden, William, 702 fn. 64
Marsh, Thomas B., received back into church, 636

Shurtliff (Shirtliff), L. A., 193; cut off church, 268
Shurtliff (Shirtliff), Vincent, 345; councilman S.L. City, 387 fn. 51; granted herd ground, 577, 580
Sidneyism, *see* Rigdon, Sidney
Silver, A. L., dist. atty. 2nd Dist., 429; notary public San Pete Co., 429
Silver Grays, *see* Nauvoo Legion
Simmons, ..., 465
Simmons, J., 639
Simmons, Joseph, 605
Simmons, Samuel, petition to extend Spanish Fork boundaries, 618
Simmons, W. B., 411, 598
Simmons, William, killed, 639
Simonds, James, 530, 530 fn. 30
Simons (Simonds), Ben, 516 fn. 16, 646, 654; Indian messenger, 646 fn. 17
Simpson, George B., 554, 555, 557, 562, 563
Sinclair, Charles E., 666, 678, 697, 700 fn. 61, 702 fn. 64, 704; judge Utah court left for Fillmore, 663; returned S.L. City, 664; explained why troops in S.L. City, 689; left for Camp Floyd, 694; returned S.L. City, 695
Sioux Indians, 170, 190, 233, 270, 282, 298; attacked Omahas, 216, 217, 219, 273; attacked Ottowas, 273; attacked Mormons, 262, 262 fn. 44, 281; destroyed property, 280; friendly, 318; *see also* Indians
Slayton, ..., 432, 433
Sleater, ..., 729
Sloan, James, 628; bio. sketch, 15 fn. 33; dist. clerk Pottawattomie Co., 307 fn. 71
Smith, ..., 408 fn. 78, 669, 670 fn. 39
Smith, Abigail Demont, 369 fn. 39
Smith, Abner, 372
Smith, Alexander, son J. Smith, 729, 729 fn. 32
Smith, Alfred, Gladdenite, 444
Smith and Donald's Store, 299, 304
Smith, C. M., 688, 689
Smith, Charles, granted herd ground, 578
Smith, Daniel, 81
Smith, David, son J. Smith, 729, 729 fn. 32
Smith, Don Carlos, editor *Times and Seasons*, 111 fn. 67
Smith, Elias, 436, 440, 442, 445, 450, 451, 505, 506, 511-12 fn. 10, 513, 529, 551, 560, 590, 597, 601, 603, 625 fn. 88, 634, 695, 697 fn. 57, 700 fn. 61, 701 fn. 63, 705, 706 fn. 72, 715; capt. Carthage Grays, 72; code commissioner, 444, 535; granted herd ground, 574, 575, 579; judge S. L. Co., 580, 615, 680; regent U. of Deseret, 581; granted freedom House of Rep., 674, 674 fn. 43; editor *Deseret News*, 674 fn. 43, 689, 689 fn. 48
Smith, Emma, wife J. Smith, 729 fn. 32
Smith, G. B., 701
Smith, G. S., 424, 425, 459, 541
Smith, George A., 25, 46, 50, 58, 63, 144, 175, 178, 243, 296, 366, 380, 384, 393 fn. 60, 407, 422, 423, 426, 432, 440, 443, 459, 460, 498, 511, 536, 541, 545, 546, 547, 548, 557, 570, 572, 581, 586, 588, 589, 599, 638, 639, 649, 651, 660, 684, 688, 690, 691, 715, 731; organized pioneer co., 228; presided over Pottawattamie Stake, 307 fn. 71; letter on O. Cowdery and other apostates, 336, 336 fn. 8; arrived S. L. City, 358; judge Iron Co., 384; organized Iron Co., 390; leg. com., 422; church historian, 511; granted herd ground 577, 579; regent U. of Deseret, 581; delegate to Wash., 595; left S. L. City, 596; arrived S.L. City, 627
Smith, Hyrum, 10, 23, 512 fn. 12; Mason, 4 fn. 4; eyewitness to murder of, 6, 6 fn. 11; implicated in murder of, 20, 20 fn. 46; supervisor of interment of, 54 fn. 18
Smith, J. N., 572, 582
Smith, James, 562
Smith, Jesse N., dist. atty. 2nd Dist., 615; dist. atty. 1st Dist., 686
Smith, John, 9 fn. 18, 16, 157 fn. 34, 171, 235, 257, 393 fn. 60, 524 fn. 24, 620, 640; patriarch, 51 fn. 15, 332; capt. of Hundred, 144
Smith, John Calvin Lazelle, 497, 531; letter on J. C. Fremont's arrival in Parowan, 508 fn. 7; bio. sketch, 531 fn. 31

Smith, John Henry, 739
Smith, John L., 535, 539, 541, 542, 545, 548; door keeper House of Rep., 404; leg., 524; bio. sketch, 524 fn. 24
Smith, John P., funeral, 29-30
Smith, Jonathan, 508, 510, 727, 735
Smith, Joseph, 4 fn. 2, 9 fn. 17, 10, 23, 45, 350, 462 fn. 18, 481, 512 fn. 12, 551, 740; eyewitness to murder of, 6, 6 fn. 11; nominated for U.S. President, 8; implicated in murder of, 20, 20 fn. 46; bodyguard for, 39 fn. 71; supervisor of interment of, 54 fn. 18; plural wives, 54 fn. 18, 505 fn. 3; store, 348 fn. 19, 595 fn. 68; revealed law of celestial marriage, 450 fn. 2; discovered Book of Mormon, 593, 593 fn. 67; sons established Reorganized Church, 729, 729 fn. 32
Smith, Joseph, high councilman, 704
Smith, III, Joseph, pres. Reorganized Church, 729 fn. 32
Smith, Laura L., 626
Smith, Lott, 642, 643; capt. Nauvoo Legion, 641
Smith, Lucy Mack, 22, 23
Smith, Mary Ettie V., 507 fn. 5, 557 fn. 46
Smith, Orin, 471
Smith, Polly Clark, 369 fn. 39
Smith, S., granted herd ground, 585
Smith, Samuel, U.S. Army deserter, 296, 297
Smith, Samuel, notary public Box Elder Co., 580, 615; judge Box Elder Co., 680
Smith, Silas S., 712; judge Utah Co., 680
Smith, T. S., 508, 541, 545, 547
Smith, Warren, 30, 36. 61, 522, 523
Smith, William (brother J. Smith), 49 51, 57, 58; letter on disposition of W. Daniels, 6 fn. 11; bio. sketch, 47 fn. 8; trouble with police, 49 fn. 10; excommunicated, 57 fn. 21, 85; Mormons disapproved as apostle and patriarch, 81; implicated in Hodge murder, 147, 147 fn. 26; followed O. Cowdery, 336; supported Emma Smith's claim, 729 fn. 32
Smith, William, granted herd ground, 577, 581, 583; Parrish murder investigation, 624 fn. 87
Smithie, ..., 55
Smoot, Abram (Abraham) O., 211, 260, 389, 413 fn. 83, 627, 634, 638, 664, 667, 674, 705, 716; policeman Winter Quarters, 211; bio. sketch, 211 fn. 10; bishop 15th Ward and justice of peace, 349; leg., 384; P.E.F. co. arrived S.L. City, 450; director first P.E.F. co., 450 fn. 3; mayor S.L. City, 674 fn. 43; high councilman, 704 fn. 68
Snake Indians, troops sent against, 380; *see also* Indians
Snedeker, ..., 337
Snelgrove, ..., 733
Snell, John W., assist. messenger leg., 673
Snider, Ephraim, 623
Snow, ..., 373, 376, 377, 385, 392, 506, 534, 585, 612, 684
Snow, Eliza Roxey, 393 fn. 16; bio. sketch, 505 fn. 3
Snow, Erastus, 127, 214 fn. 12, 343, 372 fn. 41, 442, 496, 497, 498, 578, 599, 600, 628 fn. 93, 714, 715; trustee Mechanical and Mercantile Assoc., 22; bio. sketch, 22 fn. 50; organized co. for move West, 228; capt. of Fifty, 231; mission, 310, 512, 635; counselor to C. C. Rich, 332; apostle, 342; Parrish murder investigation, 692 fn. 51
Snow, Gardner, judge San Pete Co., 680
Snow, James C., 572, 573, 574, 617, 618, 672; leg. com., 610; granted herd ground, 619
Snow, Lorenzo, 142, 312, 315, 350, 505 fn. 3, 512, 537, 538, 539, 540, 543, 579; clerk of Fifty, 144; apostle, 342; committeeman poor fund, 357; leg., 524; mission, 561; regent U. of Deseret, 581; granted herd ground, 585, 587; pres. Senate, 608
Snow, Sarah, married, 498
Snow, W., 258, 353, 364, 371, 372, 375, 379, 380, 383, 386, 394, 550; committeeman poor fund, 357
Snow, Warren S., 137 fn. 10, 156, 644, 645, 652; granted herd ground, 616, 617
Snow, Willard, bishop, 214; bio. sketch, 214 fn. 12; policeman Winter Quarters, 220; capt. of Hundred, 231; magistrate Potawatamie Co., 307 fn. 71; counselor to D. Spencer,